James Braden

History of Trumbull and Mahoning counties

Vol. I

James Braden

History of Trumbull and Mahoning counties
Vol. I

ISBN/EAN: 9783742888716

Manufactured in Europe, USA, Canada, Australia, Japa

Cover: Foto ©ninafisch / pixelio.de

Manufactured and distributed by brebook publishing software (www.brebook.com)

James Braden

History of Trumbull and Mahoning counties

HISTORY

OF

TRUMBULL AND MAHONING

COUNTIES,

WITH

ILLUSTRATIONS AND BIOGRAPHICAL SKETCHES.

VOL. I.

CLEVELAND:
H. Z. WILLIAMS & BRO.
1882.

PREFATORY NOTE.

This work was undertaken in answer to the invitation of many citizens of the Mahoning Valley. It originated in their laudable appreciation of the deeds of their ancestors and the desire that the record of the lives of those who laid the foundation of civilization on the Reserve, and have brought to its successful accomplishment the work of developing the resources of this favored valley, should be embodied in permanent form. The publishers have aimed at accuracy and completeness, and trust they have been reasonably successful. The material used in the compilation of these two volumes was mainly gleaned from interviews with more than one thousand individuals. The editors have been at great pains to eliminate errors, but they can not hope in every instance to have avoided inaccuracies. It is believed, however, that their work is essentially correct.

In the compilation of the General History original manuscripts and records were usually relied upon, but in addition to these, published works have furnished valuable information. The following volumes were consulted: Bancroft's History of the United States, Parkman's Conspiracy of Pontiac, Whittlesey's History of Cleveland, Henry Howe's History of Ohio, Abbott's History of Ohio, Taylor's History of Ohio, Historical Collections of the Mahoning Valley, Geological Survey of Ohio, various State reports, files of the local papers, and other publications. "The Mahoning County Bar" is the contribution of John M. Edwards, Esq., of Youngstown. "The Trumbull County Bar" was prepared in part by Jefferson Palm, Esq., and in part by David Jameson. The first two chapters of the history of Youngstown were written by J. M. Edwards, Esq., whose special qualifications are well known. The history of Hartford township was written by T. A. Bushnell, and of Greene by James Braden. The editors were received everywhere with cordiality and treated with kindness. It is impossible to make special acknowledgments, but all who rendered assistance are assured that their favor was appreciated.

CONTENTS.

HISTORICAL.

GENERAL HISTORY.

CHAPTER.	PAGE.
I.—Indian Occupation	9
II.—European Explorations	13
III. Ownership of the Northwest	17
IV. Sale of the Western Reserve	22
V. Connecticut Land Company	26
VI.—Progress of Western Settlement	33
VII.—Settlement of the Reserve	40
VIII.—Indian Abdication	50
IX.—The Pioneers	56
X. Civil Government	63
XI.—Mahoning County	76
XII.—Militia Organization and War of 1812	83
XIII.—Geology	92
XIV.—Transportation Facilities	100
XV.— County Societies	107
XVI.—The Rebellion Record	115
XVII.—The Bar of Trumbull County	174
XVIII. Mahoning County Bar	208

CITY OF WARREN, OHIO.

CHAPTER.	PAGE.
I.—The Village and Village Life	241
II.—Business Growth	251
III.—Religious Organizations	259
IV. The Press	268
V. Schools	273
VI. Civil History	280
VII. Physicians of Warren	289
VIII. Warren Lodges	293
IX.—Leavittsburg	305
X. Biographical Sketches	306
XI.—Biographical Notes	335

CITY OF YOUNGSTOWN, OHIO.

CHAPTER.	PAGE.
I. Initial Events	359
II.—Industrial Growth	368
III.—Religious Societies	378
IV. Public Schools	394
V.—Physicians	401
VI.—Soldiers' Monument	414
VII.—The Press Secret Societies	416
VIII.—Biographical Sketches	424
IX.—Notes of Settlement	449

Sketch of the Life of James A. Garfield . . 485

BIOGRAPHICAL.

	PAGE		PAGE
Asper, Joel F.	189	Burkey, Moses H.	223
Abell, Arot	195	Butler, John L.	230
Adams, Whittlesey	201	Bents, William Carey	232
Arrel, George F.	220	Brown, William I.	233
Anderson, William S.	224	Brown, Cornelius M.	233
Ashbaugh, William N.	226	Blockson, James B.	234
Angell, Elgin A.	233	Blockson, Ensign Church	234
Arms, Freeman O.	444	Brown, Ensign N.	236
Birchard, Matthew	177	Beardsley, Frederick W.	237
Beaver, John F.	187	Brindley, Rev. Edward A.	350
Brown, George F.	189	Baldwin, Caleb	426
Buttles, Joel B.	190	Brownlee, Alexander B.	441
Barnes, Buel	190	Brownlee, John	440
Belden, David D.	191	Curtis, Benjamin F.	191
Bright, W. J.	191	Cox, Jacob D.	193
Barnes, Riverius Bidwell	200	Cowdery, Julius N.	203
Bragh, Petler	211	Calhoun, Marlen Anderson	204

CONTENTS.

	PAGE
Craig, Samuel Baxter	204
Correll, Servetus A.	206
Canfield, Henry J.	214
Campbell, Walter L.	221
Clark, Stephen L.	226
Clark, John H.	226
Callahan, William H.	229
Cassidy, Henry C.	230
Case, Halbert B.	232
Camp, Henry	233
Canfield, Edward G.	234
Coffee, Isaac E.	235
Church, John W.	235
Cracraft, John W.	238
Case Family	334
Crowell, General John	192
Dawson, William B.	237
Davies, Rev. J. L.	322
Dabney, Nathaniel G.	434
Drown, A. A.	203
Ensign, Erastus Humphrey	200
Edwards, John M.	217-221
Evans, Mason	223
Eddy, Burdette O.	224
Estep, Ephraim James	234
Ewing, Harrison J.	236
Eaton, Dan	432
Edwards, William Johnson	439
Edwards, John S.	1820
Fuller, Ira L.	185
Forrest, William O.	189
Fee, William Thomas	207
Freer, Charles Smith	208
Ford, David Tod	226
Ferguson, William	231
Freeman, Judge Francis	325
Glidden, Charles E.	186-237
Gillmer, Thomas Irwin	203
Gilbert, David Revilla	205
Gillmer, Thomas H.	206
Gilson, Joseph Wilber	207
Gibson, William T.	224
Gillies, Patrick F.	228
Gibson, Samuel W.	235
Gibson, James and descendants	435
Humphrey, Nathan O.	184
Harris, Sidney W.	187
Hutchins, John	194
Hart, Melancthon C.	195
Harrington, Charles Adams	197
Hutchins, Francis Edwin	198
Hunter, George Preston	202
Hulse, Richard K.	203
Hyde, Washington	204
Hunter, Lafayette	205
Herzog, John Lafayette	206
Huntington, Samuel	210
Hine, Homer	211
Hoffman, Benjamin F.	216
Hine, Cecil D.	223
Huxley, Jared	224
Howells, William E.	226
Hatch, George C.	228
Hansard, Thomas F.	229
Hine, Homer H.	231

	PAGE
Hutchins, Francis E.	232
Hutchins, John C.	233
Harrington, Charles A.	235
Haines, Seldon	236
Higley, B. S.	238
Harmon, John B. and family	313
Hoyt family	327
Hapgood, George	331
Hughes, Rev. William	391
Hillman, James	424
Holcomb, John R.	439
Higley, Brainard Spencer	442
Hoffman, Benjamin F. and family	447
Ingersoll, Jonathan	190
Izant, Robert T.	206
Iddings, Richard	309
Jones, Hon. Lucian Curtis	200
Jameson, David	208
Jones, Asahel W.	218
Justice, Isaac A.	221
Johnson, Monroe W.	222
Jacobs, Frank	225
Jackson, Sidney DeLamar	230
Johnston, Joseph R.	238
Knight, William L.	190
Kennedy, Edwin Doud	206
Kyle, Otis W.	222
Knight, Addis E.	225
Kennedy, James	228
King, Lewis N.	229
Knight, Robert E.	232
King, John H.	232
Knight, William	236
Knowlton, Emery E.	237
King, Leicester	309
Kinsman, Frederick	311
Leet, George W.	185
Leggett, General M. D.	193
Lawthers, William J.	223
Ladd, John A.	228
Leslie, Henry G.	232
Lewis, John H.	237
Logan, Albert B.	238
Lane, Henry, and Family	307
Morgan, Orlando	191
McLain, Thomas Jefferson	196
Moran, William B.	205
Metcalf, William L.	205
Moore, Albert Freeman	206
McLain, Frank David	206
Myers, Edward	208
Moore, William G.	217
Moses, Halsey H.	219
Murray, Robert B.	220
Miller, L. Barclay	226
Maline, William A.	227
McGehan, William B.	227
McNabb, Melvin Cary	227
Mastin, London	236
Moore, Alexander H.	236
Moore, John J.	236
Mygatt, Comfort	313
Mygatt, Hon. George	326
Marvin, Joseph	331
Meiser, Rev. G. F. H.	390

CONTENTS.

	PAGE		PAGE
McCay, James	428	Stewart, Homer E.	203
Montgomery, Robert	429	Sloan, Merrick John	205
Montgomery, Robert M.	430	Struck, Charles H.	207
Mackey, James	430	Sanderson, Thomas W.	218
Maxwell, Rev. Samuel	449	Strong, Sidney	223
Norton, Homer	201	Smith, Eugene	227
Newton, Charles Bostwick	205	Smith, Clate A.	227
Newton, Eben	215	Swanston, Edward	228
Nesbit, Frances C.	236	Swanston, George	228
Nash, James M.	238	Servis, Francis G.	234
Olcott, Charles	190	Stevens family	332
Osborn, William M.	232	Seltzer, Rev. Charles M.	388
O'Connor, Patrick	445	Shelby, Daniel	434
Osborn Family	448	Sutliff, Milton	178
Pease, Calvin	174-210	Tayler, James D.	185
Parker, Alexander C.	191	Tayler, Robert W.	189-215
Palm, Jefferson	197	Tyler, Judge Joel W.	195
Porter, William	201	Tuttle, Hon. George Merrill	196
Pickering, John Everton	207	Taylor, Hon. Ezra B.	1828-201
Powers, Ridgeley J.	231	Taylor, John Warren	206
Powers, Willis Waring	231	Thayer, Albert Anson	207
Porter, William	233	Tod, George	207-219
Perkins, Simon	310	Tod, Governor David	171-214
Perkins, Henry Bishop	311	Thomas, Leroy D.	220
Perkins, Jacob	323	Truesdale, Charles R.	221
Quinby Family	306	Taylor, Hallett K.	228
Reed, Philo Ellsworth	185	Thomas, Daniel L.	229
Ranney, Rufus P.	192	Tayler, Matthew B.	318
Ratliff, General Robert Wilson	198	Tayler, George	328
Reeves, Hon. Wilbur Asahel	203	Van Gorder, James I.	307
Rogers, Ikio	204	Van Hyning, Giles	238
Rogers, Volney	229	Wilson, James F.	207
Rogers, Disney	229	Woolford, Marshall	208
Rockwell, Edward	230	Whittlesey, Elisha	213
Rice, Theron M.	235	Wilson, David M.	217
Ruggles, Charles	235	Woodworth, Laurin D.	219
Ruggles, Horace G.	235	Woolf, Albert Jacob	225
Ruggles, Edwin C.	236	Wilson, Elliott M.	226
Roller, John S.	236	Wilson, James P.	227
Rayen, William	427	Wirt, Benjamin F.	228
Sutliff, Calvin G.	182	Ward, George J.	232
Stone, Roswell	182	Whittlesey, William W.	233
Sutliff, Levi	183	Wordbridge, John E.	433
Smith, Charles W.	184	Wick, Colonel Caleb B.	437
Spaulding, Rufus P.	192	Webb, Thomas Denny	181
Scull, John M.	199	Young, Garretson I.	235
Spear, Hon. William T.	201	Wood, George L.	191
Sanderson, Matthew Dille	202	Young, John	434
Snyder, George W.	202	Yeomans, Hon. Albert	197

ILLUSTRATIONS.

	PAGE.
Portrait of James A. Garfield	Frontispiece
Portrait of Hon. E. B. Taylor	between 182 and 183
Portrait of General John Crowell	facing 192
Portrait of Judge Benjamin F. Hoffman	facing 216
Portrait of James Hoyt	facing 265
Portrait of Joseph Marvin	facing 280
Portrait of George Hapgood	facing 288
Portrait of Samuel Quinby	facing 306
Portrait of James L. VanGorder	between 308 and 309
Portrait of Elizabeth S. VanGorder	between 308 and 309
Portrait of Dr. John B. Harmon	between 312 and 313
Portrait of Mrs. John B. Harmon	between 312 and 313

	PAGE.
Portrait of Judge Francis Freeman	facing 325
Portrait of Matthew B. Tayler	facing 328
Portrait of Benjamin Stevens	between 332 and 333
Portrait of Mrs. Benjamin Stevens	between 332 and 333
Portrait of Governor Tod	facing 359
Portrait of John M. Edwards	facing 368
Portrait of R. S. Higley	facing 384
Portrait of John Brownlee	facing 392
Portrait of Freeman O. Arms	facing 400
Portrait of John R. Holcomb	facing 408
Portrait of Caleb B. Wick	facing 437

GENERAL HISTORY

OF

TRUMBULL AND MAHONING COUNTIES, OHIO.

CHAPTER I.

INDIAN OCCUPATION.

Early Occupation of Northern Ohio—Indian Traditions and Tribal Conflicts.

There hangs over America an impenetrable veil of mystery, tradition, and silence. Mounds and fortifications bear evidence of habitation by a race whose annals have never been written, whose history will never be known. The origin of the Indian race, whose warlike nations were found by the European explorers, is involved in the most vague and untrustworthy tradition. The dawning of Western history may be dated about the middle of the seventeenth century, when the first white adventurers followed shaded streams far into the unbroken forest and carried back to civilization some knowledge of the vast extent of the Western continent. But even for a century later the narrative of these nations is so intermingled with fable and legend that little can be relied upon as the simple record of truth.

The Indians of Northwestern North America were embraced in two generic divisions, the Algonquins and the Iroquois. The Iroquois family, consisting of the Eries, Wyandots, Andastes, and six tribes of Western New York (known as the Six Nations), were confined to the regions about Lakes Erie and Ontario. All around them was the vast expanse of Algonquin population extending from Hudson's bay on the north to the Carolinas on the south, from the Atlantic on the east to the Mississippi on the west.

Soon after the first permanent white settlement on the Atlantic coast the Mohawks, Oneidas, Onondagas, Cayugas, and Senecas formed a confederation and were governed by the decrees of a common council. The Tuscarawas joined the union early in the seventeenth century and the confederacy became known as the Six Nations. Their government had the rude elements of a republic and was the only Indian power on this part of the continent deserving of the name.

The Eries dwelt on the southern shore of the lake which bears their name. Their tribal seat was on the Sandusky plains. They were known to the early French explorers as Felians or Cat Nation, a name indicating fierceness and stealth.

The Hurons or Wyandots inhabited the eastern shore of Lake Huron and the peninsula between Lakes Erie and Huron. Their warriors were strong and brave, but not so numerous as the armies of the other two powers.

The Six Nations having grown arrogant in consequence of long years of confederation and undisputed supremacy, determined upon a campaign against their Western neighbors. The Wyandots were their first victims. The campaign had already commenced when Champlain entered the upper lakes, and that enterprising officer accompanied one of the hostile parties against the enemy. Crossing the Niagara river they marched westward until the Huron country was reached. The encounter was desperate; on one side the battle was for victory; on the other for existence. The invaders triumphed, and then pursued their retreating foes with relentless fury. Driven from place to place, suffering, in addition to the cruelties inflicted by their enemy, disease and famine, a feeble remnant of the defeated and exiled nation at last found protection in the dominion of the Sioux. Flushed by victory the confederates returned more eager and confident than ever. Between their country and the territory of the Eries lay a wide reach of forest inhabited by wandering bands and used as a common hunting-ground by both the great nations. The valley of the Mahoning lies probably within this neutral district. It was the border country beyond which, on both sides, were villages and council seats, where assemblages feasted and offered sacrifices, and warriors held peace councils and war councils. There is where we must look for legends and traditions of the heroic race. The Mahoning valley is exceptionally devoid of associations of that character.

The confederate braves rested from their expedition against the Hurons, impatiently awaited the permission of their war council to put on the war paint and take up the tomahawk against the most powerful of their western neighbors the Eries. The Eries, on the other hand, regarded the situation with the greatest apprehension. Never doubting the personal superiority of their warriors, they dreaded the power of the allied tribes on account of overwhelming numbers. The destruction of the Hurons was suggestive of the possibility of their fate, however the character and disposition of the confederate warriors were unknown. It was resolved to put them to the test.

To cope with them collectively they saw was impossible. Their only hope, therefore, was in being able by a vigorous and sudden movement to destroy them in detail. With this view a powerful party was immediately organized to attack the Senecas, who resided at the foot of Seneca lake (the present site of Geneva) and along the banks of Seneca river. It happened that at this period there resided among the Eries a Seneca woman who in early life had been taken a prisoner and had married a husband of the Erie tribe. He died and left her a widow without children, a stranger among strangers. Hearing the terrible note of preparation for a bloody onslaught upon her kindred and friends, she formed the resolution of apprising them of their danger.

As soon as night set in, taking the course of the Niagara river, she traveled all night, and early next morning reached the shore of Lake Ontario. She jumped into a canoe, which she found fastened to a tree, and boldly pushed into the open lake. Coasting down the lake, she arrived at the mouth of the Oswego river in the night, where a large settlement of the nation resided. She directed her steps to the house of the head chief, and disclosed the object of her journey. She was secreted by the chief, and runners were dispatched to all the tribes, summoning them immediately to meet in council, which was held in Onondaga hollow.

When all were convened, the chief arose, and, in the most solemn manner rehearsed a vision, in which he said that a beautiful bird appeared to him and told him that a great party of the Eries was preparing to make a secret and sudden descent upon them to destroy them, and that nothing could save them but an immediate rally of all the warriors of the Five Nations, to meet the enemy before they should be able to strike the blow. These solemn announcements were heard in breathless silence. When the chief had finished and sat down there arose one immense yell of menacing madness. The earth shook when the mighty mass brandished high in air their war-clubs, and stamped the ground like furious beasts.

No time was lost. A body of five thousand warriors was organized, and a corps of reserve, consisting of one thousand young men who had never been in battle. The bravest chiefs of all the tribes were put in command, and spies immediately sent out in search of the enemy, the whole body taking up their line of march in the direction whence they expected the attack.

The advance of the party was continued several days, passing through, successively, the settlements of their friends, the Onondagas, the Cayugas and the Senecas; but they had scarcely passed the last wigwam, now the fort of Can-an-du-gua (Canandaigua) lake, when the scouts brought in intelligence of the advance of the Eries, who had already crossed the Ce-nis-se-u (Genessee) river in great force. The Eries had not the slightest intimation of the approach of their enemies. They relied on the secrecy and celerity of their movements to surprise and subdue the Senecas almost without resistance.

The two parties met at a point about half way between the foot of Canandaigua lake, on the Genesee river, and near the outlet of two small lakes, near the foot of one of which (Honeoye) the battle was fought. When the two parties came in sight of each other the outlet of the lake only intervened between them.

The entire force of the five confederate tribes was not in view of the Eries. The reserve corps of one thousand young men had not been allowed to advance in sight of the enemy. Nothing could resist the impetuosity of the Eries at the first sight of an opposing force on the other side of the stream. They rushed through it and fell upon them with tremendous fury. The undaunted courage and determined bravery of the Iroquois could not avail against such a terrible onslaught, and they were compelled to yield the ground on the bend of the stream. The whole force of the combined tribes, except the corps of the reserve, now became engaged. They fought hand to hand and foot to foot. The battle raged horribly. No quarter was asked or given on either side.

As the fight thickened and became more desperate, the Eries, for the first time, became sensible of their true situation. What they had long anticipated had become a fearful reality. Their enemies had combined for their destruction, and they now found themselves engaged, suddenly and unexpectedly, in a struggle not only involving the glory, but perhaps the very existence of their nation. They were proud, and had heretofore been victorious over all their enemies. Their superiority was felt and acknowledged by all the tribes. They knew how to conquer, but not to yield. All these considerations flashed upon the minds of the bold Eries, and nerved every arm with almost superhuman power. On the other hand, the united forces of the weaker tribes, now made strong by union, fired with a spirit of emulation, excited to the highest pitch among the warriors of the different tribes, brought for the first time to act in concert, inspired with zeal and confidence by the counsels of the wisest chiefs, and led by the most experienced warriors of all the tribes, the Iroquois were invincible.

Though staggered by the first desperate rush of their opponents, they rallied at once, and stood their ground. And now the din of battle rises higher; the war-club, the tomahawk, the scalping-knife, wielded by herculean hands, do terrible deeds of death. During the hottest of the battle, which was fierce and long, the corps of reserves, consisting of a thousand young men, were by skillful movement under their experienced chief, placed in the rear of the Eries, on the opposite side of the stream, in ambush.

The Eries had been driven seven times across the stream, and had as often regained their ground; but the eighth time, at a given signal from their chief, the corps of young warriors in ambush rushed upon the almost exhausted Eries with a tremendous yell, and at once decided the fortunes of the day. Hundreds, disdaining to fly, were struck down by the war-clubs of the vigorous young warriors, whose thirst for the blood of the enemy knew no bounds. A few of the vanquished Eries escaped to carry the news of the terrible overthrow to their wives and children and old men that remained at home. But the victors did not allow them a moment's repose, but pursued them in their flight, killing all who fell into their hands.

The pursuit was continued for many weeks, and it was five months before the victorious party of the Five Nations returned to their friends to join in celebrating the victory over their last and most powerful enemy—the Eries.

When the victorious warriors had returned to their native hills, and while the bones of the brave but ill-fated Eries lay bleaching on the cold, damp soil of a dark, unbroken forest, a wierd silence hung over the region now embraced in the State of Ohio. There were no wigwams, no camp-fires to break the desolation and gloom. The rugged valley of the Mahoning, now enrobed in smoke and noisy with industry, knew no sound save the melancholy bustle of leaves and monotonous ripple of flowing water.

But these hills and valleys, abounding in the native animals of the forest, were not long without human habitation. The Six Nations, gradually growing more numerous, sent offshoots to occupy the country they had conquered. The Senecas became the chief occupants of the headwaters of the Ohio and pushed as far west as the Sandusky river. The Wyandots or Hurons having recovered from complete and disastrous defeat, migrated eastward to recover their long lost dominion, and eventually established themselves upon the Sandusky plains and prairies. The Delawares, a branch of the great Algonquin family, occupied the valleys of the Muskingum and Tuscarawas, and the Shawnees established themselves upon the Scioto. Our first accurate and authentic information relating to Ohio Indians dates from about the middle of the eighteenth century, when French and English traders began to ply their canoes upon every stream, seeking out the denizens of the forest. The first detailed account giving the strength, character, and geography of the several tribes is found in the report of Colonel Boquet, who made a military expedition west of the Ohio in 1764. Long before this the natives saw with jealousy and apprehension the encroachment of white settlements. A common enemy and common danger created a bond of sympathy among the tribes. They had the sagacity to see that their only hope of maintaining dominion over the forest lay in unity of action and purpose. For this reason it is probable that the Six Nations made no objection to the occupation of their vast western hunting ground by former enemies. They were all of kindred race, of kindred habits and kindred interests. Their ground became in some measure common ground, and to maintain it against white encroachments was their united purpose. While to each nation was ascribed well defined limitations, they all frequented the country beyond their boundaries, and some of them, several times within the period of our definite knowledge, changed places of residence.

When Boquet made his observations the Mahoning valley was mainly occupied by Delawares. The densest population of this Indian nation was upon the upper Muskingum and the Tuscarawas. They were numerous and held possession of the greater part of eastern Ohio. The Chippewas dwelt north of them on the lake shore, and the Mingoes, an off-shoot of the Six Nations, had several villages on the Muskingum, below the present site of Steubenville. With these exceptions the country between the Beaver and Muskingum was inhabited by people of distinctively Delaware stock. The Massasaugas, a roving tribe of hunters, were most numerous on the Mahoning. They were among the last of the Delaware nation to leave the eastern part of the present territory of Ohio.

The Delaware nation, which claimed to be the elder branch of the Lenni Lenape has, by tradition and in history and fiction been accorded a high rank among the savages of North America. Schoolcraft, Loskiel, Gallatin, Drake, Heckewelder, and many other writers have borne testimony of the superiority of this tribe; and James Fennimore Cooper, by his attractive romances has added luster to the fame of the tribe. The Delawares have a tradition that many years before they knew the white man, their home was in the western part of the continent, and separating from the rest of the Lenni Lenape, migrated eastward. Reaching the Alleghany river, they joined the Iroquois in a war against a race of giants, the Allegewi, in which they were successful. From there the Delawares continued their slow migration eastward and finally settled on the river which bears their name. When Europeans first became acquainted with them, their population had spread to the Hudson, the Susquehanna, and the Potomac. There was a tradition that the Iroquois had, long before white explorations, made war upon the Delawares and conquered them by treachery, in the language of the Iroquois had "eaten them up" and "made women of them." They were less warlike than their neighbors, probably on account of their defeat. The Iroquois were a constant menace, and when at last white settlers began to encroach upon their territory the Delawares determined to return to the West. They concentrated upon the Alleghany, but again being molested by advancing white settlements, a second westward migration became necessary, this time to the valley of the Muskingum and eastern Ohio, where Boquet found them in 1764.

They had been living in the Ohio country not more than a score of years, but were a more numerous and flourishing tribe than they had ever been before. Their warriors numbered not less than six hundred, but were considered inferior in strength and courage to the Wyandots, whom they called "uncles" thus acknowledging inferiority. The Delawares accepted Christianity more readily than any other tribe. Most of their towns were in the vicinity of the forks of the Muskingum and near the mouth of the Tuscarawas. That region was the place of their tribal councils and great feasts, and is rich in Indian traditions which are called to mind by the old Indian names occurring in the local geography. The Massasaugas, who inhabited the Mahoning valley, were a band of roving hunters who made no pretensions to the honor of being warriors. They had no permanent villages, but encamped at several places in the present territory of Mahoning county and south part of this county. This region as far east as the Beaver was thinly populated, and regarded as a hunting ground. Twenty years after the expedition of Colonel Boquet, Captain Brady, the celebrated Indian fighter and adventurer, frequently crossed the territory embraced within the sphere of this history, but never met with any opposition. During the long period of border war between the Indians and the first white settlers west of the Alleghanies, and in Kentucky, until Wayne's victory at Greenville in 1794, this region as far south as the Ohio river was a belt of wilderness separating the advance posts of civilization, which were constantly harassed by predatory incursions, and the seats of the native tribes.

CHAPTER II.
EUROPEAN EXPLORATIONS.

Early Explorers—The Cavaliers—La Salle and His Discoveries.

The most stirring achievements recorded in the history of the two centuries succeeding the return of Columbus to Spain, in 1492, are embraced in the story of adventure and exploration on the newly discovered continent. Spain, France, and England were rivals in eagerness, enterprise, and daring. Greed for gold and the legendary fountain of perpetual youth, led Ponce de Leon into the everglades of Florida, where he found his grave, and made De Soto the discoverer of the Mississippi. English explorers measured the Atlantic coast and pushed up the Atlantic rivers into what was then supposed to be the far interior. The French, rounding the coast of Newfoundland, discovered the passage to the great West. Champlain passed the rapids above Montreal in 1606, and, in 1615, Priest La Caron discovered Lake Huron, and from this time, for more than a century, Jesuit missionaries were busy in their endeavors to convert the pagan Indians, and to found an empire for their king.

Cavelier La Salle is commonly supposed to have been the first white man who trod the soil of the present State of Ohio. He was the first whose name history has preserved, and whose adventure was fruitful of practical results. But, as mounds and systematic fortifications bear testimony of habitation by a race whose history can never be known, so the Western Reserve forest has preserved marks of occupation by unnamed whites, whose exploits and destiny are past finding out.

A tree was cut in the northwest part of Canfield, in Mahoning county, in 1838, which must be considered a good record as far back as 1660 at least. The tree when cut had been dead several years, and was about two feet in diameter. It was quite sound with the exception of a slight rot at the heart. About seven inches from the center were distinct marks of a sharp axe, over which one hundred and sixty years of annual growth had accumulated. The evidence was clear that when the tree was about fourteen inches in diameter, an expert chopper with an axe in perfect order had cut nearly to the center. The tree, not otherwise injured, continued to grow for a period of at least one hundred and sixty years.

Trees containing similar marks have been found in Cuyahoga, Lake, Huron, and Ashtabula counties, showing about the same date of incision. It cannot be supposed that these marks were made by Indians, for the only axes possessed by the natives when the French first became acquainted with them had narrow, dull blades, with which it would have been impossible to make the marks referred to, and they could not have possessed better tools at an earlier date. The Jesuits visited the tribes of western New York as early as 1656, but there is no written evidence of their having come as far west on this side of the lake as the Reserve. It has been inferred by some historians that La Salle, on his return from the Illinois in 1682-3, passed through northern Ohio, and that the tree marks were left by his men. Such a supposition is highly improbable. Although it is known that his return was by land, and there is no proof on which side of the lake he traveled, he could not have remained long enough on the present territory of the Reserve to leave so many mementos as have been found in widely separated localities. Besides, there must have been hundreds of trees on the Reserve on which axes have been used to furnish so many examples after the lapse of two centuries. These tree marks must remain among the mysteries which veil our early history.

The adventures of La Salle had an important effect upon western history, and fully detailed constitute one of the most romantic stories in the world's annals. Born of a proud and wealthy family in the north of France, he early imbibed the spirit of the chevaliers, but was destined for the service of the church and of the Jesuit order. His restless spirit soon broke loose from ecclesiastical restraints, and at the age of twenty-six we find him confronting the dangers of the New World in western New York, eager for romantic exploit and filled with a desire to extend the dominions of his king, Louis XIV. With a few followers and Indian guides he penetrated the country of the fierce Iroquois until, says Parkman, he reached "at a point six or seven leagues from Lake Erie, a branch of the Ohio, which he descended to the main stream," and so went on as far as the falls, at the present site of Louisville. His men abandoning him there he retraced his way alone. This was about the year 1670. There is every reason to believe that the Ohio had never before been seen by a white man. Ten years later La Salle unfurled the first sail ever offered to the breeze on Lake Erie, and in the Griffin, a schooner of forty-five tons burthen, made a voyage to Lake Huron.

In 1682 he reached the Mississippi and descended to its mouth. He then solemnly proclaimed, in the name of Louis XIV., possession of the vast and fertile valley he had explored. Meanwhile the priests had been active in establishing missionary posts and carrying the story of the Cross into the dense wilderness as far west as the Mississippi. They were not frightened by the stories of forest monsters, nor had the red man yet been taught to be jealous of and fear the pale-face. Traders were not far behind the missionaries, and they found great profit in bartering such articles as pleased the Indian taste and appetite for their peltry and fur. So industriously did the cavaliers, the religious enthusiasts, and the traders engage in seeking out the denizens of the forest and winning their friendship with rich presents, that by the opening of the eighteenth century France was deceived into the belief that her vast dominion in the New World was secure. Certainly if the right of discovery implies the right of possession the claim of France was indisputable. Of the work of her adventurous cavaliers, Irving has well said: "It was poetry put into action; it was the knight-errantry of the Old World carried into the American wilderness. The personal adventures; the feats of individual prowess; the picturesque descriptions of steel-clad cavaliers with lance and helmet and prancing steed, glittering through the wilderness of Florida, Georgia, Alabama, and the prairies of the Far West, would seem to us mere fictions of romance did they not come to us in the matter-of-fact narratives of those who were eye witnesses, and who recorded minute memoranda of every incident."

England, however, was not disposed to accede to the unqualified claims of France to this region, the vast extent of which the cavaliers and priests of France had taught her. She had quietly founded her colonies, and planted English civilization on the Atlantic coast. Colonial charters had included all the territory explored and possessed by France, but the law enacted by practice makes occupation the only basis of ownership in a newly discovered country.

Alexander Spottswood, the royal governor of Virginia, was the first Englishman to call attention to the extent and resources of the West, and the danger of its settlement by a power hostile to the English. No attention was paid to his advice by the royal government. However, the crown years afterward, realized that a wise policy had been neglected. Governor Spottswood carried his plans into partial execution upon his own authority. In 1710 he engaged in systematic explorations of the Alleghanies; four years later he discovered an available passage to the West and entered with great ardor upon a scheme for taking practical possession of the Ohio valley. He founded the Transmontane order, whose knights were decorated with a golden horseshoe bearing the inscription, *Sic jurat transcendere montes.*

The French had a very just claim to the West and Northwest, but it was destined that they should not hold it. Although the British ministry seemed indifferent, events were rapidly shaping which led to the overthrow of French authority and the vesture of title and possession in the English crown. The powerful influence of the confederate Six Nations was secured in favor of the English, and expeditions and individuals bore presents from the colonies on the Atlantic coast by which the friendship of several Western tribes was purchased. Competition between French and English traders became sharp, but the former were most successful in maintaining the confidence of the tribes. Courtly conduct, glittering dress, and rich presents convinced the Indians that the French were their friends, and would assist them to defend their hunting grounds against English encroachments. The jealousy between traders of opposing nationalities often resulted in reprisals. A French fort was established on Sandusky bay, and an English fort and trading-post on the Great Miami about the year 1750. The latter was destroyed in June, 1752, by a force of French and Indians.

A gigantic scheme of western colonization was set on foot in 1748, in Virginia, known as the Colonial Ohio Land company. There were twelve associates, among whom were Augustine and Lawrence Washington, brothers of George Washington, and Thomas Lee. Christopher Gist was employed to explore the Ohio valley. With George Croghan and Montour he traveled as far as the falls, and upon the basis of his report a royal charter for half a million acres of land was secured, located in the Ohio valley. In 1753, preliminaries having been arranged, preparations were made to establish the colony, but the French being reinforced and having secured the alliance and active co-operation of all the northern tribes, manifested an intention of determined resistance. George Washington, then a young man, was commissioned by the royal Governor of Virginia, to visit the French commander and inquire by what right the French claimed and invaded British territory.* Washington, accompanied by Indian guides and Christopher Gist, the explorer, journeyed over the mountains to the forks of the Ohio. He then remarked the site as peculiarly eligible for a military post, and then journeyed northward to French creek, where a conference with the French commander was secured. Washington received a haughty and defiant answer to the question he was commanded to bear. Returning to Virginia the failure of his mission was made known. The project of making a settlement was abandoned and preparations set on foot for the maintenance of the British claim by force of arms. The colonies, under the lead of Virginia, united in the cause and the royal government finally came to their assistance.

Benjamin Franklin had previously tried to effect a union of the colonies but had been unsuccessful, chiefly on account of jealousy and ambition for supremacy. In 1754 he proposed a plan of western settlement, suggesting that two colonies should be founded, one upon the Cuyahoga, the other upon the Scioto, "on which," he said, "for forty miles on each side of it and quite up to its head is a body of all rich land, the finest spot of its bigness in all North America, and has the advantage of sea-coal in plenty (even above the ground in two places) for fuel when the wood shall have been destroyed." The result of the war which followed, known in history as the "French and Indian war," was the defeat of the French and the vesture in the British crown of all right and title to Canada and all the territory east of the Mississippi and north of the Spanish possessions, excepting New Orleans and a small body of land surrounding it. This treaty was concluded at Paris in 1763. This highly satisfactory result cost a royal army under Braddock and many of the Colonial troops engaged. The Virginia militia had contributed most largely to success. Connecticut, knowing little of the extent and importance of the territory covered by her charter, took no interest in the struggle. It will be noted presently that this was not the only time Virginia was instrumental in preserving Connecticut's title to Western territory.

The peace of 1763 was followed by a long series of Indian troubles, preventing the consummation of any of the many schemes of Western settlement. Expedition after expedition was sent into the Western country, some attended with disaster, some partially successful, but none able to effectually quell hostilities and to render the borders of Virginia, Pennsylvania, and Kentucky safe against savage murders, and preda-

---

* The British claim was based mainly upon a treaty of cession made with the Iroquois, who claimed ownership by right of conquest.

tory incursions. Fort Sandusky fell and the garrison was murdered in 1764. Fort Pitt was saved only by the timely arrival of Boquet and his English soldiers. Lord Dunmore suffered severely on the Scioto. There were many other expeditions of less note. The war was conducted with activity and vigilance on both sides. It is estimated that twenty thousand whites were killed or taken prisoner during the cruel twelve years following the treaty of Paris.

When the outbreak of the Revolution summoned the energies of the colonies, and occupied all the attention and resources the royal government could expend in the New World, all plans of colonization and intimidation were abandoned. Western history during the Revolutionary period is almost barren of incident. There was one event, however, of immeasurable importance in American history. It was the second successful attempt, under Virginian auspices, to preserve the great West to the Eastern establishments. It was a Virginia soldier who had served under Lord Dunmore in 1774, and in 1776 settled in Kentucky, then a county of Virginia, who first foresaw the importance of destroying the military establishments of the British in the West. Had peace been concluded while the enemy was in actual occupation of the great territory, the Alleghanies would have been the Western border of the United States, and the pioneers who had crossed the mountains would be excluded from the benefits of the new Republic.

General George Rogers Clark was the realization of the ideal soldier—"cool, courageous, and sagacious, and at once the most powerful and the most picturesque character in the whole West." His clear foresight and splendid exploits have never received adequate recognition, either in the halls of legislation or in the pages of history. Firmly convinced of the necessity of striking a blow in the West, he journeyed to the capital of his State, where he argued the great importance and destiny of the West. The House of Burgesses could not be interested in the project. He next appeared before the Governor, Patrick Henry, from whom he received a commission to enlist seven companies for service in the West, subject to his orders. There was another secret commission, bearing date Williamsburg, Virginia, January 2, 1778, in which General Clark is given authority to capture, in the name of Virginia, the military posts held by the British in the Northwest. Now fully authorized, supplied with all needful authority, this patriot, to whom the Northwest is more largely indebted for the blessings of Republican government than is generally known, proceeded to Pittsburg, where he secured arms and ammunition, which he floated down the river to Kentucky. He then began the work of enlisting in his enterprise the hardy and resolute pioneers. The quota was soon filled, and in June, 1778, the Ohio was crossed and the thick wilderness of Illinois penetrated. Cahokia, Kaskaskia, and St. Vincent were successfully surprised and their garrisons captured. With tact equal to the ability of his generalship, General Clark won the friendship of the French inhabitants and made them the warm allies of the United States. By two other well directed expeditions against the Indians on the Miamis, he secured silence in that quarter.

In October, 1778, the Virginia House of Burgesses resolved that "all citizens who are already settled there, or shall hereafter be settled, on the west side of the Ohio, shall be included in the district of Kentucky, which shall be called Illinois county." Thus the northwest had been wrested from the British by George Rogers Clark in the name of Virginia, and at the close of the war the flag of the United States floated over its military posts. This subject has an important bearing when we come to consider Connecticut's claim to lands west of Pennsylvania covered by her colonial charter. In the negotiation of the treaty of 1783 at Paris, it was insisted by the British Commissioners that the Ohio should be the western boundary of the new country, and that all the territory west should remain vested in the British crown. It was found that the only tenable ground on which the American Commissioners could sustain claim to territory bounded by the lakes and the Mississippi was the fact that General George Rogers Clark had conquered the country, and the State of Virginia was in undisputed authority over it while the treaty was being made.

"The fact," says Burnet, "was confirmed and admitted, and was the chief ground on which the English commissioners abandoned their claim. The colonial charters which covered all this vast area, were wholly disregarded, because of their vagueness and conflicting character, resulting from a meager knowledge of the country at the time they were granted. We are interested in knowing what became of the adventurer and general whose name western people should write second only to Washington in the roll of Revolutionary heroes."

"It is a stain upon the honor of our country," says General Garfield*, "that such a man, the leader of the pioneers who made the first lodgment on the site now occupied by Louisville, who was in fact the founder of Kentucky, and who, by his personal foresight and energy gave nine States to the Republic, was allowed to sink under a load of debt incurred for the honor and glory of his country."

There is something pathetic in what Judge Burnet says in his notes on the Northwest Territory. He drove out twenty miles from Louisville, in 1799 (ten years after the Federal constitution had gone into exercise), to see the veteran hero whose military character he admired, and whose success was of such great consequence. "He had," says Burnet, "the appearance of a man born to command and fitted by nature for his destiny. There was a gravity and solemnity in his demeanor resembling that which so eminently distinguished the venerated father of his country. A person familiar with the lives and character of the military veterans of Rome in the days of her greatest power, might readily have selected this remarkable man, as a specimen of the model he had formed of them in his own mind; but he was rapidly falling victim to his extreme sensibility and to the ingratitude of his native State, under whose banner he had fought bravely and with great success. . . Yet the traveler who had read of his achievements, admired his character, and visited the theater of his brilliant deeds, discovers nothing indicating where his remains are deposited, and where he can go and pay a tribute of respect to the memory of the departed and gallant hero."

We have no apology for dwelling so long, comparatively, in the course of this hasty narrative, upon the achievements and character of General Clark. His achievements in behalf of liberty and republican government in the West was an individual enterprise. Washington carried the war for independence to a successful issue, but no

* Address at Burton, Ohio, 1873.

individual man was the father of the Revolution; George Rogers Clark was the originator of the idea and general of the enterprise which secured to the West the benefit of the successful issue of the war, and to the East the ownership of the fertile valley of the Mississippi and its tributaries. But for this Virginian the Congress of the Confederation would never have been embarrassed by the conflicting claims of five States to territory beyond the Ohio; Connecticut would have had no occasion to pass an act of cession in 1786, nor would she have had a reservation to dispose of in 1795 larger than the parent State; there would have been no motive for the settlement of loyal old Connecticut stock in this wealthy valley.

As soon as the Revolution had closed, schemes of Western settlement revived in all the coast States. But, before proceeding, it will be necessary to understand clearly the terms of the final settlement of the difficult problem of ownership. To that subject we will devote a short chapter.

CHAPTER III.

OWNERSHIP OF THE NORTHWEST.

The Claims of France—England's Claim—Treaty of Paris in 1763—Ohio as a Part of France and Canada—Conflicting Claims of States—The Northwest Territory Erected as Botetourt County—Illinois County—New York withdraws Claim—A Serious Evil Averted—Treaty of Fort Stanwix—Treaty of Fort McIntosh—Indian Tribes Recognized as Rightful Owners.

France, resting her claim upon the discovery and explorations of Robert Cavelier de la Salle and Marquette, upon the occupation of the country, and later, upon the provisions of several European treaties (those of Utrecht, Ryswick, Aix-la-Chapelle), was the first nation to formally lay claim to the soil of the territory now included within the boundaries of the State of Ohio as an integral portion of the valley of the Mississippi and of the Northwest. Ohio was thus a part of New France. After the treaty of Utrecht, in 1713, it was a part of the French province of Louisiana, which extended from the gulf to the northern lakes. The English claims were based on the priority of their occupation of the Atlantic coast, in lattitude corresponding to the territory claimed; upon an opposite construction of the same treaties above named; and last but not least, upon the alleged cession of the rights of the Indians. England's charters to all of the original colonies expressly extended their grants from sea to sea. The principal ground of claim by the English was by the treaties of purchase from the Six Nations, who, claiming to be conquerors of the whole country and therefore its possessors, asserted their right to dispose of it. A portion of the land was obtained through grants from the Six Nations and by actual purchase made at Lancaster, Pennsylvania, in 1744. France successfully resisted the claims of England, and maintained control of the territory between the Ohio and the lakes by force of arms until the treaty of Paris was consummated, in 1763. By the provisions of this treaty Great Britain came into possession of the disputed lands, and retained it until ownership was vested in the United States by the treaty of peace made just twenty years later. We have seen that Ohio was once a part of France and of the French province of Louisiana, and as a curiosity it may be of interest to refer to an act of the British Parliament, which made it an integral part of Canada. This was what has been known in history as the "Quebec Bill," passed in 1774. By the provisions of this bill the Ohio river was made the southwestern, and the Mississippi river the western boundary of Canada, thus placing the territory now constituting the States of Ohio, Indiana, Illinois, Michigan, and Wisconsin under the local jurisdiction of the Province of Quebec.

Virginia had asserted claims to the whole territory northwest of the Ohio, and New York, Massachusetts, Connecticut, and Pennsylvania, had claimed title to portions of the same.

In order to understand what follows, it will be necessary to state the basis of these several claims. It would be hard to find a section of territory so covered over with conflicting titles of ownership. When the royal charters were issued under which colonies were planted on the Atlantic coast, there was entire ignorance of the inland extent of the continent, which was the cause of overlapping of prescribed boundaries. Sir Francis Drake had reported during the reign of James I, that from the top of the mountains on the Isthmus of Panama he had seen both oceans. Upon this statement was based the belief that America was only a narrow strip of land, "the South sea," by which appellation the Pacific was known, not being very far removed from the Atlantic. It seems that the French explorations and discoveries did not become sufficiently known in England to correct these false notions of Western geography, for as late as 1740 the Duke of Newcastle addressed a letter to the "Iland of New England."

Virginia's colonial claim takes precedence of all the others. The London companies' charter, granted by James I., in 1609, commenced its boundaries at Old Point Comfort, on the Atlantic coast, and extended two hundred miles south and two hundred miles north from this point. The southern boundary was a line drawn from the southernmost point on the Atlantic, due west to the Pacific; the northwestern boundary was a line drawn diagonally across Pennsylvania and western New York, touching the eastern bend of Lake Erie, and continuing to the Arctic ocean; the Pacific ocean, then called the mythical South sea, constituted the western boundary. More than one-half the North American continent is embraced within these lines including the whole of the Northwest Territory. A charter was granted to the council of Plymouth, by James I., in 1620, upon which Massachusetts based her claim to lands in the West. This charter covered all the territory from the Atlantic to the Pacific between the fortieth and forty-eighth parallels of north latitude, an area of more than a million square miles, embracing all the present inhabited British possessions to the north of the United States, all of what is now New England, New York, one-half of New Jersey, nearly all of Pennsylvania, more than the northern half of Ohio, and the States and Territories west and north of the fortieth parallel. In 1664 Charles II. ceded to his brother, the Duke of York, a vaguely defined tract of country from Delaware bay to the river St. Croix, which it was insisted extended westward to the Pacific.

The same monarch issued a charter to William Penn, in 1681, covering, to some extent, the territory embraced in all the others and including a part of the present State of Ohio. Connecticut's charter, in which we are specially interested, dates two years earlier than that of New York, 1662, and was also granted by Charles II. The boundaries were Massachusetts on the north, Narragansett bay on the east, the sea on the south, and the Pacific ocean on the west; being a strip of land sixty-two miles wide extending from Narragansett bay to the Pacific, between latitude 41° and 42° 2' north—the north and south boundaries of the present Western Reserve.

George III. virtually repudiated all these charters in so far as they related to lands west of the Ohio, by issuing a proclamation forbidding all persons from intruding upon lands embraced within the valley of the Ohio. Some of them had been wholly or partially annulled by legally constituted courts. During the negotiation of the treaty of 1783, by which the independence of the States was confirmed, the American commissioners were unable to base any tenable claim to the West upon these charters, for when they were granted that region was actually occupied by a foreign power, and the legitimate ownership was not vested in the English crown until after the treaty of 1763 at Paris. This is why the American commissioners had to rely upon the conquests of George Rogers Clark and the actual occupation at that time by Virginia, as the only ground upon which their claim to the great territory of the Northwest could be maintained.

These claims had been for the most part held in abeyance during the period when the general ownership was vested in Great Britain, but were afterwards the cause of much embarrassment to the United States. Virginia, however, had not only claimed ownership of the soil, but attempted the exercise of civil authority in the disputed territory as early as 1769. In that year the Colonial House of Burgesses passed an act establishing the county of Botetourt, including a large part of what is now West Virginia and the whole territory northwest of the Ohio, and having, of course, as its western boundary the Mississippi river. This was a county of vast proportions—a fact of which the august authorities who ordered its establishment seem to have been fully aware, for they inserted the following among other provisions of the act, viz:

WHEREAS, The people situated upon the Mississippi in the said county of Botetourt will be very remote from the court-house, and must necessarily become a separate county as soon as their numbers are sufficient, which will probably happen in a short time, be it therefore enacted by the authority aforesaid that the inhabitants of that part of the said county of Botetourt, which lies on the said waters, shall be exempted from the payment of any levies to be laid by the said county for the purpose of building a court-house and prison for said county.

It was more in name than in fact, however, that Virginia had jurisdiction over this great county of Botetourt through the act of 1769. In 1778, after the splendid achievements of General George Rogers Clark—his subjugation of the British posts in the far West, and conquest of the whole country from the Ohio to the Mississippi—this territory was organized by the Virginia Legislature as the county of Illinois. Then, and not until then, did government have more than a nominal existence in this far extending but undeveloped country, containing a few towns and scattered population. The act, which was passed in October, contained the following provisions:

All the citizens of the Commonwealth of Virginia who are already settled, or shall hereafter settle on the western side of the Ohio, shall be included in a distinct county which shall be called Illinois; and the Governor of this Commonwealth, with the advice of the council, may appoint a county lieutenant or commander in chief, during pleasure, who shall appoint and commission so many deputy commandants, militia officers, and commissaries, as he shall think proper, in the different districts, during pleasure, all of whom before they enter into office, shall take the oath of fidelity to this Commonwealth, and the oath of office, according to the form of their own religion. And all officers to whom the inhabitants have been accustomed, necessary to the preservation of peace and the administration of justice, shall be chosen by a majority of citizens, in their respective districts, to be convened for that purpose by the county lieutenant or commandant, or his deputy, and shall be commissioned by the said county lieutenant or commandant in chief.

John Todd was appointed a county lieutenant and civil commandant of Illinois county, and served until his death (he was killed in the battle of Blue Lick, August 18, 1782), being succeeded by Timothy de Montbrun.

New York was the first of the several States claiming right and title in Western lands to withdraw the same in favor of the United States. Her charter, obtained March 2, 1664, from Charles II., embraced territory which had formerly been granted to Massachusetts and Connecticut. The cession of claim was made by James Duane, William Floyd, and Alexander McDougall, on behalf of the State, March 1, 1781.

Virginia, with a far more valid claim than New York, was the next State to follow New York's example. Her claim was founded upon certain charters granted to the colony by James I., and bearing date respectively, April 10, 1606,

May 23, 1609, and March 12, 1611; upon the conquest of the country by General George Rogers Clark; and upon the fact that she had also exercised civil authority over the territory. The General Assembly of Virginia, at its session beginning October 20, 1783, passed an act authorizing its delegates in Congress to convey to the United States in Congress assembled, all the right of that Commonwealth to the territory northwest of the Ohio river. The act was consummated on March 17, 1784. By one of the provisory clauses of this act was reserved the Virginia Military District, lying between the waters of the Scioto and Little Miami rivers.

Massachusetts ceded her claims without reservation, the same year that Virginia did hers (1784), though the action was not formally consummated until the 18th of April, 1785. The right of her title had been rested upon her charter, granted less than a quarter of a century from the arrival of the Mayflower, and embracing territory extending from the Atlantic to the Pacific.

Connecticut made what has been characterized as "the last tardy and reluctant sacrifice of State pretensions to the common good"* on the 14th of September, 1786. She ceded to Congress all her "right, title, interest, jurisdiction, and claim to the lands northwest of the Ohio, excepting the Connecticut Western Reserve," and of this tract jurisdictional claim was not ceded to the United States until May 30, 1800.

The happy, and, considering all complications, speedy adjustment of the conflicting claims of the States, and consolidation of all rights of title in the United States, was productive of the best results both at home and abroad. The young Nation, born in the terrible throes of the Revolution, went through a trying ordeal, and one of which the full peril was not realized until it had been safely passed. Serious troubles threatened to arise from the disputed ownership of the Western lands, and there were many who had grave fears that the well-being of the country would be impaired or at least its progress impeded. The infant Republic was at that time closely and jealously watched by all the governments of Europe, and nearly all of them would have rejoiced to witness the failure of the American experiment, but they were not destined to be gratified at the expense of the United States. As it was, the most palpable harm caused by delay was the retarding of settlement. The movement towards the complete cession of State claims was accelerated as much as possible by Congress. The National Legislature strenuously urged the several States, in 1784, to cede their lands to the confederacy to aid the payment of the debts incurred during the Revolution, and to promote the harmony of the Union.*

The States of New Jersey, Delaware, and Maryland had taken the initiative action and been largely instrumental in bringing about the cession of State claims. The fact that they had no foundation for pretensions of ownership save that they had equally, in proportion to their ability with the other States, assisted in wresting these lands from Great Britain, led them to protest against an unfair division of the territory—New Jersey had memorialized Congress in 1778, and Delaware followed in the same spirit in January, 1779. Later in the same year Maryland virtually reiterated the principles advanced by New Jersey and Delaware, though more positively. Her representatives in Congress emphatically and eloquently expressed their views and those of their constituents, in the form of instructions upon the matter of confirming the articles of confederation.

The extinguishment of the Indian claims to the soil of the Northwest was another delicate and difficult duty which devolved upon the Government. In the treaty of peace, ratified by Congress in 1784, no provision was made by Great Britain in behalf of the Indians—even their most faithful allies, the Six Nations. Their lands were included in the boundaries secured to the United States. They had suffered greatly during the war, and the Mohawks had been dispossessed of the whole of their beautiful valley. The only remuneration they received was a tract of country in Canada, and all of the sovereignty which Great Britain had exercised over them was transferred to the United States. The relation of the new government to these Indians was peculiar. In 1782 the British principle, in brief that "might makes right"—that discovery was equivalent to conquest, and that therefore the Nations retained only a possessory claim to their lands, and could only abdicate it to the govern-

---
* Statutes of Ohio; Chief Justice Chase.

* Albach's Annals of the West.

ment claiming sovereignty—was introduced into the general policy of the United States. The Legislature of New York was determined to expel the Six Nations entirely, in retaliation for their hostility during the war. Through the just and humane counsels of Washington and Schuyler, however, a change was wrought in the Indian policy, and the Continental Congress sought henceforward in its action to condone the hostilities of the past and gradually to dispossess the Indians of their lands by purchase, as the growth of the settlements might render it necessary to do so. It was in pursuance of this policy that the treaty of Fort Stanwix was made, October 22, 1784. By this treaty were extinguished the vague claims which the confederated tribes, the Mohawks, Onondagas, Senecas, Cayugas, Tuscarawas, and the Oneidas had for more than a century maintained to the Ohio valley. The commissioners of Congress in this transaction were Oliver Wolcott, Richard Butler and Arthur Lee. The Six Nations were represented by two of their ablest chiefs, Cornplanter and Red Jacket, the former for peace and the latter for war. La Fayette was present at this treaty and importuned the Indians to preserve peace with the Americans.

By the treaty of Fort McIntosh, negotiated on the 21st of January, 1785, by George Rogers Clark, Richard Butler, and Arthur Lee, was secured the relinquishment of all claims to the Ohio valley, held by the Delawares, Ottawas, Wyandots, and Chippewas. The provisions of this treaty were as follows:

ARTICLE 1st—Three chiefs, one from the Wyandot and two from the Delaware nations, shall be delivered up to the Commissioners of the United States, to be by them retained till all the prisoners taken by the said Nations, or any of them, shall be restored.

ARTICLE 2d— The said Indian nations, and all of their tribes, do acknowledge themselves to be under the protection of the United States, and of no other sovereign whatever.

ARTICLE 3d — The boundary line between the United States and the Wyandot and Delaware nations shall begin at the mouth of the river Cuyahoga, and run thence up the said river to the portage between that and the Tuscarawas branch of the Muskingum; then down the said branch to the forks at the crossing-place above Fort Laurens; then westwardly to the portage of the Big Miami, which runs into the Ohio, at the mouth of which branch the fort stood which was taken by the French in the year one thousand seven hundred and fifty-two; then along the said portage to the Great Miami or Owl river, and down the southeast side of the same to its mouth; thence down the south shore of Lake Erie to the mouth of the Cuyahoga, where it began.

ARTICLE 4th—The United States allot all the lands contained within the said lines to the Wyandot and Delaware nations, to live and to hunt on, and to such of the Ottawa nation as now live thereon; saving and reserving for the establishment of trading posts six miles square at the mouth of the Miami or Owl river, and the same at the portage of that branch of the Miami which runs into the Ohio, and the same on the cape of Sandusky, where the fort formerly stood, and also two miles square on the lower rapids of Sandusky river; which posts, and the land annexed to them, shall be for the use and under the Government of the United States.

ARTICLE 5th—If any citizen of the United States, or other person not being an Indian, shall attempt to settle on any of the lands allotted to the Wyandot and Delaware nations in this treaty, except on the lands reserved to the United States, in the preceding article, such persons shall forfeit the protection of the United States, and the Indians may punish him as they please.

ARTICLE 6th—The Indians who sign this treaty, as well in behalf of all their tribes as of themselves, do acknowledge the lands east, south, and west of the lands described in the third article, so far as the said Indians claimed the same, to belong to the United States, and none of the tribes shall presume to settle upon the same or any part of it.

ARTICLE 7th—The post of Detroit, with a district beginning at the mouth of the River Rosine on the west side of Lake Erie and running west six miles up the southern bank of the said river; thence northerly, and always six miles west of the strait, till it strikes Lake St. Clair, shall be reserved to the sole use of the United States.

ARTICLE 8th—In the same manner the post of Michilimackinac, with its dependencies, and twelve miles square about the same, shall also be reserved to the use of the United States.

ARTICLE 9th—If any Indian or Indians shall commit a robbery or murder on any citizen of the United States, the tribe to which such offenders may belong shall be bound to deliver them up at the nearest post, to be punished according to the ordinance of the United States.

ARTICLE 10th—The Commissioners of the United States, in pursuance of the humane and liberal views of Congress, upon the treaty's being signed, will direct goods to be distributed among the different tribes for their use and comfort.

The treaty of Fort Finney, at the mouth of the Great Miami, January 31, 1786, secured the cession of whatever claim to the Ohio valley was held by the Shawnees. George Rogers Clark, Richard Butler, and Samuel H. Parsons[*] were the commissioners of the United States. James Monroe, then a member of Congress from Virginia and afterwards President of the United States, accompanied General Butler, in the month of October preceding the treaty, as far as

[*] General Samuel H. Parsons, an eminent Revolutionary character, was one of the first band of Marietta pioneers, and was appointed first as associate and then as chief judge of the Northwest Territory. He was drowned in the Big Beaver river, November 17, 1789, while returning to his home in Marietta, from the North, where he had been making the treaty which secured the aboriginal title to the soil of the Connecticut Western Reserve.

Limestone† (now Maysville, Kentucky). The party, it is related, stopped at the mouth of the Muskingum and (in the words of General Butler's journal,) "left fixed in a locust tree" a letter recommending the building of a fort on the Ohio side. By the terms of this treaty the Shawnees were confined to the lands west of the Great Miami. Hostages were demanded from the Indians, to remain in the possession of the United States until all prisoners should be returned, and the Shawnees were compelled to acknowledge the United States as the sole and absolute sovereign of all the territory ceded to them, in the treaty of peace, by Great Britain. The clause embodying the latter condition excited the jealousy of the Shawnees. They went away dissatisfied with the treaty, though assenting to it. This fact, and the difficulty that was experienced even while the treaty was making, of preventing depredations by white borderers, argued unfavorably for the future. The treaty was productive of no good results whatever. Hostilities were resumed in the spring of 1786, and serious and wide-spread war was threatened.

Congress had been acting upon the policy that the treaty of peace with Great Britain had invested the United States with the fee simple of all the Indian lands, but urged now by the stress of circumstances the Government radically changed its policy, fully recognizing the Indians as the rightful proprietors of the soil, and on the 2d of July, 1787, appropriated the sum of $26,000 for the purpose of extinguishing Indian claims to lands already ceded to the United States, and for extending a purchase beyond the limits heretofore fixed by treaty.

Under this policy other relinquishments of Ohio territory were effected through the treaties of Fort Harmar, held by General Arthur St. Clair, January 9, 1789, the treaty of Greenville, negotiated by General Anthony Wayne, August 3, 1795, and various other treaties made at divers times from 1796 to 1818.* The Cuyahoga and the portage path between it and the Tuscarawas, constituted the boundary line between the Indians and the United States upon the Reserve,

† General Butler's Journal in Craig's Olden Time, October, 1847.

*It is a fact worthy of note, and one of which we may well be proud, that the title to every foot of Ohio soil was honorably acquired from the Indians.

until July 4, 1805. On that day a treaty was made at Fort Industry, by the terms of which the Indian title to all the lands embraced in the Reserve was extinguished.

CHAPTER IV.
SALE OF THE WESTERN RESERVE.

The Hesitancy of Purchasers—Fear of Title—Sale of the Salt Spring Tract—Death of General Parsons and Failure to Pay for Lands—Sale to the Connecticut Land Company.

Connecticut was the most persistent of all the States in the assertion of her claim to the territory within the boundaries described in her charter. The first decisive contest was with Pennsylvania, more than half of which lies within these limits. Both States strove for occupancy of the disputed soil, and Connecticut went so far as to sell to certain individuals seventeen townships situated on the Susquehanna river. The tract was organized into a civil township called Westmoreland, and attached to the probate district and county of Litchfield, Connecticut. Representatives from Westmoreland occupied seats in the Connecticut Legislature. Popular feeling in Pennsylvania ran high; the Legislature protested the legality of the titles, and when the Revolution had closed sent an armed force to drive the Connecticut settlers from their homes. This radical procedure was carried so far as to involve the shedding of blood. A softer method of settlement was, however, finally resorted to, the controversy being submitted to commissioners appointed by Congress, as provided for in the articles of Confederation. The court sat at Trenton, New Jersey, in 1787, and soon reached a decision favorable to Pennsylvania. The title to lands lying west of Pennsylvania was not involved and consequently remained in dispute.

It has been already noted that Connecticut a year previous to this decision had yielded to the appeal of Congress and in some degree imitated the patriotic example of Virginia, Massachusetts, Pennsylvania and New York, by releasing all claim to territory west of a north and south line one hundred and twenty miles west of the established west boundary of Pennsylvania. The decision of the Trenton commission left the tract sixty-two miles wide and one hundred and twenty miles long, which at that time was first designated the Connecticut Western Reserve, the only territory beyond New York to which the State retained the shadow of a title. The deed of cession of 1786 can not be construed to have been a settlement of the ownership of the Reserve. It was only the relinquishment of a part of a claim which nowhere outside of Connecticut was believed to have a valid basis. The State's claim to land in Pennsylvania was far more tenable, yet it was overthrown by a legally constituted court. These facts have an important bearing upon the history of the Reserve. A good system of land titles is more necessary to the permanent prosperity of a country than well organized civil government.

People are loath to run any risk involving the security of their homes. This is why Connecticut begged purchasers at fifty cents an acre while great corporations were offering double that amount for tracts bordering the Ohio. Having been shorn of her pretensions in Pennsylvania, the State made haste to secure her reserved claims in Ohio by actual occupation. A resolution was passed by the Legislature, authorizing the appointment of three persons who should cause a survey to be made of the tract as far west as the Cuyahoga and Tuscarawas branch of the Muskingum. This committee was also authorized to negotiate a sale. It was provided that five hundred acres in each township should be reserved for the support of the gospel ministry, and five hundred acres for the support of schools. The first minister who settled in a township was entitled to two hundred and forty acres. The General Assembly agreed to guarantee the preservation of peace and good order among the settlers.

The only sale made under this act prior to the purchase by the Connecticut Land Company in 1795, was executed in 1788, to General Samuel Holden Parsons, of Middletown. This purchase embraced a tract of twenty-five thousand acres, and soon became known as the Salt Spring tract. The existence of a saline spring, or more properly a salt lick, on this tract had long been known. It is marked on Evans' map, which was drawn in 1755, and during the Revolution the pioneers of Western Pennsylvania erected cabins and works. The cabins were soon after destroyed by Indians, but the works remained until after the Reserve was permanently settled. Judge Augustus Porter, who was one of the surveying party in 1796, found at this point "a small piece of open ground, say two or three acres, and a plank vat sixteen or eighteen feet square by four or five feet deep, set in the ground, which was full of water and kettles for boiling salt; the number he could not ascertain, but the vat seemed full of them. An Indian and a squaw were boiling water for salt, but from appearances with poor success."* The first settlers in 1799 found the foundations of destroyed log cabins and ruins of stone furnaces.

The Indians, in all this part of the country, had large iron kettles for boiling maple sap and making sugar, the kettles being similar to those found at the salt works, and probably taken from there. From this it appears that the industry was at one time carried on quite extensively, but could not have been otherwise than laborious and unprofitable. Soon after the first settlement of the Connecticut pioneers in the Mahoning valley, not only the high price of salt, but also the great difficulty of obtaining it at any price, led to an effort to revive its manufacture; but the solution of salt in the water was found to be so small that it cost more than six dollars per bushel, the price of the commercial article. How toilsome it must have been, therefore, for the Pennsylvania pioneers to travel nearly a hundred miles, breaking their own path through a forest, and guarding against attacks of savage enemies, and here in the midst of an inhospitable wilderness, by the slow process of evaporation in kettles in rude furnaces, obtain enough salt to supply the needs of their families! What must have been the anxieties and fears for the safety of wives and children left in the cabins at home, liable at any time to fall victims to the merciless denizens of the forest!

There is no evidence that General Parsons established works or revived those already established. It is probable that he did not. He was doubtless aware of the existence of these springs before the Revolution, for, as a member of the committee on colonial land claims, it was his duty to examine into the geography of the West as well as old charters. As a member of that committee he did his State good service, for

*Barr Mss.

he was one of the best lawyers in New England. It was very largely through his management, both before and after the Revolution, that a policy was adopted which finally resulted after his death in the procurement of a secure title. It was this same General Parsons who first suggested the advisability of calling a colonial congress, and Samuel Adams, acting upon his suggestion, issued the call which resulted in the formation of that historic body which is perpetuated in the present constitutional Congress. At the outbreak of the war he entered the army as colonel and continued in the service until the establishment of peace, having been promoted to the rank of major-general. In 1786 he made a journey to the mouth of the Miami as one of three commissioners to treat with the Indians in that quarter. The route of travel at this time was overland to Pittsburg, thence down the Ohio. He probably made inquiry at this time in Pennsylvania concerning the resources of the Reserve and the salt springs which the settlers were accustomed to visit.

General Parsons was made one of the first three judges of the Northwest Territory, and subsequently became chief justice. He had taken active interest in advancing enterprises of western emigration, and his knowledge of the resources and destiny of the wilderness west of the Ohio, probably had more influence in determining him to engage in speculation than the hope of making a fortune out of a salt spring. The salt water might have its influence upon the development and settlement of the country; hence the location by Parsons of his purchase in its vicinity. The description given in the patent reads as if the survey had been made, although no lines had been run, at least under official direction. The description is as follows: "Beginning at the northeast corner of the first township in the third range, thence northerly on the west line of the second range to forty-one degrees and twelve minutes north latitude; thence west three miles, thence southerly parallel to the west line of Pennsylvania two miles and one-half, thence west three miles to the west line of said third range; thence southerly parallel to the west line of Pennsylvania, to the north line of the first township in the third range; thence east to the first bound."

This tract lies in the civil townships of Austintown, Lordstown, Jackson, and Weathersfield. The description was made out with reference to townships six miles square, as originally contemplated in the act authorizing the survey. General Parsons proceeded to make sales and deeds to several parties of portions of his tract. His patent was recorded in the office of the Secretary of State at Hartford. In July, 1788, the whole Northwest Territory was erected into the county of Washington and the deeds issued by General Parsons were recorded at Marietta, where he lived. When Trumbull county was erected they were again recorded at Warren, as doubts existed as to the validity of the jurisdiction of Governor St. Clair and authorities created by him over the lands claimed by Connecticut. The whole tract, however, was destined to revert to Connecticut. Judge Parsons left Marietta in the fall of 1789 to act as commissioner for the State of Connecticut, to conclude a treaty with the Indians on the Reserve. Where the conference was held is not definitely known. He started on his homeward journey in a canoe, but was drowned in attempting to pass Beaver Falls November 17, 1789. His heirs, either on account of inability or lack of confidence in the speculation, failed to make the back payments, so that the patent, with all the deeds based upon it, was returned to the State.

The Salt spring or Parsons tract was the only sale made under the resolution of 1787. There were two reasons for this; one—the inability of the State to give a perfect title—has already been noted. The second reason was the great difficulty of access to the Reserve. The French war had opened roads to Fort Pitt, and after that the Ohio was more or less a highway of travel, especially so after the settlement of Kentucky. Washington, before the Revolution, described the fertile bottoms touching the river. The Ohio Land company had previously received extensive grants in the immediate valley, and other projects of companies and settlements in that locality attracted or more properly absorbed the discussion of western affairs. After the Revolution had closed, while Connecticut was stingily and jealously nursing her feeble claim to the northern wilderness, unexplored except by traders, scarce known in the east, Congress was industriously preparing the way for immigration and settlement upon the lands on the Ohio

Virginia was also opening the way for settlers on the Scioto. It was the reports which United States surveyors carried back to New England in 1785, which determined the Ohio Company to locate its purchase at the mouth of the Muskingum. When a colony was planted there in 1788, the Reserve was without a white inhabitant if we except the few traders who were temporarily stationed at the mouth of the Cuyahoga and on the lake shore. All was a wild, weird, desolate, damp wilderness.

The Connecticut Legislature, in 1792, made an important grant of half a million acres off the western end of the Reserve to those persons or their heirs who had suffered losses in consequence of British raids and depredations in the State during the Revolution. Upwards of two thousand of the inhabitants of Greenwich, Norwalk, Fairfield, Danbury, New Haven, New London, Richfield, and Groton had suffered severe losses, mainly by fire. The tract for this reason was called the "Fire Lands." Each sufferer received a part of the whole tract in proportion to the estimated amount of his loss. The Fire Lands embrace all of Huron and Erie counties and the township of Ruggles, in Ashland county.

As no one except Parsons had purchased lands under the resolution of the Connecticut Legislature of 1787, it was determined to adopt a new mode of disposing of the western lands in May, 1795.

Wild land speculation fever had for ten years been epidemic in New England, and for seven years had been sweeping to the West the flower of her veteran soldiery. Serious difficulties with the Indians had in some measure repulsed the tide of emigration between 1771 and the fall of 1794, but the victory of General Wayne at Fallen Timbers, by which the Indian power was effectually broken, had the effect of the destruction of a dam ; the accumulated energy of four years rushed wildly westward until it expended itself upon the rugged forest. Connecticut could have selected no better time to conclude a favorable sale. The Resolution of May 30th read as follows:

RESOLVED by this assembly that a committee be appointed to receive any proposals that may be made by any person or persons, whether inhabitants of the United States or others, for the purchase of lands belonging to this State lying west of the west line of Pennsylvania, as claimed by that State, and the said committee are hereby fully authorised and empowered in the name and behalf of this State to negotiate with any person or persons on the subject of such proposals. And also to form and complete any contract or contracts for the sale of said lands and to make and execute under their hands and seals to the purchaser or purchasers a deed or deeds duly authenticated, quitting in behalf of this State all right, title, and interest, judicial and territorial, in and to the said lands, to him or them and to his or their heirs forever. That before the executing of said deed or deeds, the purchaser or purchasers shall give their note or bond payable to the treasurer of this State, for the purchase money, carrying an interest of six per centum, payable annually, to commence from the date thereof, or from such future period not exceeding two years from the date, as circumstances in the opinion of the committee may require and as may be agreed upon then, and the said purchaser or purchasers with good and sufficient sureties, inhabitants of this State or with a sufficient deposit of bank or other stock in the United States or of the particular States, which note or bond shall be taken payable at a period not more remote than five years from the date, or if in annual installments so that the last installment be payable within two years from the date, either in specie or in six per cent., three per cent., or deferred stock of the United States, at the discretion of the committee. That if the committee shall find that it will be most beneficial to the State or its citizens to form several contracts for the sale of lands, they shall not consummate any of the said contracts apart by themselves while the others lie in a train of negotiation only, but all the contracts, which, taken together, shall comprise the whole quantity of said lands shall be consummated together, and the purchasers shall hold their respective parts or proportion as tenants in common of the whole tract or territory, and not in severally. The said committee, in whatever manner they shall find it best to sell their lands, whether by entire contract or several contracts, shall in no case be at liberty to sell the whole quantity for a principal sum less than one million dollars in specie, or if the day of payment be given, for a sum of less value than $1,000,000 in specie, with interest at six per centum per annum from the time of such sale.

The committee of eight, one from each of the eight counties in the State, appointed to carry this resolution into execution, consisted of John Treadwell, James Wadsworth, Marvin Waite, William Edmonds, Thomas Grosveno, Aaron Austin, Elijah Hubbard, and Sylvester Gilbert. It will be seen that Connecticut did not offer to guarantee a clear title to any purchaser, but merely offered a quit claim deed. Connecticut people did not consider this a serious obstacle, for they had no doubt of the tenability of the State's claim. But the situation was viewed in a different light outside of the State, Connecticut's pretensions being everywhere doubted and in some States ridiculed. Nevertheless the speculation fever prevailed so generally that several parties entered the field as purchasers. Benjamin Gorham and Oliver Phelps owned an extensive tract in Western New York which they sold to

Robert Livingston, of Philadelphia. Phelps being a Connecticut man subsequently made the heaviest investment in the Reserve. He had several years before, when the New York purchase was made, advocated the advantage of striking deeper into the forest. Robert Livingston, having disposed of the New York purchase to a Holland company, entered as a competitor of the Connecticut men, but was persuaded to accept for the Philadelphia company which he represented all the surplus over three million acres. The Reserve at that time was supposed to contain more than four million acres. The summer was spent in negotiations, which were terminated in a bargain September 2, 1795. Forty-eight persons had presented themselves who were willing to take the entire tract at the sum of $1,200,000. The names of the purchasers and the respective proportions subscribed are:

Joseph Howland } Daniel L. Coit	$30,461
Elias Morgan } Daniel L. Coit	51,402
Caleb Atwater	22,846
Daniel Holbrook	8,750
Joseph Williams	15,231
William Low	10,500
William Judd	16,250
Elisha Hyde } Uria Tracey	57,400
James Johnson	30,000
Samuel Mather, Jr	18,461
Ephraim Kirby } Elijah Boardman } Uriel Holmes, Jr.	60,000
Oliver Phelps } Gideon Granger	80,000
Solomon Griswold	10,000
William Hart	30,462
Henry Champion (2d)	85,675
Ashur Miller	34,000
Robert C. Johnson	60,000
Ephraim Root	42,000
Nehemiah Hubbard, Jr	19,039
Solomon Cowles	10,000
Oliver Phelps	168,185
Asahel Hathaway	12,000
John Caldwell } Peleg Sanford	15,000
Timothy Burr	15,231
Luther Loomis } Ebenezer King, Jr.	44,318
William Lyman } John Stoddard } David King	27,730
Moses Cleveland	32,600
Samuel P. Lord	14,092
Roger Newberry } Enoch Perkins } Jonathan Brace	38,000
Ephraim Starr	17,415
Sylvanus Griswold	1,683
Jabez Stocking } Joshua Stow	11,423
Titus Street	22,846
James Bull } Aaron Olmstead } John Wyles	30,000
Pierpont Edwards	60,000
Amounting to	$1,200,000

No survey had yet been made, so that it was impossible to determine the number of acres to which each was entitled. The committee of eight made out deeds to each of the purchasers or association of purchasers, of as many twelve-hundred thousandths in common of the entire tract as they had subscribed dollars.

These deeds and the subsequent drafts were recorded in the office of the Secretary of the State of Connecticut and afterwards transferred to the recorder's office at Warren. They are very long, reciting the substance of the resolution authorizing the sale and mode of sale to the grantees. It does not appear that any part of the consideration was paid in hand.* Thus the State made final disposition of all her western lands except the tract purchased by General Parsons, which reverted in consequence of non-payment of this stipulated price. This tract was divided up as follows and afterwards sold by order of the legislature, the deeds being issued by the Secretary of State.

The whole purchase is surveyed into thirteen tracts, of different sizes and forms, numbered from four to sixteen inclusive, and a four thousand acre reservation lying in the vicinity of tract sixteen, is subdivided and allotted into lots, with two series of numbers. One series—number one to number twenty two inclusive,—lies part in Lordstown and part in Jackson, and the other series, number one to number thirty seven inclusive, lies part in Weathersfield and part in Austintown, besides a gore of said tract number sixteen, about fifty seven rods wide, along the west side of the four thousand acre tract. The four thousand acre salt spring reservation tract is subdivided and allotted into lots, numbered from one to twenty-four inclusive.

CHAPTER V.
CONNECTICUT LAND COMPANY.
Terms of the Association—Survey and Division—Proceedings of the Directors.

The number of original parties to the purchase of September 2, 1795, was thirty-five, although there were forty-eight individuals. There

*Webb MSS.

were, however, other persons who did not appear as purchasers whose capital was represented, so that the whole number of persons was fifty-seven. These constituted the Connecticut Land company.

The members of this company effected an organization on the 5th day of September, 1795. This was done at Hartford, Connecticut. They adopted articles of association and agreement, fourteen in number. Their first article designated the name by which they chose to be known. Article number two provided for the appointment of a committee, consisting of three of their number—John Caldwell, John Brace, and John Morgan—to whom each purchaser was required to execute a deed in trust of his share in the purchase, receiving in exchange a certificate from these trustees showing that the holder thereof was entitled to a certain share in the Connecticut Western Reserve, which certificate of share was transferable by proper assignment. The form of this certificate is given in Article IX.

Article III. provides for the appointment of seven directors, and empowers them to procure an extinguishment of the Indian title of said Reserve; to cause a survey of the lands to be made into townships containing each sixteen thousand acres; to fix on a township in which the first settlement shall be made, to survey the township thus selected into lots, and to sell such lots to actual settlers only; to erect in said township a saw-mill and a grist-mill at the expense of the company; and to lay out and sell five other townships to actual settlers only.

Article IV. obliges the surveyors to keep a regular field book, in which they shall accurately describe the situation, soil, waters, kinds of timber, and natural productions of each township; said book to be kept in the office of the clerk of said directors, and open at all times to the inspection of each proprietor.

Article V. provides for the appointment by the directors of a clerk, and names his duties.

Article VI. makes it obligatory upon the trustees to give each of the proprietors a certificate as named above.

Article VII. imposes a tax of ten dollars upon each share to enable the directors to accomplish the duties assigned to them.

Article VIII. divides the purchase into four hundred shares, and gives each shareholder one vote for every share up to forty shares, when he shall thereafter have but one vote for every five shares, except as to the question of the time of making a partition of the territory, in determining which every share shall be entitled to one vote.

Article X. fixes the dates of several future meetings to be held.

Article XI. reads: "And, whereas, some of the proprietors may choose that their proportions of said Reserve should be divided to them in one lot or location, it is agreed that in case one-third in value of the owners shall, after a survey of said Reserve in townships signify to said directors or meeting a request that such third part be set off in manner aforesaid, that said directors may appoint three commissioners, who shall have power to divide the whole of said purchase into three parts, equal in value, according to quantity, quality, and situation; and when said commissioners shall have so divided said Reserve, and made a report in writing of their doings to said directors, describing precisely the boundaries of each part, the said directors shall call a meeting of said proprietors, giving the notice required by these articles; and at such meeting the said three parts shall be numbered, and the number of each part shall be written on a separate piece of paper, and shall, in the presence of such meeting, be by the chairman of said meeting put into a box, and a person, appointed by said meeting for that purpose, shall draw out of said box one of said numbers, and the part designated by such number shall be aparted to such person or persons requesting such a severance, and the said trustees shall, upon receiving a written direction from said directors for that purpose, execute a deed to such person or persons accordingly; after which such person or persons shall have no power to act in said company."

Article XII. empowers the company to raise money by tax on the proprietors, and to dispose, upon certain conditions, of so much of a proprietor's interest, in case of delinquency, as shall be necessary to satisfy the assessment.

Article XIII. provides for the appointment by the company of a successor to a trustee who may have caused a vacancy in the office by death.

Article XIV. places the directors in the transaction of any business of the company under the control of the latter "by a vote of at least three-fourths of the interest of said company."

The following gentlemen were chosen to constitute the board of directors: Oliver Phelps, Henry Champion (2d), Moses Cleaveland, Samuel W. Johnson, Ephraim Kirby, Samuel Mather, Jr., and Roger Newbury. At a meeting held in April, 1796, Ephraim Root was made clerk, and continued to act in this capacity until the dissolution of the company, in 1809. A moderator was chosen at each meeting, and changes of directors were made from time to time.

NAMES OF MEMBERS OF THE CONNECTICUT LAND COMPANY.

The following are the names of the persons who subscribed to the "Articles of Association and Agreement constituting the Connecticut Land Company":

Asher Miller,
Uriel Holmes, Jr.,
Ephraim Starr,
Luther Loomis,
Solomon Cowles,
Daniel L. Coit,
Pierpont Edwards,
Titus Street,
R. C. Johnson,
Ephraim Kelley,
Gideon Granger, Jr.,
Moses Cleaveland,
Elijah Boardman,
Samuel Mather, Jr.
Nehemiah Hubbard, Jr.,
Joseph Williams,
William M. Bliss,
William Battle,
Timothy Burr,
Joseph C. Yates,
William Law,
Elisha Hyde,
William Lyman,
Daniel Holbrook,
Thaddeus Leveett,
Roger Newbury,

Roger Newbury for Justin Ely,
Elisha Strong,
Joshua Stow,
Jabez Stocking,
Jonathan Brace,
Joseph Howland,
James Bull,
William Judd,
Samuel P. Lord,
Oliver Phelps,
Zephaniah Swift,
Enoch Perkins,
William Hart,
Caleb Atwater,
Lemuel Storrs,
Peleg Sandford,
John Stoddard,
Benajah Kent,
Eliphalet Austin,
Samuel Mather,
James Johnson,
Uriah Tracey,
Ephraim Root,
Solomon Griswold,
Ebenezer King, Jr.,
Elijah White.

In behalf of themselves and their associates in Albany, New York.

Before this organized body of men lay the important work of obtaining a perfect title to their purchase; of causing a survey of the lands to be made; of making partition of the same; and then of inducing colonies of men to undertake the settlement.

To these tasks the purchasers addressed themselves in right good earnest. In order to make sound their title they must obtain from the United States a release of the Government's claim—a very just and formidable one—and to extinguish the title of the Indian, whose right to the soil rested upon the substantial basis of actual occupancy. Whatever interest Virginia, Massachusetts, and New York may have had in the Western Reserve had passed to the United States, and if none of the claiming States had title, the dominion and ownership were transferred to the General Government by the treaty made with Great Britain at the close of the Revolution. There was, therefore, a very reasonable solicitude upon the part of the Connecticut Land company lest the claim of the United States would, if issue were made, be proven to be of greater validity than that of Connecticut, the company's grantor. Another difficulty made itself felt. When an attempt was made to settle the Reserve, it was discovered that it was so far removed from Connecticut as to make it impracticable for that State to extend her laws over the same, or to make new ones for the government of the inhabitants. Congress had provided in the ordinance of 1787 for the government of the Northwestern Territory; but to admit jurisdiction by the General Government over this part of that territory would be a virtual acknowledgment of the validity of the Government's title, and therefore an indirect proof of the insufficiency of the company's title. The right to such jurisdiction was therefore denied, and Connecticut was urged to obtain from the United States a release of the Governmental claim. The result was that Congress, on the 28th day of April, 1800, authorized the President to execute and deliver, on the part of the United States, letters patent to the Governor of Connecticut, releasing all right and title to the soil of the Reserve, upon condition that Connecticut should, on her part, forever renounce and release to the United States entire and complete civil jurisdiction over the Reserve. Thus Connecticut obtained from the United States her claim to the soil, and transmitted and confirmed it to the Connecticut Land company and to those who had purchased from it, and jurisdiction for the purposes of government vested in the United States.

THE EXTINGUISHMENT OF THE INDIAN TITLE.

At the close of the Revolution the General Government sought by peaceable means to acquire the red man's title to the soil northwest of the Ohio. On the 21st of January, 1785, a treaty was concluded at Fort McIntosh with four of the Indian tribes—the Wyandots, Delawares, Chippewas and Ottawas. By this treaty the Cuyahoga and the portage between it and the Tuscarawas were agreed upon as the boundary on the Reserve between the United States and the Indians. All east of the Cuyahoga was, in fact, ceded to the United States. The Indians soon became dissatisfied, and refused to comply with the terms of the treaty.

On January 9, 1789, another treaty was concluded at Fort Harmar, at the mouth of the Muskingum, between Arthur St. Clair, acting for the United States, and the Wyandot, Delaware, Chippewa and Sac nations, by which the terms of the former treaty were renewed and confirmed. But only a short time elapsed before the Indians violated their compact. Peaceful means failing, it became necessary to compel obedience by the use of arms. Vigorous means for relief and protection for the white settler were called for and enforced. At first the Indians were successful; but in 1794 General Wayne, at the head of thirty-five hundred men, encountered the enemy on the 20th day of August, on the Maumee, and gained a decisive victory. Nearly every chief was slain. The treaty of Greenville was the result. General Wayne met in grand council twelve of the most powerful northwestern tribes, and the Indians again yielded their claims to the lands east of the Cuyahoga, and made no further effort to regain them.

The Cuyahoga river and the portage between it and the Tuscarawas constituted the boundary between the United States and the Indians upon the Reserve until July 4, 1805. On that day a treaty was made at Fort Industry, by which the Indian title to all the Reserve west of the Cuyahoga was purchased. Thus the Indian title to the soil of the Reserve was forever set at rest, and no flaw now existed in the Connecticut Land company's claim to the ownership of the lands of the Reserve.

SURVEY OF THE WESTERN RESERVE.

The title having been perfected, the company made preparations to survey the portion of the Reserve lying east of the Cuyahoga. In the early part of May, 1796, the company fitted out an expedition for this purpose, of which Moses Cleaveland was the leader of a company—all told of about forty men—five of them surveyors, one a physician, and the rest chainmen and axemen.

By previous arrangement they commenced their journey, ascending the Mohawk in four flat bottomed boats, proceeding by way of Oswego, Niagara and Queenstown to Buffalo, reaching the soil of the Reserve on the 4th of July.

ARRIVAL OF THE SURVEYORS.

The records of the Ashtabula Historical and Philosophical Society contain an interesting narrative made by Judge Stow of the journey of the surveying party, and from this we gather what follows in relation to the expedition.

At the time the party commenced its journey, Fort Oswego, which they were compelled to pass, was garrisoned by the British. They anticipated difficulty in being able to get beyond the fort. At Fort Stanwix, however, they had the good fortune to be overtaken by Captain Cozzens, who had been sent by the British Minister, Mr. Bond, with open dispatches to all His Majesty's officers and subjects, announcing the ratification by both Governments of Jay's treaty, and that the navigation of the lakes should henceforth be free to all American vessels. They now anticipated no trouble. Captain Cozzens took passage on board Judge Stow's boat, and they ascended Wood creek toward Lake Ontario. When arrived at Oswego, however, permission to pass the fort was denied on the ground that his instructions were positive, and without the sanction of his superior officer, then at Niagara, he was powerless to grant the request.

Mr. Stow's instructions from the Land company were not to attempt to run by the fort in any event; but, if permission were withheld, to lie in wait until further orders from the company should be received. But the climate was unhealthy; the soldiers in the garrison were many of them sick, and some of them dying; time was precious, and the anxiety to reach the Reserve was great. After much deliberation, it was almost the unanimous voice of the party to attempt the passage. The boats were floated down to within four miles of the fort, when they were hauled into a small bay and secreted among the bushes. One of the boats was then relieved of the greater part of its cargo, manned with double oars, and, with the agent, Mr. Stow, on board, moved down to the fort. The British officer in command of the fort evidently supposed that the boat was on its way to Fort Niagara to obtain the consent of the officer in command at that point to make the passage, and the crew were not disturbed. The garrison was thrown off its guard by this stratagem, and, at dead of night, the other boats passed the fort unobserved, and joined their companions on the waters of Lake Ontario. The following incident of the voyage will be of interest:

The first boat had proceeded as far as to Sodus, where the little fleet intended to make a harbor. A sudden storm arose and overtook the boats before they could reach Sodus. Night had come on, and the darkness was intense; the storm became more and more violent, and the situation was one of eminent peril. Beacon-fires were built by the crew of the boat which had landed, but it was impossible for the rest of the boats to make the harbor. The situation of the agent at this moment was intensely painful. His companions were in a perilous situation, and it was out of his power to afford them any relief. They were but a short distance from a dangerous shore, and the next billow might dash their little bark in pieces. Besides, he had assumed the responsibility of running by the fort, and, although successful in that attempt, yet if the boats were cast away or lost, the whole responsibility of the catastrophe would rest upon him. In this state of suspense and alarm, a man from one of the boats came running from the beach with the intelligence that all was lost. No anxiety could be greater or suffering more intense than that of the men on shore. They ran up and down the beach to see if it were not possible to render some assistance or gain some tidings from their companions. They found thrown upon the shore a gun and oar, which they recognized as belonging to Captain Beard, who was in charge of one of the boats. This increased their alarm. The next moment, however, they met Captain Beard himself, and anxiously asked if all were lost. He replied that nothing was lost but a gun and an oar! No lives were lost. The boats sustained much injury, and one was so badly damaged it could not be repaired, and was abandoned.

Without more adventure worthy of note Mr. Stow and his comrades reached the mouth of Conneaut creek in the early part of July, 1796.

The names of this surveying party, a company of fifty-two persons, all told, are as follows: Moses Cleaveland, the Land Company's agent; Joshua Stow, commissary; Augustus Porter, principal surveyor; Seth Pease, Moses Warren, Amos Spafford, Milton Holley, and Richard M. Stoddard, surveyors; Theodore Shepard, physician; Joseph Tinker, principal boatman; Joseph McIntyre, George Proudfoot, Francis Gray, Samuel Forbes, Elijah Gunn, wife and child, Amos Sawtel, Samuel Hungerford, Amos Barber, Stephen Benton, Amzi Atwater, Asa Mason, Michael Coffin, Samuel Davenport, Samuel Agnew, Shadrach Benham, William B. Hall, Elisha Ayers, George Gooding, Norman Wilcox, Thomas Harris, Timothy Dunham, Wareham Shepard, David Beard, John Briant, Titus V. Munson, Joseph Landon, Olney F. Rice, James Hamilton, John Lock, James Halket, Job V. Stiles and wife, Charles Parker, Ezekiel Morley, Nathaniel Doan, Luke Hanchet, Samuel Barnes, Daniel Shuley, and Stephen Burbank.

It is a noteworthy coincidence that this advance-guard of the army of civilization that was soon to people the territorial limits of the Reserve first touched its soil on the anniversary of America's independence. Thus in this signal manner did a new colony, destined to play so important a part in the future of the Nation, begin its existence on the same day of the same month in which the Nation itself began to exist. Nor were these sons of Revolutionary fathers oblivious of the day which not only commemorates the birth of their country's freedom, but should henceforth be to them and their posterity the anniversary of the day on which their pilgrimage ended, and on which began their labors, toils, and sufferings for the establishment in the wilderness of Ohio of homes for themselves and their children. Animated with emotions appropriate to the occasion, these Pilgrim Fathers of the Western Reserve celebrated the day with such rude demonstrations of patriotic devotion and joy as they were able to invent.

They gathered together in groups on the eastern bank of the creek now known as the Conneaut; they pledged fidelity to their country in liquid dipped from the pure waters of the lake; they discharged from two or three fowling-pieces the National salute; they ate, drank, and were merry, blessing the land which many of them had assisted in delivering from British oppression; and they may have indulged in glowing predictions as to the future greatness and glory of the colonies they were about to plant. Could one of their number who shared their fancies, but who lived to see no part of them realized, behold to-day the changes which have proceeded in so wonderful a manner, we think that he would admit that the boldest anticipations of the little party of 1796 were but a feeble conception of the reality. However difficult it might be for him to understand the stages of the process by which so great a transformation has taken place, the actual truth would still present itself for his contemplation. What would astonish him most would be, not the conquest of forests, but that they have been succeeded by the numerous thriving cities and villages and the multitudinous homes of the prospering farmer, established on nearly every quarter-section of land in this country; that distance has been annihilated by the use of steam and the consequent acceleration of speed; that wealth and population have been so rapidly accumulative; that the community is so opulent and enlightened; that education is fostered by so admirable a system of free schools; that intelligence is universally diffused by so many representatives of a free press; that moral opinion has gained such ground; that religion is sustained by the convictions of an enlightened faith, and that the happiness of the people is universal and secure.

They christened the place where occurred these demonstrations of patriotism and joy Fort Independence, and the following are the toasts which they drank:

1. The President of the United States.
2. The State of Connecticut.
3. The Connecticut Land company.
4. May the Port of Independence and the fifty sons and daughters who have entered it this day be successful and prosperous!
5. May these sons and daughters multiply in sixteen years sixteen times fifty!
6. May every person have his bowsprit trimmed and ready to enter every port that opens!

The surveyors proceeded to the south line of the Reserve, and ascertained the point where the forty-first degree of north latitude intersects the western line of Pennsylvania, and from this line of latitude as a base, meridian lines five miles apart were run north to the lake. Lines of latitude were then run five miles apart, thus dividing the Reserve into townships five miles square. As the lands lying west of the Cuyahoga remained in possession of the Indians until the treaty of Fort Industry, in 1805, the Reserve was not surveyed at this time further west than to the Cuyahoga and the portage between it and the Tuscarawas, a distance west from the western line of Pennsylvania of fifty-six miles. The remainder of the Reserve was surveyed in 1806. The surveyors began, as we have seen, at the southeast corner of the Reserve, and ran parallel lines north from the base line and parallel lines west from the Pennsylvania line' five miles apart. The meridan lines formed the ranges, and the lines of latitude the townships.

THE APPOINTMENT OF AN EQUALIZING COMMITTEE.

After this survey was completed the Land company, in order that the shareholders might share equitably as nearly as possible the lands of the Reserve, or to avoid the likelihood of a part of the shareholders drawing the best, and others the medium, and others again the poorest of the lands, appointed an equalizing committee, whose duties we will explain.

The amount of the purchase money, $1,200,000, was divided into four hundred shares, each share value being $3,000. The holder of one share, therefore, had one four-hundredth undivided interest in the whole tract, and he who held four or five or twenty shares had four or five or twenty times as much interest undivided in the whole Reserve as he who held but one. As some townships would be more valuable than others, the company adopted, at a meeting of shareholders at Hartford, Connecticut, in April 1796, a mode of making partition, and appointed a committee of equalization to divide the Reserve in accordance with the company's plan. The committee appointed were Daniel Holbrook, William Shepperd, Jr., Moses Warren, Jr., Seth Pease, and Amos Spafford, and the committee who made up their report at Canandaigua, New York, December 13, 1797, were William Shepperd, Jr., Moses Warren, Jr., Seth Pease, and Amos Spafford.

The directors of the company, in accordance with Article III. of the articles of association, selected six townships to be offered for sale to actual settlers alone, and in which the first improvements were designed to be made. The townships thus selected were numbers eleven in the sixth range; ten, in the ninth range; nine, in the tenth range; eight, in the eleventh range; seven in the twelfth range; and two in the second range. These townships are now known as Madison, Mentor, and Willoughby, in Lake county; Euclid and Newburg, in Cuyahoga county; and Youngstown in Mahoning. Number three in the third range, or Weathersfield in Trumbull county, was omitted from the first draft made by the company, owing to the uncertainty of the boundaries of Mr. Parsons' claim. This township has sometimes been called the Salt Spring township. The six townships above named were offered for sale before partition was made, and parts of them were sold.

Excepting the Parsons claim, and the seven townships above named, the remainder of the Reserve east of Cuyahoga was divided among the members of the company as follows:

MODE OF PARTITION.

The four best townships in the eastern part of the Reserve were selected and surveyed into lots, an average of one hundred lots to the township. As there were four hundred shares, the four townships would yield one lot for every share. When these lots were drawn, each holder or holders of one or more shares participated in the draft. The committee selected township eleven in range seven and townships five, six, and seven in range eleven, for the four best townships. These are Perry, in Lake county, Northfield, in Summit county, Bedford and Warrenville, in Cuyahoga county.

Then the committee proceeded to select from the remaining townships certain other townships that should be next in value to the four already selected, which were to be used for equalizing purposes. The tracts thus selected being whole townships and parts of townships were, in number, twenty-four, as follows: Six, seven, eight, nine, and ten in the eighth range; six, seven, eight, and nine in the ninth range; and one, five, six, seven, and eight, in the tenth range; and sundry irregular tracts, as follows: Number fourteen in first range; number thirteen in third range; number thirteen in fourth range; number twelve in fifth range; number twelve in sixth range; number eleven in eighth range; number ten in tenth range; number six in twelfth range; and numbers one and two in the eleventh range. These tracts are now known as Auburn, Newbury, Munson, Chardon, Bainbridge, Russell, and Chester townships, in Geauga county; Concord and Kirtland, in Lake county; Springfield and Twinsburg, in Summit county; Solon, Orange, and Mayfield, in Cuyahoga county. The fractional townships are Conneaut gore, Ashtabula gore, Saybrook gore, Geneva, Madison gore, Painesville, Willoughby gore, Independence, Coventry, and Portage.

After this selection had been made, they selected the average townships, to the value of each of which each of the others should be brought by the equalizing process of annexation. The eight best of the remaining townships were taken, and were numbers one, five, eleven, twelve, and thirteen, in the first range; twelve, in the fourth range; eleven, in the fifth range; and six, in the sixth range. They are now known as Poland, in Mahoning county; Hartford, in Trumbull county; Pierpont, Monroe, Conneaut, Saybrook, and Harpersfield, in Ashtabula county; and Parkman, in Geauga county. These were the standard townships, and all the other townships of inferior value to these eight, which would include all the others not mentioned above, were to be raised to the value of the average townships by annexations from the equalizing townships. These last named were cut up into parcels of various sizes and values, and annexed to the inferior townships in such a way as to make them all of equal value, in the opinion of the committee. When the committee had performed this task, it was found that, with the exception of the four townships first selected, the Parsons tract, and the townships that had been previously set aside to be sold, the whole tract would amount to an equivalent of ninety-three shares. There were, therefore, ninety-three equalized townships or parcels to be drawn for east of the Cuyahoga.

THE DRAFT.

To entitle a shareholder to the ownership of an equalized township, it was necessary for him to be the proprietor of $12,903.23 of the original purchase of the company, or, in other words, he must possess about three and three-tenths shares of the original purchase.

The division by draft took place on the 29th of January, 1798. The townships were numbered from one to ninety three, and the numbers, on slips of paper, placed in a box. The names of shareholders were arranged alphabetically, and, in those instances in which an original investment was insufficient to entitle such investor to an equalized township, he formed a combination with others in like situation, and the name of that person of this combination that took alphabetic precedence, was used in the draft. If the small proprietors were, from disagreement among themselves, unable to unite, a committee was appointed to select and classify them, and those selected were compelled to submit to this arrangement. If, after they had drawn a township, they could not agree in dividing it between them, this committee, or another one appointed for that purpose, divided it for them. That township designated by the first number drawn belonged to the first man on the list, and the second drawn to the second man, and so on until all were drawn. Thus was the ownership in common severed, and each individual secured his interest in severalty. John Morgan, John Caldwell, and Jonathan Brace, the trustees, as rapidly as partition was effected, conveyed by deed to the several purchasers the land they had drawn.

OTHER DRAFTS.

The second draft was made in 1802, and was for such portions of the seven townships omitted in the first draft as remained at that time unsold. This draft was divided into ninety shares, representing $13,333.33 of the purchase money.

The third draft was made in 1807, and was for the lands lying west of the Cuyahoga, and was divided into forty-six parts, each representing $26,087.

The fourth draft was made in 1809, at which time the surplus land, so called, was divided, including sundry notes and claims arising from sales that had been effected of the seven townships omitted in the first drawing.

QUANTITY OF LAND IN THE CONNECTICUT WESTERN RESERVE, ACCORDING TO THE SURVEY THEREOF.

Land east of the Cuyahoga, exclusive of the Parsons tract, in acres				2,002,970
Land west of the Cuyahoga, exclusive of surplus land, islands, and Sufferers' lands				827,291
Surplus land, so called				5,286
Islands	Cunningham or Kelley's			2,749
	Bass, or Bay No. 1			1,322
	"	"	2	709
	"	"	3	709
	"	"	4	403
	"	"	5	32
				5,924
Parsons, or "Salt Spring tract"				25,450
Sufferers', or Fire Lands				500,000
Total acres in Connecticut Western Reserve				3,366,921

CHAPTER VI.
PROGRESS OF WESTERN SETTLEMENT.
First Settlements West of the Ohio—Colonies on the Ohio River—First Settlement on the Reserve.

Next to a broad, national feeling and interest, patriotism manifests itself most in State love and State pride. These evidences of good citizenship are not wanting in Ohio, nor is there any reason why they should be. This State has a worthy history, civil organization based upon the equitable and catholic policy of the ordinance of 1787, a social fabric woven of the most hardy and substantial material the old colonial establishments could furnish, and rich natural resources have been a firm and unyielding basis of prosperous development. Although during the Revolution there was not a permanent white settlement within the present limits of Ohio, that struggle has a deep and important interest in the history of the State, aside from its effect upon the ownership of the soil. When British oppression became no longer endurable, the liberal, generous-spirited, courageous, resolute citizens of every colony hurried to the standard of independence and freedom. They literally and in fact pledged "their lives, their fortunes, and their sacred honor" to the holy cause. Their honor was gloriously vindicated, but the result was the wreck and ruin of their private estates. The war closed leaving most of its participants with nothing but physical strength, ambition, and courage. For them passages to a western wilderness were open. After experiencing the hardships of the camp and dangers of battle, the Western forest and its savage inhabitants had no terror for these brave fathers of our national independence and hardy founders of our State. A fearless spirit, coupled with necessity, made them eager in the task of subduing a wilderness.

One of the first measures forced upon the consideration of the Congress of the Confederation was a plan for disposing of the western domain. Congress had pledged, in 1776, and by several succeeding acts, liberal bounties to the Continental soldiers. A major-general was entitled to eleven hundred acres, a brigadier-general to eight hundred and fifty, colonel to five hundred, lieutenant-colonel four hundred and fifty, major four hundred, captain three hundred, lieutenant two hundred, ensign one hundred and fifty, and privates and non-commissioned officers one hundred acres each. These claims had considerable influence in keeping alive the "western fever," as it was called, and the spirit of adventure.

Immediately after the peace of 1783, General Rufus Putnam, of Massachusetts, transmitted to Washington a memorial, asking for an appropriation of land in the Ohio valley sufficient in extent to supply these bounties; but the title was yet involved, and action was postponed. After, however, this obstruction had been removed by the voluntary cession of all the States having claims except Connecticut, Congress, in May, 1785, passed an ordinance, directing Thomas Hutchins, the United States geographer, to make a survey of lands lying northwest of the Ohio river, beginning with the west line of Pennsylvania. One-seventh of the land was reserved to satisfy the bounty claims of Continental soldiers. The whole tract, except the Connecticut claim and the undefined reservation of Virginia, lying between the Scioto and the Miami rivers, was to be surveyed into townships six miles square, and each township to be divided into thirty-six sections containing six hundred and forty acres each. Four sections of each township were reserved for future sale; the balance was to be apportioned to the several States, and sold by them at not less than one dollar per acre, with the additional cost of survey and sale.

The survey was commenced under this ordinance in the spring of 1785, seven range lines being run from north to south between the south line of Connecticut's claim (now the Reserve) to the Ohio river, when Indian hostilities prevented further operations. Five townships in Mahoning county are included in this first survey made within the limits of the present State of Ohio. The provision that the land should be partitioned to the several States was in perfect accord with the States sovereignty establishment under the old Articles of Confederation, but it proved an ineffectual measure and was destined to be displaced by a more mature and encouraging policy.

It is a source of congratulation and pride to the settlers on the Reserve that their ancestors, nearly a century ago in old Connecticut, co-operated with their kindred over in Massachusetts in taking steps toward the planting of law and civilization in the western wilderness. The colony at the mouth of the Muskingum was sometimes designated "New Massachusetts." Western New England would have been a more appropriate title, for although Massachusetts stock predominated in the original settlement, many from Connecticut joined the westward train whose descendants are to be found among the inhabitants of the present day.

General Rufus Putnam continued to take a deep interest in Western colonization, particularly in securing for the veterans of the war the bounties promised them, a promise which Congress was slow to fulfil. Colonel Benjamin Tupper was appointed to assist Thomas Hutchins make the survey authorized by the resolution of 1785, and in May of that year came West and remained until difficulties with the Indians made further prosecution of the work impossible. He, however, remained long enough to form a very favorable opinion of the Ohio country, and on returning to Massachusetts in the early part of 1786, joined General Putnam in a plan for the organization of a colony. General Samuel H. Parsons had also been West, and joined heartily in the enterprise. He doubtless looked forward to the founding of a New Connecticut in that part of the wilderness touching the great lake, but the time was not ripe for such an undertaking. Generals Putnam and Tupper published an address to the people of New England setting forth the attractions and advantages of the new country, and inviting all interested in the project of forming an association with a view to emigration to meet in Boston, March 1, 1786.

The convention which assembled in pursuance of this call represented the best elements of New England society. Articles of association were agreed upon which fixed the capital stock of the company at $1,000,000; Continental certificates being accepted as money. It had been provided that these certificates should be accepted at par in payment for public land. Three directors—General Samuel H. Parsons, of Connecticut; Manasseh Cutler, of Massachusetts; and General Rufus Putnam, of Massachusetts—were elected, with instructions to procure a private grant in the Ohio valley. Another meeting was called a year later, when it was found that less than one-third the stock had been subscribed, but it was resolved to go on with the enterprise as rapidly as possible. A company was being organized in New York, with William Duer at its head, for the purpose of making a purchase at the mouth of the Scioto. Dr. Cutler found great difficulty in making a favorable contract with Congress. Coupled with this was the additional difficulty of securing the establishment of a civil government agreeable to the New England political creed. The fight was on slavery, which Dr. Cutler insisted should be rigidly prohibited from the territory, and on this issue hung the fight. Several members of Congress were interested in the Duer project, and it was found that their influence could be secured by combining the two schemes. Dr. Cutler had further desired to have General Parsons appointed Governor of the Territory, but he was compelled to yield this point and consent to the appointment of General St. Clair, who was a representative from Pennsylvania and President of Congress.

It will be seen that political methods did not differ much in 1787 from the fashion of the present time. Complete, elevated, and equitable as the ordinance of 1787 is, the founders of our State lobbied its passage by bringing to bear upon members of Congress personal influence even to the extent of making the governorship a part of the price. A contract was finally agreed upon in July, 1787, for an extensive tract at the mouth of the Muskingum, and extending to the Scioto. In this the Duer company purchase was included. Dr. Cutler had brought to bear upon Congress the threat that unless his proposition was accepted, the New England Ohio company would purchase from Connecticut her reserved lands. This was one of the most potent arguments in favor of immediate action. The ordinance providing for Territorial government was lobbied through in connection with the bill authorizing a grant of land. Jefferson, in 1784, had submitted an ordinance for the government of all the Western Territory, which contemplated an ultimate division into seventeen States. It also contained a proviso against slavery which was stricken out before the final passage of the bill by Congress. This omission from the bill as finally passed was an insuperable objection in sturdy old Puritan New England even in 1787. This was the main reason why the directors of the Ohio company refused to sign the contract concluding the purchase until a revised ordinance for civil government was adopted.

On the 13th of July, 1787, was passed the celebrated ordinance of 1787, organizing into a single territory all the country northwest of the Ohio river and eastward of the Mississippi, subject to future division, if deemed expedient by Congress, into two districts. This fundamental law, enacted before a solitary freeholder raised his cabin in the territory it was intended to govern, has been characterized as a fit consummation of the glorious labors of the Congress of the old Confederation. It established in the Northwest the important principle of the equal inheritance of intestate estates and the freedom of alienation by deed or will. After prescribing a system of territorial civil government, it concludes with six articles of compact between the original States and the people of the States in the territory which should forever remain unalterable unless by common consent. The first declares that no person, demeaning himself in a peaceable and orderly manner, should ever be molested on account of his mode of worship or religious sentiments. The second article prohibited legislative interference with private contracts, and secured to the inhabitants trial by jury, the writ of *habeas corpus*, a proportionate representation of the people in the Legislature, judicial proceedings according to the course of common law, and those guarantees of personal freedom and property which are enumerated in the bill of rights of most of the States. The third article provided for the encouragement of schools, and for good faith, humanity and justice toward the Indian. The fourth article secured to the new States to be erected out of the territory the same privileges with the old ones, imposed upon them the same burdens, including responsibility for the Federal debt, prohibited the States from interfering with the primary disposal of the soil of the United States or taxing the public lands; from taxing the lands of non-residents higher than residents; and established the navigable waters leading into the Mississippi and the St. Lawrence and portages between them common highways for the use of all citizens of all the States. The fifth article related to the formation of new States within the Territory, the divisions to be not more than five nor less than five. By the provisions of this article the west line of Ohio was a line running northward from the mouth of the Great Miami until it intersected a line running eastward from the southern bend of Lake Michigan. The sixth article provided "that there shall be neither slavery nor involuntary servitude in the Territory otherwise than in the punishment of crime whereof the party shall have been convicted." The ordinance included the Reserve under the jurisdiction of the Northwest Territory. Federal jurisdiction was also extended over the Virginia Military District and accepted in after years by the settlers without dispute.

The ordinance of 1787 gave the greatest encouragement to immigration and offered the fullest protection to those who became settlers. "When they came to the wilderness they found the law already there. It was impressed upon the soil while yet it bore up nothing but the forest."

The foundation was now laid, the purchase was made and civil government provided. All was anticipation among the members of the Ohio company. Advertising circulars pictured a land of boundless resources and fertility, and raised expectations to the highest point. There was, however, a conservative element that ridiculed the whole idea of making a home in a wilderness inhabited only by wild animals and wild men far more dangerous than wild animals. But the heroes of the Revolution were not to be influenced by the ridicule coming mainly from the neutral or Tory element, which held aloof from the war for independence.

In October, 1787, Congress ordered seven hundred troops for the protection of the frontiers, and on the fifth of that month appointed territorial officers: Arthur St. Clair, Governor; Winthrop Sargent, Secretary; Samuel H. Parsons, James M. Varnum, and John Armstrong judges. Judge Armstrong declined the office, and John Cleves Symmes was appointed to fill the vacancy. On the 7th of April, 1788, a company of forty-eight men, from Massachusetts and Connecticut, with General Rufus Putnam at their head, disembarked from their boats at the mouth of the Muskingum and planted civilization—New England civilization—on the soil of Ohio. Civil government was formally inaugurated on the 15th of July with impressive ceremonies. The secretary, judges, and inhabitants assembled on the site of the destined city of Marietta, where the Governor was welcomed by General Parsons in behalf of the residents of the Northwest Territory. Under a bower of foliage contributed by the surrounding forest, the ordinance of 1787 was read, congratulations exchanged, and three hearty cheers echoed and re-echoed from the surface of two rivers, high surrounding hills, and the dense forest.

Marietta was the first permanent settlement on the soil of Ohio. Its immigrants for a quarter of a century were from New England, and the town to this day bears the impress of its early history. The elements of society found in the Muskingum and Ohio bottoms in southeastern Ohio are almost identical with the prevailing elements in the Reserve. These two sections have always been united in the great moral and political movements in the State. Descendants from the same East, inheritors of the same traditions, New England on the Ohio and New England on the lake have joined hands in every crisis against the opposing civilizations which predominate in other sections of the State.

In the spring of 1789 an association made a settlement at Belpre, opposite the mouth of the Little Kanawha, and another on the Muskingum river at Waterford. During the same summer a third located at Big Bottom, on the Muskingum, but this group all belonged to one colony—the Ohio company—and together constitute one of the five distinct centers of early settlement.

The New England emigrants of 1788 had scarce got settled in their first cabins and blockhouses when a people of different stock cut into the forest and established themselves between the Miamis of the Ohio. In October, 1788, John Cleves Symmes, a native of New Jersey, and one of the judges of the Northwest Territory, negotiated a purchase on behalf of himself and associates, of one million acres extending northward from the Ohio, between the Great and Little Miamis. He, however, failed to make full payment according to the contract and a large part of the purchase reverted to the United States, the patent when issued covering only about three hundred thousand acres. Opposite Licking river was a large forest amphitheater—one of the most beautiful and picturesque products of the great artist, Nature, within the present bounds of Ohio. A large tract taking in the adjoining hills and the whole bottom was purchased by Matthias Denman, of New Jersey, who entered into a contract with Colonel Patterson and Mr. Filson, of Kentucky, for laying out a town. Filson was killed by the Indians, and his interest became the property of Israel Ludlow. Patterson and Ludlow, accompanied by a party of Kentucky woodsmen and surveyors, arrived on the Denman purchase December 26, 1788. This may be considered the date of the foundation of Cincinnati. They erected a stockade and a few blockhouses, then surveyed a city which was named Losantiville, a barbarous compound meaning opposite the Licking, which a few years after was dropped for the present name.

Colonel Stiles, in the preceding November, had erected block-houses and laid out a town at the mouth of the Little Miami, which he named Columbia. It was evident that the locality was favorable for a large city, when the country on both sides of the Ohio should be developed. Judge Symmes, having made the original purchase, was ambitious to be the founder of the destined metropolis, and accordingly, in February, 1789, he descended the Ohio, with a company of soldiers and citizens, as far as the mouth of the Great Miami, where a third city was marked out by blazes on the trees; but the spring floods came and cruelly destroyed the day-dream of a great western emporium at this point. This untimely inundation did not prove fatal to Symmes's hopes. A fourth city was marked out upon the trees, extending from the northernmost bend of the Ohio to the Miami, and named, from its location, North Bend. The three villages, Columbia, Losantiville, and North Bend, were rivals for supremacy, until Fort Washington was located, in June, 1789. The post was occupied by General Harmar with three hundred soldiers, many of whom belonged to the Revolutionary order of the Cincinnati, and they conferred the name of that honorable society upon the village, which their presence made permanent, in place of the pedantic compound its founders had given it. Most of the original settlers of all these villages came from New Jersey, and they were recruited, for a number of years, from the same State. All together constituted a settlement which gave to that part of the State a characteristic civilization. New Jersey came to Ohio, and qualities of Hollander and English,

tinctured with Swedish blood, are yet perceptible in the old inhabitants of the country around Cincinnati, extending a considerable distance up the Miamis.

The third settlement in Ohio was a foreign colony planted opposite the mouth of the Big Kanawha in the summer of 1791. It has never had any bearing upon State history at large, but is interesting as showing the speculative spirit of the time. The Ohio company's patent covered the contemplated purchase of Duer's company. According to previous contract, two days after Congress confirmed the grant, the Ohio company issued a patent to William Duer and others to all the land west of the seventeenth range as far as the Scioto river and south to the Ohio. The Scioto company was composed of speculators, none of whom became or desired to become settlers. The Ohio company associates and Symmes and his associates made purchases for themselves. Both flourished and became influential elements in the State. The Scioto company was a pure speculation, the failure of which is to be regretted only on account of the misery it inflicted upon the poor foreigners who were deceived by fraudulent representations. European colonization was the scheme adopted by these companies as the most profitable for disposing of its western purchase.

France was at that time completely harrowed up by revolution and discontent, a circumstance greatly favoring the formation of an American colony. Joel Barlow, the poet, was sent to France. A better agent could not have been selected. He was courtly and elegant in dress and manner; was a florid talker and graceful writer. Such a man at such a time could not fail to become the average Frenchman's friend, philosopher, and guide. He went to Paris with a map of the Ohio valley printed in high colors, and prepared to issue deeds on paper with artistically decorated border. The term Ohio was never used, La Salle's *La Belle Riviere* being much more musical to a Frenchman. The map marked towns and cities, the largest of which was happily named Fair Haven. The accomplished poet pictured an Acadia with noble forests, consisting of trees that spontaneously produce sugar, and plants that yield ready made candles. To complete the picture he added streams of pure water abounding in excellent fish of vast size; venison is plenty, "the pursuit of which is uninterrupted by wolves, foxes, lions, and tigers," and to cap the climax he added "a couple of swine will multiply themselves a hundred fold in two or three years without taking any care of them." What a paradise! A land not only adorned by nature but furnished with food and raiment, and amusement for its inhabitants "who should have no taxes to pay, no military duty to perform." This glowing description had its effect chiefly upon light *artistes*,—carvers, gilders, coachmakers, frisures, and barbers, a large company of whom received deeds to lots, and embarked in the enterprise with characteristic French enthusiasm. Less than a dozen heavy laborers joined the colony. They embarked for America with the wildest anticipations.

Something had to be done for their reception. The wooded hills which present a bleak and rugged front to the river abounded in savage animals, and were frequented by bands of men more dangerous. General Rufus Putnam, of the Ohio company, was employed to locate a village and prepare homes for the immigrants on their arrival. The location of the visionary Fair Haven was found to be below high-water mark, which induced General Putnam to locate Gallipolis four miles below on a high bank. A small tract of land was cleared and block-houses built. The Ohio company had also contracted to furnish the emigrants with provisions the first winter, but in default of payment for services already rendered the contract was cancelled. The foreigners finally arrived at the American Acadia. Howling wild animals made their hearts leap with fear, and the sight of many trees to be cut almost brought blisters on their tender hands. Worse than all, they were without food, and by reason of former life and occupation were without the means of doing for themselves. The hardy New Englanders who had passed through the battles of the Revolution could subsist on the products of their rifles and seines, but the poor Paris Frenchman knew nothing about these most elementary instruments of backwoods life. To add to their misery and disappointment, they soon learned that the Scioto company had not paid for the land, and consequently the highly-colored deeds issued in France were worthless. Despondent, in constant danger of an Indian attack,

suffering from sickness, without food and without money, many of them sought lodgments in other settlements, and a few dragged out a miserable existence as best they could. Congress granted to these unfortunate immigrants a tract at the mouth of the Scioto in 1798, but not many took advantage of the offer.

The fourth settlement in Ohio was made in the Virginia Military district. Virginia's claim to the Northwest was more valid than that of any other State, and we cannot refrain from expressing an admiration of that patriotic spirit in which she yielded her pretensions. She had promised liberal bounties to her troops engaged in the French and Indian war and in the Revolution, and to fulfil her obligation she reserved the large tract between the Scioto and Miami, from the Ohio river as far north as the centre of the State. General Nathaniel Massie was appointed by Virginia to make a survey of the district. The work was at first carried on by making expeditions through the district of Kentucky, then a part of Virginia, but this method was laborious and unsatisfactory. In the winter of 1790-91, encouraged by the flourishing condition of the settlements at the Muskingum and Miamis, he determined to plant a Virginia colony north of the Ohio. Such a settlement would afford his party protection while prosecuting the survey, and enhance the State's lands in value. A site was chosen and a town laid out in out-lots and in-lots, which took for its name Massie's Station, afterwards changed to its present name, Manchester. He gave general notice throughout Kentucky of his intention to found a town, and offered to the first twenty-five families to announce their intention to become permanent settlers, one out-lot and one in-lot and one hundred acres of land. Upwards of thirty families quickly announced their willingness to accept the proposition. The company arrived at the site of the town, whose streets had already been marked on the trees, in March, 1791. Every man—all strong Kentucky frontiersmen—went to work with a will, and in a short time each family had a cabin, and the whole village was enclosed by a strong stockade with block-houses at each angle. The Indian war was then being carried on with savage fierceness; but this little station "suffered less from depredation and even interruption by Indians than any settlement previously made on the river Ohio. This was no doubt due to the watchful band of brave spirits who guarded the place—men who were reared in the midst of danger and inured to peril—as watchful as hawks."*

Marietta, Cincinnati, and Manchester were the first three permanent lodgments of civilization in the Ohio wilderness. A great expanse of dark forest lay between the river and the lakes uninhabited, untraversed except by native red men and an occasional trader. But it was a land possessing every element of loveliness to its wild, romantic occupants. They had watched with apprehension and resisted with firmness the westward march of cultivation and improvement. Though steadily driven back they had hoped to maintain the Ohio river as the boundary between the white man's fields and their loved hunting-ground. But the barrier had now been crossed. Hundreds of busy axes sent through the forest an alarm of approaching destruction, of ultimate extinction. The natural human feeling of self preservation impelled the tribes to make a united, determined, persistent effort to resist further encroachments. The Virginia borderers and Kentuckians in the long years of preceding strife had shown them examples of diabolical cruelty. A reign of danger and blood was in store for the Ohio settlements which brought to a pause the movement of westward emigration and speculation.

The war burst upon the frontiers of the Ohio company's settlement with sudden fury. For three years the colony had been growing and enlarging its improvements without molestation or cause for anxiety. The first attack on the north side of the Ohio was at Big Bottom, on the Muskingum, on the night of January 2, 1791.

The settlers were aroused from their repose in fancied peace and security, to be made the victims of savage butchery. But two inmates of the block-house escaped; fourteen were slain and five taken captive, who, while being led into the forest saw the building in flames, tumbling over the bodies of their friends and relatives. From this time there was safety nowhere. General Harmar made a campaign against the savage braves, but with only partial success; we should rather say with partial failure, for nothing permanent was accomplished toward allaying hostilities. St. Clair met a disastrous defeat which gave the native braves renewed courage, and it was not until the battle of Fallen Timbers that hostilities ceased. For four years the progress of improvement was hampered by the necessity imposed upon the settlers of living in garrisons and the danger of making new settlements. The report of Wayne's victory on the Maumee was a joyful message to those already in the West and revived the spirit of emigration at the East. War is not an unmixed evil. It has its compensations, by making people hardier, braver, more enterprising, but chiefly in a new country by carrying back from long expeditions into unfrequented regions, a knowledge of the geography, geology, and resources of the soil. Wayne's troops opened up a road into the heart of the Northwest Territory, and the reports which they carried back reaching the old coast States, together with the assurance that the Indian power was forever broken, had the effect of bringing scores of emigrants to the West.

The old garrisons were thrown open and every valley resounded with the woodman's axe and the crash of falling timber. "Never since the golden age of the poets," says an old writer, "did the siren song of peace and farming reach so many ears or gladden so many hearts as after Wayne's treaty in 1795." Then it was that the incalculable task of hewing a great State out of a dense forest was entered upon in earnest. The village of Cincinnati, which in 1792 had a population of less than two hundred, numbered by the close of 1796 more than sixteen hundred souls; besides, her characteristically Jersey population had spread northward along the Miami valleys. Hamilton, Butler county, was laid out in 1794, and settled the following year; Dayton, Montgomery county, and Franklin, Warren county, were settled in 1796.

General Massie's first attempt to found a town in the heart of the Virginia Military district was made in 1795, but proved a failure on account of Indian hostilities. A more favorable result attended his effort the following year. Chillicothe was laid out early in 1796 and soon became by far the largest town in the district, and one of the three largest in the Territory. At the end of two years it had attained sufficient importance to be made the seat of civil government. The Virginia Military district rapidly increased

* McDonald's Western Sketches.

in population and was an early rival of each of the older settlements—Marietta and Cincinnati. Like a long peninsula, Virginia population extended through Kentucky into Ohio half way to Lake Erie. The pioneers came through the passes of the Blue Ridge mountains to Kentucky, thence across the Ohio, bringing with them the institutions of the Old Dominion, except slavery, which the ordinance of 1787 fortunately prohibited.

There was a striking contrast between the settlements on the Scioto, and on the Muskingum; as striking as the difference between the social status in Virginia and in Massachusetts. The Scioto Virginian proudly traced his ancestry to the English nobility, and claimed the blood of Norman and cavalier; his neighbor, the Muskingum New Englander, followed up his line of descent to the Puritan non-conformist, who came to America for religious freedom. The Virginian was Episcopal in religion and Jefferson Republican in politics; the New Englander was Calvinist and Federalist. They were, from the first, opposing political forces, and are to this day.

As soon as the Indian war had closed, settlers came over from Pennsylvania and entered land in the seven ranges surveyed in 1785. Many of the first settlers were Quakers, but by far the larger proportion were of that mixed blood which, for want of a better name, we call Pennsylvania Dutch (or German). Settlements in the seven ranges extended northward from the Ohio to the Reserve. The settlement of the Reserve may be said to have commenced in 1797, though very little was accomplished in the way of improvement before the close of 1798.

Settlements were scattered through the central part of the State as early as 1797, but really nothing in the way of clearing and cultivating had been done anywhere by the close of that year except along the Ohio river and its principal tributaries, the Miamis, the Scioto, and the Muskingum. The region west of the Cuyahoga had never been entered with a view to settlement even by surveyors. When the settlement of the Reserve began, the whole Northwest Territory contained less than twenty thousand white inhabitants, scattered from Marietta to Cincinnati and north as far as Columbus and Vincennes. Altogether they would have made a community smaller than the city of Youngstown.

Governor St. Clair, in 1788, for purposes of civil government, proclaimed the erection of Washington county, embracing about half the present State of Ohio,—all that part east of the Cuyahoga and Scioto. Marietta was the county seat. Hamilton county was erected in 1790, with Cincinnati as the county seat. Detroit was occupied by American troops in 1796, and made the seat of a new county, Wayne, which embraced the whole Territory of Michigan, northwestern Ohio, and northern Indiana. Adams county embracing the whole of the Virginia Military district, was erected in 1797. Washington county was divided the same year, the northern part constituting Jefferson, with the county seat at Steubenville. Ross was carved off of Adams in 1798, and considerable territory, including the present county of Franklin, added on the north side.

CHAPTER VII.
SETTLEMENT OF THE RESERVE.

Early Settlement of the Reserve—Ownership of Trumbull and Mahoning Counties—First Families with Date of Arrival.

We have had a glimpse of the Reserve and its inhabitants when white explorers first trod its damp soil in the thick shade of an unbroken forest. We have witnessed the bloody conflict which resulted in the extinction of those inhabitants; then followed the advent of other tribes and nations of the same great human family—a family whose history will forever be an interesting mystery. We have seen the westward advance of civilization and the Indian's gallant and heroic conflict with destiny for the maintenance of his forest and his home. The foundations of a State have been laid, and all conflicting claims settled except in so far as relates to the territory reserved by Connecticut in her act of session of 1786. We have reviewed the purchase of Connecticut's claim to the Reserve by a company of individuals known as the Connecticut Land company. It must be borne in mind that their deed did not give them an unincumbered title, for other States had held claims covering the Reserve, at least as valid as

Connecticut's, and Virginia's was far more so. These had all been quit-claimed to the United States while the Land company's title was based upon Connecticut's old charter and actual possession. We have followed the surveyors from Schenectady to Conneaut, and watched them from the distance of eighty-six years celebrating Independence day. The task which lay before them involved difficulties which at present can only be imagined, and what was accomplished during the first season fell far short of the company's expectations. About $14,000 had been expended, and the work was little more than half completed, although the field books show rapid work, lines being run at the rate of eight, ten, and sometimes even twelve miles a day.

It appears from the field-books that Warren, after whom the county seat of Trumbull county was named, was less energetic than the others, but he was continued in the service, from which we may conclude that the company was satisfied with him. The south or base line had been run no farther than the east line of Berlin township, Mahoning county; none of the six townships intended for sale to actual settlers had been platted except Newburg and Cleveland. This unexpected delay was embarrassing to the company, for the directors were under obligations to pay for their lands, but until the survey was completed it was impossible to effect a partition among the stockholders, and consequently no sales could be concluded. But the delay involved more than an extraordinary outlay of money without any income. The western spirit had reached almost every eastern home and was rapidly reducing the number of those who might be expected to emigrate to the Western forests. Under such circumstances the directors had good excuse for being impatient, nevertheless they had no cause to find fault with the surveyors, whose work was prosecuted under most unfavorable circumstances. Their instruments were imperfect and trees and underbrush, to say nothing of swamps, interfered with running at long sights. The old-fashioned compasses then in use required frequent correcting of deviation.

There were other circumstances tending to retard progress. Provisions were not always promptly delivered to surveying parties, so that there were frequent interruptions. Woods life was at first a novelty to the axmen, chainmen, packhorsemen, and other laborers who comprised a large percentage of the party, but they soon lost their enthusiasm in work in which they had no interest except the small wages paid, and became lazy and indifferent. After the first few weeks there was very little romance left in their employment. Every day was toil and drudgery with surroundings most uncomfortable and distressing. Ravenous mosquitoes were never idle day or night, and vegetable gas rested like a layer of poison on the surface. In clear weather the heat was oppressive, and, in wet weather, water from the underbrush and damp soil drowned out every germ of buoyancy. Meals did not always come regularly, and long intervals sometimes passed without a drop of spirit-sustaining old New England rum. Their clothing became ragged from climbing over logs and through thickets; their constantly worn shoes rapidly gave way, and there were no cobblers to mend them. The surveyors were borne up by hope of financial gain. They were learning the country, and foresaw its future wealth. Their wages invested in lands would return rich profits. Hope and anticipation of wealth made their task light. The common laborers, disgusted and discouraged, expecting nothing but their pay and hardship, naturally became discontented. There is no evidence that an open rupture ever occurred with the surveyors, but the progress of the work was hindered by dissatisfaction, which was somewhat lightened by the agents promising grants of land to such as proved to be faithful.

The surveying party gave to New England the first accurate and detailed description of the Reserve. It has been remarked that "it is due to the general system of New England education that her sons are able wherever they go in unexplored countries to record intelligibly what passes under their observation." Most of the surveyors and some of the laborers kept regular journals of their daily experiences, and these, taken back to Connecticut had considerable influence in determining the location of settlements.

The east line of the Reserve was surveyed under direction of Mr. Holley and Seth Pease, whose journals give a very satisfactory description of the country through which they passed, and it is not presuming too much to say was the means of calling attention to the Mahoning valley, making Youngstown one of the first and the leading early settlement on the Reserve.

Mr. Holley, Seth Pease, Augustus Porter, and five other men left Conneaut, the headquarters of the party, on Thursday, July 7, 1796. Without difficulty they found the west Pennsylvania line, which had been run and cleared only a few years before. They proceeded southward five or six rods west of the Pennsylvania line, measuring as they went in order to assist them in finding the forty-first parallel, which, by the old charter, is the south line of the Reserve, and also to determine the variation of their compasses. For the first eight miles from the lake the land is described as "not well watered;" from the eighth to the thirteenth mile "the land has every appearance of being overflowed in wet seasons." Further south the surface rises and falls and the soil "of course is better;" "to the end of the nineteenth mile" the land "is ridgey and better watered, covered with all kinds of timber." "On the twentieth mile an open tamarack swamp, twenty-eight chains wide; to the end of the twenty-third mile the land is indifferent, swampy."

The party encamped over Sunday near an excellent brook, which was considered a favorable circumstance. Their line next day to the end of the twenty-fifth mile was "through the most abominable swamp in the world." On the twenty-seventh mile they came to a creek—"a smooth stream five or six feet deep and navigable for batteaux." "The land on each side is rich, but to all appearance is covered by water the greater part of the year." On this creek was a beaver dam, which Mr. Holley says was "quite a curiosity." The dam consisted of some large sticks of trees thrown across the stream and filled in with thousands of willows and other small wood, which was so compact as to make considerable of a pond above, "from which through a rich soil was cut several channels and arms, where they live now, as is evident from fresh tracks, newly-cut chips and brush." We quote the journal of July 12th in full as a specimen of the many hard experiences recorded in these early records:

In the morning we breakfasted in our camp by the little brook and left the packhorsemen to come on after us, but when we had proceeded about a mile we sent back a hand to tell the men to go round the swamp with the horses, but the swamp continued and we ran on till night. Here being a hemlock ridge we were in hopes the horses would find us, but alas! we were obliged to make a camp of boughs, strike up a fire, and go to bed supperless. In the daytime I had eat raspberries, gooseberries, wintergreen berries, and wintergreens and in the night I began to grow sick at my stomach and soon after vomited up everything I had in me. Mr. Pease, too, had a turn of the cramp in consequence of traveling all day in the water. We all rose early in the morning with meager looks and somewhat faint for want of eating and drinking, for where we camped there was no water though we had a little rum.

Provisions arrived in about two hours after dawn, but most of the pack-horses were three miles behind, being mired in the swamp. The day was spent in fishing, waiting, and assisting the horses along. Mr. Holley describes the thirty-second mile from the lake as "fine land for wheat; timber chestnut, white oak, and maple, rises and descends." From the thirty-fourth mile "to the end of the thirty-seventh mile the land is good, level, and timbered maple, beach, oak, whitewood, and herbage." We now enter the present limits of Trumbull county. "The land to the end of the forty-first mile is gentle, rises and descends, good, and timbered with white oak, chestnut, black oak, pepperidge, cucumber, and whitewood." They encamped at the end of the forty-second mile, where, says Holley, "we had a most pleasing prospect, a hill at the distance of four or five miles (in Pennsylvania), with the valley that lay between covered with stately trees and herbage which indicated an excellent soil, altogether exhibited a delightful landscape, the beauty of which I suppose was enhanced from its being the first time we could overlook the woods." What a relief it must have been to rise above the dark shade of a dismal forest to the full view of a picturesque landscape. The next mile "the soil is rich, timbered with black and white oak, chestnut, and white walnut, undergrowth of the same, hung together with grapevines. There are three fine springs in this mile."

The Pymatuning at the end of the forty-fourth mile is thus described: "We crossed a large, smooth stream one chain and twenty-five links wide, course east, stony bottom, banks tolerably high; as far as we could see it was good boating; we waded the stream; it was about two feet and a half deep, but an uncommon dry time." For a mile south of the creek "land rises and descends; timber, oak and hickory; soil good for grain." Having left Pymatuning creek five miles behind, the next four miles are covered with the sentence: "very abrupt ridges, stony and poor land, oak timber, and whittleberries." On the next mile "there are large stones which appear like grindstones." The western bend of the Shenango was struck on the fifty-third mile, described as "a large creek or river about two chains and fifty links wide, bottom gravelly, current brisk, abounds with fish, course southwest. We waded this and found the depth at this dry season to be more than waist high. We supposed this stream to be the same we crossed on the forty-fourth mile, with the addition of all the others that we passed. On this creek is good bottom land, timbered with red elm, cherry, crabapple trees, plum and thorn bush." When they recrossed the Shenango on the following day it appeared navigable for boats. Mr. Holley judged the land passed over the next four or five miles good for grain. They reached on the sixty-fifth mile from the lake, or about one mile north of the Mahoning, the "Old Indian Path," which passed east and west from New York, through northern Pennsylvania and the Reserve to Sandusky. This was a common Indian highway even as late as the time of which we write, 1796, between the Eastern and Western tribes. It is highly probable that the following page from Holley's diary caused township two, range two, to be selected as one of the places for first permanent settlement.

On the sixty-sixth mile we encamped at five chains north of a river. This we find to be the Big Beaver river (it was the Mahoning, mistaken by the surveyors for the Big Beaver). The course is east, current gentle but brink, gravel bottom, and low banks. It is about four feet deep. We have measured across by trigonometry and find it to be about fifteen rods wide. After we came away Landon said he saw two men in a canoe at the opposite shore and called them to him. They told him they had been at work there (about fifty rods down the river on the Pennsylvania side) for about three years; that the salt springs were about eighteen miles up the river and they were then going there to make salt. They had not got their families on yet but would ere long; that about twelve miles below the line on Big Beaver there was an excellent set of mills, and about twenty-five miles below the line there was a town building rapidly, where provisions of all kinds could be procured, and carried from thence up the river into the heart of the Connecticut Reserve. There are no falls to the source and it is but sixty miles from the line down to Pittsburg.

They had heard at Pymatuning creek a cow bell and looked for a settlement in the neighborhood, but did not succeed in finding it; the Pennsylvanians in the boat informed them that there was a family living on the creek near the line.

On Thursday afternoon, July 21st, the party arrived at the southeast corner of New Connecticut, where they took the variation of their compasses by the polar star. On Saturday following Moses Warren, with a party of thirteen, arrived and a chestnut post sixteen inches by twelve was placed at the corner of New Connecticut on which was inscribed; west side: "New Connecticut, July 23, 1796 ;" north side, "Sixty-eight miles Lake Erie ;" and on the east side, " Pennsylvania."

After two days delay the party distributed to run the range lines back to the lake. Holley ran the first range, Spafford the second, Warren the third, and Pease and Porter the fourth. Some of the meridians converged while others diverged, causing a variation of half a mile before reaching the lake. This variation was found to make considerable difference in the size of the townships. The same difficulty was experienced in the United States surveys, and, before the invention of better instruments than the old fashioned compass and quadrant, it was found necessary to make a correction of each township line before proceeding with the next. In the survey of the Reserve the directors were in too great haste to permit the surveyors to take these precautions against fluctuations of the compass. The amount of this fluctuation will appear from the variation in the size of the townships of Mahoning and Trumbull counties; the number of acres in each of the townships is as follows:

Poland...16,140
Coitsville..15,804
Hubbard..15,274
Brookfield...15,305
Hartford..17,217
Vernon..16,539
Kinsman..16,664
Boardman..15,912
Youngstown...15,560
Liberty...15,858
Vienna..14,715
Fowler..16,551
Johnston...15,914
Gustavus...15,646
Canfield..16,324
Austintown..16,377
Weathersfield......................................15,798
Howland..15,558
Bazetta...17,247
Mecca..16,873
Greene...16,558
Ellsworth..16,168
Jackson..15,500

Lordstown	14,492
Warren	14,606
Champion	16,419
Bristol	16,331
Bloomfield	16,039
Berlin	15,907
Milton	15,757
Newton	14,946
Braceville	15,004
Southington	16,692
Farmington	17,157
Mesopotamia	16,833

It must be borne in mind that the parallel lines defining the townships varied also so that it can not be determined from the size of the township whether the lines converged or diverged. It was intended that each township should embrace just sixteen thousand acres. The fact that there is not a township in the whole Reserve measuring exactly that amount indicates the inaccuracy of the survey. It made no difference in the final partition, for by that time the area of each was known, and all deficiencies either in quality or quantity, were compensated by tracts in other localities.

While the survey was in progress the directors of the Connecticut Land company were sowing broadcast extravagant circulars describing "the enchanting beauty and inexhaustible fertility of New Connecticut." Advertisements, in 1797, even in orthodox old Connecticut, differed very little from advertisements in New Connecticut in 1882. The successful composer of that sort of literature must be oblivious to defects and wear glasses which magnify attractions and advantages. But those who contemplated making heavy purchases were not deceived by overflowing rhetoric. They either consulted the surveyors' notes, which were taken back at the end of the first season, or managed to be chosen on the surveyors' corps for the next year.

The destined capital of New Connecticut was Cleaveland, or Cleveland, as it is spelled now. The town was laid off in lots, in the fall of 1796, and a few families remained in the place over winter. The lots were small and could be purchased only by permanent settlers.

John Young, in 1797, under the provisions of Article III. of the Land company's constitution, purchased township two, range two, and gave his own name to the settlement which grew up in that township. The locality was singularly fortunate, and Young's settlement took early precedence in the Reserve, and held it for a long term of years. When the partition of land was made among the stockholders, in 1798, it is estimated that there were but fifteen families on the Reserve; ten of these were at Youngstown, three at Cleveland, and two at Mentor. The best road to the West continued to be through Pennsylvania to Pittsburg. From the falls above Pittsburg, batteaux and even flat boats could be pushed up the Mahoning, making Youngstown the most accessible point in New Connecticut.

There was little real activity on the Reserve until after the partition of lands, in 1798. It then became a personal object for each owner to find purchasers who would, by making actual settlement, improve and enhance in value adjoining tracts. For three years the company had been reaching into their pockets to keep up the expense account and interest on their obligation to the State. It was becoming an utter necessity to some of them to find purchasers at some price. We insert a copy of the original drafts of the townships included in Mahoning and Trumbull counties, as at present constituted:

Hubbard township was included in draft No. 12 to Joseph Borrell, $7,000*; Joseph Borrell and William Edwards, $17,406.46; William Edwards, $1,400.

The record shows that several transfers of stock had been made before the regular partition took place. William Edwards eventually became owner of the entire township, which he sold, April, 1801, to Nehemiah Hubbard, whose name its bears. The first conveyances issued by Hubbard were to John P. Bessell and Samuel Tyler.

Brookfield township (surveyed township four, range one) was drawn by Samuel Hinkley, together with other lands, his stock in the company being $12,903.23. The first conveyance by him was one lot to James McMullen, issued in January, 1801.

Hartford (surveyed township five, range one) was drawn by Uriel Holmes, stock $6,452, and Ephraim Root, stock $6,451.23. The first conveyance, by Holmes and Root, was to Edward Brockway, in September, 1799, of a tract of 3,194 2-160 acres, in consideration of $500,

---

* The proportion of each proprietor is expressed by the number of dollars invested.

showing considerable loss on the part of the original proprietors.

Vernon (township six, range one) was drawn by William Shepard, Jr., stock $4,000; William Whetmore, $6,000; Jeremiah Wilcox, $2,903.23. William Whetmore, having mortgaged his interest to Jonathan Dwight and Gideon Granger, and being unable to redeem it, the deed for the whole purchase was made to Shepard, Wilcox, and Granger, the latter having purchased Dwight's interest. The township was divided into three tracts, bearing the names of the then owners.

Kinsman (township seven, range one) was drawn by Uriah Tracy and Joseph Coit, stock $4,838.61; and John Kinsman, $8,064.61. Coit and Tracy subsequently conveyed their interest to John Kinsman, who thus became sole owner of the township in 1804. The first conveyances of small tracts in Kinsman were in 1802; 202½ acres to David Randall, $405; 800 acres to Ebenezer Reeves, $2,000; 106 acres to Martin Tidd, $212.

Liberty (township three, range two) was drawn by Moses Cleaveland, stock $3,298.92; Christopher Leffingwell, $2,778.31; Daniel Lathrop, $3,626; Samuel Huntington, $3,200. The greater portion of this township was purchased by the Erie company, of which all these proprietors were members. A later transfer was made by the Erie company to Simon Perkins, Daniel L. Coit, Samuel Huntington, and others.

Vienna (township four, range two,) was drawn by Timothy Burr, A. Hitchcock, Uriah Holmes, Jr., and Ephraim Root. By several transfers made from time to time Ephraim Root became owner of nearly the entire township.

Fowler (township five, range two) was drawn by Samuel Fowler, whose stock in the company amounted to $12,903.23.

Gustavus (township seven, range two) was drawn by Henry Champion, stock $93,087; Lemuel Storer, $8,154; David Waterman and Nathaniel Church, 0.34; Joshua Stow, $808; Oliver Phelps and Gideon Granger, $1,176.50. Henry Stores, in August, 1800, became sole owner of the township. He transferred, in 1801, to Josiah Pelton five thousand one hundred and ninety-eight and one-fourth acres for $6,382.25. This was the first deed executed by Stores after he became sole owner of the township.

Weathersfield (township three, range three) was drawn as follows: Caleb Atwater, stock, $333.33; Daniel Holbrook, $2,000; Turhand Kirtland, $4,750; F. J. B. Kirtland, $5,000; Levi Tomlinson, $1,250, drew tract number seven, containing eight hundred and forty-seven acres. James Lathrop, stock, $8,125; Daniel Lathrop, $3,626; John Kinsman, $1,279.67; Lynda McCurdy, $302.66, drew tract number nine, with considerable additions. This township was considered of more value than the others on account of the salt springs. The whole of Weathersfield township was not placed among the first drafts, because the boundaries of the salt spring tract were not yet defined.

Howland (township four, range three) was drawn by Joseph Howland, stock, $12,903.23. The first conveyance was made by Howland to John H. Adgate in 1799 of one thousand six hundred acres in consideration of $1,600.

Bazetta (township five, range three) was drawn by David Huntington, stock, $300; Nathaniel Shalor, $5,096.77; Samuel P. Lord, $1,188.46; Sylvester Mather, $3,300; Richard McCurdy, $3,018.

The original proprietors of Johnston township were Judson Canfield, stock $4,796.25; David Waterman, $2,640; James Johnston, $2,661; Nathaniel Church, $997.50; Frederick Walcott and Elijah Wadsworth, $131.15; Judson Canfield, James Johnston, David Waterman, and Nathaniel Church, $452.33; Samuel Canfield, $344; Eliza Wadsworth, $1,504. After numerous conveyances the township was partitioned and the greater part purchased by James Johnston, after whom it was named.

Greene (township seven, range three) was drawn by Joseph Howland, stock $12,903.23. In 1811 the whole township was conveyed to Gardner Greene. The first transfers made by him were in 1825 to Benjamin Pruden, David Rice, and Noah Bower, at prices ranging about $1.50 an acre.

Lordstown (township three, range four,) was drawn by Samuel P. Lord, stock $12,903.23. Five thousand acres were soon after deeded to his son, Samuel P. Lord, Jr., who was also a resident of Connecticut. The tax on these five thousand acres in 1806 amounted to $20.24, and in default of payment, James Hillman, district tax collector, offered the land for sale as the law directed. The manner of conducting delinquent tax sales was the same as at present—the sale being confirmed to the party offering to pay the tax in consideration of the least number of acres. Eli Baldwin, of Boardman, bid 4,273 acres, which was the lowest, and upon payment of the $20.24 tax he received a deed to that number of acres, being almost the entire tract.

The draft which included Warren (township four, range four,) fell to Reuben and Andrew Bardwell, Ebenezer King, Jr., David and Fidelia King, Joseph Pratt, Luther Loomis, John Leavitt, Jr., Timothy Phelps, Martin Sheldon, Asabel King, Simon Kendall, Erastus Granger, Oliver Sheldon, Sylvester G. Griswold, and Matthew Thompson. The same stockholders drew three other townships outside of the present limits of this county.

Champion (township five, range four) was drawn by Henry Champion, stock, $93,087; Lemuel Storer, $8,154; Judson Canfield, James Johnston, David Waterman, and Nathaniel Church, $0.34; Joshua Stowe, $808; Oliver Phelps and Gideon Granger, $1,176.50.* By successive conveyances Henry Champion became exclusive owner of this township in December, 1798. William Woodrow made the first purchase from Henry Champion in 1818. In 1825 he deeded a large tract to his grandson, Henry C. Trumbull.

Bristol (township six, range four) was drawn by Nathaniel Gorham and Worham Parks, stock $12,803.43. From them it was transferred to Benjamin Gorham who sold in 1801, 12,609 acres, being the whole of the township except a square containing 3,722 acres, to Calvin Austin and Oliver L. Phelps. Benjamin Gorham conveyed in 1803 his remaining lands to Justus Ely and O. L. Phelps so that the ownership was finally vested in Austin, Phelps and Ely.

Bloomfield (township seven, range four) was drawn by Peter C. Brooks, stock $6,000, and Nathaniel Gorham, $6,923.23. Nathaniel Gorham the following year transferred his interest in the township to Peter C. Brooks. Brooks sold to Thomas Howe and Ephraim Brown. Brown in 1815 became owner of the entire township. In 1828 Brown sold seven hundred acres to E. Goodrich, Jr., and Aristarchus Champion. A large part of this township is embraced in what was known as the tamarack swamp.

Mecca (township six, range three) was drawn by Turhand Kirtland, Jared Kirtland, Belius Kirtland, Seth Hart, Elnathan Smith, Jr., Abiatha Hall, stock $10,000; Asa Rising, Francis Pierce, $200; William F. Miller, $2,600; Caleb Atwater, $98.08; Seth Hart, $5.15. After various transfers the title to this township was in 1801 vested as follows: Rising and Pierce, 384 acres; Kirtland Brothers, 7,185 acres; Solomon Cowles, 3,760 acres; Andrew Kingsburry, 2,581 acres; William Ely tract, 3,347 acres.

Newton (township three, range five,) was drawn by Jonathan Brace, stock $2,047.23; Justin Ely, $5,428; Elijah White, $5,428.

Braceville (township four, range five,) was drawn by Jonathan Brace, stock $2,047.23; Enoch Perkins, $5,428; Newburry, $5,428. The first conveyance made by the original purchasers of this township was a tract of 2,402 acres in 1802. Deeds were issued to H. Benedict, Joshua Stowe, and Samuel North in 1810.

Southington (township five, range five) was drawn and apportioned as follows: Solomon Cowles, $5,000; William Ely, $3,757; Ephraim Robbins, $4,126.23; Joseph Barrell and William Edwards, $20. After several conveyances and an equitable division of the land the township was divided into three parts and was owned by William Ely, John Bowles, and Solomon Cowles.

Farmington (township six, range five) was drawn by Joseph Borrell and William Edwards, stock $1,503.46; Samuel Henshaw, $8,400; Joseph Pratt, Luther Loomis, David King, John Leavitt, Jr., Ebenezer King, Jr., Timothy Phelps, and Fidelia King, $1,316.77; Sylvester Griswold, $1,683. Several transfers followed, which placed John Caldwell, Ephraim Kirby, Solomon Bond, John Eaton, and Lemuel Forbes in possession of the entire township.

Mesopotamia (township five, range seven) was drawn by Pierpont Edwards, stock $12,903.23. The first transfer of lands in this township was made by John S. Edwards (recorder for Trumbull county), attorney for Pierpont Edwards, to Seth Tracy, then a resident of Pittsfield, Massachusetts. The conveyance is dated September 27, 1800.

Poland (township one, range one) was drawn

---

* In this case as in many others the same association of persons made several drafts on the basis of their united stock.

by Benjamin Doolittle, Jr., stock $1,592; Samuel Doolittle, $80; Titus Street, $6,943; William Law, $6,923; T. Kirtland, $3,750; Andrew Hull, $2,268.46; Daniel Holbrook, $2,000; T. Kirtland and Seth Hart, $1,000; Levi Tomlinson, $1,250.

Coitsville (township two, range one) was drawn by John Kinsman, stock $3,040.15; Tracy and Coit, $5,761.39; Zephaniah Swift, $3,260; Christopher Leffingwell, $841.69. Daniel Coit subsequently became owner of the greater part of this township, and when it was erected into a civil township it was named in his honor.

Boardman (township one, range two) was drawn by Elijah Boardman, stock $7,500; Homer Boardman, $1,025; David S. Boardman, $1,250; Jonathan Giddings, $325; Stanley Griswold, $1,023.38; Elijah Wadsworth and Frederick Wolcott, $979.82; William Ely, $800.

Canfield (township one, range two) was the draft of Judson Canfield, stock $4,769.25; David Waterman, $2,064; James Johnston, $2,661; Nathaniel Church, $997.50; Elijah Wadsworth and Frederick Wolcott, $131.15; Judson Canfield, James Johnston, David Waterman, and Nathaniel Church, $432.33; Samuel Canfield, $344; Elijah Wadsworth, $1,504.

Youngstown was purchased by John Young, from the directors, under Article III. of the Land company's agreement.

Austintown and Jackson townships were drawn by the same stockholders—Gideon Granger, Jr., $12,700; Oliver Phelps, $47,201; Oliver Phelps and Gideon Granger, Jr., $30,421.61. They also, on the basis of the capital here represented, drew a township in the present county of Ashtabula. Part of General Parsons' purchase, known as the Salt Spring tract, lay in each of these townships, and was excepted in the original deed.

Berlin (township one, range five) was originally owned and drawn by George Blake, stock $790.31; Samuel Mather, Jr., $7,354.54; William Hart, $1,752.31; Richard W. Hart, $3,000; Samuel Mather, Jr., $6.07.

Milton township was drawn by Joseph Borrell and William Edwards, stock $5.08; Ezekiel Williams, Jr., $96.77; Ralph Pomeroy, $8,125; Nathaniel G. Ingraham, $3,000; Ozias Marvin, Stephen Lockwood, Taylor Sherman, and Phineas Miller, $1,600; Pierpont Edwards, $0.08; Samuel P. Lord, $0.31; Ebenezer, David, and Fidelia King, $0.39; Elijah Wadsworth and Frederick Wolcott, $0.51; Uriel Holmes and Ephraim Root, $0.31; Ichabod Ward, $74.78.

We have now given the original purchasers from the Connecticut Land company of all that part of the Reserve lying within the present counties of Trumbull and Mahoning. All deeds from the company were of the character of the deed of the State of Connecticut to the company—merely quit-claims, so that the tenability of all titles rested after the partition of 1798 as before, namely, upon the validity of Connecticut's claim as against the claim of all other States vested by cession in the United States. However, the influence of actual occupation and improvement was rapidly clearing up all doubts as to what the final result would be. The permanent settlement which began at Youngstown and on Mill creek in 1797, spread rapidly up and down the river and over the more favored and accessible portions of the county in 1799. In 1800 Youngstown was the largest town on the Reserve, and Warren, which was laid off in the beginning of that year, was second in size, and as we shall see became first in importance. A settlement was made at Harpersfield in Ashtabula county, in 1798, and the Mentor settlement grew from three families in the spring of 1798 to ten by 1800. Cleveland, which dates its settlement from the fall of 1796, had at the end of the first year a population of fifteen souls. Three years from that time there were but seven permanent settlers at the mouth of the Cuyahoga, and in 1810 only fifty-seven. Both Warren and Youngstown had by that time become brisk pioneer villages. The following list gives the name of the first settlers in each township of the Reserve included in Trumbull and Mahoning counties, and the date of their settlement. For further details the reader is referred to the township histories:

Youngstown, 1797, by John Young and Daniel Shehy.

Canfield, June, 1798, by Champion Miner, from Connecticut.

Vernon, 1798, by Thomas Giddings and Martin Smith.

Liberty, 1798, by Henry and Jacob Swager.

Brookfield, 1798, by James McMullen, Sr.

Howland, 1799, by John Adgate.

Boardman, 1799, by Nathaniel Blakeley, John McMahon, and a Daniels family.

Warren, 1799, by Ephraim Quinby, Henry Lane, et al.

Vienna, 1799, by Isaac Fowler and Dennis Palmer.

Poland, 1799, by Jonathan Fowler, from Connecticut; and John Struthers, from Pennsylvania.

Coitsville, 1799, by Amos Loveland, from Vermont.

Fowler, 1799, by Abner Fowler, from Westfield, Massachusetts; and Levi Foote, from Massachusetts, in 1801.

Weathersfield, 1800, by Reuben Harmon, from Vermont.

Austintown, 1800, by John McCollum, from New Jersey.

Hartford, 1799, by Asahel Brainard, and in 1800 by Edward Brockway and Isaac Jones.

Hubbard, 1801, by Samuel Tylee, from Connecticut.

Mesopotamia, 1800, by Hezekiah Sperry, from Connecticut.

Newton, 1802, by Ezekiel Hover and Alexander Southerland.

Gustavus, 1802, by Jesse, Elias, and Josiah Pelton, from Connecticut.

Kinsman, 1802, by John Kinsman and Ebenezer Reeves, from Connecticut.

Braceville, 1803, by Ralph Freeman.

Johnston, 1803, by James Bradley, from Connecticut.

Jackson, 1803, by Samuel Calhoun, William Orr, Andrew Gault, and Samuel Riddle, from Pennsylvania.

Milton, 1803, by Nathaniel Stanley and Aaron Porter.

Ellsworth, 1804, by James Reed, from Pennsylvania; Joseph Coit and Philip Abner.

Bristol, 1804, by Abraham Baughman, from Virginia.

Bazetta, 1804, by Edward Schofield.

Southington, 1805, by Luke and David Veits and James Ghalker, from Connecticut.

Champion, 1806, by William Rutan, from Pennsylvania.

Farmington, 1806, by Zenas Curtis, David Curtis, and Elihu Moses.

Berlin, 1809, by Garrett Packard, Virginia.

Mecca, 1811, by Joseph Davidson and John Rose.

Bloomfield, 1815, by Leman Ferry, from Vermont, and Ephraim Brown, from New Hampshire.

Greene, 1817, by Ephraim Rice, John Wakefield and Ichabod Merritt.

Lordstown, 1822, by Henry Thorn.

RESIDENTS IN 1801.

The following is a list of resident tax-payers as returned by the collector in 1801, in the several townships included within the scope of this work:

POLAND—William Beech, George Brierly, John Crag, William Cowden, Joseph Cowden, Joseph Craycraft, William Campbell, William Dunlap, John Dinow, Thomas Dawson, Jacob Dawson, Jonathan Fowler, James Flemming, Thomas Gordon, William Guthrie, John Hineman, Francis Henry, John Jordan, Jered Kirtland, Isaac Kirtland, James Keys, Benjamin Leach, William Moore, John McGill, William McConnell, W. and John McCombs, John McConnell, John Miller, Thomas McCullough, McIwers & Landon, Finton McGill, Archibald Nelson, Henry Ripple, Robert Smith, John Struthers, John Sheerer, Peter Shauf, William Stewart, John Treusdell, William Treusdell, Andrew and Mary Vane, Samuel White, John Wishard, James Webb, Nathaniel Walker.

COITSVILLE—James Bradford, David Cooper, Andrew Fitch, John Gwin, Amos Loveland, James Muns, William Martin, Samuel McBride, Alexander McGreffy, John Potter, Rodger Shehy, James Shields, James Smith, John Thornton, William Wicks, James White, Francis White.

BOARDMAN—Ebenezer Blakesby, Nathan Blakesby, Caleb Baldwin, Isaac Cook, James Canady, Joseph Comyus, Noah Chamberlain, William Dree, Oswald Dutchen, Henry Dunsman, Benjamin Fisher, Eleazer Fairchild, Jonathan Fowler, Thomas Kizzarty, James McMahon, John McMahon, Archibald McArthy, John Stevens, Allen Scroggs, Michael Simons, James Stull, Andrew Simons, Beach Somers, John Thornton, Jr.

YOUNGSTOWN — Lineas Brainard, William Beer, Samuel Calhoon, Alexander Clarke, James Caldwell, Joseph Carr, Christopher Coleman, Aaron Clarke, Thomas Dree, James Davidson, John Dimmick, Nathan G. Dabney, John Dunier,

Thomas Ferrell, Michael Fitzjerald, James Gibson, James Hillman, Henry Hull, Samuel Haydon, Joshua Kyle, John Kyle, Thomas Kirkpatrick, Andrew Kirkpatrick, Moses Latter, John Musgrove, James McCoy, John McCrary, John McDowell, John McWilliams, Daniel McCartney, Jesse Newport, Jeremiah Norris, David Randall, Josiah Robbins, Benjamin Ross, John Rush, William Rayen, John Swager, Robert Stevens, Daniel Shehy, Robert M. Scott, Matthew Scott, Henry Swager, Sefford Thompson, Joseph Williamson, James Wilson, Joseph Wilson, Alfred Wolcott, A. Wolcott, John Young.

CANFIELD—Ichabod Atwood, James Bradley, Charles Chittenden, Aaron Coller, Calvin Crane, Timothy Chittenden, William Chittenden, James Dowel, Polly Doud, Jonathan Everett, Henry Faulkner, Samuel Gilson, Nathaniel Gridly, Joshua Hollister, Raphael Hulbert, Jacob Harrington, Homer Hern, Archibald Johnson, Zibai Loveland, Zebulon Merwin, Champlin Miner, Nathan Moore, James Neil, Joseph Pangbourn, Wilder Page, Phineas Reed, James Reed, Matthew Steel, Jonah Schovil, Ira Sprague, William Sprague, John Sintox, Calvin Tobias, Reuben Tupper, Trial Tanner, Isaac Wilson, Elijah Wadsworth, Bradford Waldo, Benjamin Yale.

AUSTINTOWN — William Bayard, Benjamin Bayard, John Dunier, Samuel Furgerson, Windall Grove, Robert Kirkpatrick, Alexander McAllister, Thomas Morgan, John McCullom, Samuel Miller, Frederick Mauchaman, Thomas Parkard, David Parkhurst, Calvin Pease, Gilbert Roberts, George Stanford, James Sisco, Benjamin Sisco, William Templeton, Nathaniel Walker, William Whethington.

HUBBARD—Jonathan Carr, Walter Clark, John Clark, Daniel Cary, Cornelius Dilley, William Erwin, Samuel Ewart, George Frazier, James Frazier, John Gardner, Jesse Hall, William Hanna, Thomas Hanna, Hugh Harrison, Absalom Hall, Moses Hall, Henry McFarlane, Benjamin Mars, John McCrary, James Minary, Robert McKey, James Milihettree, Alexander McFarlane, William McFarlane, John Porter, William Parvin, Joseph Porter, Zehiel Roberts, David Reed, Henry Robertson, Edward Scovil, Amos Smith, John Snyder, Samuel Tylee, Sylvester Tylee, William Veach, Samuel White.

LIBERTY—Thomas Barr, Ezra Brant, Thomas Camden Cleaveland, Francis Carlton, John Dennison, Justus Dunn, H. Eikman, Joseph Gowdy, James Hill, Barker King, James Matthews, Samuel Menough, John McGee, Neil McMullen, Joseph Miller, Thomas Potts, William Potter, Valentine Stull, William Stewart, Henry Swager, Jacob Swager, William Wilson.

VIENNA—Isaac Flower, Isaac Flower, Jr., Levi Foote, James W. Foster, Samuel Hutchins, Daniel Humison, Dennis C. Palmer, Epinctus Rogers, Darius Woodford, Simon Wheeler, Isaac Woodford.

JACKSON—Joseph McInrill, William Orr, Samuel Riddell.

WEATHERSFIELD—Reuben Harmon.

HOWLAND—John H. Adgate, David Cooper, John S. Edwards, Edward Jones, John Kinney, Asa Marriner, William McReady, Joseph Quigley, Jacob Reese, David Wells.

WARREN—Zopher Carnes, William Crooks, Meshach Case, John Daly, Benjamin Davidson, Charles Daly, Samuel Daniels, William Hall, Henry Lane, Henry Lane, Jr., John Leavitt, Enoch Leavitt, Phineas Leffingwell, Thomas Prior, Ephraim Quinby, Eleazer Sheldon, Simon Perkins.

BRACEVILLE—David Moore, Phineas Palmer.

HARTFORD—William Bushnell, Aaron Brockwell, Josiah W. Brown, A. Brainard, Thomas Dugan, Henry Hayes, George Hall, William C. Jones, Martha Merry, Aaron Rice, Elijah Woodford.

VERNON—Titus Brockwell, Obed Crosby, Joseph DeWolf, H. C. DeWolf, Thomas Giddings, Abner Moses, Ambrose Palmer, Warren Palmer, Martin Smith.

MESOPOTAMIA—Griswold Gillette, Otis Guile, Joseph Noyes, George Phelps, Hezekiah Sperry, Seth Tracy, Elam Tracy, Joel Thropp.

CHAMPION—Jonathan Atwater.

BRISTOL—Thomas Dick, D. M. and A. Fenton, Francis Martin, J. Martin, Jeremiah Norris.

GUSTAVUS — Calvin Judd, Joseph Pelton, Luther Plumb, Thomas Thompson, Asa Thompson, Samual Thompson.

It has previously been noticed that the first clearing made by white men was at Salt Springs, in Weathersfield, where several cabins were found by the surveyors. We have also seen that the Pennsylvanians used the water of these springs for making salt as early as the Revolution, and when the surveyors first saw the Mahoning river they met with two men on their way to make salt. The McMahon family settled in the county as early as 1797, and were engaged at making salt in 1800. An appropriation was made by the Land company to open the springs and improve the works, but nothing was accomplished of any material value.

There were squatters in the Reserve, besides the salt-makers, before the Connecticut emigrants arrived. They were mostly hunters and trappers, who lived a semi-civilized life. There is something attractive in the character of these squatters. They were, at least many of them were, fugitives from the civil and economical laws of aggregated communities where prolonged and systematic labor is a necessity, and where the rights of property are enforced. With his dog and gun the squatter was at home wherever he slept, and satisfied with whatever came within range of his steady rifle, always apparently happy, always roving, his wife was his slave, his life was all he cared for. His geographical, as well as ethnological, place was between the Indian and the white settler. Occupying the border ground which both used for hunting, he was always on good terms with both, but dependent very little on either. His hut was generally located near some Indian clearing, where a small patch of ground could be prepared for a little vegetable garden and corn enough to supply the family with meal occasionally. Game was his staple table fare.

The names of few of this class of the overflow of civilization have been perserved. James McMillen, senior, of Brookfield, was probably a squatter, though if he was, he belonged to the more persevering and better class. When the land came in market he purchased and improved a farm. Mr. Merryman was at Warren when the first settlers arrived, an old gray haired man. Whence he came, or whither he went, is no where recorded. Sixty winters had bleached his hair and unsteadied his step, but a faithful gun was his only reliance for the future. For years nature had provided his home, his food and his enjoyment; in all probability his death bed comforter was the howling of wolves and the cheerless whistle of the wind. Others of this class of white adventurers pushed on farther into the wilderness, when rattling axes gave notice of the opening of the drama of clearing and improvement.

From the list of settlers we have given, it will be noticed that Poland, Boardman, Canfield, Youngstown, Coitsville, Hubbard, and Warren were the advance settlements in the Reserve. The pioneers were not all Connecticut people; there were among the number Pennsylvanians, both of Irish and of Dutch descent. There was a large Irish settlement along the east border as will be seen by the number of names beginning with "Mc."

Having now seen the forest surveyed, platted and placed upon the market, also having seen openings made and here and there smoke issuing from cabin chimneys, it follows in order to detail the organization of civil government. To that subject the next chapter will be devoted.

CHAPTER VIII.
INDIAN ABDICATION.

Origin of Difficulties—The Captain George Tragedy—James Hillman's Exploits.

Although the Indians had released all claim to that part of the Reserve lying east of the Cuyahoga, wandering bands still camped and hunted here till many years after the Connecticut settlers had arrived. They were remnants of broken tribes, and were in general harmless but often provoked to crime. They did not possess that proud loftiness of character which commands our admiration in the earlier and farther removed inhabitants of the forest. Conscious of their inferiority and of their inability to maintain possession of their hunting grounds, they degenerated and became discouraged, objectless wanderers, ready to absorb any vice with which they came in contact. A passion for strong drink obtained a mastery over them, and was a prevailing cause of crime, from the responsibility of which the whites can not claim entire absolution.

The Massassaugas, a tribe of the Delaware nation, were the last dwellers of the race in the Mahoning valley. The name signifies "rattlesnake," and probably originated from the great numbers of that reptile formerly found in this region. It was certainly not because of fierceness or venom of character. When the first settlers arrived these followers of a defeated and dying race lingered in considerable numbers, but gradually grew fewer and weaker until they finally disappeared entirely. No serious difficulty affecting the community at large is recorded in the early annals of this region, with a solitary exception. A number of incidents, however, have survived the lapse of time, which are interesting in themselves and enable us to fill out the picture of pioneer life on the Reserve.

The religion of these Indians was that pagan spiritualism so generally believed in by the American tribes. Their worship involved the offering of sacrifices, and such occasions were always made their grand religious jubilees, to which the settlers were invited. The annual sacrifice consisted of a white dog. For days before the appointed time a search was made throughout the settlement for an animal without spot or blemish of any kind, and for such any price might be demanded. At early dawn the whole tribe gathered upon a sacred spot, their solemn countenances expressive of rigid and simple faith. The chiefs, with great ceremony bound the legs of the victim with thongs in such a way that it could be easily suspended on a pole. A torch was applied to the wood which had been carefully placed in a rustic rack. The living dog, by means of the pole to which he was fastened, was raised over the fire, while the head chief, acting as priest, scattered through the flames herbs and spice-wood. While this ceremony was in progress the assembly moaned and shouted and sang. Slowly the poor, howling, tortured victim was raised in and out of the fire until death finally relieved it of excruciating pain. The worshipers grew more and more demonstrative, finally terminating in a spasmodic dance around the dying fire and charred body of the victim. A feast of sugar, hominy, and whiskey terminated the religious festival, by which a great and angry spirit, it was supposed, had been appeased.

On the 27th of July, 1800, there occurred a tragedy at the Salt spring in Weathersfield township, which produced a profound sensation in the settlement, and threatened to interrupt that peace which had thus far aided the pioneers in their struggle with nature.

Joseph McMahon, with a family consisting of a wife and children, had lived in the vicinity of Warren for three years, and perhaps longer, among the Indians, subsisting on the victims of his rifle, and a small patch of corn planted each year in one of the old Indian clearings along the river. During the year 1799 he lived at the southwest corner of Howland, and the following spring removed with his family to one of the cabins which had been left standing by the salt makers. He planted about four acres of cleared land in the vicinity in corn. The land belonged to Richard Storer, by whom McMahon was employed during the summer. About sixty rods up the ravine was an old Indian camping ground, where a large number of the tribe gathered in July, and as not infrequently happened on such occasions, they were joined by a number of whites, and a drunken frolic was the result. McMahon was a member of this party. When the Indians' supply of whisky was exhausted, the whites clandestinely sent to Warren for an additional supply which they refused to share with the Indians, denying that they had succeeded in getting any.* On the following Tuesday McMahon left home to work for Storer. The Indians were still at the camp, and soon after McMahon left two or three of them visited his cabin, began to tease his wife, and insulted her with brutal proposals. On being indignantly denied, they finally threatened to kill her and her children. Mrs. McMahon fearing violence, took her child in her arms, and hurried to Storer's to inform her husband. They both returned to the springs on Thursday, and had a consultation with the Indians, who promised to give no further cause for anxiety. But when McMahon returned to his work, the Indians again threatened his wife and children. Their threats were even carried to the extent of striking one of the children on the head with a tomahawk.

The situation became more and more alarming, until Saturday, when Mrs. McMahon again took her family and started for Storer's, near Warren. She met her husband on his way homeward, and told him the whole story. They returned to Storer, and the first impulse of the two men was for blood. Upon consideration, it was determined to lay the difficulty before Captain Ephraim Quinby, of Warren, who bore the

* Another account says Richard Storer chastised Spotted John for stealing his whiskey.

reputation of being a mild and judicious man. That the difficulty might be permanently settled, Mr. Quinby advised a conference with the Indians, but thought it wise to go in sufficient numbers for self-defense, should any violence be attempted. Accordingly, on Sunday morning, all the young men and middle-aged men in the community, among whom were Henry Lane, Jr., Captain Ephraim Quinby, John Lane, Asa Lane, Richard Storer, William Carlton, William Fenton, Charles Daily, John Bently, Jonathan Church, Benjamin Lane, McMahon, Storer, and others, were mustered out. Each man had a gun, though it was not expected that there would be any occasion for using it. Leaving Warren, they passed along the old winding trail leading to Youngstown, by way of the springs. They were in a jovial mood, and engaged in practical jokes and light conversation until the run below the camp was reached. There Captain Quinby, who was looked upon as leader, called a halt, and a council was held. It was agreed that they should remain while the Captain went to the camp and learned accurately the real state of affairs.

Mr. Quinby found the Indians lolling about the camp. Among them were Captain George, a Tuscarawas, and John Winslow, called Spotted John because he was partly white. The former could speak English fluently, and on that account was the first addressed. Captain Quinby inquired the difficulty between the Indians and McMahon and his family. "Oh, Joe damn fool!" said George. "The Indians don't want to hurt him or his family. They (the whites) drank up all the Indians' whiskey and then would'nt let the Indians have any of theirs. They were a little mad but don't care any more about it. They (McMahon and family) may come back and live as long as they like. The Indians won't hurt them."* After this assurance Captain Quinby felt satisfied that no difficulty was necessary about so trivial a matter, nor no danger need be apprehended. He started back expecting to find his comrades where they had halted. But in the meantime they had sauntered up the ravine and were ascending to the plain where the Indians were when Mr. Quinby met them. They all halted to hear the result of the conference, except McMahon, who passed on.

*Case MSS.

Quinby called to him to stop, but was not heeded. While Quinby was relating his conversation at the camp they all slowly ascended the hill from the ravine into plain open view of the Indian camp about fifteen rods distant. There was only an occasional tree between them and the Indians. McMahon and two boys who had accompanied the party were already at the camp.

Captain George, a large, muscular man, was sitting on the root of a tree leaning his body against the trunk, when McMahon approached him. Five or six other Indians and several squaws and pappooses were lolling about the camp. McMahon saluted George: "Are you for peace? Yesterday you had your men, now I have mine." George sprang to his feet, seized a tomahawk, which was sticking in a tree over his head, and was swinging it when McMahon, having sprung back and brought his rifle to bear, fired, the ball piercing George's breast. The blood spurted almost to McMahon, who turned instantly and called to the men in open view: "Shoot, shoot." The other Indians by this time had seized their guns, took refuge behind trees, and were aiming at the whites. Several flints on both sides snapped, but, the morning being damp and rainy, missed fire. Storer saw Spotted John aiming at him and without a second's reflection brought his sure rifle to bear and fired. John's squaw was directly behind him endeavoring to screen herself and pappooses by the same tree. The ball passed through John's hip, which was the only part of his body exposed, and passing on broke a boy's arm, passed under the cords of the neck of his girl, and grazed the throat of his squaw. The wildest confusion prevailed both on part of the Indians and whites. The two boys* who had followed McMahon when the first shot was fired fled, and doubled their exertion after the second. When they arrived at Davidson's, three miles and a half distant, they were so overdone that "shoot" was all they could gasp between breaths. When Spotted John (Winslow) fell the whole Warren party hurried away at quick pace. The Indians were terror stricken but remained to bury their dead, then hastened westward on the old trail to the Cuyahoga and Sandusky. The widowed squaw of Spotted John took her wounded children in her arms and hastened to James Hill-

*Thomas Fenton and Peter Carlton.

man's, where she arrived, it is estimated, in one hour and a half—a distance of nine miles, or six miles an hour.*

McMahon was severely chastised for his conduct and shortly after put under arrest. No one who accompanied the party had anticipated any difficulty. They went as peace makers, and none of them meditated violence nor entertained an idea that McMahon did. They were men of high standing, and no blame of criminal intent or even want of discretion was ever attached to them. McMahon, under guard, was taken to Pittsburg, at that time the nearest place where a prisoner could be kept. It will be remembered that no jail was provided until after the session of court in August. The news of the tragedy had spread rapidly, and all the settlers along the river were soon in consultation in Warren. Shortly after McMahon's arrest, discussion turned to the propriety of arresting Storer also. Quietly observing what was going on, and keeping his own counsel, Storer, about 4 o'clock in the afternoon, walked into his cabin, put on his hat, took down his rifle, remarking that he must go out to hunt his cows, and unmolested by the excited settlers, he made his escape to the woods. A few months afterwards he returned, and is reported having said that he knew he had done nothing criminal; he had gone to the salt spring only and entirely with the intention of settling a difficulty, but suddenly found himself in imminent danger of being shot and therefore acted in self defense. The fact that Connecticut had ceded political jurisdiction over the Reserve, and that Trumbull county had been erected, was not known by common people about Warren at the time of this tragedy. Storer not knowing by what law or by whom he was to be tried, thought discretion the better part of valor, and absented himself from the power of those who were seeking to bring him into a trial which might imperil his life. On the day following her husband's departure, Mrs. Storer, with her two horses and three children, started for her former home in Washington county, Pennsylvania. Such property as she could carry was taken along; friendly neighbors took charge of what was left. Storer has never been seriously blamed for his part in the tragedy.

Among the pioneers of Youngstown was one of those brave, judicious, and useful characters whose life is an oft-told story of "the early days." Possessing the sterling qualities of a romantic borderer, James Hillman exercised his hard sense and used his ripe knowledge of Indian character in such a way as to become the hero of our frontier legend.* Mr. Hillman had been a trader long enough to foresee the possible result of this unfortunate quarrel, and on Monday started toward Sandusky, the route they were supposed to have taken. He came up with them on Wednesday, but found it difficult to obtain an interview on account of their suspicions toward the whites. But finally making known his mission to them, he offered, first $100, then $200, and so on until he had reached $500, if they would treat with him on just terms, and return to their homes; but this they would not listen to, only saying that they would go to Sandusky and hold a council with the chiefs there. Hillman replied, "You will hold a council there, light the war torch, rally all the warriors throughout the forest, and with savage barbarity come and attempt a general massacre of all your friends, the whites, throughout the Northwest Territory." They rejoined, "that they would lay the case before the council and within fourteen days, four or five of their number should return with instructions on what terms peace could be restored."

Upon Hillman's return it was thought best to prepare themselves for defense in case they should be attacked, and accordingly all the white settlers from Youngstown and the surrounding country garrisoned at Quinby's house at Warren, opened port-holes through the logs and kept guard night and day. The fourth or fifth day after, a circumstance took place which shows the

---

*Another account furnished by descendants of McMahon says that when Quinby left the party to go to the Indian camp he directed Lane to follow with his company in case he should not return in half an hour, and engage in battle. Quinby did not return at the stated time, and they proceeded rapidly to camp. On coming out of the woods they observed Quinby in close conversation with Captain George. He told Captain George that his tribe had threatened to kill McMahon and his family and Storer and his family, while Captain George had said that if the whites had come down the Indians were ready to fight them. The whites marched immediately up to the camp—McMahon first and Storer next to him. The chief, Captain George, snatched his tomahawk, which was sticking in a tree, and flourishing it in the air, walked up to McMahon, saying: "If you kill me, I will lie here. If I kill you, you shall lie there!" and then ordered his men to prime and tree.

*See Youngstown.

fear and caution of the settlers. John Lane went out into the woods a little distance one cloudy day, and missing his way gave some alarm. In the evening a voice known to be his was heard several times, and in the same direction twelve or fourteen successive reports of a gun. It was judged that the Indians had returned, and catching Lane confined him and compelled him to halloo with threats of death if he did not, with the hope thus to entice the whites into an ambush where they might massacre them. In the morning as the noises continued, a man of strong nerve, named William Crooks, went out very cautiously to the spot and found that Lane had dislocated his ankle and was not able to get back to the fort without assistance. The little party continued to keep guard until the fourteenth day, when according to promise four or five Indians returned with proposals of peace, which were that McMahon and Storer should be taken to Sandusky, tried by the Indian laws, and if found guilty, punished by them. This they were told could not be done, as McMahon was already a prisoner under the laws of the United States, in the jail at Pittsburg, and Storer had fled out of the country.

It was finally agreed on August 23d to hold a peace conference at Youngstown, and there was a prospect of speedy settlement of the "unhappy and unprovoked breach."* Wednesday, August 30th, was the day agreed upon by both parties and an interpreter was engaged for the occasion. At the appointed hour about three hundred assembled whites were met at Judge Young's by ten Indians. After a friendly conference all expressed themselves as anxious for peace, and the Indians, having exchanged tokens of friendship, departed.

By order of Governor St. Clair McMahon was sent to Youngstown under a strong guard to stand his trial at a special court ordered for that purpose by the judges, Return J. Meigs, and Benjamin Ives. Gilman, Backus & Tod were attorneys for the people, and Mr. Simple, John S. Edwards, and Benjamin Tappan for the prisoner. The court was attended by persons from a great distance, and it was generally believed that many had come with a determination to rescue McMahon in case he should be found guilty. He was acquitted, however, principally

*Judge Kirtland's Diary.

upon the testimony of a man by the name of Knox, who swore that McMahon retreated a step or two before he fired, which was probably not true, and was not believed by those who visited the spot on the day after the affair took place. Captain Peters was upon the bench during the whole trial, and was satisfied that the trial had been fair and he should be acquitted. After this it is said the settlement increased rapidly. McMahon afterwards served in the War of 1812 in the Northwestern army under General Harrison. In the battle with the Indians on the peninsula north of Sandusky bay, on the 29th of September, he was wounded in the side. After his recovery he was discharged in November and started for home. Being alone he fell a victim to the Indians.

An incident occurred a few years after the McMahon tragedy, which illustrates the degenerate character of the Massassaugas. James Hillman was passing a salt spring, some nine miles west of Youngstown, where people were wont to come from long distances to manufacture salt. They generally came with two kettles swung across a horse, and on one occasion a man came to this spring alone and was murdered by the Indians, and full two weeks after James Hillman was passing as above noted, when being attracted to a spot where his dog was barking and scratching in search of game, as he supposed, found upon going to the place a man buried about one foot deep and covered with dirt and brush. He went to Youngstown and reported the case to George Tod, Dr. Dutton, and others, and after consultation it was determined upon bringing the Indians to justice. It was also noticed that these Indians, about three hundred in number, who had for some time been around Youngstown, Canfield and Ellsworth, had lately disappeared and it was found after considerable search that they had gone to Chillicothe. James Hillman followed them some days himself, and not far from old Chillicothe he overtook them and after holding a council and stating his business, told them they had to return, that one of their number had killed a man. After a council of one day they agreed to return. The chief of this tribe stated that one of his men had killed the man; that he had stopped at the camp of the salt-maker, and that the latter had a small jug of whiskey and gave him a drink. The Indian wanted more, which was refused and the Indian had killed him and took the whiskey. He then dug a hole with his knife and tomahawk, buried him, and afterward covered the grave with brush. James Hillman, alone and by himself, brought the whole tribe back to Youngstown. The accused was tried on the bluff back of the Mahoning, between George Tod's residence and Mr. Horsye's, and opposite the old mill. It was stated that Simon Perkins, of Warren acted as judge and Alvin Pense, of Warren, as counsel for one party, and George Tod for the other. After a trial of two days they thought best to acquit the Indian by the chief going his security for his future conduct.

Mr. Roswell M. Grant, brother of Jesse Grant and an uncle of General Grant, relates an incident, in the Historical Collections of the Mahoning Valley, where a Mr. John Diven, who lived in Deerfield, had traded horses with an Indian, who concluded, after the trade had been made, that Mr. Diven had cheated him, and wanted to trade back; but his request was refused. At that time there were some four hundred Indians near Ravenna, Deerfield, and Atwater, of all ages and sizes. On Christmas night there was a ball at the house of Judge Day. John Diven and his brother Daniel were there. The former had married a Miss Ely, of Deerfield, and Daniel was to be married New Years day. All the parties were at the ball. About dark the Indian came to the door, and wanted to see John, who refused to go out. His brother told him to swap coat and hat, and he would go out. They did so. Just as Daniel stepped out of the door the Indian shot him through both eyes, laying the eyeballs on his cheeks. The Indians all left that night. It was twenty-five miles to Youngstown; but two messengers came to James Hillman, in the night, and told their business. After feeding their horses and eating something themselves, they left for Deerfield before daylight.

Upon arriving there they joined some fifty or sixty men ready to start in pursuit of the Indians. Mr. Hillman told them if they wanted to go they could do so, but if he went he went by himself. They had to consent, and he started alone. There was no snow, but the ground was very rough, and he could track them, as their feet were cut and bleeding, and they were without moccasins, the rough ground having worn them out. After a hard day's ride he came upon their camp, but fell back, and, keeping out of sight, encamped for the night. Early next morning he made preparation, and went up to them, finding the squaws getting breakfast, but the men all asleep. The Indians had a small fork stuck in the ground, with their guns leaning on it, and their shot-pouches and powder-horns hanging in the fork. The squaws did not see him until he came within fifty yards of them, when they gave the alarm, and in a moment every Indian was on his feet. He drew his gun upon the chief, told him to order every man to stack his gun against a certain tree or he would pull the trigger. The chief knew the colonel so well that he gave the order. So soon as their guns, knives, and tomahawks were stuck against a tree, Colonel Hillman took possession of the tree. He then told them his business; told them that one of his men had shot Daniel Diven; that they had to return; that he knew the man that had committed the murder; that if they would return peaceably and give up the guilty man none of the rest would be hurt, and that they all knew him. If they refused, he would kill at least twenty before they could recover their arms; that the chief would be the first man to fall. He told them to eat their breakfast; after that he would hear what they had to say.

After breakfast the chief told him that they would have to hold a council before they could give him an answer. They went off some two hundred yards, and after being absent some two hours, they returned in the war paint. As soon as the colonel saw their decision, and when they came near enough, he raised his gun, ordered the chief to halt, or he was a dead man. He then told them to go back and take off the war paint. After a parley of half an hour they returned to hold another council which lasted for some time, then came back with the emblem of peace. Then he told them to send out hunters for meat, to mend their moccasins, and to remain where they were until morning. The fourth day after he brought the whole party into Warren, where the authorities put the chief under guard. They remained there for some time until the matter was finally settled. Daniel Diven lived many years after he was shot.

The first missionary among the Indians on the

Western Reserve was Rev. Joseph Badger, who came to Northern Ohio in 1800. He was born at Wilbraham, Massachusetts, in 1757. When eighteen years of age he entered the Revolutionary army, in 1775, and again in 1777, his time expiring the 1st of January, 1778. He graduated from Yale college in 1785, and in 1787 was ordained as minister over a church in Blandford, Massachusetts, where he remained fourteen years.

In 1800, at the instance of the missionary societies of the Eastern States, Mr. Badger made a visit to this part of the country, spending a year among the various tribes, and returned for his family. He divided his time among the Wyandots and the tribes bordering on the Sandusky and Maumee, going from place to place, as duty seemed to call.

Great trouble was experienced in securing books for families. Mr. Badger writes: Bookdealers forwarded many unsalable books. The war coming on at the time, increased the difficulty and expense of transportation, and books soon fell below the former price. Rev. Thaddeus Osgood made a collection of books and pamphlets, to be forwarded to Oswego, just as the war began. June, 1812, the forwarding company took them back to Schenectady.

The war created great expense and difficulty in getting anything from the east of Buffalo. Salt was from $12 to $23 per barrel, and all other articles of merchandise in proportion. Soon after the first of October, "General Harrison came. Without being consulted, I was appointed chaplain to the brigade and postmaster for the army. There soon came on a chaplain's commission from the Government. I could not get away honorably, and concluded to stay. Some time in November we were ordered to march for Sandusky. There was no one in the camp that had ever been through, but myself. I observed to the General that, to pass through to Sandusky on the Indian path with teams, would be impracticable on account of the deep mire and swampy ground. He replied: 'Can you find a better route?' I told him I could, mostly on dry ground. He proposed I should take a guard of about twenty men, and several axmen, and mark through where I supposed the army could pass with their heavy teams. I went through in five days, marked out the road, and returned. On the last day was a heavy snow storm. I then piloted the army through in three days. The Indians were then scouting through that section of country. They killed a man, about a mile below the fort, the day I arrived there, after marking the road."

Mr. Badger returned home the early part of July. His wife died in 1818. April 18, 1819, he married Miss Abigail Ely, who survived him but six months, his death taking place in 1849, in his eighty-ninth year, closing a life of honor and usefulness.

That most loathsome of diseases, the small-pox, became epidemic among the Indians, in 1810, and greatly reduced their numbers. They were ingeniously persuaded that the disease was an indication of the Great Spirit's anger with them for not going West to lands assigned them. The war of 1812 brought to a final close their visits to the eastern part of the Reserve. A straggling hunter was occasionally seen after the restoration of peace, but such visits were few and unwelcome.

CHAPTER IX.
THE PIONEERS.

Their Toils, Privations, and Hardships—Amusements and Successes.

Begin at the old house in Connecticut, about the opening of the present century. On a farm of forty acres, of uncertain productiveness, lives a large family. The father is a strong, resolute, determined man, whose courage was fully tested twenty years before in the Revolution, and whose body bears the scars of battle. The mother's strong impulse is devotion to her family. Accustomed to share her husband's toil, her life and destiny is inseparably linked with his, and her hopes are swallowed up in solicitude for her children, who are fast growing to maturity. How to give them a start in life is a prevailing subject of anxious thought and conversation. The mail brings a pamphlet giving a map and graphic description of the Western Reserve, which, when nightfall has driven all within the plainly furnished cottage, is read aloud. The romantic, unrestrained life it suggests is vividly impressed upon the imagination of the young people, while an idea of accumulation and gain haunts the minds of parents. The pamphlet is read and re-read, and its most picturesque and sanguine paragraphs dwelt upon until they become real pictures. It is finally resolved to emigrate. The old farm is disposed of, the old furniture sold, except so much as is needed for the journey, and a great canvas-covered wagon is purchased. As the time for starting approaches mingled feelings of doubt, regret, and anticipation burden the overworked mother's mind. The father's preparations consume his thinking, and the children, buoyant with hope, are impatient for the day of starting.

A few articles of furniture, necessary cooking utensils, a month's supply of provisions and a jug of old New England rum were packed into the covered wagon, where the family took their places, with four horses to the wagon and several head of cattle, started on ahead, the long dreary journey was commenced. The mountains offered the greatest obstacle, roads were as yet unimproved, and winding, dangerous tracks, through passes and over steep ridges were slowly followed day after day until at last the valleys of the Ohio's tributaries were reached. The road from Pennsylvania into Ohio then lay along the Mahoning as far as Youngstown. By this time other immigrant families had been joined and the procession of white covered wagons moved beneath green trees through a belt of solitary wilderness which separated the Reserve from Pennsylvania settlements. Youngstown was finally reached. This was the place to which nearly all who owned land or desired to own land came. It was the center and mustering ground for the early settlers and proprietors of the Western Reserve, the place at which they rested and from which they branched off into the wilderness, following and guided by township lines marked by blazed trees, to the tracts purchased from the Land company.

It is not to be inferred that the circumstances of Western emigration were the same in every instance. We have given one instance somewhat typical of all. In many cases grown up children urged their parents to leave the homes in which they were contented, and comfortable; ambitious young wives, willing to meet any hardships in the race for fortune, urged their husbands to emigrate, some being willing to share with him his toils from the start, others remaining till a house and lot had been provided. But among the ambitious, generous, and worthy-minded, there were a few who came to escape the restraints of rigid laws or social unhappiness. Neither were all the pioneers from Connecticut, although most of the first ones were. Some came across the mountains from Pennsylvania, a few from New York, and fewer still from Virginia. The primitive Reserve presented a great variety of soil and scenery. A green robe of tightly matted forest, broken only here and there by a stream or Indian clearing, protected the virgin soil from the rays of the sun.

Streams were all larger then than now, not because the annual fall of water was greater, but because nearly all that did fall was poured into the channels which nature provided. Deep umbrage chilled the surface and destroyed the conditions of evaporation. In addition a compact, unstirred vegetable soil prevented the water from penetrating the earth. When the country came to be cleared up and stirred up, courses were opened, by the plow and decaying roots, to coarse, porous formations beneath the surface, which now freely admit and carry off a large proportion of rainfall. In a previous chapter we gave the surveyor's measurements of the Mahoning and Shenango rivers and Pymatuning creek. From their statements it is safe to estimate that all these streams were twice their present volume. In 1806 the Ohio Legislature declared the Mahoning a navigable stream as far up as Holliday's mill, in Newton township. By 1829 this stream had so far decreased in volume that Warren was declared the head of navigation. Batteaux and even flat boats, at an early period of the settlement, were paddled from Beaver falls to Warren without difficulty at all seasons of the year, excepting at two or three shoals where slight lifting was required. The commissioners were at one time empowered by the Legislature to declare Musquito creek a public highway, but no record of action in the matter exists.

When the first settlers arrived the flat lands were wet and swampy, and were consequently neglected by those seeking locations for homes. There was an ample choice for those who came with the idea of purchasing, for nearly every stockholder was anxious to dispose of part of his land in order to make back payments due the State of Connecticut on the original purchase. Many of those who owned land back at considerable distance from the centers of settlement, traded for or purchased tracts where civilization had already been planted.

Those in this part of the Reserve, having arrived in Youngstown and settled on a location, left the family with friends or at a public house of entertainment. Several men in company then selected a site for a cabin with that enthusiasm which cheerfulness always creates. They then set to work. Neighbors for miles around were there to lend a friendly lift. One of the party was appointed captain, whose business it was to direct the work of the day. He was generally a man of strong character and commanding presence, one whose word was law and yet whose directions were without the semblance of command. A jug of rum or home-made whiskey was always "on tap," and contributed its strength to the spirit of the day. First the ground was cleared. The trunks of large, straight-grained trees were split into clapboards for roof or puncheons for the floor. Smaller trees were cut down and logs of suitable length prepared for the walls of the cabin. Flat stones were placed at each corner for the foundation, on which two heavy logs were adjusted, one at each side of the building. These were notched at distances of about four feet, and straight poles laid across to serve as joists or sleepers for the puncheon floor. A skilled axeman then took his place at each corner, and as log after log for the walls tumbled into place it was notched near the ends so that the next, crossing at right angles, would rest more firmly. Thus log by log the cabin was raised to the height of about eight feet; another row of joists was then placed across for the upper floor. One or two logs more and then the gable was commenced, which was built up of smaller timber secured by poles running the whole length of the building at intervals of about three feet. On these, clapboards four feet long were laid in such a way as to make a tight roof.

The very best timber was always used for making clapboards, and, considering the tools used, they were split out with surprising accuracy. The roof was fastened down with weight poles instead of nails, which were at that time scarce and expensive. Weight poles were kept in position by blocks at the ends running from one to the other. It took persons skilled in woodcraft to dress puncheons for the floor. One side was hewn smooth, and the other notched, so that their surface, when laid, was exactly even. A good workman could make a floor as smooth as one made of plane-dressed boards. Less care was taken with the second, or loft floor. When the floors had been laid, and the roof weighted down, the heavy work was finished, and the neighbors left the proprietor to complete the structure with his own hands. With an axe he dressed down the rough edges of logs inside, and filled the cracks with sticks and mortar made of mud, mixed with leaves and grass. An opening was cut in the gable end, four feet long and six feet high, for a fire-place. On the outside a chimney was built, on a foundation of flat stones, of small puncheons thickly interlaid with clay. It was four or five feet deep at the base, but tapered rapidly toward the top. A fire-chamber was made of flat stones to keep the wood from burning. Near the top of the large opening was placed a pole of some kind of hard wood, to which chains were attached for hanging kettles, ovens, and other cooking utensils, over the fire.

An opening about five and a half feet high and four feet wide was made in one side of the building for a doorway. The door was made of puncheons, pinned to cleats at each end, and was hung on heavy wooden hinges. A window was made by cutting out a piece of one or two logs, pinning strips of lath across, and fastening over the opening greased paper. Glass was rarely seen in the West at that period, and sold at prices far beyond the most well-to-do pioneer's means. The family generally moved in before all these details were completed. Cabin furniture corresponded with the simplicity of the building. A bedstead was made by tying together the ends of two poles, one reaching to the end the other to the side of the cabin. A block placed under the corner stood in place of a bed post. Strips of bark fastened to pins at each side of this rude frame work formed a matting on which a husk and straw bed was thrown—in some instances leaves took the place of these materials. A neat linen curtain was hung around the bed, the space underneath being utilized in stowing away various articles. Few cabins afforded more than one or two chairs, benches made with the auger and broad-axe being used in their place. A table was brought from the East by most pioneers, though it was also sometimes a home made article. The cooking furniture consisted of a spider, a "Dutch oven," and a couple of kettles. Everything was cooked over an open fire. The table fare was extremely plain, and sometimes even scant. Wheat was scarce, and it was often impossible to obtain it at all. Corn, therefore, became the staff of life. Game was plenty, and few meals passed without its appearance on the table. Potatoes, after the first season, were plenty, and it was not uncommon to see the family sitting on stools and benches around the table, on which stood two pots, one containing boiled potatoes, the other a boiled haunch of venison. Pastry was little used, and it is not improbable that people were the better for it. "The first 'minced pie' I ate on the Reserve," says Hon. J. R. Giddings, "was composed of pumpkin instead of apple, vinegar in place of wine or cider, bear's meat instead of beef. The whole was sweetened with wild honey instead of sugar, and seasoned with domestic pepper pulverized, instead of cloves, cinnamon, and alspice, and never did I taste pastry with a better relish."

Most of the pioneer women were skilled, before leaving their Eastern home, in the art of cheesemaking, and no sooner had they become settled in their new cabins than preparations were made for producing this Yankee luxury. The press consisted of a home-made cheese-hoop fitted to a bench or block. The necessary weight was brought to bear by fastening one end of a pole between two logs of the cabin and hanging on the other a heavy stone. The dairy product was, however, very poor, on account of an unpleasant flavor given to the milk by leeks, which covered the damp forest pastures and were greedily eaten by cows. The product improved, and cheese-making increased as the land was cleared and cultivated pastures took the place of wild feed.

To increase the acreage of tillable land was the main object of every well-to-do pioneer. He girdled the trees and cut out the underbrush and logs of a small patch, probably ten acres, for the first season's planting. During the second year he more than doubled the "girdling" and began to cut or burn down the dead trees on the first opening. Those that were hollow or partially decayed burned readily, but large, solid timber had to be cut and "logged," that is, piled up to dry. Straight oak, walnut, and some hickory was split up into rails for fencing fields under cultivation. All the small trees and the rougher parts of larger ones were cut into logs of such size as to make them easily handled, and when several acres had been thus reduced a frolic was made to which all the neighbors turned out. Log rollings were not regarded burdensome, but on the other hand occasions of great pleasure. It was a real privilege for people to be given occasions for coming together to exchange jokes and news, and to encourage each other in the severe struggle in which all were engaged. On occasions of these neighborly gatherings axes and handspikes were handled with a lightness and enthusiasm indicative of the temper of the party. There is something inspiring, too, in the traditional "heave, oh heave" which has come down to our own generation. Competition gives earnestness even to amusement, and is the most ingenious device ever used for facilitating and lightening work.

Men at these log rollings were divided off into parties and each party into two sides, thus complicating the trial of strength and endurance in which all were ambitious to excel. Hearty, merry hurry and laughter excluded fatigue, and well-filled jugs of New England rum or homemade corn whiskey added to the hilarity. These pleasant social gatherings often terminated most joyously in a way that the sweethearts, sisters, and wives of those strong men could participate. During the day, while the clearing resounded with masculine shouts and calls, gentle voices enlivened the cabin. The assembled ladies, with needles keeping time to merry laughter and innocent gossip, rivaled the men in industry. Rags were worked into warm quilts and linens into clothing. The clearing party concluded their labors by triumphantly carrying the captain on their backs; the cabin party enfolded their hostess in a quilt, a steaming supper of wild meats, corn, cheese and whiskey; and then a squeaking fiddle announced the programme for the night. Round dancing was not indulged in by our forefathers, but they were proficient in many varieties of plain movements. High stepping was in great favor, a circumstance peculiarly adapted to the solid though irregular puncheon floor. Every movement was performed with hearty enthusiasm. The dancers were lost in their amusement and pursued it through pure love of the art and their beaux. Far into the night the dance was protracted, and then along forest paths all sought their humble homes, happy, hopeful, contented.

We have hinted at the free use of whisky in the olden days. Every pushing settler had a copper still which was capable of producing a sufficient quantity of the beverage to supply his family and friends. It is an old witticism, as old as the Reserve, that "corn was the only successful crop, but there was no market for the corn, so it was made into whisky; there was no market for the whisky so they drank it." We have no disposition in this connection to preach temperance, nor on the other hand to praise this old-time custom. The fact is presented because it is a matter of history, but those who seek to draw from it material for argument on either side of the temperance issue should carefully determine attendant circumstances. It cannot be maintained that there was no drunkenness then, as is sometimes asserted. Most men, it is true, were temperate as they are now, but every community had its inebriates and it was no unusual occurrence for fights, caused by over stimulated temper, to disturb frolics or public gatherings. The pioneers deemed it parsimony, approaching wickedness, to neglect to offer a guest liquor or to limit the quantity. It was as free as water in the harvest field, clearing, and cabin, at public dinners and on election days. It was about the year 1830 when a reaction took place, temperance societies were organized, and from that time to the present public opinion has been undergoing a gradual change.

In the early years of settlement, cattle, hogs, and other domestic animals were turned to pasture in the fenceless woods. Every cow wore a heavy, coarse-toned bell under her neck, which, at evening time, guided the direction of a search. Cattle were very fond of the leeks which covered the ground in all wet places, and flavored the milk, making it, in all its manufactured forms, revolting to the taste. Sheep were also belled, and, at first, always kept in fields to keep them from wandering far in the forest, where they would have been made the prey of wolves. At night time they were penned in high enclosures, made secure against the bold denizens of the forest. The gun was a constant companion of all the men, and hunting was an employment rather than amusement. The elk and deer were hunted for their meat. They were plenty, and at first easily obtained. A few deer were found in the swamps as late as 1850. The hunter frequently met with bears, black and gray foxes, raccoon, wild cats, opossum, porcupine, polecat, black, gray, red, and ground squirrels, and wolves. The last named animal was the most plentiful and bothersome. Being entirely useless, they had escaped the Indians' notice, or, rather, his gun, and were bolder and less cautious in consequence. They killed hogs and sheep, and sometimes even attacked travelers after night. Their dismal howl could be heard on all sides, and their glassy eyes sometimes peered through cracks in the cabin. Panthers were the most ferocious animals found by the early settlers. They soon, however, disappeared after clearing fires broke the spell which so long reigned over the forest. Fur-bearing animals were plentiful. The streams abounded in muskrat, and otter and beaver dams crossed the channel of almost every creek. Wild turkeys were common in the early period of settlement, and furnished much support to the inhabitants. Wild geese and ducks occasionally visited this region. Game and fur-bearing animals rapidly disappeared, but wolves kept up a guerilla warfare until as late as 1835, in spite of the fact that liberal bounty was paid for their scalps by the civil authorities. Red foxes did not appear until about 1815, and rabbits came about the same time, showing that these animals belong to agriculture and civilization.

At an early day rattlesnakes abounded in large numbers. One adventure which occurred in Braceville township is worthy of record. A Mr. Oviatt was informed that a considerable number of huge rattlesnakes were scattered over a certain tract of wilderness. The old man asked whether there was a ledge of rocks in the vicinity, which way the declivity inclined, and if any spring issued out of the ledge. Being answered in the affirmative, the old man rejoined, "We will go about the last of May and have some sport." Accordingly they proceeded through the woods well armed with cudgels. Arriving at the battle-ground they cautiously ascended the hill step by step, in solid column. Suddenly the enemy gave the alarm, and the men found themselves completely surrounded by hosts of rattlesnakes of enormous size, and a huge squadron of black snakes. No time was lost. At a signal of the rattling of the snakes the action commenced, and hot and furious was the fight. In a short time the snakes beat a retreat up the hill, our men cudgeling with all their might. When arrived at the top of the ledge they found the ground and rocks in places almost covered with snakes retreating into their dens. Afterwards the slain were collected into heaps and found to amount to four hundred and eighty-six, a good portion of which were as large as a man's leg below the calf, and over five feet in length.

The discovery of this den of venomous serpents being spread it was agreed that the narrator, Cornelius Feather, and two more young men in Warren and three in Braceville, should make war upon it until the snakes should be exterminated, which was done. Mr. Feather stated that in snake hunting he procured an instrument like a chisel with a handle eight or nine feet long. With this he went to the ledge of rocks alone, placed himself on the body of a butternut tree lying slanting over a broad crevice in the rocks seven or eight feet deep, the bottom of which was literally covered with the yellow and black serpents. He held his weapon poised in his right hand, ready to give the deadly blow, his left holding to a small branch to keep his balance, when both of his feet slipped and he came within a hair's breadth of plunging headlong into the den. He came near in this adventure to meeting with a most terrible death, as he could not have gotten out had there been no snakes, the rocks on all sides being nearly perpendicular.

One of the most celebrated American paintings figures a wife and mother spinning. Both hands are busy with the fabric; one foot is on the treadle which drives the whirling wheel, and the other is rocking a cradle in which is an innocent child lulled by the rythmic hum. The subject of that picture might have been found in almost every cabin in pioneer New Connecticut. Articles of dress were almost exclusively of home manufacture. Cotton and woolen fabrics were expensive and beyond the reach of the poor pioneers, who had no market for their simple products. Carding, spinning, and weaving was a slow process, but it was the best that could be done under the circumstances. A little patch of flax was planted every year, and at the proper season the crop was pulled, dried, bleached, and hackled. It was then beaten into fine tow ready for the spinning-wheel. Raw cotton was imported and exchanged for flax or wool. This had to be hand-picked and hand-carded, and then, like the flax, passed into the wife's hands for spinning. Every settler had a few sheep, whose wool was treated in much the same way as the cotton. It will appear that there was plenty of work to be done inside the house, for clothing was not only home-spun but home-woven. For summer clothing cotton was mixed with the flax, and for winter clothing wool was used for filling. Pantaloons were mostly made of deerskin tanned by hand. In wet weather they would stretch and become sloppy; in dry weather, shrink and become hard. Home-made shirts and jackets were worn until a comparatively recent period. Hon. Joshua R. Giddings made his first appearance before the supreme court of Ohio thus attired. What busy activity characterized the life of the pioneers! From daylight till far into the night the hum of a whirling wheel and thud of a ponderous loom accompanied the echoing stroke of axes, the crash of falling trees, and the roar of clearing fires.

The great distance and incapacity of mills was a serious inconvenience, and settlers were often reduced to the extremity of pounding their own corn. Roads were extremely bad, and at times impassable. At such times the spring-pole and pestle were resorted to for pounding corn. This apparatus was made on the plan of the contrivance used by the Indians. A solid stump was hollowed out, by cutting or burning, into a huge mortar, one end of a piece from the butt of a hard-wood tree was then rounded off, and the whole suspended by the other end from a pole balanced across a high stump. Handles were inserted in the pestle with which it could be brought down on the corn in the mortar with great force. In this way a man could crack enough corn in half a day to last his family a week.

But the mills were depended upon when it was possible to get to them. Oxen were largely used as beasts of draft. Deep mud-holes, short turns, brush, and poles, made the roads unsuitable for horses. If the distance was considerable bells were thrown into the wagon for use at night when they were turned out to pasture. They seldom rambled beyond the sound of the bell. These journeys were often tedious and sometimes dangerous. A single incident recorded by Leonard Case will give a good idea of the general character of this feature of pioneer life.

In February, 1801, Benjamin Davidson, Esq., of Warren township, his son Samuel, a lad of seventeen, and Ebenezer Earle, a bachelor, agreed to take a sled load of grain to the mill on Mill creek, in Boardman. The sled was provided with a new wood-rack and drawn by two yoke of oxen. The sledding was rather thin, the distance twelve miles. Soon after they started it became warmer and began to thaw. They reached the mill safely but did not get their grist till after dark. Fearing that the road would soon break, particularly the ice which bridged the streams, they started homeward in the dark. The oxen trudged along slowly, patiently bearing the impatient lash. The ice over mud-holes soon began to give way. The old gentleman took the lead on foot and so thin did the ice become that he occasionally broke through. Calling back, "Turn out, boys, turn out," he waited till the oxen dragged the sled around and then went on as before exploring the way. By the time they reached Meander creek it had risen above their sled beams, and in order to save their load from getting wet they placed chains crosswise over the top of their rack and laid poles on the chains. They piled the meal bags on top of the poles and plunged into the stream. At a little more than half-way across the weight crushed down the rack precipitating themselves with the meal into the water more than knee deep. They traveled on, however, allowing the water to drip out on the way. At about four o'clock they were heard coming half a mile from Warren, and an hour later were safely lodged by a warm fire at the Case cabin. The meal-bags had not been wet more than a couple of inches from the surface and the loss was consequently not large.

An interesting picture of the olden time may be drawn of a church gathering in a little log school-house or the forest shade. Nearly every one walked to church. Leather was expensive and shoes hard to get. The ladies economized by carrying their foot wear to the meeting-house, where it was a common sight to see them sitting on logs drawing on their heavy shoes without stockings. Few of the men wore shoes at all. There were neither fulling mills nor tailors. Imagine, then, a muscular frame, rough, tanned face, brawny hands, and large bare feet, with no other clothing than a tow shirt and pantaloons. That is the pioneer young man. Now draw another picture on the other side of the aisle—a smiling face, fresh but dark, a full head of smoothly combed hair tied up behind in a twist knot. A dress made out of seven yards of linsey-woolsey closely fits the natural form and reaches to within six inches of the floor. It is fancifully and uniquely striped with copperas, butternut and indigo alternating. The pioneer mothers made as great effort to look pretty as their more comfortably situated daughters, and considering the circumstances were as successful in their efforts. The belt is made of homespun, but is colored with imported dye, and a row of buttons down the back are also set on a bright stripe. Heavy cowhide shoes conceal substantial feet and shapely ankles. That is the pioneer young lady.

The pioneer preachers of this region were mild, moderate, men and conducted worship quietly and impressively. The worshipers, though lightly attired, were as earnest and devout as their descendants in handsome churches and rich dresses.

But pioneer life was not all burden, and care, and privation; not all chopping, and rolling logs, and grubbing, and plowing among roots, and going to mill; nor was woman's life all toil, spinning, weaving, pounding corn, hunting cows in the fenceless woods, milking, making butter, and pressing cheese; there were social joys, amusements, and pleasures which gave variety to and lightened the weight of drudgery. The hospitality of the early days is dwelt upon with fondness by all the survivors. The pioneer felt at home wherever he found a cabin. An expressive symbol of welcome survives the wreck of the log cabin to which it belonged. The ponderous puncheon door of a cabin was fastened by a wooden latch on the inside, to which a string was fastened. The other end of the string passed through a hole in the door above, and hung down outside. By pulling the string the latch was raised, and the door, creaking the tune of welcome, turned upon great wooden hinges, admitting whoever came to a bright crackling fire of logs in an open hearth, over which was steaming a kettle of hominy and roasting a haunch of venison. A traveler was treated in precisely the same hospitable spirit as a friend of the family. The best was shared with him, and his team cared for as well as it was possible. If it was evening, he was expected to remain till morning, and his visit was made interesting. Conversation dwelt upon the progress and prospects of settlement, the crops and incidents of the day; on events which transpired in the East months back, which were listened to with all the interest of current news. In the morning the stranger guest waited for his breakfast, and then departed with the best wishes of the family, whom he never offended by offering pay for his entertainment.

If a pioneer visited his neighbor, he was always invited to remain to partake of a meal. Whiskey was always offered, even though potatoes and meat were sometimes scarce. Strong friendships existed between neighbors, which gave zest and enthusiasm to social intercourse. There were few contentions, feuds or strifes to interrupt good feeling. People then could not afford to do without each other, and consequently, could not afford to quarrel.

Such in outline was life on the soil of New Connecticut four score of years ago. Bancroft has described the Connecticut of 1676, and while we are dwelling on the toils and pleasures of the pioneers of our own county, it will be interesting to look back a century farther to the scene of their ancestors conquering wild nature; "there was venison from the hills, salmon in their streams and sugar from the trees of the forest; for foreign market little was produced besides cattle, and in return for them few foreign luxuries stored in. The soil had originally been justly divided, or held as common property, in trust for the people. Happiness was enjoyed unconsciously. Beneath the rugged exterior humanity wore its sweetest smile. There was for a long time hardly a lawyer in the land. The husbandman who held his own plow and fed his own cattle, was the great man of the age. No one was superior to the matron who, with her busy daughters, kept the hum of the wheel incessantly alive, spinning and weaving every article of their dress. Fashion was confined within narrow limits and pride aimed at no grander equipage than a pillion, and could exalt only in the common splendor of the blue-white linen gown with short sleeves, and in the snow white flaxen apron, which, firmly starched and ironed, was worn on public days, by every woman in the land. There was no revolution except from the time of sowing to the time of reaping; from the plain dress of the week day to the more trim attire of Sunday. Every family was taught to look up to God as the fountain of all good; yet life was not sombre. The spirit of frolic mingled with innocence, and religion itself wore the garb of gayety and the annual thanksgiving was as joyous as it was sincere."

Nobly did the pioneers of old Connecticut do their work, and in this respect history repeated itself in the Connecticut of the West. There was a conquering spirit in the hearts of the New England founders, which was inherited by the New Connecticut founders. Both generations met savage beasts and savage men to be driven back by the exercise of resolution, perseverance and courage. The results to civilization are immeasurable.

CHAPTER X.
CIVIL GOVERNMENT.
Organization of Trumbull County—Official Vote—Civil List—County Buildings.

Simple, economical and judiciously executed civil government lies at the foundation of human progress. So important did the Ohio company associates consider a perfected civil establishment that they refused to confirm the contract of purchase until Congress had ratified the ordinance of 1787. The fact that "when they came into the wilderness, the law was already there" offered the greatest encouragement to immigration, and the greatest assurance of protection. But the Connecticut Land company had no such provision to aid their uncertain speculation. For five years everything, even to the validity of their title to the soil, was doubt and uncertainty. The National Government was at that time in its formative period. The old colonial ideas which made each State separate and independent of all others was giving way to the National idea which made the jurisdiction of Congress paramount to that of any State. The ordinance of 1787 covered the reserved territory of Connecticut, but to have admitted the political jurisdiction of the United States might, according to the crude notions of the time, have been interpreted as a release of claim to the soil. Besides, the members of the Land company had anticipated the erection of a new State to be known as New Connecticut, to the head of which they as original proprietors would naturally be called. To admit the jurisdiction of the Northwest Territory would preclude the realization of these hopes, which was an additional reason for continuing to assert absolute independence. Soon after the Connecticut associates had concluded their purchase in 1795, they made application to Congress to have a Territorial government erected over their territory as a preliminary step to the consummation of the idea of a Utopian State. There is no record of Congress touching the prayer of this petition; we only know that it was not granted. It could not have been granted without amending the ordinance of 1787, under which flourishing settlements were rapidly growing.

The need of a civil organization for the regulation of real estate operations early made itself felt. At length, despairing the hope of favorable action by Congress, the proprietors, in January, 1797, resolved to apply to the Legislature of Connecticut to elect the Reserve into a county, with proper and suitable laws to regulate the internal affairs of the territory for a limited time, and to be administered at the sole expense of the proprietors. The stockholders found Connecticut as tardy as Congress to come to their relief. In October, 1797, at their annual meeting, the directors gave the trustees full power to pursue such measures as they deemed efficient to procure legal and judicious government over lands of the company, but these resolutions were as ineffectual as the first. Neither the Legislature of Connecticut nor Congress could be persuaded to act. Meanwhile there was no legal power by which to regulate the sale of lands or to enforce payment. Settlers had already erected their cabins, but there was no law to restrain the avaricious nor to punish common crime. During the whole of the year 1798 immigration continued and the embarrassments resulting from the entire absence of government multiplied. The directors urged the necessity of immediate action, pleading heavy losses as the consequence of delay, and finally, in May, 1799, the State was prevailed upon to abate the interest due on their payments. The inhabitants continued to reject the jurisdiction of Governor St. Clair and the officers of Jefferson county. When Zenas Kimberly, an officer of Jefferson county, came into the Reserve for the purpose of assessing taxes, he was treated with ridicule and retired. From that time the jurisdiction of the Northwest Territory over the Reserve was merely nominal until the final settlement of claims in 1800.

Laws for the regulation of society were not so much needed as legal officers for the transfer of property and collection of debts. Communities, by making a legislative and executive officer, are able to protect themselves against imposition. In some places rules mutually assented to amounting to a municipal code came into use and were rigidly executed. Such social self-imposed laws were as much respected at Canfield and Youngstown as the State laws afterwards in operation.

The Connecticut Land company at length, in April 1800, secured the attention of Congress. John Marshall, the great lawyer and subsequently chief justice of the United States, made a masterly argument on the question of ownership and political jurisdiction of land covered by old colonial charters, and the Connecticut Western Reserve in particular. The deliberations of Congress resulted in a proposition to the State of Connecticut, to the effect that if the State would accept the jurisdiction of the United States over the Reserve, the United States in turn would forever quit claim all right, title and interest in the soil. This agreement was ratified by the Governor of Connecticut, on the 30th of May, 1800. Thus was confirmed to the Connecticut Land company and all purchasers under their deed, a clear and indisputable title to the soil, and at the same time was secured efficient and equitable civil jurisdiction under the fundamental law of the Northwest Territory, which Chief Justice Chase styled "a pillar of cloud by day and of fire by night in the settlement and government of the Northwest States."

No sooner did the report of the confirmation of this highly desirable compact reach the West, than was commenced that vigorous and sometimes bitter strife for the location of the seat of government, which lasted for a period of forty-five years in Trumbull county, and seventy-five in Mahoning county. Youngstown was in 1800 the largest and most prosperous village on the Reserve, and Warren probably ranked second. While Warren was nearer the center of the territory Youngstown was nearer the center of population. It was apparent that Jefferson county would not long continue to extend its jurisdiction as far north as the Reserve. Warren representatives were the first to secure the ear of Governor St. Clair in regard to the new county project. On the 10th of July, 1800, the Governor proclaimed that all the territory included in Jefferson county, lying north of the forty-first degree, north latitude, and all that part of Wayne county included in the Connecticut Western Reserve, should constitute a new county to be known by the name of Trumbull, and that the seat of justice should be at Warren. It will be seen that the county thus constituted was coextensive with the Reserve or the New Connecticut of five years before.

No better name than Trumbull could have been selected for this western Connecticut. The name is imperishably stamped on almost every phase of the history of the parent State, and represents distinguished achievement in statesmanship, law, art, divinity, and literature. While the name for the county was undoubtedly chosen as a compliment to the staunch soldier and statesman who was at that time Governor of Connecticut, three others of the name and kin were at the time distinguishing their State. Benjamin Trumbull, a divine of reputation, had just published a history of the Connecticut colony, which has obtained a permanent place in our historical literature. John Trumbull was distinguished as a lawyer and judge, as well as a poet. His poem, "McFingal," passed through thirty editions. But more distinguished than either of these was John Trumbull, the painter, whose career was just beginning when the name was conferred upon New Connecticut. Having served with credit as aide-de-camp to General Washington, and having spent considerable time in England under the celebrated painter West, he made himself known as an artist by the production of "The Battle of Bunker Hill" in 1796. His most important works are the pictures in the rotunda of the capitol at Washington, which every visitor stops to admire. His brother was Governor Jonathan Trumbull, Jr., in whose special honor the county was named. Their father, Governor Jonathan Trumbull, was one of the most distinguished men of his time, having held the office of Governor fourteen years from 1769. His conduct during the Revolution was highly praised by General Washington. Jonathan Trumbull, Jr., was born at Lebanon, Connecticut, in 1740. He served during the Revolution as a paymaster, and afterwards as aide-de-camp to General Washington. He was elected to the first Congress after the adoption of the Federal Constitution, and in 1791 was chosen speaker of that body. In 1795 the Connecticut Legislature elected him to the United States Senate, where he distinguished himself as a Federalist and supporter of Washington's administration. In 1798 he was elected Governor of his State, an office which he held until his death in 1809. If there is anything in a name to direct aspiration or give inspiration, it would have been difficult to find a more significant gift for a political division of territory. There are few names in American history possessing an equal range of meaning.

Governor St. Clair's proclamation of July 10th, erecting the Reserve into a county, was a surprise to most of the settlers on the Reserve. All the leading citizens had foreseen such a measure at an early day, but those especially interested in Youngstown, which had already become the commercial center, disappointed by the loss of the county-seat, characterized the action of the Governor as indecent haste, and resolved upon keeping up the fight. When we remember the names and character of the men who were especially interested in Warren at that time, the action of Governor St. Clair will be readily understood. Judge Calvin Pease, who received the appointment of clerk of the court, owned land at Warren, and was probably the most popular and influential resident on the Reserve at that time. In addition to Mr. Pease's own personal influence, he was the brother-in-law of Hon. Gideon Granger, Postmaster-General of the United States, whose position gave him influence with the Administration under which Governor St. Clair held his commission. Mr. Granger, besides his interest in Pease, held title to several large tracts which were enhanced in value by the location of the seat of government at Warren. Then there were John Leavitt and Ebenezer King, Jr., to make the lobby for Warren more formidable.

Under the old Territorial law the Governor had authority to appoint officers for any new county which he might choose to erect. The justices of the peace constituted the general court of the county, five of their number being designated justices of the quorum, and the others associates. They met quarterly, and were known as the "court of quarter sessions." In this body was vested the entire civil jurisdiction of the county, local and legislative as well as judicial.

Governor St. Clair appointed the following to act as officers for Trumbull county: John Young, Turhand Kirtland, Camden Cleveland, James Kingsbury, and Eliphalet Austin, Esqs., justices of the peace and quorum; John Leavitt, Esq., judge of probate and justice of the peace; Solomon Griswold, Martin Smith, John Struthers, Caleb Baldwin, Calvin Austin, Edward Brockway, John Kinsman, Benjamin Davison, Ephraim Quinby, Ebenezer Sheldon, David Hudson, Aaron Wheeler, Amos Spafford, Moses Park, and John Minor, Esqs., justices of the peace; Calvin Pease, Esq., clerk; David Abbott, Esq., sheriff; John Hart Adgate, coroner; Eliphalet Austin, Esq., treasurer; John Stark Edwards, Esq., recorder.

The sheriff was directed by the Governor to call a meeting of the court of quarter sessions at Warren, August 25, 1800. Having been duly qualified, the justices and officers of the county met in the afternoon of that day, on the common just south of Liberty street. It was 4 o'clock when the session was called to order by the clerk. That hour marks the beginning of practical government on the Reserve. The court room was a bower of native trees standing between two large corn-cribs. The capital city consisted of a dozen log cabins surrounded by a wall of trees, with here and there a gate opening to a distant settlement. The session continued five days, transacting such business as was necessary to guarantee peace, order, and equity in the administration of the laws of the Territory. We will give a synopsis of the record, which is preserved in the handwriting of Judge Pease.

TRUMBULL COUNTY, } ss.
August term, 1800. }

Court of general quarter sessions of the peace begun and holden at Warren, within and for said county of Trumbull, on the fourth Monday of August, in the year of our Lord eighteen hundred, and of the independence of the United States the twenty-fifth. Present, John Young, Turhand Kirtland, Camden Cleveland, James Kingsbury, and Eliphalet Austin, esquires, justices of the quorum, and others, their associates, justices of the peace, holding said court.

The following persons were returned, and appeared on the grand jury, and were empanneled and sworn, namely: Simon Persons, foreman; Benjamin Stow, Samuel Menough, Hawley Tanner, Charles Daly, Ebenezer King, William Cecil, John Hart Adgate, Henry Lane, Jonathan Church, Jeremiah Wilcox, John Partridge Bissell, Isaac Palmer, George Phelps, Samuel Quinby, and Moses Park.

The court appointed George Tod, Esq., to prosecute the pleas of the United States for the present session, who took the oath of office.

The court ordered that the private seal of the clerk shall be considered the seal of the county and be affixed and recognized as such till a public seal shall be procured.

The court appointed Amos Spafford, Esq., David Hudson, Esq., Simon Perkins, John Minor, Esq., Aaron Wheeler, Esq., Edward Payne, Esq., and Benjamin Davidson, Esq., a committee to divide the county of Trumbull into townships, to describe the limits and boundaries of each township and to make report to the court thereof.

The committee divided the county into eight townships to be known as Youngstown, Warren, Hudson, Vernon, Richfield, Middlefield, Painesville, and Cleveland. Youngstown embraced the present townships of Poland, Coitsville, Boardman, Youngstown, Canfield, Austintown, and Ellsworth in Mahoning county, and Liberty and Hubbard in Trumbull. Warren township embraced the present township of Berlin and Milton in Mahoning county, Lordstown, Weathersfield, Howland, Warren, Braceville, Bazetta, Champion, and Southington in Trumbull county, and Nelson, Windham, Paris, Palmyra, and Deerfield in Portage county. Vernon township included Greene, Mecca, Gustavus, Johnston, Fowler, Vienna, Brookfield, Hartford, Vernon, and Kinsman in Trumbull county, and Andover, Williamsfield, Cherry Valley, Wayne, New Lyme, and Colbrook in Ashtabula county. Middlefield township embraced the present townships of Bristol, Bloomfield, Mesopotamia, and Farmington in Trumbull county, together with portions of Portage, Geauga, and Ashtabula counties as at present constituted. Hudson township lay west of Warren and extended to the Tuscarawas and Cuyahoga rivers. Painesville and Cleveland lay north of the townships we have named. That part of the county lying west of the Cuyahoga and Tuscarawas was still occupied by the Indians and not laid off in townships.

The court accept the report of the committee appointed to divide the county of Trumbull into townships and confirm and establish the boundaries and names of the townships as reported by said committee.

The court appointed Turhand Kirtland, John Kinsman, and Calvin Austin, and Amos Spafford, Esquires, a committee to view and lay out a proper extent of ground for the liberties of the prison, and to make a report thereof to the court.

The committee aforesaid, having viewed, report that the boundaries of the liberties of the prison in this county shall begin at a soft maple tree marked, standing about ten rods northeast of the prison-house; thence running north forty-four degrees west twenty rods to an elm tree, marked; thence south four degrees east twenty-six rods to a large white oak tree, marked; thence east twenty rods to a stake standing on the west side of the road; thence south by said road twelve rods to a soft maple tree; thence east to a white oak sapling standing on the east side of the road; thence north on the east side of the road sixty-six rods to a stake; thence west to a white oak sapling standing on the west side of the road near the northeast corner of James Fenton's house; from thence to the place of beginning.

The boundaries of the jail limits cover the ground between Main and Liberty streets, extending north and south from just below Market street to William street; also embracing the land around the jail and west about twenty rods from Main street. These limits were the bounds within which a prisoner on good behavior and his parole was allowed to walk. The house referred to was the one undoubtedly occupied by William Fenton, on the river bank, and owned previously by James Fenton.

The report of this committee on the boundary of the jail limits was accepted.

The following persons were appointed to serve as constables within their respective townships: James Hillman, for Youngstown; Jonathan Church, for Warren; Heman Oviatt and Amsi Atwater, for the town of Hudson; Titus Brockway, for Vernon; Simon Rose and Rufus Grinell for Middlefield; John A. Harper and Mills Case for the town of Richfield; Charles Parker for the town of "Paynesville;" Stephen Gilbert and Eleazer Carter for the town of Cleveland.

Ordered by the court, on motion of Mr. Edwards, that Ephraim Quinby, Esq., be recommended to the Governor of this Territory as a fit person to keep a publick house of entertainment in the town of Warren on his complying with the requisites of the law.

On motion of Judge Kirtland, the court ordered that Jonathan Fowler be recommended to the Governor as a suitable person to keep a publick house of entertainment in the town of Youngstown on his complying with the requisites of the law.

Personally appeared in open court Benjamin Davison, Esq., Ephraim Quinby, Esq., John Bentley, millwright, and John Lane, yeoman, all of Warren, in Trumbull county; James Hillman, yeoman, and William Hall, yeoman, both of Youngstown, in said county, and acknowledge themselves severally indebted to the United States in the bond of recognizance in the penal sum of two hundred dollars each, to be levied on their lands, tenements, goods, and chattels, and bodies if a default be made in the condition of their recognizance, which condition is that the said Benjamin Davison, Ephraim Quinby, John Bentley, John Lane, James Hillman, and William Hall be each one in his proper person, before the next court of oyer and terminer, which shall be holden within the county of Trumbull, whenever the same shall be, there to testify the truth between the United States and Richard Storer, on an indictment of murder.

The court ordered that the clerk be authorized to procure a public seal for the county of Trumbull, of such size and with such devices as he shall deem proper, at the expense of the county.

Thus ended the first session of the court on the Reserve.

Governor St. Clair issued a proclamation September 22d, directed to David Abbott, sheriff, commanding him "That on the second Tuesday in October he cause an election to be held for the purpose of electing one person to represent the county in the Territorial Legislature." Under the Territorial government all elections were held in the county seats of the respective counties. Elections were held according to the English, or town-meeting mode. The sheriff, by virtue of his office, presided over the assembly of electors, and received their votes *viva voce*. The first election in Trumbull was held in Warren on the day specified. In a county so large as the whole Reserve a full vote could not be expected, some citizens having to travel sixty miles to the place of holding elections. Only forty-two persons participated in the election of 1800. Such general gatherings were necessarily of a rollicksome character, for it was not often that so many came together,—all brave, strong men, who feared neither the forest nor its inhabitants. There was great unanimity of choice, thirty-eight out of the forty-two votes being cast for General Edward Paine. General Paine took his seat in the Territorial Legislature in 1801, and continued to represent the county until a State government was established in 1803.

During the May term of the following year, the county of Trumbull was divided into districts for the purpose of carrying into effect the Territorial tax upon land. The county was also divided into two election districts. The towns of Middlefield, Richfield, Paynesville and Cleveland, constituted the northern district, and the house of Mr. Simon Perkins, at the intersection of Youngs road and the Lake road, was the place appointed for holding elections in the northern district.

The towns of Warren, Hudson, Vernon and Youngstown constituted the southern district, the elections being held at the house of Ephraim Quinby, Esq., in Warren.

The committee appointed to draft a plan of a jail, reported as follows:

We, being a committee appointed to report to the General Quarter Sessions of the Peace a plan of a building which will accommodate the county for a "gaol," beg leave to lay before the court a plan of a building of the following dimensions, to wit: Thirty feet long and twenty-two feet wide in the inside, to consist of two rooms, one of sixteen feet by twelve for criminals, the other sixteen by eighteen feet for debtors, the lower floor to be made of hewn timber fifteen inches in thickness to be laid double, a space say, to extend the whole length of the building, and the doors to be from the space way into each room, the sides of the prison room to be made of hewn timber, fifteen inches thick and to be laid double, and well locked in at the corners, to be laid in the following manner: The first stick to be on the floor, the next and outside timber to rise half of the width of the first stick above it; the outside wall from the space way to be laid up with square timber fifteen inches thick. The building to be raised in this manner, so as to be eight feet high between the joints; the upper floor to be lain double with hewn timbers twelve inches thick so as to break joints. The building then to be covered with a good roof to be made of rafters and covered with chestnut shingles eighteen inches in length; the foundation of the building to be a large white oak stick of timber hewn upon one side and buried in the ground; we think proper that all the timber be of white oak. Two small windows in the debtors' room and one in the criminals', well guarded with iron gates.

DAVID ABBOTT,
SAMUEL WOODRUFF,
URIEL HOLMES, JR.,
SIMON PERKINS,
Committee.

COUNTY OF TRUMBULL. March 27, 1801.

The court accept the report of the committee with the following alterations, namely: The roof to be covered with long oak shingles of the common length of long shingles, and order that a public gaol be built agreeably to the plan reported by said committee, with the aforesaid alteration, and appointed Mr. Simon Perkins to superintend the building of the said gaol, and to carry into effect such contract as the court of quarter sessions shall make with any person or persons for the building thereof.

CALVIN PEASE, Clerk.

Until the time of the occupancy of the first court-house, which was placed where the present structure stands, the courts were held first in the corn-cribs, next in a log house built by James Scott in 1805, on the corner of Mahoning avenue and High street, long known as the Greater House, and on the lot now owned and occupied by Warren Packard, and lastly in the third story of a log and frame house built by William Cotgreave, on the site of the Van Gorder block, familiarly known as Castle William. A room on the first floor was used for many years as a jail, until, in fact, the old log jail was built, which must have been about 1815. It stood on or near the site of the present structure. The old brick jail which followed it was erected in 1825. The room in Quinby's house was used until "Castle William" was occupied. In 1802 a jail was commenced according to the elaborate specifications approved by the court in May, 1801. The structure had almost reached completion in February, 1804, when it caught fire and burned to the ground. This fire was the signal for a general county-seat war. Mutterings of discontent had been growing louder and more distinct each year from the first day of the county's existence, and an opportunity for a change seeming to be open, all parties raised the battle-cry. Settlements in the southeast corner of the Reserve increased most rapidly and were able by casting a solid vote to elect a State Representative and commissioner favorable to Youngstown. It was also supposed that George Tod, the State Senator, was in favor of a change, but he seems to have taken very little interest in the contest. Youngstown was not the only place clamoring for the county-seat. John Kinsman wanted it near Girard and Ephraim Root advocated a point near the east line of the Reserve, and Elias Tracy wanted it farther north at New Lyme, where his largest interests lay. Youngstown, however, seemed to have the best of the fight, having the commissioners and representatives in the Legislature. The Warren men had had enough experience in legislative matters to know the value of personal influence. They accordingly appointed two or three lobby representatives, whose duty it was to stay in Chillicothe during Assembly sessions to see that no law was passed infringing upon the interests of their town.

Youngstown accomplished the first step in 1805, by having Geauga county set off, embracing all the settled western part of the Reserve, thus depriving the argument that Youngstown was too far from the center, of much of its force for Youngstown was now indisputably the center of population.

Every election was contested on the county-seat issue. The rivalry between the claimants became so animated, even bitter, that it was carried into business, social life, and sports. A striking incident illustrating the the spirit of the times, has been furnished by R. M. Grant. There was in Warren a brag racehorse named Dave, of which the whole village was proud. A number of leading citizens conceived the idea of humiliating Youngstown by bantering to run Dave against any piece of horse-flesh the latter place could scare up, for a stake of a thousand dollars. George Tod (afterwards judge) at once accepted the wager, and covered the money put up by the Warren party. It happened that Tod at that time was keeping a little bay mare owned by James Hillman, which he selected to match with Dave. It is said that Tod spent every night for two weeks in the stable grooming Fly. A track one mile long in the vicinity of Crab creek was selected for the race, and at the appointed time Youngstown and Warren turned out en masse to witness and to cheer. The result would have an effect upon the ensuing election something like a torch-light procession in a modern campaign. Anxiety raised both sides on tip-toe; all for Warren on the north side, and all for Youngstown on the south side of the track. The lines were filled at an early hour, and the passion for betting reigned supreme. What little cash each one had was soon staked on the result; watches and penknives followed next, and then off came hats, coats, vests, and even shoes, to show faith in their respective towns and cause. An expert rider was mounted on each animal, and at a signal both bounded forward exactly even. This was a fortunate circumstance, for had one got the advantage of a leap the start a general fight would probably have closed the track. Side by side the two trained beasts darted on, while the neighboring forest received a continuous roar of cheers. At last Fly gained a length, and the Youngstown side redoubled their cheering. Dave's rider applied his whip faster and harder, bringing Warren's favorite again even. Side by side they dashed on, the riders whipping and yelling. Near the end of the course Fly bounded ahead, now leading by four lengths, now by six; Fly continues to gain; the race is won, and Youngstown captures the stakes.

This is only one instance of the rival towns being thus pitted against each other. Every log-rolling or raising near the half-way line was a contest between Youngstown and Warren. Even dog-fights and bull-fights were interpreted as having some relation to the location of the county-seat.

The necessity for county buildings gave fuel to the flames. In 1808 Ashtabula and Portage counties were erected with their present western and southern boundaries. This action gave Warren a decided geographical disadvantage, nevertheless it was believed that if aliens who had always been allowed to vote were excluded from the election, Warren could carry her ticket. The election resulted in the choice of Richard J. Elliott and Robert Hughes, with the aid of the alien vote, but without their vote Thomas G. Jones, Warren's candidate, was ahead. It was resolved by the Warren party to contest the election. Mr. Leonard Case, of Warren, and William Chidester, of Canfield, justices of the peace, were selected to take testimony. The aliens were nearly all Irishmen, and the commotion which the attempt to throw out their votes caused can be imagined by those acquainted with Irish character. They considered the whole project a direct blow at their liberties—a sentiment dear to that nationality. Youngstown partisans encouraged boisterousness, and took care to keep up the excitement.

The justices first sat at Hubbard; Homer Hine appeared for the respondents, John S. Edwards for the contestants. There was a general turnout of partisans on both sides, all interested, all excited. Daniel Sheehy made a flaming speech one hour and a half long, which had the effect of increasing the general disturbance. He was at last forced to silence, and the justices proceeded to take depositions. "Many of those summoned," says Mr. Case, "refused to testify until about to be arrested and sent to jail. Then they agreed to give their testimony. About one hundred depositions were taken." On the following day the justices sat at Youngstown, where similar scenes were witnessed. Sheehy was more violent and noisy, and his hearers more clamorous, but the same coaxing, arguing, and threatening was necessary to get evidence. Before the day closed the Irish orator was committed to keepers. Another boisterous day at Poland ended the local comedy. About four hundred depositions had been taken, which it was supposed would be sufficient to give Jones a place in the House of Representatives. When the Legislature met at Chillicothe in December, 1809, Messrs. Hughes and Elliott were regularly admitted to seats on proper credentials. A memorial was then presented by Matthias Corwin, of Warren county, contesting the election of Robert Hughes in favor of Thomas G. Jones. The memorial was referred to the committee on privileges and elections, which reported in favor of Hughes. The report was made the special order for the following day, both contestor and contestee being invited to be present in person and with counsel. Three days were consumed in discussion, which ended in the resolution that "Robert Hughes is entitled to his seat in the present General Assembly." Jones was given leave to withdraw his memorial.

The Youngstown members, however, were not disposed to take advantage of the result, for they made no move toward changing the county-seat, and even permitted the passage of a bill setting off towns number eight in ranges one to five from Ashtabula county and annexing them to Trumbull, making Warren the geographical center of the county. These towns were soon afterwards set back to Ashtabula. Their inhabitants were reasonably disgusted with so many changes, making them weapons in a war in which they had no interest. Judge Solomon Griswold expressed the prevailing feeling when he said: "They have no privileges in either county, and are sued in both."

The Jones contest had the effect of making the Youngstown people more politic and less confident and dependent upon numerical strength. The north part of the county had been growing rapidly, and Warren, in consequence of having the county-seat, was rapidly gaining in prestige. Besides, some of the keener heads at Canfield foresaw the prospect of a new county and were on that account indifferent to Youngstown's desires. It seems that in 1810 both Youngstown and Warren were afraid to stake the issue on a straight fight, for Aaron Collar, of Canfield, a neutral candidate, was chosen to the Legislature.

In 1811 the old issue again presented itself and resulted in the choice of Thomas G. Jones, candidate for Warren, and Samuel Boyson, candidate for Youngstown to the House of Representatives, and George Tod, of Youngstown, to the Senate. It was currently reported after the election that Judge Tod, though supposed on account of his location to be favorable to Youngstown, had given the people of Warren to understand that their interests would be safe in his hands. However this may be, Warren had no cause to complain of Tod's course in the Senate. The first chapter in the history of this bitter and selfish sectional conflict came to a close in 1813. The erection of county buildings could no longer be delayed under any pretense, and the commissioners that year contracted for a court-house in Warren. General politics during this interval of local strife had received scarcely any attention. Affairs affecting the most vital interests of the Nation could scarce be seen through the mist and storm of a faction's local conflict. The announcement of Hull's surrender of Detroit and Michigan, and the consequent exposure of Ohio to Indian forces and British guerillas, suddenly poured such a violent stream of patriotism into the community as to produce a shock. Local conflict and pride were forgotten in the broader and nobler impulse to shoulder a rifle and march to the music of the Nation in defense of home and family and the country's flag. The war was doubtless an efficient cause in the temporary settlement of the county seat.

The first court-house was built by James Scott and completed in 1815. A log jail was built about the same time near the site of the present structure. It was replaced by a brick building in 1824. The contract with Seth Thompson for its construction is dated in 1822. It was accepted by commissioners December 9, 1824, and the contractor given an order on the treasury for $2,943.

In 1835 the county commissioners first took means toward providing for the poor and unfortunate. A farm of two hundred and eighty-five acres, located about three miles from Warren, was purchased for the sum of $3,000. Three years later one hundred acres more was purchased for $1,700. In 1839 the contract was let for the erection of suitable buildings at a cost of $4,445. In 1874 an additional building was erected at a cost of $7,000. The institution has always been managed upon economical though liberal principles and is worthy the reputation of the Reserve for benevolence and advancement. It is a worthy commentary upon the superiority of republican institutions, that the prosperous and wealthy are always willing to provide for the impoverished and imbecile, and the perfection and fullness to which such provision is carried may be considered a fair measure of the intelligence and culture of ruling in the community. There are in the Trumbull county infirmary about one hundred inmates, some of them hopelessly insane, some idiotic, some decrepit men and women and poor, helpless children. It is unfortunate that all are thrown together. Bright, spirited children, should not be compelled to witness day after day the misery of feeble old men and women or the raving of maniacs. It is to be hoped that as the county grows richer and more benevolent the example of several other counties in the State will be followed, of providing a Children's Home where young minds and bodies will have entirely healthful and elevating surroundings.

About the year 1840 the dilapidated courthouse became an object of general remark. Its floors were shaky, roof leaky, offices cold, and its appearance unworthy the growing pretensions of Warren. Leading citizens of the county-seat, lawyers, and others particularly interested—petitioned for a new building. Youngstown and other southern townships protested against further improvements for the benefit of Warren. Again a strife between envious sections was launched upon the county. The issue was at first confined to the erection of new buildings. This spark was the origin of a flame which enveloped the whole county in its light. The subject of a new court-house was soon lost sight of among the multitudinous projects proposed in every section of the county. Warren was soon forced from the offensive on the subject of new buildings to a vigorous defense of her rights to retain the county-seat. There were at least four propositions for dividing the county in such a way as to leave Warren without the seat of government. In this way Youngstown had no difficulty in electing officers committed against the new court-house project. The first newspaper started in Youngstown was called 'The Olive Branch and New County Advocate, issued in 1843. In the number of December 20th of that year we find the following resolutions embodied in the report of a meeting held at Newton Falls—a previous meeting had been held at which a special committee to frame these resolutions was appointed:

WHEREAS, Vigorous efforts have been made and are now making by the citizens of the south part of Trumbull county, circulating memorials for signatures to be presented to the Legislature now in session at Columbus, praying for a new county in the southeast part of said county of Trumbull; therefore,

Resolved, That the diversity of interests which has been shown in the efforts of those in the east, north, and south parts of the county, demands a division, and that that division should be made with reference to the interests and future prospects of an increased population which may in a few years be safely estimated at double the present number.

Resolved, That whenever a division of Trumbull county should be deemed expedient, the following would be most convenient and beneficial to the several sections named in this division to wit: a new county to be formed from the south part of Ashtabula county and the north part of Trumbull county consisting of the townships of Hartsgrove, Rome, Cherry Valley, New Lyme, Andover, Windsor, Orwell, Colbrook, Wayne, and Williamsfield, in Ashtabula county, and Mesopotamia, Bloomfield, Greene, Gustavus, Kinsman, and Vernon, in Trumbull county. A new county in the east part of Trumbull county, consisting of Mecca, Bazetta, Howland, Weathersfield, Austintown, Canfield, Boardman, Youngstown, Liberty, Vienna, Fowler, Johnston, Hartford, Brookfield, Hubbard, Coitsville, and Poland with county seat at Youngstown. The townships of Windham, Palmyra, Nelson, and Paris, in Portage county, to be annexed to Trumbull county with the county seat at Newton Falls.

Resolved, That the foregoing division would be far more beneficial than the one proposed by the citizens of Youngstown, as it would leave to each of the proposed counties about the constitutional amount of territory and would forever afterwards prevent any necessity for any further alteration in the counties of Ashtabula, Trumbull, and Portage, and would leave the contemplated counties in a compact and favorable form and with a location for county seats, particularly at Youngstown and Newton Falls, in the heart of flourishing townships with facilities for commerce by the Pennsylvania and Ohio canal and with water privileges among the best in northern Ohio and which can be improved to any desirable extent.

Youngstown finally petitioned for a division of Trumbull county as it then existed into two counties, the south division part having the county-seat at Youngstown, and the northwest, which should retain the name Trumbull, retaining the county-seat at Warren. Canfield further complicated matters by petitioning for the erection of a new county out of the ten southern townships of Trumbull and five northern townships of Columbiana. This last proposition received the support of the Warren people, and was finally confirmed by the Legislature in 1846, the new county being designated "Mahoning."

Thus ended the tedious contest for the county-seat so far as Trumbull county is concerned. The main source of opposition to a new courthouse at Warren had been removed, and Time's dilapidations were making the necessity for such a structure more and more apparent. However, six years elapsed before definite measures were taken to supply this pressing need. A contract for building the new structure was awarded early in 1852 to Richards and Logan, of Poland, and work was commenced that summer. Two years were occupied in its construction and completion, the contract being formally discharged by the commissioners in 1854. The total cost appears from bills allowed to have been $23,658. It was considered at that time one of the finest public county buildings in the State.

That public spirit, too often absurdly extravagant, which demands that the hall of justice should be a palace, dates its birth in Ohio not more than a score of years since. Twenty-two thousand dollars was in 1852, as much complained of as five times that amount is now.

In 1871 it was determined to replace the old jail with a modern structure. Plans were submitted and the building contract awarded Epersom and Favorite at the designated sum of $30,694. Several changes were made while the work was in operation, making the total cost in round numbers $35,000.

CIVIL OFFICERS OF TRUMBULL COUNTY.

The first State constitution was adopted in 1802, creating substantially the present system of civil administration, except in the judiciary branch. The State was divided into circuits, a presiding judge being elected for each circuit, whose duty it was to hold regular terms of court. Each county had a board of three associate justices, whose duty it was to sit with the presiding judge during the trial of causes, and also to transact the probate business of their county. Lawyers were seldom ever called to this office, the duties of which were mostly routine. The new constitution of 1850 created the office of probate judge and abolished the system of associates. With the present population the old system would be wholly inadequate. Under the Territorial system the office of clerk of court was filled by appointment of the Governor. Upon him exclusively devolved the clerical duties of the county government. This office was appointive until the adoption of the present constitution in 1850.

CLERKS OF COURT.

The constitutional term under the old constitution was seven years; under the present constitution it is three years. The office has been filled as follows:

Calvin Pease, 1800 to 1803 ; George Phelps*, 1803 to 1806; George Parsons, 1806 to 1838†, John Huchins, 1838 to 1844‡; Clayton Harrington, 1844 to 1846; Warren Young, 1846 to 1852 ; Jonathan Ingersoll, 1852 to 1855§; Almon D. Webb, 1855 to 1861 ; C. A. Harrington, 1861 to 1867 ; Edward Speer, Jr., 1867 to 1873; M. C. Hart, 1873 to 1879; O. A. Caldwell, 1879‖.

Clerks of the court of common pleas also served in similar capacity for the supreme court of their respective counties under the old constitution, and under the present constitution for the district court.

RECORDERS.

John S. Edwards, 1800 to 1813; Alexander Southerland, 1813 to 1821; William Quinby, 1821 to 1831; Lyman Potter, 1831 to 1837; Vincent Webb, 1837 to 1843; John Veon, 1843 to 1846; Charles R. Hunt, 1846 to 1849; Sands Bonteu, 1849 to 1852; James D. Watson, 1852 to 1855; S. M. Corter, 1855 to 1861; Alexander A. Adams, 1861 to 1867; Elmer Moses, 1867 to 1873; Wells A. Bushnell, 1873 to 1879; H. J. Barnes, 1879.

COUNTY COMMISSIONER.

This office was created by the State Constitution in 1802. No journal of the board's official acts in a general way appears until 1822, then came William Ripley, who having been duly elected and qualified, took the oath of office; John C. Woodruff, elected in 1827; Rufus Beeman, 1829; Benjamin Stevens, 1829; Tracy Bronson and Cornelius Thompson, in 1833; Joel Smith, in 1835; Charles Woodruff, Joel Smith, and Amadeus Brooks formed the board in 1836; James King succeeds in 1838; in 1839 came James

*Died in October, 1806.
†Resigned October, 1838.
‡Resigned in May, 1844.
§Elected October, 1852.
‖Re-elected in 1881.

Coit and John Stewart; in 1840 came Daniel Shehy; in 1841 came Jonathan Osborn; 1842 Augustus Stevens; 1843, James Millikin; 1844, Isaac Lee; 1845, E. V. Kellogg; 1846, A. I. Ford; 1847, Edward Beaver; 1848, E. V. Kellogg; 1849, Thad. Bradley; 1850, Abner Osborn; 1851, E. V. Kellogg; 1852, Thad. Bradley; 1853, Abner Osborn; 1854, Edmund Smith; 1855, Edward D. King; 1856, B. P. Jameson; 1857, J. W. Pattingell; 1858, N. E. Austin; 1859, Jacob S. Smith; 1860, Aaron Davis; 1861, H. T. Mason; 1862, Jacob S. Smith; 1863, Aaron Davis; 1864, H. T. Mason; 1865, Orlando K. Wolcott; 1866, E. A. Reed; 1867, J. B. Payne; 1868, O. K. Wolcott; 1869, E. A. Reed; 1870, J. B. Payne; 1871, Charles Harshman; 1872, N. A. Cowdery; 1873, Addison Randall; 1874, Charles Harshman; 1875, N. A. Cowdery; 1876, Addison Randall; 1877, William Bronson; 1878, A. V. Crouch; 1879, John Sampson (appointed to fill vacancy, unexpired term of Randall, resigned); 1879, John I. Smith; 1880, William Bronson; 1881, A. V. Crouch.

AUDITORS.

William Rayen, 1802 to 1805; Edward Paine, Jr., 1805 to 1806; J. W. Brown, 1806 to 1807; Richard Hayes, 1807 to 1810; Simon Perkins, 1810 to 1812; Lyman Potter, 1812 to 1817; Roswell Mason, 1817 to 1821; Jacob H. Baldwin, 1821 to 1839; Henry Baldwin, 1839 to 1841; James G. Calender, 1841 to 1845; Hiram Austin, 1845 to 1849; George Hapgood, 1849 to 1851; Theodore Webb, 1851 to 1855; Charles R. Hunt, 1855 to 1859; O. L. Wolcott, 1859 to 1863; Junius Dana, 1863 to 1865; Charles A. Bugdon, 1865 to 1869; James D. Kennedy, 1869 to 1873; George B. Kennedy, 1873 to 1877; Ralsa C. Rice, 1877.[*]

PROBATE JUDGES.

Office created by the constitution of 1850.

I. L. Fuller, 1852 to 1855; George T. Brown, 1855 to 1861; J. W. Tyler,[†] 1861 to 1864; Albert Yeomans, 1864 to 1879; Wilbur A. Reeves, 1879.[‡]

TREASURERS.

Samuel Tylee, 1803 to 1812; John Leavitt, 1812 to 1815; Francis Freeman, 1815 to 1831; Martin Bently, 1831 to 1833; Ralph Hickox,[*] 1833 to 1834; B. N. Robbins, 1834 to 1842; Lewis I. Iddings, 1842 to 1846; Francis Barclay, 1846 to 1848; Augustus Stevens, 1848 to 1850; Zalmon Fitch, 1850 to 1852; John M. Hezlep, 1852 to 1856; John Reeves, 1856 to 1858; D. B. Gilmore, 1858 to 1862; William Ritczel, 1862 to 1866; Edward Hays, 1866 to 1870; Thomas A Brierly, 1870 to 1874; A. A. House, 1874 to 1878; T. W. Case, 1878 to 1882; Clinton O. Hart, elected 1881. The treasurer's bond for the year 1803-4 was $4,000.

PROSECUTING ATTORNEYS.

George Tod, 1833 to 1835; William I. Knight, to 1839; R. B. Taylor, to 1841; William I. Knight, to 1843; N. V. Humphrey, to 1847; Joel F. Asper, to 1849; I. N. Fuller, to 1851; N. V. Humphrey, to 1853; D. B. Belden, to 1855; Charles W. Smith, to 1859; John M. Stull, to 1861; E. H. Ensign, to 1865; John M. Stull, to 1869; William B. Porter to 1871; W. T. Spear, to 1875; Thomas J. Gillmer, to 1879; Washington Hyde, re-elected 1881.

SURVEYORS.

Alexander Southerland, from 1832 to 1835; F. E. Storrs, to 1838; Bethel Beaman, to 1841; F. E. Stowe, to 1843; Joseph Barkley, to 1846; E. Leffingwell, to 1848; W. S. Darley, to 1851; Homer M. Lut, to 1854; J. K. Burnham, to 1857; F. Trunkey, to 1860; Amos D. Fell, 1863; F. W. Messerschmidt, to 1866; Samuel F. Dickey, 1872; C. W. Tyler.

SHERIFFS.

David Abbott, 1800 to 1804; Elijah Wadsworth, 1806; James Hillman, 1809; Trial Tamer, 1813; John Struthers, 1815; Benjamin Austin, 1819; Lemuel Reeves, 1822; Andrew Bushnell, 1826; Cyrus Bosworth, 1830; George Mygatt, 1834, [executed the sentence of death by hanging passed upon Ira Gardner, who killed Miss Mary Buell in his yard about mid-day by stabbing her with a knife, near the junction of South street with Red run. This was the only murder ever committed in Warren]; Henry Smith succeeded Mr. Mygatt, and served until 1838; Warren Young, 1842; James Hezlep, 1846; Benjamin V. Robbins, 1848; William Williams, 1850; Benjamin N. Robbins, 1852;

---

*Present incumbent.
†Resigned.
‡Re-elected 1881.

[*] Appointed to fill vacancy caused by resignation of Martin Bently.

Isaac Powers, 1854; H. R. Harmon, 1858; A. B. Lyman, 1862; J. G. Butler, 1866; S. M. Laird, 1870; G. W. Dickinson, 1874; S. A. Corbin, 1878; S. F. Bartlett, 1882; John Hoyt (elected 1881).

VOTE OF TRUMBULL COUNTY.

Total vote in 1803, 1,111.

VOTE FOR GOVERNOR.

(Those marked * were the successful candidates.)

1807, Return J. Meigs* 603, Nathaniel Massie 75.

1808, Samuel Huntington* 178, Thomas Worthington 124, Thomas Kirker 407.

1810, Return J. Meigs* 658, Thomas Worthington 118.

1812, Return J. Meigs* 790, Thomas Scott 1.

1814, Thomas Worthington* 622, Othniel Looker 214.

1816, Thomas Worthington* 715, Ethan A. Brown 264.

1818, Ethan Allen Brown* 1,083, James Dunlap 79.

1820, Ethan A. Brown* 1,690, Jeremiah Morrow 27, W. H. Harrison 67.

1822, Jeremiah Morrow* 150, Allen Trimble 1,364, W. W. Irvin 12.

1824, Jeremiah Morrow* 404, Allen Trimble 1,136.

1826, Allen Trimble* 1,969, John Bigger 16, Alexander Campbell 167, Benjamin Tappan 47.

1828, Allen Trimble* 1,968, John W. Campbell 995.

1830, Duncan McArthur* (National Republican) 1,742, Robert Lucas (Democrat) 1,346.

1832, Robert Lucas* (Democrat), Darius Lyman (Whig), vote not given.

1834, Robert Lucas* (Democrat) 2,370, James Findlay (Whig) 2,504.

1836, Joseph Vance* (Whig), Eli Baldwin (Democrat), vote not given.

1838, Wilson Shannon* (Democrat) 3,269, Joseph Vance (Whig) 3,356.

1840, Thomas Corwin* (Whig) 4,031, Wilson Shannon (Democrat) 3,420.

1842, Wilson Shannon* (Democrat) 3,025, Thomas Corwin (Whig) 3,364, Leicester King (Abolition) 456.

1844, Mordecai Bartley* (Whig) 3,696, David Tod (Democrat) 3,611, Leicester King (Abolition) 745.

1846, William Bebb* (Whig) 2,953, David Tod (Democrat) 2,939, Samuel Lewis (Abolition) 471.

1848, Seabury Ford* (Whig) 3,069, John B. Weller (Democrat) 2,028, scattering 15.

1850, Reuben Wood* (Democrat) 1,649, William Johnston (Whig) 1,389, Edward Smith (Abolition) 1,550.

1851, Reuben Wood* (Democrat) 2,232, Samuel F. Vinton (Whig) 1,584, Samuel Lewis (Abolition) 1,616.

1853, William Medill* (Democrat) 2,028, Nelson Barrere (Whig) 1,165, Samuel Lewis (Abolition) 1,447.

1855, Salmon P. Chase* (Republican) 3,109, William Medill (Democrat) 1,474, Allen Trimble (Know Nothing) 31.

1857, Salmon P. Chase* (Republican) 2,311, Henry B. Payne (Democrat) 1,595, Philip Van Trump (Know Nothing) none.

1859, William Dennison* (Republican) 3,143, Rufus P. Ranney (Democrat) 1,791.

1861, David Tod* (Republican) 4,028, Hugh J. Jewett (Democrat) 833.

1863, John Brough* (Republican) 5,334, C. L. Vallandigham (Democrat) 1,618.

1865, Jacob D. Cox* (Republican) 3,989, George W. Morgan (Democrat) 1,851.

1867, Rutherford B. Hayes* (Republican) 4,525, Allen G. Thurman (Democrat) 2,189.

1869, Rutherford B. Hayes* (Republican) 4,621, George H. Pendleton (Democrat) 2,144.

1871, Edward F. Noyes* (Republican) 4,345, George W. McCook (Democrat) 1,766, Gideon T. Stewart (Prohibition) 120.

1873, William Allen* (Democrat) 1,927, Edward F. Noyes (Republican) 3,698, G. T. Stewart (Prohibition) 353, Isaac Collins (Liberal) 23.

1875, Rutherford B. Hayes* (Republican) 5,653, William Allen (Democrat) 3,301, Jay Odell (Prohibition) 96.

1877, Richard M. Bishop* (Democrat) 2,584, William H. West (Republican) 4,763, H. A. Thompson (Prohibition) 123, Stephen Johnson (Greenback) 478.

1879, Charles Foster (Republican) 5,997, Thomas Ewing (Democrat) 3,054, Gideon T

Stewart (Prohibition) 130, A. Saunders Piatt (Greenback) 278.

VOTE FOR GOVERNOR, 1881.

	Charles Foster.	John W. Bookwalter.	Abram Ludlow.	J. Seitz.
Warren City	664	244	30	17
Warren township	130	110	2	1
Weathersfield	601	265	34	40
Vienna	180	58	63	
Vernon	139	38	10	3
Southington	100	74	3	3
Newton	183	149	3	2
Mesopotamia	148	30	8	
Mecca	146	54	8	
Lordstown	54	100	6	3
Liberty	480	132	63	19
Kinsman	196	40	0	8
Johnston	95	42	11	3
Hubbard	271	216		4
Howland	124	57	3	1
Hartford	177	71	33	4
Gustavus	172	21	14	8
Greene	141	33	10	10
Fowler	150	46	1	
Farmington	190	47	21	5
Champion	101	86		13
Brookfield	135	100	54	
Bristol	201	54	9	3
Braceville	125	49	12	2
Bloomfield	123	26		
Bazetta	195	66	23	5
Totals	5,012	2,208	439	187

VOTE FOR PRESIDENT, 1880.

	Garfield.	Hancock.	Weaver.	Dow.
Warren (city)	766	302	10	3
Warren (township)	146	139		
Weathersfield	807	375	31	10
Vienna	265	117	14	10
Vernon	192	58	6	
Southington	151	91	1	
Newton	193	183	4	
Mesopotamia	184	25	7	2
Mecca	196	73	1	1
Lordstown	72	127		
Liberty	494	217	18	18
Kinsman	237	67	8	1
Johnston	152	71		3
Hubbard	482	375	44	8
Howland	138	69		1
Hartford	335	227	80	2
Gustavus	224	28	8	4
Greene	175	51	4	4
Fowler	195	62		
Farmington	252	45	1	3
Champion	119	100	9	
Brookfield	232	180	23	12
Bristol	249	70	5	1
Braceville	159	73	4	2
Bloomfield	171	30		
Bazetta	244	121	8	
Totals	6796	3248	208	85

Total vote, 10,237.

Members elected from districts in Ohio comprising Trumbull and that part of Mahoning county included in the Western Reserve, with date of service:

STATE REPRESENTATIVES.

Ephraim Quinby, March,	Walter Johnson
Aaron Wheeler } term 1803	Thomas Robbins } 1833
David Abbott } Decem- 1803	Jared P. Kirtland } 1834
Ephraim Quinby } ber term	William A. Otis
Amos Spafford	Eli Baldwin
Homer Hine } 1804	Tenuard R. DeWolf } ..1835
Homer Hine	Seth Hayes
James Kingsbury } 1805	Tracy Bronson } 1836
James Kingsbury	John C. Woodruff
John P. Bissell } 1806	Tracy Bronson } 1837
John W. Seely	Tracy Bronson
James Montgomery } 1807	Thomas Howe } 1838
Rich. J. Elliott	Isaac Powers
Robert Hughes } ..1808-1809	Thomas Howe } 1839
Aaron Collar	Peter Allen
Thomas G. Jones } 1810	Josiah Robbins } ... 1840
Thomas G. Jones	John Briggs } 1841
Samuel Bryson } 1811	Jacob H. Baldwin
Samuel Bryson	Nathan Webb } 1842
Benjamin Ross } 1812	Henry Manning
Benjamin Ross	Asahel Medbury } 1843
Samuel Leavitt } 1813	Buell Barnes } 1844
Wilson Elliott	Burll Barnes
James Hillman } 1814	Henry Boyd } 1845
Samuel Bryson	Joseph Truesdale } 1846
W. W. Colgreve } 1815	Joseph Truesdale
Homer Hine	John Harrington } 1847
Henry Lane } 1816	Isaac Lee
Eli Baldwin	Albert G. Riddle } 1848
Edward Scoville } 1817	(For Trumbull and Geauga).
Henry Lane	John Hutchins
Edward Scoville } 1818	Albert G. Riddle } 1849
Henry Lane	(For Trumbull and Geauga).
Henry Manning } 1819	More C. Bradley } ..1850-1851
Dan Eaton	Gamaliel H Kent
Elisha Whittlesey } 1820	(For Trumbull and Geauga).
Thomas Howe	Franklin E. Stowe..1852-1853
Elisha Whittlesey } 1821	Matthew Birchard..1854-1855
James Mackey	Ralph Plumb } ..1856-1857
Cyrus Bosworth } ..1822-1823	G.T. Townsend
Homer Hine	G.T. Townsend } ..1858-1859
Ephraim Brown } 1824	George H Howe
Ephraim Brown	Robert H. Walker..1860-1861
Eli Baldwin } 1825	George H. Howe..1862-1863
Henry Lane	Austin D. Kibber..1864-1865
Roswell Stone } 1826	Austin D. Kibber..1866-1867
Titus Bockway	William Ritezel....1868-1869
William Ripley } ..1827-1828	William Ritezel
Jared P. Kirtland	J. K. Wing } ..1870-1871
George Swift } 1829	J. K. Wing......1872-1873
Benjamin Allen	Thomas J. M'Lain,
Richard Iddings } 1830	Jr...........1874-1875
Calvin Pease	T. J. M'Lain. Jr } ..1876-1877
Jared P. Kirtland } 1831	D. Edwards
Jedediah Fitch	E. A. Reed........1878-1880
Benjamin Allen } 1832	Stephen Laird.... pres. Inc.

REPRESENTATIVES FROM MAHONING COUNTY AFTER BEING TRANSFERRED FROM TRUMBULL.

David Huston......1849	Reuben Carroll...1864-1865
George Pow.&......1850-1851	Joseph Bruff......1866-1867
Joseph Montgomery.1852-1853	George W. Brook..1868-1869
Jacob Musser.......1854-1855	George W. Brook..1870-1871
Joseph Truesdale...1856-1857	Cook F. Kirtland..1872-1873
Samuel W. Gilson...1858-1859	Sheldon Newton..1874-1875
Jesse Baldwin	Joseph Barclay...1876-1877
Joseph Bruff } ...1860-1861	Robert Mackey...1878-1879
Robert Montgomery.1862-1863	Thomas H. Wilson, pres.inc.

FOR MEMBERS OF CONGRESS.

*John S. Edwards, Warren, Trumbull county..1813
Reein Beall, Wooster, Wayne county.........1813 to 1814
David Clendenin, Trumbull county............1814 to 1817
Peter Hitchcock, Burton, Geauga county......1817 to 1819
John Sloan, Wooster, Wayne county...........1819 to 1823

* Died before the time for taking his seat.

Elisha Whittlesey, Canfield, Trumbull county...1823 to 1838
Joshua R. Giddings, Jefferson, Ashtabula Co....1838 to 1843
Daniel R. Tilden, Ravenna, Portage county....1843 to 1847
John Crowell, Warren, Trumbull county ... ...1847 to 1851
Eben Newton, Canfield, Trumbull county.....1851 to 1853
Joshua R. Giddings, Jefferson, Ashtabula Co....1853 to 1859
John Hutchins, Warren, Trumbull county......1859 to 1863
James A. Garfield, Hiram, Portage county......1863 to 1881
Lauren D. Woodworth, Youngstown, Mahoning
county..... ....1873 to 1877
William McKinley, Stark county..............1877 to 1881
E. B. Taylor.., ...1881

NOTE—Joshua R. Giddings represented the Lake Shore district through the periods occupied by Tilden, Crowell, and Newton, in the Trumbull district; the main part of the Lake Shore (both previous and after) was attached to the Trumbull district. The two years service of members of Congress commence on a year after election.

STATE SENATORS.

Samuel Huntington,	William Ripley....1830-1831
March term......1803	Ephraim Brown,...1832-1833
Benjamin Tappan,	Leicester King.....1834-1837
December term...1803	David Tod........1838-1839
George Tod...:.....1804-1805	John Crowell......1840-1841
Calvin Cone ,,....1806-1809	Eben Newton..... 1842-1843
George Tod 1810-1811	Samuel Quinby....1844-1845
Calvin Pease,......1812	John F. Beaver....1846-1849
Dan Eaton........1813	Milton Sutliff.....1850-1851
Turhand Kirtland..1814	Jonathan I. Tod....1852-1853
Eli Baldwin........1815	Ira Norris........1854-1855
John W. Seely....1816-1817	Robert W. Tayler..1856-1859
Eli Baldwin........1818-1821	J. Dolson Cox.....1860-1861
Samuel Bryson.....1822-1823	Samuel Quinby.....1862-1863
Thomas D. Webb...1824	Eben Newton 1864-1865
Seat contested and	George F. Brown...1866-1867
given to Henry	L. D. Woodworth..1868-1871
Manning........1825	J.. C. Jones......1872-1875
Eli Baldwin........1826-1827	J. R. Johnson.....1876-1879
Thomas D. Webb...1828-1829	H. B. Perkins.... 1879-1883

CHAPTER XI.
MAHONING COUNTY.
Erection and Civil History of Mahoning County—County Seat Controversy.

We have reviewed the toil and trouble, sectional strife, and multiplied projects which finally resulted in the erection of Mahoning county. The county seat war cloud, however, was not dispelled but only intensified by being confined to a smaller territory. Canfield found it necessary in order to secure the adoption of a plan of division favorable to her interests, to make substantial pledges, which were incorporated in the legislative act of February 16, 1846. The law is headed "an Act to create the county of Mahoning." The first section declares the creation of the county and defines the boundaries as they have since continued to exist. The section concludes that the county "shall be known by the name of Mahoning, with the county seat at Canfield." In the fifth section it is provided that "the court of common pleas and supreme court of said county shall be holden at some convenient house in the town of Canfield until suitable county buildings shall be erected." In section eight it is provided "that before the seat of justice shall be considered permanently established at Canfield, the proprietors or citizens thereof shall give bond with good and sufficient security payable to the commissioners of said county, hereafter to be elected, for the sum of $5,000, to be applied in the erection of county buildings for said county, and that the citizens of Canfield shall also donate a suitable lot of ground on which to erect public buildings."

James Wallace, of Springfield; James Brownlee, of Poland; and Lemuel Brigham, of Ellsworth, were designated by the Legislature to act as associate justices until an election should be held. They convened for the first time March 16, 1846, in the office of Elisha Whittlesey, in Canfield. Hon. Eben Newton, at that time presiding judge of the circuit, administered the oath of office. Henry J. Canfield was chosen clerk and duly qualified. The only business transacted was a division of the county into four assessment districts and the disposition of probate business. The first assessors were Thomas McGilligen, James McClelland, Samuel Hardman, and Herman A. Doud. May 11th was the time appointed for holding the first regular court of common pleas. The trustees of the Methodist Episcopal church tendered their building for the purpose, there being no public hall in Canfield. Few petitions were filed and no business of importance was likely to be called, yet the occasion of opening court is one of the historic days in Canfield. The organization and dignified conduct of a court of justice is always an impressive spectacle, to which on this occasion novelty gave additional interest.

For days before that 11th of May it would have been easy to detect from street conversations and an air of preparation that some event of consequence was catalogued for the near future. On the morning of the day people began to fill the streets, and lawyers from neighboring towns and counties made hotel bar-rooms ring with sportive revelry. Citizens opened their houses to friends and acquaintances, and for several days the streets presented a scene of bustle and stir entirely new to that quiet village. At the appointed hour James Powers, the sheriff, took his position on the church steps with a dinner bell in hand, the sound of which, as he waved it back and forth, called together lawyers, officers, and spectators, who packed the room to its utmost capacity. The surroundings were no doubt strange to a majority of the professional class assembled. The presiding judge, Hon. Eben Newton, with great dignity took his place in the pulpit and the associate justices took chairs by his side. Judge Newton, having given directions, Sheriff Powers, with a voice pitched in that tone which indicates an exalted idea of dignity, proclaimed: "Hear ye, hear ye, hear ye, all persons who have business before the honorable court of common pleas of Mahoning county, Ohio, now give your attendance and you shall be heard. Court is now opened according to law." Thus was organized the first court of common pleas.

It will be noticed in the act erecting the county, Canfield was pledged to donate a suitable lot and $5,000 toward public buildings. A committee of citizens of Canfield, soon after the passage of the act of February 16, 1846, duly executed and delivered to the commissioners a bond guaranteeing the payment of the prescribed amount, which was accepted. By private arrangement, however, between the commissioners and a committee of citizens known as the building committee, it was understood that a court-house constructed on a lot set apart for the purpose by Eben Newton, according to plans and specifications submitted by the committee, should be accepted in discharge of the bond or money obligation. Funds were at once raised by private subscription to the amount of $10,000, and contracts for the erection of a building let. Work progressed rapidly, so that by June, 1848, the committee submitted the following report:

To the Commissioners of the County of Mahoning and State of Ohio:

We, the undersigned, a committee duly chosen to erect a court-house for the use of the county of Mahoning and the State of Ohio, under the name of a building committee, having discharged the duty thus imposed upon us, do hereby offer and tender for the use of said county, the court-house situated in the town of Canfield in said county, and which has been erected by us with funds subscribed by the citizens of said Canfield in compliance with the law erecting the county of Mahoning and in discharge of the sum of $5,000, which by said law the citizens of Canfield, in said county, were required to secure before the county seat of said county should be permanently located at said Canfield.

You will also take notice that a deed duly signed, sealed, and delivered, conveying an acre of land, upon a part of which said court-house now stands, by Eben Newton and Mary his wife, is hereby signed, tendered, and offered to said commissioners for the use of said county of Mahoning.

JOHN WHITMORE,
JOHN R. CHURCH,
JOHN CLARK,   } Committee.
NATHAN HARTMAN,
EBEN NEWTON.

CANFIELD, June 29, 1848.

It was then ordered by the commissioners, James Justice, Daniel Parshall, and Isaiah Bowman, that the land tendered by Judge Newton, and the building standing thereon, should be accepted as the property of the county, and also "that said building be accepted in lieu of the $5,000 which the citizens of Canfield were required to pay, or secure to be paid, to the commissioners by the act erecting said county, and that said lot of ground and building thereon be accepted in satisfaction of the enactment of the eighth section of said act." The citizens of Canfield esteemed themselves particularly fortunate in securing the county seat on terms apparently so favorable to themselves. They interpreted this acceptance of their court-house as the conclusion of a specific contract that Canfield should be permanently considered the county seat, and that interpretation was accepted in all parts of the county, even in Youngstown. The offices were duly occupied by the proper officers and the commissioners took steps toward erecting a jail, which was completed in the course of a few years. A large addition to the court-house was subsequently built at considerable expense to the county.

From 1848 the county seat agitation rested till about the year 1872. Youngstown had by that time become a city, and was the seat of more than half the litigation in the county courts, paid one-fourth the taxes, and being a railroad center was more accessible to all parts of the county than Canfield. The question of removal became an open subject of discussion, though Canfield flattered herself on being secure in consequence of the contract implied in the act of 1846.

Early in the year 1873 a large, enthusiastic

meeting was held in Arms' hall in Youngstown, to consider the subject. John Stambaugh was chairman, and George Rudge was secretary. The meeting was addressed by T. W. Sanderson, M. Logan, A. W. Jones, William Powers, G. Rudge, J. Stambaugh, D. M. Wilson, and others; all agreeing upon the main question as to the expediency and necessity for removal.

The result of this meeting was the resolution passed to elect a Representative favorable to their interest in the coming fall election, without regard to party, and the appointment of a committee to take such action in regard to removal as they deemed proper and wise. At a subsequent meeting this committee, consisting of Dr. T. Woodwridge and others, reported—first, in substance that the removal of the county seat was to the interest and convenience of a large majority of the people of Mahoning county; second, that to attain this end it was necessary to unite upon some man to represent them in the State Legislature, irrespective of party, who was fully committed in favor of removal; third, that the city and township of Youngstown pledge themselves to build the necessary county buildings, to be twice as valuable at least as those in Canfield, and in addition donate a site for such buildings.

This report was adopted, and after business of the meeting was disposed of letters from Dr. Brooke and Mr. Wilson, the candidates of the two political parties for the constitutional convention, were read, expressing their views in regard to the constitutional provision relative to Mahoning county seats, both gentlemen favoring the provision as it stood, giving the power of removal to the majority of voters.

Acting upon the feelings of the citizens here indicated, there met in Excelsior hall the largest nominating convention ever held, on Saturday, June 30, 1873, to nominate a county ticket favorable to the removal of the county seat, the following being the ticket: Sheldon Newton, of Boardman, representative; James K. Bailey, of Coitsville, auditor; Isaac Justice, of Youngstown, Jonathan Schillinger, of Springfield, commissioners; J. Schnurrenberger, of Green, infirmary director, Henry M. Boardman, of Boardman, surveyor; Dr. Ewing, of Milton, coroner; Sheldon Newton being Republican and the other gentlemen on the ticket in their political affinities were part of them Democrats and part Republicans. This convention passed the usual number of resolutions. Conspicuous were the first two whereases, which were:

FIRST. The Constitution of the State of Ohio provides for the removal of county-seats by a vote of the majority of the voters of a county; and

WHEREAS, The township of Youngstown contains over one-third of the inhabitants, and pays nearly one-half of the taxes of Mahoning county, resolved, etc.:

On August 19th, a convention of those friendly to the retention of the county-seat at Canfield was held in that village, and the following ticket was nominated, composed partly of Democrats and partly of Republicans: Representative, C. F. Kirtland of Poland; auditor, James M. Dixon, of Jackson; prosecuting attorney, Jared Huxley, of Canfield; commissioner, James Williams, of Ellsworth; infirmary director, Isaac G. Rush, of Coitsville; coroner, Dr. E. G. Rose, of Austintown; Surveyor, Daniel Reichart, of Milton.

G. Van Hyning, Esq., of Canfield, as chairman of the committee on resolutions, reported the following, which were unanimously adopted:

Resolved, That we deprecate the issue forced upon us by the convention held at Youngstown; that said convention is directly and wholly responsible for rupturing long established and valued political associations for the probability of engendering local and neighborhood strife and division, the consequence of which will be to injure one portion of our citizens in the uncertain expectation of benefiting them.

Resolved, That this convention, representing every township in the county, deny the truthfulness of the Youngstown convention of June 30th, they being a gross exaggeration and misrepresentation of the facts, but on the contrary we claim the seat of government, being now centrally located, of convenient access from all portions of the county, and having good and ample buildings for the accommodation of the public, the removal of it to one corner of the county largely for the benefit of a few capitalists, and to satisfy uneasy political agitation would be an act of gross injustice to the greater portion of the county, and

Resolved, That we deem it of vital importance to the citizens and tax-payers to have economy prevail in the administration of public affairs, and demand, as far as practicable, the reduction of taxation in a ratio corresponding to the decline in prices of mercantile and agricultural products, etc., etc.

The first two resolutions of this convention state the issue made between the removal to Youngstown and retention at Canfield. After these conventions the contest waxed warm and the question was fully discussed by the papers of each locality and among the people at large.

The election of October, 1873, resulted in the choice of Mr Newton to the Legislature by a large majority, and was consequently a triumph of the removalist party. At the following session Mr. Newton offered a bill "to remove the seat of justice in Mahoning county from the town of Canfield to the city of Youngstown, in said county," which was passed April 9, 1874, chiefly through the influence of the Mahoning representative. The act reads as follows:

SECTION I. That from and after taking effect of this section of this act, as hereinafter provided, the seat of justice in the county of Mahoning shall be removed from the town of Canfield to the city of Youngstown in said county.

SECTION II. That the foregoing section of this act shall take effect and be in force when and so soon as the same shall be adopted by a majority of all the electors in said Mahoning county voting at the next general election after the passage thereof, and when suitable buildings shall have been erected as hereinafter provided.

Sections three and four make provisions for submitting to the votes of the electors of the county the question of removal. Then follows section five, which provides:

That in case a majority of electors of said county shall vote for removal as heretofore provided, the seat of justice and county seat shall be deemed and taken to be removed from Canfield, in said county, to the city of Youngstown, in said county, and be located in said city of Youngstown; provided, however, that nothing in the act shall be so construed as to authorize the removal of the seat of justice to said city of Youngstown until the citizens and township of Youngstown shall have donated a lot or lots of land in the city of Youngstown and of sufficient size and suitably located to accommodate the court-house, jail, and necessary offices for said county, and shall have erected thereon and completed thereon suitable buildings for court-house, jail, and all other offices and rooms necessary for the transaction of all public business for said county, at a cost for said buildings of not less than $100,000, and to the satisfaction and acceptance of the commissioners of said county, and all such buildings shall be completed within two years from the date of the election at which said act shall be ratified; and said commissioners shall not nor shall any other authority of said county levy any tax on the taxable property of said county for said lands or buildings: provided that the citizens of Youngstown may within two years build said buildings and tender the same to said commissioners.

Shortly after the passage of this act Youngstown citizens called a convention and appointed a building and soliciting, and also an executive committee, whose duty it was to manage the campaign in favor of removal. General politics were lost sight of. The odds were against Canfield, however, from the first. A county removalist convention was held at Youngstown, August 10, 1874, to which the building committee reported that $100,000, the sum required of the city and township of Youngstown for public buildings, had been subscribed, but that the committee desired to increase the subscription to $200,000. It was also reported that the city council was prepared to donate two lots on the corner of Wick avenue and Wood streets, which were valued at $40,000. The vote in October resulted in a large majority in favor of removal. The building committee then made preparations for the erection of buildings. The city council in March, 1874, authorized the mayor to convey to the building committee in consideration of the nominal sum of $10 the two lots mentioned above. Contracts were let and workmen began the construction of a court-house, which it was estimated would cost upwards of $100,000.

But Canfield was not disposed to submit to the results of the strife thus far, and the consummation of Youngstown's victory lay beyond a long line of litigation. Eben Newton and other citizens of Canfield, filed a petition in the district court enjoining the commissioners against removing the county seat to Youngstown on the ground that the law of 1874 was unconstitutional, because it contemplated the violation of a contract between Canfield and the State, which guaranteed to that village the "permanent" location of the county seat. There were other grounds stated in the petition, but none entitled to consideration. The defense or Youngstown party set up the claim that the law of 1846 could not be construed to mean that Canfield should be the county seat forever, for such a construction would take out of the hands of the Legislature the authority of regulating the government of the State, and would consequently make the act of 1846 unconstitutional. It was further argued, that the word permanent meant "without any intention of changing."

The case went from the district court to the supreme court of Ohio, where it was decided in 1876. It was held that the power to establish and remove county-seats is one which cannot be parted with by legislative contract. It is not the subject of contract, and consequently the Legislature had no authority to pass an act in 1846 making Canfield the perpetual county-seat. But the act of 1846 was not in the nature of a specific contract; a contract or grant cannot be made by the State to rest upon implication; the words of the act must be certain and direct, and must clearly show the legislative intent. Such is by no means the language of the act of 1846, which merely creates the county "with the county-seat at Canfield, and then provides that it shall not be considered as permanently established at Canfield" until donation of lot and $5,000 shall have been made toward county buildings. But further, even though the act of 1846 imply a specific contract and such a contract be constitutional, the validity of the act of 1874 would not be impaired, for the court held that by the word "permanently," as used in the act of 1846, it was not intended to specify that the county-seat was to remain forever at Canfield. The word is capable of a different and narrower meaning which the subject matter requires should be applied in this case. "Permanently established," as used in the act of 1846, was interpreted to mean simply "established as other county-seats are established." "Until the donation should be made," said Judge Welch, "or the commissioners provided for in the general law for locating county-seats in new counties should act in the matter, the seat of justice was to be temporarily or provisionally established at Canfield, but subject as all other county-seats were subject to be changed by future legislation. If, therefore, we are to regard this as a contract it has been fulfilled on the part of the State. The supposed contract was that the citizens should make the donation in consideration that the county-seat should remain at Canfield until removed by subsequent act of the Legislature. The donors have had thirty years enjoyment under this supposed contract, and I suppose when the county-seat comes to be removed their property will revert to them again. I do not see on what ground they can justly complain. If there was a contract they have had its full benefit."

The other counts in the petition of the citizens of Canfield were of a technical character. The court, five judges concurring, failed "to see any good reason for granting the injunction sought," and therefore dismissed the petition.

The case did not stop with this decision of the supreme court of Ohio. The plaintiffs appealed to the supreme court of the United States. The case was reached at the October term, 1879. James A. Garfield appeared for the citizens of Canfield, who stood as plaintiffs in the case, and Thomas W. Sanderson, of Youngstown, for the commissioners, or rather the people of Youngstown. General Garfield, in his argument, relied upon the proposition that the eighth section, relating to donation of property, when complied with by the citizens of Canfield amounted to a specific contract, and the constitution of the United States protects contracts made between any State and its citizens. "The question for this court is to determine whether the act of the General Assembly of Ohio of February 16, 1846, worked a contract for the permanent location of the county seat at Canfield."

General Sanderson's most weighty argument in reply was that the word "permanently," as used in the statutes at that time, did not mean "forever," but "the phrase permanently established is a formula in long and frequent use in Ohio with respect to county seats established otherwise than temporarily." "This practical interpretation of the phrase, though by no means conclusive, is entitled to grave and respectful consideration." The court affirmed the judgment of the State courts, thus leaving the commissioners free to change the location of the seat of justice, or rather confirming the county seat at Youngstown.

The Youngstown Register and Tribune, in the issue following the decision of the Ohio supreme court in August, 1876, said:

> The agony is over. The thirty years' contest is ended. The prize so long coveted is at last secure, and Youngstown is the county-seat. It could not but be that a contest extending through so many years should beget much bitterness. It is but natural that Canfield and the southwest should cling to the location which was so convenient of access to them. The county-seat they had obtained not without a struggle and, considering the times, at considerable expense and sacrifice. They were reluctant, of course, to see it taken away. On the other hand, Youngstown, the center of population and of business, where two-thirds of all the litigation in the county had its origin, justly felt that it was asking too much that so great a majority of the people and so large a proportion of the business interests should be compelled to contribute to Canfield and to be sacrificed to the convenience of the comparatively small minority. Both parties were earnest and determined in their aims, Canfield to retain, Youngstown to secure the county-seat; so through many years ran the conflict. Saturday saw it ended. . . . Now that these indirect advantages may be as great as possible in order to reap to the full the advantages of our good fortune, it is necessary that feelings of amity and good will shall be cultivated with distant parts of the county. It is on every consideration of policy and prudence, as well as magnanimity, that all disposition to keep up the controversy should be banished. We want the people of Smith, Green, Goshen, and Canfield to feel that Youngstown is their county-seat, and that the beautiful temple of justice that has been built here is *their* court-house. We would have them appreciate the

truth that we are actuated by no spirit of hostility against their section, but throughout the controversy have only desired that the claims of the majority shall be heeded, and that we should have what is justly ours.

In another article the same paper says:

It is but just to C. H. Andrews to say that to him more than any other man the success of removal is due. It was largely his energy and tact that secured the enabling act, and it was his indomitable perseverance that pushed the building through to completion. He had the nerve to sign the contracts and become individually responsible for the large sum required for their erection.

The public buildings of Mahoning county are among the best of their class in the State. The court-house, including basement, is three stories high, and is fitted throughout with modern conveniences and fire-proof vaults. The jail and sheriff's residence is well adapted to the uses of such a structure, being healthy, commodious, and secure. Certainly Youngstown can never suffer the reproach of having in any particular failed to comply, not only with the obligations imposed by the act of 1874, but also with the promises which her citizens made in order to secure the location of the county seat. The dedication of such buildings to the uses of the county was a fitting consummation of the struggle she had made for the seat of county government since the organization of New Connecticut into a civil division of the Northwest Territory, in the year 1800. We will close this chapter with a list of the officers of the county since 1846.

AUDITORS.

The auditors are also clerks to the board of county commissioners. Their terms begin on the second Monday in November of alternate years. Andrew Fitch served from March 1, 1846, to March 1, 1848; Benjamin Votaw, 1848 to 1850; Thomas Roller, 1850 to 1852; S. C. Clarke, 1852 to 1855; Jackson Truesdale, 1855 to 1859; Timothy D. Baldwin, 1859 to 1863; David Simon, 1863 to 1867; B. G. Wilcox, 1867 to November 1871; James K. Bailey, 1871 to 1875; James B. Hughes, 1875 to 1880; Freeman H. Scherer, 1880.

SHERIFFS.

The sheriff's term begins on the first Monday in January of every alternate year. The sheriffs of Mahoning county have been as follow: James Powers, from March 1, 1846, to January, 1848; William Schmick, 1848 to 1850; William Meeker, 1850 to 1852; Erastus Platt, 1852 to 1856; Albert Cook, 1856 to 1858; Samuel Smith, 1858 to 1862; Mathew Logan, 1862 to 1864; N. P. Callahan, 1864 to 1868; Charles Townsend, 1868 to 1872; John R. Davis, 1872 to 1876; James B. Drake, 1876 to 1880; George W. Ludwick, 1880.

COUNTY COMMISSIONERS.

The first county commissioners were: Robert Turnbull, who was elected for one year from March 1, 1846; Isaiah Bowman, elected for two years, and James Justice, elected for three years. All their successors were elected for terms of three years each.

In 1847 Daniel Parshall took Turnbull's seat. In March, 1848, Jacob Leyman was elected. At this time the court extended the terms of those then in office from March to November, and thereafter these officials were elected at the regular October elections. On November 1, 1849, John Cowden took the place of James Justice. On December 2, 1850, Daniel Thoman took Daniel Parshall's place. On the first Monday in December, 1851, Jacob Brunnstetter took Jacob Leyman's place. On the first Monday in December, 1852, John Stewart took John Cowden's place. On the first Monday in December, 1853, Furman Gee took Daniel Thoman's place. On the first Monday in December, 1854, John R. Kennedy took Jacob Brunnstetter's place. On the first Monday in December, 1855, Alexander Pow took Stewart's place. On the first Monday in December, 1856, Conrad A. Bunts took Furman Gee's place. On the first Monday in December, 1857, John Warner took John R. Kennedy's place. On the first Monday in December, 1858, John Shields took Alexander Pow's place. On the first Monday in December, 1859, Conrad A. Bunts became his own successor. On the first Monday in December, 1860, William A. Miller took John Warner's place. On the first Monday in December, 1861, James Duncan took John Shields' place. On the first Monday in December, 1862, Stephen Case took Conrad A. Bunts' place. William A. Miller was elected in 1863. Lewis Templin in 1864. In 1865 Stephen Case was his own successor. In 1866 Robert Lowry succeeded William A. Miller. In 1867 Shelden Newton succeeded Lewis Templin. In 1868 William Johnson succeeded Stephen Case. In 1869 Robert Lowry was re-elected. In 1870 Lewis Templin succeeded Newton. In 1871 William Johnson was re-elected. In 1872 Samuel Wallace succeeded Robert Lowry. In 1873 Jonathan Schillinger succeeded Lewis Templin. In 1874 J. M. Jackson succeeded William Johnson. In 1875 Shelden Newton succeeded Samuel Wallace. In 1876 J. H. Blackburn succeeded Jonathan Schillinger. In 1877 George Wetzel succeeded J. M. Jackson. In 1878 Frank McMaster succeeded Shelden Newton. In 1879 J. H. Blackburn was re-elected. In 1880 A. D. McClurg succeeded George Wetzel. In 1881 Frank McMaster was re-elected.

TREASURERS.

John H. Donald, from March, 1846, to December, 1847; Hosea Hoover, 1847-51; John Wetmore, 1851-53, Singleton King, 1853-55; Lewis Ruhlman, 1855-59; James W. McClennand, 1859-63; Robert M. Wallace, 1863-67; John R. Truesdale, 1867-71; James Barclay, 1871-73; Alexander Dickson, 1873-75; Henry Flickinger, 1875-77; Alexander Dickson, 1877-81; William Cornelius, 1881-83. The treasurer's term begins in September.

RECORDERS.

Saxon Sykes, from March 1, 1846, to October 18, 1849; George Hollis, from October 18, 1849, to October 23, 1856; A. P. Flaugher, from October 23, 1856, to June 1, 1863; J. B. Leach, from June 1, 1863, to the second Monday in January, 1865; J. V. McCurley, from the second Monday in January, 1865, to January, 1868; F. M. Simon, from January, 1868, to January, 1875; S. B. Rieger, from January, 1875, to January, 1878; Thomas H. Ward, from January 8, 1878, to January, 1881. Recorder Ward was re-elected in October, 1880, as his own successor. The recorders are elected every three years.

PROSECUTING ATTORNEYS.

William Ferguson, from 1846 to 1848; James B. Blocksom, from 1848 to 1850: E. G. Canfield, from 1850 to 1852; R. J. Powers, from 1852 to 1856; T. W. Sanderson, from 1856 to 1858; R. J. Powers, from 1858 to 1860; William C. Bunts, 1860 to 1862; James B. Blocksom, from 1862 to 1863; F. G. Servis, from 1863 to 1867; H. G. Leslie, 1867; Asa W. Jones, from 1867 to 1869; W. G. Moore, 1869 to 1871; A. W. Jones, from 1871 to 1873; I. A. Justice, from 1873 to 1875; C. R. Truesdale, from 1875 to 1877; M. W. Johnson, 1877 to 1881; C. R. Truesdale, from 1881 to 1883. James B. Blocksom and H. G. Leslie died while in office.

PROBATE COURT.

The probate court of Mahoning county was organized on March 8, 1852. The time of service of the judges dated from the second Monday in February of each year. William Hartsel served until February 12, 1855; Garretson I. Young until February 9, 1861; Giles Van Hyning until February, 1867; Joseph R. Johnston until February 10, 1873; M. V. B. King until February 14, 1876; Leroy D. Tohman until 1879; Louis W. King until February, 1882.

Judge King became his own successor at the election held in October, 1881.

VOTE FOR GOVERNOR—MAHONING COUNTY.

1848—Seabury Ford (Whig), 1,269; John B. Weller (Democrat), 2,069.

1850—Reuben Wood (Democrat), 1,862; William Johnston (Whig), 828; Edward Smith (Abolition), 477.

1851—Reuben Wood (Democrat), 1,546; Samuel F. Vinton (Whig), 484; Samuel Lewis (Abolition), 633.

1853—William Medill (Democrat), 1,360; Nelson Barrere (Whig), 381; Samuel Lewis (Abolition), 1,004.

1855—Salmon P. Chase (Republican), 1,592; William Medill (Democrat), 1,495; Allen Trimble (Know Nothing), 60.

1857—Salmon P. Chase (Republican), 1,891; Henry B. Payne (Democrat), 1,825; Philip Van Trump (Know Nothing), 2.

1859—William Dennison (Republican), 2,424; Rufus P. Ranney (Democrat), 2,041.

1861—David Tod (Republican), 2,505; Hugh J. Jewett (Democrat), 1,566.

1863—John Brough (Republican), 3,206; C. L. Vallandigham (Democrat)—

1865—Jacob D. Cox (Republican), 2,504; George W. Morgan (Democrat), 2,184.

1867—Rutherford B. Hayes (Republican), 2,898; Allen G. Thurman (Democrat), 2,602.

1869—Rutherford B. Hayes (Republican), 3,003; George H. Pendleton (Democrat), 2,552.

1871—Edward F. Noyes (Republican), 3,087; George W. McCook (Democrat), 2,602; Gideon T. Stewart (Prohibition) 160.

1873—William Allen (Democrat), 3,003; Edward F. Noyes (Republican), 3,460; G. T. Stewart (Prohibition), 48; Isaac Collins (Liberal), 16.
1875—Rutherford B. Hayes, 3,788; William Allen, 3,947; Jay Odell, 27.
1877—Richard M. Bishop (Democrat), 2,820; William H. West (Republican), 2,947; H. A. Thompson (Prohibition), 34; Stephen Johnston (Greenback), 1,339.
1879—Charles Foster (Republican), 4,179; Thomas Ewing (Democrat) 3,854; G. T. Stewart (Prohibition), 16; A. Saunders Piatt (Greenback), 219.

VOTE FOR PRESIDENT IN 1880 IN MAHONING COUNTY.

	Garfield.	Hancock.	Weaver.	Dow.
Youngstown (city)	1693	1265	68	5
Youngstown township	528	408	32	....
Springfield township	160	432	....	....
Smith township	295	81	44	6
Poland township	390	144	16	1
Milton township	54	136	....	....
Jackson township	112	163	....	5
Greene township	209	207	22	3
Goshen township	264	78	7	17
Ellsworth township	221	89	....	....
Coitsville township	160	126	3	....
Canfield township	189	206	3	....
Boardman township	140	88	4	....
Berlin township	131	112	10	....
Beaver township	214	201	2	....
Austintown township	295	218	30	5
Totals	4943	4044	241	41

Total vote, 9,269.

CHAPTER XII.

MILITIA ORGANIZATION AND WAR OF 1812.

The Need of Watchfulness—Hull's Surrender—General Wadsworth and Perkins go to the Front.

Behind the fringed border of settlement and frontier cabins was a power which gave constant apprehension of danger. Although weakened by defeat at Fallen Timbers and pledged to peace by Wayne's treaty at Greenville, in 1795, there was reason for distrusting the Indians, and every able-bodied man held himself in readiness for defense at any time. An Indian is always prepared for war. The tools with which he secures his daily food are his implements in battle; he needs no commissary, the trees are his fortifications and hidden forest paths his army roads. Besides his slyness and shyness and deep-seated hatred of the whites there were active influences at work which made the situation especially alarming. The revolution and treaty of 1783 was not a final settlement of affairs between England and the United States. The British crown had been forced to recognize American independence, but continued to cherish jealous resentment and neglected no opportunity to throw obstacles in the way of the young nation's growth. The Indian tribes of the West were found ready and useful instruments in carrying out this line of public policy. British agents were tireless in their efforts to incite insurrection and instigate savage cruelty as a means of checking the growth and development of the Northwest. By making the Indian warriors a standing army of enemies to the United States England preserved a formidable ally when the inevitable conflict should come. The magnificent and complete success of Wayne's expedition frustrated for a time these inhuman foreign intrigues. But jealousy is an active force and while it exists cannot long be restrained.

The rapid progress of western settlement was explained to the Indian to mean the extinction of his race. His pride, his prudence, and his hope were appealed to in persuading him to rally once more to the defense of his home and hunting ground. British agents found in Tecumseh an agent whose talents made him able, and whose ambition made him willing to serve their purpose. As early as 1805 this wily chief began to organize a confederacy of tribes, ostensibly at first for the purpose of effecting much-needed reforms. He sought to soften tribal prejudices and to re-establish original manners and customs. By reuniting hostile nations his influence became almost imperial. He was unceasing in his toil. His reputation as a sagacious counselor and warrior secured for him everywhere considerate attention. Having succeeded in effecting a general union, he proceeded to his second step in a manner which compliments his cunning. Superstition was summoned to his aid. The Prophet, his brother, began to dream dreams and see visions. The fame of his divine commission spread throughout the forest, and believing pilgrims received British teaching at the shrine of the Prophet. Meanwhile, Tecumseh's activity was simply wonderful. One day he was pleading loyalty to the United States at Governor Harrison's office at Vincennes, Indiana, and the same week arranging war plans in the valley of the Wabash and on the plains of Sandusky. His canoe was seen crossing the Mississippi, and before any were aware he was addressing Cherokee councils in Georgia and Alabama. The whole West was thus aroused to war, which began openly at Tippecanoe in 1811. The fact that British and Indians were relying upon each other for aid could no longer be concealed.

Meanwhile diplomatic affairs between England and the United States had become threateningly complicated. The former country and France had long been active belligerents. American vessels were accused of receiving British deserters, and under a pretended right of search merchant ships were plundered of their sailors on the high seas. Hundreds of Americans were in that way impressed into the severe service of the British navy. The crown was appealed to in behalf of American rights, but without avail. Not only did past injuries go unrepaired, but fresh insults were added till war became the only honorable course.

Standing armies are the reliance of the Old World monarchies; the patriotism and courage of its citizens has always proved adequate for the defense of our Republic. A vigilant and ready militia have responded in every emergency to the bugle notes of danger, and an industrious citizenship is converted by the presence of an enemy into a valiant soldiery. Thus we have all the safety of a standing army without the expense of its maintenance. Western settlers were well qualified for the camp and battlefield. Pioneer labor had toughened their muscles; frontier dangers had hardened their courage and made them accurate marksmen; hardships and privations they were accustomed to. The first constitution of Ohio provided for a thoroughly organized defensive force ready to be called into action whenever occasion might demand. At the second session of the Legislature of the State in Chillicothe in 1803-4 specific laws were passed providing for an effective militia. The State was divided into four divisions. John S. Gano, of Cincinnati, was elected major-general of the first, Nathaniel Massie, of Chillicothe, of the second; Joseph Beall, of Marietta, of the third, and Elijah Wadsworth, of Canfield, of the fourth. The fourth division comprised the north half of the State, including Trumbull, Columbiana, and Jefferson counties. The first division order issued by General Wadsworth is dated April 6, 1804, and reads as follows:

GENERAL ORDER.

FOURTH DIVISION OHIO MILITIA.

The fourth division of militia of the State of Ohio is divided into five regiments, which for the purpose of facilitating the election of officers and until further arrangements are made by the commander-in-chief, will be numbered as follows: The first brigade including the county of Trumbull in two regiments; the second brigade, including the counties of Jefferson and Columbiana in three regiments; the first regiment of the first brigade includes all that part of the county of Trumbull lying north of the line of township five in the survey of said county; second regiment includes all that part of the county of Trumbull lying south of the first regiment; third regiment includes the county of Columbiana, the fourth and fifth regiments include all of Jefferson county, of which all persons concerned are to take notice and govern themselves accordingly.

Benjamin Tappan and John Sloan, Esq., are appointed aides-de-camp to the major-general of the fourth division and are to be obeyed and respected accordingly.

ELIJAH WADSWORTH,
Major-general Fourth Division O. M.

A general military election was held May 7, 1804, at which the following officers were chosen for the first and second regiments of the fourth division of Trumbull county, which at that time included the whole Western Reserve.

FIRST REGIMENT.

COMMISSIONED OFFICERS.

Captain Nathaniel King.
Captain George W. Hawley.
Captain Martin Smith.
Captain Solomon Griswold.
Captain James A. Harper.
Captain Charles Parker.
Captain Josiah Cleveland.
Captain Lorenzo Carter.
Lieutenant Seth Harrington.
Lieutenant Stephen Brown.
Lieutenant David Randall.
Lieutenant Thomas Martin.
Lieutenant Ebenezer Hewens.
Lieutenant Joel Paine.
Lieutenant Jedediah Baird.
Lieutenant Nathaniel Drane.
Ensign Daniel Sawtell.
Ensign John Henderson.
Ensign Zopher Case.
Ensign Skene Sackett.
Ensign George Caldwell.
Ensign Ela S. Clapp.
Ensign Lyman Benton.
Ensign Samuel Jones.

SECOND REGIMENT.

Captain Homer Hine.
Captain Eli Baldwin.
Captain John Struthers.
Captain Barnabas Harris.
Captain George Todd.
Captain Samuel Tylee.
Captain James Applegate.
Captain George Phelps.
Captain William Bushnell.
Captain Henry Rodgers.
Captain Thomas Wright.
Captain Ezra Wyatt.
Captain John Oviatt.
Lieutenant Aaron Collar.
Lieutenant Josiah Walker.
Lieutenant John Russell.
Lieutenant James Lynn.
Lieutenant Moses Latta.
Lieutenant Edward Schofield.
Lieutenant Henry Hickman.
Lieutenant James Heaton.
Lieutenant Daniel Huminco.
Lieutenant John Diver.
Lieutenant William Chard.
Lieutenant Gersham Judson.
Lieutenant Aaron Norton.
Ensign Jacob Parkhurst.
Ensign Nathaniel Blakesley.
Ensign William Henry.
Ensign James Struthers.
Ensign Henry Hull.
Ensign John Smith.
Ensign John Elliott.
Ensign John Ewalt.
Ensign Ebenezer N. Combs.
Ensign John Campbell.
Ensign David Moore.
Ensign Thomas Kennedy.
Ensign James Walker.

The county of Trumbull was constituted one brigade. The second brigade consisted of the then regiments from Columbiana and Jefferson counties. Martin Smith and Lorenzo Carter were chosen majors for the first and second battalion respectively of the first regiment, and James Applegate and Henry Rodgers of the two battalions of the second regiment, all being promoted from the captaincy. Between 1804 and 1812, owing to increase of settlement, the fourth division was divided into four brigades, commanded by Generals Miller, Beall, Perkins, and Paine. The third brigade, commanded by General Simon Perkins, embraced the present counties of Mahoning, Ashtabula, and Trumbull; the fourth brigade (General Paine's) embraced all the Reserve west of the third.

In 1812 Cleveland, Mansfield, and Urbana were the frontier towns in Ohio. There were a few scattered settlements west of the Cuyahoga in the Reserve, but they were totally unable to make defense, even against the Indians.

General Perkins' brigade consisted of three regiments, commanded by Lieutenant-colonels William Rayen, J. S. Edwards, and Richard Hayes. The Ohio militia before the War of 1812 followed the example of the Continental establishment after the Revolution, and had no colonels, the command being vested in lieutenant-colonels, who by courtesy were generally called, except in official correspondence, colonels. The regiment numbered about five hundred men. Congress, anticipating war, passed an act in February, 1812, increasing the United States army. It provided for a regiment of volunteers from Ohio and Kentucky, of which Samuel H. Wells was commissioned colonel, and John Miller, of Steubenville, lieutenant-colonel. George Tod was subsequently appointed major of the regiment, which was listed as the Seventeenth United States. Tod previous to his commission in the regular army had been brigade-major and inspector to General Perkins. The news of the war preparations caused considerable apprehension on the frontiers on account of the open hostility of the Indians. General Perkins' first significant document was the following:

BRIGADE ORDERS.

Third brigade, Fourth division, Ohio militia, issued 28th of April, 1812, to Lieutenant-colonels William Rayen, Richard Hayes and John S. Edwards.

SIR: You are hereby required to cause to be raised within the regiment over which you have command, if they can be raised by voluntary enlistment, twenty-three good and able-bodied men, to serve in the service of the United States as a detachment from the militia of this State. If that number of men cannot be attained by voluntary enrollment, you are required to cause to be raised by draft and on your regiment thirteen men of the above description, to be taken from the respective companies composing the same, in proportion to the numbers in each. In whatever way the detachment from the Third brigade, Fourth division, Ohio militia, may be raised, it is to be officered in the manner as the law directs. On the execution of this order, you are to make the brigadier of the aforesaid brigade a return of the men enrolled or drafted by the 9th day of May next. The above order is issued in consequence of recent and pressing orders from the President of the United States, through the major-general of Fourth division of Ohio militia. The detachment from your regiment shall rendezvous at some convenient place in your regiment, as you shall order, on the 14th of May next, when it will receive further orders.

The above orders are to be executed with the greatest possible promptitude and dispatch.

For information you are referred to a statute of the United

States, passed the 6th day of February, 1812, entitled: "An act authorizing the President of the United States to accept and organize certain volunteer military corps;" likewise to the statute of the State of Ohio regulating the militia thereof April 27, 1812. By order of

SIMON PERKINS, brigadier.
GEORGE TOD, brigade major and inspector.

There was at that time considerable opposition to the policy of the administration at Washington. The old-line Federalists accused President Madison of fostering war for political purposes, and in place of encouraging enlistments endeavored to cultivate a popular feeling against a resort to arms. It was on the eve of a Presidential election, when the Federalists were making a last desperate effort for existence as a party. Their only hope of success lay in their appeal for peace. Gideon Granger wrote from Washington in February:

The Ohio delegation have recommended General Miller for colonel and George Tod for major. I am astonished at Tod's entering the army. If I could see him I could change his mind.

The recruiting and enlisting service was difficult until war had actually been declared. Major Tod wrote from Zanesville on June 29, 1812:

I have just received a file of newspapers from Washington city giving intelligence of a declaration of war by the Congress of the United States against Great Britain. This event will give a new aspect to affairs, and it is really to be hoped that it will produce a union of sentiment and action.

The war was expected for more than a year before Congress passed a formal declaration, and during this time the militia was kept in steady drill. The following order of General Wadsworth to the brigade commanders was sufficient to enable them to anticipate what they might at any time expect:

CANFIELD, September 14, 1811.

I am directed by the commandant of the Fourth division of the militia of this State to call your attention to the subject of making returns of the brigade under your command. It is important that the government of this State and that of the United States should know at a time *when war almost appears inevitable*, their actual strength. There is little or no doubt but that "the weighty and important matters" which the President has to lay before Congress, by reason of which it is called to meet earlier than usual, relate to our differences with foreign powers.

Should Congress deem it expedient to declare war against one or both of the belligerents, its information must necessarily be drawn to ascertain the force they could compel to take the field. This information cannot be derived from any other quarter than the returns made from the several States, and their neglecting to make returns at the adjutant-general's office dries up the source of information on this subject. The adjutant-general has heretofore complained of the remissness of this department, and it has been impossible for the commandant of this division to be more punctual in the discharge of the duties assigned to him, as the returns from the brigades under his command have in some instances been partially, and in others wholly withholden from him, and they have been made months after it was his duty to have forwarded them. The general expects from your attention and exertions, that a return of your brigade will be duly made and transmitted to him, agreeable to the 27th section of the militia law of this State.

With esteem and regard I am your obedient and humble servant,
ELISHA WHITTLESEY,
Aide-de-Camp.

In response to Governor Meigs' order of April 27, 1812, calling for one company from each brigade, under date of May 11, Brigadier-general Perkins says in a letter to Major-general Wadsworth:*

DEAR SIR: On the 9th inst. I received returns from the several colonels, complying with my order of April 28th. From two regiments volunteers were returned, and in one a draft was made. The volunteers returned here have been sufficient in this regiment to form a company, but they were from two regiments. I have issued an order for drafts to those regiments which returned volunteers, and my return will no doubt be complete in the course of the present week.
SIMON PERKINS.

The following was subsequently returned as the quota of the Third brigade:

WARREN, June 12, 1812.

SIR: In compliance with your order of the 27th day of April last I have caused to be drafted, and who now hold themselves in readiness for your further order, the following list of officers and men:

COMMISSIONED OFFICER.
Captain John W. Seely.
Ensign James Kerr.

NON-COMMISSIONED OFFICERS.
First Sergeant Samuel Bill.
Third Sergeant Zadock Howell.
First Corporal John Cherry.

PRIVATES.
Asa Lane, Peter Lanterman, Miller Blackley, William Strader, Joseph Nettlefield, William Crawford, James Chalpin, Robert Brewer, Nathaniel Stanley, Alexander Hayes, David Kiddle, William Martin, Conrad Knale, James Anderson, John Strain, Matthew Dobbins, Ezra Buell, Solomon Wartrous, Peter Yatman, Urial Burnett, Hugh Markee, Amos Rathburn, David Fitch, Joseph Walker, Michael Crumrine, Barnabas Slavin, Martin Tod, Jr., Justin Fobes, William Mecker, James Mears, Aaron Scroggs, Andrew Markee, Jr., Esthen Newman, Daniel Fowler.

SIMON PERKINS,
Brigadier-general Third brigade, Fourth division, Ohio militia.

Congress took early steps in 1812 to provide for the protection of the northwestern frontier. The plan was to seize upon Upper Canada as soon as war should be declared, thus throwing a

*General Perkins' order to the lieutenant-colonels is given above under date of April 28.

strong force between the British army and the hostile Indians. The plan was prudent and gave the Ohio frontier an assurance of safety; its execution was, perhaps, the most contemptible exhibition of military imbecility in American history. President Madison as a statesman and diplomat was the peer of any man of his time, but he lacked the executive energy necessary to make a successful war president. His war secretary deserves scarce less reprobation than Brigadier-general Hull, of whom we shall presently have occasion to speak. Although for four years war was anticipated as the probable issue of international complications, and while provisions were made for increasing the army and for taking possession of Canada, no marine force whatever was equipped for guarding the upper lakes and intercepting a free approach of the enemy by water. Canada projects into the United States like a wedge, the extreme point of which is Malden, where the British had a fort. Governor Hull, of Michigan, in April, two months before war was declared, was commissioned a brigadier with an army of about two thousand men, half of whom were raised in Ohio. He was stationed at Detroit, with instructions to cross the river, seize Malden, and invade Canada as soon as war should be declared. He was on the Maumee giving attention to the erection of works of defense, when a common mail communication informed him of the declaration of war. The British on the opposite shore had received the important news three days earlier by express messenger. The action of the Secretary of War in trusting to the doubtful course of mails, through a dangerous wilderness, the delivery of a message upon which depended a military campaign, has never been accounted for.

General Hull, after being notified, passed with his two thousand men in sight of Malden, which was defended by one hundred British regulars and one armed schooner, without making an attack. The entire British force, including Indians and local militia, did not exceed five hundred. Hull crossed the Detroit river, but on being informed that General Brock with the British regulars from Niagara was approaching, and that all the Indians of the Northwest were preparing for a descent upon his army, retreated to his fortifications at Detroit. This movement lost him the confidence of his army,

who were anxious for action and ambitious for glory. A few days later General Brock arrived at Malden, and assumed command of the whole British army. On the 16th of August, with 300 regulars, 450 Canadians, and 600 Indians, he crossed the river below Detroit under cover of several armed vessels and at once moved toward the fort. Advance parties of the garrison annoyed their approach, while the front line of batteries were planked in such a way as to sweep the advancing columns with grape-shot. Every one within the fort was sanguine of a successful resistance, but at a critical moment, when an order of fire was expected, General Hull, seemingly frightened, to insure civility hoisted the white flag, surrendering to the British the garrison, stores, public property, and the whole of Michigan; besides laying bare to British cruelty and Indian bloodthirstiness the whole Western frontier. Hull was afterwards exchanged for thirty British prisoners, court-martialed and sentenced to be shot for cowardice, but in consideration of his revolutionary sevices was pardoned by President Madison.

"Hull," says General George Sanderson, who was one of the humiliated army, "was an imbecile, not a traitor or a coward, but an imbecile caused by drunkenness. He was an ardent drinker. On the day before his surrender his son, Captain Abraham F. Hull, came among my men in a beastly state of intoxication. . . . On the day of the surrender I saw Hull frequently. His face about the mouth and chin was covered with tobacco juice and I thought in common with other officers that the general was under the influence of liquor. He was surrounded by a military family, the members of which were fond of high times, wines and liquors. After his surrender and before the enemy had entered, many of the officers begged Colonel James Findlay to take command of the American forces and resist the enemy, but he declined to take command. Colonel James Miller was also urged to take command, but he refused to assume the responsibility, saying 'matters had gone too far, but had Hull signified to me his intention of surrendering, I would have assumed command and defended the fort to the last.' Miller would have done so, too."

The disaster at Detroit was totally unexpected

on the Reserve, where the danger it threatened was greatest. The news reached General Wadsworth at Canfield, August 22d. The situation was alarming, and without waiting for instructions from any source he issued an order at once for the whole military force under his command to rendezvous at Cleveland. "The orders," says Colonel Whittlesey, "were received in the third and fourth brigades like the calls of the Scottish chiefs through the highlands." "As soon," says the Trump of Fame newspaper, "as the news of the fall of Detroit was confirmed, every man ran to arms, old and young, without distinction of politics, and repaired to the post of danger. None waited for the formality of orders, but every one, whether exempt from military duty or not, put on his armor." Messengers pressing hard on the track of those who brought the news from Detroit, brought the appalling report that boats were seen rounding Avon point at Cleveland, supposed to be freighted with British and Indian invaders. Women and children from about the Cuyahoga and westward deserted their homes and fled in desperate fright toward the interior, and couriers, taking up the cry of appeal for help, rode day and night spreading it. It was on Sunday, while people were assembled in forest arbors, in barns or log houses for public worship, when these messengers reached Trumbull county. At the same time General Wadsworth's messengers were spreading the summons to arms. Meetings were dispersed, hasty preparations were made for the field by cleaning hunting rifles, sharpening their knives, and filling their powder horns and bullet pouches with ammunition.

Colonel Richard Hayes' regiment, consisting of men from the north part of Trumbull and south part of Ashtabula, mustered at Kinsman's store, August 26th. This regiment embraced eight companies from Hubbard, Vernon, Brookfield, Vienna, Kinsman, Williamsfield, Gustavus, Wayne, Johnston and Fowler. Colonel Rayen's and Colonel Edwards' regiments were already on the way. So general was the uprising that Major-general Wadsworth gave directions that half of the volunteers should be sent home to act as a reserve or second guard in case of an emergency. We have traditionary authority for saying that this order was received with regret by many detailed to return. At Cleveland the immediate cause of alarm was found to be a mistake. The boats supposed to contain enemies were found to be transports with dejected victims of the surrender returning on parole. The self-organized militia met them as friends and gave them the sympathy they needed. But the danger of an invasion was still apparent, and prudence advised thorough organization. General Wadsworth, with the assistance of General Perkins, at once began organizing the troops who were massed together without the semblance of military order. The force was ample so far as pertained to numbers, courage, and ardor, but their equipment was insufficient, and their knowledge of discipline deficient. The following letter, found among General Wadsworth's papers, will give some idea of the situation.

HEADQUARTERS, CAMP AT CLEVELAND, O., August 26, 1812.

SIR:—On the instant that I received information that General Hull had capitulated with the British commander for the surrender of Detroit; that our army were prisoners, and the British and Indians in possession of the Michigan territory, and on their march to this State, I immediately ordered out all the militia under my command, consisting of the first brigade, commanded by Brigadier-general Beall; the second brigade, commanded by Brigadier-general Miller; the third brigade, commanded by Brigadier general Perkins, to repair immediately to Cleveland, with their arms and ——— days provisions. My orders have been promptly complied with, about ——— troops have already arrived and others are continually coming in from all quarters. I expect in a few days to have a sufficient force to repel any force that the enemy can at present bring against us, but I am destitute of everything needful for the use and support of an army. The troops are badly armed and clothed, with no provisions or camp equipage, or the means of procuring any. But the dangerous situation of the country obliges me to face every difficulty, since my command arrived at this place, on the ———th instant, and established my headquarters. Since my arrival at this place about ——— prisoners have been landed here by the British. Yours with respect,
ELIJAH WADSWORTH.
To Secretary of War.

That the people at home had entire confidence in the troops gone to the front is shown by the following item from the Trump of Fame:

Major-general Wadsworth has established his headquarters at Cleveland, and pushed forward a body of troops under the command of Brigadier-general Perkins to Huron. The detachment, from the brigade under the command of General Beall, has been ordered to Mansfield. The unfortunate prisoners belonging to this State, who surrendered at Detroit, are daily coming into Cleveland. All accounts concur in the establishment of the treachery of General Hull. But we trust, if the Government of the United States will put arms in our hands, that the patriotic militia of Ohio will soon take abundant satisfaction.—[September 2, 1812.

We have been unable to find more than fragmentary information of the events which followed. A block-house known as Camp Avery had been erected at Huron, near the present site of Milan. General Perkins was given command of the army at the front, with large discretion, and Colonel Richard Hayes, with the Trumbull and Ashtabula troops, led the advance westward from Cleveland. By September 6th, General Perkins had reached camp at Huron, where he had command of about four hundred men.

No order had yet been issued at Washington by the War department, and it is probable that Hull's surrender was not known there when the Reserve troops reached the line of frontier defenses. Colonel Rayen's regiment from the south part of Trumbull county joined the front ranks about September 15th. A poisonous malaria filled the valleys of the rivers and produced distressing sickness among the troops. The month of September is especially sickly when fever and ague prevail. Captain Burnham estimates that by September 15th, there were not more than two hundred and fifty fighting men at Huron, and Joshua R. Giddings has noted :

The billious fever had reduced our effective troops until we were able to muster only two guards, consisting of two relieves, so that each healthy man was compelled to stand post one-fourth of the time.

Prior to September 15th Major Austin and Lieutenant Allen, returning from an expedition to Kelly's Island, found the body of Michael Guy, of Colonel Rayen's regiment, and a native of Warren, on the peninsula. He had been scalped. A soldier of the command was shot on the way. The only engagement known to have taken place on the Reserve occurred on September 29, 1812. Colonel J. S. Edwards informed Colonel Hayes, who was in command at Huron (General Perkins having been called to Cleveland to consult with General Wadsworth), that he had four hundred bushels of wheat on the Ramsdale place on the peninsula which he was requested to secure for the troops. Several days had been passed in inactivity and in the usual Yankee amusement of practical joking. But on the evening of the 28th of September drumming and fifing announced more important business. Volunteers were called for to march against the Indian depredators. Sixty-four responded with Captain Joshua A. Cotton and Lieutenants Ramsey and Bartholomew in command. The party started that evening, and on the following day met a large body of Indians. A spirited engagement took place, in which six volunteers were killed, viz.: James S. Bills, Simon Blackman, Daniel Mingus, Abraham Simons, Lieutenant Ramsdale, and Alexander Mason. Ten were wounded, among the number Joseph McMahon, who escaped, but was killed on his way home.

The President on September 5th ordered a draft of one hundred thousand men for the regular service. Three regiments were required of the fourth division, which General Wadsworth reported ready for service, as will be seen by the following letter to the Secretary of War:

HURON, November 28, 1812.

SIR: I have organized three Regiments from the Division under my command, comprising the number of men you require me to order to take the field, and have placed them under the command of Brigadier-general Simon Perkins, agreeable to instructions from General Harrison. One regiment has advanced to Sandusky bay, where they occupy the Fort. Parties are detached daily to gather corn and other forage, and every means are made use of to prepare for a continuous campaign. I trust, Sir, that the men will signalize themselves when they engage with the enemy. I have drawn three several Bills of Exchange on you to defray a part of the expenses incurred in organizing this detachment and keeping it in the field. The draft that I mentioned in my letter of November 8th was not forwarded by Lieutenant Church from Pittsburg, owing to his having been informed by Major Stoddard that the subsistence of the provisions from Detroit was improperly embraced in his estimate on which my draft was predicated. It would accommodate the public creditors if some person in the Western Country should be authorized to purchase bills on the War Office.

General Wadsworth having rendered the Government, and particularly the Reserve, patriotic and useful services in defending the frontier, returned to his home in Canfield early in December. He had gone ahead from the beginning promptly, efficiently, and fearlessly, according to orders when he had them, without orders when it was necessary. He did not stop to ask until his work was finished "how the expense accrued in this business was to be defrayed." He had spared no pains in the discharge of duty, and had involved himself in ruin should the Government neglect him. His strong confidence in the administration did not permit him to entertain the thought of being allowed to suffer. He explained the situation on his return from the army in the following letter:

CANFIELD, December 30th, 1812.

SIR: Having on the 29th ult. completed the force ordered by you from my division by your letter of September 5th, and placed them under the immediate command of General Harrison, reporting to him the whole force, it seemed that my service was no longer necessary or required by Government, and accordingly on the 30th I left the headquarters of the right wing of the Northwestern army at Huron and returned home.

Various causes combined, which were altogether beyond my control, has in some measure lengthened the time in completing the organization of the detachment. However, no time has been lost. The extensive new settlements have been saved from savage barbarity, and the detachment equally ready to go forward with the main army. Doubtless you are sensible of the great disadvantages I have labored under to equip, support, and march into the field such a detachment of men without money. Although the credit of the United States may be good, there are a class of citizens that will not lend any assistance or support to the war. Of course it is more difficult to procure supplies for a military force, and in the present case has fallen heavy on the real friends of the Government. You will see I am placed in a critical situation. By my orders great expenditures have accerued. I am daily called on for payment and several suits have been actually commenced, although I do not conceive myself personally holden, yet it will make extra expense and, Sir, I do conceive it necessary as well for the honor of the Government as the good of the creditors, that some effectual measures be immediately adopted to save expense. Would it not be advisable to appoint some person within the limits of my Division to audit and pay off those demands?

I can assure you, Sir, that many of the creditors are much embarrassed for want of their just dues.

Yours very respectfully,
ELIJAH WADSWORTH.

It must have taken the raw frontiersmen some time to discard their notions of social equality and conform to the severe strictures of military etiquette. One of the first orders issued by Judge Tod after his promotion to the majority was the following:

The non-commissioned officers and privates at the barracks are required, when not on parade, to salute all commissioned officers whenever they meet them by raising the right hand as high as the eyes, with palm of the hand turned toward the officer. They are never to come into a room where there are any commissioned officers but with hats off. Soldiers on duty, when having arms in their hands, without any command, on the approach of a commissioned officer, will carry their arms. Any soldier or other person belonging to the barracks, who shall be found drunk or intoxicated with liquor, when called on parade, shall be immediately arrested by the officer or non-commissioned officer commanding on parade and put in confinement, and as soon as the parade has been dismissed, such offenders shall forthwith be reported to the major or other commanding officer at the rendezvous.

The major hopes these orders will be attended to with cheerfulness. If not, offenders will be punished.

GEORGE TOD,
Major United States army.

PERSONAL SERVICE.

We have been unable to obtain full rosters of all the regiments, the records at Columbus having been destroyed, and those at Washington burned in the capitol in 1814, when the British captured and burned that building. Neither have we been able to learn the companies which continued in the army after February, 1813, the date of the expiration of original enlistments. It is known, however, that many soldiers from Trumbull county participated in the campaign of 1813, which terminated with Harrison's brilliant victory of the Thames in the fall of that year. That victory left the Northwest secure, the Indians having been brought to peace and the British arms driven from Upper Canada.

Colonel J. S. Edwards, a prominent citizen of Trumbull county and an efficient officer, died early in the campaign of malarial fever, contracted in the swamps. He enjoyed the friendship of General Wadsworth, General Perkins, and Governor Meigs.

Elijah Wadsworth, though born at Hartford, Connecticut, November 4, 1747, was a resident of Litchfield, in the same State, when the Revolutionary war broke out. He was a lieutenant in Captain Benjamin Tallmadge's troop of horse, in Elisha Sheldon's regiment, serving to the end of the war with honor. Like many Revolutionary heroes, he obtained little promotion. Tallmadge's promotion to be major allowed Wadsworth to be captain, beyond which he did not rise. Major Andre was placed in his custody soon after his arrest by Williams, Paulding, and Van Wert, on the 23d of September, 1780. In 1802 Mr. Wadsworth removed to Canfield, then in Trumbull county, Ohio, where he owned largely of wild lands. In 1804 he was elected by the Ohio Legislature to be major-general of the Fourth division, embracing the northeastern part of the State. The promptness, perseverance and patriotism displayed in this command, at the outset of the War of 1812, may be inferred from this correspondence. He was long embarrassed by personal debts, contracted for the Government in raising supplies for the troops. He died at Canfield, on the 30th of December, 1817, where his grave is marked by an appropriate stone.

General Perkins came to Ohio in 1798, as an agent, explorer, and surveyor of lands on the Western Reserve, being then an energetic young man of twenty-seven years. Surveyors, engineers, and explorers are the material of which first-class military men are formed. In 1804 he settled at Warren, in Trumbull county, and was appointed postmaster. By General Wadsworth's influence he was commissioned as brigadier in 1808, our relations with Great Britain having already given premonitions of trouble. When the war occurred he was at full maturity of mind and body, and having the unlimited confidence of General Wadsworth, was immediately entrusted with the troops and posts at the front. When the term of service of the Ohio volunteers had expired, and their place was filled by the new regiments of the regular army, he was offered a colonelcy in the United States infantry. On account of the care of a growing landed estate this was declined, much to the regret of General Harrison and the administration, who were sadly in need of good officers. General Perkins died at Warren on the 19th of November, 1844.

Judge Tod, of Youngstown, was commissioned a major of the Nineteenth regiment of United States infantry (Colonel John Miller), July 6, 1812. He performed a gallant and important part in the sortie from Fort Meigs, in May, 1813, in which the British were driven from their guns in a position across the ravine, near the fort on the southeast. On the 1st of January, 1815, he was promoted to be lieutenant-colonel of the Seventeenth United States infantry. The Nineteenth regiment was raised in Ohio. After the evacuation of Malden by the British, on the approach of General Harrison in September, 1813, Major Tod was left in command of that post. He was the father of Governor David Tod, late of Briar Hill, and a very prominent character in northeastern Ohio during the first thirty years of the present century. Before the war he held the position of justice of the supreme court.

One of the most efficient men in the northern Ohio service was Calvin Pease, of Warren. He entered the service under the following order from General Wadsworth:

HEADQUARTERS,
CAMP AT CLEVELAND,
August 28, 1812.

CALVIN PEASE, ESQ.:

SIR:—You are hereby ordered and instructed to repair with all convenient speed to the middle or western parts of this State, to ascertain what number of troops are raised, or about to be raised, where stationed and by whom commanded; to gain all possible information respecting the forces of this State and of the United States, and of the enemy; to ascertain the best route for a line of communication from this camp to such other camps or posts as shall be established, and confer with the commanding officers of posts upon the means of establishing such line of communication until the commander-in-chief shall give orders respecting the same, and transmit to me at my headquarters without delay such information as you shall obtain.

You are hereby authorised if necessary to impress any horses necessary for this service, and the citizens of this State are requested to afford the said Calvin Pease all necessary assistance, and all military officers are requested to give him full credence in the premises.

ELIJAH WADSWORTH,
Major-general Fourth Division Ohio Militia.

Mr. Pease was afterwards commissioned by Governor Meigs to direct the express mail and commissary service in the Northwest.

Rev. Joseph Badger, at Camp Huron, filled the places of postmaster, chaplain, and nurse. Dr. Thompson, of Hudson, filled the place of surgeon, with a scant supply of medicines, no sanitary assistants, and scarcely any hospital accommodations. For delicacies to soothe their collapsed and nauseated stomachs, "Parson Badger made in a mortar made of a stump, by pounding corn, meal for 'hasty pudding.'" This he called "priest-craft." He was more popular than the surgeon with his calomel prescriptions.

RETURN OF DRAFT

from First regiment, Third brigade, Fourth division, made 5th of September, 1812.

I do certify this to be a true return of drafts from First regiment, Third brigade, Fourth division Ohio militia, as made to me. WILLIAM RAYEN,
Lieutenant-Colonel.

FIRST COMPANY.

COMMISSIONED OFFICERS.

Captain Joshua T. Cotton.
Lieutenant George Monteith.
Ensign Jacob Irwin.

NON-COMMISSIONED OFFICERS.

Sergeant John Cotton.
Sergeant John Myres.
Sergeant George Wintermute.
Sergeant Abraham Wintermute.
Corporal John Carlton.
Corporal Boaudwin Robins.
Corporal John Russell.
Corporal Jesse Graham.

PRIVATES.

Henry Peter, Daniel Shatto, James Crooks, Matthew Guy, John McCollum, Henry Bronstetter, Robert Kerr, Henry Crum, Nicholas Vinnemons, William McCrery, Joseph Osburn, Adam Swazer, Henry Thom, John Parkust, Samuel White, Seneca Carver, Jacob Hull, John White, John Muskgrove, George Smith, John Hayes, Thomas McCrery, John McGlaughlin, Michael Storm, John Truesdale, Francis Harvey, Anthony Whittenstay, Thomas Cummons, Jacob Parkust, Isaac Parkust, Samuel Ca'houn, George Gilbert, Abraham Simons, Thomas Craft, Archibald Maurace, James Fitch, Henry Foose, Abraham Leach, Daniel Stewart, Joseph Carter, Isaac Fisher, Jacob Powers, Thomas Irwin,

William Munn, Nathan Angue, Philip Kimmel, Abraham Hoover, Benjamin Roll, John McMahon.

SECOND COMPANY.

COMMISSIONED OFFICERS.

Captain Samuel Denison.
Lieutenant David A. Adams.
Ensign William Swan.

NON-COMMISSIONED OFFICERS.

Sergeant Amos Gray.
Sergeant William Carlton.
Corporal James Walton.
Corporal Robert Stewart.
Corporal Mathew I. Scott.
Corporal David Ramsey.

PRIVATES.

John Dunwoody, Ephraim Armitage, Samuel Ferguson, Conrad Miller, Jacob Fight, Sr., Jacob Oswalt, James Eckman, Andrew Boyd, John Moore, David Kays, John Day, Robert Walker, Thomas Wilson, John Tulley, James Lynn, William Crawford, David Willson, David McConnell, David McClellan, Isaac Lyon, Samuel Mann, John McMurry, William McMurry, William Bell, John Nelson, Peter Carlton, Jacob Fight, Jr., David Stewart, Joseph Baggs, William McKnight, Thomas Fowler, Sampson Moore, John Poynes, John Brudon, Daniel Augustine, John Polly, John Yast.

THIRD COMPANY.

COMMISSIONED OFFICERS.

Captain Warren Bissell.
Lieutenant Alexander Rayne.
Ensign Nicholas McConnell.

NON-COMMISSIONED OFFICERS.

Sergeant A. Stilson.
Sergeant Asa Baldwin.
Sergeant Parkus Woodrough.
Sergeant Simon Stall.
Corporal William Hamilton.
Corporal Jacob Dice.
Corporal Amanuel Hull.
Corporal Isaac Blackman.

PRIVATES.

David Noble, Aaron Dawson, David Coniser, Henry Rumbel, John Riddle, James Moody, Joseph Mearchant, John Bucannon, John Dickson, John Moore, Joseph McGill, Phillip McConnell, Richard McConnell, Robert Goucher, Thomas Combs, William Bucannon, William Reed, William Shield, Alexander Crase, David McComba, George Mockerman, John Dowler, Josiah Bearsley, John Murphy, Josiah Walker, John Earl, John Ross, John Cowdan, John Brothers, Robert McGill, Renalds Cowdan, Samuel Love, William McGill, Walter Bucannon, William Cowdan, John Zedager, William Frankle.

A RETURN OF CAPTAIN HINES' COMPANY.

COMMISSIONED OFFICERS.

Lieutenant Edmund P. Tanner.
Ensign Thomas McCane.

NON-COMMISSIONED OFFICERS.

Sergeant Julius Tanner.
Sergeant Silas Johnson.
Sergeant Daniel Fitch.
Sergeant John Hutson.

Corporal Christopher Razor.
Corporal Joseph Bruce.
Corporal John McMullen.

PRIVATES.

Henry McKinney, John Turner, John Young, John Chub, James McDonald, Jacob Shook, Samuel Green, Conrad Osburn, Benjamin Manchester, William Thomas, William Leonard, John Hill, William Steel, Robert McCrary, Nicholas Leonard, Henry Ripley, James Moore, George Leonard, Robert Cain, Henry Boyd, William McKinnie, George Hester, Henry Hock, James Saxeton, James Polluck, John McConnell, Arthur Anderson, Elijah Stevenson, Henry Stump, John McCully, Francis Henry, John McKey, James Jack, Garrett Peckard.

CHAPTER XIII.

GEOLOGY.

Physical Features and Economic Resources—Geological Formation.

The geological features of Trumbull and Mahoning counties are too intimately associated to be separated in our discussion of that subject. No minute and scientific treatise will be expected or would be in place in a work of this character. We shall, in a general and popular manner, endeavor to trace the origin and determine the extent of the subsurface resources, in the development of which half the capital and one-fourth the population of both counties are employed.

The whole surface area of Trumbull and that part of Mahoning counties embraced in New Connecticut may be described as an undulating plain, sloping toward the north, with a deep furrow or trough running transversely from northwest to southeast, declining toward the south. Topographically this plain belongs to the lake basin, the southern rim of which passes through the northern part of Columbiana county. Why is the water-shed separating the lake from the river streams thirty-five miles north of this rim, is a question which confronts us at the outset. This is a question, too, which involves the whole theory of geological formation. The process of rock making was necessarily slow, and can be understood only by those who have given some attention to the elements of the science. Rock strata or layers are formed of sand and gravel deposits worn by water from solid formations and transported by water, or, as in the case of coal and limestone, of animal or vegetable deposits.

The starting-point of surface geology in this region is a kind of sandstone known as the Berea grit, which is the surface rock of Farmington, Southington, Mecca, Johnston, and part of Kinsman townships. Immediately beneath this lies a soft shale—the Mecca oil rock which is exposed at several places in Trumbull county. Still deeper lies the Cleveland shale, Erie shale, and Huron shale, the last being an oil-producing rock. It is to be supposed that when the sands of the Berea grit had hardened, another inundation brought a drift of a different character, which, in turn, solidified, and has been named by geologists, Cuyahoga shale. Over this was thrown a layer of coarse gravel forming a hard conglomerate rock which is the foundation of our block coal. During the thousands of years occupied in this building-up process, it is not to be supposed that the surface was level. There were water-channels, and hills and valleys, which were constantly being washed down and filled up, so that none of these rock layers form a continuous sheet. The surface, in geological ages, bore a general resemblance to the surface at present, though there may be hills now where there were valleys or lakes then. In fact, we know that this is true, for coal beds were nothing more than swamps which gave growth to luxuriant vegetation year after year, perhaps for centuries, and then came another deluge of water and earthy matter, burying these peat beds for the use of man. It is probable that these bogs and swamps, in which was deposited the vegetable matter for coal, extended as far northward as Ashtabula county.

There is good evidence that the coal measures of western Pennsylvania continued in one unbroken sheet across the county. But during the drift period of geological history, great gorges of snow and ice from the north, carrying at their base boulders broken from hard ledges in Canada, ploughed out the deep valleys of the Grand and Mahoning rivers. The northern rocks are softer than those to the south, so that through Trumbull a broad and even valley was scooped out by the moving mountains of ice and rock. On approaching the present territory of Mahoning county, heavy conglomerate and sandstone was encountered. The eroding force naturally concentrated, cutting out a channel comparatively narrow, bordered near the State line by abrupt bluffs three hundred feet high. It was by these old glaciers that a channel to the Ohio river was formed through a region which belongs to the lake depression. It would be useless to attempt to compute the amount of coal mined by natural forces during the glacial period. Part of it was ground up and mingled with the soil of the county. The balance has been washed to the alluvions of the Ohio and Mississippi. Fragments of this coal are often found by farmers, and the mistake has sometimes been made of supposing they indicated the presence of a coal bed in the vicinity. They are, rather, indications of the opposite, for the forces which prepared the soil for agriculture have transported them from a much higher level.

The lower or block coal and rocks associated with it underlie the surface except in the immediate valley of the Mahoning and its tributaries. In Trumbull county, the whole of Hubbard and Brookfield townships, the greater portion of Hartford, Vienna, and Liberty, small parts of Lordstown, Newton, and Weathersfield, and patches in Vernon and Fowler are covered with coal rocks. It would be impossible to give the black coal areas of Mahoning county, for reasons which will be given further along. The coal and coal rocks are everywhere covered with drift, making it impossible to determine from surface indications the exact limit of the area. Block coal in the Mahoning valley lies in veins and beds, never in sheets of unvarying thickness or quality. The outline of deposits are extremely irregular, showing great unevenness of surface when the vegetation of which it was formed was deposited. It seems from present exploration to have been a surface covered with scattered swamps and marshes, sometimes running into a long-connected chain, and sometimes quite isolated, just as in low lands of the present day. A search for coal is a search for these old swamps, hidden under newer layers of sandstones, and shales, and drift, and soil. At places a current of water has ploughed a ravine through these overlying materials, exposing a vein or section of coal. Where Nature has not taken this advance in exploring, the search is often difficult and expensive. A practical geologist can determine the greatest limit of the coal area, but the location of a profitable shaft can be determined only by piercing the ground. The distance between the edges of the old swamps was at places considerable. The swamps themselves in many cases seem to have filled old channels with entering tributaries, so that a drill may be sunk in the vicinity of a profitable vein without showing any indication of the presence of coal.

The relative location and form of deposits will be best understood by supposing the drainage of a large irregular area to be suddenly checked and the lower portions of the surface become marshes. This is what happened in the coal age. Peat formed to the depth of fifty or sixty feet, covering the irregular rock bottom. The highlands between the marshes or elevations and crags rising up out of them like islands were not covered. After the lapse of time this region subsided and overflowed with water. The inundation was at first quiet, gradually arresting the growth of vegetation and then covering the peat marshes with fine clay. Under the weight of this sediment the spongy peat was compressed so that the upper coal surface shows a marked subsidence toward where the deposit is deepest. The strata of coal and shale is found dipping downward from the feather edge along the old water line. At a later date streams of water rushed over these deposits, cutting channels through the clay and peat, these channels in them filling up with sand and gravel, which now appear like walls of hard rock through the coal beds and still further complicate explorations and mining. How far these irregular and branching coal basins are connected has not yet been determined. The different sections lie in belts which have a general direction of a little east of north and west of south. The mineral ridge belt in Mahoning county extends from the old Warner & Co.'s mines in Weathersfield to the southern part of Austintown, including eight workable slopes. A similar belt extends through Vienna and Liberty townships, in Trumbull county, and Youngstown in Mahoning county.

Along the west side of Youngstown township is another belt of mines reaching into Coitsville. Even within these belts a large number of the shafts have failed to strike coal, and between them explorations have entirely failed, though there may be other rich belts entirely untouched. Several times the deposit has seemed almost exhausted, when more diligent search and closer borings resulted in new discoveries. The geological structure of this region will not permit an abandonment of the mining enterprise till every acre is thoroughly proved. The fine quality, high reputation, and prices of Mahoning block coal justify considerable expense in searching for it as long as there is a reasonable prospect of success. The northern townships of Mahoning county have been explored much more thoroughly than the middle and southern tier. It is doubted with good reason whether coal exists at all in the middle and southern parts of the county. If found at all it will be much deeper than farther north, and consequently will involve more expense. No thorough exploration of that section may be looked for until the workable northern beds are so far exhausted as to increase the demand and price. It is estimated by Professor Newberry that in those townships with producing mines not one out of ten drillings passed through veins of workable thickness. With this experience before them, it will be some time before operators invest their money in doubtful projects in unexplored and difficult regions. Block coal has been found in all five of the northern townships of Mahoning county, but is not mined in Jackson or Milton. In Canfield township a block coal seam was found of workable thickness at the depth of one hundred and sixty feet, and in Ellsworth at the depth of one hundred and fifty feet it was found two feet thick.

Coal veins in the Mahoning valley are rarely found more than four feet thick, and lie below the surface as far in some instances as one hundred and fifty feet. Mines are worked by sinking shafts, then tunneling. A peculiar structure is found in one of the mines in Hubbard township. Near the center of the bed is an island of cannel coal, which is rejected in mining. This probably represents open water in the center of the old peat marsh, in which the vegetable matter became so largely mixed with earthy material as to make it worthless. The good coal represents the parts of the marsh where vegetation grew through and gradually formed peat beds from the edges toward the center.

"The quality of coal," says Professor Newberry, "obtained from the lower seam in the Mahoning valley, has now been so fully demonstrated and understood that words would be wasted in its praise. It has been shown by a great number of analyses and by long and varied trials to be one of the purest and most valuable coals known in the world. Its open burning character, its comparative freedom from sulphur and small amount of ash it contains especially fit it for the smelting of iron, of which properly managed it gives a product scarcely inferior in quality to that obtained with the use of charcoal. Bessemer pig and car-wheel iron ore are constantly made with it, which can hardly be said of any other coal. It has been largely used for forge and mill purposes, but this has been to a degree a sacrifice, since cheaper coals would have served these purposes nearly as well. The interests of iron manufacturers of the Mahoning valley would probably have been best served in the past as they will be in the future by using the block coal only for smelting."

The Mineral Ridge coal and blackband iron belt deserves special attention. Over a bed of block coal, about two feet in thickness, lies a band of shale and iron ore ten inches thick; covering this is another bench of coal nearly three feet thick and of inferior quality. It is soft, pitchy, and contains a much larger percentage of bitumin than average block coal. So different in character was this upper layer, that geologists for a long time supposed it to belong to a different seam from that mined in the Mahoning valley. It was for a long time known as the blackband coal. They have been proved, however, essentially the same in kind, the quality being affected by the date of formation. Professor Newberry supposes the history of this deposit to be about as follows: The belt of Mineral Ridge coal mines was a shallow basin of variable breadth, in which peat, of limited thickness, accumulated, which, under peculiar conditions or from the nature of the vegetation, produced block coal. When the basin had accumulated peat sufficient to form one or two feet of coal, the water rose, smothered out vegetable life, and covered the peat deposit with a carbonaceous mud. The water contained a strong solution of iron, which was precipitated into this mud. This became the blackband ore, lately mined and worked with profit. Subsequently there was a second growth of vegetation, which formed a peat bed thicker than the first, but probably of a different character; the physical conditions may have also been different. The fact that iron was precipitated, shows evaporation of standing water. The iron of bog, found in the basin of swamps at the present day, was precipitated in the same way.

A piece of slate rock, which must have been transported from Canada, was found some years ago imbedded in this blackband. It is not rounded like the boulders drifted from the north during the later periods of geological formation, but seems to have been bound up in the roots of a tree and floated with the trunk. If this hypothesis be correct there must have been a strong water current bearing southward. It should be borne in mind that the depression now forming the lake basin was then a plain with hills and valleys much like other parts of the continent.

Overlying coal number one, or "block coal," is a soft shale. Then comes a heavy sandstone of good quality, having a thickness in some places of one hundred and sixty feet. Sandstone, like all other rock strata, lies in patches of variable thickness, depending upon the surface when the sand was washed in and deposited in beds and bars. Alternating layers of sandstone and shale cover coal number one, or block coal, to an average depth of eighty feet. Then is found another layer of coal which geologists have called number two. It is nowhere of workable thickness, but is frequently passed through in drilling for the lower and better deposit. In Trumbull county it is found nearer the block coalseam, the distance between being at some places not more than thirty feet. The value of this seam consists in the iron deposits with which it is associated. Near the Mahoning county line, just south of Weathersfield, is a splint of semi-canal coal in two benches, four feet thick, containing a workable variety of nodular ore.

Further north in Trumbull county the shales above this coal contain iron nodules. In Hubbard township is a compact layer of this iron eighteen inches thick, which has been successfully worked by the Hubbard Iron company. It is mixed with lime and bituminous matter. The out-crop of this ore covers considerable area in Hubbard and Liberty townships. It is the source in Brookfield township of the iron paint deposit found at a series of springs about one mile south of Brookfield center. The bed is about four feet deep and covers one acre of land. It is saturated with water, which empties out at the spring highly charged with iron in solution. The iron on coming in contact with the air is precipitated in the form of yellow hydrated oxide—the basis of ordinary mineral paint. In Trumbull county no coal is found higher than number two, which associated with nodular ore, spreads over a considerable part of Mahoning. The early smelting furnaces on Mill creek and in Poland probably used this nodular ore In Mahoning county there are four coal measures above number two. About one hundred and fifty feet above the lower or block coal is found a seam in Ellsworth, Austintown, and Canfield townships varying in thickness from one to four feet; some of it is of fair quality, but it is generally slaty. It is used for ordinary heating purposes, and mined in some localities with profit. Overlying this seam is a limestone bed of great profit. It is the most constant bed of stone in the county, and is exhaustively used in the furnaces, for building stone, and lime. It is from two to three feet thick, at some places resting on the coal, and at places thirty feet above it. The stone is covered with a layer of iron ore of variable thickness appearing as a series of flattened nodules.

Forty or fifty feet above this limestone is another series of coal beds of an inferior quality. In the south part of the county west of the Niles & New Lisbon railroad it is four feet thick, but is of an inferior quality, and consequently not worked. The fourth seam from the bottom is second in importance only to the block coal, which lies lowest. It is a valuable seam so far as regards thickness and character, but is almost always present in localities where it belongs. In some places it is six feet in thickness, all cannel coal of good quality; in other places it is remarkably pure bituminous coal from two to three feet thick. It is generally found to have a thickness of three feet bituminous with six inches cannel on top. This vein was first opened in the southwest corner of Canfield by J. and W. Whetmore, where it is five feet thick, all cannel. A mine was afterwards opened on the Ewing farm in the same locality, the vein being two feet bituminous and six inches cannel. This coal approaches the surface near the center of Canfield, lying immediately under the surface rock of sandstone, on Academy hill. The most extensive mines are near Green village, New Albany, and Washingtonville. In the southern part of Mahoning county is a fifth seam, nowhere more than a foot and a half thick, and of no economic value, except for forge fuel.

The higher points of the southern part of Mahoning county are capped by white limestone. The most northward extension is midway between Green village and Canfield. It is used extensively in the manufacture of lime and for flux in the furnaces. From the place of the first development of the coal resources of the valley, the old Brier Hill mine, near the north line of Youngstown township, the search for coal has radiated in every direction. The country about Youngstown has been more thoroughly explored than any other part of the county. A number of extensive basins have been struck in that neighborhood and profitably worked. The mines in Trumbull county have been found among the most profitable in the valley, but seem to be on the decrease. It is evident that south in place of north of the Mahoning line affords the most encouraging field for exploration. In considering the probability of early coal exhaustion and its consequent effect upon industries the following document will be of interest :

AUDITOR'S OFFICE,
WARREN, OHIO, March 3, 1881.

To A. S. Macintosh, Member State Board Equalization.

DEAR SIR: I herewith transmit for your consideration a statement showing the condition of our mining interests in 1881 as compared with 1870. In the items of coal furnaces and rolling mills in previous statements sent you we have claimed a great reduction in valuation in 1880 as compared with 1870. But we fear we were not sufficiently explicit in statements sent. We have therefore prepared this statement, compiled from the best authority, giving names and locality. In 1870, there was in Hubbard township: Carbon valley, mined out; Mayers Coal company, abandoned; Hubbard Coal company, Tod & Stambaugh, and Crawford, Davis & Co., mined out; P. Jacobs & Sons, abandoned; Eureka Coal company, Chestnut Ridge company, Owen & Co., Mahoning Coal company No. 1, and Mahoning Coal company No. 3, mined out; Stewart Coal company, abandoned; all together averaging about 200 tons per day when run. There was in 1880: Burnett Coal company No. 1, averaging 40 tons per day; Burnett Coal company No. 2, 200 tons; Mahoning Coal company No. 3, 200 tons; Applegate mine, 250 tons; Andrews & Hitchcock, 280 tons, as reported by A. K. Price, Esq.

Brookfield—1870: Curtis & Boys, 100 tons per day, worked out; Chew & Co., 25 tons per day, worked out;

Brookfield company, 300 tons per day, operation let; Otis Coal company, 150 tons per day, operation let. In 1880 there was: Brookfield Coal company, 200 tons per day, fair condition; Otis Coal company, 100 tons per day, nearly out.

Hartford township—1870: Woodchuck, 10 tons per day, played out; reported by T. W. Case, Esq.

Liberty township, reported by T. W. Case, Esq. In 1870: McCurdy Coal company, 200 tons per day, mining let; Church Hill Coal company, 400 tons per day, mining let; Arms, Wick & Co., 50 tons per day, mined out. In 1880, Kline Coal company, 200 tons per day, fair condition; Church Hill company, 300 tons per day, fair condition; McCurdy company, 200 tons per day, fair condition.

Vienna township, reported by J. B. Payne, Esq. In 1870: Moore slope, 30 tons daily, abandoned; Cork and Bottle, 250 tons daily, mined out; Vienna shaft, 250 tons daily, mined out; Shoo Fly, 150 tons daily, abandoned; Blackberry, 100 tons daily, abandoned; Holliday, nearly done; Strip-and-at-it, 50 tons daily, abandoned. In 1880, McMasters shaft, 80 tons daily, worked only part of time; Holliday shaft, 100 tons daily, worked only part of time; Andrews shaft, worthless.

Weathersfield, reported by H. H. Mason and C. P. Whitney—1870: Peacock Coal company, Morris & Rice, Arms, Warner & Co., Campbell bank, and Fulk Coal company, all mined out; Weathersfield bank, drawing pillars 1880. 1880: Osborn Coal company, nearly out, 90,000 tons mined in 1880; Weathersfield shaft, 5,000, nearly done for; Williams & Co., 20,000, nearly done for.

FURNACE AND ROLLING-MILL PROPERTY.

There was running in Hubbard, "Andrews & Hitchcock," two furnaces in 1870, in good condition and doing good business. In 1880: Jesse Hall & Son, poor condition, fair business.

In Liberty—1870: Corns Iron Company rolling-mill, good condition, one furnace doing fair business. 1880: There is the same one running, not doing as well.

Weathersfield—1870: James Ward & Co.'s mill, Russia mill, Falcon Iron & Nail company's mill, Niles Iron company's mill, William Ward's furnace, and Jonathan Warner's two furnaces, all in flourishing condition. 1880: Ward & Co.'s old mill, Russia mill, and Niles Iron company, doing fair business; Falcon Iron & Nail company, doing good business; Thomas & Co.'s furnace, doing middling business.

Warren city, reported by auditor—1870: Richards & Co.'s rolling-mill, good condition; Richards & Co.'s furnace, fair condition. 1880: Torn down furnace, and rolling-mill burned; repaired, and valued by appraiser at $8,000; former valuation of mill and furnace, $40,000.

Thus we had of coal banks, 1870, thirty-nine, and all in very good condition, with a mining capacity of about 7,500 tons daily, upwards of 2,000,000 tons annually. In 1880 there were but fourteen in operation, mining about 420,000 tons coal. At this rate of decrease there can be but little left in 1885.

Furnace and mill property.—Fine furnaces are now *cit*, and mills greatly depreciated.

I am, sir, with profound respect,

R. C. RICE,
County Auditor.

The geological structure of the central and northern parts of Trumbull and Mahoning counties remains to be treated.

Underlying the coal formations is a massive conglomerate which thins out as it approaches the coal beds. It is composed of water-worn pebbles and quartz, and is generally found to contain solutions of salt and iron. It is the source of the salt springs in Weathersfield and the mineral springs in Howland. It is an excellent building stone in the counties west of Trumbull, but is not available here for anything more than bridge or foundation work. Coal is never found below this formation. So that in Trumbull county any explorations north of where it appears in the surface rock is useless. This line extends through Vernon, Hartford, Vienna, Howland, Weathersfield, Lordstown, and Newton townships.

The Berea grit, with the shaly rock below it, deserves special attention because it is the only accessible oil producing rock in northern Ohio. In Mesopotamia and Farmington townships it is finely exposed and affords excellent quarries. A good quality of grindstones and coarse whetstones are made from it. As a building stone it is unequaled by any other variety. It forms a belt of surface rock passing through Southington, Champion, Mecca, Johnston, Gustavus, and Wayne. In the first it is deeply covered with tough clay. In Vernon, on Pymatuning creek, it is exposed in massive layers, from which blocks of any desired size can be taken. It is, however, damaged for building purposes by nodules of iron which color the stone. Petroleum is found on the ridges on the east and west sides of Musquito creek. Many wells have been bored in Mecca township, and a few in adjoining townships. The sand rock is soft and porous, and is underlaid with carbonaceous shale, which is the source of oil. The carbon vapors escaping from the shale penetrates the pores of the sand rock, and there condenses to a liquid. It is a circumstance deserving attention that the wells east of Musquito creek are more productive than those west. Oil is found in nearly all the wells on the east side, but is soon exhausted by pumping. After the lapse of a few months the crevices have filled up again and another supply can be pumped out. The reason oil is more plentifully obtained east of the creek is because there are fewer crevices for its escape, having over the sand rock a heavy pasty covering of clay. On the other side there are seams which gradually drain the crevices. There is a second oil-producing rock twelve hundred feet deep, but it lies too compactly to afford profitable wells in this locality. In Pennsylvania, where this stratum is disturbed the most productive wells in the world have been struck.

In the northwest part of Trumbull county may be seen how coal fields were formed hundreds of centuries ago. The extensive swamp in Bloomfield township, covering several thousand acres, was evidently once an old lake basin which gradually filled with peat. This varies in thickness from six to ten or more feet, and is now covered with grasses, mosses, and cranberry vines, in some parts, and in other parts with tamarack trees and small shrubs. This store of carbon may sometime be utilized for fuel, but not until wood is exhausted and coal becomes expensive. The chief present value of peat is for fertilizing clay land. It is equal in a hard compact soil to barnyard manure. It ought not be used directly from the swamp, however, but should be exposed to the atmosphere and sun till its acid properties are lost; otherwise it will sour land and do more damage than good. Where it is practicable it should be mixed with lime, the two supplying properties needed for vegetables and grains. Rightly utilized peat beds are sources of great wealth.

The soil of Trumbull county is composed for the most part of stiff, tenacious clay, which is well adapted for grazing but is not sufficiently reliable for profitable agriculture. Crops are affected and often destroyed by a deficiency or excess of rain. There is more danger from oversaturation than from drought. It is remarked by many of the older farmers that crops are far less reliable now than for the two or three decades following the clearing—a fact which is easily accounted for. The old roots burrowing to great depths, decaying left holes which communicated with the lower and more porous earthy matters. They were the channels from a variable surface to a depth of constant moisture, carrying off surface over-supply and supplying surface deficiencies. These channels have by cultivation been stopped up, and if agriculture is to be relied upon by the farmer he should bring art to his rescue by making tile drains. Trustworthy experiments have proved that clay soil can be doubled in productiveness by tiling. The more advanced farmers have understood this fact for some time and profited by it. Happily for Mahoning county and parts of Trumbull the soil is of such a character as not to require artificial drainage. The surface is hilly, and has in consequence better natural drainage, besides the soil is composed of gravel and sand fertilized with disintegrated particles of limestone. Mahoning ranks high as a wheat-growing county. Trumbull county exceeds all others in the production of cheese. The alluvions bordering the Mahoning are well adapted to corn culture.

In succeeding chapters of a more local character the industries based upon geological formations are fully detailed. It would be impossible to give the number of men employed in the coal trade and iron industry in all its ramifications, nor would such a fact be essential history. The manufacture of iron began as early as 1805 or 1806 on Yellow creek, near the Mahoning river, by Daniel and James Heaton. The forest surrounding it was used for making charcoal for the blast and an ore bed in the locality furnished the iron. It was probably the nodular ore associated with coal number two. The blast was of an extremely primitive character. A square box was placed upright in a cistern of water communicating with a drain; the upper end was placed in communication by a long pipe with a dam of water, another pipe extending from the side of the upright box into the blast stack. Water suddenly turned on at the dam forced the air contained in the connecting pipe and box into the blast. Water was then shut off at the dam and allowed to escape into the cistern, air taking its place in the apparatus. This contrivance was ingenious, but was rendered unsatisfactory by charging the air with moisture, neutralizing in some measure the heat. James Heaton after a few years removed to Niles where he started another furnace. Daniel continued at the old works, making kettles, stoves, and castings. A furnace was built below Heaton's in 1814 by Robert Montgomery, with a blast made of fly fans driven by a water wheel, which proved much more satisfactory. Such was the simple beginning of an industry which employs in the valley more than ten thousand men in its various branches.

Coal, prior to the completion of the Ohio and Pennsylvania canal in 1840, was mined in limited quantities for household, mill, and forge use. A mine was opened on the Tod farm, about three miles above Youngstown, which was estimated superior coal for ordinary engines. After the Ohio and Pennsylvania canal was completed, David Tod, with his characteristic energy and foresight, opened out a bank on a hill rising up from the river valley, the surface of which was covered with briers. "Brier Hill" was therefore a natural designation for the place and the coal which has since become so famous. Lake steamers seemed the only promising source of a large market. Two canal-boat loads were shipped to Cleveland, and after a thorough test by engineers, was accepted as the standard fuel. The market from that time steadily grew, but a more economical and profitable use for open burning block coal was soon discovered. Charcoal and coke had been used exclusively in the manufacture of iron. About 1842 the attention of practical mineralogists from Pittsburgh was drawn to coal on account of its chemical composition and peculiar physical structure. These experiments led to the establishment in 1844, by Messrs. Wilkes, Wilkinson & Co., of Pittsburgh, of the first blast furnace in America for the manufacture of pig iron from bituminous coal. This furnace was located at Lowell. The Eagle furnace soon followed, built by Messrs. Philpot, Warner & Co., and after it the Brier Hill furnace, built by James Wood, of Pittsburgh. These first raw coal furnaces used the native or blackband ore. The hot-blast had not yet been invented, and the demand for iron was not one hundredth as great as at present. It has been remarked that a couple of canal-boat loads stocked the market. The general rapid progress of improvement increased the demand for iron, and invention, the handmaid of necessity, responded promptly to the demand made upon her for improved furnaces. The product of native ore was what is known as American Scotch pig, which was superior to the foreign article, but in time proved inadequate to the demands of the iron trade. Explorers in the Lake Superior region had found banks of almost pure iron. The proposition to transport this for manufacture to the coal-fields was at first ridiculed as visionary, but was soon demonstrated to be entirely practicable and profitable. The ore for more than one-half the iron manufactured in the valley at the present time is transported from the Lake Superior mines. Native ores and Pennsylvania ores are the complement. Block coal has always stood the test for blasting, but its exclusive use for that purpose has been abandoned by advanced manufacturers. The proportion of raw coal to Pennsylvania coke is about one to five. Only enough coal is used to supply the gas needed for heating purposes, not because coal is inadequate for the purpose, but because the use of coke is more economical. The celebrity of Brier Hill coal and the physical properties which adapt it to transportation have given it a price beyond its value as a furnace fuel. This circumstance has given an additional impetus to transportation industry, which will be considered in the following chapter. Along with the furnaces came rolling mills, and with the rolling mills other manufactories depending upon them, the growth of which will be elsewhere considered. There are at present nineteen furnaces of large capacity in operation in the valley. There are in the valley thirty producing coal banks yielding about one million tons annually. The coal and iron industry and the transportation industry have always been mutually dependent upon each other, and their growth is intimately associated.

The following statistics will show the importance of the mineral resources of the valley. The entire coal output for the year 1880 was 1,020,841 tons. Three thousand one hundred and fifty-seven laborers are employed in these mines.

The following rolling mills are located in Trumbull and Mahoning counties. Statistics from the census of 1880:

Firms.	Year built.	Tons annual capacity.	Puddling furn.	Nail and spike machines	Number employes.
Brown, Bonnell & Co.	1846-79	35000	53	46	900
Cartwright, McCurdy & Co.	1863-74	10000	30		600
Wick, Armes & Co.	1876	850		2	50
Mahoning Valley Iron Co.	1871		52		363
Youngstown Rolling Mill Co.	1871	6000	14		350
Corns Iron Company	1873	7000	13		30
Falcon Iron & Nail Company	1867	11000	12	44	180
Jesse Hall & Son	1872	4000	7		125
Niles Iron Company	1872	13000	19		280
L. B. Ward	1864	7500	12	5	150
Ward Iron Company	1841	14000	20		900
C. Westlake & Company	1870	9000	16		75
Total rolling mill employes					3293
Total blast furnace employes					755
Total number coal miners					3157
No. directly connected with iron and coal production					7205

There were twelve furnaces in blast, as follows:

Name.	Names of Owners.	No. men employed.
Pirier Hill.	Brier Hill Iron and Coal Co.	60
Eagle..	Eagle Furnace Co.	50
Falcon..	Brown, Bonnell & Co.	50
Grace...	Brier Hill Iron and Coal Co.	60
Heselton..	Andrews Brothers.	58
Himrod..	Himrod Furnace Co.	100
Phœnix..	Brown, Bonnell & Co.	50
Mary....	Ohio Iron and Steel Co.	50
Struthers.	Struthers Furnace Co.	80
	Mahoning Valley Iron Co.	36
Girard...	Girard Iron Co.	60
Hubbard..	Andrews & Hitchcock.	60
Thomas..	Thomas Furnace Co.	33
	Total.	755

CHAPTER XIV.

TRANSPORTATION FACILITIES.

Turnpikes—Stage Lines—Railroads and Canals.

We have already seen that Youngstown was the objective point of immigrants to the Reserve. It was accessible both by river and winding wilderness roads from Pittsburg and the Pennsylvania settlements, from which roads had been cut to the East. Many of the first settlers came in flat-boats and batteau from the falls, being able to cover the distance quicker in that way than by wagon road. From Youngstown the first settler in any direction was under the necessity of cutting his own way, the second followed the track to the nearest point to his own destination, then branching off made his way by cutting, as the first had done, and so tracks were cut out like veins through the forest. As terminal points became closer, connecting paths were opened. All were in time, as the land was cleared, straightened and removed to property lines, which follow, as a rule, lot and township limits. One road from Youngstown followed the old Indian and salt-makers' trail to the salt spring in Weathersfield, and was extended from there on to Grand river. This road was the second laid out and legally established on the Reserve. Judge Turhand Kirtland was the surveyor of this road. We learn from his diary that he arrived at Youngstown from Grand river, August 3, 1798, and then engaged to help John Young lay out Youngstown. He also surveyed Poland township during the same summer. This road was probably not cut out further than Warren for some years. Between Youngstown and Salt spring it was much traveled, being the outlet to several branches which bore the suggestive names, "salt-roads." Besides the main thoroughfare leading to Warren, branches led northeast to Kinsman, east to Hubbard, and north to the "girdled road," in Ashtabula county. This "girdled road" was the first surveyed in the Reserve, and was constructed according to specifications contained in the following report:

To the Gentlemen, Proprietors of the Connecticut Company, in meeting at Hartford Connecticut:

Your Committee appointed to inquire into the expediency of laying and cutting out roads on the Reserve,

REPORT,

That in their opinion it will be expedient to lay out and cut out a road from Pennsylvania to the City of Cleveland, the small stuff to be cut out: 25 feet wide, and the timber to be girdled 33 feet wide, and sufficient bridges thrown over the streams as are not fordable, the said road to begin in township No. 13 in the first range of the Pennsylvania line, and to run westerly through township No. 12 in the second range, No. 12 in the third range, No. 11 in the fourth range, to the Indian ford at the bend of Grand river; thence through township No. 11 in the fifth, and also No. 10 in the fifth range, No. 10 in the sixth range, No. 10 in the seventh range, No. 10 in the eighth range, and the northwest part of No. 9 in the ninth range, to the Chagrin river, where a large creek enters it from the east; and from the crossing of the Chagrin the most direct way to the middle highway leading from the city of Cleveland to the hundred-acre lots. Submitted with respect by

SETH PEASE,
MOSES WARREN,
WILLIAM SHEPARD, JR.,
JOSEPH PERKINS,
SAMUEL HINCKLEY,
DAVID WATERMAN,
Committee.

HARTFORD, January 30, 1798.

ESTABLISHMENT OF A MAIL ROUTE.

Until 1801, Pittsburg was the nearest post-office to the settlers of Trumbull county. In that year General Wadsworth succeeded in getting a mail route established from Pittsburg to Warren via Canfield and Youngstown, and was himself appointed postmaster at Canfield, Simon Perkins at Warren, and Calvin Pease at Youngstown.

The correspondence between General Wadsworth and the Post-office department conclusively evinces that the Washington officials had but little geographical knowledge of the Northwest Territory at that time. April 30, 1801, General Wadsworth addressed a letter to the Postmaster-general, asking for the establishment of a mail route from Pittsburg to Warren. The reply is appended:

GENERAL POST-OFFICE, May 16, 1801.

DEAR SIR: Your favor of the 30th ult. is received. Inclosed you have an advertisement inviting proposals for carrying the mail from Pittsburg to Warren. We have no correct information of the distance on that route, and perhaps proper time for the performance of the route is not allowed; if any alteration in that respect is desired it should be stated in the proposals. The price for carrying a mail once in two weeks varies from $2 to $3.50 a mile, by the year, counting the distance one way.

I received your favor with a map of the Reserve, for which be pleased to accept my thanks.

Mr. Canfield recommended your appointment to the office of postmaster at Warren, which the Postmaster-general has concluded upon, unless you should wish to avoid the trouble.

Will you be so good as to furnish me with a list of stages or places of refreshments, and the distances from Pittsburg to Warren, and also to mention whether there is any place between Pittsburg and Georgetown where it would seem useful to establish a post-office. I presume you travel from Pittsburg to Georgetown on the south side of the Ohio, but if there are better settlements on the north side, and any villages where it would be proper to establish post-offices, it would be advisable to send the mail on that side although it may be further. I will thank you for advice on the subject. It is probable that the route will produce but little towards the expenses of carrying the mail, and any means to increase its productiveness ought to be considered to insure a continuance of the establishment. It would doubtless have been pleasing to you if the mail could have been in operation before the first of October, but this could not be done consistently with the practice of the office and the time required by law for the advertisements to appear before a contract is entered into.

I am, sir, your obedient servant,

ABRAHAM BRADLEY, JR.

Captain Elijah Wadsworth.

The address upon this letter was as follows:

Free
ABRAHAM BRADLEY JNR
Assist'g Postm Genl
CAPTAIN ELIJAH WADSWORTH
Warren in the Connecticut Reserve
near Pittsburg, Pa

If Captain Wadsworth should not be at Pittsburg Doct. Scott is requested to forward this by some private hand.

June 6, 1801, Captain Wadsworth transmitted the proposal of Eleazer Gilson, who had just arrived in Canfield, to carry the mail for two years from the following October, once in two weeks, for $3.50 a mile by the year, counting the distance one way. In his letter of that date Captain Wadsworth also took occasion to recommend the establishment of post-offices at Beaver and Youngstown. He declined the office of the postmastership at Warren, but urged the establishment of an office in Canfield, and agreed to accept the office of postmaster if the office should be established. October 14th Captain Wadsworth received notification of his appointment as postmaster at Canfield. Gilson[*] entered upon the duties of mail-carrier and on the 30th day of the month the first mail arrived upon the Reserve. The mail-route was eighty-six miles, and the offices upon it were Beaver (Fort McIntosh), Georgetown, Canfield, Youngstown, and Warren. Samuel Gilson, son of Eleazer, carried the mail the principal part of the time, very often traversing the entire route on foot. The mail-bag, doubtless a light one, he carried upon his back.

The mail route until 1815 was through Warren to all parts of the Reserve. At that date a route was established from Erie to Cleveland through Ashtabula, and three years later the first stage-coach made its appearance over this route. In 1819 the Ashtabula and Trumbull turnpike was constructed. This was esteemed an important public improvement, for it connected the lake at Ashtabula with the Ohio at Wellsville by a substantial wagon road. Coaches were run as far as Poland in 1824.

Aaron Whitney, of Conneaut, was probably the first projector of a stage-coach line on the Reserve. He conceived the idea of starting a passenger line from Erie, Pennsylvania, to Cleveland, in opposition to the mail line owned by the Harmons, who used exclusively covered wagons. Whitney was a wagon-maker, and consequently had the facilities for building his own coaches. He secured the services of Charles Barr, afterwards a citizen of Youngstown, to make the bodies. When the first coach was completed, Whitney, Barr, and several others made a triumphal excursion to Ashtabula, where they were received with great *eclat*. A company was soon afterwards organized to run a coach line from Conneaut to Poland, composed of Aaron Whitney, Caleb Blodget, Samuel Helvering, John Kinsman, General Martin Smith, Seth Hayes, and Philip Kimmel. This line was put

---

[*] The statement that Gilson was the contractor is perhaps incorrect, for a part of a published letter from General Perkins, Warren's first postmaster, to Hon. Elisha Whittlesey, says: "A Mr. Frithy, of Jefferson, Ashtabula county, was contractor on the route which came and terminated at Warren, the terminus for two or four years before it went on to Cleveland. Eleazer Gilson, of Canfield, was mail carrier, and made a trip once in two weeks."

in operation in 1824. Poland was the southern terminus, Warren and Youngstown being the chief objective points on the route.

The following appeared in the Western Reserve Chronicle in 1828:

Best route for Western travelers.—We presume that many travelers arriving in Buffalo and bound for the West are unacquainted with the fact that the shortest, cheapest and most expeditious route between the lake and Ohio river is to land at Ashtabula, where excellent coaches start every day for Wellsville on the river, a distance of less than one hundred miles, and traveled in about twenty hours at an expense of $4. The traveling public have an interest in a knowledge of these facts. Nothing can be required to insure to the enterprising stage proprietors extensive patronage.

As early as 1827 a project began to be agitated for uniting the Ohio river with the lake by a railroad. The enterprise looked visionary at that time, and when a pike road was completed many wise heads predicted that no better facilities for transportation would be provided, unless it might be a canal. The railroad scheme was pushed however, so far as obtaining a charter, which fixed the capital at $1,000,000, and designated that the road should run from a point on Lake Erie between Lake and Ashtabula counties, and terminate at some point on the Ohio river in Columbiana county. The leaders in this inceptive enterprise found less difficulty in locating the road than in raising the required capital. Their project failed. The second railroad enterprise affecting Trumbull county was instituted in 1836, under the name of Ashtabula, Warren & East Liverpool company, with a capital of $1,500,000. This was substantially an Ashtabula county enterprise, the Mahoning valley towns being engrossed in another enterprise, regarded as of paramount importance. Work was already commenced on this road, but was brought to a stop by the panic of 1836-37, and never revived. Business depression had an adverse effect upon Warren's nursed enterprise—the Ohio and Pennsylvania canal, which was talked of as early as 1825. No sooner had the Ohio canal and Erie canal been projected than the construction of a connecting link was looked upon as a promising scheme. Philadelphia merchants were especially interested, for it would open up to them northern Ohio, and place them on a fair competing basis with New York, which had the advantage of lake commerce.

The following appeared in the Western Reserve Chronicle, August 9, 1832:

Mahoning Canal.—Merchants and capitalists during the last winter gave strong assurances that the stock in this important work of internal improvement should be taken whenever the books were opened for subscriptions. Knowing, as we did, the arrangements they had made, and the deep interest they felt in the subject, we flattered ourselves that it would be engaged in as early as the ensuing autumn, or at least the following spring. We now, however, have the regret to learn that President Jackson's veto is producing so much depression and derangement in the moneyed concerns of the country, that all hopes of obtaining subscriptions are abandoned. The pressure upon the business men in that city is represented as extreme.

It is stated in the same paper a few weeks later that stock subscription books were soon to be opened, and the work was to be pushed rapidly to completion. Nothing was actually done, however, till business began to revive, in 1838; then, with that surprising activity which generally follows repressed energy, the old project was carried forward. Surveys were made and the bed located from Beaver run to Akron, Ohio, its terminal points being the main north and south highways of Ohio and Pennsylvania. Work was at once commenced and completed as far as Warren in May, 1839. A public reception was tendered the first packet. That the local importance of a public work of this character was appreciated, is shown by the following newspaper correspondence:

WARREN, OHIO, May 28, 1839.

Pennsylvania and Ohio Canal Celebration—On Thursday last, May 23d, our citizens were greeted with the arrival of a boat from Beaver. The packet Ontario, Captain Bronson in charge, came into town in gallant style, amid the roar of cannon and the shouts and hearty cheers of our citizens. The boat was crowded by gentlemen from Pennsylvania and along the line, and accompanied by four excellent bands of music. On arriving at the foot of Main street they were greeted by the Warren band, and a procession formed which marched through the square to the front of Towners' hotel, where a neat and appropriate address was made to the passengers by John Crowell, Esq., mayor of the town, giving them a hearty welcome in the name of the town authorities and citizens, which was responded to by B. B. Chamberlain, of Brighton. The rest of the day was past in hilarity, and on Friday the boat left for Beaver, carrying about forty citizens of Youngstown, who were highly delighted with the excursion. The boat is owned by Clark & Co., of Beaver, who are entitled to all commendation for their exertions in pushing their boat through to the head of navigation, notwithstanding unlooked for and unavoidable obstructions. These obstructions will all be removed in a few days, leaving the canal in good navigable order. Arrangements have been made by Messrs. Clark & Co. for running a daily line of packets from this place Beaver. Three boats, the Ontario, Huron, and Hudson, are fitted up in superior style to carry fifteen tons of freight and sixty passengers, and will leave Warren daily at noon, arrive at Beaver next morning, and proceed by steamer Fallston to Pittsburg. Returning will leave Pittsburg at 4 P. M., Beaver at 7 P. M., and arrive at

Warren about noon the next day. We trust and believe that the enterprising proprietors of this line will reap a rich reward for their labor.

The Western Reserve Chronicle contains a two column report of the "opening celebration," which was participated in by about forty people from Pennsylvania, a large number of citizens of Youngstown, and all the leading men in Warren. A. M. Lloyd, Lieutenant J. Ingersoll, C. C. Seely, James Hoyt, and J. D. Taylor acted as committee of arrangements, having been appointed by the town council. They had raised sufficient money to entertain the guests royally. Major John Crowell, in his address of welcome, said touching the history of the enterprise:

> The charter of the company passed the Legislature of Ohio in January, 1827, and was approved and concurred in by the Legislature of Pennsylvania in April of the same year, but it remained for several years afterward a dead letter on the statute book.
>
> The convention of November, 1843, first breathed into it the breath of life. This convention assembled in this place and was composed of distinguished citizens of both States interested in the work, and after several days spent in deliberation and examination of the route described by the charter, it was resolved to commence the undertaking. Books for the subscription of stock were subsequently opened, the requisite amount subscribed and the company was organized in May, 1835.
>
> Since that time the work has progressed as rapidly as the embarrassed state of the funds of the company would permit, under the superintendence of able and skillful engineers whose whole energies have been devoted to the work with the most untiring industry; and now we have the pleasure of beholding as the result of their labors, the completion of this great work to this place and the arrival of the first boat that has floated on the bosom of its waters.

The response of Mr. Chamberlain on part of the visitors is not reported. At four o'clock a banquet was served. General J. W. Seely presided, being assisted by General Crowell. A few of the toasts responded to may be of interest. Wine flowed freely and spirited music was rendered by the bands in attendance.

"Pennsylvania & Ohio — Pennsylvania, the keystone of the arch, and Ohio the stone which supports the arch."—Hail Columbia.

"The Pennsylvania & Ohio canal—a new link in the chain of sisterhood between two States whose interests can never be severed."—Twin Sisters.

"The Pennsylvania & Ohio Canal company— May the prosperity of the company equal the zeal and energy with which the objects of its creation have been pursued."—Grand Canal March.

"The officers of the canal company—Patriotic in their designs, efficient in their execution, and faithful to their trust."—Washington's March.

"The engineer corps of the Pennsylvania & Ohio canal, faithful and competent in the discharge of the duties devolving upon them."—Lafayette's March.

"The packet Ontario—the first boat that ever floated the waters of the Pennsylvania & Ohio canal."—The Bonny Boat.

"The owners and captain of the packet—May they reap a rich return for their toil."—Yankee Doodle.

F. J. Clark, of Beaver, after expressing the thanks of the visitors for their splendid reception, offered, "The Village of Warren—We admire it not more for its own beauty than for the liberality and enterprise of its citizens."—In the Green Village (by Youngstown band).

General Crowell remarked that while celebrating on this festive occasion the distinguished and meritorious services of the living, we ought not to be unmindful of departed worth. He therefore offered "The Memory of General Abner Lacock, the first president of the Pennsylvania & Ohio canal. His memory will long be cherished by the friends of the enterprise." Drank standing.

Colonel David Tod, after remarking on the services of a distinguished citizen of Warren, in procuring the charter, and who now sleeps with the dead, offered "The Memory of General Roswell Stowe. Peace be to his ashes."

Mr. Gould, of Beaver county, Pennsylvania, after a brief preliminary speech in behalf of Beaver and Mercer counties as represented by himself and associates on this occasion, tendered the citizens of Ohio the congratulations of Pennsylvania upon the opening of navigation from the Big Beaver to Warren. He then proposed "The Triple Union—The rivers of the South with the lakes of the North; the Cuyahoga with the Big Beaver; western Pennsylvania with eastern Ohio; by the cross-cut canal, through Warren, the center of the Union." This rather spread eagle toast was followed by a lively flourish of all the bands, to the tune, Come Haste to the Wedding.

The canal was completed to Akron by the fall of that year, and another excursion and jollification took place at that terminus. Among those especially interested in the enterprise who accompanied the party was Dr. Seely of Warren, who died at Akron through over jubilance.

The Ohio and Pennsylvania canal was a work of inestimable importance to Warren, Youngstown and Cleveland, by creating a market for coal, iron and produce. Inadequate and unsatisfactory as it was, it demonstrated the possibilities of the region, and its few boats were the inception of an immense carrying trade. In a sense the canal may be considered the foundation of a railroad system which penetrates every valley and reaches to every coal, iron, and limestone bed, but it is a foundation which the superstructure has pressed out of existence, leaving only a dry bed and an occasional wrecked hull as souvenirs of its existence. Even the bed in many places has become the track of locomotives.

RAILROADS.

The Cleveland & Mahoning railroad was the product of a long-felt need, and became an accomplished fact in spite of a series of obstacles and embarrassments almost equally long. The project was a revival of the old Ohio & Erie road, its route being changed to accommodate the coal and iron trade developed by the canal. But this trade was the inspiration of the enterprise. While the canal afforded cheap transportation, it was too slow for a heavy iron and coal trade.

This first successful railroad enterprise was born in Warren, and was mainly nurtured at the same place. A charter was granted February 22, 1848, and books at once opened for stock subscriptions. The directors were Jacob Perkins, Frederick Kinsman, and Charles Smith, of Warren; Reuben Hitchcock, of Painesville; Dudley Baldwin, of Cleveland, and David Tod, of Youngstown. A proportion of the stock was subscribed by Eastern capitalists through the influence of the Ohio directors, and when it was supposed sufficient amounts had been pledged to guarantee success, work was commenced in 1853. The work of construction was not half completed when the treasurer reported the stock subscription exhausted, and a depressed money market dispelled hope of enlisting Eastern capital in the enterprise. The alternative presented itself to the directors of abandoning work and bankrupting the company, or staking their own private fortunes on ultimate success. Mr. Perkins, the president, took the lead, and all the other directors followed him in offering their own estates as security for mortgage loans. So confident of success was President Perkins that he guaranteed to pay the first $100,000 loss. A financial panic made the situation extremely embarrassing. English capital was solicited in vain, but the directors, relying upon their own resources, pushed the enterprise as expeditiously as their straitened circumstances would permit. The company was fortunate in having a superintendent who carried on its operations at once efficiently and economically. We refer to Charles Rhodes, now of Cleveland.

The road bed was finally completed as far as Youngstown, but the debt-ridden company's embarrassment was not yet over. Locomotives and cars had to be purchased before it could be made to earn anything. Two of the directors spent two weeks in Philadelphia trying to borrow $20,000, with which to purchase two locomotives, at last succeeding only through personal friendship, and on personal credit. Cars were run between Cleveland and Youngstown in 1856, when there began to be a small but steady income. Railroad stock was traded for canal stock until the company had control of both lines of transportation. The directors experimented with a policy of high freights, but were compelled to abandon it, or drive the coal and iron which were chiefly depended upon for business, out of the market. Two dollars per ton was at one time charged for carrying coal from Youngstown to Cleveland. Stock began to rise in value as soon as the first train had passed over the rails.

The frightful debt which threatened even private houses was year by year scaled down, and, contrary to the usual rule of railroading, was eventually discharged without loss to creditors or stockholders. President Perkins, whose hard labor had been so efficient from the beginning, did not live to see this splendid consummation. However, even at the time of his death in January 1859, enough had been accomplished to insure success. It would be useless to enter into an estimate of the benefits derived from this road by Youngstown, Warren, and Cleveland, nor does the public spirit, energy, and sagacity of the directors who carried it to a successful completion need our poor words of praise. At the beginning the enterprise was looked upon as an experiment. The success of that experiment, under the circumstance, is sufficient comment upon those interested in its execution. Eighty miles of track from Cleveland to Youngstown, and from Youngstown to the State line, called the Hubbard branch, was constructed by the Cleveland & Mahoning company. Two tracks were laid from Cleveland to Leavittsburg, and the road was paying a satisfactory dividend, when, in 1863, it was leased to the Atlantic & Great Western Railroad company for the term of ninety-nine years. At the same time was transferred to the lessee all the company's machinery, rolling stock, tools, etc., for the sum of $405,802.45. The annual rental of the road proper was fixed at $273,072. All liens and mortgage bonds at the date of this lease amounted to $2,300,000.

In 1853, with a capital of $1,000,000, the Ashtabula & New Lisbon Railroad company was chartered. By surveying two lines between Ashtabula and Warren, one along the third range, the other on the fourth, a competitive feeling was created, which had its effect upon stock subscriptions but did not secure the required amount. The road was divided into two divisions, one from Ashtabula to Niles, the other from Niles to New Lisbon. Subscriptions on the former amounted to $274,600, on the latter, $126,175. Robert W. Griswold was chosen president in 1854. He was succeeded in 1856 by Eben Newton, of Canfield, who served three years. Henry Hubbard was chosen to that position in 1859. Like nearly all enterprises of this kind success was secured by a series of failures. The projected road was only partially constructed. In 1864 the uncompleted roadbed south of Niles was leased by a new organization, known as the New Lisbon Railroad company. This company's charter gave it authority to complete the road from New Lisbon to Niles, or some other point on the Cleveland & Mahoning railroad; ten miles to be completed within two and the balance within five years. Under its charter and lease from the Ashtabula & New Lisbon company, the New Lisbon Railroad company proceeded mortgaging the road for its completion; but failing to carry out the terms of the lease, and becoming financially embarrassed, the mortgage was foreclosed, and the road, thirty-five miles in length, was sold in 1869 to private parties, who organized the Niles & New Lisbon Railroad company, and operated the road until 1872 under that title.

A road was built under charter granted the Liberty & Vienna Railroad company in 1868 from the Church Hill Coal company's road in Liberty township to Vienna. In 1870 this company increased its capital $300,000, and extended its line through Girard to Youngstown. The line from Girard to Youngstown was sold in 1871 to the Ashtabula, Youngstown & Pittsburg company, the remainder being retained by the Liberty & Vienna company.

August 14, 1872, by previous articles of agreement, the Cleveland & Mahoning, the Niles & New Lisbon, and the Liberty & Vienna consolidated and became the Cleveland & Mahonhoning Valley Railroad company, its capital stock being the aggregated stock of the several companies, amounting to $2,759,200. The branches continued to be known as the Niles & New Lisbon and the Liberty & Vienna railroads until 1880, when they were leased to the lessee of the Cleveland & Mahoning for the unexpired term of the lease of 1863. The stipulated annual rental for the branches is $72,980. Under the lease of 1880 all the lines of the Cleveland & Mahoning Valley Railroad company, Reuben Hitchcock, president, are operated by the New York, Pennsylvania & Ohio Railroad company.

It remains in this connection to trace briefly the subsequent history of the Ashtabula & New Lisbon company. A company known as the Ashtabula, Youngstown & Pittsburg Railroad company was chartered in 1870 and entered into a contract with the Pittsburg, Fort Wayne & Chicago company to construct a line from the terminus of the Lawrence branch of the Pennsylvania road at Youngstown to Ashtabula Harbor. The partially constructed line of the Ashtabula & New Lisbon company was adopted from Niles to Ashtabula. Five and a half miles of the track of the Liberty & Vienna company, from Youngstown to Niles, was purchased for $200,000, and the missing link from Niles to Girard was constructed. A contract was made with the Pennsylvania company by which it was to operate the road in harmony with its other lines, and divide the net earnings pro rata. The road was sold in 1878 to a company known as the Ashtabula & Pittsburg Railroad company, and is now operated by the Pennsylvania company under a ninety-nine year lease. The Lawrence Railroad and Transportation company was chartered in Pennsylvania and Ohio in 1864, and lines constructed from Lawrence, Pennsylvania, to Youngstown, Ohio. The line, in 1869, was leased to the Pittsburg, Fort Wayne & Chicago company for the term of ninety-nine years. The Lawrence branch from the Newcastle & Beaver Valley railroad to Youngstown is eighteen miles. In addition to this there is a branch four and one-half miles long, from Canfield Junction to the coal fields, all now controlled by the Pennsylvania company, which, by the Newcastle & Beaver Valley, the Lawrence, and the Ashtabula, Youngstown & Pittsburg, has a continuous line from Ashtabula Harbor to Pittsburg, giving both Youngstown and Warren competing lines from Lake Erie to the Ohio river. Thus the visionary project of 1826 is doubly accomplished.

The New York, Pennsylvania & Ohio company, which now has precedence in the trade of the Mahoning valley, is the product of gradual growth and consolidation. We have already traced the history of the Cleveland & Mahoning valley consolidation, whose lines are now operated under a lease dated in 1880, for the term of eighty-two years. It remains to speak of the main line reaching from Salamanca, New York, to Dayton, Ohio. In 1851 a charter was granted to the Franklin & Warren railroad company to construct a railroad from Franklin, Portage county, via Warren to the State line, with power to continue the same from its place of beginning in a westerly or southwesterly direction to connect with any other railroads within this State, which the directors may deem advisable. Under this authority a line was constructed from Dayton to the State line, crossing the Cleveland & Mahoning at Leavittsburg. The length of this line is two hundred and forty-six miles. The name in the meantime had been changed (in 1855) to the Atlantic & Great Western Railroad company. In 1857 the Meadville Railroad company was chartered in Pennsylvania, and purchased of the Pittsburg & Erie company, chartered in 1846, its property, rights, and franchises in Mercer and Crawford counties, embracing the proposed line of the Meadville company therein. The name of the Meadville Railroad company was changed in 1858 to the Atlantic & Great Western Railroad company of Pennsylvania.

The Erie & New York City Railroad company, chartered in 1852, failing to complete its proposed line, in 1860 sold thirty-eight miles of its road from Salamanca, to the Atlantic & Great Western Railroad company in New York, chartered in 1859. The Buffalo extension of the Atlantic & Great Western Railroad company was chartered in 1864, and in 1865 the four companies consolidated under the name of Atlantic & Great Western Railway company, and in that name operated the through line from Dayton to Salamanca and the branch from Jamestown to Buffalo. In consequence of suits brought for foreclosure the property of the consolidated company was turned over to a receiver April 1, 1867, General R. B. Potter receiving the appointment. After passing through several receiverships and being leased as often, it was finally sold at foreclosure sale in January, 1860, an association of mortgage bondholders being the purchasers. In March of the same year it was conveyed to five corporations, in consideration of $45,000,000 capital stock and $87,500,000 mortgage bonds. They organized the New York, Pennsylvania & Ohio Railway company, taking out charters in Ohio and Pennsylvania. The road was originally constructed with a wide or six-feet gauge, but a few months after it passed under its present management it was reduced to what is known as the standard guage. Its business has since rapidly increased, and the road is now supposed to be operated on a solid basis.

The Painesville & Youngstown railroad was the first narrow gauge line in the State attempted for general transportation business. The company was organized in 1870. The partially constructed Painesville & Hudson road was purchased for $60,000, and by January, 1873, cars were running over a three-feet gauge road from Painesville to Chardon. The company, after expending $265,000 received from stock subscriptions in grading, etc., entered into a contract for the construction of the entire line and full equipment, the contractors to receive the bonds of the company and its capital stock. The road was completed to Niles by January, 1874, and is now extended to Youngstown, being 61.8 miles in length. In 1877, in consequence of foreclosure proceedings, the road was placed in the hands of M. R. Martin, receiver, and was sold at master commissioner's sale in 1879 to H. B. Payne, W. J. Hitchcock, and M. R. Martin, who transferred it to the corporators of a new company, styling itself the Painesville & Youngstown Railway company, in consideration of $1,249,775 in stock and mortgage bonds. It is an interesting fact that this first narrow gauge experiment is soon to be abandoned for the standard guage. The dependence of one road upon another makes uniformity of track necessary, and it is probable that the day of experimenting with either wide or narrow guages is past. Warren has seen the practical failure of both.

The Mahoning Coal Railroad company filed its certificate of incorporation in 1871 to build a road from Youngstown to a point in Brookfield township, the capital being $70,000. In 1871 a supplementary certificate was filed to construct a track from the main line in Liberty township to the Ashtabula branch of the Lake Shore and Michigan Southern railroad, thirty-eight miles, and increasing the capital to $1,500,000. A branch was subsequently built from Youngstown to Struthers, in Mahoning county, and another to the Foster coal mines, making the company's lines 41.58 miles in length. The whole is leased to the Lake Shore & Michigan Southern company for ninety-nine years from May 1, 1873, at an annual rental of forty per cent. of the gross earnings.

The construction of the Alliance & Lake Erie railroad was commenced by the Lake Erie, Alliance & Wheeling Railroad company, in 1876, the proposed line running from Fairport to Wheeling. Trains were run from Alliance to Newton Falls by January, 1877, and to Braceville, on the New York, Pennsylvania & Ohio, before the close of the summer of that year. Operations were stopped in November under foreclosure proceedings, and in May, 1878, the line was sold to the Alliance & Lake Erie Railroad company, a new organization. Trains resumed running in August of that year. The constructed line was lengthened to Phalanx, on the Cleveland & Marietta branch of the New York, Pennsylvania & Ohio, in 1879. The principal freightage of the road is coal procured at Palmyra, where it is said the best coal in the State is mined.

Two new roads are in process of construction.

The Pittsburg, Youngstown & Chicago will connect at Pittsburg with the Baltimore & Ohio, run through Youngstown, Warren and Akron to Chicago Junction, where it connects with the Chicago division of the Baltimore & Ohio. Of this road C. H. Andrews, of Youngstown, is president. The Pittsburg & Western branches from present construction lines at Niles.

CHAPTER XV.
COUNTY SOCIETIES.

Early Fairs—Organization of an Agricultural Society in 1846—First Year's Exhibition—Mahoning County Agricultural Society—Its Constitution and Gradual Growth—Pioneer Reunion at Youngstown—Formation of a Pioneer Society—Publication of a Volume of Historical Collections.

TRUMBULL COUNTY AGRICULTURAL SOCIETY.

The first agricultural fair in Ohio was held in Youngstown in 1818 or 1819, and a county society was at that time regularly organized. A more detailed account of these meetings will be found in the history of the city of Youngstown. Stock shows were for a long time fashionable among the farmers of this county, and these in course of time led to the formation of a regularly organized agricultural society. The initiatory steps were taken at a meeting held in the summer of 1846, at which time J. F. Beaver was chosen President. A premium list was arranged and October 23d appointed as the day of exhibition. The first fair was held accordingly in the court-house and on the park in Warren. The day was a success even beyond expectation. Cattle and horses were tied to trees in the park, where they were gazed upon by crowds of people with that interest which novelty always gives any occasion. Grains, fruits, flowers, and manufactured articles were exhibited in the court-house. The day closed in the healthful and old-fashioned way, with an address on the subject of agriculture and farming by Hon. J. F. Beaver.

The Western Reserve Chronicle said in the issue following this first exhibit:

The 23d was a proud and glorious day for old Trumbull. The fair under the auspices of the Trumbull Agricultural society far exceeded the expectations of its most sanguine friends and supporters. It being the first fair of the kind ever held in Trumbull county, or at least the only one for quite a number of years, it was feared by some that there would be a small turn out, that there would be but little if any competition for the premiums offered by the society. All were happily disappointed. Notwithstanding the day opened with dark, lowering clouds and rain, a general rush was made from all parts of the county. The persevering farmers came up feeling a deep and abiding interest in the enterprise, which if carried out, cannot fail to benefit them materially. They came not alone, or empty-handed, but with their beautiful horses, with their cattle from the field, blooded Durham down to the best of their common stock, their sheep, their hogs, their cheese and butter and fruit, and also with their implements of husbandry. The ladies manifested their interest, and gave the enterprise their presence and the society their all-powerful influence, by bringing forward elegant specimens of the labor of their own hands. From the handiwork of their grandmothers in the cradle-spread manufactured one hundred and fifty years ago and the magnificent patchwork quilt, down to the pin-cushion made by a child four years old, all were exhibited to add to the general interest of the occasion. Many, rich, and valuable were the articles exhibited; many of them useful, and some of them ornamental.

* * * * *

We feel pretty sure that the spirit of improvement has taken deep root among the farmers of old Trumbull. The interest this day shown is not a spark struck for a moment to die, but it is the outbursting of a hidden stream, just bursting from a long confinement, to flow on, and as it goes become deeper and wider.

The highest premium paid was $4. The largest number of entries came under the head of "cattle." Draft-horses were exhibited, but trotting had not yet come in fashion. Draft-horses and draft-cattle were paraded around the square and tested on the public street. In those practical days people took more interest in testing strength than speed. There was, however, a class of people who loved horse-racing, but they took no part in the fair. Youngstown was always the resort for that kind of amusement. The following list embraces the names of successful exhibitors in 1846:

The following persons were awarded premiums on exhibits of cattle: George Heslep, Gustavus; George W. Cowden, Gustavus; Jacob H. Baldwin, Champion; Thomas Kinsman, Simpson Cowden, Greene; David H. King, Howland; Seth A. Bushnell, Hartford; Andrews Bushnell, Hartford; C. C. Beardsley, Lordstown; Hiram Harvey, Greene; Lucius Graham, Gustavus; Linus D. Sheldon, Vernon; Simeon Baldwin, Champion; Chauncy Taft, Farmington; Boswick H. Finch, Warren; Samuel Kennedy, Howland; Lyman Andrews, Kinsman; Simon R. Estabrook, Warren; Peter Struble, Bazetta; C. N. Prindle, Vienna; Samuel Merry, Vernon; total money premiums, $24.

HORSES—John Bronsteller, Weathersfield; Hiram Hutchins, Vienna; John Hadger, David Adams, Isaac Van Gorder, Warren; Henry B. Perkins, Lysander Pelton, Gustavus; James Bishop, Gustavus; Harrison Austin, Warren; Thomas Pew, Warren; total money premiums, $10.

SHEEP—Silas A. Palmeter, Brookfield; Jacob Harshman, Lordstown; Lyman P. Andrews, Kinsman; Joseph Perkins, Warren; Gustavus Adams, Weathersfield; George Heslep,

Gustavus; Harris Ewalt, Howland; B. H. Finch, Warren; premiums, $6.
SWINE—Frederick L. Taft, Braceville; John Lamb, Lordstown; John W. Seely, Howland; premiums, $4.
CROPS—Collins Atwood, Howland; David B. King, Howland; premiums, $2.
BUTTER—Maxwell Kennedy, Howland; Thomas Creed, Vienna; Chester Andrews, Hartford; first premium, $3.
CHEESE—Stephen P. Robbins, Gustavus; Oliver Mills, Gustavus; Samuel H. Furguson, Farmington; premiums, $6.
PLOWS—Sheldon H. Reed, Vienna, for the Diamond plow, $2.
PLOWING MATCH—Ox team, Purdy & Fuller, Howland; horse team, John Tibbetts, Weathersfield; John Reeves, Jr., Howland; premiums, $10.
APPLES—Isaac Van Gorder, Harris Ewalt.
GRAPES—Frederick Kinsman, $1; John Harsh.
FULLED CLOTH—David S. Fitts, Gustavus; premium, $2.
FLANNEL—Isaac Lee, $2.
SUNDRY ARTICLES—Mrs. E. W. Welt, Warren, vest and regalia; Mrs. Hiram Iddings, Warren, red quilt; Rufus Beeman, Gustavus, woolen sheets; Miss Elizabeth Iddings, Warren, carpet; Mrs. Sarah C. Bosworth, Warren, carpet; Mrs. E. S. Tait, Warren, rag carpet; Mrs. Mary Stevens, diaper table cloth; Mrs. Coates, Warren, traveling bag; Miss Lucy Stevens, Warren, lamp rug; L. W. Case, Gustavus, patent bedstead; Charles Pease, Warren, coop of fowls; Mary Hoadly, Hartford, pin cushion; Lorenzo Potter, Warren, press.

Total amount paid in premiums $74.

The following were chosen officers for the year 1847-48: J. F. Beaver, president; George Heslep, vice-president; Jacob H. Baldwin, treasurer; George Hapgood, secretary; Major Churchill, Andrew Bushnell, Josiah Robbins, Jr., Cyrus Bosworth, Israel B. Sheldon.

Two exhibitions were held on the park in Warren, but on account of the rapid increase, both of the exhibit and of the attendance, a larger tract had to be selected. The necessity of owning grounds on which permanent improvements could be made soon became apparent to the managers. A committee consisting of B. N. Robbins, W. H. Hutchins, and O. H. Patch, was appointed to make investigations with a view to purchasing land suitably located. The movement seems to have made little progress, for two years elapsed before a practical method was adopted for making the purchase. In 1858 it was proposed to organize a joint stock company, shares being fixed at $25, for the purpose of purchasing grounds.

It was provided that stock should be paid up in instalments, and draw interest after five years. The whole property was to revert to the company in case the association failed to purchase the stock, with interest, within a period of ten years. It seems the company's advance for the grounds was in the nature of a loan to the association, which was dependent for money upon its ordinary and somewhat doubtful resources.

The committee appointed to solicit stock subscriptions at the meeting in November, 1858, reported in February, 1859, that Warren township had responded to the amount of $2,400, and Howland to the amount of $875. B. N. Robbins was appointed to make a thorough canvass of the whole county, with a view to raising the amount of stock to $6,000. By May the amount was deemed sufficient to warrant making a purchase, and the committee on grounds was accordingly called on to report. Several tracts were deemed eligible, but twenty acres of the farm of William Peck was esteemed most desirable, and accordingly purchased at $150 per acre. The title was made in trust to three trustees: Frederick Kinsman, Warren; Franklin E. Stowe, Braceville; and Maxwell Kennedy, Howland. Franklin Stowe deceased in 1872, and H. F. Austin was appointed to his place. Measures were at once taken to improve the grounds and prepare facilities for an exhibition on a more elaborate scale than had hitherto been possible. Franklin Stowe, C. A. Adams, and Frederick Kinsman were appointed on the committee to construct a track for racing, which it was deemed expedient to introduce. The premium list under the head of "Trotting" is sufficient commentary upon the importance attached to that feature of the fair compared with the present policy. We quote from the advertisement:

Best trotting stallion.................................. $5 00
Best trotting mare or gelding.......................... 5 00
Best trotting pair matched mares or geldings........... 5 00
Best walking horse..................................... 5 00
Horses will be allowed to trot in harness or under saddle.

The judges of the race were James E. Leffingwell, of Ravenna, Seabury Ford, of Burton, and Norman E. Austin, of Youngstown. There was considerable though not brilliant competition for these trivial prizes. Several supporters of the fair doubted the expediency of this innovation upon precedent, but the interest it added to the occasion made the managers more liberal in succeeding years, until the race-track became the chief attraction to more than one-half of the visitors. We have no disposition to comment upon public taste, to which all sorts of entertainments are aimed to be adapted. It is doubtful whether a quiet show of live stock, grain, fruits, and fabrics, and a speech would attract many people in this age of railroads and graphic newspapers, which respectively take people in a few hours to great exhibitions and bring world's fairs on paper into their own homes. Yet there is an honest doubt, and well-grounded, too, as to the propriety of advertising a menagerie when the show is understood to be a circus, as is the case some places. The managers of the Trumbull association have no doubt acted wisely by avoiding extreme policies—providing objects of interest and a field for competition for all.

The following list of officers since 1855 is furnished us by H. F. Austin, secretary of the association:

Presidents—1855, F. E. Stowe; 1856-57, J. F. King; 1858, R. H. Walker; 1859, Harmon Austin; 1860, H. B. Perkins; 1861-62, Josiah Robbins; 1863, S. R. Estabrook; 1864, R. H. Barnum; 1865, H. B. Perkins; 1866-67, F. Kinsman; 1868-69, D. Harrington; 1870-71, Harmon Austin; 1872, William Bronson; 1873, B. J. Jameson; 1874, S. M. Laird; 1875, B. P. Jameson; 1876-77, J. F. King; 1878, F. N. Andrews; 1879-80, A. Wheeler; 1881, J. F. King; 1882, M. S. Clapp.

Vice-presidents—1855, J. F. King; 1856, Abner Rush; 1857, R. H. Walker; 1858, Harris Ewalt; 1859, ———; 1860, Josiah Robbins; 1861, Leman Palmer; 1862, John Ratliff; 1863-64, Harris Ewalt; 1865-67, Harmon Austin; 1868-69, J. F. King; 1870-71, H. B. Perkins; 1872-75, A. Wheeler; 1876-77, O. B. Deling; 1878-80, M. S. Clapp; 1881-82, S. F. Bartlett.

Secretaries—1855, Philo E. Reed; 1856-60, J. D. Cox; 1861, Junius Dana; 1862, I. L. Fuller; 1863-82, H. F. Austin.

Treasurers—1855, ———; 1856, U. H. Hutchins; 1857-1860, B. N. Robbins; 1863-64, B. P. Jameson; 1865-72, Almon D. Webb; 1873-82, Peter L. Webb.

MAHONING COUNTY AGRICULTURAL SOCIETY.

Pursuant to a call for that purpose, a convention was held at Canfield on the 22d day of February, 1847, to deliberate upon the propriety of organizing an agricultural society for Mahoning county, under the provisions of an "act for the encouragement of agriculture," passed by the General Assembly of the State of Ohio, February 27, 1846. The call for said convention was signed by Hon. Elisha Whittlesey, Judge E. Newton, George Pow, Henry Manning, Asa Baldwin, Warren Hine, Silas C. Clark, and other prominent business men of the county.

The convention was well attended, and organized by appointing Judge E. Newton, chairman, and Silas C. Clark, secretary. The meeting was addressed by Hon. Elisha Whittlesey, who delivered an able speech on Competitive Exhibitions as a means of awakening more active inerest in all Industrial Pursuits.

At this meeting it was unanimously

Resolved, That we, the subscribers, agree to form ourselves into an agricultural society, to be known as the Mahoning County Agricultural society, in conformity to the rules and regulations established by the State board of agriculture, and pay the sum of $1 annually, during the existence of said society, or during the time we are members thereof; and to be subject to such constitution and by-laws as may hereafter be adopted by the society.

Whereupon one hundred and eleven names were placed upon the roll of membership. A committee was appointed to draft a constitution for the society, and report at an adjourned meeting.

The society next met April 7, 1847, when fifty-nine more names were added to the roll of membership. The committee appointed at the previous meeting reported the following constitution, which was adopted:

CONSTITUTION.

ARTICLE I.

SECTION I. This association shall be styled the Mahoning County Agricultural society.

SECTION II. It shall be the object of this society to elevate the standard and character of the husbandman, and to promote the true dignity of labor, to encourage domestic industry and enterprise in such agricultural, horticultural, and manufactural improvements as may incite an improved rural and home-adorning tastefulness throughout this community, and tend to the developement of the vast and manifold resources of Mahoning county.

ARTICLE II.

SECTION I. The officers of this society shall consist of a president, vice-president, secretary, treasurer, and five managers, who together shall constitute a board of government, and have the general administration of the affairs of the society; they shall be elected on the adoption of this constitution, and thereafter at the annual meeting, by the members of the society by ballot, and hold their office until their successors are appointed.

SECTION II. The president shall be chairman of the board of government, shall superintend the various departments, countersign all claims on the treasurer audited by the committee on accounts, sign all diplomas and certificates, and may, by giving suitable notice, convene the society or the board of government, at such time and places as he may deem expedient.

SECTION III. In the absence of the president the duties of his office shall devolve on the vice-president.

SECTION IV. The secretary shall keep a record of the proceedings of the society, and of the board of government, and shall countersign all diplomas and certificates relating to premiums. He shall also preserve all letters and papers appertaining to his department, and shall conduct the correspondence of the society with the advice and under the supervision of the president or managers; and deliver to his successor all books, papers, documents, etc., belonging to the society.

SECTION V. The treasurer shall collect and receive all funds due and belonging to the society, and disburse them only on the joint authority of the president and committee on accounts. He shall keep his accounts in a book kept for that purpose, and shall exhibit to the board of government on the first Wednesday of November of each year a statement of the receipts and expenditures of the current year, together with a list of members in arrears to the society, and the amount due from each. He shall also perform the duties of depository, and shall receive and distribute, under the direction of the managers, all minerals, seeds, plants, implements, books, animals, models of machinery, etc., that may be committed to his care; and deliver to his successor everything in his possession belonging to the society. He shall give bond with security, to the society, in the sum of $5,000, for the faithful performance of his duties, which bond shall be deposited with the secretary and recorded by him.

SECTION VI. The managers shall constitute a committee on accounts, whose duty it shall be to audit all accounts and if found just to approve them. They shall also make all the necessary arrangements for the annual show and fair.

ARTICLE III.

SECTION I. The board of government shall meet statedly at Canfield on the first Wednesday of April and November, and five of them shall constitute a quorum for business. They shall annually appoint a township committee consisting of one from each township in the county, and awarding committees, each consisting of three members; also fill all vacancies in the offices or committees that may occur by death or otherwise. They shall also make out the premium list and publish the same on or before the first Wednesday of May, annually.

SECTION II. It shall be the duty of the township committee to co-operate with the managers to promote the interests of the society in their respective townships. Their correspondence shall be addressed to the secretary.

SECTION III. It shall be the duty of the awarding committee to judge between the several articles or animals offered in competition, belonging to the class assigned to each committee respectively, and to award premiums to those entitled to them. But no premiums shall be awarded by the committees unless they deem the articles presented meritorious.

SECTION IV. No premiums shall be paid to any person except members of the society and their families, nor to any member who is in arrears to the society for his subscription; and in order to be entitled to premium awarded the person must have been present at the exhibition unless prevented by some cause satisfactory to the board of government.

ARTICLE IV.

SECTION I. Any citizen of the county may become and remain a member of this society by signing the constitution and paying the treasurer one dollar, and thereafter one dollar per annum for the use of the society, which amount shall be due on the 1st day of January of each year. Any member may withdraw by giving notice to the treasurer and paying all his arrearages.

SECTION II. The annual meeting shall be held at Canfield on the first Tuesday of October and the day following, at which time and place the cattle show and fair shall be held. But at the discretion of the board of government a later day may be appointed for the exhibition of such classes of articles as may not be ready at the time of the stated annual meeting.

ARTICLE V.

SECTION I. This society, its officers, and committees, shall be governed by this constitution and the rules and regulations prescribed by the Ohio State Board of Agriculture.

SECTION II. This constitution may be amended by the concurrence of two-thirds of the members present at any regular meeting, provided that an exact manuscript copy of the proposed alteration or amendment be submitted a proper time for deliberation prior to any decisive action thereon by the society.

No changes were made in the above constitution till 1856, when it was altered by increasing the number of managers from five to seven; and the number of days of fair from two to three.

In 1868 the constitution was amended by increasing the number of managers to eight, dividing them into two classes, and providing for the election annually of four to serve two years, and also by vesting in the board of government instead of the society the election or appointment of secretary and treasurer.

Again in 1878 the constitution was amended so as to allow persons living out of the county to become members and compete for premiums in all articles except domestic manufactures and field crops and gardens; also, the compensation of the secretary was fixed at $100 per annum, and treasurer at $50.

The business meetings of the society, in the first year of its existence, were held in the Congregational church at Canfield, and at the court house the second and third year. The stock on exhibition was shown on the streets of the village and adjoining fields. The Fourth annual fair of the society was the first one held on its own grounds. In 1851 the society bought five acres, enclosed it with a board fence, and charged all persons, except children under eight years, an admission fee of twelve and a half cents. Since that time additions have been made until the society now owns twenty-two acres, enclosed with a substantial fence, and furnished with a good half-mile track, and all the buildings and other improvements necessary to facilitate the convenient transaction of its business, and to accommodate exhibitors. The grounds and improvements are valued at $5,000.

FAIRS OF THE SOCIETY.

First, October 5, 1847; second, October 3, 4, 1848; third, October 2, 3, 1849; fourth, September 25, 26, 1850; fifth, October 7, 8, 1851; sixth, October 5, 6, 1852; seventh, October 4, 5, 1853; eighth, October 3, 4, 1854; ninth, October 2, 3, 1855; tenth, October 7, 8, 9, 1856; eleventh, October 6, 7, 8, 1857; twelfth, October 5, 6, 7, 1858; thirteenth, October 4, 5, 6, 1859; fourteenth, October 2, 3, 4, 1860; fifteenth, October 1, 2, 3, 1861; sixteenth, October 7, 8, 9, 1862; seventeenth, October 6, 7, 8, 1863; eighteenth, October 4, 5, 6, 1864; nineteenth, October 3, 4, 5, 1865; twentieth, October 2, 3, 4, 1866; twenty-first, October 1, 2, 3, 1867; twenty-second, October 6, 7, 8, 1868; twenty-third, October 5, 6, 7, 1869; twenty-fourth, October 4, 5, 6, 1870; twenty-fifth, October 3, 4, 5, 1871; twenty-sixth, October 1, 2, 3, 1872; twenty-seventh, October 7, 8, 9, 1873; twenty-eighth, October 6, 7, 8, 1874; twenty-ninth, October 5, 6, 7, 1875; thirtieth, October 3, 4, 5, 1876; thirty-first, October 2, 3, 4, 1877; thirty-second, October 1, 2, 3, 1878; thirty-third, October 7, 8, 9, 1879; thirty-fourth, October 5, 6, 7, 8, 1880; thirty-fifth, October 4, 5, 6, 1881.

PRESIDENTS.

Hon. Eben Newton, 1847-48; Hon. George Pow, 1849; Asa Baldwin, 1851-52; David Haynes, 1853-54; C. C. Brainerd, 1855-56; Martin Allen, 1857-58; Hon. Elisha Whittlesey, 1859-60; Hon. George Pow, 1861-70, inclusive; Richard Fitch, 1871-74; John M. Sears, 1875-76; Ward Dean, 1877-78; J. H. Shields, 1879-80; D. I. Richards, 1881-82.

VICE-PRESIDENTS.

Jacob Cook, 1847; George Pow, 1848; Asa Baldwin, 1849-50; David Haynes, 1851-52; C. C. Brainerd, 1853-54; George Pow, 1855-58; Alexander Pow, 1859-60; G. N. Brainerd, 1861; Richard Fitch, 1862-70; J. H. Shields, 1871; John M. Sears, 1872-74; C. S. Haynes, 1875; John M. Osborn, 1876; H. C. Beardsley, 1877; J. H. Shields, 1878; N. S. Baldwin, 1879-80; Peter Fullwiler, 1881-82.

SECRETARIES.

Silas C. Clark, 1847-49; J. M. Edwards, 1850-51; G. I. Young, 1852-53; H. B. Brainerd, 1854; T. M. Rice, 1855-58 (now Member of Congress from Missouri); A. P. Flaugher, 1859; J. M. Edwards, 1860; C. S. Mygatt, 1861; F. C. Nesbit, 1861-63; H. G. Ruggles, 1864; J. J. Moore, 1865-66; F. C. Nesbit, 1867-68; F. W. Beardsley, 1869-74; Jared Huxley, 1875-79; G. F. Lynn, 1880; Philo Huxley, 1881; Rev. C. L. Morrison, 1882.

TREASURERS.

William Little, 1847-52; Alexander Pow, 1853-57; F. G. Servis, 1858-60; Huwa Hoover, 1861-64; John S. Wilson, 1865-66; J. W. Canfield, 1867-74; F. W. Beardsley, 1875; G. F. Lynn, 1876-77; H. A. Manchester, 1878-82.

MANAGERS.

Joseph Wright, David Hanna, Jacob Baird, Asa Baldwin, John Cowden, 1847; Henry Manning, Cornelius Tomson, Joseph Wright, David Hanna, Asa Baldwin, 1848; Joseph Wright, David Hanna, Henry Manning, David Haynes, Cornelius Tomson, 1849; David Haynes, Joseph H. Coult, Francis Henry, David Bonsall, Warren Hine, 1850; Edwin Morse, Lemuel Bingham, Alexander Pow, Francis Henry, Warren Hine, 1851; Francis Henry, John Bingham, C. C. Brainerd, Warren Hine, Alexander Pow, 1852; Philo Beardsley, G. Lanterman, J. R. Truesdale, J. Gordon, Richard Fitch, 1853; G. Lanterman, J. R. Truesdale, Martin Allen, D. Bonsall, D. Thoman, Warren Hine, A. Moherman, H. K. Morse, 1854; G. Lanterman, David Bonsall, Martin Allen, B. P. Baldwin, H. K. Morse, 1855; David Bonsall, H. K. Morse, Martin Allen, James Predmore, M. Swank, G. Lanterman, B. P. Baldwin,

1856; B. P. Baldwin, James Predmore, David Haynes, Thomas Mead, Furman Gee, G. N. Brainerd, Francis Henry, 1857; Furman Gee, B. P. Baldwin, Andrew Shields, Robert Manchester, James Predmore, Thomas Mead, David Haynes, 1858; Furman Gee, Abram Ohl, David Haynes, Robert Manchester, James Predmore, Nathan Hartman, Thomas Mead, 1859; David Weikart, Nathan Hartman, Robert Manchester, Thomas Mead, Roswell Matthews, Abram Kline, Philo Beardsley, 1860; Robert Manchester, Roswell Matthews, Peter H. Bean, Robert Montgomery, L. T. Foster, Isaac Kirkpatrick, Abram Kline, 1861; Robert Manchester, L. T. Foster, Andrew Shields, Robert Montgomery, Roswell Matthews, Abram Kline, G. N. Brainerd, 1862 and 1863; Robert Manchester, Abram Kline, L. T. Foster, Roswell Matthews, Robert Montgomery, Nathan Hartman, G. N. Brainerd, 1864; L. T. Foster, David Lower, G. N. Brainerd, Abram Kline, Andrew Shields, Robert Manchester, Roswell Matthews, 1865; Robert Manchester, David Lower, J. H. Shields, W. H. Moherman, Roswell Matthews, L. T. Foster, Abram Kline, 1866 and 1867; L. T. Foster, John M. Sears, J. H. Shields, Abram Kline, David Lower, Roswell Matthews, Mathias Swank, 1868 and 1869; L. T. Foster, M. Swank, C. S. Haynes, Samuel Thoman, J. H. Shields, David Lower, Roswell Matthews, John M. Sears, 1870; L. T. Foster, M. Swank, C. S. Haynes, James M. Sears, David Lower, Ward Dean, John M. Sears, N. S. Baldwin, 1871 and 1872; J. M. Osborn, Lyman Schnurrenberger, C. S. Haynes, Clark Osborn, N. S. Baldwin, Samuel Thoman, David Lower, Ward Dean, 1873; J. M. Osborn, Lyman Schnurrenberger, C. S. Haynes, Clark Osborn, N. S. Baldwin, Moses Webber, David Lower, Ward Dean, 1874; Moses Webber, D. I. Richards, Ira M. Twiss, H. C. Beardsley, N. S. Baldwin, Clark Osborn, Lyman Schnurrenberger, J. M. Osborn. 1875; David Lower, Lyman Schnurrenberger, Clark Osborn, William Lasserman, D. I. Richards, Ira M. Twiss, H. C. Beardsley, N. S. Baldwin, 1876; N. S. Baldwin, D. I. Richards, H. N. Lynn, Peter Fullwiler, Lyman Schnurrenberger, David Lower, Clark Osborn, William Lasserman, 1877; David Lower, William Lasserman, C. S. Haynes, N. S. Baldwin, D. I. Richards, H. N. Lynn, Peter Fullwiler, Lyman Schnurrenberger, 1878; D. I. Richards, Peter Fullwiler, H. N. Lynn, Philo Huxley, David Lower, William Lasserman, Lyman Schnurrenberger, F. M. Moore, 1879; D. I. Richards, Peter Fullwiler, H. N. Lynn, Philo Huxley, David Lower, F. M. Moore, Alfred Peters, J. K. Wilson, 1880; J. W. Canfield, John Cronick, B. P. Baldwin, John Kirk, Alfred Peters, J. K. Wilson, F. M. Moore, David Lower, 1881 and 1882.

The darkest period of the association's history, in a financial point of view, was during the war, from 1861 to 1864, inclusive. Debts were created that burdened and crippled the society for years. Finally, by good management, the entire debt was liquidated, and soon thereafter followed the most prosperous years, financially, that the society has experienced. From 1872 to 1875, inclusive, the receipts were the largest they have been since the fair was organized. A full treasury led to increased expenditures, investments in permanent improvements on the grounds of the society, and a large increase of premiums offered. Diminished receipts since those years have somewhat embarrassed the society, with a debt of over $1,600. The present board of managers, however, are sanguine of a prosperous future.

The receipts from all sources have been as follows:

1847	$ 308 00	1865	$1585 36
1848	520 42	1866	1554 71
1849	516 82	1867	2218 20
1850	615 32	1868	2061 44
1851		1869	3123 61
1852	400 82	1870	2338 70
1853	414 90	1871	2875 26
1854		1872	4397 92
1855		1873	4204 99
1856		1874	4600 45
1857	768 04	1875	4372 73
1858	846 66	1876	3136 89
1859	1109 06	1877	2678 80
1860		1878	3818 43
1861		1879	3207 74
1862	596 48	1880	3338 79
1863	896 81	1881	2441 75
1864	1363 74		

The amount offered in premiums annually has gradually increased from $150—amount offered in 1847—to $2,500.

The amount awarded and paid annually has increased from $131.50 in 1847 to over $2,000 in 1880.

PIONEER SOCIETY.

The first attempt to organize an historical society for Trumbull county was made as early as 1840. The subject was discussed in the local press, but no definite action was taken, and the time passed when such a society could have made itself of much service to the historian. Much that has already become vague tradition, and can only be given as such, would have been preserved as true and indisputable history. The pioneers did not anticipate the interest a future generation would take in the story of their conflict with nature. Could all have foreseen what the very few yet remaining on the field of their early toil now see, there would be a wealth of material at hand from which to select our data.

The Mahoning Valley Historical society, though of recent organization, has taken vigorous hold of the labor of making a collection of record and reminiscence. Its inception was in May, 1874. In a conversation of three persons who casually met, old-time reminiscences were interchanged, and it was decided to call a meeting of old citizens for pleasure and a mutual exchange of traditional and actual knowledge. The following call was published in the papers:

> All who are in favor of a reunion of those who have been for thirty-five years or more residents of Youngstown, are requested to meet at the Tod house, Saturday, May 30 (1874), at 7 o'clock, to make arrangements for a reunion of old settlers.

This call was signed by Timothy Woodbridge, H. B. Wick, William Powers, G. King, J. M. Edwards, Madison Powers, Alex Kinnie, John Manning, J. Van Fleet, Joseph Barclay, and Henry Tod. A number of persons responded to this call on the evening of May 30th, and made preliminary arrangements for a pioneer reunion at the opera house on the 10th of September following. Dr. Timothy Woodbridge was selected chairman, C. B. Wick and W. G. Moore secretaries, and a committee of five, consisting of Timothy Woodbridge, J. R. Squire, J. M. Edwards, R. Holland, and Asahel Medbury, to collect historical facts. There was also appointed an executive committee, consisting of William Powers, Joseph Barclay, Henry Tod, John Stambaugh, and A. J. Woods.

The following general invitation was published in the papers in July:

> At a meeting held in the Tod house May 30th, by a number of our citizens who were residents of this township thirty-five or more years ago, it was resolved to hold a grand reunion of those who were then citizens on Thursday, September 10, 1874, and committees were appointed to make suitable arrangements. The committee on invitation and reception cordially invite all, whether now residents here or elsewhere, without further or special notice or invitation to meet with us on that day, namely, September 10, 1874, at 10 o'clock A. M., at the opera house in this city, and participate in the reunion. Ample accommodations will be provided for all. Those who can meet with us are requested to notify us by letter, or otherwise, previous to that time. Those who cannot meet with us are requested to communicate to us their present residence, with sketches of the history and reminiscences of the olden-time citizens, etc.

A second invitation was published in the papers September 1st, together with the order of exercises for the day.

The reunion was all the most earnest of the preliminary committeemen could have wished to make it. The following report appeared in one of the city papers:

> The reunion of old citizens, which took place here on Thursday, the 10th inst., transcended in interest all that had been anticipated from it. Quite early in the day the streets began to be thronged with men and women of the olden time. There were those here who had seen Youngstown when scarcely a score of houses stood to indicate the future that was in store for her. The greetings on all sides were interesting to hear, and the jokes that had not been told for many and many a year were revived and provoked a laugh as fresh and hearty as if they had happened but yesterday.
>
> Of those that gathered on that day there were not a few who had not seen the business and hum of life for many years. Weighed down with age, they had remained at home, passing in quietness and rest the close of lives which had begun amid the excitements, and toils, and vicissitudes of settling a new country. Some could tell of Indian wars and massacres, of the hard battle for existence which was fought in an unsubdued wilderness with the savage foe. There were here on that day soldiers of the War of 1812, and men who had lived in Ohio while she was yet a Territory. It is the story of three-quarters of a century—the history of the Western Reserve.
>
> The oldest man present was William Smith, now living in his township, near Lanterman's mill, about ninety years of age. Of the veterans of 1812, there were present James Foster, aged eighty-three; Samuel Fitch, eighty; Jacob Vail, and Rev. Wilson. Of the widows of soldiers of 1812 there were Mrs. Polly Jackson, Mrs. William McFarland, and Mrs. Polly Smith. Among the oldest persons, Jacob H. Baldwin, aged eighty-four, now of Kinsman; William Rice, aged eighty, now of Painesville; John Kimmel, aged seventy-nine; Philip Stambaugh, aged seventy-nine; Alexander McKinnie, aged seventy-five; Peter Kline, aged seventy-two; Dr. Lemuel Wick, aged seventy-one; J. F. Hogue, aged seventy; R. B. Baldwin, aged seventy-three; Ray Noble, aged seventy. The oldest native of Youngstown was Osirus Case, born in 1804. The oldest lady present, Mrs. Nancy Hine, of Painesville, aged eighty-four.

Mr. Edwards' welcome address was a well-timed outline of the early history of Youngstown. We reproduce a few of the first paragraphs. The historical part is all embodied in different chapters of this volume.

> MY FRIENDS:—The pioneers of the West, of this land we now inhabit, were a race of heroes. Less than one hundred years ago the State of Ohio, and more especially the Western Reserve, was an almost unbroken wilderness, the haunts of savage men and savage beasts. To subdue this wilderness, to convert the pathless forests into fertile fields, to replace the wigwam of the Indian with the comfortable abodes of civilization, and eventually to make this wilderness to blossom like the rose, those noble pioneers, taking, as it were, their lives in their hands, left their homes of comfort and luxury in the East, and, with stout hearts and strong hands, struck their axes into the huge growths of the forest, and prepared for us, their descendants and successors, a land whose superior in all the resources which, properly used, may make men prosperous and happy, is not to be found in any other portion of country on this earth.
>
> Those men and women have mostly passed away. To cherish their memory; to recall the history of those early days; to renew ancient friendship; to greet, as of old, companions and acquaintances from whom we have been long parted, we, their successors and early settlers of this, one of the earliest settled townships of the Reserve, have assembled here to-day. To all those present, to those who were residents of this township thirty-five or more years ago, to our invited guests and visitors, and those, as well, who have become residents at a more recent period and are here as spectators, we extend a cordial welcome.
>
> I have said that within one hundred years this country was a wilderness. I might have said, with truth, that it was so

within three-quarters of a century, within the lifetime of many now living, and, perhaps, of some here present. And yet it seems to the more youthful portion of those now on the stage of active life as if the period of the settlement of the Reserve, so recent, in fact, comparatively, was an event so remote in time that its facts and incidents are among the dim and hazy memories and traditions of antiquity.

A large portion of the history of the settlement of the Reserve is unwritten, and exists only in tradition. It is peculiarly so of this township. And yet this history is well worth collecting and preserving in durable form. We trust that this will be one of the results of our reunion to-day. I have gathered a few facts and incidents of this history, partly from records and documents, and partly from conversations with the pioneers and with our early settlers, which may be of interest, and propose to occupy your attention for a short time in their narration.

This occasion closed with a dance at the Tod house, in which all, old and young, participated. It was a joyful ending of a pleasant day.

This first reunion, which was primarily a Youngstown affair, led to the organization the following year of a society embracing in its membership the entire valley. The proposition to form an organized society took shape early in May, 1875. It was generally agreed that the society should not be confined to any one township or county, since the fundamental history of the whole valley was essentially the same in the whole territory included. It was agreed that the first annual reunion of the pioneers of the Mahoning valley should be held September 10, 1875, just one year after the reunion of the pioneers of Youngstown. The meeting, in accordance with this arrangement, was held in the opera house. The following officers and committees had previously been selected: H. B. Wick, chairman; William Powers, chairman committee of arrangements; John M. Edwards, secretary; Benjamin Weaver, stenographer. German Lanterman, Youngstown; James Brown, Lowell; Madison Powers, Liberty; Fred Kinsman, Warren; Charles Smith, Warren; T. W. Kennedy, Struthers; H. B. Wick, Youngstown; Sheldon Newton, Boardman; John M. Edwards, Youngstown; Warren Hine, Canfield, directors. Miss Grace Tod, chairman; Mrs. Richard Brown, Mrs. Mary Bentley, Mrs. John Besore, Mrs. William Breaden, Mrs. M. T. Jewell, Mrs. William Barclay, Mrs. James Ford, Mrs. W. H. Wick, Mrs. A. J. Williams, Miss Lute Van Fleet, Miss Eliza Powers, Miss Sarah Reno, John Kimmell, Joseph H. Brown, R. M'Millan, W. W. M'Keown, William Pollock, committee on reception.

The day was spent in the reading of narratives, the response to toasts, and in social amusements. The following is a list of old people present on that occasion, with their ages:

Poland, John Guthrie 67; William Logan 68, Mary A. Logan 66, James Moore 71, Joseph Seaton 80, George Dickson 67; Warren, John Harsh 81, Benjamin Stevens 88, Z. Van Gorder 70, E. D. King 70, Isaac C. Powers 70, Edward Potter 82, Boardman, John Zediker 82, Asa Baldwin 78, Henry Fankel 80, Sheldon Newton 69; Hubbard, Mrs. —— Osborn 67, Nathaniel Mitchell 72, Mrs. N. Mitchell 71, Catherine Hunt 69, Mrs. George Hagar 70, Daniel Shively 70; Youngstown, Elizabeth Lanterman 96, William Smith 91, A. Ritter, 92, Jonas Foster 83, Mary Woods 72, Sarah Ague 70, Henry Osborn 73, Parkhurst DeCamp 76, Jane Wick 84, Joseph H. Brown 65, James Orr 76, Elizabeth Woods 72, Thomas Davis 72, Asahel Medbury 76, Thomas Polly 69, Anna Goff 77, Alexander McKinnie 76; Kent, Christian Cackler 84, John V. Gardner 86; Sharon, Fanny Jackson 78; Bridgewater, Mary Briggs 82; Canfield, Eben Newton 80; Roy's Corners, Samuel Beaver 70; Cleveland, Hon. George Mygatt 73, N. C. Baldwin 74; Gustavus, Zephania Stone 82; Girard, David Goodwillie 73, George Hood 68; Paris, Amos Osborn 65; Newcastle, J. T. Duchane 77; Sandy Lake, Fletcher Houge 73; Coitsville, Elizabeth McFarland 85, Betsy Augustine 73, John Augustine 75, Polly Jackson 79, Mary Augustine 62, Nicholas Jacobs 65, James Davidson 73, Barbara McFall 66, William McClelland 72, Polly Kyle 77, Partridge Bissell 72, John Shields 72, William Stewart 68, Catherine Hurst 69, Tobias Kimmell 73.

At a meeting held at 8 o'clock in the evening a constitution was approved for the Mohoning Valley Historical society, and officers elected for the ensuing year as follow: President, William Powers; vice-president, Dr. T. Woodbridge; corresponding secretaries, John M. Edwards and A. B. Cornel; recording secretary, W. A. Beecher; treasurer, H. K. Wick; directors, H. B. Wick, Asa W. Jones, Reuben McMillan, A. J. Packard, and Henry Tod. It was provided in the constitution that the officers of the society shall consist of a president, and one vice-president for each township of the counties of Trumbull and Mahoning. These vice presidents were subsequently selected as follow:

Trumbull county—Warren, Frederick Kinsman; Braceville, George Stowe; Newton, Dr. J. F. Porter; Lordstown, Thomas Duncan; Weathersfield, Irwin Moore; Liberty, Boyd McClelland; Hubbard, Nathaniel Mitchell; Howland, Z. T. Ewalt; Vienna, Alexander S. Stewart; Mesopotamia, Charles A. Brigden; Bazetta, Aaron Davis; Gustavus, Miss Phebe M. Barnes; Bloomfield, Dr. George W. Howe; Fowler, Dr. Beach; Champion, Henry Rutan; Southington, Homer Norton; Bristol, A. A. House; Johnston, Josiah A. Hine; Vernon, E. A. Reed; Greene, Walter Bartlett; Kinsman, Rich. K. Hultz; Mecca, W.

S. Benton; Farmington, A. K. Woolcott; Hartford, T. A. Bushnell; Brookfield, J. E. Stewart.

Mahoning county—Youngstown, T. Woodbridge; Coitsville, John Shields; Austintown, William Porter; Milton, Francis R. Johnson; Berlin, George Carson; Ellsworth, Richard Fitch; Canfield, Eben Newton; Boardman, F. A. Boardman; Poland, Samuel McBride; Smith, William Johnson; Goshen, Joseph Bruff; Green, Lewis Templin; Beaver, I. B. Ruhlman; Springfield, Hiram Macklin; Jackson, David Anderson.

The work of preparing for publication a volume of historical collections was commenced in the fall of 1875. A neat volume of more than five hundred pages was issued the following year. It contains much that is valuable. It was the intention to publish successive volumes until the entire field was covered, but so far nothing further than the first issue has appeared.

The society has held annual reunions since its organization in 1876, and has been the means of bringing together the old citizens of the valley, of preserving and formulating traditions and innocent gossip of former years, of strengthening the bonds of friendship and creating a love and pride of home. Robert M. Montgomery succeeded Mr. Powers as president.

CHAPTER XVI.
THE REBELLION RECORD.

Beginning of the War—Contribution of Trumbull and Mahoning Counties—Organization of Regiments and Outline of their Service in the Field.*

This is not the place to tell the causes of the rebellion which cost the country a million of her

*NOTE.—The introductory regimental sketches are compiled mainly from Whitelaw Reid's History of Ohio in the War. It has been the object of the editor to give merely an index to the services of each regiment, which will enable the reader, with the aid of any amplified history of the rebellion, to trace the history of any organization in which he may be interested. The rosters have been compiled from the records in the Adjutant-general's office, at Columbus. If there are mistakes it is the fault of the records. There are, no doubt, omissions, particularly in the list of officers, drafted men, and substitutes, since the records are in such shape that it is impossible to trace these three classes to their addresses at the time of entering the service. The names of those whose original enrollment occurred in camp will, in many cases, be found omitted from the rosters. With these unavoidable exceptions the record will be found generally accurate.

bravest citizens. Such a discussion would involve the whole constitutional history of the United States. Conflicting civilizations, conflicting interests, and conflicting ideas concerning fundamental principles of government had several times threatened the disruption of the Union. During all this time the insolent pretensions and arrogant demands of the South were met by the loyal people of New England stock, with quiet determination to resist the growth of slavery and to cripple the power by which it was supported.

The winter of 1860-61 was employed at the South with busy preparations for the impending conflict; at the North it was a period of waiting and doubt. On the 5th of October, 1860, the initial step toward actual secession was taken, by the Governor of South Carolina addressing a confidential circular to the Governors of other cotton States asking their advice and counsel on the proposition to secede from the Union. Florida supported the proposition with something like enthusiasm. The other Governors were unwilling to commit their States to a proposition so glaring and extravagant. But defeat at the polls in November changed the attitude of Southern leaders. It became apparent that if an aristocracy was to be maintained an independent government must be established. Military companies were formed and equipped. The rabble, conspicuously indolent, found occasions for drill capable of being converted into hilarious holidays. The vanity of wealthy leaders and indolence of ignorant plebians hurried rebellion to a crisis while the Government was handicapped by an inactive Executive and deluded by the hope of a peaceful compromise. The whole North watched with most intense interest the operations at Charleston harbor, and at the same time the proceedings of the peace convention in session at Washington. At length all doubts, and all fears, and all hesitation came to an end when the telegraph spread on the 12th of April, 1861, the news of the first gun fired upon Sumter. The conflict was at hand, and the need of the hour was clear. A few days later President Lincoln published a call for seventy-five thousand soldiers, which was answered with an alacrity worthy of the great cause in which they were to take part. Camps were established in different parts of the State for organization. Cleveland was a place of rendezvous, where, by the close of April, four thousand men had collected anxious to go to the front. Of these one company was from Trumbull county, one from Mahoning, and a detachment of light artillery from both counties. Here begins the history of the Seventh Ohio Volunteer infantry known, in history as the "Bloody Seventh."

SEVENTH OHIO REGIMENT VOLUNTEER INFANTRY.

Out of the men collected at Camp Taylor on April 30, 1861, this regiment was organized. Three companies were from the city of Cleveland, one from Oberlin, one from Painesville, one from Warren, one from Youngstown, one from Norwalk, and one from Franklin. They were men who obeyed their first impulse, and were consequently ready—adventurous spirits whose hearts were in the cause. Many of them were men of culture, and came out of the refined professions; among them were merchants, and the ranks were filled with mechanics and laborers. The Seventh had perhaps fewer farmers than any of the later organizations. The news of war first reached the towns, and the first call for men was largely filled from the towns. It was on Sunday morning, early in May, that this regiment left Camp Taylor, and marched into Cleveland. They were dressed in citizens' clothing, and bore no arms. Indeed, only the self-conscious step of the raw soldiery and the rattling measures of martial music distinguished them from the accompanying crowd. Every soldier bore the hard expression of fixed resolution, while the multitude—men, women, and children—expressed their feelings by prayers and cheers, by exultation and tears. The regiment, more than one thousand strong, took the cars at Cleveland, and was soon in Camp Dennison, near Cincinnati. That wretched camp, bordered on the Miami river, was a cultivated field, and the rich loam soaked with water. No provision had been made for the reception of the regiment, but all set to work, and by evening huts had been built in which to bivouac for the night. The regiment was organized at Camp Dennison by the election of E. B. Tyler, of Ravenna, Ohio, colonel; William R. Creighton, lieutenant-colonel; John S. Casement, major. The regiment was placed under severe military discipline. By the time they had mastered the manual of arms and regimental and battalion movements the President issued a call for three years troops, or during the continuance of the war. The Seventh held a meeting, and almost unanimously voted to enter the three years service. Up to this time no uniforms had been supplied to the men; the citizen's dress was exchanged for the army blue. After a six days' furlough the regiment was mustered into the three years service. We are unable to give a roster of the three months men, the records not having been preserved.

This regiment began full duty in Western Virginia, having left camp June 26, 1861. The first camp was at Clarksburg where a stand of colors was received as a present from a Cleveland society. The first regular march of this regiment was to the village of Weston, June 29th. Before three miles had been covered, exhaustion required a reduction of baggage. Canteens had not been supplied, and as the day was oppressively hot there was much suffering from thirst. Weston was finally reached on the following morning, and the object of the march accomplished, which was to capture $65,000 in gold that had been deposited in the bank at that place by the Virginia government. The next march was to Glenville, where the Seventeenth Ohio was beleaguered by a force of rebels. By the time the Seventh arrived the rebels had fled. Supplies were by this time exhausted, and confiscation was the only means of subsistence. This was a severe trial upon the consciences of many of the Seventh, but hunger soon made a conquest of conscience, and confiscating became part of the regular daily duty of the regiment.

General Cox was at that time moving up the Kanawha valley, and the Seventh was ordered to establish communication with his division. While the regiment was encamped at Cross Lanes an order was received from General Cox ordering it to join him at Gauley bridge. When the regiment reached a position near General Cox it was ascertained that rebel General Floyd, with four thousand men, was preparing to cross the Gauley at Cross Lanes, the camp so recently vacated by the Seventh. A countermarch was ordered, and within seven miles of the old camp the enemy's pickets were encountered but easily driven back. The regiment bivouacked near Cross Lanes and stood on picket duty all night. At daybreak firing commenced, and in a short time a strong force of the enemy appeared in line of battle. The companies of the Seventh held different positions and acted independently of each other. They held their position bravely until forced back by an overwhelming force. One hundred and twenty men—killed, wounded, and prisoners—were left upon the field. The regiment was divided on the retreat, half finding its way back to Gauley, and the other coming into the National lines near Charlestown, several miles below.

While at Gauley the regiment received a present of a handsome stand of arms from the people of the Western Reserve. In October Colonel Dyer assumed command of the Seventh. The regiment participated in the pursuit of Floyd through West Virginia. It was then returned to Charlestown and thence transferred to Central Virginia and in close proximity to the rebel army. Rebel General Jackson anticipated an attack planned against him, by advancing against the Federal forces. General Lander, under whom the Seventh was serving, retreated, leaving Jackson to occupy Romney, and after several attempts to intercept Jackson bivouacked on Hampshire Heights for a period of ten days. This was in mid-winter; the winds were boisterous, the snow ten inches deep, and the cold intense. There was scarce any protection from the cold and rations were short, circumstances which caused great suffering. The only protection from storms was a hut made of rails and brush, and huge bonfires of logs. Pawpaw Station was next occupied, and the regiment remained there till the opening of spring. While in camp General Lander died, and General Shields succeeded to the command.

The battle of Winchester was the first general engagement in which the Seventh participated. On March 7, 1862, when Shields broke up winter quarters Banks had already occupied Winchester, Jackson having retreated without offering resistance. Shields made a reconnoissance to Strasburg, where a few rounds of artillery were exchanged. But little opposition being offered, the division returned to Winchester, covering the distance from where it started in four hours. Jackson stationed his army within four miles of Winchester, and on March 23d the rebel artillery opened a general engagement. Shields' division was early thrown to the front. The lines became furiously engaged about three o'clock in the afternoon, and until dark the battle raged. The Seventh performed a conspicuous part. Its loss was fourteen killed and fifty-one wounded, also several prisoners. Colonel Tyler was promoted to the rank of brigadier-general. Lieutenant-colonel Creighton succeeded to the colonelcy of the regiment.

From Winchester General Shields moved up the Shenandoah valley to Harrisburg, and from there falling back took a strong position near New Market. A few days later an order from the War department required the Seventh, with the remainder of Shields' division, to join General McDowell at Fredericksburg. The troops arrived at their destination May 21st, nine days having been consumed on the march, a distance of one hundred and thirty-two miles. When Shields' soldiers arrived at McDowell's camp they were completely exhausted, and threw themselves upon the ground to rest. On the following day President Lincoln and other officials arrived at McDowell's camp, and another day of toilsome review increased the discomfort of the wearied men.

Rebel General Jackson, as soon as Shields' division was withdrawn from the Shenandoah, pushed up the valley, and finding little opposition from Banks' army, made direct march toward Washington. It had been the Federal plan to march Shields' division toward Richmond, but this bold move on part of the opposition, required a change of arrangements. Shields hurried toward Jackson's rear, and the Third and Fourth brigades reached a point opposite Port Republic. Colonel Carroll was driven back, and by the time General Tyler came up a heavy force was prepared to meet him. Jackson began an assault at five o'clock on the following morning, and was promptly met with resolute resistance. The Seventh and Fifth Ohio became the center of the fight, and bore their conspicuous part with honorable bravery. The odds against General Tyler compelled him to meet the cunning Jackson with tactics of strategy. A wheat-field lay near the enemy's center. Under cover of standing wheat the Fifth and Seventh were double-quicked from point to point along the line, halting at intervals to pour a galling fire into Jackson's forces. For five long hours this movement was kept up, three thousand muskets repelling fourteen thousand of the flower of the rebel army. When a retreat was ordered by General Tyler, the Seventh was made the rear guard. The retreat was toward Washington, the Federal forces being hard pressed by the rebels. The Seventh never broke line, and sometimes halted to repel the enemy's advance. Jackson finally fell back toward Richmond.

Shields' division reached Alexandria, on the Potomac, and thence took steamer to the Peninsula to join McClellan, then operating against Richmond. In consequence of the Third and Fourth brigades being greatly reduced in numbers, they were ordered to disembark and go into camp near Alexandria. The First and Second brigades joined McClellan. In July the Third and Fourth joined Bank's forces near Little Washington. While at this point General Geary succeeded General Tyler as brigade commander. The latter was promoted to the rank of major-general.

General Pope assumed command of the army of Virginia, to which General Banks' corps belonged. The Seventh was placed in Banks' corps. On August 9th General Banks arrived at Cedar Mountain, which was held by Stonewall Jackson. Banks commenced the attack about 3 o'clock. The Federals were at great disadvantage, having to stand in an open field, while the rebels were protected by thick woods. The Seventh was advanced to the front in full range of the enemy's guns. The Federal ranks marched boldly to the woods and were engaged in a hand to hand struggle when night closed in on the bloody scene. The Federals retired a short distance for the night. Over three hundred men of the Seventh were engaged, of whom only one hundred escaped unhurt. The approach of General Lee required a retreat on part of the Federal forces, to Washington. A month of fighting and laborious marching followed. On September 17th was fought the bloody battle of Antietam. The Seventh was present but did not actively participate, except as a reserve force. In the fall of 1862 the Seventh was recruited by two hundred men. The original one thousand had been reduced by disease, in battle, and from other causes, to less than three hundred. In December the regiment went into winter quarters and was only once disturbed—by Stuart's cavalry, which was easily repulsed. The camp remained quiet until April 30, 1863. On that date a ten days' march was begun toward Chancellorsville, with eight days' rations; the march consumed ten days. On the day following the arrival of the Seventh the battle of Chancellorsville began. The Seventh was thrown into the hottest of the fight, being ordered first to support a battery and then a line of skirmishers. The latter soon fell back to the main line, but the Seventh continued the advance till ordered to retreat. Early on the following morning the Seventh occupied a line of rifle pits exposed to a terrible fire from the enemy. About noon it was transferred to its former position. While here it was left in the most hazardous situation. All the Federal forces withdrew, leaving the Seventh and two other regiments to cover the retreat. The conduct of the Seventh, both in action and retreat, was highly meritorious. Its entire loss was 14 killed and seventy wounded.

After a few days spent in reorganization, both armies began the race through Maryland into Pennsylvania. The Seventh reached Gettysburg on June 1, 1863, after a laborious march, and took a position on the left of the National lines. During that terrible battle the Seventh was hurried from point to point where reinforcements were most needed. It had the protection of breastworks during the hottest of the fight. It was consequently saved, only one man being killed and seventeen wounded.

After the battle of Gettysburg the Seventh was ordered, with other regiments, to New York to quell the riots, and on August 26th went into camp on Governor's Island. In September, the drafts being over and all disturbances being quieted, the Seventh returned to the Rapidan. While there the Twelfth army corps, to which it was attached, was consolidated with the Eleventh army corps, and formed the Twentieth army corps under Hooker, which was ordered to the Western department. They passed from Washington, over the Baltimore & Ohio railroad, through Columbus, Indianapolis, Louisville, and thence to Nashville and Bridgeport, Alabama, where they went into winter quarters. General Grant, then in command of the Western department, determined to drive the rebels from Lookout Mountain, and for that purpose concentrated his forces at Bridgeport. The Seventh was ordered to leave its comfortable winter quarters and join in the service. It was not brought under fire until the foot of the mountain had been reached, where the conformation of the ground gave ample protection. The enemy on top of the mountain, unable to bring their guns into range, attempted to resist the ascent of the Federal troops by shooting off the tops of the trees. A heavy fog soon enveloped the whole mountain, and the firing ceased. At dawn the enemy had disappeared, and the flag of the Union was planted on the highest pinnacle of that lofty and rugged mountain.

The enemy was hotly pursued across the plains of Chattanooga and up the sides of Mission Ridge, where but feeble resistance was met. This retreat cost the rebel army two thousand prisoners. On the 27th of November the enemy made a stand on Taylor's Ridge, to prevent the Federals from going through Thompson's Gap. Geary's brigade was ordered to storm the height. It formed in two columns on the railroad, the Seventh occupying the left of the rear column. Before advancing the gallant Colonel Creighton made a speech to his men, in which he said: "Boys, we are ordered to take that hill. Now I want to see you walk right up and take it." They advanced in face of a merciless fire on the front and on the left. Colonel Creighton, finding it impossible to advance directly, turned his men into a ravine, but they were still subject to a galling fire. The line approached a fence and while Creighton was facing the enemy's bullets, waiting the advance of his command, a rifle ball pierced his body. He gasped "My dear wife," and expired. Lieutenant-Colonel Crane had also fallen, and the regiment, bearing their loved commanders, made hasty retreat. Only one commissioned officer of the Seventh escaped uninjured. Nineteen were killed and sixty-one wounded. The regiment retreated to Chattanooga. Creighton and Crane were both from Cleveland, the former a printer, the latter a ship carpenter. Both were characteristically brave and admired. The loss to the regiment was severe and discouraging. It is no wonder that on the 1st of January, when the roll for re-enlistment was presented, these battle-worn troops were indisposed to join the service.

The winter was spent quietly at Bridgeport, Alabama, until May 3d. On that date the regiment left winter quarters and met the enemy at Rocky Face Ridge. Hooker's corps easily overcame opposition, and followed in pursuit until June 11th, with but slight loss on either side. The recruits of the Seventh were consolidated with the Fifth, and with that regiment served with Sherman through Georgia. The veterans' term of service having expired, they were sent North by rail to Nashville, thence by steamer to Cincinnati. On Saturday, June 24, 1864, the regiment took its departure for Cleveland, and on July 8th was mustered out of the service.

The Seventh had served more than three years, during which time more than one thousand eight hundred men had served with it. It had served in more than a score of battles, and, except about sixty new recruits, only two hundred and forty men remained to bring home the colors, riddled by shot and shell. It had served East and West, was always in the van, and participated in the hottest battles of the war.

COMPANY H.

COMMISSIONED OFFICERS.

Captain Joel F. Asper, promoted to lieutenant-colonel May 20, 1862, *vice* Creighton promoted.
First Lieutenant George L. Wood, promoted to captain of Company D, January, 1862, *vice* Captain Dyer.
First Lieutenant Holbert C. Case, promoted to first lieutenant January, 1862, *vice* Wood promoted; resigned February 1, 1862.
Second Lieutenant James P. Brisbine, promoted from first sergeant to second lieutenant January 1, 1862; promoted to first lieutenant Company E.

NON-COMMISSIONED OFFICERS.

First Sergeant Joseph Pollock, mustered out with company.
Sergeant John L. Davis, mustered out with company.
Sergeant Ellis Fox, wounded at Ringgold, Georgia.
Sergeant John A. Choffee, mustered out with company.
Sergeant John Pollock, mustered out with company.
Corporal Henry H. Pierce, mustered out with company.
Corporal David L. Hurst, mustered out with company.
Corporal Samuel M. Vance, mustered out with company.
Corporal Charles Glendening, wounded at Ringgold, Georgia.
Corporal Joseph Kincaid, wounded at Ringgold, Georgia.
Corporal Davis Wintersteen, wounded at Ringgold, Georgia.
Wagoner James Mosier, wounded at Ringgold, Georgia.

PRIVATES.

Mustered out with Company—Stephen Burrows, Reuben W. Bower, Seth J. Coon, William Hunter, Willard A. Levens, Jacob A. Mohler, Eurasius C. Palmer, George W. Parker, Salmon S. Pelton, Hiram Shaffer, William H. Tracey, Alfred Webster, Benjamin Wilson, Addison White, Henry A. Weir.
Killed in Battle—William Vanary, at Ringgold, Georgia; William H. Bennett, at Ringgold, Georgia; Ambrose C. Trimmer, at Chancellorsville, Virginia; Henry Bacon, at An-

tietam, Maryland; Malcolm Eckenrhoad, at Cedar Mountain; Frederick Groth, at Winchester, Virginia; William H. McClurg, at Cedar Mountain; Calvert C. Miller, at Cedar Mountain; James H. Merrill, Ringgold, Georgia; Maney Smith, at Chancellorsville, Virginia; George B. Swisher, at Cedar Mountain.

Died—William Bowman, 1861; Joseph J. Bonegh, 1861; Harrison P. Bower, 1863; Owen Gregory, 1862; James Hunt, 1862; Wesley Harkelrode, 1863; Homer P. Raynor, 1862; Selby C. Starlin, 1861; Harrison P. Shaffer, 1860; Charles H. Tenney, 1863.

Not Reported—Louis J. Clark, John Daws, Thomas McMullen, Williams H. Overmire, Louis T. Phillips, Samuel J. Wise.

Discharged before expiration of service.—Charles A. Brooke, Robert S. Bower, James P. Brisbine, William D. Bradon, Stanley M. Casper, George W. Moor, Frederick H. Roberts, Hiram J. Bell, Stephen E. Bishop, William C. Baldwin, George W. Bower, Nelson Chaffee, Alfred Combs, Arthur A. Cavanah, Charles L. Campbell, Horace H. Downs, John C. Fox, Charles Garnard, Israel H. Gregg, Reuben R. Hine, Henry W. Hescock, Alonzo Inskeep, John Lentz, James M. McWilliams, John Moyer, Monroe L. Miller, Hiram McQuiston, Robert V. Murray, John C. Osborn, Morris Osburn, Daniel O'Conner, Alpheus J. Packard, William Perkey, Charles Perkey, William S. Reed, Russell Stone, David W. Summerville, Frederick S. Swisher, Chauncy B. Scott, John C. Scott, John S. Williams, Archibald Wise, Riley White, Hubbard J. Wolden, Edwin Wood.

Transferred.—William H. Bannister, Daniel D. Owen.

COMPANY I.

COMMISSIONED OFFICERS.

Captain William R. Sterling, detailed on staff of Major-general D. Butterfield in 1862; rejoined the regiment July 8, 1864, and mustered out of service July 11, 1864, per order of Major-general Starr, Sixth cavalry.

First Lieutenant Samuel McClellan, transferred to company H, by reason of promotion to captain May 20, 1862.

First Lieutenant Seymour S. Reed, promoted to captain November 25, 1862, and mustered by Captain De Russey.

First Lieutenant Leicester King, promoted to second lieutenant of company I, December 17, 1861, vice Fitch resigned; promoted to first lieutenant June 1, 1862, vice McClelland promoted; dismissed the service for drunkenness, by order of the Secretary of War, December 22, 1862; order revoked, and allowed to resign to date December 23, 1863.

Second Lieutenant Edward F. Fitch, resigned November 23, 1861.

Second Lieutenant Joseph Cryne, transferred from company B to company I, by order of W. R. Creighton, commanding regiment, May 25, 1863; vice King, killed in action at Ringgold, Georgia, November 27, 1863.

NON-COMMISSIONED OFFICERS.

Sergeant Edward J. Couch, promoted and mustered out with company.
Sergeant William Christy, mustered out with company.
Sergeant William Crowley, reduced to ranks, and mustered out with company.
Sergeant Hiram B. Deeds, promoted and mustered out with company.
Corporal John S. Ray, mustered out with company.
Corporal William J. Jones, mustered out with company.
Corporal Stephen Willock, mustered out with company.
Corporal Reynolds Cowden, mustered out with company.
Corporal Gebhard Seibold, mustered out with company.
Corporal Charles Smith, mustered out with company.

PRIVATES.

Mustered out with company.—William H. Duncan, James Decker, John C. Deboll, George A. Earle, William J. Evans, John Evans, William Fraher, Richard M. Freeman, Anthony Gordon, Frederick Hall, Jacob Heisley, William Kelley, Henry Lewis, Robert M. Patton, Adam Schneider, James Snider, Bustament Sims, John Smith, Allen Walker, John Wilson.

Killed in battle.—Robert McClelland at Dallas, Georgia; James Bisp at Winchester, Virginia; Alonzo H. Burton, George Fox, James P. Ray, and James D. Stephenson at Cedar Mountain, Virginia.

Died.—William W. Houck and Andrew J. Kelley, 1862; Charles S. Cowden, 1864; John D. Dicks, 1861; Alfred Jackson, 1862; Abraham D. Crooks and Lemuel J. Cecil, 1861; Joseph B. Deeds, 1864; Jacob Marlett, 1863; John McFadden and John Shannon, 1862; James C. Shaaff, 1861.

Not reported.—William Andrews, Caleb L. Bryant, Henry Clemens, Joseph Cuffman, Henry G. Edwards, Robert J. Ferguson, Christopher G. Gail, Michael H. Salley, John McKenzie, Samuel Pierce, Charles E. Rice, Francis L. Vanamburg, Thomas D. Williams.

Missed in action.—Charles Berrett and Charles Bustine at Cross Lanes, Virginia; Michael Campbell at Port Republic, Virginia; Ferdy Larkin, Morgan Llewllyn, and George V. W. Thompson at Cross Lanes, Virginia; William Waldorf at Cedar Mountain, Virginia.

Discharged before expiration of service.—Joseph H. Ross, James Housel, James A. Bell, John C. Jackson, John J. Manning, William Burch, John V. Brown, Maskel Bispham, David M. Daily, Benjamin Davis, William W. Earle, John Fishcorn, John N. Fredenburg, Henry Garlo, James R. Greer, Garvin Jack, James Johnson, Daniel H. Johnson, Clark Knox, Samuel P. Kemp, Hugh Moore, Martin V. Owrey, Richard Phillips, Randall B. Palmer, Henry Sower, Michael Sower, Anthony Williams, David Williams, Paul C. White, William G. Wilson, Lewis Wood, John Weir.

Transferred.—Stephen Mosier, John Beiler, Alfred Conelley, Thomas B. Doran, William Fairgrieve, George Metcalf, Theodore W. Pratt, Thomas J. Williams.

COMPANY B.

PRIVATES.

John Stone, Thomas Walker, Benjamin F. Williams.

COMPANY C.

PRIVATE.

Jeremiah Reeve.

NINETEENTH REGIMENT OHIO VOLUNTEER INFANTRY.

Just two weeks after the Seventh left Camp Taylor for the field, a sufficient number of full companies had reported at the same place to form another regiment, which was mustered into the three months' service as the Nineteenth Ohio volunteer infantry. Three companies of this regiment, B, C, and G, were mainly from Trumbull and Mahoning counties. They were transferred to Camp Jackson, near Columbus, May 27, 1861, and at once proceeded to the election of officers. The old militia rules were then practiced which gave regiments the privilege of choosing their own officers. In the later days of the war such democratic management was not tolerated. Samuel Beatty was chosen colonel, Elliott W. Hollingsworth lieutenant-colonel, Lewis P. Buckley major. Companies A and B were placed on guard duty, and the other eight companies sent to Camp Goddard to master the manual of arms and drill. The regiment was united at Bellaire June 21st, and arrived at Parkersburg on the 23d. The Eighth, Tenth, and Nineteenth were organized into a brigade and placed under command of William S. Rosecrans for service in West Virginia. The brigade reached a position in front of the rebel fortifications at Rich Mountain July 7th. General Rosecrans, in his report of the battle, said: "Seven companies of the Nineteenth deployed into line and delivered two splendid volleys, when the enemy broke." And again: "The Nineteenth distinguished itself for the cool and handsome manner in which it held its position against a flank attack, and for the manner in which it came into line and delivered its fire near the close of the action." Three men were wounded in this battle.

By September 26th nine companies had re-enlisted for the three years' service, and by November 7th the regiment was at Camp Dennison fully armed and equipped for the full term. Trumbull and Mahoning's contribution to the second organization will be found at the close of this sketch. November 16th it took steamer for Louisville, and was the first regiment to occupy Fort Jenkins, near Louisville. The first death was that of David Clunk, whose team ran over him.

The Nineteenth was brigaded under command of General Boyle, and marched to Columbia, where it encamped. January 16th it moved up the river for the purpose of intercepting Zollicoffer, but the rebel defeat at Spring Mills rendered a force on the Upper Columbia unnecessary, and the regiment returned to Columbia. While lying at that place typhoid fever made sad havoc among the men. From Columbia the regiment marched to Nashville early in March, one hundred and twenty miles of the distance being covered with shoes in such condition that they might be termed barefooted. On March 18th the regiment took steamer at Nashville for Savannah, and on Sunday, April 6th, was within fourteen miles of that place. It set out on double-quick in the direction of the booming cannon. At dark the regiment was on the boat that was to transport it to Pittsburg Landing. Thousands of stragglers and wounded men lined the river bank, and the army was driven almost to the river. The dreary, rainy night which followed was passed upon the field, and daybreak opened with a sharp rattle of musketry, and the enemy appeared pursuing the advantage gained on the previous day. A published report says:

The colonel and Captain Manderson held their men steady and deported themselves, as did their officers and men, with coolness and courage until the colonel ordered them back to a position from under the enemy's battery. Major Edwards was shot dead from his horse, and a number of privates were killed and wounded.

The success of the second day at Pittsburg Landing is well known. The next ten days were spent upon the field, without tents or camp equipage, in mud and rain, and the terrible stench of the battlefield.

The regiment participated in the approach to Corinth. It was while on this march in April, 1862, that Captain Franklin E. Stowe, of company G, died of disease. On May 29th it entered Corinth after the enemy and followed the enemy in pursuit as far as Brownsboro. It subsequently joined the army under Buell and marched to Florence, Alabama, and to Battle Creek, at which place Lieutenant David W. Hildebrand died of disease.

The Nineteenth was present at Bardstown Turnpike, but did not participate. It afterwards engaged in a running skirmish at Crab Orchard, where it captured a rebel gun. The regiment marched through Somerset, Glasgow, Gallatin, and Nashville into camp on the Murfreesboro turnpike. December 26th, the regiment, under command of Major Manderson, began the march toward Murfreesboro. On the last day of the year it was thrown across Stone river, on the left, for the purpose of swinging around into Murfreesboro, but the disaster to McCook's right wing compelled a withdrawal. The river was recrossed and by determined resistance the rebel advance was checked.

On January 2d the Fourteenth and Twenty-third brigades, to which the Nineteenth was attached, recrossed the river and received the full charge of the rebel column under Breckinridge. They were forced to retreat, but the rebels coming into range of the massed batteries were driven back with great slaughter. The Nineteenth Ohio and Ninth Kentucky were the first across the river in pursuit. More than a mile was gained, four pieces of artillery captured, and, had not darkness interfered, the pursuit would have been carried into Murfreesboro. But this success was accomplished with great cost. Captain Bean, of company E, Lieutenant Bell, of company C, Lieutenant Donovan, of company B, and Sergeant-major Tylee were killed. Lieutenants Southerland and Keel were severely wounded. The regiment entered the battle with four hundred and forty-nine men, and lost in killed, wounded, and missing two hundred and thirteen, nearly one-half. Murfreesboro was occupied on January 4th, and the Nineteenth went into camp on Liberty turnpike. Lieutenant-colonel Hollingsworth resigned, Major Manderson was promoted to his place, and Captain H. G. Stratton made major.

The whole army remained in camp till June 28th. In August the Nineteenth crossed the Cumberland mountains, and in September, at Craw-fish Springs, had a brisk skirmish with the enemy, in which two men in company D were killed. On September 18th the Nineteenth, supported by two other regiments, made an advance upon the enemy. With a cheer the regiment advanced upon the enemy, drove them back, and captured several prisoners and a battery. Compelled to retreat by a superior body of rebels they were mistaken for a detachment of the enemy and fired upon. This mistake cost several lives. September 20th, the second day of the battle of Chickamauga, the regiment held an important position and performed an important share of the fighting till nightfall, when the whole army retreated to Chattanooga. During the siege the regiment remained at Chattanooga, and on November 23d made an advance on Orchard Knob, in which twenty men were lost. On November 25th it charged on the rebel works at Mission Ridge, and without orders scaled the rugged mountain and aided in driving the rebels down the opposite side.

The Nineteenth marched with Sherman to Knoxville. This was a most arduous march, the men being only half clothed and half shod.

They left tracks of blood on the snow. Finding that Longstreet had raised the siege of Knoxville the forces moved to Flat creek, where over four hundred of the Nineteenth re-enlisted in the veteran service. The regiment returned to Chattanooga, and thence to Ohio, reaching Cleveland February 16th.

The veterans were promptly in camp at Cleveland by March 17th, and reached Knoxville on the 24th, where they awaited the opening of the Atlanta campaign, in which the regiment participated throughout. The loss in the campaign was 2 commissioned officers and 28 privates; wounded 6 officers and 96 men; missing, 13 men. After leaving Atlanta the Nineteenth, under Thomas, started northward to arrest the advance of General Hood. It participated in the battle of Nashville and in the subsequent pursuit of Hood. The regiment was employed at Huntsville and Chattanooga, and between these points till July, 1869, when it was ordered to Texas.

October 31st the Nineteenth was mustered out of the service at San Antonio, Texas, and started on its return home. It reached Columbus, Ohio, November 22d, and was paid off and finally discharged at Camp Chase, November 25, 1865, having performed nearly five years of honorable service.

COMPANY B.
COMMISSIONED OFFICERS.

Captain Lewis R. Fix, promoted from second lieutenant to first lieutenant of company E, August 1, 1862; promoted to captain March 24, 1864, and transferred to company B; was wounded at Atlanta, Georgia, in right hand, August 4, 1864; mustered out with company.

Captain James M. Nash was captain of company B from original enrollment; was promoted to major July 27, 1863, and transferred to field and staff; promoted to colonel of regiment.

Captain James R. Percival was first lieutenant of company B from original enlistment to December 2, 1862; promoted to captain and transferred to company K; rejoined by transfer from company K July 27, 1863; resignation accepted November 25, 1863.

First Lieutenant Wesley Upson, promoted from private to sergeant of company K September 25, 1861; promoted to second lieutenant April 14, 1863; was transferred to company E July 28, 1863; was promoted to first lieutenant and transferred to company B August 4, 1864; in command of company B to May 17, 1865; mustered out with company.

First Lieutenant Daniel Donovan, promoted from second lieutenant of company B to first lieutenant, December 3, 1862; was killed in action at Stone River, December 31, 1862.

First Lieutenant Calvin T. Chamberlin, promoted from sergeant to first sergeant December 31, 1861; promoted to second lieutenant December 31, 1862; promoted to first lieutenant February 5, 1863.

Second Lieutenant Henry M. Fusselman, promoted to second lieutenant from sergeant April 14, 1863, and assigned to company D; rejoined by transfer May 12, 1863; was promoted to first lieutenant August 4, 1864, and transferred to company F.

Second Lieutenant Jacob Bidaman, promoted to sergeant from corporal June 1, 1862; promoted to first sergeant July 27, 1863; promoted to second lieutenant August 4, 1864; promoted to first lieutenant March 8, 1865, and transferred to company I.

Second Lieutenant Onesimus P. Shaffer, promoted from private to hospital steward February 18, 1862, and transferred to field and staff; promoted to second lieutenant March 8, 1865, and assigned to company B; resignation accepted May 19, 1865.

NON-COMMISSIONED OFFICERS.

Sergeant Reynolds I. Cowden, mustered out of service, promoted from private.

Sergeant James Beatty, mustered out with company, promoted from private.

Sergeant Gideon Fusselman, mustered out with company; promoted from private.

Sergeant Daniel F. Lentz, mustered out with company; promoted from private.

Sergeant Robert A. Rolston.

Corporal David Hogg, promoted from private.

Corporal Mark Godward, promoted from private.

Corporal Joseph F. Smith, promoted from private.

Corporal Augustus Dilly, promoted from private.

Corporal Former T. King, promoted from private.

Corporal Giles C. First, promoted from private.

Corporal Richard Duke, promoted from private.

Corporal William Meyers, promoted from private.

Musician Clark Snyder.

PRIVATES.

Mustered Out with Company.—Daniel H. Brown, Dillon P. Gardner, John Green, George S. Gillum, Paul W. McDonald, John A. McDonald, Adam Mathews, Washington Sexton, William Stanley, Ammi Stilson.

Recruits.—George Ague, William J. Bartlett, Frank Burt, William Calhoon, Charles W. Higgins, Harvey T. Keller, William N. Landon, Alexander Martin, John P. McFetridge, Boston M. McEwen, Peter M. Warner, George Washington.

Killed in Battle.—Daniel Cooper, John Marks, Henry Ague, James Bohmer, at Stone River; Benjamin Bohmer, Lovejoy Station, Georgia; Mathew G. Courtney, James Jewell, Stone River; Charles Jacobs, Chickamauga; John A. Johnson, Stone River; James W. Johnson, Picketts Mills, Georgia; William Mitchell, Lovejoy Station, Georgia; George Parish, Chickamauga; Andrew J. Porter, Kenesaw Mountain, Georgia.

Missing in Action.—Charles Hume, disappeared before Corinth; Alexander Burrows, disappeared before Chickamauga.

Died.—Stephen W. Allerton, 1862; Joshua Beatty, 1863; James P. Brownlee, 1863; John A. Brownlee, 1863; Isaac Davis, 1863; James F. Gardner, 1865; John E. M. Hindman, 1862; Albert Hively, 1862; Peter F. Hively, 1863; James H. Mathews, 1863; Charles T. Murphy, 1862; Russel Roberts, 1864; Jesse Smith, 1863; Emery Stacy, 1862; John S. Stewart, 1864; Zacharias Sisco, 1865; Samuel Vogon, 1864; Hosea H. Weyle, 1862.

Not Reported.—Early Bartlett, Allan W. Forney, Adam Hum, Oliver Macklin, Moses Sisco.

Discharged Before Expiration of Service.—Christian Felder,
Aaron R. King, John W. Vaninker, Thomas L. Sexton, George S. Boak, Charles S. Burr, Calvin M. Klingan, Charles R. Caner, William Ague, Albert L. Augustine, Joel Bailey, Thomas Brisbine, John Burnett, James H. Clark, Willis Clark, Samuel Clark, Calvin M. Chrigan, Henry Crum, John A. Dickson, William M. Dubes, James Dobbins, Hughey Dorian, John W. Early, Alonzo Early, John Evans, Connell Gallagher, James Godward, John Godward, Joseph Hively, Otis Hulbert, John O. Hubler, Alfred W. Humes, Hudson Hulbert, Lewis Howlett, Albert Howlett, George T. Hinchliff, Adam Hum, Iria Ransom, Martin V. B. King, Albert King, Rufus Kirk, Levi Leach, Hiram S. Lyon, Joshua Mathews, Milton Mathews, Joshua Mathews, Benjamin Mathews, Samuel R. Lindsay, Harmon McFall, John C. McConnell, John McLaughlin, William McCurdy, James B. McCrone, Oliver Musser, Reuben D. Rauch, David Roland, Samuel F. Sexton, Moses Sisco, James D. Shields, Daniel J. Sheehy, John A. Stevens, William P. Stewart, David L. Stambaugh, James Truster, Jacob Truster, James W. Thornton, George W. Veasey, Henry M. Vail, John O. Wilkson, Isaac Zigler.

Transferred.—James Alexander, James K. Bailey, Ephraim Koblentz, Ephraim Echelinman, George King, John Lemont, William Lewis, Samuel A. Shaffer, Lyman Tyler, John Zeigler.

COMPANY C.

COMMISSIONED OFFICERS.

Calvin F. Chamberlin, promoted from sergeant to first sergeant company B, January 1, 1862; promoted to second lieutenant, November 23, 1862; promoted to first lieutenant; December 31, 1862; promoted to captain; transferred to company C, August 4, 1864; mustered out with company.

Henry G. Stratton, captain, discharged to accept promotion as major, January 16, 1863; wounded in battle of Stone River, December 31, 1862.

Uriah W. Irwin, captain, died of wounds received in action at Chickamauga, Georgia, December 6, 1863; was first lieutenant of company H; promoted to captain April 14, 1863, and transferred to company C.

James G. Bailey, first lieutenant, promoted from sergeant to first sergeant July 27, 1863; to first lieutenant March 9, 1865; mustered out with company.

Oscar O. Miller, first lieutenant, transferred to company I, March 5, 1862, by order of Colonel Beatty.

Job D. Bell, first lieutenant, promoted from second to first lieutenant December 31, 1862; killed in battle of Stone River, January 2, 1863.

James S. Kettle, first lieutenant, promoted from private in company F, to first lieutenant and transferred to company C, April 1, 1862; resigned June, 1863.

First Lieutenant Homer C. Ried, promoted to captain and transferred to company K, March 9, 1865.

Second Lieutenant John C. Culbertson, promoted from sergeant to first sergeant April 14, 1863; to second lieutenant July 27, 1863; to first lieutenant and transferred to company A, January 6, 1865, by order of Colonel Stratton.

Second Lieutenant Homer J. Ball, promoted from private in company I to sergeant, December 7, 1861; promoted to second lieutenant and transferred to company C, February 19, 1862; resigned April 18, 1862.

NON-COMMISSIONED OFFICERS.

Sergeant Asahel Adams, promoted to first sergeant; mustered out with company.

Sergeant Newton Gregg, promoted to sergeant; mustered out with company.
Sergeant Newell Mead, promoted to sergeant; mustered out with company.
Sergeant Alvin T. Smith, promoted to sergeant; mustered out with company.
Sergeant Marcellus O. Musser, promoted to sergeant; mustered out with company.
Corporal Ira A. Haight, promoted to corporal; mustered out with company.
Corporal George W. Allen, promoted to corporal; mustered out with company.
Corporal William W. Henry, promoted to corporal; mustered out with company.
Corporal William Dean, promoted to corporal; mustered out with company.
Corporal Dallas Burnett, promoted to corporal; mustered out with company.
Corporal Robert L. Carson, promoted to corporal; mustered out with company.
Corporal Charles Freas, promoted to corporal; mustered out with company.
Corporal Harvey Myers, promoted to corporal; mustered out with company.

PRIVATES.

Mustered out with company.—Joseph Fisher, Daniel Glaspy, Jacob Hilliard, Joseph Landers, Frederick Lewis, Jonas Rader, Joseph Scott, Alfred Wilson, Milo Wilson, James F. Wilson, John F. Foonderlin, Warren Draper, Israel I. Lewis Adam Lyons, Abraham Van Wye, Jacob White, Robert Percell, James Arnold, Noah J. Cummins, William A. DeLong, B. Grephart, Daniel Horn, Isaac W. Holloway, Jeremiah Miller, William Smith, Gottlieb Silley, Thomas J. Cummins.

Killed in Battle.—William E. Haight at Chickamauga, Georgia; Henry S. Sheffer, Stone River; Peter C. Allison, Chickamauga, Georgia; Horace H. Bailey, Shiloh, Tennessee; Barney Laughron, Kenesaw Mountain, Georgia; Ira F. Powell, Shiloh, Tennessee; Hiram Hader, Kenesaw Mountain, Georgia; Lucius J. Scott, Peach Tree Creek, Georgia; Seldon S. Truesdall, Stone River, Tennessee; Peter Wilson, Kenesaw Mountain, Georgia.

Deaths.—John Aldridge, 1862; John Thomas, 1862; William Anderson, died in Andersonville prison; George Bennett, 1864; James Boyd, 1863; John Barth, 1865; Noah J. Dolly, 1863; James Evans, 1864; Clark Latin, 1863; Charles Lander, 1862; Charles E. Masters, 1862; William Masters, 1863; George Parsons, 1862; Daniel Powell, 1864; David Rease, 1864; Reuben Remalin, 1862; Jesse D. Reed, 1862; Mathias Stoneroek, 1865, Charles J. Tallister, 1862; Addison Trimble, 1863; David Vandermulin, 1862.

Not Reported.—Bonner King, Henry Brazelle, Andrew S. Cuther, Henry Henson, Thomas Jenkins, William Reiter, William Sanders, Jefferson Shaw.

Discharged Before Expiration of Service.—John B. Lewis, Thomas A. Beerly, Benjamin F. McCarty, Henry H. Townsend, Albert W. Haight, Andrew Arnett, Nerus J. Anthony, Henry W. Allen, William F. Barnett, Alex B. Burnett, Charles G. Burton, Nehemiah S. Baldwin, Washington Brown, Milo Burnett, Aaron Crispen, John B. Cottrill, Nathan Draper, John H. Dunn, Richard Danford, John L. Davis, William J. Davis, Lorenzo Darling, Silas S. Ernest, John Evans, William W. Flower, Homer W. Folsom, Warren Finn, William P. Gartman, Kidder Hulin, Simonson Hulin, Thomas Howell, William M. Horn, James A. Hardy,

Thomas L. Harris, David Jones, Joseph Jewell, John D. King, William Leavitt, Joseph Leavitt, Albert H. Lewis, Horace M. Miller, Joseph R. Milikin, Thomas G. McClain, John W. Masters, Samuel Miner, William F. Mahony, Jonathan D. Miller, Daniel McVay, Joseph S. Nelson, Almond M. Pool, Abner Rush, Robert Reed, Wayne M. Richmond, Henry K. Speckler, James Smith, William H. Sheffer, Byron L. Setterfield, Henry Spunse, John L. Smith, Theodore Seivering, Winfield Thompson, James J. Truesdall, Charles Humphreys, James F. Wilson, John Wilson, James Wooley, Albert B. Allen.

Transferred.—George M. Hall, William P. Friend, Jefferson H. Hall, Henry King, Albert Miner, William J. Miller, James Nelson, Elisha Robins, John H. Reiter, John N. Weeks, Wilson Miller.

COMPANY D.

NON-COMMISSIONED OFFICER.

Corporal James Shingleton, appointed July, 1865.

PRIVATES.

Wallace Shoemaker, killed near Marietta, Georgia; James A. Barber, died January, 1865; Benjamin Reiehard, died June, 1863; Joseph Miner, deserted from stockade; Hiram Forney, Nathan Smith, John W. Crise, John Davis, Samuel Hardinger, Emery Smith, discharged.

COMPANY E.

PRIVATES.

Thomas Kincaid, Phillip McCall, Christian Miller, Thomas J. Rupp, Ferdinand Smith, discharged; William H. Stock, transferred.

COMPANY F.

PRIVATES.

Harvey H. Shipley, David M. Rainsburg, J. D. Gouser, promoted to corporals; Enos Swan, W. H. H. Agler, Jacob Cunningham, Mirah Hipsher, Jacob Kirk, veteran recruits; Charles F. Somers; Allen H. Stamlaugh, Charles Frankle, Christ Stuckey, Daniel J. Wilhelm, Godfrey Zangg, recruits wounded; Winfield Wyandt, killed at Picketts Mills; N. M. Fugate, died March, 1863; Jesse Vanies, died May, 1864; William Agler, not reported; John F. Cook, Edward L. Hall, John Bush, Levi Cunningham, John R. Ross, Peter Soverland, discharged.

COMPANY G.

COMMISSIONED OFFICERS.

Captain Almon K. Roff, promoted from corporal to sergeant, company I, March 20, 1862, to second lieutenant April 14, 1863, to first lieutenant, and transferred to company G January 21, 1864; promoted to captain January 7, 1865, mustered out with company.

Captain Franklin E. Stowe, died at Pittsburg Landing, Tennessee, April 30, 1862, from disease contracted in camp.

Captain Cyrus Trease, promoted from first lieutenant, company F, to captain April 14, 1863, and transferred to company G; resignation accepted December 18, 1862.

Captain Correl Smith, promoted from first lieutenant to captain April 14, 1863; discharged October 4, 1864, on account of wounds received in action.

First Lieutenant Phillip C. Meek, promoted from corporal, company D, to sergeant January 1, 1864, to second lieutenant March 9, 1865, and transferred to company G; promoted to first lieutenant October 1, 1865; mustered out with company.

First Lieutenant William A. Knapp, promoted to first lieutenant from second lieutenant, company A, and transferred to company G April 14, 1863; promoted to captain January 21, 1864, and transferred to company F.

First Lieutenant George M. Hull, promoted from corporal, company C, to sergeant-major, and transferred to field and staff January 12, 1863; promoted second lieutenant, and assigned to company A, August 5, 1864; promoted to first lieutenant, and assigned to company G January 1, 1865; transferred to company D September 30, 1865.

Second Lieutenant Ambrose C. Scheffer, discharged September 15, 1862, by order of Secretary of War.

Second Lieutenant Russell Case, resignation accepted March 26, 1863.

Second Lieutenant Jason Hurd, promoted from first sergeant to second lieutenant April 14, 1863; promoted to first lieutenant August 4, 1864, and transferred to company A.

NON-COMMISSIONED OFFICERS.

First Sergeant Lauriston Lane, promoted from private to corporal.

Sergeant Azariah R. Kelly, promoted from private to corporal.

Sergeant Joel Johnson, promoted from private to corporal.

Sergeant Robert Cridebring, promoted from private to corporal.

Sergeant Manning Anderson, promoted from private to corporal.

Corporal William J. Helsdey.
Corporal John C. Roberts.
Corporal Jacob Reep.
Corporal Thomas C. Carson.
Corporal Henry S. Green.
Corporal William C. Parks.
Musician Ulysses J. Adgate.

PRIVATES.

Veteran Private.—Daniel Cutting.

Recruits.—Franklin M. Peter, John H. Murry, Tracy R. Green, Charles McGeary, William H. Pugh, Stewart Robinson.

Killed in Action.—Charles Castinore, at Stone River; Robert J. Presho, killed on skirmish line.

Died.—John C. King, 1862; Robert Truesdell, 1862; John Adams, 1864; John Cravat, 1862; William Caley, 1863; Richard Hunt, 1863; Moses Hedrick, 1863; Thomas Hatcher, 1864; Franklin S. Hicok, 1864; Orange F. Merwin, 1862; John Moore, 1863; Lester S. Oviatt, 1862; William A. Park, 1863; David W. Park, 1864; John K. Rodgers, 1862; Abraham Segar, 1862.

Not Reported.—George Peck, Boal Andrew, William H. Fenton, John W. Green, William Jones, Hamilton McGill.

Discharged Before Expiration of Service.—William F. Hurst, John Brown, Cyrus L. Worth, John H. Clark, William L. Dailey, Allison J. Hatheway, Sanford Lawton, Evan Price, James Athinson, Thomas B. Blair, John J. Brister, Charles Benedict, Samuel Cravat, Ebenezer Champlain, Michael Casey, Harvey Cramer, Ezra Cutting, Isaac Crawford, John Chaisty, Sylvester Doty, Lyman Dunn, James R. Dowley, Hiram G. Duff, William Evans, Alexander Evans, George W. Elliott, Eli Fulwiler, Benjamin A. French, Theodore Finney, George F. Gordon, Richard Gorman, George W. Grost, Alonzo Harrington, John Hurst, Jr., James S. Hicok, Walter Hincheliff, Adam Hoffman, Edmund Hitchcock, John Jenkins, Robert J. Kincaid, John Kelly, Lester Lane, George W. Lawson, Riley D. Miller, Gilbert Merwin, Richard McReady, William S. Worth, Ansel M. Worth,

Erastus E. Oviatt, Albert Parker, Thomas Phelps, Herman Potter, Thomas Richards, Samuel Rex, George Reiter, Thomas Stephens, Dwight Sherman, Edmund Stewart, Eli Segar, Charles Steven, Henry Townsend, Robert L. Taft, Joseph Widnoleee, Hiram Willbee, Judson C. Wilmulth, Alexander Walker. George Taucer, Eli Teagley, George Teagley.

Transferred.—Owen L. McCarty, Peter Shafer, Benjamin T. Battles, James C. Graham, Plimpton Kyneth, David Ort, Francis Sheler.

NINETEENTH OHIO VOLUNTEER INFANTRY.

FIELD AND STAFF.

Sergeant Lyman Tyler, killed at Stone River.
Musician Henry J. Couch, mustered out 1862.
Musician James A. Hogue, mustered out 1862.
Musician Cornelius E. Simmons, mustered out 1862.
Musician Lewis M. Pollock, mustered out 1862.
Musician Truman Palmer, mustered out 1862.
Musician Theodatus G. Harber, mustered out 1862.
Musician Dwight Kimmel, mustered out 1862.
Musician Oliver W. Weiner, mustered out 1862.
Musician Wilkes Stigleman, mustered out 1862.
Musician Samuel E. Holland, mustered out 1862.

TWENTIETH REGIMENT OHIO VOLUNTEER INFANTRY.

The Twentieth Ohio volunteer infantry was organized in response to the first call for three months' troops in May, 1861, with Colonel Charles Whittlesey as colonel, and Manning F. Force as lieutenant-colonel. Colonel Whittlesey had graduated at West Point and made considerable reputation as an engineer and geologist. He had performed important service in the Lake Superior region, and when thrown into active service at the head of a regiment gave his attention to constructing works for the defense at Cincinnati. While engaged on these works the regiment was under direct command of Lieutenant-colonel Force, by whom they were trained for field duty. Colonel Whittlesey resigned April 19, 1862, and Lieutenant-colonel Force was promoted to colonel and subsequently to brigadier-general. Harrison Wilson was the third colonel of the Twentieth regiment. First-lieutenant John C. Fry was promoted to captain and with that rank entered the three years' service. He was promoted to colonel of the regiment in January, 1864.

On the 14th of February the Twentieth arrived before Fort Donelson and was under heavy fire during the following day. It was then ordered to the extreme right and held in reserve during the remainder of the battle. Though not drawn into the heat of the fight the regiment deported itself creditably in this first action in which it was called. After the surrender of the fort the Twentieth was sent north in charge of prisoners and became scattered all over the country. By the middle of March seven companies of the regiment were collected on the Tennessee river. While in camp at Adamsville, on April 6th, the booming of cannon was heard at Pittsburg Landing. At three o'clock the regiment started for the field and took a position on the right of the army. In the next day's fight the regiment participated with considerable loss and a full share of honor. It was in command of Lieutenant-colonel Force, Colonel Whittlesey being in command of a brigade. During the advance on Corinth the Twentieth remained on duty at Pittsburg Landing, where sickness and death made terrible ravages. At one time less than one hundred men were able to appear on parade duty. After the fall of Corinth it was transferred to Bolivar, where it was left on garrison duty. At this point the health of the regiment greatly improved. In August, 1862, rebel General Armstrong with thirteen regiments was repulsed by the Twentieth and two other regiments, but with the loss of two companies, G and K, by capture. Of so much importance was this affair considered that several officers were promoted for gallantry.

In the fall of 1862 the Twentieth was assigned to General Logan's division of the Seventeenth army corps. It proceeded southward and reached Memphis on January 23, 1863. In May the Thirteenth corps moved towards Raymond, where the Twentieth Ohio lost in an hour's struggle 12 killed and 15 wounded. At the conclusion of this fight three cheers were given for the "Twentieth Ohio boys." It then moved on through Clinton, Jackson, and Champion Hills, where the regiment was placed in advance position in a ravine, and held it against the massed advance of the enemy till its ammunition gave way. It then fixed bayonets and prepared to charge, but the timely arrival of the Sixty-fifth Ohio relieved it of such desperate action. By May 21st the regiment reached the rear of Vicksburg. It performed an honorable part in the Vicksburg campaign. More than two-thirds of the men re-enlisted in January, 1864, and in March returned to their homes on veteran furlough. They again rendezvoused at Camp Dennison, May 1st, and from there were transferred to Clifton, Tennessee.

On the 23d of June the regiment arrived at Kenesaw mountain. In the battle which followed it performed a dangerous part. It participated in the battle of Atlanta, and subsequently accompanied Sherman to the sea. Its service was concluded in that direction by the surrender of Savannah. After some skirmishing and fighting in Carolina it reached Raleigh, and on April 15th, when it became known that Johnston had asked terms of surrender, the men were crazy with joy. They stood on their heads in the mud, threw their knapsacks at each other, and hugged each other in mad delight.

From Raleigh the regiment marched via Richmond to Washington; it participated in the grand review of May 24th, and from Washington was transferred to Louisville. June 18th the Twentieth Ohio was returned to Columbus and mustered out.

COMPANY H.

COMMISSIONED OFFICERS.

Captain James Powers, resigned February 9, 1862, at Cincinnati, Ohio; promoted from first lieutenant December 5, 1861.

First Lieutenant Henry M. Davis, promoted April 14, 1863, and transferred to company C.

Second Lieutenant Henry O. Dwight, promoted to first lieutenant April 12, 1863, and transferred to company G.

Second Lieutenant Herman H. Sherwin, promoted from sergeant February 19, 1862; resigned March 31, 1862, and honorably discharged.

Captain Edward C. Downs, appointed first lieutenant October 9, 1861; promoted to captain February 19, 1862; promoted to major February 20, 1864; transferred.

Captain Peter Weatherer, promoted to major April 23, 1865, and transferred to field and staff.

Captain William M. Barrington, promoted from first sergeant company I to captain July 5, 1865; mustered out with company.

First Lieutenant Jesse S. Felt, mustered out with company.

NON-COMMISSIONED OFFICERS.

First Sergeant James M. Wonder, mustered out with company.

Sergeant James E. Bader, mustered out with company.
Sergeant Wesley Craig, mustered out with company.
Sergeant Solomon F. Henninger, mustered out with company.

Corporal Lorain Ruggles, mustered out with company.
Corporal Daniel Brobst, mustered out with company.
Corporal Lewis Ginn, mustered out with company.
Corporal Colgate J. Busey, mustered out with company.
Corporal James J. Starley, mustered out with company.
Corporal George Hoagland, mustered out with company.

PRIVATES.

Mustered Out with Company.—David Barringer, John Barringer, George W. Boyd, Daniel Buck, Peter Bush, Lester Cook, John Crum, Jupiter P. Fusselman, Daniel E. Goodheart, Michael Gillen, Benedict B. Hashman, Alfred

Hunt, Levi Hood, Heston O. Kyle, John Longaberger, Franklin Lucas, Martin Craig. Hiram Mace. Christopher Martin, Willis Maxfield, John Le McIlersh, William Moran, John Moore, George C. Seward, Israel Stihle, Benjamin F. Taylor, John Wickline, Amos Wright.

Discharged Before Expiration of Service.—William G. Downs, Hiram Ohl, James Quackbush, Will J. Grinnell, Jonathan Lodwick, Samuel Hughes, William F. Hughes, Albert G. Black, Gottlieb Bock, Alfred Boyd, Charles Flick, John A. Fulk, William Goodheart, Samuel Hookney, James K. V. Horn, Emery Kilbert, John Lawrence, David Longaberger, George Lawrence, Ensign Lawrence, James B. Miller, William Ohl, John Owry, Isaac Owry, George Richmond, Nathan Smith, Jacob W. Snook, James Snider, Samuel B. Spears, Jacob P. Simon, James Winans.

Transferred.— Hezekiah Chryst, Russel Lee.

Not Reported.—Franklin Hart, Henry Lee, William McCarty, Thomas Morand, Frederick Myers, David R. Bright, Peter Grim, David Gilmore, Thomas Gilmore, Samuel Goodheart, Harrison Glendenning, Mason Hamon, John Hamon, Samuel Hood, Alexander Longimore.

Discharged Before Expiration of Service. – Theodore Muirenberger, John S. Smith, Nelson Strock, Frank Van Arne, Lemuel White, Amos Wright.

Died.—Alexander Biel, 1862; Granville Caswela, 1863; Solomon Fulk, 1861; Uriah T. Fulk, 1863, Dorsey E. Huxley, Addison J. Leach, 1862; Henry Lawrence, 1863; Isaac McNelly, 1862; Uriah N. Oviatt, 1862; Franklin Richards, 1862; Charles Sechler, 1862, Henry Shively, 1863; William Taylor, 1862; Eleazer Quackenbush, 1864; Joseph Fusselman, 1864; Nathan Hensinger, 1864; Benjamin Knos, 1864; Isaac Stock, 1864; Lester C. Robbins, 1864; James M. Thomas, 1864.

Not Reported.—Benjamin D. Elliot, John Hogin, William M. Ray.

TWENTY-THIRD REGIMENT OHIO VOLUNTEER INFANTRY.

A part of company E, of the Twenty-third Ohio volunteer infantry, was recruited in Mahoning county. The regiment organized at Camp Chase in June, 1861, with W. S. Rosecrans in command as colonel. October 15, 1862, E. P. Scammon succeeded to the colonelcy and he was succeeded by R. B. Hayes, who had enlisted as major. After the promotion of Colonel Hayes to the rank of brigadier-general, James M. Comly succeeded to the colonelcy. Few regiments were favored with better commanders. It bore through the entire conflict an honorable part, and takes high rank among Ohio organizations. It served in West Virginia, bore a conspicuous part at South Mountain and at Antietam, Barryville, North Mountain, and Cedar Creek.

The Twenty-third was mustered out of the service at Cumberland July 26, 1865, and was transferred to Camp Taylor and discharged.

COMMISSIONED OFFICERS.

William W. Cracraft, promoted second lieutenant January 2, 1863.
William McKinley, Jr., promoted commissary sergeant April 15, 1862; promoted second lieutenant April 24, 1862.
Surgeon John McCurdy, appointed surgeon Eleventh Ohio volunteer infantry November, 1862.

COMPANY B.
PRIVATES.
Oscar Bosley, Horace A. Olmsted, mustered out with company.

COMPANY C.
William S. Crowell, substitute.

COMPANY E.
NON-COMMISSIONED OFFICER.
Corporal Ezra J. McComb, mustered out with company.

PRIVATES.
Mustered out with company.—W. D. Courtney, Joseph H. Dumars, Daniel Eberhart, Dwight D. Kimmel, William O. Logan, Charles W. McNabb, Henry J. Nannah, Jered D. Porter, Joseph T. Shaffer, John G. Spears, Israel Cisco, A. J. Tindy, recruits.
Prisoners.—David M. Cobb, John A. Livingston, John Reed, Benjamin B. Stilson, recruits.
Died in prison 1864.—Daniel Blackman, recruit.
Died from wounds 1864.—B. Whitmore, recruit.
Discharged. –Thomas Carter, Thomas Crow, Alfred W. Pain, John H. Smith, recruits.

COMPANY G.
Not reported.—William M. Brandle, John Coffman, James Ryan, drafted; William H. Love, substitute.

COMPANY I.
COMMISSIONED OFFICER.
Corporal John N. Chamberlein, appointed captain 1865.
NON-COMMISSIONED OFFICER.
William M. Stokes, appointed corporal 1865, drafted.
PRIVATE.
Calvin B. Whitmore, transferred to company F.

TWENTY-FOURTH OHIO VOLUNTEER INFANTRY.

This regiment was organized under the first call of President Lincoln for three years troops. Company F was recruited in Trumbull county; Huron, Muskingum, Sandusky, Columbiana, Adams, Montgomery, Highland, and Cuyahoga counties contributed the other nine companies. The regiment left Camp Chase for the field July 24, 1861, and was placed on guard duty at Cheat Mountain, Virginia. The enemy was in force only fifteen miles distant. September 11th it was drawn into an engagement, in which it conducted itself with coolness and order. In the spring of 1862 the regiment was assigned to the Western department, and in February went into camp in Nashville. Early in April it marched towards Pittsburg Landing, and on the 5th reached Savannah, five miles from that place. On Sunday morning the roar of artillery was heard, and the regiment at once placed in readiness to move. There being no boats to transport it across the river, it marched through the deep swamp and arrived in time to take part in the closing action of the first day. On the second day of the battle the regiment bore a brave part, though the loss was fortunately small. Major Albert S. Hall, who enlisted from Warren, was severely wounded. From Pittsburg Landing the Twenty-fourth marched to Corinth and participated in several skirmishes on the way. It was one of the first regiments to enter Corinth. It followed in pursuit to Alabama, and in July was encamped at McMinnville, Tennessee.

In December, 1862, when Rosecrans left Nashville, the regiment was reduced to three hundred men. With this strength it went into the battle of Stone River. The regiment was assigned to an important post, and held it faithfully. Colonel F. C. Jones, Major Terry, and Lieutenant Harmon were killed the first day. Four commissioned officers were killed in this engagement, and the regiment lost one-fourth of its strength. The Twenty-fourth participated in the battle of Woodbury, Tennessee, January 24, 1863; at Lookout Mountain, at Mission Ridge, at Chickamauga, at Taylor's Ridge, and at Ringgold. Company D re-enlisted in the veteran service.

The remaining companies were mustered out at the expiration of their term of service.

COMPANY A.

COMMISSIONED OFFICER.

Second Lieutenant Charles R. Harmon, assigned to company A December, 1861; to company H February, 1862; killed at Stone River.

PRIVATE.

Cassius M. Giddings, recruit.

COMPANY B.

COMMISSIONED OFFICER.

John W. Brooks, enlisted May, 1861; transferred from company F January, 1862; appointed captain company B, August 11, 1862.

COMPANY F.

COMMISSIONED OFFICERS.

Captain Albert S. Hall, promoted to major December 20, 1862 (appointed colonel of One Hundred and Fifth Ohio volunteer infantry).

Captain Warrington S. Weston was mustered in with the company June 16, 1861, as first lieutenant; promoted captain December 20, 1861, and resigned by reason of disability July 19, 1862.

First Lieutenant Emerson Meris was mustered in with the company as second lieutenant June 16, 1861; promoted to first lieutenant, and transferred to company G December 16, 1861.

Second Lieutenant Daniel Reynolds was mustered in with the company as corporal, and appointed fifth sergeant October 12, 1861; appointed first sergeant December 16, 1861; promoted second lieutenant March 1, 1862; resigned July 12, 1862.

Second Lieutenant Willard J. Stokes was private from enrollment till January 25, 1862, when promoted second lieutenant; resigned October 12, 1862.

NON-COMMISSIONED OFFICERS.

First Sergeant John J. Musser, mustered out with company.
Sergeant James D. Burnett, mustered out with company.
Sergeant Emmons T. Gray, mustered out with company.
Sergeant Michael Barron, mustered out with company.
Sergeant Daniel O. Sewalt, mustered out with company.
Corporal Allen H. Long, mustered out with company.
Corporal Aaron Robbins, mustered out with company.
Corporal William Manly, mustered out with company.
Corporal Jacob Fox, mustered out with company.
Corporal Hugh Quinn, mustered out with company.
Musician Thomas Hall, mustered out with company.

PRIVATES.

Mustered out with company.—Leonard Blessing, William Adams, John W. Brown, James Chisholm (wounded at Stone River), Thomas Church, Edward Cox, Peter Donnelly, Hugh Dunnelly, Wilkinson Douglass (taken prisoner at Chickamauga), Wallace W. Drake, Michael Finnegan, David Greenwalt, John Given, Samuel Henery, William Kysett, John Kelly, Jackson Lenhart, Theodore A. Lockwood, Hiram Patten, Almon S. Sackett, Samuel S. Sackett, Daniel Seagraves, Edward Sholder (taken prisoner at Chickamauga), William Smiley, Philip Stansfield, Joseph Williams.

Died.—Egbert Andrews, 1863; Robert Ewing and James Quigley, 1862; John Beck, 1864; John H. Cowen, 1863; Charles Delong, Willard Goodwin, William Sanders, and Irwin Star, 1862.

Not reported.—Francis M. Wood, Henry Erwin, David C. Chadwick, Joseph Drsler, Albert Fox, John Grummit, Joseph D. Harris, William R. Ludlow, Thomas Latimer, Frank E. Lyman, Barney McBride, Joshua Martin, Matthew Sergeant, James Wood, Thompson Hall.

Discharged before Expiration of Service.—John P. Lake, Amzi C. Williams, Charles Raymon, Richard Elliott, William S. Fuller, George H. Gibson, Alanson Kennedy, Gilbert S. Lane, Thomas Paradine, Jacob H. Robinson, John Supple, Jerome Stoll, Henderson Smith, William R. Spear, Doctor B. Sherman, Lewis C. Smith, Martin Tyrell, William Tague, John E. Tuttle, John Q. Wilson.

Transferred.—Charles G. Harman, William R. Townsend, William Olmstead, Charles Hayward, John W. Brooks.

TWENTY-SIXTH REGIMENT OHIO VOLUNTEER INFANTRY.

Company G, of this regiment, was organized in Mahoning county. The other companies were from the counties of Ross, Delaware, Butler, Guernsey, Champaign, Scioto, and Madison. It was mustered in July, 1861, at Camp Chase, and was soon after sent to the Kanawha valley. It remained on scouting duty until January. In

Rosecrans' advance on Sewell Mountain the Twenty-sixth led the movement and guarded the retreat. The service of this regiment in the early part of the war was laboriously severe, although no opportunity was offered to try its powers on the field of battle. In January, 1862, the Twenty-sixth was transferred to the Department of the Ohio, afterwards known as the Department of the Cumberland. It was under General Buell through the whole campaign of 1862, and suffered with his army the hardships of forced marches, but had no opportunity to display courage on the field. It bore a reputation for order and discipline, and in those particulars was a model. In a slight engagement with Forest at McMinnville, Tennessee, Colonel Young and the Twenty-sixth, supported by three other regiments, repelled the enemy and made the important capture of General Forest's battle horse, which was subsequently shot under Colonel Young on the battle of Perryville, while in the command of the Fifty-sixth. The first general engagement in which the Twenty-sixth participated was at Murfreesboro, December 26, 1862. On that day the command devolved upon Major Squires; several gallant and successful charges were made on the enemy, one of which was of great advantage. The enemy's retreating rear guard was driven back and the fire of a burning bridge extinguished. Major Squires was presented with an elegant sword as a mark of appreciation of his services on that day.

The Twenty-sixth performed a gallant part in the battle of Stone River. It was one of several regiments which stood firm against rebel General Bragg's dashing columns, while the Union army on the right and left gave way. The Twenty-sixth was the apex of a convex line of battle which stood immovable for several hours. On that day nearly one-third of the regiment was either killed or disabled. This regiment was present at Tullahoma, at Shelbyville, and at Chattanooga. Its bloodiest day was at Chickamauga, where it was in the thickest of the fight. Three-fifths of all engaged were killed, wounded, or captured. One company (H) lost twenty-one out of twenty-four men engaged. There was no surrender of wounded men.

We copy from Reid the conduct of this regiment at Mission Ridge:

It occupied nearly the center of the front line of assault,

and was there called upon to sustain the concentrated force of the rebel circular line of forty cannon and thousands of muskets. The assault was made in the face of this terrific fire, and the column worked its way slowly and painfully, yet steadily and unfalteringly up the long and rugged slope of that blazing, smoking, jarring, blood-drenched, and death-laden mountain, fighting its way step by step, every minute becoming weaker by the exhaustive outlay of strength in so prolonged a struggle, and thinner from the murderous fire of the foe from above, until with less than half the command, with the entire color guard disabled, the colonel, bearing his own colors, spurred his foaming and bleeding horse over the enemy's works, and they threw down their arms, abandoned their guns, and gave themselves to precipitous flight. In this action the Twenty-sixth captured fifty prisoners and two cannon. Later in the day the Twenty-sixth Ohio and Fifteenth Indiana, under command of Colonel Young, captured a six-gun battery the enemy were attempting to carry off in their retreat, and flanked and dislodged a strong body of the enemy, who, with two heavy guns, were attempting to hold in check the National forces until their trains could be withdrawn. These guns also were captured. In token of their appreciation of Colonel Young's gallantry his command presented him with a splendid sword.

The Twenty-sixth, after the fight on Mission Ridge, could muster few more than two hundred men out of the one thousand who two years before had entered the service. The Twenty-sixth, half fed, half clad, battle-scarred, and worn out by marching and fighting, almost to a man re-enlisted on January 1, 1864. It was the first regiment of the Fourth army corps to re-enlist for the veteran service, and the first to arrive home on veteran furlough.

After the expiration of its furlough the Twenty-sixth rejoined the Fourth corps at Bridgeport, Tennessee, whence it joined under Sherman in his Atlanta campaign. It maintained its splendid fighting reputation at Resaca, Kenesaw, Peach Tree creek, Jonesboro, and all minor engagements. It participated in the pursuit of rebel General Hood to Nashville and in the successful battle which followed. It again participated in the pursuit of the defeated rebels to Alabama, and reaped a full share of the spoils of victory. The Twenty-sixth participated in the Texas campaign in the summer of 1865. It suffered greatly in consequence of heat, thirst, and other annoyances. It was mustered out of the service October 21, 1865, and at once transported to Camp Chase, where it was paid off and discharged.

COMPANY G.
COMMISSIONED OFFICER.

Captain Samuel C. Rook, enrolled as captain; resigned March 6, 1863.

First Lieutenant William H. Ross, enrolled as first lieutenant; promoted to captain and assigned to company I July 20, 1862.

First Lieutenant David McClellen, promoted from second lieutenant and assigned to company D; transferred to company G July 19, 1862; killed December 31, 1862, at battle of Stone River, Tennessee; was second lieutenant from enrollment.

PRIVATES.

Veterans.—George Brown, John Adams, James Daily, Elijah G. Graham, Myers Horn, Frank Lyons, Theodore Lehman, Callender McFadden, Benjamin R. Moss, John Stever, James L. Thompson, Lewellyn Williams.

Killed in Battle.—John Jennings, at Stone River; Joseph Fullerton, Chickamauga; Nicholas Krichbaum, Stone River; Robert M. McCauley, Chickamauga; William Crum, Chickamauga; James F. Evans, Chickamauga; John Karn, Stone River; John Lewellyn, Chickamauga; Daniel Mitchell, Chickamauga; James McEvay, Chickamauga; John Tagg, Stone River; Daniel Williams, Chickamauga.

Missing in Action.—Joseph Reese, Isaac Ritter.

Died.—James Cochran, 1864; John F. Woods, 1864; Luman Parmelee, 1864; John Smith, 1865; Samuel Hirch, 1861; William Brown, 1864; Cornelius Deasy, 1864; Francis Jones, 1863.

Not Reported.—Thomas Clark, Thomas G. Davis, Deedare Gushard, John Lytle, John Hoover, Joseph Price, Joseph Thomas.

Discharged Before Expiration of Service.—Edmund C. Miller, Thomas Legget, Joseph A. Eager, Timothy Deasy, James Walker, George W. Bear, John Moore, Charles Barclay, John Bush, Richard Coyle, John F. Davis, Thomas Edmunds, Arthur Glenn, John Gale, Washington Gardener, George W. Griffith, Lewis Hughes, Isaac Jenkins, George W. Jenks, Charles A. Jones, William W. Kendall, Barney Lafferty, George Laughlenbaugh, John Maburn, Jacob Moser, Daniel McFadden, Erasmus Montgomery, Thomas F. Mahar, Hugh McClellen, Reuben Maburin, Thomas Morgan, Charles Madden, Andrew McGraw, Thomas McCormic, Thomas M. Morgan, Joseph T. Moore, William Noe, Rufus B. Parker, William Quinn, Morgan Reynold, John Riddle, John O. M. Rosser, Edward Turner, Charles Wellheffer, David Williams, Andrew B. Wagoner, John S. Williams, John Wilkins.

Transferred.—Thomas E. Davis, Christopher C. Hollingsworth, Edward Matthews, Thomas D. Paston.

TWENTY-NINTH OHIO VOLUNTEER INFANTRY.

The Twenty-ninth Ohio infantry was recruited mainly in Ashtabula county, and mustered into the service at Camp Giddings, near Ashtabula, in August, 1861, being one of the first regiments to respond to the call for three year troops. A few volunteers from the north part of Trumbull county joined this regiment. Their names will be found below. The Twenty-ninth participated in the battles at Winchester, Virginia, March 23, 1862; Port Republic, June 9, 1862; Cedar Mountain, August 9, 1862; the second Bull Run, at Chancellorsville, May 1 and 3, 1863; at Lookout Mountain, November 24 and 25, 1863; and in the several engagements of Sherman's Atlanta campaign. The regiment was discharged from the service July 22 and 23, 1865.

FIELD AND STAFF.

Lieutenant-colonel Edward Hayes, promoted major August, 1863.

COMPANY A.

PRIVATE.

Robert Monger, not reported.

COMPANY B.

PRIVATES.

George Gale, died April, 1863; Walter Nelson, not reported; Lewis Bane, discharged; Samuel R. Emases, transferred.

COMPANY E.

PRIVATE.

William Truman, died February, 1864.

COMPANY F.

NON-COMMISSIONED OFFICER.

Musician F. A. Helwig.

PRIVATES.

Jabial Maltby, discharged; Lorin Frisby, transferred; Elmore Stevens, died on field, Chattanooga; Iremus M. Foote, promoted to corporal; D. E. Humphrey, discharged; A. W. Hardy, Luther C. Hawley, discharged.

COMPANY G.

PRIVATES.

James L. Smith, died in 1863; Lewis Inman, not reported; Henry Edson, Jacob Gates, Richard Riley, discharged; George C. Gurst, promoted to corporal; James Gale, Charles E. Griffin, Andrew B. Holman, Corwin Spencer, Justice Townsley, John C. Kendrick, recruit; W. G. Stephen, discharged; Thomas White, appointed corporal.

COMPANY K.

PRIVATE.

S. B. Emms, discharged.

THIRTY-SEVENTH REGIMENT OHIO VOLUNTEER INFANTRY.

The German citizens of Ohio showed no want of patriotism when troops were required to preserve the Union. The third German regiment from the State, which took rank as the Thirty-seventh Ohio, was recruited from the counties of Cuyahoga, Ross, Lucas, Mahoning, Auglaize, Franklin, Tuscarawas, Erie, Wyandot, and Mercer. Company I was partially enrolled at Youngstown. Colonel E. Siber was an accomplished soldier, having been in the service in Prussia and Brazil. The regiment was mustered into service October 2, 1861, at Camp Dennison, and assigned to the Department of West Virginia, then in command of General Rosecrans. The service through West Virginia was dangerous and laborious, though it did not afford the opportunity for participation in great battles. An affair at Wyoming Court House, in which two Youngstown soldiers lost their lives, was somewhat characteristic of the service in that locality. While on an expedition to destroy a railroad, a detachment fell into an ambuscade and was surrounded by the enemy. Besides the two killed, one officer and seven men were taken prisoners. On September 10, 1862, the regiment engaged in a fight on the Princeton road, which lasted six hours. Colonel Siber displayed great gallantry in protecting a valuable train of provisions and equipage on a retreat which a superior force of the enemy made necessary.

Early in 1863 the Thirty-seventh was transferred to the Mississippi to engage in Grant's Vicksburg campaign. It was one of the regiments detailed to construct a canal which was to change the course of the river and leave Vicksburg an inland town. During the siege the regiment lost nineteen killed and seventy-five wounded. After the fall of Vicksburg the Thirty-seventh marched to Jackson, Mississippi, and participated in the capture of that place. It then pursued rebel General Forrest to Chattanooga and assisted in the capture of Mission Ridge November 25, 1863, at which place Joseph Zedaker, of Mahoning county, was killed.

Three fourths of this gallant German regiment re-enlisted in the veteran service, and on returning to the field in March, 1864, it was detailed for the Atlanta campaign, and subsequently followed Sherman to the sea.

The Thirty-seventh was mustered out in August, 1865.

COMPANY I.

PRIVATES.

Charles Hagerman, Jacob Walter, Ferdinand Wellendorf, mustered out with company.
John Lump, promoted to sergeant, killed at Vicksburg.
Henser Ignaz, Henry Loewer, killed at Wyoming Court House, West Virginia.
Joseph Zedaker, killed at Missionary Ridge.
David Friegel, drowned in the Kanawha, February, 1862.
Frederick Fessman, Jacob Rapp, not reported.
Discharged.—Eugene Ritter, George Penaenger, Philip Haas, Gottlieb Lidle, John Loler, John Rahn, Walter Benedict, John Rushi, John Buhrle, David Frankforter, Gottlieb Limel, Joseph Seibold, Frank Sufert, Gustav Urnstein, John Wellendorf, Schorder Conrad.
Charles B. Ramser, promoted lieutenant 1862.
Frederick Lennig, promoted lieutenant 1863.
Joseph Leifert, promoted lieutenant 1865.
John Altinger, John Andregg, transferred.

THIRTY-EIGHTH REGIMENT OHIO VOLUNTEER INFANTRY.

This regiment, of which Edwin D. Bradley, Edward H. Phelps, and William A. Choate were the successive colonels, was organized at Defiance, Ohio, in September, 1861. In the original muster no Reserve men were included. The regiment was afterwards recruited by transfers from other regiments. The following, from the One Hundred and Fifth Ohio, originally enlisted from Trumbull and Mahoning counties:

COMPANY B.

PRIVATES.

Lafayette H. Lake, George Lane, Martin B. Rowdren, Morrison P. Shaffer, Charles C. Stoores.

COMPANY C.

PRIVATES.

Thomas Hire, recruit; George Hire, John B. Richard, John B. Thomas, recruit.

COMPANY D.

PRIVATES.

George M. Dice, Morgan Davis, Guillmun Davis, William H. Johnston, James Kline.

COMPANY F.

PRIVATES.

William Bailey, Jesse M. Sweat, Samuel Stambaugh, Edward Whitehouse.

COMPANY G.

PRIVATES.

Lewis Witmer, Benjamin Witsman, Henry Manderman.

FORTY-FIRST REGIMENT OHIO VOLUNTEER INFANTRY.

The nucleus of the Forty-first Ohio volunteer infantry was a company of volunteers recruited in Trumbull county, by Seth A. Bushnell and Emerson Opdyke. The defeat of Bull Run had fired the patriotic North, and men responded to the call to arms with alacrity. More than the full quota of one company enlisted from Trumbull, which made it necessary for several volunteers to be assigned to other companies. At the regimental organization, September 1, 1861, the Trumbull company was ranked A in recognition of its priority of enlistment. William B. Hazen, of the United States infantry, was appointed colonel. He was succeeded in November, 1862, by Aquilla Wiley, and Colonel Wiley in June 1864, was succeeded by Ephraim S. Holloway. The successive lieutenant-colonels were John J. Wiseman, George S. Mygatt, Aquilla Wiley, Robert Z. Kimberly, E. S. Holloway and Ezra Dunham. The successive majors were George S.

Mygatt, William R. Tollars, Aquilla Wiley, Robert Z. Kimberly, J. H. Williston, Ephraim S. Holloway, Ezra Dunham and James McCleary.

An officers' school was instituted at Camp Taylor and rigid military discipline practiced. By the time the rolls of all the companies were filled the regiment was ready for the field. It was formally mustered into service at Camp Dennison, near Cincinnati, October 31, 1861. Occasional raiding excursions into Virginia was the only relief from the monotony of daily drill, until the latter part of November, when it joined the forces then being organized into the Army of the Ohio, by General Buell. The winter was spent at Camp Wickliffe, where the Forty-first, by its neatness and precise conduct, became conspicuous. It became the nucleus of the Nineteenth brigade, placed under command of Colonel Hazen, and in February moved up the Cumberland to Nashville.

About the middle of March the army to which the Forty-first belonged moved up the river to Savannah, and on Saturday, April 5th, encamped within two miles of Pittsburg Landing. The roar of heavy firing announced the opening of the battle. On Sunday morning, April 6th, about 1 o'clock, the army began to move toward the field. At 5 o'clock it arrived opposite the battlefield, and Hazen's brigade was second to cross the river. That terrible night was spent in the beating rain on the field strewn with dead, dying, and wounded soldiers. When in the morning the enemy was discovered to be advancing, Hazen's brigade was ordered to the charge. The Forty-first occupied the front line and steadily advanced through a thicket of underbrush to an open space where a murderous fire saluted the steady line. The advance was continued till the rebels were driven beyond their fortification and their guns captured. The brigade in turn was driven back to its orignal line, where it readily re-formed. Three officers and three men who at different times carried the colors were shot down, and of the three hundred and seventy-three members of the regiment who entered the engagement one hundred and forty-one were either killed or wounded in half an hour's desperate action.

From Pittsburg Landing, the Forty-first accompanied the army as far as Corinth. It had in the meantime occupied miserable quarters on the field of Shiloh, which had seriously affected the health of the men. After the evacuation of Corinth, the regiment was employed at skirmishes and forced marches, continuing with the army under Buell. It marched from Louisville in October against Bragg, and participated in the battle of Perryville. Its next engagement was at Murfreesboro, in which it performed a conspicuous and dangerous part. It had entered the battle with four hundred and ten officers and men, of which number one hundred and twelve were killed or wounded. It was engaged in marches, rest and skirmishing until September 19th, when the battle of Chickamauga commenced. In the first charge on that day one hundred men were killed or wounded. General Hazen's brigade participated in the last charge of the day, which determined the issue of the battle. At Lookout Mountain the Forty-first maintained its reputation for gallantry. After the battle, while Generals Grant and Thomas were reviewing the field, General Thomas said to Colonel Wiley: "Colonel, I want you to express to your men my thanks for your splendid conduct this afternoon. It was a gallant thing, Colonel—a very gallant thing."

At Mission Ridge the conduct of the Forty-first was in harmony with its former reputation; one hundred and fifteen men were lost in that battle.

On January, 1864, there were only one hundred and eighty-eight of the veteran regiment left. All but eight re-enlisted in the veteran service. It reached Cleveland on veteran furlough February 2, 1864. With one hundred recruits, the regiment was reported for service at East Tennessee, March 26th. During the summer of 1864 the regiment was with Sherman on his Atlanta campaign. After the fall of Atlanta the Forty-first accompanied Thomas' army in pursuit of Hood. At the battle of Nashville the regiment captured some prisoners, four pieces of artillery and two battle flags. The latter were captured by private Holcomb, of company A, and Sergeant Garrett, of company G, who were afterwards sent to Washington by General Thomas to bear their trophies. The regiment followed in pursuit of Hood after the demoralization of his army at Nashville, as far as Huntsville, Alabama. The Forty-first was detailed on the Texas campaign and mustered out at San Antonio in November, 1865. It reached Columbus, Ohio, and was finally discharged November 26, 1865, having been in the service four years and one month. In this regiment Dr. A. G. Hart volunteered and was commissioned surgeon.

COMPANY A.

COMMISSIONED OFFICERS.

Captain Seth A. Bushnell, resigned November 27, 1861.

Captain Emerson Opdyke, promoted to captain January 9, 1862; mustered out October, 1862, to become colonel of One Hundred and Twenty-fifth Ohio volunteer infantry.

Captain James McCleery, promoted to first lieutenant January 9, 1862; promoted to captain October 31, 1862; transferred to company H in 1865.

Captain Seward S. Palmer, promoted to sergeant February 9, 1862; to first sergeant July 17, 1864; to first lieutenant December 6, 1864; promoted to captain March 27, 1865; mustered out with company.

First Lieutenant Davis C. Fuller, promoted to second lieutenant December 21, 1862; promoted to first lieutenant February 9, 1863; mustered out August 1, 1863.

First Lieutenant Calvin C. Hart, promoted to second lieutenant January 9, 1862; killed in action at Stone River December 31, 1862.

First Lieutenant Edwin B. Ashwood, promoted to second lieutenant January 21, 1862, and assigned to company G; promoted to first lieutenant company A, October 31, 1862; transferred to company G in 1862.

First Lieutenant James McMahon, promoted to second lieutenant company I, February 13, 1863; promoted to first lieutenant company A, April 19, 1864; mustered out December 5, 1864, to accept appointment as captain company I, December 6, 1864.

First Lieutenant Phillip A. Bower, promoted to corporal December 29, 1862; to sergeant May 1, 1863; to first sergeant December 6, 1864; to first lieutenant March 27, 1865; mustered out with company.

Second Lieutenant Charles W. Hill, promoted to second lieutenant company A, February 7, 1863; mustered out 1864, per order War department on surgeon's certificate of disability.

NON-COMMISSIONED OFFICERS.

First Sergeant Andrew C. Parker, promoted from corporal and mustered out with company.

Sergeant Joseph Jackson, promoted from corporal and mustered out with company.

Sergeant George F. Haynes, promoted from corporal and mustered out with company.

Sergeant Charles Settle, promoted from corporal and mustered out with company.

Sergeant Sheldon Crooks, promoted from corporal and mustered out with company.

Corporal Daniel J. Holcomb, promoted to corporal and mustered out with company.

Corporal Sullivan D. Ralph, promoted to corporal and mustered out with company.

Corporal Alfred J. Henry, promoted to corporal and mustered out with company.

Corporal Isaac A. Gamber, promoted to corporal and mustered out with company.

Corporal Adolphus Flint, promoted to corporal and mustered out with company.

PRIVATES.

John Goodsell, Jacob Lynn, Henry Miner, Finley McDonald, Alexander Wilson.

Killed in action.—Horace B. Ames, Shiloh; Wallace W. Bruddon, Chickamauga; Charles R. Smith, Picketts Mills, Georgia; George L. Barnes, Picketts Mills, Georgia; Samuel Bennett, Shiloh; Albert McFarland, Stone River; Milo Ritchie, Mission Ridge; Thomas Saddler, Brown's Ferry; John Waggoner, Stone River; John Ward, Shiloh.

Died.—Charles H. Bennett, 1863; Henry H. Brown, in Andersonville prison; Avory Bennett, 1863; Daniel W. Brockway, 1864; Clinton Bacon, 1863; Carilin Beck, 1862; Frank Curus, 1862; Virgil Holcomb, 1863; Judson B. Holcomb, 1864; Marquis D. Holcomb, 1864; Loftus L. Murry, 1863; George L. Norton, 1862; James Pelton, 1862; Albert L. Parker, 1865; William Ratliffe, 1861; Ralph Ransum, 1863; John Settle, 1863; Owen Spencer, at Reedsville, Tennessee; William Shirey, 1863; James Wadsworth, 1862.

Discharged Before Expiration of Service.—Elmer Moses, Augustus D. Drury, Lester W. Perham, William W. Carnahan, Harrison Daily, Julius A. Cutler, Charles H. Gallup, Thomas Snyder, Orlando W. Haynes, Henry Barber, Daniel Beneit, Joseph Bennett, James L. Bird, Edmund Burr, George Braden, George A. Clark, Robert Chambers, Augustus T. Dryer, Albert V. G. Ducher, Jeremiah Davis, Robert Eakin, Leroy Ely, James Fansher, Benjamin Flint, John Gamber, Homer Gridley, Morgan Hall, Elijah Harness, Orlanda Hayes, Thomas Huey, George Huey, Samuel Huey, Augustus C. Hills, Albert Jones, Hiram Keesler, Henry Keis, Allen P. Kepner, Enos Lane, Thaddeus Lehman, Addison Lincoln, Jacob Linn, George R. Miner, Archibald McCann, Benjamin Nephen, Walter C. Paitegrew, David E. Pierce, Edward Plouts, Dwight Shepherd, Abraham Shull, John M. Smith, Joseph Tolman, Almon Webb, John A. Webber, Joshua Webber, William Webber, John C. Williams, Richard Worts, Jr., William Wright, Robert A. Johnson, George Hall.

Transferred.—James J. Mattocks, Lyman Allen.

Prisoner of War.—Asbury E. Hewitt.

COMPANY B.

Fletcher Andrews, John M. Hamilton, recruits.

COMPANY F.

Mahlon Stacy, killed at Chickamauga.

Samuel J. Ewing, fatally wounded at Stone River.

Alfred Miller, promoted to corporal.

Discharged.—John Reed, David Akins, Robert P. Bellard, Benjamin M. Hoffman, Peter Lawrence, Robert Lowry, Lewis Ludwick, David Messerman, Rodney Orr, Reuben Shoemaker.

Discharged for wounds.—David F. Johnston, Samuel Shisler.

COMPANY K.

Harvey Burr, Levi Foot, Robert Miserer, died in hospital, 1862.

John Decker, killed at Picketts Mills, Georgia.

Discharged for disability.—B. H. Lake, William Dickinson, Walter Dickinson, William Galdner.

Discharged.—John L. Hutchins, Charles Hitchcock, Seth Taft, Reuben Taft, James Tompkins, James Tryon.

Transferred to Veteran Reserve corps.—Andrew Winters, Mark Keith, J. C. Whitney, R. M. Whitney, H. W. Jones, A. R. Williams, S. N. Palmer, Philip A. Bowers, James Dilly, Harrison Allen, Irving Holcomb.

FIELD AND STAFF.

Quartermaster Sergeant Lyman Allen, appointed June 1863.

Sergeant James J. Mattocks, appointed sergeant December, 1862.

FORTY-SECOND OHIO VOLUNTEER INFANTRY.

This was Colonel Garfield's regiment. Colonel Garfield had been a candidate for the colonelcy of the Seventh Ohio, but was defeated by E. B. Tyler, of Ravenna. We are enabled to trace but three enlistments in this regiment to Trumbull county, viz:

COMPANY F.
PRIVATES.

Andrew Smith, Edward Shriver.

COMPANY G.
PRIVATE.

Aaron Faus.

FIFTIETH OHIO VOLUNTEER INFANTRY.

The Fiftieth Ohio infantry was recruited from the State at large, and mustered into the service at Camp Dennison, August 27, 1861. Of the originally enrolled members none were from this county. Among the recruits the following names are found:

PRIVATES.

Herbert M. King, Henry J. Bailey, Philander Church, and George V. French.

FIFTY-FIRST OHIO VOLUNTEER INFANTRY.

The following recruits to the Fifty-first Ohio infantry were from Trumbull and Mahoning counties:

PRIVATES.

Edward G. Armstrong, Homer Beardsley, William Curtis, John W. Grant, Alvin Green, Amos Sears, John C. Tucker, William Ames, Myron Mills, Isaac Phelps, Charles E. Sherman, and Daniel R. Weatherton.

FIFTY-SECOND OHIO VOLUNTEER INFANTRY.

Several attempts to organize a regiment to rank as the Fifty-second had failed, and the number remained unfilled until the summer of 1862. In May, 1862, Governor Tod issued a commission to Captain Daniel McCook, and by August the quota was full. It was recruited from all parts of the State. The following names were enrolled in the counties embraced in the field of this volume:

PRIVATES.

Wesley W. Williman, Blair H. Puffenburg, Levi Walters, Andrew Weisfoot, John Sickles (died at Louisville), and D. W. Woodard.

SIXTY-FIFTH OHIO VOLUNTEER INFANTRY.

NON-COMMISSIONED OFFICER.

William Case was appointed corporal and transferred to the Sixty-fifth in 1865.

EIGHTY-FOURTH REGIMENT OHIO VOLUNTEER INFANTRY.

This was one of the regiments which was organized in response to the call of 1862 for men to serve three months. The general field officers were: Colonel William Lawrence, Lieutenant-colonel John J. Wiseman, Major John C. Groom, Surgeon Benjamin B. Leonard, Assistant Surgeon James W. Thompson, Chaplain Abraham R. Howbert. Two companies, one enrolled at Youngstown and the other in several of the townships of Trumbull and Mahoning counties, are given below. The regiment was organized at Camp Chase, near Columbus, June 7, 1862, and four days later ordered to Cumberland, Maryland. From this point the regiment was variously employed on expeditions, cutting off rebel communications, capturing mail and mail carriers, and beating down guerrilla bands. Shortly before the expiration of its term of service, the Eighty-fourth anticipated an engagement with the enemy at New Creek, and made preparations accordingly. The enemy, however, retired without striking a blow, after which the Eighty-fourth and Eighty-seventh were sent to Camp Delaware and there mustered out of the service. Governor Tod in an address complimented both officers and men upon the efficiency of their service, which covered a period of nearly a month longer than the time of their enlistment.

There were several of these three months regiments. The President in May, 1862, perceived the urgent need of an increased army to guard the Northern States against threatened raids. General Banks had retreated down the Shenandoah valley, and Rebel General Jackson, the most energetic commander in the field, was evidently planning a northern expedition. But a couple of weeks elapsed between President Lincoln's call for seventy-five thousand men and the arrival at the front of Ohio's quota.

COMPANY B.

COMMISSIONED OFFICERS.

Captain Roswell Shurtleff.
First Lieutenant John Sourbeck.
Second Lieutenant Hiram M. Fifield.

NON-COMMISSIONED OFFICERS.

First Sergeant Charles E. Patrick.
Sergeant Christopher C. Mendeker.
Sergeant Levellette Battelle.
Sergeant Leonard Dobbins.
Sergeant John W. Brothers.

First Corporal Thomas B. McKee.
Corporal Robert Geddes.
Corporal Robert A. Polluck.
Corporal Charles L. Fitch.
Corporal Charles F. Selliman.
Corporal Mahlon B. White.
Corporal Henry D. Seymour.
Corporal George J. Margerum.
Corporal Joseph B. Couch.
Corporal John C. Johnston, not on muster out roll.
Musician Daniel W. Hiltabiddle.
Musician John K. Potter.

PRIVATES.

Archibald Armstrong, John Barbour, Andrew A. Buchanan, William Beatty, Sylvester F. Barker, Spencer Bradford, Joseph A. Bell, James Burt, Edgar Bresden, John W. Blackman, Charles H. Beck, Allen Cowden, Simeon Carlton, Newton Carlton, Charles C. Coats, Wells Clark, James A. Clark, John Q. A. Conant, Charles B. Dumer, John C. Duringer, William G. Davis, Charles G. Drake, Richmond M. Elliot, James L. Edwards, Matthias Falkenstien, John K. Fitch, Milton D. Fellows, Henry Gans, Chauncey D. Hamilton, Frederick F. Hoffman, William Hanmoor, Horatio Herbler, George W. Holland, Edward T. Higgs, James Hinson, Anthony Howells, Jr., George Jennings, Bruce Jackson, John K. Johnston, John C. Johnston, Edward Kyle, Stephen Lampman, Rievard W. Lundy, Robert M. Montgomery, George C. McKee, William McClure, Henry Moore (or Moon), Arthur McKiever, Edward Moffatt, Thomas R. Mahan, Joseph A. Osborn, Joseph B. Park, William Pauley, Harvey Pyle, Edward Powers, John S. Pollock, William F. Pitman, John F. Powers, Henry C. Reno, Louis A. Roberts, Charles H. Ray, Henry Schlong, Robert Stewart, Charles Sebright, Charles B. Stoddard, William Thomas, William D. Tod, Seth H. Truesdale, Joseph W. Van Wye, Milton A. Wilder, Charles E. Wick, James Wooley, James T. Wick, David Williams, Anthony Weleb, Jesse Williams, Martin Winderbas, William Wilson, Josiah S. Zimmerman.

Discharged before Expiration of Service—Ambrose Eckman, George Fraek, Ralph Sutlifl.

COMPANY C.

COMMISSIONED OFFICERS.

Captain Hulbert B. Case.
First Lieutenant John B. Irwin.
Second Lieutenant Charles S. Abell.

NON-COMMISSIONED OFFICERS.

First Sergeant J. Phil Hurlburt.
Sergeant Allen L. Moffat.
Sergeant Horace L. Miller.
Sergeant Hugh C. Williamson.
Sergeant John C. McLain.
Color Sergeant Jefferson Wilson.
Corporal Jesse B. Luce.
Corporal Wallace W. Tracy.
Corporal Jeffrey Tribbey.
Corporal Horace S. Fuller.
Corporal William H. Woodrow.
Corporal Jeremiah Bowker.
Corporal James H. Morrow.
Corporal Joseph M. Lewis.
Musician William Birchard.
Musician Robert Gamble.

PRIVATES.

Abner C. Allison, Bryson Brown, Oliver Brooks, John Bell, Ephraim Byers, John Burnett, John E. Brockway, George W. Bissel, Hiram L. Brown, Allen H. Barr, William A. Camp, Lewis S. Carter, Harold Cordes, John A. Cannon, William Crawford, John Davis, Allison C. Dilley, Ward Deihl, John Ditheridge, Henry C. Ewart, Josiah Enos, Walter Ensign, Porter G. Eastman, Hezekiah M. Ford, Lumen R. Fobes, Warren Fuller, Christian Fudrow, Allen D. Ferguson, Harmon K. Graeter, Claudius J. Giddings, Jr., John O. Hewitt, Richard Hannon, John Hall, Aaron Hayes, Evan Harris, Samuel Harny, Joseph Hickey, Michael Hannon, John S. Hoyt, Richard Holcomb, David Jones, Allured L. Jones, Flavel E. Jones, Philip Leonard, Reuben P. Leisenring, Frank J. Mackey, John McConnell, Theodore McConnell, John McWhorter, Jud Morrow, Dan Morse, Theophilus Morses, Calvin Osborn, Thomas F. Paden, John Rayen, James Roberts, Joseph Lewis (not on muster out roll), James L. Randall, Alfred P. Shaffer, Dell Swindler, Jacob J. Shaffer, Scott N. Wick, Jefferson Wilson (not on the muster out roll), George W. Snyder, Henry C. Smith, James Stuart, Homer J. Stanley, Alfred G. Sturgis, John Spear, Jules J. Vantrot, Jr., James P. Williams, Corvin V. Wilson, Thomas Waterland, Justus H. Woodburn, William D. Woodburn, Alvin S. Wilcox, William H. Watkins, Henry A. Wise, James S. Weir.

First Lieutenant James Cromdon, resigned June 8, 1862.
Sergeant James M. Scott, appointed hospital steward June 15, 1862.
Private William McCracken, deserted July 26, 1862.
Private William Byerly, died August 11, 1862, at Cumberland, Maryland.
Private Levi Bartholomew, died August 8, 1862, in Cumberland, Maryland.

COMPANY G.

Privates John W. Dakin, Francis M. Smith, George Shield.

COMPANY K.

NON-COMMISSIONED OFFICERS.

Hospital Steward James N. Scott.
Musician Daniel W. Hillbiddle.

PRIVATES.

James Bentler, H. M. Boon, Benjamin F. Cambell, John Fireman, Matthew Hill, George Heller, William Miller.

EIGHTY-SIXTH OHIO VOLUNTEER INFANTRY.

[Six Months Organization.]

There were two organizations known as the Eighty-sixth Ohio infantry. The first was a three months regiment, recruited under the call of May, 1862. That regiment served chiefly in West Virginia. At the expiration of its term of service the danger of rebel raids into the Northern States had not abated, and a reorganization was effected for six months longer. Wilson C. Lemert, the former major, was commissioned colonel of the new regiment, and but a short time elapsed before the companies were all full. Captain Seth H. Truesdale, with a company from Mahoning county, was first to report.

The organization was opportune, for the men had scarce been equipped when the famous rebel guerilla, John Morgan, crossed the Ohio and began an expedition through our own State. The Eighty-sixth, then in Camp Tod, was ordered to join in pursuit of the invaders. Morgan had been defeated at Buffington's island in an attempt to cross the river at that point, and turned toward the Northwest with a view of making his escape in that direction. The Eighty-sixth was ordered to Zanesville, and a detachment under Lieutenant-colonel McFarland at once sent to Eagleport, where it was supposed Morgan would cross the river. It arrived just in time to see the rear guard clear the stream. McFarland's force not being sufficient to attack, he endeavored to delay the enemy by skirmishing until the force in pursuit should come up. Having executed his orders McFarland returned to Zanesville. In the meantime Major Kraus, with the remainder of the Eighth-sixth, had gone to Cambridge to intercept Morgan at that point. In this he was unsuccessful, the raiders having passed through the town before Kraus arrived. Pursuit was continued until the capture of Morgan's forces in Salineville, Columbiana county.

The Eighty-sixth returned to Camp Tod, whence after a short rest it was ordered to Kentucky. The regiment was permitted to participate in one achievement, which was accomplished without the loss of a single man. The Eighty-sixth and One Hundred and Twenty-ninth Ohio, the Twenty-second Ohio battery, and detachments of two Tennessee cavalry regiments arrived before Cumberland Gap on the 8th of September, on the Kentucky side. Simultaneously General Burnside's division appeared on the Tennessee side, thus throwing the rebel garrison between the two forces. After a judicious disposition of the troops the garrison, under command of General Frazier, was summoned to surrender, which was readily acceded to, though spirited resistance might have been offered. The Eighty-sixth Ohio was first to march into the fort and raise the National colors. The fruit of the capture was 2,800 prisoners, 5,000 stand of arms, 13 pieces of artillery, and large quantities of commissary stores and ammunition. The Eighty-sixth Ohio was retained at Cumberland Gap as part of the garrison till the expiration of its term of service. It started for Ohio January 16, 1864, and arrived at Cleveland, January 26th. The regiment was mustered out February 10, 1864, at Cleveland.

COMPANY A.

COMMISSIONED OFFICERS.

Captain Seth H. Truesdale.
First Lieutenant Lewis N. Pollock.
Second Lieutenant Charles E. Patrick.

NON-COMMISSIONED OFFICERS.

First Sergeant Josiah Zimmerman.
Sergeant John S. Pollock.
Sergeant James T. Wick.
Sergeant Hugh R. Moore.
Sergeant John D. Dickson.
Corporal Stewart Truesdale.
Corporal John I. Wilson.
Corporal Lewis L. Campbell.
Corporal Joseph L. Shunk.
Corporal Isaac P. Cowden.
Corporal Edgar Crandon.
Corporal Samuel Hobbs.
Corporal Samuel Holland.

PRIVATES.

Henry H. Glendening, William Welch, William D. Courtney, Anderson Thomas, Arkwright Delaney, George Ague, Seth Augdon, Ashburn J. Nelson, Thomas Ammous, George H. Bellard, Daniel Blackman, Clayton T. Brainard, Edgar Breaden, William Bailey, James I. Clewell, Charles Dean, Charles B. Diemer, James Fussleman, Charles W. Guenther, Henry T. Guring, Isaiah Greegor, John Goddard, Horation E. Hubler, Francis Hayne, William L. Hall, Henry Hubbard, Judson L. Hubler, Albert Howlette, Jerome F. Hill, Edward Hollinbaugh, James M. Holton, Charles R. Holton, William Ipe, Samuel Jewell, Henry I. Jones, Howell Jones, Leander Kegarice, David Kelly, George W. King, Thomas S. Livingston, Edwin Lee, David Llewllyn, William McKale, Lazarus Moherman, William B. Moore, Darius B. McNabb, William I. McFarland, David Montgomery, Alexander C. McDonald, Malcom McFall, Lewis Moherman, Thomas H. Pollock, Charles Parker, George Phillips, John A. Pfeisder, Lovenin Packard, Henry Roberts, Israel Redinger, Henderson Reed, Henry Reed, Henry H. Rader, Clayton Randolph, David Rollen, John S. Struthers, Joshua Simons, Deemer Simons, Durham Stacy, Samuel Stambaugh, Hiram Smith, Henry Toolman, Henry Thompson, Robert Welch, John W. White, Solomon Zedaker.

Discharged Before Expiration of Service.—Henry C. Reno.
Transferred.—William Kraus, promoted to major; Rufus P. Manning, Charles B. Stoddard.
Died.—Manly Partridge, 1863; Emmett Parthour, 1863; Lewis Moherman, 1864.

COMPANY G.

COMMISSIONED OFFICERS.

Captain William F. Millikan.
Second Lieutenant Virgil N. Weir.

NON-COMMISSIONED OFFICERS.

First Sergeant Addison L. Wolcot.
Sergeant Henry L. Masser (or Muser).
Sergeant Albert H. Smith.
Corporal Henry C. Smith.
Corporal William A. Bascon.

Corporal Harlem P. Waters.
Corporal William T. McCracken.
Corporal Austin Lee.
Corporal Romeo H. Freer.
Corporal John Combs.
Musician Seymour Lee.
Musician Charles E. Adams.
Wagoner John Combs.

PRIVATES.

William H. Anderson, Charles H. Anstadt, Aaron D. Baird, Irwin Budgen, John P. Bateman, Jacob H. Bestwick, Adolphus C. Bower, Albert H. Browning, John H. Burnes, Almond H. Clark, George W. Euler, William Freeburn, Norman A. Gilbert, Elbert Gilbert, Jasper N. Griffith, Henry Hoffman, Simeon E. Harrington, Thomas Hayward, Henry C. Hall, Charles R. Knight, Thomas C. Lee, David E. Liblondge, Robert Martin, James McCardell, Henry Mease, Julius K. Nims, Addison F. Osmer, Cassius M. Pierce, Merick Sloan, Frank C. Taylor, Peter L. Webb.

Died.—John Jackson and Charles E. Richard.
Discharged.—John N. Harrington, William H. Johnson.

COMPANY I.

PRIVATES.

Transferred to company A, July 16, 1863.—John Goddard, Josiah Moherman, Louis Moherman, Hiram Smith, Turham Tracy, Samuel Stambaugh, John W. White.

COMPANY D.

NON-COMMISSIONED OFFICERS.

Corporal Benjamin Campbell.
Musician Warren T. Marks.

PRIVATES.

Joseph Dean, George Dean, Edward France, Jacob H. Hartz, Milo C. Hunter, James M. Marks, Edward Morrison, William Walling, George W. Ward, George H. Malone.

FIELD AND STAFF.

Major William Karns, promoted from company A July 17, 1863.
First Lieutenant and Quartermaster Rufus P. Manning.
Quartermaster Sergeant Charles B. Stoddard.

EIGHTY-SEVENTH REGIMENT OHIO VOLUNTEER INFANTRY.

This regiment was organized in response to the call of President Lincoln in May, 1862, for three months' men. H. B. Banning was commissioned colonel. It left for the field June 15th, and was stationed at Harper's Ferry, where it remained until the siege of that place by rebel General Jackson, and was surrendered with the National forces, although the term of its enlistment had expired. When this circumstance was made known the regiment was permitted to return home. It was mustered out at Camp Chase September 20, 1862. The following were enrolled in Trumbull and Mahoning counties:

COMPANY I.

NON-COMMISSIONED OFFICERS.

Edward G. Whitsides, promoted sergeant June, 1862;
James Whipps, appointed corporal June, 1862.

PRIVATES

Silas W. Alford, Thomas S. Chapin, Joseph H. Trew, Henry Kropp, Edward E. Kelly, William S. Love, John W. McCord, John McConnahay, Robert G. Rhodes, Robert Wallace.

COMPANY K.

NON-COMMISSIONED OFFICER.

Musician Charles E. Adams.

EIGHTY-EIGHTH OHIO VOLUNTEER INFANTRY.

Next to pure, patriotic feeling the love of glory and applause is the soldier's most powerful incentive to noble action. There is in consequence a feeling of disappointment if the opportunity of attaining distinction is not afforded. The Eighty-eighth Ohio was peculiarly unfortunate in the position it was required by stern military discipline to occupy. The nucleus of this regiment was the First battalion, Governor's Guards, Independent volunteer infantry, organized in June, 1862. It was placed on guard duty at Camp Chase, then filled with rebel prisoners. This service was both arduous and monotonous. Both officers and men urgently solicited a change of duty, in which they were successful to the extent of being transferred to another quarter. It was made part of the guard back of Covington to prevent the threatened attack on Cincinnati. In this position the battalion did efficient service. Frequent applications had been made for authority to recruit a full regiment, which was finally granted.

June 26, 1863, just one month later, the regiment was completed. Company D was enrolled in Mahoning county. George W. Neff, lieutenant-colonel of the Second Kentucky infantry, who had shortly before been released from a thirteen months imprisonment, was appointed to the colonelcy of the regiment. He placed it under severe discipline and joined his men in the hope of being ordered to the front. There was great disappointment, therefore, when the main body was ordered on the dreaded guard duty at Camp Chase. A small detachment was sent to West Virginia, but was soon recalled by the presence of the rebel raider, John Morgan, on this side of the Ohio river. It was correctly surmised that Morgan would attempt the destruction of Camp Dennison, one of the most important posts in the West. Colonel Neff was placed in command and ordered to take every precaution against being surprised by the enemy, or overcome in a conflict with him. The invalids were armed and the Governor's Guards stationed at proper places. The people of the surrounding country were pressed into the service, and were of great use by obstructing the roads with timber, thus delaying Morgan's movements. One small squad of the raiders forced its way to within a mile of the camp, but was driven back by a force of invalids. After the Morgan excitement was over the regiment returned to Camp Chase, where it suffered the monotonous routine of guard duty most of the time until finally mustered out, July 3, 1865. Reid says in his history: "The Eighty-eighth Ohio was a complete and well drilled regiment, and if given a chance would immediately have performed good service in the field."

COMPANY D.

COMMISSIONED OFFICERS.

Captain John M. Green.
First Lieutenant John S. King.
Second Lieutenant William L. Brown.

NON-COMMISSIONED OFFICERS.

First Sergeant Patterson T. Caldwell.
Sergeant Edward L. Howard.
Sergeant Benjamin B. Stilson.
Sergeant William M. Kerr.
Sergeant Philip Miller.
Corporal Calvin M. Keefer.
Corporal Samuel H. Meys.
Corporal Alfred Beck.
Corporal James D. Caldwell.
Corporal George Z. Cockell.
Corporal Hiram F. Dirkson.
Corporal Hoel Delia.
Corporal Hugh P. Wilson.
Musician John F. Keefer.
Musician Edwin Tidball.

PRIVATES.

Transferred to Eighty-eighth regiment Ohio volunteer infantry.—James C. Allen, David Anderson, Robert Anchuiz, Baker Wrilby, Albert Bannon, James Bannon, Bela Barber, Andrew Barger, Cornelius Butt, Bruce Brownlee, John Carr, Lucius J. Chandler, James Christy, William Cole, William Cever, Edwin Cress, Richard D. Dayton, Henry Funkrll, John S. Galbraith, Samuel S. Garver, Tobias A. Greenamyer, David H. Hall, James M. Holton, Charles R. Holton, Ira Hoover, Converse B. Hunt, Solomon Ipe, James D. Jones, Leffert T. Kyle, Henry M. Kirkpotsch, Thomas S. Kerr, Martin Kimman, Levi Kistler, John Lanrgen, Edward Lee, Jacob W. Lewcuse, Alexander B. Love, John W. Lucket, Seth Marshall, William I. Marshall, Augustus Mendell, Joseph Miller, Jacob Morse, George Murphy, Jefferson McCleary, George McAdams, Alexander McConnell, Stanly McGittigan, George McKinnie, Hiram M. Osborn, William Osborn, Charles Parker, Joseph Parke, James Quest, Israel Rediner, George G. Roberts, Alfred W. Robinson, Albert H. Robinson, Jonas Rollar, Peter H. Roach, William P. Rose, Edward H. Sampson, Willis G. Sampson, Thomas Skinner, John F. Smith, Samuel Strong, Jonathan Taylor, John Thomas, Edgar M. Toor, Ira W. Wallace, Joseph D. Wallans, William C. Warnock, Frederick Weyman, John Weaver, Eugene A. Weiler, Joseph B. White, Cassius Zedaker, Solomon Zedaker, Martin V. Turner, Ichabod Whitaker, Leister S. Cone, Royal Jacobs, Peter Lahrents (not reposted).

ONE HUNDRED AND FIFTH REGIMENT OHIO VOLUNTEER INFANTRY.

The One Hundred and Fifth was recruited wholly in the eastern part of the Reserve. Companies A and H were from Mahoning county, the former being made up largely of miners. Company C was from Weathersfield township, and was also composed of miners. Company B was from different parts of Trumbull county, and company I from the northern townships of Trumbull, and southern townships of Ashtabula. G and K were mainly recruited in Lake county, and F in Geauga. Albert S. Hall, who had entered the service at the first call for troops as captain in the Twenty-fourth, was commissioned colonel. A full roster of the field and staff will be found below. We give from Reid's Ohio in the War a sketch of this regiment carried out in greater detail than that of other regiments, because one-half of the One Hundred and Fifth was enrolled within the particular field of this volume.

"The last company was mustered in at 10 o'clock on the morning of August 21st (1862), and in one hour the regiment, 1,013 strong, was on the march to the depot of the Cleveland & Cincinnati railroad, under orders to leave the State. It arrived at Covington, Kentucky, on the morning of August 22d, being the first regiment to leave the State under the call of August 4, 1862. Its first company rendezvoused at Camp Taylor, August 11th, and ninety-five per cent. was enlisted after August 1st. It remained at Covington three days, the men receiving their advance bounty and one month's pay. Having been fully armed and equipped for the field, the regiment left Covington August 25th by railroad for Lexington, where it arrived the same day. At Lexington it was assigned to a brigade commanded by Colonel Charles Anderson, of the Ninety-third Ohio. Much confusion and excitement prevailed around Lexington at the time of the arrival of the One Hundred and Fifth, and the regiment had every prospect of an immediate encounter with the enemy. General Kirby Smith was advancing from Cumberland Gap toward

Lexington, and the most energetic preparations were being made to meet him.

"On the 30th of August the One Hundred and Fifth, with several other regiments, received orders to march for Richmond, Kentucky, with all possible dispatch for the purpose of reinforcing General Nelson. Before reaching that place, however, the battle had been fought and lost. A halt was made at the Kentucky river until the remnants of Nelson's command could come up, when they returned to Lexington. The rebels in large force menacing Lexington, it was ordered that that city should be evacuated. Hasty preparations were made for the departure of our forces. On the night of September 1st the last column left for Louisville. The march was a forced one. Colonel Hall, of the One Hundred and Fifth, asked the privilege of bringing up the rear, and was allowed to do so. The troops were all new, and, as usual with that class of soldiers, were loaded down with baggage. The weather was intensely warm. There had been a drouth in the country marched over, and water was exceedingly scarce; and such was the supposed urgency of the retreat that the column was pushed on with great haste, giving the men little or no time to quench their thirst when water was found. The One Hundred and Fifth, being in the rear, fared badly, for those in front almost invariably exhausted the wells and creeks, leaving nothing but the muddy dregs for their companions in the rear. At times the thirst was overpowering, and each day men fell down from sunstroke apparently dead. However, the march was completed, the One Hundred and Fifth faithfully performing its duty as rear guard, not only to the retreating force, but acting as a support to a section of artillery totally unprovided with ammunition. All along the weary, dusty way scares occurred, and frequently stands were made against a supposed but invisible foe, involving detours across corn-fields, always, of course, on the double quick. This march was the baptismal campaign of the One Hundred and Fifth, and it told sadly on officers and men. As no tents had been drawn men were compelled to lie down upon the naked ground after enduring the terrible heat and dust of the day. The march was completed September 5th, the men arriving at Louisville footsore and exhausted. Many were afflicted with chronic diarrhea and fevers, the majority of whom never recovered, but were discharged or died in the hospital. At Louisville the regiment was assigned to a brigade commanded by General Terrill, in a division commanded by Brigadier-general Jackson, which afterwards became the Thirty-third brigade, Tenth division of the army under General Buell. Much apprehension was felt at Louisville at the time on account of rebel General Bragg's invasion of Kentucky, and the troops were ordered at once to throw up works and prepare for vigorous defense.

"General Nelson, recovering from his wound received at Richmond, took command of the army, and the utmost vigor and watchfulness were manifested, and every precaution taken to prevent surprise. The arrival of the army under General Buell allayed all fears, and the remainder of the time at Louisville was spent at drilling and making preparations for an early campaign against the rebel forces under General Bragg. Still, the One Hundred and Fifth entered upon this fall campaign with comparatively little knowledge of tactics and field maneuvering.

"Leaving Louisville October 1st, the regiment marched via Taylorsville and Bloomfield to Perryville, where it was engaged October 8th, in the battle at that place. After marching some eight or ten miles on the morning of the 8th, making frequent halts, the vicinity of the contest was reached, but it was not until afternoon that the battle commenced at the point where the One Hundred and Fifth was stationed. The regiment moved rapidly forward and formed at the base of a ridge, where it awaited orders. Two companies had been sent out as skirmishers, but they joined the regiment at this point. Another regiment, the One Hundred and Twenty-third Illinois, and Parsons' battery, had been assigned to a position farther to the front and left. The regiment and battery soon became engaged, and the One Hundred and Fifth was ordered to their support. Moving by the right flank and on the double-quick, it passed in rear of the battery for the purpose of forming on its left. Before reaching its position it received a volley from a rebel regiment at short range and at once halted, faced by the rear rank and opened fire. The smoke from their guns had hardly cleared away before another rebel regiment, within fifty yards, rose up out of the tall grass that completely concealed it and fired another volley. Parsons' battery had been posted without any support near it, and within fifty yards of the nearest concealed lines of rebel infantry. At the time the One Hundred and Fifth came up, most of the guns of Parsons' battery had been silenced, more than half its horses shot down, and many of its men killed and wounded. At the first volley from the One Hundred and Fifth the rebel lines, three or four deep, gradually moved forward, firing as they advanced, and swept the ridge where the battery and the One Hundred and Fifth stood.

"In the rear of the rebel lines of infantry, on another ridge, were posted their batteries, which did terrible execution. General Terrill, seeing the gradual advance of the enemy, ordered Major Perkins to have the men fix bayonets, move forward, and try to save the guns. The enemy seeing this movement opened fire with renewed vigor. Fresh troops sprang up, new volleys smote the advancing National line. It faltered, wavered, and then fell back to its former position. The enemy rushed forward and succeeded in taking the guns. The lines were now almost within pistol shot. A second time, led on by the gallant Terrill and Major Perkins, the left wing moved forward against the foe now swarming around the silenced guns, and with exultant cheers pouring their destructive volleys into our line. On the left the enemy had forced back the One Hundred and Twenty-third Illinois, turned the flank of the One Hundred and Fifth Ohio and turned the guns on the National lines. The line again wavered but the men were still unwilling to retreat. At length General Terrill, seeing that further resistance was hopeless, gave the order to fall back. The order was obeyed; the men retired slowly at first, but under the merciless fire of the rebels the ranks broke, the companies scattered and order was lost. General Terrill and Colonel Hall succeeded in keeping together a few hundred men from different regiments, and these fell back from one position to another until they finally formed in rear of a battery, which they supported until night closed the contest. Here fell General Terrill, mortally wounded. General Jackson had been killed early in the engagement and Colonel Webster, commanding the other (Thirty-fourth) brigade, having been mortally wounded, Colonel Hall being the senior officer in the division took command. Before the battle commenced Lieutenant-colonel Tolles had been sent out in charge of a skirmish line to protect the left flank and did not rejoin the regiment until it had fallen back from its first position where the battery stood. Thus closed the first battle in which the regiment engaged. How well they fought the long list of killed and wounded will show. Captain I. D. McKee was killed, several other officers were wounded, one captain, Robert Wilson, mortally. Forty-seven men were killed and two hundred and twelve wounded, many of whom afterward died.

"After the battle the regiment, under command of Lieutenant-colonel Tolles, marched via Harrodsburg to Danville. Colonel Hall was relieved of the command of the division by General Robert S. Granger, and took command of the brigade. At Danville the brigade was detached from the main army and ordered to Mumfordsville, where it arrived October 25th, and remained there till November 30th, performing post and guard duty. Time being had for drill at this place great proficiency was acquired, and the regiment now became fairly organized. On leaving Mumfordsville it marched to Glasgow, thence to Carthage, Tennessee.

"After leaving Kentucky the brigade was ordered to Hartsville, on the Cumberland river, where a brigade of Northern troops had just been captured by the rebel John Morgan. Remaining at Hartsville but one night the regiment marched to Bledsoe's creek, about six miles from Gallatin, and encamped. While here the brigade was assigned to the Twelfth division, commanded by Brigadier-general J. J. Reynolds, and participated with the division in the pursuit of John Morgan, going as far as Cave City. The division was then ordered to return and join the main army at Murfreesboro. This diversion after Morgan prevented the One Hundred and Fifth Ohio from being present at the battle of Stone River. The division reached Stone River January 11, 1863, marching through Bowling Green and Nashville. A permanent assignment was here made, making Hall's the Second and Reynold's the Fifth brigade, soon afterward the Fourth division of the Fourteenth corps.

"The One Hundred and Fifth remained at Murfreesboro until June, frequently accompanying the brigade and division in reconnoissances.

On the 20th day of March the brigade was engaged at Milton, about fourteen miles from Murfreesboro, with John Morgan's command, and inflicted on that rebel chieftain a severe chastisement. This engagement had a most favorable effect upon the men of the One Hundred and Fifth, who fought at Perryville. They learned that by a judicious disposition of forces men may be able to stand their ground though largely outnumbered. When the enemy made his assault, which was bold and impetuous, it was met with a steadiness that hurled him back in the utmost confusion; and a second and a third attempt resulted in the same way. The engagement finally settled down into a spirited artillery duel, which lasted nearly the entire afternoon.

"On June 24th the regiment broke camp to participate in the Tullahoma campaign. Colonel Hall and Lieutenant-colonel Tolles were both left at Murfreesboro sick, and Colonel Hall died there on the 10th of July. Lieutenant-colonel Tolles obtained leave of absence and returned home to recruit his health. Colonel Robinson, of the Seventy-fifth Indiana succeeded to the command of the brigade, and Major Perkins to the command of the regiment. In common with the rest of the army, the One Hundred and Fifth shared the fatigues of the brief campaign which resulted in driving Bragg from his position at Tullahoma, and sending him across the Tennessee river. It lay encamped at University Mountain some time during the warmest weather. At this place Colonel King was assigned to the command of the brigade.

"On August 30, 1863, the regiment crossed the Tennessee river at Shellmound and moved with the army to intercept Bragg and compel the evacuation of Chattanooga. Lookout Mountain was crossed September 11th and 12th. September 19th and 20th the regiment was engaged at Chickamauga. On Saturday it followed the fortunes of the day, meeting with no decided success or repulse, but did hard fighting. At two different times the regiment on its right gave way without apparent cause, and once, also, the regiment on its left fell back some distance, but the One Hundred and Fifth remained quiet and was complimented by the brigade commander, who was an officer of mature years and extensive experience. On Sunday, September 20th, in consequence of General Wood's withdrawing his division, a gap was made in the line, which the enemy took advantage of. The troops of Brannan's division were flanked and fell into confusion. Reynolds's division was posted next on the left of Brannan's. General Reynolds seeing that his flank would soon be exposed and wholly unprotected, ordered Major Perkins to change front with his regiment and charge the rebels on the flank as they advanced. The regiment was at this time in the second line of battle and was lying down. The danger was imminent, and the task anything but inviting. The rebels on the right were cheering each other on, and evidently thought to follow up their success by throwing our line into confusion. At the word of command the regiment sprang to its feet, executed the change of front with as much precision as though on parade, and started forward with deafening yells, on the double-quick to what seemed certain destruction. The suddenness of the movement, the thick growing underbrush which prevented the enemy from estimating the light force coming against them, the unevenness of the ground, which compelled the enemy to extend its front, all operated favorably. The desired object was accomplished and the first line of the enemy was thrown back upon the second, upon reaching which the One Hundred and Fifth opened fire in gallant style, keeping it up for several minutes. Major Perkins soon discovered that his left flank was exposed, and he was compelled to withdraw by the right flank in haste. However, the onset of the enemy was checked, and time given to General Reynolds to make such disposition as secured his right flank and prevented further disaster to the army. This prompt movement of the One Hundred and Fifth was highly commended by General Reynolds at the time, and afterwards by General Rosecrans. Its gallant commander, Major Perkins, was wounded in this charge and conveyed to the rear, and was rendered unfit for duty for nearly four months. The other casualties of the regiment were: E. A. Spaulding, captain, mortally wounded; 3 other officers seriously wounded, and 75 men killed, wounded and prisoners. Two of the largest companies were not in the engagement, so that in proportion to the number engaged the casualties were very heavy.

"Chattanooga was reached September 23d,

and the regiment lay there with the army, doing heavy fatigue duty and living on short rations, until November 23d. Lieutenant-colonel Tolles had rejoined the regiment, from sick-leave. At this time General Grant arrived at Chattanooga, General Sherman's army had arrived from Memphis, and General Hooker's command lay at Lookout valley. On November 23d the old army of the Cumberland moved out of camp and took a position in front of the town. The One Hundred and Fifth took part in the maneuvering of the 23d and 24th, and on the 25th participated in the battle of Mission Ridge. Baird's division, to which it belonged, formed the extreme left of the army of the Cumberland. It occupied the second line, while advancing up the hill, but the first line on reaching the top deployed as skirmishers. The One Hundred and Fifth, on reaching the top, halted to re-form the line, which had become disordered by climbing the hill. As soon as formed, it moved forward, and was the first regiment in the division that moved forward in regular line of battle to the support of the troops of the first line, who were deployed. The other regiments came up promptly, and the entire division being massed in a small compass, it concentrated a heavy fire on that portion of the rebel army remaining on the ridge, which after a few volleys broke and ran down the other side of the ridge. The loss of the regiment in this engagement was comparatively slight. After having joined in the pursuit as far as Ringgold, Georgia, it returned to Chattanooga and went into camp. Major Perkins, who had been absent on account of disability, rejoined the regiment in January, 1864."

William R. Tolles succeeded to the colonelcy after the death of Colonel Hall. He resigned in January, 1864, and was succeeded by George T. Perkins, who commanded the regiment until the close of the service. The One Hundred and Fifth participated in the Atlanta campaign under General Sherman. It performed an honorable part, although not thrown into the heaviest engagements. Colonel Perkins obtained leave of absence in September, and the regiment under Major Edwards joined in the pursuit of Hood as far as Galesville, whence it returned to Atlanta. The remaining months of the year were employed in tearing up railroads and on forced marches on various expeditions. Until the latter part of March the regiment was moving almost constantly. At Goldsboro the troops were reviewed by Generals Sherman and Schofield. The sight was imposing. Full twenty-five per cent. of the men were barefooted; they were ragged and dirty, many in citizens dress and some in rebel uniform. Having received clothing and other necessary supplies the army left Goldsboro April 10th, and after four days' skirmishing with the rebel cavalry arrived at Raleigh. Before General Johnston had made any proposition for a cessation of hostilities a prompt pursuit was ordered, and on the morning of the 14th the Fourteenth corps took the advance toward Charlotte. It was halted at Cape Fear river and remained there until Johnston surrendered.

The corps to which the One Hundred and Fifth belonged arrived in Richmond May 7, 1865. The several corps, exultant in victory, contended for the honor of reaching Richmond first. Some days as many as thirty-five miles were covered. Several deaths was the result of this intemperate haste. The regiment took part in the grand review at Washington May 24th, and was mustered out June 3, 1865. It reached Cleveland June 5th, and was paid off and discharged June 8th, having been in the service nearly three years. It was the first regiment organized under the call of August 4, 1862, and the first disbanded from Camp Cleveland in 1865.

FIELD AND STAFF.

Colonel Albert S. Hall, died of disease at Murfreesboro, Tennessee, July 10, 1863.

Lieutenant-colonel William R. Tolles, resigned January 29, 1864.

Lieutenant-colonel George T. Perkins, promoted from major January 31, 1864.

Major Charles G. Edwards, promoted from company A January 31, 1864, vice Perkins promoted.

Surgeon Charles N. Fowler, mustered out with regiment on special rolls to facilitate final payment.

Assistant-surgeon Joseph G. Paulding, resigned; resignation accepted by special field orders number twenty-five, Department Cumberland, April 8, 1863.

Assistant-surgeon Harvey S. Taft, dismissed.

Assistant-surgeon John Trumbull, mustered out with regiment on special service; appointed vice Paulding resigned.

Quartermaster Marshall W. Wright, resigned; resignation accepted April 13, 1864, by special field order number one hundred and four, Department Cumberland.

Quartermaster Stanley B. Lockwood, appointed regimental quartermaster vice Wright, resigned June 8, 1864, regimental order number twelve.

Adjutant Ambrose M. Robbins resigned; resignation accepted March 28, 1863, by special field order number eighty-four, Department Cumberland.

TRUMBULL AND MAHONING COUNTIES, OHIO.   143

Adjutant Albert Dickman, appointed regimental adjutant vice Robbins, resigned March 29, 1863, by regimental orders number twenty-five; mustered out with regiment.

Chaplain Aaron Van Nostrand, died of disease at Painsville, Ohio, February 27, 1863.

NON-COMMISSIONED STAFF.

Sergeant-major Lester D. Taylor.
Quartermaster Sergeant George W. Cheney.
Commissary-sergeant William J. Gibson.
Hospital steward, John Mehaag.
Sergeant-major Albert Dickman, discharged, to date December 15, 1862, to accept appointment as second lieutenant, by special field order number seventy, Department Cumberland.
Sergeant-major Irwin Butler, discharged, to date February 26, 1863, to accept appointment as second lieutenant, by special field order number seventy, Department Cumberland.
Sergeant-major Porter Watson, discharged, to date June 19, 1864, to accept appointment as first lieutenant, by special order number one hundred and fifty-two, Fourteenth army corps.
Quartermaster-sergeant Horatio M. Smith, discharged, to date February 17, 1863, to accept appointment as second lieutenant.
Private musician Horace Ranown, reduced to musician, and transferred to company I, September 14, 1864, by regimental order number twelve.
Private musician William Doty, veteran volunteer, transferred to Thirty-eighth regiment, Ohio veteran volunteer infantry, June 1, 1865, by special order number thirty-six, Fourteenth army corps.

COMPANY A.
COMMISSIONED OFFICERS.

Captain Charles G. Edwards, mustered out January 30, 1864, to accept promotion as major in same regiment.
Captain Richard J. See, joined from company K, by transfer per regimental order number six, vice Edwards promoted and transferred to company G by regimental order number fourteen, September 20, 1864.
Captain Daniel B. Stambaugh, promoted to captain vice See, transferred.
First Lieutenant Richard J. See, promoted to captain February 16, 1863, and assigned to company K.
First Lieutenant Daniel B. Stambaugh, promoted to captain August 3, 1864; assigned to company A, vice See transferred to company G per regimental order.
First Lieutenant Norman D. Smith, appointed first lieutenant from first sergeant of company F, and assigned to company A, August 3, 1864, by regimental order number fourteen; mustered out on special rolls.
Second Lieutenant Daniel B. Stambaugh, promoted to first lieutenant February 16, 1863, vice See promoted.
Second Lieutenant Patten Himrod, promoted to first lieutenant February 24, 1863, and assigned to company C by regimental order number twenty.
Second Lieutenant William H. Castle, promoted to first lieutenant March 31, 1864, and assigned to company E by regimental order number eleven, June 20, 1864.

NON-COMMISSIONED OFFICERS.

First Sergeant Robert Kay.
Sergeant James Brown.
Sergeant Isaiah J. Noble.
Sergeant James Morris.
Sergeant Robert C. Porter.

Corporal William Phillips.
Corporal William G. Davis.
Corporal James Allen.
Corporal Samuel Alexander.
Corporal Michael Burns.
Corporal Henry B. Bailey.
Corporal Thomas Bowen.
Corporal Hugh Cooley.
Corporal James Files.
Corporal Thomas George.
Corporal Dixon Holloway.
Corporal Frederick Heiliger.
Corporal William Jones.

PRIVATES.

Frederick James, Thomas Jarrs, Mahashalal Kelley, Andrew Knox, Wesley Kyle, Thomas Sally, Ashley Moore, Francis Moore, John Miles, Simon P. McFall, Dennis McKanna, John B. McDonald, John Phillips, John T. Parker, James T. Rayen, John E. Stambaugh, Jonathan Wise, Lewis Young, Nathan W. King, William H. Craig, Joseph Applegate, Albert Miller, Michael McGinhl, Henry Niblock, James William, Emmons Sparrow, Lafayette McCoy, George Walser, Alexander Barr, John A. Boyle, James C. Coulter, Richard Houston, Benjamin B. Lewis, Isaac Morris, William B. Price, Reuben B. Keep, William W. Stewart, John Shingledecker, John B. Thomas, Cyrus Williams, Henry Witherstay, John H. Webb, David Edmunds, Frank Hulburt, Richard Williams, Himrod Patten, James Crays, John D. Jewell, Joseph Torrence, John Cliugensmith, George S. Anderson, George Conklin, John Flecker, Charles Fielding, Emanuel Fair, James Hunter, John J. Kandy, David D. Jones, Thomas H. Morris, James F. Knox, James O'Hara, Richard Rega, Daniel Robbins, John W. Keen, Samuel M. Stewart, Thomas Tyrell.

Transferred —Porter Watson, John F. McCollum, Dugala Cook, John C. Foster, Aaron Harber, Stephen T. Kelley, James Malcomsom, Robert McKibben, Porter Lewis, Daniel A. Smith, Jacob Stien, John Allen Stewart, John Alex Stewart, Charles C. Stover, William Briley.

To be Transferred.— George Baker, James Chisty, Oscar C. F. Heiliger, Leonard K. Hothum, Frederick Harrington, Anthony Kaine, Edward L. Howard, Patrick McCambridge, John O'Donal, James Patterson, Elijah B. Russell, Eli S. Reed, James Rowe, Samuel A. Stambaugh, James Stewart, Cyrus Stewart, David C. Whetstone, William L. Jones.

COMPANY B.
COMMISSIONED OFFICERS.

Captain Ephraim Kee, died of disease January 19, 1863, Murfreesboro, Tennessee.
Captain Andrew D. Braden, promoted from first lieutenant company B, February 24, 1863, vice Captain Kee, died; mustered out on separate rolls.
First Lieutenant Andrew D. Braden, promoted to captain and mustered out February 24, 1863, vice Kee, died.
First Lieutenant Albert Dickerman, promoted from lieutenant company H; mustered out November 30, 1863; Dickerman transferred.
First Lieutenant Ira F. Mansfield, promoted from second lieutenant company H; mustered out November 30, 1863, vice Dickerman, transferred.
Second Lieutenant Henry D. Niles, resigned; resignation accepted by special field order number forty, Department of the Cumberland.
Second Lieutenant Merit Emerson, promoted to Second Lieutenant and mustered out April 19, 1863, vice Niles, re-

signed; assigned to duty April 19, 1863, order number twenty; died of disease January 13, 1865.

NON-COMMISSIONED OFFICERS.

First Sergeant John S. Williams.
Sergeant Noah J. Pound.
Sergeant Wilson S. Hulls.
Sergeant Charles Stewart.
Sergeant Osman B. Tuttle.
Corporal James B. Ramsdell.
Corporal Henry E. Finney.
Corporal Hubert E. Hillman.
Musician Aaron J. Merritt.

PRIVATES.

Clusky Ballard, Enos Bare, Abner Bare, Francis Colton, John P. Davidson, William Ensign, James E. Fanrot, Ephraim Grim, Seth Hart, Simeon Hart, Edwin Hadsell, Lattin Wright, Hugh Lowery, Charles H. Mason, Alexander Mackey, Benjamin H. Mayhugh, John A. Murphy, Dwight R. Philips, Lauren A. Purty, Ralph E. Ragow, Homer Stephenson, William J. Shaffer, Charles Shaffer, Jacob Shaffer, Benjamin F. Smith, John Smith, Hugh J. Snodgrass, George M. Thomas, Albert P. Tuttle, John E. Wildman, William H. Welch.

Killed at Perryville, Kentucky.—Jonas E. Wanneper, Jonathan Bellaret, John Drennon, John F. Helsley, Benjamin F. Kennedy, Jacob Ryan, Christopher F. Ricker, William C. True.

Died.—Edward S. Palfreeman, 1864; John A. Ewalt, 1863; Hiram J. Scott, 1863; Marcus Berlingame, 1862; Calvin Caldwell, 1863; James A. Crawford, 1865; Heman Dilly, 1862; Albert Grim, Joseph Hartman, Adelbert Hart, 1863; Henry Hurst, 1862; Henry Heath, 1862; Hugh R. Kelly, 1864; Perkins Addison, 1862; Daniel Rush, 1864; James Sage, 1864; Samuel K. Gaft, 1862; Newton L. Wolcott, 1865.

Not reported.—Henry I. Beebe.

Discharged before Expiration of Service.—William H. Forbis, Merritt Emerson, Norval B. Cubb, George F. Center, James M. Dickerman, George W. Granger, Michael E. Hegs, Daniel Ladwick, Edward M. Bell, Henry H. Center, Joseph Card, Marshall Davis, Jasper C. Downs, James W. Hathaway, Edwin J. Kinner, Isaiah S. Kitiage, John J. Landon, Edwin D. Lewis, Harry Mahanah, Stephen Prudens, Edward W. Sager, Harmon W. Stow, Martin W. Ulrick, Dwight R. Phillips (prisoner of war), William C. Welch (prisoner of war).

Transferred.—William Hughes, Lewis Long, Mayer William, Cyrus Oliver, Edward Printons, Albert Printions, Lawrenson H. Sparks, Charles R. Dayton, William Decker, William H. Johnson, Hugh W. Jackson, Lafayette Lane, Calvin L. Randon, Martin B. Randon, Morrison R. Shaffer, Samuel Wierman, William Harver.

COMPANY C.

COMMISSIONED OFFICERS.

Captain Ambrose C. Mason, died of disease August 27, 1864; promoted to captain, vice Gilbert, resigned.

First Lieutenant James H. Bond, resigned; resignation accepted March 12, 1863, by special field order number sixty-eight, Department of the Cumberland.

First Lieutenant Himrod Patten, promoted from second lieutenant company A; assigned to company April 19, 1863, vice J. H. Bond, resigned; promoted to captain company E December 1, 1863.

First Lieutenant Reuben G. Margaridge, promoted to captain; assigned to company D December 21, 1864, vice Baker, resigned.

First Lieutenant William C. Old, appointed from first sergeant company G; assigned to company C December 21, 1864, vice Reuben G. Margaridge, promoted.

Second Lieutenant James H. Bond, promoted to first lieutenant; mustered July 24, 1863, vice A. C. Mason, promoted.

Second Lieutenant Irwin Butler, resigned; resignation accepted May 8, 1863, by special field order number one hundred and twenty-five.

NON-COMMISSIONED OFFICERS.

First Sergeant Clinton F. Moore.
Sergeant John B. Miller.
Sergeant Jacob Tinney.
Sergeant John Geddes.
Sergeant Robert Dalton.
Corporal Albert Jasatt.
Corporal Samuel Rupper.
Corporal Robert A. Rowles.
Corporal Austin Tibbits.
Musician Christian Hughes.
Musician Thomas C. Hogle.
Wagoner Charles E. Miller.

PRIVATES.

William F. Adams, James Culler, C. L. Casper, John W. Davis, James Donovan, Aseriah Evans, James L. Edwards, John F. Edwards, Charles C. Fowler, George W. Green, John W. Green, Michael J. Hood, Joseph Healy, Thomas Jessop, William Jones, Caleb Lewis, William Lewis, Evan Lewis, Theron S. McKinly, John M. Mackey, William Morris, Alfred Osborn, Nilson S. Powers, John P. Rosser, John Roberts, George L. Keis, James Rodgers, William R. Reese, Lafayette Seaton, I. Senchrist, Samuel Netton, John Sinclair, David J. Shealor, Thomas A. Thomas, Homer B. Walker, Samuel Walker, William Evans, William H. Godshall, Lawrence Kelley, Lemuel Moser, Lemuel B. Miller, Richard H. McLain, Lemuel Power, Nelson Stewart, Cornelius Shook.

Not reported.—Morgan Mannering, Joseph K. McKinsie, Thomas Robinson, William T. Richards.

Discharged before expiration of service.—James Bolter, Samuel Blackmore, John Burgess, Morgan W. Davis, Benjamin Esgarr, Harvey A. Fuller, John H. Frazier, Isaac Frazier, Reuben B. Heidands, Joel Hanley, Thomas Jones, William Jack, Jasper B. Kingsley, Henry Lawrence, Phillip H. Moser, Charles E. Moser, John Powers, Joseph Phillips, David P. Richard, Horace Sconife, Robert J. Stewart, James A. Stewart, Thomas Smith, James G. Townsend, Charles W. Townsend, Austin W. Wilson.

TRANSFERRED.

First Sergeant Irwin Butler to lieutenant on commissioned staff December 18, 1862.

John B. Brandt to Veteran Reserve corps April 11, 1864.

William Cowan to Veteran Reserve corps, February 7, 1864.

William P. Graham to Engineer corps, July 18, 1864.

Hiram T. Hull to Veteran Engineer corps, July 18, 1864.

Thomas Quigley, to Veteran Reserve corps, September 1, 1863.

John Wambaugh to Veteran Reserve corps, September 1, 1863.

Died.—Erastus Bartholomew, 1864; William R. Davis, 1864.

To be transferred.—George M. Dice, Morgan Davis, Gaylum Davis, Thomas Heis, George Heis, John B. Richards, John B. Thomas, Daniel Webster, Edward Whitehouse.

Killed.—Adolphus Vally, Andrew N. White.

COMPANY H.

COMMISSIONED OFFICERS.

Captain Robert Wilson, died of wounds received in action at Chaplain Hills, Kentucky, October 8, 1862.

Captain William R. Tuttle, promoted from first lieutenant company E, and assigned to company D, December 15, 1862, by regimental order No. 29.

First Lieutenant William H. Clark, transferred to company F, February 24, 1863, by regimental order No. 8, February 27, 1863.

First Lieutenant John C. Hartsell, on detached service February, 1864, by special field order No. 43, February 12, 1864.

Second Lieutenant Ira F. Mansfield, promoted to first lieutenant, and mustered out February 24, 1863, vice Clark, transferred.

NON-COMMISSIONED OFFICERS.

First Sergeant George M. Dull.
Sergeant Abram S. McCurley.
Sergeant John W. Nesbit.
Sergeant James S. Caldwell.
Sergeant George J. Smith.
Corporal Jason W. Silsern.
Corporal William K. Mead.
Corporal Manasses Miller.
Corporal Andrew Geddes.
Corporal John H. Bellard.
Musician Samuel Bright.
Musician William M. Taylor.

PRIVATES.

Joseph S. Allen, Jesse F. Allen, Frederick Brown, Jacob Buchecker, Constantine Brenaman, Sylvester Baker, Joseph Carbaugh, John W. Cessna, Amos Cobbs, John F. Ellinger, Zimri Engle, Joseph H. Flansher, Solomon Fishel, Joseph Grussman, Jeremiah Harrison, Joshua Hartzell, Daniel Hayes, Frank Kaiser, Robert A. Kirk, William T. Marton, Edmund H. Mathias, William H. Middleton, James Naylor, John Ovington, James Park, Charles D. Price, Samuel K. Raub, George W. Shinck, Homer J. Shields, Charles D. Strawn, Jesse Stutler, Allen Silvers, George J. Spitters, Peter Spiller, Charles A. Van Norden, Peter Vanable, Francis White, Samuel Weldy, Moses Weldy, Jeremiah Whitestone, Samuel Wire, David A. Wilson.

Killed.—William T. Armstrong, Chaplain Hills, Kentucky; Horace Roughton, Chaplain Hills, Kentucky; Alfred Hunt, Atlanta, Georgia; Nathan Hartman, Chaplain Hills, Kentucky; Joseph Rummel, Jonesboro, Georgia; Eri Stratton, Chaplain Hills, Kentucky.

Died.—William H. Baker, 1862; Benjamin Deem, 1863; Eben B. Fishel, 1863; William D. Ingling, 1863; Usher Kirkbride, 1863; John C. McCurley, 1863; Homer Noble, 1863; William H. Naylor, 1862; Eli G. Owens, 1864; Isaac C. P. Raub, 1863; Albert A. Sherman, 1863; Daniel W. Umstead, 1863.

Not Reported.—Henry Hutton.

Discharged Before Expiration of Service.—Thomas Bennett, David Bricker, George V. Boyle, Joseph Kirkbride, James T. Mathers, Jonathan Myers, Addison Miller, Horace G. Ruggles, Florensine M. Simeons, Alexander T. Watson, Ears Yosder.

Transferred.—Frederick Courtney, Almon Eastman, Chancey M. Hunt, Hornstine Rasilla, James Kirkbride, John Meharv, Rezol M. Stewart, John Young.

To be Transferred.—James Shaffer, Lewis Witmer, Benjamin Witeman.

COMPANY I.

COMMISSIONED OFFICERS.

Captain S. Dwight Kee, killed in action at Perryville, Kentucky, October 8, 1862.

Captain Henry C. Sweet, dismissed by special field order.

Captain William Wallace, promoted from second lieutenant company I, and mustered September 6, 1863, vice Sweet, dismissed.

Charles A. Brigden, resigned; resignation accepted by special field order No. 18, Department Cumberland, Tennessee, January 21, 1863.

First Lieutenant William H. Osborn, transferred from company K February 27, 1863, by regimental order No. 9, vice Brigden, resigned.

Second Lieutenant William H. Osborn, promoted to first lieutenant, and assigned to company K December 15, 1862, by regimental order No. 27.

Second Lieutenant Albert Dickerman, promoted to first lieutenant, and assigned to company B February 27, 1863, by regimental order No. 9, vice Braden, promoted.

Second Lieutenant William Wallace, promoted to captain, and assigned to duty with company I September 6, 1863, by order of regimental commander, vice Sweet, dismissed.

NON-COMMISSIONED OFFICER.

Corporal Orris Udall.

PRIVATES.

Anderson Thomas (honorably discharged from hospital at Cleveland, June 24, 1863), Gabriel P. Barb, John M. Bower, David Bower, Hezekiah H. Hescock, Salethiel Harrison, Homer Halbut, Benjamin Joslin, John Kellogg, Edgar A. Kelly, Lucius Perkins, John P. Stoner, William F. Triloff, Jeremiah M. Tidd, William R. Wilcox, Robert Winnram, Ezra Yokes, John S. Cook, Seymour A. Cox, Henry Collar, Edwin A. Whitcomb.

Died.—Edwin H. Andrews, 1862; Ambrose J. Bailey, 1864; William Creighton, 1863; Manuel J. Harrison while prisoner of war, Hyran T. Knight and Harvey W. Partridge, 1863; Esau A. Sealy, 1864; Whitman B. Talcott, 1862; George Thomas, 1863.

Not reported.—Ira W. Beckwith, John W. Lyman, Milan H. Merrit.

Discharged before expiration of service.—Collins E. Bushnell, William S. Caldwell, Miloe G. Heath, Robert N. Holcomb, John Haddock, William J. Haine, Samuel Hark, Chancy W. Lattimore, Horace A. Leonard, Phillip Reynolds, Albert H. Smith, William Wallace, Salethiel Harrison.

Transferred.—Robert S. Abell, George Haine, Edgar Lockwood.

To be transferred.—George Lane.

COMPANY K.

PRIVATE.

A. N. Parker.

COMPANY F.

RECRUITS.

Levi B. Cousins, Charles Gray, Warren Hobert, Daniel Ketcham, John Sadler, J. B. Scott.

ONE HUNDRED AND TWENTY-FIFTH REGIMENT OHIO VOLUNTEER INFANTRY.*

Six companies of the One Hundred and Twenty-fifth regiment were organized at Camp Cleveland during the months of October, November, and December, 1862, under the immediate supervision of Colonel Opdycke. Two companies enlisted for the Eighty-seventh Ohio infantry at Camp Mansfield, Ohio, as place of rendezvous, were transferred to the One Hundred and Twenty-fifth on the 6th day of December, and were mustered shortly afterwards. On the 27th of December the regiment was ordered to be ready to leave the State by the 1st day of January, 1863. It did not march, however, until the 3d, when with three days' rations in haversack the men waded through almost impassable mud to the Cleveland & Columbus depot and were then transported by railroad to Cincinnati.

By order of Major-general Wright, requiring Colonel Opdycke to report with his command to Brigadier-general Boyle, the regiment took boat at Cincinnati on the 4th and arrived at Louisville, Kentucky, on the following day. They were ordered into camp at the southern outskirt of the city, where, crowded into tents without stoves and even without straw to lie on, they passed the remainder of the month. The weather was severe, snow at one time covering the ground to the depth of twenty-two inches. Yet the men were healthy and cheerful and the memory of "Camp Opdycke" (named in honor of the colonel) will ever be cherished as a happy epoch in their soldier history. While at Louisville the One Hundred and Twenty-fifth was called on to do final honor to two of Kentucky's gallant sons by escorting to the grave the remains of Colonel Forman, of the Fifteenth, and Colonel Samuel McKee, of the Third Kentucky infantry.

By order of Brigadier-general Boyle, January 2, 1863, the One Hundred and Twenty-fifth was transferred to the command of Brigadier-general C. C. Gilbert, commanding division, and on the 1st day of February it started with the rest of the command by boat for Nashville, Tennessee, where it arrived without interruption on the 9th, and went into camp near the city. At 1:30 A. M. of the 12th the command took up the line of march for Franklin, eighteen miles distant. The One Hundred and Twenty-fifth was placed in advance, and after a sharp skirmish, in which it sustained no loss, the small force of rebel cavalry which was occupying the place fled and they took possession of the town. The rest of the division not crossing the river (Harpeth), Colonel Opdycke was placed in command of the post, which place he continued to occupy until the 15th of March. On the 9th and 10th of March the regiment marched to Rutherford's creek, the rebels retiring as it advanced. It returned on the 11th and encamped near Franklin till the 2d of June, meantime taking part in a severe skirmish on the 10th of April, in which the enemy was repulsed with a loss of 25 killed and 40 to 60 wounded and prisoners. June 2d it marched to Triune, Tennessee. June 11th assisted in repulsing a sharp attack of the enemy, which lasted two hours; sustained no loss. By order of Major-general Granger, June 19. 1863, the One Hundred and Twenty fifth was ordered to report to the commander of the department at Murfreesboro.

The regiment marched on the 21st of June and was assigned by General Rosecrans to the Third brigade, First division, Twenty-first army corps. June 24th it took part in the general advance, which resulted in driving Bragg from Tullahoma, Manchester, and beyond the Tennessee river. During this march it rained almost incessantly, and the regiment suffered much on account of heavy roads and excessive labor until it went into camp at Hillsboro, Tennessee, on the 9th of July; remained at Hillsboro until August 16th, when a general advance was again ordered; crossed the mountains, and arrived at Thurman on the 20th; went into camp until September 1st, and marched to Jasper on the the 2d, to Shell Mound on the 1st and 3d, and to Lookout Station on the 5th and 6th. By order of General Crittenden, September 7th, the One Hundred and Twenty-fifth, with the rest of Harker's brigade, was ordered up Lookout valley on a reconnoissance; returned at dark, having developed the enemy's batteries, and accomplished what was termed by General Wood one of the most dangerous expeditions of the war. On the 8th, 9th, and 10th it marched to Chattanooga, and to Gordon's mills on the 11th and 12th; remained at Gordon's mills until

---

* Official record.

the 18th, and was in the hottest of the battle of Chickamauga on the 19th and 20th. It was in the battle on the 20th of September, where it led in three successive charges which checked the advance of the enemy, broke his ranks, struck terror into his seemingly invincible columns, and saved the Army of the Cumberland from destruction, that General Wood applied to the One Hundred and Twenty-fifth regiment the name of "Ohio Tigers." The regiment went into the engagement with 11 officers and 298 men, of which it had 1 officer and 11 men killed, 2 officers and 71 seriously, and 10 slightly wounded. Several subsequently died of their wounds; others were maimed for life. On the 21st of September the One Hundred and Twenty-fifth retired with the rest of its brigade to Rossville, and during the night fell back to Chattanooga, where it arrived at 2 o'clock A. M., of the 22d, and went into camp. The work of fortifying the place commenced immediately, and was pursued vigorously night and day. Although the men were on less than one-third rations, subsisting part of the time almost entirely upon parched corn, they endured it without a murmur, and went cheerfully at their daily task until Chattanooga was encircled with impregnable fortifications. They remained in camp at Chattanooga until the 23d of November, when a forward movement was again ordered.

During that day and night the enemy's outposts were driven in, and the regiment intrenched one mile from the base of Mission Ridge. The One Hundred and Twenty-fifth was on picket the 24th, and on the 25th was engaged in the hottest of that memorable battle. In spite of the shower of shot and shell that rained upon it, the One Hundred and Twenty-fifth regiment was among the first to reach the summit of the ridge and charge the enemy from his breastworks, capturing 100 prisoners, 1 fine Whitworth gun, 1 wagon and mules, and a large quantity of small arms. Our loss in the engagement amounted to 3 killed, and 1 officer and 26 men wounded.

The regiment pursued the enemy to Chickamauga creek on the night of the 25th, and returned to Chattanooga on the day following. All baggage arrived at Knoxville December 8th. After a rest of four days they marched to Blair's Cross-roads on the 12th and 13th,
where they remained in bivouac, poorly clothed and worse fed, until the 15th of January, 1864. January 15th and 16th they marched to Dandridge, went on picket on the 17th, were attacked at 2 o'clock P. M. by a brigade of dismounted rebel cavalry, and skirmished sharply until dark. They repulsed the enemy, but lost during the day 7 officers and 5 men killed, and 12 men wounded.

They retreated at night, and returned to Strawberry plains on the 18th and 19th, and to Knoxville on the 20th and 21st. They marched again on the 23d, and arrived at London, Tennessee, on the 25th of January, where they built winter quarters and spent the remainder of the winter comfortably. The spring was spent in East Tennessee until June, when the regiment was ordered to Louisiana, and thence to Texas, where it was mustered out September 25th. Returning to Ohio it was discharged at Camp Chase October 17th.

FIELD AND STAFF.

Colonel Emerson Opdyke, appointed brigadier-general January, 1865; appointed major-general; received leave of absence while commanding Second division, July 5, 1865.
Lieutenant-colonel David H. Moore, resigned September 20, 1864.
Lieutenant-colonel Joseph Bruff, mustered out on separate rolls.
Major George L. Wood, resigned April 20, 1863.
Major Joseph Bruff, promoted to lieutenant-colonel January 23, 1865.
Surgeon Henry McHenry, resigned June 1, 1865.
Assistant Surgeon Porter Yates, resigned May 6, 1863.
Assistant Surgeon James G. Buchanan, resigned January 25, 1865.
Assistant Surgeon John E. Darby, promoted to surgeon colored regiment, May 18, 1864.
Assistant Surgeon William E. McKim, mustered out on separate rolls.
Chaplain John W. Lewis, resigned January 20, 1865.
Adjutant Edward G. Whiteside, promoted to captain company A, March 1, 1864.
Adjutant Ridgley C. Powers, promoted to captain company B, July 7, 1864.
Adjutant Wyman Phillips, appointed adjutant from regimental quartermaster July 7, 1864.
Quartermaster Abner B. Carter, resigned May 4, 1864.
Quartermaster Wyman Phillips, transferred to regimental adjutant July 7, 1864.
Quartermaster William H. Crowell, mustered out June 9, 1865.
Sergeant-major Seabury A. Smith.
Sergeant-major Henry A. Bell.
Quartermaster-sergeant Melvin E. Hillis.
Quartermaster-sergeant William H. Crowell.
Quartermaster-sergeant Henry Lord.
Commissary-sergeant Hezekiah H. Steadman.
Commissary-sergeant Thomas E. Trimble.
Hospital Steward Simon S. Herring.

Hospital Steward George W. Dietrick.
Principal Musician Peter Damund.
Principal Musician Samuel Sidlinger.
Principal Musician Benjamin F. Young.

COMPANY A.
COMMISSIONED OFFICERS.

Captain Joseph Bruff, mustered out as captain February 29, 1864, to accept appointment as major One Hundred and Twenty-fifth Ohio volunteer infantry.

Captain Edward G. Whiteside, promoted from adjutant One Hundred and Twenty-fifth Ohio volunteer infantry to captain company A, March 1, 1864.

First Lieutenant Robert B. Stewart, mustered out as first lieutenant June 19, 1865, to accept appointment as captain company D, same regiment.

First Lieutenant Alexander Dickson, mustered out as first lieutenant August 1, 1864, to accept appointment as captain company K, same regiment.

First Lieutenant David K. Blyster, promoted from second lieutenant company C to first lieutenant company A October 11, 1864; resigned April 11, 1865.

First Lieutenant Thomas R. Mahan, promoted from second lieutenant company C to first lieutenant company A, May 2, 1865.

Second Lieutenant Alexander Dickson, promoted from second lieutenant company A to first lieutenant same company March 2, 1864, vice Stewart promoted.

NON-COMMISSIONED OFFICERS.

First Sergeant Daniel K. Bush, promoted from corporal to first sergeant September 16, 1864; mustered out May 29, 1865.

Sergeant Nathan J. Thomas, mustered out May 29, 1865.
Sergeant William J. Townsend, promoted sergeant March 8, 1865, mustered out May 21, 1865.
Corporal Dighton Young, mustered out with company.
Corporal Luther S. Calvin, mustered out with company.
Corporal Silas Coy, mustered out with company.
Corporal James R. Dickson, mustered out with company.
Corporal Irvin Thomas, mustered out with company.
Corporal Charles Wagner, mustered out with company.

PRIVATES.

George Arbuckle, George W. Balis, George Beeman, John S. Blim, Silvanus Baker, Albert Callahan, Mathias C. Callahan, Jeremiah Creps, David B. Erb, Henry Hilton, Joseph D. Hartzell, Eli C. Kelly, Samuel A. Miller, James P. Ramsey, Jacob W. Ruppert, Albert Stone, Jerred Shenefield, Thomas Spickler, Nicholas Winning, George W. Weekart, Richmond Thomas.

Discharged Before Expiration of Service.—Bernard J. Sheridan, Thomas Freeman, Josiah H. Blackburn, Joseph B. Naylor, Michael Wilford, Robert P. King, George Hoffman, Joshua Crouse, William Hutton, Jacob Baughman, John Boner, Henry L. Barricks, John P. Calvin, Solomon Color, Joshua Callahan, Simon S. Coy, Emery Fasnaucht, John Gety, Orrin L. Lazarus, John Steves, Aaron Schroy, Jonathan Wining.

Died.—James B. Morris, Alexander D. Pollock, Ephraim Snyder, Horace Bunnell, Reuben Bunnell, Jacob B. Calvin, George W. Calvin, Jacob Creps, Jeremiah Callahan, Cornelius J. Detchon, William L. Dickson, John Danforth, James Flack, Isaac Goodman, Sylvester Harriff, Cornelius Infildt, David Loyd, Alexander Miller, Samuel Morningstar, John C. Naylor, William Osborn, Lewis Welsh, Isaac Wilson.

Transferred.—Benjamin F. Rhodes, Thomas G. Stradford, John H. Stamp, Amos V. Baily, Jacob Blim, Andrew Cook, James G. Crawford, Peter Meiger, Marian Parker, Benjamin F. Stover, Francis Tool, Thomas Richmond.

Not Reported.—Edward Carr, John Shoff, Charles F. Timble, Henderson Lee.

COMPANY B.
COMMISSIONED OFFICERS.

Captain Albert Yeoman, resigned May 7, 1864.

Captain Rigley C. Powers, promoted from adjutant to captain company B, July 7, 1864; mustered out.

First Lieutenant Elmer Moses, mustered out to receive promotion as captain company E, January, 1864.

First Lieutenant Rolse C. Rice, mustered out to receive promotion as captain company H, April 15, 1865.

First Lieutenant Henry Glenville, promoted from second lieutenant company H, to receive promotion as first lieutenant company B, April 16, 1865.

Second Lieutenant Charles Hackman, resigned June, 1863.

NON-COMMISSIONED OFFICERS.

First Sergeant Rufus Woods.
Sergeant Albert Mathews.
Sergeant Fredrick H. Knight.
Sergeant William Fitch.
Corporal Lyman Root.
Corporal Sylvester T. Hashman.
Colonel Wallace J. Henry.
Corporal Isaiah Brown.
Corporal John Thompson.

PRIVATES.

Oliver Brown, Walter Brown, James Cranston, Jasse H. Cary, Caleb French, Warren H. Fisher, Franklin J. Fobes, Harvey Giddings, Porter A. Goff, John Gilin, Emory Gilmore, Thomas Louzanhisen, George Murdock, John C. Mossman, Morris Meacham, Apollos P. Morse, Alnson Peck, James M. Pollock, Henry N. Tracy, Edwin C. Woodworth, Patrick Welch, James K. Warren.

Killed.—James M. Murdock, Franklin, Tennessee; William M. Johnson, Chickamauga; Adrian Fitch, Nathan B. Hatch, Kenesaw, Georgia; Rufus P. Mossman, Chickamauga; Robert F. Rice, Kenesaw Mountain, Georgia.

Died.—Thomas M. Burnham, 1863; William A. Covert, 1864; William A. Dana, Ethan C. Briggs, Orvin F. Gates, 1863; Charles W. Henry, 1864; Asa Hagan, Thomas T. Heath, Levi Spiltsone, George Stroubble, James M. Tidd, Elmer H. Waters, Joel N. Williams, John W. Welch, Perry Fitch, 1863.

Discharged before expiration of service.—Richard K. Huber, Rollin P. Barner, William Vesey, Darwin F. Allen, William H. Lee, Emerson Brainard, Michael Perringer, Dennis J. Adkins, Charles A. Austin, Morgan Brown, George French, James Floody, Wesley C. Fishel, Henry B. Gildard, John P. Gertner, Dudley D. McMichael, William T. Smith, Francis Sprague, Harrison Turner, David B. Wood.

Not reported—William Fenton, Andrew Moffat, Robert K. Simpkins.

Transferred.—Seabury Smith, William H. Crowell, Hezekiah N. Steadman, George P. Davis, William Wasson, Orlando Bundy, James N. Burnett, Thomas Brown, Darius Britten, Gilbert L. Cook, William E. Davis, Orsamus Fitch, Samuel Fenn, Hezekiah L. Griffith, Washington Jones, John W. King, Seth T. Moses, Ephraim E. Peck, James Paden, Theophile Panquett, George Pigott, Edwin M. Reynolds, Gideon A. Robinson, William M. Smith, George Stratton.

COMPANY C.

COMMISSIONED OFFICERS.

Captain Edward P. Bates, received commission as major February 28, 1865.

First Lieutenant Heman R. Harmon, resigned April 16, 1863.

Second Lieutenant Alson C. Dilley, received commission as first lieutenant May 9, 1864; was killed in action at Kennesaw, Georgia, June 27, 1864.

Second Lieutenant David Blyston, mustered out to accept commission as first lieutenant company A, October 10, 1864.

Second Lieutenant Thomas R. Mahan, mustered out to accept commission as first lieutenant company A, May 17, 1865.

NON-COMMISSIONED OFFICERS.

First Sergeant Mark Kieth, promoted from sergeant August 6, 1865.

Sergeant Sidney Higgins, promoted from corporal March 5, 1864.

Sergeant Clinton H. Phelps, promoted from corporal September 6, 1864.

Sergeant John Murphy, promoted from corporal July 10, 1865.

Sergeant Yalmon F. Morris, promoted from corporal August 6, 1865.

Corporal William F. Thorn, appointed November 1, 1862.

Corporal James Sanner.
Corporal Robert Parker.
Corporal Rees C. Davis.
Corporal Clark Van Wie.
Corporal Archibald Hill.
Corporal Thomas Comerford.
Wagoner Ralph H. Porter.

PRIVATES.

Sanford Armstrong, William R. Arnold, Simon H. Andrews, John T. Bell, Truman Borden, Edward Brima, Enoch Boyd, Jared Bouton, Charles Brown, Walter Chreney, Gilbert S. Cook, James Corcoran, Bernard Comerford, Leonard H. Curtis, Thomas Fay, Onamus Fitch, Leroy Fuller, John Hall, John Handley, Hiel Higgins, Kinomel K. Harrison, Chancy B. Hayden, Avery Harwood, Frederick Keck, John W. King, James W. Seet, Quincy Satin, John D. Mahan, William McKinvley, Samuel Machem, Joseph Miller, William M. Orr, John C. Osborn, George Perkins, Thomas R. Pinks, George Pigot, Minor Radcliff, Edward M. Reynolds, Seneca St. John, Jeremiah Swinehart, Warren Sandy, George Simston, Michael Swartz, William Thompson, Alexander Vesey, Lewis Williams, Nathan C. Warden, Cassius M. Zedaker, George Rummage.

Died.—Joseph Andrews, 1863; Edwin Y. Abrams, 1863; Henry Baker, 1863; Simeon Carlton, 1864; Lolin B. Cowdry, 1862; Joseph Custer, 1864; Jonathan Dilley, 1863; Anson E. Hayford, 1864; David Jack, 1863; Nicholas Keck, 1863; John W. Powers, 1863; Jesse Sample, 1864; George W. Simpson, 1864; Eli Swinehart, 1864; Fratus G. Tylee, 1864; Sylvester Waterman, 1864.

Discharged before Expiration of Service.—Howard Bascom, Erastus Brainard, Chancy Brainard, Linus H. Brocket, Anthony Burrow, John Campbell, John A. Canon, Charles E. Cole, Cassius Coats, Charles William, Alson C. Dilley, Samuel Fenn, Shawn French, Morgan Gray, Levi H. Hall, Asael B. Hall, Benjamin Hall, Elbert R. Higby, George Justice, Harvey W. Lamb, Lafayette Sake, Leronse Bates, Jesse B. Luse, Thomas R. Mahan, Samuel T. Morrison, Cornelius McNutt, Philander Odell, Hiram Phillips, Lorenzo Row, William D. Todd, Chester Tuttle, William H. Watkins, George Waterman, Wilmer J. West.

Transferred.—Henry Bell, Jason Case, Christopher Clark, John Fenton, Silas H. Jones, Mark Shields, Thomas M. Thompson, John Williams.

Not Reported.—Thomas Belden, Joseph Bell, Napoleon Blanchert, Thomas Brown, Meghair Choplop, Charles Chodier, John Dubois, George Gulliver, William H. Lynn, Robert Osborn, Thomas Osborn, Joseph Ominet, Charles Parker, Theophile Paguett, Gilbert Richardson, Gideon A. Robison, William Neaborn, John Trudell, Moses Trudell, James Wilson, Joseph Wilson.

ONE HUNDRED AND FIFTY-FIFTH REGIMENT, OHIO NATIONAL GUARD.

The fear of northern raids and the inadequacy of the force left on guard duty along the border, the strength of the National army being employed in the interior of the Confederacy, induced the President to issue a call for one hundred days' volunteers. Ohio's quota was thirty thousand, which was soon filled, chiefly from the ranks of the Ohio National Guards. The Forty-fourth battalion, a Mahoning county organization, composed of four companies, was consolidated with the Ninety-second Ohio volunteer infantry, and formed the One Hundred and Fifty-fifth Ohio volunteer infantry. Company A, of the Forty-fourth battalion, became company B of the One Hundred and Fifty-fifth; company B of the Forty-fourth was with the exception of its commandant, Captain F. O. Arms, distributed among the companies of the Ninety-second; company D of the Forty-fourth retained its letter, and company C became company G of the One Hundred and Fifty-fifth. A roster of companies B, D, and G will be found below.

The One Hundred and Fifty-fifth was mustered into the service May 8, 1864, and on the following day started for New Creek, West Virginia. It was at once, upon arrival in the field, placed on garrison and escort duty at Martinsburg, where it remained until June 10th, at which time it left under orders for Washington city. From there it proceeded to White House, thence to Bermuda Hundred, and to City Point, where it remained till the 29th. The regiment was then placed on garrison duty in an entrenched camp near Norfolk, Virginia. On July 26th five hundred men of the One Hundred and Fifty-fifth, with other troops, marched to Elizabeth City, North Carolina, where the infantry was held in check while the cavalry raided the country, securing horses, cotton, and tobacco. The expedition returned to Norfolk, where the regiment remained till August 19th, when it was ordered to Ohio for muster out. It arrived at Camp Dennison August 24th, and was discharged from the service August 27th. Its casualties were light, although the men suffered considerably from sickness.

FIELD AND STAFF.

Colonel Harley H. Sage.
Lieutenant-colonel Roswell Shurtleff.
Major Peter Lutz.
First Lieutenant and Adjutant Thomas J. Watkins.
First Lieutenant and Quartermaster Joseph Walker.
Surgeon A. S. Strawburg.
Chaplain Samuel H. Brigh.
Sergeant-major Charles H. Dodd.
Quartermaster Sergeant Archibald Armstrong.
Commissary Sergeant Joseph B. Dunlap.
Hospital Steward William R. Elder.

COMPANY B.
COMMISSIONED OFFICERS.

Captain Christopher T. Meadeker.
First Lieutenant Joseph B. Couch.
Second Lieutenant Thomas Brown.

NON-COMMISSIONED OFFICERS.

First Sergeant Abraham Harris.
Sergeant James L. Edwards.
Sergeant Henry Whitehouse.
Sergeant Mathias Faulkinstein.
Sergeant Anthony Stefauski.
Corporal Thomas W. McClelland.
Corporal Robert Wiseman.
Corporal Christopher C. Wiseman.
Corporal Alexander K. McClelland.
Corporal Lewis J. Jacobs.
Corporal Francis J. Jacobs.
Corporal Chancy Hamilton.
Corporal Cornelius Thomas.
Musician Thomas A. Jacobs.
Musician William Barker.

PRIVATES.

Archibald Armstrong, Darius M. Alford, Christian Didemar, Robert C. Beatty, William F. Brannan, John L. Branyan, Nathaniel Croell, William Crawford, David B. Calhoun, Benjamin C. Cunningham, John Doyle, David R. Darrow, Robert Dugan, Owens Evan, John H. Eatler, William J. Ewing, Charles S. Fitheau, Charles Fry, Sebastian A. Fitheau, Casper Gerlah, James Gibson, George Goodwin, Valentine S. Holnaugh, Hiram G. Hiltabiddle, Alfred W. Hubler, David Hartley, Law Hellawell, Francis Hardy, Solomon Holland, Solomon Helsel, Thomas Jacobs, Sheldon Jacobs, George E. Jensing, David Jones, David D. Jones, Thomas S. Knox, David Kay, James A. Lockhart, Horace O. Nette, James Morgan, Robert M. Megowen, John McEwan, Andrew McEwan, Thomas Meltale, Henry Moore, George Oldham, John E. Powers, Charles W. Platt, John Reep, Michael Reeble, Theodore Rowan, Jacob Stanilaugh, Robert Turner, Henry Toulman, Thomas W. Williams, Henry B. White, Milton A. Wilder, Thomas Wilson, Benjamin Wilhelm, Thomas Wood, Frank Williams, Andrew Wiseman, Randolph J. Welsh, William Welch, Henry G. Fisher.

COMPANY D.
COMMISSIONED OFFICERS.

Captain Frederick S. Whitslar.
First Lieutenant Augustus D. Cornell.
Second Lieutenant Justice M. Silliman.

NON-COMMISSIONED OFFICERS.

First Sergeant John W. Brothers.
Sergeant Thomas B. McKee.
Sergeant Nathoniel B. Miller.
Sergeant Wilson F. Calvin.
Sergeant Joseph B. Park.
Corporal Baxton Myers.
Corporal John W. Beede.
Corporal Emery Miekesell.
Corporal John Brenner.
Corporal George S. Baldwin.
Corporal James Satch.
Corporal Brainerd S. Higley.
Corporal William H. Darrow.
Musician Moses Combs.
Musician John Satch.

PRIVATES.

Myron J. Ames, Laurence Baker, Phillip Borts, Stephen H. Benson, Robert Buchanan, Sherman Blackman, George Converse, Joseph Cunningham, Charles Campbell, Augustus Craft, Hugh F. Cowden, William S. Corer, William W. Cover, William Dennison, William H. Dubes, William R. Elder, John W. Ellis, Job Freeman, James Fusselman, George B. Gizie, Augustus Gerloh, Jesse Hamilton, Virgil Hoffman, Frederick Huffman, Thomas W. Johnston, Richard Jones, Samuel W. Jewell, Hugh King, Joseph C. Kennedy, William H. Kennedy, Henderson G. Kennedy, Edward Kyle, William D. Lyons, George Lasterman, Ferdinand Lee, William O. Logan, Manuel Leopard, James Murray, Azariah D. Marriner, John McKay, James C. Miller, James Maxwell, Joel McCollom, John McClare, Thompson McCullom, Samuel Maxwell, James P. McGown, William McClure, James Miller, Darius McNabb, James H. McCunda, James Orr, Calvin Osborn, Lewis N. Pollock, George W. Porter, John J. Park, Leander D. Robinson, Almon Rany, David M. Simpkins, John G. Stewart, William Stuart, Robert Shelby, Levi J. Simonton, Enoch Shaffer, Isaac Thomas, Charles D. Viall, Perry Wehr, Robert Wilson, Solomon Zedaker.

COMPANY G.
COMMISSIONED OFFICERS.

Captain Richard B. Engle.
First Lieutenant Leonidas Carson.
Second Lieutenant Abraham Miller.

NON-COMMISSIONED OFFICERS.

First Sergeant James P. McNely.
Sergeant Alexander Baker.
Sergeant Benjamin P. Baldwin.
Sergeant Solon Day.
Sergeant David Carson.
Corporal Aaron Fink.
Corporal William E. Lancaster.
Corporal Jacob Slock.
Corporal Allen Fogg.
Corporal Charles F. Shinn.

Corporal James M. Whigan.
Corporal Joseph H. Chamberlain.
Corporal David Cramnel.

PRIVATES.

David Boner, Freeman Beel, Jefferson Blossom, Elias Besanger, Dickson M. James, John Dustman, John Davis, Abraham Dustman, John Eastman, Michael Eadler, David Eadler, Josiah Fogg, Frank Fitch, Daniel Floor, Hiram Floor, Archy Boly, Solomon E. Greenemyre, Tobias Greenemyre, Francis Gee, James Gault, William Hawkins, Hiram Hull, Uriah Holeman, Samuel Hahn, Oscar E. Hammond, Jacob Helsel, J. Hartsell, Comfort Hoil, Jacob B. Hawkins, Joseph C. Cowden, Andrew Kale, Joseph King, John Kump, Mahlon Kirkbride, Elias Martz, Solomon Martz, Eli Mock, John Mock, David Mock, George W. Martin, Joel Middleton, Thomas Mitchell, Sampton McNutt, John B. Mellinger, Evan Middleton, Samuel Nailer, Thomas Powell, Samuel Phillips, Edgar Ripley, John A. Ripley, Henry Rummell, John Rummell (first), John Rummell (second), Jonathan Sell, Hugh Swartz, William Smyth, Thomas Scott, David Shafer, Madison Trail, John Teets, Lisly G. Valan, John M. Witte, William Q. Weldy, Alva Weldy, Samuel D. Warton, William Warton, Joseph Yaney, Jared P. Reed.

COMPANY I.

PRIVATES.

Henry D. Seymour, William Parker, T. L. Peterson, Frederick R. Probert, James A. Ranny.

ONE HUNDRED AND SEVENTY-FIRST OHIO VOLUNTEER INFANTRY—NATIONAL GUARD.

This regiment of one hundred days' men was mustered into the service May 7, 1864. It was composed of seven companies of the Forty-first Ohio National guard from Trumbull county, and filled up from Portage, Geauga, and Lake counties. Rosters of companies A, B, C, D, G, H, and I, from Trumbull, will be found below. The regiment was organized and mustered into the service at Sandusky, Ohio, and was at once placed on guard and fatigue duty on Johnson's island. It soon became noted for proficiency in drill and the neatness of its camp.

The One Hundred and Seventy-first regiment left Sandusky for Covington, Kentucky, on the 9th of June, and upon its arrival reported to General Hobson. Morgan and his guerilla followers were in the vicinity of Cynthiana. The railroad bridge across Kellar's creek had been destroyed, and a Northern raid was anticipated. Considerable anxiety was felt at Covington, and there was even fear for the safety of Cincinnati. The One Hundred and Seventy-first regiment was placed on board cars and ordered to proceed to Kellar's bridge, which was one mile from Cynthiana, and there await orders. Sentinels were placed on the cars and company officers charged to remain with their men. When the wrecked bridge which, was one mile from Cynthiana and sixty-five from Cincinnati, was reached, the regiment debarked, one company was sent out on sentinel duty and a "handful of men" detailed to serve as cavalrymen. The trains which had brought them were backed down the track and burned. Upon their arrival, the men of the One Hundred and Seventy-first regiment were supplied with ammunition, and then proceeded to eat their breakfast. We take from the Cincinnati Commercial the description of what followed:

Suddenly their quiet was disturbed by the rattle of musketry at Cynthiana, telling that hot work was going on there between the One Hundred and Sixty-eighth Ohio and the rebel forces; and in a few minutes, to their great surprise, they ascertained that the fields around themselves were alive with rebel forces. A volley of musketry was poured in upon them by a squad of the enemy massed behind the fence of a clover field. From the first it was evident to General Hobson and Colonel Asper that their little force was completely surrounded, and from the disposition of the rebel troops it was evidently their design to conduct the fight in the bushwhacking style from the bush should our forces resist, which they probably did not believe would be the case, as they evidently were two to their one in the first of the fight.

Under these circumstances the regiment was divided into several squads, and sent to both east and west of the railroad, occupying such positions as they might secure. The rebels then appeared on every hand, displaying great activity in firing and considerable skill in keeping under cover from the fire of our troops. Throughout, the affair was as between sharpshooters, each man firing as he could obtain sight of one of the enemy. This continued about five hours, the loss on both sides being heavy. That of the rebels was much greater than our own, as much so, perhaps, proportionately, as their force was superior in numbers—we having 700 men, and they, with their re-inforcements, 2,000. Against these odds the resistance made was desperate and determined. General Morgan who, when the fight here commenced, was at Cynthiana (the rebel force being in command of General Getty), had supposed the Union force would surrender immediately. He considered his great odds, the greenness of our forces, and wondered with impatience how it occurred that the fighting continued. He had expected an immediate surrender, and sincerely desired it, as he did not wish to lose any of his men. He certainly had not expected this desperate resistance. He was astounded when at 9 o'clock A. M., a carrier dashed up to him at Cynthiana, and gave General Getty's message: "Re-inforcements, or give it up!" Several hundred troops were immediately sent down the pike, Morgan at their head, and with these the line was drawn still closer around the little band until General Hobson was forced to accept the flag of truce and Morgan's conditions of surrender, that the private property of the troops should be respected and that the officers should retain their side-arms. General Hobson, so all accounts agree in saying, had done all that could be done, himself displaying the greatest personal courage; and in thus surrendering, he decided for the best.

After the surrender General Morgan directed that the officers should be allowed to retain their horses, but a rebel colonel had taken a fancy to Lieutenant-colonel Harmon's horse, and being already in possession, insisted on keeping it, which he finally did, but gave Colonel Harmon another, though much inferior one. In this engagement the regiment lost 13 killed, and 54 wounded, 4 of whom subsequently died.

It was not for prisoners that the rebel raider made this attack upon the Union forces, but rather to remove opposition to his northward progress. To detain his captives as prisoners was impracticable, consequently he planned to dispose of them on the most advantageous terms. Morgan proposed to effect an exchange of prisoners, and with that view paroled General Hobson and staff, Colonel Asper, and Lieutenant-colonel Harmon, and Major Fowler, to go to the nearest point affording telegraph communication with General Burbridge (then commanding the district of Kentucky) under escort of three rebel officers. It was understood that if an exchange could not be effected they should return as soon as possible. Falmouth was reached June 12th, but before that time General Burbridge had pressed Morgan so closely that the latter was compelled to parole his prisoners, who made their way to Augusta, whence they were taken on boats to Covington and from there to Camp Dennison, Ohio. General Burbridge replied to General Hobson's communication concerning an exchange of prisoners, with an order to General Hobson and staff to report at Lexington, Kentucky, for duty, and also that his escort of rebel officers should be taken with him as prisoners of war; the other Ohio officers were ordered to Cincinnati. The One Hundred and Seventy-first was transferred from Camp Dennison to its old camp on Johnson's island, in Lake Erie, but being paroled no duties were required till the War department declared the parole invalid, when the regiment was again equipped and placed on duty. It remained on Johnson's island till the expiration of its term of service, when it was mustered out August 20, 1864. Reid says of the encounter with Morgan June 9th:

The results of the fight at Kellar's Bridge was greater than they at first appear to be. Morgan had planned his raid into Kentucky for the purpose of obtaining recruits, horses, and money, intending at the same time to sweep down the Licking valley, to capture the small garrisons on the route in detail, and, if possible, to ride into Covington at Kellar's bridge. He was delayed twenty-four hours and General Burbridge was enabled to meet him. The citizens of Falmouth, Kentucky, held a meeting and thanked General Hobson and the officers and men under him for the gallant manner in which they defended the valley from invasion; the citizens of Covington also thanked General Hobson, Colonel Asper, and the men in their command for the protection they had afforded the city.

And the Cincinnati Gazette said:

There is little doubt that the stubborn resistance of the One Hundred and Seventy-first saved Cincinnati from visitation. After the capture General Hobson, in a letter to Colonel Asper, expressed his entire satisfaction with the conduct of the One Hundred and Seventy-first, and General Heintzelman and Governor Brough both declared to Colonel Asper personally their gratification at the bravery and courage displayed by the regiment.

FIELD AND STAFF.

Colonel Joel F. Asper.
Lieutenant-colonel Heman R. Harmon.
Major Manning A. Fowler.
Surgeon Frederick C. Applegate.
Assistant-surgeon Benjamin F. Pittman.
First Lieutenant and Adjutant J. P. Hurlbut.
First Lieutenant and Regimental Quartermaster Jacob Stambaugh.

NON-COMMISSIONED STAFF.

Sergeant-major Jacob J. Shaffer.
Hospital Steward Albert G. Miner.
Quartermaster Sergeant John J. Lyde.
Lyman P. Andrews.
Hospital Steward Myron N. Clark.
Drum-major George Stiles.
Fife-major Sylvanus Oviatt.

COMPANY A.

COMMISSIONED OFFICERS.

Captain Francis E. Hutchins.
First Lieutenant F. Kinsman, Jr.
Second Lieutenant F. J. Macky.

NON-COMMISSIONED OFFICERS.

Sergeant Hezekiah M. Ford.
Sergeant Charles C. Benton.
Sergeant George N. Hapgood.
Sergeant William A. Camp.
Sergeant James H. Smith.
Corporal Henry J. Lane.
Corporal Jefferson Wilson.
Corporal Jules Vautrot.
Corporal George W. Pond.
Corporal William B. Brown.
Corporal Kirtland M. Fitch.
Corporal Charles Burton.
Corporal Amasa Hoyt.
Musician William H. Butt.
Musician William H. Dunn.

PRIVATES.

Edwin C. Andrews, Andrew J. Archibald, Phillip Artman, George W. Bissel, Ensign Baldwin, Adolphus Bishop, Addison J. Bishop, Oliver Belden, Nelson Clark, Samuel P. Drax, Oresimus Dunlap, John Drihl, John J. Edwards, Erastus H. Ensign, Henry Fitts, Charles T. Fussleman, Romeo H. Freer, Clement B. Gilbert, James Gaskell, Wallace Gilmore, Delorma S. Garwood, Curtiss M. Goucher, Byron Hank, Albert B. Heslop, George Hervey, Thomas Hervey, George Holland, William H. Harmon. Henry Iddings, George Jamison, Andrew G. Kibler, William Knighton, John Kinsman, Harrison H. King, Kline Lake, Theodore McConnel, Andrew J. Martin, Henry A. Potter, Edward K. Patch, Benjamin H. Peck, Henry C. Pitcher, William Peffers, John H. Park, William W. Powell, George K. Phillips, Henry Ricksicker, Francis Rowan, John Rowan, Rodolphus Row, Benjamin Root, John Rush, Jr., James Smith, Thomas C. Snyder, George M. Stiles, Ezra B. Taylor, Frank C. Tayler, George H. Tavler, Allison Truesdell, George Van Gorder, Amzi C. Williamson, George M. D. Woods, Sylvanus S. Williams, Hugh Watson, Edward Woodrow, John Woodrow, Washington Webb, Byron A. Winnagle, Henry A. Wolcott, John Ricksicker, Albert Root.

COMPANY B.

COMMISSIONED OFFICERS.

Captain Richard O'Dell Swindler.
First Lieutenant James McGrath.
Second Lieutenant John P. Lepley.

NON-COMMISSIONED OFFICERS.

Orderly Sergeant Robert Gedden.
Sergeant Abner C. Allison.
Sergeant John Davis.
Sergeant Joseph Hickey.
Sergeant John Rager.
Corporal John Ditheridge.
Corporal Wilson Beard.
Corporal H. R. Swindler.
Corporal James Draw.
Corporal Hiles G. Butler.
Corporal J. Louis Will.
Corporal William B. Mason.
Corporal Jacob Shelar.
Musician Henry Harriff.
Musician Charles Galleur.

PRIVATES.

Christoph Adams, Thomas Adams, James Brogan, Lafayette Bear, John Bottles, Arthur M. B. Brockwav, Frank M. Beard, Nelson Brooks, Cyrus Cochran, Edward Cunie, Albert A. Cleveland, John Crum, Mahlon Cope, Wallace Coffin, Alfred W. Crosby, William Davis, Jr., William Delph, Alexander Erwin, Eli C. Ferguson, Martin Fulk, Robert Fuller, William Getts, Harrison H. Glendenning, Charles Green, Almog A. Green, Arthur B. Gilbert, Scott Hood, John Haller, Matthew Halfpenny, James M. Holton, Milo Hudson, Frederick D. Haller, William B. Hood, John Jenkins, John F. Kingsley, Charles Knight, William Kincaid, Ferdinand Lee, George Ludwig, John C. Miller, John H. Merrills, Joseph Mills, John Matthews, Joseph Miller, James McGinley, Jacob Neathammer, Adam Neis, James Orwig, Austin G. Parker, Reese Parker, Henry Rester, Jesse Rose, George Shelar, John Stow, Henry Stine, John Stevenson, Jacob Stevenson, Philip Shamoun, George Scarlet, Peter Swindler, Mortimer C. Thompson, Thomas Turnbull, John M. Tyler, Jackson Whipple, Samuel Wallace, James G. Wilson, Lemuel White.

COMPANY C.

COMMISSIONED OFFICERS.

Captain Joseph M. Jackson.
First Lieutenant Milton Mathews.
Second Lieutenant Benjamin Veach.

NON-COMMISSIONED OFFICERS.

First Sergeant Mahlon B. White.
Sergeant Alfred W. Hume.

Sergeant Andrew R. Bailey.
Sergeant Jesse Hoover.
Sergeant Robert A. McMurrain.
Corporal John Applegate.
Corporal John Randall.
Corporal John Mitcheltree.
Corporal John Himmel.
Corporal James Treester.
Corporal Hiram S. Stephens.
Corporal Samuel Kennedy.
Corporal Cyrus B. Leyde.
Wagoner Hugh Veach.

PRIVATES.

Samuel Brunstetler, Martin Bensley, John V. Buck, Ephraim Blackburn, Leander W. Burnett, John Barringer, Byron Clark, William W. Crawford, Milo Crawford, Hewett Clingan, Lorenzo F. Clingan, Wesley Calhoon, Lewis G. Campbell, Jonathan Dilley, James Dilley, Thomas Dixon, James H. Davidson, Joseph Everhart, Solomon Everett, Edward Fusselman, Harvey Gregory, Vincent Hollenbeck, Howard Hultz, William C. Hall, James S. Hoover, William H. Hoover, John S. Huff, Enos S. Harrington, Eno. M. Housel, Robert H. Jewell, William J. Jackson, John G. Jackson, Smith Kimmel, Daniel Kashner, Hugh A. Love, Delos Luce, John G. Leitch, Abner McClury, John C. McCreary, Andrew J. McMurrain, Eli McFall, Samuel McCowen, Joseph McCulley, Thomas J. Matthews, William H. Marshall, James A. Murphy, Joseph Menard, James M. Porterfield, William H. Porterfield, Benjamin S. Pierce, William Robinson, James F. Stephens, Findley Stewart, Joseph A. Starkey, Samuel H. Tyler, Samuel Tyler, Emmanuel Treester, Reuben Taylor, William Ulps, Levi Williams, Jesse Williams, Henry Waldorf, Jr., James M. Wakefield, Albert G. Werriek, Crawford White, John M. White.

COMPANY D.

COMMISSIONED OFFICERS.

Captain Evan Morris.
First Lieutenant Austin W. Wilson.
Second Lieutenant John Sampson.

NON-COMMISSIONED OFFICERS.

Sergeant Robert Strawhan.
Sergeant Charles Goodwin.
Sergeant R. L. Walker.
Sergeant S. H. McCartney.
Sergeant James G. Jones.
Corporal George Phillips.
Corporal Daniel E. Moyer.
Corporal Morris Theopholis.
Corporal Joseph A. Osborn.
Corporal John H. McKean.
Corporal Aaron H. Westlake.
Corporal Edward Powers.
Corporal Freeman Reapsmeur.
Musician Lauriston L. Miller.
Musician George Todd.
Wagoner Samuel Esgar.

PRIVATES.

A. A. Adams, Homer S. Adams, Charles H. Adams, David Andrews, Joseph S. Bell, George H. Bowen, Richard Bowen, John Bodin, John Burgess, John Breew, Newton B. Carlton, John M. Cook, John L. Cussord, Rosser Davis, Benjamin Davis, Edward Davis, Jacob Davis, William Davis, Ambrose Eckman, Evan J. Evans, Edward Evans, Zenas Evans, George B. Frazier, Fredrick Fatchell, George M.

Frank, David Griffith, Harvey Gilbert, Hiram K. Goist, Nicholas H. Green, Talbot Gridley, John Harris, George Harper, Benjamin F. Hull, Amos S. Hood, John Jeffreys, William G. Jones, Thomas D. Jones, Jonathan Keefer, John B. Lewis, Lewis D. Lewis, John E. Lewis, Charles S. Miller, Ezra B. Miller, William W. Miller, Evan W. Morgan, Isaiah Morris, Andrew McCartney, Samuel Mansell, James D. Morris, Augustus Neal, John C. Nelson, William Perkins, James Parker, Joseph Rayen, George N. Rodgers, Thomas Reynolds, Robert Roberts, Theodore Richmond, John Shults, Simon Schopp, Robert Taylor, David Williams, Thomas Williams, John Woodbridge.

COMPANY H.

COMMISSIONED OFFICERS.

Captain Harlan H. Hatch.
First Lieutenant Harrison A. Lee.
Second Lieutenant James B. Barnard.

NON-COMMISSIONED OFFICERS.

Sergeant Benjamin F. Waters.
Sergeant Rodney Miller.
Sergeant Alonzo Bundy.
Sergeant Henry M. Kildsoe.
Sergeant Robert R. Moore.
Corporal Milo Griffith.
Corporal Harmon Osborn.
Corporal James Roberts.
Corporal Henry A. Haughton.
Corporal Arlington J. Hatch.
Corporal Josiah W. Belden.
Corporal Chester Stowe.
Corporal John W. Wilcox.
Musician John J. Steadman.

PRIVATES.

George T. Anderson, Oliver R. Anderson, Ephraim Asper, Austin H. Bright, Hamlet B. Belden, Selnight M. Bowers, Henry Beecham, Austin H. Belden, Dwight H. Baldwin, Edward E. Byrnes, Henry H. Byrnes, George F. Brooks, Silas L. Curtis, Corwin S. Curtis, Judson S. Curtis, George Canon, David Canon, James H. Dubbs, Carsey O. Easson, Clark Flick, Norman A. Gilbert, Alonzo W. Greer, Henry Hall, Edward B. Hall, William Harklerode, Marcus B. Haughton, Lester J. Haughton, Melancthon C. Hart, James M. Hulbert, Ervin I. Hatch, Homer U. Johnson, Joseph M. Jackson, Hubbard Joy, Almon L. Lew, Frank K. Lewis, Almon G. Lee, Seymour Lee, William D. Lamberton, George W. Moffitt, Austin McKay, Robert Martin, Albert Morrison, William Mahan, Ezvil C. Osmer, Addison Osmer, Emery D. Reeves, Thomas Reid, Howard C. Reynolds, Chester Steel, Wilbur Strickland, Johnson J. Sadler, Abraham W. Spitler, James H. Snow, Jacob Strohm, Chauncy Travis, William Taylor, George B. Worrell, Leander H. Wolcott, Lyman B. Wolcott, Darwin B. Wolcott, Benson E. Wildman, Ezra G. Wildman, Joseph Wilson, Albert Wilson, Isaac Williams, John B. Browning, George A. Waters, George Davis, Addison S. Wolcott, James A. Waters.

COMPANY I.

COMMISSIONED OFFICERS.

Captain Cyrus A. Mason.
First Lieutenant William H. Earl.
Second Lieutenant Frank H. Snow.

NON-COMMISSIONED OFFICERS.

Sergeant William R. Little.

Sergeant Sheldon F. Higley.
Sergeant Wilson S. Messenger.
Sergeant Alvan Smith.
Sergeant Edward W. Williams.
Corporal Edwin D. Earl.
Corporal Jason B. Johnson.
Corporal Francis D. Snow.
Corporal Henry B. Waklen.
Corporal Alfred M. Higley.
Corporal Spencer G. Tracy.
Corporal Charles W. Goodsell.
Corporal Henry J. Noble.
Musician Samuel Sharp.
Musician James A. Snow.
Wagoner Chaffee Wolcott.

PRIVATES.

Francis R. Alderman, Thomas O. Angel, Hiram G. Allen, Elijah Alford, Charles E. Alford, Levi Bush, Harvey M. Buck, Warren L. Barter, Frederick Bristol, Nathan E. Birchard, Oscar Bond, Perry E. Beckwith, Henry W. Bradley, Gideon C. Boswick, James C. Brooks, Charles J. Bow, William C. Bowers, Eleazer A. Curtis, Myron S. Clark, William B. Cline, Isaac H. Ensign, George R. Fay, Oscar D. Freeman, George G. Goldie, William A. Higley, Philander R. Higley, Francis B. Harmond, George Hilderhof, Ranson F. Humiston, Ephraim F. Jagger, William Johnson, Orville A. Kirkham, George R. Long, James Murray, Henry A. Millikan, William A. Messenger, Ephraim H. Millard, Van B. Merwin, J. W. Pike, Daniel H. Pike, Henry Palmer, Francis Poor, Samuel A. Pardee, George S. Pinney, Benjamin Pitman, William S. Russell, Alanson R. Russell, William W. Reed, Roswell J. Reed, Alvan V. Rudd, James Rouse, Lowell Roberts, Emerson W. Scott, William W. Stewart, Minor G. Spencer, Justin E. Snow, Horatio N. Strong, William E. Strong, Samuel Springthrop, Harmon M. Stevens, Woodworth E. Smith, John A. Wadworth, Philander Waters, Sherburn O. Willer, Davison Ward, Reuben L. Wait, Oscar L. Whiteford.

ONE HUNDRED AND SEVENTY-NINTH REGIMENT, OHIO VOLUNTEER INFANTRY.

This regiment was organized at Camp Chase, September 28, 1864, and consisted of men from all parts of the State, many of whom were veterans. It was discharged at Columbus June 27, 1865. Five members of company A were from this county—Samuel Combs, Henry I. Lepper, Corwin T. Lee, Cassius M. Pierce, and Fernando C. Peck.

ONE HUNDRED AND EIGHTIETH REGIMENT, OHIO VOLUNTEER INFANTRY.

The One Hundred and Eightieth was one of a series of one year regiments, recruited in the fall of 1864. Only one name on the muster roll is traced to the field of this history, Edward Fitch, a corporal in company G.

ONE HUNDRED AND EIGHTY-FOURTH REGIMENT, OHIO VOLUNTEER INFANTRY.

The One Hundred and Eighty-fourth was one the regiments recruited under the call of President Lincoln for one-year troops, and was organized at Camp Chase February 21, 1865. One company, C, is given below; immediately after muster, it received orders to move to Nashville, where it was placed on garrison duty. From Nashville it proceeded by way of Chattanooga to Bridgeport, Alabama, to guard an important bridge over the Tennessee river. It also guarded the track of the railroad, between Bridgeport and Chattanooga, a distance of about thirty miles. Detachments of the regiment frequently encountered bands of rebel guerrillas and squads of rebel cavalry. Several prisoners were taken at the expense of some casualties. From July 25th till the expiration of its term of service, the One Hundred and Eighty-fourth was on duty at Edgefield. It was mustered out of service September 20, 1865, and finally discharged at Camp Chase, Ohio, September 27th. This regiment was composed largely of men who had been in the service with other regiments.

COMPANY C.

COMMISSIONED OFFICERS.

Captain Joseph Allen, appointed captain from civil life.
First Lieutenant Alexander M. Duck, appointed lieutenant from civil life.
Second Lieutenant Hiram Reed, appointed second lieutenant.

NON-COMMISSIONED OFFICERS.

Sergeant Joseph S. Shunk.
Sergeant Samuel Hobbs.
Sergeant Thomas Hanna.
Sergeant John Ellis.
Sergeant Charles E. Strauss.
Corporal Isaiah Greegor.
Corporal Franklin Reed.
Corporal William R. Black.
Corporal George W. Duck.
Corporal George W. Wilhelm.
Corporal Albert Hurtow.
Corporal George W. Shirrs.
Corporal John Crow.
Musician Josiah Shunk.
Musician Edward Stoder.
Wagoner Nathaniel Oaks.

PRIVATES.

Henry Adams, George Adams, George W. Ashtons, Philip Bash, John Bowers, Levi Barnet, Arthur G. Barnes, John Baker, Lewis Beiskler, Joseph Bowquin, Francis Cooper, William A. Cramer, Joseph Cross, Daniel Dorsey, William R. Deeds, James E. Duncan, Michael Eckert, Martin C. Egner, Eugene L. Firestone, Julius Gleitsman, Lewis Gauclat, George W. Hile, George W. Hines, William Hudnut, James B. Hutchison, John Hoover, Abraham Hoover, Wilkam H. Hall, Albert J. Harry, Henry Imler, Frederick Ish, John Korn, John B. Lytle, William Miller, Peter Maylaugh, Adolphus Menner, John H. Muma, Benjamin Milligan, William S. Porter, Francis M. Porter, Albert Pherson, Henry Prizer, John A. Pfeiner, Samuel Patrick, John M. Robinson, Haman Rohn, Levi Rohn, Jinsey H. Rogers, Christian Reichenlaugh, James M. Reese, George Ralston, Adam Stanlarger, George W. Sparkle, William H. Senr, Jacob Swark, Solomon Spring, Clark Spidle, Matthew Shark, George B. Sweringen, Godfrey Smith, Harman Shultz, Marion Tenters, Isaac Tom, Ephraim Teeple, John W. Tracy, William Thompson, Daniel B. Voorhes, Earnest Voltz, Uriah Weimer, George W. Wilkinson, Levi Wilkinson, John Weaver, Joseph Wolgomot, William Wright, William Zutervan.

Discharged Before Expiration of Service.—Leonard Heider, John Druhot, John I. Arnabaugh.
Not Reported.—Isaac Fink, John H. Maltz.

COMPANY H.

PRIVATE.

Lester J. Haughton.

ONE HUNDRED AND NINETY-SIXTH REGIMENT OHIO VOLUNTEER INFANTRY.

This regiment, of which two companies and part of a third were recruited in Trumbull and Mahoning counties, was mustered into the service under the last one-year call of President Lincoln, March 25, 1865. Like the One Hundred and Eighty-fourth, most of the officers and many of the men had seen service in other regiments. Its first service was in West Virginia, when it was assigned to the Ohio brigade at Winchester. While there it was thoroughly drilled and disciplined. In July the regiment was ordered to Baltimore and placed on garrison duty in the fortifications around the city. A detachment was detailed to Fort Delaware. The One Hundred and Ninety-sixth was mustered out of the service September 11, 1865, at Baltimore. The body of the regiment was composed of young men. It was especially complimented on its fine soldierly appearance.

FIELD AND STAFF.

Colonel Robert P. Kennedy.
Lieutenant-colonel Eben S. Coe.
Major Thomas C. Thoburn.
Surgeon H. B. Noble.
Assistant Surgeon J. W. Driscoll.
Assistant Surgeon Charles J. Shields.
First Lieutenant and Adjutant Joshua M. Yeo.
First Lieutenant and Regimental Quartermaster Thomas Reber.
Sergeant-major Edgar O. Miller.
Quartermaster-sergeant Charles D. Baltzell.
Commissary-sergeant Pensler F. Kissane.
Henry B. McComsey.
Henry Hatfield.
Thomas K. Bisbee.

COMPANY D.

COMMISSIONED OFFICERS.

Captain George B. Kennedy.

First Lieutenant James H. Harbogast.
Second Lieutenant Samuel Lee.
Henry Iddings.

NON-COMMISSIONED OFFICERS.

Sergeant John C. Fox.
Sergeant Robert Martin.
Sergeant John H. Hatch.
Sergeant Orvel C. Osmer.
Corporal William H. Dunna.
Corporal Homer J. Wolcott.
Corporal Alfred W. Crosby.
Corporal William F. Danner.
Corporal William H. Hunter.
Corporal William R. Harper.
Corporal Dayton Kelso.
Corporal Hiram W. Kirk.
Musician Uriah Foust.
Musician Weller P. Brewer.

PRIVATES.

John M. Barb, Alonzo Brooks, William H. Bren, Henry Burgett, Joseph Burgett, George Brewster, William Bradford, James A. Benedict, Samuel Cather, Lewis C. Crain, Judson C. Cutler, William B. Cline, Charles Cain, William H. Downs, Chauncey Dabney, John H. Eaton, Joseph English, Smitzer Ellis, James E. Filkins, Harris C. Gleason, Charles F. Harrington, William Hughes, Jacob Hoffman, George L. Hohn, Marvin J. Dawson, Daniel R. Lynn, William F. McElroy, Edward McElroy, Francis H. Martin, William H. Macklin, Frank B. Merrill, Milton Miller, Oscar A. Maxwell, Marshall B. Mayhew, Uriah Metts, Austin G. Parker, Lewis Peters, Levi Pettie, Samuel Painter, Lycurgus W. Patton, Ordell S. Roberts, John H. Reiter, Nelson Reel, Josiah S. Ratliff, Andrew J. Reese, Arthur E. Sheldon, Plumb Sutliff, Lewis Stroek, Solomon Scoville, Jr., Gillyard Scoville, Aaron Strong, Samuel Shick, Manasses Somers, James Ligue, Charles S. Thorpe, James K. Thompson, Samuel F. Thoman, Freeman R. Woodworth, John Wagner, John Wulse, Henry A. Welke.

Discharged before expiration of service.—Walter S. Ensign, Lewis Crestinger, Thomas Hayden, George W. Hardy, Samuel Lee, William D. Morrison, Eli C. Northrop, Henry Rathbun, William Raynor, Andrew J. Shively.

Transferred.—Reuben W. Carl, Elias M. Carter, William H. Lewis, Almeron S. Lynn.

Died.—Hiram Ewell, 1865; Lowell Roberts, 1865; Ezekiel J. Wolfcale, at Camp Chase, date unknown.

Not reported.—Martin Daniels, James Harris, Valentine Johnson, George Johnson, John Miller, Daniel Ryan.

COMPANY E.

COMMISSIONED OFFICERS.

Captain Francis M. Baker.
First Lieutenant William H. Allauck.
Second Lieutenant William B. Brown.

NON-COMMISSIONED OFFICERS.

First Sergeant Robert W. Raynor.
Sergeant Charles Purcell.
Sergeant George A. Woodworth.
Sergeant Thomas G. Peppard.
Sergeant Horace C. Burgess.
Corporal Swelia Fradenburg.
Corporal Wilson H. Beary.
Corporal George Hash.
Corporal Alfred C. Dillen.
Corporal Lemuel White.

Corporal John F. Fuller.
Corporal Frederick W. Hickox.
Corporal Hiram W. Gridley.
Drummer Eli Baker.

PRIVATES.

Henry W. Anson, Robert Anderson, Marcus Bankraft, John Brown, Robert Ballis, William H. Bomk, Charles Burdick, Moses Brown, Austin H. Beldin, George W. Blake, Arthur M. B. Brockway, Wellington Baker, Christian Boots, Amos J. Coy, Daniel Coy, Rafaelle Cehens, Albert A. Cleveland, William Drew, Edward Donohoe, Wilkin H. Davis, James Enger, Adolphus Eggleston, Samuel Fenton, Sylvester Tadley, Edway E. Grant, James E. Gaskell, Levi W. Gaskill, James W. Galleher, Melvin S. Gillett, John Hoffman, William Hohn, Charles W. Hyde, Dallas Hull, Edwin Johnson, Avery B. Jones, Gideon Kearns, Orange S. Krivney, Patrick W. McGuire, Frank M. Merril, George D. McIntosh, Franklin Osborn, Reuben Penny, William H. Pattison, Steven W. Parker, William W. Painton, George Ryder, John D. Raub, Perry G. Rodgers, Albert Ruger, Clark Richard, Isaac St. Clair, Horace L. Smith, George W. Stouffer, Robert Smith, Aaron Simpson, James H. Tidd, Daniel Tiffany, Eber H. Finkham, Colwell Waggoner, John O. Wood, Sylvanus Williams, Nelson R. Wood.

Discharged before Expiration of Service.—David Bullfrich, Daniel H. Brooks, Samuel Ball, Ebenezer Champlain, Charles E. Cook, Charles M. Grower, John J. Musser.

Died.—Daniel D. Dewey, 1865; Jerome W. Newman, 1865; Virgil Coburn, 1865; Charles Stark, 1865.

Not Reported.—John Berry, George Burnstuttle, Louis Devots, George Hilderhof, James Keller, Charles M. McKenzie, Abner Stapleton, John Sank.

COMPANY K.

PRIVATES.

Bacchus G. Alderman, John E. Burbank, Andrew Coy, Myron F. Clover, Nathan Colban, George A. Earl, Alonzo D. Kent, William F. Quinn, Eliuer Smith, George W. Bolster, Henry Frazier, Frank E. Barnes, John E. Baker, Augustus Meister, Isaac Pinney.

ONE HUNDRED AND NINETY-SEVENTH REGIMENT, OHIO VOLUNTEER INFANTRY.

Companies A and K of the One Hundred and Ninety-seventh Ohio were partially recruited in Mahoning county. This was the last regiment organized in the State (eight companies of the One Hundred and Ninety-eighth were mustered in, but never organized). Company A was mustered in at Camp Chase March 28, 1865, and the regimental organization was completed April 12th. Nearly half of the men and all except five of its officers had previously been in the service. The regiment left Camp Chase April 25th, for Washington city, at which place it learned of the surrender of rebel General Johnston. It had no prospect of participating in active service. The time was spent in camp and garrison duty until July 31st, when it was mustered out of the service.

COMPANY A.

NON-COMMISSIONED OFFICERS.

Sergeant Henry R. Thompson.
Corporal William Ipe.
Corporal W. Rader.
Corporal David Llewellyn.
Corporal Jonathan Shearer.

PRIVATES.

William Ashman, Alexander Black, Samuel Burton, Abraham Cover, Leigh R. Crouse, William Cover, John Coil, Thomas Chiles, Norman Church, Irwin G. Duncan, Albert Eldridge, John Graham, David Windman, James C. Hall, William M. Irwin, Eli Mack, George McQuinn, David L. Sweeter, Austin VanAmburgh, James Whaler, Solomon Zedaker.

Not Reported.—Jacob Harding, Sweetling Zedaker, and Thomas Thomas.

COMPANY K.

NON-COMMISSIONED OFFICERS.

Second Sergeant Henry K. Amer.
Corporal Arthur S. Donaldson.

PRIVATES.

Columbus B. Justice, Henry N. Lincoln, Thomas G. Shannon, George Thomas.

Not Reported.—Henry Wilcox.

SECOND OHIO VOLUNTEER CAVALRY.

One of the finest military organizations recruited in the summer of 1861 was the Second Ohio cavalry. Soon after the war had actually begun, Hon B. F. Wade, of Jefferson, and Hon. John Hutchins, of Warren, were commissioned by the War department to supervise the recruiting service in this part of the State. The enlistment rolls were filled with the names of men of wealth, intelligence, and culture. It is natural that that class of men should join the cavalry service rather than the infantry, for it involves more adventure and less monotonous labor.

The last company of the Second Ohio volunteer cavalry was mustered in October 10, 1861. From Camp Wade it went to Cleveland, where it was uniformed, mounted, and partly drilled. About December 1st it was ordered to Camp Dennison, where sabers were supplied, and, while orders were awaited from the War department, the practice in drill and arms continued. Early in January, 1862, the regiment proceeded under orders to Platte City, Missouri, by rail. A small detachment, under Lieutenant Nettleton, had served about two weeks in Kentucky while the regiment was stationed at Camp Dennison. The first duty of the Second cavalry in Missouri was to raid the State. On February 22d, while on the march through the border counties toward Fort Scott, Kansas, a scouting party encountered a detachment of rebels equal in number to themselves, under command of the infamous Quantrell. The fight which ensued lasted fifteen minutes, and resulted in the complete rout of the enemy with a loss of fourteen men. The Second lost one killed and three wounded. Sabers, navy pistols, and Austrian carbines constituted the arms of the regiment at that time. The months of March and April were mainly spent in breaking up guerrilla bands in the border counties of Missouri and in Kansas. The Western army concentrated at Fort Scott about the middle of May, and early in June marched south into Indian Territory. While the infantry halted at Spring river, the cavalry and artillery moved forward and drove the Indian rebel Sandwaitie from his camp at Baxter Springs, Indian Territory. Three regiments of Indians, mounted on ponies and armed with squirrel rifles, joined the army. These proved a great relief to the otherwise dreary monotony of the march.

After participating in the attack and capture of Fort Gibson, the Second returned to Fort Scott, where it arrived and went into camp August 15th. Although little opportunity of meeting the enemy had been afforded, the Second had seriously suffered from sickness; many had died on the march from a peculiar brain fever, caused by the heat. It was also found that only two hundred and fifty serviceable horses were available to the regiment. Near the close of August the regiment shared in a forced march, occupying ten days and nights, in pursuit of a rebel band of raiders. About this time there was a pressing need for artillerymen, and one hundred and fifty men and two officers of the Second were detailed as a light battery and were soon after transferred and regularly organized as the Twenty-fifth Ohio battery, which will be noticed subsequently. The Second participated in the fall campaign under General Blunt and fought at Carthage, Newtonia, Cow Hill, Wolf Creek, White River, and Prairie Grove, Arkansas, at which place, December 3, 1862, a splendid victory was won. In September Captain August V. Kautz, of the Sixth United States cavalry, was made colonel of the Second, Colonel Charles Doubleday having been promoted to brigadier-general. Colonel Kautz at once took measures to have the regiment transferred to the East, and in this he succeeded before the year closed.

January, February, and March were spent in Camp Chase, Ohio, where the regiment was refurnished and reorganized, the original twelve companies being consolidated into eight, and four new companies added. Early in April it left Camp Chase, and until June 27th, with the exception of occasional raids, was in camp at Somerset, Kentucky. During this time it engaged with the enemy twice at Steubenville, twice at Monticello, and once at Columbia, Kentucky. Colonel Kautz's brigade, of which the Second was a part, began a spirited pursuit of John Morgan, July 1st, and followed the great raider one thousand two hundred miles through three States, traveling five-sixths of the time and living for twenty-seven days wholly upon the gifts of the people. This celebrated chase resulted in the capture of Morgan at Buffington's Island. In recognition of the regiment's endurance and gallantry in this expedition it was highly complimented at Cincinnati by General Burnside.

In August, 1864, the Second having reassembled moved with the army to East Tennessee. The brigade to which it belonged, commanded by Colonel Caster, met its first resistance at London Bridge, over the Tennessee river, but easily weighed down opposition. After the surrender of Cumberland Gap it marched to Knoxville and soon afterward joined the Army of the Cumberland under Rosecrans. The Second bore an honorable part in the battle of Blue Springs, and was with the mounted force which defeated the rebels at Blountsville and Bristol. It engaged the enemy's cavalry near Cumberland Gap and participated in the siege at Knoxville and the subsequent pursuit of the retreating force. On December 2d it engaged Longstreet's cavalry at Morristown and two days later fought eighteen regiments at Russellville, in which forty men were killed and wounded. For the next six days it was under almost constant fire. Until January 1st the regiment was fighting or marching with little rest. It was under these circumstances that when the rolls for veteran enlistment were presented, January 1st, four hundred and twenty out of four hundred and seventy volunteered to continue in the service. A veteran furlough was granted and the regiment arrived at Camp Chase February 16th, when it disbanded for thirty days. One hundred and twenty recruits joined the regiment on reassembling at Cleveland March 20th. On April 4th it was encamped at the Chesapeake, and on May 3d, having been reviewed by Lieutenant-general Grant, it reported to General Burnside at Warrenville Junction. During the terrible campaign of the Wilderness the Second was engaged almost constantly. On May 29th it was transferred to Sheridan's famous cavalry corps, in General J. H. Wilson's brigade. It sustained the heaviest of the charge at Hanover Court House. It was actively employed along the Potomac until early in August, when it moved through Washington to the Shenandoah valley, where on August 17th was fought the battle of Winchester, in which the Second cavalry took a conspicuous part and sustained considerable loss. At Summit Point on the 19th, at Charlestown on the 22d, and at Harper's Ferry, the Second sustained its reputation for gallantry. On August 30th this regiment assisted in driving the enemy from Berryville, Virginia, and on September 13th captured one of rebel General Early's regiments in front of Winchester. The Second was engaged at Waynesboro, where it saved itself from capture by a gallant charge through the rebel column. During the subsequent march down the valley the regiment acted as rear guard. It performed hard work during the battle of Cedar Creek, and was subsequently constantly employed and frequently engaged with the enemy until going into winter quarters December 28th near Winchester. On February 27th the Second joined Sheridan's cavalry in the last raid of the war, and on March 2d assisted in the capture of Early's army near Waynesboro. Between March 27th and Lee's surrender the Second captured eighteen pieces of artillery, one hundred and eighty horses, seventy army wagons, nine hundred prisoners, and large quantities of small arms. After the surrender it was ordered to North Carolina, and from there to Washington to participate in the grand parade. In June the regiment was transferred to Missouri, where it served until mustered out September 1st. It was finally disbanded at Camp Chase, Ohio, September 11th, having served four years.

It is estimated that the regiment marched an aggregate distance of twenty-seven thousand miles, and participated in ninety-seven engagements. It served in the Army of the Frontier, of the Missouri, of the Potomac, of the Ohio, and of the Shenandoah. Few military organizations were composed of better material, few made a better record.

FIELD AND STAFF.

Colonel Charles Doubleday, resigned June 16, 1862.
Colonel August V. Kautz, promoted brigadier-general in April, 1865.
Colonel A. B. Nettleton, promoted brevet brigadier-general for gallantry.
Colonel Dudley Seward, mustered out with regiment.
Lieutenant-colonel Robert W. Ratliff, resigned June 25, 1863.
Lieutenant-colonel George A. Purington, promoted colonel but not mustered.
Lieutenant-colonel Dudley Seward, promoted lieutenant-colonel in May, 1864, colonel in 1865.
Lieutenant-colonel A. B. Nettleton, promoted lieutenant-colonel in November, 1864, colonel in 1865.
Lieutenant-colonel David E. Welch, promoted lieutenant-colonel in June, 1864.
Lieutenant-colonel Albert Burnitz, promoted lieutenant-colonel in 1865.
Major George G. Miner, promoted lieutenant-colonel in September, 1862.
Major Henry F. Wilson, resigned March 10, 1862.
Major George A. Purington, promoted to lieutenant-colonel.
Major Henry L. Burnet, promoted major March 10, 1862, resigned in August, 1863.
Major Dudley Seward, promoted major September 18, 1862.
Major A. B. Nettleton, promoted major June 25, 1863.
Major D. E. Welch, promoted major August 15, 1863.
Major Manford F. Weeks, promoted major May 9, 1863; revoked.
Major Albert Burnitz, promoted major in December, 1863; mustered out with regiment.
Major Hyman N. Eastman, promoted major in May, 1864; mustered out with regiment.
Major R. E. Lawder, promoted major in June, 1864; mustered out with regiment.
Surgeon Alfred Taylor.
Surgeon Joseph T. Smith.
Surgeon William H. McReynolds.
Surgeon N. B. Bristine.
Assistant Surgeon Joseph T. Smith.
Assistant Surgeon H. B. Noble.
Assistant Surgeon William H. McReynolds.
Assistant Surgeon Matthias Cook.
Chaplain G. B. Hawkins.
Chaplain Edwin F. Brown.
Sergeant-major James K. Elder.
Hospital Steward Reuben D. Bennett.
Hospital Steward James S. Tod.
Saddler John Misner.

COMPANY B.
PRIVATES.

Cyrus Allen, Peter Landen, Emory Snodgrass, Dean W. Sterling (recruit).

COMPANY C.
COMMISSIONED OFFICERS.

Captain Henry L. Burnet, promoted major March 10, 1862.

First Lieutenant Robert L. Hart, resigned in October, 1861.
Second Lieutenant L. D. Bosworth, promoted to second lieutenant.
Lieutenant Daniel Coates, promoted to lieutenant.
Lieutenant William W. Randall, promoted to lieutenant.
Lieutenant George B. Hayden, promoted to lieutenant.

NON-COMMISSIONED OFFICERS.

Commissary-sergeant Byron M. Peck.
Commissary-sergeant Leonard Pfouts, promoted sergeant in 1865.
Commissary-sergeant Sylvester Barber, promoted sergeant; captured.
Corporal James Sherman.
Corporal Alfred Morrison.
Corporal Silas Laughlin.
Corporal Marshall J. Madison.
Corporal Andrew Colbit.
Farrier David O. Barber.
Farrier Eben Hulste.
Saddler William C. Corbin.
Wagoner Frederick Brice.

PRIVATES.

Quincy Bradley, Seth Comin, Martin V. Cole, Freeman Darling, William A. Finley, Hatton P. Forbis, John L. Manchester, Osnian McIntosh, Solomon Morris, Charles Richmond, Enos Smart, George Stubble, Jasper Stubble, Sylvester J. Sanford, Richard Tiner, Richard M. Ball (killed at Five Forks, Virginia), Samuel C. Trescott (died in prison), Henry Burgess (missing in action), Lucius C. Fox (discharged at hospital), Henry C. Hart (died in Andersonville), Taylor Jones (died in Andersonville), Joseph Jones.

Discharged before Expiration of Service.—Elisha F. Humason, Edwin Buell, Edsell R. Feil, Alfred Jordan, Franklin G. Peck, Hubert Beers, Elias Stahl, Charles J. Montgomery, George W. Kennedy, Byron M. Peck, Henry Fullwiler, Sylvester Loveland, Francis Lewis, George W. Hoffman, Samuel Barnes, James E. Beech, Albert S. Bennett, Cornelius Bentley, James H. Brown, John Probst, Orin J. Chalker, George W. Chae, Levi Craver, Benjamin Craver, Clark Leman, Thomas J. Carew, John Extell, Thomas C. Hart, Samuel M. Huff, John H. Hultz, Amos Hunter, Joseph A. Hunter, Edmund Hudson, Charles H. Johnson, William H. Jones, William Jones, Milton R. Kinney, Alfred Kinney, Otis Martin, S. C. Montgomery, Aver A. Parker, Thomas R. Peabody, John Peterson, C. George Riesel, Calvin R. Rinear, George W. Roxburry, Anderson Root, Nelson Root, James A. Russell, Lorin Scott, William Shoemaker, Jacob Smallseed, Warren Soul, Luther P. Spaulding, Robert C. Spencer, Emery D. Still, Lucius H. Thomas, Cyrus Trunky, Daniel W. Tresser, William S. Tuttle, Alvin Vincent, Hiram Walker, John Warren, Charles L. Willis, Thomas L. Wood.

COMPANY D.

This company was recruited chiefly in Farmington township.

COMMISSIONED OFFICERS.

Captain James Caldwell, resigned May 15, 1862; re-commissioned September 20, 1862; discharged February, 1863.
Captain Henry Clay Pike, appointed second lieutenant January 4, 1862; promoted first lieutenant January 8, 1862; promoted captain January 22, 1863. Mustered out with the regiment.

TRUMBULL AND MAHONING COUNTIES, OHIO.

First Lieutenant James D. Kennedy; resigned January, 1862.
First Lieutenant Alonzo McGowen, commissioned second lieutenant September 14, 1861; promoted first lieutenant January 8, 1862; resigned February 4, 1863.
First Lieutenant Timothy R. Spencer, appointed February, 1863; promoted to captain and transferred to company F.
First Lieutenant John B. Dutton; enlisted as private; promoted sergeant October 30, 1861; second lieutenant February, 1863; first lieutenant November, 1863; transferred to company C.

NON-COMMISSIONED OFFICERS.

First Sergeant William D. Hickox.
First Sergeant William Wolcott.
Sergeant John A. White.
Sergeant Lorin Roberts.
Sergeant Homer Dillon.
Corporal Robert A. Wilcox.
Corporal Edward H. Herrendon.
Corporal Joseph B. Johnson.

PRIVATES.

Ed. P. Holcomb, Alva R. Harshman, Christopher Kincaid, Stephen Lampman, Levi J. Terrill, George W. Wilcox.
Killed.—First Sergeant John O. Caldwell, Quartermaster Sergeant John B. Williams, at Ashland Station; George L. Seymour, at Harper's Farm, Virginia.
Died of wounds.—Hiram A. France, 1864.
Died in prison.—Frank G. Palmer, August, 1864.
Discharged before mustering out of company.—William Wilcox, Velorous M. Hart, Daniel W. Myers, Edward F. Rinear, James C. Edner, Adam Echenrod, Cushman Pelton.
Discharged for disability.—Joseph W. Anderson, William Henderson, Henry McAfoos, Edwin Outley, Joseph Bradford, Charles A. Spauldwin.
Transferred to Seventh Ohio volunteer cavalry.—James K. Elder, Lyman C. Wolcott, David W. Halstead, Rodney Lest, Thomas Warlow, William W. Moore, Lewis B. Holt, Stewart R. Nample, J. A. Cummings, Chauncy Dabney, Ed L. Freeman, A. P. Oviatt, Homer H. Troop, John C. Watts, Franklin Wilhelm, James D. Thompson.
Other transfers.—Madison P. Headley, Frank H. Knapp, H. T. Bushnell, Freeman Thorp.
*Names not on muster-out roll.—Jacob Strohm, John P. Ritter, Edward P. Merwin, Benjamin C. Waggoner, Henry G. Wolcott, L. B. Montgomery, Job Reynolds, Emery E. Knowlton, James B. Burnard, Samuel Lee, George W. Brown, Oliver Johnson, Ed T. Barton, Joseph J. Brown, George M. Bailey, Ed J. Caldwell, Sperry C. Clark, A. H. Chaffey, Robert Evans, Thomas J. Evans, Egbert E. Ensign, Abraham Ford, Harrison H. Gee, George B. Hamilton, Jacob Herriff, Charles E. Horns, A. E. Hanford, John W. Johnson, William L. Jones, John A. Johnson, Amiel Kincaid, George B. Kennedy, John A. Long, Frederick D. Lepper, Jacob Leroy, Benjamin Misner, Charles Munson, John L. Mahaney, John A. Newton, George A. Prindle, Sanford R. Pratt, William Quiggle, Rulsa C. Rice, Wilbur A. Reeves, Frank B. Richards, Daniel B. Rhodes, John C. Watts, Homer J. Wolcott, George Wilson, Frank Wilhelm, William C. Woods, George W. White, William H. Wildman.

* The larger part of these were discharged at the reorganization of the regiment at Camp Chase in February, 1863.

COMPANY E.

COMMISSIONED OFFICERS.

Captain Hiram A. Hall, mustered out February 15, 1863.
Captain Baylis R. Fawcett, promoted to captain December 20, 1861, from first lieutenant company E; resigned May, 1862.
Captain Crawford W. Stewart, promoted to captain February 23, 1863; died April 26, 1864.
Captain Warner Newton, promoted to Captain November, 1864; died of wounds at City Point, Virginia.
Captain William Smith, joined by transfer.
First Lieutenant Peter L. Rush, promoted to first lieutenant December, 1861; resigned January, 1863.

NON-COMMISSIONED OFFICERS.

First Sergeant Charles E. Bostwick, promoted to first sergeant August, 1865.
Sergeant Henry Phillips, promoted to sergeant January, 1865.
Sergeant James F. Johnston, promoted to sergeant March, 1865.
Sergeant John A. Johnston, promoted to sergeant July, 1865.
Sergeant Franklin Keiper, promoted to sergeant August, 1865.
Sergeant Solomon C. Wise, promoted to sergeant November, 1864.
Sergeant Thomas C. Grist, discharged.
Sergeant Henry D. Sayler, discharged.
Corporal Isaac Gause, promoted to corporal July, 1865.
Corporal James J. Winans, promoted to corporal January, 1865.
Corporal Orin B. Hopkins, promoted to corporal March, 1865.
Corporal Franklin Ackley, promoted to corporal June, 1865.
Corporal George F. Woodbourn, promoted to corporal June, 1865.
Corporal William Cramer, promoted to corporal July, 1865.
Corporal Oliver D. Bannon, promoted to corporal August, 1865.
Corporal Charles R. Truesdale, discharged.
Corporal James E. Newton, discharged.
Farrier John L. Huffman.
Farrier Robert W. McGrew.
Wagoner Nelson Russell.

PRIVATES.

Mustered out September 11, 1865.—Cyrus C. Brainard, Simon B. Carlton, Charles H. Dickinson, Edward Folley, Henry M. Fowler, John Gleghorn, John F. Hobbs, Henry Lanterman, William H. Lute, John Marton, William H. Miller, George C. Mygatt, James Nesbitt, Henry C. Newman, Park Matthews, Noah Pile, Napoleon B. Platt, James G. Reed, Jacob R. Reed, Thomas G. Reese, Seth Robinson, Thomas C. Sherman, John W. Thatcher, Hugh B. Wilson, William H. Wiggins, Ansel D. Wood.
Killed.—John R. Johnston, at Winchester, Virginia.
Died.—Zabad C. Bissell, in Andersonville; John W. Addison, at Washington, 1864; Philip Laisier, drowned at Cincinnati; Henry T. Truesdale, in rebel prison; Noble D. Thorne, at Savannah, Georgia, 1864; William Wakefield, at Washington, 1865; John W. Williams, drowned at Cincinnati, Ohio.
Discharged.—Richard R. Baird, Robert B. Brooklin, Lewis

W. Goodwin, William D. Moore, John Platt, Levi W. Sechler, George Tow.

Transferred.—George A. Wilkins, John O. McConnell.

Names Not On Muster-out Roll.—Daniel H. Arnold, Horace M. Lord, Joseph R. Johnston, Augustus H. Harris, William H. Arnold, Henry M. Meeker, officers; William E. Williams, David B. Corning, James W. Earl, William H. Akdorffer, Alvin Anderson, John Antibus, John Brandeburg, John Brown, James Campbell, Lewis Campbell, Theodore Campbell, Alfred Dotchon, Abraham Ernest, Charles Etre, John H. Fullerton, Reuben Hahn, Stephen Hudson, James J. Johnson, John Z. Johnson, James Kelly, Julius Kincaid, Isaac Kissinger, George W. Lanterman, Albert J. McAulis, James McArthur, Robert T. McMahon, Park Irwin, Robert W. Pennell, Seely Platt, Samuel H. Reaker, James Robbins, George W. Robins, James Rummage, James Shaffer, John C. Sheets, John Strang, Titus Thomas, Steve J. Tod, James R. Truesdale, James L. Truesdale, E. H. Tullis, Alex Whetstone, Robert Williams, Robert Wilson.

COMPANY T.
PRIVATES.

Mustered out with Company.—Leslie C. Benson, Henry Cleveland, George W. Eastwood, James P. Hull, Julius Howard, William L. Roach, Albert H. Rice, Henry B. Wright.

Not Reported.—Emery M. Haskins.

Discharged.—Charles H. Bliss.

COMPANY G.
PRIVATES.

John Thompson, mustered out with company; Abram Williams, died at Saulsbury, North Carolina, in 1865; John A. McDonald, not reported; Henry Steel, not reported; Samuel B. Foster, discharged for disability; Charles H. Mead, discharged for disability.

COMPANY H.
PRIVATE.

Mustered Out with Company.—Warren W. Whitney.

COMPANY I.
NON-COMMISSIONED OFFICER.

Saddler M. Ernst, mustered out with company.

PRIVATES.

James Bruce, John L. Wager.

COMPANY M.
PRIVATES.

John H. Mason, died in hospital; Michael Clark, discharged; Joseph Jones, discharged.

SIXTH OHIO VOLUNTEER CAVALRY.

The second cavalry company recruited by Hon. B. F. Wade and John Hutchins was organized at Warren in October, 1861, and on being mustered into service was ranked as the Sixth Ohio cavalry. The camp, which was near the city, was named in honor of Hon. John Hutchins. During the months of October, November, and December the daily exercise in drill and arms was witnessed by scores of interested visitors. It was with considerable regret that in January, 1862, the order to move to Camp Chase was received. The regiment had been recruited on the Reserve, and nearly one-third of its members were residents of the county in which they were camping.

The regiment was employed at Camp Chase guarding rebel prisoners until early in May, when complete equipments were furnished, and on the 13th the cars were boarded for Wheeling, West Virginia. It joined General Fremont at Strasburg, and started in pursuit of Jackson down the Shenandoah valley. Its first engagement was at Strasburg, and all the way down the valley it was skirmishing until Cross Keys was reached, where it was regularly engaged with the enemy June 7th. It was also engaged at Luray Court-house and Cedar Mountain. At this point the regiment came under command of General Pope, who contested with Jackson the passage of Rappahannock. For fourteen consecutive days it was under fire. After the second battle of Bull Run, August 29, 1862, the regiment was compelled to retire to camp at Hall's farm to rest the horses, exhausted by almost constant action. After driving the enemy from his position at Warrenton the Second joined Burnside in his advanced upon Fredericksburg. The winter of 1862-63 was spent in camp and guarding the Rappahannock. It joined Hooker's army in the spring, and in March vindicated the standing of the National cavalry at Kelley's ford. In Lee's movement toward Maryland the Sixth was in several actions. At Aldie, June 17th, led by Colonel Steadman, the Sixth made the most gallant charge in the record of cavalry service.

Following Lee into Maryland the Sixth cavalry participated in the battle of Gettysburg and made several important captures. During the retreat, Kilpatrick's brigade, to which it belonged, captured one thousand five hundred of the defeated enemy at Falling Waters. At Culpeper Courthouse, Rapidan Station, Sulphur Springs, and Auburn Mills battles were fought. In the last Captain Rowe was mortally wounded, Captain Richart and Lieutenants Bingham and Miller seriously wounded, and thirteen men killed and wounded.

When the army went into winter quarters at Warrenton, the Sixth was detailed to general guard and picket duty. This was an arduous task and required constant watchfulness, for during the whole winter the wary guerilla Moseby and his chivalric band of freebooters harrassed the camp. On January 1st about two hundred of the Sixth re-enlisted and were furloughed. Upon reorganization in the spring the companies were well filled with recruits, and the regiment entered the campaign with nearly its maximum number of men. It was made a part of Sheridan's famous cavalry. It participated in the battle of the Wilderness. At Owen's church, May 28th, Captain Northway was killed, whose gallantry was the pride of the regiment. At Cold Harbor, May 31st, Captain Loveland was wounded. June 6th the Sixth started on Sheridan's raid on Gordonsville, and was engaged at Trevillian Station, where Henry M. Baldwin was killed June 24th. The Sixth was active during the whole seige of Petersburg, and participated in several close contests, in one of which, at Hutchins' Run, October 27th, Captain E. S. Austin was killed. He was distinguished for coolness and perception in battle.

It has been remarked that in all these movements there was one place which the Sixth was destined to fill—that of advance guard. Any point they failed to carry while in this position was not designated for any other regiment (either cavalry or infantry) to attack. The year 1864 did not end the service of this veteran regiment. In February it left camp, and the same bloody fields were again traversed. At Hutchins' run, Dinwiddie Court-house, and Five Forks it participated in spirited engagements. It led in the pursuit of Lee, fighting at Farmville and Sailor's creek. "At the battle of Appomattox Court-house, on April 9th, this regiment had the honor of opening the engagement, it having marched during the night to a position across the only road left for the retreat of the rebel army. Soon after daylight on that memorable morning an attack was made on our line, which had been fortified with a rail breastworks, and after a spirited resistance the regiment fell back only to show to pursuing rebels our strong line of infantry who had come up during the early morning. The attack was ended, a white flag was flying across the rebel front, and the work for which they had fought so long and so well was accomplished."

The Sixth acted as General Grant's escort from Appomattox to Burksville station. After going to Petersburg it was ordered to North Carolina. Johnston having surrendered, it was divided into detachments and stationed in the District of Appomattox. In August, 1865, the regiment was ordered to Cleveland, and mustered out of the service.

FIELD AND STAFF.

Lieutenant-colonel Frank C. Loveland, appointed second lieutenant October 28, 1862, promoted captain August 1, 1864; promoted lieutenant-colonel April 20, 1865, and to colonel September 4, 1865.

Surgeon Alphonzo D. Rockwell, appointed assistant surgeon April 18, 1864; promoted surgeon December 14, 1864.

Assistant Surgeon Cano Kilrie, April 16, 1865.

Adjutant Williams M. Davis, entered service as private, November 6, 1861; promoted sergeant December 14, 1861; promoted from sergeant to first sergeant July 14, 1864; promoted first lieutenant February 6, 1865.

Commissary Dwight Cory, entered service as private October 8, 1861; promoted corporal October 14, 1861; promoted regimental commissary sergeant October 1, 1862; promoted first lieutenant November 18, 1864.

[Died].

Major Benjamin Stanhope, 1863.
Assistant Surgeon Zenas A. Northway, 1864.
Adjutant Henry M. Baldwin, 1864.

[Discharged Before Expiration of Service.]

Colonel William Stedman.
Lieutenant-colonel Norman A. Barrett, wounded at Malvern Hill.
Lieutenant-colonel George W. Dickinson.
Major William Stedman.
Major John H. Cryer.
Major James C. Richart.
Major George W. Dickinson.
Surgeon William B. Reyner.
Assistant Surgeon Augustus L. Knowlton.
Assistant Surgeon Alphonzo D. Rockwell.
Adjutant Richard I. Wright.
Adjutant Alcimis Ward Fenton.
Quartermaster Uriel H. Hutchins.
Quartermaster John R. Parshall.
Commissary Charles C. Baker.

[Resigned].

Colonel William R. Lloyd.
Major Richard B. Treat.
Major Matthew H. Cryer.
Assistant Surgeon James C. Marr.
Adjutant W. H. Haskell.
Adjutant William T. Reynolds.
Quartermaster Charles R. Hunt.
Quartermaster Charles Bostwick.
Quartermaster Joel A. Clark.

[Dismissed].

Major Amander Bingham.

[Detached].

Lieutenant-colonel William O. Collins.
Major William O. Farrell.
Quartermaster William Woodrow.

NON-COMMISSIONED STAFF.

Sergeant-major Henry M. Baldwin.

Veterinary Surgeon Pelton Winthrop.
Regimental Quartermaster Sergeant George M. St. John.
Regimental Quartermaster Sergeant Frank Trunky.
Regimental Quartermaster Sergeant Samuel Cassill.
Regimental Quartermaster Sergeant John G. Carson.
Regimental Quartermaster Sergeant Dr. F. Burgess.
Regimental Commissary Sergeant Daniel E. Hedden.
Hospital Steward Caleb L. Lising.
Saddler Sergeant Ethen More.
Chief Bugler John Morey.
Regimental Commissary Sergeant Madison Hedley, transferred.
Sergeant Major George T. Keller, reduced.

COMPANY A.
PRIVATES.

A. C. Brockway, William R. Joiner, Addison Harrington, Charles S. Plumb, Gottlieb Bazer, P. E. Goodrich, Chauncey G. Hutchins, Nathan Pool, Thomas Vokes.

COMPANY B.
PRIVATES.

Boursel Brown, Hugh Kennedy, Charles Feidler, Sidney G. Hickox.

COMPANY C.
PRIVATES.

Albert King, Orlando Beckwith, Wilson Galloway, Arthur E. Fenton, Collins W. Fenton, Lewis Wiley, Andrew McCracken, Robert Mason, Thomas H. Mahany, William H. Parmelee, Alfred Webster, Henry Willey, William E. Wilson.

COMPANY D.
PRIVATES.

George W. Gilbert, Allen W. Barr, Franklin Bennett, George Chapman, Wesley M. Hall, S. A. Condray (died of wounds at Jettersville station).

Discharged.—John B. Clark, A. R. Fell, William J. Hicks, Horace Pardee, Benjamin Robbins, William Sheffleton, Alfred H. Pierce, Charles W. Patterson, Robert W. McCartney, Matthew K. King, Oliver B. Hall, Henry H. Burns, P. Cook, Anson E. Hudson, George Hopkinson, Colonel E. Allen, Harrison Lee, Allen Wallace, Daniel Brobst, Levi Bonesteel, Isaac Bridges, Richard Clark, Thomas Forley, Robert Force, Royal Force, Dwight Goff, Jacob C. Hoover, George Hayes, Samuel B. Hartshorn, F. Hartshorn, Riley Hall, Cleveland Hudson, James Johnson, Irwin Kincaid, George Loveless, Harmon B. Osburne, Homer Oviatt, William Peterman, Myers S. Patterson, Joshua Ramalia, James Roberts, Ira Smith, John Sweezy, Joseph Sutliff, James Saunders, Charles Tucker, Richards Watterman, Charles W. Wade, Lewis P. Weight.

Transferred.—Robert Dabney, Charles Hamlin, Daniel E. Hedden, Picton Hayes, Caleb Rising.

Died in the Service.—Joseph Brown, George T. King, Horace A. Prior, Frank Downes, Gibbs Great, Thomas Hull, Robert W. Lorenz, Deming Renier, Amos Ramalia, Allen Robbins, Cassius A. Thompson.

Not Reported.—James R. Ormsby, Theodore S. Wolcott.

COMPANY E.
NON-COMMISSIONED OFFICER.

Commissary Sergeant Charles W. De Witt.

PRIVATES.

Christopher C. Garn, John C. Lawson.

Not Reported.—Benjamin Applegate.
Discharged.—William Marlow, Ransom J. Knowles.

COMPANY F.
NON-COMMISSIONED STAFF.

Quartermaster Sergeant George E. Davis.

NON-COMMISSIONED OFFICER.

Sergeant Lyman W. Dickerson.

PRIVATES.

Silas Cox, David Fult, William Gilbert, B. H. Jackson, George A. Layer, C. Larve, William Lawrence, David Morris, William H. Price, Andrew J. Sharp, John P. Frank, William W. Baldwin, Henry C. De Wolf, Alanson Kennedy, David Lewis, Jacob Harshman, John H. Grate, Edward Herst, Hamilton Johnson, Leroy A. Sogus, Hosea Trowen, Joseph Oviatt, Leavitt W. Robbins, Dwight Seamons, Seneca Tracy, Wallace Williams, Lafayette Williams, Guy H. Washbourn, George F. Gordon.

Died.—Erastus Emerson in Salsbury prison; Peter Bailey, in 1864 at home; John Demming died of wounds.

Not Reported.—Timothy Wierants.

COMPANY G.
COMMISSIONED OFFICERS.

Captain William K. Miller, entered as second lieutenant December 27, 1863; commissioned captain December 8, 1864, and mustered to date December 8, 1864.

Captain James C. Richart, commissioned major January 1, 1864; mustered March 20, 1864.

Captain Euselius S. Austin, commissioned captain May 9, 1864; mustered in company G, May 14, 1864; killed October 27, 1864, near Boydton Plank Road, Virginia.

First Lieutenant John N. Roberts, commissioned captain August 3, 1863; mustered in company D, Sixth Ohio Volunteer cavalry, April 27, 1864, to date November 7, 1863.

First Lieutenant Josiah E. Woods, commissioned first lieutenant May 9, 1864; mustered in company G, May 14, 1864; discharged by special order number four hundred and thirty-nine, War department.

Second Lieutenant George L. Wilton, service expired October 11, 1864.

NON-COMMISSIONED OFFICERS.

First Sergeant William S. Saighman.
Quartermaster-sergeant Isaac N. Crooks.
Sergeant Gilbert L. Medley.
Sergeant James H. Miller.
Sergeant John F. Smith.
Sergeant Luther B. Shueliff.
Corporal Hiram Hull.
Corporal John Lafferty.
Corporal Bernard Derring.
Corporal Silas Warring.

PRIVATES.

Joseph Battenfield, Milton Darwin, Peter Franeen, Erwin Hurst, William Moore, Birney McGilligan, William Shieble, George S. Thurp, Josiah Zimmerman.

Killed.—John S. Keen, near Boydton Plank Roads, Virginia; William Borte, at Enon Church, Virginia.

Died.—John W. Dunlap, 1863; Frank L. Shaffer, 1863; Clarence L. Anderson, 1864; George Williams, 1863; Robert T. McClain, 1864; Robert Barrett, 1864; Edwin Elliott, 1862; Curtis O. Harshman, 1862; John Jack, at hospital, date unknown; Thomas Kincaid, 1862; Benjamin F. Kline, 1863; James Rourk, 1864.

164   TRUMBULL AND MAHONING COUNTIES, OHIO.

Not Reported.—Christian Dladogne, James Fendon, John Hickey, Charles Keeler, John Keeler, Samuel Miles, John O'Connor, Allen Patterson, David D. Tracy.

Discharged Before Expiration of Service.—Charles G. Miller, William M. Davis, Miles G. Butler, Ralph Fowler, Truman Reeves, William Barrett, George W. Gillis, Edwin D. McKee, William Phillips, William H. McClure, Lemuel Granger, Stewart Groscost, David M. Musser, Samuel Treep, Henry Kinnaman, Alfred Whеiеr, Edward W. Tanner, John Gilmore, Henry Vanhout, Nathan C. Tylor, Freeman Ague, Wilson Henry, John Black, Isaac Brister, William Brown, John Brister, John Cameron, Richard Cooley, Ismer C. Chase, George Caven, Lorenzo Darrow, Isaac Devense, John L. Evans, George K. Fowler, James Gannon, Shannon Harmon, Bernard Harrison, Thomas Hank, Joseph Holden, Enos H. Hake, Gideon V. Holstead, Charles B. Jones, William Jack, John Kay, Thomas S. Knox, George T. Keller, George A. Kellogg, Hugh Leonard, Lucas Libus, Joseph Mawley, Joseph D. Miller, Thomas Morris, William McCormick, Hugh O'Donnell, Emory Osborn, Orlando M. Pratt, Samuel Parks, John Rader, David Rice, William Richard, David S. Sears, Hiram Smith, John S. Thorp, Benjamin F. Thornton, Charles Taylor, Joseph Traxler.

Transferred.—Henry M. Baldwin, Myron A. Barker, Julius Hill, Albert J. Criss, Patrick Whitty.

COMPANY I.

COMMISSIONED OFFICERS.

Captain Reuben E. Osgood, entered as private November 1, 1861; promoted to sergeant December 16, 1861; promoted second lieutenant December 1, 1862; promoted first lieutenant August 1, 1864; promoted to captain January 1, 1865.

Captain James S. Abel, killed May 9, 1864.

Captain John L. Miller, discharged October 6, 1864.

First Lieutenant William J. Haight, resigned October 6, 1862.

First Lieutenant Elias Shepard.

Second Lieutenant Jeremiah H. Phillips, died September 9, 1864.

Second Lieutenant Jacob R. Templin, discharged by reason of wounds received October 27, 1864.

NON-COMMISSIONED OFFICERS.

Sergeant Ezra A. France.
Sergeant Edwin Sale.
Corporal Pomroy E. Bancroft.
Corporal Henry Boneham.
Corporal Henry Beaker.
Corporal Moses Cole.
Corporal James Chaffee.
Corporal Isaac France.
Corporal Faunce Parmenas.
Corporal Ishamus Haskins.
Corporal Nelson P. Lease.
Corporal Shofer Mowery.
Corporal Thomas McKritchie.
Corporal Jeremiah Morey.
Corporal Darish H. Petro.
Corporal Charles Stark.
Corporal John S. Schmidt.
Corporal Gilbert G. Woldorf.
Corporal Irwin Warner.
Corporal John McKellep.
Corporal Eli Fenshmacer.
Corporal John Park.

Corporal Francis J. Goldsmith.
Corporal John Mowry.
Corporal Ira Morey.
Corporal John Stroup, killed.

PRIVATES.

Curtis Cook, Charles A. Greene, Robert H. Mackey, John Mummert, William Rose, John Sheparitson, Sylvester M. Scoville, Quinby Shafer, Charles D. Ayres, George W. Rale, Charles H. D. Baker, James Burnes, Charles H. Brum, Joseph Barnes, Milo Burnett, Isaiah Craig, Seymour Covert, Samuel Crooks, Richard Canfield, Sherbon H. Chaffee, Byron N. Crundle, James H. Crooks, Curtis Bennett, Seth Cook, Andrew Cook, Warren J. Dice, John H. Dilly, Delormay Detrick, Evan Davis, Dennis Dwyre, Loyd W. Irwinger, Peter Fenstimacer, John Griffith, Madison Sowers, Daniel M. Hilliard, James Hayhusk, Albert Houge, Perry Hosmer, William E. Hill, Christopher C. Hively, George Hoffman, Orlo Jordan, Peter Jacobs, Josiah A. Kestler, Baily D. Keefer, Arnard Leash, Thomas Leary, Jacob Lease, Charles F. Mason, Andrew Martin, Porter L. Morse, Sylvester Morgan, Miles McManus, Irwin D. Miner, Albert H. Measham, William Near, Willius H. Palmer, Winthrop Pelton, Taylor Randolph, Amos C. Reede, Joseph Ribager, Albert Ropke, Christopher Switz, Samuel Shafer, Charles D. Smith, Isaac Swager, Calvin Stevens, James Sirrine, Gotlieb Stark, Nelson Struble, William Smith, George Smith, Henry S. Truesdale, Ims Templeton, Uriah Williams, James M. Webber, Lemon F. Wright, Edward Wilber, John A. Wheeler, William Wolf, Melvin G. Wakeman, Andrew Weaver, Isaac S. White, Oliver H. York.

Killed.—James Stewart, May 28, 1864; Peter H. Dubendorf, January 24, 1864; John Robertson, Jacob Oppenlander.

Died.—Emory H. Dice, 1865; Washington A. McCormick, 1864, Frank Crooks, 1862; Theodore F. Davison, 1865; William S. Kilby, 1862.

Not Reported.—John R. Fenton, Henry Mason.

Discharged Before Expiration of Service.—Orivel M. Burnell, Edward Sodon, William Knead, Benjamin F. Bloomer, Jacob Mesiner, Francis B. Miner, George C. Shepard, Michael Stewer, James Trimble, Milton O. Jayrs, Samuel M. Castle, Franklin Basford.

Transferred.—John Hamuel, Michael Kegan, Henry Kellogg, John McDowell, Levi J. Richardson.

COMPANY K.

COMMISSIONED OFFICERS.

Captain Charles R. Rowe, died November 2, 1863.

Captain John E. Wyatt, discharged March 3, 1865.

First Lieutenant Wallace H. Bullard, entered as private October 7, 1862; promoted to general muster sergeant company B, December 10, 1862; promoted to regimental quartermaster-sergeant November 10, 1864; promoted from regimental quartermaster-sergeant to first lieutenant April 20, 1865.

First Lieutenant Reuben E. Osgood, promoted to captain and mustered in company I, Sixth Ohio volunteer infantry, January 1, 1865.

Second Lieutenant Josiah D. Freer, resigned May 15, 1862.
Second Lieutenant Hiram G. Suiter, promoted to captain and mustered in company C, April 21, 1865.

NON-COMMISSIONED OFFICERS.

Sergeant Charles B. Blakesley.
Corporal Albert McEwen.

PRIVATES.

George W. Amos, William Hamond, William Hamilton,

John King, Nelson Loomis, Charles B. Olcott, Perry Osendorf, David Palmer, William N. Porter, Norris Root, Nehemiah Viers, Homer Young.

Killed.—William E. Dunlap, 1865; George Cutshaw, Lester Blood, 1865; Daniel Brown, William Harris, 1864; Wellington Parker, Norman B. Stowe, 1862; William Stewart, 1865.

Died.—William H. Smith, in hospital, 1862; William F. Tousley, Cassius C. Starr, 1865; Charles L. Murray, 1863; Enoch Morse, Elons Hannan, 1864; Henry Fieldhouse, 1863; Phillip Kesey, 1862; Henry Leopoldi, Patrick McGee, Warren L. Sprague, 1864.

Not reported.—Justin Allen, George H. Tousley.

Discharged before expiration of service.—Simon D. Young, Jerome Pickett, Thomas S. Bark, Newton J. Allen, Harry A. Young, Horace Cole, Frank M. Arnold, Anderson M. Basquin, Elhanen W. Grover, Jabez H. Hunt, Martin V. Oviatt, Daniel S. Robertson, Alman A. Sheffield, Jesse Willshir, Willard B. Wurriner, Harvey Bartram, Horace Edgerton, William Elliot, Lucius Hollenbeck, James Mullen, Edwin Pentis, Orrin M. Wilcox, John S. Case (blacksmith), George Hopkins, Christopher House, Nelson Brown (bugler), Albert J. Criss, Sumner Stoughten, Luman S. Holt, Roswell G. Thomas, Gould Nickerson (wagoner), Oliver Basquin, Seymour Brown, Hiram Brown, Joseph K. Bratten, Newton D. Boyd, Henry L. Campbell, Henry Combs, Hiram W. Cowles, Wallace Clark, William H. Day, James J. Day, Ambrose Fenton, Joseph W. Fairbanks, Simon H. Gould, Ralph Hale, Lester Knapp, John Kent, Andrew J. Lamb, Michael Lally, John Larr, Carlos P. Lyman, John Mehrling, Thomas J. Myars, James L. Osgood, Philemon Perry, Calvin Sprague, Monroe Thomas, Thomas Jefferson, William H. Thomas, Bruce Tracy, Napoleon B. Wing, Harrison Winters, William Wheeler, Manville Wintersten, Ezra F. Wyatt.

Transferred.—George M. St. John, David Johnson, David Martin, Melmoth D. Trimmer.

NON-COMMISSIONED OFFICERS.

First Sergeant, Jacob B. Temple, promoted to first sergeant.
Bugler David A. Musser.
Blacksmith Nelson K. Gunder.

PRIVATES.

William D. Ware (recruit), Joseph Whitcomb (recruit), Jeremiah Culler, James Grim, Jacob Hoover, Harmon Minard, George K. Mead, Robert McKim, William Peterman, Benjamin T. Peterman, John A. Ripley, John Reed, Henry H. Spickler, William H. Stratton, Henry W. Wick, Robert Underwood, Henry Vernon, Jr., Daniel Winchell, John White, Henry Wilson, Hazel Brook, John G. Carson, David Harmon.

Died.—Daniel Crist at Camp Chase, John Pyle in hospital, David L. Shelter in hospital.

Not Reported.—John L. Wagar, James Cassad, James E. Amer, Ephraim Hayes.

COMPANY H.
PRIVATE.
Charles McCoy.

COMPANY M.
PRIVATES.
John M. Chamberlain, died 1864; Samuel C. Boice, discharged.

TWELFTH REGIMENT, OHIO VOLUNTEER CAVALRY.

The War department issued an order to Governor Tod, in August, 1863, authorizing him to recruit for the United Stated service a regiment of cavalry. The regiment was intended particularly for the protection of the southern State border, "but," said the order, "the force will be liable to serve elsewhere should the public service demand it." It was necessary that the regiment should be in the field as soon as possible. All the offices were consequently tendered to persons already in the service. Lieutenant-colonel Robert W. Hatliff, of the Second Ohio volunteer cavalry, was commissioned colonel, which was a guarantee of the proficiency to be expected of the regiment. The first company was reported by Captain E. C. Moderwell October 2, 1863, at Camp Taylor. The bounty at that time was so small that there was no pecuniary inducement to enlist, so that the Twelfth cavalry, like the regiments of 1861 and 1862, was composed of men who went to war out of motives of real patriotism. This fact gave to the organization high merit as a body of men and efficiency upon the field. Squadron E was recruited mainly in Mahoning and Highland counties.

The organized field and staff was as follows: Colonel Robert W. Ratliff, Lieutenant-colonel Robert H. Bently, of Richland county; Majors J. F. Herrick, of Cuyahoga, Mills J. Collier, of Akron, Erastus C. Moderwell, of Crawford; Surgeon George W. Brooke, of Mahoning; Assistant Surgeons Abram H. Hunt, of Wayne, and W. K. Hughes, of Mahoning county; Adjutant Frank H. Mason, of Trumbull county; Quartermaster William S. Wood, of Geneva; Commissary Milton W. Parsons, of Hamilton county; Chaplain Thomas W. Roberts, of Trumbull county. Colonel Ratliff was already a tried officer, having served two years in the Second Ohio cavalry. Lieutenant-colonel Bently had served as an officer of the Thirty-second infantry. Major Herrick had been a captain in the Eighty-seventh Ohio, and Major Moderwell in the Eighty-sixth. Major Collier had served with Colonel Ratliff in the Second Ohio cavalry. Adjutant Frank H. Mason, of Niles, had entered the service as private and had attained to the rank of staff captain for valiant conduct on the field.

The Twelfth cavalry, soon after its first regimental parade, was ordered into service. It was a fortunate circumstance that so many of its officers were trained soldiers, for months would have been required to prepare a green cavalry regiment for the field. Six companies were sent to Sandusky bay, in November, to guard the prison stockade on Johnson's island, upon which an attack was threatened. The winter was spent by these six companies on guard duty, while the other six companies were drilling for field service. When, in March, the order came to report at Louisville, it was greeted with a cheer by men weary of camp life and the monotony of guard duty. The 30th of March found the regiment encamped on the plains in the rear of Louisville.

Little of importance transpired until the latter part of May, when it became evident that John Morgan was making a northern raid and had already entered Kentucky. The first engagement with the rebels was at Mount Sterling, on June 9, 1864, when the Twelfth acted with great gallantry. Morgan was again overtaken at Cynthiana, Kentucky, and his forces scattered by the daring charge of the cavalrymen. On Septemper 20th, the enemy was again encountered at Saltville, and a half day's hard fighting followed, during which the Twelfth charged the enemy's works and drove him from his position.

In the forty hours' fight at Marion which resulted in the defeat of rebel General Breckinridge by General Stoneman, the Twelfth cavalry performed a conspicuous part. One charge in particular was praised by the officers in command. The men bearing sabres, rushed upon the enemy's cavalry, achieving a complete victory. Saltville was captured in December, closing a successful raid, which resulted in the capture of four boats, one hundred and fifty miles of railroad, thirteen trains, lead mines, salt works, iron foundries, and a large quantity of stores.

By February, 1865, the regiment was again thoroughly armed, equipped and mounted, ready for the service. Early in March it reached Nashville, and from there hastened to Knoxville and Murfreesboro. The spring and summer was employed chiefly in making raids and destroying railroad communications through Virginia, the Carolinas, and Tennessee. It aided in the capture of Jefferson Davis, and overtook and captured, in Alabama, Generals Bragg and Wheeler.

September 1st the regiment went into quarters at Pulaski, the several companies being engaged in enforcing law and order in the neighboring counties. In November the regiment rendezvoused at Nashville, and on the 14th was mustered out of the service. On arriving at Columbus, Ohio, the men were paid and discharged November 22 and 23, 1865, having been in active service two years.

FIELD AND STAFF.

Colonel Robert W. Ratliff, brevetted brigadier-general March 13, 1865.
Surgeon George W. Brooke.
Assistant-surgeon Wallace K. Hughes; promoted to surgeon August 16, 1865, vice Brooke resigned.
Chaplain Thomas Roberts.
Adjutant Frank H. Mason; promoted to captain of company L August 19, 1864.

NON-COMMISSIONED STAFF.

Hospital Steward Chauncey Stewart.

REGIMENTAL BAND.

Edward B. Reeves (cymbals).

COMMISSIONED OFFICER.

Captain John W. Johnston.

NON-COMMISSIONED OFFICERS.

Sergeant John A. Young.
Sergeant James A. Fenton.
Sergeant John W. Christy.
Corporal Charles W. Townsend.
Corporal Wallace C. Howard.
Corporal Newton J. Burnett.
Trumpeter Baldwin Chew.
Farrier Harvey Sea.

PRIVATES.

David Anderson, Perry Aikers, Henry H. Brumsterrer, George H. Belland, William Brown, Al Bartlett, John S. Burnett, George B. Chisly, Aaron J. Callahan, John Crawford, Emery J. Clark, Tiberias Clipper, Allen D. Ferguson, Augustus H. Ferguson, Isaac W. Frazier, Charles R. Gilbert, David Hill, James Howells, Michael M. Howard, George W. Lyman, Robert R. Miller, Washington Miller, Daniel Perry, Sylvanus Pennel, James C. Randolph, John C. Randolph, Jonathan R. Randolph, Edward B. Reeves, Chauncey Steward, Nelson Shaffer, Joseph W. Tuttle, Ira Wilcox, John H. Witherill, Leonard Plouts, G. W. Bear, G. Bear, C. S. Brainard, E. F. Bear, Abner Bear, Reuben Shull, Robert Gamble, Lafayette Carnahan.

FIRST OHIO LIGHT ARTILLERY.

Of this regiment James Barnett was colonel till October, 1864; C. S. Cotter succeeded him. It was first organized under the militia laws of Ohio in 1860, and consisted of six companies, each having one gun. It was the first organization called into service after the firing on Sumter, being reported at Columbus for service April 22d. It served on guard and active duty during the summer and was mustered into the United

TRUMBULL AND MAHONING COUNTIES, OHIO.   167

States service in September, 1861, for three years. The following volunteers were from these counties:

BATTERY B.
PRIVATES.

George Ruggles, Alonzo Walpmin; Edgar R. Lucas, died; Henry C. Sawyer, died; John M. Warner, died on field; Calvin Allen, missing in action at Chickamauga; Elias Dwyer, to veteran reserve corps.

BATTERY C.
PRIVATES.

Ross Montgomery, James O'Connor, Warren Clark (died in hospital), Dennis Aikins, Samuel W. Billings, John Foster, Albert L. Hardy, Luther D. Henry, James M. Saunders, James E. Stevens, James Wisenor.

BATTERY E.
PRIVATES.

John W. Smith, Isaac Sidall, Russell O. Watkins, Isaiah Cleveland (died at Bridgeport), Albert Brainard, Milton F. Rose.

BATTERY F.
PRIVATES.

Recruits.—Byran C. Coon, George L. Coon, William Oliver, William A. Powell, John Purtee, George W. Richards, Henry T. Sexton, Morris S. Vail, Allen T. Wright; Samuel Billingsly, died in hospital; William O. Suters, died in Alabama; Amacia Martin, transferred.

SECOND OHIO HEAVY ARTILLERY.

In 1863, the Union army having captured several important forts, it became necessary to garrison them with heavy arms. The One Hundred and Seventeenth Ohio volunteer infantry was the nucleus of the First Ohio heavy artillery. The Second consisted of twenty-four hundred men, and was recruited in all parts of the State in July and August, 1863. The following roster belongs to the field of this history:

COMPANY A.
PRIVATES.

Hiram A. Rockwell, Riley Falkner, Charles R. Bliss, Charles M. Foot, John Jones, Harvey W. Parker.

COMPANY B.
PRIVATE.

Washington Lovelace.

COMPANY C.
PRIVATE.

William H. Curtis.

COMPANY D.
PRIVATES.

James Green, William Green.

COMPANY E.
PRIVATES.

Andrew Meade, Richard McDonald, William Stoliker, Orson Stoliker.

COMPANY G.
NON-COMMISSIONED OFFICERS.

Sergeant Almond C. Lodwick.
Sergeant William Rutan.
Corporal Ebenezer Thomas.
Corporal Ephraim H. Smith.
Corporal Bostwick Parker.
Corporal Isaac H. Benedict.
Musician John W. Howett.
Musician George W. Lenox.

PRIVATES.

Abraham Angles, Chester H. Buck, John Ballard, Jacob H. Baldwin, Thomas Dawson, Homer C. Dice, Joseph M. Heard, John W. Houts, William Kinman, James A. Laird, Alfred Lamphier, Washington Lovelace, William H. Monroe, John Moore, Stanley L. Meachem, Cyrus L. North, William L. Pierce, George Peabody, Franklin Rhodes, William Sharpnack, William H. Seagraves, Hiram Sheldon, George Seagraves, William St. John, William Underwood, Thomas B. Wilson, Wesley W. Wilson, Napoleon B. Wing, Isaac N. Woodrow.
Died.—John A. Drake, in Cleveland hospital; John W. Lenox, died at Strawberry Plains.
Not Reported.—David Pierce, Clark Royal, John Wilson.
Discharged.—Emery B. Cook, James A. Davidson, John H. Waterson.

COMPANY I.
NON-COMMISSIONED OFFICERS.

Sergeant Walter Hawler.
Sergeant Freeman W. Barr, died at Cleveland.

COMPANY L.
PRIVATES.

David W. Colbourn, Cornelius Eames, Simon S. Mecklin, mustered out with company.
Transferred.—Gustavus Bumgardner.

COMPANY M.
NON-COMMISSIONED OFFICERS.

Sergeant Jacob M. Pound.
Sergeant Perry C. Wagner.
Musician Robert B. Lewis.
Corporal Thomas D. Chase, died in hospital.

PRIVATES.

Henry M. Buck, John Buckley, Evelyn Dutton, Jacob Gould, Ira H. Morey, John W. Moore, Alexander Marvin, Alexander McNutt, Edgar W. Wilson, mustered out with company.
Died in Hospital.—Abel W. Riley.
Discharged.—John Beaty, Francis B. Fulton, Francis A. Kinnear, Cyrus Palmer, Samuel Quigley, Ira A. Squires.

SECOND OHIO INDEPENDENT BATTERY.

This battery was organized in the northeastern part of Ohio in July, 1861, and mustered into service at Camp Chase August 9th, for a period of three years. It re-enlisted in 1864, and was mustered out in July, 1865.

COMMISSIONED OFFICER.

Second Lieutenant Isaac W. Wheaton, promoted second lieutenant.

168   TRUMBULL AND MAHONING COUNTIES, OHIO.

NON-COMMISSIONED OFFICERS.

First Sergeant Levi T. Robeson, promoted first sergeant.
Corporal John D. Tichnor.
Artificer Edwin W. Beckwith.
Artificer Joseph I. Colby.
Artificer John G. Beard.

PRIVATES.

John G. Beard, Christopher Ford, Hiram E. George, William R. Handy, Lucius Hill, George A. Lilley, Ashley O. LaBundy, William Mead, Patrick Murphy, Harvey C. Meddaugh, Charles L. Patterson, Henry W. Titus, George Weatherston.

THIRD OHIO INDEPENDENT BATTERY.

This battery was organized at Canton in the fall of 1861.

PRIVATE.

Newton J. Barnett.

NINTH OHIO INDEPENDENT BATTERY.

Henry S. Whitmore was captain of this battery, which was organized at Camp Wood in October, 1861. It was recruited in several counties. The following were enrolled in our territory:

COMMISSIONED OFFICER.

First Lieutenant Leonard B. Burrows.

NON-COMMISSIONED OFFICERS.

Sergeant William H. Chapman.
Artificer Edward H. Tinkham.

PRIVATES.

Luther S. Barton, Perry W. Foote, Desmond J. Goodsell (died at Bridgeport, Alabama), Frederick E. Bills, Samuel N. Barnes, Abel J. Seeley, J. E. Walton.

FOURTEENTH OHIO INDEPENDENT BATTERY.

This battery was recruited by Wade and Hutchins in July and August, 1861, mainly in Ashtabula, Lake, Trumbull, and Geauga counties. It consisted of two hundred and forty-nine men, who were mustered into the service for three years at Cleveland, September 10, 1861. Its first engagement was at Pittsburg Landing, when, owing to the failure of its infantry support, its guns were captured. They were recovered, however, on the following day.

At the expiration of its term of service about three-fourths of the Fourteenth re-enlisted and served till the conclusion of the war. Colonel Jerome B. Burrows resigned August 26, 1864, and was succeeded October 12th by Seth M. Laird. The following is the roster so far as it relates to Trumbull county:

COMMISSIONED OFFICERS.

Captain Seth M. Laird, commissioned second lieutenant July, 1862; promoted to first lieutenant June 10, 1863, and to captain October 12, 1864.
First Lieutenant William H. Smith, commissioned second lieutenant September 10, 1861; promoted to first lieutenant January 1, 1864; resigned April 16, 1864.
First Lieutenant Homer H. Stull, commissioned September 10, 1861; died May 17, 1863.
Second Lieutenant Walter B. King, commissioned April 16, 1864; mustered out April 22, 1862.

NON-COMMISSIONED OFFICERS.

Sergeant DeWitt C. Ackley.
Sergeant Isaac W. Parker.
Sergeant George Housh.
Corporal Curtis R. Waters.
Corporal Lester Woodford; died in 1862.
Artificer Thomas Douglas.
Artificer Philo Maltby.
Artificer John Pixley.
Artificer Oscar F. Hoskins.

PRIVATES.

Mustered out with battery.—Albert Abbatoy, Eugene P. Bennett, William J. Bower, John S. Hunter, Cassius N. Hadsell, John Shively, Jacob A. Kagey, Truman E. Coffee, William Downey.

Died in the service.—John Arnstadt, 1862; Levi Kittinger, 1862; Austin W. Lane, 1862; William McCullum, 1862; Enoch Phillips, 1862; George C. Sprague, no record; George Sprague, 1862; Leicester Sprague, 1862; Rosse W. Sanderson, 1862; James B. Thorp, 1862.

Discharged.—Andrew J. Atwood, William Bick, Elijah Bower, Seldon W. Burr, Austin H. Beldin, Lorin Clark, Henry H. Cowles, Marshal C. Clark, Richard H. Cadwell, Floyd Farmington, Jacob W. Grim, John S. Hunter, Henry L. Musser, William S. McCombs, Charles D. Prouty, Reese Rowe, William Rutan, Joseph M. Richards, Sevalia T. Vadenburg.

Transferred.—Edward Spear, Alonzo P. Fish.

FIFTEENTH OHIO INDEPENDENT BATTERY.

Captain J. B. Burrows and First Lieutenant Edward Spear, Jr., of the Fourteenth Ohio Independent battery, recruited the Fifteenth battery of Ohio light artillery, late in the fall of 1861. It rendezvoused at Camp Dennison, where Edward Spear, Jr., had been transferred to command. The men were mostly from Trumbull, Ashtabula, Cuyahoga, and Lorain counties. It was attached to the army of the Tennessee, and its first general service was in the seige of Corinth.

The roster for Trumbull county is as follows:

COMMISSIONED OFFICERS.

Captain Edward Spear, Jr., commissioned first lieutenant of the Fourteenth Ohio Independent battery, September 10, 1861; promoted to captain and transferred to the Fifteenth January 1, 1862; discharged at expiration of service September 20, 1864.
First Lieutenant Adrian A. Burrows, commissioned January 1, 1862; resigned December 31, 1862.

NON-COMMISSIONED OFFICERS.

Corporal Elisha Schorville.
Corporal Barrett Pennell, discharged.
Bugler Peter Burk.

Artificer Thomas McGrusion, died at Corinth, Mississippi.
Artificer Russell C. Darling, discharged.
Artificer Benjamin Williams, discharged.

PRIVATES.

Mustered Out with Battery June 20, 1865.—James Burt, John Burk, George Bidgelow, George E. Day, James Fullerton, Joseph W. Gailes, Moses Geer, William Henry, George Hann, Daniel Haren, William Kale, Cornelius Miller, James Nixon, Jewett B. Poor, Samuel Parker, Mansfield Stanley, John M. Stanton, Almon Sager, Daniel Thornton, Charles Van Kirk, Lewis Williams, Leander Warren.

Died.—James D. Andrews, at Pittsburg Landing; Jesse Day, Savannah, Georgia; Milton D. Fellows, Vicksburg; Richard E. Newman, Cincinnati; Ambrose Smith, Cincinnati.

Discharged.—Bower Heman, Daniel H. Barr, James L. Beebe, Albion Creed, Frank Murray, Francis O. Robbins, Samuel H. White, William Ward, Jr.

TWENTY-FIRST OHIO INDEPENDENT BATTERY.

PRIVATE.

Chauncy Covel, recruit.

TWENTY-SECOND OHIO INDEPENDENT BATTERY.

PRIVATES.

Ross S. Augenbaugh, John Burnett, Hedep Powers (died in hospital), Andrew S. Cramer.

TWENTY-FIFTH OHIO INDEPENDENT BATTERY.

As has been previously noted, this battery was formed of a detachment from the Second Ohio cavalry, which was transferred and permanently organized as a battery at Crane Creek, Missouri, February 17, 1863. It had been detached from the Second cavalry in August, 1862, while the regiment was at Fort Scott, Kansas. There was at that time a pressing need for artillerymen. Captain Job B. Stockton was given command, and General Blunt gave it the name of Third Kansas battery. The detail petitioned to be restored to the regiment but in this it failed, but upon reorganization as a permanent battery it was properly accredited to Ohio. Trumbull county was represented as follows:

NON-COMMISSIONED OFFICERS.

Sergeant Robert W. Pennell.
Corporal George W. White.
Corporal Harrison H. Gee.
Corporal Edmund Hudson, discharged.
Corporal Robert McMahon, discharged.
Corporal William H. Andorffer, discharged.

PRIVATES.

John Autibus, George Alders, Buell Butler, John Burke, Theodore Campbell, James Crozier, William De Puye, Charles Fire, Calvin C. Goodheart, Stephen Hudson, Henry H. Hulse, Milton Irwin, William M. Jones, James Kelley, Isaac Kinsinger, Amiel Kincaid, James McArthur, James Matthias, George O. Otterman, Thomas Peabody, Azor A. Parker, Henderson D. Rosier, William Shoemaker, John Strong, Aaron A. Sperry, Rodger E. Smith, Josiah Smith,

William S. Tuttle, Daniel W. Tresler, Charles L. Willis, William H. Wiklman, George W. Whipps.

Died in Hospital, 1864.—Nathaniel Ague, Robert J. Blunt, Thomas C. Brown, Daniel Lutz, Alexander S. Pruden, William Whitmore; Isaac Stanley died at home, 1865.

Not Reported.—William K. Ague, Daniel Crays, Thomas Morris, Luman Robinson.

Discharged.—Robert Brown, John Brandeburg, John A. Newton, Lyman W. Niece, James A. Russell, Jasper Struble, Fred P. Shipman, Alvin S. Vincent, Robert Williams, George Tompkins.

The following from Hartford township are known to have enlisted and joined Pennsylvania regiments. There were probably others from other townships, but we are unable to give names:

PRIVATES.

Fred K. Patterson, Alfred Patterson, Allen Patterson, Sylvester Mountain, Hubbard Mountain, Daniel Hay, Henry Messenger, George W. Dutcher, William Shirey, R. D. Patterson, Elliot S. Gilky.

THIRTY-FOURTH REGIMENT, OHIO VOLUNTEER INFANTRY.

PRIVATE.

William S. Fuller.

ONE HUNDRED AND NINETY-FIRST REGIMENT, OHIO VOLUNTEER INFANTRY.

PRIVATES.

Lucian Hays, Abner B. Loomis, Wick Loomis, William Anderson.

SIXTH NATIONAL GUARDS.

PRIVATE.

William Law (colored), died 1864.

WARREN HOME COMMITTEE.

Henry B. Perkins, Junius Dana, Matthew B. Tayler, Charles R. Hunt, John M. Stull, James Hoyt.

The board of enrollment for the Nineteenth Congressional district, then comprising the counties of Ashtabula, Geauga, Trumbull, Mahoning and Portage, was organized under the conscription act of Congress at Warren, in May, 1863, by the appointment, by President Lincoln, through Edwin M. Stanton, Secretary of War, of following officers: Darius Cadwell, of Ashtabula county, as provost marshal, with the rank and pay of captain of cavalry, having charge of enlistment, and as president of the board; Charles S. Field, of Geauga county, as commissioner of the board, having in charge the enrollment of all men subject to the provisions of the act, to supervise and direct the drafting of such when required under the calls of the President; and George W. Howe, of Trumbull county, surgeon, having the medical examination of all volunteers, drafted men, and all claiming exemption from the draft on account of physical disability. These two last-named officers had the rank and pay of lieutenants of cavalry, and all three were placed on the general staff of the president.

Ambrose M. Robbins, of Niles, Trumbull county, was chief clerk in the captain's department; Edward C. Wade, of Jefferson, Ashtabula county, in that of the commissioners, and Mathews, of Trumbull county, in the surgeon's. John A. Hervey, also of Jefferson, was chief clerk in the quartermaster's department for the issuing of clothing, etc., to volunteers and drafted men. The business of the board required from six to thirty clerks.

The provost marshal had to assist him one deputy in each of the counties of the district, and a detail of soldiers from the veteran invalid corps. No data can now be obtained short of the War department at Washington as to the number of men enlisted at this office or the number drafted. The commissioner had, in addition to his corps of clerks, an enrolling officer in each of the towns in the district, one hundred and five in number, bearing upon the roll of the district over seventeen thousand men between the ages of eighteen and forty-five, as subject to military duty, and consequently to the draft. Warren was often full and running over with excited fathers or mothers, or both, looking anxiously for an enlisted son, or seeking to get one exempted from the draft, or to find a substitute for one already drafted. Many pathetic, many affecting, and many humorous scenes were enacted, but amid all the sorrow, amid all the suffering and all the excitement above, and controlling all other feelings, patriotism, pure and holy, held fast supremacy over all, and led to final victory.

Under all the calls of the President for men, and during every draft, Warren, as did many of the townships of Trumbull county, displayed her patriotism by zeal and dilligence, by hard work and liberal bounties procuring volunteers by enlistment, thereby saving the burden and, as it was then by some considered, the disgrace of being drafted. After the defeat and surrender of Lee's army, the board was, about the 1st of May, 1865, honorably discharged from the service of the United States, carrying with them a tribute of which they may well be proud. The Secretary of War shortly before their discharge, in an official letter, says: "The board of enrollment of the Nineteenth Congressional district of Ohio, in its efficiency and in the prompt and able discharge of the onerous and delicate duties imposed by the law and general order, is excelled by none in the United States." At the conclusion of the war and after the board was discharged the members returned to their several avocations. The provost marshal, Captain Cadwell, being a lawyer, resumed his profession, and is now, and has been for some years past, one of the common pleas judges of Cuyahoga county, having his residence in Cleveland. Commissioner Charles S. Field was a merchant, and remained in Warren, where he now resides, on Mahoning avenue, carrying on the business, on Main street, of clothing and gentlemen's furnishing goods. Surgeon George W. Howe resumed the practice of medicine on his return to his home in Bloomfield, where he now resides (a biographical sketch of his life will be found elsewhere).

The township and city military committee, composed of Charles R. Hunt, James Hoyt, John M. Stull, Humphrey Horsh, Alonzo Truesdell, and others whose names do not now occur, were indefatigable in their efforts to raise money to procure and pay local bounties to volunteers, and to them much of the honor belongs of procuring for the city and township exemption from the draft. Warren's quota was kept always full, with a surplus to their credit to apply on future calls of the President for more.

No accurate account of the amount of money raised and expended for this purpose can now be obtained; but the best estimates, founded on the number of volunteers furnished and the sums paid each, increasing largely as the war continued, would aggregate at least $100,000, and with all this the patriotism of the people kept even pace.

GOVERNOR DAVID TOD.

The most illustrious representative of the Mahoning valley in military affairs was Governor David Tod. Upon Governor William Dennison devolved the task of inaugurating war measures and of initiating their execution. To him is due the credit of placing Ohio in the front rank of States that patriotically responded to the President's call for assistance in the first period of the Union's peril. But during the year 1861 no great battles were fought, in which Ohio troops were engaged; no distressing defeats had made the newspaper a daily messenger awaited in almost every loyal home with the most anxious solicitude. Knowing nothing of war, of the dangers of battle, of the heart-rending suffering of the hospital, or of the squalid distress of prison confinement, the anxious volunteers of 1861 went to the field with buoyant cheers, as fast as the Government would accept their services. But there came a time, and that speedily, when enlistments were procured with more difficulty. It was the lot of Governor Tod's administration to meet the first reaction of defeat, to recruit the depleted ranks of regiments in the field, and to raise new regiments after the State had contributed its bravest, most loyal, and most ardent citizens; and what was, perhaps, more difficult than either, to resist seditious political influences. In addition to all these embarrassing executive tasks, the State was in constant danger of invasion, requiring at all times watchfulness, and in frequent emergencies, prompt and vigorous action. Governor Tod was a man well fitted by temperament, talent, and training for the peculiarly difficult and responsible place he was called by the people of Ohio to fill.

Judge George Tod, a sketch of whom will be found in this volume, was a man of marked ability and character, but did not possess the faculty of accumulating wealth. Mrs. Tod was a gentle, amiable, lovable woman who was always mentioned by her son in her mature years with the most reverent affection. It will appear, therefore, that David Tod had the good fortune of having been well born. He inherited character and ability, and had the example of a father and the precept of a mother to inspire a worthy ambition.

David Tod was born in Youngstown township February 21, 1805. His early education was not extensive, being limited to a term or two at the academy. It was not the fashion at that time for every aspiring boy to go to college, but had he desired more preliminary training, pinching financial circumstances would probably have prevented the attainment of that end. He was admitted to the bar in 1827 and at once began practice at Warren. Though but twenty-two years old, his frank, dignified manner, and clear way of looking at things soon attracted attention and brought him clients. His active practice covered a period of fifteen years, until after the death of his father in 1841. He gained the reputation of being a successful and skilful practitioner, and was a good lawyer though not particularly able. The secret of his success was an almost faultless judgment of men with whom he came in contact. His tact in the examination of witnesses was not surpassed, if it was equalled, by any of his colleagues. He always succeeded in placing himself on friendly terms with the jury, and once having their confidence held it by a frank, direct, clear, and earnest statement of argument. He had the faculty of making the trial of cases interesting by throwing into them his own buoyancy of spirit and happy, quick wit.

After the death of his father, Mr. Tod came into possession of the old Brier Hill farm near Youngstown. He had really owned it for some time before, having gained the title through a circumstance highly creditable to his generous character. It dates back to almost the beginning of his professional career, when he was yet a briefless barrister, and what was more embarrassing, was in debt for the means which gave him an academic and professional education. His father's creditors, after long and patient waiting, became importunate, and it became certain that unless assistance from some source intervened the old farm would be sold. The full-, affectionate-hearted young lawyer could not think of allowing his mother to be turned out of house and home without an effort, at least, to avert it. There were fortunately friends who had confidence in the young man's courage and honor and were affected by the beauty of his filial devotion. By their aid the debt was lifted and he became the owner of the farm, which remained the home of his aged parents. This farm thus acquired became the source of great wealth, and the starting-point of a great and profitable industry which has made the valley one of the wealthiest in Ohio. This property is located about two miles above Youngstown, on the north side of the valley. It bore the name of Brier Hill while yet the home of Judge Tod, on account of the abundance of wild blackberries growing there. Coal had been mined in limited quantities for several years, but the local consumption was so light that the deposit was not deemed of any great value. But it remained for David Tod to find a market for the deposits, the great value of which he was acute enough to perceive. The canal had two years before opened direct transportation to Cleveland. The open-burning character of Brier Hill coal had previously been noticed, which seemed to commend it for steamboat navigation. Two canal-boat loads were sent to Cleveland and engineers urged to accept it as an experiment. The offer was refused by some, but others, less cautious, were willing to test its efficiency, and were soon convinced of its great utility.

Having opened a market Mr. Tod met a second difficulty which, however, the confidence inspired by pluck, determination, and keen business insight, enabled him to quickly overcome. Early personal debts, rather extravagant habits, and the relief of his parents by making a timely purchase of their farm, had consumed his income at the bar and left him without the means of taking advantage of the splendid opportunity he saw before him. Timely aid a second time came kindly to the rescue. The old friend of his father, Colonel William Rayen, and his uncle, James Ford, of Akron, promptly secured his obligations, which enabled him to proceed with the development of his plans. The Brier Hill coal mine was opened and another one adjoining it. The market expanded faster than mines could be developed, and in due time came the introduction of raw coal blast furnaces, making the almost exhaustless deposits still more valuable.

Mr. Tod possessed great self-confidence and was always sanguine of success. He had the faculty, too, of making others share his confidence. During the early years of his business operations he was once approached by Colonel Rayen, who said in a kindly way, "David, if you fail to meet the obligations upon which I am security, you will break me up." "Give yourself no trouble about that, Judge," replied Tod, and the old gentleman went away satisfied that he had no cause for solicitude.

Soon after the Cleveland & Mahoning railroad enterprise was inaugurated by Warren capitalists, Mr. Tod became interested and was subsequently chosen to a directorship. His zealous labor and confidence in ultimate success were of material value to the embarrassed company. It was mainly through his influence that a loan was negotiated for the purchase of the first locomotives.

In tracing Mr. Tod's professional and business career we have thus far omitted his political inclinations and honors. During his boyhood Andrew Jackson was the great popular hero. Young Tod, during the bitter campaign of 1824, not yet having reached his majority, fell in with the popular party of the day. The joy and patriotic pride with which Jackson's triumph at New Orleans thrilled the country, was among his earliest recollections of current history. Admiration of a great leader made his inherited love of politics more ardent, so that we are not surprised to find him early in his professional career an energetic partisan of the Democratic faith. He publicly avowed his convictions in the presidential campaign of 1828, and remained earnest, zealous, steadfast, until the secession movement in 1861. He belonged to the agreeable rather than the eloquent class of popular political orators. His speeches were direct, clear, and interesting. They were of the type generally described by the word "clever." In 1838 he was elected to the State Senate, running several hundred votes ahead of his ticket. During the campaign of 1840 he made speeches all over the State, leaving everywhere a good impression. Judge George Tod had served under General Harrison and entertained a warm friendship for his old comrades. He is said to have been somewhat grieved at the course his son chose to pursue.

By 1844 Mr. Tod had attained such prominence in his party that he was the unanimous choice for Governor. His Whig opponent in that campaign was Mordecai Bartley, whose majority was only one thousand, while Clay carried the State a month later by six thousand.

In 1847 Mr. Tod was tendered by President Polk, and accepted, the office of minister to Brazil. During the five years of his residence in that country he negotiated several important commercial treaties, and treaties involving Government claims of over thirty' years standing. The farewell address of the Emperor was highly flattering to the minister. During the administration of Pierce and Buchanan he continued to do effective party service, but sought no office from either.

Mr. Tod was first vice-president of the convention which met at Baltimore in 1860 to nominate a candidate for President. He was an enthusiastic Douglas man. It soon became evident in the convention that the Southern representatives had preconcerted a bolt, and with them was Caleb Cushing, chairman of the convention. The bolt began early in the proceedings, the hall became a scene of wild confusion, in the midst of which the chairman abandoned his post. Tod preceived the situation in an instant, hurried to the deserted chair, stamped firmly upon the platform, and appealed for order, which was restored and the convention proceeded with the business for which it had been called. Tod's conduct at this convention was warmly applauded by his party at the North. He entered zealously into the campaign which followed, giving Douglas his warm and unqualified support. He was one of the Northern Democrats who was opposed to allowing the South to frame the party's policy, and doubtless preferred the election of Lincoln to the success of the Breckinridge wing of his own party.

When the result of the election was known and the secession movement started in the Southern States Mr. Tod was active in his endeavor to restore peace. He urged, both before the peace congress and after, that every honorable means to avert civil war ought to be brought to bear upon the rebellious section. But when all effort proved futile and traitors had inaugurated open treason Mr. Tod saw but one course for loyal men to pursue. The last echo of belligerent guns at Sumter had scarce died away until his voice was ringing clear warning of the Union's peril and arousing his patriotic neighbors to action. The first company of troops organized at Youngstown, a company of the Nineteenth Ohio volunteer infantry, was recruited largely at his expense, and before leaving for camp each received from him, as a present, an army overcoat, which were known in the service as "Tod coats," and some of them were brought home after four years' service.

The movement which resulted in Tod's nomination to the Governorship started in Cleveland among men who esteemed country higher than party. They sought to break down former lines in the hope of uniting all loyal citizens, who believed in prosecuting the war, in one party. Tod was known as a conspicuous war Democrat, and the suggestion of his nomination by the Republicans was well received throughout the State. The convention was unanimous in its choice, and his majority in the State was about fifty-five thousand. The limits of a short sketch forbid anything like a review of Governor Tod's war administration. In every emergency he was found prompt. At all times courteous, but independent. He was always jealous, not only of the honor, but also of the care of Ohio troops in the field. On one occasion his request for tents and other equipments for Kentucky troops was delayed. The Governor angrily telegraphed: "It is well I don't know whose fault it is, or I would whip the fellow if he were as strong as Sampson." Again he telegraphed: "For God's sake send our troops, in Kentucky, canteens."

Such telegrams as the following had the effect of stiffening Ohio pride, though critics of our war management pronounced it indiscreet:

The gallant people of Ohio are mortified to death over the rumored cowardice of Colonel Rodney Mason, of the Seventy-first Ohio, and in their behalf I demand that he have a fair but speedy trial; and should he be convicted of cowardice, that the extreme penalty of the law be inflicted upon him, for in that event we can not endure even his foul carcass upon our soil.

These quotations from official dispatches show the character of the man. It was Governor Tod who proposed permitting soldiers in the field to vote, on the ground that there was no reason why a man should be disfranchised because he was brave enough to fight the battles of his country. He ordered several arrests of members of the anti-war party for seditious utterances, and is known to have countenanced the arrest of Vallandingham in 1863. This and other official and political conduct made him a special object of hatred in the Vallandingham element of the Democratic party. George E. Pugh said, at the convention which nominated Vallandingham for Governor:

If we had an honest man for Governor my rights and liberties would have been preserved. That creature, who has licked the dust off the feet of the administration, is less than the dust in the balance. We have no Governor. We have a being, and he has the audacity to say, and has said to my face, after this war is over he will come back into the Democratic party and put such men as Vallandingham and Olds to the wall. I told him if he would show his face in a Democratic convention I would move to suspend all business until he was expelled. I can pardon an honest man who might have been misled, but the man who not only sold himself, but sold the birthright of Democracy, his crime is infamous.

This bitter utterance, considering the time, place, and circumstances, must be looked upon as a compliment. While Governor Tod's administration was generally commended, he had made many enemies, as any man controlling hundreds of appointments necessarily will. In view of the fact that the State had the year before gone Democratic, and the peculiar appeal of Vallandingham for vindication, it was deemed advisable by Republican leaders to bring out a new man. John Brough was accordingly nominated, somewhat to the disappointment of the Governor, who, however, cordially and enthusiastically supported the nominee.

After retiring from office, January, 1864, Governor Tod returned to his Brier Hill farm, and from that time until his death devoted his energies to business, continuing to retain at the same time an active interest in politics.

He died suddenly November 13, 1868. The announcement was received with sorrow all over the State, and deepest regret among his old neighbors and life-long friends.

CHAPTER XVII.
THE BAR OF TRUMBULL COUNTY.

[The following sketches, preceding that of General John Crowell, have been furnished by Jefferson Palm, Esq., of Warren. Sketches of members of the present bar have been prepared by David Jameson.]

To say nothing in disparagement of Trumbull county's bar as it is now, in the early history of the State and county it had none superior in the West. Early, Benjamin Tappan and Edwin M. Stanton practiced at Warren. A little later, Andrew W. Loomis, Joshua R. Giddings, Rufus P. Spalding, John Crowell, Benjamin F. Wade, Rufus P. Ranney, Van R. Humphrey, Peter Hitchcock, and others of little less distinction, made their mark and reputation in Trumbull county. What bar in the State can boast of such a galaxy of names? We do not intend to omit the distinguished gentlemen, Elisha Whittlesey and Eben Newton, but complete sketches of them, together with Governor David Tod, will appear in another part of this work.

A volume could be written and read with profit concerning each of the learned gentlemen named above. Most of them have passed away, but their memories are cherished and dear to the members of Trumbull county's present learned and able bar.

CALVIN PEASE.

The city of Warren has the distinction of furnishing four judges of the Supreme Court of Ohio, namely, Calvin Pease, Matthew Birchard, Rufus P. Ranney, and Milton Sutliff, and outside of the city, in Trumbull county, one more, George Tod. Of the first named, Judge Pease, we ought, in justice to his memory, speak more fully than of some of the others, because he was in all respects a pioneer in Ohio, in putting on, and wearing with credit to himself and the State, the judicial ermine.

Among the lawyers who at an early day emigrated from the State of Connecticut to the Western Reserve, and afterwards attained great distinction was Calvin Pease, the subject of this brief sketch. He was born at Suffield, in the county of Hartford, and State of Connecticut, on the 9th day of September, 1776. The place of his birth was originally under the jurisdiction of the State of Massachusetts, but was annexed to Connecticut in 1752. It is not known whether the distinguished judge, in his youth, received any other education than the schools of his native town afforded. He studied law in the office of his brother-in-law, the late Gideon Granger, who was Postmaster-general under Thomas Jefferson. Benjamin Tappan, who was distinguished as a United States Senator from Ohio, was his fellow-student. Mr. Granger, who is well known as a very able man, died at his residence in Canandaigua, Ontario county, New York, on the 31st day of December, 1822.

The young Pease, after completing his studies,

was admitted to the bar in Hartford county, Connecticut, in 1798, and commenced the practice of the law in New Hartford, in that State, where he was quite successful; but being desirous of going West, where young men make fortunes and reputation, he removed to Ohio. He first settled at Youngstown, then in Trumbull county, and was the first postmaster of that town, which office he held until he removed to Warren in 1803. He was admitted to practice law by the general court of the territory northwest of the Ohio river, in Marietta, on the third Tuesday of October, 1800. At the same time George Tod (father of the late Governor Tod), John S. Edwards, Samuel Huntington, and Benjamin Tappan were also admitted.

The first court of common pleas and general quarter sessions held on the Western Reserve was at Warren, August 25, 1800. At that term Mr. Pease was appointed clerk and George Tod prosecuting attorney. This court was not exactly held in the "vast temple of the firmament," for it sat between two corn-cribs, with split logs thrown across for a roof, on the southwest corner of Main and South street, very nearly the place where the Cleveland & Mahoning depot now stands, in said city.

At the first session of the Legislature, held at Chillicothe, after the admission of Ohio into the Federal Union, Mr. Pease was elected president judge of the court of common pleas, which was then the third circuit, composed of the counties of Washington, Belmont, Jefferson, Columbiana, and Trumbull, which office he held, and the duties of which he discharged, with marked ability, until the 4th day of March, 1810, when he sent in his resignation to Governor Huntington. At the time of his election he was not quite twenty-seven years of age.

The office was afterwards tendered to David Abbott, Thomas D. Webb, Mr. Potter, Peter Hitchcock, John S. Edwards, and Mr. Austin; but on the 14th of March, 1810, he sent a commission to Sampson King. Surely these men belonged to a past generation, as such indifference to office is not characteristic of the present day. They were all honorable men — distinguished in their profession — and rest in graves their descendants are proud to keep green.

Judge Pease was married in 1804 to Miss Laura G. Risley, of Washington city. She was an estimable lady, and by her exemplary and faithful discharge of every duty — domestic, social, and religious — made his home pleasant, which was proverbial for hospitality.

After leaving the common pleas bench, and a short vacation, he was elected by the Legislature one of the judges of the supreme court. He entered upon his duties in 1816. During his term of office as judge of the court of common pleas, many interesting questions to the legal profession were presented for adjudication. Among them was the constitutionality of some portions of an act of the Legislature, passed in 1805, defining the duties of justices of the peace. He held and decided that so much of the fifth section of said legislative act as gave justices of the peace jurisdiction exceeding the sum of $20, and so much of the twenty-ninth section of said act as prevented plaintiff from recovering costs in actions commenced by original writs in the court of common pleas, for sums between $20 and $50, were repugnant to the Constitution of the United States and the constitution of the State of Ohio, and therefore null and void.

The grounds of the decision that created the excitement, which was intense, were that sections five and twenty-nine of the act of 1805 were in conflict with the seventh amendment of the Constitution of the United States, which provides that in suits at common law, where the amount in controversy exceeds the sum of $20, the right of trial by jury shall be preserved; and the eighth section of the constitution of Ohio, which declares that the right of trial by jury shall be inviolate.

The clamor and abuse to which this decision gave rise, was not in the least diminished or mitigated by the fact that it was concurred in by a majority of the judges of the supreme court, Judges Huntington and Tod. Nothing could furnish more conclusive evidence of a clear and vigorous mind, of unbending integrity and judicial independence, than the prompt and fearless manner with which, after he and a majority of the court had arrived at the conclusion that the act before mentioned was unconstitutional, they pronounced and maintained their decision. Popular fury was wholly impotent to make the majority of the court hesitate or falter or turn Judge Pease or his associates aside from the faithful discharge of their duty. He cared nothing for the consequences that might follow doing right, as his conscience and legal obligation required; but he did not escape the blows aimed at him and Judge Tod by the advocates of legislative supremacy.

At the session of the Legislature of 1807-8, proceedings were taken to impeach him and the other judges of the supreme court who concurred in the decision that was so offensive to the law-making power. A resolution was introduced into the House of Representatives, but not acted upon during the session. However, the advocates of impeachment waxed warmer and at the commencement of the next session a committee was appointed to inquire into the conduct of the offending judges, with leave to exhibit articles of impeachment, or report otherwise as the facts might warrant. The committee without delay reported articles of impeachment against Judges Pease and Tod, but not against Judge Huntington, who had, the fall preceding, been elected Governor of the State.

The charges against Judge Pease were three, and as follow:

1. That on appeal from the judgment of a justice of the peace for a sum exceeding $20, he had, as president judge of the third circuit, reversed that judgment on the ground that the justice had no constitutional jurisdiction of the case.

2. That in an action for a sum between $20 and $50, commenced by original writ from the court of common pleas, he had allowed the plaintiff his costs of suit upon recovering judgment, contrary to the twenty-ninth section of the justices' act and the fifth section of the act organizing the judicial courts.

3. That sitting as president judge of the third circuit, he had decided, on various occasions, that the court had full power to set aside, suspend, and declare null and void the fifth section of the act defining the duties of justices of the peace.

The articles of impeachment were preferred by the House of Representatives on the 23d day of December, 1808, by the following vote, to-wit: Article one, yeas thirty-five, nays eleven; article two, yeas thirty-five, nays ten; article three, yeas thirty-five, nays eleven. Thereupon he was summoned to appear before the Senate, forthwith, as a high court of impeachment. He promptly obeyed. The managers of the prosecution were Thomas Morris, afterwards a United States Senator from Ohio, Joseph Sharp, James Prichard, Samuel Marrett, and Othniel Looker.

Judge Pease, in his answer to the charges preferred against him, admitted that in his judicial capacity he had decided that the fifteenth section of the act of the Legislature, giving to justices of the peace jurisdiction in cases exceeding $20, was unconstitutional and void; asserting his right to make such a decision, and insisted that it was his duty to try and determine cases brought before him as a judge, according to his convictions of the law, and vindicated the purity of his motives and his sincere desire to faithfully administer the law.

Several days were consumed in the investigation of the charges; but at the conclusion he was completely vindicated and acquitted. There were some votes for conviction, but the requisite two-thirds could not be obtained.

To lawyers and judges of the present time, it seems as though such things could not have transpired in Ohio, even in its early history. Now, courts of limited jurisdiction even, pass on the constitutionality of many acts of the Legislature, as is their province and duty, and Judge Pease and his associates are entitled to very great credit for their independence in determining what the law was. Under our system of government it is the duty of the Legislature to pass the laws by which the conduct of the citizen is to be governed; but it is as much the duty of the judicial branch of the government to execute or nullify it as it may appear to be constitutional or unconstitutional. To-day, every student of the law, as well as every intelligent citizen, will say that Judge Pease was right, and are proud that he had the manhood to stand firm.

My Lord Coke, of England, long before the subject of this sketch was born, said that "when an act of Parliament was against common right and reason, or repugnant, or impossible to be performed, the common law controls it, and adjudges such act to be void." Lord Holt, much later, occupying a seat on the same bench in Westminster hall, said that "Lord Coke said not an extravagant, but a very reasonable saying." The question is no longer debatable in England or this country; Lords Coke and Holt were right —and so was Judge Pease.

Judge Pease was chosen a Senator to the State Legislature in 1812, a very important position during the late war with England, and like his judicial duties afterwards, he performed the duties of Senator well.

The last office that Judge Pease held was Representative in the Legislature from Trumbull county, being elected in 1831. Dr. Kirtland, then of Poland, in Mahoning county, was elected to the House with him. Together, they rendered invaluable services to the State and public, by urging the construction of a new penitentiary, and improving prison discipline.

The judge was a great wit and humorist, and often very sarcastic. Frequently on the bench he was severe—not, however, intending any offense—but it cut the young lawyers, especially, very keenly. He was the Nestor when in his retirement. He met his old friends and acquaintances at the Western Reserve bank in Warren, of which he was a director, among whom were Judge Leicester King, Dr. John B. Harmon, Judge Freeman, Dr. John W. Seely, General Perkins, George Parsons, and others. He died on the 17th day of September, 1839. He left a family of five children, only two of whom are now living, Mrs. Judge Van R. Humphrey and Charles Pease, both now of Cleveland. He was a man of fine presence—full six feet in height, and corpulent, with a strongly marked face, indicating kindness and humor. He was a pure man and a just judge.

MATTHEW BIRCHARD.

The Hon. Matthew Birchard was born in Becket, Massachusetts, January 19, 1804. His parents were Nathan and Mercy (Ashley) Birchard, and he was the seventh of ten children born to them. The family is of English extraction, the founder of the family being Thomas Birchard, who arrived in Boston, September 16, 1635. In 1812 his father settled in Windham, Portage county, Ohio, where he became one of the original proprietors of that township, when the subsequent judge was a young lad. Judge Birchard was educated in the common schools of that period, with some academical advantages at Boston, Portage county, and Warren, Trumbull county. At the age of twenty years he commenced the study of law with General Roswell Stone, in Warren. He was admitted to the bar in 1827, and at once entered into partnership with the late Governor Tod, who was admitted to the bar about the same time, under the firm name of Birchard & Tod.

In 1829 he was appointed postmaster at Warren, under General Jackson's administration, which office he held until 1833, when he resigned to accept the position of president judge of the court of common pleas of the circuit in which he lived, which at that time embraced nearly the whole of the Western Reserve. In 1836 he resigned the judgeship to accept the office tendered him by General Jackson of solicitor of the general land office at Washington, which position he filled for three years. His capacity and ability being appreciated, he retained his position until the coming in of President Van Buren, when he was promoted to the office of solicitor of the treasury, where he remained until the Harrison administration came into power in 1841.

While Judge Birchard was solicitor of the Treasury, the celebrated "Florida claims" were pressed upon the Government, in the adjustment of which Judge Birchard took a leading part—his management of the same being so able and honorable that leading men of both political parties gave him high credit.

In the autumn of 1841, upon his retirement from the Treasury department, he married at Washington the eldest daughter of Lieutenant William A. Weaver, of the United States Navy, one of the survivors of the memorable engagement between the Chesapeake and Shannon; being wounded and taken prisoner in that action by the British. His widow and two children survive him.

Returning to Warren he resumed his law practice with Mr. Tod, continuing it until 1842, when he was elected by the Legislature to the supreme bench of the State; holding this position for seven years, being chief justice for the last two.

At the expiration of his term on the bench he resumed the practice of the law in Trumbull county, and continued therein until 1853, when he was nominated by the Democratic party for Representative in the General Assembly, and was elected in what had been one of the strongest Whig counties in the State.

After the expiration of his legislative term, Judge Birchard devoted the greater portion of his time to the practice of his profession, finding peculiar delight in the pursuit of that which was so congenial to his feelings and tastes.

As solicitor of the land office and of the treasury, he made an excellent record, instituting in these departments numerous beneficial changes and practices, which proved to be of the highest importance in the administration of the Government.

As a lawyer Judge Birchard ranked high in his profession. His knowledge of the fundamental principles of the law was exceedingly clear, whilst his tact in their application was not surpassed by his colleagues on the bench. His cool reflection and matured judgment made him eminently safe as a counsellor. In the preparation of his cases he used the greatest care. As an advocate he confined himself to the presentation of the law and the evidence, presenting both in a calm, lucid, and logical manner, ignoring all emotional appeals to a jury, relying for a verdict rather on their intelligence and good sense than on any biased appeal to their passions or prejudices. This course he regarded as the true mission of the advocate.

The possession of these qualities peculiarly adapted him to the bench, and we are not surprised to find that in the office of judge he achieved his greatest success. Being a man of sober reflection, sound judgment, mature deliberation, not easily swayed by prejudice or emotion, together with high integrity, and possessing an innate perception of what constituted justice and equity, he became a model judge.

His decisions were always made with the greatest circumspection, prudence, and diligent research. He did nothing hastily, but supported every decision with such copious, standard authorities, and such sound, logical reasoning, that they stand to-day as authority. In fact, but few of his decisions, which were made with the majority of the court, have been reversed.

In political belief and action Judge Birchard was a Democrat of the old school, casting his lot with that party in its earlier and palmier days —the days of Jackson, Van Buren, and Wright. Conscientiously believing in the principles of his party, he clung to it with marked fidelity through all its vicissitudes; working earnestly and faithfully for its success, always standing high in the councils of its leaders. But not alone as a political leader, or his ability as a judge, did the deceased stand high in the opinion of the people. As a good citizen, a kind neighbor, and an honest man, he had a strong hold on his fellow men.

He was public spirited, working for the advancement of the educational, the religious, and material interests of the community. His kindness of heart, his sympathy for the suffering or afflicted, his generosity to the poor, and his leniency towards his debtors, were proverbial. His word was as good as his bond. His integrity and honesty were never doubted at home or abroad.

Although descended from pious parents Judge Birchard never connected himself with any church, and for many years he regarded himself as inclined to infidelity; but was an habitual student of the Bible and led a moral and upright life. However, during the last six months of his life, his religious feelings experienced a change, and his end was the quiet, cheerful, trusting death of the Christian—of one who unreservedly trusted to the atonement of Jesus Christ for the pardon of his sins—looking forward with implicit confidence to the blessed immortality of the faithful.

During the last three years of Judge Birchard's life his health gradually declined; but he had a wonderful tenacity of life, and an indomitable will that resisted the attacks of disease which would long before have undermined a less vigorous constitution. He peacefully expired at his residence in Warren on the 16th of June, 1876.

On the 17th of June a meeting of the Trumbull county bar was held, at which appropriate resolutions were passed, and his funeral was attended in a body by his brethren.

MILTON SUTLIFF.

The following memorial of Hon. Milton Sutliff, for the necrology of alumni at the Commencement of the Western Reserve college was prepared by an intimate friend of his, in 1878, and is inserted by permission of the writer as part of this history:

Hon. Milton Sutliff was born in Vernon, Trumbull county, Ohio, October 16, 1806. His parents were Samuel and Ruth (Granger) Sutliff, who removed from Hartland, Connecticut, and finally settled in Vernon, in 1804. His father was a man of strong sense and intelligence; of limited education, but had taught school and understood surveying. His mother was a cousin of Gideon Granger, Postmaster-general under Thomas Jefferson. She was largely endowed with strong sense, resolution, and piety; was a woman of remarkable memory and of much reading, into which largely entered the Bible, and such as Paradise Lost and Pilgrim's Progress. His father was a man of piety, and held the office of deacon in the church of his neighborhood. Milton Sutliff was the fourth of six sons, of whom four, including himself, became lawyers. His early education was in the common schools, and afterwards, in preparation for college, was with Rev. Harvey Coe, pastor of his parents' church, and subsequently one of the trustees of Western Reserve college. Of more than average size, height, and strength, quick in perception and movement, and endowed with great physical energy, he was himself fond of athletic sports and exercises, and was a great admirer of those who excelled in them, a trait which he retained to his latest age. At seventeen he taught school and afterwards went to the South, and there taught some years. Doubtless his observations there intensified those sentiments toward slavery which characterized his later life. While there he formed friendships and attachments which lasted to his death; and after the war of the Rebellion, he rendered kindness to some who had suffered from the war; and a very late act of his life, known to the writer, was to write to a lady there, on behalf of her mother and family, none of whom he had seen for nearly fifty years, enclosing a check for a considerable sum of money, and accompanying the gift with explanations of characteristic delicacy and consideration.

Judge Sutliff entered Western Reserve college in 1830. With his previous acquirements he accomplished the course of two years in that college year, and graduated in 1833.

At that time slavery had begun to be more pointedly discussed at the North, and opposition to it to assume organized action. Its discussion entered college halls, and entered Western Reserve college. The results of it there, at that time, are known to the public. Judge Sutliff had been an active and efficient participant in such discussions. Soon after he left college he received an agency from the Western Reserve Anti-slavery society to travel and promulgate its sentiments. This agency he performed faithfully for nearly nine months. He had many public discussions, which he was very able to hold; and in December, 1833, he attended, with others, the formation of the American Anti-slavery society at Philadelphia. But a more frequent and favorite mode of promulgation seems to have been by private and individual interviews, and his diary makes frequent mention that he called upon such and such a person, conversed, and left tracts. This undertaking does not appear to have been in the expectation of pecuniary reward, and it could hardly have been in the prospect of honor. He appeared to have been in the necessity of depending upon his own resources for the payment of his expenses.

He was admitted to the bar in Warren in August, 1834, and directly began the practice of the law at that place. There were giants in those days. Judge Sutliff began the practice with such men, already established in the field, as Giddings, the two Wades, Horace Wilder, Samuel Wheeler; occasionally when off the bench, Peter Hitchcock; Calvin Pease, David Tod, John Crowell, R. P. Spaulding, Elisha Whittlesey, Eben Newton, and Andrew W. Loomis. Judge Sutliff soon took high rank among them. For many years he was second to none in the extent of his practice. In 1840 Judge Sutliff acted with the Anti-slavery party organized for political action. He continued this until the formation of the Free-soil party in 1848. To the formation of this party he largely contributed, and with it and its successor, the Republican party, he acted until the election in 1872. In the spring of 1850 he was nominated by the Free-soil party of Trumbull and Geauga counties, as one of the three candidates for the Constitutional convention. The Whig and Democratic parties, each in a minority in those counties, proposed that each party should nominate but one candidate. The Free-soil party declined, and the former nominated two Whigs and one Democrat. Judge Sutliff, with an average majority of eleven hundred and ninety-five against him, fell short of an election by only two hundred and twenty-three votes.

In October, 1850, he was elected to the Ohio Senate. In this place he exerted important influence, not only by his speeches, but by his less public and more informal counsels. He introduced joint resolutions expressive of his views of the fugitive slave law, then recently enacted, and supported them by a most able, learned and exhaustive argument. The result of the discussion there had, was the passage of two joint resolutions strongly condemning the law. At this session Judge Wade was elected to the United States Senate. The controversy attending this election was, at the time, highly interesting. The views of the members were widely divergent upon the subject. Two conventions and thirty-seven ballotings were had before an election was made. It was at the first evident that the candidate to be elected must be acceptable to the Free-soil members; it also became very evident that such a candidate would not be presented by the Democrats. From the first to the last they steadily adhered to their candidate, Henry B. Payne. The Whigs at different times presented Hiram Griswold, Thomas Ewing, Thomas Corwin, Benjamin F. Wade, Sherlock J. Andrews, Ebenezer Lane, and again Benjamin F. Wade. The small minority, generally composed of the Free-soil members, at first presented Joshua R. Giddings, and afterwards successively, Edward Wade, John C. Vaughn, Milton Sutliff, Reuben Hitchcock, and Samuel Williamson. Mr. Wade was highly objectionable to some of the Whigs on account of his anti-slavery principles, and for other reasons to one or two of the Free-soil members, who for a long time refused to vote for him. It was apprehended by his especial friends that some of the Whigs would only vote for Mr. Wade when they believed he could not be elected. The plan acted upon by his friends was, that the Free-soil members should generally withhold their votes from him until a sufficient number of them would vote for him to secure his election. This was done for several successive ballotings, till one hitherto recusant Free-soil member signified to his colleagues his readiness to vote for Mr. Wade, when all did so, and he was elected. In accomplishing this result, Judge Sutliff not merely rendered important assistance, but it is believed that without him Mr. Wade could not have been elected. At the same time Judge Sutliff showed his discrimination and ability to act independent of mere party grounds, by supporting and largely aiding the election of Rufus P. Ranney to the supreme bench. The constitution of 1851 put an end to Judge Sutliff's term of office. He was never a member afterwards nor had been before. In several notices of his life, and among others in a register of the graduates of Western Reserve college, there is an error in this respect. He was never, at any other time, a candidate for the place after the accession of the Free-soil party He, however, at other times gave very important assistance to particular public measures, and it is believed he did so at the third election of Mr. Wade, and was of great service to him there.

In 1857 Judge Sutliff was elected to the supreme bench of Ohio. Judges of the supreme bench are *ex-officio* judges of the district court, and at that time the supreme judges usually sat and presided in the district court. It was to the duties of the supreme court that the qualities of Judge Sutliff most fitted him. He had to a great degree the very important talent of applying principles. He was thorough in research. His opinions are logical, learned, and masterly. During his term the cases of *ex parte* Bushnell and Langston came before the judges of the supreme court at Columbus upon a writ of *habeas corpus*. The case arose upon a conviction in the United States circuit court for Northern Ohio under the fugitive slave law. Judge Sutliff, with Judge Brinkerhoff, dissenting from the other three judges, held that the prisoners ought to be discharged; and he embodied his reasons in a most able and thorough argument. Of this opinion Mr. Sumner, in a letter replete with expressions of admiration and commendation of the argument, and declaring his confidence that its doctrines were law and must finally be adopted, said: "In delivering your opinion on this subject you have erected a monument to yourself in the judicial history of the country." The question has since been settled in another manner. In 1860 Judge Sutliff attended the Chicago convention at which Mr. Lincoln was nominated. The unfortunate rejection by the convention of a resolution offered by Mr. Giddings, which some in the convention thought unnecessary, and others perhaps thought little about, will be recollected, and the leaving of the convention by Mr. Giddings. The consideration which Mr. Giddings received during his attendance on the convention made it obvious how large a space he filled in the general estimation and how important might be the consequences of his withdrawal. Judge Sutliff saw the great moment of the occasion and made haste to avert the danger. Exercising the influence of his advice and persuasion with the New York delegation, he caused another resolution, embracing the substance of Mr. Giddings', to be offered from that quarter, and the convention appreciating the exigency, immediately passed it. Mr. Giddings was informed of the fact and returned to the convention with the welcome of cheers and the waving of handkerchiefs; and the breach was repaired.

At the end of his judicial term Judge Sutliff returned to the practice of his profession, and continued that with his other business to the end of his life. He did not cease to take an interest in public affairs. During all the war he took great interest in the progress of our arms. He urged and in many ways promoted energetic and efficient action, and was an intelligent and attentive observer of the course of events, and of the part borne in them by the different actors. He formed judgments of men who wished prominent place in the service, and who sought the influence of his recommendation to enable them to attain it. Many who had the benefit of his influence in their favor rose to high places, and results justified the appreciation of those he undertook to aid. It was a favorite sentiment with him that when the war was ended it would not be said that this general or that statesman had accomplished it, but the American people.

After the war he supported the ensuing constitutional amendments, but was in favor of a liberal policy toward the South, and a continuance of the paper money policy which the Government pursued during the war. He supported Horace Greeley in 1872, and he was himself the candidate of the Democratic party for Congress in opposition to General Garfield. He continued the practice of law until his death. That event occurred very suddenly on the 24th day of April, 1878.

Judge Sutliff was a man of very remarkable qualities. He was a man of extraordinary ability. When aroused, and especially, speaking upon any favorite topic, he exhibited unsurpassed power. In moments of his inspiration the writer has heard him when it seemed as if he spoke as never other man spake. He had a large acquaintance with the classics, and with that highest of all classics, the Bible. He was especially fond of Shakespeare and Wordsworth. He had great delicacy of sensibility, and rarely offended against good taste or propriety. He had a lively sense of humor and of wit, which he could use with readiness and effectively. His friendships were most enduring; no man could feel more deeply the ingratitude of a friend, and yet no man could overlook with more charity. He had a large liberality, but which sought no blazonment. With very few did fraternal regard embrace so wide a range of objects. He had great self-control and rarely, if ever, failed in a just courtesy to others. He was exceedingly indisposed to pretensions for his own advancement. The writer believes that he fully realized an ability in himself to act in great affairs; but this indisposition kept him back, and public places were taken by others. He was always ready to enlist his services for the poor and needy, and was ever faithful in his service. Few have higher claims to a grateful remembrance, and there are few who will not sooner be forgotten.

THOMAS DENNY WEBB.

Thomas Denny Webb, son of Peter and Tamasin (Denny) Webb, was born in Windham, Connecticut, on the 10th day of May, 1784. His wife, Betsey Stanton, was born at Montville, in the county of New London, Connecticut. They were married at Warren, Ohio, January 13, 1813. Mr. Webb was prepared for college at the academy in Leicester, Massachusetts, the place of his mother's nativity, graduated at Brown university, in 1805; studied law under that distinguished jurist, Hon. Zephaniah Swift, afterwards chief justice of the State of Connecticut, and was admitted to the bar of that State.

Immediately after this he left New England with the intention of going into what is now the State of Indiana, and locating himself near the Falls of the Ohio, but was induced to change his plan, and in December, 1807, took up his abode in Warren, then the county seat of Trumbull county, and the most flourishing town in eastern Ohio. There he practiced law until 1857, when the infirmities of age compelled him to desist. During this time, though not a printer, he established in Warren the first newspaper ever issued in Northern Ohio, called The Trump of Fame. A few copies are still preserved and occasionally exhibited at festivals and society meetings.

In 1813 Mr. Webb was appointed a collector

of internal duties for the Eighth district of Ohio. He was twice elected a member of the Senate of Ohio. In one instance he forebore to take his seat in that body. In the other he served the constitutional period of two years. About 1832 he was a candidate for Congress, with Hon. Elisha Whittlesey for competitor. He had a majority in one county, but Mr. Whittlesey obtained majorities in two counties, and gained the seat. Mr. Webb was known as the anti-masonic candidate. The Morgan excitement, which had not died out, probably lost him many votes.

On the first day of December, 1811, his right leg was amputated above the knee, in consequence of an injury received at the raising of a log building near where the Austin stone quarry in Howland now is. Notwithstanding this serious inconvenience he attended to his professional duties until within a few years of his decease.

Mr. Webb was in some respects quite peculiar and was easily irritated. When the custom was in this judicial district for the lawyers to "ride the circuit," half a dozen or more would go together on horseback. Of course Mr. Webb was compelled to use a crutch, and sometimes when they stopped for the night at some inn, some of the waggish members of the bar, like Judge Pease or Judge Wood, after most were pretty soundly asleep, would take Mr. Webb's crutch and walk with it into rooms of the house where strangers and guests were not expected to go, and father Webb had to take all the blame, and the others had their sport at his expense.

Mr. Webb died March 7, 1865, in the eighty-first year of his age. He left two children, Adaline and Laura. The former was never married, the latter was married to Dr. Warren Iddings, of Warren. They are now both dead.

ROSWELL STONE.

General Roswell Stone was born in Burlington, Hartford county, Connecticut, in 1794. He had excellent educational advantages, graduating with honor in the class with Rufus P. Spalding, at Yale college, in September, 1817. He received the degree of master of arts, at Yale college in 1821. After his graduation he went to Port Tobacco, in Maryland, and for a year taught school. This did not entirely suit the ambition of young Stone, so he sought his fortune in what was then in the East denominated "the Far West" coming to Warren, Ohio, in 1822. The next year he went back to Connecticut and married Caroline, daughter of Dr. Titus Merriman, and returned with her to Warren, where he remained until he died in 1834.

General Stone was a man of ability and prominence. He was elected from Trumbull county to the Legislature, and was prosecuting attorney for the county in 1833, at the time of the trial and conviction of Ira West Gardner for murder in the first degree. Gardner was executed in November, 1833, the only execution which ever took place in Trumbull county.

CALVIN G. SUTLIFF.

Calvin Granger Sutliff was born in Vernon, Trumbull county, Ohio, on the 17th day of April, 1808. He was a brother of the late Judge Milton Sutliff; was a lawyer, and for some time was a partner of his brother in the practice of law in Warren. Afterwards he formed a partnership with Hon. John Hutchins, now of Cleveland, and they continued the practice of law together for some time.

Calvin G. was a laborious worker, very industrious, had a good practice, but in the very prime of life, when everything looked auspicious, was cut down. Physically, he was a powerful man; about six feet two or three inches in height, with tremendous muscular power. Perhaps relying too much on his ability to resist the effect of our winter's severity, not taking the necessary precautions, he went in a cutter to Geauga county, on professional business, but returning late, and the weather being intensely cold, he contracted an influenza, or some kindred disease, which terminated in his death, on the 2d day of February, 1852.

Mr. Sutliff was married to Miss Hannah Bennett, of Hartford, Trumbull county, Ohio, on the 18th day of September, 1844. He died, leaving a widow, one son and two daughters, all grown to man and womanhood, three of whom are married, and all with bright prospects for the future.

Mr. Sutliff was a great lover of music and an excellent vocalist. After his day's work was done, with his musical friends, he would often spend the evening—we mean before the cares of married life came upon him—in some friendly house, where, with others of like tastes, a most pleasant hour would be spent.

JOHN STARK EDWARDS was born in New Haven, Connecticut, August 23, 1777. He was a son of Pierpont and Frances (Ogden) Edwards. His birth occurring shortly after the battle of Bennington, Vermont, his father gave the name of General Stark, the hero of that battle and an old friend, to his son. He graduated at Princeton college, New Jersey, in 1796, studied law with his father, who was a distinguished lawyer, attended the lectures of Judge Tappan Reeve, at the celebrated Litchfield law school, and was admitted to the bar at New Haven in the spring of 1799. Shortly after he left New Haven for Warren, Ohio, where he arrived in June of that year. He was probably the first lawyer who settled in the Reserve. His father was one of the members of the Connecticut Land company, and in the division of the Reserve among the members, the township of Mesopotamia was allotted to him. To take charge of this and other land of his father, in other parts of the Reserve, was one object of the son in coming to Ohio. He soon began a settlement in that township by making a clearing and erecting a log house. Here he resided, nominally, until about 1804, although to give attention to his professional business and official duties he passed a good part of his time in Warren. His name appears, as attorney, in the first case on the docket of the court in Trumbull county, in 1800. He was commissioned by Governor St. Clair, in July, 1800, recorder of Trumbull county, which office he held until 1813. In March, 1811, he was commissioned colonel of the Second regiment, Third brigade, Fourth division, Ohio militia. On the receipt of the news of the surrender of General Hull, at Detroit, in August, 1812, he, with others, made strenuous endeavors to put the country in a state of defence, a general and great alarm being felt, as by that surrender the whole country lay exposed to the dangers of incursion by the British and Indians. He marched with a portion of his regiment to Cleveland. After being there for a period, new arrangements were made by the military authorities, and his services as an officer being no longer required he returned to Warren.

In October of the same year he was elected Representative in Congress from the sixth district, comprising the counties of Trumbull, Ashtabula, Geauga, Cuyahoga, Portage, Columbiana, Stark, Tuscarawas, Wayne, Knox, and Richland, and was the first member of Congress elected who resided on the Reserve. He did not live to take his seat.

In January, 1813, in company with George Parsons and William Bell, he left Warren with the intention of going to the Put-in-Bay islands, where he owned lands and had a large number of sheep, to look after his property. When at Lower Sandusky, a thaw coming on, they thought best to return and started for home. He got wet, was taken ill on the road, and died on February 22, 1813, during the journey.

Hon. John Crowell, of Cleveland, formerly a lawyer of eminence at Warren, in a sketch of the life and character of Mr. Edwards, as a member of the bar and a citizen, accords to him the highest traits and all that could recommend him to the esteem of his associates and acquaintances, and to the warmest regards of his relatives and friends. His death was deeply felt, and, says Mr. Crowell, "shed a sadness and gloom over the whole country." He is described as a man of fine appearance, over six feet in height, stoutly built, and muscular; of a florid complexion and commanding presence.

He was married February 28, 1807, at Springfield, Vermont, to Miss Louisa Maria Morris, born April 13, 1787, daughter of General Lewis and Mary (Dwight) Morris, of that place. In the spring they came to Warren, Ohio, and there resided. In 1814 she was married a second time to Robert Montgomery, of Youngstown, whom she survived several years and died December 24, 1866. She was a woman of fine intellect, well educated, with a good physical organization, active and energetic, and well calculated to encounter the trials and hardships, and assist as a pioneer in the settlement of a new country. She was "a mother in Israel and known far and wide for her many personal excellencies." By Colonel Edwards she was the mother of three children, only one of whom, William J. Edwards, grew to adult years. He is now living in Youngstown, one of its most respected citizens. By Major Montgomery she was the mother of three children, Robert Morris, Caroline Sarah, married to Dr. M. Hazeltine, and Ellen Louisa, who was married to Samuel Hine.

HON. EZRA B. TAYLOR.

In the year 1814 Elisha Taylor removed from Massachusetts to Ohio and settled in what is now Nelson township, Portage county. Here he and his family struggled with the difficulties and hardships incident to pioneer life. The most common blessing of the poor, a household of children, came to Elisha Taylor, and in 1823 the subject of this sketch, Ezra B., was born.

School privileges and literary opportunities were few in those days, and there were only a few sons of poor and hard-working farmers who undertook the difficult task of preparing themselves for professional life. Among the few, however, was Ezra Taylor, who showed marked ability in the acquisition of knowledge, and was prepared at an early age to begin the study of law. He studied with Judge Payne, now of Cleveland, who then resided in Garrettsville; and in 1845 he passed a creditable examination and was admitted to the bar by the supreme court of Ohio, in Chardon. He removed to Ravenna and opened a law office there in 1847. He continued in the practice of law at Ravenna until 1862, when he removed to Warren, where he has since resided. In 1864 he enlisted as a private in the One Hundred and Seventy-first Ohio National guard, which served three months. He was exceedingly popular in the regiment, which, on its return, elected him colonel.

In 1877, after the death of Judge Servis, a member of the Warren bar asked Colonel Taylor if he would accept an appointment to fill the vacancy on the bench of the common pleas court. He answered emphatically, "No." "But," said his friend, "would you accept the office if all the bar of the sub-district ask for your appointment?" "Yes," he said, not supposing, however, that any such action would be taken. A few days afterwards he was surprised to learn that nearly every lawyer, Republican and Democrat, in the sub-district composed of Mahoning, Trumbull, and Portage counties, had signed a petition for his appointment, and it was immediately made.

Judge Taylor's eminent fitness for the office was demonstrated at once when he entered upon the discharge of his judicial duties. Clear-headed, impartial, quickly discerning the merits of every case, and conscientiously opposed to the waste of time and money in useless wranglings and irrelevant proceedings, he dispatched business with such accuracy and promptness as courts are not often accustomed to, and soon became known as one of the ablest judges who has ever presided in our courts.

At the October election of 1877 he was elected to the office by the people. He honored the office, and has the profound respect and confidence of the bar.

Judge Taylor has been an earnest and efficient Republican from the foundation of the party. As a political speaker he has few equals. His clear, strong common sense, the strength and purity of his diction, and his skill and force in the presentation of facts and arguments, make his addresses attractive and powerful. Cool and sagacious in council, and eloquent and convincing on the stump, he has rendered the most valuable service to his party in many hard fought campaigns.

Judge Taylor has a wonderfully retentive memory, and his ability at the bar and on the stump to make all his points with unerring skill and accuracy, without the use of memoranda, is often a subject of remark by those who hear him. His extraordinary memory and his logical mind, in connection with his mastery of pure English speech, fit him for eminence as a debater of political questions.

In the winter of 1880, when General Garfield was elected United States Senator, the Warren Tribune suggested that Hon. Ezra B. Taylor should be his successor in the House of Representatives. The suggestion was received with great favor and the Tribune continued to advocate Judge Taylor's nomination until he became the leading candidate. His competitors were Hons. S. A. Northway and W. P. Howland, of Ashtabula county; Hon. Peter Hitchcock, of Geauga county, and Hon. J. B. Burrows, of Lake county—all good and popular men. Judge Taylor took no part in the canvass preceding the nominating convention, but confined his attention solely to the duties of his office as a judge of the court of common pleas. His friends, however, made the contest lively, and the result was his nomination by the District Congressional convention, held in Warren August 12, 1880. He then resigned his seat on the bench and took an active part in the brief but earnest campaign which preceded General Garfield's election to the Presidency. Mr. Taylor's majority at the October election for the regular term in the Forty-seventh Congress was over twelve thousand. He was then nominated, without opposition, to fill the unexpired term of General Garfield in the Forty-sixth Congress.

Mr. Taylor is a quiet and modest member of the House, who seldom makes speeches. Nevertheless he is a steady and efficient worker, and does more to shape legislation than many members who make more noise. At this time (1882) he is a member of the committee on the judiciary and the committee on claims. In both these committees important questions of law constantly arise, and Mr. Taylor is called upon to do a large amount of work in the examination of such questions. For such important duties he is regarded by his fellow-members as one of the ablest and most efficient of committeemen. He is always at his post, and uses all his influence to prevent unnecessary delays in the transaction of public business.

During the discussion of the bill to restrict Chinese immigration, Mr. Taylor delivered a speech against the bill which attracted more attention and called forth more praise than any other speech delivered during the long and able debate on the Chinese bills.

Hon. Ezra B. Taylor.

LEVI SUTLIFF.

The subject of this sketch was born in Vernon, Trumbull county, Ohio, on the 12th day of July, 1805, and at his death was nearly fifty-nine years old. He was a brother of Judge Milton Sutliff, and was the third son in a family of six, all of whom have passed away. Flavel Sutliff, another brother, and a lawyer, died young. Their ancestors were of Puritan stock, the leading doctrines and principles of which were embraced by the sons of Deacon Samuel Sutliff, the father of the subject of this brief sketch, in a modified form.

Pioneer life on the Western Reserve was attended with hardships of every description. The following incident in the early life of Mr. Sutliff will serve to illustrate the trials of this pioneer boy, as well as test his powers of endurance and faithfulness:

When a small boy, under ten years of age, his father sent him to mill with a bag full of grain. This was a trust of no small moment for a boy of such tender years. The mill to which he was to go was upon the Shenango river in Mercer county, Pennsylvania, was distant from Vernon about twelve miles, and was reached only by a bridle or blazed path through a dense forest for most of the distance. The bag was balanced on the saddle upon the family horse and the boy mounted on the top. In the woods several miles east of Kinsman, the horse, in attempting to escape the deep mud in the path, brought the bag against a tree with so much force as to throw the boy and bag to the ground. He was unable to replace the heavy bag on the horse, and it would not do to leave it. The wheat was worth two dollars per bushel, and it had cost his father several days hard labor to obtain it. He then watched beside it, waiting and hoping that some one would pass who would be able to assist him. He watched on through the night, and into the next day till near the meridian—a faithful sentry—but no one came. It was a dreary watch and one full of peril to so young a boy, and well calculated, in that primeval forest, to test the nerve and bravery of any boy, and indeed many men. At length the sharp crack of a hunter's rifle was heard by him in the distance, when, after hollowing at the top of his voice for some time, the hunter's attention was arrested and he came to the assistance of the boy. The bag was lifted to its place, the boy mounted as before, and he continued on to the mill.

On arriving at the mill he related his misfortune, when the miller, who was a good, kind-hearted man, took a grist from the hopper, turned in the boy's grist, and sent him to his house and had him cared for. When the grist was ground and ready it was again placed upon the horse, the boy again mounted on top, and started for home. It was dark before he came to the opening where the village of Kinsman now is, but soon he saw before him at a distance a dancing light dodging among the trees, and on meeting it found it was a lantern carried by his father, who had started to look for him. He was so overjoyed at the sight that it was difficult for him to sit on his horse, while his father was affected to tears on the relation of the story.

Such was pioneer life in the boyhood days of Mr. Sutliff. His experience was rather the rule, not the exception.

The advantages for education in that unbroken wilderness were meagre, indeed, therefore his early education was quite limited; but by assiduous study he was able to remedy the defect measurably. Later in life he was a man of fair culture and extensive reading.

In middle life he turned his attention to the law, and was frequently called upon to assist his neighbors in justice courts. In 1840 he was admitted to the bar. In 1850 he removed to Warren, and formed a partnership with Judge Birchard, with whom he remained for two or three years; but at that time being possessed of a good deal of real estate which required his constant attention, he substantially retired from the profession.

Like all of his brothers, Mr. Sutliff was a very strong anti-slavery man, and in the opinion of a good many of his neighbors and friends, went in that direction a little too far. But that is all past now.

Mr. Sutliff was twice married. His first wife was Miss Mary Plumb, of Vernon, who died soon after. For his second wife he married Miss Phebe L. Marvin, of Bazetta, on the 1st day of October, 1840. She and three children survive him. He died on the 25th of March, 1864, at Warren, Ohio.

CHARLES W. SMITH.

Charles W. Smith was born October 10, 1821, in Yates county, New York. His parents were Philander W. and Martha F. Smith. With them he removed to Bazetta, Trumbull county, Ohio, in 1835. His early education was such as could be had at the common schools in his district, save two or three terms at the West Farmington academy. From 1840 to 1846 part of his time was spent in teaching school and reading law. He commenced the study of the law with the writer of this notice, and completed the same in the office of Herman Canfield, Esq., in Medina, Medina county, Ohio, and was admitted to the bar in 1846. On the 22d of October, 1846, he married Rachel Ann Park, daughter of John Park, of Weathersfield; opened a law office in Niles, Trumbull county, in 1847, and remained there, with good practice, three years. In 1850, he removed to Warren, and was soon after elected prosecuting attorney of the county, which office he held for two terms, after which he was twice elected mayor of the city of Warren.

In 1861 he enlisted in the military service and served as captain during the war. After the termination of the war he removed to Charlestown, West Virginia. He was elected a member of the Legislature of that State in 1869, and made judge of the Fifth judicial district in 1871. In 1874 he was the Republican candidate for Congress, but was defeated. By his popularity and recognized ability, he cut down the usual opposition majority from three thousand to three hundred. He afterward removed to Huntington, West Virginia, where he continued in the successful practice of the law until his decease, June 29, 1878.

On the decease of Judge Smith, the Wheeling Standard, a leading paper of that city, said of him:

He filled the position of judge with general acceptability to all parties. He was in every respect an extemporaneous man and a recognized power on the stump. In a joint discussion of the political issues of the day, was a formidable antagonist. People would ride miles through the heat or rain to hear him speak.

When Judge Smith was a young man he endured hardships that young men of the present day are strangers to. For a time he worked in James L. VanGorder's flouring-mill, in Warren, and while engaged in studying law in Warren clerked in the post-office.

The world was better for his being in it. He died, leaving three daughters, Sophie, Ida, and Angie E. His remains were brought to Warren and interred in Oakwood cemetery. The Masonic fraternity, of which order he was a member, and the Trumbull county bar paid their last tribute of respect to a worthy man, by attending his funeral in a body.

NATHAN O. HUMPHREY.

Nathan O. Humphrey was born in Braceville, Trumbull county, Ohio, on the 16th day of November, 1816. His father, Oliver Humphrey, was from Goshen, Connecticut, and was one of the pioneers of Braceville township, purchasing the land upon which he lived and died when it was an unbroken wilderness. This was in 1815. He married Miss Anna Birchard, daughter of Nathan Birchard, of Windham, Portage county, Ohio. Miss Birchard taught the first school in Windham, and also the first in Braceville. He had two sons—Nathan O., the eldest; the other died in infancy. At that time educational facilities and privileges were very limited. The district school and one term at Farmington academy, then taught by Rev. Daniel Miller, were all he ever had. At the age of sixteen he taught one winter term of school in the township of Milton, then in Trumbull county, but now in the county of Mahoning, at $8 per month, and another term in Howland, Trumbull county, receiving $16 per month.

At the age of twenty-one years he entered the office of the Hon. David Tod, as a student at law, and was admitted to the bar in 1838. He was soon after nominated by the Democrats for the office of prosecuting attorney, but, his party being in the minority, was defeated by Robert W. Taylor. In 1842 and 1844 he was elected to that office, and in 1852 he was again elected. His father dying in 1847, he returned to Braceville to take charge of the homestead farm and care for his widowed mother and young sisters.

For many years he was chosen township treasurer, and in 1870 was elected justice of the peace, which office he held until his decease on the 3d day of July, 1879.

During several years of his later life his health was poor, but he did not complain. He was a very honest and upright man. He lived seven miles from the county seat, and died while the court of common pleas was in session. The court adjourned and the members of the bar attended his funeral in a body.

GEORGE W. LEET.

George W. Leet, we believe, was born in Brookfield, but after being admitted to the bar settled in Vienna. He was a young man of much promise. His health failed, and he died soon after. Had he lived he would undoubtedly have made his mark in the profession.

PHILO ELLSWORTH REED.

Philo E. Reed, son of Garry C. and Amanda (Hart) Reed, was born in Hartford, Trumbull county, Ohio, on the 20th day of June, 1831, and lived there until he was seventeen years of age. In addition to the common schools in the vicinity of his home, his father sent him for a short time to the academy at West Farmington. After that he taught school for a year at Altoona, Pennsylvania. He then entered the office of Leggett & Cox, in Warren, as a student at law, and after pursuing a regular course of studies, was admitted to the bar in 1854. After a short practice in Warren he married, November 22, 1855, when he removed to Monmouth, Illinois, where he continued the practice of his profession until August, 1862, when, willing with others to maintain the integrity of the Government by arms, enlisted in the Eighty-third Illinois volunteer infantry, and was elected captain of company A in that regiment. His regiment was soon ordered to the front, and detailed for garrison duty at Fort Donelson, Tennessee, and in February following was attacked by Forrest and Wheeler's raiders, when young Reed was slain at the head of his men.

IRA L. FULLER.

Ira Lucius Fuller was born at Lisle, Broome county, New York, on the 21st day of November, 1816. His father, Ira, and Sally, his wife, together with the family, consisting of several children, among whom was the subject of this brief notice, desiring to benefit their family, emigrated to Brookfield, Trumbull county, Ohio, in 1833. He, like most young men of his time, was educated mainly in the common schools of the country; but we would like to say here that the common schools of that day were fully as good if not superior to what is denominated the graded school of the present. At least we find as many scholarly young men emanating from the country school-house as graduate from our city high schools.

When Mr. Fuller was about nineteen years of age he went to Warren to clerk in the post-office, when David Tod was postmaster. As opportunity offered he would study law, and after reading the necessary time, he was admitted to the bar in 1840. He was twice elected to the office of prosecutor in Trumbull county, first in 1849. After the adoption of the second constitution in Ohio, by which the probate court was created, he was elected judge of that court, which office he held with credit for three years. On the expiration of his term he resumed the practice of the law, in which he continued until his decease on the 16th of October, 1874.

Judge Fuller was a man of high moral character; but we believe that he never attached himself to any church, though his parents were very consistent Baptists. He died as he lived, highly esteemed by his acquaintances, and an upright, honorable man.

JAMES D. TAYLER.

James Douglas Tayler was born in the township of Youngstown, Mahoning county, Ohio, on the 24th day of November, 1816. He was the fifth child of James Tayler and Jane (Walker) Tayler, whose parents came to America from the north of Ireland.

The father of James D. removed from Harrisburg, Pennsylvania, to Beaver Falls, Pennsylvania, in 1814, and from thence to Youngstown the year following. Mr. Tayler's early education was obtained in such common schools as were in the vicinity of his home in that early day. His father carried on at Youngstown a woolen factory, in which young James D. was frequently an efficient helper. As we learn, his parents were more than ordinarily careful in the mental and moral training of their children, as may be well assumed when it is stated that he was the brother of George Tayler, who died cashier of the First National bank of Warren, after many years' service in that capacity, Robert W. Tayler, who died at Washington First Comptroller of the United States Treasury, and Matthew B. Tayler, who also died cashier of the First National bank of Warren.

On the 10th day of May, 1831, he went into the clerk's office of Trumbull county, George Parsons at that time and for many years afterwards being clerk. Here he remained until 1839, writing in the office, and studying law at intervals, when he was admitted to the bar at a term of the supreme court held in Gallia county, on the 23d day of March of that year. At the same term Henry W. King, son of Judge Leicester King, of Warren, was also admitted. Mr. Tayler immediately opened an office in Warren, and very rapidly grew into a good practice, notwithstanding at that time his health was none of the best. In September following he formed a partnership with Sidney W. Harris, and together they continued the successful practice of the law until 1844, when he went to Akron and formed a law partnership with his friend Henry W. King, where he remained until 1849. He was married on the 2d of May, 1848, to Miss Isabella Florilla Howard, of Akron. In July, 1849, he removed to Peru, Illinois, practicing in LaSalle and adjacent counties. Here his health entirely gave way and he was compelled to abandon the practice and seek relief in the "Sunny South."

On the 18th of January, 1855, he went to Enterprise, in east Florida, but he obtained no relief, and died of consumption on the 22d day of March following. He left a wife and three children. His remains were brought to Warren, the home of his youth and the residence of his brothers and sisters, for interment. His brethren of the bar called a meeting, at which the following proceedings were had :

The members of the bar met on Friday evening, the 13th instant, at the office of the probate judge, to take into consideration the course proper to be pursued by them in view of the recent death of James D. Tayler, Esq., in Florida, and the return of his remains to this place.

Upon motion of J. Hutchins, Esq., the Hon. Matthew Birchard was called to the chair, and upon motion of M. Sutliff, Esq., J. D. Cox was appointed secretary. The chairman, upon taking his seat, briefly addressed the meeting as to the cause which had assembled them, and the business which would be before them. J. Hutchins, Esq., then moved the appointment, by the chair, of a committee of five to draft appropriate resolutions, and report the same to the meeting; and the motion being sustained, the chairman appointed M. Sutliff, J. Hutchins, G. F. Brown, M. D. Leggett, and J. D. Cox as the committee. The meeting then adjourned to meet at Judge Birchard's office the following morning at 9 o'clock.

On Saturday morning, pursuant to adjournment, the Bar met, and the committee on resolutions made the following report, which was adopted :

Resolved, That the members of the bar of Trumbull county have heard with sorrow and regret the death of James D. Tayler, who was formerly a member of this bar.

Resolved, That by this afflictive event, the legal profession has been deprived of an efficient, able, and honorable practitioner; the community in which he resided, of an exemplary citizen; the interests of humanity, of a generous, laborious, and upright man; and his family, of a kind and affectionate husband and father.

Resolved, That the chairman of this meeting convey to the bereaved family and to the bar of Peru, Illinois, the sentiments of high regard entertained by this bar for the memory of the deceased, and of sympathy with them in their affliction.

Resolved, That the chairman of this meeting present these resolutions to the court of common pleas at the term next to be holden in this county, with a request that they be entered on the journals.

Resolved, That as a bar we will attend the funeral of the deceased in a body, and that a committee of three be appointed by the chair to make the necessary arrangements therefor.

Upon the adoption of the report the chair appointed Messrs. R. F. Hoffman, Ansel Atwell, and T. E. Webb a committee of arrangements for the funeral, by whose direction the funeral procession was placed under the charge of the chairman and marshal, and the order of the same arranged as follows, viz : 1st, the clergy in a carriage; 2d, the bar in double file; 3d, the hearse with four pall-bearers on each side, Messrs. Sutliff, Ratliff, Hutchins, Fuller, Buttles, Leggett, Brown, and Ranney being appointed to that duty ; 4th, the mourners, followed by the friends and citizens generally. The procession was arranged to move from the house of M. B. Tayler, Esq., at half past ten, and proceed to the cemetery, where appropriate services would take place.

The members of the bar then adjourned to meet at the place and hour appointed for the funeral, which took place in accordance with the above arrangements.

M. BIRCHARD, Chairman.

J. D. COX, Secretary.

Similar proceedings and resolutions of respect were adopted by the bar of Peru, Illinois, and entered on the journals of the court at that place.

CHARLES E. GLIDDEN.

Charles E. Glidden was born in New Hampshire; but when quite a young man came to Ohio and located in Poland, Mahoning county, where there was then a law school of considerable celebrity. We believe that Mr. Glidden graduated at that institution. A short time he practiced law in Mahoning county, and in 1861, at the age of twenty-six, was elected judge of the court of common pleas for the district that had predecessors like Governor Wood, Luther Day, Benjamin F. Hoffman, Van R. Humphrey, and earlier, George Tod, the father of Governor Tod. He performed his duties with such acceptability to the profession and the public, that after a lapse of five years he was again elected to the same position.

Judge Glidden was a young man of more than ordinary ability in his profession; but by reason of his being elected judge in early life, never acquired great reputation at the bar.

Notwithstanding Judge Glidden's youth when he went on the bench, his judgment seemed well matured, and his charges to the jury and his opinions in chancery cases, gave satisfaction to the profession.

Judge Glidden was a man of fine presence—nearly or quite six feet tall, and by reason of his "make up," if we may be allowed to use that expression, was very popular with the people.

During his last term on the bench his health failed, and he was compelled at its close to seek medical aid. Being an Eastern man he naturally turned to the East. Of course he obtained the best medical skill in the country, but at this writing he is in Boston and quite infirm. His wife is still living, and a most estimable lady, whom he married in Poland. They have one son, now about twenty years of age, who, with his mother, devote their attention almost exclusively to the care of the invalid.

SIDNEY W. HARRIS.

Sidney W. Harris was born in Addison county, Vermont, about 1815. His father was Henry Harris, and his mother Harriet (Stevens) Harris. He came to Warren, Ohio, with his mother and Augustus Stevens, his uncle, in 1825, and lived in the family of Mr. Stevens about six years, going to school most of the time. Mr. Stevens sent him to Western Reserve college, at Hudson, for a time, but he did not graduate. Afterwards he clerked in the store of H. & C. Smith, in Warren, for about a year.

Mr. Harris had a taste for the legal profession, and through the aid rendered him by his uncle commenced the study of the law with Hon. John Crowell, then in full practice in Warren. Young Harris afterwards attended the law school at Cincinnati, an institution of high repute, with Judge Walker at its head. He was well qualified for the profession of his choice, and was admitted to the bar about the same time Mr. James D. Tayler, also of Warren, was admitted. They soon after formed a partnership and opened an office in Warren. Having much ability and many friends they soon acquired a good practice, which they retained while they remained in Trumbull county, but like most young men, whether in professions or in other employments, they were ambitious to take the positions they and their friends thought they were capable of filling. Mr. Harris went to Cincinnati and Mr. Tayler to Akron. Mr. Harris remained in Cincinnati about five years, but thought he had better go farther West, and removed to Morris, Grundy county, Illinois, where he commenced the practice of the law and was very successful. In 1862 he was elected judge of the court of common pleas for that county and district, which office he filled for several years with credit and ability, but the salary being small, he resigned and again commenced the practice of the law, in which he continued with great credit to himself and good results to his clients, until his decease in 1876.

Mr. Harris was a self-made man, a fine speaker, had a strong liking for the profession, and availed himself of all the advantages within his reach. He married Mary Freeman Bronson, daughter of Dr. Tracy Bronson, of Newton, by whom he had three children, now all married and living in the State of Illinois. Mrs. Harris is also deceased.

JOHN F. BEAVER.

John F. Beaver was born in Stoyestown, Somerset county, Pennsylvania. There he acquired an education, while laboring under many difficulties. Having a desire for the legal profession, he went to Greensburg, Westmoreland county, Pennsylvania, and entered himself as a student at law in the office of Colonel J. B. Alexander. The greatly distinguished lawyer and judge, Jeremiah S. Black, was also a student of Colonel Alexander's, and at the same time. By close application, and an enduring perseverance, he thoroughly mastered the rudiments of the law, was soon after married, and devoted all of his energies to its practice. He pursued his chosen avocation in the courts of Westmoreland and neighboring counties until 1841, gaining no little distinction, in a local way, as an able and successful advocate. We believe that at one time he was a law partner of the Hon. Edgar Cowan, late United States Senator from the State of Pennsylvania.

Mr. Beaver sought a broader field of operations than Westmoreland county afforded, and removed to Pittsburg, where he practiced his profession for three years; but the habits and social requirements of city life not agreeing with his peculiar tastes and temperament, and having already accumulated, by economy and patient toil, a comfortable competence, he came to Ohio in 1844, and purchased a valuable farm and mill property at Newton Falls, in Trumbull county, and for a time abandoned the active practice of his profession, but occasionally aided his neighbors in the adjustment of controversies in the courts of justices of the peace and in the common pleas. His talents won for him a proud prominence in his new home. He attracted so much attention, that in 1845 he was elected to the State Senate, an honor of no low distinction, which position he filled with very great credit to himself and his constituents, for three terms (six years), and was considered one of the most ready debaters and learned parlimentarians in that body.

It was at the beginning of his first term in the Senate that he became prominently known to the country by the appellation of "Beaver's Boots," a name applied to him, not disrespectfully, but rather to commemorate an adventure of which he was the hero. It occurred before the days of many railroads in Ohio, and when the Democrats and Whigs were a tie in the Senate, so that the absence of one member from either side would give the opposite party the organization of that body. It was therefore very essential to each party that every one of their members should be present at the beginning of the session. Mr. Beaver went to Cleveland and designed taking a boat to Sandusky, from whence he could travel by rail to Newark; but no boat could be obtained, and he was obliged to take a wagon to Columbus. The roads were very muddy and progress was slow and difficult. When within twelve or fifteen miles of the capital the wagon broke down and left the party sticking in the mud. This mishap occurred about 3 o'clock in the morning, and as the Legislature met at 9 o'clock the same morning, Mr. Beaver determined that his party should not suffer on his account, and accordingly started on foot, through mud almost unfathomable, for the capital. At five minutes before 9 o'clock the Whigs were gathered in groups about the capitol, deploring the absence of Mr. Beaver, and lamenting among themselves the triumph the Democrats would enjoy in ten minutes, in the election of the officers of the Senate. A member rushed out and declared that "Mr. Beaver ought to be killed," to which Mr. Dennison, afterwards Governor, replied that Mr. Beaver had come, at the same time eyeing a man so covered with mud as to be scarcely recognizable. "No," said the member, "he has not come." "Yes," replied Dennison, "that's him," pointing to the approaching mud-pile. "What, them boots?" From this "Beaver's boots" became a by-word, and furnished the opposition with an almost inexhaustible amount of ridicule during the balance of Mr. Beaver's term.

The politicians of middle life well remember the "hard cider" campaign of 1840. It was a campaign of songs and cider. Among the distinguished poets of that time was John Greiner. His verses in celebration of "Beaver's Boots" were copied into almost every newspaper in the country, and won for their hero, as well as their author, a considerable notoriety. So that, instead of the famous boots becoming a source of ridicule to the wearer, they were a source of pride. We reproduce the song as it was originally written:

BEAVER'S BOOTS.

- Strike, strike the harp—come sweep the lyre!
Kindle and blaze, Promethean fire;
Tune up your sweetest dulcet notes,
My ponderous theme is Beaver's boots.

Old Trumbull's bull—a bull whose hide
Grew thick and tough—took sick and died.
Its soul went with all the other brutes,
His hide went into Beaver's boots.

Millions of creeping things lie dead,
Mangled and crushed beneath his tread,
Two insect smashers—Death recruits
His ranks in following Beaver's boots.

When first they thundered up the aisle,
Filled inside—outside with Free-soil,
The Senate hushed their fierce disputes,
And speechless gazed at Beaver's boots.

The tangled hair of Whitman rose,
And pale with fear grew Graham's nose;
Byers alarmed and backward shoots,
Aghast, amazed at Beaver's boots.

The Chase was up, the Swift grew lazy,
The Burns grew Cold, the Payne grew easy;
E'en Cunningham's white head salutes
The high-soled man in Beaver's boots.

That well filled vest with pride displays
The guard chain red of other days,
That unshaved honest face denotes,
A Governor stands in Beaver's boots.

Many worse Governors has Ohio had than John F. Beaver would have made; but more ambitious men, whose work was not always done with clean hands, pushed integrity and worth aside.

Early in life Mr. Beaver developed a taste for reading quite unusual; in fact, his entire time, in the latter years of his life, when he was not engaged in hunting, was spent in the study of choice works of history and biography. His memory was really wonderful; a faculty that stayed with him when he became advanced in years; in fact, up to the time of his decease.

Mr. Beaver was very fond of hunting as well as of books. Having some wild land in the western part of Ohio, he would every winter, until his advanced age and declining health prohibited him from doing so, put on his buckskin armor and spend a month in his comfortable log cabin hunting deer, which his friends well know he was very successful in getting. His evenings were employed in reading the books he brought with him, by the light of a tallow dip, or often the fire that cheerfully blazed from the cabin hearth.

A correspondent of the Cleveland True Democrat visited Mr. Beaver at his home in Newton, and wrote to his paper as follows:

"On being introduced to him he stretched out his huge paw, and such another shake of the hand I never had. His whole heart was in it, and it said, 'I am glad to see you.' In that hand-shaking there was no disguise; it was one of the evidences of his true character."

While a member of the Senate he was his party's candidate for speaker, and was defeated by one vote, he refusing to vote for himself.

Mr. Beaver was not ambitious for office; he cared more for the comforts of home life than for the best office in the gift of his fellow citizens. He was plain and unostentatious in his manners and habits, caring little or nothing for display, and never sought to render himself conspicuous. He was the unpolished diamond, but possessing all of the elements of value and genuine merit. He possessed a strong constitution, but it succumbed to the infirmities of age—his mind remaining clear to the end. At the age of seventy-seven years he passed away - one of the truest of men, the soul of honor, and a man of unimpeachable integrity.

ROBERT W. TAYLER.

Robert W. Tayler, an elder brother of James D. Tayler, now also deceased, was formerly of the Trumbull county bar; but many years since went to Youngstown and from there to Washington, where he occupied the position of first comptroller of the treasury until his decease. A full sketch of him will be found in another part of this work.

JOEL F. ASPER.

Colonel Joel F. Asper died in the State of Missouri. He was admitted to the bar in Trumbull county, where he practiced his profession until the breaking out of the war of the Rebellion, when he volunteered in the service. He soon reached the position of colonel, which he filled throughout the entire war. On its termination he located in Missouri, and resumed the practice of the law. He was elected to Congress from his adopted State for one term, and soon after died. He left a widow and several children, who reside in Missouri.

WILLIAM O. FORREST.

William O. Forrest, now engaged in a successful practice of law in Mexico, Missouri, studied his profession with Hon. John Crowell, in Warren, and was there admitted. He was esteemed a good lawyer, and had a good practice in Trumbull county. At one time he was a partner of F. E. Hutchins. Mr. Forrest's ambition led him to the West, where he now is.

GEORGE F. BROWN.

George F. Brown now resides east of Topeka, in Kansas, and practices his profession of the law. When a young man, and about the time he commenced the practice, he became a partner of the Hon. John Crowell. Their practice was large and lucrative, being retained in most of the important litigation. In 1855 he was elected to succeed Ira L. Fuller to the office of probate judge of Trumbull county, which office he filled for two terms of three years each, discharging his duties to the satisfaction of the public. In 1866 Judge Brown was elected to the State Senate for one term, at the conclusion of which he went to Mississippi and engaged in the practice of his profession there, and not long after was elected a judge of the court of common pleas. Losing some of his family by reason of the unhealthy part of the country in which he had settled, he determined to change his place of residence, which he promptly did by going to Kansas, where his family enjoy excellent health and he a good practice.

JOEL B. BUTTLES.

Joel B. Buttles studied law and was admitted to the bar in Trumbull county. He removed from Brookfield to Warren about 1840. His practice was not very large, as he soon after went into the newspaper business with the Hon. E. B. Eshelman, now of Wooster, Ohio.

While a resident of Warren Mr. Buttles was appointed warden of the Ohio penitentiary, which place he filled for some time. Soon after, he removed to Iowa City, where he still resides, engaged mostly in dealing in real estate.

BUEL BARNES.

Buel Barnes was born in Farmington, Connecticut, in 1797, on the 6th day of October. He settled in Gustavus, Trumbull county, Ohio, on the 8th day of June, 1820. Mr. Barnes was a leading and influential man in Gustavus. His first commission as justice of the peace was dated April 23, 1835, and he held the office continuously until April 15, 1871. He was twice elected to the State Legislature, in 1844 and in 1845; was an honorable member and faithful in the discharge of the trust the people of his county placed in his keeping. He did not come to the bar until quite late in life, and, being a man of ample fortune, did not care to enter the arena with younger men, and therefore had not much practice in the county courts.

Mr. Barnes was highly esteemed by his neighbors and acquaintances, and died at the ripe age of eighty-seven years, in 1880.

WILLIAM L. KNIGHT.

William L. Knight was born in Massachusetts, and was graduated at Amherst college. He had the best advantages of education, and came to Warren about 1831 and opened an office, where he acquired a good practice. He was elected prosecuting attorney of Trumbull county in 1835, and re-elected in 1837. After his term of office expired he continued the practice of law until failing health admonished him that he must desist. His father lived in Poland, Mahoning county, where he went for kindly care, but he soon after died.

A full sketch of Mr. Knight appears in another part of this work.

CHARLES OLCOTT.

Charles Olcott came to Warren, Trumbull county, in 1821, and commenced the practice of the law. He was graduated at Yale college and took the highest honors of his class; remained in Warren but a short time, having such practice as a young lawyer would be likely to obtain, when he removed to Medina county, a new county then just created by the Legislature, and continued the practice of his profession there until his decease, which was about the year 1840.

JONATHAN INGERSOLL.

Mr. Ingersoll was born about 1802, and belonged to the distinguished family of that name who early settled in the State of Connecticut. He was educated for the United States navy and entered its active service on the old Constitution when but a boy. He went wherever the old Constitution went; around the globe, in fact. He was engaged in a skirmish on land, in the East Indies, at the head of a corps of marines, which has gone into history, much to his credit for valor.

About 1838 he married Catharine Seely, daughter of Dr. Sylvanus Seely, of Warren, having about two years before that time resigned the position of lieutenant in the United States navy and devoted his time to the study of the law.

Mr. Ingersoll commenced the practice of the law in Warren, and was soon after appointed clerk of the court of common pleas, which office he filled for seven years, and was then appointed clerk of the supreme court of Trumbull county. After his term of clerkship expired he returned to the bar and formed a partnership with Nathan O. Humphrey, a sketch of whose life appears in this work, and continued the practice of his profession until his health failed him.

Mr. Ingersoll was an upright and honorable man, and had the confidence not only of his intimate friends and neighbors, but of the entire community. He died in 1875, and was interred in Oakwood cemetery, at Warren. Mr. Ingersoll had five children to lament his loss. His wife died before him.

On the decease of Mr. Ingersoll the bar of Trumbull county met and passed resolutions of respect and condolence, and attended his funeral in a body. The funeral rites were in Christ church, Warren, where his friends and neighbors assembled in great numbers. Let the writer of this say of him: he was a true man.

DAVID D. BELDEN.

David D. Belden received most of his academic education at the West Farmington seminary. After getting through with his academic course he commenced the study of the law in Warren; was admitted to the bar, and commenced the practice of his profession. He had not been long at the bar when he was elected prosecuting attorney of Trumbull county, which office he filled with credit until the close of his term. Soon after that he went to Omaha, and from there to Denver, where he now resides engaged in mining and practicing his profession.

BENJAMIN F. CURTIS.

We believe that Benjamin F. Curtis came to Warren from Geauga county, Ohio. He opened an office here and commenced the practice of the law. He was well educated and read in his profession.

After a little time he went in the county clerk's office, under Warren Young, where he remained for some time, and was afterwards appointed collector of customs at Warren, on the Pennsylvania and Ohio canal. After his retirement he again resumed the practice of law, which he continued with much ability and success to the time when he removed to Grand Haven, Michigan. There he acquired a good reputation as a lawyer, and was very successful.

While in Warren he married Lucy, the daughter of John Williams, by whom he had one son. In 1880 Mrs. Curtis went on board a steamer bound for Chicago, and when not far from the middle of Lake Michigan the boat sunk, and Mrs. Curtis and all the other passengers on board perished. None of the bodies have since been recovered.

GEORGE L. WOOD.

George L. Wood was admitted to the bar, we believe, in Geauga county, Ohio. He soon after came to Warren, Ohio, and commenced the practice of law, and afterwards became the law partner of C. W. Smith, and was once elected mayor of the city of Warren.

On the breaking out of the war, Mr. Wood volunteered his services to the Government—went to the front and was severely wounded. He returned to Warren on furlough, and when he sufficiently recovered resumed his profession, and after the close of the war, he and his wife, Jane Tod, daughter of Dr. Jonathan I. Tod, removed to the State of Mississippi, where he opened an office and commenced the practice of his profession. He did not, however, long remain there, as declining health admonished him that he had better return to the North. He accordingly went back to Warren, where he soon after died, leaving a wife and one daughter, who now survive.

Mrs. Wood afterwards intermarried with General Robert W. Ratliff, who, together with the daughter, now reside in Warren.

ALEXANDER C. PARKER.

Alexander C. Parker was the son of William Parker, and was born in Bloomfield, Trumbull county, Ohio. He was a very studious young man, and we believe graduated at Farmington academy. Afterwards studied law in the Cleveland Law college, where he graduated, and was admitted to practice law in the State of Ohio, about 1872. By reason of ill health, Mr. Parker practiced but a short time, and was compelled to succumb to the fatal destroyer, and died of consumption in 1876. Mr. Parker was well educated and thoroughly read in the profession of his choice. He was a very conscientious and exemplary man and a great student.

W. J. BRIGHT.

W. J. Bright lived in Hartford, Trumbull county, Ohio, during his minority. When he grew up he studied law and was admitted to the bar about 1850 or 1851 in Trumbull county. He had a good many suits before justices of the peace, but not much practice in the higher courts in Trumbull county. Soon after he was admitted, he went West, where we learn he was quite successful in his profession and died in Indianapolis about 1880. He was an energetic man and of very considerable ability.

ORLANDO MORGAN.

Orlando Morgan was born in Windsor, Ashtabula county, Ohio, in 1818; went to Warren and studied law with John Erwin, now of Cleveland, but who then resided in Warren, and was admitted to the bar in 1843.

He practiced but little, and soon after his admission, went into the mercantile business with H. L. Steele, under the firm name of Morgan & Steele. The firm did not continue long until Mr. Iddings was added to it and the firm name changed to Iddings, Steele & Co. The last named firm did not last very long when Mr. Steele went out and the firm reorganized under the name of Iddings & Morgan, which continued in successful business for thirty years, and until both members deceased.

Mr. Morgan was married on the 27th day of June, 1849, to Miss Harriette C. Sheldon, of Martinsburg, New York. She still survives him and resides at Warren. They had no children.

GENERAL JOHN CROWELL

was born in East Haddam, Middlesex county, Connecticut, September 15, 1801. His father Samuel Crowell, was the first settler of Rome township, Ashtabula county. He was a carpenter, and, like most of the early pioneers, had scanty means for the education of his children. John attended school a couple of months in the winter, and worked on the farm all the rest of the year, so that at his majority his education was very meager. In November, 1822, he came to Warren on foot for the purpose of attending the academy, then in charge of E. R. Thompson, a graduate of Cambridge university, and an excellent teacher. With the exception of short intervals, Mr. Crowell attended school here until February, 1825, at which time he began the study of law in the office of Hon. Thomas D. Webb. While preparing for his profession he devoted a portion of his time to teaching, being for about six months principal of the academy. In 1827 he was admitted to the bar, and immediately began the practice of his profession. About this time he purchased an interest in the Western Reserve Chronicle, his partner being George Hapgood. Mr. Crowell did most of the writing during his connection with the paper. His editorials were vigorous and convincing. In 1840 he was elected to the State Senate. He took high rank as a debater and sagacious politician. It was the reputation he made in the Senate, in addition to his success at the bar, which secured for him the Whig nomination for Congress in 1846. His competitors were John Hutchins, Abolitionist, and Judge Ranney, Democrat. Crowell was elected by a large majority, and again elected in 1848. In Congress he took grounds with the anti-slavery wing of the Whig party. After his retirement from Congress he removed to Cleveland and resumed the practice of law in 1852. In 1862 he was chosen president of the Ohio State and Union Law college, at Cleveland, a position which he held for fourteen years. He was also for a number of years editor of the Western Law Monthly, published in Cleveland. Mr. Crowell was married in 1833 to Eliza B. Estabrook, and has a family of four children.

RUFUS P. SPAULDING,

now aged eighty-three years and the oldest lawyer in Cleveland, was for many years a citizen of Warren and a member of the Trumbull county bar. He was born on the island of Martha's Vineyard, Massachusetts, in the year 1799. At the age of eighteen he graduated from Yale college, and there prepared himself for the bar. After being admitted he came West and finally located at Warren. He united with his law practice school teaching. His name occurs at two different times among the teachers in the old academy. Although he was severe in enforcing discipline he is kindly remembered by his pupils. At the bar he worked his way to the foremost rank, and had a large practice in Trumbull and adjoining counties. In 1849 Mr. Spaulding was chosen to a seat on the supreme bench of the State. After retiring in 1852 he began practice in Cleveland, where he has since resided, being regarded as one of the leading practitioners in Northern Ohio. Judge Spaulding was elected to Congress in 1862, and continued to represent his district with acknowledged ability for three consecutive terms. Though sixty-five years old when he entered Congress, for punctuality and close attention to public business he was conspicuous. Johnson, in his History of Cleveland, says:

After passing the age of seventy he retired from public life, but did not abandon his interest in public affairs, and even yet the voice of the octogenarian lawyer, judge, and congressman is occasionally heard in favor of the policy he considers to be sound and the principles he believes to be right.

RUFUS P. RANNEY

was twice, during the earlier period of his practice, connected with the Trumbull county bar. He was born in Hampden county, Massachusetts, October 30, 1813. His father, a farmer of

John Crowell

moderate means, exchanged his land in Massachusetts for a larger tract in Portage county, and removed to the West in 1824. Like most country people of the period, Mr. Ranney had no means with which to send his son to school. But relying upon himself young Ranney found a way of overcoming difficulties. He chopped wood to pay for his first Latin dictionary and Virgil, and begun receiving private instructions from Dr. Bassett, of Nelson, working at odd intervals to pay his tuition. Subsequently by teaching school and manual labor he earned money enough to go to college. Before graduating he began the study of law in the office of Giddings & Wade, at Jefferson, and in the fall of 1836 was admitted to the bar. He opened an office in Warren but remained in the county but a short time. Mr. Giddings having been elected to Congress, Mr. Wade invited young Ranney to enter into partnership with him. This partnership continued nearly ten years, during which time they acquired the reputation of being the leading advocates in northeastern Ohio. They were also leading politicians in their respective parties, Mr. Ranney being a Democrat and Mr. Wade distinguished as a radical Whig. When the senior partner was elected common pleas judge in 1845 Mr. Ranney removed to Warren, where he already had a full practice. He had been a candidate for Congress in 1842 in the Ashtabula district, and was again a candidate in the Trumbull district in 1846, and a third time in 1848. These nominations, however, were accepted only "for the party's sake," there being no hope of election on the Democratic ticket. In 1850 Mr. Ranney, Jacob Perkins, and Peter Hitchcock were chosen to represent Trumbull and Geauga counties in the convention to draft a new State constitution. He took an active part in the debates before the convention and, as chairman of the committee on revision, drafted a large part of the instrument which, at the succeeding election, was adopted as the fundamental law of the State. While serving as a member of the convention he was elected by the Legislature to the supreme bench of the State. The same Legislature elected his former partner, Judge Wade, United States Senator. After the adoption of the new constitution Judge Ranney was re-chosen supreme judge by the people of the State, and filled the position with credit until 1856, when he resigned and began the practice of his profession in Cleveland, of which city he has since been a resident. Judge Ranney is ranked among the leading lawyers of the country.

GENERAL M. D. LEGGETT,

who distinguished himself in the army, and has since made a reputation at the bar, practiced law in Warren six years, between 1851 and 1857. He was born at Ithaca, New York, April 19, 1831. His parents were Friends, and educated their children in the doctrine of non-resistance and other peculiar creeds. In 1847 they removed to Geauga county, Mortimer D. being at that time sixteen years old. He was a diligent student, though given little opportunity of attending school. He was self educated, but well educated. Upon the organization of the Warren schools in 1849, under the "Akron school law," Mr. Leggett was chosen superintendent and teacher of the high school at a salary of $700 a year. This position he filled until succeeded by Mr. Cox in 1851. While teaching he had pursued the study of law, and was admitted to the bar soon after retiring from the schools. He had a very promising practice in this county, and at the same time gave considerable attention to educational matters. In 1857 he removed to Zanesville to accept the superintendency of the public schools at that place. In the fall of 1861 he was authorized by Governor Dennison to recruit a regiment. In the fall of 1862 he was commissioned colonel of the Seventy-eighth Ohio volunteer infantry. In November, 1862, he was promoted to the rank of brigadier-general, and breveted major-general July 22, 1864. In January following he was promoted to the rank of full major-general. It is said that while in the army he abstained strictly from drinking and playing cards, and permitted neither at his headquarters. After the war General Leggett held the position of United States commissioner of patents under President Grant's administration, and as a patent lawyer has acquired a high standing. His present residence is at Cleveland, Ohio.

JACOB DOLSON COX

is prominent among former members of the Trumbull county bar who have made for themselves national reputations. He is a native of

Montreal, Canada, but his parents were both citizens of the United States, his father, who was a master carpenter, being employed temporarily at Montreal during the year 1828, the year of General Cox's birth. His childhood and youth were spent in New York until 1846, when he entered Oberlin college, where he graduated in 1851. In the fall of that year Mr. Cox removed to Warren, having been chosen superintendent of the schools. He served as superintendent and principal of the high school three years, and at the same time pursued the study of law. Having in the meantime been admitted to the bar, he began practice in 1854. His oratorical ability made him somewhat of a political leader. Having a radical character of mind, and being the son-in-law of the radical president Finney, of Oberlin college, he was the choice of the sturdy Reserve Abolitionists for the position of Senator in the State Legislature in 1859. Political controversy was at its highest pitch, and the principles of the new Republican party were not yet settled. There were three members of that Senate distinguished for their radicalism—Professor Monroe, of Oberlin, Mr. Cox, and Professor Garfield, of Hiram. Before the close of the second session of that Legislature the fall of Sumter had made them leaders of the Assembly. Senator Cox had for some time been a general officer in the State militia, and in that capacity had demonstrated military talent. After the bombardment of Fort Sumter he abandoned all professional and official duties, and devoted himself to organizing the Ohio contingent. He was on April 23, 1861, commissioned brigadier-general of Ohio volunteers. With the opening of the Rebellion General Cox's connection with Trumbull county was severed. On the field he maintained an honorable standing, attaining to the rank of major-general of volunteers. In the fall of 1865, while in command of the Department of Ohio with headquarters at Columbus, General Cox was elected Governor of Ohio, to accept which he resigned his position in the army. After the war General Cox became a leader of the conservative wing of the Republican party, and in the earlier part of the unfortunate controversy between President Johnson and Congress he took open ground on the side of the President. The fact of his being Governor made his position on this engrossing political issue conspicuous. He declined to be a candidate for re-nomination for the Governorship, and retired to the practice of his profession. He was chosen by President Grant, upon the organization of his first cabinet, Secretary of the Interior. He resigned on account of differences with the President, and has since been a resident of Cincinnati.

JOHN HUTCHINS,

though now a resident of Cleveland, must be classed among the public men from Trumbull county. He was for more than twenty-five years connected with the Warren bar ; was during all that time an active politician, and represented for four years the district to which the county was attached in the Congress of the United States. His father, Samuel Hutchins, and his mother, whose maiden name was Flower, were both natives of Connecticut. They removed to the Reserve in 1800, making the whole journey from Connecticut with an ox team, and settled in Vienna township. John, the fourth child, was born July 25, 1812. He worked on the farm and attended the common school until twenty years old. He subsequently attended Western Reserve college. In 1835 Mr. Hutchins began the study of law in the office of David Tod and was admitted to the bar in 1838 at New Lisbon, Columbiana county. After practicing about one year he received the appointment of clerk of the courts for Trumbull county, which position he filled five years. Upon resuming practice Mr. Hutchins was received into partnership with Tod & Hoffman. He was afterwards associated with J. D. Cox until official positions interrupted the practice of both. Mr. Hutchins had been a pronounced anti-slavery man from the beginning of his career, and became a radical Republican after the organization of that party. Hoffman, Sutliff, King, Hutchins, and a few others were avowed promoters of the "Underground Railroad" emancipation project, and when at last there was a political movement which gave hope of the triumph of freedom, these same men were found in the front ranks. Mr. Hutchins was nominated in 1858 to succeed the venerable and honored Giddings in Congress. He was active in defending the honor of the Government before secession, and when rebellion broke out bent his energies in Congress to provide for our armies and at home to recruit those armies. He was succeeded in Congress at the end of his second term by General Garfield, and again devoted himself to the practice of his profession, never, however, losing an opportunity to promote the Union cause as long as the war lasted. In 1868 he removed to Cleveland, and has since been practicing in that city. While in Warren he took an active part in educational matters, and was one of the leading advocates in 1849 of the graded school system. He married Rhoda M. Andrews and has a family of five children.

MELANCTHON C. HART,

son of Joseph C. Hart, of Farmington township, Trumbull county, was born December 15, 1846. He received his preliminary education in the schools of his native town, Western Reserve seminary, West Farmington, and at Allegheny college, Meadville, Pennsylvania. In the spring of 1869 Mr. Hart began the study of law in the office of Hutchins, Tuttle & Stull, and was admitted to practice in June, 1871. He opened an office in Hubbard, Trumbull county. Mr. Hart was elected clerk of Trumbull county in October, 1872, and was re-elected in 1875. Retiring from office January 1, 1879, he removed to Cleveland, and has since been practicing in that city. He married in 1872 Miss Mary Camp, of Akron, Ohio.

JUDGE JOEL W. TYLER,

now of Cleveland, was born in Portage county, Ohio, January 21, 1823. He was educated at the Western Reserve college at Hudson, taking a classical course. He engaged in teaching school when quite young, was engaged in teaching many years, and was principal of an academy in Geauga county. He received much valuable instruction from Dr. P. C. Bennett, in Geauga county. He studied law with Mr. Wheaton, in Hudson, two years, and one year with Tilden & Ranney, of Ravenna; was admitted to the bar at Ravenna, and commenced practice in Garrettsville, in 1846 or 1847. In the fall of 1850 he removed to Kent, where he soon after became connected with the Atlantic & Great Western railroad, and subsequently filled the position as attorney for the road for many years, rendering it in that capacity valuable and efficient service, which was appreciated and gratefully acknowledged by the company. In 1856 he removed to Mansfield, where he resided until 1858, when he came to Warren, forming a partnership in the practice of law with Judge Birchard. In 1860 he was elected to the office of probate judge of Trumbull county. The office came to him wholly unsolicited, and he declared his purpose in accepting the position to resign in favor of the first wounded soldier of the county who should be capable of discharging the duties of the office. He was re-elected in 1863, but after serving one year, and on the return of Judge Yeomans from the army, he resigned in favor of Yeomans, who was appointed his successor. During his incumbency of this office Judge Tyler invariably gave his services to soldiers, their wives or widows, without charge. After his resignation of the office of probate judge, he resumed his former position as attorney for the Atlantic & Great Western, removing to Cleveland in 1865. He continued to act as attorney for the road until its foreclosure, and upon the organization of the Cleveland & Tuscarawas Valley railroad, accepted the same position for that road, which he still holds. He has also a large private practice.

Judge Tyler was married in 1847 to Miss Sarah A. McKinney, and has two sons, Charles W., editor of the Sunday Voice, and William W.

AZOR ABELL

is the oldest among the living members of the bar of the county, having been in practice here for nearly fifty years, Judge Newton, of Canfield, being, perhaps, the only lawyer his senior in this part of the State. Mr. Abell is of English descent and was born at Bozrah, London county, Connecticut, January 17, 1794. His father, Jesse Abell, was a farmer, but Azor was not required to do very much farm work. He attended district school and at the age of fourteen began to teach. He continued teaching and studying for several years. In 1822 he removed to Ohio, reaching Canton May 10th. He had already been reading law in Norwich, Connecticut, for some time. After being at Canton eighteen months he was admitted to practice in this State. In the fall of 1823 Mr. Abell removed to New Philadelphia. While at New Philadelphia he was appointed by the county commissioners to fill out an unexpired term of a deceased auditor. He was subsequently elected to the office for two terms. About this time he spent between two and three years on a collecting tour in the South. In the spring of 1834 he removed to Trumbull county, locating in Warren. He has made Warren his home since that date, practicing law, with the exception of a few years spent in mercantile business, until incapacitated by age. In 1838 he formed a partnership with John Crowell, which continued six years. He practiced alone during the rest of the time. "Father Abell," as he is called among the members of the bar, is now eighty-eight years of age. Until very recently he had been in good health, and within the past year argued with all the vigor of youth a case in the common pleas court.

Since the above was written Mr. Abell departed this life. His death occurred in Warren, March 23, 1882.

THOMAS JEFFERSON M'LAIN

was born during Jefferson's administration, October 23, 1801, in Huntingdon county, Pennsylvania. He came to Ohio in 1828; settled in Warren in 1830. He studied law under Judge Fuller and J. M. Edwards, and was admitted to the bar in 1842. Very little of his life has been devoted to the exclusive practice of his profession, and during much of his time he has been actively engaged in other business. From 1830 to 1839 he edited the Warren News Letter. From 1842 to 1845 he was postmaster at Warren. From 1840 to 1876 he was engaged in the banking business. He was also mayor of Warren for several years. In 1845 he became an active member and ardent admirer of the fraternity of Odd Fellows, and during his membership he has been honored with some of the highest positions in the order. From 1852 to 1853 he served as grand patriarch; from 1855 to 1856 he was grand master, and for a series of years was grand representative to the Sovereign Grand lodge of the world. He is also a prominent member of the Masonic order and other kindred organizations, whose tendency is to elevate mankind and bring men into closer relations with the brotherhood of man and the fatherhood of God.

HON. GEORGE MERRILL TUTTLE

was born June 19, 1815, at Torrington, Litchfield county, Connecticut, near the birth-place of John Brown. He is of English descent. His ancestor, William Tuttle, landed in America a few years after the Pilgrims. Common labor upon his father's farm occupied the subject of our sketch until in his sixteenth year. Then mechanical matters began to interest him, and from that time until twenty-one he was a clockmaker. The winter he was twenty years old he taught school. He had studied at home, in the fields, in the clock shop, and at the schools to which he had access. At the age of twenty-one he quit the clock business, and during the following winter he attended school. In the spring of 1837 he commenced his legal studies in the office of William S. Holaviard, district attorney of the United States for the district of Connecticut, and postmaster at Winsted. He read here about eighteen months, clerking in the postoffice at the same time. His health failing, he went home and spent the summer in recuperating. In the fall of 1838 his people removed to Ontario county, New York. Here he taught select and district schools until their removal to Ohio, in the following May. The family settled in Colebrook, Ashtabula county. After working there about a year, he attended school for a few months at Austinburg. He soon after resumed his law studies with Wade & Ranney, of Jefferson.

After reading about ten months he was admitted to the bar September 1, 1841. He began the practice of his profession at Windsor, where he taught select school during the winter of 1842–43. He remained there until January, 1844, when he removed to Warren, where he has since remained. He first formed a partnership with Judge Humphrey, then with Alexander McConnell and William Whittlesey, then with Hon. M. Sutliff, then with J. M. Stull, then with both Sutliff and Stull. In October, 1866, he was elected judge of the court of common pleas. January 1, 1862, six months before the expiration of his term of office, he resigned the judgeship and formed a law partnership with F. E. Hutchins. This partnership continued until January 1, 1882. In 1873 he was one of the most learned and laborious workers in the State constitutional convention.

Judge Tuttle has been from early youth a great lover of books. We have heard him relate an account of a visit, made by him when a boy, to the home of a clergyman of his town. The library of the latter, containing probably two hundred volumes, stood open, and, upon what appeared to him as most magnificent facilities for the acquirement of knowledge, he feasted his famished vision. With access to such a library he would be happy. Books were few with him, but those obtainable were eagerly devoured and thoroughly digested. His early ambition is gratifying itself, and he is now the possessor of probably the largest library of law and miscellaneous books in Trumbull county.

JEFFERSON PALM

was born November 22, 1821, in Cumberland county, Pennsylvania. His parents were Adam and Nancy (Askew) Palm. His father was descended from John Palm, who emigrated from Germany in 1760. Adam Palm settled in Trumbull county in 1822. Jefferson attended the common schools of that day until nineteen years of age, when he commenced the study of law with William L. Knight, of Warren. He finished his studies with John M. Edwards, and was admitted to practice in 1844. During his practice here he has held the office of justice of the peace twelve years. In 1862 he commenced the publication of the Warren Constitution. After editing this paper for five years he sold it to Judge Birchard. Mr. Palm was commissioned postmaster of Warren by President Johnson, holding the office during his administration. Upon the suspension of the savings bank of T. J. McLain & Son, he was made the assignee of its effects, and much of his time since then has been occupied in the settlement of its affairs.

CHARLES ADAMS HARRINGTON

was born June 16, 1824, upon a farm in Greene township, where his parents, William and Helena (Bascom) Harrington, have resided since 1817. Until twenty-one years of age he remained at home, at intervals teaching and attending school. He began to teach when seventeen years old and continued for many winters. He attended Western Reserve seminary at Farmington, Grand River institute at Austinburg, and in 1845 entered Oberlin college. Here he remained until the last term of his junior year. Being unwilling to study Hebrew he left the course which he had intended completing. Soon after this he opened a select school in Greene. This school he continued with good success for about six years. While here he began to study law. In 1846 he commenced to read with Crowell & Abell, of Warren. In 1848 he was admitted to the bar. He continued teaching in Greene, practicing his two professions together. In 1860 he was elected clerk of courts. He held the office two terms. About this time President Johnson had appointed Alexander McConnell assessor of internal revenue for the Nineteenth Congressional district. The Senate refused to confirm his appointment. The President then consented to appoint an assessor upon the recommendation of the Republicans of the district.

A consultation held in some haste among some of the leading Republicans resulted in the choice of Mr. Harrington. He was notified and his consent obtained. The appointment was made and confirmed. In March, 1867, the month following the expiration of his term of office as clerk of courts, he assumed the duties of assessorship. He continued to hold this office until it was abolished in May, 1873. In the following winter he went into the office of W. T. Spear to assist him in the management of his business. Two years later, in 1876, the law firm of Spear & Harrington was formed. This partnership continued until Mr. Spear's elevation to the bench in 1878.

With the exception of a very few years Mr. Harrington has been a valued and faithful member of the board of education of Warren, and much of the time its president, since 1867. He has also held the office of city solicitor in that city. At the organization of the Second National bank of Warren, he was one of the incorporators, and a member of the first board of directors.

HON. ALBERT YEOMANS

is the son of Joshua and Harriet (Cole) Yeomans. He was born at Kinsman, Trumbull county, Ohio, November 14, 1826. The youthful intellect of the future probate judge was cultivated and matured in district school, Kinsman academy, and Grand River institute at Austinburg. In 1845, at the age of nineteen, he went to Warren and commenced the study of the law with General Crowell. He had expected to follow the life of a farmer; but after his return to it he was so frequently called from the field to attend to legal business, that he decided to go to

Warren and make application for admission to the bar. His application was successful, and he immediately engaged in active practice. During the civil war he was a soldier in the Union army for upwards of two years. At the battle of Chickamauga he received a wound from a minie ball, which he carried a year, causing a permanent lameness.

After the war he returned to Trumbull county, and in the fall of 1864 was elected probate judge. His chief claim to public notice was earned by his able conduct of the business of this office during his long administration. From his election, in 1864, he held the office of probate judge continuously until February 9, 1879. Since then he has been engaged in practice in Warren.

FRANCIS EDWIN HUTCHINS

was born in Huntington township, Litchfield county, Connecticut, September 16, 1826. His parents were Myron M. and Mary M. (Porter) Hutchinson. The subject of our sketch, when a young man, upon the suggestion of friends, dropped the last syllable of his family name. When quite young his parents removed to Portage county, Ohio. After a residence of two years in Ohio, they removed to Kalamazoo county, Michigan, settling upon a farm in the backwoods. A hut of rough logs was superseded in a few years by a more pretentious house of hewed logs. Their nearest neighbor was a mile away, and the nearest school house two miles farther, through an almost unbroken forest. Here, in "God's first temples," young Hutchinson passed the days of his youth. He attended school altogether about six months. Much of his time was spent in the manufacture of split shingles, in which he became very expert, and in attendance on an "up and down" saw-mill; hunting raccoon, deer, and bear for diversion. In the fall of 1844 the Hutchinson family removed to Youngstown, Ohio, driving through from Michigan. Young Hutchinson brought with him $45, earned during the previous summer. He learned upon arriving within the pale of civilization that his summer's work had availed him nothing; his barbarous employer had paid him in counterfeit notes. For a short time during the following winter he attended school at Boardman, working nights and mornings to pay expenses. In the summer of 1845 he attended Poland academy, working the garden of the principal for board and tuition.

During the next summer he ran on a canalboat between Youngstown and Cleveland; first as man-of-all-work, and then as captain of the T. S. Morely, owned by John Kirk, of Youngstown. In the winter of 1845-46 he attended school in Youngstown, at the old brick school-house called "Science Hill," Hiram A. Hall, preceptor. Here he studied the principles of the Latin language. An incident will illustrate the proficiency of the class in this department. A member, afterwards a well-known business man in Youngstown, being called upon to translate the sentence, *anima corpore major est*, did so as follows: "The major is a greater animal than the corporal."

During the summer of 1847 Captain Hutchinson ran the canal-boat Abbey Kelly. Upon his birthday, in the fall of 1847, he became an apprentice at the carpenter's trade. He continued a hewer of wood until the spring of 1849, when he began to read law with William Furgeson, Esq., of Youngstown. In company with his fellow student, T. W. Sanderson, he was examined before a committee of twenty-one at Canfield, and admitted to the bar in 1851.

Forming a partnership with Mr. Furgeson, and subsequently with Mr. Sanderson, he practiced in Youngstown until 1859, when he removed to Warren, where he has been located ever since, He has been a partner in the following firms: F. E. & W. H. Hutchins, Hutchins, Ratliff & Forrest, Hutchins & Forrest, Hutchins & Glidden, Hutchins, Glidden & Stull, Hutchins & Tuttle, Hutchins, Tuttle & Stull, and later Hutchins & Tuttle.

During the Rebellion Mr. Hutchins was captain of company A, One Hundred and Seventy first regiment, hundred days' men. He served first at Johnson's island as superintendent of the rebel prison; but was subsequently detailed, by General Heinzelman, as judge advocate of a military commission at Cincinnati. While in service he endured a severe siege of typhoid fever, which has seriously and permanently affected his hearing.

He was married December 11, 1851, to Elizabeth M. Sanderson.

GENERAL ROBERT WILSON RATLIFF

is one of the most prominent of Warren's soldier lawyers. He was born June 30, 1822, in

Howland township, and is the son of John and Elizabeth (Wilson) Ratliff. He worked on the homestead farm, attending district school during the winter until eighteen years of age. The next three or four years were spent in teaching and attending select school. About 1844 he began to read law with H. Canfield in Warren. His law studies proper were concluded in the office of Wade & Ranney. In 1846 he was admitted to the bar. While pursuing his legal studies he taught school during two terms in a school-house located upon a part of the lot now occupied by his residence. After his admission to the bar he was book keeper and teller in the Western Reserve bank for a period of six years. He afterwards formed for a short time a law partnership with Hon. B. F. Hoffman, which lasted until the latter's election to the judgeship. Mr. Ratliff then went into partnership with John Hutchins and J. D. Cox. Two years later, upon the election of Mr. Hutchins to Congress, the firm became, by the accession of W. T. Spear, Cox, Ratliff & Spear. This firm continued in practice here until Mr. Ratliff entered the army. The day after Fort Sumter was fired on he went to Columbus and upon his return assisted in organizing military companies in this county and in Cleveland until August, 1861, when he was made lieutenant-colonel of the Second Ohio cavalry. He accompanied that regiment to Kansas, and made the Indian expedition to the Cherokee nation, assisting in restoring the Union Cherokees to their territory. Early in 1863 he was ordered with his regiment to Columbus, where it was remounted and rearmed, and from there sent into Kentucky, and thence into Tennessee. After the battle of Jackson's Farm Colonel Ratliff resigned and came home, raising the Twelfth Ohio cavalry, of which he was made first lieutenant-colonel October 12, 1863. On the 20th of the November following he was promoted to the colonelcy. With this regiment he served until mustered out. On March 13, 1865, Colonel Ratliff was made brigadier-general "for gallant and meritorious service in the expedition under Generals Burbridge and Stoneman in southwest Virginia." Colonel Ratliff was severely wounded at Duck Creek, Tennessee. In 1867 General Ratliff resumed his law practice in Warren. He was one of the incorporators of the Second National bank of Warren.

JOHN M. STULL

was born in Liberty township, Trumbull county, Ohio, May 16, 1823. His father, James Stull, was of German descent. His mother's maiden name was Catharine McIlree; although born in Scotland, she was of Irish origin. His parents removed from Liberty to Farmington when he was six years old. When he was twelve years old his father died, leaving him to care for and be cared for by his mother. At the age of nineteen he went to learn the blacksmith's trade with Abraham Anxer, of Hamden, Ohio. He worked with Anxer two years and then returning to Farmington opened a shop there. About six months after his return to Farmington, while shoeing a horse by lamplight, he received injuries which disabled him from longer pursuing this occupation. Young Stull had, up to this time, only a very limited education; but, his body disabled, his intellect began to prepare to assert itself. He attended Farmington academy, studying during the summer, and teaching in the South in the winter. While in the South he established at Nashville, Tennessee, a business college. He began his law studies at the age of twenty-seven, with Judge Barbee, of Campbellsville, Kentucky. His studies were continued through the various vicissitudes of a southern schoolmaster's life, until his return to Ohio. He was admitted to the bar of Warren, in May, 1853. The same month he was married to Florilla W. Wolcott, daughter of Deacon Lewis Wolcott, of Farmington. He immediately began the practice of his profession at Warren. He has been associated in partnership with Hon. G. M. Tuttle, Hon. M. Sutliff, F. E. Hutchins, and Hon. C. E. Glidden.

In the fall of 1858 Mr. Stull was elected prosecuting attorney of Trumbull county. He served in that office one term at that time, but four years later was re-elected, holding the office two terms longer. In the spring of 1858 he was elected mayor of Warren. He has ever been one of the most active and influential politicians of this section. During several of the most exciting campaigns in the experience of the party he was chairman of the Republican central committee of his county. For the last ten years he has been an active worker in the Methodist Episcopal church. To him and a few others of similar liberality and activity this denomination is largely indebted for the magnificent church edifice, which is the pride of its congregation in Warren.

HON. LUCIAN CURTIS JONES

has always been a resident of Trumbull county. He was born in Hartford township December 25, 1822. His father, Elam Jones, and his mother, Sarah (Hyde) Jones, were both Connecticut people of Puritan blood. His mother belonged to a family very remarkable for longevity. Of nine children the one dying youngest was upwards of ninety and the oldest one hundred and two. Lucian grew up upon a farm, attending district and select schools, and beginning a classical course under Rev. Wells Andrews. He attended Western Reserve college at Hudson, Ohio, taking an optional course. He attended this college several years but did not graduate. Most of the time he was compelled to support himself, in doing which he learned while there the chair painters' trade. Upon leaving college he studied medicine with Dr. Robert M. Beebe, of Hartford, attending lectures at Columbia Medical college, in Washington, District of Columbia, and reading in the office of the famous Professor Sewal. After taking the degree of M. D. he practiced in Hartford for about eighteen months. The practice of this profession did not please the young man as had the study of its science, and he soon quit it and engaged in mercantile business. The mismanagement of his partner made this business as unsatisfactory as the practice of medicine had been. At the solicitation of John Crowell he commenced the study of law with him. He was admitted to practice in company with H. C. Ranney and M. D. Leggett in 1854.

He practiced law in Hartford until the spring of 1862, when, in company with E. B. Taylor, of Ravenna, he located in Warren. This partnership continued until 1876; soon after its dissolution Judge Taylor went onto the bench. He practiced alone for four years, and in May, 1880, formed a partnership with T. I. Gillmer.

Mr. Jones has held many positions of trust and honor, but none to which he points with more pride than to the office of justice of the peace, to which he was elected just before his twenty-first birthday, attaining his majority before receiving his commission. He was draft commissioner during the war. In the fall of 1871 he was elected to the State Senate, holding the office two terms. Among the important measures originated by Senator Jones are the present mining law of Ohio, drafted and carried through by him; the bill providing for the late revision of the statutes of Ohio, which he succeeded in passing through a Democratic Legislature; and the present law governing the appropriation of private property for public use. On the committees and in the discharge of his other duties he was known as a hard-working legislator.

In politics he is an active Republican, outspoken and independent. He has been the attorney for the Atlantic & Great Western railroad company, and its successor, since its organization. He held the office of registrar in bankruptcy, except while in the Legislature, from 1867 until the repeal of the bankrupt law. He was the first city solicitor of Warren, and in that position was largely instrumental in bringing about the construction of many of the extensive public improvements which are the pride of that city.

Mr. Jones was married in January, 1860, to Sallie C. Stiles, daughter of Henry Stiles, and a member of one of the oldest families in Warren.

RIVERIUS BIDWELL BARNES

was born at Gustavus, October 26, 1827. He is the son of Connecticut parents, Buell and Marietta (Bidwell) Barnes. He was admitted to the bar April 21, 1854, having studied under N. L. Chaffee, of Jefferson, Ohio. Mr. Barnes is located at Gustavus.

ERASTUS HUMPHREY ENSIGN

was born at Simsbury, Connecticut, August 5, 1821. He was of English descent, his parents being Eri and Lucretia (Humphrey) Ensign. "Mack's" early life was devoted to agricultural pursuits and the tinner's trade, which he learned. He attended district school, and during one term the academy at Westfield, Massachusetts. In 1844, his father having died, he removed with his mother to this county. In 1846 he was married to Lucinda Shell, of Newton Falls. In 1853 President Pierce appointed him postmaster at Newton Falls. He continued in charge of this office, conducting in connection with it a drug store, during a period of eight years. His law studies were pursued with D. D. Belden and J. D. Cox. In 1858, at the age of thirty-seven, he was admitted to the bar. He had, however, been practicing in Newton Falls previous to his admission. In 1861 he was elected prosecuting attorney for the county upon the Union ticket. In the spring of 1862 he removed to Warren. In 1863 he was re-elected to the office of prosecuting attorney. During his practice here he has been associated as a partner with Hon. Mr. Birchard and Hon. L. D. Woodworth. While with the former he was for a little more than a year one of the editors of the Warren Constitution.

HOMER NORTON,

one of the oldest members of the Trumbull county bar, has in past years been in charge of a large practice in justice, probate, and common pleas courts. He came into the practice after a long time of service as justice of the peace, and has resided and had his office in Southington. A detailed sketch will be found in the history of that town. As a practitioner Mr. Norton has always been found reliable.

WILLIAM PORTER

was born near Meadville, Crawford county, Pennsylvania, October 10, 1806. During the first twenty years of his life, he worked on his father's farm, attending such schools as the country at that time afforded. From 1826 to 1828 he held a position on the public works of Pennsylvania. From 1828 to 1829 he was employed as bookkeeper for James Hezlep, of Youngstown. In 1829 he removed to Austintown, becoming a partner in the firm of J. Hezlep & Co. in the dry goods business. April 25, 1832, he was commissioned captain of the first company, First regiment of Ohio militia, and on September 19th following he was appointed adjutant of the Fourth regiment, Colonel David Tod commanding. In March, 1833, he removed to Newton township, opening a dry goods store in Milton. In May, 1836, he was elected justice of the peace. To this office he was subsequently several times re-elected. January 21, 1840, he was commissioned associate judge of the court of common pleas for Trumbull county. October 24, 1851, he was appointed postmaster at Milton. In September, 1859, he was admitted to the bar, and has since then been engaged in practice in this and adjacent counties. His present home is in Bristol.

HON. WILLIAM T. SPEAR

was born at Warren, June 3, 1833. He is the son of Edward and Ann (Adgate) Spear. His common education was obtained in the excellent public schools of his native city. He commenced the study of law with J. D. Cox in 1856, and was sworn in as an attorney in 1858. After his admission he spent eighteen months in Cambridge Law school, graduating there. He began the practice of his profession in Warren in 1860, as a partner in the firm of Cox, Ratliff & Spear. Later the firm became Cox & Spear. After his dissolution with Governor Cox he practiced alone until 1876, when he formed a partnership with C. A. Harrington. In September, 1864, he was married to Frances York. In the fall of 1871 he was elected prosecuting attorney of the county. He performed the duties of this office acceptably during two terms. In the fall of 1878 the term of office of Hon. P. B. Conant as judge of the court of common pleas in the Ninth judicial district expired. The subdivision was composed of the counties of Portage, Mahoning, and Trumbull. Portage county presented to the Republican convention for re-nomination Judge Conant. Mahoning county presented several candidates, among them A. J. Van Hyning, A. W. Jones, and Robert E. Knight. Trumbull county brought forward the name of W. T. Spear, and after a persistent effort, prolonged through the day, secured his nomination. He still holds this office, and is regarded as a very accurate and just judge.

WHITTLESEY ADAMS,

a member of the Adams family so well known in this part of the State, is the son of Asahel and Lucy (Mygatt) Adams. He was born at Warren, November 26, 1829. He graduated at Yale college in 1857; was admitted to the bar in 1860 at Springfield. In 1864 he received an appointment as paymaster in the United States army. Although designing to follow the law as a profession he unconsciously drifted into insurance. In this business he has been very successful.

HON. EZRA B. TAYLOR

is of New England stock. His parents, Elisha and Theresa (Couch) Taylor, came from Massachusetts, Berkshire county, settling in Nelson, Portage county, in 1814. Nine years afterwards,

July 9, 1823, Ezra B. was born. His parents were poor, but he attended school during the winter months until seventeen years old, studying a great deal at home. He had early set his heart upon a professional life, and his law studies were begun when quite young. He read law with Judge Robert F. Payne, then of Garrettsville, afterwards of Cleveland, and was admitted to practice in 1845. He immediately began practice, and in 1847 removed to Ravenna and opened an office there. In 1849 he was married to Harriet M. Frazier, of Ravenna. In 1854 he was elected prosecuting attorney of Portage county. He continued to reside in Portage county until the spring of 1862, when he removed to Warren, forming a partnership with L. C. Jones. He has ever since resided in Warren. In 1864 he enlisted as a private in the One Hundred and Seventy-first regiment, Ohio National guards, serving three months. On its return home the regiment elected him colonel. The firm of Taylor & Jones dissolved in 1876.

In 1877, upon the petition of nearly every member of the bar in this sub-division of the judicial district, he was appointed by the Governor to succeed Judge Servis, who had died shortly after his election to the judgeship. At the election held in October of the same year the people continued Judge Taylor in the position to which the Governor had appointed him. Judge Taylor remained upon the bench until the fall of 1880. General Garfield having been called to a higher place, it became necessary to select his successor as Representative of the Nineteenth Congressional district. The Republican convention met in Warren, August 12, 1880. The friends of Judge Taylor took his name into the convention backed by the almost solid delegation from Portage and Trumbull counties. From Ashtabula county came Hon. S. A. Northway and Hon. W. P. Howland with a powerful following. From Geauga county came Hon. Peter Hitchcock, Captain J. B. Burrows, of Lake county, G. H. Ford, of Geauga, and B. A. Hinsdale, of Portage county, were also mentioned in the convention. The contest was an exciting one, and lasted until late in the evening, resulting in the nomination of Judge Taylor. At the election following he was triumphantly elected. In politics he has been since the organization of the party an uncompromising Republican, and his oratorical powers, which at the bar distinguished him as an advocate, have enabled him to do upon the stump signal service for his party.

GEORGE PRESTON HUNTER

was born at Lowellville, now Mahoning county, Ohio, August 31, 1841. His parents removed to Howland, Trumbull county, where he grew up a farmer's boy. It was during these years that the resolution to become a lawyer was formed, and during the years of preparation, as a student and teacher, it was never forgotten. The ups and downs, struggles and privations of a boy determined to rise, with no one to point out the way or render him much assistance, were all beneficially experienced.

From the position of common school teacher, "boarding 'round," he was advanced to the more desirable position of superintendent and principal. He was elected superintendent of schools at Newton Falls, Ohio, for a third year, and at the same time, without consultation with him, principal of the grammar school at Warren. He declined both positions.

A good common school education had been supplemented by a five years' course in Oberlin college. This course was now continued for a year at the University of Rochester.

The study of law was formally entered upon at Albany, New York, in 1864. He was admitted to the New York bar May 26, 1865. The payment of debts accumulated in obtaining an education compelled him to resort once more to teaching. Two years later the practice of law was begun in Warren, November 27, 1867. He served as county school examiner during seven years.

MATTHEW DILLE SANDERSON

was born at Youngstown, Ohio, July 6, 1843. His parents were Matthew Dille and Mary M. Sanderson. He began the study of law in 1861, with Sanderson & Moore, at Youngstown. From 1862 to 1865 he was a soldier in the Union army. He completed his law studies with Hutchins & Glidden, at Warren. He was admitted to the bar in 1867, and the same year began the practice of his profession at Niles.

GEORGE W. SNYDER

was born in Hartford township in the year 1839. His educational advantages were such as the schools of the times afforded. He read law with Hon. L. C. Jones, at Warren, and was admitted to the bar in 1867. He located in Orangeville, in which village he has successfully held the positions of justice of the peace, mayor, and postmaster.

HOMER E. STEWART

is the tallest member of the Trumbull county bar, being six feet two and one-half inches in height. He was born at Coitsville, then Trumbull county, Ohio, May 21, 1845. He graduated at Westminster college in 1867, and began the study of law with Hon. Milton Sutliff, at Warren, the following fall. He afterwards attended Albany Law school, graduating in 1869. In September, 1869, he became a member of the bar of Ohio, and immediately began the practice of his profession. For about nine months he was employed by Judge Sutliff in his office He then formed a partnership with him, which continued until Judge Sutliff's death, April 4, 1878. Since then Mr. Stewart has not been associated with any partner. September 7, 1870, he was married to Kate L. Sutliff, daughter of Calvin G. Sutliff, deceased.

JULIUS N. COWDERY

is the son of William W. and Mary A. Cowdery, of Mecca township, and spent his early life on a farm, attending common school, Cortland academy, Western Reserve seminary, and Western Reserve college, graduating in the latter institution in the class of 1865. In the autumn following he began the study of law with Tuttle & Stull, of Warren. After reading a year he entered the law department of the University of Michigan. He was admitted to practice, at Warren, in April, 1868. In January, 1869, he located in Hubbard, removing to Niles, his present location, in November, 1871. In June, 1873, he was married to Helen Marvin, of Atwater, Ohio.

RICHARD K. HULSE

is the son of Henry K. and Rhoda (Rowley) Hulse. He was born in Bazetta township, Trumbull county, Ohio, February 7, 1829. His father, Henry K. Hulse, came to the county in 1807, raising a family of thirteen children, of whom the second son, John, was the first white child born in Bazetta. At the age of fifteen Richard entered Farmington academy for two years. At about this time he also taught school for several terms. He learned the blacksmith's trade in Warren. In 1847 he went to Kinsman, continuing to work at his trade until 1862. He was married to Hannah Payton, of Chautauqua county, New York July 4, 1850. In 1862 Mr. Hulse enlisted in the One Hundred and Twenty-fifth Ohio volunteer infantry. Among the battles in which he fought were those of Rocky Face Ridge, Resaca, Atlanta, Mission Ridge, and Chickamauga. He served until after the close of the war, being mustered out with the rank of captain at Victoria, Texas, in October, 1865. Returning to civil life, he studied law, and was admitted to the bar in 1869. He has ever since been located in Kinsman.

THOMAS IRWIN GILLMER

is of German-Scotch descent, the son of William and Catherine (Miller) Gillmer. He was born in Newton township, Trumbull county, Ohio, May 13, 1844. His father died when he was eight years of age, leaving him in the care of his mother, who is still living at the advanced age of eighty-two years. At the age of twelve years Thomas took charge of and managed the business of an improved farm of one hundred and sixty acres, in the winter attending district and academic schools. In the spring of 1868 he graduated from Iron City Commercial college at Pittsburg, Pennsylvania, and in May, 1868, began to read law with Hon. John F. Beaver. He was admitted to the bar in May, 1870, and began practice immediately in company with his late preceptor, at Newton Falls, continuing with him until his death. In September, 1873, he was admitted to practice in the United States supreme court. In September, 1874, he located in Warren, and in the fall of 1875 received the Republican nomination for prosecuting attorney. He was elected and took the oath of office January 1, 1876. Mr. Gillmer filled this office during two terms with great success. In May, 1880, he formed a partnership with Hon. L. C. Jones, under the firm name of Jones & Gillmer. He was married to Helen Earl, of Newton Falls, January 26, 1870.

HON. WILBUR ASAHEL REEVES

was born in Freedom, Portage county, Ohio, August 5, 1840. His parents, Rev. Asahel and Lydia (Phelps) Reeves, came from Lewis county,

New York, to a farm in Nelson, Portage county, Ohio, in 1849. From there they removed to Farmington, Trumbull county. Here the subject of this sketch resided until the breaking out of the war. In August, 1861, he enlisted as a private in company D, Second Ohio cavalry. He remained with that company until 1862, when he was detailed with others into the Twenty-fifth Ohio battery, with which command he remained until near the close of the war. Re-enlisting January 1, 1864, for three years he was detailed as drillmaster, and, toward the close of the war, to the command of detachments of heavy artillery and United States infantry, being promoted to the rank of captain. He returned home October 10, 1865. Captain Reeves had previously attended district schools and Western Reserve seminary at Farmington, and he now took a course in Allegheny college, at Meadville, Pennsylvania, graduating in 1869. He commenced the study of law immediately with Hutchins, Glidden & Stull, of Warren, and was admitted to the bar May 4, 1871. After practicing in Canton for three years in partnership with A. D. Braden, he returned to Warren, forming a partnership with John M. Stull, with whom he remained until elected probate judge of Trumbull county in October, 1878. In 1881 Judge Reeves was re-elected.

MARLEN ANDERSON CALHOUN

is the son of Andrew and Mary J. (Anderson) Calhoun. He was born in Edinburg, Portage county, Ohio, January 8, 1849. In the September following, his parents removed to Weathersfield, Trumbull county. Until about seventeen years of age he remained upon his father's farm, obtaining during that time a common school education. He then attended for two years Oberlin college. After spending a few years in the West he returned to Trumbull county and began the study of law October 22, 1869. In April, 1872, he was admitted to the bar and began practicing in Niles. Up to the time of his admission to the bar Mr. Calhoun had been a follower of several trades. He was an exceedingly expert broom-maker, and of the masons' and carpenters' trade had learned enough to be able to build his own law office. February 19, 1874, he was married to Matt I. Tucker, of Silver Creek, New York. While in practice in Niles he held the office of solicitor during two terms. In April, 1880, Mr. Calhoun moved to Warren.

WASHINGTON HYDE

is the son of Julius E. and Ann (Oatley) Hyde. He was born at Farmington May 7, 1847. By a great personal effort he was enabled to attend school at Farmington, during part of his course officiating as bell-ringer boy. He graduated in 1867. Afterwards he attended Michigan university at Ann Arbor, taking the degree of Ph. B. in 1870; spent two terms in the law department of the same institution, graduating in 1872. During the summer months he had been in the office of Palmer & DeWolf, Cleveland. He was admitted to the bar of this State at Ashland July 5, 1872, and immediately, in Warren. In the fall of 1879, after a lively contest, he obtained the nomination for the office of prosecuting attorney. He was elected, served two years, and in October, 1881, re-elected for a term of three years. He is a faithful political worker on the side of his convictions, and has served during several campaigns as secretary of the Republican county central committee.

SAMUEL BAXTER CRAIG

came from Irish stock; his parents were Samuel and Margaret (Darling) Craig. Samuel, Jr., was born in Braceville township October 2, 1844. He attended school in Warren and in Farmington, and subsequently, by his own labors, earned means enabling him to take a course in Allegheny college at Meadville, Pennsylvania. He graduated there in 1871, and began the study of law the same year in the office of Hutchins, Glidden & Stull; was admitted to the bar in April, 1873, and opened an office in Warren the following August. He was married to Mary E. Forbes October 14, 1874.

DIO ROGERS

is the son of James and Elizabeth D. (Jaureson) Rogers; he was born at East Palestine, Columbiana county, Ohio, April 24, 1850. His common school education was confined to the English branches. He taught school during three years at his native village. He read law with Rogers & Rogers, his brothers, and was admitted to practice in April, 1874. In the summer of 1874 he opened an office in Hubbard, where he has ever since remained.

WILLIAM R. MORAN

is the son of Francis and Bidnigh E. (Taylor) Moran, and was born in Leitrim county, Ireland, July 11, 1846. He emigrated to America with his parents in 1852, locating in Trumbull county. By his own efforts Mr. Moran secured a good education, afterwards spending some time in teaching. In 1870 he began the study of law, and in 1872 entered the office of Hutchins, Tuttle & Stull. He was admitted to practice September 28, 1874, locating in Vernon. He has once or twice been a candidate before the Republican convention for the nomination for prosecuting attorney.

LAFAYETTE HUNTER

was born in Howland township, Trumbull county, Ohio, June 28, 1846. He remained upon a farm, attending district school, a school at Newton Falls, and the McNealey Normal at Hopedale, Ohio, until 1872. He then went to commercial college at Cleveland. In September, 1873, he entered Albany Law school, where he graduated May 5, 1874. He was admitted to practice in Ohio September 28, 1874, and soon after located in Warren.

WILLIAM I. METCALF

was born in Yorkshire, England, September 4, 1844. When he was ten years of age his parents emigrated to America, settling in Grand county, Wisconsin. William continued on his father's farm, having, from the time he was fourteen years old, entire charge of it for three years, up to the spring of 1863. He then started out in the world to seek his fortune; landing in the oil regions of Pennsylvania when the oil excitement ran high. Good wages being obtainable, he was soon able to save considerable money. In September, 1864, he was married to the youngest daughter of S. P. McFadden, Esq., of Liberty, Trumbull county, Ohio. In the winter of 1864-65 he gratified an early ambition to become a book-keeper, and took a course in Duff's commercial college. As a book-keeper he occupied several responsible positions. He was appointed assignee in bankruptcy of the large estate of Jonathan Warner, of Mineral Ridge, discharging the duties of the trust acceptably and well. In 1871 he decided to study law. He pursued his studies under the direction of General T. W. Sanderson, and was admitted to practice September 13, 1875, locating in Mineral Ridge.

MERRICK JOHN SLOAN

was born September 23, 1844, in Greene township. His parents were Isaac and Martha C. (Cooley) Sloan. His early life was passed in the usual juvenile employments of a farmer's boy. Leaving the farm in June, 1863, he enlisted in the Union army, serving under two enlistments until the close of the war; he was finally discharged in July, 1865. The greater part of his education was obtained subsequently at schools in Greene, at the Normal at Orwell, and at Oberlin college. He was at Oberlin, earning his own way, about three years. His law studies had been begun before going to Oberlin. From 1866 until 1871 he was compelled to spend much of his time in teaching. In April, 1871, he married Stella S. Fisk, of Oberlin. His office reading was done in the office of John C. Hale, of Elyria. He was admitted to the bar in 1874. In the following year he located in Niles, remaining there until 1880, when he removed to Warren.

A. A. DROWN,

son of Calvin and Jennett (Baxter) Drown, was born in Nelson, Portage county, Ohio, August 13, 1850. He attended public schools and Hiram college. He read law with Taylor & Jones; was admitted to the bar August 20, 1875. September 7, 1875, he was married to Luella V. Tait, of West Farmington. She died of consumption March 15, 1879.

DAVID REVILLA GILBERT

was born October 22, 1846, in Vernon township. When ten years of age his parents removed to Gustavus. His father was a cabinet-maker; and this trade the young man learned. He attended district schools, and afterwards Oberlin college. He came to Warren in 1871, and began the study of law, reading in the office of Taylor & Jones. He was admitted to practice by the district court at Canfield, September 29, 1873. He opened an office in Warren in the spring of 1875. In the fall of 1880 he entered into partnership with Hon. E. B. Taylor, with whom he still continues to be associated.

CHARLES BOSTWICK NEWTON

was born April 11, 1851, in Tallmadge, Summit county, Ohio. He attended the public schools of Kent, and for two years studied in private under the instruction of Professor F. T. Suloit. He began the study of law with Simon P. Wolcott, of Kent, and qualified as an attorney April 1, 1874. Mr. Newton then read for a year with W. B. Thomas, of Ravenna, locating in Newton Falls, May 18, 1875.

EDWIN DOUD KENNEDY

is a descendant of the old Kennedy family, whose record can be traced back one hundred and fifty years. His parents were Maxwell and Eveline (Doud) Kennedy. He was born in Howland township, November 15, 1850. He attended district school, Courtland academy, Western Reserve seminary, and Hiram college. At the age of sixteen he began teaching. In 1873 he began his law studies with Ratliff & Moses in Warren. He was admitted to the bar September 13, 1875, and opened an office in Warren in the following spring. Mr. Kennedy is somewhat famous as a speller, an ability in this direction being hereditary in the family.

ALBERT FREEMAN MOORE

was born in Mahoning county October 2, 1856. He attended public schools, studied under a private tutor, and subsequently attended Oberlin college. His law studies were begun with Judge Birchard in 1874, during a college vacation. Later he read with J. M. Stull and with Hutchins & Tuttle, being admitted to the bar April 13, 1877. He was married the same year to Susie Robinson. He has been in practice here since 1877, two years of the time in partnership with E. H. Ensign. In 1877 he was a candidate for the office of prosecuting attorney on the Democratic ticket. During the famous controversy concerning water works in Warren he was a candidate for city solicitor, running one hundred votes ahead of his ticket.

THOMAS H. GILLMER

was born in Newton township July 15, 1849. His parents were James and Jane (McKibben) Gillmer. Mr. Gillmer attended district school, Newton Falls high school, and the National Normal at Lebanon. During the fall and winter, from 1870 to 1878, he taught school. His law studies began in 1876, with General R. W. Ratliff and T. J. Gillmer. He was admitted to practice April 9, 1878, and opened an office in Newton Falls the same month.

JOHN WARREN TAYLOR

was born in Mecca township, November 10, 1851, and is the son of William and Mary A. (Moran) Taylor. His mother died when he was two years of age, and to his step-mother, Roxa A. (Rhodes) Taylor he is indebted for the greater part of his early education. Young Taylor attended Western Reserve seminary, that educator of so many Trumbull county lawyers, a little more than a year. In 1875 he commenced to read law, clerking in a store and reading whenever an opportunity offered. About six months of his student life were spent in an office with Hon. L. C. Jones and D. R. Gilbert. He was admitted to practice at Warren April 13, 1877. He then took a course in Ann Arbor Law school, graduating there March 27, 1878. He opened an office in this city a few weeks later. He was elected justice of the peace September 15, 1878, holding the office three years.

FRANK DAVID M'LAIN,

the son of General T. J. and Harriet (Doughton) McLain, was born in Warren September 12, 1854. He completed a course in the public schools of Warren, graduating in 1873, subsequently attending Western Reserve college at Hudson. He read law with Spear & Harrington, and was licensed to practice in 1878, locating in Warren.

ROBERT T. IZANT

was born at Great Elm, Somersetshire, England, March 18, 1855. His parents emigrated to America, arriving in Warren in the spring of 1872. In the September following he became a clerk in the office of John M. Stull. He afterwards studied law in the same office, and was admitted to the bar April 8, 1878. He still continues in the employ of Mr. Stull.

JOHN LAFAYETTE HERZOG

was born February 9, 1857, in Warren, Ohio. His parents are William H. Herzog and Lucia Heiner. His studies were pursued under Sutliff & Stewart. April 9, 1878, he was admitted to practice, locating in Warren. In October, 1881, he was elected justice of the peace.

SERVETUS A. CORRELL,

son of Martin and Maria (Weaver) Correll, was born in Newton July 17, 1849. His early educational advantages were not the best. Later he attended Hiram college, Alliance college, and the National Normal at Lebanon, graduating at the latter place. His law studies commenced at home. He afterwards read with C. B. Newton and E. B. Taylor. He was sworn in at Cleveland September 10, 1877, opening an office in Warren in the spring of 1878.

JOSEPH WILBER GILSON,

son of Robert M. and Sarah Hannah (Gilson) Gilson, was born at New Derry, Westmoreland county, Pennsylvania, September 20, 1851. His mother died when he was quite young. He attended district school, and at the age of seventeen went to an academy at Elders Ridge, Pennsylvania. Here he prepared for college. After teaching two years he entered the University of Wooster, graduating in 1873. Within a year he began to read law at Canfield, reading afterwards in the office of Hutchins & Tuttle, at Warren. He attended Albany Law school, graduating in 1877. He was admitted to practice in this State early in 1878, and April 11, 1878, located in Warren. In June, 1879, he formed a partnership with A. A. Thayer.

JAMES F. WILSON

is of Irish-German descent. He was born April 30, 1843, the son of James and Nancy (Welty) Wilson, the former said to have been the first male child born in Youngstown, Ohio. James, Sr., was one of the first settlers in Warren township, and having cleared a farm in a wilderness of woods, reared there a family of ten children, of whom James F. is the fourth son. The subject of this sketch lived on the farm until eighteen years old, attending district schools in the winter season. In 1861 he enlisted in company C, Nineteenth regiment, Ohio volunteers, for three years. This regiment was commanded by Colonel H. G. Stratton. Mr. Wilson afterwards re-enlisted as a veteran, and was finally discharged in October, 1865. He spent the next few years attending school and teaching alternately. In 1871 he graduated from Allegheny college, subsequently he was superintendent of public schools in Chagrin Falls three years and in Ashtabula four years. He was admitted to the bar at Jefferson in March, 1878, and in the August following located in Warren, for which city he is now solicitor. December 18, 1872, he was married to Hattie R. Larned, of Chagrin Falls.

ALBERT ANSON THAYER

was born at Freedom, Portage county, Ohio, February 12, 1850. His parents were Charles A. and Mary (Nisetter) Thayer. His law studies were begun with H. C. Ranney, of Ravenna, in 1868. He afterwards read in the office of F. R. E. Cornell, attorney-general of Minnesota. After reading here a year and a half he was admitted to practice in Minnesota in 1871. In the following year he was admitted to the bar of this State, after being admitted and practicing in a number of the southern States. Mr. Thayer located in Warren in the fall of 1878. Shortly afterwards he associated himself with J. W. Gilson. The firm of Thayer & Gilson subsequently united with General R. W. Ratliff under the firm name of Ratliff, Thayer & Gilson. Mr. Thayer was married in September, 1881, to Miss Lizzie B. Williamson, of Youngstown.

WILLIAM THOMAS FEE

is the son of Dr. William M. and Mary M. (Barnheizel) Fee. He was born at Niles, May 6, 1854. Five years later his parents removed to Franklin, Pennsylvania. He attended the State Normal school at Edinboro one year, Oberlin college four terms, and subsequently Lafayette college, where he graduated in 1876. He then went to Germany, attending, during two years at Goetingen. He returned home in 1878, and began the study of law at Lancaster, Pennsylvania, under M. Brosius, concluding his studies in Niles. He was admitted at Warren April 3, 1879, locating in Niles in the following July; he was elected solicitor there. In the spring of 1880 he located in Warren.

JOHN EVERTON PICKERING,

the son of Barzilla and Eliza Pickering, was born in Worcestershire, England, March 4, 1852. He came to America with his parents in 1865, settling in Trumbull county; attended Western Reserve seminary six years, graduating in 1876. He commenced to read law in his senior year, reading under the tutorship of Judge Tuttle and Washington Hyde. He was admitted to practice at Cleveland, and subsequently opened an office in Trumbull county in October, 1879.

CHARLES H. STROCK

was born in Newton township November 10, 1849. His parents, Gideon and Sarah Strock, separated in 1865, and Charles started out in life for himself. He worked at farming and lumbering until 1870, when he began to teach. He attended normal schools at Lebanon and at Medina, and continued teaching. In 1878 he entered the law office of T. H. Gillmer at Newton Falls. In the following spring he entered the office of Jones & Gillmer, at Warren. He was admitted to practice May 5, 1880, opened an office at Niles August 1, 1880, and was elected solicitor of Niles the following spring.

CHARLES SMITH FREER,

the son of Josiah D. and Caroline P. Freer, was born at Courtland, August 18, 1848. He graduated from Warren union schools in 1867; read law with General R. W. Ratcliff; was admitted to the bar August 29, 1869; practiced one year in Licking county as a member of the firm of Dennis & Freer; left practice to engage in other business in Niles in 1870, and resumed practice in 1881 in Warren. He has served six years in the Ohio National guard, and is now captain of the Second battery of artillery.

MARSHALL WOODFORD

was born in Hartford township, March 15, 1847, and was the son of Almon O. and Nancy J. (Parsons) Woodford. He took the degree of bachelor of arts at Oberlin college in 1872. Until 1876 he was superintendent of public schools at Van Wert, Ohio. He commenced to read law in 1875, spending a year of his studentship in the office of Hon. L. C. Jones; he was admitted in 1877. From 1877 until 1881 he was principal of the Warren high schools. He began the practice of law in Warren in September, 1881. During the war Mr. Woodford served as an hundred days' man in the Fortieth Wisconsin.

DAVID JAMESON

was born July 24, 1856, in Bazetta township. His parents were B. P. and Sarah A. (Blair) Jameson. He attended Allegheny college, and the University of Victoria college at Cobourg, Ontario. He studied law under Hutchins & Tuttle at Warren, and was admitted to the bar March 1, 1880.

EDWARD MYERS,

son of Dr. E. and Mary Rabhalld Myers, born at Newcastle, Pennsylvania, December 27, 1855, read law with W. A. Reeves and J. W. Taylor. He was admitted October 4, 1881, and opened an office here immediately.

CHAPTER XVIII.
MAHONING COUNTY BAR.[*]

Among the early settlers of the southeastern part of the Western Reserve, now Trumbull and Mahoning counties, were five young lawyers from the State of Connecticut, who gained distinction in their profession and became prominent and honored citizens of Ohio. They were John S. Edwards, who came in 1799 from New Haven; George Tod and Calvin Pease, in 1800, from Suffield; Homer Hine, in 1801, from New Milford, and Elisha Whittlesey, in 1806, from Danbury.

Mr. Edwards became a resident of Warren, was the first recorder of Trumbull county, and was elected a member of Congress and died in 1813 before taking his seat. The others became residents of (the present) Mahoning county. Mr. Pease came to Youngstown in 1800, was its first postmaster in 1802, resided there for about three years, removed to Warren and died there in 1839, aged sixty-three years. Mr. Tod came to Youngstown, made it his permanent home, and died there in 1841, aged sixty-seven years. Mr. Hine came to Canfield, removed to Youngstown in 1806, resided there until his death in July, 1856, aged eighty years. Mr. Whittlesey came to Canfield in 1806, resided there until his death in January, 1863, aged nearly eighty years. Another young lawyer, Samuel Huntington, afterwards the third Governor of Ohio elected by the people, came from Norwich, Connecticut, to Youngstown in 1800, remained there a few months, and after visiting other parts of the State removed his family in 1801 from Connecticut to Youngstown, resided there some time and then removed to Cleveland, where he resided until 1809, when he removed to Painesville, where he died in 1817, aged fifty-two years.

ORGANIZATION OF COUNTY AND FIRST COURT.

The county of Mahoning was organized in 1840, with the county seat at Canfield. The first regular term of the common pleas court was held in the Methodist Episcopal church, in Canfield, on May 11th of that year. Eben Newton, of Canfield, was president judge, and James Wallace, of Springfield, James Brownlee, of Poland, and Lemuel Bingham, of Ellsworth, were associates. James Powers, of Milton, was sheriff,

[*] By John M. Edwards, Esq.

and William Ferguson, of Youngstown, prosecuting attorney. Henry Canfield, of Canfield, who had been appointed clerk *pro tem.* at a prior special court, held by the associates, was clerk. On the last day of the term, William W. Whittlesey, of Canfield, was elected clerk for five years, and gave bond in the sum of $10,000.

There were nineteen cases on the docket when it was called on the opening of the court. The term continued three days, and upon the adjournment of court there were thirty-seven cases on the docket. No case was tried to a jury; one judgment was rendered on confession. Partition of real estate was ordered in one case, and, on petition of a guardian in another, real estate was ordered to be sold. Eight wills were proved, and the executors therein named received letters testamentary. Administrators were appointed on eleven estates, and eight guardians of minors were appointed. By request of the sheriff, Ransford Percival and John C. Fitch were appointed his deputies. The court appointed John M. Edwards, Robert W. Tayler, and James B. Blocksom master commissioners in chancery; Hiram A. Hall, John M. Edwards, and Reuben McMillen school examiners, and John Kirk and Andrew Gardiner auctioneers.

This first term of court in the new county was attended not only by the lawyers of the county, but by citizens from all parts of the county, and lawyers and others from neighboring counties; and during the three days of the term the town presented an appearance of great bustle and business activity. The terms of court following were held in that church until the fall term of 1847, which was held in the court-house erected by the citizens of Canfield and then ready for occupancy.

In August, 1876, the county-seat was removed to Youngstown, a full account of which is given in chapter XI.

FIRST COURT AFTER REMOVAL.

The first term after the removal of the court of common pleas was held in the new court-house at Youngstown. It commenced September 10th, and adjourned December 19, 1876. Hon. Philip B. Conant, of Ravenna, was judge; Henry B. Shields, clerk; John R. Davis, sheriff, and Charles R. Truesdale, prosecuting attorney. The number of civil cases on the docket, when court opened, were six hundred and seventy-four, criminal cases forty-eight, total seven hundred and twenty-two. At the close of the term, including those disposed of, the number of civil cases was nine hundred and fifty-three, criminal cases one hundred and thirty-five, total one thousand and eighty-eight. The total number of civil cases commenced since the organization of the county, at the opening of the September term, 1881, was twelve thousand and twenty.

GEORGE TOD,

the pioneer lawyer of Youngstown, and one of the earliest lawyers of the Reserve, was born in Suffield, Connecticut, December 11, 1773. He was a son of David and Rachel (Kent) Tod. He graduated at Yale college in 1795. Subsequently he taught school at New Haven, Connecticut; read law at the law school of Judge Reeves, in Litchfield, Connecticut, and was admitted to the bar. He was married at New Haven in October, 1797, to Miss Sally Isaacs, who was born January 12, 1778, and was a daughter of Ralph and Mary Isaacs. Their two oldest children, Charlotte L. and Jonathan I. Tod, were there born. In 1800 he came to Youngstown, Ohio; returned to Connecticut, and in 1801 he removed with his wife and children to Youngstown.

At the first territorial court of Trumbull county, held in August, 1800, he was appointed prosecuting attorney. The following is a copy of the record of the court journal: "The court appointed George Tod, Esq., to prosecute the pleas of the United States the present session, who took the oath of office."

At that term of the court the grand jury returned a bill of indictment for murder against Joseph McMahon, for shooting Captain George, an Indian, at the Salt springs, on the 20th of July preceding, and he was tried at a special court held at Youngstown in September following, Mr. Tod appearing in behalf of the United States as prosecuting attorney.

During the first year of his residence in Ohio he was appointed, by Governor St. Clair, Territorial secretary.

In April, 1802, at the first township election held at Youngstown, upon the admission of Ohio as a State into the Union, he was elected township clerk, and re-elected in 1803 and 1804. In 1804–05 he was Senator from Trumbull county in the State Legislature, and again in 1810–11. In 1806 he was elected a judge of the supreme court of the State. In the War of 1812 he was commissioned major and afterwards colonel of the Nineteenth regiment of Ohio militia, and served with distinction at Fort Meigs and Sackett's Harbor. In 1815 he was elected president judge of the court of common pleas of the old third circuit, which then comprised a large part of the counties of the Reserve, and held the office until 1829. He was elected prosecuting attorney of Trumbull county in 183— and held the office for one term.

After leaving the bench, except when attending to his duties as prosecutor, he retired in a measure from practice and devoted his attention to the care of his large farm, at Brier Hill, in the north part of the township of Youngstown; the farm which afterwards became so celebrated for its deposit of fine mineral coal, developed by his son, the late Governor David Tod.

He died at Brier Hill April 11, 1841. As a lawyer and a judge he ranked among the first in the State of Ohio; as a citizen he was held in the highest regard. His estimable wife survived him a few years, and died at Brier Hill September 29, 1847.

SAMUEL HUNTINGTON

was born in Norwich, Connecticut, in 1765. He graduated at Yale college in 1785. He read law, was admitted to the bar, and practiced law several years in his native town. In 1800, at the instance of owners of land on the Reserve, he visited Ohio, reaching Youngstown the 25th of July, making the journey on horseback. He visited different portions of the Reserve east of the Cuyahoga river, and was so well pleased with the country that he determined to settle there. He also visited Marietta, Ohio, the official residence of Governor St. Clair, and the Territorial court being in session he was admitted to the bar of Ohio. He was present, as tradition says, with Governor St. Clair at the trial, in September, 1800, in Youngstown, of Joseph McMahon, for shooting Captain George, an Indian, at the Salt Springs, as counsel, but on which side, or as advisory counsel with Governor St. Clair, it does not relate. He returned to Norwich on horseback in the fall. Early in the following spring he returned to Youngstown with his wife, who was a daughter of Andrew Huntington, of Norwich, to whom he was married about 1793, and his young family, in a covered wagon. He remained a year or more in Youngstown, and then removed to Cleveland, Ohio. During his residence in Youngstown in 1801, he was appointed by Governor St. Clair lieutenant-colonel of the Trumbull county militia, and on January 19, 1802, was commissioned a justice of the court of quarter sessions, of which, at the request of the other judges, he became the presiding officer. In 1802 he was elected a member from Trumbull county of the convention which formed the first constitution of Ohio, and on the adoption of the constitution he was elected Senator from Trumbull county, in the first General Assembly, which convened in Chillicothe, in March, 1803. On April 2, 1804, he was elected by the Legislature a judge of the supreme court, then newly formed, his commission, signed by Governor Tiffin, being the first issued in the name of the State of Ohio. He was elected Governor in 1808, and served one term of two years, when he retired to his farm near Painesville, which he had purchased in 1807. He was Representative from Geauga county in the State Legislature in 1811-12. He was appointed district paymaster with the rank of colonel in 1812, and remained two years with the Northwestern army, after which he returned to his farm. He died of consumption at Painesville in February, 1817. A biographer says: "His business capacity was of a high order, as was shown by his executing so well the duties of many responsible offices. He bore the reputation of being a man of spotless character."

CALVIN PEASE

was born in Suffield, Hartford county, Connecticut, September 9, 1776. He was admitted to the bar in Hartford in 1798; practiced law in Connecticut until March, 1800, when he removed to Youngstown, Ohio, and commenced practice. He was appointed postmaster of Youngstown January 1, 1802; was the first postmaster of that place, and held the office until his removal to Warren in 1803. He was also, in 1802, elected township trustee of Youngstown. He was appointed clerk of the court of common pleas of Trumbull county, at its first session in August, 1800, and held the office for a few years. He was subsequently elected judge of the common pleas and of the supreme court, and Representative and Senator in the Ohio Legislature. In 1804 he was married to Miss Risley, of Washington city. He died at Warren, Ohio, September 17, 1839. A more full biographical notice will be found in the history of the bar of Trumbull county.

PERLEE BRUSH

was a pioneer lawyer of the Reserve, and a man of considerable note in the early days, yet authentic and definite information as to his early history appears in a great measure wanting. He was born in Connecticut, graduated at Yale college in 1793, read law in Connecticut, and was there admitted to the bar. He removed to Ohio at an early day, was a member of Trumbull county bar, resided for many years at or near Youngstown, and afterwards in Hubbard, Trumbull county. We learn, by tradition, that he taught a school at the center of Youngstown prior to 1805, and it is said that he was the pioneer school teacher of Youngstown. There are persons now living in Youngstown, or who were born there, who were his pupils in a log school house in the southern part of the township as early as about 1814. They remember that in addition to his duties as a teacher, he practiced law in justices' courts in the vicinity, and also to some extent in the higher courts at Warren.

In 1826 he purchased a farm of about one hundred acres of land in Hubbard, on which he afterwards resided. A gentleman of that place thus writes concerning him:

A small stream, called Yankee Run, flowed through his land, on which there was an old-fashioned carding machine and fulling mill, which he operated for about a year, and then turned his attention to his farm. He lived exclusively by himself and boarded himself until his health began to fail when he went to board with a neighbor, still lodging at home. He was a fine scholar; could talk, read, and write the Greek, Latin, and Hebrew languages as well as he could English, and it was said he was well versed in the principles of law. He died in 1852, aged about eighty-four years.

HOMER HINE

was born in New Milford, Connecticut, July 25, 1776. His great-grandfather, who was among the early settlers of Milford, in New Haven county, Connecticut, is said to have emigrated from Ireland, and the family were supposed to have settled in Ireland during the time of Cromwell, from Scotland or England, and were of the class known as Scotch-Irish. His grandfather, James Hine, was born in Milford in 1696, removed in early manhood to New Milford, among the first settlers of that place, and there married Margaret Noble, who was carried there when quite a child, and was the first white female that set foot in that place. James Hine was a respectable farmer, lived to the age of seventy-eight years, and died in 1774, leaving two sons, Austin and Noble, and several daughters. Noble was a fore-handed farmer, and, during the Revolutionary war, was a colonel of the Connecticut militia. He died in 1795, leaving three sons, one of whom was Homer, the subject of this sketch, and six daughters, the youngest of whom, Sophia, was afterwards the wife of Rev. Charles A. Boardman, a clergyman of eminence, and for many years pastor of the First Presbyterian church of Youngstown, Ohio.

Homer Hine, after a preparatory course in the schools of New Milford, entered Yale college, and graduated in 1797 in a class of thirty-seven. Among his class-mates were Horatio Seymour, United States Senator from Vermont; Henry Baldwin, judge of United States Supreme court; Rev. Dr. Lyman Beecher, and many others of prominence. The first year after his graduation he spent pleasantly at Stockbridge, Massachusetts, as preceptor of an academy. Miss Catharine Sedgwick, a celebrated authoress, was one of his pupils. He read law during that year with Judge Sedgwick, her father. The next year he read law with P. Ruggles in New Milford, and during the year 1800 he attended the law school of Judges Reeve and Gould at Litchfield, Connecticut. He was admitted to the bar in Litchfield in 1801.

In June, 1801, he removed to Canfield, Ohio. The journey was made on horseback over the mountains and through Pittsburg, carrying his wardrobe in his saddlebags. His small library of law books were brought in an ox-wagon which was bringing out the household goods of Benjamin Tappan, who, with his wife and sister-in-law, Miss Wright, were moving from New England to locate a new home in Ravenna, Ohio.

The whole Reserve then formed one county, and contained six or eight hundred inhabitants. In view of its wonderful growth in population and improvement otherwise, in 1848 Mr. Hine, writing to an old classmate, Rev. Dr. James Murdock, says:

I feel constrained to bear testimony to the beneficial effects of home missionary labor in the new settlements. At first it was the general custom for the settlers to spend the Sabbath in hunting, or to come together for a drinking frolick and engage in all kinds of sport. Even those who had left New England as professors of religion seemed so far carried away by the influence of example as to conclude that the Sabbath was not binding in the wilderness." The missionaries immediately commenced forming churches in the principal settlements and persuaded the people to assemble on the Sabbath and perform public worship by singing, prayer, and reading printed sermons. This, together with occasional visits from the missionaries, soon produced a radical change in the inhabitants for good, both in a religious and moral point of view. The few hundred dollars expended on the Reserve for missionary services has profited the country to the amount of millions. But the real benefit is not to be measured in dollars and cents.

In 1806 Mr. Hine removed to Youngstown, where he continued to reside until his death, in July, 1856, aged eighty years. He commenced the practice of law on his first arrival on the Reserve and continued it with good success until the age of sixty. He then declined to engage in new cases, but attended the courts for about three years in order to dispose of the cases in which he was engaged. Terms of court, in those early days, were more matters of general interest than now. The members of the bar followed the circuit on horseback over roads that were merely underbrushed and marked by blazed trees through the unbroken forests, fording rivers and streams, and giving chase occasionally to a bear or wolf, enjoying with cheerful zest the adventures of rough roads and rude fare, the latter often composed of wild game from the forests.

The courts were frequently held under trees, or in barns, or in other rude buildings. The lawyers, sometimes with the judges, lodged in the hay-mow of a barn. Then with such companions as Judges Tappan, Pease, Tod, and others, and often the free circulation of a whisky decanter, they had lively, or jolly times.

Mr. Hine was not naturally fond of litigation and, where it was practicable, advised his clients to settle, compromise, or arbitrate. This trait of character, which many of the legal profession might regard as a weakness, was frequently of service to him when trying cases. Many jurymen and justices of the peace, when cases were on trial before them, gave more than ordinary weight to his arguments and summing up of evidence from having faith in his disposition to be just and fair in the settlement and preventing of suits at law, believing that he would be fair in his statements on the trial.

He was four times elected to the office of Representative in the Ohio Legislature—in 1804, 1805, 1816, 1824. He held the office of non-resident tax collector for five years, until the office was abolished, about 1812. He was a soldier in the War of 1812, under Colonel William Rayen. In 1805 he was appointed, by the Legislature, a commissioner to lay out a State road from Warren to such point on Lake Erie as, in his judgment, would make the most feasible route from Pittsburg to Lake Erie. After examining the different routes, ending between Cleveland and Conneaut, he selected a route with the terminus at the mouth of Grand river, in Painesville township, Lake county, regarding that as the easiest on which to construct a road, and the river at Fairport, at that time, as affording the best natural harbor, on that part of Lake Erie.

He was always a regular attendant at the meetings of the Presbyterian church, and, in the absence of a clergyman, the duty of reading a printed sermon usually devolved on him. He was a fine reader, and he probably read more sermons to that congregation than any single clergyman ever preached to it. He was always interested in all useful reforms, and was one of the earliest workers in the temperance reform, and from its start and for many years was president of the Youngstown Temperance society. He was open and generous in his hospitality, especially to clergymen, so much so that among them his house was known as "The Minister's Tavern."

On removing to Youngstown in 1806, he purchased a frame house and two acres of land, east of the Diamond, of Robert Kyle. This was, probably, the third frame dwelling then in the present city. It is still standing, and occupied, although removed to another site. On October 5, 1807, he was married to Miss Mary Skinner, daughter of Abraham Skinner, of Painesville, Ohio, an emigrant in 1801 or 1802 from Connecticut, where she was born in Glastonbury, in Hartford county, September 20, 1789. In May, 1808, they began housekeeping in that house, and there resided until 1818, when he purchased a farm of one hundred and ten acres at the mouth of and on the east side of Crab creek, on which was a house large for those times, into which they removed. It was a two-story frame dwelling, built by Colonel James Hillman, and had been occupied by him as a tavern. It had a double front, one to the south overlooking a long reach of the Mahoning river, the other to the westward, looking through the entire length of Federal street and of the village, as it then was, to the residence of Colonel Rayen at Spring Common. It was then, and still is one of the land marks of Youngstown, and few who have traveled through that city towards Pittsburg, will fail to recollect its position and peculiar appearance. It is now surrounded by railroad tracks, and has been sold to a railroad company, and is occupied by it.

Mrs. Hine, after the death of her husband in 1856, resided in that old homestead until 1872, when she removed to Painesville, where she resides with a son. She is now (1881) in her ninety-third year, and although feeble physically is in full possession of all her mental faculties and senses, enjoys seeing her relatives and old friends, enjoys conversing about old times, takes a lively interest in the welfare of her children and descendants, as well as in politics and the progress and prosperity of her country, and is calmly and peacefully passing the evening of her days with the happy satisfaction of looking, in retrospect, on a well-spent and useful life.

ELISHA WHITTLESEY

was born in Washington, Litchfield county, Connecticut, October 19, 1783. He was the son of John and Molly Whittlesey. His father was a descendant of John Whittlesey, who emigrated from England to Saybrook, Connecticut, about 1630. In his youth he labored on the farm, attending school in the winters. One of his instructors was Rev. Jeremiah Day, afterwards president of Yale college. In 1792, his father having sold his farm in Washington and purchased one in Salisbury, Connecticut, the family removed to that place. In the fall of 1798 he attended school in Danbury, Connecticut, residing with his brother, Matthew B. Whittlesey, a lawyer of that place, returning in the spring to his father's farm to work, and in years following attended school in Danbury, alternating with farm work at home.

In 1803 he commenced the study of law with his brother, and was admitted to the bar at Fairfield, Connecticut, at the March term, 1805. He commenced practice in New Milford, Connecticut. On January 5, 1806, he was married in Danbury to Miss Polly Mygatt, at the residence of her father, Comfort S. Mygatt, who afterwards removed to Canfield, Ohio. Prior to their marriage they had decided to emigrate to Canfield, and on June 3, 1806, in company with Miss Gesie Bostwick, sister of Mrs. Herman Canfield, who with her husband were among the pioneers of Canfield, they started on their journey. Their means of transportation were a Jersey covered wagon and a good pair of horses. In a manuscript found among the papers of Mr. Whittlesey, after his decease, he describes the incidents of his journey, which, although somewhat eventful, was safely accomplished. They made a short stay at Pittsburg, at Mr. Peeble's, at the sign of the bear, at the northwest corner of the diamond. "The town then," he says, "was comparatively a small affair, and there were not half a dozen houses in what is now Allegheny city." The mouth of the Beaver was forded by taking the deposit of sand formed by the meeting of the water of the Beaver with that of the Ohio. The journey was ended and they arrived in Canfield on June 27, 1806, having been twenty-four days on the road.

In the following August he was admitted to the bar of Ohio by the supreme court at Warren. At the first term of the court of common pleas thereafter he was appointed prosecuting attorney of the county, and held the office until he resigned in 1823.

Shortly after his arrival in Canfield he was elected ensign of a military company, and elected and commissioned as captain in 1808. In 1810 General Elijah Wadsworth, of the Fourth division, Ohio militia, appointed him his aide-de-camp, and August 22, 1812, as aide-de-camp, he entered into the service of the United States in the war with Great Britain. He was afterwards appointed brigade major and inspector under General Perkins, and remained as such in the military service until February 25, 1813, when the troops that had served six months and more were discharged. He continued in service a few months longer as aid and private secretary of General Harrison, at his request.

In 1820 and in 1821 he was elected Representative in the State Legislature. In 1822 he was elected Representative in Congress from the district composed of Trumbull, Portage, Geauga, and Ashtabula counties, and re-elected seven times, and resigned in 1838, making his Congressional term about sixteen years, during a great part of which he was chairman of the committee on claims, one of the most important committees of the House.

In 1822 he formed a law partnership with Eben Newton, which continued until 1841, when he was appointed by President Harrison auditor of the treasury for the postoffice department, which required his continued residence in Washington. The name of the firm was Whittlesey & Newton. It enjoyed a large practice, and was favorably and extensively known. Mr. Whittlesey, in the Congressional vacations, and after his resignation from Congress, devoted his time to the professional business of the firm.

He resigned the office of auditor September 30, 1843, and returned to Canfield, engaging in practicing law and in other business. In 1847 he was appointed general agent of the Washington Monument association, which office he resigned May 31, 1849, when he was appointed by President Taylor first comptroller of the treasury. He held this office through the Taylor and Fillmore administrations. When President Pierce was inaugurated Mr. Whittlesey resigned, having opposed the political party which elected General Pierce; but so strongly was the President impressed with the value of his services, that he entirely disregarded his political opinions, and insisted upon his remaining. He acceded to the President's request, and remained until President Buchanan's inauguration, when he again for the same reason tendered his resignation, and it was accepted.

In May, 1861, he was appointed to the same office by President Lincoln, and performed its arduous duties to the day of his death, January 7, 1863, being stricken down at his post in his office at Washington city.

In regard to his appointment to his first office, prosecuting attorney, in 1806, and subsequent practice, in an autobiographical sketch, he says: "The appointment was unsought and wholly unanticipated. My practice extended into each county on the Reserve as they were organized. In several of the counties the courts of common pleas therein appointed me special prosecutor, and I think in each indictments will be found in my handwriting."

In regard to his Congressional career a Washington paper since his death justly remarks:

In that day it required talent, moral worth, and personal energy to secure a position of responsibility and influence in Congress. Mr. Whittlesey possessed a systematic business mind and an enthusiasm of character which soon won for him the chairmanship of the committee on claims. Although of trifling political consequence, and for that reason never receiving much consideration at the hands of the people, that committee, nevertheless, is one of the most important of the House. There is, perhaps, no committee which requires more unremitting industry or minds capable of deciding nicer points of equity. He was peculiarly qualified for the chairmanship of that body. He was gifted with that admirable courage which never quailed before the seductive blandishments of wealth or the threatening importance of power. He never hesitated to espouse the cause because it was weak. Strong combinations by men of position to carry a point which he believed to be wrong had no terrors for him.

We add, as a summary of his character, the remark of one who knew him well: "During his long career in public life Mr. Whittlesey had established a national reputation for untiring perseverance and scrupulous honesty."

HENRY J. CANFIELD

was born in Connecticut. He was son of Judson Canfield, a distinguished lawyer of that State and one of the proprietors of the township of Canfield, Ohio, to which he gave his name. Henry J. graduated at Yale college in 1806, studied law at the celebrated law school of Judge Reeve, in Litchfield, Connecticut, was admitted to the bar in Connecticut, and shortly afterwards came to Canfield, Ohio, to take charge of his father's lands. He was admitted to the bar of Ohio at Warren, devoted some attention to practice, but was principally engaged in farming and land surveying, in which he was skilled. He was a large sheep grower, and published a work of great merit on The Sheep.

On the organization of Mahoning county in 1846, at the first special court held by the judges, he was appointed clerk pro tem. of the court of common pleas, and held the office until the appointment of the clerk for the full term at the first regular term of the court held May 11th of that year. From his arrival in Ohio his residence was in Canfield. He there died in 1856.

DAVID TOD

was born in Youngstown, February 21, 1805. He was a son of George and Sally (Isaacs) Tod, who emigrated to Ohio from Connecticut, and were among the earliest pioneers of the Reserve. He was admitted to the bar in Warren, Ohio, in

1827; resided there engaged in practice until 1844, when he returned to the old Brier Hill farm in Youngstown, and resided there until his death on November 23, 1868. He was elected Governor of Ohio in 1861, and held other civil and military offices. He was married at Warren, Ohio, July 24, 1832, to Miss Maria Smith, of that place, the daughter of early settlers. She survives him. Although he resided in Mahoning county at the time of its organization, and was a member of its bar during his after life, he had virtually during that time retired from practice, and was engaged in extensive mining and manufacturing business.

A more full biographical sketch appears elsewhere in this book.

ROBERT W. TAYLER

was born in Harrisburg, Pennsylvania, November 9, 1812. He was son of James and Jane (Walker) Tayler. His father removed with his family to Youngstown in 1815, and there settled and there died in 1834. His mother died December 11, 1844. The means of his father were limited, but he gave his children as good an education as could be obtained in our common schools, and from his own instruction, being himself a man of much reading and intelligence; and he trained them in the path of industry, truth and honesty.

In the winter of 1830-31 Robert taught school, and afterwards officiated as deputy to George Parsons, clerk of the courts of Trumbull county, Ohio. In the summer of 1833 he accompanied Calvin Cone, appraiser of real estate for taxation, as his secretary, through Trumbull county, displaying, as was said by those who had business with them, on that tour, a knowledge of the value of real estate and the matters connected with the duties of the office of appraiser remarkable in one so youthful in appearance and in fact.

He studied law with Whittlesey & Newton, of Canfield, and was admitted to the bar at Warren, Ohio, in August, 1834, and commenced practice in Youngstown. He resided there in practice until 1860, when he removed to Columbus, Ohio, on commencing his duties as State auditor. He was in law partnership for a time with John Crowell, of Warren, Ohio, and afterwards with William G. Moore of Youngstown, Ohio.

In 1839 he was elected prosecuting attorney of Trumbull county, holding that office two years and ably performing its duties. In 1850 the Mahoning county bank at Youngstown, Ohio, was organized. At the earnest solicitation of the board of directors he became its cashier, retaining the privilege of attending courts and continuing the practice of his profession. In 1855 he was elected State Senator on the Republican ticket, for the counties of Mahoning and Trumbull, and re-elected in 1857. During his term of service in the Senate his eminent abilities as a lawyer and financier, and his character as a judicious and honest man became so well known that he was nominated by his party, almost without opposition, for the office of auditor of State, and elected in 1859. His term commenced in 1860, and he served in that office until, upon the death of Elisha Whittlesey, his former legal preceptor, first comptroller of the United States treasury in 1863, he was called by President Lincoln, at the suggestion of Salmon P. Chase, then Secretary of the United States Treasury, who knew his eminent fitness, to fill the vacancy in the office of first comptroller. For nearly fifteen years he faithfully discharged the duties of that office and death found him at his post as the honest and incorruptible watchman of the treasury. His health had been failing for some time and only a few weeks before his death he had been spending a short time at Youngstown for a partial rest from labor. He improved apparently and returned to Washington. He was at work at his desk in his office, on February 25, 1878, when he was stricken with paralysis and only lived two hours. Funeral services were held in Washington, and afterwards at Youngstown, where he was buried on March 1st, his funeral being one of the largest ever held in that city.

He was married on March 24, 1840, to Miss Louisa Maria, daughter of John E. Woodbridge, of Youngstown. She died February 11, 1853. He was again married, on January 12, 1854, to to Miss Rachel Kirtland, daughter of Colonel Caleb B. Wick, a son of Henry Wick, who was one of the early settlers of Youngstown. She survives him.

EBEN NEWTON

was born in the town of Goshen, Litchfield county, Connecticut, October 16, 1795. He was a son of Isaac Newton, a farmer who died at Goshen, and of Rebecca Newton, who removed to Ohio in 1820, and died at the home of her son, in Canfield, in 1833. In his early years he worked on his father's farm and attended the schools at Goshen. In May, 1814, he emigrated to Portage county, Ohio; worked on a farm, and about two years prior to 1820 was a clerk in his brother's store, where he began to read law in the office of Darius Lyman at Ravenna. In 1822 he returned to Connecticut, read law a short time, returned to Ravenna, read law with Jonathan Sloan, and was admitted to the bar at Warren, Ohio, in August, 1823.

Before his admission to the bar, he received an invitation from Elisha Whittlesey, who had been elected a member of Congress, to enter into a partnership with him, which he accepted and removed to Canfield, which since then has been his place of residence. The partnership of Whittlesey and Newton continued twenty years, fifteen years of which time Mr. Whittlesey was in Congress. Their business extended all over the Reserve and into other parts of the State, and the reputation of the firm was among the highest in the State.

In the fall of 1840 he was elected to the State Senate, and during his term he was elected president judge of the Third judicial district, and filled that office with marked ability. He resigned the judgeship in 1846 and returned to his law practice.

In the fall of 1850 he was elected to Congress and served two years, and then resumed practice. In 1863 he was again elected to the State Senate. After the expiration of his Senatorial term he took charge of the settlement of the estate of the late Simeon Jennings, in which he has been engaged since then. This involved much litigation in many States, and required extensive travel in this country and two visits to Europe. Except when employed in official duties he has practiced law in our courts; has kept an open office, and to some extent is still, at his advanced age of eighty-six years, engaged in legal business.

Besides his official and legal business other business enterprises have occupied his time and attention. He was for some years president of the Ashtabula & New Lisbon Railroad company, now Niles & New Lisbon, and to his exertions it owes, in a great measure, its existence. He has always taken great interest in agricultural improvement, and, for several years, was president of the Mahoning County Agricultural society. He has been a practical farmer on a large scale, imported and raised thoroughbred stock, and is extensively known as a leading stock-breeder and well-informed agriculturist.

During the time he practiced law, before he entered Congress, he had thirty and more law students, and for many years the Canfield Law school of Whittlesey & Newton had a wide and deserved celebrity. Among its graduates were Senator Benjamin F. and his brother Edward Wade, Joshua R. Giddings, Ralph P. Buckland, and others, who became members of Congress, and several who became judges and distinguished lawyers.

He was married at Canfield on May 10, 1826, to Miss Mary S. Church, a native of that place and daughter of Ensign Church, an early pioneer and son of Nathaniel Church, one of the proprietors of the township.

BENJAMIN F. HOFFMAN

was born January 25, 1812, in Chester county, Pennsylvania. His parents were Joseph and Catharine (Stitcler) Hoffman, both natives of Chester county. He received his primary education in the common and select schools of West Chester and Stroudsville, Pennsylvania. He removed with his parents to Trumbull county, Ohio, in 1833. Hon. David Tod, afterwards Governor of Ohio, was his law instructor at Warren, Ohio, for two years; and then for six months in 1835-36 he attended the Cincinnati Law school, conducted by Wright, Benham & Walker, at which he graduated in 1836 as bachelor of law, and immediately thereafter was admitted to the bar by the supreme court at Cincinnati. He then returned to Warren, and practiced law there for several years as a member of the firm of Tod, Hoffman & Hutchins. He was appointed postmaster at Warren in October, 1838, and held the office until about June, 1841.

He was elected judge of the court of common pleas for the second sub-division of the ninth judicial district of Ohio at the annual election in October, 1856, entered on the term February 8, 1857, and held the office until February 9, 1862. He was the private secretary of Governor Tod from February 9, 1862, until the expiration of the Governor's term of office in January,

Judge B. F. Hoffman.

1864. He then returned to Warren, resumed the practice of law, and there resided until 1870, when he removed to Youngstown, where he has since resided engaged in the practice of the law. He was married in December, 1837, at Akron, Ohio, to Miss Elizabeth A. Cleveland, a native of Rutland, Vermont. She died at Warren in November, 1869. He was again married at Youngstown on July 20, 1870, to Mrs. Alice W. Hezlep, whose maiden name was Higgins. She was a native of Cuyahoga county, Ohio.

A more full biography will be found in another department of this work.

JOHN M. EDWARDS

was born in New Haven, Connecticut, October 23, 1805. He was the son of Henry W. and Lydia (Miller) Edwards, of that city. He removed to Ohio in 1832; admitted to the bar in New Haven in 1826, and afterwards at Warren, Ohio. He is now practicing in Youngstown, Ohio. A more full biography will be found in another part of this work.

WILLIAM G. MOORE

was born January 7, 1832, at Freedom, on the north bank of the Ohio river, in Beaver county, Pennsylvania. His parents were Edwin and Mary A. Moore. They were natives of Balnamore, county Leitrim, Ireland, and emigrated to the United States in 1829, resided a few years in Pennsylvania, and then removed to Youngstown.

In March, 1845, he commenced the study of law in the office of John Crowell, in Warren, Ohio, and subsequently read law with Robert W. Tayler, late first comptroller of the United States treasury, at Youngstown. He was admitted to the bar by the supreme court in 1847, and in December, 1854, was admitted to the bar of the supreme court of the United States.

In 1847 he commenced the practice of law at Youngstown as partner of R. W. Tayler, which partnership continued until Mr. Tayler assumed the office of cashier of the Mahoning County bank, in 1850. He afterwards was a partner of General Thomas W. Sanderson, which continued until Mr. Sanderson joined the army in 1861. He was afterwards in partnership with William C. Bunts, deceased, and afterwards a short time with William J. Lawthers.

He was elected mayor of Youngstown in April, 1854, and re-elected in 1856. In 1869 he was elected prosecuting attorney of Mahoning county, and served two years.

He was married March 18, 1852, to Miss Laura A. Andrews, born in Vienna, Trumbull county, daughter of Norman Andrews, an early settler of Trumbull county, but for many years a citizen of Youngstown, Ohio.

DAVID M. WILSON

was born in Guilford, Medina county, Ohio, July 21, 1822. He was the second son of David and Abigail (Porter) Wilson. His father was a native of Virginia, of Scotch-Irish descent, and his mother a native of Connecticut, of English descent. His grandfather, Porter, was a drum-major in the war of the Revolution. His grandfather Wilson was also a Revolutionary soldier. His father was a soldier of the War of 1812.

He was raised on a farm, attended the common schools until he was about sixteen years old, and then attended the Norwalk seminary, in Huron county, Ohio, for several terms, and taught school one term. He read law with Hiram Floyd, at Medina, Ohio, and was there admitted to practice in 1844. In 1845 he removed to Warren, Ohio, and commenced practice, and in 1846, on the organization of Mahoning county, he removed to Canfield and commenced practice. While there, for a few years, he was a partner of John W. Church, afterwards a judge of the court of common pleas, as Wilson & Church. In 1858 he removed to Youngstown, there practicing for a period in partnership with James B. Blocksom, as Wilson & Blocksom. He was afterwards a partner of Robert G. Knight as Wilson & Knight, and then of Halsey H. Moses as Wilson & Moses, and for a few years partner of James P. Wilson, his nephew, as Wilson & Wilson.

In 1863 he was nominated for attorney-general of Ohio by the Democratic State convention, and in 1874 he was nominated for Representative in Congress by the district Democratic convention. He was not elected to either office, the ticket on which he was nominated being in the minority in both instances, but his personal popularity at home secured him many votes for each office ahead of the general ticket.

He was married, in 1846, to Miss Nancy Merril, a native of Orangeville, Wyoming county, New York. She died in 1851. He was again married, in 1871, to Miss Griselda Campbell, of Trumbull county, Ohio. He died February 11, 1882, at Youngstown.

THOMAS W. SANDERSON

was born in Indiana, Indiana county, Pennsylvania, October 17, 1829. His father, Matthew D. Sanderson, was of Scotch descent. His mother, Mary (Wakefield) Sanderson, was daughter of Thomas Wakefield, who was born in the town of Wakefield, England, which locality Oliver Goldsmith has immortalized as the scene of his world-famous tale, The Vicar of Wakefield.

M. D. Sanderson was a farmer, and in 1834 he removed with his family to Youngstown, Ohio, where he continued the business of farming. He died in 1864.

T. W. Sanderson attended the schools at Youngstown, and afterwards attended a college at Bardstown, Kentucky. He read law with William Ferguson at Youngstown, and was admitted to the bar by the district court at Canfield in August, 1852. During the period of his reading law he spent part of the time in land surveying and civil engineering, and, for a period after his admission to the bar, he followed the profession of civil engineer. In 1854 he commenced the practice of law at Youngstown in co-partnership with his brother-in-law, Frank C. Hutchins, now of Warren, under the firm name of Hutchins & Sanderson, and continued this partnership for a few years. In 1856 he was elected prosecuting attorney of Mahoning county, and served one term.

In 1861 he left the practice of law and entered the United States army as lieutenant and adjutant of the Second Ohio volunteer cavalry. He remained in the service over four years, passing through the several grades of promotion, and was made brigadier-general in 1864. During the last two years he commanded brigades and divisions all the time. He was with General Rosecrans from Stone River, and participated in nearly all the actions in which the army of the Cumberland was engaged. He continued with this army when it passed under the leadership of General Thomas, and fought at Chickamauga and Lookout Mountain. When General Thomas was superceded by General Sherman he was connected with it until the fall of Atlanta, and then on Sherman's march to the sea, and again through Georgia and the Carolinas until the surrender of Johnston and the close of the war. During these years of blood and battle he was always in the field. It is worthy of remark that he was made brigadier-general for gallantry in action. At Bear Creek station, south of Atlanta, on the second day of Sherman's march to the sea, with one brigade of Federal cavalry against three divisions of Wheeler's cavalry, he fought the enemy and won the victory.

On leaving the army he returned to the practice of the law in Youngstown, and stands high in the profession. He refuses to enter the political arena as a candidate for civil office, yet is decided in his political preferences. In 1872 he served as a delegate-at-large from the State of Ohio in the National Republican convention which nominated General Grant for re-election as President.

He was married December 19, 1854, to Miss Elizabeth Shoemaker, of Newcastle, Pennsylvania, a member of one of the oldest families of that State.

ASAHEL W. JONES.

Asahel W. Jones was born at Johnstonsville, Trumbull county, Ohio, September 18, 1838. His father, William P. Jones, was born in Hartford, Trumbull county, Ohio, July 11, 1814. His father and grandfather removed there from Burkhamstead, Connecticut, in 1801, and there they reared the second cabin in the township. His mother was Mary J. Bond, born at Avon Springs, New York, February 26, 1816, and emigrated to Hartford in 1833. She died in Youngstown, Ohio, March, 1882. On his father's side he was of Welsh descent, on his mother's of English or Irish, two Bond families, one from England and one from Ireland, being among the early emigrants to America, and it being uncertain to which his mother owes her descent.

He read law with Curtis & Smith at Warren, Ohio, and was there admitted to the bar September 27, 1859, practiced there a few years, and removed to Youngstown in 1864, where he is now practicing as a member of the firm of Jones (Robert B.), Murray & (Elliot M.) Wilson. His practice is largely, at present, for railroads and corporations. He held the office of prosecuting attorney for two terms, the first by appointment on the death of Henry G. Leslie, in 1868, and the second by election. In 1874 he took an active part in the organization of the Second National bank of Youngstown, and has since been one of its directors. In 1878, with the change of management in the corporation of Brown, Bonnell & Co., extensive iron manufacturers, he became a director of that company and has given some attention to the industries carried on by it.

He had the honor, in connection with Judge Tripp, to represent the Seventeenth Ohio Congressional district in the Republican National convention held at Chicago in 1880.

He was married September 24, 1861, at Hampton, Geauga county, Ohio, to Miss Annette J. Palmer, who was born at Kingsville, Ashtabula county, Ohio, June 23, 1840.

LAURIN D. WOODWORTH

was born in Windham, Portage county, Ohio, September 10, 1837. His father was William Woodworth, a substantial and highly respected farmer. He was educated first at Windham academy, and then at Hiram college. He read law in the office of O. P. Brown, in Ravenna, Ohio. He was admitted to the bar in 1859, but being desirous of perfecting himself he then took a course at the Ohio State and Union Law college at Cleveland, and then formed a partnership with Mr. Brown, which continued until the fall of 1861, when he practiced alone for some months. In 1862 he was appointed major of the One Hundred and Fourth regiment Ohio infantry volunteers. This regiment was ordered into Kentucky, where it was actively engaged for about ten months carrying on a guerrilla warfare. His exposure and hard service having brought on a disease which disabled him from further service in the field, he resigned, and for the next two years traveled, under medical advice, to various places in the endeavor to recover health. He attempted to re-enter the service, but was rejected on account of physical disability, having lost the sight of his right eye. About 1865 he removed to Youngstown and resumed the practice of law. In October, 1867, he was elected to the Ohio Senate for the Mahoning and Trumbull district, re-elected in 1869, and was chosen by his fellow Senators president *pro tem.* of that body. At the close of his second term he declined a re-nomination, and resumed his law practice. In October, 1872, he was elected representative in Congress from the Seventeenth Ohio district, composed of Mahoning, Columbiana, Stark, and Carroll counties, and he was re-elected in October, 1874. At the expiration of his second term he resumed the practice of law in Youngstown.

He was married October 6, 1869, to Miss Celia Clark, of Windham, his native place.

GEORGE TOD

(second) was born in Warren, Ohio, in 1841, and was the son of David and Maria (Smith) Tod, and grandson of George Tod, the pioneer lawyer of Youngstown. He removed, with his parents to Briar Hill, near Youngstown, in 1844. In April, 1861, in response to the call of President Lincoln for volunteers, he enlisted as a private in the Mahoning Rifles, one of the first companies which reported for duty to the Governor. On May 20th, at Cleveland, the Rifles were made part of the Nineteenth regiment as company B. As a private in that company and regiment he served gallantly during the term for which he enlisted. He returned to Youngstown, read law, and was admitted to the bar at Canfield, in 1865. He has devoted but little attention to the practice, but is, and for several years has been, largely engaged in coal and manufacturing business.

HALSEY H. MOSES

was born July 12, 1830, in Morgan, Ashtabula county, Ohio. His parents were Jonathan and Abigail (Plumley) Moses, both born in Norfolk, Litchfield county, Connecticut, from which place they emigrated to Morgan in 1814. He was a student of the Grand River institute, and read law with C. L. Tinker, of Painesville, and was admitted to the bar at Jefferson, Ohio, in August, 1861. He practiced law for a few years in Ashtabula county, and then removed to Warren, Ohio. He was a partner of Matthew Birchard, former judge of the supreme court, from 1862 to 1867; of Ira L. Fuller, from 1867 to 1870; and of General Robert W. Ratliff, from 1870 to 1880. In 1872 he removed to Youngstown, still retaining his law practice in Warren in the firm of Ratliff & Moses. In 1877 he became a partner with George F. Arrell, in the firm of Moses & Arrell, which continued until 1880, when the latter became judge of the common pleas, since which time he has practiced without a partner. He was married in Morgan in March, 1852, to Miss Mary J. Murdock, of that place, who was a native of Mesopotamia, Trumbull county, Ohio.

ROBERT H. MURRAY

was born in Youngstown, Ohio, March 6, 1843. He was the youngest son of Ira and Hannah (Carothem) Murray. He attended the public schools in Youngstown, and afterwards was a student at Allegheny college, Meadville, Pennsylvania, and was also a student at Ann Arbor university, Michigan, for about two years. He followed the profession of teaching for about six years, during which time he was principal of the union school at Mercer, Pennsylvania, and of an academy at Meadville, Pennsylvania. At an early age he commenced reading law and pursued it at intervals. He was admitted to the bar at Canfield in September, 1867, and immediately commenced practice in Youngstown. In March, 1870, he entered into partnership in the practice of law with Asa W. Jones, under the name of Jones & Murray, and the firm still continues in practice in Youngstown. He was married in 1870 to Miss Sophia Bond, a native of Geneseo, Livingston county, New York. He is a prominent member of the Methodist Episcopal church.

LEROY D. THOMAN

was born in Salem, Columbiana county, Ohio, July 31, 1851. His father was Jacob S. Thoman, one of the early pioneers, who came when quite young, with his parents to Springfield township, Mahoning county, Ohio. His mother was a daughter of Rev. Henry Sonnedecker, a man of extraordinary power in his day in the ministry. She was born in Wooster, Wayne county, Ohio, and moved with her parents to Springfield, in 1827. His early education was at the common schools, with one year academic. He read law with Joseph H. Adair, of Columbia, City, Indiana, and was admitted to the bar there August 13, 1872, and to the bar of Ohio in Mahoning county in September, 1873.

He was deputy prosecuting attorney of the Ninth judicial district of Indiana from August 14, 1872, until February, 1873, when he resigned and removed to Youngstown, Ohio, where he formed a partnership with Isaac A. Justice, in the practice of law. He was elected probate judge of Mahoning county in October, 1875, and re-elected in 1878. Having served two terms of three years each, at the annual election in 1881 he declined being a candidate for re-election.

He is now practicing law in Youngstown, and is also engaged in publishing and editing the Youngstown Vindicator, of which he is part proprietor.

He was married in Youngstown March 29, 1876, to Miss Mary E. Cripps, of Youngstown. She died December 4, 1876.

GEORGE F. ARREL

was born in Poland, Ohio, October 1, 1840. His parents were David Arrel, born in Poland May 6, 1803, and Martha (Moore) Arrel, also born in Poland; she died June 25, 1872, in her sixty-third year. They were both children of the early pioneers. He graduated at New Wilmington college, Lawrence county, Pennsylvania, in 1865. He studied law with Francis E. Hutchins, at Warren, Ohio, and afterwards attended the Albany Law school. He was admitted to the bar at Canfield, Ohio, August 20, 1867, and then removed to Youngstown, commenced the practice of law, and has since resided there. Part of the time he was in partnership with Halsey H. Moses, under the firm name of Moses & Arrel.

About July 1, 1870, he was elected city solicitor of Youngstown, to fill the vacancy occasioned by the resignation and removal from Youngstown of Joseph Harris. He was re-elected at the expiration of his term, and biennially thereafter until 1878, when he declined a further re-election. In September, 1880, he was appointed by the Governor judge of the court of common pleas, to fill the vacancy made by the resignation of Judge E. B. Taylor, and until a judge should be elected and qualified. At the annual election in October, 1880, he was elected for the remainder of Judge Taylor's term, which would expire in February, 1882. At the annual election in October, 1881, he was re-elected for the full term of five years. The vote in Mahoning county resulted in a majority in his favor of 981 in a total vote of 7,551, in the judicial district comprising Mahoning, Trumbull, and Portage counties a majority of 4,743 in a total vote of 20,751. He was married, October 18, 1870, to Miss Grace Tod, daughter of the late Governor David Tod, at the Tod family residence at Brier Hill in the township of Youngstown. He resides in the city of Youngstown.

ISAAC A. JUSTICE.

Isaac A. Justice was born in Austintown, Mahoning county, Ohio, March 16, 1837. He was a son of John and Nancy (Sexton) Justice. They were both born in Washington county, Pennsylvania, and removed with their parents to Ohio about 1805, and were among the earliest pioneers of Mahoning county. They both died at Austintown in 1881, after having spent together over sixty peaceful and prosperous years of married life.

The subject of this biography was educated at the Mahoning academy, in Canfield. He spent his summers from 1856 to 1860 in attending school and his winters in teaching. He read law with S. W. Gilson, Esq., at Canfield, and was admitted to the bar in the fall of 1867, at the session of the district court in Canfield. He soon entered into partnership with Mr. Gilson, which continued for a short time. About 1872 he removed to Youngstown, Ohio, and has been engaged in the practice of law there since that time.

In October 1873, and during the contest for the removal of the county seat to Youngstown, he was elected, on what was called the "removal ticket," prosecuting attorney, and held the office for one term, commencing on January 7, 1874, and terminating January 7, 1876.

During the term of office of L. D. Thoman as probate judge, he tendered to Mr. Justice the appointment of school examiner of Mahoning county, a position he was amply qualified to fill, but the appointment was declined because of want of time to perform the duties of the office. He has taken a very prominent part in the temperance movement for the past five years, and has spent much time in lecturing, and otherwise, at home and abroad, in attempting to persuade men to live sober lives. He is now president of the Ohio Christian Temperance union.

He was married in 1860 to Miss Dorcas Hitchcock, of Canfield, a class-mate of his at the academy, by whom he had two children, both now living. She died in December, 1870. He was again married in 1871, to Miss Helen A. Warner, of Lorain county, Ohio. She was also his class-mate. She died in 1881, leaving a bereaved husband and four interesting children to mourn her loss.

CHARLES R. TRUESDALE

was born in Boardman, Mahoning county, Ohio, September 15, 1841. His parents were, Alexander, born in Washington county, Pennsylvania, and Harriet (Leach) Truesdale, born in Morristown, New Jersey. He graduated at Western Reserve college in the class of 1871, read law in the office of Taylor & Jones at Warren, Ohio, and was admitted to the bar at Warren in April, 1872.

He served in the war of the Rebellion in company E, Second Ohio cavalry, from July, 1861, to July, 1865, and participated in the battles of the Wilderness, Spottsylvania, Cold Harbor, Reams Station, and many others.

He was married at Youngstown, June 19, 1872, to Miss Louisa M. Jacobs, of that city.

He was elected prosecuting attorney of Mahoning county in 1875, and held the office for two years.

WALTER L. CAMPBELL

was born in Salem, Columbiana county, Ohio, November 13, 1842. His parents were John and Rebecca P. (Snodgrass) Campbell, old citizens of that place. When in his fifth year one eye was accidentally injured. Inflammation in both eyes ensued, and when he was five years old he was totally blind. In his ninth year he entered the Ohio Institute for the Blind, at Columbus, Ohio, and left it when sixteen years old. During his attendance at the institute, in addition to the education he acquired in the branches usually taught, he became a proficient on the organ. After leaving the institute he taught music for nearly a year, and then, with a view of perfecting his musical education, he entered the Pennsylvania Institute of the Blind, at Philadelphia, where he remained five months. He now determined to acquire a collegiate education, left Philadelphia and entered the Salem, Ohio, high school, for the purpose of preparing for college. He entered Western Reserve college, in Hudson, Ohio, in 1863 and graduated in 1867, standing second in his class, and delivering the salutatory oration. During his freshman year he took the prize for best written translation, in Latin. In his sophomore year he took the prize for best English composition, and at the junior exhibition delivered the philosophical oration.

He studied law for one year with Judge Jacob

A. Ambler, at Salem, and then, for a year, attended the law school of Harvard university, at Cambridge, Massachusetts. He was admitted to the bar of Massachusetts, by the supreme court, at Boston, June 17, 1869. He then went to Wyoming Territory, then just organizing, and of which his brother had been appointed Governor. He was appointed United States commissioner and practiced law for some time in the Territory. He returned to Ohio and was admitted to the bar, at Warren, in May, 1873. In May, 1874, without having engaged in practice in Ohio, he purchased an interest in the Mahoning Register, of Youngstown, Ohio, and was the editor of that paper and the daily that grew out of it, and other papers with which it was consolidated, until the latter part of January, 1882. He then returned to the practice of law.

For several years past he has been organist of the First Presbyterian church of Youngstown. He is a good and ready speaker, and on several occasions has delivered addresses, evincing much thought and study, which received great commendation. His memory has become remarkable, and is so well trained the he is a very accurate reporter, being able after listening, to dictate to an amanuensis, or reproduce on a type writer, testimony and arguments in a law trial, political speeches, etc. This faculty he often exercised advantageously in his editorial career.

Although totally blind, with only the aid of his cane he visits all parts of the city, turning corners and entering doors without hesitation or mistake; and not only this, but unattended he makes journeys on railroads, visiting other cities, traversing their streets and reaching the buildings he seeks with the ease and facility, apparently, of one in full possession of his eyesight. He was married at Youngstown, April 4, 1877, to Miss Helen C. LaGourgue, of that city, formerly of Cleveland, the daughter of a French gentleman and a lady of New England ancestry.

OTIS W. KYLE.

Otis W. Kyle was born in Austintown, Mahoning county, Ohio, March 21, 1843. He is the oldest son of Joshua and Elizabeth Kyle. When eighteen years old he entered Hiram college as a student, remaining four years and graduating in 1864. He engaged as bookkeeper for the New Lisbon, Ohio, Coal company for several years. During his residence in New Lisbon he assisted in organizing the First National bank, of which he was the first cashier. He had been reading law at intervals for some time previous, and was admitted to the bar at New Lisbon in 1876. He removed to Youngstown in 1879, and has since been engaged in practice in this city.

He was married in 1871 to Miss Charlotte M., daughter of William and Almira Tibbits, and has a family of three daughters.

MONROE W. JOHNSON

was born in Pymatuning township, Mercer county, Pennsylvania, June 28, 1840. He was a son of William and Hannah (Harris) Johnson. His father was born in Pulaski, Mercer county, Pennsylvania, of Scotch-Irish descent. His mother was born in Coitsville, Ohio, on the father's side descended from a French Huguenot, on the mother's side she was a Poe, and a descendant of that great Indian fighter.

He attended Westminister college, Lawrence county, Pennsylvania. Early in the war of 1861 he enlisted in company E, Twenty-third Ohio volunteers, President Hayes' regiment, and served three years; was engaged in the battles of Carnifax Ferry, West Virginia, South Mountain, and Antietam, Maryland, and in the last battle was severely wounded and afterwards discharged on account of his wound. At the time of the battle he was serving in the quartermaster's department, but when the battle commenced he shouldered his musket and went into the ranks. After recovering in a measure from his wound he went again into the quartermaster's department, and was at the battle of Gettysburg, in which he participated. He established a post in the quartermaster's department at Reading, Pennsylvania, and another afterwards at Harrisburg, Pennsylvania, and remained to the close of the war.

In 1867 he came to Lowellville, Mahoning county, Ohio; studied law with T. W. Sanderson at Youngstown, Ohio; was admitted to the bar at Canfield, Ohio, in 1868, and commenced practice in Youngstown, where he has his office, but resides in Lowellville. He held the office of prosecuting attorney of Mahoning county for two terms from 1878 to 1882.

In September, 1869, in Pittsburg, Pennsylvania, he was married, by Rev. Noble, of the First Presbyterian church, at his residence, to

Henrietta Book, of Poland, Ohio, who was born there in 1833. They are the parents of three children, two of whom were twins and one of whom survives. She was a teacher of colored people at Fortress Monroe during the war, and had her quarters in ex-President Tyler's house, near the Fortress. Her father, John Book, merchant and milliner, was a leading anti-slavery man during the agitation on that subject.

WILLIAM J. LAWTHERS

was born in Leesburg, Carroll county, Ohio, October 17, 1837. His parents were Colonel Garvin and Mrs. (Price) Lawthers. His father, a physician of repute, is of Scotch and Irish descent; his mother is of Irish and Welsh descent. He attended the public schools at his home. During the war of 1861 he was for several months in the army, and was discharged in December, 1864, at Camp Zanesville, Ohio. He read law at Cleveland, Ohio, with R. E. Knight, Esq., and was admitted to the bar in Carrollton, Carroll county, Ohio, in 1866. He commenced practice in Carroll county, and removed to Youngstown, Ohio, in the spring of 1868, where he has since resided, engaged in practice. At Youngstown he practiced for a short time in partnership with H. B. Case, as Case & Lawthers, and afterwards with William G. Moore, as Moore & Lawthers. For several years past he has had no partner. In 1876 he was admitted to the bar of the district court of the United States at Cleveland, Ohio. In 1880 he was elected mayor of the city of Youngstown, and re-elected in 1882.

He was married at Cleveland, Ohio, September 20, 1870, to Miss Josephine, daughter of Captain William Wilson, of that city, and niece of the late Hon. David M. Wilson, of Youngstown.

MASON EVANS.

Mason Evans was born in Philadelphia, Pennsylvania, November 24, 1849. His father, Owen Evans, was born in Montgomery county, Pennsylvania, and resided in Philadelphia until his death in 1859. His mother, Sarah Roe Evans, was born in Cincinnati, Ohio, and now resides in Philadelphia. He was a graduate of the law department of the University of Pennsylvania, class of 1869. His law instructor was Aaron Thompson, of Philadelphia. He was admitted to the bar in Philadelphia, November 23, 1870. He removed to Youngstown, Ohio, September 19, 1871, and was admitted to the bar of Ohio at Warren, in 1875, and is now practicing law in partnership with General Thomas W. Sanderson, firm of Sanderson & Evans. He was married June 8, 1876, at Youngstown, Ohio, to Miss Lucy E. Gerwig, daughter of Frederick Gerwig, of German nativity, an iron manufacturer now deceased.

SIDNEY STRONG

was born in Strongsville, Cuyahoga county, Ohio, June 12, 1839. He read law at Columbus, Ohio, with C. N. Olds, and was there admitted to the bar in 1867. He came to Youngstown shortly after, commenced practice, in which he still continues.

He was married at Youngstown, Ohio, December 10, 1872, to Miss Mary A. Gerlick, of that city.

CECIL D. HINE

was born August 3, 1849, in Hubbard, Trumbull county, Ohio, where his parents then resided. They were Samuel Hine, now of Poland, Ohio, who was born in Youngstown, and was a son of Homer Hine, one of the earliest lawyers of the Reserve, and Ellen L. (Montgomery) Hine, of Coitsville, Ohio, daughter of Robert Montgomery, an early settler, and who, in 1806, built and operated in Poland, Ohio, a furnace for making iron, one of the first furnaces in Ohio.

He attended the Western Reserve college to the beginning of senior year. That college has since conferred on him the degree of A. M. He read law two years with Taylor & Jones, at Warren, Ohio, and was there admitted to the bar, by the district court of Trumbull county, April 15, 1872. He soon after commenced practice at Youngstown, where he now resides, engaged in practice. He was married at Poland, Ohio October 9, 1872, to Miss Lizzie W. Woodruff, a native of that place.

MOSES H. BURKEY

was born in Berlin, Mahoning county, Ohio, September 15, 1846. His parents were Jacob and Catharine Burkey, of German ancestry. He read law with F. G. Servis and G. Van Hyning, at Canfield, Ohio; was there admitted to the bar April 19, 1869, practiced his profession there from that date to August 20, 1876, when he removed to Youngstown, where he has since resided engaged in practice. He was elected mayor of Canfield in April, 1871, and held that office by subsequent elections to April, 1875. He was married at Berlin, October 23, 1870, to Miss Mary A. Burkey, of that place.

WILLIAM S. ANDERSON

was born in North Jackson, Mahoning county, Ohio, December 31, 1847. His father, David Anderson, was born in Ireland. His mother, Hannah L. (Shaw) Anderson, was of Irish descent. He read law at Warren with Hutchins & Glidden; was admitted to the bar there April 7, 1870, commenced practice shortly after in Canfield, Ohio, and removed to Youngstown in 1877, where he practiced for several years in partnership with Louis R. King, until February, 1882, when the latter commenced his term as probate judge, as Anderson & King.

He was married October 6, 1864, to Miss Louisa M. Shields, of Boardman, Ohio, daughter of Andrew Shields, one of the early citizens of the Reserve.

JARED HUXLEY

was born in Ellsworth, Mahoning county, Ohio, July 23, 1840. His father, Socrates I. Huxley, was born in New Marlborough, Berkshire county, Massachusetts. His mother, Pauline (Spaulding) Huxley, was born in Pomfret, Litchfield county, Connecticut. They emigrated, in early life, to Ellsworth, where they now reside. He graduated at Oberlin in 1867, read law with Charles W. Palmer in Cleveland, Ohio, and was admitted to the bar at Norwalk, Huron county, Ohio, April 3, 1871.

During the war of 1861 he was clerk in the quartermaster's department at Nashville, Tennessee, and at Mobile, Alabama. For two years immediately preceding his admission to the bar, he was professor of mathematics and theory of accounts in Felton & Bigelow's Business college at Cleveland, and for a year prior held the same position at Star City Business college at Lafayette, Indiana. On his admission to the bar he commenced practice at Canfield, and on the removal of the county-seat to Youngstown he removed to that city, where he is now engaged in the practice of law.

WILLIAM T. GIBSON

was born in Youngstown, Ohio, December 20, 1850. His parents were: Samuel Gibson, born in Youngstown, March 17, 1819, son of one of the earliest pioneers, and Nancy J. (Gault) Gibson, born in Mercer county, Pennsylvania, September 25, 1825.

He graduated at the Rayen school, of Youngstown, June 20, 1872, and at Western Reserve college, Hudson, Ohio, June 25, 1876. He read law with George F. Arrel at Youngstown, and was admitted to bar at Warren, Ohio, September 3, 1878. He has since resided in Youngstown, and engaged in practicing law.

BURDETTE O. EDDY

was born in Windsor, Ashtabula county, Ohio, April 11, 1846. He was the son of Lorenzo S. and Elizabeth (Eaton) Eddy. They were natives of Connecticut. On the father's side he is of Scotch descent, his paternal ancestor being an emigrant to the United States about the year 1700. His great grandfather was a soldier of the Revolution. His grandfather was a soldier in the War of 1812. His mother was of English descent. Her ancestors came to the United States shortly before the Revolutionary war.

Mr. Eddy graduated at the Orwell, Ohio, Normal institute in June, 1870, and in the law department of the Michigan university at Ann Arbor, Michigan, in the class of 1874. His law instructors were Judge T. M. Cooley and other law lecturers in the university. He was admitted to the supreme court of Michigan in Lansing in April, 1874, to the United States district court at Detroit in the same month, and to the bar of Ohio at Canfield in September, 1874. He then removed to Youngstown and commenced the practice of law, and has since resided there engaged in practice.

When quite a young man he was elected constable of his native town, and held the office for one year. In October 1880, he was appointed, by the court of common pleas, official stenographer of the courts of Mahoning county.

He was married September 17, 1874, at Orwell, Ohio, to Miss Sarah Day, a native of the place, and by her had two children, the oldest of whom, a son, died January 13, 1879. She died December 17, 1878. On August 17, 1879, he was again married at New Castle, Pennsylvania, to Miss Vella Sunderlin, a native of that city.

In the war of 1861 he was a private in battery G, Illinois light artillery, which was attached to the Sixteenth army corps, and participated in the following engagements, viz: Union City, Coffeeville, Tupelo, Old Town Creek, Hurricane Creek, Siege of Vicksburg, all in Mississippi; Nashville, Tennessee (the two days' action); the sieges of Spanish Fort, Blakely, and Mobile, Alabama, from March 27th to April 12, 1865. He was mustered out at Camp Butler, Springfield, Illinois, September 4, 1865. After being mustered out of the United States army he went on to the plains of Nebraska, Dakota, Colorado, and Wyoming, where he acted for three years in the capacity of train boss, scout and hunter to various trading parties in that section, and was captain of the vigilance committee of the Laramie valley for over a year. He was wounded in a single-handed combat with a party of Indians at Cooper creek, Wyoming Territory, in August, 1868. He returned to Ohio in that year, where he has resided since, except when pursuing his law studies in Michigan.

ADDIS E. KNIGHT

was born in Leesville, Carroll county, Ohio, October 29, 1852. His parents were Robert E. and Mary E. (Lawthers) Knight, both natives of Ohio. He removed with his parents to Youngstown in 1869, graduated at the Rayen school in Youngstown, read law with his father, then a practicing lawyer in Youngstown, was admitted to the bar at Canfield September, 1874, and has since practiced law in Youngstown. He was elected justice of the peace of Youngstown township April 5, 1880.

He was married April 19, 1879, at Youngstown, to Miss Grace Johnson, a native of that city.

ALBERT JACOB WOOLF

was born in Berlin township, Mahoning county, Ohio, April 26, 1852. His father, Jacob Woolf, was born near Martinsburg, Virginia, July 25, 1819, but his home, the greater part of the time, until he reached manhood, was near Hagerstown, Maryland. His mother, whose maiden name was Christina Reichard, was born near Mount Alto, Guilford township, Franklin county, Pennsylvania. They were both of German descent. They were married December 9, 1847, migrated to Ohio in May, 1848, and settled in Berlin township, on the east bank of the Mahoning, nearly opposite the village of Frederick, and there resided until the spring of 1861, when they removed into the adjoining township of Milton, where his mother still resides. His father died January 14, 1874. The name of the family, as written by his ancestors, is Wolf, but his father, Jacob, about 1850, commenced using two o's, which orthography has always been used by his children, although his other relations still practice the old way of spelling the name Wolf. This departure from the old way of spelling was the result of a spirit of originality rather than any other cause.

The subject of this sketch entered Mount Union college in the fall of 1872 and graduated in 1876. He also attended and completed a commercial course at Hiram college in 1871, and in 1874 he attended, part of the year, at Wittenberg college, in Springfield, Ohio. Prior to entering college, and during part of the time of his collegiate course, he taught school at intervals in Mahoning county, and in the fall and winter of 1873–74 he taught school in Johnson county, Missouri. He prepared for the bar in Youngstown, Ohio, studying with Van Hyning & Johnston part of the time, and the residue with C. R. Truesdale. He was admitted to the bar by the supreme court at Columbus, Ohio, June 4, 1878, and has practiced law at Youngstown since that time. He is a member of the board of school examiners of Mahoning county, and has served in that office for over three years past. He was the Democratic candidate for probate judge of Mahoning county in the fall of 1881, but was not elected.

FRANK JACOBS.

Frank Jacobs was born in Youngstown, Ohio, May 22, 1855. His parents were Philip Jacobs, born in Pennsylvania, and Sallie (Kimmel) Jacobs, who was daughter of Betsey (Kirkpatrick) Kimmel, who was born in Youngstown in 1800, and one of the first white children born in the township. She was granddaughter of Caleb Baldwin, one of the earliest pioneers, and the first justice of the peace in the township. He read law, in part, with Anderson & King, at Youngstown, graduating at the Albany law school May 26, 1877, and was admitted to the bar of Youngstown, Ohio, March 26, 1878, where he has since resided practicing his profession, in partnership with John S. Roller, of Canfield, in the firm of Roller & Jacobs.

DAVID TOD FORD.

David Tod Ford was born in Cleveland, Ohio, October 21, 1854. His parents were James H. and Arabella (Stambaugh) Ford, the former a grandson of the late Judge George Tod, and the latter descended from an early pioneer of Youngstown of German ancestry. He came with his parents to Youngstown several years since, and there read law with Sidney Strong, Esq., and was admitted to the bar at Columbus, Ohio, February, 1876, commenced and is in practice in Youngstown. He was married May 15, 1878, to Miss Carrie L. Arms, of Youngstown, daughter of Freeman O. Arms, for many years a prominent merchant of that city.

ELLIOTT M. WILSON

was born January 17, 1846, at Shalersville, Portage county, Ohio. His parents were Charles and Esther S. (Hancock) Wilson, who were from Massachusetts. He read law at the Ohio State and Union Law college in Cleveland, Ohio, and in the office of John Crowell, president of the college. He was admitted to the bar at Cleveland in September, 1874, but did not immediately commence practice. He removed to Youngstown in 1877, and engaged in practice, in which he has since continued at that place.

STEPHEN L. CLARK

was born in Williamsfield, Ashtabula county, Ohio, June 8, 1849. His parents were Allen and Mary Clark, of that place. They were natives of Lawrence county, Pennsylvania. He received an academical education at Jamestown, Mercer county, Pennsylvania. He graduated in the Law department of the Michigan university at Ann Arbor, March 20, 1874. His legal instructors were Stephen A. Northway at Jefferson, Ohio, in the code practice of Ohio, and Professor Thomas M. Cooley at Ann Arbor, on common law practice. He received certificates for two years' study from each. He was admitted to the bar at Toledo, Ohio, April 8, 1874. He removed to Youngstown, Ohio, May 13, 1874, where he commenced the practice of law, and now resides. He was married February 21, 1878, at Greene, Trumbull county, Ohio, her then residence, to Miss Addie A. Noble. She was born in Gustavus, Trumbull county, Ohio.

JOHN H. CLARK

was born at New Lisbon, Ohio, September 18, 1857. His parents were John and Melissa (Hessin) Clark. His father was, for one term, judge of the court of common pleas, and is one of the oldest lawyers of that place. John H. graduated at the Western Reserve college at Hudson in 1877. He read law with his father and was admitted to the bar at New Lisbon in 1878, and commenced practice. He removed to Youngstown April 1, 1880, purchased an interest in the Vindicator, a weekly newspaper, Democratic in politics, and is engaged in the editing and publishing of that paper and also in practicing law in partnership with Leroy D. Thoman, late probate judge of Mahoning county, under the firm name of Thoman & Clark.

I. BARCLAY MILLER

was born in Youngstown, Ohio, January 18, 1850. He was the son of Joseph and Jane (Jones) Miller. His father was from Charlestown, West Virginia, a farmer; for many years a resident of Youngstown. His mother was born in Austintown, Mahoning county, Ohio. He graduated at the Rayen school, read law with General T. W. Sanderson, was admitted to the bar at Canfield in 1873, and has since practiced his profession in Youngstown. He was married in Youngstown October 7, 1874, to Miss Ella J. Coombs, of that city.

WILLIAM N. ASHBAUGH

was born May 14, 1854, at Freeport, Armstrong county, Pennsylvania. His parents were William and Eliza A. (Metz) Ashbaugh. He removed with them to Youngstown, Ohio, in October, 1874. He read law with David M. Wilson and William J. Lawthers, and was admitted to the bar by the district court at Youngstown, April 3, 1877, and has since resided there engaged in practice.

WILLIAM E. HOWELLS

was born in Youngstown, Ohio, March 10, 1857. His parents were Anthony and Elizabeth Howells, of Welsh nativity, but who early in life emigrated to Youngstown. They now reside in Massillon, Ohio. His father held the office of State treasurer for one term and is now and has been for several years largely engaged in coal minnig and furnace business, at and near Massillon.

He read law with William S. Anderson, at Youngstown, was there admitted to the bar

March 17, 1879, and resided there since in practice.

WILLIAM A. MALINE

was born in Canton, Ohio, September 1, 1852. His parents were John Maline, deceased, and Catharine (Pirrong) Maline, now of Youngstown. They emigrated from Bavaria to Ohio, and resided some years in Canton, Ohio. He read law with Henry A. Wise in Canton, and afterwards with M. W. Johnson and Isaac A. Justice in Youngstown. He was there admitted to the bar April 3, 1877, commenced practice, and has since resided there. In 1882 he was elected city solicitor of Youngstown.

He was married June 24, 1880, at Youngstown, to Miss Louisa Rudge, daughter of George Rudge, a native of England, who came to Ohio about 1848.

WILLIAM B. M'GEHAN

was born in Coitsville, Mahoning county, Ohio, June 8, 1838. His parents were Thomas McGehan, born in New Bedford, Lawrence county, Pennsylvania, and Charlotte (Bissell) McGehan, born in Coitsville, a daughter of one of the first settlers. He attended the schools in Coitsville and Youngstown, read law with David M. Wilson, and afterward with Samuel W. Gilson at Canfield, and was admitted to the bar at Canfield, May 8, 1862. He resides at Coitsville, but his law office is in Youngstown.

He was married at Coitsville, October 4, 1865, to Miss Anna Brownlee, of that place, whose parents were of Scotch nativity.

JAMES P. WILSON

was born February 6, 1857, at Lyons, Iowa. He came to Cleveland with his parents in 1863, and to Youngstown, September 1, 1878. His parents were James Wilson, born at Wilson's corners, Medina county, Ohio, and Harriet (Hawes) Wilson, born at Chester, Geauga county, Ohio. He graduated at Cleveland high school in 1875; studied law in the office of Rufus P. Ranney at Cleveland in 1876, and in 1877-78 with Theodore W. Dwight, of Columbia Law college, in New York city, and graduated there in 1878. He was admitted to the bar of New York in New York city by the supreme court in 1878, and to the bar of Ohio in August of the same year. He practiced in Youngstown for some time with D. W. Wilson, now deceased, in the firm of Wilson & Wilson, and resides in Youngstown engaged in practice.

MELVIN CARY M'NABB

was born in Poland, Mahoning county, Ohio, October 14, 1852. His parents were L. B. and Mary McNabb, both natives of Poland. He graduated at Poland Union seminary in 1870, and then removed to Salem, Ohio. In 1874 he commenced the study of law in the office of Brooks & Laubie, under the tuition of L. L. Gilbert. He removed to Youngstown in November, 1876, and continued the study of law in the office of William M. Osborn. He was admitted to the bar by the district court at Youngstown, April 3, 1877, and immediately commenced the practice of law in that city. In 1881 he was practicing in partnership with Wyllis W. Powers, now deceased, as McNabb & Powers.

He was married April 21, 1880, to Miss Clara P. Stambugh, daughter of Martin Stambaugh, at his residence near Vienna Junction, Liberty township, Trumbull county, Ohio. She was born in Hubbard, Ohio, October 8, 1854, and died in Youngstown, April 7, 1881.

EUGENE SMITH

was born in Bucks county, Pennsylvania, October 25, 1844, and removed to Ohio with his parents in 1856. He received his early education in the district school and in the high school at Salem, Columbiana county, Ohio, and taught district school a few terms. He studied law with J. C. Stanley, Esq., of Alliance, Ohio, and was admitted to the bar in March, 1879. He commenced practice in Youngstown in September, 1879, and has since resided there, continuing the practice of his profession.

CLATE A. SMITH

was born in Canfield, Ohio, in September, 1850. His parents were Edwin E. and Jane E. (Crane) Smith, of that place. He removed, when quite young, with his parents, to Youngstown, Ohio, which has since been his residence. He read law with Jones & Murray at Youngstown, and was admitted to the bar at Warren, Ohio, in April, 1872, and then commenced practice. He has been connected, editorially, with the Evening News, since changed to News-Register, a daily and weekly newspaper, published in Youngstown for the past three years. He was married at Youngstown, in 1870, to Miss Melinda, daughter of Boston Myers of that city.

BENJAMIN F. WIRT

was born in West Middlesex, Mercer county, Pennsylvania, March 26, 1852, and removed with his parents to Youngstown, Ohio, in December of that year. He was a son of William Wirt, a native of Youngstown, and Eliza Jane (Sankey) Wirt, a native of Pennsylvania. He was a graduate of the Rayen school, of Youngstown. His law instructor was L. D. Woodworth, of Youngstown, and he was admitted to the bar in Columbus, Ohio, March 11, 1871, and commenced the practice in Youngstown, where he now resides, engaged in practice in partnership with his former preceptor, under the firm name of Woodworth & Wirt. He was married on the 23d day of June, 1881, at New Bedford, Pennsylvania, to Miss Mary M. McGeehen, a resident of that place and a native of Pennsylvania.

JAMES KENNEDY

was born in Poland, Ohio, September 3, 1853. He was a son of Thomas W. and Margaret (Truesdale) Kennedy. His early education was in the common schools. He prepared for college at the Poland Union seminary, and graduated at Westminster college, Pennsylvania, in 1876. He read law at Youngstown with General T. W. Sanderson, and was admitted to the bar March 16, 1879, and commenced practice in Youngstown, where he resides and engaged in practice.

GEORGE C. HATCH

was born in West Farmington, Trumbull county, Ohio, June 24, 1857, and is the son of H. H. and Jennett (Lane) Hatch. He graduated at the Western Reserve seminary in 1877, and at Oberlin college in 1878, read law with Jones & Murray at Youngstown, was admitted to the bar in 1879, practiced his profession for a short time at Warren, Ohio, and then removed to Youngstown, Ohio, where he has since resided, and engaged in practice.

EDWARD SWANSTON

was born in the county of Fermanaugh, Ireland, November 2, 1848. He was the son of William and Eliza (McCurdy) Swanston. He came to the United States and to Mahoning county, Ohio, with his parents in 1851. He attended the Union seminary at Poland, Ohio, and afterwards entered the Western Reserve college at Hudson, Ohio, but left before finishing the course. He studied law with Anderson & King, Youngstown, Ohio, and was admitted to the bar at Youngstown, Ohio, March 17, 1879; commenced practice there, where he is now in practice, in partnership with his brother George, as Swanston Brothers.

GEORGE SWANSTON

was born in Coitsville, Mahoning county, Ohio, January 5, 1852; is a son of William and Eliza (McCurdy) Swanston, natives of Ireland, who came to the United States in 1851. He was a graduate of Poland Union seminary, class of 1876. His law instructor was William S. Anderson, of Youngstown, Ohio, and was admitted to the bar in that city March 17, 1879. Since his admission has there practiced law in partnership with his brother Edward, under the firm name of Swanston Brothers.

JOHN A. LADD

was born at Newton Falls, Trumbull county, Ohio, January 17, 1848. He was the son of William P. and Letitia (Clark) Ladd. His father was a blacksmith and a native of Vermont. His mother was a native of New Jersey. He came to Youngstown in 1865, was engaged in drug business five years and then in insurance and collecting business. He read law with Jones & Murray, at Youngstown, and was admitted to the bar at Jefferson, Ashtabula county, March 19, 1878, and then commenced practice in Youngstown in which he is now engaged.

PATRICK F. GILLIES

was born in Airdrie, Lanarkshire, Scotland, July 27, 1854. He came to the United States in 1871, making his home at Chicago, where he resided until 1874, when he removed to Lowellville, Mahoning county, and soon after to Youngstown. He read law with Isaac A. Justice, at Youngstown, and was there admitted to the bar March 17, 1879, where he immediately commenced practice, and now resides.

HALLETT K. TAYLOR

was born in Ravenna, Ohio, November 2, 1857. He was a son of Ezra B. and Harriet M. (Frazer) Taylor, both natives of Portage county, Ohio. His father was for several years judge of the common pleas of the second subdivision of the ninth judicial district, and is now (1882) Representative in Congress from the nineteenth Ohio Congressional district. H. K. Taylor was a graduate of the Western Reserve college, at Hudson, Ohio, class of 1879. Read law with his father at Warren, Ohio, and was admitted to the bar at Columbus, Ohio, in June, 1881. He then commenced practice in Youngstown, Ohio, where he now resides.

VOLNEY ROGERS

was born in Middleton, Columbiana county, Ohio, December 1, 1846, and was a son of James and Elizabeth D. Rogers. He read law with Andrews & Rogers, at Mt. Gilead, Morrow county, Ohio, and was admitted to the bar by the supreme court at Columbus, Ohio, in December, 1871. He commenced practice in Youngstown, Ohio, where he now resides, in February, 1872. In 1874 he formed a partnership in law practice with his brother Disney, under the firm name of Rogers & Rogers, which still continues. In 1878 he was elected city solicitor of Youngstown and re-elected in 1880.

DISNEY ROGERS

was born in Middleton, Columbiana county, Ohio, December 19, 1844. He is a son of James and Elizabeth D. (Jameson) Rogers. His father is of Welsh descent; his mother of Scotch descent. He attended the public schools at Middleton and the high school at New Lisbon, Ohio; read law with James L. Smith at New Lisbon, and was admitted to the bar by the district court at St. Clairsville, Belmont county, September 12, 1866. He practiced in Mt. Gilead, Morrow county, Ohio, from 1866 to 1874, in partnership with Bertrand Andrews, as Andrews & Rogers. In 1874 he removed to Youngstown, Ohio, and has since practiced there in partnership with his brother Volney, as Rogers & Rogers. While residing at Mt. Gilead he was a member of the council for five years, and was appointed by Judge Sherman, of the United States district court, a commissioner for the northern district of Ohio, which office he now holds. In the Presidential campaign of 1880 he was chairman of the Republican central committee of Mahoning county. He was married at Mt. Gilead, Ohio, February 13, 1869, to Miss Ida S. Andrews, daughter of Bertrand Andrews, his former law partner.

WILLIAM H. CALLAHAN

was born in Green, Mahoning county, Ohio, in 1851. He was a son of Nathan P. (for some time sheriff of Mahoning county) and Mary Callahan. He read law with S. W. Gilson, Esq., at Canfield, and was there admitted to the bar in 1870. He practiced there until 1876, when he removed to Youngstown, where he is engaged in practice.

THOMAS F. HANSARD

was born near Hudson, Summit county, Ohio, June 28, 1855. He was a son of John and Mary Hansard, natives of Ireland. He attended at Notre Dame university, Indiana, but left without graduating, and commenced studying law with E. M. Brown, in Cleveland, Ohio, in 1877. He taught school part of the time while studying law, finished his law studies with Daniel Babst, Jr., at Crestline, Ohio, was admitted to the bar at Columbus, Ohio, December 7, 1880, and then commenced practicing law at Youngstown, Ohio, where he now resides.

DANIEL L. THOMAS

was born October 2, 1848, in Palmyra, Portage county, Ohio. His parents were John D. and Sophia C. (Lewis) Thomas. His father was a native of Wales, his mother was a daughter of Frank Lewis, an early pioneer from New England, and a well-known and popular inn-keeper, at Palmyra, prior to the advent of railroads in eastern Ohio, on the old stage road from Cleveland to Pittsburg. He came, with his parents, to Youngstown in 1863, graduated at the Rayen school in 1870; was, for a time, in mercantile business; then read law with H. H. Moses, at Youngstown; attended a course of law lectures at the Michigan university, at Ann Arbor, and was admitted to the bar at Canfield, Ohio, in 1875. He has since practiced in Youngstown.

On May 14, 1874, he was married, at Waukegan, Illinois, to Miss Elizabeth A. Turner, of that place.

LEWIS W. KING

was born November 24, 1854, at Unity, Columbiana county, Ohio. His parents were Eleazer and Margaret (Mollenkopf) King. His father was of Irish ancestry, his mother of German ancestry, and the daughter of one of the earliest settlers of that township. He removed to Canfield, Ohio, in 1873, and officiated as clerk in the office of the probate judge until January, 1875, and then as assistant to the clerk of the court of common pleas until February, 1877. During the time he was in the probate and clerk's offices he studied law with Anderson & Roller, and was admitted to the bar. He commenced practice in 1877, in partnership with William S. Anderson, in the firm of Anderson & King. In October, 1881, he was elected probate judge for three years, and commenced his official term February 9, 1882.

JOHN L. BUTLER

was born in Cambridge, Massachusetts, January 9, 1848. Here he was schooled and educated until his sixteenth year, when, having caught the war fever, he enlisted in the regular army, serving under the late General Myer in the signal corps. He participated in several battles and skirmishes, principally the famous passage of the forts in Mobile bay, under the leadership of Admiral Farragut; and again in the reduction of Mobile city, under the leadership of General Canby. After the war he returned to his native city, where he remained until 1867, when he embarked in the oil business in Pennsylvania. Here he remained until 1875, having in the meantime been admitted to the Warren county, Pennsylvania, bar. In 1877 he was admitted to the supreme court of Pennsylvania. In 1878 he returned to Boston, Massachusetts, intending to pass the remainder of his days in his native city. But owing to the severity of the climate the health of his wife to whom he was married while in Pennsylvania, failed, and this necessitated a removal to a more inland State.

In 1881 Ohio was chosen as the field of his labors, particularly on account of his wife, who was Miss Josephine Swisher, a native of Petersburg, Mahoning county, a woman well known in literary circles. She at one time wrote for the Youngstown papers and other county publications, under the *nom de plume* of "Rose Wilde." In politics Mr. Butler is independent, his voice and pen always ready to denounce sham and fraud, no matter what par · suffers. He has the confidence of many of the ablest leaders in each party. As a lawyer he came highly recommended. He resides in Youngstown, engaged in practice. His father and mother are still living in Boston, Massachusetts, hale and hearty. His father was born in Tipperary, Ireland, and is first cousin of General B. F. Butler. His grandfather emigrated to Canada when the father of the subject of our sketch was an infant in arms. The B. F. Butler branch of the family emigrated from Ireland to New Hampshire. Another branch of the family settled in South Carolina. The family is descended from the Fitzwalter family of Normans, who invaded Ireland. In personal appearance Mr. Butler appears rather young for a man of his age. In height he is about five feet nine inches, dark complexion, of slender build, smooth, clean shaven face. He has no facial resemblance to his celebrated kinsman of Massachusetts, but bears, it is said, a striking resemblance to United States Senator Butler, of South Carolina.

HENRY C. CASSIDY.

Henry C. Cassidy was born in Butler county, Pennsylvania, February 22, 1856. His parents were Charles and Mary (McGillop) Cassidy. His father was a native of Ireland, his mother of Tyrone, Blair county, Pennsylvania. He removed with his parents to Youngstown, Ohio, in November, 1858. He graduated at Notre Dame university, Indiana, read law with Moses & Arrel of Youngstown, was admitted to the bar at Columbus, Ohio, in May, 1880, and has since practiced in Youngstown.

SIDNEY DE LAMAR JACKSON

was born in Hubbard, Trumbull county, Ohio, April 9, 1855. His parents were Joseph M. and Rebecca L. Jackson. His father was born in New Bedford, Pennsylvania; his mother in Hubbard, Ohio. They reside in Coitsville, where he received his early education. He read law in Youngstown with Hon. David M. Wilson. He was admitted to the bar at the district court in Canfield, Ohio, April 3, 1877, and commenced practice in Youngstown, where he is now practicing in partnership with William T. Gibson.

He was married at Fredonia, New York, December 14, 1880, to Miss Mary E. Cushing, of that place.

EDWARD ROCKWELL

was born in Connecticut. He graduated at Yale college in 1821, read law at the Yale law school in New Haven, Connecticut, and was there admitted to the bar. About 1827 he moved to Youngstown, where he practiced several years. During his residence he held the office of justice of the peace. He removed to Cleveland about 1855, and was secretary and treasurer of the Cleveland & Pittsburg railroad company. Prior to his removal to Youngstown he was married, at New Haven, Connecticut, to Miss Matilda D. P. Salter. He died in Cleveland in 1874; his wife died in Youngstown, April 4, 1847.

HOMER H. HINE

was born in Youngstown, Ohio, February 15, 1823. He was a son of Homer and Mary (Skinner) Hine, both early pioneers of the Reserve. He graduated at Western Reserve college, read law with his father, and afterwards with Hitchcock, Wilson & Wade, at Cleveland, and was admitted to the bar at Warren in the fall of 1846. He commenced practice in Youngstown in 1847, in partnership with Milton Sutliff, of Warren, as Sutliff & Hine. In 1849 he removed to Painesville, Ohio, where he still resides, on the farm cleared up and in the house built by his grandfather, Abraham Skinner, in 1805, in which house his parents were married in 1807. He is engaged in farming and occasionally attending to cases in court. He was married April 3, 1845, to Miss Julietta Rue, daughter of Jonathan Rue, of Harrodsburgh, Kentucky.

WILLIAM FERGUSON

was born in Trumbull county, Ohio, about 1820. He read law with Tod, Hoffman & Hutchins at Warren, Ohio, and was there admitted to the bar about 1844 and then commenced practicing in Youngstown, Ohio. In 1846 he was elected prosecuting attorney of Mahoning county, at the first election held after the organization of the county, in April, being a special election. He was re-elected at the annual election held in October, and held the office one term. In 1853 he removed to DeWitt, Clinton county, Iowa, and entered into practice. He was for a time attorney for a railroad company. He died at DeWitt in 1862. He was married about 1850 at Youngstown, to Miss Prudence Murray, daughter of Lewis Murray, of that place.

RIDGELEY J. POWERS

was born in Youngstown, Ohio, April 17, 1822. His parents were Jacob and Nancy Powers, the former born in Westmoreland county, Pennsylvania, the latter in Wheeling, Virginia. He graduated at Alleghany college, Meadville, Pennsylvania, in 1843; studied law with Tod, Hoffman & Hutchins, at Warren, Ohio, and was admitted to the bar at that place in 1844. He commenced the practice of law at Youngstown, Ohio, as a member of the firm of Hoffman, Hutchins & Powers, in which firm he continued for a short period. He resided in Youngstown several years and then removed to Pittsburg, Pennsylvania, where he is now engaged in the practice of the profession as senior member of the firm of Powers, Force & Powers. He was elected prosecuting attorney of Mahoning county, and served three terms, viz: during the years of 1852-53, 1854-55, and 1858-59. The two first terms he was elected as a Democrat and the last as a Republican.

He was married, at Meadville, Pennsylvania, June 15, 1843, to Mary Henderson Waring, then a resident of that place. She was born at Louisville, Kentucky.

WILLIS WARING POWERS

was born in Warren, Trumbull county, Ohio, February 2, 1848. He was a son of Ridgeley J. and Mary Henderson (Waring) Powers. His father was born in Youngstown, Ohio, and practiced law in that city from 1844 until 1867, when he removed with his family to Pittsburg, Pennsylvania, where he now resides, engaged in practice. His mother was born in Louisville, Kentucky.

He entered Allegheny college, Pennsylvania, in 1865, and graduated in 1869. For several years prior to his graduation his father had instructed him in the elementary principles of law, and in 1870 he was admitted to practice in the various county courts of Alleghany county Pennsylvania, and a few years later to the supreme court of that State, and to the United States courts. He resided in Pittsburg, as a member of the law firm of R. J. & Willis W. Powers until 1880, when, after being admitted to the bar of Ohio at Columbus, Ohio, he removed to Youngstown, Ohio, and shortly after there commenced practice in partnership with M. C. McNabb as McNabb & Powers.

While residing at Pittsburg, he received an appointment and commission from Governor Hartranft, of Pennsylvania, as major and aide-decamp, Sixth division National guard of Pennsylvania, and served, with his division, in the suppression of the great riots in the anthracite coal regions of Pennsylvania in the summer and fall of 1876.

Immediately following his admission to the bar in 1870, he was married to Ella S. Powers, of Youngstown, daughter of Abraham Powers, of that city, one of the most prominent business men of the Mahoning valley. He died September 8, 1881.

FRANCIS E. HUTCHINS

was born in Pennsylvania, came when a youth with his parents to Youngstown, Ohio, attended the schools there, read law with William Ferguson, and was admitted to the bar, at Canfield, in 1850. He practiced law at Youngstown a few years and then removed to Warren, where he now resides, engaged in practice. He was married at Youngstown, December 11, 1851, to Miss Elizabeth Sanderson, of that place.

ROBERT E. KNIGHT

was born in Carroll county, Ohio, about 1831, was admitted to the bar at Carrollton, Ohio, practiced there some years, and removed to Youngstown, Ohio, in 1869; practiced there for a short time in partnership with David M. Wilson, as Wilson & Knight, and in 1873 removed to Lincoln, Nebraska. He remained there three years and returned to Cleveland, where he is now engaged in practice.

He was married, in 1850, to Miss Mary E. Lawthers, of Leesburg, Carrol county, Ohio, daughter of Colonel G. Lawthers, an old citizen of that place.

JOHN H. KING

was born in Youngstown, Ohio, about 1827. His father was Singleton King, who removed to Youngstown in 1805, and was for many years a prominent business man. He was admitted to the bar at Canfield in 1852, and practiced law in Youngstown several years, during part of which time he held the office of justice of the peace. He died August 5, 1858.

GEORGE J. WARD

was born in Austintown, Ohio, in 1850. His parents were George and Hannah (Smith) Ward. His father was born in England; his mother in Wales. He read law at Canfield with S. W. Gilson, Esq.; was there admitted to the bar in 1874, practiced there a short time, and removed to Youngstown in 1876, where he continued to practice. He died March 5, 1877.

WILLIAM CAREY BUNTS

was born in Berlin, Mahoning county, Ohio, was admitted to the bar in 1856, and practiced law several years in Youngstown. He was elected prosecuting attorney of Mahoning county in 1860, and served one term. He then joined the Union army as a volunteer, and after leaving the army he removed to Cleveland, Ohio, where he died several years since. He was married about 1859 to Miss Clara Barnhisel, daughter of the late Henry Barnhisel, of Liberty, Trumbull county, Ohio.

HENRY G. LESLIE

was born in Poland, Ohio, March 17, 1839. He was a son of John G. Leslie, a merchant of that place. He was admitted to the bar at Canfield in 1862, and commenced practice in Youngstown, Ohio, where he continued in practice until his death. He was elected city attorney of Youngstown in 1864, and was elected prosecuting attorney of Mahoning county in 1867, and died March 2, 1869, during his term of office.

He was married in Cleveland in 1865, to Miss Amelia Burton, daughter of Rev. Lewis Burton, of Cleveland, Ohio, a distinguished minister of the Protestant Episcopal church.

HALBERT R. CASE

was born in Mecca, Trumbull county, Ohio, about 1838. He attended the Western Reserve seminary at Farmington, Ohio, and the college at Oberlin. He read law at the Michigan university, and was admitted to the bar in Trumbull county, Ohio, in 1863. Prior to his admission to the bar he had served as a soldier in the war of 1861, in the Seventh Ohio regiment, in which he was captain of a company. He removed to Youngstown about 1864, and practiced law there for a few years, part of the time in partnership with Asa W. Jones, as Jones & Case, part of the time in partnership with William J. Lawthers, as Case & Lawthers, and part of the time without a partner. About 1870 he removed to Alba, Iowa, afterwards to DesMoines, and then to Chattanooga, Tennessee, where he now resides, engaged in practice. He was married, about the time he came to Youngstown, to Miss Carrie, daughter of Austin D. Kibbee, of Farmington, Ohio. She died at DesMoines. He was afterwards married at Chattanooga to Miss Jennie Spooner, who had removed there from Ohio with her parents after the close of the war.

WILLIAM M. OSBORN

was born in Youngstown, Ohio, in 1842. He

is a son of Abner and Abby (Allison) Osborn. He attended the Poland, Ohio, academy, and shortly after the beginning of the war of 1861 he enlisted in the Twenty-third regiment, Ohio volunteer infantry, and served several months. He contracted a fever which nearly cost him his life, disabling him from further service, and he was discharged. He read law with Judge Glidden at Poland, and afterwards attended the law department of the University of Michigan at Ann Arbor. He was admitted to the bar in Warren, Ohio, about 1869, and commenced practice in Youngstown, Ohio, at first alone, and then in partnership with General T. W. Sanderson, as Sanderson & Osborn, and then alone. He was elected mayor of Youngstown in 1874, and served one term. He removed to Cleveland, Ohio, in February, 1878, and commenced practice there.

He was married in Boston, Massachusetts, on April 29, 1878, to Miss Fanny Hastings of that city, adopted daughter of Walter Hastings, since deceased, and niece of Judge Glidden. Mr. and Mrs. Osborn, with Mrs. Hastings, visited Europe in December, 1880, and are still there on an extended tour.

WILLIAM L. BROWN.

William L. Brown was born in New England, and removed to Canfield with his mother, a widow, when quite young. He attended the academy there, read law and was admitted to the bar in 1863. Shortly after, he went to Montana, remained there a few years, returned and located in Youngstown, where he engaged in practicing law and in publishing the Youngstown Vindicator, a democratic weekly journal. About 1879 he purchased an interest in the New York Daily News, sold his interest in the Vindicator, and removed to New York city, where he now resides, engaged in editing and publishing the Daily News. In December, 1878, he was married at Washington city to Miss Henrietta Jeffries, daughter of General M. L. Jeffries of that city, formerly a lawyer of Ravenna, Ohio.

HENRY CAMP.

Henry Camp was born in Jackson, Mahoning county, Ohio. He was son of Captain John Camp, a former justice of the peace, militia officer and hotel-keeper of that place. He was for several years a Disciple preacher in Ohio and Pennsylvania. He read law and practiced for a time in Pennsylvania. He removed to Youngstown, Ohio, in 1875, and there commenced practice. In February, 1877, during a strong, popular Murphy excitement, he joined the Murphy ranks. He was a ready and forcible speaker and his services as a temperance lecturer were soon in demand. He removed to Cleveland, and in the spring of that year engaged actively in a Murphy revival there, and has been largely engaged since in different parts of the State as an advocate of temperance.

WILLIAM PORTER

was a native of Ireland, came when a youth to the United States, and resided several years in Milton, Ohio. He was elected, about 1840, an associate judge of the court of common pleas of Trumbull county under the old constitution. He was admitted to the bar at Canfield, Ohio, in 1859, practiced a few years in Milton, Ohio, and removed to Youngstown about 1870, where he practiced a few years, and about 1879 removed to Bristol, Trumbull county, and engaged in other business.

ELGIN A. ANGELL

was born in the State of New York, was admitted to the bar at Canfield in 1876. He practiced a short time thereafter in Youngstown and removed to Cleveland, where he now resides, engaged in practice.

JOHN C. HUTCHINS

was born in Warren, Ohio, son of John Hutchins, a lawyer, now of Cleveland, Ohio. He was admitted to the bar at Canfield, Ohio, in 1866, commenced practice in Youngstown, remained there a short time and removed to Cleveland, where he now resides, engaged in practice.

CORNELIUS M. BROWN

was born in Youngstown, Ohio, was there admitted to the bar in 1878. He practiced in Youngstown a short time and removed to Springfield, Ohio, where he is now engaged in practice.

WILLIAM W. WHITTLESEY

was born in Canfield, Ohio; was a son of Hon. Elisha Whittlesey; read law with Whittlesey & Newton; was admitted to the bar about 1840, at Warren, Ohio, and practiced law a few years at Canfield in partnership with Hon. Eben Newton, as Newton & Whittlesey. At the first term of the court of common pleas of Mahoning county, in May, 1846, he was appointed clerk and held the office until 1855. He practiced in Canfield for a few years thereafter, when he was appointed a clerk in the United States Treasury department, and removed to Washington city, where he now resides. He was married at Canfield about 1840, to Miss Jerusha Lockwood, daughter of Stanley C. Lockwood of that place.

JAMES B. BLOCKSOM

was born in New Lisbon, Columbiana county, Ohio, July 19, 1821. He was a son of Fisher A. Blocksom, a native of Wilmington, Delaware, and a pioneer lawyer of Ohio, who settled in New Lisbon about 1800, became a man of high repute as a lawyer, held several public offices, and died at a very advanced age. His mother, Margaret (Graham) Blocksom, was born in Chambersburgh, Pennsylvania. James B. received his early education at the public schools. He read law with his father, and was admitted to the bar at Zanesville, Muskingum county, Ohio, in 1842, commenced practice in New Lisbon, resided there until 1846, when he removed to Canfield, shortly after the organization of Mahoning county. He was elected prosecuting attorney of the county in 1848, and served for one term. He was elected justice of the peace of the township of Canfield in 1861, and for several years was mayor of the village of Canfield. He was again elected prosecuting attorney in 1862, and died January 15, 1863, during his official term. Shortly after he came to Canfield he formed a law partnership with John M. Edwards, under the firm of Edwards & Blocksom—which continued some time. In 1858 he was a partner of David M. Wilson, who then resided in Youngstown, Ohio, as Wilson & Blocksom, which continued a short time. He was married in Canfield, January 9, 1849, to Miss Frances M. Church, daughter of John R. Church, one of the early settlers of that township, and granddaughter of Nathaniel Church, one of the proprietors of the township. Her parents were natives of Connecticut, and of English descent.

ENSIGN CHURCH BLOCKSOM,

son of James B. and Frances M. (Church) Blocksom, was born in Canfield, Ohio, August 1, 1855. He read law in the office of Van Hyning & Johnston at Canfield, and was admitted to the bar about 1877. He practiced law at Canfield about two years, and afterwards at Canton, Ohio, as a member of the firm of Bond & Blocksom. He went to San Francisco, California, in the fall of 1880, where he resides at present, but is not now practicing law.

EPHRAIM JAMES ESTEP

was born in Wellsville, Columbiana county, Ohio. He was a son of Henry and Abigail Estep, who were residents of Ohio from 1806. He studied law with James Mason in New Lisbon, Ohio, and was admitted to the bar at that place in 1845. On the organization of Mahoning county in 1846 he removed to Canfield, Ohio, and was engaged in practice there for several years, and then removed to Cleveland, where he still resides engaged in practice. At Canfield he was a partner with James Mason of New Lisbon, under the firm of Mason & Estep, and afterwards at Cleveland, under the same firm, Mr. Mason having removed to Cleveland. At Cleveland, subsequently, he was a partner of Reuben Hitchcock as Hitchcock & Estep, of F. T. Backus as Backus & Estep, of Stevenson Burke as Estep & Burke, and of Andrew Squire, his present partner, as Estep & Squire.

He was married in May, 1851, at Canfield, Ohio, to Miss Julia M. Peffers, a native of that place and granddaughter of Eli T. Boughton, one of the early settlers.

EDWARD G. CANFIELD

was born in Portage county, Ohio, and was there admitted to the bar and practiced for a short period. He removed to Canfield, Ohio, soon after the organization of Mahoning county, in 1846, and engaged in practice for some time in partnership with John L. Ranney, Esq., of Ravenna, Ohio, as Canfield & Ranney. He was elected prosecuting attorney of Mahoning county in 1850 and served one term. Several years ago he removed to Trumbull county, Ohio. He was married while residing in Canfield to Miss Ritter, daughter of Henry Ritter, an old citizen of that place.

FRANCIS G. SERVIS

was born in New Jersey in 1826, and, at an early age, came, with his parents, to Berlin, Mahoning county, Ohio. His father, Abraham Servis, was a farmer, but, although not a member of the bar, practiced law to a considerable extent before justices of the peace in Berlin and neighboring townships, and, as such practitioner, had quite a reputation for shrewdness and ability. Francis G. received a common school education, then taught school and was clerk in a store. On March 9, 1852, he was appointed clerk of the probate court of Mahoning county and officiated as such until 1855. During this time he read law; was admitted to the bar, and, after leaving the probate office, he commenced practice in Canfield. In 1863 he was appointed, by the court of common pleas, prosecuting attorney to fill the vacancy occasioned by the death of James B. Blocksom, and was elected to that office in 1864, and re-elected in 1866. In 1872 he was appointed, by President Grant, judge of Montana, which office he held for a few years and resigned and returned to Canfield and resumed practice. In 1876 he was elected judge of the second subdivision of the Ninth judicial district of the court of common pleas, but died March 6, 1877, without taking his seat on the bench.

He was married, at Canfield, September 11, 1853, to Miss Martha E. Patten. She survives him.

GARRETSON I. YOUNG

was born in Columbiana county, Ohio, and read law with S. W. Gilson, Esq., at Canfield, Ohio, and was there admitted to the bar in 1851, and then commenced practice. He was elected probate judge of Mahoning county in 1854, and was re-elected in 1857, and served in that office six years. After the expiration of his term of office, he returned to Columbiana county and resumed the practice of law. He was elected Representative in the Ohio Legislature from that county in 1869, and died at Columbus in 1870, while attending his legislative duties. He was married at Ellsworth, Ohio, March 27, 1856, to Miss Susan Bingham, of that place.

ISAAC E. COFFEE

was born in Salem, Columbiana county, read law with S. W. Gilson, Esq., at Canfield, was there admitted to the bar in 1855; practiced law there in partnership with Mr. Gilson, and died at Canfield in September, 1859. He was married to Miss Kate Hine, of Canfield, November 19, 1857.

CHARLES A. HARRINGTON

was born in Trumbull county, Ohio, and there admitted to the bar. He practiced for a time at Canfield, and returned to Trumbull county and resumed practice at Warren. He there held the office of clerk of the courts for several years.

THERON M. RICE

was born in Trumbull county, Ohio; addmitted to the bar, and removed to Canfield, Ohio, about 1855; practiced there a few years and removed to Missouri, where he was elected a judge of the common pleas, and in 1880, a Representative in Congress for the seventh district.

SAMUEL W. GILSON

was born in Pennsylvania. He graduated at Washington college in that State, taught school, read law, and was admitted to the bar in Columbiana county, Ohio. He removed to Canfield soon after the organization of Mahoning county, and there resided, in the practice of law until his death.

He was elected representative in the Ohio Legislature from Mahoning county in 1858, and served one term. He died at Canfield in May, 1874.

JOHN W. CHURCH

was born in Canfield, Ohio, was a son of John R. Church, an early settler of that township, for many years a merchant, and for one term an associate judge of the court of common pleas of Trumbull county. He was admitted to the bar about 1850. He practiced in Canfield a few years in partnership with David M. Wilson as Wilson & Church, and removed to Massillion, Stark county, Ohio. He was there elected judge of the common pleas, and died some years since. He was married about 1856, to Miss Frances Pease, daughter of Samuel Pease, Esq., a lawyer of Massillon.

CHARLES RUGGLES

was born about 1806, and was a son of an early pioneer of Canfield. He was raised on a farm, became a practical farmer and surveyor. He read law and was admitted to the bar at Warren, Ohio, about 1840. He practiced law in Canfield, in addition to surveying, for many years, but has now retired from law practice, in a great measure, and is engaged in other business.

HORACE G. RUGGLES,

son of Charles Ruggles, was born in Canfield; attended the Mahoning academy; read law and was admitted to the bar about 1860. He practiced in Canfield a few years and removed to the West. He was married, December 24, 1863, to Miss Amanda C. Hoyle, of Berlin, Ohio.

EDWIN C. RUGGLES

is a son of Charles Ruggles. He was admitted to the bar at Canfield in 1869, practiced there a few years and removed to Cuyahoga falls, Summit county, Ohio, where he resides engaged in practice. He was married April 20, 1859, to Miss Catharine McFarland, of Canfield, Ohio.

JOHN S. ROLLER

was born in Green, Mahoning (then Columbiana) county, Ohio, September 27, 1839. His parents were Simon and Mary Ann (Weikert) Roller, whose parents were early settlers of that township. He attended the Mahoning academy at Canfield, read law and was admitted to the bar in Portage county in May, 1871. He commenced practice in Leetonia, Columbiana county, in November, 1871. In April, 1874, he removed to Canfield, where he has since resided, in practice, part of the time in partnership with William S. Anderson as Anderson & Roller.

He was married January 15, 1868, at Canfield, to Miss Asenath A. Fitzpatrick.

LANDON MASTIN

for a number of years was a resident of Smith other, Mahoning county, Ohio; engaged in other business. He read law with F. G. Servis, Esq., of Canfield, and was there admitted to the bar in 1870. He resides there now, practicing occasionally, but engaged in other business. He was married November 15, 1850, to Miss Harriett Santee of Smith township.

ENSIGN N. BROWN

was born in Canfield December 9, 1854. He is son of Richard and Thalia F. (Newton) Brown, then of New York city, and grandson of Eben Newton, of Canfield, a lawyer of distinction, and one of the oldest on the Reserve. In 1878 he removed to Canfield, Ohio, with his parents, who were former residents of that place. He read law with Judge Newton, and with VanHyning & Johnston, and was admitted to the bar at Columbus, Ohio, in 1880, and commenced practice in Canfield, where he is still in practice.

FRANCIS C. NESBIT

was born in Pennsylvania, attended the academy at Canfield, Ohio, read law, and was admitted to the bar of Ohio about 1860, and commenced practice at Canfield. He was a justice of the peace of that township from 1866 to 1869, and removed West about 1870. He was married in October, 1861, to Miss Ellen Wright, of Tallmadge, Ohio.

HARRISON J. EWING

was born in Milton, Ohio, was admitted to the bar at Canfield in 1876, practiced a short time in the county, and removed to Cuyahoga county. He was married November 23, 1866, to Miss Sarah Patterson, of Milton, Ohio.

ALEXANDER H. MOORE

was born in Milton, Mahoning county, Ohio, was admitted to the bar at Canfield in 1859, practiced there a few years, and afterwards in Youngstown, and removed back to Milton, where he is engaged in other business, occasionally attending to law practice.

JOHN J. MOORE

was born in Milton, Ohio, was admitted to the bar at Canfield in 1863, practiced some time in Canfield, and removed to Ottawa, Putnam county, Ohio. He resumed practice there, and in 1878 was elected judge of the court of common pleas of the Third subdivision of the Third judicial district.

He was married at Milton, Ohio, May 19, 1859, to Miss Elizabeth Patterson, of that township.

SELDEN HAINES

was the son of parents who removed from New England to Vernon, Trumbull county, Ohio, and were among the early settlers of the Reserve. He was born about 1806. He graduated at Yale college in 1826, read law and was admitted to the bar in Trumbull county about 1828, and commenced practice in Poland, Ohio. In July, 1832, he was colonel of the First Rifle regiment, First brigade and Fourth division, Ohio militia. He practiced law several years at Poland, and then entered the ministry of the gospel. He removed from Poland and was, in 1882, the pastor of a Presbyterian church in Rome, New York. In 1872 he received from the college at Maryville, Tennessee, the honorary degree of S. T. D.

WILLIAM KNIGHT

was a citizen and lawyer of Wilbraham, Massachusetts, and had been a Representative in the

Legislature of that State. About 1840, having a son, the late William L. Knight, settled at Warren, Ohio, as a lawyer, he removed to Ohio, purchased a residence in Poland, then in Trumbull county, and commenced practice, and there resided during his life. He died in Poland in 1852.

CHARLES E. GLIDDEN

was born at Claremont, New Hampshire, December 4, 1835. His parents were Erastus and Diantha Glidden, of that place. He prepared for the bar at the New York State and Union Law college at Poughkeepsie, New York, and graduated at that college in 1855. He removed to Poland, Ohio, September 10, 1855, and was admitted to the bar at Ravenna, Ohio, in 1856. He practiced law at Poland, Ohio, from 1856 to 1862, in which year he was elected judge of the court of common pleas in the second subdivision of the ninth judicial district of Ohio. His term expired in 1867, when he resumed the practice of law at Warren, Ohio, with F. E. Hutchins and John M. Stull, under the firm name of Hutchins, Glidden & Stull. He continued in practice until 1872, when he was again elected judge of the common pleas of the same subdivision and district. His term expired in 1877, when he resumed practice at Warren, but his health failing, he retired from practice and removed to Roxbury, Massachusetts, where he now resides.

At the time he was first elected judge he was not quite twenty-seven years of age, and, probably, was the youngest man ever elected judge in the district, and, perhaps, in Ohio. As a lawyer he ranked high in his profession, and he retired from the bench with the reputation of a learned, able, and upright judge.

He was married at Poland, Ohio, December 10, 1856, to Mrs. Eliza K. Morse, of that place.

FREDERICK W. BEARDSLEY

was born in Canfield, and is a son of Philo Beardsley, a farmer and pioneer of that township, from New England. He attended the academy at Canfield and afterwards taught school. He was elected clerk of the court of common pleas in 1860, and served, by re-election, six years. He was admitted to the bar at Canfield in 1866. After the expiration of his term of office as clerk, he practiced in Canfield a short time and removed West.

He was married October 25, 1860, to Miss Jacqueline P. Gee, of Mahoning county.

WILLIAM B. DAWSON

was born in West Union, now Calcutta, Columbiana county, Ohio, June 6, 1831. His parents were Augustine and Maria (Bever) Dawson. He attended the academy in his native village, studying Latin and Greek and the higher branches under different teachers, then read law at Canfield, Ohio, with S. W. Gilson and afterwards with D. M. Wilson and John W. Church, and was admitted to the bar at Canfield in May, 1853, and commenced practice and still resides there.

He was married in Canfield, October, 1853, to Miss Maria C. Wadsworth, who was born in that place. She was a daughter of Colonel George Wadsworth, and granddaughter of Major-general Elijah Wadsworth, who acquired distinction on the northern frontier in the War of 1812, and was one of the proprietors and first settlers of Canfield.

JOHN M. LEWIS

was born at Gwynnedd, Montgomery county, Pennsylvania, July 2, 1814. His parents were Jesse and Susannah Lewis, natives of that place. He graduated at Gwynnedd high school in 1835, removed to Greenford, then in Columbiana county, Ohio, September 18, 1841; read law with Umbstaetter & Stanton in New Lisbon, Ohio, and was admitted to the bar at New Lisbon in the spring of 1843. He practiced at Greenford until the spring of 1846, when he removed to Canfield on the organization of Mahoning county. He practiced there about eight years and then removed to Cincinnati, and remained about eight years engaged in practice. He then returned to Greenford, where he has since resided, engaged in other business, and also practicing law to some extent.

EMERY E. KNOWLTON

was born in Ashtabula county Ohio. He was left an orphan at an early age, and was adopted and raised by Isaac Griffin, of Farmington, Ohio. He attended the Western Reserve seminary at that place. He entered the army soon after the commencement of the war in 1861, and served with credit during the war. After his return from the army and about 1866, he was appointed deputy clerk of the court of common pleas, of Mahoning county, Ohio, was elected clerk in 1872, and served in that office until his death. He died January 6, 1875. While officiating in the clerk's office he read law and was admitted to the bar at Canfield in 1869. He was married in October, 1871, to Miss Mary E. Nash, of Canfield.

GILES VAN HYNING

was born in Summit county, Ohio, in 1834. He is a son of Henry and Julia Van Hyning, now of Canfield, Ohio. He studied law at the Ohio State and Union Law college, at Poland, Ohio, and was admitted to the bar at Canfield, Ohio, in 1858, and immediately commenced practice in that place. In 1860 he was elected probate judge of Mahoning county, and re-elected in 1863, holding the office six years. At the expiration of his term he resumed the practice for a time in partnership with Francis G. Servis, as Servis & Van Hyning, and for several years past and now in partnership with Joseph R. Johnston, as Van Hyning & Johnston, with offices at Canfield and Youngstown.

On October 30, 1860, he was married to Miss Hannah K. Newton, daughter of Judge Eben Newton, of Canfield.

R. S. HIGLEY,

a native of Portage county, began practicing law in Youngstown in 1861, and has been in constant practice since that time with the exception of about four months, during which he was in the army, and a period of eight years, during which he resided at Marietta, Ohio. As a full biographical sketch is given of Mr. Higley elsewhere, further mention of him is omitted here.

JOSEPH R. JOHNSTON

was born at Jackson, Mahoning county, Ohio, September 12, 1840. His father, John Johnston, removed there from Armstrong county, Pennsylvania, in 1811. His mother was from Fayette county, Pennsylvania. He attended academies at Jackson and at Canfield. He enlisted and served in the Second Ohio volunteer cavalry from September, 1861, to February, 1863, when he was transferred to the Twenty-fifth Ohio battery, and remained with the battery until he was mustered out of the army, September, 1864, at Little Rock, Arkansas.

On returning from the army he commenced studying law with Judge G. VanHyning at Canfield, and was admitted to the bar in September, 1866. He was elected probate judge of Mahoning county in October, 1866, and re-elected in 1869. Since the expiration of his term as probate judge, in 1873, he has practiced law in Canfield in partnership with G. VanHyning, under the firm of VanHyning & Johnston. He was elected to the Ohio Senate for the counties of Mahoning and Trumbull in October, 1875, and re-elected in October, 1877.

He was married at North Benton, Mahoning county, Ohio, June 9, 1868, to Miss Mary S. Hartzell, a native of that place.

ALBERT B. LOGAN

was born in Poland, Ohio, (read law) and enlisted and served during part of the war of the Rebellion in the Union army; afterwards read law and was admitted to the bar at Canfield, in 1866; practiced for a time in Mahoning county, and removed to Missouri.

JOHN W. CRACRAFT

was born in Poland, Ohio, November, 1839. He was son of Joseph and Sarah Ann (Craver) Cracraft. He read law at the Ohio State and Union Law college in Poland, and was admitted to the bar at Canfield, Ohio, in 1860. He practiced law at Lowellville, Mahoning county, until after the commencement of the war of 1861, when he enlisted in the Twenty-third regiment of Ohio infantry volunteers, and served with great credit during the war. After its close he removed to Charlestown, West Virginia, where he now resides, engaged in the practice of his profession.

JAMES M. NASH

was born about 1832. In early life he worked in a printing office, becoming a proficient practical printer and acquired readiness, skill, and tact as a reporter and editor of a newspaper. This was his vocation in Youngstown at the commencement of the war of 1861. In response to the call of President Lincoln for seventy-five thousand men he enlisted as a private in the Mahoning Rifles, one of the first companies formed in Youngstown or in Ohio. He was elected by his fellow-soldiers to the rank of orderly sergeant and left Youngstown with the company on May 20, 1861, for Cleveland, where the Rifles was incorporated into the Nineteenth Ohio regiment as company B, and soon left for the field of action. In this regiment he served gallantly during the war and returned at the close the colonel of the regiment. During his services in the field he received a wound in the hand which disabled him from type setting, but on his return he was again employed in his old occupation as reporter and assistant editor. In 1866 he was elected clerk of the court of common pleas of Mahoning county, Ohio, and re-elected in 1869, holding the office six years. During his term as clerk he read law and was admitted to the bar about 1870. He was married to Miss Mary Church, daughter of John R. Church, of Canfield, June 19, 1859.

POLAND LAW COLLEGE.

Hayden, King & Leggett, a firm composed of Chester Hayden, Marcus A. King and Mortimer D. Leggett, about 1856 established a law school at Poland, Ohio, styled the Ohio State and Union Law college, which they conducted there for a few years, when it was removed to Cleveland, Ohio. We find on the records of the Mahoning county district court, at its April term, A. D. 1857, on application of Chester Hayden, president, the appointment by the court of Eben Newton, S. W. Gilson, J. M. Edwards, R. J. Powers, and F. E. Hutchins a committee to attend the annual commencement and examine students for admission to the bar. Some students were admitted to the bar at that and subsequent terms.

Of the two first named members of the firm our biographical information is limited. Chester Hayden and Marcus A. King removed from Poughkeepsie, New York, where they had conducted a law school, to Poland, Ohio. Several of their pupils came with them. Mr. Hayden was an elderly man, a lawyer of ability, and had been a judge of one of the circuit courts of the State of New York. Mr. King was a young man and had not been long in practice. They were both admitted to the bar of Ohio at the district court in Canfield at the april term, A. D. 1857. When the college was removed to Cleveland they removed from the county. Judge Hayden died several years since.

Mortimer D. Leggett was born April 19, 1831, in Ithaca, New York, and removed with his parents, who were Friends, to Geauga county, Ohio, in 1847. He was admitted to the bar in 1853, and practiced a few years in Warren, Ohio, in partnership with J. D. Cox, afterward Governor of Ohio, as Leggett & Cox. When the law school was removed from Poland he removed to Zanesville, Ohio, where he continued the practice, and was also superintendent of the public schools. In the fall of 1861 he raised the Seventy-eighth regiment Ohio volunteer infantry, and, on January 11, 1862, was commissioned colonel, and on November 29, 1862, brigadier-general. He was engaged at Fort Donelson, Pittsburg Landing, the siege of Corinth, in the battles of the Atlanta campaign, and in other battles, in some of which he was wounded, and in one severely. He was with Sherman in his march to the sea, commanding the Third division, Seventeenth corps. He was breveted major-general July 22, 1864, and commissioned major-general January 15, 1865. After leaving the army he resumed the practice of law. He was appointed United States commissioner of patents June 13, 1871. He held that office a few years and then resumed the practice of law at Cleveland, Ohio, his present residence, making a specialty of patent cases.

The following gentlemen, admitted to the bar in Mahoning county, practiced in the county for longer or shorter periods, but are now deceased, have removed from the county or have discontinued practice. The dates of admission are added to their names: J. W. Stanley, 1860; W. V. S. Eaton, 1867; N. A. Gilbert, 1867; W. R. Brownlee, 1869; Augustus L. Heiliger, 1869; John B. Barnes, 1870; Hiram Macklin, 1870; Robert W. Tayler, Jr., 1877; David Burden, 1853.

The following gentlemen, admitted elsewhere, have practiced for longer or shorter periods in Mahoning county, but have removed. The state or county whence from and present residence, if known, are added to their names: Thaddeus Foote, from Massachusetts to Michigan; Andrew J. Dyer, to St. Louis; Charles F. Abell, from Ashtabula county to New York State, was married at Youngstown, November 12, 1879, to Miss Ada Murray of that city; Edwin S. Hubbard, from New York State to a western State; Cornelius Curry, from Salem, Columbiana county, to a western State, now deceased; J. R. Clarke, from Kansas to Pennsylvania; William Collins, F. S. Rock and D. T. Hervey, from Pennsylvania and returned to Pennsylvania; M. D. Tanneyhill, William Case, to a western State.

CITY OF WARREN, OHIO.

WARREN.

CHAPTER I.
THE VILLAGE AND VILLAGE LIFE.

We begin with the scene presented to the first earnest adventurers who came to prepare a home for civilization in the gloomy Western wilderness. A winding path through the dark swampy forest led to an open, undulating alluvion covered with a soft carpet of green leeks. The outline of this open space was irregular but clearly defined, and embraced an eligible mill-seat. It had evidently been an Indian clearing and had many years previously been a field for primitive agriculture. There were several such fields in the Mahoning valley, the site of Youngstown being one; but no account has been preserved of any so large or favorably located as the one which determined the settlement of the immigrants whose names are preserved as the founders of Warren.

It was for a temporary residence and storehouse that John Young built the first house on this clearing in 1798. He owned no interest in the land, but took squatters' occupation because of its fertility and preparation for the plow. He lived in the cabin during the spring and summer, while the crop required attention, and again in the fall while harvesting. At gathering season his residence was converted into a crib in which the crop was stored until winter, and was then drawn in sleds to Youngstown. In itself Mr. Young's enterprise was a trivial circumstance, but is worthy of this prominent mention because of its effect upon succeeding events. The eastern part of Warren township was partitioned to Ebenezer King, Jr., one of a syndicate of stockholders in the Connecticut Land company, which drew four townships. Mr. John Leavitt received in the apportionment a large tract in the western part of township four, range four, now embraced in the organized township of Warren. It was on King's land that John Young raised his crop of corn in 1798.

Joseph McMahon lived in the vicinity, occupying a rude hut which he probably built about the time Young built his. In the fall of 1798 two citizens of Washington county, Pennsylvania, Ephraim Quinby and Richard Storer, made a trip on horseback up the Mahoning for the purpose of viewing the country, and if found favorable, of selecting land on which to make settlement. They crossed the low flat country called the swamp, in Poland township, to Yellow creek, thence through dark woods covered with logs and underbrush to Youngstown, the headquarters of immigrants at that time. From there they took the salt spring road to Weathersfield, and then again plunged into the deep shade of the wild and uninviting forest through which lay their course to the broad, sunny Indian meadows. Such contrast was the rich alluvial soil, dried by exposure to heat, light, and air, and bearing the ripening fruit of a summer's industry, to the somber clays bearing aggravating underbrush and rugged beech and elms, lying behind and beyond, that the promised land seemed to have been reached. Both the visitors were satisfied, and both made selections. Mr. Quinby's choice was lot number twenty-eight and part of lot number thirty-five, making in all four hundred and forty-one acres. Mr. Storer selected land on both sides of the river further down, sixty acres of which was cleared, and has in late years been known as the Fusselman farm. Rarely in a new country do settlers find an opening more auspicious,—good land already cleared, a house ready to receive their goods and families, and a noble stream offering unlimited water power. Hardships and inconveniences were of course to be expected, but with half the battle won in advance, the future looked promising.

Messrs. Storer and Quinby, full of enthusiasm, with samples of soil packed in their saddle-bags, returned to their homes in Washington county. Negotiations for a purchase of the lots selected were at once entered into with Ebenezer King, Jr. The enthusiasm with which the new country was described had the effect of popularizing the enterprise, so that by spring the emigration fever became contagious. As soon as the opening of spring permitted, a party consisting of Mr. Quinby, Mr. Storer, William Fenton, wife and child, Francis Carlton and family—three sons and one daughter—and some hands, making a party of about fifteen persons, left Washington county in wagons, and after a tedious journey reached their destination April 17, 1799. These were the first settlers of Warren: though no town was laid out, and we have no evidence that there was at that time any intention of laying one out.

A busy summer followed; houses were to be built, crops planted and attended to, and provisions made for more extended operations during the year to follow. McMahon had removed his family to the southeast corner of Howland township, leaving his cabin on the Indian meadows empty.

Thus the new comers had two places of temporary abode. Mr. Quinby began the erection of a house on the site of the present Cleveland & Mahoning railroad depot. This house was designed to contain three rooms, two of which were finished during the first summer. The third, about ten feet square and built of heavy hewn logs, was not finished until the newly erected county required a jail, for which purpose this room was generously donated by Mr. Quinby. Mr. Storer built a cabin on his farm soon after the party's arrival, and Mr. Fenton continued to occupy for several years the cabin deserted by McMahon. Each of the families broke ground for corn, and everything progressed prosperously. The first settlers were closely followed by their Pennsylvania neighbors, Henry Lane, Sr., and Meshach Case, accompanied by John Lane and his half brother, Edward Jones.

Henry Lane purchased that part of the bottom on which the Young cabin stood. Leaving the young men to occupy the cabin and plant a crop of corn, Messrs. Case and Lane returned to Washington county. Mr. Case did not purchase land at that time, but in August following he came back to the settlement and took a deed for one hundred and ninety-eight acres a short distance below Storer's farm. He cleared about two acres and put up a cabin—a mere shell composed of walls and roof. He then again joined his family in Pennsylvania. Thus far the proprietors, Ebenezer King, Jr., and John Leavitt, had not seen their lands, on contracted portions of which settlement was progressing with such promising rapidity. Four or five cabins and several corn fields in the midst of thick wilderness must have been a pleasing spectacle on the occasion of their first visit during that first summer of the settlement.

There is some authority for believing that the township was divided up into lots at this time, and the name of their friend, Moses Warren, who had been one of the surveyors for the Land Company, was memorialized in the name of the settlement. Warren's home was at New Lyme, Connecticut, where, says an old manuscript, he was "much respected." One of the surveyors speaks of him as being somewhat tardy in the performance of duty, but it is evident that he was held in high esteem by at least two members of the Company. William Crooks and wife had accompanied the proprietors on their visit, and remained to make an improvement; Messrs. King and Leavitt returned after a short stay. Crooks cleared about eighteen acres west of the site of the present city, on which he built a cabin. He seeded several acres in wheat that fall, which was the first wheat sown in this township. He was also the first Connecticut settler in the township, all the others having come from Washington county, Pennsylvania. By fall sufficient accommodations had been prepared for the families of those who had left their wives at the old home. Among the first to come was Mrs. Edward Jones, who was accompanied by Henry Lane and Benjamin Lane, a lad of fourteen. It was evident that the Lanes were earnest about making settlement, for two large bundles of young apple trees were strapped on the horse which the lad was riding. The trees were at once planted, and for many years bore fruit after the scattered community had grown to the proportions of a city. These were the first fruit trees, so far as is known, planted in the present limits of Trumbull county.

Jones and his wife continued to occupy the Young cabin (which stood opposite the present upper mill dam) during the winter. Mr. Lane returned to his family in Washington county in December, accompanied by John and Benjamin. Richard Storer and Ephraim Quinby also returned to Washington county, when their corn crop had been harvested. As soon as sufficient snow had fallen that winter to make traveling easy, they started with their families for the new home on the Mahoning. Mr. Storer's family consisted of a wife, two sons, and a daughter; Mr. Quinby's family consisted of Mrs. Quinby and four children—Nancy, Samuel, Arabella, and William. It will be noticed that all the settlers of the first year except Mr. Crooks' were from Washington county, Pennsylvania. They were, however, of New England descent; that county having been settled originally mainly by Massachusetts people. Before the close of the year 1799 Benjamin Davidson, Esq., of Huntingdon, Pennsylvania, came to Warren with a view of making a purchase. He selected a lot adjoining the Case and Storer farms, and built a cabin on the surveyed road to Beavertown. He returned to Pennsylvania to spent the winter. The nearest neighbor to the Quinby settlement was John Adgate, who lived in the southwest corner of Howland, where he owned a large tract of land. His family consisted of Mrs. Adgate and nine or ten children —Sally, Belinda, Caroline, John H., Nancy, Charles, Ulysses, James, and one or two more, also Caleb Jones and wife. There were also a few others, hands and single men living in the neighborhood, whose names have not been preserved in the annals of the time.

It is estimated that the first year of the settlement brought thirty souls. No town had yet been laid out, but Mr. Quinby's keen business eye was not slow to detect the success of such a project. Youngstown contained, at that time, about twenty houses compactly located, giving the place a village appearance. It was the stopping place of westward bound emigrants, and consequently well-known in the East, where Quinby's settlement was unknown, and even at Youngstown no one anticipated the importance which one more year was destined to give this frontier collection of cabins. The settlers employed the winter by fencing their fields, increasing the acreage of cleared land, improving and adding to their houses, and making whiskey of a part of the summer's corn crop. The early settlers, whether they came from Pennsylvania or Connecticut, or Massachusetts, habitually and regularly used that stimulating beverage. Few of their fields or farms had been fenced during the first season; they had no domestic animals, and deer and other wild animals did little damage.

The year 1800 was characterized by great activity, and increased Warren from a scattered and unknown settlement to the most prosperous town in New Connecticut. Youngstown may have been larger, but its population was transient and was inferior, both in intelligence and earnestness of purpose, to the Warren community. It appears from the county records that no deeds were issued until February 22, 1800 (Washington's birthday). On that day at Suffield, Connecticut, Ebenezer King, Jr., conveyed and transferred to Ephraim Quinby, Henry Lane, Sr., and Benjamin Davidson, tracts for which they had previously contracted.

Mr. Quinby's purchase was four hundred and forty-one acres, for which he paid the sum of $1,625 or $3.69 per acre. Mr. Lane's farm embraced the same number of acres. It is probable the price named in the deed was agreed upon the year before Quinby established his Washington county colony. Other lands were at that time selling at from fifty cents to $2 per acre. The Indian clearings had probably increased the price of this purchase, but it appears from the figures not in proportion to the value.

An interesting event occurred in February, 1800; made interesting as an historical item because it was the first event of its kind to occur in the new settlement. A daughter was born to Mr. and Mrs. Edward Jones, who had been living here a little less than a year. This may have been the first birth within the present limits of the county, but our information does not warrant a definite statement to that effect. The child grew to womanhood and became the wife of William Dutchin, for many years a highly respected citizen of Warren.

The opening of spring brought a large increase to the settlement. On the 18th of April there arrived from Pennsylvania six families, viz: Meshach Case and his wife Magdaline, with six children, Elizabeth, Leonard, Catharine, Mary,

Reuben, and Sarah; Henry Lane, Sr., with his wife and five children. John, Asa, Benjamin, Catharine, and Ann; Henry Lane, Jr., and his wife Elsie; Charles Dally and his wife Jennie, with several children; Isaac Dally and his wife Effie, with several children; and John Dally and his wife with one child. These names are from a memorandum made by Mr. Leonard Case. It is inferred that they all came together from the same place, though Mr. Case is not clear on this point. From the same source we have a brief but interesting account of the journey, which applies to the Case family at least, and probably to the whole party whose names we have given. April 10, 1800, was the day of starting from Fallowfield township, Washington county. At Beavertown, which was reached by land, they were detained three days. Poland was reached on the 17th, and Warren on the following day, about 4 o'clock. We give Mr. Case's own language:

The usual incidents attended the journey until crossing the south line on 41° north latitude. From there to Poland was a very muddy road called "the swamp." In Poland the settlement was begun, Judge Turhand Kirtland and wife living on the east side and Jonathan Fowler and wife, a sister of the Judge, keeping tavern on the west side. From there our way was through woods to where there was a family named Stevens, who had been there three years or more. The wife's name was Hannah. With her our family had been acquainted. She said she had been there three years without seeing the face of a white woman. There our party and cattle stayed over night. Next morning we passed up the west side of the river, for want of means to cross it, to James Williams', and then through the woods to the old road made by the Connecticut Land company to the salt spring. There were some settlers, Joseph McMahon among the rest, engaged in making salt. From there we passed through the woods to the clearing and cabin of Benjamin Davidson, on the north half of lot number forty-two in Warren, in town four, range four, then one-quarter of a mile to a path that turned east to the Fusselman place on the south half of lot number thirty-five, and then to the residence of Richard Storer, arriving there about four o'clock on the afternoon of April 18, 1800. After our passage through the woods and mud the leeks on the Indian field on Mahoning bottom made a most beautiful appearance.

It has been noted that Benjamin Davidson visited the settlement and built a cabin in the summer of 1799. It was occupied by the family in the latter part of April; the family consisted of eleven children, viz: George, Liberty, Polly, Prudence, Ann, Samuel, William, Walter, James, Betsy, and Benjamin.

In May, 1800, the family commenced their labors for a crop. In June following John Leavitt arrived with his family, consisting of his wife Silence, and children, William, John, Jr., Cynthia, Sally, Henry F., Abiah, and Humphrey. Some hired men also accompanied them, including Elam and Eli Blair. Soon after them came Phineas Leffingwell and family. The settlers thus far, except the Leavitt and Crooks families, were all from Pennsylvania, most of them from Washington county. It was from there that the first preacher came who held services in Warren —Rev. Henry Spears. He belonged to the Baptist denomination. It was merely to visit his old neighbors and friends that he had come, but while here they determined to make use of him, and arranged for a preaching service one Sunday morning in June. In the shade of a natural bower on the river bank an audience of more than fifty assembled for instruction and for worship. The eye of our imagination lingers enviously on that meeting, in which all joined with that enthusiasm and heartiness characteristic of frontier communities. All around them was beauty, and bountiful nature, suggestive of the character of the King whom they had assembled to worship and praise. "With respectful attention" they heard the pious words of the preacher, and at the conclusion joined him in a chorus of thanksgiving. No religious service was held after this, so far as is known, till the fall of that year, when Rev. Joseph Badger, by order of the Connecticut Missionary society, visited the settlement.

The improvements were scattered for a considerable distance along the river. The present business center of Warren had not yet been cleared, except small tracts in the vicinity of cabins. Grading and paving has made a great change in the surface of the south and southeast part of the city. No change was made where the court-house stands, and the land north and northeast of it retains its original elevation. From the court-house towards the south the slope was rapid, with an undulating and irregular surface, dipping to a swamp where Main and Market streets meet. The surface at that point was about ten feet lower than at present. This swamp overflowed during high water and in winter time was covered with a sheet of ice. It has been stated that the river channel coursed through it at one time, but this is only a supposition. For several years after the settlement it remained a deep, soft mire, in which venturesome domestic animals sometimes stuck fast. A cow belonging to Mr. Jacob Harsh one day waded into the mire, and being discovered, the whole village was called to her rescue. After much labor she was drawn out, but in such an exhausted condition that she died on the following day. The west side of Main street has been graded down. The ground was high at the corner of Liberty and Market streets, and sloped east to a deep ravine through which a small stream poured into the swamp below. The eastern side of the ravine was so steep that considerable effort was required to climb it.

There was a second swamp east from the corner of Elm and Market streets; low lands extended to the mouth of Red run. This stream, like all other water courses, was larger then than since the surface it drains has been cleared. It derives its name from the fact that a kind of red moss covers its mucky bed, and also that the water is tinged red by mineral and vegetable matter from the bogs and swamps above. There is a current myth which gives a tragical significance to the name. The story runs, that before any white settlers had come to the Reserve, a band of Indians committed savage depredations on the white settlement at Greensburg, Pennsylvania, which led the settlers to take summary measures for avenging the offence. An armed party started in pursuit and overtook another marauding band at this place, on the banks of a small stream, where a conflict ensued. The Indians were defeated and their blood, mingling with the flowing water, suggested the name Bloody or Red run. But it is more probable that the name suggested this fiction, than that any such action was the origin of the name.

So much swampy and low land, and the fact that no regular roads had been constructed, made travel extremely difficult during most of the year, and at times impossible. This circumstance made the need of a mill in their own community almost imperative. Mill creek was the nearest point where grinding was done, and even there two or three days were at times occupied in waiting till the primitive little concern had ground out the grain of those ahead. The enterprise of building a mill at Warren was undertaken first by Henry Lane, Jr., and Charles Dally. They be-

gan work on the dam in June, 1800. Receiving considerable assistance from time to time from the neighbors, the work progressed satisfactorily until winter. Cold weather stopped operations, and the spring floods tore out the newly constructed dam. Though this was very discouraging, the pioneers were not of the class to be baffled by such a reverse. As soon as spring opened in 1801 they again set to work with the increased energy which previous experience had taught them was necessary. By hard work and frequent frolics the dam was completed before winter, but in spite of their utmost exertions another winter passed before the grinding machinery was ready for work, and then it was little more than a "corn-cracker." Each customer had to bolt his own grist. Notwithstanding these inconveniences it answered a very good purpose and was greatly appreciated after three years' dependence upon the stump mortar and spring-pole, and an inadequate concern fourteen miles away. The old dam has since been repaired and strengthened but is still at the same place, and has been the head of constant water-power ever since. The old dam was sold by Dally & Lane to Royal Pease, and the property has since successively belonged to Justus Smith, Gideon Finch, and James L. Van Gorder. It was burned in 1839, but soon after rebuilt. The last structure was burned in 1881.

Another mill was built two or three years later by George Lovelace, in which Ephraim Quinby was interested. The dam was built just below the present Market Street bridge. A woolen mill was connected with it by Levi Hadley, and afterwards owned and operated by Benjamin Stevens. James L. Van Gorder subsequently came into possession of the mill property, and after the canal was built moved the structure further down the river. These mills had the effect of encouraging immigrants to settle in this locality, and consequently aided materially in building up the town.

The year 1800 closed with a survey of the town by Captain Quinby. On December 10th, Caleb Palmer, surveyor, platted all that part of Mr. Quinby's property east of the river. The plat sets apart streets and a square for "publick uses," the general plan being in imitation of New England villages. The streets on Mr. Quinby's plat are numbered. Main street and Mahoning avenue is denominated No. 1; High street, No. 2; Market street, No. 3; South street, No. 4; and Liberty street, from the square south, No. 5; no northern continuation was laid out.

The final settlement of the county seat at Warren, gave the town a prestige which accelerated its growth and affected its character. The first settlers were strong, industrious, and earnest; the seat of county government supplemented this element with a superior order of intelligence and increased wealth. It attracted such men as Judge Pease, Colonel Edwards and General Perkins—men capable of giving direction to energy and elevating the social plane. The seat of government made Warren the center of public information and public interest. With all its natural and political advantages, it took considerable time to make Warren even comfortable for a place of residence. The square designated for a park had an irregular, broken surface, full of ugly knolls and repulsive mud-holes. The forest trees with which it had been covered were chopped down in 1801, and left lie to decay. For about twenty years the place was left in an unseemly condition. About 1820 Simon Perkins, Jr., assisted by other public-spirited citizens, graded the ground and planted the trees which now furnish refreshing shade and make the plat a delightful summer lounging place.

During the primitive village years, before a thick, drear forest had given place to cultivated fields, native animals were extremely troublesome and destructive. Cattle and hogs were in constant danger, even in daylight, of being attacked by wolves and bears; and domestic fowls were a constant prey of smaller animals and vermin. Wolves are the boldest, most persistent, and most destructive of all wild animals. It was not uncommon for a hungry wolf to come into the village, even before nightfall, and seize a pig in some cabin dooryard. So ravenous were their appetites that it was almost impossible for a while to raise hogs or sheep. They were always boldest in winter when food was scarcest, and at such times frequently made attacks on grown cattle. Mr. Case has recorded an illustrative incident which took place in February, 1801. A severe storm had been in progress, and the night was cold and blustering. A large number of the settlers' cattle were gathered together on the bottom protecting themselves from the storm by standing close to each other. A pack of wolves approached with frightful howls. With that instinct, which even in brutes impels the strong to protect the weak, the larger cattle bellowed and pitched ferociously at their savage enemies. In the morning it was evident that a severe encounter had taken place, the oxen having buried their horn's to their skulls in soft mud, and several of the weaker cattle being badly bitten. Hogs were the favorite prey of bears. They frequently carried away shoats weighing as much as one hundred and fifty pounds, but preferred smaller pigs. Mr. Case testifies that it was six or seven years before sheep could be effectually protected from wolves. Vermin destroyed all kinds of domestic water fowl. Hunting was not only a delightful amusement, but useful employment. It became profitable, too, after the county began paying a bounty on wolf scalps. Venison and bears' meat made healthful and delicious food. The skins of the deer were indispensible for clothing in those rugged times, and bear skins commanded a fair price in Eastern markets. The river abounded in excellent fish, it appears from the traditional accounts, almost waiting to be caught. The early settlers found enticing amusement in shooting and gigging fish. Some were of immense size. A story is told of how, in 1801, Henry Lane and Ephraim Quinby welcomed a friend to the village. James Scott, who had just arrived, was given temporary entertainment at Fenton's cabin. In the morning, when he opened the cabin door to refresh himself before meeting his hostess, a monster pike, "fully six feet long," pitched head first into the room. Quinby and Lane, both practical jokers, had been out fishing during the night, and left their largest catch suspended upon a stake, leaning against the stranger's door.

New England people of the old school never permitted anything to interfere with the proper celebration of the anniversary of the declaration of Independence. Many of the Warren people in 1800 remembered the enthusiasm which followed the announcement of that ever glorious day. There were a few who had borne arms in the struggle for independence and liberty. The mighty significance of "the day we celebrate" had not yet been lost sight of, nor, indeed, ought it ever to be lost sight of, for the principles enunciated on that day lie at the foundation of all our American history. There should be no sentimental sneering at real patriotic utterances on these annually recurring occasions. There is danger in these latter days of business and rapid growth in population and wealth of our forgetting the American eagle and the stanch heroic characters who made that wide-winged bird a sacred national emblem. But there was no lack of patriotic enthusiastic demonstration at Warren on the 4th of July, 1800. John Young, Calvin Austin, and others from Youngstown, General Edward Paine and Eliphalet Austin from Painesville, were present to participate in the occasion. When the crowd assembled, it was found that no musical instruments had been provided for. In the ebullition of their enthusiasm it is supposed the Warren people overlooked these indispensable articles of Fourth of July furniture. But Yankee wit is always ready, and the anniversary was not to be a failure for want of stirring old martial music. Eli and Elam Blair, twin brothers, came to the front; one was a drummer, and the other a fifer. The latter found a large, strong elder stem which he soon whittled into a fife. The other, with equal readiness but with more difficulty, set to work, making a drum. He cut down a hollow pepperidge tree, and with only a hand-axe and jack-plane made a drum cylinder. William Crooks in the meantime killed a fawn, and brought the skin for a drum head; Mr. Case gave a new pair of plow lines for cords and snares. But a short time elapsed before the instrument constructed from these materials was rolling Yankee Doodle to the entire satisfaction of the assembly. Everybody had guns which, of course, they fired early and often, adding noise to the demonstrative music. In addition to this, several members of the party came loaded with characteristically American speeches. It is mildly recorded by one of the participants: "Toasts were duly given and honored with the needful amount of stimulus. All went off merrily."

During these early years a mysterious character paid frequent visits to the settlement. "Old Merryman" was the only name by which he was ever known. Whence he came or whither he went was past finding out. Always modest and peaceable, he traded his deer skins and furs for whiskey and meal, asking no questions or making no answer to inquiries touching himself. He avoided notoriety, and seemed to have no other object in life than to eat, drink, move, and have his being. His visits finally ceased, and the mystery remained a subject of fruitless conjecture.

Merchandise was at first retailed to the settlers from a canoe by James E. Caldwell. Early in 1801 he commenced making periodical trips up the Mahoning. His stock consisted of groceries, calico, and notions. The demand for calico was, of course, light, owing to the high price at which it was held. The quality which now retails at five cents a yard, was sold at the canoe store for fifteen times that amount. The women purchased only in limited quantities "for fine dresses" and trimmings. This nautical store generally made its appearance fortnightly at Warren, which was the terminus of its route. It announced its arrival by blowing a tin horn, inviting all who desired to make purchases to the river bank. But the settlement was not long dependent upon the accidents of a water craft for such necessities as the soil, the forest, or their own hands did not produce. George Lovelace, in the fall of 1801 or spring of 1802, opened a small shop on the east side of Main street near South street. This was the beginning of a permanent mercantile business, the gradual expansion of which, during the eighty years to the present time, is elsewhere sketched.

Warren remained the capital town of the whole Reserve until 1809, and for more than a quarter of a century was the principal town in it. Mr. Louis M. Iddings compiled for the "Mahoning Valley Historical Collections" a map of the town in 1816, which fixes the location of fifty-two houses. It is safe to infer that the population at that time enumerated two hundred souls. In 1810 the population exceeded one hundred. There were eight houses on or near Mahoning avenue at that time, a continuation of street number one, now Main street. Beginning at the upper end on the west side was the mill owned by James I. VanGorder, and then in their order were the VanGorder residence, the house of Mrs. Rowe, the residence of Jacob Harsh, General Simon Perkins' residence (where Hon. H. B. Perkins' residence now stands), and a house built by George Phelps. On the east side of the avenue there were but three houses, one occupied by a Mr. McFarland, the residence of Mr. Reeve with blacksmith shop adjoining, and a log house built by a Mr. Scott on the site of Warren Packard's residence. Continuing from this point east on High street (number two on the old plat) were the residences of Dr. John B. Harmon, George Parsons, and James Scott; the jail was also built on the site of the present structure a few years later. David Bell lived some distance northeast, just across the line in Howland township, but within the present corporate limits. The first court-house proper was being built at the time on the site of the present structure. East of the park, on Liberty street, were the Shook house, and Asahel Adams' store, afterwards the Franklin house.

The Western Reserve bank building was in process of erection where the First National bank building now stands; further south stood the residence of Mrs. McWilliams, and a shop. On the opposite side stood the residences of Elihu Spencer and Zebina Weathersby. East of Liberty street were scattered several houses, John Jerrodell's cabin, Judge Pease's office, residence of Richard Iddings, cabins of George Mull and Mark Wescott; and on East South street were the residences of Captain Oliver Brooks, Thomas D. Webb (this house was built in 1807 by Colonel J. S. Edwards, and is still standing), Mr. Hake, and Jonathan Rankin. Near the corner of South and Liberty streets stood the residence of James Quigley, with a tannery in the rear. South of the square on Market street, beginning at the crossing of Liberty, were the residences of Samuel Chesney, store of William Bell and James Quigley, the Cotsgreave house, familiarly known as Castle William, and on the corner of Main and Market was the old hotel stand. South of Market, on the east side of Main street, were five houses, residences of Tony Carter and Jeduthen Rawdon, the Western Reserve bank, and Judge Freeman's house, now the eastern part of the Austin house. This is the oldest structure in the city. On the west side of Main street were the residence of Judge Calvin Austin, the Leavitt house, for many years one of the leading hotels, Adamson Bentley's store, and Jeremiah Brooks' residence. It was in the Bentley building that the Trump of Fame was printed, and the Brooks house was built by Mr. Quinby in 1799, and served the purpose of a jail for some time after Trumbull county was erected. Below Market street bridge, on the north river bank, stood Mr. Stevens' carding machine, built some years before by Levi Hadley. In the bottom were two cabins in which a Mr. Morris and James Ellis lived. Mr. Ephraim Quinby and Mr. Burnett lived on top of the hill.

The first graves were on a knoll on South street, where the late residence of Thomas D. Webb stands. In the memoranda at our command the time or names of the first burials are no where noted, neither were any tombstones erected, the spot probably being marked by boards which soon rotted away. Colonel Edwards built the Webb residence in 1807; his workmen paying no attention to graves concealed there beneath the kitchen floor. There is a stone in the old cemetery, on Mahoning avenue, bearing date 1804, from which it is inferred that the place of interment was changed about that date.

Frontier village life had its inconveniences, toils, privations, and loneliness, but these asperities were so completely compensated by amenities that we can scarce help, at times, regretting the fate which has placed us eighty years in the rear of the pioneer army. But perhaps we derive more pleasure in employing an idle hour in the contemplation of the "good old times" than the pioneers did in the years of actual experience. The old Cotgreave house was the scene of many interesting events during Warren's village years. This building was at first a log cabin built by Henry Harsh, in 1802. About 1807 William W. Cotgreave, who had purchased the property, made an extensive, but extremely homely, addition, which served for court-house, jail, church, public hall, and saloon for some years. The lower story was built of logs in block-house fashion, the two upper stories were frame with gabled roof. The lower story was designed and used for a jail until the special building for that purpose had been completed. Court was held in the second story until the court-house was built, and the whole building furnished accommodations for school on weekdays and church on Sunday, and at night masonic meetings and dances. Dancing was a fashionable amusement before "Castle William," as the roomy pile just described was called, was built. Warren people were noted for their hospitality and social grace, making public balls very popular and very agreeable affairs.

In a letter to Connecticut in July, 1803, John S. Edwards says:

I was at Warren on the 4th of July, when I attended a ball. You may judge of my surprise at meeting a very considerable company, all of whom were dressed with neatness and in fashion, some of them elegantly. The ladies generally dressed well. Some of them would have been admired for their ease and grace in a New Haven ball room. It was held on the same spot where four years since there was scarcely the trace of human hand, or any where within fifteen miles of it. We improved well the occasion; began at two in the afternoon of Monday, and left the room a little before sunrise on Tuesday morning. We dance but seldom, which is our apology.

We add one other account from the same pen, but of three years later:

WARREN, OHIO, July 7, 1806.

We are but just well through the 4th of July. It was celebrated at Warren with great splendor. About one hundred citizens of Trumbull sat down to a superb dinner provided for the occasion. Seventeen toasts were drunk in flowing bumpers of wine under a discharge of fire-arms. The whole was concluded with a *feu de joie* and a procession. The greatest harmony and hilarity prevailed throughout the day. In the evening we attended a splendid ball, at which were present about thirty couples. You would have been surprised at the elegance and taste displayed on the occasion, recollecting that within seven years, on the same spot of ground, the only retreat from the heavens was a miserable log house, sixteen feet square, in which I was obliged to take my lodgings on the floor, wrapped in my blanket. But further, not satisfied with dancing one evening, we assembled again on the 5th, and had a very agreeable and pleasant ball. Before we dined on the 4th we had an oration. So much for New Connecticut. Do you think now we live in the woods, or is it surprising we forget that we do? The emigrations into this part of the country have been very large this spring.

Mr. Tod is made a member of the supreme court of Ohio.

The dances in Castle William were more than annual affairs. The monotony of long winter was frequently interrupted by joyful tripping to the time of hurrying music. On stated occasions the young from far and near joined in the dance. From early in the afternoon till sunrise next morning Uncle Tony's fiddle measured time for the tireless company. Tony, an eccentric colored chap, presided at the fiddle for many years, his presence being as happy in its effects upon the company as his music. Isaac Ladd was caterer for the gentlemen, his quarters being in the third story. It was reached by a door from the ballroom communicating with the stairs. Thither the gentlemen repaired for their drinks between dances. While Benjamin Towne kept tavern in Castle William a dancing master named Gitchel gave lessons in the hall. One of his invitations for a public ball was headed as follows:

A public ball at B. Towne's hall,
This night will be attended;
The ladies fare being something rare,
Which makes our joy more blended.

A favorite chorus of the time was as follows:
And since we're here, with friends so dear,
Let's drive dull cares away.

But amusement was not confined to parties, and dancing, and celebrations. We have some account of a sporting club composed of twelve members, two of whom were from Warren, Calvin Pease and Simon Perkins; other members were: General Wadsworth and Mr. Mygatt, of Canfield; Dr. Tyler, of Tylertown; Messrs. Montgomery and Clendenen, of Coitsville; some one from Poland, and four from Youngstown—Judge George Tod, William Rayen, John E. Woodbridge, and James Hillman. Racing on the Mahoning was a sport much indulged in by this club, in winter time. All starting abreast at Youngstown; their course was to Warren, where a royal dinner had been ordered, to be paid for by the six last of the party to arrive. Their fixed price for dinner was $24, from which it will appear that they were well served. Two dollars a plate was a big price for meals in those early days. About 1809 this club instituted a unique diversion. It was agreed that each should choose a pig and keep it two years, at the end of which time all the hogs chosen were to be weighed. The owners of the six lightest ones were to pay for a banquet. Who the defeated parties were is not recorded, but the two heaviest hogs belonged to James Hillman and Dr. Tyler, and weighed over 500 and 700 pounds respectively. The combined weight of Colonel Rayen and his wife exceeded the heaviest hog more than twenty pounds.

Militia training days were epochs in the social life of the times, nor were such regimental maneuverings all for parade and show. The military spirit of the Revolutionary period was not yet dead; a dangerous neighbor occupied the bordering forest and the mighty power of Great Britain was menacing the general peace. Under such circumstances, simple prudence as well as the higher feeling of patriotism appealed to the strong and brave who had come to make homes, also to prepare to preserve them against an invasion by a desolating foe. The time came quickly, when their courage and patriotism was put to a test. Their ready and prompt action on that occasion will protect the military character of our pioneer fathers from any indignity, and at the same time vindicate the old militia system. On general training days all the regiments in the county gathered at the county-seat, where they were inspected by General Perkins, brigade commander, and after a general drill, a dinner was served by the ladies, followed by a grand ball. It is but natural that a day which furnished such practical education and discipline as the times made essential, and at the same time a day of revelry and rollicking and feasting, followed by a night of dancing and courting, should have been anticipated with interest and was recollected with pleasure.

CHAPTER II.
BUSINESS GROWTH.

We have seen that in 1816 there were six stores in Warren besides a number of shops and smaller places of business. An interesting peculiarity of the mercantile development of a village is the fact that stores do not increase in number proportionate to the increase of population. Indeed, the number decreases between the period of the hasty and temporary at the beginning, and the solid and endurable which follows. So universal is this fact of history that it might with propriety be called a law. The wants of a new community are few and simple, relieving stores of the necessity of keeping a large variety of goods. Any one with a couple of hundred dollars and a house could carry on trade by converting one room of his dwelling into a store. The profits of these little establishments footed up to a considerable amount, for prices were high and no rent, clerk hire or incidentals cut down expenses. But the time came quickly when these little concerns did not meet the public demand. Greater variety and better quality was wanted, making larger rooms a necessity. With the change came increased incidental expenses, besides new buildings, so that although there was more trade and larger stores the number of them did not increase. This continued until business began to divide and run in its natural channels.

We are unable to give the census enumeration of Warren previous to 1830, at which time the "town plat" supported a population of five hundred and one individuals. In the year 1828 there were on Liberty street two stores, Daniel Gilbert's and Asahel Adams', and opposite Adams' store the Western Reserve bank was doing business. Market street presented a dilapidated appearance, the houses being old and homely. Horace Stevens had a hatter's shop near the crossing of Liberty, in which he manufactured wool and felt hats to order, and at the same time keeping a small stock on hand for sale to transient customers. The hatter was at one time a tradesman of as much importance to the community as the tinner or the carpenter. During dull seasons he traveled the country soliciting work, but in spring and fall he was kept profitably busy filling orders which came to his shop. Mr. Stevens is yet living, and a further notice of him will be found elsewhere. Next to the hatter's shop stood a two-story building, in which Samuel Chesney lived and had a cabinet shop. The shop was up-stairs and could be reached by an outside stairway. Mr. Chesney's work was manufacturing a general line of furniture and coffins. This trade has gone the way of the hatter's—into large establishments. The third building going west was Jacob Harsh's blacksmith shop, with its blazing forge and noisy anvil. Next was Van Gorder's hotel, known as the "Pavillion House," or more generally as Castle William—a comfortable abode for strangers, and a place of rollicking amusements for the villagers. On the corner was another tavern, the Rodden house, Horace Rodden, proprietor. This was an old stand.

On the west side of Main street stood a row of five stores. Daniel and Leicester King were at the corner, both were prominent men and highly esteemed merchants. The second store belonged to William Quinby. Then in order was Harmon & Brother, at that time young and energetic merchants. Henry & Charles Smith held the fourth place in this row. The Smiths came to Warren in 1817 and have been up to the present time leading citizens. The fifth store was managed by William McCurdy & Brother. Further southward Henry Stiles had a saddle and harness shop. The word saddle has long since been discarded from the style of corresponding concerns. Harness shops we yet have, but saddles have almost gone out of use and the name is now seldom seen upon signs. The last shop on Main street was occupied by Walter King, silversmith and watchmaker. Repairing clocks constituted the chief part of his employment. George Mygatt also had a store in Warren at that time, which he soon afterwards removed from the lower part of town to the south side of the park. He removed to Norwalk in 1834 and afterwards removed to Cleveland, where he yet resides, surrounded by the accumulations of a busy life.

A building was erected on Main street in the year 1828, which is still standing, though in a shattered condition. We refer to the old three-story brick below the opera house. It was built by Charles R. Harmon and Walter King for store rooms, and the lower story is a good specimen of the appearance of business rooms at that time. Small windows, small doors, and low ceilings. There were three store rooms which when finished were occupied by H. R. Harmon, Henry Stiles, and Walter King. The upstairs apartments were at first used for shops, but erw ards converted into school-rooms.

Between 1830 and 1840 the growth of Warren was steady and of a substantial character. The wealthiest business men on the Reserve lived here, and had enough confidence in the future of the place to make them enterprising. Sanguine expectation had always been characteristic of Warren settlers. An illustrative incident occurred about 1820. Mr. Leonard Case, who settled in Cleveland in 1816, came to Warren to borrow some money, his object being to make an investment in real estate at Cleveland. General Perkins endeavored to convince Mr. Case that he was making a great mistake by not investing at Warren in place of Cleveland, "Here is the place," said he, "to put your money, here is a growing town." It was this sort of confidence that made Warren men conspicuous in enterprises of public improvement, particularly the Ohio and Pennsylvania canal project, and the Cleveland and Mahoning railroad. Had it not been for the liberality and activity of Warren merchants, the canal would probably never have been built, for it was Warren subscriptions, and Warren encouragement that pushed that enterprise to a successful termination. Youngstown eventually harvested the chief benefit, but it was the fruit of Warren's sowing. The canal, however, had the effect of throwing new life and vigor into trade here. Old store rooms became too small for the increased stock, and new buildings began to be erected. Prices fell on manufactured articles, and farm products increased in value; circumstances which advanced real estate, encouraged settlement, diminished the difficulty of living and encouraged more liberal expenditure, all of which increased trade, and built up the town. Manufacturing soon outgrew the little shops in second-story rooms, and found quarters in special buildings. But this department of industry did not attain to full growth and expansion until after the railroads were in operation.

In 1838, according to the return of William Williams, marshal, the town contained a population of 928 whites and ten negroes—two males and eight females. There were fourteen lawyers, twenty-seven merchants and clerks; five doctors, nine cabinet-makers, eighteen joiners, twelve saddlers, seven hatters, thirteen blacksmiths, fifteen shoemakers, two painters, fourteen tailors, three silversmiths, three tool-makers, four clothers, one glove maker, three wagon-makers, three coopers, three plasterers, eight printers, and seven tinners.

Ten years later Henry Howe, the historian, wrote of Warren:

It is a well built and very pleasant town, through which beautifully winds the Mahoning. In the center is a handsome public square, on which stands the court-house. In June, 1846, this village was visited by a destructive fire which destroyed a large number of buildings facing the public square; since built up with beautiful stores. Warren was laid out in 1801 by Ephraim Quinby, Esq., and named from Moses Warren, of New Lyme. The town plat is one mile square, with streets crossing at right angles. Warren contains one Presbyterian, one Episcopal, one Baptist, one Methodist, and one Disciple church; about twenty mercantile stores, three newspaper printing offices, two flour-mills, one bank, one woolen factory, and a variety of mechanical establishments. In 1840 its population was 1,066; it is now estimated at 1,600.

The firm of D. & L. King built a block on Main street in 1828, into which they moved their store the following year. Edward F. Hoyt purchased their establishment in 1832, and effected a consolidation with Charles R. Harmon. This was then the largest store in the town. In 1837 the Harmon interest was purchased by Lewis and James Hoyt, brothers of Edward E. Hoyt. Until 1864 business was conducted by the firm of E. E. Hoyt & Co., when it was terminated by the death of the senior partner. James Hoyt retired in 1864. Twice during the quarter century of this firm's existence, its property was consumed by fire, in 1849 and in 1860.

T. H. Best had a store on Market street about 1830. He sold to Isaac F. Reeves, an excellent citizen, but he proved an unsuccessful business manager. He remained in trade only about three years. Lewis J. Iddings began business on Market street in 1837. His store and trade steadily increased, until he became one of the leading merchants. Mr. Iddings remained in business until his death in 1879.

Henry Stiles continued in business until his death in 1869, since which time his son, William R. Stiles, has managed the business. Park & Wentz came to Warren in 1846. Their store was a conspicuous trading place until 1869, when Park retired. Mr. Wentz is still a resident of the city.

In the year 1851 Warren Packard, who had commenced business as clerk in Harmon's store, opened a small establishment on the east side of Main street. He has been in the hardware trade until recently, variously associated with other merchants, S. Z. Freeman, R. H. Barnum, and J. G. Brooks being among the more prominent.

Patch & Allison were among the earliest saddlery hardware dealers in the place. They began as saddle and harness makers, and gradually enlarged their facilities by manufacturing supplies in their line for country shops. Mr. Allison retired and Emerson Opdyke, of New York, took his place. S. M. Park subsequently became a partner. Mr. Opdyke retired at the opening of the war, to enter the army. Business has since been conducted under the firm name of Park & Patch.

It is impossible to trace out every line of business succession up to the present time, nor would such a record be of interest in a work of this character. We have mentioned the old merchants of recognized standing, and will conclude this subject with a roster of the several departments of mercantile trade in 1881:

MARKET STREET.—Truesdell & Townsend, furniture; Thad Ackley, jewelry; H. Stiles & Sons, dry goods; A. Wentz, dry goods; James Reed's Sons, stoves; Edward A. Smith, drugs; C. C. Adams & Co., clothing; Hall & Mackey, harness and trunks; Freer & Smith, groceries; A. Nuhrenberger, notions; Lamb Brothers, boots and shoes; Vautrot & Hull, jewelry and notions; S. W. Park, harness hardware; Pew & Brother, crockery; Feister & Lingo Brothers, groceries; George Adams, books; S. R. Brown, dry goods; Hart Brothers, clothing; Peck & Brother, dry goods; Pond & Camp, clothing; Gunelfinger & Brother, dry goods; H. G. Stratton & Co., drugs; Kirk & Christie, hardware and tinshop; Babbitt, Brooks & Smith, hardware; W. Porter, books and news.

MAIN STREET.—A. L. Tash, boots and shoes; James C. Rogers, clothing; Bradford & Van Gorder, drugs; Mrs. L. Green, notions; Peter Melony, dry goods; Masters Brothers, groceries; William Hapgood, drugs; James McConnell, bakery; Brainard & Trew, agricultural implements; C. S. Field, clothing; Spear & Voit, furniture; George Gleachel, boots and shoes; David Byard, drugs; Peter Gross, cigar factory; S. W. Derr, tobacconist; M. B. Tyler, gun store; McCombs & Ross, wholesale grocers; William & Young, flour and feed; G. O. Griswold, flour and feed; D. Hecklinger, groceries; William Oldecker, butcher; H. H. Coe, butcher; James Morrison, groceries; William Thomas, wholesale liquor dealer; Wilhelm, butcher; Cond & Cook, butchers.

PARK AVENUE.—Weir Brothers, groceries; Dr. Heard, oculist; Kneeland Brothers, books and news.

Eating houses, saloons, and smaller shops are omitted.

.BANKING.

The Miami Exporting company, of Cincinnati, was the first corporation in Ohio to which banking powers was granted. The charter of this corporation was taken out in 1803. The Bank of Marietta, chartered in 1808, was the first corporation to do exclusively banking business. Charters were soon afterwards granted to banking associations at Chillicothe, Cincinnati, and other places. In 1816 a law was passed by the Legislature regulating the manner of establishing banks, and providing for State supervision over their management. This law required a certain share of the profits to be paid into the State treasury. It remained in force with various modifications until 1845, when a system of State banking was established. The first bank on the Western Reserve was chartered in the winter of 1811-12, and was located at Warren. We give a very full sketch prepared a few years since by Judge Frederick Kinsman.

The original corporators of the Western Reserve bank were: Simon Perkins, Robert D. Parkman, Turhand Kirtland, George Tod, John Ford, C. S. Mygatt, Calvin Austin, William Rayen, and John Kinsman. The corporators soon after organized and by subscription secured the required amount of stock, $100,000, as is shown by the following list:

	SHARES.	AMOUNT.
Calvin Austin	200	$ 5,000
David Clendennen	200	5,000
John Ford	300	7,500
Turhand Kirtland	300	7,500
* John Kinsman, Sr.	800	20,000
Simon Perkins, Sr.	300	7,500
William Rayen	300	7,500
Asahel Adams, Sr.	20	500
Seymour Austin	20	500
John Andrews	20	500
John Brainard	4	100
William Bell, Jr.	50	1,250
Adamson Bentley	20	500
Mary Bentley	10	250
David Bell	20	500
Oliver Brooks	20	500
Richard Brooks	10	250
David Bell	12	300
Benjamin Bentley, Jr.	2	50
John Leavitt	25	650
Lydia Dunlap	8	200
John Doud	20	500
Charles Dutton	75	1,875
Ann Jane Dutton	25	625
Edward Dras	4	100
Dan Heaton	20	500
Francis Freeman	25	625
Otis Guild	20	500
Lois Guild	5	125
Jerusha Guild	10	250
Peter Hitchcock	10	250
John B. Harmon	20	500
Ira Hudson	20	500
Benjamin J. Jones	10	250
Thomas G. Jones	10	250
Jared Kirtland	20	500
Abraham Kline	30	750
Samuel King	40	1,000
Charles King	20	500
Samuel Leavitt	40	1,000
Henry Lane	20	500
Wheeler Lewis	20	500
Lambert W. Lewis	20	500
Comfort S. Mygatt	100	2,500
Calvin Pease	20	500
Laura G. Pease	10	250
George Parsons	20	500
Francis M. Parsons	5	125
Ephraim Quinby	100	2,500
James Quigley	20	500
Samuel Quinby	20	500
Nancy Quinby	20	500
Plumb Sutliff	20	500
Samuel Tyler	50	1,250
Tryal Tanner	8	200
Mary Tanner	2	50
John E. Woodbridge	20	500
Elisha Whittlesey	10	250
Fanny Weatherby	5	125
Josiah Whetmore	4	100
Henry Wick	60	1,500
David Webb	4	100
James Healey	20	500
E. T. Boughton	12	300
Robert Montgomery	50	1,250

* John Kinsman, Sr., died before the bank was organized for business.

The first board of directors was composed as follows: Simon Perkins, Turhand Kirtland, Francis Freeman, John Ford, William Rayen, Calvin Austin, Comfort S. Mygatt, Calvin Pease, Henry Wick, Leonard Case, David Clendennen, William Bell, Jr., and Richard Hayes. General Simon Perkins was chosen president, and remained in that position until he resigned in 1836. Zalmon Fitch was chosen to the position of cashier.

On November 24, 1813, the business of this corporation began in a house at one time used by Robert Erwin as a store.

This was the only gambrel-roofed house ever built in Warren, and it stood on the east side of Main street, north of where McQuiston's grocery now stands.

What was known as the old Western Reserve Bank building was erected in 1816 and 1817, upon the lot now occupied by the beautiful structure of the First National bank. The lot formerly belonged to Mrs. Justus Smith, of whom it was purchased. The Western Reserve bank, original capital of $100,000, was latterly increased to $300,000, being nearly the present capital of the First National. It went into liquidation in December, 1843, the charter having been extended from 1816 until that time. In July, 1845, it was reconstructed under the independent banking law, and extended until 1866.

Although among the first banks chartered in the State, it was the only one that continued solvent until the end of the State Bank organization.

Mr. Fitch, the cashier, was promoted to the presidency April 5, 1836, to fill the vacancy caused by General Perkins' resignation. Ralph Hickox succeeded to the cashiership. Mr. Fitch resigned the presidency January 21, 1838, and was succeeded by George Parsons, who held the office till the close of the business existence of the bank, a period of a quarter of a century. George Tayler succeeded Mr. Hickox after the death of the latter in 1840. Mr. Tayler remained cashier through the existence of the Western Reserve bank, and was chosen to the same position in the First National, which succeeded in 1863. In the year 1814 business was seriously prostrated and capital embarrassed as a result of the war. Banks all over the country suspended specie payments, this one with the others being compelled to yield to the pressure for a few months. In 1836 another general panic paralyzed business. A second time the old Western Reserve bank was forced to suspend specie payments, but resumed as soon as the New York banks resumed. A few weeks later the New York banks suspended a second time, but the Western Reserve continued paying specie until a general suspension caused by the war. An incident is told which shows the good credit of this bank in 1816. Banks were allowed at that time to issue paper circulation based upon coin reserve. Much of this paper was received by the United States bank chartered by Congress, and in 1816 Mr. Thaw, as agent for the National bank, started through the West with a wagon making settlements and requiring many banks, especially doubtful ones, to resume their paper. This operation had the effect of closing up many Western concerns. On the collector's arrival at Warren he proceeded at once to the bank and called for a balance of accounts, at the same time presenting a large amount of paper for redemption. He was promptly informed that the bank was ready for settlement and that the specie was ready for the balance. The settlement was at once made, but Mr. Thaw concluded to leave the specie balance where it was.

After the passage of the National banking act of 1863 the directors decided to wind up its business under the State charter, which would have expired in 1866, and to take out a charter under the new National law. The following is quoted from a Cleveland paper:

Fifty years are not many, but it is a long life for a bank to live and then die an honest death. In these days of financial inflation and contraction, monetary chills, and monetary fevers, which exhaust and collapse, a bank, being a soulless corporation, may not seem entitled to an obituary notice. But the case of the Western Reserve bank, with which so many of the old-school men have been connected, seems exceptional. This corporation, through its half-century career, has not only made good quarterly returns, on paper, but has deservedly enjoyed a good repute among men. The Western Reserve bank has really gone out of existence. It seems it did not wait the expiration of its charter. Although it did not take its own life, yet it was so anxious to depart and be at rest that it sort of "gin out," consenting not for its own sake, but out of pure regard for others, to keep breathing until it should legally expire in May, 1866.

We give all the directors with the date of their election: Simon Perkins, Turhand Kirtland, Francis Freeman, John Ford, William Rayen, Calvin Austin, Henry Wick, Leonard Case, Comfort S. Mygatt, Calvin Pease, David Clendennen, William Bell, Jr., and Richard Hayes, elected in 1813; Adamson Bentley, 1814; Charles Dutton and Samuel W. Phelps, 1815; Samuel Leavitt, John Kinsman, and Samuel Quinby, 1817; Dillingham Clark, 1820; Leicester King, 1824; Jared P. Kirtland, 1825; David L. King, 1826; Seabury Ford, 1829; William Quinby, 1831; Daniel Gilbert, 1834; Asahel Adams, 1835; Simon Perkins, 2d, and Frederick Kinsman 1836; Ralph Hickox, 1839; Henry Kirtland, 1840; Elisha Whittlesey, Seth Hayes, and Lemuel Wick, 1841; Joseph Perkins, 1845; Ralsa Clark, 1847; Jacob Perkins and Henry Wick, Jr., 1848; Matthew B. Tayler, 1849; Samuel L. Freeman, 1852; Henry B. Perkins, 1853; John Hutchins, L. J. Iddings, 1855; G. O. Griswold, and B. P. Jamison, 1859.

FIRST NATIONAL BANK.

An organization with the above title was effected in July, 1863, under the National Banking act of 1863. The capital stock was placed at $125,000, with privilege to increase to any amount not exceeding $300,000. At the first election of officers the following directors were chosen: Samuel Quinby, Frederick Kinsman, L. J. Iddings, B. P. Jamison, M. B. Tayler, H. B. Perkins, and J. H. McCombs. H. B. Perkins was elected president, and at a subsequent meeting, George Tayler was elected cashier. Books and business under the new charter were opened September, 14, 1863. In May, 1864, Matthew B. Tayler was chosen to the position of cashier, George Tayler having deceased. The bank increased its capital stock in March, 1865, to $200,000, and in 1868-69, erected a large three-story block, on the site of the old building, in which business had been conducted for half a century. The capital stock was further increased in 1872, to $300,000, the limit fixed by its charter. A serious loss was sustained in November, 1880, in the death of M. B. Tayler, the cashier. In January, 1881, J. H. McCombs was chosen to fill the place thus made vacant. Mr. McCombs had previously filled the office of vice president.

Of the first directors of this bank, four are dead: Samuel Quinby, died February 4, 1874; L. J. Iddings, March 5, 1879; B. P. Jameson, June 10, 1876; M. B. Tayler, November 23, 1880. The present board of directors are: H. B. Perkins, Frederick Kinsman, William R. Stiles, Edward A. Smith, Junius Dana, Thomas Kinsman, and J. H. McCombs.

THE TRUMBULL NATIONAL BANK

was started January 1, 1866, ex-Governor David Tod being one of the original movers in the enterprise, and his family now has quite an interest in it. The original officers were Charles Smith, president; Kirtland M. Fitch (who was succeded by the present officer, Edward C. Smith), cashier. The directors are Harmon Austin, Charles Smith, Henry W. Smith, John M. Stull, G. O. Griswold, Warren Packard, and S. W. Park. The capital stock, $150,000, is divided between thirty-five shareholders. The bank has a surplus of $31,000.

THE SECOND NATIONAL BANK

was organized May 16, 1880. The officers then chosen were D. J. Adams, president; A. Wentz, vice-president; K. M. Fitch, cashier. The directors were, K. M. Fitch, C. A. Harrington, R. W. Ratliff, A. Wentz, I. O. Hart, L. F. Bartlett, E. Finney, Mr. Brown, I. N. O. Lynn, D. J. Adams, A. A. Drake. The stock taken was $100,000, $100 being the amount of each share, and there being in number eighty members representing several millions of dollars.

HOTELS.

To meet the demands of the traveling public, upon motion of J. S. Edwards as a suitable person "to keep a house of public entertainment" Mr. Ephraim Quinby was recommended to Governor St. Clair. In the May term (1801) it was ordered that license be given Mr. Quinby upon the payment by him into the county treasury of the sum of $4. This was the first license taken out, and evidently less expensive than was expected, for the court ordered that $12, which Mr. Quinby advanced at the time of his application, should be returned to him.

In August, 1801, Mr. James Scott also received a license "to keep a public house of entertainment," but neither he nor Mr. Quinby opened regular inns. They merely entertained strangers with such fare as they had themselves. John Leavitt took boarders as early as 1801. He lived on Smith's corner, but did not receive a license until 1803, when he opened a regular hotel. This was the first house in the town, and was also the first house that could boast of a brick chimney. It was situated on the corner of Main and Market streets, and was the grand hotel of the town for many years, the successors of Mr. Leavitt being Jesse Holiday, John Reed, Andrew McKinney, and Horace Rawdon, from whom about 1836 Messrs. H. W. & C. Smith purchased the property.

There was also a Leavitt house on the west side of Main street, near the present depot building, that was used for many years as a hotel. This property was afterwards known as the Walter King place.

The house and store of Asahel Adams, who came to Warren in 1803, was built in an early day and known as the Franklin house. The house was built on the corner of Park avenue and Market street, and is still standing. Old Uncle Billy Williams kept hotel in this house for a long term of years.

Cyrus Bosworth, who came to Warren in 1811, had purchased of John Love one half of lot thirty-three, containing one-fourth acre, April 2, 1817, and erected the National hotel, the present building now known as the Park hotel, and owned by Clark and Hedding. The successors of Bosworth to this property are John Love, William Fearing, Benjamin Towne, Almon Chapman, Phineas Chase, George Parks (December 1, 1879), who erected the present addition, and Clark Hedden.

The new Crescent hotel was started by Messrs.

Fusselman & Stone in 1874, and afterwards purchased by the former, C. F. Fusselman, who still owns the property. It has a good frontage of fifty feet, is two stories in height, and contains commodious apartments for parlors, sleeping-rooms, etc.

The Austin house was one of the original houses of Warren, and was formerly a frame structure and simply a boarding-house. It was kept by Francis Freeman, and under his management lawyers and the public generally attending court would stop there.

The Clifford hotel was originally a store-room and used by Mr. Kamp as a hotel, was sold in 1866 to Mr. Gilmore, who kept it for four years and then sold it to Mr. D. C. Thompson, and after some years it was purchased by Jennie Smith, the present owner, and is now under the management of J. P. Pancoast. It has thirty-five bed-rooms, and is 85 x 40, with an addition of 37 x 35.

MANUFACTURING.

Mr. Benjamin Stevens, born in Litchfield county, Connecticut, 20th of July, 1788, came to the Reserve in 1816, and after making a tour to Chillicothe on horseback, from Cleveland, and also seeking elsewhere, came to Warren in July of that year and purchased a carding machine of Levi Hadley, who had used the machine during the previous summer. Mr. Thomas Wells was then contemplating the erection of a manufactory for cloth; Mr. Stevens also bought out Mr. Wells' interest and put in operation an establishment for making satinet and fulled cloth. This was the first establishment of the kind in Warren, although a carding machine had been in operation in Youngstown.

The site of Mr. Stevens' building was near the west end of the bridge across the Mahoning river, and at the foot of Market street. Mr. Stevens afterward purchased a machine and a shuttle in Pittsburg, and associated with himself in the business his brother Augustus, who remained in partnership with him for many years. The original building was burned down in 1826, and they then removed further down into a brick building, but the dam, built in 1839, drowned them out, and they again moved, going to where the VanGorder property is, into a building still standing.

The manufacturing of wool into cloth was afterwards carried on by Horace Stevens, a nephew, until 1868, when Mr. R. P. McClellan bought out all interests. Mr. McClellan's mill was burned on the 3d of May, 1881, his loss being complete. He has re-established himself on the original site, just west of the Mahoning bridge. He has now a complete set of manufacturing machinery.

The furniture establishment of Truesdell & Townsend had its origin in 1845 with the firm of Truesdell & Hitchcock. The building was then a frame, two stories high, 20 x 40 feet on Main street, near the Mahoning depot. In 1847 Mr. Hitchcock retired, and in 1859 G. T. Townsend, who had been in the furniture business in Girard for eighteen years previous, became a member of the firm, and the next year a small factory owned by them on Fulton street was burned, which was immediately rebuilt and enlarged. The original being one story, was replaced by a two story frame, having double the capacity. In 1867 the store on Main street was burned, followed in two weeks by the burning of the factory on Fulton street. Sixteen thousand dollars' worth of property was thus destroyed, on which there was an insurance of only $4,000. New buildings were erected, three in number, two stories high. The store was then moved to the frame on Main street, and in 1869 two doors below, occupied by John Waldeck. In 1873 the store, three stories, 22 x 95 feet, was built. The consumption of lumber for chairs, bedsteads, bureaus, stands, tables, etc., is over one hundred thousand feet yearly. They give employment to twenty men, having a pay-roll of about $275 per week. Their goods are almost wholly of their own manufacture, and they do a wholesale and retail business.

Edward Spear fitted up machinery in 1848 on the corner of Market and Pine streets, for the manufacture of doors, sash, and blinds. In 1854 it was removed to its present site on Canal street. Spear & Son had it in charge until 1862, when it was sold to Warren Packard. It was destroyed by fire in 1872. It was rebuilt by McBerty & McCormick, who occupied it until 1876, when W. B. Payne took possession August 21, 1876.

Two members of the present firm of H. C. Reid & Co. commenced work alone in a small way on the corner of Park avenue and Fulton street in 1865, with two lathes and one planer.

Next year they bought a stove foundry adjoining, and in three years they had a force of ten hands and a capital of $18,000. At this time they were burned out, but the works of Hill & Medbury, corner of Park avenue and South streets, were purchased at an expense of $14,000, and a force of twenty-five men employed. In 1873 the works were again burned, by a drunken moulder who lost his place, but this fact was not known until all trace of him was lost. The loss this time was about $50,000, on which there were but $20,000 insurance. Mr. Reid, after some time, built again, increased the number of hands to fifty.

The main building is 40 x 90 feet, three stories high; the foundry is 40 x 80, one-story, twenty feet in height. The buildings are all brick, with slate roof. The machine-shop is well equipped, with a number of planes, lathes, drills, saws, etc., etc., and numerous minor fixtures. They buy car-loads of coal and iron weekly, to the amount of thousands of dollars, and which goes directly to the remuneration of laboring men.

The Warren Machine works was established about the year 1850, under the superintendence of W. H. Hall. It was in a frame building, occupying the lot on which the present works are located. Important changes were made from time to time until 1878, when the concern was purchased by Judge Kinsman, and is now controlled by his son, F. Kinsman. The main structure of these works is of brick, two stories high, 90 x 40 feet in size. The foundry department is a one-story brick, 40 x 60 feet, while the boiler shop is 20 feet square. They employ from twenty to twenty-five men. These works are now among the largest industries of the city.

The C. Westlake Rolling-mills originated about twenty years ago, in a steam-hammer, operated by Mr. Packard, who did a large business for the oil trade. The increase of business induced Packard & Co. to build furnaces. This was in 1871, when the company built in all six puddling furnaces and an eighteen-inch train-roll, but in 1873 the firm failed and the mill was sold to William Richard, who increased the puddling furnaces in number to sixteen, and added two heating furnaces, one ten-inch train of rolls. In 1877 the mill was partly burned, and in 1879 bought by Covington Westlake, who is now manager and proprietor. Mr. Westlake has added link and pin machinery, of which he manufactures two tons per day. He makes all sizes of muck bar, and also manufactures finished iron in large quantities. The business gives employment to about one hundred and seventy-five men.

The manufacturing company of Camp & Randall stood among the largest establishment of the kind in the State. The large mill burned down in the summer of 1881, after the company had just refitted it and put in new machinery at a cost of some $20,000.

The business to which we refer was originally started by Mr. D. W. Camp in 1859, and continued until 1867, when Mr. J. F. Randall became a partner. In 1878 a joint stock company was formed with a capital of $200,000. The firm in Warren operated flouring and bagging mills. At Farmington, in this county, they have a flax mill, at which they make a part of the tow used for bagging at the Warren mill. They have also a brick flax mill at Richmond, in this State, with a large frame warehouse connected with it. This place is used as a purchasing depot for grain used at the Warren mill.

In 1830 Messrs. Davison & McCleery started a carriage manufactory. They seldom had more than three or four hands, and after a few years they dissolved, each doing business for himself. About 1845 H. C. Belden became a partner with McCleery, and he continued at the head of the firm for twenty-four years, at times employing thirty to fifty hands, and having a pay-roll footing up from $50 to $60 per day. This was in the period embraced from 1855 to 1865, after which date he seldom employed more than twenty men. In 1869 two of his employes, Messrs. Belden and Guist, bought out the establishment, keeping the full force until 1874, when Mr. Goist sold out. Mr. Drenner is now sole proprietor. He keeps three forges in blast, employs two wood workers, one trimmer, and five painters, and uses over $20,000 worth of stock yearly, the bulk of this expense being in the painting and trimming department. He keeps the best of Norway and common iron, and wood, and manufactures wagons and vehicles of every description. The manufactory embraces four buildings, the blacksmith shop, the wood shop, the warerooms, and the paint shop. The buildings are large and commodious, and are well equipped with all needful machinery of every description.

Bartlett & Corbin, manufacturers of and dealers in buggies and carriages, are an enterprising firm, started up since June, 1880. They give employment to about fifteen men, and are doing a good business.

The first attempt made in Warren to establish a steam saw- and grist-mill was made about the year 1838, by Liberty Reymond. The experiment proved a failure. Daniel Derr was more successful about twenty years later. He built a mill and distillery, but the latter was closed by the whiskey tax in 1861. The mill did a remunerative business until it was destroyed by fire in 1869.

After the canal was built the old VanGorder mill, commonly known as the "lower mill," was removed to its present site. It is now owned and operated by A. & G. VanGorder, and is the only flouring establishment in Warren.

WEBB'S OPERA HOUSE.

was built by A. D. Webb, in the year 1861, and was known for a long time, as Webb's hall. The destructive fire in 1860 burned out most of that street, at which time Mr. Webb bought this lot, and erected a substantial three-story brick block, 45 x 98 feet, having store rooms below and office rooms in front, on the second floor. The opera hall proper, has a seating capacity, of about six hundred, has a stage 20 x 16 feet, with necessary scenery.

INSURANCE.

The citizens of Trumbull county, as early as the year 1830, realized the benefits arising from insuring against loss by fire, and about that time the Trumbull Fire Insurance company was established, with George Parsons as president and Jacob H. Baldwin as secretary. By an old policy issued by this company, November 28, 1832, the property of Roswell Stone, of Warren, was insured against loss by fire, to the amount of $1,100, $800 on his dwelling house situated on lot number six, in the town plat of Warren; $100 on his law office on the north side, adjoining the dwelling; and $200 on the furniture of his office and house.

This company was a stock affair, having a capital of about $30,000. They did a close business for a few years, and then closed out.

In 1843 The Trumbull County Mutual Fire Insurance company was organized, but the great fire which occurred in Warren in 1846, left the company in such a depleted condition that about fifty-two cents on the dollar was paid, and this amount only after some litigation had ensued.

Of this company, Lewis J. Iddings was president, Jacob H. Baldwin was secretary, and T. J. McClain treasurer.

In addition to these attempts, a farmers' company in Lordstown township is running on a limited scale, as is also the Grangers, who organized a few years ago, having John Dunlap as president and William Thomas, of Kinsman, as treasurer.

About the year 1846, the eastern companies commenced operations, and established agencies at Warren. Charles Pease was the first agent. T. J. McLain also started about this time carrying a full line of companies. Among that list may be mentioned the Liverpool, London & Globe, The Phœnix, and others. In 1857 Mr. Whittlesey Adams embarked in the business and has been a successful agent during all the years since that time, and is doing a large business. Swager & Post have also been successful in the business during these many years. D. R. Gilbert and John W. Taylor represent some good companies and are doing an active business. Mr. T. J. McLain is now the oldest representative in this department of business, and represents a good list of insurance houses, as do Whittlesey Adams and others.

By an examination of the county auditor's report for 1880, the amount of money this county paid out to foreign companies alone for that year will be found to aggregate the net sum of $15,631.21. This is exclusive of the amount paid to any other but foreign insurance companies.

It is due to the business men of Warren that further mention should be made of their public spirit and liberality exercised in procuring railroad facilities. The Cleveland & Mahoning railroad was substantially a Warren enterprise. The project originated and was set on foot here, and it was mainly Warren determination, backed by Warren capital, that carried it to successful completion. We have seen that when an exhausted treasury seemed to threaten failure and total loss to all who had invested in stock, three of the Warren directors—Jacob Perkins, Frederick Kinsman, and Charles Smith—together with three of their associates—David Tod, of Youngstown, Reuben Hitchcock, of Painesville, and Dudley Baldwin, of Cleveland, made themselves personally responsible for the floating debt, never less than $500,000, and at times reaching almost $1,000,000. Through the able management and fidelity of the directors, all stockholders, both heavy and light, were not only fully repaid, but reaped large dividends. The stock sold at twenty per cent. premium in 1863, and a dividend of fifteen per cent. had previously been declared.

While Warren business men were yet embarrassed with the burden of debt incurred by the Mahoning road, the managers of the Atlantic & Great Western railroad began to push work on their line. The directors were disposed to resent Warren's failure to make liberal donations for the road by locating their line three miles north of the city. The survey had been made and work was about to be commenced when the injurious effects of such an action began to be anticipated by capitalists and business men. A subscription was at once started and right of way donated for a distance of six miles, together with ample depot grounds in the city. In addition to this gift of property worth at least $16,000, $24,000 in cash was presented to the company in consideration of running the road through Warren. It was expected, of course, that the company would provide at least comfortable depot facilities. Upon this point Judge Kinsman, in a communication to the Chronicle, says:

Instead of occupying the depot grounds for depot purposes, they built a shanty for freight and passengers on the right of way, remote from the depot grounds, but located so that every train stopping blocked one of our leading streets, and proves a great and dangerous annoyance. Very soon after the building became very rickety and too small for freight, and a new freight building was located on the remote corner of the depot grounds donated, and a new passenger shanty was built, much less, and not as good as the first, but on the same ground, about twenty-five rods from the depot grounds donated. This building was erected by Sweetzer, superintendent, at the same time with a freight depot on the old canal bed.

Soon after the new Atlantic & Great Western freight depot was burned, and its place was supplied by the removal of the freight depot built by Sweetzer on the old canal bed, west of town, and on the then Mahoning branch, supposed to have been done to keep some other projected road from occupying that location.

The donated grounds are now occupied by that freight depot and several shanties in use by the trackmen and employes of the road, not giving a very tidy or comely appearance.

After the location and completion of the road and transfer of the Mahoning road, an effort was made to connect the Mahoning branch at that point and remove the connection at Leavittsburg to Warren, to connect here with the main line of the Atlantic and Great Western railroad. A plan was matured and the company engineer laid out about eighteen acres of ground, which was secured, and a subscription of about $10,000 made to carry out that object. A resolution of the board was passed and recorded on the company's books at New York, that they would accept the proposition of the citizens and transfer the connection from Leavittsburg to Warren.

About two months after this arrangement the road failed, and went into the hands of Jay Gould and others. The arrangement was placed before them and they looked over the ground, but took no action upon it, and it failed from want of attention by the company.

Warren gave $50,000 to the Ashtabula road, or rather subscribed that amount in stock, which is now worthless. It will be seen that $90,000 has been given to railroads, from which no direct return has been realized. Liberal assistance has been given private enterprises, many of which failed. The capitalists of few cities can show a better record than those of Warren, when compared on the basis of liberal expenditure for the public good. If growth latterly has been slow and unsatisfactory, the blame cannot be laid upon business men or capitalists, but it is not difficult to find a satisfactory reason.

CHAPTER III.
RELIGIOUS ORGANIZATIONS.

The early settlers seemed to incline toward the Baptist or Presbyterian societies. According to the best authority the first services held in Warren were by Rev. Henry Speer, a Baptist minister from Washington county, Pennsylvania. He visited Warren in June of 1800. The settlers were no doubt glad to hear a sermon once more, and soon cleared a little spot under an arbor of trees where about fifty persons gathered to listen. In the fall of this same year the Rev. Joseph Badger came. He was sent out by the Connecticut Missionary society. Mr. Speer was an acquaintance of some of the settlers of Warren. The Baptists were a little in advance of all others in their first service, and also a little in advance in organizing.

It is thought that the first regular services conducted in Warren were by the Rev. Thomas Jones, a Baptist minister who resided east of Brookfield, on the Shenango. This was not later than 1801 or 1802. Mr. Jones continued his services until some time in 1807. The Rev. Joseph Badger visited Warren in the fall of the same year (1800) in which the Rev. Henry Speer came.

These two churches were first represented in the place the same year, and the organization of the congregations occurred near the same time, that of the Baptist preceding the Presbyterians only by a little over two months, the one being in September and the other in November of 1803.

FIRST BAPTIST CHURCH.

The First Baptist church of Warren, Ohio, was organized September 3, 1803. Its constituent members were ten in number, as follows: Isaac Dally, John Leavitt, Jr., Caleb Jones, Samuel Firtner, Samuel Burnett, Henry Firtner, Effie Dally, Jane Dally, Nancy Burnett, and Mary Jones. The first preacher of the Baptist faith who preached in Warren, was the Rev. Henry Speers, of Washington county, Pennsylvaian. He visited the place in June, 1800, and preached his first sermon to about fifty persons, assembled under the shade of the trees along the road south of the Mahoning river. From the time of its organization until 1810, the church had no settled pastor, but was supplied at intervals by the Rev. Thomas G. Jones, a resident of the Shenango valley east of Brookfield. In May, 1810, Adamson Bently was ordained to preach the gospel, and in 1811 was settled as pastor. He continued in this relation until he changed his views, and the great schism occurred which well nigh destroyed the church. Until 1821 there was no meeting-house, and meetings were held from house to house. During the years 1820 and 1821, the meeting-house was built, which stands on the north side of the public square, and now occupied by the Disciple church. A few years later Alexander Campbell came upon the ground and succeeded, with the aid of Rev. Walter Scott, in carrying almost the entire church over to his peculiar views. Only four or five continued fast in the faith of their fathers, still retaining the Baptist name and holding the church property. Little can be said concerning the history of the church from 1828 to 1834, when seven members came together at the house of Ephraim Quinby, father of the late Samuel Quinby, and reorganized themselves into a church. On the following Sunday they held communion service in the old meeting-house, where they occasionlly held services for some time afterwards. At a meeting held February 14, 1835, at which Elder Jacob Morris presided, a resolution was passed to withdraw the hand of fellowship from all those who had departed from the faith of the regular Baptist church in Warren, called "Concord."

For some time after this, meetings were held from house to house. Attempts were made from time to time to get possession of the church property, but to no purpose. The meeting-house and church records are still in possession of the Disciple church.

On December 4, 1845, the house of worship on Pine street, now in use, was dedicated. Since then the history of the church has been varied. At times it has enjoyed remarkable prosperity. Up to the period of the war, during the ten years' pastorate of Rev. E. T. Brown, lately deceased, the church became strong and influential.

The war took away some of its noblest and bravest young men who, alas! never returned. Besides this, it has lost heavily by removals to the West and other places.

The following persons have served the church as pastors: Rev. Jacob Morris, from 1835 to 1836; John Winter, 1841-48; Lewis Ranstead, 1849-53; John D. Melson, 1854-58; E. T. Brown, 1856-66 (one year of this time was spent in the army as chaplain); George Pierce, 1866-1869; R. Tilford, 1869-72; J. P. Stevenson, 1873-76; W. T. Whitmarsh, 1876-79. Rev. J. S. Hutson is the present pastor. His labors began November 1, 1879. The present membership is one hundred and forty-one, embracing some of the oldest and most highly esteemed citizens of the place. Its deacons are Samuel Sidels and E. A. Palmer; trustees, G. O. Griswold, F. A. Palmer, and C. W. Tyler; finance committee, George E. Day, William J.

Kerr, and M. J. Sloan, Esq. Solomon Mountain is sexton.

The church sustains a flourishing Sabbath-school. E. A. Palmer is the efficient superintendent, and J. B. Mills secretary.

The current expenses of the church are met by voluntary weekly contributions. The pastor's salary is paid promptly every week. Missionary collections are taken up every two months. The seats are free. The church is free from debt, and its prospects for the future are hopeful.

PRESBYTERIAN CHURCH.

The history of the Presbyterian church of Warren dates back to the earliest days of the city, its organization having been effected by the labors and through the instrumentality of the old pioneer missionary, Rev. Joseph Badger. It seems unnecessary to speak particularly of him in this connection, for his name is to be seen in all parts of the history of the Western Reserve.

This congregation when organized was under the Congregational form of government, and was called the "Church of Christ of Warren." In the organization of churches at this early day it was frequently the case that what was called a "plan of union" was adopted, and the church composed of members from both the Congregational and Presbyterian churches.

In the organization of this church Rev. Mr. Badger was assisted by the Rev. Messrs. Lait and Wick, of western Pennsylvania. Rev. Mr. Lait was from Mercer, Pennsylvania; Rev. Mr. Wick was formerly pastor of the church at Neshannock, Pennsylvania, and later of the Congregational at Youngstown, and of Hopewell, Pennsylvania. [See biography in connection with the church history of Youngstown.]

In the year 1803 six persons, after due consideration, and with a sense of the obligations resting upon them, met together for the purpose of conference and action in the matter of church relations. This meeting was held on the 18th of November, 1803.

The names of these six persons were Thomas Prior, Betsy Prior, Thomas Ross, Rosalinda Ross, Polly Lane, and Elizabeth Davidson. After prayer for direction in all their deliberations, and for guidance in the important work in which they were engaged, an examination was held respecting the Christian character of those who proposed entering into church relations.

This examination in regard to their knowledge of the fundamental docrines of the gospel, and of the evidences of their Christian hope was satisfactory. It now only remained necessary to adopt a "confession of faith" and to determine upon rules and regulations for the practice of the members. They met again on Saturday, the 19th day of November, and completed the organization by adopting a "confession of faith" and determining upon rules of practice, and upon a covenant to be entered into. Those persons uniting in fellowship and covenant, and standing as a church of Christ in this place were: Thomas Prior, Betsy Prior, Thomas Ross, Rosalinda Ross, Polly Lane, and Elizabeth Davidson.

As a matter of history and for the benefit of those who may wish to understand more particularly the peculiarities of those organizations, it may be well to quote from the original documents, in which we find that they were "solemnly charged to walk in the ordinances of the Lord, and to keep covenant with each other, looking for divine assistance to the great head of the church, to whose grace they are committed." The church adopted the regulations of the general assembly of the Presbyterian church, and the general association of Connecticut, respecting the organization of churches in the new settlements.

The church adopted this standing rule, "that no person shall be admitted a member in this church, by letter or otherwise, without an examination, that a unity of sentiment and practice may be promoted and preserved with the members of this church. Attest, Joseph Badger, missionary from the Missionary society of Connecticut."

In March, of 1804, the Rev. Mr. Badger, at a meeting of the church, presented a confession of faith similar in principle, but different in some respects from the one previously adopted. A vote was taken and the same adopted. Some changes were also made in the articles of practice. At this meeting it was also voted to choose the Rev. Thomas Robbins moderator of the church.

The first pastor was the Rev. James Boyd, who was installed October 21, 1808. He died March 8, 1813. One-half of his time was spent with this church and the remainder with the church in Newton. Previous to his pastorate the Rev.

Jonathan Leslie was engaged as an occasional supply. He labored in this capacity during the three years from 1805 to 1808.

After the death of Mr. Boyd the Rev. James Duncan acted as stated supply for a period of two years.

Rev. Mr. Curtis came to Ohio in 1817, under the appointment of the Hampshire Missionary society of Massachusetts. He acted as missionary for some months, and then became stated supply for this church, laboring in that capacity for about eighteen months previous to his installation. He was installed pastor of this church by the Grand River Presbytery on the 4th of February, 1820. He was a faithful and acceptable pastor, the church prospering under his ministry. In June, of 1831, at his own request, Mr. Curtis was dismissed on account of failing health. Rev. George W. Hulin labored as stated supply for two months, beginning in December, 1831, and was followed by the Rev. J. A. Woodruff, in the same capacity, for a term of eighteen months. The Rev. Josiah Towne became a candidate for the pastorate in May, 1834, and was installed as pastor, by the Trumbull Presbytery, in May, 1835. He was dismissed in October, 1839.

The Rev. Nathan B. Purington received a call from the congregation and was installed pastor by the Presbytery of Trumbull in May, 1840. He remained in the discharge of his pastoral duties nearly eight years, being dismissed by Presbytery on the 12th of April, 1848. Mr. Purington was a native of Newburyport, Massachusetts. He graduated from the Ohio university in 1837, and took his theological course at Lane seminary. On leaving Warren, in the spring of 1848, he removed to Rock Island, Illinois, where he died, after a long illness, on the 22d of May, 1850.

After the close of Mr. Purington's labors, the Rev. William C. Clark was invited to supply the pulpit. He began preaching on the 18th of February, 1848. The church extended a call to him to become their pastor, which he accepted, and was installed pastor by the Presbytery of Trumbull, November 15, 1848. His resignation was tendered to the church on the first Sabbath of January, 1863, and his labors closed on the 1st of July of that year. He went immediately to Sturgis, Michigan, but on account of ill health he was obliged to give up all labor, and he moved to Detroit, where he died on the 30th of June, 1870.

On the 5th of July, 1863, Mr. Henry Richard Hoisington took his place here as stated supply for six months. He was a graduate of Auburn Theological seminary, and a licentiate of the Presbytery of Auburn. He was ordained as an evangelist the last week in April, 1864, by the Presbytery of Trumbull, and on the 14th of December following was installed as pastor of the church. He retired from the pastorate on the 1st of June, 1867. Afterwards he became pastor of the First church in Circleville, Ohio.

Rev. Benjamin St. John Page immediately began the work as supply, in which capacity he remained until his death, which occurred on the 9th of November, 1868.

In September of 1869 the Rev. Nathaniel P. Baily, of Painesville, was invited to fill the pulpit as a supply. This he continued to do from Sabbath to Sabbath the greater part of the time until March of 1870, when he accepted a unanimous call from the congregation to become its pastor. On the 11th of May of the same spring he was installed by the Presbytery of Trumbull. The church remained Presbyterian, but under the Congregational form of government, until 1838, and on the 1st of February of that year the church, by resolution, adopted the Presbyterian form. On the 10th of March, 1845, the society was incorporated as the First Presbyterian church of Warren, Trumbull county.

In the fall of 1830 a house of worship was begun, which was dedicated the 10th of May, 1832. The dedication sermon was preached by Rev. Charles B. Storrs, president of Western Reserve college. In 1849 this house was repaired and improved. In 1850 the lecture room was built. This house was known as the "Old Presbyterian church" and did good service until 1875, when it was taken down to give place to the new and beautiful edifice now occupied by the church. This house was situated at what was known as High street and the "turnpike" (now Mahoning avenue). The location is fine and the building an ornament to the town. The Sunday-school in connection with this church is in a flourishing condition. At present the school numbers three hundred and fifty-six, an increase of one hundred and six over last year. In connection with the congregation is a Young People's Christian association, which was organized on the 18th of September, 1871, with constitution and by-laws governing the association, the objects being the development of Christian character, of usefulness and activity in its members, with the improvement of the mental, moral, and spiritual condition of our young people, etc. The officers consist of president, secretary, and treasurer, with a board of managers. The total membership of the church at the close of the year was three hundred and twenty-nine, being an increase of twenty-four during the year. On March 25, 1848, the church voted to adopt the principal of a rotary eldership.

The present pastor, the Rev. Alexander Jackson, is a young man of great promise, a native of Glasgow, Scotland. His father died when Alexander was in his tenth year. He was the second of six children. His widowed mother had a very moderate competence and it was thought necessary for Alexander to be taken out of school and placed in an office, where he could earn a livelihood. He served a seven years' apprenticeship in a book-bindery, spending his evenings and spare moments in study, laying the foundation for a thorough education. By diligent use of such advantages as he enjoyed in evening classes at Dr. McNair's normal school he was prepared to enter college.

After spending some time in the University of Glasgow, he went to Edinburgh, at the age of twenty-one, and formed a connection with a business house, with the privilege of using a part of his time in study. Under this arrangement he was enabled to pursue his studies, for four years, in the University of Edinburgh, and one year in the Divinity school. He excelled in philosophical studies, and in a class of two hundred, was one of fifteen who won high honors. A Duke of Hamilton scholarship was awarded him, and he returned to Glasgow university, where he graduated. Afterward, he spent a year in London filling a position in the library of the British Museum. He married Agnes, eldest daughter of John Armstrong, of Townhead, Dumfrieshire, Scotland, while in London.

Mr. Jackson came to America in 1872, and continued his studies in the Theological seminary at Auburn, New York. He then entered the ministry and served the Presbyterian church in Amenia about three and a half years. Afterwards he supplied pulpits in Newark, New Jersey, and in Chicago, until he was called to the church in Warren. By the foregoing we see that Mr. Jackson is a self-made man, having earned the means to pay for his own education. He has had contact with business people, in the work-shop and in the business office, and is eminently fitted for the discharge of the responsible duties resting upon him in his ministry over his people in Warren, while his sermons and his labors in general are highly appreciated by the church and people of this place.

METHODIST EPISCOPAL CHURCH IN WARREN.

During the summer of 1819 Methodism was established in Warren. Mr. John Bridle, a member of the Methodist Episcopal church, a resident of Warren, being anxious to secure Methodist preaching in this place, went on foot to Youngstown to a quarterly meeting the first week in November, and during the meeting made arrangements with both elder and pastor in charge to visit Warren and preach to them. Accordingly, at the time appointed Elder Swayze and Mr. James McMahon came to Warren, and on Thursday evening Elder Swayze preached in an old log school-house, and the next day Mr. McMahon formed a class in the old log jail, consisting of John Bridle (leader) and wife, Sarah Towen, A. Stewart, R. Brockway, Achsa Knapp, and John Barnes and wife.

Preaching was held in the court-house on Sunday evenings, and the following spring several persons were converted and added to the class, Josiah Soule, Nancy Harsh, Betsy Hall, Ebenezer Rodgers, and Benjamin Stevens and wife. Mr. Stevens is probably the only representative of this class now living, and was born in Litchfield, Connecticut, July 20, 1788, came to Warren in 1816, and for three score years and over has been identified with this church, as one of the first class leaders, and ever thereafter as one of its most prominent and active members.

Rev. William Swayze, the presiding elder, was born in Sussex county, New Jersey, November 8, 1784, near the village of Asbury, named after the venerable Bishop Asbury. He was a young minister, talented and zealous, and was styled a "son of thunder," attracting great crowds of people to his ministry, and with a power and pathos but few have equaled. He was tall and straight in person, with great powers of endurance. His complexion was dark, his black eyes deeply set and very expressive, while his voice possessed great compass and was perfectly under his control.

The church was favored with a most glorious revival, which commenced in January of 1819, and spread into the surrounding country until nearly a hundred were converted, which were finally consolidated with the village class. Rev. Joseph McMahon was the first circuit rider who preached in Warren. He continued in the work, calling at the village about once every two weeks for a period of about two years, and was succeeded by his brother John. The two McMahons were brothers, and were of Irish origin.

These men were succeeded in their charge at this place by the now noted Alfred Bronson, formerly of Danbury, Connecticut, who was born in that place February 9, 1793. He was received into the Ohio conference in 1820, and subsequently removed to the Mahoning circuit. He was a very large, compactly built man, possessing a bold, fearless spirit, ambitious and resolute, and sure to keep something astir whereever he was. In all he was well adapted for his work among early settlers, and has won for himself a name in the history of his church.

Alfred Bronson was assisted in his work by his colleague, the Rev. Ezra Booth. The first sacrament was administered by Mr. Bronson and Father Bostwick at a two days' meeting which was held in a grove on the bank of the river, in or near the village.

At a quarterly conference held in Youngstown November 24-25, 1821, Mahoning circuit, we find present Rev. William Swayze, presiding elder, Rev. Charles Elliott, Rev. Dermis Goddard, circuit preacher, Rev. John Crawford, Shadrack Bostwick, L. C., William Veach, L. D., Elias Morse, L. D. Circuit stewards: Isaac Powers, Titus Hays, and Henry Stowe. Exhorters: Chauncey Hickox, William Burnet, Hezekiah Reeder, Asa Walden, and Joseph Davis. Class leaders: Shadrack Bostwick, Benjamin Flint, Benjamin Stevens, Isaac Powers, Chauncy Merry, Freeman Parcy, David Leroy, Titus Hays, Roger Perkins, Peter Hought, John Bates, Henry Stowe, William Carish, Tillinghouse Moorey, Robert Patrick, Samuel Clark.

The first quarterly meeting was held in Warren February 10, 1827. Charles Elliott was the presiding elder; Revs. R. C. Hutton and Robert Hopkins assisted. The meeting was held in the court-house, there being an unusually large number in attendance. The membership of the church had increased to sixty in number, and on that occasion an addition of seventeen more was made. The two ministers who officiated at that time were noted for their zeal and power in the good work.

The first protracted meeting was conducted in 1836, in a room in the old academy building, which had been used by the denomination for some eight years.

The first meeting house was a large, commodious frame building, 40x60, and was erected on the bank of the river as early as 1837, and dedicated in November of that year. It was built with Gothic windows, a suitable cupola and basement.

A subscription paper* was circulated, and the following are some of the names of persons who subscribed to that fund: Benjamin Stevens, David Tod, Milton Graham, Charles Smith, Garry Lewis, Henry W. Smith, Warren R. Quinby, Frederick Kinsman, Samuel Quinby, Ralph Hickox, Simeon L. Hunt, Simon Perkins, John Ewalt, Henry Lane, James L. VanGorder, E. H. Allison, James Scott, Leicester King, Edward Potter, Lyman Potter, George Parsons, Joshua Henshaw, Edward Hoyt, Walter King, Robert Craig.

In the latter part of 1839 Warren was made a station and Lorenzo D. Mix was appointed to the charge. In 1841 Bishop Roberts presided over the first annual conference that was held in Warren. In 1851 the second annual conference, and in 1868 the third. Bishop Morris presided at the second one, and Bishop Kingsley at the third, and in 1880 Bishop Bowman presided.

In 1866, the church having increased in numbers and the old edifice beginning to show signs of decay, the members resolved to erect a more modern and convenient building. Accordingly a subscription paper was put in circulation and the people responded liberally. A lot on High street was purchased at $5,000, and work began. Soon the new structure that now adorns the city was seen gradually nearing completion, and on

---

*This paper is still in the possession of Mr. Benjamin Stevens.

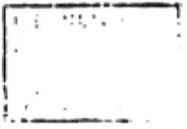

the 21st of June, 1874, the house was formally dedicated to the worship of God. Dr. B. I. Ives conducted the dedicatory services, preaching the sermon. In these service she was assisted by E. W. Schon, D. D., of the Methodist Episcopal Church South, a former pastor.

The church is commodious and is elegantly finished and furnished, costing in all some $50,000.

No debts encumber the church. They have adopted the envelope system, which has thus far been successful. The annual expenses are about $2,000. The membership is about four hundred.

The trustees hold the title to the church property. The stewards are expected to look after the finances. The leaders are expected to see all the members once every week. The prayer meetings are well attended. The young people of the church have a literary society which is well attended, and is the means of some mental improvement. This meets once in two weeks.

The Sunday-school is the largest in the city, and is growing in interest. At present it numbers about three hundred, with one superintendent and an assistant, who are further assisted by a corps of eighteen teachers. The Bible class is under the care of the pastor, Rev. A. H. Norcross. Mr. John M. Stull is the efficient superintendent.

CHRIST CHURCH.

The actual date of the first service of the Protestant Episcopal church in Warren is not known, but records of the church show that services were held in the court-house at different times by various clergymen of the Protestant Episcopal church. The ministers who held such services were the Rev. Bishop Chase, and the Rev. Messrs. Serle, M. T. C. Wing, and J. L. Harrison. So far as can be definitely ascertained, the first service held was by Rev. Mr. Serle, in the court-house, about the year 1813. At this time only one communicant of the church resided here—Mrs. Lavina Rowe, the grandmother of Messrs. Henry and Charles Smith, two of the present vestrymen. Bishop Chase visited here once, or perhaps twice, officiating in the court-house. Rev. M. T. C. Wing, D. D., afterwards professor of ecclesiastical history in the Theological seminary at Gambier, Ohio, was here with Bishop Chase, and probably at other times.

The following "article of association" we append, with names in full:

We, whose names are hereunto affixed, deeply impressed with the importance of the Christian religion, and earnestly wishing to promote its holy influence in the hearts and lives of ourselves and families, and our neighbors, do hereby associate ourselves together under the name, style, and title of the Parish of Christ church, in the township of Warren, county of Trumbull, State of Ohio, and by so doing accept the constitution and canons of the Protestant Episcopal church in the diocese of Ohio, in communion with the Protestant Episcopal church in the United States of America.

John Crowell, Charles Wolcott, Jacob H. Baldwin, Hiram Baldwin, Edward E. Hoyt, John Veon, M. B. Taylor, Oliver H. Patch, James Hoyt, John B. Canfield, Thomas H. Best, John L. Frazier, Henry W. Smith, William L. Knight, Addison Weatherbee, John Supple, William Johnson, James Chesney, Edwin Leffingwell, Lyman Potter, R. P. Ranney, Henry Curtis.

This organization was effected sometime during the year 1836, under an act of the General Assembly of the State of Ohio. Some time after this the organization was given up.

There was occasionally preaching in Warren by the Rev. J. L. Harrison, at that time rector of the church in Boardman, and also that of Canfield. In August, 1841, the parish was reorganized by the Rev. C. C. Townsend, and at the winter session of the Legislature, 1842, it was incorporated by petition of J. Crowell, Esq., now of Cleveland, Ohio.

This parish, in connection with St. Marks, of Newton Falls, remained under the pastoral care of Mr. Townsend until June 25, 1843. Up to the date of re-organization (the winter of 1842) there were twenty-six communicants enrolled, nineteen of whom were added during Mr. Townsend's pastorate. After the withdrawal of Mr. Townsend the church was without a regular pastor until November, 1848, but during this time regular service according to the use of the church was performed, first by S. D. Harris, and afterwards by W. G. Darley, lay readers, licensed by the bishop.

The minutes of vestry meetings previous to Easter Monday of that year have not been preserved, and it is impossible to learn the names of all the early vestrymen. Those we can learn were: Mr. Lewis Iddings, Judge Matthew Birchard, Lieutenant Ingersoll, Mr. J. Baldwin (now of Kinsman), Judge R. P. Ranney, and General Crowell (now of Cleveland).

Of the first confirmation class the names and the number are unknown. This class was presented by Rev. C. C. Townsend, the service being held in the old Methodist church on the river bank. About this time the old court-house was torn down. Mr. Townsend, who taught school in addition to his duties as rector, had a schoolroom in a building at the corner of Main and Franklin streets; service was held in that schoolroom.

At a parish meeting held in 1843 the following officers were elected: S. D. Harris and C. I. Van Gorder, wardens; John Crowell, H. Hubbard, George Parsons, U. B. White, I. Canfield, vestrymen.

At about the first service held, the only man who stood up to make responses was Mr. Jacob Baldwin, and at the expiration of Mr. Townsend's pastorate there were twenty-six communicants enrolled. The vestry comprised some of the most substantial men in the town, while the congregation embraced the families of many of the best citizens. This was in a great measure due to Rev. C. C. Townsend.

In 1846 it was proposed to purchase a lot on Bunker Hill for the erection of a church, at a cost of $300. Two weeks later a committee consisting of U. B. White, C. I. Van Gorder, and S. D. Harris was appointed by the vestry to circulate a subscription paper for the purpose of raising funds to erect a church building. This was successful, and on the 11th of February, 1846, a contract was made with Mr. Blatchly for the lot on the corner of Liberty street and Franklin alley, for which he was to receive $600 in gold on or before the 20th of April. A contract for the building was soon after made with Mr. U. B. White, and the corner-stone was laid September 1st.

June 16, 1848, it was unanimously resolved to invite Rev. Mr. Hughes, of Oneida, New York, to accept the office of rector of this parish. The call was duly signed, but the minister not accepting, a call was addressed to Rev. G. W. Dubois, who came, at a salary of $250. He held the first service in the new church, which was formally consecrated on September 23, 1849, by the Right Rev. C. P. McIlvaine, bishop of the diocese of Ohio.

During the pastorate of Rev. Mr. Dubois, extending over a period of nearly five years, eighteen persons were confirmed, several were added to the church by transfer, and in all, thirty-five families are recorded as having been added to the parish. During the early part of his ministry the Ladies' society was organized, doing then, as ever after, most effective service. This is the oldest church benevolent society in the town of Warren.

In 1850 Judge Mathew Birchard, Messrs. Lewis Iddings, Charles Smith, and Edward Smith were added to the vestry. This year, according to the records, this parish was first represented in the diocesan convention. The delegates chosen were Messrs. Francis Granger and George Parsons, Jr. After repeatedly asking to be released from the charge, the parish very reluctantly consented to part with their pastor, Rev. Mr. Dubois.

The Rev. Mr. Ryan entered upon his duties here in October, 1855, the church having been without a pastor two years. During this time the church lost heavily in members.

August 2, 1858, a call was extended to Rev. C. S. Abbott, who entered upon his duties in September of the same year.

The following spring J. H. McCombs and C. C. McNutt were added to the vestry. The lot upon which the church now stands, was purchased in April, 1862, for $700. In February, 1863, plans were secured from an architect of Cleveland, and a building committee consisting of E. A. Smith, I. I. Iddings, Charles Smith, and S. L. Weeks appointed. Charles Smith and his brother Henry were made vestrymen in 1861. In 1863 J. R. Woods, William L. Porter, and T. J. McLain, Jr., were elected vestrymen. On Ascension day, May 14, 1863, the corner-stone was laid for the present house of worship. The religious ceremonies were conducted by the Right Rev. G. T. Bedell, assisted by the rector. The next year (1864) the old church property was sold to the Romanists for $1,200. On Wednesday, May 24, 1865, the new church was consecrated to the worship of God by the Right Rev. C. P. McIlvaine. The rector and clergymen took part. This year the name of Mr. Frederick Kinsman came upon the roll as vestryman, and in 1867 Mr. S. L. Hunt became vestryman. On the 27th of May, 1867, Rev. Abbott resigned after a pastorate of nearly nine years. Rev. Charles T. Steck entered upon the duties of rector of this church in September, 1867. His stay was short, he only remaining as their pastor until the following June. The next pastor was the Rev.

Henry L. Badger. He resigned July 30, 1871, to go away as a missionary.

A call was immediately extended to Rev. Thomas Taylor. He began his labors October 15, 1871. His resignation took place in April, 1873.

In March, 1874, Rev. A. R. Kieffer was called to the rectorship.

Mr. Kieffer was born in Heidelberg, Pennsylvania, in the year 1842. When eighteen years of age he completed his literary course in college, and then went into the army where he remained one and a half years. He afterwards attended Gambier college, and took a course in theology, from which institution he was graduated in 1871. He was ordained deacon by Bishop Bedell in 1871, and was afterwards in Ironton, Ohio, nearly three years. He came here in 1874. On December 25th he married Lessie Hall, daughter of Alexander Hall, a prominent Disciple preacher and author.

The church in Warren, under Mr. Kieffer's rectorship, is in a flourishing condition, and the utmost good will and kindly feeling exists between the pastor and people. The church is beautiful and pleasant, and all things combine to further the interests of Christ church. The present officers are: E. A. Smith, senior warden; S. L. Hunt, junior warden; Charles Smith, Frederick Kinsman, John H. McCombs, John R. Woods, Henry Smith, A. Wentz, E. A. Wise, and Samuel Iddings, vestrymen.

THE DISCIPLE CHURCH

was born in March, 1841, in the agonies of fierce contention. The establishment of this church developed considerable opposition. It was brought about by a discussion held between J. Hartzel and Rev. Mr. Waldo, a Congregationalist, which made a profound impression. Conversions followed, and a number of Mr. Waldo's friends were baptised into the church. As usual in the history of this church, a malignant opposition arose to its principles of reformation, and Mr. Waldo also encountered other ministers in the issues involved. The Rev. Dr. Boardman, pastor of the Presbyterian church, and J. J. Stedman, of the Methodist Episcopal church, and others still held discussions which served to awaken a feeling for the organization, and helped to establish the church having for its corner-stone—"Is baptism in any case necessary to the forgiveness of sins."

In August, 1842, Mr. Campbell, the founder of the doctrine advocated by this church, came to the Western Reserve, touching Warren, Youngstown, and other places, and helped to establish the church. J. W. Lanphear was secured as its first pastor, but in March, 1843, he resigned and returned to New Lisbon. The annual meeting for Trumbull county was held in 1843 in Youngstown—a brother of John Henry being president of the meeting—which was large, and estimated at from six to ten thousand persons, and the number of Disciples probably two thousand. This effort on the part of the church was attended by an ingathering of some fifty into the church. The membership is now over three hundred. M. L. Streater, the late pastor, is a gentleman of culture and ability. He came from New Castle, Pennsylvania, to this charge in May, 1866. His ministry was very successful during his stay, and the church has grown in numbers and cleared itself of all incumbrances. The present pastor, Rev. Mr. Smith, came to the charge in 1881. Their beautiful brick church is situated on Wood street, the lot, building, etc., costing the church $28,752.88.

GERMAN REFORMED CHURCH.

During the earlier days of Warren the Germans held service together, irrespective of denomination, but after a time, as they grew in numbers, they separated into different societies.

The German Reformed church probably held their first service in Warren about the year 1841. This first service was held by the Rev. Nathan Paltzgroff, in the McFarland block, at the corner of Park avenue and South streets. Mr. Paltzgroff only continued his services a few months, after which no service was held for a long time, but in 1846 he resumed the work in King's block, on Main street, when the society was regularly organized. A lot was bought in 1848, on Vine street, and soon after a suitable building was erected. Mr. Paltzgroff, while in charge, became identified with the English Evangelical synod, the greater part of the congregation going with him.

Mr. Guenter succeeded in the pastorate, remaining some years. He also had charge at Lordstown. After his retirement, in 1857, services became irregular, and, in 1866, the building was sold to the German Lutherans, and to members of the German Reform who still adhered to their views as formerly.

The Evangelical congregation became scattered, some uniting with the Methodist church.

The German Lutheran services were held in Empire hall, about the time the old court-house was torn down. After this they held service in the basement of the Baptist church. They afterwards bought the building on Vine street, where they continued joint owners until the fire of 1868, when it was destroyed. They then divided, when the Lutherans rebuilt, and the German Reform again worshiped in the basement of the Baptist church. They are few in number, however, and they have but little prospect of increasing.

THE ROMAN CATHOLIC CHURCH.

The first rite of this church was preformed by Rev. Prudiprat, and was that of baptism, administered July 3, 1849. The first mass was celebrated by Rev. J. Ringale, at the house of John Lowry, November 12, 1850. For a period of three years, about this time, Father Ringale made three or four visits annually to Warren. In the winter of 1853, Father McGown held mass and service in the house of Mr. McNally. In 1855 the building of the Mahoning railroad brought quite an accession of those of Catholic faith, and services were held monthly by Fathers Stoker and O'Connor, succeeded in 1856 by Rev. Mr. Pendergrast. In 1857 William O'Connor resumed his ministrations. In the year 1863 the Episcopal church was bought, and mass was celebrated therein April 1, 1864, by Father O'Callaghan. Father Sidley succeeded, preaching alternately in Warren, and Niles. E. Conway became the first resident priest in 1868. He was followed by F. E. Murphy, October 3, 1869, who established a Catholic school, October 4, 1871, at his own expense. He was succeeded July 6, 1873, by Father Paginini, who had the full confidence of the church, and who succeeded in making some considerable additions to the building. He was succeeded in 1879, by Father Manning, who is a late graduate of the St. Mary's seminary at Cleveland. The church membership comprises about thirty-one or two families, or probably one hundred and fifty persons.

A. M. E. CHURCH.

Warren has had a number of negro residents since the year 1830, most of them emancipated, or escaped slaves. The number has since increased very slowly, and at present, does not exceed thirty. A practical writer has observed that people of African descent are "naturally religious, and naturally need religion." No church was formally organized in Warren until 1874, when Rev. J. F. Lee, of the A. M. E. conference, visited the brethren of Warren, and formed a congregation. His successors have been, John Bell, C. Arbury, T. H. Cyrus, — Weir, — Smith, P. Ralph, James Jones, — West, Jesse Smith, and A. Waldon. A frame meeting-house was built west of the river in 1875.

CHAPTER IV.
THE PRESS.

American journalism has been passing through a crude, unstable, and experimental period. Whether it has yet reached a permanent plane and become an established system we leave to the future historian to record. The system, however, as it exists, is no longer crude. It is the product of development according to the law of adaptation, and is in perfect accord with the character of civilization as it exists. The transatlantic press differs widely from our own, and is led by journals far surpassing in excellence any published in this country. Larger, better, and cheaper papers are made in London than in New York, because they have a more extended sale. They circulate and are read all over England. The same may be said of the capital journals of other advanced and enlightened nations. All law emanates from the capital where the nation's most vital interests are centered so completely that papers devoted to strictly local affairs are supported only in the larger provincial cities. But the American journalist is governed by conditions entirely different. Every community in the United States is a component part of the Nation, and has a voice in all its affairs. It is therefore desirable and essential that each should have a mouthpiece through which its interests and opinions reach the public at large. The true American journalist makes his own town the center of the universe, and spares no effort to make the influence of his paper felt. Local pride and local feeling support a paper in almost every village, and no party feeling or other influence should interfere with its support of such measures as would be of advantage to the region or element of society of which it is the recognized organ. On all general questions public opinion is divided, making an organ for each party necessary. The local paper has nothing to fear from its larger city contemporary. Americans are not content to know the leading news, but want details concerning their own neighborhood, and they want them presented in the home familiar spirit by some one with whom they are acquainted and in whom they have confidence. The impersonal character of city papers does not admit of such a spirit.

The complete files of Warren newspapers furnish an excellent example of the mutations and gradual development of the rural press. The first paper issued in the Western Reserve made its appearance June 16, 1812, with a pretentious name, Trump of Fame; Thomas D. Webb, editor and publisher. It was a folio sheet, with pages little larger than the pages of this volume, and was set in small pica type. News from Washington was just then of absorbing interest, and three-fourths of all the reading matter consisted of speeches in Congress and discussions relating to foreign affairs. No reader of the first issue would have been led to anticipate the declaration of war two days later, for it took Washington news more than a week to reach Warren, and when we remember that the editor depended upon Washington weekly periodicals for his information, the Trump of Fame needs no apology for publishing news two weees old. The local historian who consults the files of this paper with the hope of finding current reports of important local events will be disappointed. People at that time were supposed to know everything going on around them. Even the great excitement following Hull's surrender, described in a previous chapter, receives in Mr. Webb's paper only an incidental notice, written with less energy and occupying less space than one of the present enterprising journals would devote to a dog fight, or a big pumpkin. During the war no effort seems to have been made to collect news from the field where soldiers from the Reserve were engaged. The entire file contains less than a dozen references to military affairs of a strictly local character. David Flemming was Mr. Webb's printer, and considering his limited facilities did neat and commendable work. A heavy kind of paper was used, and ink was distributed on stuffed balls, one held in each hand. A small quantity of ink was dipped up from the ink-board and evenly distributed over the surface of each ball by rubbing them together, and then patting them vigorously on the form. At a later day the inking was done with a hand roller. The editor in those days had no correspondents, did little writing, and had few exchanges, but Congressional speeches and diplomatic overtures, reprinted from capital organs, were no doubt appreciated by people hungering and thirsting for knowledge.

James White became associated with Mr. Webb as a partner in 1813, and the following year Samuel Quinby purchased an interest, Mr. Webb retiring. The paper struggled along and increased in circulation under the firm name of James White & Co., until 1816, when Fitch Bissel became proprietor. Bissel was an energetic fellow, and gave considerable attention to his publication, yet its appearance was out of all proportion to the high sounding name which it bore. This is evident from an incident connected with the change of name. It is not strange that a recent arrival should be first to notice and speak of this incongruity, for old settlers had become accustomed to it. One day in September Benjamin Stevens, recently from Vermont, met the editor at the post-office, and conversation turned upon the paper. Mr. Stevens thought a less high sounding title would be more appropriate for a paper in this new country, and advised the proprietor to "call it the Western Reserve Chronicle, or Gazette, or something of that sort." Editors are characteristically self-willed and love to appear original, but at the same time are always watching for suggestions from which to profit. Mr. Bissel repudiated this suggestion, but three weeks later the paper came out headed Western Reserve Chronicle, "Vol. 1, No. 1," "October 4, 1816." At the head of the first column was the announcement in italics:

The *Western Reserve Chronicle* is printed every Thursday

at $2.00 a year if paid in advance; if payment is neglected till the end of the year, $2.50.

Papers transmitted by mail are at the expense of subscribers.

Letters and communications addressed to the editor must be post paid or they will not be attended to.

On changing the name it was enlarged to a four-column, four-page paper, the whole sheet being 18 x 22 inches. The file for nearly a year contains no local news and very few editorial items. The contents averaged about as follows: Advertisements, six columns; congressional speeches and national news from Washington, six columns; foreign news, two columns, and one column of State Legislative news. In 1817 the Chronicle changed hands again, being purchased by Samuel Quinby and Elihu Spencer. Editorial work devolved upon the latter, who was in every way qualified for the task, being a gentleman of liberal culture. He introduced the practice of devoting a column, more or less, to comments on public affairs, and occasionally to local events of importance. Mr. Spencer was not spared long to his task. He died in 1819 and was succeeded by George Hapgood. Mr. Hapgood was a native of Brattleboro, Vermont, where he served an apprenticeship at the printer's trade, then came west in search of his fortune. He first found employment as compositor in the Chronicle office until the death of Mr. Spencer left the editorship vacant. A printing office cost very little in those days, making it possible for any industrious fellow to earn a partnership in a year or two. Mr. Hapgood brought to the place excellent qualifications, having decided convictions and the ability and stamina to maintain them. Short editorials on political affairs appeared from time to time after the presidential election of 1824 divided the country into contending factions. The first vigorous political writing appears in the Chronicle during the campaign of 1828. Mr. Hapgood had defended the administration of John Quincy Adams and opposed the popular wave which carried Jackson into the Presidency. The Chronicle's position during the canvass, and strong prejudices of its editor committed it to anti-Jackson principles. It supported Harrison in 1836 and again in 1840. So strong and pronounced had the editor's course been that the Jacksonian Democrats started in 1830 an organ devoted to the administration, called the

NEWS-LETTER.

T. J. McLain, editor, and J. G. McLain, publisher. The News-Letter was not a venture, for fidelity to the party gave it a sustaining patronage. It was larger than the Chronicle, and being the only Democratic paper on the Reserve, acquired a paying circulation, and was extensively quoted as the Jackson organ of Northern Ohio, and was made an official medium for the publication of United States laws. The Messrs. McLain sold out in 1839 to Christopher Columbus Seeley and William Baldwin, who changed the name to Trumbull Democrat, and continued its publication. During the Jackson and Van Buren administrations, the News-Letter and Chronicle frequently discussed public questions from the standpoints of their respective parties. Opposition seems to have had a good effect upon both journals, for the Chronicle, as soon as an opponent entered the field, began to show more vigor. It was about this time that we begin to find local items, not details or trivial pleasantries, but a brief summary of important occurrences. Mr. Hapgood's fidelity to Whig principles was recognized by General Harrison after his inauguration in 1841, by an appointment to the postmastership. He retired from the paper in June, 1841. His associates in its publication during the twenty-two years of his editorship, were Otis Sprague, E. R. Thompson, William Quinby, John Crowell, Calvin Pease, Jr., and A. W. Parker, who purchased an interest in 1832, and became editor on the retirement of Mr. Hapgood. After the death of President Harrison the old Whig editor lost the post-office. He was subsequently offered the nomination for county auditor by the Free-soil party, but his strong Whig affiliations and feeling prevented his acceptance. Mrs. Matthew Tayler, the editor's oldest daughter, worked at the case on the Chronicle for a number of years, and had the reputation of being the fastest compositor in Warren.

Between 1845 and 1861 was a period of intense political agitation and frequent change. The Chronicle, under Mr. Parker, energetically condemned Tyler's apostasy and opposed with vigor in 1844 Polk and the annexation of Texas. It condemned every measure calculated to provoke war with Mexico, and when the war was actually in progress, severely criticised the manner in which it was conducted.

In other words, it was consistently and radically Whig, and found little outside of politics worth its attention. The year 1848 dates the beginning of the political catastrophe which ultimately ended in the disruption of one party and paralyzation of the other. The cause was a conflict between a strong, healthy anti-slavery sentiment on one side and the avarice of the slave power on the other. General Taylor, a conservative Whig, General Cass, an aggressive Democrat, and Martin Van Buren, a Democrat, but an opponent of the extension of slavery, were the Presidential candidates. The latter was the nominee of an independent party styled the Free-soilers, made popular on the Reserve because of its advanced position on slavery issues. The Chronicle deserted its old moorings and espoused Van Buren and his Free-soil platform. The old line Whigs, indignant at what they called apostasy, erected a press, purchased type, and before their wrath had cooled

THE TRUMBULL COUNTY WHIG

made its appearance, filled with enthusiastic praise of Taylor, and repeating the story of his achievements in Mexico. A triumphant Whig victory that year gave this paper considerable prestige, while the Chronicle was practically without a party after election day. There was, however, a strong element in the Reserve opposed to both old parties, which sustained it during the doubtful period of political shifting. E. D. Howard purchased the paper of Mr. Parker in 1853. The Whig had in the meantime changed its name to

WESTERN RESERVE TRANSCRIPT.

It was conducted with fair ability, but found itself in a more dangerous condition after the election of 1852 than the Chronicle had held since 1848. The repeal of the Missouri compromise by the passage of the Kansas and Nebraska bill in 1854, effected a union of Northern sentiment. Both Chronicle and Transcript were brought upon the same political platform, and were soon united under the name of Western Reserve Chronicle and Transcript. James DeMars, editor of the Transcript, continued to edit the consolidated paper for a short time. In 1855 George N. Hapgood and C. A. Adams purchased the establishment and restored to the paper its time-honored name. We shall now have to turn back a few years to trace the fortune and fate of contemporaries.

While the compromise measures of 1850 were pending, a small weekly, named the Liberty Herald, made its appearance. Its editors were J. B. Tait and A. B. Walling. It was a weak experiment and soon failed.

We left the Trumbull Democrat in 1839 in the hands of Messrs. Seeley and Baldwin, neither of whom were printers. Mr. Seeley had built the Hope cotton factory at Pittsburg, and after coming to Warren devoted his attention to general business. William Baldwin, upon whom the management of the paper devolved, was a son of Eli Baldwin, Democratic candidate for Governor in 1836 against Joseph Vance. He came here a young man from Meadville college. He died in Warren. Dr. D. B. Woods and Sharon Cotton were Democratic managers at that time, and purchased the paper not so much for the profit in it as for the good of the party. During their proprietorship John M. Edwards was editor and manager, and the paper had considerable vitality. Frequent changes followed. Mr. Harrington owned the paper for a short time; then J. B. Buttles and E. B. Eshelman became joint proprietors. The former was a young lawyer, the latter a practical newspaper man, who has since acquired a State reputation in politics. Mr. Eshelman retired from the management after a short period. Mr. Buttles was appointed warden of the penitentiary, and disposed of the paper in 1854 to Messrs. Ritezel and Mills. The latter retired after a short connection. Mr. Ritezel was a practical printer, and soon developed editorial ability which brought his paper into favor among all classes, and satisfied his party friends until secession, treason, and rebellion forced upon the North questions before which party affiliations and associations dwindled into insignificance.

The sense and sentiment of the North was for saving the Union at all hazards, but there were honest differences of opinion as to how that end was best to be accomplished, and as to the constitutionality of the methods which the party lately come into power proposed to employ. When complications resolved themselves to the question of peace and disunion, or war and union, there was practically but one party on the

Reserve, however much the elements of that party may have differed concerning those measures which led to the dread question. As the vicissitudes of general politics had united the Chronicle and Transcript in 1854, so the new Chronicle and Democrat were united in 1861. We see in this how intimate is the relation between papers and parties. When some great issue effects a union of sentiment, and eclipses factious interests and minor divisions, a union of papers, which are organs of opinion, may be expected.

The union of the Chronicle and Democrat took place in February, 1861, the name of the former being retained. It was published and jointly edited by Messrs. Adams, Hapgood, and Ritezel. Mr. Adams retired during the war, and Mr. Hapgood died in 1865, leaving Mr. Ritezel sole proprietor and editor. It was during the war that the paper developed to the vigor and usefulness which it has since retained. It adopted and followed the policy of giving its readers such information as they sought most anxiously. It sifted out and published such news from the field as pertained to Trumbull county soldiers, and at the same time vigorously and courageously exerted its influence in support of the Government. Since the war the Chronicle has been the organ of the Republican party, steadily and faithfully supporting its candidates and upholding its policy. Its local columns have been well filled.

In 1877 Mr. Ritezel associated with himself as partners, B. J. Taylor and F. M. Ritezel, William Ritezel & Co. being the present style of the firm. Mr. Taylor, upon whom the management now chiefly devolves, learned the printing trade in the office more than twenty years ago, and has been connected with the establishment in various capacities ever since. The senior proprietor represented Trumbull county in the Legislature two terms—1868-69 and 1870-71.

In 1862, Jefferson Palm, Esq., encouraged by his Democratic friends, brought out the Warren Constitution. Mr. Palm had been a compositor on the old News-Letter, and in 1840 started, for John G. McLain, a small periodical named the Mercury, mainly devoted to light literature. On the accession of Tyler to the Presidency, the type, fixtures, etc., were removed to Youngstown, to be used for printing the Olive Branch, the first paper in Youngstown. The Mercury was discontinued. Mr. Palm, however, became known as a Democratic leader. Through the campaign of 1861 the party had been without a paper, in consequence of the coalition of the Chronicle and Democrat. Early in 1862, a subscription paper was circulated and more than a thousand names entered on the list. Thus the Constitution had an advance assurance of success. The Democratic party at that time consisted of several factions, ranging in opinion from outright Southern sympathizers to loyal Union men who opposed the Administration party's measures, but were at the same time in full sympathy with its object—the restoration of the Union. The Constitution carried at the head of its editorial page during the war Crittenden's famous resolution, introduced into the "peace convention" at Washington in 1861:

Congress, banishing all feeling of passion or any resentment, will recollect only its duty to the whole country. That this war is not waged on their part in any spirit of oppression, or for any purpose of conquest or subjection, or purpose of overthrowing or interfering with the rights and established institutions of these States [slave States], but to defend and maintain the supremacy of the Constitution and to preserve the union with all the dignity, equality and rights of the several States unimpaired, and that as soon as these objects are accomplished the war ought to cease.

The Constitution was purchased in 1867 by Judge Matthew Birchard and Erastus H. Ensign, both lawyers. It was subsequently transferred to William Birchard, who continues publisher and editor.

THE WARREN RECORD

was established at Warren on the 14th of January, 1876, at the solicitation of a large number of prominent Democrats in the county, who entertained the view that the establishment of a Democratic paper was a political necessity to maintain party organization in the county. Its editor, S. B. Palm, is a son of Jefferson Palm, Esq., the founder of the Constitution, who was connected with the first Democratic paper published in Trumbull—the Warren News-Letter. The Record enjoys a good circulation, and pays considerable attention to town and county affairs.

THE WARREN TRIBUNE

is the most recent applicant for public favor. Mr. W. S. Peterson, the editor-in-chief, is a native of Indiana. After a proper course of study he was admitted to the ministry of the Congregational church. In the year 1874, having retired from the ministry, he purchased the Canfield (Mahoning county) News, which he published for nearly two years until the removal of the county seat seriously crippled his patronage. He then removed to Warren and established the Tribune. The first number made its appearance in August, 1876. O. M. and A. M. Peterson have lately been associated in its management. The Tribune makes a specialty of local county news. Politically it is in accord with the Republican party, but reserves the right of exception to local candidates.

The aggregate circulation of Warren newspapers is about five thousand. This number is more than fifteen hundred in excess of the aggregate circulation in 1870. It appears from this that the local press is not greatly influenced by the increased enterprise of neighboring dailies, but is gaining patronage in proportion to its development in efficiency.

CHAPTER V.
SCHOOLS.

As soon as the Warren pioneers had got themselves comfortably housed, their land under a productive state of cultivation, they made provision for the education of their children. A log school-house was built on the river bank north of the park. We have no record nor even traditional knowledge of who the first teacher was. George Parsons states in his memoranda that he taught "the first man's school in the place," from which it may be inferred that a school taught by a lady had preceded his. The second school-house was also a log building and stood on the present site of the Park hotel. John Leavitt, Jr., was the first teacher in this house, but it was not long used for school purposes. Not many years elapsed before a comfortable frame house was built near the old log building, on the river bank, which was used for a considerable period. Among the teachers who whipped and taught the village youth in it were Alexander Southerland, Samuel Forward, Miss Mary Case, and Colonel Cyrus Bosworth.

About the year 1816 efforts began to be made to raise the standard of education above what was possible to be attained in the general and mixed common school which was taught by any one who happened to be fortunate enough to secure a sufficient number of pupils. A young lady's seminary was opened by Miss Boswick, in the third story of old "Castle William." A public exhibition given by this school is remembered. The ladies read essays and spoke "pieces," rendering a programme similar to school performances of the present time. Following Miss Boswick's school, or perhaps at the same time, a select school was conducted on Main street by Mr. Olcott, a graduate of Yale college and a fine scholar. A school was kept by Mr. Tower about 1822–25 in a frame building on the present site of Stiles' block and about the same time Miss Norton (afterwards wife of General Curtis, of Sharon) taught in a small room on Market street. A similar select school was afterwards taught by Miss McNeal. In these schools there was no authority higher than the teacher, who was in no way indebted to any civil power or to the community. They were wholly irregular, the teacher paying his own rent and charging his pupils tuition. The inefficiency of this system and a sense of the importance of thorough common education and discipline, characteristic of New England people, led to the formation, in 1818, of the "Warren School association." Articles of incorporation were taken out and preparations made for erecting an academy building.

THE ACADEMY.

The academy directors purchased a lot of Ephraim Quinby, on the north side of the public square. The trustees in whose name the deed was made were: James Quigley, Richard Iddings, Samuel Leavitt, Francis Freeman, and George Parsons. A brick building, which is yet standing, was erected and ready for occupation about the year 1820. The plan upon which it was founded was admirably adapted to the public wants. Provision was made for four departments, two for pupils of each sex—the boys' primary and girls' primary on one floor, and the boys' high school and girls' high school on the other. This plan of systematic division was probably never carried fully into effect, but the primary pupils were generally separated from those of the upper grade or high school.

The first board of examiners were Dr. Eaton, Mr. Olcott, and George Swift, the two last being Yale college graduates. The necessity for a change in the management of school affairs had a tendency to make that change radical. Loss of time and injustice to pupils had resulted from the absence of any authority to test the competency of teachers before entering upon their work. Now, when a board for that purpose was provided, the test was made severe. Among the first applicants was W. H. McGuffey, a young man just out of college. He failed to pass the rigid examination, and consequently lost the position of teacher. Mr. McGuffey, as is well-known, became one of the best educators Ohio has produced, being the author of a popular series of school text books, and for a number of years president of Miami university. He attributed his success in life to the incentive for study which the mortification of his defeat at Warren gave him. Few of the academy teachers remained more than two years, and most of them not longer than one year. The first teachers were Messrs. Cunningham and Johnson. Succeeding teachers were: Rufus P. Spalding, Reuben Case, Jacob Osborn, Captain Thompson, Miss Clarissa Norton (Mrs. General Curtis), David L. Coe, Ralph Hickox, Miss Irene Hickox (late Mrs. Scranton, of Cleveland), John Crowell (General Crowell, of Cleveland), R. P. Spalding (a second time), Mr. Babbitt, Seldon Haynes, A. Cadwallader, Mr. Harlow, Anderson Dana, Morris Iddings, and Francis Gillett. Among these some were good, some were indifferent, and some were poor teachers. They were well trained scholars as a rule, but many of them cannot be commended for governing ability. Rufus P. Spalding is remembered as a successful teacher. Some men seem to have been born to succeed. Mr. Spalding has since won a place in the very front rank of Ohio lawyers. Corporal punishment was at that time not only the usual, but the necessary way of enforcing obedience, even though it was an academy. Along one wall there was a bench about eighteen inches from the floor. Boys were punished by being required to kneel and place their heads under this bench. A whole row might sometimes be seen thus bowed down and resting on their hands and knees. Vigorous and unexpected use of a long ruler as the master walked back and forth along the repentent line sent one head here and another there, thumping against the wall.

Anderson Dana, father of Junius Dana, bore the reputation of being one of the best teachers. Francis Gillett was a graduate of Yale college. He was extremely rigid in discipline, and severe in enforcing unreasonable rules. He always carried a ferrule in his hand and used it freely on the hands of his pupils. One of his rules was that every lesson must be recited perfectly; the punishment for one error was one stroke, for the second two, and so on, each succeding error receiving double the punishment of the last. All other misdemeanors were punished in the same way. It is said that John B. Harmon reached as high as sixty-four raps for a single offense. This master naturally is conspicuously remembered on account of his unpopularity.

Miss Lathrop was for a number of years teacher of the primary department of the academy. There were other teachers, whose names are forgotten. The course of study compared very favorably with that of similar institutions in the West. The common branches were taught, and the higher mathematics and languages were pursued far enough to enable the student to enter any American college. Among the old academy boys the names of five Yale graduates are recalled — Alfred Perkins, Milton Sutliff, Henry King, Jacob Perkins, and John B. Harmon. Julian Harmon graduated at Western Reserve college. There probably were others whose names are not remembered. The academy did not survive Mr. Gillett's principalship, but the building continued to be used for school purposes for some time.

SELECT SCHOOLS.

Miss Estabrook taught a school for young ladies, being assisted by Miss Dickinson. Miss McNeal's primary school on Market street prospered for some time. It was conducted on the modern kindergarten plan. The academy building was occupied during the winter of 1834-35 by I. N. Gray, to whose school pupils of all grades were admitted.

During the winters of 1835-36, and 1836-37, James D. Callender conducted a school of high grade in the old King building, until lately standing on Main street. He demonstrated the important truth that order could be maintained without the use of the rod. He was always strict and decided, but congenial and kind. His qualities commanded respect to a degree which made the fear of punishment a useless instrument. Mr. Callender was an excellent teacher and scholar. Perhaps no better compliment can be written than the record of two of his pupils. During the two terms Dey's algebra was mastered, and Adams' arithmetic reviewed; and Latin and Greek, to which no attention had been given previously, were pursued far enough to pass the entrance examination at Yale.

Daniel Jagger kept a school in the winter of 1837-38 in a frame building which stood on the present site of Reid's machine shop. Two years later he taught on High street, in an abandoned store-room, which stood on the site of Warren Packard's residence. Junius Dana was the next teacher, occupying the academy building one term and then moving to the basement of the Methodist church, where he had classes in the higher mathematics and ancient languages, which were taught by W. S. Kennedy.

We are indebted to Hon. T. J. McLain's Centennial Sketch for the greater part of what follows. Succeeding Junius Dana the principal instructors were Prof. Bronson, William G. Darley, Martha Callendar, Martha and Fanny Dickey, Lucy Clark, S. D. Harris, Dr. J. R. Woods, and Rev. Mr. Brown, of whom Mr. McLain says, "by his persistent and merciless use of the rod, strap, and ferrule acquired a reputation for brutality which has never been equalled in the history of our schools. Being now dead, we will say to his remains what he never said to a pupil: *Requiescat in pace.*" He was a Baptist clergyman.

About the year 1844 Prof. Bronson established an Episcopal female seminary in a building on South street. The project soon proved a failure and was abandoned. Prof. Bronson then opened a select school in the basement of the Methodist church, on the river bank. "Junius Dana, who was a leading educator from 1840 till 1848, generally taught a select school in the summer and a district school in the winter." Daniel Jagger was associated with him part of the time. They occupied, at different times, the academy, the King block, and the McFarland block. William G. Darley taught two terms, 1846-47 and 1847-48, in the King block. His school was quite popular. Prior to 1844 Warren had depended entirely upon private schools. That year three district school-houses were erected, one on the corner of School and Prospect streets, another on east High street, and a third south of the canal. These additional facilities, and the organization of a legal board, greatly increased the efficiency of the educational machinery. The employment of school teaching, under the old system, offered almost as doubtful means of support as the efficiency of the system itself for giving instruction. Yet it appears that teachers were generally qualified and pupils could find instruction almost any time. Those who desired could pursue the ordinary academic studies here as well as any where.

Prior to the Legislative act of 1848 school taxes were not collected as they now are, by being placed upon the duplicate and paid as other taxes, but the directors were made collectors, and in case of a refusal to pay they were empowered to sue and collect just as other debts are collected. So many claims naturally gave rise to considerable litigation. Mr. McLain tells of a case of this kind in Warren. Three of the wealthiest citizens refused to pay their quota because of dissatisfaction with the teachers. The directors levied upon the harness of one, the fatted calf of another, and the wagon of the third, and exposing these articles at the front door of the court-house, sold them to the highest bidder to the amusement of the taxpayers who had responded to the demands of the directors. This case stood as an example for a number of years.

As soon as legal provisions were made for more thorough organization of the educational machinery, Warren was ready to embrace the opportunity. The remainder of this chapter will be devoted to the establishment and growth of graded schools.

GRADED SCHOOLS.

On February 21, 1849, a general act was passed by the Legislature, the provisions of which seemed to meet the approval of many of the citizens of Warren. A public lecture was delivered by John Hutchins upon the subject, and on March 31, 1849, a legal call was made for an election to decide whether the village should adopt the act mentioned above. This call was signed by six resident free-holders, viz: Matthew Birchard, Leicester King, John B. Harmon, R. P. Ranney, Milton Graham, and I. J. Iddings. The election was held at the court-house on April 10, 1849, B. F. Hoffman acting as chairman, Joseph Perkins as assistant chairman, and I. I. Fuller as clerk. The vote stood one hundred and thirty-four for the law and twenty-two against; so the law was adopted. On the 23d of the same month, at an election, R. P. Ranney and George Tayler were elected to serve as members of the board of education for one year; M. Birchard and B. P. Jameson for two years, and Joseph Perkins and John Hutchins for three years. The board organized on the 30th of April, choosing Mr. Birchard for president, John Hutchins for secretary, and George Tayler for treasurer. School examiners were appointed as follows: Julian Harmon for one year, Jacob Perkins for two years, and Rev. W. C. Clark for three years. In a very short time the board proceeded to organize the schools under the new law. A high school under the charge of Miss Martha Dickey was put in operation in a two-story frame building, which stood on the site of the present brick on Monroe street.

The frame buildings, which have been previously spoken of were utilized, and other rooms were rented, so that six primary and secondary rooms were put in operation during the summer months, taught by Fanny Dickey, Mary Brown, Amanda Brown, Elizabeth A. Tuttle, Mary Tillotson, and Frances Janes. The salaries paid the teachers at this time were $4.00 per week in the high school, and $3.50 per week in the others. The price of tuition for foreign scholars was fixed at $3.00 per term in the high school and $1.50 per term in the primary. The following course of study was established: For primary and secondary school—Eclectic Spelling Book, Eclectic First, Second, and Third readers, Wells' Elementary grammar, Thompson's Mental and Practical Arithmetic, Parley's and Morse's Geographies, Wilson's History of the United States; for the high school, McGuffey's Fifth Reader, Mandeville's Course of Reading, Morris' Geography, Wells' School Grammar, Thompson's Practical and Higher Arithmetic, Loomis' Algebra, Davies' Legendre Geometry, Smith's Illustrated Astronomy, Parker's Natural Philosophy, Davies' Surveying, Gray's Chemistry, Ackerman's Natural History, Cutler's Physiology, Woods' Botany, Wilson's American History, Hitchcock's Geology, Ollendorf's French Grammar, and Arnold's Latin and Greek series. During the summer of 1849, arrangements were made so that upon the 10th of September the first regular session of all the schools opened with the following corps of teachers, viz: Superintendent and principal of the high school, M. D. Leggett, at a salary of $700 per annum; Miss Lucretia Wolcott, assistant in the high school, with a salary of $200 per annum; Miss Lucretia Pomeroy, principal of the grammar school, with a salary of $175 per annum; Martha Dickey, M. A. Booth, Lucia Cotton, Frances Janes, Amanda Brown, and Marietta Leggett in the primary and secondary school, at $3.50 per week.

At the close of first year Mr. J. D. Cox was elected to fill the place made vacant by the resignation of M. D. Leggett. Mr. Cox began his labors as superintendent September 1, 1851, continuing three years at a salary of $600 per annum.

Rev. James Marvin began the work of superintendent at the close of Mr. Cox' administration, September 1, 1854, remaining in the position for eight years. His salary at first was $900, afterward advanced to $1,000, and finally $1,200 per annum. At this time it was evident that more room was necessary to the proper accommodation of pupils, and a meeting of the electors was held on the 9th of May, 1854, at Empire hall, at which it was voted that $6,000 should be raised by taxation for the purpose of purchasing sites and building school-houses. During the summer of 1854 the high-school lot, including the old building, was bought from Joseph Perkins for $1,400.

A lot was purchased of Anna J. Gordon, on Quinby hill, for $500. In the following spring the Liberty street lot, including frame building, was bought of E. E. Hoyt & Co., for $900, also a lot on Vine street for $400. The Liberty street lot gave the district two comfortable school-rooms, with only a little expense for repairs and fitting up.

During this time the Quinby Hill school was conducted in the residence of Peter Gaskill, Mrs. Gaskill being the teacher. This was about the time the library was established in connection with the high-school, books being received from the State.

On the 9th of June, 1855, a meeting of the

electors was held; it was voted to raise $8,000 by taxation for the purpose of building a new high-school edifice, the old one being entirely too small for the greatly increased number of pupils. Soon after this contracts were made with Richard Craven and Messrs. Soule and Johnson, for the erection of the present building, which was completed and occupied during the summer of 1856. The old building, which had been used first as a carpenter-shop, a select school, and the high school, was sold for $148, removed to Park avenue, and is now used as a private dwelling. Sometime during the year 1859 the limits of the district were enlarged by the addition of some territory from the east of Howland and the west of Warren township.

In the following spring a petition was presented to the board by the residents of the west side, asking that a meeting be called to vote upon the question of building on the lot on the west side of the Mahoning, purchased from Anna Gordon. The electors voted to raise $3,500 by taxation for this purpose, and a two-storied brick building was completed in 1864. In the summer of 1862 Rev. James Marvin resigned the position of superintendent to accept a professorship in Allegheny college at Meadville, Pennsylvania; J. H. Caldwell being elected to fill the vacancy, served until 1886. His salary at first was $800, then $1,000, and later $1,300 per annum. During the year 1865 the intermediate grade of school was established. Excepting on the west side, the houses in which the primary and secondary schools were held had by this time become so dilapidated as to demand new buildings. The electors were again called together on January 18, 1867, to vote upon this matter, when it was decided to levy a tax of $5,000 per annum for four years, making $20,000 in all, for the purchase of sites and the erection of proper buildings. As the demand was urgent for immediate action in the matter, the board was authorized to borrow money in anticipation of the tax. Two years and a half passed by and the sum of $7,279 had accumulated, but no lots had been purchased or buildings begun; in the meantime the schools were still held in buildings that were small, dilapidated, badly heated, and almost devoid of ventilation, and, of course, unhealthy. Considerable feeling among the citizens had been engendered in consequence of such a state of affairs, and a spirited election for members of the board was held on July 21, 1869, when four new members were elected: I. N. Dawson, T. J. McLain, Jr., J. S. Edwards, and Julian Harmon.

The new board, composed of the members just elected, together with C. A. Harrington and M. B. Taylor, proceeded promptly to carry out the wishes of the electors. Two months after organization, advertisements were made for proposals to build on the Liberty street lot; consequently a brick building was erected with two rooms during the fall and winter. This was followed by other and similar structures, which was the inauguration of a new era in school building in Warren. The architect was Joseph Ireland, of Cleveland, and the contractors Messrs. Green & Co., of the same city. The building committee were Julian Harmon and M. B. Taylor. The superintendent was I. N. Dawson. The cost of the building, when completed, with all its surroundings, was about $8,000.

J. J. Childs acted as superintendent during the year ending September 1, 1867, and W. H. Pitt during the two years following, each at a salary of $1,200. On September 1, 1869, H. B. Furness was elected superintendent at a salary of $2,000 per annum, acting one year. In March, 1870, the new board sold the lot on High street, and bought a fine double lot of J. L. Smith, on East Market street, for $1,400. During that summer and fall a substantial building was erected at a cost of $10,500, and fitted for two schools.

The architect was Joseph Ireland, and the contractors William Ernst and Joshua R. Seeley. The building committee was Messrs. Dawson and Harmon; the superintendent was I. N. Dawson. The funds already voted for the erection of buildings being almost exhausted, and at least two other buildings needed, another meeting of electors was held on March 15, 1871, at which it was voted to levy $10,000 per annum for two years, making a total of $20,000, for the purpose of buying lots and erecting two buildings, one in the north and one in the south part of the city. During the ensuing fall and winter the school lot, on the corner of School and Prospect streets, was enlarged by an additional purchase, and a fine brick house was erected suitable for two schools. Walter Blythe, of Cleveland, was architect; Messrs. Downs, Elliott & Co., and Wilkins and Sidles were the builders; T. J. McLain, Jr., and Julian Harmon were the building committee; I. N. Dawson was superintendent. The cost when completed, including the lot, was about $11,000.

The next year the fourth building was completed, in south Warren, on the corner of Liberty and Fulton streets; it is very similar in style and size to those preceding it.

The architect, contractors, committee, and superintendent were the same as those connected with the erection of the north building, the cost about $10,500. In the summer of 1874 about $3,000 was spent in repairing and improving the high-school building.

Since that time a lot in the southwest part of the city was bought, and a convenient frame house was built, suitable for one school, the whole cost of lot and building being about $1,500. Owing to the great number of pupils in the primary schools, on Prospect and East Market streets, it became necessary to organize another primary school in the eastern part of the city. A building belonging to Mrs. William P. VanGorder, on Pine street, was secured at a rental of $10 per month, where a school of fifty-four pupils, taken from Pine and East Market streets, was established under the care of Mrs. Dorcas Gaskill, who had previously occupied the building as teacher of a private school. This was in the spring of 1879. Again in the spring of 1880, the intermediate school being too much crowded, an unoccupied room in the building on First street was furnished and forty pupils were transferred from the intermediate school to this room, and Miss Turnball was installed teacher. With an increase of two hundred and thirty-six pupils since 1874, only three additional schools have been organized, with no additional school building except the one room rented on Pine street, and it is not well fitted for school purposes. The subject of building has been under discussion for some time, but as yet no plan has been decided upon.

Some of the former superintendents have attained eminence in other positions since leaving Warren. The following is a list of the superintendents in regular order since 1849: Mortimer D. Leggett, Jacob D. Cox, James Marvin, Hugh J. Caldwell, J. J. Childs, William J. Pitt, H. B. Furness, J. C. Barney, and E. F. Moulton, the present incumbent.

The school library contains in all between six and seven hundred volumes, about one hundred and seventy-five having been added during the past year. The Ohio Legislature in 1873 passed a law granting to boards of education in cities permission to appropriate $150 annually for the purpose of purchasing books for a school library, and this board has made three appropriations in accordance with this provision. Every year shows an increase in the number of pupils who take books from the library, and a better class of books is called for than heretofore, showing that a taste for good reading is being cultivated.

The parents in Warren show their appreciation of the public schools by their frequent visits to the different departments of the schools. The number of visits made during the past year by parents and others not officially connected with the schools, is stated to have been seven hundred and seventy-nine. The number made by the superintendent seven hundred and seventy-one, and by the members of the board of education seventy-three. The course of study in the grades below the high school is about the same as in all schools of the better class. The new course has been in some respects changed from the old to suit the more advanced ideas of the manner of instructing, and also, so far as is possible, to meet the wants of children of average capacity, and in such a way as to admit of promotion whenever a case may demand it, and also to allow a pupil to fall back into a lower grade, when not able from any cause to keep pace with his class.

The high school course has been prepared upon such a basis as to meet as nearly as possible the wants of the different classes of pupils in the school, the greater number of whom expect to finish their education in the high school. It has been thought best to introduce what are usually called practical studies, as far as could well be done without sacrificing what are considered the higher objects of an education—mental discipline and culture. The course prescribed will admit of either a fair or a very liberal common school education.

In 1857 the system was first adopted of granting diplomas to scholars who should complete the prescribed course of study, and at the close of that year three pupils graduated. The whole number of graduates since that time has been one hundred and eighty-two. Of these one hundred and forty were females and only forty-two males. In salaries paid to teachers Warren is not behind her sister cities. A few cities of her class pay larger salaries, but many pay much smaller.

The schools are felt to be in good condition, harmony prevails and good and efficient work is being done in the different departments by both teachers and pupils. While a large increase in attendance is attended by a great decrease in the number of cases of tardiness, especially during the past four years, in the six years preceding the close of 1880, there has been an increase in the number enrolled of one hundred and thirty-seven, in the average number belonging of two hundred and nine, and in the average daily attendance of two hundred and thirty-six, and during the same time there has been a decrease of thirty-five in the enumeration.

It is said that during these six years just past, the number of cases of tardiness has been reduced from over four thousand to less than one thousand, and also that the cases of truancy and absence have diminished proportionally.

M. D. Leggett, the first superintendent, soon after resigning his position removed to Zanesville, where he pursued his legal profession. At the outbreak of the war he entered the service of the United States, and served during the war, being promoted to a general's command, and during President Grant's second term he received the appointment of commissioner of patents. He is now practicing law in Cleveland. J. D. Cox, the second superintendent, studied law while in the city of Warren, and soon after his resignation was elected to the State Senate. Subsequently he entered the service, served through the war, making a fine record, and before the close became a major-general. In 1865 he was chosen Governor of Ohio, serving two years, and declining a second nomination. On the organization of President Grant's first Cabinet, he was appointed Secretary of the Interior. He has, since his resignation of that office, been practicing law in Cincinnati.

Rev. James Marvin was the third superintendent, and resigned to accept a professor's chair in Meadville college, and afterwards became president of the University of Kansas, situated at Lawrence in that State.

The following is a complete list of the gentlemen who have served as members of the board of education since 1849:

Matthew Birchard, Rufus P. Ranney, Joseph Perkins, George Taylor, B. P. Jameson, John Hutchins, Azor Abell, Zalmon Fitch, Matthew B. Tayler, Ira L. Fuller, Henry B. Perkins, Julian Harmon, T. E. Webb, William Ritezel, J. H. McCombs, John L. Weeks, Charles A. Harrington, Thomas J. McLain, Jr., Isaac N. Dawson, John S. Edwards, O. H. Patch, J. J. Gillmer, Julius King, Charles C. Adams, George B. Kennedy, Seth M. Laird, S. F. Dickey, Kennedy Andrews, A. F. Spear, Dr. I. A. Thayer, William M. Lane, Charles Augstadt, Henry C. Christy.

The names of the teachers for the year 1880-81: High school, Marshall Woodford and Mrs. H. W. Woodford. In the other grades: Emma Way, Lottie M. Sackett, Ella M. Estabrook, Emma Way, E. M. Moore, E. E. Bierce, Libbie Graham, Mary F. Kinney, Nellie C. Bierce, Charlie A. Bennett, Mary L. Selkirk, Ella M. Ward, Minnie M. Howard, Alice I. Hall, Louise Andrews, Mary C. McNutt, Fannie Foote, Laura Bartlett, Jennie M. Landers, Mabel L. King, Gertrude Campbell. Special teacher of music: A. J. Phillips.

School officers.—Samuel F. Dickey, president; Frank J. Mackey, clerk; Kennedy Andrews, treasurer.

Edwin F. Moulton, the superintendent of the Warren schools, was born at Moulton Hill on St. Francis river, Ascott township, Canada, in 1836. His great grandfather, Calvin Moulton, was in the War of 1812, and his great grandfather and two brothers on his mother's side were in the same war, but fought on the other side. The father of Professor Moulton removed to Iowa, when he was ten years of age, where Edwin F. Moulton worked on a farm until he was fifteen years old, and then clerked in a store until twenty years of age, when he entered the Grand River institute, and prepared for college, after which he attended Antioch college, and finished his course, taking his degree of A. B. in 1865. In 1869 he took charge of the schools of Oberlin, and continued as superintendent until the year 1876, when he was called to Warren, where he has had charge as superintendent of the schools ever since. Mr. Moulton is a pleasant, agreeable gentleman, and is scholarly and well fitted by education and experience to manage the educational interests of this city.

DANA'S MUSICAL INSTITUTE.

Dana's Musical Institute is one of the many interesting places in Warren, an institution of which the little city has just reason to be proud. It is wholly their own. Its president, a native of the place, conceived the plan upon which he, with a corps of six or eight professors and teachers, are now working with very marked success. The school was opened in October, 1869, in rooms on the third floor of the building at the corner of Main and Market streets, and now occupied by the Knights of Pythias. Before the close of the year it became evident that greater accommodations were needed, and accordingly, in July of 1870, the large building at the corner of Park avenue and High street was bought and fitted up for the use of the institute. Forty rooms in all are used for the various departments. The building is a substantial brick, four stories high above the basement. The basement contains the fuel, tank, boiler, and closet rooms. On the first floor are the reception rooms, president's room, business office, and the piano and organ rooms, in which is a magnificent pipe organ. The second floor is occupied by the vocal class room and piano practice rooms. The third floor has the violin and theory class rooms, and organ and piano practice rooms. The organ practice rooms are on the fourth floor. The entire building is used for school purposes. The rooms throughout are kept in excellent condition. It is heated by steam and lighted with gas. Everything required in the study and practice of music is supplied. Pianos, organs, violins, and other stringed instruments, and every conceivable kind of wind instrument are to be seen in their appropriate places.

The president, William H. Dana, is meeting with success in his profession, is ambitious to excel, and devotes his time to his profession. He is now visiting the northern countries of Europe. Junius Dana, Esq., a gentleman of ample means, is the financial head of the institute. He was born in southwestern New Hampshire, in 1821, and at the age of seventeen he came to this State with his father, spending the first five years on the farm; afterwards he attended school, then taught six years. In 1863 he was elected county auditor, and has been successfully engaged in a number of enterprises. In 1844 he was married to Miss Martha Parker.

CHAPTER VI.
CIVIL HISTORY.

In the winter of 1834 the citizens of Warren sought corporate powers and privileges under the laws of Ohio. Their petition to the Legislature was granted March 3d, by an enactment which defined the village limits as follows:

Beginning at a point one hundred and sixty rods due west of the center of the public square, thence running north one hundred and sixty rods, thence east three hundred and twenty rods, thence south three hundred and twenty rods, thence west three hundred and twenty rods, thence north to the place of beginning.

It will be seen that these limits embraced an area one-half mile square.

Municipal government was formally organized on the 5th of April by the election of officers. The election was held at the court-house and presided over by Liberty Reymond and Henry Lane; Lyman Potter was clerk. The following officers were elected: George Parsons, mayor; Edward Spear, recorder; Charles White, Charles Smith, John Roberts, A. W. Porter, Walter King, Asahel Adams, and Richard Iddings, trustees; George Mygatt, marshal; and Samuel Chesney, treasurer. It appears from the records that the first measures considered by the council related to the park, which had not yet become much of an ornament to the town. It was resolved to sell to the highest bidder the use of the park for "mowing land, but not to be used for pasture," for the term of one year. The fences, gates, trees, etc., were to be taken care of by the purchaser. The records of April 19th show that Mark Wescott was the purchaser of the mowing privilege, his bid being $12; pretty high rent for a tract so small, leaving out of account the fact that it was exposed to the boys.

In 1868 the corporate limits were enlarged, making each side of the square five hundred

Rev. Joseph Marvin

and twenty rods, having the center of the park for its center.

The municipal council since 1834 has been composed as follows:

1835—George Parsons, mayor; Edward Spear, recorder; Walter King, Charles White, Asahel Adams, Daniel Gilbert, Richard Iddings, and Rufus P. Spalding, trustees.

1836—Edward Spear, mayor; Azor Abell, recorder; Frederick Kinsman, Zalmon Fitch, Garry Lewis, Charles Smith, Horace Howard, Daniel Gilbert, and Eben Blachley, trustees.

1837—George Parsons, mayor; Charles Stevens, recorder; Horace Howard, Walter King, John Harsh, Liberty Raymond, James Gibson, David Tod, and George Brewster, trustees.

1838—David Tod, mayor; James Hoyt, recorder; George Hapgood, Walter King, George Austin, Liberty Raymond, John Crowell, Daniel McCleery, and John Harsh, trustees.

1839—John Crowell, mayor; George Tayler, recorder; Liberty Raymond, Daniel Gilbert, Charles White, Daniel McCleery, Frederick Kinsman, Richard Iddings, and James L. Van Gorder, trustees.

1840—Alexander McConnell, mayor; George Tayler, recorder; Heman R. Harmon, Samuel Chesney, Charles Stevens, William McFarland, Azor Abell, Frederick Kinsman, and Lewis J. Iddings, trustees.

1841—Alexander McConnell, mayor; William N. Porter, recorder; Benjamin Stevens, John Brown, Walter King, Augustus Greater, David Ernst, James Hoyt, and William Williams, trustees.

1842—Jonathan Ingersoll, mayor; W. F. Porter, recorder; John Brown, Frederick Kinsman, Robert M. Miller, David Ernst, Zalmon Fitch, Albert VanGorder, and John Hutchins, trustees.

1843—Frederick Kinsman, mayor; George Hapgood, recorder; Benjamin Stevens, Azor Abell, J. L. VanGorder, David Hitchcock, George R. Brewster, Charles Pease, Lewis Hoyt, trustees.

1844—Samuel Quinby, mayor; Comfort M. Patch, recorder; John R. Canfield, David Hitchcock, Edward E. Hoyt, Edward H. Allison, Heman R. Harmon, W. N. Porter, and James Scott, trustees.

1845—James Hoyt, mayor; Comfort M. Patch, recorder; Edward Spear, Alanson Camp, John B. Canfield, Charles Messenger, David Hitchcock, Heman Canfield, Zalmon Fitch, second, Sullivan D. Harris, trustees.

1846—James Hoyt, mayor; George Hapgood, recorder; Freeman Howard, S. D. Harris, O. H. Patch, Anthony Luke, J. B. Canfield, C. Messenger, David Hitchcock, Albert Van Gorder, trustees.

1847—James Hoyt, mayor; George Hapgood, recorder; Zalmon Fitch, B. R. Jameson, Charles Messenger, Joseph Perkins, Albert Van Gorder, O. H. Patch, A. Luke, F. Howard, J. B. Canfield, trustees.

1848—James Hoyt, mayor; George Hapgood, recorder; Samuel Quinby, E. H. Allison, Anthony Luke, George Tayler, Zalmon Fitch, B. P. Jameson, Jacob Perkins, and C. Messenger, trustees.

1849—Oliver H. Patch, mayor; Junius Dana, recorder; Henry Stiles, Azor Abell, M. B. Tayler, John Brindle, E. H. Allison, and George Tayler, trustees.

1850—George F. Brown, mayor; D. D. Belden, recorder; Charles Howard, Joseph Perkins, I. S. Kibbee, James Hoyt, John Brindle, Henry Stiles, Azor Abell, and M. B. Taylor, trustees.

1851—George F. Brown, mayor; D. D. Belden, recorder; Charles Howard, Henry Stiles, Joseph Perkins, D. B. Gilmore, L. S. Kibbee, E. H. Allison, James Hoyt, and William H. Weeks, trustees.

1852—John L. Weeks, mayor; Azor Abell, recorder; Henry Weeks, D. B. Gilmore, R. S. Parks, E. H. Allison, Charles Howard, G. O. Griswold, J. S. Kibbee, and George Hapgood, trustees.

1853—John S. Weeks, mayor; B. N. Robbins, recorder; Charles Howard, David B. Gilmore, R. S. Parks, John S. Kibbee, Giles O. Griswold, trustees.

1854—John I. Weeks, mayor; B. N. Robbins, recorder; G. O. Griswold, Zalmon Fitch, William G. Darley, C. M. Patch, and C. R. Wisell, trustees.

1855—E. W. Weir, mayor; Henry B. Reeves, recorder; Zalmon Fitch, C. M. Patch, Samuel Quinby, William Williams, and Edward Spear, Jr., trustees.

1856—R. W. Ratcliff, mayor; C. M. Patch, recorder; Edward Spear, Jr., George O. Griswold,

Lewis J. Iddings, James G. Brooks, and R. S. Parks, trustees.

1857—T. J. McLain, mayor; C. M. Patch, recorder; Daniel H. Warren, Lewis Hoyt, Cornelius Maser, A. Wentz, and James G. Brooks, trustees.

1858—T. J. McLain, mayor; George N. Hapgood, recorder; E. H. Allison, James G. Brooks, Lewis Hoyt, R. A. A. Baldwin, and C. C. McNutt, trustees.

1859—John M. Stull, mayor; G. N. Hapgood, recorder; C. B. Darling, J. C. Johnson, A. VanGorder, C. R. Hunt, and R. W. Ratcliff, trustees.

1860—C. W. Smith, mayor; G. N. Hapgood, recorder; C. R. Hunt, A. VanGorder, R. W. Ratcliff, C. B. Darling, and B. P. Jameson, trustees.

1861—G. L. Wood, mayor; G. N. Hapgood, recorder; C. R. Hunt, B. P. Jameson, C. B. Darling, A. VanGorder, Samuel Quinby, Louis Hoyt, trustees.

1862—A. B. Lyman, mayor; G. N. Hapgood, recorder; John R. Woods, G. T. Townsend, James G. Brooks, Horace Stevens, W. D. Hall, trustees.

1863—A. D. Webb, mayor; G. N. Hapgood, recorder; Albert Wheeler, J. R. Woods, Horace Stevens, J. G. Brooks, and Benjamin Cranage, trustees.

1864—Almon D. Webb, mayor; G. N. Hapgood, recorder; James G. Brooks, Albert Wheeler, Albert VanGorder, G. T. Townsend, W. B. Gorton, trustees.

1865—Almon D. Webb, mayor; T. J. McLain, Jr., recorder; Fred Kinsman, R. S. Parks, J. G. Brooks, W. B. Gorton, and I. N. Dawson, trustees.

1866—John L. Weeks, mayor; Henry H. Townsend, recorder, Fred Kinsman, W. B. Gorton, I. N. Dawson, R. S. Parks, and James G. Brooks, trustees.

1867—I. N. Dawson, mayor; H. H. Townsend, recorder; Fred Kinsman, J. G. Brooks, L. J. Hoyt, T. J. McLain, and John Anderson, trustees.

1867—I. N. Dawson, mayor; H. H. Townsend, recorder; F. Kinsman, I. G. Brooks, L. J. Hoyt, T. J. McLain, John Anderson, trustees.

1868—I. N. Dawson, mayor; H. H. Townsend, recorder; F. Kinsman, J. J. Gillmer, A. Wheeler, A. Truesdell, H. B. Perkins, trustees.

In 1869 Warren became a city, and was divided into three wards.

1869—*I. N. Dawson, mayor; E. W. Hoyt, clerk; Charles R. Hunt, Alonzo Truesdell, C. C. McNutt, J. J. Gillmer, Henry J. Lane, and Albert Watson, council.

1870—B. P. Jameson, A. Truesdell, James Hoyt, H. H. Lane, C. C. McNutt, and Albert Watson, council.

1871—I. N. Dawson, mayor; E. E. Hoyt, clerk; Albert Wheeler, Leonard Burton, David B. Gibbons, James Hoyt, B. P. Jameson, and A. Truesdell, council.

1872—Albert Wheeler, L. Burton, D. B. Gibbons, B. P. Jameson, A. Truesdell, James Hoyt, council.

1873—I. N. Dawson, mayor; E. E. Hoyt, recorder; Jered N. Green, James H. Smith, John Wheatley, B. P. Jameson, A. Truesdell, and James Hoyt, council.

1874—B. P. Jameson, Alonzo Truesdell, James Hoyt, Jered N. Green, John Wheatley, and James H. Smith, council.

1875—I. N. Dawson, mayor; E. E. Hoyt, clerk; Jered N. Green, James H. Smith, William G. Watson, B. P. Jameson, A. Truesdell, and James Hoyt, council.

1876—Jered N. Green, James H. Smith, W. G. Watson, Warren D. Hall, Alonzo Truesdell, and James Hoyt, council.

1877-78—I. N. Dawson, mayor; E. E. Hoyt, clerk; W. D. Hall, A. Truesdell, James Hoyt, Robert S. Wilkins, James H. Smith, and Warren Finn, council.

1879—Columbus Ward, mayor; E. E. Hoyt, clerk; James Hoyt, W. D. Hall, A. Truesdell, Robert S. Wilkins, Thaddeus J. Reed, George H. Quinby, council.

1880—James Hoyt, A. Truesdell, Daniel W. Camp, R. S. Wilkins, T. J. Reed, and G. H. Quinby, council.

1881—Columbus Ward, mayor; E. E. Hoyt, clerk; James Hoyt, A. Truesdell, R. S Wilkins, T. J. Reed, George H. Quinby, H. S. Pew, council.

TOWNSHIP OF WARREN.

The court of general quarter sessions of the peace, held at Warren on Monday, August 4, 1800, appointed Amos Spafford, Esq., David

*Two years.

Hudson, Simon Perkins, John Minor, Aaron Wheeler, Edward Payne, and Benjamin Davidson, a committee to divide the county of Trumbull into townships, to describe the limits and boundaries of each township, and to make report to the court thereof.

This committee gave the boundary lines of Warren township, which were as follows: "All that tract of country lying within a line beginning at the southeast corner of township one in the fifth range; thence running north to the southeast corner of township number three, in the fifth range; thence east to the southeast corner of township number three, in the third range; thence north to the northeast corner of township number five, in the third range; thence west to the northwest corner of township number five, in the sixth range; thence south to the southwest corner of township number one, in the sixth range; thence east along the south line of the county, to the place of beginning, shall constitute one township, and to be called and known by the name of Warren."

The first election held in Warren township was on the 6th of April, 1802, at the house of Ephraim Quinby; John Leavitt, chairman; Ephraim Quinby, clerk; Simon Perkins, Benjamin Davison, and John H. Adgate, managers. The following officers were chosen: Zopher Carnes, Thomas Ross, appraisers of property; George Lovelace, lister; Zopher Carnes, William Hall, and John Leavitt, supervisors of highways; Meshack Case and Thomas Prior, overseers of the poor; Charles Dally, Benjamin Davison, and James Wilson, fence viewers; Jonathan Church, William Crook, constables.

STREET IMPROVEMENTS.

In a previous chapter a description was given of the physical features of the tract embraced in Warren. The system of grading which was afterwards followed made some streets in spring time almost bottomless mud holes. Main and the lower end of Market were particularly bad, for near their junction is a fill of about ten feet of clay and muck, which was loosened to the bottom by the spring thaw and rains. The pasty clay in other streets gave the town an unenviable celebrity. In 1866 the long agitated subject of street improvements was taken hold of in earnest. The town had been building railroads and helping other enterprises for the public good to the comparative neglect of immediate home interests; but when the work did begin it was pushed with rapidity and thoroughness. All the principal streets have been paved and the walks flagged, while most of the avenues are well gravelled. Few small cities in Ohio excel Warren in the beauty and durability of sidewalks. The flagging stone, which is quarried near the corporation limits, is smooth, even, and fine-grained. An occasional spot colored by iron nodules adds rather than detracts from the natural beauty.

Shade trees minister to the comfort as well as appearance of Warren's avenues. These have grown to magnificent size along Mahoning avenue, and give that part of town a composed and finished appearance. A liberal estimate places the public and private cost of street improvements in Warren at $300,000. If the adage be true—"The way to improve a town is to make it look healthy"—a good foundation has been laid for the future. If external circumstances forbid rapid growth, the surroundings of comfort and ease have at least been secured.

MAIL SERVICE.

It has been seen in a previous chapter that United States mail facilities were first provided for the Reserve in the year 1801, and that General Simon Perkins was the first commissioned postmaster at Warren. We have traditional evidence that a common pocket handkerchief often served as a wrapper for the whole delivery after the carrier had passed Canfield and Youngstown. At a later day, when stages brought the mail from Ashtabula on the old pike, and several little offices were along the way, each postmaster opened the mail bag and hunted out what belonged to his office, sometimes having to look over a hundred pieces to find one or two letters, while impatient passengers were condemning his slowness, or the more considerate the arrangement which made such waiting necessary.

General Perkins gave little personal attention to the office, further than securing some one to minister to the public wants. John Leavitt kept the key and attended to the business for about one year. His boarding-house, or tavern, was the principal stopping place for strangers and chatting place for residents. When the semi-weekly mail arrived it could nearly all be delivered in the tavern bar-room.

George Phelps, clerk of the courts, was the

next deputy. George Parsons, Samuel Quinby, and Samuel Chesney were successive deputies. The first record of a post-office account was rendered December 31, 1807, and showed a balance due the Government of $4.76. After Jackson's inauguration to the Presidency in 1829 a general change was made in the civil service all over the country. Warren did not escape the wave of political change which swept over the country. General Perkins was succeeded by Matthew Birchard.

The following list of officers is furnished by T. J. McLain, Esq.: Simon Perkins to 1829, Mathew Birchard to 1832, David Tod to 1838, B. F. Hoffman to 1841, George Hapgood to 1842, Thomas J. McLain to 1845, John W. Collins to 1849, Comfort Adams to 1853, John S. Kibbee to 1856, Theodore Webb to 1861, C. M. Patch to 1866, Jefferson Palm to 1867, Henry Townsend to 1871, E. K. Wise, present incumbent.

Mr. Wise, the present postmaster, was born in Westmoreland county, Pennsylvania, and received common school education. He began business in Davenport, Iowa, and afterwards acted as a clerk on lower Mississippi boats, and was in the South at the breaking out of the Rebellion, but came north and enlisted under Lincoln's first call for troops for three months. Enlisted in the Eleventh Pennsylvania volunteers for three years; was in sixteen regular engagements, and numerous skirmishes; was wounded in the right arm at Gettysburgh, Pennsylvania, which necessitated amputation. After recovery he was put in charge of transport steamer Connecticut, in conveying sick and wounded from the front. He was discharged September 5, 1864. Was appointed assessor of internal revenue at Pittsburg, Pennsylvania. Soon after was elected alderman of the Sixth ward, and not long after this removed to Warren, Ohio. He was elected postmaster in 1871, and assumed the duties of his office in May; was re-appointed in 1875 for four years more. On his accepting the office in 1871 he at once set about making improvements to suit the public wants. The old office fixtures were replaced by new and improved designs, nineteen old lock boxes being replaced by one hundred and forty-seven new ones. A few hundred call boxes by twelve hundred and eighty new ones. The revenues of the office are constantly increasing. Fourteen mails are despatched and received daily.

WOODLAND CEMETERY.

It has already been noted where the first graves were located. The old cemetery on Mahoning avenue, in which Mrs. Adgate was the first person buried, has also been spoken of. It continued to be the receptacle of Warren's dead until 1848. In the year 1848 Messrs. Jacob Perkins and Frederick Kinsman took the initiative toward providing a cemetery which should be of ample size for the growing city, and so located as to admit of being beautified as becomes "the home of loving, mournful memories."

Woodland Cemetery association was organized November 15, 1849, under the act of Assembly making provision for the incorporation of cemetery associations, passed February 24, 1848, Messrs. John Harsh, L. J. Iddings, F. Kinsman, Joseph Perkins, Matthew Birchard, Richard Iddings, D. B. Gilmore, Hiram Iddings, B. F. Hoffman, Chester Bidwell, Jacob Perkins, and Orlando Morgan being the incorporators.

The original purchase of land by the incorporation was a tract of about sixteen acres, which, with the improvement made on it, has been paid for entirely by the sale of lots for burial purposes. From this source also has been accumulated a fund from which the association has been enabled to add, from time to time, to the grounds, until it is now possessed of a tract of fifty-five acres, in a compact form, separated only by the right of way of the Atlantic & Great Western railroad. The last recent purchase embraces a tract of over seventeen and a half acres upon the Niles road, immediately south of the old grounds, and a tract of about nineteen and a half acres lying immediately west of the Atlantic & Great Western railroad, all of it being well adapted to cemetery purposes. These purchases were made from the assignee of S. L. Freeman at reasonable prices, and the association had on hand funds sufficient to meet the entire purchase money except about $400, which it is expected will soon be collected from amounts due for lots heretofore sold.

It is the expectation of the officers within a reasonable time to enclose the entire tract with a suitable fence, to take out the logs, underbrush, and stumps in the new part, and to lay out drives throughout the entire tract so that visitors may have easy access by carriages to all parts of the ground, and in time, if means are afforded, to build an ornamental gateway at the entrance, and to construct within the grounds a pond or lake, to be supplied with water from Red run, which courses through the westerly part of the improved grounds.

FIRE DEPARTMENT.

Few rural cities have suffered the quick destruction of fire so frequently, and with so great loss as Warren. But this fact cannot be attributed to carelessness on part of the authorities to make reasonable provisions for preventing conflagrations. Of course, fire extinguishing apparatus, like everything else, was at first primitive, and the present efficient system is the product of steady growth. Under the act of incorporation every citizen was required to devote, in addition to his two days' road tax, two days to the construction and improvement of sidewalks. There were practically no other expenditures, so that tax levied year after year accumulated in the treasury. The levy was light, and accumulation slow, but by 1838 there was a surplus of $800. How it should be spent became a question in municipal politics. All, however, agreed upon the necessity of securing a fire engine. At a session of the council held October 31, 1838, a resolution was passed authorizing the purchase of a rotary engine at a cost of $295, which was warranted to throw one hundred gallons per minute upon a three-story building. This little machine was little better than a common force pump, such as are now used in manufacturing establishments. It was operated by eight men, four to a crank and handle on each side. Belonging to the truck was a tub, from which the water was drawn. This tub was kept filled by a bucket brigade; only a few rods of leading hose could be used. About the same time an ordinance was passed organizing a fire company, whose duty it was to manage the engine and take entire police charge during the progress of a fire. Citizens were "enjoined" in this ordinance to form themselves into bucket brigades, and carry water for the engine. The company was required to practice at least once a month. Keeping the tub full was the laborious part of these training days.

No opportunity was given this company to prove its capability in the great fire of 1846. That conflagration in a few minutes was beyond the control of any engine. Fortunately the flames were confined to the old part of the town, but for that reason they spread more rapidly. Beginning near the corner of Main and Market streets the fire made its way eastward from house to house to Liberty street, and south on Liberty until stopped by exhaustion of fuel. This occurred on June 1st. Three blocks were consumed, and twenty-two buildings. Twelve stores and shops were destroyed. Main street, which was then the center of business, was in imminent danger, and was only saved by a united effort of owners and occupants of property. The poor little engine in the hurry and excitement was not entirely forgotten, though the bucket brigade occasionally so far neglected its duty as to run directly to points of danger with water in place of keeping the engine tub supplied. The truck was finally broken and the little concern planted on boxes at the corner of Main and Market streets, where it did some useful though not conspicuous service.

The ashes of the fire of June 1, 1846, had scarcely time to cool before measures looking toward an efficient and properly equipped fire company began to be agitated. Early in July Messrs. James Hoyt and O. H. Patch were appointed a committee to go to Cleveland and purchase a Button engine at a cost of $600. This was a common hand fire engine, similar to the one owned by the company now. The embarrassing difficulty was in raising money to pay for it. The treasury was depleted and there was no authority to issue bonds. But there was a statute in existence at that time which helped them out. It authorized the treasurer to issue certificates on the treasury which were receivable for taxes. After considerable canvassing the committee in charge succeeded in selling a sufficient amount of certificates to pay for the much needed engine. The former company, of which Mr. Bridle had been chief, was disbanded, and a reorganization effected under title of Mahoning company, with Charles Messenger as chief. The council offered a standing premium of $3 to the member of the company who would reach the engine house first in case of fire. The house stood on Liberty street, back of the First National bank building. A close contest was made for this prize, on the night of the great fire of 1849, which consumed two blocks on Market street. The fire was seen apparently at the same time by W. R. Stiles and James Hoyt, both merchants. Both ran with all possible speed toward the engine house, where they arrived so nearly at the same time that at the instant Mr. Hoyt grabbed for the latch Mr. Stiles seized it, thus winning the money.

A second hand engine named the Saratoga was purchased in 1851, and a company organized for its management.

The present hand engine was purchased in 1855. It will be noticed that these purchases followed soon after fires. The burning of the VanGorder block in 1854 inspired this one.

In 1860 occurred the most destructive fire in Warren's history. It was absolutely beyond all control, and reduced to ashes with terrible rapidity nearly the whole business part of the town west of Liberty street and south of Market street. The fire started in Truesdell & Townsend's furniture factory, about mid-day, and was spread from building to building by flying sparks and shingles. The buildings for a considerable distance along Main street, on both sides, were burning at the same time, the flames forming an arch over the street. The burnt district embraced several acres, but did not long remain a desolate ruin. The final result was rather beneficial than otherwise, although more than $300,000 worth of property was destroyed. Main street was at once graded to its present level, and before a year elapsed substantial brick blocks had replaced the old structures. With a few exceptions the buildings between Liberty street and the river spared by the conflagration of 1860 were consumed in 1866 and 1867. Five frame houses on Market street, occupying the lots on which the Stiles and the Smith blocks now stand, were swept away in 1867. The King block, no longer an ornament, made two narrow escapes. There have been many smaller fires, but this last comprises all that are especially memorable.

The first steamer was purchased in accordance with an ordinance passed June 30, 1868. It cost, together with nine hundred feet of hose, $9,000. A new company was organized and named in honor of the mayor, I. N. Dawson. That name was also applied to the steamer. J. L. Smith was chosen chief of the department, and has served in that capacity till the present time. A new engine was purchased in July, 1881, at a cost of $4,000. Both are under the management of the I. N. Dawson Fire company. In 1875 a team for drawing the engine was purchased and trained. Improved equipments have been added from time to time. Efficient action may reasonably be expected of the department, should an occasion unfortunately require.

ANTI-SLAVERY DAYS.

Ephraim Brown, one of the pioneers of Bloomfield township, wrote in 1807: "I have been taught from my cradle to despise slavery, and will never forget to teach my children, if any I should ever have, the same lesson." Mr. Brown was not alone in entertaining that sentiment, for it found frequent and emphatic expression, both in words and deeds, all over the Reserve. Warren was well represented in the management of what was figuratively named the "underground railroad." A great many people fleeing from bondage passed through here, and were at times concealed in the houses of citizens. Probably the first place among Warren abolitionists should be accorded the Sutliff family—Levi Sutliff, Milton Sutliff, and Calvin G. Sutliff; then came James D. Taylor and Ralph Hickox. The former was a speaker of ability, and one of the most aggressive workers in Ohio. Judge Leicester King attained a wider reputation as an abolitionist than any other Warren man, having been placed in nomination in 1847, by the Abolitionists, with John P. Hale, for President. Both declined in favor of VanBuren and Adams, nominees of the Free-soilers. Mr. King had been the Abolitionist candidate for Governor in 1842, and presided over the National Liberty party convention in 1844. Judge Hoffman, of Youngstown, and John Hutchins, of Warren, were also aggressive workers.

POLITICAL EVENTS.

It was but natural that a majority of the freeholders of Warren, retaining the Federalist principles of their Connecticut ancestors, were, after a second division of parties, Whigs. There was, however, a practical unanimity of sentiment on the growing question of slavery, so that the New England portion of the population, with few exceptions, were ready in 1855 to march under the banner of the Republican party. Warren at once became a center of political management, and is famous throughout the State as a place for great Republican mass meetings. Ever since the war hardly-contested campaigns have never passed without great gatherings of people of the eastern part of the Reserve at Warren. A most potent influence was exerted by the meeting of 1875, when General Hayes was a candidate for Governor. That year also was marked by the largest Democratic meeting since the war. Currency expansion was a financial heresy possessing great attraction for all engaged in the coal and iron industry. The result was doubtful, and a special effort was made by the Republicans to make a greater show of enthusiasm than had been made by the Democrats. The audience which greeted Governor Hayes was the largest assembled that year in Ohio. Its effect is a part of the political history of the country.

During the campaign of 1881 the greatest political gathering in the history of the Reserve was held at Warren. It was the personal desire of General Garfield, who had so long represented this county in Congress, that the people should be given an opportunity to demonstrate their attachment. To that end it was arranged with the State and National committees that Roscoe Conkling, of New York, should be present as principal speaker, and that General U. S. Grant should preside over the meeting. September 28th was the day appointed. The local committee, with John M. Stull as chairman, made elaborate preparations. A wigwam with a capacity of twelve thousand was erected, and entertainment secured for distinguished guests.

On the eve of the day visiting delegations began to arrive. Among other distinguished men was Roscoe Conkling, then at the summit of his popularity. He was conveyed directly to the residence of H. B. Perkins, where he received a few calls during the evening and passed a nervous night preparatory to his first oratorical effort in the West. In the morning General Grant arrived, and joined Senator Conkling at Mr. Perkins' residence. General Grant at that time was the most popular citizen in America, and his presence naturally attracted thousands who were not even in sympathy with the cause. Besides Grant and Conkling there were present on that day ex-Senator Simon Cameron, of Pennsylvania; Senator John A. Logan, of Illinois; General M. D. Bradley, of Kentucky; President Chadbourne, Williams college, Massachusetts; Hon. John Beaver, of Pennsylvania, and others of National reputation. The streets were appropriately decorated and festooned. Less than half the people who thronged the little city were able to gain admission to the wigwam. There were in the city about six times its entire population. After the meeting the distinguished guests repaired to Senator Perkins' residence, and from there started on a journey to Mentor to pay their respects to the distinguished leader of the party.

CITY BUILDINGS.

The first engine house stood on Liberty street, just south of the First National Bank building. It was an insecure frame structure, but was the only building belonging to the town until 1858, when the two-story brick just west of the park and south of the present hall was erected. Engines, hose, etc., were packed into the lower story of that little building, which was then on a level with the street, since filled to a level with the second floor. The second story was used for a firemans' hall, and part of the time for council room, but it was found expedient to rent a room for the latter purpose.

The inconvenience constantly experienced from the absence of a hall for public meetings, town offices, and ample facilities for the fire company gave rise to numerous projects for the construction of a city hall. The council, yielding to public opinion, passed resolutions October 23, 1874, which resulted in the erection of the present handsome structure. Its entire cost was about $40,000.

TEMPERANCE REFORM.

It is a favorite tenet of the conservative and unprogressive East that western pioneer communities are made up of the overflow of civilization, and that only by process of long cultivation they are made comparable to the Atlantic States. But against this idea stands the historical fact to which the West, and Ohio in particular, points with pride, that the pioneers were of the best blood and most hardy muscle the East could furnish, and out of these materials have been produced the foremost men in the Nation's history. The very best families of old Connecticut were represented among the pioneers of New

Connecticut, and were strengthened by rugged contact with natural obstacles for the harder contests which followed in the public arena. They brought with them the social habits of the eastern homes, one of which was the free, in some cases inordinate use, of spirituous stimulants. Public and common indulgence in strong drinks was a vital legacy of old English life, which met with little or no restraint in New England until within the last half century. It is a fact of which the West may well be proud that radical, thorough, and conscientious reaction began in the Ohio colonies of New England. There is no evidence that the habit had become more destructive here than at the East. Warren particularly, was noted for its healthful moral tone and intelligence, but even here every store kept a pail of whiskey with a tin cup in it standing upon the counter, to which customers had free access. It was purchased by the barrel and sold freely by the gallon for home use. Every house, even to the log cabin with roof weighted down with poles, had a sideboard filled with decanters and tumblers. The kind of liquors depended much upon financial circumstances, the wealthy having wines and brandy, and all had whiskey in profusion. A guest never entered, even to call, without being offered a drink, nor was he expected to decline. Ministers, physicians, politicians, and lawyers all came together at the festive board—all drank from the same bottle. We are convinced by careful inquiry into individual history that the popular belief that "there was no drunkenness in those days" is an error. Men died from the effects of intemperance then as they do now, and always will so long as mischievous appetite exists.

The first reform movement on the Reserve was almost ineffectual, except as it served to prepare the way for a future movement. In 1830 a temperance advocate visited Warren and was well received. He held several meetings and received a few signatures to a pledge to abstain from all alcoholic beverages *except wine and cider*. He left no permanent impression.

The second movement was in 1841, and was followed by better results. Captain Turner, of Cleveland, inaugurated the movement and was chiefly instrumental in carrying it on. He had been an old sea captain, and bore the pseudonym, "Old Sea Dog." He was an interesting and forcible speaker, and understood the art of making an unpopular subject attractive. For four weeks he spoke to large audiences, and pledged the best people to abandon their sideboards and the merchants to remove from their counters the whiskey pail. Since those meetings ministers from Protestant churches have wholly abstained from spirituous beverages in public, and generally in private; none of the better class of general stores have kept whiskey, either to treat customers or for sale—for many years tavern bar-rooms were the only drinking places open to the public. Since that time abstinence and temperance have made their opposites to say the least, unpopular and unprofitable.

A supplementary movement was instituted about 1852, but did not receive substantial support, the subject of slavery at that time engrossing aggressive public sentiment. While moral sentiment on the subject of temperance was steadily improving, there was no violent movement until 1873, when what was known as the women's crusade was instituted. This was eminently a women's movement, originated by a woman, and carried into execution in every town in the West by women. Of the Warren association Mrs. Junius Dana was president. The central object was to close the saloons and other places of drinking, and for that purpose delegations of women visited, time and again, the retail dealers, and exercised the powers of prayer and persuasion to induce them to close the doors of their places of business. Mass meetings were held at night for the purpose of reviving a sustaining public sentiment. While the crusade had the effect of calling public attention to the extent of a great social evil, it was not followed by any direct permanent result. Most of the retail houses were closed for a time but were all reopened.

The Murphy movement in 1878 was more logical. It recognized the fact that supply depends upon demand, and the proper place to begin is with the antecedent. The movement instituted by Francis Murphy in Pittsburg, reached every State in the Union. A long series of meetings were held in Warren, and Mr. Murphy himself lectured here.

PUBLIC MORALITY.

The moral tone of Warren is indicative of a high order of intelligence. There are few cities of equal size in Ohio where drinking is less popular, or where drunkenness is less common. Good order prevails upon the public streets, both night and day, and the Sabbath-day is quiet and well observed. There are eight flourishing churches, which have generally been supplied by able and well-paid clergy. Warren has always, from the primitive village years, been remarked for the high character of its society. Wealth and culture have combined to make life agreeable and to stimulate an ambition which has already produced golden fruit on various fields of activity.

CHAPTER VII.
PHYSICIANS OF WARREN.

Sickness did not prevail in the Mahoning valley during the period of first settlement to the same extent as in many other parts of the State. A change of climate, and from the conditions of a long settled and long cultivated country to a wet and shaded forest, induced more or less ague and fever. In the neighborhood of Warren there was very little bilious sickness. Doctors were nevertheless needed, particularly in cases requiring surgical operations. We are unable to state positively who was the first physician located at Warren, but Dr. John W. Seeley in all probability was. He located in Howland township, on a farm, in 1801, having previously been settled at Jefferson, Green county, Pennsylvania. He removed his family to Howland in 1802. It is proper that we should speak of Dr. Seeley as a Warren physician, for his practice embraced Warren and a surrounding territory of at least ten miles. He was a man of congenial habits and affable manners. His professional attainments were respected and praised. In the spring of 1812, when the Government had lost all hope of a peaceful settlement of difficulties with England, and a call was made for troops to increase the army, Dr. Seeley was one of the most active in this part of Ohio to encourage volunteering. When the Trumbull company roll was finally full he was complimented by an election to the captaincy, and was mustered into the army before war was formally declared. We know very little of the details of Dr. Seeley's army life, further than that he attained to the rank of general. After the war General Seeley resumed his profession. He continued in active practice until the time of his death. The Ohio and Pennsylvania canal project received from him enthusiastic and valuable support. He labored from the beginning soliciting stock, and afterwards, as one of the board of directors, gave personal attention to its construction. His death occurred on the day of triumph. A delegation of Mahoning valley and Pennsylvania capitalists and citizens celebrated the completion in March, 1841, of this link between the Ohio and Pennsylvania canals, by an excursion to Akron. It was a gala day, and General Seeley was a leading spirit in the party, until seized by apoplexy. His death soon followed. The same boat brought back his lifeless body.

Dr. Enoch Leavitt came to Warren township with his father, Enoch Leavitt, Sr., about 1805. He was at the time a young man, but whether a practitioner or merely a student we are not informed. It was not many years after that date, however, when he was answering professional calls and making a reputation as a physician. He was what has has been called an "old line" doctor—a dispenser of roots, herbs, and calomel, but that was the common practice of the period. Time has added to all sorts of scientific knowledge, medicine not excepted. We learn from his gravestone at Leavittsburg, that he was born May 12, 1775, and died August 7, 1827.

The next physician in practice, and latterly a contemporary of Doctors Seeley and Leavitt was, John B. Harmon, whose office was in the village of Warren. A full biographical sketch will be found in this volume.

Sylvanus Seeley was born in Jefferson, Green county, Pennsylvania, January 5, 1795. He read medicine under his father in Howland township, this county, and in 1812, though only seventeen years old, entered the service as surgeon's mate to Dr. John D. Harmon, the friend and contemporary of his father. He was present at the attack on Fort Mackinac, and rendered Dr. Harmon efficient assistance. In the year 1814 he married a daughter of Colonel George Jackson, of Virginia, which circumstance induced him to locate in that State. After a few years he returned to Warren, and until his death stood high as a physician, his reputation going beyond the limits of Trumbull county. He died April 2, 1849. He has two surviving children, viz: Mrs. Cyrus VanGorder, of Warren, and George J. Seeley, of Cleveland.

Dr. Farrell was a physician of considerable prominence between 1840 and 1861. He was a man of very respectable culture, and possessed the confidence of a large circle of friends who regretted his departure.

Other physicians of some prominence were: Dr. Ebon Blattsley, who practiced in Warren about ten years; Dr. Kuhn was here a short period; Dr. D. W. Jameson practiced about three years, until his health failed; Dr. Nichols, a man of some promise, died of consumption; Dr. William Paine practiced some, but gave his attention chiefly to the drug trade, and came to Warren in 1845.

The oldest practitioner in Warren, the oldest, with one exception, in Trumbull county. His reputation needs no defence and his merits no praise. John Woods, father of the doctor, a Pennsylvanian of German descent, settled in Youngstown township in 1816. Of his five children four are living—Daniel B., John R., Sarah A. (Lanterman), and Clark. E. Winchester died near Youngstown in August, 1878. John Woods died on his farm near Youngstown, March 22, 1863. Daniel B. Woods, the oldest son, was born in Youngstown township, November 11, 1816. At the age of sixteen he entered Allegheny college, receiving the full course of instruction, except the last term. In 1836 Mr. Woods began reading medicine under Dr. John A. Packard, of Austintown. The degree of M. D. was conferred in 1840 by the Ohio Medical college, Cincinnati, where he had attended a regular course of lectures. In April of the same year the young physician opened an office in Warren. Since that time his energies and talent have been closely devoted to the profession. Dr. Woods has not been content to follow in the prescribed ruts, as is the case with too many medical men of talent. It is well that there are ruts for some practitioners, for their judgment would be dangerous. Those, however, who are competent to rely upon themselves generally profit by doing so. Dr. Woods was one of the first doctors in the West to use ether in surgical operations. He used chloroform before it was manufactured for commerce or sold anywhere in the country. This was about ten years after its discovery by Leibig in Germany. From the formula by Professor Simpson, of Edinburgh, Dr. Woods, assisted by Daniel Jagger, a druggist in Warren, the first chloroform used, at least in Northern Ohio, was made and administered to a patient in October, 1846. The experiment was repeated in the spring following. A few years later this valuable anæsthetic came into general use in this country. Dr. Woods' reputation as a surgeon is not confined to this State. He is practical and careful. The doctor has given some attention to politics, but is not, nor has he ever been ambitious for political preferment. He has three times been the Democratic candidate for Congress, the first time against Joshua R. Giddings, and the last time against James A. Garfield, in 1876. The latter, that year, carried the county by only two-hundred and fifty majority. Dr. Woods married, in 1842, Phebe L. Holliday, of Warren. Their family consists of five children living, William E., Dallas M., Daniel B., Emma B., and Sarah E. Julia E. (Smith), the youngest daughter is dead. Dallas M. is a practicing physician in Warren. William E. resides in Youngstown.

An extended sketch of Dr. Julian Harmon will be found elsewhere in this volume.

Warren Iddings, son of Richard Iddings, a Warren pioneer, was born March 4, 1817. In 1839 he began the study of medicine in the office of Dr. Tracy Bronson, at Newton, Ohio. The second and third years of his course were pursued in the office of Coon & Seeley, at Warren. He attended lectures at the Ohio Medical college, Cincinnati, and graduated from that institution in 1844. Dr. Iddings at once began the practice of medicine in Warren, and continued until failing health required his retirement a few years later. He engaged in general business until 1862, then removed to Mercer county, Pennsylvania, to resume his profession. For a period of sixteen years he had an extensive practice. Dr. Iddings returned to Warren in 1878, since which time he has been devoting himself especially to the treatment of the eye and ear. He married, in 1848, Laura, daughter of Hon. Thomas D. Webb, of Warren.

Dr. John Loy, son of John and Anna Loy, was born in Pennsylvania, in 1812. His parents were of German descent. They removed, with the family, to Ohio, and settled in Liberty township. He worked on a farm and attended common school until he entered upon the study of medicine in the office of Dr. Dellenbaugh, in Georgetown, New York. He removed to Buffalo, and was there during the cholera scourge in 1832, in active practice. His health was broken down by overwork, requiring his return home. After recuperating he opened an office in Liberty township, and removed to Warren in 1845. In the meantime he had attended a course of lectures at Cleveland Medical college, and subsequently a course at the Eclectic Medical institute at Cincinnati, from which a degree was received in 1850. Between 1848 and 1869 Dr. Loy was in partnership with Dr. Nelson in the practice, but suffered more or less from ill health. He was married in 1839 to Mary B. Oswald, daughter of Jonathan Oswald, of Liberty township. Since the doctor's death she has continued to reside in Warren.

John R. Woods, son of John Woods, was born in Youngstown, in 1825. His early life was spent on the farm and in the common schools. He received his preliminary education at Allegheny college, Pennsylvania, and read medicine in Warren in the office of his brother, Daniel B. Woods. Mr. Woods attended lectures, and graduated at the Cleveland Medical college in 1850, since which time he has been practicing in Warren, except for a period of about two years spent in California. He was in partnership with his brother, Daniel B., for a score of years. Dr. Woods married Julia H. Heaton, a daughter of James Heaton, of Weathersfield.

Dr. J. R. Nelson has been practicing in Warren since 1847. His father, Abram Nelson, was one of the early settlers of Liberty township, where the Doctor was born in 1813. The family is of Irish descent. He studied medicine under Dr. Loy, in Liberty, and attended lectures in Cleveland. He began practicing in Garrettsville in 1844, and in 1847 came to Warren, where he has since been located.

J. R. VanGorder, a son of J. L. VanGorder, an early settler of Warren, was born in 1825. He received his education at the old academy in Warren, and then read medicine in the office of Dr. Sylvanus Seeley. After the death of the latter he completed his studies under direction of Dr. Farrell. He attended lecturer at the University of Pennsylvania Medical college and received a degree from that institution in 1849. Dr. VanGorder has been in continuous practice in Warren since 1852. He has a family.

Frederick Bierce was born in Litchfield county, Connecticut, in 1822. In 1825 the family removed to Portage county, Ohio. He worked on a farm and taught school until a course of medical studies was entered upon at Nelson in Portage county. He began practicing in Ashtabula county in 1852, and was actively employed there until 1861. Since that date he has been in Warren. Dr. Bierce is a member of the Northeastern Ohio Homeopathic society.

Dr. Myers would be an interesting subject for a detailed biography, but the character of our work and the limits of our space requires brevity. He was born in Bavaria, Germany, in 1823. From the public schools in his twelfth year he was placed in a gymnasium at Padua, Italy, where a six years' course was pursued. A course of philosophical study covering two years, followed at Vienna. The time of medical preparation occupied five years—two years in Bardua, two years in Vienna, and one year in hospital service. At the completion of his long course of preparation, covering thirteen years from the time he left the common school, Dr. Myers received a diploma which gave him the privileges of a full practitioner. He opened an office in Vienna in the fall of 1847, but became involved in the revolution which occurred during the following winter. That year is characterized in history as the revolutionary epoch. The insurgents were mostly educated young men, unwilling longer to bear the yoke of despotism, but the time was not ripe, and the revolution proved a failure, and the participants had to flee for their lives. Dr. Myers, in company with five young friends, left Vienna in disguise and under assumed names. They traveled incognito through Germany to France, and then took ship for America, having safely evaded danger of arrest. Dr. Myers was informed at New York of the prevalence of cholera in Cincinnati, and at once started for that city. After practicing two years in Cincinnati he removed to New Castle, Pennsylvania, and from there to Alliance in 1856, thence to Cuba, Missouri. At the opening of the war he volunteered, and was made surgeon of a German battalion under General Sigel, stationed at Cuba. After the battle of Wilson's Creek he was mustered out of the service and came to Warren in the fall of that year. He has since been in active practice here. Dr. Myers married, in Cincinnati, Mary Rapbould, who died in 1858, leaving two sons. For his second wife he married Malissa Post, of Johnston township, who has borne him one child.

Dr. L. Spear was born in Austintown in 1828. His father, Dr. Alexander Spear, settled there in 1820. Mr. Spear read medicine under Dr. B. W. Spear, in Salem, Ohio, and graduated from the Cincinnati Eclectic Medical college in 1855. He began practice in 1855, and came to Warren in 1861. He accompanied the One Hundred and Seventy-first Ohio volunteer infantry as surgeon to Camp Sandusky, but did not go to the field.

Cyrus Metcalf is of English descent. His father, John Metcalf, was a native of Massachusetts, from which State he removed to Medina county, New York, where the doctor was born July 7, 1822. In 1836 his family removed to Licking county, Ohio. After spending several years in attendance at Granville academy and teaching school, he began the study of medicine at Newark, Ohio, and subsequently attended lectures at Geneva Medical college, New York, receiving a degree in 1846. He opened an office at Bristolville that year, and soon had a satisfactory practice. In 1866 he removed to Warren and is now in full practice.

Dr. H. A. Sherwood is one of the younger physicians of the homœopathic school of practice. He was born in Knox county, Ohio, in 1851. His preliminary education was received at the public schools in Frederickstown, Knox county. He commenced the study of medicine in September, 1873, and the same year entered the Homœopathic Hospital college of Cleveland, on a three years course, which was completed, and the degree conferred in 1876. While in college he was house physician at the Huron Street hospital, and physician to the college dispensary. Soon after graduating Dr. Sherwood opened an office at Warren. In 1880 he was appointed city physician and member of the board of health. He is a member of the Homœopathic Medical society of Eastern Ohio, and has served as president of that organization.

Dr. C. S. Ward is a son of Columbus Ward, and was born in Ashtabula county, in 1854. His family removed to Warren in 1865, at which time he entered the Warren public schools, and graduated in 1871. He commenced the study of medicine with Dr. H. McQuiston, completing the course in the office of D. B. and J. R. Woods. Mr. Ward attended lectures at the University of Michigan Medical college, from which institution he received a degree in 1874. In 1875, he received an *ad eundum* degree from Bellevue Hospital Medical college, New York city. He served one year as surgeon in the Ninety-ninth Street Reception hospital. Since 1876 Dr. Ward has been practicing with Dr. D. B. Woods, in Warren.

CHAPTER VIII.
WARREN LODGES.*
OLD ERIE LODGE NUMBER THREE, FREE AND ACCEPTED MASONS.

Alexander Sutherland, secretary of this lodge in A. L. 5821 and 5822, in his prefatory to the abstract made by him of the first records of the lodge says:

It is a matter of no small importance that the records and proceedings of every important and valuable institution be kept entire, and it is equally important that they be kept in such form that the readiest access may be had to the most essential particulars. The frequent meetings of our honorable institution and the multiplicity of business therein transacted necessarily renders our records extremely voluminous, while the scattered and informal manner in which they are usually kept renders them no less obscure. To remedy this inconvenience and to place important particulars in a conspicuous situation is the object of this abstract.

To this abstract made by Brother Sutherland we are indebted for very many of the facts in this sketch, while some have been obtained from other worthy and trusty sources, while some have been winnowed out of the legends and traditions of these olden times, together with the remembrance of the very few still living, who were contemporary with them.

In the year 1803, Anno Lucis 5803, a number of Free and Accepted Ancient York Masons residing in Trumbull county, within the Connecti-

* By R. A. Baldwin, past master, and Charles S. Field.

cut Western Reserve, in the State of Ohio, met at Warren (the seat of justice for Trumbull county, then comprehending the entire Western Reserve), and mutually agreed to organize and establish a lodge of the order, to be located at Warren, to-wit: Samuel Tylee, Martin Smith, Tryal Tanner, Camden Cleveland, Solomon Griswold, Aaron Wheeler, John Walworth, Charles Dutton, Arad Way, Gideon Hoadley, Ezekiel Hover, Turhand Kirtland, John Leavitt, William Rayen, George Phelps, James B. Root, James Dunscomb, Samuel Spencer, Joseph De Wolf, Daniel Bushnell, Calvin Austin, and Asahel Adams, joined in a petition to the Grand lodge of Connecticut, from which State and from the lodges thereof the most of these brothers had emigrated, praying for authority to "congregate as Free and Accepted York Masons, and form a lodge as such under their jurisdiction and protection. At this meeting Samuel Tylee, one of the brothers present, was duly appointed their representative; and clothed with the necessary authority and recommendations, entrusted with the petition, he proceeded to the city of New Haven and presented it to the Grand lodge of Connecticut, then holding its annual session there, having thirty-nine of its subordinates therein represented. After due deliberation they concluded to grant the prayer of these brothers. A charter was granted to the brothers above named, bearing date October 19, 5803, and Brother Samuel Tylee was, by the Grand lodge, appointed and installed as deputy grand master for the purpose of proceeding to Warren to dedicate the new lodge and install its officers. The charter was delivered to him, and shortly after his arrival home in Warren, on the 16th of March, A. L. 5804, at 2 P. M., he, with the *pro tem.* officers of the Grand lodge, appointed from the brethren present, went in procession to the room provided, and then, as deputy grand master, proceeded to and opened the lodge in the first three degrees of Masonry in proper form, and after due examination of the brothers, who were proposed by the petitioners as officers of the new lodge, to-wit: Right Worshipful Turhand Kirtland, master; Right Worshipful John Leavitt, senior warden; Right Worshipful William Rayen, junior warden; Calvin Austin, treasurer; Camden Cleveland, secretary; Aaron Wheeler, senior deacon; John Walworth, junior deacon;

Charles Dutton and Arad Way, stewards; Ezekiel Hover, tyler; and being fully satisfied with their character, skill, and qualifications for the government of the lodge, they having also received the entire and unconditional consent of the members thereof, did, by the authority given him by the Grand lodge of Connecticut, with the assistance of the grand officers *pro tem.*, constitute, consecrate, and solemnly install the said petitioners and their said officers by the name of Erie Lodge No. 47, Ancient Free and Accepted York Masons, agreeable to the ancient usages, customs, and laws of the craft, under the protection and jurisdiction of the Grand lodge of Connecticut. And now, having solemnly erected the lodge to God, and dedicated it to the holy Saints John, and being legally empowered as a lodge of Free and Accepted Masons, to work and act as such, in strict conformity to the ancient charges and laws of the fraternity, the usual rites and ceremonies performed, and the honors paid the Grand lodge, it, at 3:30 P. M., closed in form, with great harmony.

The members forming this lodge resided in various parts of the Reserve, brothers Walworth and Hoadley being residents of Cleveland, Rayen and Dutton of Youngstown, Tryal Tanner of Canfield, Turhand Kirtland of Poland, Samuel Tylee of Hubbard, and others from the lake shore towns.

At 5 o'clock P. M. of this day Erie Lodge No. 47, for the first time since their organization, as above set forth, convened at its lodge room in Warren, and, opening in due form, proceeded to business, and from that time continued work under the authority so granted, until considering that greater benefits would arise to the craft by the formation of a Grand lodge for the State of Ohio, they, on the 11th of March, A. L. 5807, at their annual meeting, by a solemn vote of the lodge, appointed George Tod, John Leavitt, and William Rayen (three members thereof) a committee to correspond with the other lodges in the State on the subject. This committee, faithful to their trust, carried out the object of their appointment, and, at a meeting of the lodge held November 11, A. L. 5807, reported that they had received communications in answer to theirs from lodges at Marietta, Cincinnati, Zanesville, and Chillicothe, relative to the formation of a grand lodge. When this report had been deliberately considered, the encouragement thereby afforded induced the lodge to pass a resolution appointing brothers George Tod and John W. Seeley delegates from Erie Lodge No. 47 to meet delegates from other lodges within the State in convention to be held at Chillicothe on the first Monday in January, A. L. 5808, and "confiding these our delegates full power in conjunction with the delegates from other lodges to institute a grand lodge and form a constitution and by-laws agreeable to the ancient landmarks, constitution, charges and usages. Thus to Erie lodge belongs the honor of being the first to suggest and first to take the initiative towards establishing the Grand lodge of Ohio, a distinction of which it may well be proud. The result of this move upon its part was that on the 4th day of January, A. L. 5808, a preliminary meeting of delegates from all the lodges in the State was convened at Chillicothe to deliberate on the propriety of forming a grand lodge to take Masonic cognizance of the craft within the State, and, if found expedient, to inaugurate measures for its organization. Six lodges were represented, located respectively in Marietta, Cincinnati, Warren, Zanesville, Chillicothe, and Worthington. Robert Oliver was made chairman and George Tod secretary. The convention deliberated for some days, and its labors resulted in the unanimous adoption of the following resolution proposed by brother Lewis Cass and seconded by brother John W. Seeley, of Erie lodge.

Resolved, That it is expedient to form a Grand lodge in this State.

On the next day they went into an election of officers, which resulted in the choice of Rufus Putman, of Union lodge No. 1, Marietta, Rt. W. Gr. M.; Thomas Henderson, Cincinnati lodge No. 13, Rt. W. D. G. M.; George Tod, of Erie lodge No. 47, Rt. W. S. G. W.; Isaac Van Horn, of Amity lodge No. 105, Zanesville, Rt. W. J. G. W., and the other grand officers. The lodges then in the State were chartered by the various Grand lodges of the States whence their members had emigrated to Ohio, and took their numbers therefrom. The proceedings of this convention was, by the delegates from Erie lodge, reported to its regular annual meeting held on the 9th of March, A. L. 5808, and unanimously approved, and at a meeting held December 5th following, George Tod, Samuel Hunting- ton, and John H. Adgate were, by a unanimous vote of the lodge and by warrant of the right worshipful master and warden, appointed and empowered to represent the lodge in the Grand lodge at their grand communication to be held in January thereafter. It was also resolved by the lodge, in compliance with a resolution adopted by the Grand lodge, that the charter granted them by the Grand lodge of Connecticut and the by-laws of the lodge be submitted to the care of the said 'representatives, to be surrendered to the Grand lodge of Ohio under the regulation adopted by it, and receive in its stead a warrant of dispensation. All of which being done, and the same granted by the Grand lodge, and presented to Erie lodge at its meeting March 23, A. L. 5809, and by the lodge read, considered, and approved, it was resolved to adopt under this warrant of dispensation the same by-laws that were in force under the charter granted by the Grand lodge of Connecticut, now surrendered.

The lodge thus continued to exercise the powers vested in it as well under and by authority of the charter and the warrant of dispensation by the title of Erie lodge No. 47, from the period of its first institution until at a certain regular meeting held at its lodge-room in Warren on the 2d of February, A. L. 5814, when the presiding secretary in open lodge reported that he had received from the grand secretary of the Grand lodge of Ohio a charter of constitution signed by the M. W. Henry Brush, G. M.; Rt. W. Jacob Burnett, D. G. M. *pro tem*.; Rt. W. Edward Tupper, S. G. W.; Rt. W. Levin Belt, J. G. W.; Rt. W. David Kincaid, Grand Treasurer; and attested by Rt. W. Robert Kercheval, Grand Secretary; and with the seal of the Grand lodge attached thereto, dated at Chillicothe on the 5th of January, in the year of redemption 1814, and of Masonry 5814, constituting and appointing Samuel Tylee, Francis Freeman, Elisha Whittlesey, Seth Tracy, William W. Colgreave, John Leavitt, and Calvin Austin, and their successors forever, a regular lodge of Free and Accepted Masons, to be hailed by the name and title of Erie lodge No. 3. Granting them concurred precedence with the other five original lodges convened at Chillicothe, A. L. 5808, under which charter, name, and number the lodge continued to exercise the power granted thereby. At the stated communication held June 13th, John S. Edwards and George Tod were initiated as entered apprentices. Brother Tod was passed November 13, A. L. 5804, and raised November 14, A. L. 5805. He was elected master of the lodge March 20, 1811. He was prominent in the effort made by the lodge to establish the Grand lodge; was the secretary of the convention at Chillicothe at which the Grand lodge was organized; was its first grand senior warden, to which office he was re-elected for a number of years. He served the lodge in every capacity and in all its offices. He died April 11, 1841. He was faithful in the discharge of his duties, public and private, and a true, devoted Mason to the last. (See biographical sketch).

In 1805 Joseph Coit was initiated, and in 1806 William Andrews, Eperntus Rogers, James Hillman, and George Hardman; in 1807, Alexander Campbell, John H. Adgate, and Edward Scoville; in 1808, Jonathan Church, Titus Brockway, and Elderkin Potter; in 1809, Hezekiah Knapp, and Rufus Edwards; in 1810, Elisha Whittlesey, Rev. Adamson Bentley, and Archibald Tanner. Of Elisha Whittlesey perhaps more than the brief notice of his initiation into our fraternity is due. A man who lived to ripe old age, honored and beloved; honored as being an honest public man, as a member of the National house of Representatives from the Nineteenth Congressional district of Ohio for many years. He always took an active part in the affairs of the lodge, filling most of its offices, and in them, as in all other matters, he was a just and upright man and Mason, continuing as such until at the call of the gavel of the supreme grand master of the Universe he was raised to the celestial lodge above (see biographical sketch).

In 1811 Otis Guild, Thomas McMillen, and Steven Oviatt were initiated; in 1812, Robert Bentley and Alexander Sutherland; in 1813, Solomon Oviatt, Fisher A. Blocksom; in 1814, Seymour Austin, John Brown Harmon (for a biographical sketch see another page, written by his son, Dr. Julian Harmon), Samuel Wheeler, and Robert Harper; in 1815, Lyman Potter; in 1816, James Guild and William W. Morseman; in 1817, Levi Hoadley, Wheeler Lewis, Seth Oviatt, Samuel North, Richard Iddings, and Isaac Ladd; in 1819, Israel Procter, Asa Howe, John Chambers, Charles Green, and Solomon Sweatland; in 1821, Cyrus Bosworth, Ebenezer Thompson, Charles Olcutt, Rufus Payne Spalding, Roswell Stone, and John M. Goodman; in 1822, Jacob H. Baldwin, Isaac Heaton, Alfred L. Norton, James C. Marshall, Jeremiah Brooks (2d), and Alfred Allen; in 1823, Enoch W. Heaton, Reece Heaton, Calvin Austin, Edward Spear, Benjamin Towne, John R. Barnes, W. B. Washington; in 1824, George W. Tallmadge, William McFarland, Henry Stiles; in 1826, Cornelius Ferris and James Wickersham. The records being so incomplete but a partial list of those initiated can be given, as there are gaps of more than a year that nothing but fancy can fill. Many joined the lodge from other lodges, among whom were John Harrington and the two brothers, Benjamin and Horace Stevens.

Benjamin Stevens was made a Mason in Vergennes, Vermont, in 1810, removed to Warren in 1816, was admitted to membership in Erie lodge March 19, 1817, served in all the offices of the lodge, was elected and presided in the Oriental chair in 1820, and again in 1821. He became one of the charter members of the present Old Erie lodge in 1854. He was born in Canaan, Litchfield county, Connecticut, July 20, 1788, and now at the age of nearly ninety-four resides at his home on Mahoning avenue, Warren, an exemplary man and Mason as he has ever been through life.

Horace Stevens, Sr., was born February 2, 1794, in Huntingdon, Luzerne county, Pennsylvania, removed to Warren in 1816, to Newton Falls in 1828, and back to Warren in 1867. He was made a Mason in Dorchester lodge No. 3, Vergennes, Vermont, December 3, 1815 (his diploma from that lodge now graces the reception room of Old Erie), he was admitted to old Erie August 2, 1817. He filled nearly all the offices, was diligent and zealous, ever attentive to the business on hand. He now lives with his widowed daughter, Mrs. Ira L. Fuller, on Market street, and occasionally meets with the lodge.

Of the charter members of Erie lodge No. 47 much can not now be ascertained. Some of them were members of the Connecticut Land company, who were owners of the Western Reserve, but the details obtainable are so meagre that injustice might be done in this hasty sketch should even brief mention be made, so we refrain only in justice to them and those who afterwards became members of the lodge. It should be said that it numbered among its members the best men of the day and the time—many of them becoming famous in the history of the State as judges, congressmen, legislators, counsellors, in all the professions, arts, trades, and commerce. Biographical sketches of some of them will be found on other pages of this and Mahoning county history.

Where the room was located in which the lodge was instituted, and from that time (A. L. 5804) held, its meetings cannot, from the limited data at the command of the compilers of this sketch, be ascertained. Tradition, having a foundation, no doubt, in fact, says that they met somewhere in 1810 in the gambrel-roofed, red frame building, in which the Western Reserve bank was first organized, that stood on the east side of Main street, just north of the Freeman property, and on ground now occupied by the Biggers grocery store. Afterwards and during the war with Great Britain (1812-15) they met at the Hadly tavern, built by John Leavitt, then standing on the west side and just back from Main street, in the rear of, and on the ground now occupied by the King frame block, immediately south of the old King brick block, now (April, 1882), being torn down. From this room they marched in procession, on the celebration of St. John's day, in June of one of those years, to a log building then used as a school-house, standing on the northwest corner of the park, west of Main street, and north of the present city building. Soon after this, probably in 1816, they removed to "Castle William," afterwards known as the Pavillion hotel, located on ground now occupied by VanGorder's brick block on Market street.

The room which they occupied in this hotel was used in common for the Masonic hall, court-room, public meetings, shows, exhibitions, singing-schools, balls, etc., and the log part of the house as a jail. The lodge continued to occupy this room until about 1829, when the first chapter of its prosperity comes to a close and one of darker aspect opens. Seizing on an unfortunate circumstance which occurred in a neighboring State, aspiring political demagogues took up the cry, and then, as now, pandering to the prejudices of the ignorant and uninformed for the purpose of gaining the honors and emoluments of office, raised an anti-Masonic tempest that, aided and encouraged by false brethren, who could readily make merchandise of their honor, swept over the whole country. It is not, however, our intention to repeat the story of those times, when to be an avowed Mason was sufficient of itself to brand the man with infamy, and yet an allusion must be made to those days in reference to their effect on the subject of which we are writing. Such exterminating zeal and wild fanaticism prevailed that in some towns where the lodges continued to meet, their rooms were broken into and their property publicly destroyed, and such the defection of members who before were considered "good and true," that even the really worthy could not maintain their Masonic position in an organized form without incurring the enmity of the public and social ostracism by the community in which they lived. In 1831 a national anti-Masonic convention was held in Philadelphia, and William Wirt was nominated for President of the United States and polled a considerable vote, receiving a majority in one or two States in consequence, and in obedience to public opinion, then so inflamed, and concluding to let time, reason and calm judgment determine the right, a majority of the lodges in Ohio and in most of the States ceased to work as such. Some of them voluntarily surrendered their charter, some gave them up on the call of the Grand lodge, while others, with colors still unfurled died charter in hand. The charter of Erie Lodge No. 3, was consumed in 1833, when the house of Brother Edward Spear (standing on the grounds now occupied by the First Methodist church building) on High street, was burned, and from this time forward the transactions of the lodge ceased. But it is a very dark night that is not followed by another day. After mentioning the last recorded meeting and giving a list of the officers of the lodge from its organization to this time, as far as possible, we will take advantage of the dawning light of the brighter day that again illumined the onward pathway of the fraternity.

On Wednesday evening, December 3, 1827, a regular communication was held at which were present Edward Spear, Rt. W. M.; Roswell Stone, Rt. W. S. W. pro tem; Rufus P. Spalding, Rt. W. J. W. pro tem; Henry Stiles, treasurer; Isaac Ladd, secretary pro tem; Horace Stevens, S. D. pro tem; Francis Freeman, J. D. and T. pro tem; visiting brother Isaac N. Gilson. A committee consisting of Francis Freeman and Roswell Stone was appointed to settle with the treasurer and secretary and to report at a special meeting held the next evening. They made their report, showing the assets of the lodge to be $75.83½, and all due from members either for dues unpaid or money loaned. This is the last recorded meeting of the lodge, yet it continued to meet and was represented in 1828 in the Grand lodge by Brothers Francis Freeman, R. P. Spalding, and Edward Spear, and in 1830 it is in the list of existing lodges under the Grand lodge.

Worshipful Masters—1804, Turhand Kirtland; 1805, Edward Payne; 1806, Martin Smith; 1809, George Tod; 1812, John Leavitt; 1813, Samuel Tylee; 1814, Francis Freeman; 1816, George Tod; 1818, Adamson Bently; 1820, Benjamin Stevens; 1822,* Edward Flint; 1824, R. P. Spalding; 1825, Edward Spear.

Senior Wardens—1804, John Leavitt; 1805, Martin Smith; 1806, Samuel Tylee; 1808, John Leavitt; 1810, John S. Edwards; 1811, Martin Smith; 1812, Francis Freeman; 1814, Seth Tracy; 1818, Horace Stevens; 1820, Francis Freeman; 1821, Horace Stevens; 1822, Rufus Payne Spalding; 1824, Edward Spear; 1825, Jacob H. Baldwin.

Junior Wardens—1804, William Rayen; 1805, Samuel Tylee; 1806, Solomon Griswold; 1809, Samuel Tylee; 1810, Francis Freeman; 1812, Calvin Austin; 1813, Elisha Whittlesey; 1814, Adamson Bently; 1818, John Gordon; 1820, Edward Flint; 1821, John Gordon; 1822, Cyrus Bosworth; 1823, Isaac Ladd; 1824, Jacob H. Baldwin; 1825, James C. Marshall; 1826, Cyrus Bosworth.

Treasurers—1804, Calvin Austin; 1806, Turhand Kirtland; 1807, John Leavitt; 1808, Calvin Austin; 1810, Asahel Adams; 1812, John W. Seeley; 1813, Seth Tracy; 1814, Otis Guild; 1815, John B. Harmon; 1816, Lyman Potter; 1818, Benjamin Stevens; 1820, Richard Iddings; 1825, Henry Stiles.

Secretaries—1804, Camden Cleveland; 1806, George Tod; 1808, William Rayen; 1809, John

* New by-laws changing time of election went into effect.

S. Edwards; 1810, Calvin Austin; 1812, Elisha Whittlesey; 1813, William H. Cotgreave; 1814, John W. Seeley; 1815, Seymour Austin; 1817, Edward Flint; 1820, Horace Stevens; 1821, Alexander Sutherland; 1822, Jacob H. Baldwin; 1824, James C. Marshall; 1825, R. P. Spalding; 1826, William McFarland.

Senior Deacons—1804, Aaron Wheeler; 1806, Seth Tracy; 1809, Richard Hayes; 1810, Tryal Tanner; 1812, Seth Tracy; 1813, John Leavitt; 1814, Robert Bently; 1815,George Tod; 1816, William W. Cotgreave; 1817, Alexander Sutherland; 1818, John B. Harmon; 1819, Richard Iddings; 1820, Alexander Sutherland; 1821, Francis Freeman; 1822, Roswell Stone; 1823, Edward Spear; 1824, William B. Washington; 1825, Francis Freeman; 1826, Horace Stevens.

Junior Deacons—1804, John Walworth; 1806 James Danscombe; 1808, John W. Seeley; 1809, Francis Freeman; 1810, Arad Way; 1811, Elisha Whittlesey; 1812, Edward Scofield; 1813, Calvin Austin; 1814, Eli Barnum; 1815, William W. Cotgreave; 1816, Francis Freeman; 1818, Lewis Hoadley; 1820, John Gorden; 1821, Edward Flint; 1822, Reuben Case; 1822, *Francis Freeman; 1823, Calvin Austin; 1824, William McFarland; 1826, Francis Freeman.

Stewards—1804, Charles Dutton and Arad Way; 1805, George Phelps and Edward Payne; 1806, Edward Wadsworth and Tryal Tanner; 1807, S. G. Bushnell; 1808, Richard Hayes and William Andrews; 1809, James Hillman and William W. Cotgreave; 1810, James Hillman and Camden Cleveland; 1811, William Andrews and Hezekiah Knapp; 1812, James Hillman; 1813, Hezekiah Knapp and Asahel Adams; 1814, Steven Oviatt; 1815, James Hillman and Hezekiah Knapp, 1816, Alexander Sutherland; 1817, Benjamin Stevens and Stephen Oviatt; 1818, Richard Iddings and Wheeler Lewis; 1819, Alexander Sutherland and John Shook; 1820, John Shook and Levi Hoadly; 1821, Samuel Phillips; 1822, Isaac Ladd and Charles Olcutt; 1823, Benjamin Towne; 1826, Isaac Ladd.

Tylers—1804, Ezekiel Hover; 1805, Elijah Wadsworth; 1806, Josiah W. Brown; 1807, Arad Way; 1808, Jonathan Church; 1809, William Andrews; 1810, Jonathan Church; 1812, Hezekiah Knapp; 1813, Alexander Suth-

*New by-laws went into effect, changing time of election.

erland; 1816, John Shook; 1819, Isaac Ladd; 1822, Francis Freeman; 1822, Charles Olcutt; 1824, Isaac Ladd; 1825, Edward Flint; 1826, Benjamin Towne.

Early in A. L. 5854 a number of the members of Erie Lodge No. 3, who were still living and still holding on to, and cherishing, and honoring the principles of Masonry, and having during all the years of darkness aided and counseled each other, met at the home of one of them, as they had continued to do, and agreed to petition the grand master for a dispensation to commence work. The grand master, William B. Dodds, was pleased to grant their prayer by issuing a warrant of dispensation dated June 2, 1854, to Richard Iddings, Jacob H. Baldwin, J. B. Buttles, W. H. Holloway, Henry Stiles, J. Rodgers, H. Benham, Gary C. Reed, J. Veon, Benjamin Stevens, Edward Spear, John B. Harmon, Alexander McConnell, and H. McManus, under the title of Western Reserve lodge. The committee on charters and dispensations, at the session of the Grand lodge held in Chillicothe October 17, A. L. 5854, report that they "have examined the dispensation, by-laws, etc., of Western Reserve lodge at Warren, Trumbull county, Ohio, and take pleasure in stating that but one error, and that an unimportant one, was discovered"; they recommended that a charter be issued to them. The report was adopted by the Grand lodge. The name Western Reserve lodge was adopted because during the lapse of Erie lodge another lodge of that name had been established, and under the regulations of the Grand lodge two lodges of the same name were not allowed.

On Wednesday P. M., October 18th, at the communication of the Grand lodge, Brother A. L. Holcombe, of Vinton lodge No. 131, offered the following resolution, which on his own motion was laid on the table:

Resolved, That the name of Western Reserve lodge, to which a charter has been granted at this communication, be changed to Erie, and that it take the number "three" from an old lodge of that name formerly located at the same place.

This resolution was referred to the committee on charter and dispensation, who on the afternoon of the 19th reported this resolution:

Resolved, That the name of Western Reserve lodge be changed to Old Erie, and that it be numbered three.

And so the lodge had restored to it the name, number, and precedence to which of right they belong. This charter was issued to the same brothers as named above in the dispensation.

Since the time of its re-organization its progress has been rapid and permanent, and in every way successful, paying more dues to the Grand lodge for the year A. L. 5866 than any other lodge except one in the State. It was constituted and its first officers installed in the lodge room of Mahoning lodge No. 29, Independent Order of Odd Fellows, in Iddings' brick block, on Market street, January 30, 1855, by special deputy Brother John M. Webb. The officers were the same as under the dispensation, to wit: Brother Gary C. Reed had served during that time as worshipful master, but not having taken his demit from Jerusalem lodge, he was held by Special Deputy Brother Webb as ineligible to be installed; Brothers John Veon, S. W.; H. A. Benham, J. W.; Henry Stiles, treasurer; H. W. Holloway, secretary; William Green, S. D.; Morgan Gaskill, J. D; John A. Woods, tyler. They removed from the Odd Fellows' hall to their new rooms in the Gaskill house, now the Austin house, southeast corner of Main and South street, about the month of March, A. L. 5855. The first officers elected under its charter November 20, 1855, were: Edward Spear, W. M.; Charles R. Hunt, S. W.; Jacob H. Baldwin, J. W.; Henry Stiles, treasurer; John M. Stiles, secretary; William Green, S. D.; Edward Spear, Jr., J. D.; Ebenezer H. Goodale, tyler. March 25, 1862, they removed from the Gaskill house to and held their first meeting in the hall built for them on the southeast corner of Main and Market streets, from thence in 1869 to the elegant hall and rooms over the First National bank, southeast corner of Park avenue and Market street, which rooms they have since occupied.

The following is a list of the officers of the lodge since its reorganization in 1854:

Worshipful Masters — 1855, Edward Spear; 1865, R. A. Baldwin; 1866, C. R. Hunt; 1871, T. Ackley; 1875, E. C. Cady; 1877, H. B. Weir; 1879, S. F. Bartlett; 1881, W. A. Reeves.

Senior Wardens — 1855, C. R. Hunt; 1860, R. A. Baldwin; 1865, Julius King; 1866, I. N. Dawson; 1867, P. Chase; 1868, L. Dray; 1869, F. P. Reed; 1870, T. Ackley; 1871, John Kœhler; 1873, F. Kinsman, Jr.; 1874, E. C. Cady; 1875, H. B. Weir; 1876, J. A. Thayer; 1877,

G. B. Kennedy; 1878, S. F. Bartlett; 1879, W. A. Reeves; 1881, J. Vautrot, Jr.

Junior Wardens—1855, J. H. Baldwin; 1856, W. C. Hathaway; 1857, R. A. Baldwin; 1860, Julius King; 1861, J. N. Green; 1862, Julius King; 1863, H. A. Seabrook; 1864, S. N. Kemble; 1865, W. N. Lane; 1866, E. H. Ensign; 1867, H. P. Bassett; 1868, J. G. Gilmer; 1869, T. Ackley; 1870, F. E. Hutchins; 1871, Matthew Rankin; 1873, W. T. Spear; 1874, H. B. Weir; 1875, J. I. Kennedy; 1876, J. J. Jones; 1877, C. H. Angstadt; 1878, W. A. Reeves; 1879, J. Vautrot, Jr.; 1881, G. H. Tayler.

Treasurers—1855, Henry Stiles; 1869, P. Chase; 1871, T. A. Brierly; 1874, John Koehler.

Secretaries—1855, John M. Stull; 1856, E. H. Goodale; 1857, H. W. Holloway; 1861, W. Adams; 1863, W. M. Lane; 1864, W. R. Gorton; 1865, L. Dray; 1866, H. H. Townsend; 1867, W. T. Spear; 1868, R. A. Baldwin; 1870, F. Kinsman; 1871, J. G. Baldwin; 1877, J. I. Kennedy.

Senior Deacons—1855, William Green; 1856, Edward Spear, Jr.; 1857, Julius King; 1860, J. N. Green; 1861, J. W. Tyler; 1864, I. A. Bentley; 1865, T. Van Antwerp; 1866, R. A. Baldwin; 1867, F. P. Reed; 1869, T. Van Antwerp; 1870, E. G. McOmber; 1871, C. E. Strong; 1872, R. A. Baldwin; 1873, M. Rankin; 1874, G. L. Jameson; 1875, J. J. Jones; 1876, H. B. Weir; 1877, Thad. Ackley; 1878, R. A. Baldwin; 1879, F. D. McLain.

Junior Deacons—1855, Edward Spear, Jr.; 1856, James McKnight; 1857, J. N. Green; 1859, H. Ewalt; 1860, Calvin Reeves; 1861, H. Stevens; 1863, D. D. Dunn; 1864, T. Van Antwerp; 1865, John W. Roberts; 1866, T. Van Antwerp; 1867, T. Ackley; 1869, E. G. McOmber; 1870, John Koehler; 1871, M. W. Spear; 1872, C. H. Augstadt; 1874, J. D. Kennedy; 1876, W. B. Payne; 1877, J. N. Green; 1878, John Wilkins; 1879, C. W. Field; 1880, A. B. Camp; 1881, G. K. Ross.

Tylers—1855, E. H. Goodale; 1856, Thomas Douglass; 1857, E. H. Goodale; 1858, I. Burton; 1870, G. B. Hucke; 1872, J. D. Kennedy; 1874, John Wilkins; 1875, L. Burton, 1876, E. H. Goodale.

Delegates to the Grand lodge.—1855-56-57, Edward Spear; 1858-59-60, Edward Spear and R. A. Baldwin; 1862, Edward Spear and W. C. Hathaway; 1863-64, R. A. Baldwin; 1865, Edward Spear; 1866, R. A. Baldwin and Edward Spear; 1867, C. R. Hunt and Edward Spear; 1868, C. R. Hunt; 1869, John G. Gilmer; 1870-71, T. Ackley; 1872, John Koehler; 1873-74, T. Ackley; 1875-76, E. C. Cady; 1877, ———; 1878, R. A. Baldwin; 1879, S. F. Bartlett and J. Vautrot, Jr.; 1880-81, S. F. Bartlett.

MAHONING CHAPTER ROYAL ARCH MASONS NO. 66.

A dispensation dated March 31, 1855, was granted by Most Excellent High Priest H. M. Stokes, upon the petition of Francis Freeman, Richard Iddings, Jacob H. Baldwin, Chester Bidwell, Edward Spear, Gary F. Reed, Cyrus Bosworth, Benjamin Stevens, and Alexander McConnell. At the first meeting held under it, April 20, 1855, the petitions of Charles R. Hunt, William Green, R. W. Ratliff, and I. C. Jones were received. Its first officers under dispensation were Edward Spear, M. E. H. P.; Chester Bidwell, E. King; Richard Iddings, E. Scribe. A charter was granted to it October, 1855, and the first election held under it December 19, 1855. The following officers were elected: Edward Spear, M. E. H. P.; Chester Bidwell, E. K.; J. H. Baldwin, E. S.; Richard Iddings, treasurer; R. W. Ratliff, secretary; William Green, C. H.; C. R. Hunt, P. S.; Edward Spear, Jr., R. A. C.; R. A. Baldwin, M. 1st V.; I. C. Jones, M. 2d V.; Morgan Gaskill, M. 3d V.; E. H. Goodale, guard. It now, April, 1882, has over one hundred members.

WARREN COUNCIL NO. 58, ROYAL AND SELECT MASTERS,

organized under dispensation dated March 21, A. I., 5871, and held its first stated meeting April 7th, thereafter. It was chartered September 26, A. I. 5871, and the first officers elected were Edward Spear, T. I. M.; R. W. Ratliff, D. I. M.; William M. Lane, P. C. W.; George M. Stiles, treasurer; Frederick Kinsman, Jr., recorder; E. G. McOmber, C. of G.; J. C. McLain, sentinel. It now, April, 1882, has something over thirty members.

MAHONING LODGE NO. 29 INDEPENDENT ORDER OF ODD FELLOWS.[*]

The Independent Order of Odd Fellows originated in London, England, in 1788. Claims

---

[*] By Past Grand Charles S. Field.

are made by zealous members dating its origin as far back as 1726, but its earliest written records date back only to 1788. In that year a club calling themselves the Union Order of Odd Fellows met in that city every week for convivial and social practices. Other clubs formed on its model, and taking its rules to govern them, were established, by its consent, in various places throughout England, and the same convivial practices, often carried to excess, continued, until, in 1809, when after "Victory club" (or lodge, as they were then designated) was instituted at Manchester, some of its more intelligent members, perceiving the necessity of a reform in these practices of the brotherhood, and making mutual relief and charity instead the main objects of their meetings, sought to make such a change, but finding, after several years of effort, that such a result could not be accomplished without a radical change of the order, they therefore, in 1813, called a convention of all members of the order everywhere, who were in favor of the reform sought, to meet at Manchester for counsel, advice, and action. At this meeting several lodges, including the one at Manchester, seceded from the old union order and formed the Independent Order of Odd Fellows, Manchester Unity, and under its improved practices advanced rapidly, and soon overshadowed the rival from whence it sprang forth.

Members of this new order emigrating to the United States formed self established or unchartered lodges here, and then issued charters or authority for the establishing of other ones. But the successful institution of Oddfellowship, the fountain of the present wide-spread organization in this country, dates back only to 1819.

Thomas Wildey, a blacksmith by trade, an Englishman by birth, an American by adoption, and a citizen of Baltimore, Maryland, inserted in the papers a call for a meeting of Odd Fellows. It was responded to by John Duncan, John Welch, John Cheatham, and Richard Rushworth, who, together with Wildey, organized and self instituted Washington lodge Number 1, of Baltimore, April 26, 1819, and afterwards, February 1, 1820, received a charter from the Manchester unity, with power to grant charters to other lodges, thus becoming both a grand and working lodge. This mixed or double power was soon found to be extremely inconvenient, and on February 22, 1821, its power as a grand body was voluntarily surrendered to the past grands of that and Franklin lodge, then also existing in Baltimore, and thus the grand lodge was organized, receiving a charter as such from the Manchester unity, May 15, 1826, and proceeded to grant charters as subordinate lodges to those who had so organized it. This system continued until 1847, when the present representative form was adopted. It is now composed of two representatives from the subordinate lodges, and two from the encampment branch of the order from each jurisdiction governed by a State or Territorial grand lodge, and has power to grant charters to these National, State, or Territorial grand bodies, or to subordinate lodges in counties or districts where no grand lodges have been established by it, the several grand lodges chartering subordinates within their own jurisdiction. In 1878, owing to the establishing of lodges of the order in foreign countries, and for the purpose of having uniformity in the laws and in the unwritten work of the order, representatives from those countries were admitted and it is now styled the Sovereign Grand lodge of the Independent Order of Odd Fellows, and it only furnished the general laws and unwritten work to all the grand lodges of the world, local legislation being left to the several grand bodies, the form of its government being similar to that of the United States, and the several States. It separated or seceded from the Manchester unity in 1842.

The Sovereign Grand lodge had, in 1880, under its jurisdiction 50 grand lodges, 40 encampments, 7,172 subordinate lodges, 1,857 subordinate encampments, located in the States and Territories of this country, South and Central America, Mexico, Europe, Dominion of Canada, Sandwich Islands, Australia, New Zealand, etc. The total relief granted to members during 1880 was $1,695,979; the total revenue for 1880 was $4,618,846.42; total number of members in 1880 was 456,942.

ODD FELLOWS IN TRUMBULL COUNTY.

Odd Fellowship was first established in Trumbull county by the institution of Mahoning lodge No. 29, at Warren, May 21, 1844, since which time there have been organized and instituted nine other lodges, eight of which still exist, and are progressing rapidly in members and finances. The lodge established in Gustavus was unable, for some reason, to sustain itself, and its charter was surrendered. The following table shows the name, number, when instituted, location, and night of meeting of the nine lodges now in Trumbull county, together with the amount of their capital or invested fund, annual income, amount paid for relief of members during the year 1880, and the number of past grands then holding membership in each:

Name	Number	Date when Instituted	No. Members	Where Located	Night of Meeting	Capital or Invested Fund	Annual Income	Amount Paid for Relief of Members	No. P. G.
Mahoning	29	May 21, 1844	443	Warren	Monday	$3,477.88	$1,204.88	$437.22	26
Newton Falls	335	June 14, 1856	79	Newton Falls	Saturday	1,154.86	486.87	64.22	9
Girard	433	July 20, 1869	55	Girard	Thursday	1,141.35	568.15	199.00	12
Niles	436	Aug. 7, 1869	80	Niles	Tuesday	617	419.45	264.25	8
Hubbard	495	Aug. 27, 1871	102	Hubbard	Tuesday	2,650.63	1,120.72	117.25	7
Mineral Ridge	497	Apr. 25, 1871	127	Mineral Ridge	Wednesday	3,971.63	528.78	495.88	13
Trumbull	533	July 24, 1872	59	Vienna	Saturday	1,323.16	494.86	42	5
Cortland	554	Aug. 4, 1873	68	Cortland	Saturday	1,196.16			9
Mecca	697	Nov. 8, 1881	39	Mecca*					
Total			697†			$16,132.89	$5,336.55	$1,698.00‡	93

* No report until next year. † The number of members at this time (March, 1882) is 738 in the county. ‡ These lodges have in the aggregate expended for the relief of members and for charitable purposes over $75,000 since their establishment in this county.

ODD FELLOWS IN OHIO.

Odd Fellowship was established in Ohio by the organization and institution, December 23, 1830, of Ohio Lodge No. 1, at Cincinnati. The first officers were: Jacob W. Holt, N. G.; James Brice, V. G.; Samuel Cobb, secretary; Nathaniel Estling, treasurer. The Grand lodge of Ohio, consisting of the past grands of Ohio Lodge No. 1, was organized and went into operation January 2, 1832, and has now under its jurisdiction seven hundred and eight subordinate lodges, with a membership of nearly fifty thousand. These subordinate lodges have an invested fund of $1,510,760.82, an annual income of $323,435.59, and have paid out for the relief of its members and for charitable purposes $113,708.43. These figures are for the year 1880, except the membership, which is the estimate for the present year of 1882.

MAHONING CHAPTER NO. 29, INDEPENDENT ORDER OF ODD FELLOWS.

A charter was issued to Mahoning lodge No. 29, Independent Order of Odd Fellows, bearing date May 21, 1844, the following being charter members: Charles Pease, John Benson, Josiah F. Brown, L. P. Lott, and E. W. Weir. It was signed by Samuel W. Corwin, M. W. G. M.; H. N. Clark, R. W. D. G. M.; Joseph Roth, R. W. G. W.; David T. Shelbacker, R. W. G. Secretary; and the other officers of the Grand lodge, countersigned by Albert G. Day, G. C. Secretary. The lodge was instituted in the afternoon of May 21, 1844, in the hall in Daniel Gilbert's two-story brick block, corner of Market and Liberty (now Park avenue) streets, on ground now known as the Stiles block, being situated over that part of it now occupied by A. Wentz's dry-goods store, it being the second story in that block east from Park avenue, by D. D. G. M. Gideon E. Tindall, assisted by P. G. Bro. E. T. Nichols, both of Cleveland. The following were its first officers, elected that afternoon: Lewis P. Lott, N. G.; Josiah F. Brown, V. G.; Charles Pease, secretary; E. W. Weir, treasurer. A meeting was held on that evening, and on the next forenoon, afternoon, and evening, and on the 24th following, Sullivan D. Harris, William H. Newhard, Arthur Pritchard, Adoniram F. Hunt, William I. Knight, Charles R. Hunt, O. P. Tabor, Asahel F. Adams, Levi M. Barnes, and A. W. Bliss were initiated, and at the end of the first year the membership was fifty-four.

On the night of June 1, 1846, occurred a very disastrous fire that swept away a large portion of the business part of the city, including the block in which the hall was located, and most of the furniture, regalia, emblems, wardrobe, and effects were lost. A special meeting was called by the noble grand, at the request of Brothers F. K. Hulbard, E. W. Weir, and eleven others, at the ball-room of William H. Newhard, in the American House, now Dana's Musical institute, northwest corner of Park avenue and High street. At this meeting the hall committee were instructed to get together the scattered property of the lodge, and a special committee consisting of Brothers William Williams, Alanson Camp, and F. K. Hubbard were appointed to ascertain the amount of loss sustained by each individual member as soon as practicable. No report of this committee, if any was made, is upon record.

At the next meeting Brother William Williams, from a committee that had been appointed to confer with sundry individuals in regard to the purchase of a lot whereon to build an Odd Fellows building, reported nothing definite had been ascertained, but that a room could be procured in A. Adams' brick block on Main street, now (1882) known as the King block, and being torn down, for $30 per year. Brothers I. P. Lott, A. W. Bliss, and Alexander McConnell were appointed a committee with instructions to procure the rooms of Mr. Adams, and to have the same fitted up and in proper condition for the lodge to meet in at its next regular meeting, and it was done. The lodge continued in occupancy of these rooms until July 12, 1847, at which date it removed to Iddings' new brick block on Market street, where it has since been located, nearly thirty-five years.

On June 30, 1846, a circular, issued by the authority of the lodge, was sent out to the "lodges of this and adjacent States," asking assistance for the sufferers by the late calamitous fire. They were responded to quite generally and with very liberal donations, their timely help materially assisted in forwarding the re-establishment of business. Bros. T. J. McLain, M. B. Tayler, and Z. Fitch, were a committee to distribute this fund in a uniform and just manner.

The lodge has uniformly advanced in numbers and finances, except during, and a few years preceeding and succeeding the late war of the Rebellion. During this period its membership fell from over one hundred and twenty to about fifty; its capital or invested fund was materially diminished by losses on individual loans, and by parties with whom it had been deposited, but it recovered from the reverse, and now (1882) has a membership of over one hundred and fifty, with an invested fund (Government bonds), amply sufficient to guarantee the fulfillment of all its contracts with its members.

A number of lodges have grown out of this one, located in and out of the county, composed wholly or in part of its members, they taking withdrawal cards from this to become charter members of the new one. The following list names a few of them: Ralph A. Ingersoll, March 1, 1845, for new lodge at Canton, Ohio; Wilmot Bartlett, Charles A. Hosmer, Asa Forsythe, Monroe Atkinson, April 7, 1845, new lodge at Meadville, Pennsylvania; F. L. Smith, T. Garlick, R. G. Garlick, D. J. Wick, George W. Seaton, J. O. Osborn, September 29, 1845, Hebron No. 55, Youngstown, Ohio; F. W. Hulbard, November 17, 1845, new lodge at Racine, Wisconsin; James D. Watson, March 23, 1846, lodge at Ravenna, Ohio; Joseph Hartman, June 14, 1847, lodge at New Lisbon, Ohio; Royal Dow, A. E. Ensign, Wanton Hathaway, J. S. Cleveland, July 1, Geauga, No. 171, East Claridon, Ohio. And many others since, at the institution of other lodges in this and adjacent counties, and others in various Western States, the lodge having initiated over four hundred members, and among them many who have become very prominent, if not famous, not only in the order, but in all the departments of the professions, commerce, trades, and mechanics.

The following named members have been elected and served as N. G.'s, and for such service received the rank and title of P. G.: Levi P. Lott, Josiah F. Brown, Charles Pease, in 1844; John Benson, E. W. Weir, I. P. Lott (second term), 1845; William H. Newhard, Charles R. Hunt, 1846; Charles Pease (second term), A. W. Bliss, 1847; Alexander McConnell, D. Hitchcock, 1848; Thomas J. McLain, F. K. Hurlburt, 1849; J. D. Watson, R. W. Ratliff, 1850; S. D. Harris, Joel F. Asper, 1851; C. M. Patch, M. D. Leggett, 1852; Peter Gaskill, D. B. Gilmore, 1853; James Hoyt, M. McManus, 1854; E. H. Allison, Benjamin Cranage, 1855; Warren Packard, John M. Stull, 1856; Joel F. Asper (second term), E. H. Goodale, 1857;

Jacob Goldstein, J. C. Johnson, 1858; Biven P. Jameson, Leonard Burton, 1859; Rufus Thompson, William R. Stiles, 1860; Joel F. Asper (third term), L. Burton (second term), 1861; Thomas McCormick, James G. Brooks, 1862; Josiah Soule, Daniel Bishop, 1863; L. Burton (third term), J. G. Brooks (second term), 1864; C. C. McNutt, H. D. Niles, 1865; B. Goehring, C. M. Patch (second term), 1866; W. Y. Reeves, M. C. Woodworth, 1867; Alonzo Truesdall, J. G. Brooks (third term), 1868; J. W. Hoftse, D. M. Lazarus, 1869; J. W. Hoftse (second term), E. A. Burnett, 1870; J. R. Hardy, Michael Parker, 1871; R. S. Elliott, E. W. Moore, 1872; M. B. Deane, John L. Smith, 1873; J. D. Hoon, Wilson Downs, 1874; George B. Kennedy, John Buckstein, 1875; D. S. Jackson, Robert S. Wilkins, 1876; William Dennis, J. L. Smith (second term),[*] 1877; Charles N. Van Wormer, J. W. Masters, 1878; F. J. Mackey, J. W. McMurray, 1879; A. R. Hunt, James McCormick, 1880; Charles Holman, S. W. Park, 1881; Horace P. Bassett, 1882.

The following have been admitted to membership on cards as past grands from other lodges: Charles S. Field from Geauga lodge, 1867; Milo Clapp from Orwell lodge; Charles E. Kistler, Newton Falls lodge, 1870; Thomas Chase, Chardon lodge, 1866; A. E. Lyman, Newton Falls lodge; S. J. Enclioll, Orwell, April 1, 1879.

CHARTER MEMBERS.

Lewis P. Lott was initiated in Cleveland lodge No. 13, Independent Order of Odd Fellows, took a withdrawal card from that lodge, and became the first noble grand of Mahoning lodge. He was one of the most active, zealous, and efficient workers, was re-elected noble grand in 1845, and took a withdrawal card from that lodge November 9, 1846, for the purpose of joining one in Racine, Wisconsin, where he, about that time, removed. He was a merchant, and very much respected.

Charles Pease was also initiated in Cleveland lodge No. 13, Independent Order of Odd Fellows, withdrew from there, and was one of the charter members of this lodge; was elected its third noble grand, was re-elected in 1846; was district deputy grand master in 1845, and as such, instituted Hebron lodge No. 55, in Youngstown,

[*] To fill vacancy caused by the resignation of J. W. Hillman.

and others in other localities; served two terms as representative to the Grand lodge of Ohio; was one of the charter members of Pymatuning encampment No. 4, at Warren, now (1882) residing in Cleveland, Ohio; is still a member of this lodge, never having severed his membership therewith; a genial, social, open, frank-hearted, and much respected gentleman of some seventy years of age. He quite often visits the lodge, and is always greeted with hearty hand-shakes and expressions of respect, esteem, and love.

E. W. Weir was initiated in some lodge in the city of Cincinnati, taking the third, fourth, and fifth degrees here; he was elected noble grand in 1845. He was a tailor by trade, and was expelled from the order November 28, 1859, for non-payment of dues.

John Benson.—No data can be found as to when Brother Benson was made an Odd Fellow, but the records show that he became a charter member of this lodge "on deposit of card;" he was elected noble grand in 1845. A plasterer by trade, he took a withdrawal card May 3, 1874, and removed to Philadelphia, Pennsylvania.

Josiah F. Brown.—The records do not show when Brother Brown was made an Odd Fellow. He became a charter member by deposit of card; was second noble grand of the lodge; a tailor by occupation; he was expelled from the order July 23, 1860, for non-payment of dues.

The following members of Mahoning lodge have served in the Grand lodge of Ohio in the offices named:

P. G. Thomas J. McLain, most worthy grand master in 1855, and grand representative to the Grand lodge of the United States from the encampment branch of the order in 1850, and again in 1853 and 1854. In 1852 he was elected most worthy grand patriarch of Grand encampment.

P. G. David M. Lazarus, most worthy grand patriarch of the Grand encampment in 1878; grand warden of the Grand lodge in 1874, and grand conductor in 1877.

P. G. Charles R. Hunt, grand conductor in 1853.

P. G. Benjamin Cranage, grand guardian in 1855.

October 4, 1878, Mahoning lodge No. 29 gave a reception to the most worthy grand sire of the Sovereign Grand lodge, John B. Harmon, and to the order generally throughout the State. The writer of this sketch can do no better than to copy a few words from the report of this reception, given to the Grand lodge at its next session thereafter, by the then grand master, William S. Capellar, who was present at this reception visit of the most worthy grand sire of the Grand lodge of the Independent Order of Odd Fellows:

On the 1st of October, 1878, I was notified of the visit of this distinguished brother to the home of his childhood, and invited by the officers and members of Mahoning lodge No. 29, to unite in a general demonstration of welcoming the most worthy grand sire to the hearts and homes of the brethren of this jurisdiction. Accordingly, in company with our right worthy grand warden, Brother W. H. Pearce, we arrived on the morning of the 4th of October in the city of Warren, Trumbull county, and had the pleasure of meeting the largest and most enthusiastic gathering of Odd Fellows I had seen for a long time, gathered from all points of that section of the State. The city was literally alive with gay banners and music, all in honor of one who was born and educated in their midst, and after an absence of many years was visiting them as the honored head of an institution composed of a half million of men, whose motto is "friendship, love, and truth." Here we met and were greeted by the most worthy grand patriarch, D. M. Lazarus, and Past Grand Masters T. J. McLain, C. H. Babcock, Belden Seymour, and our Right Worthy Deputy Grand Master E. K. Wilcox, and a host of P. G's., and other worthy members. Here we, for the first time, grasped the hand of the most worthy grand sire and extended to him a hearty welcome among the Odd Fellows of Ohio. The ceremonies of the reception were grand and imposing, and reflected great credit on the brethren of Mahoning lodge, and will long be remembered by the friends of the order in Warren and vicinity. The response of Brother Harmon to the address of welcome from Brother P. G. M. McLain was very interesting and characteristic of the worthy brother.

Mahoning lodge has paid out since it was instituted, for the relief of the members and beneficiaries, and for charitable purposes, over $15,000.

Past Grand James Hoyt was initiated June 9, 1845; was elected noble grand in 1854; has served the lodge as one of its trustees for a majority of the years of its existence, and in the matters pertaining to the welfare of the lodge, as to all those of public interest or policy (and he has had much to do in shaping the affairs of our city and country), he has shown zeal, energy, and ability. He now (1882) lives at the age of about sixty-eight in Warren, west side, and has been all his life an active energetic worker in the cause of right.

Past Grand Master Thomas J. McLain, initiated March 10, 1845; elected noble grand in 1849; grand master of the State of Ohio in 1855; grand patriarch in 1854; has been elected representative to Grand lodge of the United States from the encampment branch of the order in 1850, and again in 1853; also representative to Grand lodge of the State, a number of times. Has been an able and efficient help in the business, legislative and executive departments of the order, and now, at the age of eighty, holds membership in the order, and is present at most of our lodge meetings.

INDEPENDENT ORDER ODD FELLOWS, ENCAMPMENT BRANCH, TRUMBULL COUNTY.

Pymatuning encampment No. 14 was instituted at Warren, May 12, 1846, but not proving very successful was removed to Youngstown, where it is now very prosperous.

Trumbull encampment No. 147 was instituted at Warren, July 21, 1871. The charter members were Charles R. Hunt, Leonard Burton, James G. Brooks, Daniel Bishop, Phineas Chase, Robert S. Elliott, John W. Masters, M. B. Dean, and D. M. Lazarus. It was instituted by C. L. Russell, most worthy grand patriarch, and Joseph Dowdall, right worthy grand scribe. It has now (1882) about fifty members and is making rapid progress in membership and finance.

An encampment was established in Niles, but for want of support and other reasons its charter was surrendered.

OTHER LODGES.

Independence lodge No. 9, Knights of Pythias, was instituted July 27, 1875. The ceremony on that occasion was conducted by Hon. John G. Thompson, of Columbus, grand chancellor of Ohio. There were twenty-four members, which number he increased to fifty. The first officers were L. M. Lazarus, past chancellor; G. B. Kennedy, C. C.; E. A. Cobleigh, V. C.; H. A. Potter, prelate; George H. Taylor, M. of F.; T. McQuiston, Jr., M. of E.; C. L. Hoyt, K. of R. and S.; F. M. Ritezel, M. of A.

There are also in Warren recently established lodges of the Royal Arcanum and Hibernians.

CHAPTER IX.

LEAVITTSBURG.

The little railroad village of Leavittsburg, in Warren township, is situated near the original platted village which the owners of this township intended should become the mercantile center. A public square facing the present railroad switch yards was set apart and remained an open common for half a century. But no town was ever started. The open bottom and better mill-sites further down the river was more potent in fixing the place of business than plats and original owners. Yet there was at one time fair prospects for the center village.

Samuel Forward built a saw-mill, and a few years later Richard Iddings built a grist-mill. Both these industries expedited improvement and attracted settlers. It was about the time the mill was completed that the name Leavittsburg was adopted as a compliment to the three Leavitt families whose land was around the square. This park was eventually incorporated into a farm on which it joined, and no vestige of a village remained. The present railroad village has sprung up since the completion of both lines of the New York, Pennsylvania & Ohio railroad.

It is proper that a few pioneers of Leavittsburg should be sketched. They were all closely identified with Warren.

As has been elsewhere stated, the original ownership of township four, range four, was vested in Ebenezer King, Jr., and John Leavitt. The latter removed with his family from Connecticut to Warren in the summer of 1800, and erected a cabin on the west side of Main street, which he afterwards converted into a public house of entertainment. The family consisted of Mrs. Silence Leavitt, William, John J., Cynthia, Sally, Henry F., Abdiah, Humphrey, and Albert. One of the girls married Robert Erwin, one of the first merchants, and another Wheeler Lewis. Humphrey Leavitt read law, and located in Steubenville. He afterwards received the appointment of United States district judge. Albert continued to live in the village of Warren. John Leavitt, Jr., settled on a farm near the center of Warren township about 1805. He was a well-to-do farmer, and raised a respected family. John Leavitt, Jr., known as Esquire John, died in Warren in 1815, being at the time county treasurer.

Samuel Leavitt, nicknamed Esquire Sam, was born in Connecticut, February 26, 1756. He visited the Reserve for the first time in 1800, and made a purchase of land in Warren township, adjoining the farm on which John Leavitt, Jr., afterwards settled. 'Squire Leavitt with his wife moved from Connecticut to Warren in 1802, and made an improvement on his farm. His was probably the first house in the center of the township. He had married in Connecticut Mrs. Abigail Kent Austin, mother of Benajah Austin. The fruit of this union was one child, Lynda, afterwards wife of Judge Francis Freeman. Mrs. Leavitt died September 4, 1816, aged sixty-six years. Mr. Leavitt removed to Warren in 1817, into a house on Main street. He married for his second wife Mrs. Margaret Kibbee Parsons, mother of George Parsons, Sr. His home until his death, which occurred August 4, 1830, was in Warren. Mrs. Margaret K. Leavitt died at Warren, March 5, 1841.

Esquire Enoch Leavitt was the third of the name who settled near Warren center. He was born in 1746; emigrated from Connecticut with his family during the first decade of settlement, and purchased the land on which the present village stands. He died in 1815, and is buried in Leavittsburg cemetery. His only son, Enoch Leavitt, Jr., was a young man when the family settled in Ohio, and soon became popular as a physician. Dr. Seeley in Howland, Dr. Harmon in Warren, and Dr. Leavitt at Leavittsburg were relied upon in cases of sickness by all the neighborhood within a radius of ten miles. Dr. Leavitt accumulated a large property, having about one thousand acres of land in Warren township at the time of his death. His children were Virgil, Daniel, Lorinda, Emeline, Lucius, and Parinthia, none of whom are now living. Dr. Leavitt died in 1827, at the age of fifty-two years.

Benajah Austin, another of the pioneers of the neighborhood of Leavittsburg, and a son of Mrs. Samuel Leavitt by a former husband, was born in Suffield, Connecticut, in the year 1779. From Connecticut he removed to Rupert, Vermont, and from there in 1803 to the Reserve. He married that spring Olive Harmon, and settled on what has been known as the Murberger farm, which was his first purchase. He soon afterwards removed to a farm in the center of Warren township, now owned by Harmon Austin, his son. Mr. Austin was one of the early public men, having been commissioner twelve years, part of the time while the whole Reserve was embraced in Trumbull county. He also served as deputy sheriff one year, and sheriff two terms. Mr. Austin was, however, essentially a farmer, and during his whole life devoted his untiring energies to that employment. His family consisted of six children: Hiram died at Chardon; Julius, living at Braceville; Enos, living at Youngstown; Amelia (deceased March, 1876), wife of S. A. Potter; Benajah died at Warren, and Harmon residing in Warren. Mr. Austin died in February, 1849. His son Benajah read medicine, and practiced for a short time in Warren, but losing his health, he retired on a farm. He died in March, 1871, aged fifty-eight years. Harmon Austin, who succeeded to the old homestead farm, was born in 1817. He lived on the farm till 1870, and then removed to Warren, his present home. He married Minerva Sackett, of Canfield. Their family consists of three children living. Mr. Austin has been engaged in the lumber and flagstone trade. He has been president of the Warren Flagstone company since its formation in 1872. All the handsome and durable flagging of which the excellent sidewalks of Warren are made came from this company's quarry.

One of the earliest settlers on the present site of Leavittsburg was Phineas Leffingwell. His brother Jabez settled in the same neighborhood in 1818. Of the latter's family there were eight children, three of whom survive. Lucy R., widow of Alvin Fobes, resides in Warren.

CHAPTER X.
BIOGRAPHICAL SKETCHES.
QUINBY FAMILY.

Ephraim Quinby, practically the first settler and founder of Warren, was born in New Jersey, May 11, 1766. He married Ammi Blackmore, at Brownsville, in 1795, and settled in Washington county, Pennsylvania; thence removed to Trumbull county in 1799, at which time the family consisted of three childen, Nancy, Samuel, and Abrilla. Seven children were born in Warren —Elizabeth, William, Mary G., James, Warren B., Ephraim, Jr., Charles A., and George. Mr. Quinby during his lifetime was a man of considerable prominence in the community and acquired considerable wealth by the fortunate location of his land. He served several years as associate judge of the common pleas court and took an active part in organizing the county. His life was devoted chiefly to dealing in real estate and farming. His death occurred June 4, 1850. Mrs. Amma Quinby died March 16, 1833. Four of the family are yet living—Nancy, wife of Joseph H. Larwell, Wooster, Ohio; Mary G. Spellman, Wooster, Ohio; Warren B., Warren, Ohio, and George, Wooster, Ohio. Warren B. Quinby has always made his home in Warren. He married in 1840 Rebecca Hixon, daughter of Timothy Hixon, who settled here in 1812 on a farm, and died in 1868. They have had two children, both dead—Ephraim and Amma Elizabeth. Samuel Quinby, oldest son of Ephraim Quinby, was born in Pennsylvania, November 27, 1794. His name is first found in business annals in 1814, as a member of the firm of James White & Co., publishers of The Trump of Fame. He was again connected with the paper from 1817 to 1819.

Having received the appointment of receiver of moneys derived from the sale of United States public lands, Mr. Quinby removed to Wooster, Ohio, in 1819. The land office for the district of Northwestern Ohio was then located at that place. The office was abolished during Van Buren's administration and in 1840 Mr. Quinby returned to Warren. While at Wooster he had been a candidate on the Whig ticket for Representative in Congress, but the district being Democratic he was defeated. On returning to Warren he was chosen secretary and treasurer of the Ohio and Pennsylvania canal, which office he held several years. Outside of official business Mr. Quinby was otherwise actively employed. He dealt largely in real estate, and directed farming operations. He was one of the original stockholders in the Western Reserve bank, as was also his father, and was elected to the directorship in 1817. Considerable outside

business, such as the settlement of estates in probate, was transacted by him. Mr. Quinby was an active politician. He served two terms in the Ohio Senate, first in 1844-45, and again in 1862-63. He married at Steubenville, December 30, 1819, Lucy Potter. Two daughters by this marriage are living, Elizabeth (Stiles) and Abigail (Haymaker), both in Warren. For his second wife he married Mrs. Emma B. Brown, October 22, 1847. George H. Quinby is the only son living. Samuel Quinby died in Warren February 4, 1874. Mrs. Quinby remains a resident of Warren.

Elizabeth Quinby, the daughter of Ephraim Quinby, Sr., was married to Dr. Heaton, of Warren. She died in Warren. William Quinby was recorder of Trumbull county a number of years and afterwards engaged in mercantile business in Warren, where he died. James was also in trade in Warren, then removed to New Lisbon, where he died. Ephraim, Jr., settled at Wooster, Ohio, being at the time of his death the wealthiest man in the place. Charles A. died in Warren.

HENRY LANE AND FAMILY.

Henry Lane's settlement in Warren was noted at the proper place, but no idea was there given of the man. He was industrious and thoroughgoing. The first mill in Warren was built by him, and the first apple trees planted by him. In company with most of the other first settlers, he was present at the Indian tragedy at Salt Springs, but was in no way responsible for that unfortunate affair. Mr. Lane represented Trumbull county in the Legislature four terms—1816-18-19 and 1826. He was a man of extraordinary strength, which alone, in a new country, is a certificate to respectability. It was claimed that he could whip anybody in the county, and when a bully advertised himself for a fight he always excepted Henry Lane. He was considered an excellent man for the Legislature because of his strength. But he had other claims to public confidence, being a good man and citizen. His son Asa returned to Pennsylvania in 1820, and died there. Henry Lane had two daughters—Catharine, who married John Tait, a Lordstown settler, and Annie, who married Samuel Phillips, of Austintown. John, Asa, and Benjamin were the three sons. Benjamin Lane was born in Washington county, in 1785, and came with his parents to Warren in 1799. The farm on which they settled is now owned by Henry J. Lane. This farm consisted of one hundred and thirty acres. He was married in 1841 to Hannah Cook, a native of England. They raised a family of three children, viz: Henry J., born February 11, 1843, married in 1866 Anna Murdock, and has a family of two children—Harry E. and Grace M.; Benjamin F., born May 3, 1850, married in 1879 Mary Ackley, of Bloomfield, and has one child—Lina, resides in Lordstown; Mary S., born April 24, 1853, is married to Samuel Greiner, and resides in Lordstown. Benjamin Lane engaged largely in buying and selling live stock, and driving them over the mountains to Philadelphia. Mrs. Lane died in 1853, Mr. Lane in 1866.

John Lane was born in Pennsylvania in 1793. He married in Mansfield, Ohio, Mary Caldwell, and in 1821 removed from Mansfield, where he resided, to Trumbull county, and settled in Weathersfield and engaged in farming. He finally removed to Warren, where he spent the balance of his life. He died in 1854 in his sixty-second year. His widow is still living, in her eighty-eighth year.

E. C. Lane, the oldest of the surviving children, was born in 1829, in Weathersfield. He is an engineer by occupation, and is now employed in the Packard planing mill in Warren.

JAMES L. VAN GORDER.

Few men, if any, have ever lived in Warren of greater energy of character or more effective activity of life than James L. VanGorder. Some idea of the man is gained from a mere statement of the predominant fact of his life—the fact that notwithstanding heavy and embarrassing losses and with no other capital to start with than a strong, healthy body, indomitable perseverance and industry, united with a sound judgment, he accumulated an estate amounting to $125,000.

James L. VanGorder was the son of Abram and Elizabeth VanGorder, and was born in Sussex county, New Jersey, April 1, 1785. He came to Warren at the age of about twenty years, and having a ready hand for almost any kind of work, had no difficulty in finding employment. But he was not the kind of metal that hirelings are made of. After a short time of service under Henry Lane in his mill and clearing, he began boldly and with perseverance an independent career.

In 1809 Mr. VanGorder married Elizabeth, daughter of Robert Spear, who was born at Washington, Pennsylvania, February 13, 1789. Her parents having died she became a resident in the family of her grandparents, and came to Trumbull county with her uncle, John Prior, in the year 1805. As was very common at that time the trip was made on horseback. One hundred miles' journey would seem like a great task for a girl of sixteen, but it was lightened by exercise in that method of travel. Mr. Prior settled a mile and a half s southwest of Warren.

About two years after his marriage Mr. Van Gorder removed to Suffield, Portage county, and engaged in milling on an extensive scale. He ran a train of flour wagons to Cleveland harbor, and soon built up a business surpassing any of the kind on the Reserve, at that time. In 1821 Mr. VanGorder returned with his family to Warren, having become interested in the mills of this place. The upper dam and mill had been built by Henry Lane, and the lower mill by George Lovelace, the latter being just below the Market-street bridge. (The present lower dam was built by Mr. VanGorder in 1838-39. He built at the same time four of the locks in the canal adjoining, and made a mile of excavation.) The control of both of these mills, in addition to two saw-mills, did not occupy his whole attention for any great length of time. He purchased in 1828 the old Cotgreave house, more familiarly known as Castle William, and by getting the stage office and stage patronage he soon made it the leading hotel in the place. "Old Pavilion" was a familiar name among travelers, and especially among coachmen. Seven stages passed through Warren daily, giving the " regulation tavern " a good patronage outside of irregular custom. On the ground floor was a stage office, a bar-room, and a store; the second floor was used for bed-chambers, and the third for a dancing hall. This was the same building in which John S. Edwards speaks in his letters of having attended balls. The house had undergone repairs, however.

Mr. VanGorder was an extensive contractor on the Ohio and Pennsylvania canal, employing at one time as many as one hundred hands, fifty of whom were boarded at the "Pavilion." The completeness and thoroughness of his operations are shown by the fact that he had his own wagonmaker shop, his own blacksmith shop, his own tavern to board his men, and his own mills to grind the flour for their bread; and further than this, raised some of the wheat which was ground into flour. Mrs. VanGorder superintended all the cooking and baking, which was no light task, for dinners for the laborers had to be sent to their place of work. Anyone who has had any experience, even in a small way, of preparing food to be eaten in that way will readily appreciate the task of thus making dinners for fifty masons and shovelers.

One of the upper mills burned in October, 1845, but was rebuilt as quickly as was possible. In the great conflagration in June, 1846, the old Pavilion tavern was reduced to ashes. Before a year had elapsed, a block containing six stores stood in its place. This block was in turn consumed in 1854, but before the living flames had exhausted their food, a contract had been signed for rebuilding the entire block. The second block was again partially destroyed in 1860. During the five years preceding the fire of 1854, and including that conflagration, Mr. VanGorder's losses by fire, and his losses as surety, for which he had obligated himself to a large amount, aggregated over $34,000, yet he never permitted himself to be embarrassed, depending upon industry to regain what he lost through misfortune.

He was characteristically successful in the management of hired labor. His own strength being inexhaustible he was always able to lead. He seldom said "go," but "come" was a familiar command. Week after week for as long as six weeks in succession, he has stood in water covering his knees, repairing some of the mill appendages. Never did he require of a hireling what he was unwilling to do himself. In addition to other operations, he carried on merchandising for about forty years. Mr. VanGorder was a member of the Presbyterian church. Mrs. VanGorder's connection with that society antedates that of her husband. She still retains her membership. During his older years he was a

Elizabeth S. Van Gorder.

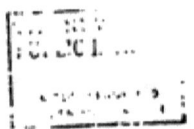

partial cripple, having met with an accident at his saw-mill. He was not incapacitated, however, for any kind of work. He was actively employed until the sickness which resulted in his death, September 14, 1858.

Mrs. VanGorder, now past her ninety-fourth year, is the oldest resident of Warren; with two exceptions she is the oldest person living in the city. Her long preservation through a toilsome life is indeed remarkable. She is clear in mind and cheerful in disposition. She has borne a family of thirteen children, and nurtured from childhood two grandchildren. Eleven of her children lived to mature age. The following is a copy of a page from the family record: Albert, born in Warren July 18, 1810; Emeline, born in Suffield November 5, 1811; Olive, born in Suffield April 26, 1813; Cyrus J., born in Suffield April 1, 1815; Martha J. (Newell), born in Suffield January 7, 1817; Ann Mary (Marvin), born in Suffield August 30, 1819; Phebe, born in Warren June 11, 1821; Betsy (Scott), born in Warren April 22, 1823; James R., born in Warren March 30, 1825; George, born in Warren May 8, 1827; Isaac F., born in Warren February 18, 1829; Charles, born in Warren March 8, 1831; Charles, (second) April 15, 1836. Albert, Cyrus J., Martha J. (Newell), Ann Mary (Marvin), James R., George, and Isaac F., are still living.

RICHARD IDDINGS

was born in Berks county, Pennsylvania, August 18, 1786. He came to Warren in September, 1805, but returned to Reading in 1808, where, in January, 1809, he married Miss Justina Lewis. In February he started for the Reserve with his wife, and reached Warren April 20th. He was in the War of 1812, and was afterwards chosen major in the militia. He was elected to the Legislature in 1830-31. His death took place March 26, 1872.

At his golden wedding, in 1859, Mr. Iddings gave the following description of his trip to the Reserve with his wife:

I first came to Warren in September, 1805, and remained here until the fall of 1808, when I returned to Berks county, my native place. I married Miss Justina Lewis, at Reading, Pennsylvania, on the evening of the 15th of January, 1809, at 8 o'clock just fifty years ago. On the 8th of February we started for Ohio in a two-horse sleigh, with our household furniture, for which there was plenty of room. When we reached the top of the Allegheny mountains the snow was four feet deep; but we learned there was no snow at the foot of the mountain, nor westward to Ohio. Therefore, we went to the house of an uncle to my wife, who resided in Fayette county, some twelve miles from Brownsville. Leaving her, the sleigh, and one horse, I proceeded to this place on horseback. Here I hired a canoe, and, engaging Mr. Henry Harsh to assist me, I went down the Mahoning and Beaver rivers to Beaverton, and up the Ohio and Monongahela to Brownsville. Taking my wife and a few household fixings on board, we floated down to Pittsburg, where I purchased a barrel of flour, and went on to Warren. The weather was quite cold, and the settlers few and scattering. Some nights we lodged in houses near the river, and sometimes on its bank, without shelter. Sometimes we had plenty to eat, and sometimes we went without food for a whole day. We were two days getting over the falls of Beaver river. Mr. Harsh and myself were most of the time in the water (frequently up to our waists), pulling up the empty canoe, while my wife sat on the shore watching the goods which we had landed. At the mill-dams on the Mahoning the same process was repeated. We reached Warren on the 20th day of April, having been twenty-one days coming from Brownsville.

LEICESTER KING

was born May 1, 1789, at Suffield, Connecticut. He married, October 12, 1814, Julia Ann Huntington, daughter of Hon. Hezekiah Huntington, of Hartford, Connecticut, and died at North Bloomfield, Trumbull county, Ohio, September 19, 1856, at the residence of his son-in-law, Charles Brown.

Mr. King removed from Westfield, Massachusetts, where he was engaged in the mercantile business for a few years, to Warren, Ohio, in 1817, where he continued the same business until 1833. At that time, becoming interested in the project of building the Pennsylvania and Ohio canal, he abandoned mercantile life, and devoted the most of his time to forwarding that enterprise; and it was mainly through his energy and labor that it was finally constructed—he being for a long time the president of the company. He filled the position of associate judge of the court of common pleas, and represented the Trumbull district for two successive sessions (1835-39) in the State Senate. He was a decided Abolitionist, although elected as a Whig, and at each session introduced and advocated a bill to repeal the infamous "Black laws," which then disgraced our statute books. After the spirited Presidential contest of 1840 he identified himself with the few who organized the

Liberty party, and was the first candidate for Governor nominated by that party in 1842; and he was renominated in 1844. As the champion of that forlorn hope he thoroughly canvassed the State, discussing its platform of principles in every county and in almost every school district. He was president of the first United States Liberty party convention, held in Buffalo in 1844, which put in nomination James G. Birney as candidate for President, and Thomas Morris for Vice President of the United States. In 1847 Mr. King was the nominee for Vice President, with John P. Hale for President; both, however, declined the nomination in favor of Martin Van Buren and Charles Francis Adams, as candidates for the Free-soil party—the Liberty party thereafter being merged into this new party of anti-slavery principles. After the death of Mrs. King, January 24, 1849, Mr. King withdrew from politics, although he continued, until the day of his death, a warm advocate of the principles for which he had declined all political preferment and personal position from the old Whig party.

The earnest zeal with which he sowed the seed through the State of Ohio required but a few years to bring forth an abundant harvest of right sentiments, and had its due share in the successful contest for human rights, which resulted in placing Abraham Lincoln in the executive chair in 1861.

SIMON PERKINS*

was born at Norwich, Connecticut, on the 17th of September, 1771. His father was a captain in the army of the Revolution, and died in camp. He emigrated to Oswego, New York, in 1795, where he spent three years in extensive land operations. A portion of the Western Reserve in Ohio having been sold by the State of Connecticut, the new proprietors invited Mr. Perkins to explore the domain and report a plan for the sale and settlement of the lands. He went to Ohio for that purpose in the spring of 1798. He spent the summer there in the performance of the duties of his agency, and returned to Connecticut in the autumn. This excursion and these duties were repeated by him for several successive summers. He married in 1804, and settled on the Reserve at Warren. So extensive

* From Lossing's Field Book of the War of 1812.

were the land agencies intrusted to him that in 1815 the State land tax paid by him into the public treasury was one-seventh of the entire revenue of the State.

For twenty-eight years he received and merited the confidence of the department and the people. At the request of the Government, in 1807 he established expresses through the Indian country to Detroit. His efforts led to the treaty of Brownsville, in the autumn of 1808, when the Indians ceded lands for a road from the Reserve to the Maumee or Miami of the lakes. In May of that year he was commissioned a brigadier-general of militia, in the division commanded by Major-general Wadsworth. On hearing of the disaster to Hull's army at Detroit, he issued orders to his colonels to prepare their regiments for active duty. To him was assigned the duty of protecting a large portion of the northwestern frontier.

"To the care of Brigadier-general Simon Perkins I commit you," said Wadsworth, on parting with the troops of the Reserve, "who will be your commander and your friend. In his integrity, skill, and courage we all have the utmost confidence." He was exceedingly active. His scouts were out far and near continually.

His public accounts were kept with the greatest clearness and accuracy for more than forty years. "No two officers in the public service at that time," testifies the Hon. Elisha Whittlesey, "were more energetic or economical than Generals Harrison and Perkins."

When, in 1813, General Harrison was sufficiently reinforced to dispense with Perkins' command, he left the service (February 28, 1813) bearing the highest encomiums of the commander-in-chief of the army of the Northwest.

President Madison, at the suggestion of Harrison and others, sent him the commission of colonel in the regular army, but duty to his family and the demands of a greatly increasing business caused him to decline it. General Perkins was intrusted with the arrangement and execution, at the head of a commission, of the extensive canal system of Ohio. From 1826 until 1838 he was an active member of the "Board of Canal Fund Commissioners." They were under no bonds and received no pecuniary reward. In the course of about seven years they issued and sold State bonds for the public improvements, to the amount of $4,500,000.

Among the remarkable men who settled the Western Reserve General Simon Perkins ever held one of the most conspicuous places, and his influence in social and moral life is felt in that region to this day. He died at Warren, Ohio, on the 19th of November, 1844. His widow long survived him. She died at the same place, April, 1862.

HENRY BISHOP PERKINS,

president of the First National bank of Warren, was the youngest son of General Simon Perkins, and was born March 19, 1824. He pursued the course of instruction provided by local schools until his twenty-first year, when the death of his father threw upon him the management of a large property. Being naturally public-spirited, and having a heavy personal interest, he naturally became identified with public affairs. But he carried this interest beyond the measure of personal advantage. When the graded school system had been organized, he accepted a position on the school board, and labored faithfully in that capacity for several years. He joined his brothers in endowing a professorship in Western Reserve college, and otherwise exerted himself to promote the cause of education. He inherited a large landed estate to which personal attention has always been given. Agricultural pursuits being particularly suited to his tastes, he served twice as president of the county agricultural society, and two times on the State board of agriculture. When the Ohio Agricultural and Mechanical college was established, he was appointed one of its trustees.

Mr. Perkins was a stockholder in the Cleveland & Mahoning railroad, and subsequently became a director. He was elected one of the directors of the Western Reserve bank in 1852, and on the organization of the First National bank was chosen president. He has served in that capacity since that time. This is the oldest bank in Northern Ohio.

Mr. Perkins inherited the Whig principles of his family, and on the organization of the Republican party he became a leading member and worker. He received the appointment in 1861 of agent for the sale of the first national loan. In 1878 he was appointed by the Governor on a commission of three persons to serve with a similar commission from Pennsylvania, to re-establish the boundary line between Ohio and Pennsylvania.

In 1879 Mr. Perkins was chosen to represent his Senatorial district in the General Assembly of Ohio, and was re-elected in 1881. He is recognized as a leading member of that body, and his advice is respected on all matters of business and public policy. His bearing in the Senate is that of a business man rather than of the politician. He is there in the service of his district and the State. In this respect he is unlike a majority of his colleagues. It is a notorious and unfortunate fact that our State Legislature is largely composed of office seekers.

Mr. Perkins is a member of the Presbyterian church, to which he has contributed liberally. Socially his standing is as high as in business circles. He is a good type of his family, dignified and honest, clear-headed and energetic.

Mr. Perkins married, in 1855, Miss Eliza G. Baldwin, daughter of N. C. Baldwin, of Cleveland. They have a family of four children. The Perkins residence is the finest in Warren, and the grounds, which embrace a number of acres, are artistically improved. It is the old family seat of Simon Perkins.

FREDERICK KINSMAN

was born in Kinsman township, Trumbull county, March 4, 1807. His education until his eighteenth year was confined to the common schools of his native township, with the exception of one summer at Geauga academy. In February, 1825, in company with his oldest brother, he rode on horseback to Connecticut, where he then sold his horse and entered Plainfield academy. After spending a year at the academy he entered the military school at Camp Partridge, at Middletown, Connecticut. A diversion of school-days' monotony which is remembered with interest, was a visit to New York on the semi-centennial of American independence (July 4, 1826). Three hundred cadets, all in bright uniform and fully armed, were conveyed to the city in a boat and participated in the parade. He remembers to have seen on that day Aaron Burr, erect, clear-eyed, and with flowing white hair, watching the ceremonies but scarce receiving any recognition. The fallen politician may be gazed upon but is never courted.

Mathematics and engineering occupied the greater part of Mr. Kinsman's time while in the military academy. Late in the year 1826 his class was detailed to make a topographical exploration of the country. While thus engaged he was prostrated by typhus fever as the result of a day of over-exertion. He had traveled one morning to a high point on the Meriden mountains to establish a flag-station—a distance of about ten miles. He reached a point from which could be seen Hartford, New Haven, Middletown, and other cities, where he set up a flag and returned to Middletown that night, completing a laborious trip of more than twenty miles through brambles, woods, and over rocks. The fever which set in on the following day confined him for some time, eventually terminating his academic career.

Mr. Kinsman, on returning to Ohio, engaged in his brother's store as clerk until the year 1830. He was then employed two years in the land office of General Perkins, at Warren, at the end of which time he married Olive D. Perkins. In 1832 he became a partner in the land business with Mr. Perkins, and eventually assumed entire charge of the office. Mr. Perkins' agency was the largest in the State, the taxes one year being one-fifteenth part of all the land taxes in the State of Ohio.

Mr. Perkins was agent for the Erie company and for Daniel L. Coit. The Erie company's business was settled up in General Perkins's lifetime, but the Coit agency business was not finally closed out until 1872, by Mr. Kinsman. This was the last of Western Reserve land agencies. Mr. Kinsman was elected to the office of associate judge in 1845—an office of little profit.

He took an active interest in public affairs, and enterprises calculated to enhance the value of property. As one of the original directors of the Cleveland & Mahoning railroad he exerted all his energy, and was one of the six to assume personal liability, that the road might be completed and placed upon a remunerative basis. The Mahoning valley owes more to Jacob Perkins, Frederick Kinsman, Charles Smith, David Tod, Dudley Baldwin, and Reuben Hitchcock, than any other six men in the Reserve. Mr. Kinsman was a director of the Western Reserve bank until its conversion into a National bank, and has continued in the same office since that time. He served several years as a member of the city council, and not only favored measures looking toward the improvement of streets, etc., but gave much time and personal attention to the work.

Mr. Kinsman has not been a politician in the ordinary meaning of that term, but has always been active in furthering the interests of his party, and has never shrunk from the obligations of citizenship. He was a delegate to the National Republican convention in 1864, and Presidential elector in 1868. During the war he aided the Union cause in a substantial way. He has long been looked upon as a leader in matters of public improvement. He is an attendant and liberal supporter of the Episcopal church. Mr. Kinsman has been a careful agriculturist and judicious stock man. He was long prominently identified with the county agricultural society, and for two years its president.

Mrs. Olive Perkins Kinsman died in 1838. Mr. Kinsman married for his second wife Miss Cornelia G. Pease, daughter of Judge Calvin Pease. She died in 1873. The children of his first wife died young. Four sons by his second wife are living—Frederick, Jr., in Cleveland; John, Thomas, and Charles P., in Warren. Mr. Kinsman is well preserved for a man of his years. He is tall, erect, and dignified. His manner is firm but clever. He possesses that keen appreciation of pure humor which characterizes a clear mind.

Mrs. John B. Harmon.

COMFORT MYGATT.

In 1807 there settled in Canfield a family, several members of which afterwards became prominent in Warren business affairs. The head of this family was Comfort Mygatt. Accompanying the party from Connecticut were three sons-in-law with their wives and families—Lewis Hoyt, Eli S. Bouton, and Elisha Whittlesey; eight daughters—Elizabeth, afterwards married to Zalmon Fitch of Warren; Lucy, afterwards wife of Asahel Adams, of Warren (the oldest lady living in the city); and Maria, who died unmarried; Amanda, who married William McFarlane, of Warren; Eleanor, who married Allison Kent, of Canfield; Hannah, who married W. S. C. Otis, of Cleveland; Juliana, and Almira; three sons—George, Comfort, and Eli, and two step-sons, Jairus and Henry Stiles.

JOHN B. HARMON AND FAMILY.

Northern Ohio is justly noted for the intelligence, energy, integrity, and thrift of her people. Her pioneers came from the best New England families. They came with the grand purpose of founding a new State in which the rights of man and the consequent happiness of the people should be amply secured. They had the knowledge and the means requisite to a greater degree than almost any other portion of the West. They foresaw the hardships they would have to endure, but had the will to face them with unswerving courage. The toils, privations, and fatigues of pioneer life fall upon none more heavily than the physician who enjoys the general support, and ministers faithfully to the wants of such a settlement. The pioneer doctors of northern Ohio were admirably fitted for their work. Strong, enduring in body, sagacious and fertile of mind, resolute and daring, they went everywhere among the settlers, lights amid darkness, beacons of hope in hours of peril, and almoners of help in time of need. Of no one of them is this more rigidly true, than of the subject of this sketch. Six feet tall, with a round, full chest, a bundle of muscle and nerve of the finest quality, a high, square forehead jutting over deep, bluish-gray eyes, whose smile could hold the love of woman at their pleasure, or whose frown could cow a fiend, he commanded the life-long respect and friendship of the early pioneers of the Western Reserve. This imposed upon him an amount of work and responsibility which very few men could ever have met so well.

His early life fitted him for the part he was to play in after life. In helping his father carry on a large farming business in Vermont, he early began a life of exposure, often going through the winter storms on foot, with his dog and gun, from the home or Valley farm to one several miles off up the mountains. His father, Reuben Harmon, Jr., was an extensive landholder, and had been a member of the Vermont Legislature or assembly for a number of terms, and had the privilege of coining copper coins upon his own responsibility, which was in those days no light distinction. In 1796 he purchased of Samuel H. Parsons, five hundred acres of land embracing the "salt springs," in Weathersfield township, and went there in the summer or fall of 1797, and began the manufacture of salt, which he continued through the winter, and returned home in the spring.

It is not known to the writer whether he left any one to continue the salt manufacture during the summer or not, but each fall and winter he returned and continued the business, and erected a cabin to become the future home of his family. In the early spring of 1800 he returned to Vermont and prepared for the final removal to the new field, which seemed to promise so much to one of his vigor and activity. An old settler of Warren, John Ewalt, said of him, "He was the smartest man I ever knew, and Doctor John B. is exactly like him. Looks like him, walks like him, talks like him, is exactly like him in all respects." He illustrated his idea of smartness by adding that "he was a general business man to draw deeds, contracts, and settle disputes. He could converse with a room full of people, fifteen or twenty, all at once, hear them tell their story, and write at the same time, and when done no word had to be erased or another to be put in. He could do as many things at a time as he needed to, and do each exactly right." While the feat is not so very difficult to one accustomed to such work, it doubtless indicates an unusual expertness and accuracy.

Having all things ready, the family started in June for the far West. Besides his wife, four daughters and four sons, the youngest, Reuben third, being a babe three months old, he brought a family with him by the name of Barnes, who afterwards settled in Fowler. While wending their slow way thither, fresh disturbances with the Indians occurred, and they halted some time at Beaver, so that they did not arrive at the salt springs till August.

Young Harmon had begun the study of medicine in 1796, with Dr. Josiah Blackmer, and was prepared to practice so far as the wants of the family and the few scattered settlers should require. In the spring of 1806 Reuben Harmon, Jr., returned to Vermont to finish settling his business there. He took with him his son to pursue study further with Dr. Blackmer, who had married his elder sister Ruth, and was a skillful physician in Dorset, Vermont. Upon his return west Reuben Harmon found the agent whom he had left in charge of the salt works had disappeared with $2,000, part of which he had collected from sales of salt, and part had been sent on before his return. Thus stripped of his means he was called to all the harder work for the support of his family. In the midst of it he was taken with fever, and died October 29, 1806, in the fifty-seventh year of his age. His loss was a sad blow to his family, and caused much inconvenience to the settlement. For nearly ten years he had made them their salt, and been a leading man among them. He had been for many years a member of the Congregational church of Rupert, Vermont, and in 1803 united by letter with the First Presbyterian church of Warren, and was noted for his decided piety, kindness to all, and rigid integrity. From a condition of independence and prospective affluence, the family were left in comparative poverty. His widow proved equal to the occasion. Ruth Rising was a daughter of Aaron and Anna Rising, of Suffield, Connecticut; was married to Mr. Harmon in September, 1774. She was a resolute, capable woman, above average height, of a broad, muscular build, sociable, cheerful, and of indomitable patience and perseverance.

During the war of the Revolution Reuben Harmon, Jr., was in the revolutionary army, and his wife either resided with his father at Sunderland, Massachusetts, or was there on a visit when it was burned by the British and Indians. Mrs. Harmon caught an unbroken colt in the field and mounted it, bare-back, with a babe three weeks old in her arms, and fled while the smoke of her husband's early home rolled up behind her. One of such pluck was well fitted to be the first white woman in Weathersfield township. Fearless amid semi-hostile Indians, and strong in every hour of trial. The babe she had carried in her arms during the long journey west was scalded to death in 1802. May 10th of that year their youngest child, Eliza, who afterwards married Reuben Allen, and died in Illinois March 2, 1856, was born. She was a lively girl, full of song and mirth, a favorite in social gatherings, and an unfailing fountain of cheer wherever she went.

One day Mrs. Harmon was left alone in the cabin and three intoxicated Indians intruded with threatening demands for more whiskey, which she sturdily refused, and had a hard day's work to keep them from violence. At dark young Harmon returned from a day's hunting. Awhile after supper the Indians became again more violent, especially one of them, "Big Bill" as he was called, who envied the young white's skill with the rifle, was determined on whiskey or a fight. Young Harmon instantly threw him, and bumped his head soundly on the hearth, and bade him lie there until morning. When he left he brought his gun to his shoulder, and pointing to Harmon gave a whoop of vengeance. After that Big Bill and the young doctor when out hunting kept one eye for deer and one eye for the "the first shot." A sudden attack of lung fever soon after ended the strife. Passing the camp toward night, Dr. Harmon heard loud lamentations. Going in he found his enemy in the last agonies of pain, and was glad that he was relieved from shooting him or being shot himself.

Such incidents disclose some of the special perils of the new settlers.

Mrs. Harmon met all her trials with rare fortitude and sagacity. She spent the last few years of her life in Warren, at the homes of Dr. Harmon and her son, Heman R. Harmon, at whose house—a brick on the corner of Main street and Franklin alley, which he had erected with the aid of his father-in-law, George Parsons, about 1829 or 1830—she died, April 10, 1836, in her seventy-eighth year, of congestion of the lungs. She kept bright, cheerful, and active, with a large share of the enjoyments of a ripe old age. She was a member of the Methodist church in Warren for many years, and died in the full hopes of such a faith. Thus much of the parents of Dr. Harmon. His grandfather, Reuben Harmon, was the sixty-fourth descendant of John Harman (so spelled in the records), who immigrated from England prior to 1644, when he settled in Springfield, Massachusetts, and died January 7, 1660. Reuben was his great-grandson, born at Sunderland, Massachusetts, or perhaps at Springfield, February 18, 1714, and married Eunice Parsons, of Suffield, Connecticut, August 25, 1739. He died at Rutland, Vermont, September 6, 1794. His widow died there November 18, 1803, aged eighty-six years. He sold his real estate in Suffield in 1759. In 1776 he became a large land owner in Rupert. In 1779 he bought one hundred and seventy acres in Rutland, and soon after moved there, and was selectman and justice of the peace in 1780. June 30, 1780, he conveyed to his son Oliver, in Rutland, ninety acres of land, and to his son Reuben, Jr., of Rupert, ninety acres. Some forty-five deeds passed to and from Reuben and Reuben, Jr., in the course of a few years. Dr. John B. appears to have had a leaning to land also, for in 1803 he bought of his father two hundred and fifty acres of the Salt Spring tract for $2,500 in currency, which was resold in 1806. He became the owner afterwards of some two hundred and eighty acres in Warren township, and carried on farming quite extensively. He devoted special care to raising thoroughbred horses, but kept also choice cattle and Merino sheep, and invested in mules also to a large extent. He made himself the first horse-rake used in this section, from a fence rail, eleven feet long, in which a few long teeth were put, and two stakes for handles. Hitching a large stallion called "Buck Oscar" (a racer who had never had harness on before) to this, he raked up in the afternoon nine acres of heavy grass. The weight of the rake and rapid gait of the horse made this a very hard feat. The stoutest of his hired men could not repeat it. When this rake was broken a few years later Hugh Riddle, who was in Warren temporarily, made him a light one, but it was not until several years later he could persuade his brother farmers to give up the hand-rake.

At an early day he established his brother, Heman R. Harmon, in trade under the firm name of Harmon Brothers. The store was on the west side of Main street, south of one formerly occupied by Ephraim Quinby. In connection with Walter King they built the three story brick in 1827-28, known as the King and Harmon block, which was, in April, 1882, torn down. Harmon Brothers occupied the north half, keeping drugs in the south end and dry-goods in the north end. It had a handsome cherry circular counter, and was regarded as a grand affair in its day. King occupied the south end of his half with a jewelry store. Henry Stiles had the north part of King's half (a separate room) for a saddlery store. There the late Edward E. Hoyt, James Hoyt, and O. H. Patch, learned the saddler's trade.

Harmon Brothers lost largely by outside business, dealing in cattle, clocks, etc., and by endorsing for others. In 1832 they failed. The debts were eventually paid, by Dr. Harmon mostly, but the loss stript him of his farms, and imposed on him the necessity of prolonged toil in his profession. He never did business in the store himself, but his surplus earnings were absorbed by it. In fact, his whole life was helpful to others far more than to himself.

Upon the death of his father, he naturally assumed the guidance of the family. While at Dorset he wrote his brothers Hiram and Heman "to be careful of their leisure hours, to shun all bad habits, study evenings, so as to fit themselves for future usefulness and honorable positions in life, and to cherish always a reverent regard for the great Author of the Universe." Afterwards he sent Heman to school at Cannonsburg, Pennsylvania, with the view of his studying medicine, but exposure led to necrosis of the femur, a large part of which the doctor removed. He was left slightly lame, and gave up the study of medicine to become a merchant, farmer, and general business man, in which he was remarkably active, industrious, and useful, but a fatality adverse to financial success hovered over him.

Of the children of Reuben Harmon, the following additional particulars may be of some interest:

Anna Harmon was born February 20, 1782, in Rupert; died March, 1841, in Bristol. She was for many years employed as a school teacher in different townships of the county, and is still remembered by some of the older descendants of the pioneers as the woman who could teach them arithmetic.

Clary Harmon was born April 12, 1785; married William Leavitt, son of John Leavitt, Esq., of Warren, from whom she was divorced because of intemperance. Afterwards she married Dr. John Brown, and moved to Lancaster, New York, where she died January 22, 1844. She was a very pleasant, agreeable, exemplary woman.

Betsey Harmon was born November 12, 1788, and died November 7, 1853; married Samuel Gilson, by whom she had a son, Reuben H. Gilson, and two daughters—Mary, who married Henry McGlathery, of Bristol, and Julia, who married Hugh Lackey, of Youngstown, who live now in Hartsgrove, Ashtabula county. After the death of Mr. Gilson, she married Albert Opdycke, and lived in Hubbard till 1836, when they moved to Pulaski, Williams county, Ohio, where they prospered greatly—one of the happiest families to be met with anywhere. Dr. Harmon prized them both very highly, and made them two visits with his wife and other relatives, which were full of pleasure to all. Dr. Harmon was an overflowing fountain of life and fun on such occasions. His last visit was in 1854. By a break in the canal they were detained a day at Toledo. At the hotel a professional checker player had cleaned out the company at a dollar a game. Dr. Harmon wore a long dressing gown and broad brimmed hat, and gravely invited the gamester to play for amusement, which was contemptuously refused. The gamester kept inquiring, "Well, old man, have you got your courage up to risking a dollar yet?" "I have never played for money, and am too old now to break my rule," was the answer. The company were anxious to take their chance on the "Old Man," but the temptation was resisted till late in the afternoon the gamester grew too impudent to be tolerated. He was relieved of five successive dollars. The broad-brim was tipped up a little, and a quizzing eye, asked if he wished to spare more. As he rose up, the hooting was more than he could stand; he paid his bill, and struck for another hotel. Dr. Harmon said he thought the scamp was worse punished than he was himself, but concluded the end justified the means. Mr. and Mrs. Opdycke had six sons and one daughter, who is the wife of O. H. Patch, of Warren.

Lucretia Harmon was born February 11, 1791, and married William Draper, of Weathersfield, who lived but a short time. She afterwards married William Frazier, of Hubbard, moved to Trenton, Ohio, and afterwards to Dearborn, Indiana, where he died in May, 1862. Mrs. Frazier died at Dillsboro, Indiana, January, 1871, and was the last of the family of eleven children—four sons and seven daughters, of whom nine were well known by the pioneers of Trumbull county.

Hiram R. Harmon was the ninth child and second son, born at Rupert, Vermont, December 18, 1793, died at Ives Grove, Wisconsin, October 15, 1852; was a blacksmith, lived in Liberty and Brookfield a few years, then moved to Bristol, and bought the Potter farm, where he kept a hotel for many years, working at his trade some, and farming extensively. He sold his farm, and moved on one a mile west of the village, but a few years later moved West, and died of apoplexy in the harvest field about three years after, an active, industrious, honest, and capable man, and a zealous advocate of temperance and antislavery.

Heman R. Harmon was born February 12, 1798, and died December 1, 1859. He began business early in Warren as a merchant, dealt extensively in cattle, taking large droves East, and carried on a large farm near the springs. He was at different times a member of the firm of Harmon Brothers, of Harmon & Stiles, and of E. E. Hoyt & Co., and of Harmon & Johnson. He served two terms as sheriff of the county, was an ardent politician, and an indefatigable worker in all that he undertook,—aided in the manufacture of the Heath mowing machine, and started the first one in the county. Liberal-minded, truthful and kind to all, he did work enough to have amassed a fortune. His losses grew out of adverse circumstances more than from special faults of his own.

Dr. John B. Harmon was born in Rupert, Bennington county, Vermont, October 19, 1780; was named after John Brown, a friend of his father in the Vermont Assembly. His early education was limited, but he was sufficiently acquainted with Latin to give him a good understanding of the Latin terms in use in the medical books of his day. He was correct in spelling and grammar, quick and accurate in arithmetic, well versed in English and American history, and was fond of speculative inquiries, such as Locke's Essay on the Human Understanding, Hume's Moral, Political, and Religious Essays, etc. He was partial to poetry also, Pope, Burns, and Shakespeare he often quoted, as well as Cowper and Watts. The Bible was at his tongue's end as much as with a Methodist or Disciple minister. In politics he was a Jeffersonian, afterwards a J. Q. Adams man and Whig. In medicine he was cautious and conservative, but progressive, so as always to adopt new views and remedies so far as reason and experience showed them to be of value. In 1814–16 he abandoned venesection in camp fever. He early adopted stimulants and cold water in fevers, and chlorate potassa, tincture of iron, and digitalis in scarlet fever. Ether and chloroform he hailed at once as boons to the suffering. At seventy years of age he was more progressive than many doctors of thirty-five. He was bold and skillful in surgical operations, having a hand which remained steady to the last. But he always studied carefully every operation of danger before he began it. His knowledge of anatomy was derived largely from books and plates, but it was accurate and minute. His observation was acute to a proverb, and his sound judgment was admitted as master of all. The late Tracy Bronson, M. D., said of him: "He had the best judgment of us all. I thought I had as much science, but when we got in a pinch and didn't know what to do, he would see at a glance, and help us out."

From 1800 to 1806 he aided his father in the salt works, which were carried on extensively, and furnished salt to the settlers at distant points, as well as those nearer. He enjoyed the common sport of the day, deer and bear hunting, and was one of the most expert at an off-hand long shot. One winter he had some twenty deer strung up on a hill a mile west of the springs. The law of hunters made such property more safe than bolts and locks now make our hams and bacon. The fat of the bear was used in cooking. Dr. Harmon used to say, "with a short cake in his bosom, made from bears' oil, he could travel further on a hunt or a ride, than on any other food." One time he treed a cub, placed his gun at the foot of the tree, and his dog to guard it, and climbing secured the cub. Its cries quickly brought the she bear from the thicket, but the sagacious dog, keeping out of her reach, quickly seized her as she essayed the tree, so at last she retreated, and Harmon descended with his cub, and regained his gun, when the bear renewed the attack. Backing off with the cub on his shoulders, and the dog at the heels of the enraged animal, while he held his gun cocked, and ready for the shot, he saw her finally give up the pursuit, and he bore his cub home in triumph.

In 1804 Dr. Enoch Leavitt settled in Leavittsburg, and Dr. Harmon resorted to him at intervals for study. In 1808 he returned from Vermont and located in Warren. His practice rapidly increased, and although the fees were low, yet they enabled him to meet his large expenses easily. Part of this time he boarded at the tavern kept on Market street, by Colonel William W. Cotgreave, by whom he was commissioned surgeon of the Second regiment, Fifth brigade, Fourth division of the militia of the State of Ohio, on the 10th day of August, 1813. This commission was repeated by Stephen Oviatt, colonel, February 5, 1817, and by Governor Worthington, July 17, 1818, only his brigade was the first, and the rank of captain was assigned to him. He was present at the attack on Fort Mackinaw in 1813. When our forces first reached the fort, Dr. Harmon urged an immediate attack, but the general delayed some three days, during which it was reinforced, and the attack was repulsed with great loss. During the fight a captain was shot with a poisoned arrow in the body. His sufferings were great, and he cried out, "Oh doctor, for God's sake give me a cup of water." A spring near by had been alternately in possession of the contending parties. The doctor got a squad of twenty men, and gained possession long enough to secure some muddy water. The captain drank a cupful and exclaimed, "Now, if I had a shot at that d—d Indian I'd die content."

On returning to Cleveland the doctor was left on the boat with his sick and wounded while the officers proceeded to the tavern. He charged them first of all to send supplies to the boat; waiting until he became impatient, he went to the hotel and found the company at table. To an invitation to a seat, he sternly replied, "He did not eat till the sick were cared for." Their needs were attended to while the feasting was delayed.

Near the close of the war he resumed practice in Warren, and from this time on his rides extended greatly, reaching to Cleveland, Painesville, Ashtabula on the lake, and a long distance in all directions, as, indeed, they had previously, but now more frequently. These rides were made on horseback, and it is no wonder that he sought out the elastic, easy-gaited racer. The fast walk, easy trot, courage, and endurance made him indispensable. One night his favorite "Buck Rabbit" broke through the ice with him in crossing Musquito creek, near Captain Joseph Marvin's. The game horse struggled through ice and up the steep miry bank. The doctor rode, with his clothes froze to him, some four miles on, sat beside a woman in labor and rode home without food the next morning.

In the winter of 1816 he laid out in the woods, three miles west of Warren, in a fierce storm, his horse chained to a sapling, and himself beside a log, while the wolves kept up their howling and snapping at his horse, who kept them at bay with his heels. He lost his watch there, but noted the spot so carefully that it was found the next spring. In riding home one night the doctor fell asleep, and his horse walked a fourteen-inch stringer laid across the Mahoning river at the "Wilmot center of the world," and as he stepped off the doctor wakened, to find how safely his favorite had carried him over. But sometimes the roads were too bad for the best of horses. Then the doctor went afoot with his saddle-bags on his arm, across the country as best he could. His light, agile step enabled him to do a vast deal of such pilgrimages. In one of these tramps he walked sixty-five miles, starting at break of day, seeing many patients, and reaching home at 10 o'clock at night.

In the winter of 1816 he attended a family of six children and the parents in Aurora, all down with the epidemic of typhoid pneumonia. He reached them each night, laid upon the hearth floor, and returned next day. Upon their recovery, he was himself taken sick. He went to the house of his mother at "Salt Springs," hired a trusty nurse, and gave her directions how to manage him in the bad turns of the disease, with the promise of his horse and saddle should he not recover. One night he was thought to be dying,

Dr. John W. Seeley was sent for, but he said "Dr. John B. will be all right in the morning," and did not visit him. The nurse tided him through, but for six months after he was so emaciated as to ride with a pillow on his saddle, and carried a cold foot, which he had to warm even in warm weather, ever after.

In 1816 he bought the frame (which had been erected the year previous) on lot forty in Warren, and in 1817 finished the story and a half dwelling, where he afterwards resided. His sisters, Mrs. Clara Leavitt and Mrs. Dunscomb, kept house for him several years. Mrs. Dunscomb was made blind by small-pox, but was a neat housekeeper; kept everything easy in her hands, could make a good shirt even, and made a good home for the doctor as well as herself, her husband having died early after his removal from Rupert to the springs in 1802. Afterwards the wife of Captain Thompson (who taught in the academy) kept house for him. In 1822, February 6th, he married Sarah Dana at Pembroke, New York. Although never engaged, an early friend had forsaken him for another, and this no doubt had led him to postpone so important an event, but at the suggestion of Mrs. Leavitt, mother of the late George Parsons, and an aunt of Miss Dana, he had obtained by letter "the promise." He drove on in a double team sleigh, was introduced to the bride to be, and the next day started for home. He could not have found one better suited to aid him in his hard toil, had he looked over New England.

Although of poor health, she kept his house in order—kept track of his patients, provided for all his home wants with economy, and left him free of all such cares as often vex men in their homes.

In the summer of 1822 Dr. Leavitt wished to operate on a Mrs. Norton for the removal of a tumor in the abdomen. Young Dr. Harmon advised against it, but Dr. Leavitt had removed a large fatty tumor from a Mrs. Gaylord some two years before, and was determined that this was like it. It proved to be a cancerous mass on the under side of the liver. He handed the knife to Dr. Harmon, who dissected out several masses from the size of a goose's egg to a small pullet's egg. Dr. Leavitt staid with her six days and nights, and she recovered so as to ride to Warren, a distance of some three miles, but died about four months after. During his attendance on her Dr. Harmon was induced by Mrs. Leavitt to adopt one of her daughters, Mitty, then a girl of eight years. She proved to be a woman of rare good sense, an elder sister to his children, and a life long faithful daughter. She was born June 23, 1814, at Hamburgh, New York; married Jacob Gimperling April 8, 1833, lived several years in Hudson, Ohio, then moved to Ravenna, where he died December 25, 1848. She returned to Dr. Harmon's, and married Rev. John McLean, then in Bristol, November 4, 1863. She died in Canfield in 1878 or 1879; was a devoted Methodist from sixteen years of age, and was highly respected by many warm friends.

In 1830 Dr. Harmon was prostrated by a severe run of fever, which nearly proved fatal. In 1833 he was pulled by a colt he was leading, from his saddle, and his horse ran, dragging him by the heels in his stirrup till the breaking of the girth released him. His back was so hurt that he could not sit down or get up for a long time without help. Years after in attempting to do so he would suddenly fall helpless. But he kept at his work. In February, 1838, his horse ran away and broke his ribs and one leg, and he lay in the snow for some time till found by John McConnell, whose son William he was visiting. He was helped in his sleigh, and went on and prescribed for his patient, and was brought home before his own injuries were cared for. About 1840 a tumor formed on his left side, beneath the deep pectoral muscle. It was opened by Dr. Delamater, and again by Dr. Bronson, and a seton put in. The inflammation was severe, and was nearly fatal. In the summer of 1845 he was again severely sick, and again in 1854 he had a congestive chill, in which for four hours he seemed to be past recovery. All of these attacks were results of excessive work and special injuries, which his iron constitution enabled him to survive.

In 1852 he returned East with his wife and visited his early home and hers also. They spent six weeks of May and June in such pleasant way. He found the remains of his father's old copper mill, still at Rupert, and several boys like himself grown to be seventy and eighty years of age.

In 1854 he foreswore practice, saying that "an old man without eyes, ears, teeth, or fingers had no business to be dabbling in medicine." This was not true of him, but it indicated his belief, that a man should quit before he becomes incompetent. His help, however, continued to be sought in counsel often, and was ever of aid to his son, who was taking his place in active work. His last case of obstetrics was in July, 1857. His practice in this branch extended over fifty-five years. He early supplied himself with a complete set of obstetrical instruments, and was expert in their use. In general surgery he was recognized as a master till the time of Ackley. In his fine sense of touch and cautious judgment he occasionally proved himself superior even to him, and the still more celebrated Mott, of New York city.

In 1838 he was sued for malpractice, in having (as was said) unnecessarily amputated a leg. The prosecution was conducted by the Hon. J. R. Giddings, with the help of Wade, Sutliff, and Ranney. The defence was made by David Tod and R. P. Spalding. The leg had been crushed by a timber rolling down from the top of a cabin which was being raised. Doctors John W. and Sylvanus Seeley were called in, on the second day as counsel, and the operation was done. They were all sued. The unquestioned ability of the surgeons, and the fame of the counsel, gave the case great notoriety. The issue was squarely made: Had an ignorant public the right to pass judgment on the action of three eminent surgeons, who had fully considered the case at the time? Giddings claimed the right, and had succeeded a few years before in obtaining a verdict against a doctor in Ashtabula county, for not properly caring, as was charged, for an injured ankle. He was a monomaniac on the subject, as it were, and left nothing undone that a zealous and able man could do, to win his case. Tod and Spalding were equally zealous and able for the defence, and were completely successful. The expense was large. It cost Dr. Harmon more than he had ever made from surgery; but it showed to the public the essential impudence of such prosecutions, and has resulted in a better understanding of medical responsibility. There is no more sense in such a suit than there would be if a doctor should assume to prosecute three eminent lawyers for losing a case they had done their best to win, and such is the feeling now with the legal profession.

Dr. Harmon was usually a silent, thoughtful man, but when occasion called expressed himself fluently and clearly. He was outspoken in all his convictions, and gave his reasons with such force and originality as to command a respectful hearing. While opposing invariably what he thought errors in religion, he yet made firm friends among the most devout of women, and the ablest of preachers. From early days until his decease Presbyterians and Methodists, Baptists and Disciples alike patronized and honored him. Said the women, "We can't see why he thought as he did, but he was surely a good man, and he has gone to heaven." He was ever at the call of the sick, whether pay was to be had or not. He sometimes swam his horse across the Mahoning, swollen with floating ice, to meet a professional engagement. A large part of his life regular sleep was unknown to him. Within the memory of his children he has gone two weeks without undressing at home, because of daily calls. He learned to sleep on his horse, or in his sulky, and when he lay down instantly fell asleep; would awake at a call, put up medicine in his bed, give directions, and be asleep before the waiter was out of the room. He had his amusements. The fleet horse must be put to his mettle, and he delighted in the race, not for gaming but for love of the beauty and fleetness of the horse. About 1830 the "Warren Jocky Club" was formed, and a mile track was made on the John Leavitt (now James Hoyt) farm in Leavittsburg. In the spring and fall one, two, three, and four mile races were held. Sporting men came with the best racers of neighboring States. Dr. Harmon kept some of the fleetest himself. The Pennsylvania & Ohio canal went through the track and ended the sport in 1839. In boyhood he began the play of checkers, at which he soon became the best of his day. In the leisure hours of later life he often met his friends, the Seeleys, Bronson, and King, in the auditor's office, where Jacob H. Baldwin presided so long, and had a ti' He had less fondness for back-gammon, but indulged in that occasionally with Judge Pease, Parsons, and Freeman, and others. He had become known as a checker player from Maine to New Orleans. Champion players from all parts came to play with him, only to find their superior. He excelled in whatever he undertook. His natural endowments were of the very highest order. One who had seen the leading public men of his age, both in this country and abroad, said: "He always impressed me as being the peer of any man I ever met." The last few years of his life were spent in quiet ease. Young in face, hair but slightly gray, and scarcely thinned, erect and straight as an arrow, he took his daily walks with a light step, read the news of the day and the last Medical Journal, and mingled with his friends, cheerful and thoughtful himself, and greatly revered by all. He was taken with an acute pleuro-pneumonia in January, and died February 7, 1858.

The Cleveland Leader said of him:

Dr. Harmon was skillful and scientific, and met the largest success to which one in his profession can attain. As a man, he was true in all his relations, a faithful husband, kind father, obliging neighbor, steadfast, generous friend, patriotic citizen, a helper in every good work, a great, good, and true man—" we ne'er shall look upon his like again."

His wife, Sarah (Dana) Harmon, was born in Enfield, Connecticut, September 24, 1796; was the seventh daughter of Daniel and Dorothy (Kibbee) Dana. Her father was born in Ashford, Connecticut, September 16, 1760, and died in Warren, November 8, 1839. He graduated at Yale college, and was a studious man of letters; of the fifth generation from Richard Dana, who immigrated from France, and died at Cambridge, Massachusetts, April 2, 1690. Miss Dana was delicate in health, barely escaping death in early womanhood by consumption; but had perseverance and energy sufficient to enable her to meet the demands of her day with ample success. She was a friend to all; her "charity covered a multitude of sins" in the erring, and her household gifts were ever at the disposal of the young, who lacked in the requisites of good housekeeping. She toiled hard to bring up the family, and was anxious to see them educated as well as possible. In the evenings her kitchen table was set for her boys to study, and with the intuitive tact of woman, she could help them to learn what she did not know herself. She was a natural cook, and delighted in surprising her family with new dishes. The love of flowers was strong within her, and she kept as many in her door-yard as economy would permit. She early became a member of the Presbyterian church, and remained a quiet, unobtrusive, but firm and consistent member. After the death of her husband, she gave up the cares of the house, and led an easy, cheerful life till its close, November 6, 1868.

They had six children. John B. Harmon, Jr., born October 29, 1822; graduated at Yale in 1842, a lawyer of San Francisco; grand master of Odd Fellows in 1878-79, to whom they gave a grand reception in Warren October 4, 1878, in which the citizens universally joined, making it by far the grandest celebration ever held in Warren, if not in the State. Six hundred and seventy-two guests sat at the table at one time in the Methodist church, details of which may be found on another page, in the History of Odd Fellowship.

Doctor Julian Harmon, born August 1, 1824; graduated at Western Reserve college August, 1846, at Cleveland Medical college February 28, 1849; practiced with his father till March 1, 1854; continued alone till June, 1860, when Dr. J. T. Smith formed a partnership with him. Smith went out, as assistant surgeon with the Second Ohio volunteer cavalry in 1861. Dr. Harmon continued his rides during the war, during which his practice became very extensive. In the winter of 1862-63 he rode horseback through snow and mud for ninety consecutive days, a trip of from thirty-two to fifty-two miles, going on foot evenings and mornings around the town. One night he walked between 8 and 11 o'clock six miles, after a ride of fifty-one miles. Small and delicate, he seemed unfitted for such work, and was induced to enter the drug business in September, 1865. He left it April 1, 1868, having lost some $16,000. His wife had died six weeks previous, and he was, in consequence, deprived of the help he relied on, which made his pecuniary loss greater. He resumed practice in his old office, with Dr. Metcalf, till April, 1875, since when he has been alone. He has acted as examining surgeon for Trumbull county, for pensions, for some twenty years; is an active member of Trumbull county, Northeastern Ohio, and the State Medical societies, and has been a trustee of the Newburg insane asylum and of the Western Reserve college.

He married J. Rebecca Swift, daughter of George and Olive (Kinsman) Swift, July 30, 1857, by whom he has two daughters and one son. He was married again, June 6, 1871, to Mary E. Bostwick, daughter of I. L. and Margaret (Wetmore) Bostwick, of Canfield, by whom he has one son living, an elder one having died October 26, 1881. He himself was severely sick from thirteen to nineteen years of age, and in 1851, and again in 1871 was nearly cut off by erysipelas of head and neck. In 1840 he was prostrated nine weeks by jaundice, and has had no light burden of infirmity to contend with a large part of his life.

The loss of Captain Harmon's son Ellis, (whom he had adopted) at thirteen years of age, and his own son, Charlie, at nine years, both by malignant diphtheria, were severe disappointments of his hopes in the future. The sudden loss of his wife, Febuary 13, 1868, made a black chasm across his pathway. Brilliant and sociable, unwearying and devoted as a wife and mother, generous and helpful, she was taken away just when she would have been of the highest value to him and their children. His sister was a close friend and intellectual companion and adviser, whose recent loss has added heavily to his burdens. Amid all, he has remained true to his manhood. Integrity unsullied, and elastic in spirits, he bids fair to keep his ship afloat awhile longer, and bring her to port in good trim at last. As a physican he has been prompt in attendance, quick to recognize and skillful in combating the dangerous forms of disease. He was eminently successful in 1854 during an epidemic of vesicular bronchitis among children. During the great prevalence of scarlet fever and diphtheria in 1861-62-63 and 1864 he lost but very few out of a large number of cases. In the gravest accidents of obstetric practice he has been prompt, skillful and successful. For many years he acted as surgeon for the Cleveland & Mahoning, and Atlantic & Great Western railroads, and has managed some desperately bad cases with most gratifying success. Unassuming in manners, devoid of all trickery, frank in speech, clear in convictions, enthusiastic in the love of his profession, he may fairly be called a chip from the granite block.

Captain Charles R. Harmon was born November 4, 1826. Active and restless as a child, he abhorred the confinement of school, but when the fit was on him, would learn in a few weeks all that his mates had spent a full term on. At thirteen he entered the store of E. E. Hoyt & Co. as clerk, and remained there till 1846, when he became a clerk with T. P. Ellis & Co., of New York city, dealers in hardware. March 5, 1848, he married Mary, daughter of James and Sarah (Heywood) Hezlep, of Girard, Ohio, and established himself in the hardware business at Warren, in company with Edward E. Hoyt, under the firm name of Harmon & Co. Mr. Hoyt withdrew their part of the business from the firm of E. E. Hoyt & Co., and Charlie pushed the business to a large extent. Warren Packard and James G. Brooks were his clerks. In a few years the firm was dissolved, and he continued the business alone. Packard was started in a separate store with $1,200 worth of goods bought by Harmon, who was a silent partner with Mr. Packard for three years.

In 1854 Mr. Harmon formed a partnership with H. A. Opdycke, but continued in business only a few months. An uncurbed passion for sport brought his business to a close. Soon after, he moved to Iowa, remained there one or two years, and returned to Warren.

With the aid of relatives he built a house on Washington avenue, published a spicy sheet in the interest of the Mecca oil business for about a year, enlisted in company F of the Twenty-fourth Ohio volunteer infantry as a private, was in the Western Virginia campaign in Colonel Ammon's brigade, served as a valuable scout, and enjoyed the hearty respect of Colonel Ammon. He was home on a recruiting furlough with rank of lieutenant. In February and March, 1862, he rejoined his regiment with his recruits immediately after the battle of Shiloh, was the first soldier over the defences at Corinth, and was in the march from Alabama to Louisville when the race was run on quarter rations. In a letter to the Spirit of the Times he gave a vivid caricature of the performance under the signature of "Reuben."

At the battle of Perryville he wrote home:

Here we are, fifty-five thousand men in arms, anxious to fight. The country is rolling and our cannon could sweep it, but we will have no order to move. Buell will let McCook be slaughtered, he will never fight unless he is forced to; then he would go in grandly to save his reputation. Our officers say it is only a skirmish, but every private as well as officer know it is death to McCook and his men.

At the battle of Stone River the lieutenant-colonel was shot at the outset. In the afternoon Lieutenant Harmon and men were ordered down flat, to cool their guns and let our cannon play over them; raising his head a little upon his hands, he encouraged his men, humming, "Who would not be a brave soldier boy?" A sharpshooter up a neighboring tree sent a bullet through his brain. While being carried back, Major Terry (then in command) said, "Halt, let me see him." As he leaned forward the same gun brought him to the ground, as he was saying "Oh, God, but it's hard." All the officers were picked off save one captain, who had more discretion than valor. The sharpshooter was seen at last, and a volley riddled him.

The commission of captain was mailed Lieutenant Harmon by Governor Tod the day he was killed, and after long discussion between Commissioner Bartlett and Dr. J. Harmon as to the pension his widow was entitled to, the commission was returned home by the valiant captain, who had kept it till after the battle at Chickamauga. The same day came the pension as lieutenant. Dr. Harmon forwarded both to Washington, and soon after President Lincoln issued an order that in all such cases the soldier should be put on the rolls as if he had received his commission and been formally mustered-in. He had been acting captain for some six months, and justice was done his widow by the effect of the order.

Captain Harmon was naturally extremely sensitive to suffering, and not till after long effort could he see blood without fainting, yet he was cool, brave, and daring in the extreme.

Although addicted to sport, he was rigidly temperate, and would not permit liquor or tobacco to the young in his employ. He was a courteous and very popular salesman, and could command a high salary. When pressed with poverty, he was offered a salary of one thousand dollars to enter a grocery and liquor store in Warren, but said "he would starve sooner than engage in such work." He was a very sociable and attractive man, correct in business, a ready writer, furnishing a play for school exhibitions, or a racy letter to the Chronicle from the army, with ease. His companions in arms honored and trusted him. Had fate spared him his career would have been one of continued and increasing success. When he arrived at Louisville from Alabama, the news reached him of the death of his twin son Ellis, by diphtheria. The blow was cruel indeed. He wrotehome, "If ever I return, I shall be looking for the dear boy, with a longing earth can not fill. If I fall, let my body rest where it falls." The cemetery at Murfresboro holds the remains of few men so brave, unselfish, and capable as was Captain Charles R. Harmon.

Edward D. Harmon was born May 1, 1831; clerked for his brother, Charles R., some time; went to California in March, 1853; returned and married Marie Metcalf, of Newark, Ohio, in the summer or fall of 1868. He is a prosperous farmer and real estate dealer in Oakland, California.

Sarah D. Harmon, their only daughter, was born April 3, 1833, and died in Warren, July 6, 1880. She was highly educated, and taught in the grammar and high schools of Warren, Dunkirk, Columbus, Elkhart, and Poughkeepsie, (Select Ladies seminary,) and also in Sanford's seminary, at Cleveland. Never robust, she overworked in her school duties, and wore herself out prematurely, but had done a good life's work with great success, and bore a year and a half of intense suffering with great courage and resignation, and the firm hope of an humble Christian woman.

Their youngest child, Willie, was born June 30, 1835, and died April 10, 1836, a pet favorite with his father, never forgotten. The stern, stoical man years after would drop a tear when, coming to his home, some incident would recall his babe. The inner feelings of such men are seldom understood. A few years before his death, a poor woman said to him, "Oh doctor, you can't imagine how I felt when my child was scalded." "Ah, mother," he said, "yes I do; my youngest brother was scalded to death, over fifty years ago, and I hear his cries again every time I am called to care for such a case." This acute sensibility, coupled with resolute courage and self control, is largely enstamped upon his children, softened in some more than in others, by the quiet tenderness of his wife.

JACOB PERKINS[*]

was born at Warren, September 1, 1822, being next to the youngest of the children of General Simon Perkins. In his early years Jacob Perkins developed a strong inclination for study, acquiring knowledge with unusual facility and gratifying his intense passion for reading useful works by every means within his power. He commenced fitting himself for college at the Burton academy, then under the direction of Mr. H. L. Hitchcock, afterwards president of the Western Reserve college, and completed his preparation at Middletown, Connecticut, in the school of Isaac Webb. He entered Yale college in 1837. While in college he was distinguished for the elegance of his style and the wide range of his literary acquirements. He delivered the philosophic oration at his junior exhibition, and was chosen second editor of Yale Literary Magazine, a position in which he took great interest and filled to the satisfaction and pride of his class. His college course was, however, interrupted by a long and severe illness before the close of his junior year, which compelled him to leave his studies and (to his permanent regret) prevented him from graduating with his own class. He returned the following year and was graduated with the class of 1842.

He entered his father's office at Warren, and was occupied with its business until upon the death of his father, some two years afterward, he became one of his executors.

During his residence at Warren he appeared occasionally before home audiences as a public speaker, and always with great acceptance. In politics he early adopted anti-slavery principles, then not the popular doctrine, and they were always freely and openly advocated.

Without solicitation he was nominated and elected a member of the convention that framed the present constitution of Ohio. His associates from the district were judges Peter Hitchcock and R. P. Ranney, and although "he was the youngest member but one of the convention, and in the minority, his influence and position were excelled by few." He was one of the Senatorial Presidential electors for Ohio on the Fremont ticket in 1856. In the intellectual progress of the young about him, and the building up of schools and colleges, he took especial interest.

[*] From Mahoning Valley Collections.

He first suggested and urged the adoption of the conditions of the present permanent fund of Western Reserve college rather than to solicit unconditional contributions, which experience had proved were so easily absorbed by present necessities, and left the future as poor as the past. In connection with his brothers he made the first subscription to that fund.

The wisdom of his suggestion was subsequently shown when, during the rupture and consequent embarrassment under which the college labored, the income of this fund had a very important, if not vital, share in saving it from abandonment, and afterwards proved the nucleus of its present endowments. He was always efficient in favoring improvements. He was associated with Hon. F. Kinsman and his brother in founding the beautiful Woodland cemetery at Warren. The land was purchased and the ground laid out by them, and then transferred to the present corporation.

Soon after his return from the constitutional convention he became interested in the Cleveland & Mahoning railroad. He was most influential in obtaining the charter and organizing the company, of which he was elected president, and became the principal, almost sole, financial manager. Owing to prior and conflicting railroad interests, little aid could be obtained for his project in either of the terminal cities, Cleveland and Pittsburg, and the work was commenced in 1853 with a comparatively small stock subscription. A tightening money market prevented considerable increase of the stock list or a favorable disposition of the stock of the road, and the financial crisis, a few years afterwards, so reduced the value of the securities of this, as of all unfinished railroads, as practically to shut them out of the market. In this emergency the alternative presented itself to Mr. Perkins and his resident directors, either to abandon the enterprise and bankrupt the company, with the entire loss of the amount expended, or to push it forward to completion by the pledge and at the risk of their private fortunes, credit, and reputations. In this, the darkest day of the enterprise, Mr. Perkins manifested his confidence in its ultimate success, and his generous willingness to meet fully his share of the hazard to be incurred by proposing to them jointly with him to assume that risk, and agreeing that, in case of disaster, he would himself pay the first $100,000 of loss, and thereafter share it equally with them. With a devotion to the interests intrusted to them, a determination rarely equalled in the history of our railroad enterprises, they unanimously accepted this proposition, and determined to complete the road, at least to a remunerative point in the coal fields of the Mahoning valley. The financial storm was so much more severe and longer continued than the wisest had calculated upon, that for years the result was regarded by them and the friends of the enterprise with painful suspense.

In the interest of the road Mr. Perkins spent the spring of 1854 in England, without achieving any important financial results. At length, in 1856, the road was opened to Youngstown, and its receipts, carefully husbanded, began slowly to lessen the floating debt—by that time grown to frightful proportions, and carried solely by the pledge of the private property and credit of the president and Ohio directors. These directors, consisting of Hon. Frederick Kinsman and Charles Smith, Esq., of Warren; Governor David Tod, of Briar Hill; Judge Reuben Hitchcock, of Painesville; and Dudley Baldwin, Esq., of Cleveland, by the free use of their widely known and high business credit, without distrust or dissension, sustained the president through that long and severe trial—a trial which can never be realized, except by those who shared its burdens. The president and these directors should ever be held in honor by the stockholders of the company, whose investments they saved from utter loss, and by the business men of the entire Mahoning valley, and not less by the city of Cleveland, for the mining and manufacturing interests developed by their exertion and sacrifices lie at the very foundation of the present prosperity of both.

Before, however, the road was enabled to free itself from financial embarrassment so as to commence making a satisfactory return to the stockholders, which Mr. Perkins was exceedingly anxious to see accomplished under his own presidency, his failing health compelled him to leave its active management, and he died before the bright day dawned upon the enterprise.

He said to a friend, during his last illness, with characteristic distinctness, "If I die, you may inscribe on my tombstone, Died of the Ma-

Judge Francis Freeman

honing Railroad;" so great had been his devotion to the interests of the road, and so severe the personal exposures which its supervision had required of him, who was characteristically more thoughtful of every interest confided to his care than of his own health.

He was married October 24, 1850, to Miss Elizabeth O. Tod, daughter of Dr. J. I. Tod, of Milton, Trumbull county, Ohio, and removed his family to Cleveland in 1856. Of three children only one, Jacob Bishop, survives him. Mrs. Perkins died of rapid consumption June 4, 1857, and his devoted attention at the sick-bed of his wife greatly facilitated the development of the same insidious disease, which was gradually to undermine his own naturally vigorous constitution.

The business necessities of his road, embarrassed and pressing as they were, united with his uniform self-forgetfulness, prevented his giving attention to his personal comfort and health long after his friends saw the shadow of the destroyer falling upon his path. He was finally, in great prostration of health and strength, compelled to leave the active duties of the road, and spent the latter part of the winter of 1857-58 in the Southern States, but returned in the spring with little or no improvement. He continued to fail during the summer, and in the fall of 1858 he again went South, in the vain hope of at least physical relief, and died in Havana, Cuba, January 12, 1859. His remains were embalmed and brought home by his physician, who had accompanied him, and were interred at Warren in Woodland cemetery, where so many of his family repose around him. A special train from each end of the Cleveland & Mahoning railroad brought the board of directors and an unusually large number of business and personal friends, to join the long procession which followed "the last of earth" to its resting-place.

One of the editorial notices of his death at the time very justly remarks of him:

> He was a man of mark and through strength of talent, moral firmness, and urbanity of manner, wielded an influence seldom possessed by a man of his years. In addition to his remarkable business capacity, Mr. Perkins was a man of high literary taste, which was constantly improving and enriching his mind. He continued, even amid his pressing business engagements, his habits of study and general reading.
>
> Mr. Perkins belonged to that exceptional class of cases in which great wealth inherited does not injure the recipient.

An editorial article in a Warren paper, mentioning his death, says:

> He was born in this town in 1821, and from his boyhood exhibited a mental capacity and energy which was only the promise of the brilliancy of his manhood. To his exertion, his personal influence, and liberal investment of capital, the country is indebted for the Cleveland & Mahoning railroad. To his unremitting labor in this enterprise he has sacrificed personal comfort and convenience, and, we fear, shortened his days by his labors and exposure in bringing the work to completion. Known widely as Mr. Perkins has been by his active part in public enterprises, his loss will be felt throughout the State; but we, who have known him both as boy and man, have a deeper interest in him; and the sympathies of the people of Warren with his relatives will have much of the nature of personal grief for one directly connected with them.

Said a classmate in the class-meeting of 1862:

> Although his name on the catalogue ranks with the class of 1842, his affections were with us, and he always regarded himself of our number. He visited New Haven frequently during the latter part of his life, in connection with a railway enterprise in which he was interested, and exhibited the same large-heartedness and intellectual superiority which won for him universal respect during his college course.

JUDGE FRANCIS FREEMAN

was a conspicuous figure in Warren business affairs for nearly half a century. He was born in Amenia, Dutchess county, New York, June 7, 1779. During his youth he acquired a good education in the schools of his native county. On leaving school he engaged for some time in the lumber trade, but western emigration and settlement had opened a more profitable field for enterprise. His first visit to Ohio was made in 1803. Warren had been made the county seat of the whole Reserve, and was regarded as having excellent prospects for growth. This fact determined Mr. Freeman's choice of location. He returned to New York to close out his business there, which was accomplished in about two years. His brother joined him in the removal to Warren, and each purchased a farm. This purchase was the foundation of Mr. Freeman's future wealth, and shows his characteristic business sagacity. A large part of his tract was within the present city limits, being that part lying south of the Cleveland & Mahoning railroad. Being a man of powerful physique and vigorous health, he was enabled to accomplish with cheerfulness the rugged labor of clearing and cultivating new land. His business qualifications and business habits were soon recognized by his neighbors. He was one of the original stockholders of the Western Reserve bank, and was chosen one of the first board of directors. He continued a director until his death, being during the whole period one of the most influential members of the board. A prominent trait of his business character was rigid and judicious economy. This he exercised both in private and public transactions, and acquired the reputation of being a "safe" man. His voice and vote in bank directors' meetings always received the respect of his associates, who were, during the whole history of the bank representative business men.

In 1832 Mr. Freeman was chosen one of the associate justices of the court of common pleas, and held the position for seven years. The three associate justices under the old judicial system transacted the probate and minor judiciary business, and during terms of court sat upon the bench with the presiding judge. Their place and subordinate dignity upon the bench gave them the appellation of "side judges." Mr. Freeman had previously served sixteen years as treasurer of Trumbull county. He succeeded John Leavitt after the death of the latter in 1815, and was regularly chosen to the position at the election following. He was successively re-elected until the expiration of his eighth regular term in 1831. It will be seen that with the exception of one brief interval he was in continuous official life twenty-three years. Mr. Freeman sold his farm to a company of capitalists, realizing a handsome profit on his original investment. During his older years he had extensive real estate interests in the vicinity of Warren, which occupied a large portion of his business energy. Physically Judge Freeman was one of the largest men in the county, being tall, round-featured, and broad-shouldered. He married January 27, 1817, Lyndia, only daughter of Samuel and Abigail Kent Leavitt. She was born at Rupert, Vermont, July 5, 1785. She was married in 1807, to Joseph Hopkins, who died a few years afterward.

The family of Francis and Lyndia Freeman consisted of three children: Samuel L., the only son, was born March 29, 1823, married in 1846, Charlotte L. Tod, and has been identified with commercial and banking business in Warren until recently; Laura Abigail was born August 24, 1819, was married to Charles Hickox in 1843, and resides in Cleveland; Olive, born October 25, 1825, was married to Albert Morley July 9, 1851, and died in Warren February 12, 1866.

Judge Freeman died in Warren September 8, 1855. Mrs. Freeman survived her husband nearly twelve years, the date of her death being April 20, 1867.

HON. GEORGE MYGATT.

This venerable gentleman, for many years a resident of Trumbull county, now residing in Cleveland, was born in Danbury, Connecticut, June 14, 1797. His parents were Comfort S. and Lucy (Knapp) Mygatt, who were among the pioneers of Canfield, now Mahoning county. They came from Danbury to Ohio in the summer of 1807, arriving in Canfield on the 7th day of July.

Comfort S. Mygatt was engaged in mercantile business in Canfield some sixteen years. Soon after coming to Canfield he entered into partnership with Herman Canfield and Zalmon Fitch, under the firm name of Mygatt, Canfield & Fitch, and opened a general store. The firm was dissolved after about two years, and the business was continued by Mr. Mygatt during the remainder of his life. He had been a member of the Connecticut Legislature before removing to Ohio. He died in October, 1823.

George Mygatt obtained his education in the common school, but enjoyed very limited advantages after the removal of the family to Ohio. He entered the employ of the Western Reserve bank at Warren in 1818. He carried on a mercantile business in Warren for about five years; was county tax collector in the fall of 1821. He was elected sheriff of Trumbull county in 1829, and re-elected in 1831, serving four years. He removed to Huron county in 1834, and was cashier of the Bank of Norwalk, residing there about two years. He removed to Painesville, and was cashier of the Bank of Geauga county for ten years. In 1846 he removed to Cleveland, where he now resides, and was subsequently elected president of the City bank of Cleveland, which position he held four years. He was a member of the firm of Mygatt & Brown, private bankers in Cleveland six years. He was elected to the Legislature from Cuyahoga county in 1855, and served two years. From 1857 to 1861 he was cashier of the Merchants' bank, of Cleveland; was afterwards secretary and treasurer of the Cleveland & Mahoning railroad company for six years, holding that position till February, 1871, when he retired from active business. This bare recital of facts in the life of Mr. Mygatt shows it to have been one of remarkable activity, and his industry and activity have been attended with equal success. He was married in 1820 to Miss Eliza Freeman, daughter of Robert Freeman, one of the early settlers of Braceville township. Mrs. Mygatt was born in New York State April 28, 1797. This union was blessed with six children, only one of whom survives, viz: Lucy, now widow of Franklin T. Backus.

THE HOYT FAMILY.

The name Hoyt occurs so frequently in the preceding pages, relating to the civil and industrial history of Warren that a brief sketch of the family will be of interest in this connection. Lewis Hoyt was a native of Norwalk, Connecticut, and was born in the year 1782. It was the custom of all well-to-do young men in those days to learn a trade. Mr. Hoyt served an apprenticeship in a hatter's shop, the manufacture of hats being a profitable branch of industry. He married, in 1804, Abigail Mygatt, whose father, Comfort S. Mygatt, soon after removed to the Western Reserve and settled at Canfield. Mr. Hoyt also began to seek a more promising field for his business, and accordingly wrote to his brother-in-law, Elisha Whittlesey, at Canfield, asking whether that would be a good point for a hatter. Mr. Whittlesey, with characteristic humor, replied that "people out West were born without hats on." In 1808 he removed from Connecticut with his family, then consisting of a wife and two children, and from that date Canfield was his home. He died in Cleveland in October, 1828. Mrs. Abigail Hoyt lived to the age of eighty-two years, the date of her death being August 27, 1867. Their family consisted of six children, one of whom, Eli, died in early manhood.

Lucy A. married John C. Smith in 1826. They lived on Long Island, New York, until after his death. She then removed to Warren.

Edward E. Hoyt was born in Danbury, Connecticut, in July, 1807. He served seven years apprenticeship at the harness and saddlery trade in Warren. In 1832 he engaged in mercantile pursuits, to which he gave exclusive attention until the time of his death, which occurred June 20, 1864. He was a man of quiet manners and close business habits. He married in Hubbard, Trumbull county, Martha L. Callander, who is living. Four children are living—two sons and two daughters. Edward W. has been city clerk for a number of years; John S. is sheriff of Trumbull county. The daughters are Abigail M. (Briscoe) and Frances A. (Jameson).

Comfort L., second son of Lewis Hoyt, was born in Canfield, August 2, 1811. He clerked in Warren for some years, and then removed to Painesville, where he was in the banking business twenty-eight years. He was married three times. His death occurred in Painesville, July 20, 1866.

For almost half a century James Hoyt has been one of the most active, vigilant, and public spirited citizens in Warren. He was born in Canfield, February 22, 1814. At the age of fourteen he began learning the saddlery trade in Warren under the direction of Henry Stiles, and served six years apprenticeship. He worked at the trade until 1851, but was also in partnership with his brother, Edward E., engaged in mercantile business, having purchased an interest in 1837. He retired from the store after the death of his brother in 1864. Mr. Hoyt married March 26, 1840, Elizabeth Brown, of Warren. Their family consisted of two sons, Eli S., who is dead, and James B., who resides in Warren. A prominent characteristic of Mr. Hoyt is the interest he takes in public affairs. He was a member of the first fire company organized in Warren, and has ever since been watchful of the public safety. Since Warren has been made an incorporated city, he has been marshal, recorder, mayor, and councilman (a part of the time being president of that body), making twelve years consecutive service. He had previously under the village government served four years as mayor, and three years in the council. He was township treasurer nineteen years, and for seven years held the office of assistant assessor of internal revenue. Mr. Hoyt is especially mentioned by the writer of the history of Mahoning lodge, I. O. O. F., as a zealous and active member. During the war he was a member of the local military committee, and in that capacity did effective work in the Union cause. A man so prominently connected with public affairs of local character could not expect to escape criticism, but his unselfish devotion to the public good has never been questioned, and on the whole his management of affairs entrusted to him has been entirely satisfactory.

Lewis Hoyt, the youngest of the sons of Lewis Hoyt, Sr., was born at Canfield, June 15, 1816. He has been in mercantile business in Warren since 1837. His specialty for a number of years was drugs, and he acquired the reputation of being an expert pharmacist. He is at present engaged in the drug business. He married in 1847, Sarah M. Spear, of Warren. They have three children, Comfort L., Abigail, and Annie.

GEORGE TAYLER.

In this register of Warren business men, more than passing notice must be made of George Tayler, who was for twenty-three years cashier of the Western Reserve bank, and on the organization of the First National bank, was chosen to the cashiership of that institution. His father, James Tayler, was born in Pennsylvania, his parents being natives of the north of Ireland. He married Jane Walker, and settled in Franklin county. In 1814 they removed to Beaver county, and in 1815 came to Youngstown township. He purchased on Mill creek a fulling mill and wool factory, which he operated for several years. In the year 1831 Mr. Tayler removed to Youngstown. His death occurred in 1834. Their family consisted of nine children, only one of whom, Jane, the oldest, is living. Robert and James D. were lawyers respectively in Youngstown and Warren, and are spoken of in other parts of this volume. John was a commission merchant at Warren; Nancy was married to Dr. Adair, of Poland, and Susannah to John B. Canfield, of Warren; Albert, the youngest son, died in Youngstown; a sketch of Matthew B., the third son, follows in this connection. George Tayler was born in Franklin county, Pennsylvania, in 1811. While his parents resided on Mill creek, in Youngstown township, he assisted in the woolen factory and on the farm, and in the meantime attended the district school. After spending a term or two at the Youngstown academy, he began the study of law, in 1832, in the office of Hurchard & Tod at Warren. Tod was postmaster at that time, and his student was employed so much of the time in the post-office, that his study was seriously interfered with. This, after all, was probably a fortunate circumstance, for it threw Mr. Tayler into a business instead of a professional channel. What he might have become as a lawyer can only be guessed; that he possessed business qualifications of a high order he proved by a highly successful career. In 1835, having left the law office and the post-office, we find him employed as clerk to the treasurer of the Pennsylvania and Ohio canal, then in course of construction. The following year he accepted a situation in the Western Reserve bank, at Warren. That he proved himself faithful and efficient is shown by the fact that upon the death of Mr. Hickox, he was the choice of the directors for the cashiership. This position he held in the Western Reserve bank, and in its successor, the First National bank, until his death, which occurred May 25, 1864. During the twenty-eight years of his connection with the bank, he proved himself worthy of the confidence which the directors placed in him. Competent, honest, and courteous, he won the confidence of all with whom he came in contact, both in business and social relations. He was a member of the Methodist Episcopal church, and practiced the faith he professed. Mr. Tayler was married April 25, 1837, to Elizabeth Woodbridge, who still survives. Six of their family lived to mature age. The monument which marks the grave of Mr. Tayler was erected by the bank directors as a tribute to his memory.

MATTHEW B. TAYLER.

Matthew B. Tayler was the third son and fourth child of James and Jane Walker Tayler, whose settlement near Youngstown has been noted. He was born at Beaver Falls, Pennsylvania, March 17, 1815. His boyhood was spent on the farm in Youngstown township, his time being divided between farm work and attendance upon the country school. After his parents re-

moved to the village of Youngstown, he became a pupil at the "academy," where he completed what may be termed a good business education. At the age of eighteen years he embarked upon a business career. From this time forward his life was one of earnest, ceaseless activity, and in that, chiefly, was the secret of his success. His life furnishes an example of the value of early discipline. It was the close application and solicitous care which he gave to every transaction in his younger years that moulded the character of the exemplary and trustworthy business man. Mr. Tayler's first experience was in the dry-goods business in the store of W. H. Goodhue, at Warren. He continued in the dry-goods trade six years, until 1839, when he entered the Western Reserve bank as teller. When the bank closed its accounts under the first charter in 1843, Mr. Tayler embarked in the forwarding and commission business on the Pennsylvania and Ohio canal. This was his first independent venture, and gave him a wider and freer field of action than he had hitherto occupied. Year after year the business grew and satisfactory gains rewarded his enterprise and labor. While not actively employed in the old bank he became connected with its business in 1849, in the capacity of director, a position which he held until the bank closed out its business in 1863. He subsequently became one of the first directors of the First National bank, and sustained that relation until his death.

Mr. Tayler, in 1856, discontinued the canal trade and became a member of the coal firm of Tod & Yates, subsequently Tod, Yates & Tayler. The office of the company was at Cleveland, but his family remained in Warren. After about five years he severed his connection with the firm.

In 1864, after the death of George Tayler, the directors of the First National bank showed their confidence in his brother, Matthew B., by choosing him to the vacant cashiership. From that time until his death he discharged the duties of that office.

Mr. Tayler was married March 17, 1841, to Miss Adaline A. Hapgood, daughter of George Hapgood. A family of eleven children blessed this union, all of whom are living. In this large and interesting family the father took great pride and interest. Always loving, always indulgent, always gentle, he found in the home circle a quieting refuge from every troubling care incident to active employments. Mr. Tayler in 1840 became a member of the Methodist Episcopal church, and during the forty years of his connection with that society he was always found pure, tender and sincere. Mr. Tayler was religious because he believed in Christianity, he was charitable because it gave him pleasure to relieve suffering and want. Many unfortunate people lost a full-hearted friend and assistant when he died.

During the month of November, 1880, Mr. Tayler complained considerably of indisposition, but with that will and determination which characterized all his conduct he remained at his post of duty. On November 22d he was compelled to yield, and at 8 o'clock on the following morning, November 23d, he died. The funeral services were held in the church of which he was a member November 26th. As a token of the universal respect in which he was held all business was suspended during the sad funeral hour.

Mr. Tayler was a man of medium height, broad shouldered, full-chested and compact body. His large face wore a settled and benevolent expression. His eyes and hair were dark. Native affability quickly won the friendship of people with whom he came in contact, qualities of character held the friendship of those with whom he associated. His manner was warm, hearty and sympathetic. No better analysis of his character or tribute to his memory can be written than the memorial prepared by his business associates:

When honored men pass away, it is well for us to consider those elements of character through which they won honor and achieved success. Mr. Tayler was a modest, retiring man, seeking not the approbation of his fellows so much as the approval of a good conscience, and yet was he honored of all who knew him, and of none so much as those who knew him best. In qualities of mind and heart he was worthy of the esteem he secured from all.

He was a man of a remarkably clear and well-poised judgment. Everything submitted to his consideration was carefully examined and well weighed before a decision was given. He had the rare faculty of retiring all extraneous questions, and personal influences, and judging of things upon their merits alone; his decisions were, therefore, accepted, and relied upon, as just, wise and conclusive. In matters of great interest, and in times of deep excitement, his equanimity was undisturbed, and his judgment unclouded.

He was a man capable of making fine moral distinctions, and was pre-eminently a lover of justice. Everything in his own conduct and life was harmoniously keyed thereto. No individual interest, no financial gains, no bias of friendship could make him deviate from the way commanded by the strictest justice, and the most uncompromising righteousness. He was as true to the claims of honesty and probity as the chronometer to the hour of midnight.

He was a man of convictions, and dared to maintain them. Such was the constitution of his mind that he loved truth, and in his eye it was of great price. He would not yield to error; he made no compromise with it. Liberal, charitable in his thinking, he nevertheless paid homage to the truth as it came to him, and refused to part with it. Unobtrusive in his opinions he was firmness itself in holding his beliefs. He regarded beliefs as the constructors of character, and character as priceless. A man of great strength of will, he was not obstinate—obstinacy seeks not for reasons; his opinions and decisions were always supported by them.

He was successful in business and gained a competence; but he used it not for selfish gratification. He was a man of benevolence and kindness of heart; a generous contributor to those institutions of society upon which its stability and excellency depend. He had an ear to hear the wants of mankind, a heart to feel for them, and an open purse to relieve them. Many were the objects of his charity who received his bounty not knowing whence it came. He was a friend of the poor, a distributor to the needy. Attentive to business and bearing heavy responsibilities, he yet found time for the discharge of those social obligations which devolve upon men in his station, and those church obligations which devolve upon the Christian. As a friend, none could be truer, more reliable, more constant.

He was a true Christian man. This is saying much, but there are none who knew him that will question it. His experience, his deeds, his life all bear witness to the great fact. He carried his religion into his business, and business into his religion. No man in the city of Warren commanded a larger share of the public confidence in his Christian integrity. He was an example of a Christian business man to whom reference may be made with great assurance. For forty years he lived in communion with the Methodist Episcopal church, of Warren, Ohio—a pillar, a wise counsellor, a safe guide. The uniform testimony of that large, intelligent church to his simple, unaffected piety, his liberality, and the wisdom of his counsels, is a witness to his character that cannot be misinterpreted. The esteem in which he was held by the citizens of Warren and the business communities adjacent, is a proof that no ordinary man has passed away. Such men are rare, and dying, they leave vacancies that go unfilled for a generation.

GEORGE HAPGOOD.

Few men become better known in the county in which they reside, than the editors of country newspapers. It is the business of the newspaper man to find out and narrate current happenings. He is consulted on matters of general information, of public opinion, and of general policy. For this reason, to the man of social temperament and painstaking habits, the position is fascinating; that it was so to Mr. Hapgood is shown by the fact that for a period of twenty-three years he remained connected with one paper. He was born in Petersham, Worcester county, Massachusetts, August 9, 1795, and died at Warren September 2, 1861. Little is known of his boyhood beyond the fact that he learned the printing trade in the office of the New England Farmer, of which Thomas G. Fessenden was editor, Brattleboro, Vermont. Having completed his apprenticeship, in the spring of 1817 Mr. Hapgood came westward, traveling on foot as far as Albany, New York, where he found employment of a temporary character. In December, 1817, he arrived in Warren, the place which he subsequently adopted as his home. He became connected with the Western Reserve Chronicle in a short time, and purchased an interest in the office in 1819. Until 1835 his work was chiefly in the mechanical department, but at that date he assumed the active editorship. The paper was strongly Whig in argument, as the editor was Whig in feeling. Glancing through the files, we find much in praise of "the gallant Harry of Kentucky"—Clay, and nothing against the Van Buren Democrat was too severe to be excluded from the Chronicle's columns. It is presumed that Mr. Hapgood's political services were brought to the notice of General Harrison, by whose administration he was chosen postmaster at Warren, though he was commissioned by John Tyler, after the death of Harrison.

Mr. Hapgood having been confirmed postmaster, sold his interest in the paper to his partner, Mr. Parker. But the tenure of a Federal office is uncertain. A sudden change of policy on part of the National administration, after the Tyler administration had become settled in the management of the Government, a gradual change began to be made in the whole civil service. Mr. Hapgood was a victim of this policy. After a service of about three months he was succeeded by General T. J. McLain, at that time an active Democrat. Mr. Hapgood received the Whig nomination for county auditor in the fall of 1842, and was elected by a complimentary majority. He failed of a re-election on account of unyielding loyalty to the Whig party, being unwilling to enter into compromise with the liberals, even though such compromise would probably have resulted in his re-election.

During his official term he engaged in the nursery business at Warren, which was under the supervision of his sons, in which he continued a number of years. The later years of his life were spent in ease and retirement.

While firmly attached to the Whig party, he desired the ultimate abolition of slavery. He belonged to that faction of the party which opposed the extension of slavery, and at the same time feared the consequences of Abolition agitation. He sympathized with refugee slaves, and whenever opportunity offered provided for them assistance. When the irrepressible conflict between slavery and freedom finally came, his sympathies were wholly with the newly organized Republican party.

Mr. Hapgood was a man of a quiet temperament, and perceptive mind, and agreeable, sociable qualities. In 1836 he became a member of the Methodist Episcopal church, and until his death remained consistent with his profession and true to his convictions. He was an officer of the church during most of the period of his membership, and had the satisfaction of seeing all of his family members of the church, all but one members of the church with which he was connected.

Mr. Hapgood was married April 6, 1820, to Adaline Adams, daughter of Asahel and Olive Adams, of Liberty township, and a sister of Asahel Adams, of Warren. The family of Mr. and Mrs. Hapgood consisted of eleven children. Three died in childhood. The remaining eight all married, and had families. George N., the eldest son, learned the printing trade in his father's office, and became one of the editors and publishers of the Chronicle in 1855, which relation continued until his death in August, 1865. Henry K., the youngest, died December, 1875. Charles is living in California. Laura (Mrs. Paul C. Ford) is living in Ashtabula county. William is a druggist of Warren. Three of the daughters, Mrs. M. B. Tayler, Mrs. George Van Gorder, and Mrs. S. R. Brown, live in Warren. Mrs. Adaline Hapgood died in the house in which she was married in Liberty township, October 26, 1871.

JOSEPH MARVIN.

The Marvin family of this county are descended from Reynold Marvin, one of the Puritan settlers of Massachusetts. Joseph Marvin, son of Matthew Marvin, was born at Lyme, New London county, Connecticut, March 26, 1772. He married in his native village in 1797. This union continued for a period of nearly sixty-eight years, until broken by the death of Mrs. Marvin, September 24, 1864, then in the eighty-fourth year of her age. Mr. Marvin lived to the remarkable old age of one hundred and one years, five months, and three days, the date of his death being August 29, 1873, at Atwater, Portage county, Ohio. On the same day of the same month, sixty-seven years before, his father, Matthew Marvin, died. He was a man of great industry and activity, being able to swing an axe even after he had passed the centennial of his birth. Mrs. Marvin, too, was strong and healthy even in her old age.

Joseph Marvin, son of Joseph Marvin, Sr., and well-known within the field of this history as teacher, merchant, and preacher, was born January 12, 1807, in Lyme, Connecticut. He accompanied his father's family in 1821 from their Connecticut home to Ohio, the journey being accomplished in the old-fashioned way, the wagon with goods being drawn by an ox-team, and the family by a horse-team. Slowly they traveled for forty days, until Musquito creek, in Bazetta township, was reached. There they settled in the midst of a woods more than five miles in extent, with all the surroundings of pioneer frontier life. Turkeys, squirrels, and raccoons destroyed crops, and wolves made night hideous with horrible howling. When the Marvin family settled in Bazetta there were only thirty-seven families in the township. All that were then married are dead, except Mrs. William Davis, who lives with her son-in-law, William Kennedy, in Bazetta, now in her ninety-eighth year.

Mr. Marvin, after having assisted his father on the farm seven years, began life for himself. A boy's work on a farm at that time was wholly unlike a boy's work since machinery has come into general use. Added to the toil of cultivating the soil was the severe labor of clearing, which was carried on year after year. Mr. Marvin engaged in teaching until 1835, and in the meantime had devoted considerable attention to the study of medicine. While at New Castle teaching, in 1834, he became interested in a religious revival, and on September 13th was soundly converted in the old Methodist style. Before the year closed he joined the Methodist Episcopal church, and was licensed to preach in 1835 by the quarterly conference held at Greenville, Pennsylvania, in October of that year. The presiding elder engaged him to labor on Salem circuit, consisting of twenty-seven appointments to be filled every six weeks. Mr. Marvin filled his appointments in regular succession, preaching as often as eleven times in eight days. There certainly was very little financial inducement for a Methodist itinerant in that day. The highest salary Mr. Marvin ever received was $142 for a year. The pay of most circuit riders was much less than that. Mr. Marvin had weakened his constitution before entering the ministry, by excessive study, so that the physical exhaustion caused by his severe itinerant labors brought on nervous prostration. He quit the circuit and resumed teaching. In 1837 he was employed in an academic department to be connected with Ohio university at Athens. He labored in his new field with success for some time. He married, December 25, 1838, Lucy Temple Dana, daughter of Joseph Dana, of Athens.

Mr. Marvin, accompanied by his wife, returned to Trumbull county in January following, having resigned his position to a young college graduate. Since that time he has been engaged in merchandising and farming, holding these employments, however, as secondary to the calling to which he devoted himself in early life. During the forty-six years of ministerial life, sometimes in conference relation, but for the most part as local preacher, he has asked or received little monetary compensation for his labor, having ample outside means of support. During all that period he has failed to meet but two appointments of his own announcement. He has traveled in his buggy more than forty miles on Sunday and preached to two congregations. It is a remarkable fact that despite the hard labor to which his life has been devoted he is yet, at the age of seventy-five years, hearty and strong. His figure does not suggest old age, nor is he w..ing to admit what the incontrovertible logic of mathematics proves, that he is an old man. Mr. Marvin, after the death of his first wife, married Ann VanGorder, daughter of James L. VanGorder, of Warren. This city has been his home since 1851.

BENJAMIN STEVENS AND STEVENS FAMILY.

The name of Stevens has been associated with the history of Warren since 1816. The advance member of the family was Benjamin Stevens, a clothier, who took charge of the works here at that date, being then in his twenty-ninth year. Mr. Stevens is yet living in Warren, as are also two of his brothers, the youngest of whom has passed his eighty-sixth year.

The ancestry of this family has been traced to General Nicholas Stevens (or Stephens) a brigadier under Cromwell in the revolutionary army of 1649. After the overthrow of the commonwealth and the restoration, in 1660, General Stevens, deeming prudence the better part of valor, came to America and settled in Taunton, Massachusetts. From his youngest son Henry, Zebulon Stevens was descended. He was a small Connecticut farmer, and had a family of seven sons, three of whom were in the Revolution— Zebulon, Thomas, and Benjamin. The seventh son, Jonathan, was born in Canaan, Connecticut, March 7, 1767. He married in Connecticut Susan Wells, and in 1789 removed his family to Luzerne county, Pennsylvania, and from there in 1799 to Addison county, Vermont. The family at that time consisted of one daughter and five sons, the daughter and eldest son having been born in Connecticut. The children were, Harriet, born in 1787; Benjamin, born July 20, 1788; William, born in 1790; Charles, born in 1792; Horace, born February 4, 1794, and Augustus, March, 1796.

The Stevens family belonged to the Jeffersonian or Democratic party, and in consequence were supporters of the war which was declared against England in 1812. The father and all the sons belonged to the militia companies, and when an invasion of New England from the north was threatened, all but the youngest son volunteered. All were engaged on the celebrated field of Plattsburg, September 11, 1814, which resulted in the complete rout of British General Provost, with a loss of 3,000 men. The American forces were mostly militia from the neighboring towns of Vermont and New York. Every boy able to carry a gun was admitted to the lines.

Jonathan Stevens came to Ohio after the emigration of his children, and settled at Newton

Falls, where he enjoyed a peaceful old age. His death occurred in 1848. Mrs. Susan Wells Stevens died in Vermont. Harriet, the only daughter, was married to Mr. Harris. She came to Ohio in 1827, and lived with her father; went finally to reside with her son, Judge S. W. Harris, of Morris, Grundy county, Illinois, where she died. William is residing in Pennsylvania, having attained the advanced age of ninety-two. Charles married Catherine Sterling, of Lancaster, Fairfield county, Ohio. He died in Warren in 1860. He was in partnership with his brother Benjamin in the manufacture of cloth. Horace came to Warren in 1817. He was a hatter by trade, and opened a shop on Market street. With the exception of an interval of a few years he has resided here ever since. Augustus came to Warren in 1816, and engaged in business with his brother Benjamin in the cloth business. He afterwards established a factory at Newton Falls which he operated for a number of years. He now resides with the family of his brother Benjamin at Warren.

Benjamin Stevens at the age of fourteen was apprenticed in a clothier's establishment in Vermont for a period of seven years—as it looks to us now, a long time to learn a trade. At the expiration of his service he was given charge of the works, but soon engaged in business on his own responsibility. He met with heavy loss at the conclusion of the War of 1812, in consequence of the demand for army clothing being suddenly stopped. Mr. Stevens started West in search of a favorable location in 1816. Warren being at that time the leading town in the Reserve, he like most other emigrants made this the objective point. Levi Hadley was operating a carding machine and Thomas Wells had just fitted up machinery for making cloth. Mr. Stevens purchased both establishments and operated a regular factory. Water-power was not adequate to a large business in all the departments of carding, spinning, weaving, and fulling, but considerable flannel was made for the Pittsburg market, and cloth was manufactured at $1 per yard.

The business mainly consisted in carding wool ready for the domestic spinning wheel. During the year 1842 Mr. Stevens worked twenty-eight thousand pounds of wool. The business began to decline about 1850 in consequence of the growth of larger establishments and increased transportation facilities. Mr. Stevens sold out and retired in 1847. He married, in 1825, Mary Case, daughter of Meshach Case. Their family consisted of five children, three of whom are living. Mary and Harriet reside in Warren; Lucy (Opdycke) in New York; Benjamin and Leonard are dead. Mrs. Mary (Case) Stevens died in Warren April 18, 1874.

He was initiated into the Masonic fraternity in Vermont and in former years attended the communications of the lodge at Warren. He is the oldest member of the Methodist Episcopal church, having been received into membership but a few months after the organization of the first class in November, 1819, composed of six persons. For more than sixty years Mr. Stevens has made the simple demands of his church a part of his life, and in his old age is comforted by the faith which has ripened with years.

Horace Stevens was born in Huntingdon township, Luzerne county, Pennsylvania, February 2, 1794. In 1808 or 1809 he went to learn the hatters trade, at which he served some six years. In the fall of 1816 he came to Warren, Ohio, and the following spring commenced at his trade in Warren, in which he continued until 1828, when he removed to Newton Falls, and with his brother Augustus built a flouring- and saw-mill, and also clothing and carding works. He resided there until 1867, when he retired from active business and removed to Warren, where he has since resided. In 1819 he married Miss Aurelia Pier, who was born in 1798. She died in 1851. Mr. Stevens volunteered in the War of 1812, and was under fire at the battle of Plattsburg. He was captain of the Rifle Grays in Warren in 1825 or 1826. His first American ancestor was General Nicholas Stevens, who came over in 1660 and settled at Taunton, Massachusetts. Of his family four daughters are living, namely: Aurelia Hall, of Philadelphia; Mary B. Fuller, of Warren; Laura A. Merwin, of Fox Lake, Wisconsin, and Frances Smith, of Waupun, Wisconsin.

Mary B. Stevens was born in Warren October 25, 1822, and married Ira Lucius Fuller December 10, 1840. Mr. Fuller came to Warren at an early day and was a clerk in the post-office and county clerk's office; read law and was admitted to the bar in Warren, and was a successful lawyer. He was subsequently elected probate judge. He died October 16, 1874. Six of the eight children of Judge and Mrs. Fuller are living—Mrs. Mary C. Harmon, Horace S., and Emily S. Tidball, of Nebraska; Lucius E., of Bradford, Pennsylvania; Harriet P., attending Cooper seminary at Dayton, Ohio; Robert P., at home. Lily S., wife of R. H. Freer, died May 22, 1873, and Ella T., at the age of twenty, in 1872.

Augustus Stevens was born in Pennsylvania in 1796. He was married to Esther C. Sherril, of Vergennes, Vermont, in 1821. She died in Newton Falls in 1860. He removed with his family to Vermont, and in 1816 made his first visit to Ohio. He stopped with his brother Benjamin in Warren, and subsequently engaged with him in the manufacture of cloth at this place. He built a grist-mill about 1822, below the present Market-street bridge, which he sold in 1828 to James L. Van Gorder. Mr. Stevens then removed to Newton Falls, where he built a gristmill and cloth factory, which he operated in partnership with his brother Horace. In 1861 he returned to Warren and has since been living here.

CASE FAMILY.

The Case family settled in Trumbull county, near Warren, in the year 1800. The name is of Dutch origin. Meshach Case was of Holland parentage on his father's side and Irish on his mother's side. He was born in New Jersey in 1752, and in 1780 he married, in Westmoreland county, Pennsylvania, Magdalen Eckstine, who was of German descent. They settled in Washington county, Pennsylvania, whence they removed to Trumbull county. Mr. Case was a farmer and shared the experiences incident to life in a new country. Mrs. Case died in 1832 at the age of seventy years. Mr. Case lived to the age of eighty-nine years, his death taking place in 1841. Their family consisted of eight children. Elizabeth was married to James Ellis, of Warren, Ohio, removed to Kentucky, and after his death she returned to Warren and died here; Leonard removed to Cleveland; Catharine was married to Daniel Kerr, of Painesville; Mary was married to Benjamin Stevens of Warren; Reuben removed to Maysville, Kentucky; Sarah was married to Cyrus Bosworth, of Warren; Jane died in childhood; Zopher, the only surviving member of the family, resides in Cleveland.

Of Leonard, the oldest son of Meshach Case, it is proper that something more should be said although his mature years were spent in Cleveland. He was born in Westmoreland county, Pennsylvania, July 27, 1786, and was consequently about sixteen years old when his parents settled in this county. A severe sickness the following year left him a cripple for life. Poor and unfitted for physical labor, his chief anxiety was how to escape becoming a burden upon his friends. He secured a few books and began the study of surveying, which at that time was considered profitable business. This was at a period of life when a whole career depends upon the little things which lead the way. Though he never became a regular surveyor he acquired a fair knowledge of the business, which was of inestimable service to him in after life. In 1806, being twenty-two years old, he obtained employment in the land office in Warren. His work attracted the attention of John S. Edwards, county recorder, who induced him to study law. In connection with other work he did sufficient reading to be admitted to the bar. His position in the land office gave him an accurate knowledge of the Western Reserve—its history and its resources. The appointment to the position of collector of taxes of non-residents on the Reserve still further increased his acquaintance.

In 1816 the Commercial bank of Lake Erie was organized and Mr. Case was appointed cashier. Cleveland was a small town at that time, and the bank did not occupy Mr. Case's whole attention. He pursued his profession and acquired the reputation of being the best authority in northern Ohio on questions relating to the law of real estate and land titles. He seldom appeared in the trial of general causes in the courts. In addition to banking and professional work he dealt extensively in real estate, which, after 1834, occupied all his time. His life was by no means devoted exclusively to the accumulation of a fortune. He was public-spirited and used his influence and wealth for the upbuilding of his adopted city. He died in Cleveland December 7, 1864, leaving one son, Leonard, who has since died without issue.

CHAPTER XI.

BIOGRAPHICAL NOTES.

George Parsons, Sr., was born in Enfield, Connecticut, April 10, 1781. He came to Ohio in 1803, and December 10, 1807, was united in marriage to Frances M. Austen. He was clerk of the county court some thirty years, and was also president of the Western Reserve bank. He died August 20, 1865, and his wife June 19, 1850. They raised two children—George, Jr., and Mrs. Heman R. Harman, who died in 1878. George Parsons, Jr., was born in Warren, September 3, 1810. He studied law at New Lisbon, Ohio, and was admitted to the bar at Cincinnati, May 3, 1834, Salmon P. Chase being one of the examiners. On account of ill health he could not practice. June 28, 1838, he married Adaline Baldwin, by whom he had five children. The oldest, George, was a member of the Nineteenth Ohio volunteer infantry, and died in camp in Kentucky, March 10, 1862, in his twenty-second year; Adaline, born December 16, 1842, Charles H., December 13, 1846, both at home; William B., May 31, 1849, residing in Bazetta; Jacob H., June 14, 1852, a resident of Dakota. Mr. Parsons' first wife died January 26, 1861, and April 26, 1865, he married Harriet M., daughter of Roswell Lee, born in Farmington township, February 27, 1822. He resided on a farm in Champion township until 1866, when he moved to Warren township, on the Hapgood place. Mr. Parsons has been a member of the Episcopal church for forty years.

Henry Stiles was born in Danbury, Connecticut, in 1798, and was nine years old when his family came to Canfield. All aspiring boys in those days were apprenticed to learn trades, saddlery being one of the most popular. There were no light vehicles, so that errands and pleasure-going called the saddled horse into use. Wheeler Lewis had the principal shop in Warren, and it was to him that Mr. Stiles was apprenticed in 1812. The usual apprenticeship at that time was seven years, but boys began so early that that they had acquired their trade and their liberty at twenty-one. It will be seen that Mr. Stiles was " bound out," as it was called, at the age of fourteen. When he had completed his trade he purchased the business from Mr. Lewis. In 1834 he sold the shop to Mr. Brewster and removed to Medina to engage in milling with his brother Jairus. A year later he removed to Norwalk, where he was one of the first to plant shade trees, for which that city is now celebrated. In 1837 Mr. Stiles returned to Warren and engaged in mercantile business in partnership with George Mygatt. In 1848 he purchased Mr. Mygatt's interest and continued in business in partnership with his sons until his death, which occurred August 13, 1869. Mr. Stiles married, in 1821, Mary Reeves. She died at Warren in December, 1859. Their family consisted of six children, five of whom are living: Henry L., Timothy M., William R., Mary E., Sarah C. (Jones), and George M. William, Mary, and Mrs. Jones reside in Warren. George M. died in 1873. William R. continues the dry goods business at the old Mygatt & Stiles corner.

Zalmon Fitch, first cashier and second president of the old Western Reserve bank, was born in 1785. He came to the Reserve from Washington county, Pennsylvania, in 1801, his parents having settled that year at Canfield. A few years later he engaged in mercantile pursuits in which he continued until the organization of the Western Reserve bank at Warren. Mr. Fitch served as cashier until General Perkins resigned the presidency in April, 1836, when he succeeded to the vacancy. About 1840 Mr. Fitch removed to Cleveland. He became a director in the Bank of Cleveland and also one of the directors of the Cleveland & Pittsburg railroad. He died at Cleveland April 28, 1860. He was a man of strong character and good executive ability. He was one of the most successful of that successful generation of early business men whose names were associated with the reliable old Western Reserve bank.

One of the oldest merchants and the oldest book dealer in Warren is W. N. Porter. He was born in New Hartford, New York, in 1804. Having learned cabinet-making, he worked in his native place until 1832, when he removed to Warren. He continued at his trade at this place until 1836. D. M. Ide some time before had started a bindery, and that year associated Mr. Porter in partnership. A general book trade was added to the bindery business. This was the first bookstore in Warren, though, of course, other stores had kept books in their general stock. Blank books were at that time made by the home manufacturer, and the trade in miscellaneous books was much larger than at present. Blank book manufacture has, of late years, been concentrated into large establishments, but why the trade in general volumes has fallen off is at first a puzzling question. The number of readers has increased, and as the country grows older, people have more time to spare from business to devote to reading. A partial explanation is found in the growth of periodical literature; easy access to large city establishments may also have some influence upon the rural trade. Mr. Ide remained in partnership with Mr. Porter about fifteen years. He then removed to New Hampshire where he died in 1880. Mr. Porter, excepting an interval of two years, has been in the book trade since 1836. He was married in New York, to Mary Ann Higby. Their family consisted of one son and one daughter. The son had a special fondness and aptitude in art. He opened a studio in Denver, Colorado, in 1875, but his health failed, and he died in May, 1876. The daughter, Mrs. D. W. Jameson, resides in Warren. Mrs. Porter died in November, 1878.

Calvin Austin was probably in Warren in 1800. He was a prominent man, and one of the first justices of the peace. He was also associate judge. His sons, Seymour and Calvin, were prominent merchants.

Asahel Adams came to Trumbull county in 1807, and to Warren about 1814. He built the old Franklin House, on the corner of Market street and Park avenue, where he lived and kept store. Later he built and occupied the Adams homestead on Mahoning avenue, and died in October, 1852, aged sixty-five years. His wife, whose maiden name was Lucy Mygatt, still survives him. Two sons reside in Warren, Whittlesey Adams, insurance agent, and George Adams, book dealer.

Adamson Bently was born in Allegheny county, Pennsylvania, July 4, 1785, and at an early age came to Brookfield, Trumbull county. He began life at nineteen years of age as a Baptist preacher, and was settled in Warren in 1810. In addition to his work in the ministry, he was a merchant, a cattle-drover, and managed a tavern. He was a director in the Western Reserve bank, and built a number of houses. About 1820 Mr. Bently became interested in the doctrines advanced by Alexander Campbell, and eventually became one of his followers. He died in November, 1864.

Cyrus Bosworth was born in Plymouth county, Massachusetts, April 12, 1791, and came to Warren in 1811. He busied himself, at first, in teaching school, but soon was employed as an express messenger between Warren and Pittsburg, and carried to the last named city the earliest news of Perry's victory. In 1813 he married Miss Serina Strowbridge, of New England. After his return to Warren he built the National hotel, and also engaged in mercantile business in a frame building standing south of the hotel, and afterwards well-known as "Stiles' Store." He attempted to start a distillery on Red run, where it is crossed by Woodland street, but the enterprise soon failed. Later, he purchased and occupied a farm in Lordstown, on the Canfield road. Having lost his first wife, he was married again to Miss Sarah C. Case, a sister of the late Leonard Case, of Cleveland. He was for many years prominent as a worker in the interests of the Disciple church. He also held the offices of sheriff and Representative. His death occurred in Warren, April 4, 1861.

David Bell occupied a farm and house where the Jacob Perkins place is, on the Bazetta road, near Red run. He came to Warren, probably, previous to 1808, and was from Ireland.

Captain Oliver Brooks came from New Jersey and occupied the old Brooks homestead, on South street.

Samuel Chesney was born in Mifflin, Juniata county, Pennsylvania, April 18, 1778. He came to the Reserve in 1803, having previously taught school near Pittsburg. He for many years held the office of deputy postmaster, and was elected justice of the peace a number of years in succession, until he declined to serve. His death occurred May 5, 1866. One son and one daughter survive—Benjamin Chesney, of Painesville, and Mrs. L. J. Iddings, Warren.

William W. Cotgreave was in Warren as early as 1807. He was one of the active men of the place, and a major in the war of 1812; but he seems to be best known through the number of buildings that he erected, conspicuous among which was a large house, standing upon what is now known as the VanGorder property, and sometimes called "Castle William." He married a daughter of John Reed, and finally, removing to Mansfield, Ohio, died there.

Henry Harsh came to Warren in 1801, and purchased the lot and built a house where Adams' book store now stands. He also built a blacksmith shop at the same place, being one of the first blacksmiths in Trumbull county. He died June 5, 1828.

Jacob Harsh was born in Lancaster county, Pennsylvania, in 1783, and came to Trumbull county, Ohio, in 1803, settling in Warren. He carried on blacksmithing for many years. He was in the War of 1812, serving three months, from Warren. He married Elizabeth, daughter of James Wilson, and reared a family of five children, of whom two sons are living. He moved on the place now owned by his son H. J. Harsh in the spring of 1832, which was then but little improved. He was a leading member of the Disciple church. He died October, 1851. Mrs. Harsh died August, 1853. Henry J. Harsh was born in Warren, Ohio, February 22, 1829; married, May 14, 1851, Jane M., daughter of Milton Rice, born in Parkman, Portage county. Milton Rice was one of the early settlers of Southington township, coming with his father, Joseph Rice, about 1808. He had a family of five children, four of whom are living. He died in Newton Falls April 10, 1863. Mrs. Maria Rice is still living at Newton Falls with her son, Dr. N. J. Rice, aged seventy-seven. Mr. Harsh still occupies the old homestead. He has dealt extensively in buying and shipping live stock, and has also paid considerable attention to stock-raising and to dairying. Mr. and Mrs. Harsh are the parents of the following children: Milton M.; Jennie E., wife of Dr. Milton Atkinson, of Cortland; J. C. Fremont; Frederick R.; William J., and Kittie P.

John Harsh was born in Westmoreland county, Pennsylvania, October, 1794. When very young he settled in Warren, learned the trade of blacksmith and followed it during his life in Warren. He was always a hardworking man and a skillful mechanic, and acquired a handsome property. He was married in 1821 to Nancy Hall, who is still living at the age of eighty-three. The issue of this marriage was eight children, six of whom are living, the oldest aged sixty-one. Mr. Harsh died April 25, 1882, having been an invalid for several years.

Humphrey Harsh, oldest child of John and Nancy Harsh, was born in Warren, Ohio, November 7, 1821. He worked at blacksmithing until twenty-five years old. In 1849 he was constable for two years and during his official service he acquired a knowledge of financial transactions, and he has since followed the business of loaning money and buying notes with much success. November 7, 1866, he was married to Mrs. John Kibbee, daughter of George Hubbard. Mrs. Harsh was born in Connecticut in 1830.

John Eckman was born in Lancaster county, Pennsylvania, March 24, 1789. In 1802 he came to the Reserve from Fayette county, Pennsylvania, with his father, a gunsmith. Although they settled in Weathersfield township, Eckman was always more or less in Warren. He helped to build the furnace on the old Eaton place, and speaks of having seen the first bar of iron manufactured there. Adam Victory, of Pittsburg, was the hammer-man. Mr. Eckman is still living (1876), at the advanced age of eighty-seven years.

The Fusselmans came early, and lived many years on what is known as the Fusselman farm—one of the earliest settled farms in Trumbull county.

Levi Hadley, who came to Warren in 1815, and followed the business of a wool carder and hotel keeper, soon left and became a judge in the Sangamon country, in Illinois. Later he committed suicide by jumping from a steamboat into the Mississippi river.

James Quigley, one of the first and most energetic merchants in Warren, was born in Cumberland county, Pennsylvania, in 1770. He came to the Reserve in 1809 or 1810, and in addition to his mercantile business he dealt in live stock. He died in 1822.

Justus Smith came to Warren from Glen Falls, Washington county, New York, in 1810, with a view of making an exchange of property with Royal Pease, who was then a citizen of Warren, and who owned the whole lot upon which the First National bank stands. An exchange was effected, and Mr. Smith returned east to settle up some business, sending out his family the next year, who took possession of the building vacated by Mr. Pease on the bank lot, and Mr. Smith returned later in company with Jacob H. Baldwin, and on foot. Mr. Smith occupied the

Pease property until 1815, in which year he died, leaving a widow and five children. Mrs. Smith then sold her lot to the bank, and purchased the lot on the corner of High street and Mahoning avenue, now owned by Warren Packard. There she lived until 1836, when she sold her property, and passed the remainder of her life with her children.

Edward Spear was born in Huntingdon county, Pennsylvania, October 12, 1792. He moved to Warren in 1818. For seven years Mr. Spear was associate judge of the common pleas, and held the office of justice of the peace until the time of his death. He was for many years prominent as an elder in the Presbyterian church of Warren, and also as a Mason. His death occurred on the 31st of January, 1873.

James Scott was born in Carlisle, Pennsylvania, March 17, 1774, and moved to the Western Reserve in 1801. Scott built the jail that stood on the bank of the river, which was burned in 1804. He also had the contract for building the old court-house, 1813-16. He died January 31, 1846.

Elihu Spencer, a gentleman of culture, came to Warren in 1816, and lived in a house which stood on Liberty street, on the present site of the building erected by Isaac VanGorder from the bricks of the old court-house. He died in 1819, leaving a wife and child, who returned to the east, where the son, although dying young, attained some eminence in the literary way.

Mark Wescott, one of the earliest inhabitants of Warren, lived for many years in a house recently torn down, but then standing on the southwest corner of Pine and Market streets.

Zebina Weatherbee, a prominent early merchant, came to Warren very early, probably about the year 1803. He died young, about 1812, leaving a widow, the sister of the late Mr. Francis Freeman. Mrs. Weatherbee died July, 1876, at the advanced age of ninety years. Mr. Weatherbee was probably the third person in Warren to engage in mercantile business, as has been previously noted. In 1803 Mr. Weatherbee had a contract to remove the trees felled upon the public square.

One of the oldest citizens of Warren is Samuel Ellwell, now in his eighty-eighth year. He was born in Salem county, New Jersey, April 18, 1795. He married February 29, 1816, Anna Reeves, and the same spring removed from Bridgeton, New Jersey, to Warren, Ohio. He had worked in a woolen factory in New Jersey, and after he came to Warren was employed in the woolen factory of Benjamin Stevens for several years. He then purchased of Noah Brockway, near Warren, a farm of eighty acres, on which he resided until his removal to Warren in 1860. His wife, Anna, died in 1856 aged fifty-seven. She was the mother of his children, of whom there were ten, seven boys and three girls, of whom six sons are living, viz: Stephen, living in Kansas; General John J. Ellwell, of Cleveland; Augustus, in Braceville; Alfred, in Willoughby; Joseph S., and William H. H., in Chicago. In 1860 Mr. Ellwell was married to Mrs. Clarissa Hall, who died January 15, 1871.

Lewis J. Iddings, son of Richard Iddings, was born in Warren in 1809. He began mercantile business in Warren in 1832, and was engaged in trade without interruption until his death in 1879. He was a man of liberal, progressive spirit, and was esteemed by his fellows both in business and in society. He was elected director in the old Western Reserve bank in 1855, and held a great many positions of trust. Mr. Iddings married, in 1840, Jane Chesney, who still survives.

James Reed was prominent among the business men of Warren. His death occurred October 12, 1880. The Western Reserve Chronicle of the next day contained the following:

Our community was suddenly shocked yesterday morning by the announcement on the streets of the death of our esteemed townsman, James Reed, of the stove firm of James Reed & Sons. He had been sick for some ten days, but on Monday seemed much better, and the most sanguine hopes were entertained of his recovery. When, therefore, as men were on their way to the polls yesterday morning, they learned of his death, all were filled with astonishment and the deepest sadness.

James Reed was born in Virginia in October, 1812, being, at the time of his death sixty-eight years old. He came to this county some forty years ago, and settled in Newton Falls. Here he engaged in the foundry business in company with Mr. Charles Boardman. He continued the business here until January, 1859, when he moved to this city. Here he purchased the foundry then owned by James Warl, and prosecuted his business until 1861, when he united in business with Jameson & Wheeler, under the firm name of Reed, Jameson & Co. In 1864 he sold his interest to Jameson & Wheeler, and returned to Newton Falls, where he engaged in the dry goods trade until 1870. In that year he returned to Warren, and bought out Jameson & Wheeler. Since that, he and his two sons, Thaddeus and William, have conducted the foundry and stove business under the firm name of James Reed & Sons.

Mr. Reed, it may be justly said, was one of the most highly respected men in this community. It is slight praise when we say that for punctuality, thoroughness, strict honesty and integrity, he stood without reproach, and without a superior.

Among business men and all who knew him, his name was a synonym of stability and honor. Upon the Disciple church, of which he was a member and a leading officer, his death is a terrible blow. In that body of Christians he stood as a pillar, and the sorrow which pervades that family of worshipers is second only to that which fills his own household; and here it is crushing. His family may be assured that they have the deepest sympathy of this whole people.

D. J. Adams, president of the First National bank, Warren, is a son of Robert and Sally (Jackson) Adams, and was born in Londonderry, New Hampshire, November 24, 1823. Mr. Adams' career has been exclusively of a business and commercial character. He lived in his native town until eleven years of age, and then went to Genessee county, New York, where he resided until twenty years old engaged in farming. He removed to Erie county, Pennsylvania, in 1843, and was engaged in the stove business until 1853. He married there, in 1850, Mary Smith, who is still living. In 1853 he came to Kingsville, Ashtabula county, and carried on farming until 1863. For a few years subsequently he was engaged in the oil business in Pennsylvania, while retaining his residence in Ohio. In 1868 he commenced trading through the Southern States, dealing extensively with sugar planters in Louisiana, which proved a profitable business. In this he continued until 1876, when he took up his residence in Warren, where his headquarters had been since 1873. On the organization of the Second National bank of Warren he was elected president, and is still filling that position.

J. H. McCombs, cashier of the First National bank, of Warren, Ohio, was born in Weathersfield, Trumbull county, Ohio, February 13, 1814, elder son of James and Elizabeth McCombs. James McCombs settled in Weathersfield in an early day and resided there until his death. He was drafted in the War of 1812, and went to Sandusky but was subsequently discharged on account of sickness. He died in 1847 and his wife the same year. They were the parents of two sons, the subject of this sketch and Milo McCombs, who died in 1879, a resident of Howland township. J. H. McCombs came to Warren in 1832, and has resided here since with the exception of two years which he spent in Youngstown. He began here in business with H. W. Smith in a general store, with whom he continued until 1868. Subsequently he was in partnership with Mr. Charles Smith, afterwards retiring from active business until the fall of 1879, when, in connection with George K. Ross, his son-in-law, he began the wholesale grocery business, in which he still retains an interest. He was elected a director of the First National bank upon its organization in 1863, and afterwards was chosen vice-president. In January, 1881, he was elected cashier. Mr. McCombs was married in 1837 to Miss Amarillis B., daughter of John Fitch, an early settler of Mahoning county. The fruit of this union was two daughters, Helen and Charlotte. Helen, who died January, 1881, was the wife of George K. Ross.

One of the oldest business men in Warren is Charles Smith, president of the Trumbull National bank. He was born in New York August 12, 1803, and was the son of Justus and Charlotte Delamater Smith. His parents removed to Ohio in 1808. He began business as clerk for Judge King, and in 1822 opened a store in partnership with his brother, H. W. Smith, with whom he continued till 1835. After the Ohio & Pennsylvania canal was opened, Mr. Smith ran a packet boat for some time. He was interested in the canal company, and became its president. He was one of the original projectors of the Cleveland & Mahoning railroad, and was a member of the first board of directors. He continued merchandising till 1861. He was the largest stockholder in the Trumbull National bank, and ever since its establishment has served as its president. By industry and economy Mr. Smith has acquired considerable property, being among the wealthiest men in Warren. Mr. Smith married in 1828, Angeline, daughter of James Scott, one of the pioneers of Warren. Their family consisted of five children: William H., resident of Vicksburg, Mississippi; Edward C., cashier of Trumbull National bank; Margaret S., wife of Whittlesey Adams, Warren; Eliza and Mary, Warren. Mr. Smith has been a member of the Episcopal church for many years. In politics he has always been a Democrat, and never voted any other ticket except for his brother-in-law, David Tod, in 1861.

Oliver H. Patch, son of John H. Patch and

Rebecca Mygatt Patch, was born in Canfield, November 18, 1812. His father, John H. Patch was a native of Danbury, Connecticut, where he married Rebecca Mygatt, sister of Comfort Mygatt. At the age of fourteen Oliver H. Patch came to Warren to learn the saddlery trade as an apprentice of Henry Stiles. He served an apprenticeship of seven years. He then worked as a journeyman saddler in Brooklyn, New York, for two years, and at the age of twenty-three began business in partnership with George R. Brewster, the firm being Brewster, Patch & Co., the stock being general saddlery, harness, and carriage supplies. This was in 1835. Since that time Mr. Patch has been in the business and the head of the store until 1882. He was married in 1845 to Elizabeth Opdyke, of Williams county. Her brother, Emerson Opdyke, was a partner of Mr. Patch at the opening of the war. The firm at this time had large interests in the trade of their line at the South and lost heavily when the guns were fired on Sumter by the seizure of a large stock at Memphis, Tennessee. Mr. Patch's family consisted of five children, two of whom are living— Lucy A., and Henry O. Mr. Patch has been mayor of Warren and served on the council several years, also the board of education and other public positions. Mr. Patch recoved the money he lost at the beginning of the war before its conclusion. He has always been a progressive business man and public-spirited citizen.

Bostwick H. Fitch, is a son of Cook and Sarah Fitch. His father came from Danbury, Connecticut, and settled at Canfield in 1802. He married at Canfield Sarah Bostwick. The family of Cook and Sarah Fitch consisted of four children—Thalia Rebecca, married to Henry F. Kirtland, of Poland; Mary, married to H. F. Kirtland after the death of Thalia Rebecca; Bostwick H., and Thomas T. The last named lives in Poland. Bostwick H. was born September 24, 1815, at Canfield. His father was a hatter and kept a hotel in Canfield until his death by cholera in 1834. Bostwick H. had gone into Kirtland's store at Poland, and remained there until 1840 when he came to Warren and engaged in mercantile pursuits until 1844, since which time he has been in the wool trade. He was married in 1840 to Frances L. Bidwell, of Poland, daughter of Chester Bidwell. They have two children, Kirtland M., cashier of the Second National bank of Warren, and Mary F.

Rev. William O. Stratton was born in Baltimore, Maryland, November 19, 1798. His early occupation was that of a morocco dresser. He left home at the age of twelve and went as cabin-boy for a short time. He was afterwards engaged in merchandise in New York city in a small way. Having united with the church he commenced to fit himself for the ministry of the Presbyterian church, and attended the academy at Bloomfield, New Jersey, for two or three years. He was licensed to preach in 1825, and officiated as minister for a few years in New Jersey and in western New York; came to Ohio as a licentiate in 1828 and was located at Canfield, Mahoning county, until 1844. He was afterwards stationed at North Benton for twenty-four years, where his labors were very successful. He then retired from active work in the ministry and came to Warren in 1866, where he has since lived, occasionally occupying the pulpit of the Presbyterian church in the absence of the pastor. Mr. Stratton was united in marriage October 9, 1832, to Anna M., daughter of Hon. Elisha Whittlesey. She was born in Canfield, Ohio, November 7, 1812. Mr. and Mrs. Stratton are the parents of seven children, of whom six are living, as follows: Rev. Howard W. Stratton, born September 9, 1833, a resident of Washington Territory; Lucy J., born April 19, 1835, now widow of Whittlesey Collins, and residing in St. Joseph, Michigan; Colonel Henry G., born March 1, 1837, a druggist of Warren; Polly A., born March 11, 1840, wife of Homer C. Reid, of Warren; Alice V., born June 9, 1848, wife of George M. Hull, residing in Virginia; Julia M., born July 10, 1855, wife of George H. Briscoe, residing in Atlanta, Georgia. Harriet A. died in infancy.

Rev. A. R. Kieffer, rector of Christ's church, Warren, was born in Alexandria, Huntingdon county, Pennsylvania, April 2, 1842; son of Rev. Dr. M. Kieffer, for many years president of Heidelberg college, Tiffin, Ohio. Mr. Kieffer graduated from Heidelberg in 1860. At the first call for troops in the spring of 1861, he enlisted in the Eighth Ohio volunteer infantry, company A, and was in the service eighteeen months, when he was discharged on account of physical disability. Returning home, he entered the theological department of Heidelberg, and completed a course of study, but declined ordination to the ministry. He was subsequently for a time a teacher in the Sandusky, Ohio, high school. In 1870, having previously decided to enter the ministry of the Protestant Episcopal church, he entered the senior theological class at Kenyon college, Gambier, Ohio, and graduated the following year. He was ordained a deacon of the Protestant Episcopal church by Bishop Bedell and sent to Ironton, Ohio, where he remained some three years, when he accepted a call to the rectorship of Christ church, Warren, delivering his first sermon here on the first Sunday after Easter, 1874. Mr. Kieffer was married December 25, 1866, to Miss Lissie Hall, daughter of Dr. Alexander Hall, a former prominent clergyman of the Disciple church and an author of a number of scientific works. Mrs. Kieffer was born in Belmont county, Ohio, March 3, 1848. Two children is the result of their marriage: Alma Kate was born December 19, 1868, and Augustus Bedell was born October 14, 1871.

Rev. Alexander Jackson, pastor of the First Presbyterian church of Warren, was born in Glasgow, Scotland, February 13, 1845. When in his tenth year his father died, and his widowed mother's circumstances were such as to make it necessary for the son to depend upon his own labor for a livelihood. He accordingly left school and sought employment in a book bindery, where he served a seven years' apprenticeship. Possessing a studious disposition, he devoted whatever spare time he enjoyed to his books, and attended the evening classes at the normal school, thus fitting himself to enter college. He attended the University of Glasgow for some time, and then entered the employ of a business house in Edinburgh, reserving a part of the time for study. This arrangement enabled him to take a course of four years in the University of Edinburgh, and one in the Divinity school. Mr. Jackson excelled in philosophical studies, and in a class of two hundred, was one of fifteen who won high honors. A Duke of Hamilton scholarship was awarded him, and he returned to Glasgow University, where he was graduated. He came to the United States in 1873, and continued his theological studies in the seminary at Auburn, New York. He then entered the ministry, and was pastor of the Presbyterian church in Amenia about three and a half years. He afterwards supplied pulpits in Newark, New Jersey, and in Chicago, until he was called to the pastorate of the church in Warren, December 28, 1879. Mr. Jackson was married September 10, 1872, to Agnes, elder daughter of John Armstrong, of Townhead, Dumfriesshire, Scotland, and has three children.

I. N. Dawson, for many years mayor of Warren, was born in Northumberland county, Pennsylvania, September 25, 1824. He came to Ohio in 1850, and entered the employ of G. O. Griswold at Warren. He afterwards became a member of the firm of Dawson, Hoyt & Co., manufacturers of oil, which business was continued several years. His administration as mayor of Warren covered a longer period than that of any other man since the organization of the municipal government, and was highly satisfactory. He also served years as justice of the peace in Warren. He was a member of the Masonic lodge and Baptist church. Mr. Dawson was married February 28, 1852, to Nancy L., daughter of John and Sarah Reeves. She was born in Howland township August 16, 1825, and liberally educated at the common schools and seminary. The family of Mr. and Mrs. Dawson consisted of four children, three of whom are living: William K., born December 21, 1852, resides in Columbus; Lewis Reeves, born June 23, 1856; and Ella R., born June 13, 1858, wife of William C. Christy, of Youngstown. Isaac N. Dawson died August 20, 1878. Mrs. Dawson resides in Warren.

G. O. Griswold, oldest son of Jesse and Fanny Griswold, was born in Meriden, Connecticut, December 1, 1810. When fourteen years old he commenced to do for himself, and was in an ivory comb factory and otherwise employed for six or seven years. In May, 1831, he was married to Eliza Ann Bailey. He engaged in the manufacture of sheet and wrought iron household implements, and then for a number of years in the manufacture of coffee-mills. For three years subsequently he had charge of a foundry. He came to Ohio in 1838, locating in Aurora. In 1842 he removed to New Castle, Pennsylvania, and engaged for some six years in the linseed oil business. Coming to Warren in 1849 he commenced the business in which he is still engaged. For the last three years it has been conducted as a branch of the Cleveland Oil works, and has done an extensive business, employing fourteen men. The products of his manufacture find a market in Cleveland and the East, the oil cake also being shipped to Cleveland. Mr. Griswold has been twice married, lastly in 1837 to Miss Maria M. Merriman, a native of Connecticut, and by this marriage has had three children, all of whom died in infancy. He has been a member of the council several terms. Mr. Griswold has made his success in life by his own efforts, having no start in life and beginning on $4 per month.

Colonel Henry G. Stratton, youngest son of Rev. William O. and Anna M. Stratton, was born in Canfield, Mahoning county, Ohio, March 1, 1839. He was brought up on a farm, attending the common schools, completing his education at Poland academy. In the fall of 1854 he entered the employ, as clerk, of F. A. Smith, druggist of Warren, with whom he remained six years, when, in January, 1860, he was admitted as partner. In May following he was burned out and the firm dissolved, but afterwards in connection with Lewis Hoyt, under firm name of Hoyt & Stratton, resumed business, and has since been engaged in the drug business in Warren, though with various partners, the firm now being H. G. Stratton & Co. April 27, 1861, he enlisted in company C, afterward attached to the Nineteenth Ohio volunteer infantry, and was elected first lieutenant under Captain N. A. Barrett; was ordered to West Virginia and was at the battle of Rich Mountain. After four months service he was mustered out at Camp Chase, Columbus, Ohio. Soon after returning home he recruited a company, raising sixty-three men in three days. He was elected captain of the company, which was afterwards known as company C, and attached to the Nineteenth Ohio volunteer infantry, and sent on detached duty to Kentucky. Colonel Stratton was afterwards in some of the fiercest engagements of the war—at Pittsburg Landing, Corinth, and at Stone River, where Colonel Stratton acted as major. The regiment suffered severely in this battle, 236 out of 456 men and officers being killed and wounded. Colonel Stratton was himself severely wounded, being shot through the right hip. He returned home on account of his injury, remaining about four months, when he returned to the army on crutches and was placed on court martial duty. He was promoted to major and subsequently to lieutenant-colonel. When the army moved from Murfreesboro he went with his regiment. At the battle of Chickamauga Colonel Stratton was in command of the regiment. He was in the engagement at Mission Ridge, and after the battle was ordered to the relief of Burnside at Knoxville, where his regiment re-enlisted as veteran volunteers, and after a brief furlough rejoined the army of the Cumberland at Dalton, Tennessee, and afterwards took part in the Atlanta campaign at Resaca, New Hope Church, Kenesaw Mountain, Peach Tree Creek (a sharp and brilliant engagement), and taking part in the siege of Atlanta. The campaign closed at Lovejoy Station, where Colonel Manderson was wounded, and the command of the regiment devolved upon Colonel Stratton. Returning to Atlanta he took part in the pursuit of Hood and subsequently returned with Thomas to Pulaski and Columbia, Tennessee. He participated in the battles of Franklin and Nashville, where the regiment suffered heavily, pursuing the enemy to Huntsville, Alabama, where they went into winter quarters. After a long and eminently successful military career Colonel Stratton, on account of physical disability, caused by his wound, resigned, and was mustered out at Huntsville, Alabama, February 13, 1865. October 14, 1868, he was married to Miss Susan R., daughter of General T. J. McLean, of Warren, and has one daughter, Flora May, born in 1873.

Samuel Fisher Dickey, son of Samuel Dickey, was born in Londonderry, New Hampshire, on the 11th of June, 1820. He attended academy in New Hampshire in 1843. He, with his father's family, came to Warren and settled on a farm. He was married in 1846 to Mary A. Parker, of Litchfield, New Hampshire. They have three children—Edward L., Fannie M. (wife of M. O. Messer), and Elizabeth L. Mr. Dickey has been city engineer since 1867, and continues to reside on his farm at Warren. He has been a member of the board of education for five years. He has been an elder in the Presbyterian church for thirty years.

Aaron Wentz was born in Pennsylvania February 22, 1817. When seven years old his parents removed to Binghamton, New York, where, after obtaining a business education, he entered upon mercantile pursuits. In 1838 he engaged in business in New York city. Nine years later he came to Warren, and in partnership with Mr. Parks, under the firm name of Parks & Wentz, opened a store. Mr. Parks retired in 1868, since which time Mr. Wentz has continued the business alone. His line is general dry goods and groceries. He married in 1847 Miss Sarah A. Hunt, who died in 1870. He married for his second wife, Julia, daughter of Hiram Baldwin, a former esteemed citizen of Warren.

Columbus Ward, mayor of Warren, was born in Ashtabula county, Ohio, May 29, 1834. His parents, William and Mary (Williams) Ward, were pioneers of Ashtabula county. He married in 1853, and has a family of four children: C. S., physician and surgeon; Augustus, William C., and Almon. Mr. Ward removed from Ashtabula county to Warren in 1865, and engaged as bookkeeper for G. O. Griswold. From 1867 till 1878 he was in the insurance business. In August, 1878, Mr. Ward was elected by the council to the mayoralty in place of I. N. Dawson, deceased. At the following spring election he was re-chosen to that office, and again re-elected in 1881. Mayor Ward gives close attention to municipal affairs, and is well regarded as a public official.

Henry C. Christy is the son of Matthias and Jane Christy, and was born in Howland township, March 23, 1847. He remained on the farm till 1867, when he entered mercantile business as a clerk for W. H. Smith & Co. The firm of Kirk & Christy was formed in 1868, composed of Isaac Kirk and H. C. Christy. Howard C. Bradley has since been admitted into the partnership. Their trade consists of hardware, house findings, and agricultural implements. Mr. Christy married in 1877, Miss Mary Hunter, of Howland township.

Cyrus J. VanGorder, son of James L. and Elizabeth VanGorder, was born in Suffield, Portage county, Ohio, in 1815. September 23, 1840, he married Miss Jane Seeley, daughter of Sylvanus and Mary Seeley. They have one daughter and one son—Mrs. John Kinsman, of Warren, and George S. Mr. VanGorder was in business with his father for many years, and was one of the originators of the Warren Gas works. In regard to his efforts in this direction the Scientific American of January 17, 1863, says:

Mr. C. J. VanGorder, of Warren, Ohio, conceiving it his duty to provide a better illumination for his fellow-townsmen, went to work and erected a coal gas manufactory, without any further knowledge of the process than that which he has derived from reading the various articles relating to it published from time to time in the Scientific American. His experience in overcoming obstacles and local prejudices has been no exception to the general rule, but he has the satisfaction of having triumphed over all of them, both material and mental, and the pleasure of seeing his scheme in successful operation, and his work appreciated by his townsmen.

James G. Brooks, oldest son of Oliver J. Brooks and Althea Gilbert, was born in Warren, Ohio, April 22, 1831. His father, who is still living, in Chicago, was born in New Jersey in 1795, and came to Warren about 1816 or 1817. Oliver Brooks, the father of Oliver J., came out several years earlier, about 1808. Oliver, Jr., was engaged in the tanning business for many years in Warren, with his brother, the firm being R. S. & O. J. Brooks. He raised a family of three sons and three daughters. James G. Brooks, in 1848, commenced as clerk with E. Hoyt & Co., where he remained some three years. In 1852 he purchased, in connection with Warren Packard, the business of Harmon & Co., and has been constantly in trade since, although the partnership has undergone several changes. In the winter of 1882 the interest of Warren Packard was purchased and the present firm of Babbitt, Brooks & Smith formed, who do an extensive business, both wholesale and retail. Mr. Brooks was married in 1855 to Miss Maria Bennett, by whom he had two daughters, Helen, wife of J. P. Stephenson, of Ottawa, Kansas, and Mary, wife of James McCormick, of Warren. His wife died in 1862, and in 1877 he married Caroline M. Pennock. By this marriage he has two children, Alice and James D.

E. P. Babbitt was born in Morris county, New Jersey, April 19, 1841. He received a common school education, and engaged in mercantile pursuits, in which he continued until coming to Ohio, in 1865. He entered the employ of Warren Packard as traveling salesman until January 1, 1869, when he was admitted to partnership. The firm name was Packark, Cook & Co., afterward Warren Packard & Co. Mr. Packard retired from the firm January 1, 1882, when the present firm of Babbitt, Brooks & Smith was formed. This firm is doing an extensive wholesale and retail business. November, 1868, Mr. Babbitt married Miss L. A. Adams, of Morris county, New Jersey. They are the parents of three children, Mary E., Edward A., and Sarah A. Mr. Babbitt is a member of the Presbyterian church and superintendent of the Sabbath-school.

Augustus L. Van Gorder, son of Isaac Van Gorder, one of the early settlers of Warren township, was born in Warren in 1823. He followed carpentering and painting for several years. In the fall of 1861 he removed to Bowling Green, Wood county, Ohio, where he remained for two years, engaged in farming. He then returned to Trumbull county, where he was engaged at farming until his death, which occurred in May, 1869. He married for his first wife Mary I. Beardsley, daughter of Curtis and Sophia Beardsley, of Canfield township, and had a family of six children, of whom three are living. His first wife died in July, 1859, and in 1860 he married Alice E. Hunt, by whom he had three children, who, with their mother, now reside in Madison, Lake county.

Henry L. Van Gorder, son of Augustus L. and Mary S. Van Gorder, was born in Warren, July 30, 1850. At the age of seventeen he commenced as clerk in the drug store of which he is now an owner, then the firm of Hoyt, Stratton & Hapgood. After an absence of two years on the home place, he returned to his former position in the same store with the new firm of Hoyt & Spear. For a couple of years he was on the road selling agricultural implements. He became a member of the firm of Hoyt, Bradford & Co. In the spring of 1882 the firm was changed to Bradford & Van Gorder, wholesale and retail drugs, groceries, etc.

Mrs. Dorcas (Boyle) Gaskill was born in Butler county, Pennsylvania, July 30, 1827. Her father, John Sullivan Boyle, was of English ancestry but of Irish birth, born in Castletown, Ireland. He came to the United States about the year 1820, and spent several years in traveling, subsequently locating in Butler county, Pennsylvania, where he engaged in teaching school. He married in Butler county, Nancy Dunlap, whose father was a large landholder there, and an early resident of the county. About 1830 Mr. Boyle removed to Warren, where he was engaged in teaching and in other pursuits, being for some time a clerk in the office of General Perkins. He died at the residence of his daughter, the subject of this sketch, in April, 1865, at the age of nearly eighty years, surviving the death of his wife only a few weeks. They were the parents of nine children, four of whom grew to mature age. Mrs. Gaskill received her early education at private schools in Warren. She was an apt pupil, and attained such proficiency in her studies that before she had reached her thirteenth year she began teaching a private school in Warren. She subsequently attended the Willoughby (Ohio) Collegiate institute, and also the Western Reserve seminary at Farmington, Ohio, where she completed her education. Her connection with the Union schools of Warren, which continued for a period of about twenty years, began under the superintendency of Mr. Leggett. She has taught in private schools in Warren for nearly an equal length of time; and so, for upwards of forty successive years, with the exception of two years—1875 and 1876—during which she was matron of the Chicago Female college, she has been thus prominently identified with the educational interests of the place. As a teacher she was very popular, and her career, pursued not without difficulties often, has been attended with much success. She was married April 5, 1848, to Peter Gaskill, of Warren, and has a family of three children.

Alonzo Truesdell was born in Hartford county, Connecticut, on the 14th of July, 1822. When nine years of age he came to Trumbull county with his parents, who settled in Vienna, where his father is still living upwards of ninety years of age. His mother died many years ago. They reared three children, of whom two are living—Ambrose in Vienna, and the subject of this sketch in Warren. Mr. Alonzo Truesdell came to Warren in 1839, where about 1850 he engaged in the furniture business, in which he has been engaged ever since. In the spring of 1859 he formed a partnership with Mr. Townsend, which has existed since. The firm manufactures furniture, selling at wholesale from the factory and retailing from the store. Mr. Truesdell was married in 1849 to Esther S. King, and has three children—Charles, a finisher in the factory; Walter K., a farmer and county surveyor in Pawnee county, Kansas; and Frank W., editor and proprietor of the Petroleum World newspaper, at Titusville, Pennsylvania.

C. A. Adams, oldest son of Asahel and Lucy (Mygatt) Adams, was born in Warren, Ohio, December 18, 1818. Asahel Adams was born in Connecticut and came to Ohio with his father, Asahel, Sr., about the year 1802. The family settled in Liberty township, Trumbull county, where they cleared up a place which is still in possession of the family. C. A. Adams received a common school and academic education and was brought up to mercantile pursuits. He began in trade in Warren in 1837, and continued there several years. He was one of the proprietors of the Western Reserve Chronicle for some ten years, firm of Adams & Hapgood, and for a time of Adams, Hapgood & Ritezel. He was postmaster of Warren four years under Taylor and Fillmore, and was deputy-collector of United States internal revenue for Trumbull county during the war of 1861-65. He resigned this position in 1865 and removed to Cleveland. After removing to Cleveland he engaged in mercantile business, organizing the firm of Adams, Osborn & Goodwillie. Mr. Osborn afterwards retired and Mr. Adams continued with Mr. Goodwillie under the firm name of Adams & Goodwillie, until 1879, when he retired from active business. He was married in 1863 to Mrs. K. E. Denis, and has a family of two daughters and two sons.

Samuel Pew came from Westmoreland county, Pennsylvania, to Trumbull county as early as 1809, and located on what is now the Dr. Woods property, west of Warren. He brought his wife and one child, and all his worldly goods with a single horse. The mother and child, with a feather bed, were carried by the horse, while Mr. Pew footed it, carrying his gun. After improving the place on which he first located, he sold out and bought where Henry Ernst now lives. He finally purchased four hundred acres where his son Seymour now lives, which was his permanent home. He died at the home of his son, S. H. Pew, about 1855. His wife's maiden name was Elizabeth Downey, whom he survived about two years. He had thirteen children, all of whom were born in Ohio, except the oldest. Only two are now living—Seymour, and Horace, who lives in Bazetta township. Seymour Pew was born on the place where he still lives in Warren township, in 1816.

He received from his father a farm of one hundred acres in Lordstown township, where he lived for some time. He then bought the home place where he has since lived. He was married December 25, 1840, to Sarah J. Snyder, and has had seven children, only three of whom survive—H. S., John, and Laura J. Swisher, who lives at New Straitsville, Ohio. The two sons are engaged in the crockery, china, and silver-plated ware business in Warren, under the firm name of Pew & Brother. H. S. Pew was married in 1865 to Julia, daughter of Richard Elliott, a resident of Champion township, and has three children—Kirt E., Addie L., and Fred C.

Jules Vautrot, son of Francis and Marie, was born in France October 17, 1819, and with his parents came to this country in 1834, the family settling near Meadville, Pennsylvania. When sixteen he commenced an apprenticeship at the jewelers' trade in Pittsburg, and afterwards worked in Louisville, Kentucky, two years. In 1849 he came to Warren, Ohio, and for nearly two years was in the employ of Walter King. He then engaged in business for himself and is still engaged in the same, having had partners at various times. The firm is now Vautrot & Hull. He was married in November, 1844, to Miss Rosella Gandillot, who was born in France in 1825, and has one son and one daughter, Jules J. and Julia. Mrs. Vautrot died in 1856. Mr. Vautrot was formerly a director in the Trumbull National bank, of Warren, and is now connected with the Second National. His son Jules was a member of the Eighty-fourth Ohio volunteer infantry in the war of the Rebellion, and was at the battle of Cumberland in 1862. In 1864 he was in the one hundred day service, being a corporal in the One Hundred and Seventy-first Ohio national guards, and was taken prisoner with his regiment at Cynthiana, Kentucky.

Caleb Peck was born in Cambridge, Massachusetts, in 1799; came to Ohio in 1820, and November 1, 1832, was married to Rebecca J. Porter, who was born in Lancaster county, Pennsylvania, January 27, 1813. Her parents, Francis and Sarah Porter, came to Ohio in 1826, settling in Howland township, afterwards, about 1831, removing to Champion, where he died in May, 1860. Mr. Peck, the subject of our sketch, was a resident of Warren from 1836 to 1860, engaged in the grocery trade, when he was burnt out, losing about $10,000. He then moved to the place now occupied by the family. He died December 3, 1880. His widow is still living. They have five children, namely: A. F., born in 1833, in Warren; George S., 1844, also in Warren; Elizabeth S., married and residing in Illinois; Alanson J., born in 1853, conducting the home place; Mary J., born in 1857, at home. Mr. Peck was a member of the Disciple church.

Benjamin H. Peck, oldest son of Harvey and Susan Peck, was born in New Haven county, Connecticut, July 18, 1824. He attended an academy at Orange and taught school for two or three years, remaining at home until of age. In 1847 he came to Mercer county, Pennsylvania, and engaged in mercantile business; went to Pittsburg in 1849, where he was engaged in business two or three years. He came to Warren, Ohio, in the spring of 1854, where he started in the dry goods business, soon after taking into partnership his brother, H. Peck, and has since done a successful business. The firm is Peck & Brother. December 26, 1876, he was married to Miss Margaret Matthews, a native of Ireland, born in June, 1845, who came to this country with her parents in 1846, the family settling in Farmington. Mr. and Mrs. Peck are the parents of one daughter and one son, namely: Lina, born March 23, 1878; Harvey, born October 29, 1879.

A. Hoelz emigrated to this country from Germany in 1854; resided in New York fifteen years; then removed to Greenville, Pennsylvania, where he remained eleven years, coming thence to Warren in the spring of 1880. He engaged in the merchant tailoring business, which he still continues under the firm name of A. Hoelz & Son, and which he has been engaged in most of the time since coming to America.

David Adams and his wife Deborah (Thorn), originally from the State of New York, removed with their family to Erie county, Pennsylvania, and thence to Trumbull county, Ohio, in 1842 or 1843. They settled first in Lordstown township, on a place now belonging to John McKee, but shortly afterwards moved into Warren township. About 1846 Mr. Adams bought of Judge King the Aaron Reeves place, in Warren township, where he lived until his death, which took place in 1871, at the age of seventy-eight. His widow is still living with other children on the old place, and is now eighty-eight years of age, though still smart and active. A. H. Adams, a son of David and Deborah Adams, was born in Galway, Saratoga county, New York, in 1821, and removed with his parents to Trumbull county. He married in 1856 Sarah E. Brockway, who had been a teacher in the public schools of Warren for three years. Her father, Noah T. Brockway, was one of the early settlers in the vicinity of Warren, where Mrs. Adams was born in 1828. Mr. and Mrs. Adams are the parents of six children, who are living—Louise M., Clara I., Marvin E., Alonzo H., Sarah E., and Charles E. Mr. Adams has been engaged, to a considerable extent, in the insurance business and also in patents. He formerly dealt largely in butter and cheese and in wool.

James H. Smith, son of Philander W. and Martha F. Smith, was born in Monroe county, New York, September 6, 1834. His father removed with his family to Ohio in 1837, and settled in Bazetta, Trumbull county, where he spent the balance of his life. He was a carpenter by trade. He raised a family of three daughters and eight sons, of whom nine are living. He died April 30, 1860, and his wife December 9, 1867. Mr. Smith was a soldier of the War of 1812. James H. Smith came to Warren in 1850 and commenced clerking in the hardware store of George K. Reynolds. He was in similar positions in New York city and Janesville, Wisconsin, for several years. Returning to Warren from New York city, he commenced with Mr. J. P. Freer, the firm name being Freer & Smith, in the grocery business. In April, 1864, he enlisted in the One Hundred and Seventy-fifth Ohio national guard; was wounded at the battle of Cynthiana, Kentucky, was mustered out at Johnson's island, August 22, 1864. He was married November 16th, of the same year, to Miss Mary A. Douglass, daughter of Thomas Douglass, and has one daughter—Zell Patti, born November 18, 1867.

G. T. Townsend was born in Youngstown, Ohio, in 1813. His father, John F. Townsend, a native of Wilmington, Delaware, came to Youngstown from Red Stone, Pennsylvania, as early as 1806. He was a hatter by trade, which he followed for many years, finally removing to a farm at Girard. He married, in Mercer county, Pennsylvania, about 1808, Anna Watson, and reared six children, of whom all but one are living. He died in Youngstown at the age of eighty-four. Mr. G. T. Townsend at the age of sixteen commenced to learn the cabinet trade in Youngstown, and afterwards worked at the trade in Pittsburg, Pennsylvania. In May, 1859, he came to Warren, Ohio, and engaged in the furniture business in partnership with Alonzo Truesdell, who had established the business some years previous. In exactly one year afterwards the firm were burned out. They immediately rebuilt, but the elements seemed determined upon their destruction. They were subsequently burned out three times, and in 1879 a tornado damaged their store and stock to the amount of $2,000. Messrs. Truesdell & Townsend have been in business together for nearly a quarter of a century. Mr. Townsend in 1836 was married to Miss Mary L. Kellogg. His family at one time consisted of three children, but only one is now living.

William S. Woodrow was born in Westmoreland county, Pennsylvania, October 2, 1807; moved to Trumbull county, Ohio, with his father in May, 1808, locating in Champion township. William and Martha, the parents of the subject of this sketch, made this their home till their deaths, which was in 1848, the mother preceding the father just twenty days. Mrs. Woodrow was a remarkable woman, quite strong and active, frequently doing the work of a man, assisting in clearing up the place and working the farm. Once upon a time she needed a pair of shears to cut out a garment for one of her boys, and not having the article, cut it with an axe. This family consisted of nine children, seven sons and two daughters. All grew up to man and womanhood except one son, who died in infancy. Only two of them are now living. A sister of W. S. Woodrow resides near Pittsburg. Mr. Woodrow was married in Warren in 1836, to Miss Eunice I. Holt. The family consisted of eight children, four daughters and four sons, only two of whom are now living. Four died when children, and two after they grew up. The survivors are William Henry, a resident of Youngstown, and Arthur, formerly a merchant in Pennsylvania. Mr. and Mrs. Woodrow have been members of the Presbyterian church since 1832, and he has been a member of the session for the past thirty years. He witnessed the installation of the First Presbyterian preacher of Warren, and every one who has been installed since. At the age of twenty-one Mr. Woodrow learned the carpenter trade, which he followed for fifty years. In August, 1881, he roofed his own house. He helped to build the old and the present Presbyterian church.

James Wilson, a native of Ohio, lived on a farm in Warren township about sixty years. Nancy, his wife, a native of Maryland, is still living. Mr. Wilson died in 1879, aged seventy-nine years. They had fourteen children, eleven of whom arrived at years of maturity. Six sons and three daughters are still living, viz: Catharine (Beach), Harriet (Curtis), Laura (Masters), William H., Corwin V., James F., Edward B., and Welty J. Five of the sons are ministers of the Methodist Episcopal church. J. F. Wilson is an attorney at Warren. Rev. W. J. Wilson, the second son, is now pastor of the Kinsman and Gustavus Methodist churches. He was born in 1839. He graduated from Allegheny college in 1866, and followed teaching six years. Four years of this time he was superintendent of the union schools in Washington, Pennsylvania. In 1872 he entered the ministry and has since labored in Trumbull and Mahoning counties. He was married, in 1866, to Emma N. Whittlesey, of Atwater, Portage county. Their four children are May M., Lou N., John W., and Roy C. Mr. Wilson's ministerial work has been greatly blessed, and he is deservedly popular.

Simon R. Estabrook was born in Holden, Worcester county, Massachusetts, in 1805, and came to Trumbull county, Ohio, in the fall of 1835. His first wife Frances (Scarborough), whom he married in Brooklyn, Connecticut, died before his removal to Ohio, leaving him one child, a daughter, now the wife of Professor Newton, of Oberlin college. He married for his second wife Mary Bushnell, a daughter of General Andrews Bushnell, of Hartford township, and resided in that township a year or two, but afterwards lived where his son James now lives, up the river in Warren township, where he owned some three hundred acres of land. He had bought the place where his daughters now live, and was improving it when, one morning

(July 7, 1871), while crossing the railroad bridge on the main line of the Atlantic & Great Western railroad, he was run over and almost instantly killed by a passenger train. He was an active and valued member of the Presbyterian church, and a highly esteemed citizen. By his second marriage he had four sons and two daughters named as follows: James A., Simon, David B., Frederick A., Mary B., and Ellen M. Simon, David, and Frederick are dead—the last named being drowned when about thirteen, while trying to save a comrade, with whom he was in swimming in the Mahoning river. James resides on the home place, married Martha Aldridge, and has four children. The daughters reside in Warren, and are unmarried. Ella has been a teacher in the public schools of Warren. Mrs. Mary Estabrook died October, 1879, aged about sixty-four.

Ulysses J. Adgate, son of John H. and Nancy (Hover) Adgate, was born in Warren, December 8, 1828. John H. Adgate was a native of New London, Connecticut, where he was born in 1791, and came with his father, John H. Adgate, Sr., to Trumbull county, Ohio, in 1800. John Adgate, Sr., was the owner of twelve hundred acres of land, southeast of and adjoining Warren. John H. Adgate, Jr., was a farmer by occupation. He married previous to the War of 1812, Nancy, daughter of Emanuel Hover, a pioneer of Warren. They raised a family of eight children, of whom five are living. He was a soldier in the War of 1812. In 1857 he moved to Kansas, where he died in April, 1861. Mrs. Adgate died in February, 1855. Ulysses J. married July 4, 1855, Jane, daughter of William A. Davidson, a former resident of Farmington township. They have had three children, of whom two are living, William A., and Margaret M., wife of Edward Bratton, a resident of Howland township. Frank died when four years old. Mr. Adgate was a resident of Kansas some four years, commencing with 1857. Returning to Ohio, he enlisted the Nineteenth Ohio volunteer infantry, and participated in the battles of Pittsburg Landing, Chickamauga, and Chattanooga; was at the siege of Atlanta, went in pursuit of Hood, and was at the battles of Nashville and Franklin, Tennessee; afterwards went to Texas, and continued in the service until after the close of the war, making in all over four years. He was mustered out at Columbus in December, 1865. Returning to civil life, he resumed his farm life on his place in Warren township, where he has since resided.

John L. Smith, son of Johnson and Susan Smith, was born in Port Patrick, Scotland, August 31, 1841. In 1845 his parents removed to Grimsby, England, where his father was a contractor on the government docks. He was killed at New Holland in 1848. In 1853 the widow, with her family, came to the United States, locating in Cleveland, Ohio, where all but the subject of this sketch still reside. He followed the occupation of gardener until learning the trade of stone-cutter. August 31, 1862, he enlisted in company C, Nineteenth Ohio volunteer infantry, and was in the battle of Stone River, and was one of the three of whom special mention was made for bravery in that battle. At the battle of Chickamauga, September 19th, he was captured and was an inmate of Libby prison and of other places, finally escaping from Danville with other prisoners was recaptured in the Blue Ridge mountains, bucked and gagged and returned to Danville. From there he was taken to Andersonville and experienced all the horrors of that place for seven months. Upon the approach of General Sherman he was removed to Florence, South Carolina. December 9, 1864, he was paroled, and returned home on furlough. Early in 1865 he joined his regiment at Nashville, Tennessee, and was finally discharged June 12th, the war having ended. Returning from the army he came to Warren and with Barnhart Goehring, under the firm name of Goehring & Smith, engaged in contracting and building, in which they did an extensive business. In 1874 Mr. Smith purchased the interest of his partner, and has since carried on the business. He was elected county commissioner of Trumbull county in the fall of 1879, and is the first officer of that kind elected from Warren township in forty-five years. He is also chief of the fire department. March 25, 1869, he married Carrie G. Tovey, of Cleveland, and has two sons, Albert C. and William T.

David B. Gilmore was born in Warren, Ohio, June 14, 1819. He is the oldest son of William and Mary Gilmore. William Gilmore, a native of Pennsylvania, came to Ohio about 1810, and settled in Warren, where he conducted the business of tanner and currier for William Quigley, on what is now Park avenue, for a few years. Of his six children but two survive, David B. and James A., residents of Philadelphia. He died in 1853. David B., when seventeen, commenced an apprenticeship at cabinet-making. He entered into partnership in 1840, with his former employer, William Williams, for one year, when he bought him out and the business was continued under different firms until 1857. He was elected county treasurer in the fall of 1857 and re-elected in 1859, serving four years. In 1862, he engaged in the boot and shoe business, under the firm of Cranage & Gilmore, for two years. From 1865 to 1871 he conducted the Gilmore house (now the Clifford house). He afterwards engaged in the furniture trade till the spring of 1879, when he retired from business. He has been twice married; in 1842, to Charlotte T. Jameson, the result of which marriage are the following children: Wallace J., born in August, 1843, and Charlotte J., born in January, 1851, now wife of William R. Case, residing in Philadelphia. Mrs. Gilmore died April 25, 1867, and March 30, 1881, he married Susan Moyer, daughter of Gideon Moyer, a former resident of Warren.

John Cratsley was born in Ontario county, New York, May 23, 1829. He was the youngest son of Frederick and Emma (Chamberlin) Cratsley. He came with his parents to Ohio in 1836. The family located in Vienna township, Trumbull county, where he remained until his twenty-fifth year. November 6, 1856, he married Mary J., daughter of Hugh and Jane (Campbell) Love. Hugh Love was born in Westmoreland county, Pennsylvania, in 1805, and came with his parents to Hubbard township, where his father was one of the pioneers. He continued to reside in the township until 1868, when (coal having been discovered on his place as early as 1840) he sold out to Chauncey Andrews and removed to Warren, purchasing the Judge Brown place, where he lived until his death, which occurred May 16, 1881, and that of his wife a year before. They raised a family of eight children, all of whom are living. He was an active member and liberal supporter of the church. Mr. and Mrs. Cratsley are the parents of two children, one son and one daughter, as follows: Albert B., born February 26, 1858, now teaching school in Hubbard; and Emma J., born in Vienna December 4, 1859. Mr. Cratsley held several township offices in Howland, of which he was a resident some sixteen years, removing from there to Warren in 1881.

Josiah Soule, Sr., was born in Plimpton, Massachusetts, in 1796. He traced his descent directly back to George Soule who came over in the Mayflower. He (Josiah Soule) came from Massachusetts in 1817 and settled in Warren. His trade was that of builder and contractor. He served in the War of 1812. He died in 1872. He married Sally Young, sister of Warren Young, born in Wareham, Massachusetts, in 1799. His widow is still living in Warren. They raised eleven children of whom four are living, as follows: Josiah, Jr., Isaac, and Harrison, in Illinois; and Miss Julia Soule, of Warren.

Josiah Soule, Jr., was born in Warren May 29, 1819; married, in 1843, Ann, daughter of John Ratliff. She died in 1857, aged about thirty-three years. She was the mother of one son and one daughter. The former died in infancy and the latter is the wife of Howard B. Weir. In 1861 Mr. Soule was again married to Malvina Kellogg, whose father, Charles Kellogg, moved from Connecticut, settling in Gustavus. By this marriage he has one son, Henry Bishop, born September 24, 1865. His second wife died June 4, 1871. Mr. Soule is a contractor and builder, having learned the trade when he was young.

Camden Cleveland was a native of Canterbury, Connecticut, and was born in April, 1778. On May 25, 1800, he married Betsey Adams, and the same year came out and located land in Liberty township, Trumbull county, returning for his wife and settling in 1801. He cleared up a farm in Liberty and lived there until 1814, when he removed to Youngstown township, locating on the place now owned by Jacob Stambaugh, where he lived until his death. He was a judge of Warren at an early day. He was an early school-teacher in Youngstown township, and had a grist-mill there known as the Cleveland mill. Judge Cleveland was a younger brother of Moses Cleaveland, for whom the Forest City was named. He died March 13, 1826. Five of his seven children are still living. Mrs. Betsey Cleveland died August, 1867.

Benjamin Newport Robbins was born in Maryland in 1799, and when about one year old removed with his parents to Ohio. He was a farmer by occupation. About 1838 or 1839 he was elected county treasurer of Trumbull county and afterwards re-elected. He was subsequently elected sheriff, which position he also filled two terms. He married, on the 3d of May, 1827, Eliza Payne, daughter of Camden Cleveland, who was born in Liberty township, Trumbull county, Ohio, August 29, 1806, and who still resides in Warren. Three children were born of this marriage—Laura Newport, wife of Homer Baldwin, of Youngstown; Charles Cleveland, of Mesopotamia; and Albert A., of Youngstown. Mr. Robbins died December 30, 1876.

Henry Waldeck, son of Jacob and Catharine Waldeck, was born in Hesse Darmstadt, Germany, May 19, 1836. When twelve years of age he commenced to learn the trade of his father, that of baker. In the fall of 1855 he came to this country, and locating in Cleveland worked at his trade until August, 1857. He afterwards lived in Wellsville, Ohio, and at New Lisbon. July 22, 1858, he married Miss Mary S. Roesinger, who was born in Bavaria, Germany, February 19, 1837. By this marriage he had six children, of whom are living Lizzie S., John Edward, Mary S., and Clara. He came to Warren in July, 1858, and commenced the bakery business, which he has continued to the present time. His first wife died May 6, 1873, and May 12, 1874, he was married to Emma Knoth, a native of Germany, born April 3, 1847. To this union three children were born—Philomena M., Frank Henry, Jacob G. Mr. Waldeck is an active member of Emerald Beneficial association, and has been presiding officer some five years.

Cyrus Bosworth was a native of Plymouth county, Massachusetts, born in 1791. He married Sina Strowbridge in Massachusetts. Coming to Ohio in the fall of 1813, he subsequently entered into mercantile business in Warren, also kept public house where the Park hotel now stands. He was elected sheriff about 1826, filling that position two terms. He also represented his district in the Legislature. He was an elder in the Disciple church. He was the father of seven children, all of whom are living. He died in April, 1861. His daughter,

Elizabeth S., born in Warren, May 12, 1821, became the wife of J. G. Calender, who was born in Poultney, Vermont, in 1815. At the time of his marriage he was residing at Newton Falls, engaged in the manufacture of stone pumps. In 1863, he purchased a flouring mill in Milton, Mahoning county. He also owned a tow mill, woolen-factory, and saw-mills, at Price's Mills, in the same township, and was an enterprising business man there for many years. He died May 24, 1872. He was county auditor of Trumbull county for two terms, elected first about 1840. In 1875, Mrs. Calender came to Warren where she has since resided.

Lemuel G. Mathews, son of James and Mary (Calhoun) Mathews, was born in Liberty township, Trumbull county, Ohio, January 2, 1815. James Mathews was born in Pennsylvania, in 1769, and came to Ohio in 1799, settling in Liberty township. In 1828 he removed to Warren township, and settled in the woods on the farm now owned by his son L. G., where he spent the rest of his life, and where he died in 1834. He was a soldier in the War of 1812. He married in Pennsylvania, previous to his removing to Ohio, Mary Calhoun who was born in 1776, and died at the age of eighty-two. They raised a family of twelve children, of whom but two survive: Betsey, widow of Loren W. Hulburt, residing in Portage county, and L. G., the subject of this sketch. Lemuel G. married in 1840, Jane, daughter of James Pew, an early settler of Lordstown. They have had six children, of whom four are living: Alfred J., born in 1841, died at the age of twenty-four; Mary Jane, wife of Carlos Williams, resides on the home place; Edward F. resides on a farm adjoining his father; Priscilla Annie, now wife of Edwin Park, a resident of Lordstown; Lottie J., still at home. Her twin brother died in infancy. Mr. Mathews owns the home place and occupies a fine residence built in 1858.

Joel Downs was born in Sandersfield, Berkshire county, Massachusetts, in 1772. He married in New York Lois Mansfield, and came to Ohio in the fall of 1816. He settled in Southington, Trumbull county, where he resided a short time; also in Howland, coming to Warren in 1818. He lived in Warren in the south part of the town until 1835, when he removed to the place on Parkman road known as Hard-scrabble, and cleared up a place there. He raised a family of seven children, of whom three sons survive. He died in the fall of 1862, his wife surviving him some nine years and dying aged about seventy-seven. Mr. Downs was a soldier of the War of 1812.

Wilson Downs, son of Joel, was born May 16, 1826. He learned the trade of stone-mason and brick-layer, and has since followed his trade, being now engaged in building and contracting. He married, November 25, 1852, Miss Elizabeth Hardman, born in Weathersfield September 13, 1831. Their children are Mary M., wife of J. R. Porter, of Warren, born March 24, 1854; Francis C., April 9, 1857; Charles W., September 15, 1859; Add E., April 24, 1862; Bert B., April 26, 1866.

James A. Blackburn, youngest son of James and Eliza (McClellan) Blackburn, was born in Canfield, Mahoning county, Ohio, February 12, 1837. James Blackburn, Sr., was born in Poland township, Mahoning county. He married April 10, 1832, Eliza McClellan, daughter of an early settler. She was born November 13, 1806. They raised a family of six children, all of whom are living. The family continued to live in what is now Mahoning county until 1840, when they removed to Braceville township, Trumbull county, where they lived until the spring of 1866, when they moved to Warren township, where they spent the remainder of their lives. Mrs. Blackburn died November 23, 1869, and Mr. Blackburn, February 20, 1872. James A., Jr., resides on the home place. He was elected justice of the peace in 1870 and re-elected in 1882.

Zebulon Van Houter, son of Isaac and Mary (Ellston) Van Houter, was born in Sussex county, New Jersey, August 1, 1806. His father was a native of New Jersey, born December 9, 1776, came to Ohio in 1817, settling in Milton township, now Mahoning county, but the following year removed to Newton township, Trumbull county. He had eight children, of whom but two are now known to be living—Zebulon and Hannah, widow of Amos Allison, residing in Niles. Isaac Van Houter died September 6, 1841, and his wife in 1838. Zebulon for four years carried the United States mail from Warren to Salem and Hudson, also from Warren to Poland, and from Warren to Painesville, on horseback. He was employed on the Pennsylvania & Ohio canal for two years, and was afterwards in the employ, for about five years, of William Quinby. January 2, 1834, he married Mary Ann Allen, a native of England, born April 3, 1816. They have had six children, of whom two survive, viz: Mrs. John W. Ernst, born August 19, 1839, and Seymour P., born June 18, 1854. After his marriage Mr. Van Houter resided in Garrettsville some three years, and also in Lordstown a short time. In the fall of 1837 he moved to Leavittsburg where he operated a grist- and saw-mill some two or three years. In the spring of 1845 he purchased the place where he now lives. His wife died April 28, 1870. Mrs. Ernst has one son, Allen B., born in Warren, August 30, 1858. Seymour Van Houter married Ellen A. Lapham, in February, 1878, and has two daughters.

Augustus Graeter was a native of Germany, born in 1803 and emigrated to this country in 1823, and settled in Allentown, Pennsylvania, where he published a German newspaper until 1836. In the spring of that year he came to Warren and engaged in mercantile business for a short time, and afterwards operated a brewery for many years. He died March 8, 1863. He was married July 17, 1832, to Sarah Hoffman, daughter of Michael and Mary M. Hoffman, who was born in Lehigh county, Pennsylvania, April 24, 1808. Mr. and Mrs. Graeter have had eleven children, of whom five are deceased. The survivors are Adolphus Frederick, and Alfred, of Montana Territory; Olivia, wife of Robert Hopkins; Frederika, wife of Sandford Bailey, of Bradford, Pennsylvania, and Isabella, wife of Frank M. Ritezel, of the Chronicle, Warren. One son, Harmon, was in the one hundred day service, and died at Cumberland Gap September 29, 1862. Mrs. Graeter is still living in Warren with her brother, Stephen Hoffman.

Stephen Hoffman was born in Lehigh county, Pennsylvania, November 5, 1813. He is a printer by trade; came to Ohio in January, 1835, and located in Jackson township, now Mahoning county. In 1840 he came to Warren and kept a hotel where the Austin house now stands, two years, then the Ohio hotel on the corner of Mahoning avenue and High street. Since 1856 he has been working at his trade, now employed on the Western Reserve Chronicle, and is probably one of the oldest compositors in the State. December 23, 1836, he married Esther Paltsgrove, born in Pennsylvania June 15, 1815, and had one son, J. M. Franklin, born July 13, 1838. He was a member of the One Hundred and Seventy-first Ohio national guard, and died May 25, 1864. Mrs. Hoffman died September 8, 1856.

William Osborn was born in Fayette county, Pennsylvania, November 1, 1804. He is the oldest son of Richard and Sarah Osburn. With his parents he removed to Stark county in 1808, and to Trumbull county in 1815, settling in Lordstown township. Richard, the father of William, raised a family of two daughters and four sons, all of whom are living. He died about 1860. He was a justice of the peace. William remained on the farm until his marriage in 1825 to Sarah, daughter of John Jordan, an early settler of Poland township. She was born in said township January 20, 1801. They were the parents of eleven children, seven of whom are living. Mrs. Osborn died September 21, 1851, and in 1855 he married Angeline Current, who was born in Howland township in 1825. By this marriage there were six children, five of whom are living: William P., a resident of Niles; Ida M., wife of Frank Rufe, of Niles; Cora M., Frank E., and Warren C. Three are still at home. Mrs. Osborn died July 4, 1874. After his marriage he settled in Lordstown township, where he cleared up a farm, and where he remained until 1848, when he removed to Warren township, purchasing the U. B. White farm. In 1876 he moved to Warren, where he now resides.

David R., son of David and Margaret Byard, was born in Youngstown, Ohio, February 1, 1857. His parents removed to Sharon, Pennsylvania, in 1862, where he entered a drug store as clerk at the age of twelve. He resided there till 1873, when he came to Warren, and in June, 1874, commenced the drug business, which he is still engaged in. His mother is still living, vigorous in mind and body.

Sands Bouton, a native of Long Island, came to Ohio about 1835, and afterwards settled in Farmington township. He was elected county recorder of Trumbull county and filled that position two terms. He married Jennette Butler and raised a family of ten children; five daughters and two sons survive. He was a long time member of the Presbyterian church; died in 1855 at Kansas City. His daughter Jennette, born in New York State March 19, 1819, married Isaac S. Scott in Warren, in 1839. Mr. Scott was born in Vienna township, Trumbull county, in 1813; he died April 30, 1879. Mrs. Scott is still living. She is the mother of one son and three daughters. The son, Lucius J., enlisted in 1861 in the Nineteenth Ohio volunteer infantry, and was in the battles of Pittsburgh Landing and Stone River. He was killed January 2, 1863. Of the daughters Olive M. is the wife of Henry B. Weir, Mary E. of Frank Van Wormer; Emma D. is still at home.

John Brown was born in Washington county, Pennsylvania, March 17, 1789. He came to Warren, Ohio, in 1805. He was a hatter by trade and engaged in that business in Warren. He was a volunteer in the War of 1812, serving six months. He married Miss Elizabeth Rankin, born in New Jersey June 23, 1799. She came with her parents to Ohio in 1806, passing through Warren and settling in Mesopotamia township, afterwards removing to Warren. Mr. and Mrs. Brown were the parents of six children, of whom five are living. He died August 24, 1861; Mrs. Brown is still living; still smart for one of her advanced age. Their daughter, Martha M., who occupies the old family residence built in 1816 by her father, was married October 26, 1838, to James Ferguson, a cabinet maker by trade, and had one daughter, Mary E., born July 30, 1839, died May 7, 1861. Mr. Ferguson died September 2, 1840.

Isaac R. Dally was born in Warren December 31, 1805. His father, I. R. Dally, Sr., came to Ohio in 1800, settling on the place now owned by the subject of this sketch, on which a small clearing had been made by a man named Edward Jones, whose daughter Hannah was said to have been the first white child born in the county. Isaac R. Dally, Sr., in 1792 married in Pennsylvania a daughter of Henry Lane, an early settler. He had a family of nine children, of whom Isaac R., our subject, is the only survivor. He resided on the home place until 1841, when he removed to Indiana, where he died August 17, 1843. Mrs. Dally died May 19, 1836. Isaac was brought up to farming. November 4, 1830, he married Margaret, daughter of John and Barbara Fusselman, early settlers of Warren, who settled in that township in 1814. Mrs. Dally was born in Perry county, Pennsylvania, June 7, 1807. They have had seven children, of whom four are living—two died when young : Henry Harrison, born August 7, 1831, now a resident of Newton Falls, Trumbull county; Noah U., November 9, 1833, enlisted in 1862 in the Nineteenth Ohio volunteer infantry, and was wounded at Murfreesboro, from which he died at Nashville, January 27, 1863; Lydia E., born February 11, 1838, at home; Effie R., born March 13, 1840, widow of Thomas M. Bradley, who died in 1863. She has one son, Thomas M., born in 1862. Minerva P., born July 19, 1847, wife of Leslie E. Osborn, a resident of Pennsylvania. The first church service in Warren was held on the Dally place. His father assisted in clearing up the public square, and in building the first jail in Warren. Charles Dally came here a year or two previous, and settled on the place now owned by Mr. Dickey.

Henry Christianar was born in Hanover, Germany, in 1825, and came to this country in 1842 and resided in Indiana with his mother and brother. In 1847 he came to Warren where he worked at his trade of wagon making and repairing. In 1852 he married Eliza Bishop, of Germany, and has six children—William, Emma, Frederick, Ella, Carrie, and Laura.

William L. Christianar was born in Warren, January 14, 1853. At the age of eighteen he commenced an apprenticeship at the blacksmith trade, afterward working as journeyman in various places for several years. In 1874 the firm of Christianar & Grim was formed. This firm now carries on the business of wagon-making, blacksmithing and repairing.

J. G. Butler, son of Joseph and Esther (Green) Butler, was born in Bellefonte, Center county, Pennsylvania, May 13, 1814. He received his education at the common school and Bellefonte academy. He married in 1835, Temperance Orwig. Of their ten children five are still living, four sons and one daughter : Ithamar M., now a resident of Youngstown; J. G., superintendent and manager of Brier Hill Iron & Coal company; Miles G., a resident of Weathersfield township; James W., residing in Warren, and Emma E. at home. Mr. Butler came from Pennsylvania in 1842 and settled at Niles. He was clerk and bookkeeper for James Ward & Co. seventeen years, when he moved to Warren.

He was elected sheriff in 1860 and re-elected in 1862. He had previously been township clerk in Weathersfield some years, also filled the same position in Warren township at a later date. He is now engaged in the flour and feed business, which he engaged in for himself in the spring of 1879. He is a member of the Independent Order Odd Fellows and now worthy chief patriarch of the encampment.

A. E. Lyman, a dentist of Warren, was born in Massachusetts, and came to this State in 1853. He practiced this profession in Newton Falls, locating there in 1855, but after several years concluded to perfect a course in dental science, which he did in the Ohio Dental college, Cincinnati, graduating from that institution in 1859. In 1866 he came to Warren, where he has built up for himself a successful business. The doctor is one of the few dentists in this city who have taken a full professional course of lectures. He is well patronized, and deservedly so. His operating chair is one of the latest improved, and his office is supplied with all the best instruments and appliances used in the profession. Dr. Lyman was married to Miss Sarah Rudolph, a cousin of Mrs. James A. Garfield.

Peter Lynn, oldest son of Adam and Rachel Lynn, was born in Trumbull (now Mahoning) county, April 20, 1828. In early life he followed the trade of shoemaking, but in later years has followed farming. In 1849 he was married to Miss Sarah Wehr, by whom he has had five children, three sons and two daughters, viz: Henry, George F., Maria, Ferdinand, and Mary E. Henry and Maria are dead. Mr. and Mrs. Lynn are members of the Reform church of Warren township. His farm contains one hundred and thirty-three acres.

Daniel Wannamaker, second son of Daniel and Catharine Wannamaker, was born in Lynn township, Lehigh county, Pennsylvania, in 1816. At the age of eighteen he came to Trumbull county, subsequently purchasing a farm of fifty acres in Southington township. This he sold a few years afterwards and served an apprenticeship at the joiners trade, which occupation he afterward followed in connection with his brother John, for twenty-five years. He married at the age of twenty-two, Miss Maria Stroup, by whom he had one son, Jonas, who was killed at the battle of Perrysville, in the war of 1861–65. He was an orderly sergeant in the One Hundred and Fifth Ohio volunteer infantry. The first wife of the subject of this sketch died about eighteen months subsequent to her marriage, and he married for his second wife Mrs. Matilda Murberger, widow of Daniel Murberger, by whom he has had one daughter, Sarah Ada, now Mrs. Edwin Odding. Mr. Wannamaker occupies a farm of one hundred and fifty-seven acres in Warren township. Himself and wife are members of the Reform church.

Isaac Brobst, oldest son of Henry and Susannah Brobst, was born in Lehigh county, Pennsylvania, September 10, 1824. Henry Brobst was born in Lynn township, Lehigh county, December 30, 1801. He came to Ohio in April, 1825, and settled in Canfield, now Mahoning county, afterwards removed to Austintown, where he resided until 1845, when he removed to Warren township, purchasing the land now owned by his sons, Isaac, William, and John. Four years afterwards he located where he first settled in 1826, and where he still lives. Isaac Brobst was brought up to farming, and remained at home until his marriage, September 26, 1848, to Miss Catharine Hardman, whose father was a well-known resident of Liberty township. Mrs. Brobst was born in Wurtemberg, Germany, May 16, 1824. To this marriage were born five sons and five daughters—William H., Mrs. Harriet Wager, Eli, Charles Edward, Isaac, Mary L., Susan M., Alice C., George F., and Lizzie J. Mr. Brobst was married a second time October 21, 1879, to Mrs. Lydia Rowe, daughter of Philip Moser, born in Lehigh county, Pennsylvania, April 3, 1836. By this marriage he has one child—Cornelia Pearl, born August 28, 1880. After his first marriage he settled on the place adjoining his present home in Warren township, building his residence in 1870. William Brobst, younger brother of Isaac, of the preceding sketch, was born in Austintown, January 16, 1836. When twenty-one he learned the trade of stonemason, remaining at home until twenty-three. January 5, 1860, he married Miss Lisette Grenekle, who was born in Hanover, Germany, September 21, 1840. This union was blessed with four children, three of whom are living—Heman Ensign, born October 1, 1860, died May 31, 1875; Horace D., born October 8, 1865; William Noble, December 20, 1874; Calvin Edward, October 24, 1877. Mr. Brobst located on his present place after his marriage, and has carried on farming, while at the same time conducting his trade of stone-mason.

Godfrey Klinite, son of Frederick and Catharine (Fisher) Klinite, was born in Wurtemberg, Germany, January 15, 1819; came to America with his parents in 1832, who settled on the place now owned by Joseph Kreitler. They afterwards lived in various places in Trumbull county. Frederick Klinite died in 1878. He had a family of nine children. Five are yet living. Godfrey, when twenty years of age, bought fifty acres of land, and September 3, 1845, was married to Mary Ann Rigle, who was born in Warren May 4, 1828. They have four children—Sarah Ann, born March 4, 1846, wife of William Moyer; Samantha C., August 3, 1849, wife of William Anderson; William B., April 4, 1852; Solomon H., April 22, 1857. After marriage Mr. Klinite continued to live in Warren township, buying the Samuel Bailey place about 1869, consisting of one hundred and twelve acres.

Ferdinand Eckenrod was born in Lynn township, Lehigh county, Pennsylvania, November 1, 1827; oldest son of George and Leah (Follier) Eckenrod. He came to Ohio with his mother in the spring of 1835, and settled in Austintown township, now Mahoning county. He was brought up to farming till eighteen, when he served an apprenticeship of a year and a half at the carpenter and joiners' trade, and afterwards followed his trade in Austintown. March 1, 1855, he married his wife Catharine, who was a resident of Green township, Mahoning county, where she was born September 4, 1838. Mr. and Mrs. Eckenrod are the parents of six children—Henry, born January 8, 1856, Franklin February 17, 1859; Mary Ellen, July 23, 1861, wife of Henry Winters; George W., October 7, 1862; John F., September 13, 1864; Sarah Ann, January 21, 1867. Mr. Eckenrod resided in Green township some four years subsequent to his marriage. He purchased the farm where he now lives, in Warren township, in 1858, formerly the William Stebbins place, removing upon it in May, 1858. Mr. Eckenrod has a finely improved farm, and one of the best and most commodious barns in the State, costing about $7,000.

Samuel Gephart was born in Shenango, Pennsylvania, September 10, 1834. His father, John A., was a native of Germany. After emigrating to this country he settled in Pennsylvania, but came to Ohio in an early day and settled in Warren township, and was afterwards engaged in trade in Leavittsburg for about thirty years. Samuel learned the blacksmith trade, but followed it only one year. In the fall of 1856 he went to Illinois and resided in that State five or six years, engaged in business. In the fall of 1864 he commenced in the mercantile business in Leavittsburg, Trumbull county, purchasing the business lately conducted by his father, dealing in dry goods, groceries, etc., which he still continues, and doing a successful business. June 10, 1869, he married Miss Matilda Smith, of Braceville, and has four children, viz: Estelle May, born August 25, 1870; Louis A., December 5, 1872; Otis Q., April 14, 1876; Clayton H., October 2, 1877.

Joseph Kreitler, youngest son of John and Bridget (Rebholz) Kreitler, was born in Hozenhollern, Germany, December 9, 1829. When fifteen years old he commenced a three years' apprenticeship at the trade of millwright, and afterwards followed his trade some six years in Switzerland. In November, 1853, he came to the United States, locating in Boston, where, or in the vicinity, he remained until 1860, engaged in the cabinet and furniture business. In May of that year he came to Ohio and located in Warren, and entered the employ of Truesdell & Townsend. In the fall of 1860 he purchased a part of the place where he now lives, in Warren township. He continued in the employ of Truesdell & Townsend until 1876, meanwhile carrying on the farm with the assistance of his boys. July 31, 1855, he married Miss Josephine Kappler, who was born in Baden, Germany, February 27, 1827. Mr. and Mrs. Kreitler have a family of eight children, as follows: J. A., born February 24, 1856, of Cleveland (conducting a printing office); George E., May 15, 1858; Josie A., December 17, 1859; Louise C., February 5, 1862; Charles F., July 5, 1863; Albert H., August 24, 1865; Rhinehart G., December 1, 1867; Walter E., November 11, 1871.

James McConnell, son of John and Nancy McConnell, of Washington county, Pennsylvania, was born in Weathersfield, Trumbull county, Ohio, June 6, 1814. John McConnell came from Pennsylvania with his family, on horseback, in 1804, and settled in Weathersfield, where he lived until his death, which occured in 1823. He raised a family of thirteen children, of whom three are now living. He was a justice of the peace for many years, and a prominent man in his community; was deacon in the Presbyterian church. James McConnell came to Warren about 1840, and was engaged in the boot and shoe trade until 1860, when he was burned out and since then has been engaged in the grocery and restaurant business. He married, June 29, 1842, Miss Sarah S., daughter of William McCombs, an early settler in Poland township, and has had eight children, of whom two daughters and four sons are living, viz: John, Maria, Hattie, William J., Frank C., Harry R. John was a member of the One Hundred and Twenty-fourth Ohio volunteer infantry, and was wounded at Mission Ridge, and was discharged on account of his injury.

William Coon was born in New Jersey, October 9, 1785. He removed to Ohio and was one of the early settlers of Brookfield township, Trumbull county. He was a tailor by trade, and also a farmer. He came to live in Warren, where he died May 15, 1871, in his eighty-sixth year. He married Catharine DeForest, and raised a family of seven children. A daughter, Mrs. Sarah C. Chapman, now resides in Warren. She was married to Almon Chapman November 24, 1841. Mr. Chapman was a native of Hartford county, Connecticut, born in 1807, but came to the Western Reserve in an early day. He resided in Deerfield, Portage county, and came to Warren in 1846 and kept hotel here for about twenty-two years. He died March 8, 1877.

D. C. Thompson was born in Mercer county, Pennsylvania, in 1825. He became a resident of Trumbull county in 1831; engaged in farming till the year 1865, when he came to Warren and purchased of William Williams the Franklin house. He kept hotel six years, when he rented the property to parties engaged in different branches of business. In 1871 he purchased the Gillmore house, kept hotel in this about seven years, known during this time as the Thompson house; did a large business. On account of his family having grown up and married off he sold to Jennie Smith. Since then the house has been owned by her and run by Mr. Pancoast. Since this Mr. Thompson has been living a retired life. In the spring of 1881 he purchased a fine residence on Elm street. In the year 1847 Mr. Thompson and Miss Minerva McMahon were united in marriage. The family consists of three daughters. Celia is the wife of Dr. Sherwood, of Warren. Clara is the wife of William Richard, and is successfully running a furnace in Virginia, using the native ore. Alice is the wife of William Willson, engaged in the iron business in Chicago.

Spear & Voit, furniture dealers, partnership formed September 1, 1878, dealers in furniture and upholstery. They occupy a room in the Spill block. Mr. Spear for the past seven years previous to this business, was engaged as salesman in the store of Truesdell & Townsend. Mr. Voit was upholsterer in the same establishment, during the same time. Mr. Spear is a native of Pennsylvania, but has been a resident of Warren seventeen years. Mr. Voit is a native of Warren. Mr. Spear married, and has a family of five children. Mr. Voit is unmarried.

A. Wheeler was born in Brookfield township, in 1826. At the age of sixteen he commenced to learn the tinners trade with Freeman & Howard, of Warren. Engaged in the business himself in Warren, in 1849, in which he continued in company with B. P. Jameson twenty-one years. Moved upon his place east of Warren in 1870, returned to Warren in 1871, and resided three years. In 1873, remodeled his house and beautified his yard, and completed a fine home. At present, is engaged in farming. Was married in 1851 to Miss Sarah J. Gaskill, has a family of three daughters, two of whom are married.

James Mullen was born in Chester county, Pennsylvania, in 1812. At the age of fourteen he learned the tailor trade, worked at it in Unionville, in Chester county, five years. Here he was married in 1833, to Miss Ann W. Robinson. In 1837 he became a citizen of Warren, and engaged in custom work tailoring, afterwards kept a stock of goods. The fire of 1860 burned his stock entirely up. After this loss he spent a year in St. Louis. Since then he has been working at custom work in Warren. Mr. Mullen's family consists of seven children, all living and married. The two oldest sons and daughter reside in St. Louis, Missouri, one in Cleveland, and one in Illinois, and one daughter in Warren. Mr. Mullen is a member of the Methodist Episcopal church.

S. F. Bartlett was born in Johnston township, Trumbull county, Ohio, June 3, 1841. His father was a farmer, though he worked at the wagon making trade. Mr. Bartlett, Sr., was a prominent citizen, and widely known for his anti-slavery convictions. In 1858 Mr. S. F. Bartlett commenced the blacksmith trade, at which he worked till 1867. From this date until 1874 he was engaged in the livery business in Warren. In the last-named year he was appointed deputy sheriff of Trumbull county. In 1877 he was elected sheriff, which position he still holds. He is also engaged in the carriage business with Mr. Corbin. Mr. Bartlett was married in 1861, and has one daughter. He is an active Republican, and a worshipful master in the Masonic order. He is a director of the Agricultural society and of the Second National bank.

S. A. Corbin was born in the State of Connecticut in 1840. In 1863 he came to Warren, where he resided until 1867 engaged in the sewing machine business. From 1867 till 1874 he resided in Niles, where he carried on the livery business. In 1873 he was elected sheriff of Trumbull county, and re-elected the following term. He married Emma C. Folsom, and has three sons. He is now engaged in the carriage business in Warren.

John Martin, youngest son of John and Mary Martin, was born in Germany February 22, 1820. After receiving a German school education, he was apprenticed at the age of sixteen to the blacksmith's trade, for a period of three years. He worked two years in Switzerland, and then returned to his native place where he worked as journeyman blacksmith till 1847, when he came to America, and settled in Youngstown. Two years later he came to Warren, and worked for the fourteen succeeding years in Belden's carriage factory, since the expiration of which time he has been in business for himself. He married in 1849 Miss Nancy Demming, who was born in New York State in 1826. They have a family of four children, viz: William Humphrey, Charles H., Emma, wife of Frank L. Brown, and Frederick, all live in Warren.

Mr. Martin is a prosperous and industrious man, and has by his own industry established a good business.

Henry Ernst was born in Perry county, Pennsylvania, August 27, 1820, and came to Trumbull county in 1833. Three years afterwards he began an apprenticeship at the carpenter and joiner's trade, which he has since followed, being one of the most extensive contractors in the county. He also for a time operated a planing-mill at Niles. He was married in 1843 to Miss Harriet Southworth, and has a family of five sons and four daughters—Silas S., George H., Clayton, John H., Olive Ann, Jessie Benton Fremont, Delmoretta, Nettie, and James Ward, all living, the oldest being married. Mr. Ernst is now living upon a farm of one hundred and seventy-four acres in Warren township.

William A. Ernst was born in Carlisle, Cumberland county, Pennsylvania, November 15, 1829, oldest son of John and Margaret (Bradley) Ernst. John Ernst was born in Pennsylvania about 1806. He came to Ohio in the fall of 1836, and settled in Warren township, where he carried on blacksmithing until 1858. He raised a family of ten children, eight of whom are living. In 1858 he removed to Illinois, where he died in 1875, and his wife in 1876. William was educated in Warren, and at the age of twenty had acquired his father's trade, which, since his marriage, he has carried on for himself in Warren, where he has resided continuously, with the exception of one year spent in Cleveland. He was married March 16, 1852, to Mary Ann, daughter of Ferdinand Artman, a former well-known resident of Warren. They are the parents of three children—Clara E., wife of J. N. Butler, of Warren; Frank H., a merchant of Warren; and Lucy M., born November 8, 1868.

Walter King was born in Suffield, Connecticut, December 26, 1792; came to Ohio in 1815, and settled in Warren. He was a silversmith by trade, and conducted that business in connection with the jewelry trade forty years. He built the King block, on Main street, in 1827 and 1828, where he was located in business for some time. March 19, 1820, he married Cynthia Halladay, who was born in Warren July 21, 1802. She is the oldest child of Jesse and Sarah (Hover) Holladay. Jesse Holladay, her father, was born in Kentucky in 1781, and married in Pennsylvania in 1801, and came to Ohio the same year and located on the premises now occupied by Porter's book store, where he built a log house which he kept as a public house and also carried on the business of hatter near the site of the present Trumbull county bank. He raised six children of whom but two are living, viz: Mrs. King, and Mrs. Dr. D. B. Woods. Mr. and Mrs. King are the parents of six children of whom but four are living, viz: Maria, residing with her mother; Esther, wife of Alonzo Truesdell, of Warren; Walter B., a resident of Chicago, and Julius, of Cleveland. Ashbel died in 1862, aged thirty-nine; Sarah, wife of R. M. St. Clair, is also dead. Walter King was an active temperance man. He died April 5, 1855. Mrs. King still resides in Warren.

# CITY OF YOUNGSTOWN, OHIO.

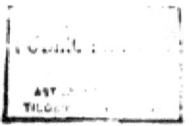

YOUNGSTOWN.

CHAPTER I.
INITIAL EVENTS.

Youngstown, the county seat of Mahoning county, is situate in the southeast part of the Western Reserve, nearly in a direct line between Cleveland and Pittsburg, about seventy miles from each city. It is intersected in a direction from the northwest to the southeast by the Mahoning river, a branch of the Beaver, a confluent of the Ohio. It derives its name from John Young, who purchased the township from the Connecticut Land company in 1796. As will appear elsewhere in this work that company purchased the Reserve from the State of Connecticut, surveyed it into townships five miles square, and after the survey made sale of a few of the townships, or parts thereof, to individuals, prior to the partition by draft among the members of the company. One of the townships thus sold was designated in the plat of the survey as number two in the second range. Its east line is five miles west of the Ohio and Pennsylvania State line, and its south line five miles north of the south line of the Reserve. The precise time of the purchase we are not able to learn. The contract cannot be found, and no public record, as we are aware, exists of the contract of purchase. But among the papers which have escaped loss or destruction, a document was found which casts some light upon the history of the purchase. From this paper it appears that a contract had been made between the directors of the Connecticut Land company of the one part, and John Young for himself and Philo White of the other part, for the sale and settling of "a township of land in the Connecticut Reserve, so-called," and which township, by agreement between said directors and said Young, was understood to be township number two in the second range. The document now spoken of, is a map of the township as divided into lots. On one of these lots, which includes about one-third of the township on the east side, is this entry:

> Five thousand five hundred acres disposed of to Hill, Sheby and others, by contract with John Young, on which they are to settle with seventeen families.

On the other lots, which are of different sizes, are entered the number of acres and names of their proprietors, Young, White, and Storrs. On the margin of the map is the following entry:

> This may certify that we, being equally interested in township number two in the second range in the Connecticut Reserve, do agree to the above sale of the five thousand five hundred acres to the actual settlers as above, and do likewise agree to the division of the remainder in the manner to which our names are annexed in the above sketch.
>
> MIDDLETOWN, January 30, 1797.

The names of those signing the agreement are cut off. They were, probably, John Young, Philo White, and Lemuel Storrs.

On the same sheet with the map is a conveyance from Philo White to John Young for the consideration of $1,050, of all his interest in the original contract, to which it refers. This conveyance is dated February 9, 1797.

In fulfillment of the terms of this contract of sale the Land company, by deed dated April 9, 1800, conveyed to John Young township number two in the second range, called Youngstown, containing fifteen thousand five hundred and sixty acres of land for the consideration of $16,085.16.

SURVEY INTO LOTS AND SETTLEMENT.

The survey of the Reserve into townships was commenced in July, 1796, at the southeast corner, consequently this township was one of the first surveyed and its border line designated, and it is probable that John Young contracted for its purchase during the latter half of that year, and it is possible that in 1796 or not later than early in 1797, the time named by tradition, he visited the township with Alfred Wolcott, his surveyor, and others as assistants, and possibly with prospective settlers. The assistants of Mr. Wolcott were Phineas Hill, of Western Pennsylvania, axeman; Isaac Powers, of North Beaver, Pennsylvania; Daniel Shehy, who, as his descendants state, came from the State of New York with Mr. Young, and probably others whose names tradition has not retained. They surveyed and laid out the town plat, upon and around which the city now stands, and the remainder of the township into great lots, as they exist at this day. Settlements on the lands surveyed were immediately commenced.

Mr. Wolcott married soon after, settled in the township, remained for a short period and returned to the East. Mr. Hill removed his family to the township, was engaged in building the first mill, of which he became the miller, remained here a few years and removed elsewhere. Messrs. Powers and Shehy, then unmarried, soon married, settled on farms, on which they resided during long, useful, and honorable lives, and died on the farms on which they settled, Mr. Powers in 1861, aged eighty-four years, and Mr. Shehy in 1834, aged seventy-five years, each leaving a numerous posterity.

FIRST SETTLER.

Tradition, as already stated, informs us that the settlement of the township commenced immediately after the visit of John Young with his surveyor and assistants, and the survey of the township into lots in 1796 or 97. But the incidents relating to this visit and the meeting of Mr. Young with the man who became the first settler, are differently related in some particulars. As the different traditionary stories may interest the readers of to-day, when all matter of pioneer history are subjects of eager research, we will recount them, leaving each one to form his own opinion as to which is most probable.

Howe's Historical Collections of Ohio, published in 1848, has this statement:

In 1796 Mr. James Hillman, when returning from one of his trading expeditions, alone in his canoe, down the Mahoning river, discovered a smoke on the bank near the site of the present village of Youngstown, and on proceeding to the spot he found Mr. Young, the proprietor of the township, who, with Mr. Alfred Wolcott, had just arrived to make a survey of his lands. The cargo of Mr. Hillman was not entirely disposed of, there remaining among other things some whiskey, the price of which, to the Indians, was one dollar per quart, in the currency of the country—a deer skin being a legal tender for a dollar, and a doe skin for half a dollar. Mr. Young proposed purchasing a quart, and having a frolic on its contents during the evening, and insisted on paying Hillman his customary price for it—Hillman urged that inasmuch as they were strangers in the country, and had just arrived upon his territory, civility required him to furnish the means of the entertainment. He, however, yielded to Mr. Young, who immediately took the deer skin he had spread for his bed (the only one he had), and paid for the quart of whiskey. His descendants, in the State of New York, in relating the hardships of their ancestors, have not forgotten that Judge Young exchanged his bed for a quart of whiskey.

This account also says that "Mr. Hillman remained with them a few days, when they accompanied him to Beavertown to celebrate the Fourth of July, and Mr. Hillman was induced to return and commence the settlement of the town by building a house. This was about the first settlement made on the Western Reserve."

George A. Young, an old resident of Youngstown, who lived with Colonel Hillman several years when a boy, and until 1824, states, as his recollection of Hillman's account of this meeting, as he has heard him relate it, that in one of his voyages up the Mahoning to trade with the Indians, he had reached the site of the future Youngstown, and had encamped on its banks; that Mr. Young arrived with his party, and seeing a smoke arising above the trees, came to ascertain its cause, met Mr. Hillman, and thus commenced the acquaintance and friendship of these two pioneers, whose names will ever be associated and identified with the settlement and early history of this township.

Another tradition relates that Mr. Young met Mr. Hillman at Beaver, on the Ohio, near which was his home, and employed him to transport Mr. Young and party up the Beaver and Mahoning rivers in his trading boat. But if this was the fact it is highly probable that the children of Mr. Isaac Powers, who was an early settler, and who, as they state from his narrations to them, was employed to assist in the survey by Mr. Young while stopping over night at the house of Abraham Powers, father of Isaac, in Beaver, when on his way to Youngstown, would have made mention, as part of that history, that Mr. Hillman transported the surveying party from Beaver to Youngstown in his boat. But they do not, and had it occurred Isaac, no doubt, would have related it, as an important event, to his children, and they would have transmitted it as part of the traditional history of the first settlement.

But whatever may be the true story of this first meeting of these two pioneers, there is no doubt that they met and their acquaintance commenced on this visit of Mr. Young, with his surveying party, and that then inducements were offered by Mr. Young, and arrangements made which resulted, shortly after, in the removal of Mr. Hillman, with his wife and a few household goods, to the new settlement, and of his thus becoming the first regular and permanent settler of the township and of the Reserve. That there were white men who had built huts or shanties, and had temporarily resided on the Reserve, particularly on the lake shore, or at the salt springs, before this time, is altogether probable, but they were merely "squatters," or "transient residents," and James Hillman, we think there is no doubt, from all the evidence we are able to collect, after a period of eighty-five years has elapsed, was the "first settler."

FIRST LOG HOUSE.

The question now rises, in what part of this vast wilderness, of which the township then was part, did he make his settlement, or, more precisely, where did he erect his dwelling; and here tradition differs. A lady now living relates a conversation held with Mrs. Hillman, in her latter days, in which she said that when they came to Youngstown they put up a shanty on the west side of the Mahoning river, between the present Mahoning avenue and the river, that in this shanty they often entertained men from the East who came to the Reserve to purchase land, and at one time as many as eighteen men slept in that shanty, lying on the floor, and so thick that it was difficult to pass over the floor without stepping on some one. What kind of a structure this was we can only conjecture. It was probably a mere temporary shelter, perhaps a hut of poles, or it may have been a shanty built by Mr. Hillman in one of his former voyages up the Mahoning, as a trading place or sort of a store, as this place appears to have been then, as well as prior and many years after, an occasional resort of the Indians.

Another tradition, which is generally accepted, also relates that soon after his arrival here Mr. Hillman, assisted by his wife and an Indian, who happened along at the time, and perhaps others, raised a log house on the northeast bank of the Mahoning, on Front street, a short distance east of Spring common, on a lot now owned and occupied by Samuel Atkins, and formerly by Moses Crawford, known as the Crawford place, and that this was the first log house erected in the township. Mr. Hillman resided here for a time, but afterwards moved across the river to a farm, now built up as part of the city, on the west side of Mill street, and Moses Crawford purchased this log house and lived in it as early as 1805, and in it, about that time, was held the first meeting for public worship, by members of the Methodist Episcopal church, about six in number, who then formed a church organization, the first of that denomination in the Reserve, and the pioneer of the present large and flourishing Methodist churches of Youngstown.

ABORIGINAL YOUNGSTOWN.

The Mahoning valley was the home of the Indian before its settlement by the white man. Indications throughout this region, found in the pioneer times and some remaining to this day, record this historical fact. Earthworks, relics, Indian trails, etc., form part of the record, and the traditions learned of the Indians by the pioneers confirm it, and show further that where Youngstown city now stands, with its vicinity, was an Indian camping ground or town. We will cite a few items of evidence in proof of our assertion:

The late William Powers, whose father, Isaac Powers, and grandfather, Abraham Powers, were among the earliest settlers, and who visited the valley on hunting or other excursions many years prior to its occupancy and settlement by the whites, states, probably as learned from them, in an article in the Mahoning Valley Historical Collections, that the place where Youngstown now stands "had once been cleared, but that the Indians had left it about twenty years before the survey (in 1796 or 1797), and at that time it had grown up to bushes about as high as a man's head riding on horseback."

In excavating for the foundation for a furnace at Hazelton, about two miles southeast of the Public square in Youngstown, on land bordering the Mahoning river on the north side, an Indian burial place was found. A large number of human bones and articles of an Indian character were exhumed. What stronger evidence can be required to prove that in the vicinity of that Indian burial place there was an Indian town? Indian arrow-heads have also been found in various parts of the township, denoting Indian battles in the former days.

Mr. William Powers, also at the pioneer reunion in 1875, in a recital of the traditions of the pioneer days, related an Indian story, as occurring in the history of Abraham Powers, his grandfather, in February, 1778, which is of interest in this connection. Abraham then lived in Ligonier valley, Westmoreland county, Pennsylvania. Here were a number of families gathered, and it was one of the most westerly settlements in Pennsylvania. The weather was cold, and the snow lay deep on the ground. About the first of the month a band of Indians entered the settlement, murdered a family, burnt their cabin, after taking such of its contents as they fancied, and left for the west. A number of the settlers, able bodied men, all mounted, Mr. Powers one of them, started in pursuit in a few hours. They followed the Indians to the Allegheny river, which they crossed about thirty miles above Pittsburg, down the Allegheny and Ohio to the mouth of Big Beaver, and up that stream and the Mahoning to the first inhabited village they saw, which was on the farm afterwards settled by Isaac Powers, son of Abraham, and in the southern part of the township of Youngstown. With their utmost exertions they cou'd travel no faster than the Indians, who were also mounted, and they usually camped at nightfall, where the Indians had camped the night before. Upon their discovery of the Indian village, they were saluted by the rapid firing of single guns. They returned a round or volley at the only Indian in sight, who fell wounded, but rising partly on his knee continued firing. At the second round from the pursuers he fell dead, with seven balls in his body. Captain Pipe was as brave an old man as ever faced an army alone. There was no one with him but his daughter, a girl about fourteen years old, concealed behind a log. She loaded the guns, of which they had several, while the chief did the shooting. The pursuing party scraped the snow away, covered the body with leaves and brush, and taking the girl with them, followed the trail of the fleeing Indians to the salt springs, a few miles further up the Mahoning, where they held a council of war, and learning from the girl that a large number of warriors were collected at Sandusky, released her and returned home, having been absent about two weeks. In 1802, when Isaac Powers settled on his farm, he and his father found the bones of the brave warrior and gave them such Christian burial as they could. The site of the town was overgrown with bushes and small trees, mostly hickory and black walnut. They cut down all but one black walnut about three inches in diameter, which they allowed to grow to mark the grave of Captain Pipe, and the site of Pipestown. This tree stands alone on the south bank of the Mahoning, opposite the mouth of Dry run, about eighty feet high, and a conspicuous object.

We add a few Indian stories of the pioneer days. Isaac Powers told that when engaged in the survey of the township, and while at breakfast in their camp near Spring common, they heard the report of a gun not far distant in a northerly direction. They were somewhat surprised at this as they supposed the Indians had all gone, and they knew of no other white men than themselves in the vicinity. Mr. Powers and another went in the direction whence had come the report to learn who had fired the gun. They soon came up with an Indian who had shot a deer, ripped it open, taken out the entrails, put part of them under his blanket and next his skin in his bosom, and was standing with both his feet in the body of the deer to warm them.

He related another and singular incident which occurred while they were building the first mill in the township, which was erected at the Mahoning falls on Mill creek, in 1797. Mr. Powers and John Noggle were in the adjacent woods felling timber for the mill. In the forenoon two squaws came from the west, one carrying a pappoose or Indian baby, fastened on a piece of bark, and the other carrying bows and arrows. They placed the bark with the pappoose upright leaning against a tree, and went into the woods, leaving the two choppers as custodians of the child. About 4 o'clock in the afternoon the squaws returned, bringing the hide and carcass of a deer they had killed, took the pappoose and returned in the direction from which they came in the morning. The child, true to its Indian nature, had not even whimpered during the several hours it was leaning against the tree.

Mrs. Edward Potter, a venerable lady formerly of Youngstown, but now residing in Trumbull county, says that in 1798 her late husband, then a boy about five years old, came here with his parents. They had put up a tent between Crab creek and the Mahoning, near the present Basin street. A band of Indians came along. One of them took hold of young Edwards, stroked his hair and raised him in his arms to the great terror of his mother, who feared they would carry him off. But after a few moments the Indian placed him on the ground without harming him, to the great relief of his parent. That good lady in relating the story in after days would add: "The Indians were very plenty round here at that time."

Roswell M. Grant, uncle of General Grant, who came with Jesse Grant, his brother, the General's father, and with their father to Youngstown in 1805, and lived several years with Colonel Hillman, writes: "I remember the Indians coming down the river in canoes and camping in Colonel Hillman's sugar camp, at the lower end of the farm, upon the river bank. They would stay some days. Also the old chief would come to see Colonel Hillman to settle some dispute between them. They would bring thirty or forty warriors with them. They would stop at the plum orchard at the upper end of the farm. These visits were often."

John Ague, one of our oldest citizens and born in the township in 1806, remembers that when he was quite young a tribe of Indians camped opposite the house afterwards the residence of the late Dr. Manning, on East Federal street, in the woods and bushes, on what is now South Walnut street; that at that time all south of Federal street in that part of the city was woods and bushes. He thinks this was before the War of 1812.

ORGANIZATION OF THE TOWNSHIP.

At the first court of common pleas and general quarter sessions of Trumbull county, held at Warren August 25, 1800, the county was divided into townships for civil purposes. Youngstown township, as then organized, comprised the territory of the townships now organized as Poland, Coitsville, Youngstown, Boardman, Canfield, Austintown, Jackson, and Ellsworth, in Mahoning county, and Hubbard and Liberty in Trumbull county. James Hillman was appointed constable of the township, and the oath of office was administered to him.

At the February term, 1802, of the court of quarter sessions, it was ordered that town meetings be held in the several townships, previously organized, on the first Monday of the ensuing April. The first town meeting was held on that day at the public house of William Rayen. The following is a copy of the record of this town meeting:

At a legal township meeting begun and held in and for the township of Youngstown, in the county of Trumbull, at the dwelling-house of William Rayen, on the fifth day of April, in the year of our Lord one thousand eight hundred and two, the following proceedings were had, viz:

The persons hereinafter mentioned were duly chosen to the offices respectively affixed to their names—John Young, chairman; George Tod, town clerk.

Voted, that there be five trustees chosen. Accordingly, James Doud, John Strouthers, Camden Cleveland, Samuel Tylee, and Calvin Pease were duly elected.

Voted, that there be three overseers of the poor chosen. Accordingly, Archibald Johnson, James Mathews, and John Rush were duly elected.

Thomas Kirkpatrick and Samuel Minough were duly elected fence viewers.

James Hillman and Homer Hine were elected appraisers of houses.

George Tod was chosen lister of taxable property.

William Chapman, Michael Simons, James Wilson, Benjamin Ross, William Dunlap, Amos Loveland, John Denison, William Perrin, and Thomas Packard were elected supervisors of highways.

Calvin Pease and Phinehas Reed were elected constables.

Voted, that the next stated town meeting be held at the house now occupied by William Rayen aforesaid.

This meeting was then adjourned without day.

    Attest, GEORGE TOD,
          Town Clerk.

Of the trustees elected, James Doud resided in the present township of Canfield, John Strouthers in Poland, Camden Cleveland and Calvin Pease in Youngstown, and Samuel Tylee in Hubbard.

The following gentlemen, in addition to those above named, have been elected township trustees at successive annual elections, up to the spring of 1830, inclusive, several of them being re-elected, and serving one or more terms, viz: Aaron Collar, Thomas Kirkpatrick, Caleb Baldwin, Turhand Kirtland, Benjamin Ross, Asahel Adams, James Applegate, Barnabas Harris, Josiah Robbins, Moses Latta, Hiranimus Eckman, Joshua Kyle, Samuel Bryson, Hugh Larimore, James Hillman, Henry Wick, William Thorn, John Beard, Isaac Powers, William Potter, John

Parkhurst, John Rush, George Hayes, James Wilson, Jonathan Stout, William Morris, Abraham Kline, John E. Woodbridge, Homer Hine, Philip Stambaugh, Thomas Farrell, James Mackey, John Gibson, Samuel Hayden, Henry Manning, William O. Rice, Robert Kerr, John Kimmell, James McKinnie, Singleton King, Benjamin N. Robbins.

The following gentlemen were elected township clerk in the years named, viz: George Tod, 1802 to 1804; William Rayen, 1805 to 1808, and 1810 to 1812, and 1816; Samuel Bryson, 1809, 1815, and 1817; Luther Spelman, 1813; James Mackey, 1814; Jabez P. Manning, 1818; Robert Leslie, 1819 and 1821; Caleb B. Wick, 1820 and 1824; William Reid, 1822, 1825, 1826, 1829, and 1830; Cornelius Tomsen, 1827; Jonathan Edwards, 1828.

The gentlemen above named were active business men and men of note in those early days. Very many of them are represented here by their descendants who are among the active business men of to-day. Only one of them is now living, William O. Rice, who was a trustee in 1826–27, now aged eighty-seven years. He is, and for several years has been, a resident of Painesville. The last survivor residing in the township was John Kimmell, trustee in 1828, who died about a year since (in 1880) aged eighty-four years.

At the first meeting of the board of trustees, held at "the dwelling house of William Rayen, inn-keeper," on April 12, 1802, they divided the township, consisting of the ten surveyed townships, into nine highway districts, and assigned a district to each of the nine supervisors recently elected. As evidencing the amount of labor required of the "pathmaster," as he was designated, in lieu of the longer statutory name, in those days, and the lucrative nature of the office, we copy from the records two accounts presented to the trustees, viz:

Township of Youngstown to James Wilson, one of the supervisors for said township for the year 1802:

Dr. To 7 days superintending persons labor-
   ing on roads........................Doll's 8.75 cts.
   " 4 do in warning hands to work......   4.00
                                        Dollars 12.75
Cr By amount of delinquencies. 6.00
                                     Balance due 6.75
Youngstown March 4, 1803—(signed) James Wilson.
   Also,

Township of Youngstown, April 4, 1803, to Benjamin Ross supervisor
Dr To 5 days warning hands to work........ D. 6.25 cts
Cr By delinquencies....... ....   1.31
                                               $4.94

The elections were held at the dwelling house or inn of William Rayen up to 1813, after which they were held at different public houses until the town hall was built about 1850. They were there held until the city was divided into wards in 1870, since which each ward has been an election precinct for those residing in the ward, and the town hall is still the place of voting for the inhabitants of the township outside of the city.

YOUNGSTOWN AS A MUNICIPAL CORPORATION.

Shortly after the settlement of the township of Youngstown, John Young laid out a town plat, which he caused to be recorded on the records of Trumbull county. This plat extended from the eastern side of the present store building of John F. Hollingsworth, on West Federal street, easterly to the east line of the Dr. Henry Manning lot, a distance of 1,752 feet, and from Cole, now Wood street, on the north, to Front street on the south. Afterwards, he extended the plat, by what he called out-lots, west to Holmes street, east to a short distance west of Crab creek, and south to the Mahoning river.

INCORPORATED.

In 1848 the citizens applied to the Legislature for a charter as a village, and an act was passed incorporating so much of the town of Youngstown as was included in the recorded town plat.

EXTENSION OF LIMITS.

No action of organization was had under this act, but we find this entry on the village records:

In accordance with the prayer of a petition from a majority of the legal voters residing within the incorporation, the commissioners of Mahoning county, at their regular session in June, A. D. 1850, and upon due notice given, extended the limits of the town so as to include therein all the territory within the following boundaries, to-wit: Beginning on the east line of the Kyle farm, so called, and now owned by William J. Edwards, in the township of Youngstown, sixty rods south of the Youngstown & Austintown road, thence east, parallel to said road, to the north bank of the Mahoning river, thence down the north bank of said river to the west bank of Crab creek, thence northerly along the west bank of said Crab creek, to the north line of William Rice's land, thence west along the south line of Bryson farm, so called, following the several courses of said line to the southeast corner of land owned by the heirs of Charles Dutton, thence continuing west along the south line of said Dutton's land to the Holmes road, and thence west across the Thomas L. Wick farm, so called, to the east line of the Dabney farm, thence south along the said Dabney's east line to the center of said Mahoning river, thence westwardly along the center of said Mahoning river to the northeast corner of said Kyle farm, thence south along the east line of said Kyle farm to the place of beginning.

ORGANIZATION.

Immediately upon the action of the county commissioners, the following notice for an election was posted in all the public places:

Notice is hereby given to the qualified electors of the borough of Youngstown, Mahoning county, Ohio, that an election will be held on Saturday, the 15th of June, instant, between the hours of 10 o'clock A. M. and 4 o'clock P. M., at the Union House, kept by W. H. Ross, in said Youngstown, for the purpose of electing by ballot one mayor, one recorder, and five trustees, to serve for one year, according to the act of Assembly in such cases made and provided.

Youngstown, June 5, 1850.

W. EDSON,	CYRUS BRENNEMAN,
JAMES FOWLER,	R. F. HEINER,
JAMES CALVIN,	A. McKINNIE,
GEORGE MURRAY,	R. W. TAYLER,
J. R. HOLCOMB,	G. G. MURRAY,
T. GARLICK,	GEORGE W. SEATON,
JOHN HEINER,	WILLIAM S. PARMELE,

BENJAMIN H. LAKE.

ELECTION.

Said notice having been duly given and posted up as required by law, an election was held at the time and place and for the purpose aforesaid. Asahel Medbury and Edward G. Hollingsworth were judges, and John H. King clerk of said election, and were severally sworn by Andrew Gardner, a justice of the peace of said county, agreeable to law, before entering upon the discharge of their respective duties. The number of votes cast at said election was 108, as follows: For mayor, John Heiner 91, Henry Manning 15; recorder, Robert W. Tayler 106, Jonathan Warner 1; trustees, John Loughridge 105, Abraham D. Jacobs 65, Francis Barclay 105, Stephen F. Burnett 106, Manuel Hamilton 104, Henry Heasley 84, Joseph Montgomery 5, William Rice, Paul Wick, Myron I. Arms, Peter W. Keller, and John F. Hollingsworth, 2 each and Richard G. Garlick, 1 vote.

FIRST CORPORATION OFFICERS.

The judges of said election thereupon declared the following persons elected, that is to say: John Heiner, mayor; Robert W. Tayler, recorder; John Loughridge, Abraham D. Jacobs, Francis Barclay, Stephen F. Burnett, Manuel Hamilton, trustees.

FIRST COUNCIL MEETING.

The first meeting of the council was held at 7½ o'clock of the evening of the same day on which the election was held, at the office of R. J. Powers, Esq., when all the officers elected were present, and the official oath was administered by proper authority to each one. On that day, thirty-one years ago, Youngstown commenced its existence as a municipal corporation, and was thenceforth styled "The Incorporated Borough of Youngstown;" afterwards under the classification, by the State laws, of municipal corporations, it became "The Incorporated Village of Youngstown."

CITY OF THE SECOND CLASS.

In June, 1867, a census of the village was taken, and the number of inhabitants found to exceed five thousand. This fact was certified by resolutions of the council to the Secretary of State, in order to the advancement of the village to a city of the second class. On reception of the certificate Youngstown was declared a city of the second class.

SECOND EXTENSION OF LIMITS.

The city having long since outgrown its boundaries, and there being nothing in the appearance of the land occupied by buildings to show where the city ended and the country began, the council passed an ordinance on March 2, 1868, to extend the city boundaries, and order a vote of the people to ratify or reject the proposed extension to be taken at the ensuing April election. A proclamation was also issued to elect, at the same time, officers of a city of the second class.

FIRST ELECTION OF CITY OFFICERS.

The whole number of votes at the election was 620, of which George McKee received 391, John Heiner 197, and a few scattering. The officers elected were George McKee, mayor; Owen Evans, marshal; Thomas W. Sanderson, solicitor; Robert McCurdy, treasurer; Joseph G. Butler, Chauncey H. Andrews, Homer Hamilton, Richard Brown, and William Barclay, councilmen. The vote on extension of city limits was yeas 593; nays 10.

The boundaries of the city, as established by that vote, and which are its present boundaries, extended north on Wick avenue a short distance beyond McGuffey street; and on Liberty street, north of J. M. Owens' house; west, to near Eagle furnace; south, on Mahoning avenue to Mill creek hill; and on Flint Hill road to south of A. S. Kyle's land; east, on East Federal street to near G. Wilson's, and on Shehy street to Riley street.

On September 13, 1870, the population having increased to eight thousand one hundred, the council divided the city into five wards. In 1880, the population of the city, as shown by the Federal census, having increased largely, and especially in the First and Second wards, these were divided. The west part of the First being made the Sixth and the east part of the Second being made the Seventh.

THIRD EXTENSION OF LIMITS.

In January, 1880, the population of the city having increased to nearly three-fold its population at the time of the second extension of limits, and the city having again not only outgrown its boundaries, but continuing rapidly to grow, a petition signed by four hundred and sixty-nine citizens, most of them prominent business men, and only a fraction of those who would have signed the petition had it been deemed requisite to obtain their signatures to accomplish the object sought, was presented to the council, asking for further extension of the city limits.

The petition included as part of the city, as proposed to be extended, the northeast part of the township, and reached west and south sufficiently to include Brier Hill, West Youngstown, Hazelton, Lansingville, East Youngstown, and other named plats. Action was had by the council, and afterwards, on February 18, 1880, the city civil engineer submitted a report upon the extension, defining its limits, but embracing much less territory than was described in the petition. This report left outside of the proposed new limits Hazelton, a prominent manufacturing locality, East Youngstown, Crab Creek, and some other thriving, growing, and booming embryo cities or clusters of houses, etc., desirable as parts of the extended city.

An ordinance was passed by the council extending the city according to the report. It then was submitted, as the law requires, to the county commissioners for approval, and the matter was discussed before them. Their decision appears in the following entry, extracted from their journal of November 18, 1880: "The board met at 10 A. M. On motion the prayer of the petition for the extension of the city limits is ordered not granted and petitioners pay the cost."

The decision caused great surprise and much bitter comment. The necessity for the extension, then plainly apparent, becomes more so day by day, as we witness our rapid increase in manufacturing works, in population, and the very large number of new houses, built and building. The extension is only a question of time, and we trust that when a petition, embracing even larger limits than that submitted to them, is again presented to the commissioners, it will receive their unanimous approval without any hesitation.

MAYORS OF YOUNGSTOWN.

The following is a list of the mayors of Youngstown, from its incorporation as a village and first election, held June 15, 1850, with the dates of election. The mayors of the village were elected for one year:

John Heiner, June 15, 1850.
Robert W. Tayler, April 7, 1851.
Stephen F. Burnett, April 5, 1852.
William G. Moore, April 4, 1853; re-elected April 3, 1854.
William Rice, April 2, 1855.
Thomas W. Sanderson, April 7, 1856.
Reuben Carroll, April 6, 1857; re-elected in April, 1858, 1859, 1860, and 1861.
Peter W. Keller, April 7, 1862.
John Manning, April 6, 1863.
Thomas H. Wells, October 16, 1863, to fill unexpired term of J. Manning, resigned.
Brainard S. Higley, April 4, 1864; re-elected April 3, 1865.
George McKee, April 2, 1866; re-elected April 1, 1867.

The following were elected mayors of the city, for two years.:

George McKee, April 6, 1868; re-elected April 4, 1870.
John D. Raney, April 1, 1872.
William M. Osborn, April 6, 1874.
Mathew Logan, April 3, 1876; re-elected April 1, 1878.
William J. Lawthers, April 5, 1880; re-elected April 3, 1882.

FIRST MARRIAGE.

The first marriage in this township, of which

we have any record or tradition, was celebrated on November 3, 1800. The following is the record in book "A" in the recorder's office at Warren, Ohio:

This may certify that after publication according to law of the Territory, Stephen Baldwin and Rebecca Rush, both of Youngstown, were joined in marriage on the third day of November, 1800.

By WILLIAM WICK, V. D. M.

Received and Recorded November 25th by me,
JOHN S. EDWARDS, Recorder.

The married pair were among the earliest settlers and had come out from Western Pennsylvania with their relatives and other pioneers. But this was not the first marriage between pioneers of the Mahoning valley. According to a record kept at Canfield, Alfred Wolcott, of Youngstown, John Young's surveyor, who had come out with him, was married to Mercy Gilson, of Canfield, February 11, 1800, nearly nine months prior. But they were married in Pennsylvania, for the reason that there was no person in the vicinity authorized to solemnize marriages. Was the marriage at Youngstown on November 3, 1800, the first marriage on the Reserve? Tradition relates that a wedding occurred at Cleveland in the log cabin of Lorenzo Carter in 1797. The parties were Mr. Clements, of Canada, and a hired girl living in Carter's family. It so happened that Rev. Seth Hart, who had at some period of his life, in an Eastern State, been a preacher of the gospel, but was not then engaged in ministerial work, was in Cleveland as an agent of the Land company or one of the surveyors. It was decided that he was minister enough for the occasion, and accordingly he officiated in "tying the nuptial knot," and a right merry wedding was had. This was, undoubtedly, the first wedding on the Reserve. But as some of the requirements of the Territorial law were absent on the occasion, it may justly be claimed that the first legal marriage on the Reserve was that of Stephen Baldwin and Rebecca Rush, at Youngstown, and there was solemnized the pioneer marriage and there was celebrated right joyously the pioneer wedding.

FIRST FUNERAL.

The first death of a white person which occurred in the township, after its settlement, of which we have any record or tradition, was that of Samuel McFarland, who had been a short time a resident of the place, engaged in teaching vocal music. He is said to have been a very estimable young man, and in his death the infant settlement sustained a great loss. He was buried in the northwest corner of the west lot of the old graveyard, as it was designated on the town plat laid out and recorded by John Young. The late Nathan Ague, then a lad about seven years of age, was at the funeral, and said that John Young and all the population were also present. The grave was a short distance east of the Disciple church on Wood street. A plain sandstone slab stood at the head. Near the top of the stone are the figures "1811," probably the date of its erection. Then follows this inscription:

In memory of Samuel McFarland, teacher of vocal music, late from Worcester, Massachusetts, who departed this life September 20, 1799, aged twenty-eight years.

Oh, how his music charmed our ears
While he was in our land;
And now we hope he sings the song
Of Moses and the Lamb.

But little more is known of his biography than is contained in this inscription. The stone, a few years since, was removed to the west part of the Mahoning cemetery.

THE FIRST SHOW.

Youngstown is a famous show place. All the great traveling circuses and menageries here spread their tents, and on show days thousands from our own city and the surrounding country fill them and enjoy the sights. A large opera house, one of the finest in the country, erected in 1874, is occupied very often by theatrical and opera companies, and the citizens have the opportunity and pleasure of witnessing the rendition of the best dramas, operatic, and other entertainments by the best artists. Joe. Jefferson, Edwin Booth, Anna Dickinson, Mlle. Rhea, Mrs. Scott Siddons, Mr. and Mrs. Frank Chanfrau, Remenyi, Buffalo Bill, John Ellsler, Effie Ellsler, Newton Gotthold, Sol. Smith Russel, Couldock, the Florences, Raymond, Edwin Forrest, and many other noted players have exhibited their great talents to large and appreciative audiences, and all carry away with them a love for the brisk and energetic iron city of the Mahoning valley, and promise other visits.

By aid of the memory of one of the oldest living native citizens we are enabled to present a reminiscence of the pioneer show exhibited in the village in its early days. John Ague, born here in 1806, when quite a small boy, with his parents and brothers and sisters saw this first show. It was a lion in a cage, attended by two men, and was exhibited in the barn of Colonel Hillman, who then kept a tavern in the house on the northeast corner of East Federal and Walnut streets, afterwards the residence of the late Dr. Henry Manning. The price of admission was twenty-five cents, and the citizens all thronged to see the show.

ARKS ON THE MAHONING.

The following item from the Western Reserve Chronicle of May 3, 1823, notes an incident in the history of Youngstown enterprise:

THE MAHONING.—The great advantages of this stream, which have hitherto been hardly observed, or but little attended to, are beginning to emerge from the lethargy of darkness, and to assume their real importance. Two arks, on the plan of those employed on the waters of the Susquehanna, have lately been constructed by Mr. Isaac McCord, of Youngstown. One was loaded on the 4th ultimo with about seven hundred bushels of wheat and fifty barrels of flour, and the other on the 23d ultimo with about eight hundred bushels of wheat. They started within nineteen days of each other, and both arrived at the Ohio river without accident in ten hours' floating. In a conversation which I had with Mr. McCord the other day, on the subject of navigating the Mahoning, he informed me that there were some mill-dams and other obstacles which still endanger the passage of boats at a middling pitch of water; but that for one thousand dollars the channel can be completely cleared, so that loaded boats might run with perfect safety on the slightest freshets, from Youngstown to the falls of Beaver, which in my opinion is a circumstance calling for the attention of every citizen who is interested in the improvement of this section of the country.

[Signed,]
A MEMBER OF THE AGRICULTURAL SOCIETY.
(Probably Judge George Tod.)

CHAPTER II.
INDUSTRIAL GROWTH.
FIRST GRIST-MILL.

The first mill for grinding grain, and with it a saw-mill, was built on Mill creek, at the Mahoning falls, about three miles southwest of the city. We give a brief sketch of this mill and its history, as written by the late William Powers, son of Isaac Powers, one of the millwrights:

One Sunday morning in August, 1797, two men assisting the surveyors, Isaac Powers and Phineas Hill, who had both joined the surveying party with the same object in view, to wit: a selection of land for themselves and friends, left the cabin near Spring common, crossed the Mahoning, following it up to the mouth of Mill creek, and then proceeded up that stream to the falls, now called Mahoning falls. It is probable they were the first white men to discover the falls. In those days a water-power, with a given amount of land suitably located, was esteemed of great value. And here, with a fall of twenty-seven feet and an apparently inexhaustible supply of water, was presented to the explorers the most valuable site for a mill they had ever seen. It was arranged between them that Mr. Hill was to have the exclusive right to negotiate with Mr. Young for the purchase of it, as Mr. Powers, although a millwright, had selected for himself and members of his father's family land above and below the center of the township, on which they afterwards settled. On their return to camp, Mr. Hill, without telling Mr. Young what they had discovered, tried to make a contract with him for three hundred acres embracing the falls. Mr. Young, led by the anxiety of Mr. Hill to purchase, arrived at the conclusion that there was something more valuable in that tract of land than he knew of, and refused to sell the land before seeing it. Mr. Hill then told him what he had seen. After an examination Hill purchased the land at a price previously talked of, with the provision in the contract, "that he, the said Hill, was to erect a saw-mill and something that would grind corn within eighteen months from the date of the contract." In pursuance of this agreement preparations were at once made to commence the building of the mill. A rude cabin was built by Abraham Powers, then of Beaver county, Pennsylvania, who, with his son Isaac, took the contract to build the mill. On being shown the contract, he informed Mr. Hill that for $50 he could put in something that would grind corn, which he did.

The mill-stones were procured and dressed by Abraham Powers and made, from a rock found in the vicinity of the crossing of Holmes street and Lincoln avenue in the city. The rock was what is called "nigger-head," in common parlance, of about the size of the ordinary three-foot stones now used, the splitting of which made the top and bottom stones.

The saw-mill was of the ordinary wheel-mill pattern, with the exception that the shaft of the gig wheel, instead of being movable at the top, as is usual, to throw into gear with the rag wheel, was stationary, and the rag wheel was movable in its stead. On the top of the shaft of the gig wheel was the spindle that connected the runner stone of the grist-mill.

It is highly probable that the first blasting by powder in the Western Reserve was at the building of this mill. It was necessary, in putting in the foundations and cutting the head race, to remove rock to some extent.

This mill experienced the fate of most of the early mills, and, in fact, of most mills in many respects. The original log mill was taken down and a frame mill erected. It was altered, enlarged, changed owners several times, burned down once or more, rebuilt, then enlarged, furnished with the latest improvements, and is now a large, handsome frame structure, doing a good business. It is known as Lanterman's mill, from the name of its owner, German Lanterman, an old, prominent, and much esteemed citizen of Youngstown, the son of an early pioneer.

The second mill on Mill creek was built some distance below the falls a few years later, and was known as the Parkhurst mill, probably from the name of the owner, and also as the White mill, probably from its color. It was a small affair and long ago was washed away by a heavy freshet or flood in the stream, which empties a large tract of country on the south, and is liable to sudden floods covering the bottoms, and, in places, widening the creek to a river.

FIRST VILLAGE MILL.

The first mill in the village was built by Caleb Plumb, a miller or millwright, probably both, from the State of New York, soon after the settlement of the township, and according to different traditions, between 1801 and 1804. It was built on a tract of about an acre of land, situated south of the road, running west from Spring common bridge and extending east to the middle of the river, which he purchased of James Hillman, it then being part of Hillman's farm, and for which he received a deed from Hillman, dated October 16, 1806. The east half of the river, and the east bank, Plumb purchased of John Young, by deed dated January 3, 1804, which recites that "for the consideration of $1, and for divers other considerations, such as to promote the interest and convenience of a new settlement by encouraging the erection of grist-mills, saw-mills, and all other useful water works in the township," he conveys to said Plumb the following tract of land "beginning in the middle of the Mahoning river on the south side of the highway leading from Spring common, in said township, across said river, and running down the middle of said river to the intersection of a line running across said river in a due west direction from the southwest corner of lot number three, in the west division of out-lots in said town plat, thence due east to the west side of Spring street, thence to the south side of the first before-mentioned highway, and then on the south side of said highway to the place of beginning."

Plumb built a rude dam and erected log buildings for saw- and grist-mills, put in the machinery, and had them in operation about 1804. Dr. Charles Dutton became connected with him in building or operating the mills, and about 1806 bought him out, and Plumb returned to New York. The saw-mill disappeared long ago.

The grist-mill had different successive owners and varying fortunes. It developed into a fair-sized frame building, and was known as the "Red mill." It was burned down in 1855.

Homer Baldwin purchased the site, rebuilt it in 1859 much larger than before, has made successive additions and improvements, and now, as the "City mill," it is a large, handsome, and conspicuous frame structure, furnished with all the latest processes invented for making the finest grades of flour, and has a capacity of two hundred barrels of flour daily.

DIAMOND MILL.

This mill, also the property of Homer Baldwin, has a history. About 185- Morse & Co. erected a large frame mill on Yellow creek, in Poland township. It was located several miles from any railroad, and was unprofitable. In 1866, a company composed of Anson Bentley, Manuel Hamilton, George Nold, James McCartney, Abraham Powers, and William Powers, under the firm of Bentley, Hamilton & Co., purchased the mill and removed it, piecemeal, to Youngstown. They re-erected it on the west side of Market street, a few rods north of the public square or diamond, and south of and adjoining the New York, Pennsylvania & Ohio railroad, naming it the Diamond mill. It was operated by this company a few years, and then by Nold, Brown & Co. In 1872 it was burned down, and its owners soon after erected a brick building on the site, as near fire proof as possible, and fitted it up with the latest and best machinery then in use for making flour. It was operated by this company, with some change of partners, until 1880, when it was purchased by Homer Baldwin, by whom it was enlarged, furnished with additional and improved machinery, and is now in full operation with a daily capacity of three hundred barrels of flour.

The Market-street mill, one at the mouth of Mill creek, and others, were built and operated for a time, but have been washed away, burned down or discontinued.

PLANING-MILLS.

William Lindsey, a carpenter and leading contractor for erecting buildings, built and put in operation the first planing-mill about 1853. It was a large frame structure located near the east end of Front street. Steam was the motive power of the machinery. It continued in operation for twenty years or more.

The second planing-mill was also started by William Lindsey, about 1859. He bought the Baldwin mill, as it was called, a flouring-mill which had been running on Mill creek in the the north part of Boardman, and moved the frame and wood-work to a site at the south end of Market street, on the north bank of the Pennsylvania and Ohio canal. Before he had finished putting in the machinery he sold it to Marstellar & Wallace, who completed the mill and ran it about four years. They then sold it to other parties, and it changed owners a few times until 1878, when John W. Ellis became its owner. In October, 1878, it was burned to the ground by a fire supposed to be accidental. Mr. Ellis immediately rebuilt in brick. The new mill, furnished with improved machinery, commenced running in April, 1879, and has been in successful operation since.

Other planing-mills, erected since 1860, are those of George Dingledy & Co., near the east end of East Federal street, on the south side, and of the Youngstown Lumber company, nearly opposite. Each of those in operation is doing a large business.

IRON MANUFACTURES—FIRST FURNACE.

Iron ore and limestone were known to be among the mineral deposits of the Mahoning valley, even before the settlement of the Reserve. In 1803 Daniel Eaton made arrangements, by obtaining right, to dig ore and make charcoal on and near the banks of Yellow creek, a small stream which flows into the Mahoning river from the south, to build a furnace on that creek, availing himself of its water power to drive his machinery. In that and the following year (1804) he built the Hopewell furnace, which was the first furnace in Ohio, or north of the Ohio river and west of Pennsylvania. This pioneer furnace was erected in the (then) township of Youngstown, although the site on which it stood, and where its ruins may be seen, is in the (now) township of Poland. The explanation is found in the fact that, at that time, the five miles square surveyed as township number one, in the first range, afterwards named Poland, with nine other surveyed townships, in the southeast corner of the Reserve, constituted the township of Youngstown, as organized for civil purposes, at the court of quarter sessions of Trumbull county, at its first term held in August, A. D. 1800.

In 1805 Robert Montgomery, who had explored the mineral resources of the Mahoning valley, before its survey into townships, and John Struthers, commenced building a second furnace on Yellow creek, a short distance below the Hopewell, on the land of Mr. Struthers. Robert Alexander, James Mackey, and David Clendenin became interested in it as partners, while it was building, or soon after. In 1807 Montgomery & Co. bought from Eaton the Hopewell furnace and all the ore, wood, and charcoal rights. It was run but a short time after they bought it. The second furnace was run until about 1812, when it went out of blast, and was never operated afterwards. They were both charcoal furnaces.

David Loveland, who was born in 1801 and lived, until his death on February 9, 1878, about a mile from these furnaces, in a reminiscence of the Montgomery furnace, written down from his dictation in 1874 by Robert M. Hazelton, a grandson of Robert Montgomery, says: "I was there often with my father, and though a small boy can remember well how it was constructed. There was a very high dam across Yellow creek, and the machinery was driven by a large overshot wheel which was attached to a walking-beam over a Sampson post (or upright pivot), very much as they drill for oil in our day. To this walking-beam was attached two plungers, and over it two large blowing-tubs, and from them the blast was transmitted to the furnace cold, hot blast being then unknown. The iron then made was cast into kettles of various kinds, hand-irons, etc."

Thomas Struthers, son of John Struthers, above named, in 1875, then seventy-two years of age, in a communication to the Mahoning Valley Historical society says: "These furnaces were of about equal capacity and would yield about two and a half or three tons each per day. The metal was principally run into moulds for kettles, bake-ovens, stoves, flat-irons, hand-irons, and such other articles as the needs of a new settlement required, and any surplus into pigs and sent to the Pittsburg market. They were, I believe, the first blast furnaces built in the State of Ohio, certainly the first on the Reserve. The former (the "Hopewell"), it is said, had for one side the natural work of the bluff against which it was built, and for that or other reasons was fickle in its working, and probably did not last long. I have no recollection of ever seeing it in blast. The latter (the Montgomery) continued to work until 1812, when the men were drafted into the war, and it was never started again."

The "Anna," a mineral coal furnace built in 1869 by the Struthers Iron company, of which Thomas Struthers was a member, on the old John Struthers' farm and but a short distance from the site of the Montgomery furnace, is its successor, and shows, in contrasting it with the latter, the wonderful improvements made in less than three-quarters of a century in iron manufacturing, by its yield of about one hundred tons of pig iron daily. It is now owned by Brown, Bonnell & Co., of Youngstown.

Those two old furnaces, the Hopewell erected in the early days of Youngstown, and the Montgomery erected in Poland, shortly after it was detached from Youngstown, were the forerunners of the great and constantly growing iron industry of the Mahoning valley, of which the Youngstown of to-day is the center, and to Dan Eaton, Robert Montgomery, John Struthers, James Mackey, Robert Alexander, and David Clendenin, should be accorded the high honor of being the pioneers of that industry. Biographical sketches of Messrs. Eaton, Montgomery, and Mackey will be found elsewhere in this work.

MILL CREEK FURNACE.

The first furnace in Youngstown, as now organized, was built about 1826, on Mill creek, a short distance below the falls, by Dan Eaton, or by him in connection with members of his family. It was a charcoal furnace. Afterwards John Kirk and Edward Rockwell, merchants of Youngstown, purchased an interest, and it was run by Eaton, Kirk & Rockwell. It changed owners, and came into possession of Pittsburg parties, and about 1846 or 1847 it was reconstructed to use bituminous coal as fuel. It was thus run for a time. But the expense of transportation, in wagons, of coal from the mines in a distant part of the township, and of ore and limestone from the canal, and of pig-iron to the canal, from two to three miles, was so great that there was no profit in running it. The furnace was blown out, the machinery removed, and the building has disappeared.

THE EAGLE, THE FIRST BITUMINOUS COAL FURNACE.

The next furnace in Youngstown, and the first erected for the reduction of iron ore by using bituminous coal as fuel, and which may properly be termed the pioneer of the iron industries now existing in Youngstown, was built in 1846, by William Philpot, Jonathan Warner, David Morris, and Harvey Sawyer, and called the Eagle furnace. The first stone coal furnace in Ohio was the "Mahoning," built in Lowellville, in Poland township, about five miles southeast from the Public square in Youngstown, in 1845-46, by Wilkenson, Wilkes & Co. By experiment they had ascertained that the coal of the Mahoning valley, termed "block coal," could be used in its raw state, and without coking, as had been the practice, for smelting iron ore. Finding abundant deposits of that coal, with limestone, ore, etc., near Lowellville, they selected that place as the site of their furnace. It was located adjoining the Ohio & Pennsylvania canal.

The "Eagle" was the second "hard coal" furnace on the Reserve, and probably in Ohio or the United States. It was located northwest of the city limits of Youngstown, and southeast of Brier Hill, on the east bank of the canal, on land purchased of Dr. Henry Manning. The coal was mined on land of Dr. Manning, adjoining the furnace lot. The contract giving the company the right to mine the coal was the first "coal lease" made in the township. The royalty paid was one cent per bushel for the first twenty-five thousand bushels, and one-half cent per bushel for all over twenty-five thousand bushels dug in any one year, and to mine not less than seventy-five thousand bushels per year, or to pay for that quantity if not mined; the money paid for coal not mined in any year to be applied on the excess mined in any other year; the bushel of coal to weigh seventy-five pounds; the lease to be in force for twenty years. This furnace has been enlarged and improved and is still in active operation. The present owners are Cartwright, McCurdy & Co., in connection with their rolling mill.

The next furnace was the Brier Hill, built by James Wood & Co., of Pittsburg, in 1847, a short distance northwest of the Eagle furnace. The coal was furnished by David Tod from his Brier Hill mines. In 1861 Mr. Tod purchased the furnace. It is now owned by the Brier Hill Iron and Coal company.

Other furnaces were built as follows: In 1859 Grace No. 1, and in 1860 Grace No. 2, by the Brier Hill Iron and Coal company, at Brier Hill; in 1854 Phœnix, by Crawford & Howard; and in 1856 Falcon, by Charles Howard, both on the flat in the southwest part of the city. Both are now owned by Brown, Bonnell & Co., and connected with their rolling mills. In 1859 Himrod No. 1, in 1860 Himrod No. 2, and in 1868 Himrod No. 3, on the line of the New York, Pennsylvania & Ohio railroad, north of East Federal street, and west of Crab creek, by the Himrod Furnace company. In 1867 Hazelton No. 1, and in 1868 Hazelton No. 2, by Andrews & Brothers, at Hazelton, on the line of the Pittsburg & Erie railroad, and near the south line of Youngstown township. They are connected with a rolling mill recently located near the furnaces by Andrews Brothers & Co. In 1879 a furnace on Crab creek, in the northeast part of the city, by the Mahoning Valley Iron company, near its rolling mill and connected with it.

FIRST ROLLING-MILL.

In 1846 the Youngstown Iron company erected the first rolling-mill in Youngstown, or on the Reserve, and perhaps the first in Ohio, in which bituminous coal was used as the fuel. It was located on the north side of what is termed the "Flat," on the north side of the Mahoning river, in the southwest part of the city, on the north side of and adjoining the canal. The stockholders of the company were Henry Manning, William Rice, Henry Heasley, Hugh B. Wick, Henry Wick, Jr., Caleb B. Wick, Paul Wick, James Dangerfield, Harvey Fuller, Robert W. Tayler, Isaac Powers, and James McEwen, only one of whom had been engaged in the iron business previously, or were practically acquainted with it. They were men of energy and enterprise, employed workmen skilled, as they supposed, in the business, and put their mill in operation in the spring of 1846. It was operated by this company a few years, and then for reasons satisfactory to the company it was suffered to remain idle for a time. In 1855 a company of practical iron workers from New Castle, Pennsylvania, consisting of Joseph H. Brown, William Bonnell, Richard Brown, and Thomas Brown, under the firm name of Brown, Bonnell & Co., purchased the mill for $25,000, and put it into operation. At that time it only consisted of the "old mill," as it is now termed, and contained four puddling furnaces, two heating furnaces, one annealing furnace, eight nail machines, one muck train, nail plate mill and a ten-inch bar train. The capacity of the works was seven tons of finished iron and nails per day.

Additions and improvements were made, new partners taken in, and, in 1875, the copartnership was incorporated as "Brown, Bonnell & Co.," by which name the business is still conducted, although not one of the original partners is now a stockholder of the company. The "old mill" constitutes but a small fraction of the present mill, whose buildings cover acres of ground, and which gives employment to about eighteen hundred hands in its various departments and the three blast furnaces connected with it, and four hundred and thirty men in its mines.

The officers of the company (in 1882) are Herbert C. Ayer, president; F. H. Matthews, vice-president and treasurer; Asa W. Jones, secretary; John J. Williams, general superintendent; H. C. Ayer, F. H. Matthews, A. W. Jones, J. J. Williams, Ralph J. Wick, D. P. Eells, C. A. Otis, Amasa Stone, W. H. Harris, directors. Daily average of pig iron, two hundred and twenty-five tons; of finished iron, two hundred and fifty tons. The mill makes bar, sheet, and plate iron, nails and spikes, fish plates, links and pins, etc.

ENTERPRISE ROLLING MILL.

The second rolling mill was built in 1863 in the northwest part of the city, and adjoining and on the east of the canal, by Shedd, Clark & Co., a firm composed of Samuel K. Shedd, William Clark, Edward Clark, James Cartwright, and Richard Lundy, who named it the Enterprise rolling mill, but in popular parlance it was known as the "Little mill" to distinguish it from the larger Brown, Bonnell & Co. mill. It is now owned and operated by Cartwright, McCurdy & Co., an incorporated company composed of James Cartwright, William H. McCurdy, Charles Cartwright, Samuel J. Atkins, William B. Hazeltine, and William R. Parmele, with a capital of $320,000. This mill has been greatly enlarged, and the "little mill" of 1863 can scarcely be found in the large mass of buildings which now constitute the works. The number of hands employed is about six hundred. Hoop iron is made a specialty, although various other kinds of merchant iron are manufactured. Other rolling mills have been built, as follow: In 1870 the Youngstown rolling mill was built by an incorporated company of that name, northwest of the city. It also makes hoop-iron a special manufacture. In 1871 the Wick & Ridgeway Iron company built a large mill on Crab creek, northeast of the city, for rolling railroad iron; but in 1875 its fires were suffered to go out in consequence of the cessation of railroad building and the demand for rails. In 1879 it was purchased by the Mahoning Valley Iron company, of which Henry O. Bonnell, W. Scott Bonnell, Richard Brown, former members of Brown, Bonnell & Co., Charles D. Arms and others are members, and has since been operated, not as a rail mill, but for the manufacture of other varieties of rolled iron.

In 1881 Andrews Brothers & Co., a firm composed of the brothers Chauncey H., Lawrence G., and Wallace C. Andrews, Lucius E. Cochrane and James Neilson, moved to Hazelton, in the southeast part of Youngstown, from Niles, a rolling mill which had there been operated by the Niles Iron company, of which part of the firm were component parts. The mill has been re-erected, with additions and improvements, and is now in operation. The number of men employed in the mill and two blast furnaces connected with it is about five hundred.

OTHER INDUSTRIAL WORKS.

Concurrent with our furnaces and rolling mills, from year to year other industrial works have been erected and are in operation. Among them we mention, without sketching their history, as prominent and extensive, the William Anson Wood Mower and Reaper works, one of the largest in the United States, and whose manufactures are exported to Europe; William Tod & Co.'s and Booth, Millard & Co.'s Foundry and Machine works, Arms, Bell & Co.'s Nut and Washer works, Morse Bridge works, Car works, Malleable Iron works, Forsyth Scale works, C. H. Andrews & Co.'s Stove works, Woodworth, Lane & Co.'s Glass Roofing works, Youngstown Carriage and Wagon works, and many others.

GROWTH IN POPULATION.

We now sketch the progress in population of the township, and, from facts and figures before us, present its growth numerically in successive periods. By public and private records and by tradition we learn the names of many, perhaps most of the earliest inhabitants. A few names of those of 1800 are familiar: John Young, James Hillman, George Tod, Isaac Powers, Daniel Shehy, William Rayen, Caleb Baldwin, John Rush, Joseph Williamson, James Gibson, James McCoy, Joshua Kyle were all prominent men, most of whom are represented at this day by numerous descendants, who are, as were their ancestors, among our active business and honored citizens, both men and women.

But we have no record of the number of those pioneers who were in 1800 laying the foundations and beginning the building of the thriving, industrious, enterprising, and rapidly-growing city and township of 1882. We have, however, a copy from the records of Trumbull county, of the list of inhabitants taxed on their chattel property in 1803, and the amount of tax charged against each. The list contains, probably, the names of nearly all the male citizens of twenty-one years of age and upwards, and is valuable, in several respects, as a part of the history of the township. It is as follows:

John Aga............	$ .09	John B. Bissell........	$ 2.54
Henry Brown........	.80	Samuel Bryson.......	1.30
William Burr........	.77	Samuel Calhoun.....	.56
Aaron Clark.........	.58	Alexander Clark.....	.40
Christopher Coleman..	.18	Michael Crummer....	.90
Nathaniel G. Dabney..	.40	Samuel Davenport...	4.62
James Davison.......	.74	John Dennick........	.00
Thomas Dice........	.40	John Duncan........	.08
Samuel H. Duncan...	.40	Andrew Donaldson...	.40
Thomas Ferrol.......	.24	Michael Fitzgerald...	.20
James Gibson........	1.15	Daniel Gray.........	.12
Samuel Hayden......	.60	James Hillman......	.37
Henry Hull..........	1.00	Andrew Kirkpatrick..	.80
Thomas Kirkpatrick .	1.36	John Kyle..........	.40
Joshua Kyle.........	3.00	Moses Lotta.........	.32
Daniel McCartney....	.30	James McCoy.......	.09
John McDole........	.40	Jesse Newport.......	.25
William Potter.......	.80	Isaac Powers........	.80
William Rayen......	.10	Josiah Robbins......	.45
Benjamin Ross.......	.80	John Rush..........	.61
Henry Sawyer.......	.20	John Sawyer........	.65
Matthew Scott.......	.60	Robert M. Scott.....	.40
Daniel Shehy........	2.09	Robert Stevens......	.80
Martin Tid..........	.12	Leffard Thompson...	.40
Joseph Williamson...	.28	James Wilson.......	1.08
Joseph Wilson.......	.32	John Young........	4.45
Total...............................			$40.41

In this connection and as the comparative

value of chattel property in each township and consequently the advancement in settlement at that time, we give the amount of tax in other townships taken from Trumbull county to form Mahoning county:

Poland .... $48.24   Canfield $36.93
Boardman .... 17.47   Coitsville 14.95
Austintown .... 9.22   Jackson 3.07

Ellsworth, Berlin, and Milton, are not mentioned in the list.

At the first pioneer reunion, held in the opera house, in 1874, a letter was read from Roswell M. Grant, who was an uncle of General Grant, and whose father was a pioneer of Youngstown, in which he gives a list of inhabitants of Youngstown village between 1805 and 1810, and the location of their places of residence or business, which we copy, adding explanations. "Commencing on Federal street, at its west end, was John E. Woodbridge, tanner." At his death the property was sold to John Smith, now deceased, and is occupied by his children. The residence built by Mr. Woodbridge has been remodeled, and on the part of the lot used for the tannery, now stands the extensive brewery of John Smith's sons. "Then coming east, John Townsend, hatter, next, on the northwest corner of Federal street and the Holmes road," then called, now Holmes street, "William Rayen, farmer and inn-keeper," and afterwards merchant and post-master, colonel in the war of 1812, and judge of the common pleas. "On the northeast corner, William Sherman, hatter, opposite, on south side of Federal street, and east of Spring common, George Tod lawyer. South of Tod was John Hogue, tailor, and Moses Crawford," both on Front street. "On Federal street, east of Sherman, Mr. Abrams, chair-maker," afterwards occupied by Richard Young. "In the log building," now boarded, next west of present town hall, "Samuel Stewart, tavern," afterwards occupied by James Hillman as a tavern. "Opposite, Dr. Charles Dutton," a one-story frame building, one of the first built in the township, still standing some distance south of the street, but not now used as a residence. "Then on north side of Federal street, east of Stewart's," and on the site where McGillin's store now stands, "Caleb Baldwin," farmer, innkeeper and justice of the peace. "Then Kilpatrick, blacksmith, Henry Wick, merchant,"

near present Wick's banking house. "Then Hugh Bryson, merchant," east of Diamond, on north side of Federal street. "Homer Hine, lawyer," south side of Federal street, between Champion and Walnut streets; the house, frame, is still standing, but removed to back of lot, site now occupied by a brick store building. "John P. Bissell, northeast corner Federal and Walnut streets," now known as Dr. Manning's house. "Then east, — Bruce, shoe-maker, and Rev. Mr. Duncan, Willian Thorn, cabinet-maker" where Tod house stands. In addition to the above houses, in the village, there were a few houses on the west side of the river, now in the city, and several farm houses in different parts of the township.

Dr. Jared P. Kirtland visited Youngstown in 1810. In a letter addressed to the managers of the first pioneer reunion, he describes its appearance at that time, and relates events which are interesting historically, and as comparing with the present, we quote from his letter:

June 11, 1810, dined with Dr. Charles Dutton in Youngstown, a sparsely settled village of one street, the houses mostly log structures, a few humble frame buildings excepted; of the latter character was the dwelling house and store of the late Colonel Rayen.

Dr. Kirtland was then on his way from Wallingford, Connecticut, to Poland, Ohio, and had spent the night previous at Adams' tavern in the township of Liberty, making his journey on horseback. After dining, Dr. Dutton mounted his horse, and accompanied him to Poland. Dr. Kirtland says:

No bridges then spanned the Mahoning. We passed over at Powers' ford (now Hazelton); the water high, and muddy from recent rains, but the doctor (Dutton) pointed out a rock in the river with its top barely above the water, which he said was an index that when the top appeared, it was safe to ford the stream. A small frame house, one story high, and painted with indigenous red ocher, stood near the present residence, a substantial brick house, one of the first built in the township, on the Isaac Powers farm. It was then occupied by him. Since, it has been moved down to the creek, and still serves as a dwelling place.

On the Stambaugh farm, at the four corners of Youngstown, Boardman, Poland, and Coitsville, a small clearing, a fine young orchard, and a log house were observed. A view over the Mahoning valley, taken at this point, embraced, at that day, an unbroken wilderness. The public highway to the village of Poland had been already effectually cleared, and parts thrown up as a turnpike, but a universal bed of muck and mud.

Early in September, 1810, I attended a regimental muster in Youngstown. A war with Great Britain was in anticipation, and the Indians on the frontier were committing depredations. A thorough military spirit pervaded the county.

and a full turnout of every able-bodied man was evident on the occasion. It was a matter of surprise to see an apparent wilderness furnish some six or seven hundred soldiers. The regiment formed with its right near Colonel Rayen's residence, and marched to a vacant lot between the main street and the Mahoning river, and was there reviewed. Simon Perkins was brigadier-general, John Stark Edwards brigadier-major and inspector, William Rayen colonel, George Tod adjutant, and John Shannon and McConnell were majors. A heavy fall of rain, after mid-day, seriously interrupted the exercises. No one, at that period, was disposed to evade his duties, and two years afterwards the efficiency and patriotism of that body of men was thoroughly and favorably tested.

The census of 1810 records the population of Youngstown township at 773, being the third township in population on the Reserve. Warren, with 875 inhabitants, was the first; Poland, with 837, second; Hudson, with 693, fourth; Hubbard, with 674, fifth; Painesville, with 670, sixth; and Cleveland, with 547, was seventh.

In the Trump of Fame, the first newspaper of the Reserve, and published at Warren, of date of November 4, 1812, the vote of several of the townships, at the Presidential election held October 31, 1812, is given. Youngstown polls 76 votes, Warren 71, Poland 52, and Hubbard 46 votes.

In the Western Reserve Chronicle of October, 1819, a statement is published of the number of white males of twenty-one years of age and upwards, of several of the townships, and the vote at the previous election.

	No. of white males.	Vote.
Youngstown	138	116
Warren	173	104
Poland	195	76
Canfield	151	103
Coitsville	89	40
Boardman	87	37
Ellsworth	92	54

The census of Trumbull county in 1820, as taken by Jacob H. Baldwin, and published in the Western Reserve Chronicle of January 18, 1821, shows the following results:

White males	8,140
White females	7,352
	15,492
Free black	50
	15,542
Number of inhabitants in 1810	8,671
Increase in ten years	6,871

We add the census of several townships in the order of population:

Youngstown	1025	Austintown	720
Poland	990	Milton	673
Hubbard	843	Boardman	604
Canfield	787	Coitsville	541
Warren	774	Ellsworth	508
Jackson	188		

HOUSEHOLDERS IN 1826.

On May 22, 1826, James Hillman, Henry Manning, and William O. Rice, trustees, divided the township into seven school districts and two fractional districts connected with districts in other townships. The township records describe the boundaries of those districts and enumerate the householders in each. The location we state generally, without giving the boundaries, and the names of the householders:

First district, included the village, a short distance north, farther to the south and east, in part to the township line. Number of householders—Richard Holland, Solomon Holland, Daniel Shehy, James Davidson, Homer Hine, John Loughridge, Peter Repsher, Margaret Mordock, Henry Manning, James McCartney, Henry Wick, Josiah Polley, Samuel Bryson, Abraham Lackey, Solomon Chapman, Mrs. Widow Fitch, Wilson Thorn, Jeremiah Scannel, William Wick, James Hezlep, Peter Kline, Philip Kimmel, Rev. M. Harned, Daniel S. Morley, Robert Pollock, William Morris, Charles Dutton, Singleton King, George Hardman, Jonathan I. Tod, William Rayen, Jonathan Smith, James M. Smith, John Day, Moses Crawford, William Curts, Jonathan Edwards, John E. Woodbridge, Alexander McKinnie, George Cook, John Bissel, John Hayes, Robert Kyle, David LeRoy, Jacob B. Heaton, Levi Morley, Andrew McKinney, Daniel McDaniel, Samuel Hayden, Christopher Hayden, Josiah Polley, Jr., Mary Dabney, Peter Everett, Frederick Ague—Total fifty-four.

Second district, northeast part of township, including Crab creek. Householders—John Swauger, John Derrick, James Moore, Robert McDonald, Michael Storm, Isaac Swauger, Joseph Rees, Adam Swauger, Joseph Kerr, Thomas Watt, James Wilcox, John Kimmel, Daniel Thornton, Richard Young, William O. Rice, Joseph Meglathery, Dorcas Caldwell, Noah Chamberlain, Thomas Pauley, Elizabeth Baldwin, Jeremiah Allen, Joseph Cartney, Erastus Cowdry, James Mackey, Edward Boyd, Christopher Sowers, Noah Chamberlain, Jr., Byron Baldwin, Neal Campbell, Kitty Bryson, Henry Matthews—Total thirty-one.

Third district, north middle part of township, including Briar Hill. Householders — George Tod, Archibald Beggs, James Wilson, Andrew Wilson, James H. Protzman, James Beard, John Stambaugh, Justus Dunn, John Murburger, Peter Wurtz, Solomon Kline, Christopher Hollingsworth—Total twelve.

Fourth district, west middle of township. Householders—Thomas Ferrell, Alexander Kinkead, Marmaduke Bright, James Rayen, John Rush, John Rush, Jr., Eli Rush, John Madden, Joseph Williamson, James McKinnie, Stephen Baldwin, John Kyle, Cornelius Tomson, George Rastler, Philip Mikesel, Jacob Phister, John Gibson, Robert D. Gibson, James Gibson, Henry Meglathery, Thomas Kirkpatrick, Jonathan Stout, James Hillman, George Snider, Matthew Pool, Martha Knox, Francis Wooldley, Samuel Gibson, Pyatt Williamson—Total twenty-nine.

Fifth district, northwest middle of township. Householders — John Beard, John Bentley, James Tayler, William Smith, William Reid, Robert Holroyd, Elener Lightbourn, Anthony Ague, James Kyle, Josiah Robbins, Hugh Beard, Peter Wansetler, John Dougherty, Michael Rayen, Alida Ransom, Jonas Foster, David Arner, Amos A. Stoddard, Joseph Paul, Daniel Schell, John Frederick, Jedediah Fitch, Moses Dray, Jacob Wycuff—Total twenty-four.

Sixth district, southwestern part of township. Householders—John Woods, William West, William White, Elisha Blake, John White, Joshua Kyle, James Price, William Hetfield, Mrs. Cleveland, James Fitch, John McCorkle, Joseph Osborn, George Stall, Phebe Cook, Anthony Osborn, Widow Ross, Thomas Potts, Isaac Heaton, James Beggs, James White, Luther Babbit, George Hull, Thomas Woodard, Jonathan Shores, Martha Woodard—Total twenty-five.

Seventh district, northwest part of township. Householders — John Hogge, Abram Powers, Jacob Powers, Joseph Willson, Eli Philips, Aaron Philips, Christopher Erwin, Robert Kinkaid, —— Crowell, Samuel Whice, John Browher, Aaron Osborn, Jr., Thomas Erwin, Abram Osborn, Aaron Osborn, Jacob Erwin, David Vestle, Lewis Swaney, Robert Kerr, Humphrey Goff, Widow Rigall, Thomas Davidson, Jesse Bailey, Robert Patrick, William Near — Total twenty-five.

Fractional district, at Cornersburgh. Householders—Henry Hull, Jacob Hull, Samuel Turner, Nathaniel Swift, Abram Leach, Joseph Strock, Michael Hamson—Total seven.

Fractional district, southeast corner of township. Householders—Isaac Powers, John Shannon, Frederick Hake, Joseph Kennedy—Total four.

The total number of householders enumerated in the township is two hundred and eleven.

In August, 1830, the householders in the several school districts were again enumerated and the number had increased to two hundred and forty-five.

We add a few more figures showing the vote and population, at intervals of time, up to 1880, when the last census was taken. In 1832, at the State election Youngstown polled 256 votes, and in 1843 were polled 360 votes. In the census of 1850, Youngstown enumerates 2,802 inhabitants; 5,377 in 1860, an increase of 2,575, or nearly doubling; 10,837 in 1870, an increase of 5,460, or more than doubling; and 21,171 in 1880, an increase of 10,334, or nearly doubling. The increase in population for the thirty years from 1820 to 1850 was 1,057; for the thirty years from 1850 to 1880, it was 18,369. The population of the city in 1880 was 15,431, of the township outside of the city 5,740. Since the census was taken in June, 1880, the population of both city and township has been rapidly increasing, and at this time (June, 1882) it is estimated at not less than 30,000.

BANKS AND BANKERS.

The well-known banking house of Wick Bros. & Co. was organized in 1857, by Paul Wick, his brother Hugh Bryson Wick, and a few others. Mr. H. B. Wick was formerly a member of the well-known Cleveland firm of Wicks, Otis & Brownell, afterwards H. B. & H. Wick. This last organization was dissolved in 1859, two years after starting here, since which time the Wick brothers have devoted their time to the banking business in Youngstown. Hugh Bryson Wick died April 22, 1880, leaving the charge of the house in the hands of his surviving brothers. The bank has always had its location at 38 Federal street; is a private partnership, and has always had a sound business reputation.

The First National bank of Youngstown was

organized June 2, 1863, and is a reorganization of the Mahoning County, bank. It is one of the first organizations under the National banking system, being the third in number. The first organization was constituted in its management of Henry Manning president, William S. Parmelee vice president, John S. Edwards cashier. June 9, 1866, the following changes were made: William S. Parmelee was elected president, John S. Edwards vice president. In 1865, Robert McCurdy was elected cashier, which position he filled until January 1, 1877, when he was elected its president, William H. Baldwin taking the former's place as cashier and Sheldon Newton that of the vice presidency. The bank started with $150,000, but has since increased its capital from time to time until it now amounts to $600,000.00.

The Second National bank was organized in the month of January, 1875, having for its officers at that time Henry Tod for president, T. K. Hall vice-president, G. J. Margerum cashier. Mr. Tod has continued its president ever since its organization, but about one year after that date Mr. C. H. Andrews became vice-president and H. M. Garlick cashier. The board of directors consists of the following gentlemen: Henry Tod, C. H. Andrews, William B. Sampson, William B. Pollock, A. W. Jones, H. M. Garlick, J. A. Smith, Andrew J. Vanness, Jonas Cartwright, T. W. Kennedy, John R. Grist.

The Youngstown Savings and Loan association was organized in October, 1868, under State law, Hon. David Tod being one of the prime movers in the enterprise, with a capital of $600,000, about one-third paid in. David Tod, president; J. H. McEwin, secretary and treasurer. David Tod died about one month after its organization, when Freeman O. Arms was elected to the office, who, resigning, was succeeded several years afterwards by Joseph H. Brown. The Youngstown Savings and Loan association was changed into the Mahoning National bank in February, 1877, with Joseph H. Brown president, and J. H. McEwin cashier. J. H. Brown resigned several years after, and Henry O. Bonnell was elected, and is now president. The present officers are: H. O. Bonnell, president; George Tod, vice president; J. H. McEwin, cashier; J. F. McEwin, assistant cashier.

The Commercial National bank of Youngstown is one of the most recent banks organized in the city, having a date for that event May 23, 1880. It began with a capital stock of $130,000, but on the 1st of July, 1881, increased this amount to $200,000. The officers elected are as follows: C. H. Andrews, president; T. W. Sanderson, vice president; G. J. Margerum, cashier.

MAHONING VALLEY MUTUAL RELIEF ASSOCIATION.

There was formed in Niles, April 4, 1877, a life insurance company under the above title. The following were chosen officers of the company: H. T. Mason, of Niles, president; A. G. Bentley, of Niles, vice-president; J. H. Fluhart, secretary; H. H. Mason, of Niles, treasurer; Elder N. N. Bartlett, of Niles, manager of agencies; Hon. L. D. Woodworth, of Youngstown, attorney, and Dr. D. B. Woods, of Warren, medical director. About the 1st of January, 1878, the office of the company was removed to Youngstown.

J. R. Seagrave was made secretary and still holds that position. The company has been growing steadily since its organization, and its field of operations extends over all northeastern Ohio. It is a peculiarity of this company that every applicant must undergo a rigid medical examination, and only those of sound body are admitted. The medical board are all men of known character and fitness—D. B. Woods, of Warren; A. P. McKinley, of Niles; and M. S. Clark, of Youngstown, are the physicians composing it. It is the policy of the company to afford cheap insurance by avoiding hazardous risks.

PUBLIC BUILDINGS.

The Tod house, the principal hotel in Youngstown, was built by John Stambaugh, Nelson Crandall, and the sons of the late Governor Tod, in the year 1870. It is a brick structure, four stories in height, above a stone basement surrounded by an open area. It stands on the corner of Market street and the southeast corner of Diamond square, fronting fifty feet on the former street, and seventy-five on the square, then contracting to forty-four feet in width. It extends seventy-two feet farther east, making a total length of one hundred and forty-seven feet. It has a good entrance from Market street, and contains, on each floor, office, halls, suites of parlors with connecting rooms, and forty-eight bedrooms in all. There are also baggage rooms, together with reception and reading rooms, billiard halls, etc.

The gas works of Youngstown were constructed during the years 1866-67. The works with tank, gasometer, and the retort house (brick), and machinery, were soon built, and main pipes laid in the principal streets, with branch pipes and fittings in most of the business houses, and in many of the private residences. The return to the assessor of internal revenue for the first two months showed the amount of gas consumed to be 163,000 feet, not enough to pay expenses. In 1872 the works were greatly enlarged. A pit was made for a new gas receiver to be twenty feet in height by sixty feet in diameter, and in all about $30,000 were expended by the company. They had at this time about two miles of pipe, and a capacity of manufacturing about 200,000 feet of gas per day.

The opera house stands near the southwest corner of the Public square, in rear of the new bank building. Its dimensions are one hundred and ten feet in length, by seventy-eight feet in width. The walls rest on solid stone foundations, and are forty-six feet high and twenty-two inches thick. The front is of iron and the exterior appearance is very tasty and attractive, and as well as the interior arrangements, reflects great credit upon the architect. The auditorium is seventy-four feet square; the seating is admirably arranged, having a capacity of about fourteen hundred, with room for six hundred more on extra occasions. The parquette, dress circle, and family circle, are all provided with folding seats, of the Nolan patent. The frescoing is elaborate and beautiful; the ceiling of the dome is decorated with allegorical figures representing the drama, music, poetry, comedy, history, tragedy, painting, etc. The stage is thirty-six feet wide, and forty feet in depth, and is well supplied with scenery. Commodious and neatly furnished dressing rooms are connected with the stage, and every thing there, as elsewhere, is marked with a degree of perfectness.

The Youngstown Opera House company was organized in July, 1872. The officers of the company then were: William Powers, president; Henry Tod, vice-president; J. H. McEwen, secretary and treasurer.

STREET RAILWAY.

The street railroad in Youngstown extends from Watts street along Federal street to Brier Hill, and is something over two miles in length. It was built in 1875 and has since done a paying and increasing business. The officers are James Mackey, president; James Cartwright, vice-president; Alfred Smith, secretary and treasurer, and Joseph O'Neal, superintendent.

CHAPTER III.
RELIGIOUS SOCIETIES.
FIRST PRESBYTERIAN CHURCH.

The year 1800 dates the beginning of Presbyterian worship on the Reserve. William Wick and Joseph Badger were the first regular preachers on the Reserve. The latter was sent West by the Connecticut Missionary society, and held the first Presbyterian service at Warren in the fall of 1800. Baptist services had previously been held at that point, but no church society was organized. Mr. Wick was licensed to preach August 28, 1799, and was ordained pastor of the churches at Neshannock and Hopewell, Pennsylvania, in September, 1800. He had previously supplied these churches, and, it is probable, occasionally visited Youngstown. The exact date of the organization of this church is not known, the early records being lost and the first members all dead. The first recorded mention of a church in Youngstown appears in 1801, when Mr. Wick was released of the pastorate at Neshannock by the Presbytery of Ohio, and installed pastor at Youngstown. The Hopewell charge was retained until his death in 1815, his time being divided between the two. The first elders were Caleb Baldwin and William Stewart. The former died in 1813, the latter October 28, 1831. Other elders elected during the pastorate of Mr. Wick were William McClelland, elected in 1806, withdrew in 1839; Samuel Bryson, elected in 1806, died April 3, 1832; John Duncan, elected in 1806, resigned in 1813; and John Nelson, elected in 1811, dismissed in 1832. The Youngstown church was connected with the Presbytery of Ohio until 1802, when it was in cluded in the newly formed Presbytery of Erie. Hartford Presbytery was formed in 1808, and included in its limits Youngstown. No change was made until the division in 1837.

The first meeting-house was erected in 1802. It was built of logs, and stood on the northwest corner of Wood street and Wick avenue, directly opposite the present church. This house was occasionally used for public meetings, and also for the village school. It served a useful purpose until 1835, when a new structure was built on Federal street. Mr. Wick was a faithful minister, and the church prospered under his care, though the increase in membership was slow; but rapid growth could not be expected in a new and sparsely populated country.

*William Wick was of Puritan descent. He was the son of Lemuel and Deborah Wick, and was born on Long Island, New York, June 29, 1768. In 1790 he removed to Washington county, Pennsylvania, and four years later married Miss Elizabeth McFarland, youngest daughter of Colonel Daniel McFarland, an officer in the Revolutionary army. He was one of the first settlers on what was known as lower Tenmile creek. Mr. Wick had settled down to farming, but an acquaintance with Dr. McMillan, an earnest Presbyterian divine, changed his course of life. There was an urgent call for ministers, especially in the West, and Mr. Wick was finally prevailed upon to enter upon a course of study, preparatory to the work for which his talents and piety designated him. He completed an academical course at Cannonsburg in 1797, and read theology in Dr. McMillan's log cabin. He was finally licensed to preach by the Presbytery of Ohio, August 28, 1799, and soon after became pastor at Neshannock and Hopewell, subsequently at Youngstown. Mr. Wick was an intimate friend of Joseph Badger, his contemporary on the Reserve. Mr. Wick's labors did not extend further west than Youngstown. He received aid from the Connecticut Missionary society for about two years, at the end of which time his charge became self-supporting. He took a warm interest in missionary work, and associated with Revs. McCurdy, Marquis, Badger, Hughes, and other early divines in devising means for religious service in border settlements. About 1803 there was an awakening of religious interest, which greatly strengthened the church at Youngstown.

The tendency of new communities is to become absorbed in material interests to the neglect of the spiritual, but this founder of the church at Youngstown seems to have had the ability, in a measure at least, to counteract this natural influence. The period of his ministry was brief. Before leaving the farm he had experienced delicate health, and on that account hesitated to enter the ministry. There was no cause for alarm, however, until 1814, when, in October, a severe cold affected his lungs. He continued to preach during the winter, but continued rapidly losing strength till spring. His death took place at Hopewell, Pennsylvania, on the 29th day of March, 1815, in the forty-seventh year of his age, and sixteenth of his ministry. At his own request he was buried at Youngstown. From his tombstone it is learned that he preached during his ministry one thousand five hundred and twenty-two sermons, and married fifty-six couples. The Wick family consisted of eight sons and three daughters, some of whom have been among the most prominent citizens of Youngstown.

We are unable to state who served the church during the year succeeding Mr. Wick's death. Rev. John Core was licensed to preach in 1816, and was ordained pastor at Youngstown, June 25, 1817. Mr. Core, at the time of his ordination, was thirty-two years old. He served Vienna and Brookfield churches. Mr. Core was a successful pastor and served in this field six years. During that time more than one hundred were added to the church at Youngstown. A Sunday-school was formed in 1820, Elder Samuel Bryson being superintendent. This Sunday-school has ever since—more than three-score years—been a successful nursery of the church. The school was superintended successively after Mr. Bryson by Dr. Manning, Elder John Laughridge, and William Rice. No new elders were chosen during his pastorate. Mr. Core died in Clarion county, Pennsylvania, May 17, 1854.

The church was dependent from the time of the resignation of Mr. Core in April, 1823, till 1830, upon stated supplies. Rev. Enoch Bouton served as stated supply from 1824 till 1826, and from 1826 till 1829 Rev. Nathan Harned acted

---
* Our information is derived from Eaton's History of the Erie Presbytery.

in that capacity. Mr. Harned was a native of Rockingham county, Virginia, and was born in 1789. His name first appears on the records of the Erie Presbytery in 1824. The following year he was ordained pastor of the Warren, Great Brokenstian, Lottsville, and Sugar Grove congregations in Pennsylvania. In 1826 he joined the Hartford Presbytery, and was called to Youngstown as stated supply. Failing health compelled him to resign this charge in 1829. His ministerial labors really ceased here, although he frequently preached and acted as a supply whenever his health would permit. He died in New York in 1854, of disease of the heart, cancer of the stomach and hydrothorax. In 1827 Abraham Nelson and John McMurray were chosen to the eldership. Both were dismissed in 1832.

Rev. Ward Stafford was called to the pastorate at Youngstown in January, 1830, and April 5th, following, was ordained pastor by the Presbytery of Hartford. Rev. James Wright preached on that occasion; Rev. James Satterfield delivered the charge to the pastor and Rev. Thomas E. Hughes the charge to the people. Mr. Stafford was born in 1789, and entered the ministry in 1815. Until 1829 he had engaged in missionary work in and around New York city, gathering together and preaching to the poorer classes. During his seven years pastorate in Youngstown about one hundred members were added to the church. He resigned his charge in 1837. His death occurred in 1851. A new church was built in 1835 on Federal street, which was used until the present building was erected in 1866.

The subject of building, as is often the case, caused considerable discord in the congregation. This, added to previous differences on the subject of choir singing, threatened serious trouble. Some were opposed to building at that time, and others opposed building on Federal street. The feeling against choir singing on part of a considerable faction of the congregation was strong. This difference reached its climax three years before a church was finally built, but the difficulty was happily solved by the organization of the church in Liberty. Forty-three members of the Youngstown church were dismissed. Among the number were three of the four elders composing the session. Their places were filled by Dr. Henry Manning, John Laughridge, and James Thorn. Dr. Manning died January 11, 1869, aged eighty-two; John Laughridge, December 13, 1856, aged sixty-two; and James Thorn March 10, 1845, aged forty years. Those who attached themselves to the Liberty church were generally opposed to choir singing. When the Presbyterian church was disturbed by the unfortunate division into Old-school and New-school, Youngstown was almost unanimous in its adherence to the New-school. One member, William McClelland, chose the Old-school, but was refused admittance by the Liberty church on a letter from the Youngstown church. This incident shows the bitterness of feeling then existing between these two branches of Christians. The period of Mr. Stafford's pastorate was the most embarrassing in the history of the congregation, but by the time his successor was installed all differences had been settled. The questions which had divided the congregation were of a general character, and no blame for their intrusion upon the peaceful growth of the church can be attached to the pastor. He is rather entitled to credit for preserving unity.

Mr. Stafford was succeeded in the pastorate by Rev. Charles A. Boardman. He was born in Connecticut in 1788. He was ordained in 1818 at Preston, Connecticut, the charge being delivered by Rev. Lyman Beecher. During his pastorate at that place Horace Bushnell, the late noted New England divine, was converted. After leaving New Preston, and before coming to Youngstown, Mr. Boardman preached at New Haven and Westport, Connecticut, and as agent for the Western Reserve college. He was installed pastor at Youngstown, August 6, 1839, by the Presbytery of Trumbull, which had lately been formed. "It was largely, indeed, owing to his influence," says the Church Manual, "that the church voted to attach itself to the New-school wing, as he positively refused to become its pastor while it remained an Old-school congregation." The same publication says: "He was much more than an ordinary man, and during his pastorate here, and since his release and decease, it has been an occasion of surprise to many that this church was permitted to have his services so long. He was a man of fine intellect, and universally beloved for his many virtues, both as a man and a Christian."

Mrs. Boardman died in Youngstown in 1851.

In 1854 he asked the congregation to unite with him in a petition to the Presbytery to release him from the charge. The congregation reluctantly consented to a dissolution of the pastoral relation which had been so beneficial to the church. From this time until his death in 1860 he resided with his son-in-law, S. B. McEwin, at Monroe, Wisconsin. His body was brought to Youngstown for burial. Funeral services were held July 29th in the Presbyterian church. Two thousand persons came to pay a last tribute to one held in high regard as pastor, friend, and citizen.

During the year 1843 three elders were elected —William Rice, dismissed July 1, 1872; James Buck, died April 12, 1856; and Lemuel Wick, dismissed December 23, 1846.

From 1855 to 1859 Frederick H. Brown supplied the church. He assumed full pastoral charge and lived within the bounds of the charge. He never was, however, regularly chosen pastor but employed as stated supply. Mr. Brown was never held in favor as an orator, but in a measure compensated for lack of ability in that direction by tact and energy as a pastor. He was in feeble health and was finally compelled to abandon ministerial labors. He died at Elyria, July 31, 1861.

Dr. Levi B. Wilson was the fifth regular pastor of this church. He was born at Plymouth, Ohio, in 1821, was apprenticed to the shoemaker's trade, and subsequently attended school at Milan academy and at Western Reserve college, where he graduated in 1848 from the literary department, and from the theological department in 1850. He had charge of Central college, Blendon, Ohio, till 1855, when he began devoting his time exclusively to the ministry. before coming to Youngstown he served as pastor to the Central College church, (consisting of six members, one of whom was his wife), and the Congregational church, Windham, Ohio. His call to Youngstown was received and accepted in September, 1859. Just ten years later he resigned the charge and removed to Atchison, Kansas, and from there, in 1873, removed to Grasshopper Falls, Kansas. It was during Dr. Wilson's ministry that Youngstown began its rapid growth. This church, which had not increased in the number of members since 1830, increased in wealth and numbers, making the erection of a new meeting-house a necessity. The present structure on the corner of Wood street and Wick avenue, was completed in 1866. Mr. Wilson found one hundred and fifty members when he came to Youngstown. He left two hundred and eighty.

Three elders were chosen in 1857: Jonathan Warner, dismissed January 3, 1863; Robert M. Montgomery, and John Gibson. In 1865 William Bonnell, Augustus B. Cornell, and Reuben McMillen, were chosen to the eldership. The present pastor, Rev. Daniel H. Evans, began his labors in Youngstown in February, 1870, and was installed pastor by the Presbytery of Trumbull, May 5, 1870; Rev. F. A. Noble, of Pittsburg, preached the installation sermon, Rev. B. Y. Sharp delivered the charge to the pastor, and Rev. Xenophon Betts, the charge to the people.

Mr. Evans was born in Ripley, Ohio, April 16, 1838. He entered Miami university in 1855, and was graduated in 1859. He commenced his theological course at the Western Theological seminary, at Allegheny, Pennsylvania, and graduated from Andover, Massachusetts, in 1860. He was ordained in 1863, on his twenty-fifth birthday, and settled as pastor at Grand Haven, Michigan, in 1866. He was afterwards stationed at Pittsburg, Pennsylvania, some eight months. He came to Youngstown in 1870, where he has since officiated as pastor of the Presbyterian church. In 1877-8, he was abroad for nearly a year, visiting the Holy Land. Mr. Evans married Sarah J. Livingston, in January, 1863, and has had three daughters and five sons, seven of whom are living.

The following elders have been chosen during his pastorate:—1873, Gideon Cornell, died 1877, aged seventy-seven, and Thomas H. Wilson. In 1877, George Cornell, and Robert McCurdy were elected.

THE SECOND PRESBYTERIAN CHURCH.

This church was an outgrowth of the Mission Sabbath-school work started in Youngstown in the year 1872 by a few of the enterprising church members of this and other denominations', Henry B. Shields, J. F. Wilson, Henry A. Evans, and I. A. Justice being among the chief actors of the number. The Sabbath-school grew in numbers, and has continued growing in interest since its first organization. The school at the present time, in proportion to the size of the congregation of the church, is very large, it numbering about one hundred and fifty pupils, while the membership of the church is about one hundred. The growing demands of the town for a second church for this congregation necessitated action on the part of its membership, and in 1874 steps were taken to secure a place for worship. The membership of the new church consisted of eighteen persons. This small number secured a building first on Covington street, where they remained until the year 1879, when they removed to their new meeting-house on the corner of Rayen avenue and Liberty street. This is a frame structure, 35 x 60 feet, tastefully furnished.

The first pastor, Rev. Robert Scott, was a graduate of Auburn college. He began his ministry preaching to the Mission school of this place, and upon the organization of the church was installed its first pastor. He remained with the church until the fall of 1879, having been very successful in his pastorate. He was followed by Rev. S. G. Hair, who is a successful Christian laborer, and has accomplished a great work for the church. His efforts are much assisted by Mrs. Hair, who is an earnest worker. She is an accomplished organist, and, with the assistance of I. A. Justice as leader of the choir, contributes to an important feature of the church service.

The officers of this organization have changed but little since its inception. The elders are H. B. Shields and J. F. Wilson; deacons, Robert M. Aughenbaugh and J. W. F. Plug; trustees, John M. Owens, I. A. Justice, and Mansfield Milton.

The first death which occurred in this congregation was in October, 1876, in the person of J. B. Sheldon. He was one of the old pioneers of the city, coming to this place from Portage county, this State; was an active laborer in the church, and died much lamented. Mr. George M. Brainard, one of the original members of the organization, died February 13, 1880, about sixty-five years of age. He was an active member, was influential and highly esteemed by his brethren. Mrs. Lizzie Nicholl, another original member, departed this life January 10, 1879. Also Mrs. Lizzie Caldwell and Mrs. Helen Justice, both original members, are greatly missed from the society. The former

died in the fall of 1880, and the latter April 19, 1881.

FIRST METHODIST CHURCH.*

Methodism began its career with the present century in the wilderness of Western Pennsylvania and Eastern Ohio. The itinerant preacher followed close behind the pioneer settler. Shadrach Bostwick was appointed in 1803 by the Baltimore conference to take charge of this field, then under the care of Thornton Fleming, presiding elder for the Pittsburg district. Dr. Bostwick was a practicing physician, but had devoted twelve years to preaching in New York and New England. He located with his family at Deerfield, Ohio, that point being near the center of his circuit. He penetrated the forests in different directions, established appointments, and organized societies. He visited Youngstown for the purpose of forming a class, this being one of the leading points on the Reserve. The doctor had some difficulty to find a place to preach, but was finally offered the use of Judge Rayen's barn. After preaching several times, he succeeded in forming a class composed of six persons—Moses Crawford and wife, John Hogue and wife, Isaac Powers and Mr. Braden. Judge Rayen's barn continued to be used for public worship, and Mrs. Rayen joined the church. We quote from a published letter:

Moses Crawford and wife deserve more than passing notice. Anterior to the forming of the class in Youngstown, a class was formed in West Hubbard. Father Crawford was leader, and lived in Youngstown. It was the custom of the old couple on Sunday morning, after they had breakfasted, to set their house in order and start on foot for Hubbard, generally carrying an infant child, to attend meetings and hold class, returning again the same evening.

The Youngstown class soon secured the use of the old school-house on the present square for services, and from there Mr. Crawford's house was made the place of meeting. Mr. Hogue's house was afterwards the place of meeting except on quarterly meeting occasions, when the ball-room of Mr. Holland's tavern was used. Dr. Bostwick continued to serve the Deerfield circuit during the year 1804, and then settled in Youngstown to practice medicine and serve the church as local preacher. In 1807 he removed to Canfield, where he resided until his death in 1837. In 1805 the Erie and Deerfield circuits were combined; James Hunter was appointed

*From the Church Manual.

presiding elder, and David Best and J. A. Shackelfield preachers. The former was soon after exchanged for Robert R. Roberts, who was a young man of unusual vigor and in after years became a bishop. Mr. Gregg's history of Methodism gives some idea of the work of itinerants of that period:

The Erie and Deerfield circuit at this time was more than four hundred miles around, and this journey, to be accomplished every four weeks, was along blind paths found by marked trees, across swollen, unbridged streams, over rugged precipices and high hills, now winding around steep, rocky mountain sides and then plunging through deep, miry morasses, sometimes camping in the woods all night, weary and hungry, resting his head upon the root of some forest tree, while his faithful horse stood up without a mouthful to eat, and not unfrequently encountering wild beasts, rude, savage men, and venomous serpents.

Mr. Gregg's grammar in this sentence is badly involved, but the picture is no less vivid and we have reason to believe accurate.

There is no information obtainable to fix the precise time of the erection of the first meeting-house built by this congregation. It was probably about 1810-12. The deed for the sale is given in 1814 to Amos Smith, John Hogue, Abraham Powers, and William Morris, trustees of the society. Twenty dollars was the amount paid for the site, which was the lot nearly opposite the present church on Phelps street. This meeting-house was a small frame building, sided and ceiled inside with matched boards. It was lighted by candles contributed by the members, the class leader performing the additional office of chief candle snuffer. An addition was built in 1818 on the south end, in which a gallery was commenced but never completed. The old church was sold about 1828, and a part of it converted into a dwelling. A new brick house had been built on the opposite side of Phelps street on the site of the present church. It had a gallery on both sides and at one end, and accommodated a large congregation. About 1840 the walls of this house began to be considered unsafe and were torn down. A frame building the same size was occupied the following year, but was not finally finished till several years later. The pulpit was between the entrance doors, and the floor descended regularly toward the pulpit.

The present meeting-house was built in 1861, and at its completion was the best Protestant church building in the city. It has long since been inadequate to the large and growing congregation. A new structure will soon take its place.

The Sunday-school connected with this church is the oldest in the city. It grew out of the custom of holding young people's meeting in the church, at which the Bible was read verse in turn. In the year 1826 a regular school was organized with William H. Fitch superintendent, and A. W. Upham and Samuel Black teachers.

Youngstown was made a station in 1842. Coitsville, Erwin, Crab Creek, and Girard were connected with it for some years. We append a list of circuit and station preachers:

1803-04—Shadrach Bostwick. 1805—J. A. Shackelford, David Best, and Robert R. Roberts. 1806—R. R. Roberts and James Watts. 1807—C. Reynolds, C. Daniels, and A. Divers. 1808—Job Guist and William Reuter. 1809—J. Charles, J. M. Hanson, and J. J. Decellum. 1810—James Charles and James Ewen. 1811—William Knox and Joshua Monroe. 1812—The circuit was changed to Trumbull; Thomas J. Crockwell, J. Somerville, and James McMahon. 1813—John Shannon, Oliver Carver. 1814—James McMahon, Lemuel Lane. 1815—John Waterman and Shadrach Ruark. 1816—Henry Baker. 1817—D. D. Davidson and Ezra Booth. 1818—Calvin Ruter and John Stewart. 1819—James McMahon. 1820—James McMahon and Ezra Booth. 1821—Charles Elliott and Dennis Goddard. The former subsequently became well known in the church, was an editor, college professor, and college president, and an author of ability. 1824—John Somerville and Alfred Bronson. 1825—Edward H. Taylor and William R. Babcock. 1826—Robert C. Hatton and Robert Hatton. 1827—R. C. Hatton and S. Adams. 1828—B. O. Plimpton and E. W. Shehan. 1829—B. O. Plimpton and Richard Armstrong. 1830—Alfred Brunson and T. Carr. 1831—Cornelius Jones and John Luccock. 1832—Philip Green and Caleb Brown. 1833—John Preston and John I. Holmes. 1834—John W. Hill and B. Preston. 1835—J. W. Hill, Thomas Stubbs, and Henry Elliott. 1836—Thomas Stubbs and J. Robinson. 1837—John Luccock and J. E. Aiken. 1838—John Luccock and J. C. Ayres. 1839—Ira Eddy and Dennis Goddard. 1840—B. O. Plimpton and L. Clark. 1841—Dillon Prosser, E. B. Lane and J. M. Plant. 1842—

Dillon Prosser. 1843—A. G. Sturgis. 1844—Bryon S. Hill. 1845—Thomas Stubbs. 1846—W. W. Maltby. 1847—Ira Norris. 1848—J. R. Locke and Roderick Norton. 1849—J. R. Locke and J. H. Tagg. 1850-51—James Greer. 1852—William Bevins. 1853—Thomas Guy. 1854—Thomas Guy and Ira Norris. 1855—J. D. Norton. 1856-57—John Tribbey. 1858-59—H. N. Stearns. 1860-61—G. W. Maltby. 1862-63—R. H. Hurlbut. 1864—G. W. Clark. 1865—J. E. Wilson.* 1866-67—John Peate. 1868—J. S. Lytle. 1869-70—William F. Wilson. 1871—E. S. Gillette. 1872-73-74—John Peate. 1875-76-77—T. M. House. 1878-79-80—W. H. Locke. 1881—C. V. Wilson. The present membership is about five hundred.

THE SECOND METHODIST EPISCOPAL CHURCH of Youngstown, is located on the corner of West Rayen avenue and Henrietta street. The building was ready for occupancy on January 20, 1878. The necessity for the organization of this church was acknowledged by the Methodists of Youngstown and by many ministers of the conference. For a half-score of years there was not to the extent desired that substantial growth in the old church, and there seemed to be a falling off of probationers and members, notwithstanding the frequent revivals.

The responsibility of organizing a new society was thrown upon Henry A. Evans, who was appointed by the officials of the church to select two other members to co-operate with him (Robert Wilson and Walter Campbell were chosen) and perfect arrangements, all of which was done, and as a result of the enterprise there is now (1882) a society of one hundred and sixty-five members.

Early in the spring of the year 1878 there was

---

*Mr. Wilson died before the close of his first year. We quote from the Church Manual of 1870: "He labored twenty years in the ministry, during which time he was called to fill some of the most important stations in the church, among which were Milwaukee, Wisconsin; St. Louis, Chicago, Pittsburg, and Wheeling. He was re-admitted to the Erie conference in May, 1865, and appointed to this station. The conference minutes say of him: 'He entered upon his work with joyful earnestness. Great expectations had been kindled among the people, for his fame had preceded him. To him the field seemed just ready to brighten into a harvest of saved souls.' But before these expectations were realized the Master called him from labor to rest, on the 24th of September following his appointment to the station, at the residence of brother Cramer Marsteller, on Wick avenue."

organized the Young People's association, under a brief constitution and by-laws, a copy of which may be found in the Appendix of the Historical Record of this church.

In 1877 the Eastern Ohio conference at Cleveland considered the demands of the work, and G. F. Oliver, just admitted to conference on trial, was appointed to the Second church, Youngstown then existing only in name. His first year's labors resulted in a membership to the church of fifty-six.

By the annual conference, held in Alliance September 18-23, 1878, G. F. Oliver was re-appointed, and during his pastorate the church succeeded in relieving themselves of the church debt, the building and lot costing $3,485.10. In 1879 Rev. Mr. Oliver was succeeded in this charge by Rev. O. W. Holmes, a graduate of Franklin, Ohio, and of Drew Theological seminary. In the fall of 1880 he was reappointed, and is still in charge.

The Sabbath-school children's class is a new feature in the history of Sabbath-school work. The class meets every Sabbath evening at 6 o'clock.

PROTESTANT EPISCOPAL CHURCH.

A few of the pioneers were members of the Protestant Episcopal church. Mrs. George Tod, wife of the pioneer lawyer of 1800, was one of them. This estimable lady came from New Haven, Connecticut, where, with her parents and other relatives, she was a member of Trinity church, one of the oldest Episcopal churches in the United States. Others came from time to time. Among those of a later date was Mrs. Rachel Wick, first wife of Colonel Caleb B. Wick and daughter of Jered Kirtland, of Poland, Ohio, an early pioneer from Wallingford, Connecticut.

In September, 1809, the members of this church residing in Boardman and adjoining townships formed a church organization. That church was supplied at intervals with a pastor, and services were occasionally held by him in Youngstown. The Presbyterians had there erected a church edifice, about 1800, and the Methodists about 1810. It is remembered by the elderly inhabitants that Episcopal services were held in one or the other of these churches on the occasion of these visits, their use and occupancy being kindly offered by the respective

pastors and members, and the citizens generally attending the services. Rev. Jackson Kemper, afterwards missionary bishop of the Northwest, and subsequently bishop of Wisconsin, in 1814, it is believed, was one of the earliest and perhaps the first who held services here. Rev. Roger Searle was here in 1817, and subsequently Rev. Philander Chase, bishop of Ohio, elected in 1818, visited Youngstown in 1820. He preached at Canfield, Boardman, and Poland, but, his time being limited, did not preach here. In 1825 he again visited Youngstown and preached here. We extract a part of his journal of his visitations in 1825.

September 8th. Rode to Warren, and in the evening preached and performed divine services in the court-house. The audience was very large and attentive.

9th. Proceeded to Youngstown. Here, also, in the midst of a respectable congregation, the same duties were performed.

10th. At Poland, in addition to the evening services and a sermon, I baptized two children.

11th, Sunday. Rode to Boardman, where I officiated morning and evening, administered the communion to twenty-six, and confirmed three persons, baptized four adults and four children. The congregation, though so crowded as scarcely to admit the administration of the ordinances, was most attentive and reverential during the great length of the services and two sermons. In the intermission I administered the communion to a sick woman.

12th, Monday. Rode to Canfield, performed divine service and preached, and baptized one child and visited a sick person.

13th. At New Lisbon, my horse being injured, a friend, Mr. Blocksome, kindly provided me with a wagon, in which I rode with great comparative ease to Steubenville.

Rev. M. T. C. Wing settled for a time at Boardman, afterwards professor in the Theological seminary at Gambier. Revs. John Bryan, J. T. Eaton, T. L. Harrison, Joseph Adderly, C. C. Townsend and others are remembered as holding services here. Bishop McIlvaine visited the place, held services and administered the ordinance of baptism about 1853.

Rev. Gregory T. Bedell, then assistant bishop of the Diocese of Ohio, visited Youngstown in 1859, and preached in the Presbyterian church to a large audience. After the services he held a consultation with those members of the Episcopal church present, and it was decided to proceed in forming a church organization, and to erect a church edifice. Mr. and Mrs. Francis Reno, Miss Sarah McCoy, Mr. and Mrs. Joseph B. Wilder, Mr. and Mrs. William J. Hitchcock, Mrs. R. J. Powers, Mrs. Dr. Henry Manning, Mr. and Mrs. Henry Manning, Jr., Mr. and Mrs. John Manning, Mr. and Mrs. Freeman O. Arms, Mr. and Mrs. John Smith, Mr. and Mrs. M. T. Jewell, Mr. and Mrs. James Mackey, Mr. and Mrs. David Mackey, James M. Reno, and John Ellis were among those who displayed great interest, and were active in forwarding the measures proposed, and many citizens, not connected with the church, assisted by their means in the erection of an edifice. As the result of the consultation with the assistant bishop, the parish of St. John's church, of Youngstown, was organized December 15, 1859. The first wardens were Francis Reno and Henry Manning, Jr. Both served in their office until they died; Mr. Reno in 1863, Mr. Manning in 1881.

A hall was procured, in which to worship until the building could be erected, and Rev. A. T. McMurphy, officiating at Boardman and Canfield, and Rev. C. S. Abbott, officiating at Warren, frequently officiated here. The corner-stone of the present church building, on East Wood street, was laid May 27, 1861, by Right Rev. G. T. Bedell, and the same bishop consecrated the edifice on October 21, 1863. This was the first church in the diocese with which Bishop Bedell had been associated in all the important steps of its history. On October 1, 1861, the Rev. Wyllis Hall accepted a call to the rectorship of the parish. On September 15, 1865, he presented his resignation, which was accepted, and took effect September 25, 1865. On March 23, 1866, the Rev. Samuel Maxwell accepted an unanimous call to the parish, and entered upon the rectorship May 1, 1866, and is still (1882) the rector of the parish.

The number of communicants for the convention year ending June, 1865, was fifty-eight; the present number, March, 1882, is two hundred and fifteen.

In the fall of 1879, it became necessary, on account of the growth of the parish, to enlarge the building. Under the supervision of the rector, Rev. Samuel Maxwell, many desirable improvements were made, a Sunday school chapel built below the chancel, new altar, and church furniture procured, and the whole interior of the building tastefully frescoed. The church thoroughly remodeled, was opened with appropriate ceremonies, by Bishop Bedell, on May 20, 1880.

A commodious rectory adjoins the church, built in 1869 for the present incumbent.

BAPTIST CHURCH.

Regular Baptist worship was not instituted in Youngstown until 1860, although there were a number of members of that church living in the vicinity. In July, 1859, Mrs. Young, an aged lady, succeeded in having a Sunday school organized, and it is probable that the formation of a church was the outgrowth of this movement. The Sunday-school was formed with thirty-seven scholars, in a hall over Theobold's clothing store. Rev. E. F. Brown, of Warren, was present on the occasion. B. F. Parks, now of Cedar Rapids, Iowa, was chosen superintendent.

A meeting of Baptists in regular communion was held in the Protestant Methodist church June 6, 1860, which resulted in the formation of a church society. The following were enrolled as members: Stephen Stewart, Lucinda Young, Sophia Stewart, Carlos Stewart, George A. Young, Almira Young, Betsy Stewart, Cordelia Hughes, William Geddes, Eliza Geddes, Margaret Geddes, Laura S. Cornan, Mary A. Williams, Martha Williams, W. M. Ingersoll, Benjamin F. Parks, J. C. Johnston, Isabella Johnston, Katie Moore, Sidney Case, Aaron DeCamp, Nancy DeCamp, J. S. Edwards, James Shields, Rebecca Couch, Elmira McCready, Hannah Prill, Ann Hull. John S. Edwards was chosen first clerk of the session, and W. M. Ingersoll was ordained first pastor. He resigned in 1872 and B. F. Ashley succeeded in 1873. C. F. Nicholson was ordained pastor in the fall of 1875, and D. B. Simms in October, 1879. The present pastor, John A. Snodgrass, assumed pastoral relations in June, 1881. The Sunday school has grown steadily with the congregation. The successive superintendents since Mr. Parks have been A. J. Williams, H. Dillon, Disney Rogers, J. B. Couch, and Thomas Goodridge.

The first meeting-house was built on Hazel street in 1861. The present house was dedicated in 1869. There are at present about two hundred and eighty members.

We append a short biographical sketch of the present pastor.

REV. JOHN A. SNODGRASS was born in Noblestown, Pennsylvania, December 22, 1836; the only child of Dr. James and Jane (Nesbit) Snodgrass. He was educated under a private tutor until eighteen years of age, when he entered an academy at Mansfield, Pennsylvania. His father meeting with reverses in business about this time he was thrown upon his own resources and he began teaching school. He continued his studies and fitted himself as a teacher in the higher branches of mathematics, and of Latin and Greek. In 1862, with nine other teachers in the McKeesport school, he enlisted in the One Hundred and Forty-ninth Pennsylvania volunteer infantry, and became the first lieutenant. Of his associates who went out with him only four returned. He was mustered out at Harrisburg, Pennsylvania, in 1865. Upon his return he took charge of the union school at McKeesport. March 29, 1866, he was united in marriage to Miss Eva J. Haney, of Allegheny City, Pennsylvania, who has been his efficient assistant in the various schools of which he has been the head. Soon after his return from the army he began the study of theology, and September 10, 1868, he was ordained in the Sanduskystreet Baptist church of Allegheny City. His labors in the ministry have been more of a missionary character than those of a settled pastor. He has been very successful in organizing new societies and building up old ones, and in this work he has been ably assisted by his wife, to whom he feels a large share of his success due. Mr. Snodgrass came to Youngstown in January, 1880, and as pastor of the First Baptist church, has added about one hundred names to the membership and discharged a debt of $6,000. Mr. and Mrs. Snodgrass have one daughter, Sadie Jennie.

DISCIPLE CHURCH.

The Disciples organized a society in Youngstown July 18, 1841, with twenty-seven members. They had the old academy on the Diamond fitted up for church purposes, and continued to use it until 1873, when the basement of the present church was ready for occupancy. Of the twenty-six original members none are living. The present meeting-house was commenced in the summer of 1872, and completed and dedicated in 1874. The total cost was $27,000. The pulpit was supplied by the following preachers: Wesley Lamphere, John Henry, John Applegate, Henry Brocket, W. S. Gray, O. Higgins, Walter Haden, James Calvin, F. S. Whistlar, Orwin Gates, Jasper Hughes, R. E. Davis, C. C.

Smith, M. L. Streator, and J. N. Monroe. The present membership is about four hundred.

UNITED PRESBYTERIAN.

Twelve communicants of the United Presbyterian church held a meeting October 10, 1859, and were organized into a church by Rev. J. W. Logue, of Northfield, Ohio. Soon after organization a call to the pastorate was extended to G. K. Ormand, who accepted and was duly installed pastor. Under his preaching the church grew in wealth and membership. He resigned February 1, 1870, leaving a congregation of more than one hundred members, provided with a comfortable house of worship. The second pastor, Rev. J. M. Wallace, was installed February 7, 1871. He remained pastor until 1882, a period of about eleven years. Mr. Wallace was a native of Beaver county, Pennsylvania. He graduated at Allegheny seminary, and soon after accepted a call to Viola, Illinois, where he remained until called to Youngstown. As a pulpit orator he has few equals, being pleasing, persuasive, and logical. During his pastorate the membership was more than doubled. The meeting-house, which was built in 1867, was repaired in 1877, and again in 1881. An additional lot was added to the church property last year at an expense of $1,700. The pastorate is at present (1882) vacant.

ROMAN CATHOLIC.

St. Columba's Catholic congregation, whose church is on the corner of Wood and Hazel streets, is of comparatively recent origin. From a membership of about twenty families in 1855, it has within the past ten or twelve years made a most astonishing increase, and it now counts a membership of some five or six hundred families, or about two thousand souls. Though the congregation proper has but a recent existence, the first settlement of Catholics in this neighborhood extends back a great many years. As early as 1826 a Catholic priest came here to minister to the few early settlers of that time. We learn of Father Thomas Martin, a Dominican, coming here in that year from Somerset, Perry county, this State. His missionary duties brought him to the Catholic settlement at Dungannon, Columbiana county, and learning that there were some Catholics here, he extended his labors, and came to visit them in the year above mentioned.

Father Martin came once more, and then from that time until 1831 there is no record of a priest coming here. In the latter year Father McGrady, also a Dominican from Somerset, made a pastoral visit.

Fathers Martin and McGrady, and other priests who succeeded them for many years, offered up the holy sacrifice of the mass, either in the house of Mr. William Woods, whose relict, Mrs. Mary Woods, still lives in an honored old age, or in that of Mrs. Woods' father, Daniel Sheehy, who with Neal Campbell, must have been the earliest settlers of these parts. About 1835 Father James Conlan was stationed permanently as resident pastor at Dungannon, and from that year he came here frequently. Father Conlan was for many years vicar-general of this diocese before his death. After more than forty years of hard missionary labor he died universally respected by all classes, his memory being deeply revered to-day by all.

The number of Catholics was somewhat increased soon after 1835 by the laborers on the canal, and in consequence the visits of the priests became more frequent. In 1843 James Moore and his family settled here, and about the same time some members of the Kessiker family became converts to the church, so that from that time the first nucleus of a congregation may be said to have been formed.

From 1843 to 1848 Youngstown was made one of the missionary stations, and was visited by Fathers Howard, Monaghan, Kennedy, and others. Howard and Monaghan were living a short time since, and frequently came here to assist the priests in hearing confessions of the old Irish people who were unable to make confessions in the English language.

In 1848 or 1849 the first attempt was made by Father McGann to build a church. A subscription was started on one of his visits, and the result was $30 subscribed. This was amongst a few who had assembled at Mrs. Wood's house to hear mass. About six years afterward a modest little edifice was brought to completion. This was on the same site as the new one.

About 1853 the old church, which is now used as the priest's residence, was brought to completion. Fathers Megan, Stroker, and Pendergast did duty in the intervals between 1848 and 1854. In 1854 Rev. William O'Connor was appointed resident pastor of Youngstown. In 1861 or 1862 he was succeeded by Father O'Callaghan, and in 1863 he laid the cornerstone of St. Columba's, the present church, and in 1864 had it ready for use, which was then thought unnecessarily large and commodious, but to-day, in order to accommodate the congregation, four masses must be said on every Sunday.

About 1870 or 1871 Father O'Callaghan began the foundation of the large parochial school on Rayen avenue, and, like the church, it was thought large, but there is now an average daily attendance of some six hundred children. It is found that the school building is not large enough to accommodate comfortably the great crowds that daily assemble within its walls.

Father Gibbons, who succeeded Father O'Callaghan, was, in turn, succeeded by Father Mears in 1877—the present pastor.

Within ten years the flourishing congregations of St. Joseph's, of which Father Eiler is pastor, and St. Ann's, of Brier Hill, presided over by Father McGovern, have been formed as offshoots of St. Columba's, and therefore, taking them into account, the Catholic population of Youngstown and Brier Hill at the present time can not be far from eight or nine hundred families.

During the last year there were in Columba's two hundred and one baptisms, of which some ten were adults from Protestant denominations.

REV. CHARLES M. SELTZER, now in charge of St. Joseph's Catholic church, Youngstown, Ohio, is a native of Lorraine, France, born July 15, 1845. He came to America in 1864 and until the spring of 1868 was a student of St. Mary's seminary, Cleveland, engaged in the study of philosophy and theology. May 16, 1868, he was ordained and was first settled at Landeck, Allen county, Ohio, where he built a fine residence and parochial school. He was afterwards at Milan, Erie county, where he discharged a debt of $3,000 in a little over one year. September 24, 1871, he located at Doylestown, Ohio, where he erected a fine school building, and also made preparations for the erection of a church to cost some $20,000, on which a debt of only $1,100 remained when he left there. June 18, 1881, he severed his connection with the Doylestown society and came to Youngstown and immediately commenced the erection of a new church to take the place of the old one occupied by St. Joseph's society, costing some $17,000 or $18,000. Father Seltzer, it will be seen by the above, was a successful church builder.

REV. MICHAEL B. BROWN was born in Clinton county, New York, September 20, 1840. With his parents he came to Ohio in 1852, the family locating in Sandusky. He took private instruction in Latin, and in 1857 became a pupil of St. Mary Preparatory seminary, continuing two years. In 1859 he went to University of Notre Dame, graduating therefrom in 1862. During the following years until 1872 he occupied the chair of theology and philosophy. He was ordained as priest in 1867. In 1872 he was elected vice-president and director of studies of the University of Notre Dame, which position he filled two years. In 1874 he was transferred to the position of vice-president of the college of Our Lady of Sacred Heart at Watertown, Wisconsin, where he remained until 1876. He then came to the diocese of Cleveland; was stationed at Youngstown one year. In 1867 he took charge of St. Joseph's church, Crestline, where he remained till March, 1881, when he was transferred as assistant pastor of St. Columba's church, Youngstown. Recently, during the absence of Father Seltzer in Europe, Father Brown took charge of St. Joseph parish.

MARTIN LUTHER GERMAN EVANGELICAL LUTHERAN CHURCH.

Among the early settlers who at the beginning of the present century came to Mahoning county, were many Germans, whose ancestors were members of the church of the reformation, that is, of the Evangelical Lutheran church. Anxious to retain in their midst the preaching of the Gospel, and the administration of the sacraments according to the confessions of their ancestors, they in different parts of the country called pastors, and organized congregations. Thus many years ago Lutheran congregations were organized in Boardman and Crawford townships. Ministers served from ten to fifteen congregations, and some traveled over several counties. The few German Lutherans in Youngstown attended services in the surrounding Lutheran churches. The first attempt to gather a Lutheran congregation in Youngstown was made by Rev. G. Kranz, in 1857, then living in North Lima. He visited this place and frequently preached here, in connection with a Lutheran congregation which he served in Boardman. In 1858 the Lutherans and some members of the German Reform church called the Rev. Fehr as their pastor, in Youngstown. He was a Reform minister, but he proposed to the two parties that they should build a union church. The church was built, but afterwards was claimed to be a Reform church. The Lutherans, finding themselves deceived, resolved to organize themselves as a German Evangelical Lutheran congregation. This was done August 1, 1859, they numbering at that time twenty-two members. Rev. F. C. Becker, from Jackson, served them temporarily. Rev. L. Krebs, of Brookfield, was called to be their pastor July 31, 1859. After the congregation had held its services in different localities in town for some time, they bought the lot where the church now stands. The lot is 45 x 120 feet, and is located at the corner of Wood and Champion streets. March 2, 1862, the corner-stone was laid, and an ordinary brick house was built, 35 x 50, and sixteen feet high, and fifteen feet more of ground was purchased in order to enlarge the yard. In the spring of 1862 the corner-stone of the present building was laid, and November 2, 1862, the church was dedicated. The congregation then numbered fifty members. The Rev. L. Krebs moved to Youngstown in 1862, and served them as their regular pastor. January 1, 1869, the congregation called their present pastor, Rev. G. F. H. Meiser. During this year a piece of ground near the church was purchased and a parsonage erected thereon.

In the year 1876 a teacher, Prof. A. W. Lindemann, formerly serving one of the parochial schools of the Evangelical Lutheran St. Paul's congregation at Pittsburg (S. S.), Pennsylvania, was called by the congregation, and, after having accepted the call and being orderly dismissed from the congregation he served, was installed by Rev. G. F. H. Meiser as teacher for the parochial school in the congregation. The object of the congregation in establishing a parochial school for its children instead of sending them to the public schools was to train them in the German and English languages, and to combine with secular study instruction in the Bible with a view to educating them to become Christian citizens and faithful members of the church.

At first this school was held in the church building. In the following year, however, the congregation erected a school-house on the lot belonging to it. The congregation grew rapidly in numbers, mostly in consequence of the great emigration from Germany. It thus soon numbered some two hundred families and one hundred and twenty scholars.

In the year 1880 the congregation bought a pipe organ for its church. A year afterwards (1881) it became more and more apparent that the present church- and school-buildings had become entirely too small for the number of church visitors and scholars. For this reason the congregation consulted in its congregational meeting, whether to build a larger church and to enlarge the school-house at their present location, or to divide the congregation and build a new church and school-house at Brier Hill, where about one-half of the members are living. The congregation finally came to the conclusion that it would be the best for the Lutheran church at large, in this region, to make a division, which has been done. Members of the congregation living west of the present city limits were advised to organize the new congregation; those living east of said limits to remain in connection with the old congregation. In May, 1881, those members west of the city limits assembled in the public school-house at Brier Hill, and organized themselves as the German Evangelical Lutheran St. Paul's congregation of Brier Hill, Mahoning county, Ohio. They adopted a charter and constitution by which their church organization is to be ruled, and erected at once a proper church and school-house. The building plat was donated to the congregation by Messrs. David James and Robert Mackey. The plan for the building was drawn by Rev. L. A. Detzer, Evangelical Lutheran pastor of Hubbard, Trumbull county, Ohio.

On the 10th of July the corner-stone of the new church building was laid with appropriate ceremonies by the pastor of the congregation, Rev. G. F. H. Meiser, assisted by the Revs. A. H. Schmidt, of Meadville, Pennsylvania, and L. A. Detzer, of Hubbard, Ohio. St. Paul's congregation has also already called a teacher for its school, and will call a pastor of its own as soon as expedient. Until then, however, Rev. G. F. H. Meiser will serve both the Martin Luther and St. Paul's congregations.

REV. G. F. H. MEISER is a native of Prussia, born in the city of Brieg, district of Silesia, the 22d of May, 1838. He was yet a small boy when his father, Rev. Ferdinand Meiser, who was the head clergyman of St. Nicholas church at Brieg, died. His mother, descending from a family whose ancestors during many years back were serving the Lord in the Holy Trinity, did not spare any trouble or expense to give him a thorough theological and scientific education. At first he was instructed by a private tutor, then he entered the college of his native city, and after that two colleges in Breslau, the capital of Silesia. In the year 1857 he emigrated into this country, where some members of his family were living already. After becoming acquainted with the state of things in America he went to Columbus, Ohio, to finish his course of study in the Theological seminary of the Evangelical Lutheran joint synod of Ohio and adjacent States. At the end of the year 1859 he received a call from the German Evangelical Lutheran charge of Galion, Ohio, which he accepted, and was thereupon ordained and installed by Rev. H. Lang, of Fremont, Ohio, on the 4th of December. In the year 1864 he accepted the repeated call of the Evangelical Lutheran congregation in Butler, Pennsylvania, and remained there until the year 1869, when a repeated call from the Martin Luther church in Youngstown induced him to return to this city, where he has now been laboring for thirteen years. He, as well as his congregation, stand in connection with the Evangelical Lutheran joint synod of Ohio and adjacent States, one of the largest Lutheran bodies in this country.

THE METHODIST PROTESTANT CHURCH.

The "Brown Church," as the Methodist Protestant church building has always been called, was erected in 1841, and was then one of three church edifices in Youngstown. It was most prosperous while under the charge of its first pastor, Rev. William Reeves, to whom it is indebted for its existence. The principal members then were Philip Kimmel, Abraham Powers, Jona Stout, and Wilson Thorn. Owing to internal dissensions, caused largely by unfortunate pastoral relations, the average attendance had dwindled to twenty in September, 1881, when the Rev. E. W. Brindley took charge. The average number present at regular services is now one hundred and fifty. Alexander Hendry is the treasurer; Ida Mansell, secretary; and James Mansell, Thomas and John Morgan, and J. W. Daniels are the trustees. The Sunday-school has a membership of thirty-four. According to the rules governing the Methodist Protestant churches the pastors are changed every two or three years. The house of worship is a plain frame building, 24 x 50 feet, and has a frame parsonage attached. The lot is now worth $10,000.

REV. EDWARD A. BRINDLEY (present pastor, 1882) was born in the county of Kent, England, about thirty miles from the city of London, on the 4th of March, 1817. His father, Thomas Brindley, was a ship architect, and took large contracts from the English Government. After experiencing reverses of fortune, he emigrated to this country in the year 1828. The family consisted of three boys—Frederick, Edgar, and Edward. All have passed away but the youngest. Mr. Brindley received his education at Bristol college, situated on the Delaware river, twenty miles above Philadelphia. After leaving college he engaged in teaching school, both public and private, for a period of sixteen years, when he turned his attention to the ministry, and was ordained deacon in the Methodist Protestant church in the city of Steubenville, Ohio, August 31, 1850. He was ordained elder in 1854, in the town of Cadiz, Ohio, and became connected with the Muskingum conference of the Methodist Protestant church. In 1860 he was transferred to the Pittsburg conference of the Methodist Protestant church, of which he is still a member. For three years he was associate editor of Clark's School-day Visitor, published in Cleveland, Pittsburg, and subsequently in Philadelphia. He has had charges in various places in Ohio, Pennsylvania, and West Virginia, and is still able to perform ministerial work.

THE WELSH BAPTIST CHURCH.

This society was organized at Brier Hill, December 10, 1846, by Rev. David Probert, the pastor, and Rev. William Owens, of Pittsburg. The original membership consisted of nine persons, as follows: Rev. David Probert and his wife Ellen, Thomas Edwards and wife, David

Jones and wife, Mary Jones, Thomas Probert, and John Edwards. A house of worship was built at Brier Hill in 1847. The society at Brier Hill largely consisted of coal miners, most of whom finally moved to Youngstown and engaged in other business. Hence the society was transferred to the city in 1866. Services were held in a hall for some six months, and then a house of worship was built. It was dedicated January 1, 1867. Rev. Mr. Probert officiated as pastor for twenty-five consecutive years, and was followed by Rev. William L. Evan for eleven months. Mr. Evan was succeeded by Rev. David R. Jones, who remained two years, when (January, 1877) Mr. Probert, the former pastor, again took charge, and has been pastor since. The number of members at the present time is about one hundred and fifty. The Sunday-school has an average attendance of about one hundred, Mr. Thomas Jones being superintendent.

EVANGELICAL PROTESTANT REFORMED CHURCH.

This church resulted from the uniting of two entirely distinct religious bodies—the Evangelical Protestant and the Reformed congregations. The first was organized in 1855 in the Brown Methodist church, and in 1858 removed to its own church building, a frame structure on Mahoning avenue, near Springbottom bridge. The pastors were the Revs. Kranz, Fehr, Baur, Seiple, Fromm, Wagner, Seybold, Moench, and Lobschiedt.

The Reformed church was organized in 1859 or 1860, and has ever since occupied its present quarters on Wood street, between Phelps and Hazel. Its pastors have been the Revs. H. Fehr, who began his pastorate in 1859; I. M. Gretcher, from 1865; and John C. Zumpe, who resigned on January 1, 1881; since that time the Rev. Julius Herold has officiated as pastor. The consolidation took place on January 1, 1880, at which time the Evangelical Protestant church was sold, as the members now worship in the Reformed church building, which is a frame structure, painted white, and 35x45 feet. There are sixty members. The choir of ten members is led by George A. Krichbaum. The church officers are: Adam Oswald, treasurer; Joseph Yeger, secretary; Jacob Stein, Alex Boucsin, and Adam Oswald, elders. The Sunday-school has eighteen teachers and one hundred and forty-eight scholars. Mr. Charles B. Ramser is the superintendent.

CALVINISTIC METHODIST CHURCH.

The organization now known by the above title has reached its present position after surmounting difficulties of a character never to be forgotten by those who have had to combat them. For many years they met in an ordinary frame building on Hazel street, between Federal and Wick, and services were held there from 1857 to September, 1881. In 1857 there were thirty-five members; now there are sixty members in good standing. The congregation is composed of rolling-mill men and their families. At present service is held in a room in the court-house building, but a handsome gothic structure is being erected for their use at the northwest corner of Walnut and Rayen streets. The clergymen officiating have been as follows: T. C. Davies, 1857-58; Isaac Blackwell, 1858-60; from 1860 to 1872 there was no regular pastor; Ebenezer Evans, 1872-80; William Hughes, 1880. William Davies and Reese Thomas were the first deacons and T. C. Davies was the first organist. The trustees now are: Job Evans, Benjamin Reese, D. T. Davies, and D. T. Williams.

REV. WILLIAM HUGHES is a native of Wales, born in 1814. He was engaged in the occupation of quarryman until nineteen, enjoying but limited advantages for the acquirement of an education. He went to Liverpool, England, and commenced to prepare himself for the ministry, and in 1847 was ordained a minister of the Welsh Calvinistic Methodist church, and accepted a call from Birmingham. He came to this country in 1859, and was located in New York State for three years. He then removed to Racine, Wisconsin, where he was in charge of a church for some fourteen years. The loss of his voice compelled him to relinquish his charge, but after three years it was restored and in the fall of 1880 he came to Youngstown, accepting the pastorate of the Welsh Calvinistic Methodist church of that city, which he still continues to fill. Mr. Hughes was united in marriage, in 1835, to Elizabeth Davis, and has had a family of seven children, three of whom survive.

WELSH CONGREGATIONAL CHURCH.

The sturdy Welshmen, who are so numerous in this section, are well cared for spiritually, there being three church edifices in which they worship regularly. In 1840 a few Welshmen inaugurated a series of religious meetings, according to the rites of the Congregational church, in the district school on the land of Peter Worts, at Brier Hill. Rev. Thomas Evans was their first pastor, and the membership was composed of coal diggers and their families. In 1861 a church building for their use was erected on Elm street, between Wood and Rayen avenues. It is a plain frame structure, 35 x 40 feet. When Mr. Evans left in 1861, Thomas Davis took charge and was succeeded in 1867 by David Davis, whose successors have been Locke Lake, John Morgan, Thomas and John Lewis Davies. There are two hundred members and one hundred and five Sabbath-school scholars. James Llewellyn, Rees Herbert and John Hughes are among the more prominent men of the church.

REV. J. L. DAVIES, pastor of the Welsh Congregational church, Youngstown, was the only son of the late Rev. Evan Davies and Mary, his wife, of Tyn Rhos, Gallia county, Ohio. Mr. Davies was forty-five years a minister in the Welsh Congregational denomination. He was a strong man mentally and physically, earnest and loyal in the advocacy of evangelical truth, very acceptable as a preacher, and greatly honored and much beloved as a pastor. He moved with his family to America in the year 1855, and was for two years pastor of the Welsh Congregational church in Blossburg, Tioga county, Pennsylvania. Thence he moved in 1857 to Tyn Rhos, Gallia county, Ohio, and labored there as pastor of the Tyn Rhos and Nebo churches. He died in September, 1875. The subject of this sketch was born in Aberaman, Glamorganshire, South Wales, on the 16th of March, 1848. He was seven years old when he emigrated with his father to this country. After enjoying the advantages of the common schools of the rural district in which his father's parish lay, he went to the Gallia academy, and there spent two or three terms in the study of the common branches. He taught a common school in his own neighborhood when he was but fourteen years of age, in the fall and winter of 1862. In the autumn of 1864, while he was a student in the Ewington academy, he enlisted and entered the service of the Government as a private soldier in company D, One Hundred and Seventy-ninth, Ohio volunteer infantry. After his return from the army he prepared himself for college. He would study at times at the Gallia academy, and then defray the expenses of his tuition by teaching in the common schools of his neighborhood. In the spring of 1868 he entered the preparatory department of Marietta college. He entered the collegiate department of the same institution in the fall of that year. He graduated thence in 1872 with the highest honors of his class. He was employed as tutor in the preparatory department of his *alma mater* for two years after his graduation. Having studied Hebrew and church history in the interval, he entered the middle class of Lane Theological seminary in 1874. He studied there one year. Owing to his father's death in the fall of 1875, he was obliged to suspend his theological course, and was called to the pastorate of the Congregational church in Paddy's Run, Butler county, Ohio. There he labored very acceptably until the second Sabbath of October, 1881, when he resigned the pastorate of that church to take charge of the Welsh Congregational church in Youngstown. The church in the latter place is thriving, and gaining strength and influence through his labors, and pastor and people are greatly pleased with each other.

THE WELSH METHODIST CHURCH

of Youngstown, was organized some twenty years ago by William Davis, Rees Thomas, Howell Thomas, and others. Their first pastor was Rev. C. C. Davis, now in charge of a congregation at Pittsburg. He was followed in his ministry here by Isaac Blackwell, William Evans, and E. Evans, the last of whom was in charge of the congregation from 1872 until September, 1880. He was succeeded by William Hughes, the present pastor. The church building formerly used by the Baptists on Hazel, between Federal and Wick streets, not being in a desirable location, will soon be removed and a more suitable building erected.

ENGLISH LUTHERAN CHURCH.

This society was organized in September, 1877, by Henry Beard, F. Karcher, Henry Wendler, F. Arnold, and others, Rev. Jacob Meisner, pastor. The church, in its incipiency, has encountered considerable opposition, yet notwithstanding this fact it has continued to grow, having now a membership of about sev-

enty. It started with a membership of about twenty persons.

Rev. Jacob Meisner, the pastor, is a graduate of the Evangelical Lutheran seminary and college, Columbus, Ohio. In addition to Youngstown he is also pastor of the same churches at Girard and Boardman.

The members of this organization have their rooms over the Reading rooms, East Federal street. The church is now erecting a building at the corner of Wood and Liberty streets, in dimension 30 x 52 feet, including tower projection.

The elders of this church are F. Arnold and H. Wendler; H. Wendler, L. Bergman, and H. Smith, deacons, and H. Smith, secretary and treasurer.

The church at Girard was organized in 1876, the building being the old Salem church, one mile from the village. F. Kreahl, L. Hauser, D. Hauser, Mrs. S. Shook, Mr. J. Bishop, Mr. F. Workman, and J. Fouser are some of the leading members.

COLORED CHURCHES.

The colored citizens of Youngstown organized what is known as the Third Baptist church in December, 1874. Their church building is a small frame structure near Mill street. Rev. Robert Holmes was their pastor, but in a year following was succeeded by Rev. H. C. Clark. The church prospered until the year 1878, when dissensions arose in their midst and during the month of November nine of their members withdrew, and with the consent of the Baptist association authorizing the same formed the

MISSION BAPTIST,

with Rev. H. Clark as their spiritual head. Not having a place for worship a house and lot were purchased on Mahoning avenue by William Nelson, H. Clark, and Richard Wanser. The property does not belong to the church, but is used by this people until other accommodations can be had. The membership at this time, of the Mission Baptist, is not more than about twelve in number; that of the Third Baptist church is about twenty-eight.

ROD OF SHOLEM CONGREGATION.

On May 12, 1869, the following gentlemen, D. Theobald, Morriss Ullman, A. Walbrun, F. Ritter, William Jonas, Charles Ritter, S. Loewenstein, A. Ritter, A. Shaffner, A. Pruetz, Ed. Ritter, S. J. Lambert, E. Guthman, Henry Theobald, A. Goldstein, and A. Shwab, being Jewish residents of Youngstown and vicinity, met to organize a Jewish Reform congregation. Committees on constitution and by-laws, as well as organization, were appointed to report at an early date. On May 19, 1867, the organization was perfected by electing David Theobald president, Edward Ritter vice-president, Abraham Wallbrun treasurer, and E. Guthman secretary. The congregation have furnished as neat a church, on third floor, southeast corner of West Federal and Hazel streets, as there is in the city, and own their own burying-ground on the Brier Hill road; present membership, twenty-two. The present officers are M. Weinberg, president; E. Guthman, vice-president; E. I. Guthman, secretary; A. Louer, treasurer.

BURIAL PLACES.

In the original plat of Youngstown two lots were set apart and reserved for places of public burial. One of these lots is occupied at present by the county buildings, the other is the side hill lot on the opposite side of Phelps street. It was in this latter lot that the first white person, so far as is known, was buried in Youngstown. He was a music teacher, and the inscription on his tombstone is characteristic of epitaph literature:

> In Memory of
> SAMUEL McFARLAND,
> Died
> September 19, 1799,
> Aged 28 Years.

> Oh, how music charms our ears
> While he was in our land,
> And now we hope he sings a song
> Of Moses and the Lamb.

This stone was erected in 1811, and removed to the new cemetery in 1869. It soon became apparent, even before Youngstown had outgrown its village limits, that provision would have to be made for a place to bury the dead. The limits of two lots admitted of little adornment, and their close proximity to business and residences, where the quiet and solemnity of funeral rites were always liable to be disturbed. Besides, some people imagined the water affected by saturation into their wells from the graveyard.

Steps toward forming a cemetery association were taken about 1850, and resulted successfully two years later. Dr. Henry Manning was the leader in this enterprise, and was chosen president of the association after its incorporation in 1852. Sixteen acres of land were purchased off the farm of Dr. Manning and improved at considerable expense. This tract is picturesquely located on the summit of a high hill rising from the south bank of the Mahoning. It is in plain view from nearly all parts of the city, and from its undulating surface, whitened by tombs and shaded by evergreen, high above the smoke which hangs over the valley, may be seen an interesting stretch of country. The tract was laid off in lots, which were sold at auction. The remains of those who had been buried in the old cemetery were removed from time to time, but this labor was not finally completed until excavations were made for the new court-house. Mr. John Brenner was employed to superintend the grounds in 1865 and has continued in that position ever since. He has given special attention to the art of adornment, the result of which is highly satisfactory.

CHAPTER IV.
PUBLIC SCHOOLS.*

The first authentic information of any attempt to establish a school in the village of Youngstown dates as far back as between the years 1802 and 1805, by which latter date the first school-house was erected. It was a log building, one story high, with but one room, and stood upon the Public square, about where the soldiers' monument now stands. The first teacher whose name has been remembered is Perlee Brush. Whether he was the first teacher is not positively

*For the history of the public schools of Youngstown the editor of this volume has made free and almost verbatim use of the chapter devoted to this place in the Centennial History of the Public Schools in Ohio. Although there are defects and errors in that compilation, we have no warrantable guide for making corrections. The names of a few teachers have been added, but what follows is substantially copied from that volume.

known, but he was in charge of the school as early as 1806. This date is fixed by an account with Robert Montgomery, who resided just east of the village, by whom he was charged with (October 6, 1806) cloth for a coat, and corduroy for a pair of pantaloons, with trimmings, amounting to $11.72; and on the 17th of the same month with two skeins of thread, four cents; and again on the 9th, six yards of linen (probably for two shirts), leather for shoes, and four skeins of thread, $3.66. This probably constituted his outfit for teaching during the winter of 1806-7, and was also advance pay; for on September 12, 1807, nearly one year afterwards, his account amounted to $18, and he is then credited with "schooling, $18."

Other entries in the books indicate that this credit of $18.00 was made up of the school bills of the furnace hands of Mr. Montgomery, which he had assumed. It is impossible to tell what proportion this $18.00 was of the whole amount paid to Mr. Brush as a salary, for there is no record. By the same books it is shown that laboring men received about $10.00 or $11.00 a month, and clerks about $13.00 "and found."

There were from twenty to thirty scholars in attendance during the summer months, and about forty during the winter months. The usual charge for tuition was, for ordinary instruction—reading, spelling, writing, and arithmetic—$1.50, and for the higher branches of grammar and geography, $2.00 per quarter. For a long time these six branches were the only studies pursued in the school, no mention being made of others until the year 1838.

Mr. Brush continued teaching in the neighborhood of the village of Youngstown for a number of years, and many persons now living remember him. He was familiarly known as "Old Perlee;" not because of his advanced age, but on account of old acquaintanceship.

Perlee Brush was followed by James Noyes, "a tall, slim man from Connecticut." Of his personal history there is no record. In speaking of the condition of the school in 1811, the date of his coming to Youngstown, the late Dr. Manning said:

There was a log school-house on the Diamond. There was another building used as a school-house near the residence of Isaac Powers, one that served both as a church and school-house at Cornersburg, and another near Parkhurst mills. The qualifications for a school teacher in those days were few and moderate. If a man could read tolerably well, was a good writer, and could cypher as far as the rule of three, knew how to use the birch scientifically, and had firmness enough to exercise this skill, he would pass muster.

In 1818 Jabez P. Manning occupied the school-house on the Public square, and the following copy of the contract made between him and the subscribers will be of interest, as tending to show in what manner educational facilities were secured and offered at that early date:

This article, between the undersigned subscribers of the one part, and Jabez P. Manning of the other, witnesseth: That said Manning doth, on his part, engage to teach a school at the school-house near the center of Youngstown, for the term of one quarter, wherein he engages to teach reading, writing, arithmetic, and English grammar; and furthermore, that the school shall be opened at 9 o'clock A. M. of each day, and closed at 4 P. M. of each day of the week (Saturday and Sunday excepted), and on Saturday to be opened at 9 and close at 12 o'clock A. M. And we, the subscribers on our part, individually engage to pay unto the said Manning $1.75 for each and every scholar we subscribe, at the end of the term; and we furthermore engage to furnish, or to bear the necessary expense of furnishing, wood and all other things necessary for the use of the school. Furthermore, we do engage that unless by the 6th day of April of the present year the number of scholars subscribed amount to thirty-five, that said Manning is in no way obligated by this article.

"Furthermore, we allow the said Manning the privilege of receiving five scholars more than here specified.

J. P. MANNING.

Youngstown, March 31, 1818."

"Subscribers names, and number of scholars: George Tod, 3; John E. Woodbridge, 4; Homer Hine, 2; Henry Wick, 2; Philip Stambaugh, 1½; Samuel Vail, 2; Robert Kyle, 2; George Hardman, 1; James Davidson, 2; Polly Chapman, 1; Jerry Tibbitts, 3½; John F. Townsend, 2; Henry Manning, 1; William Bell, 1; Jonathan Smith, 1; Moses Crawford, 1; William Cleland, 1½; Margaret Murdock, 1; William Potter, 2; William Rayen, 1½; William Morris, 1; Noah Chamberlain, 1; Richard Young, ½; James Duncan, 1; Mrs. McCullough, ½; Byram Baldwin ½. Total 40½."

This probably was the first regular and complete organization of a school in the village. In 1819 Fanny Roth, or Ross, was a teacher, either in Youngstown, or just south of the village. There were no regularly defined districts in those days, but the teachers occupied positions in various localities, and were supported by a general subscription. Consequently it is difficult to positively locate the fields of labor of the various persons whose names have been remembered, but they all filled places comprised within the expression, "the village of Youngstown and vicinity." In 1820 Miss Phebe Wick taught the school on the Public square. Miss Mary Case (Mrs. Benjamin Stevens) also taught in Youngstown about this date.

At this time money was an exceedingly scarce commodity, every species of exchange of value being done by trading. Nearly all the corn and rye were reduced to whiskey, and periodically teams would haul it to Pittsburg or the lake shore, and the money received at these two points for the whiskey was all that came into the village. There is an entry in an ancient ledger charging Miss Phebe Wick, in July, 1820, with three bushels of wheat; in September with one hundred pounds of flour, which amounted to $2.43. Then in October of the same year she is credited with "School bill, $3.34." This was the proportion to be contributed towards the general tuition fund by the party with whom she was dealing. Thus she still had a credit of ninety-one cents, which was discharged, not by paying her that much money, but by giving her an order upon Thomas Kirkpatrick, another merchant of that day.

About 1822-23 we find it possible to obtain a little more definite general information with regard to the character of the schools. As a general rule there were three months of winter term—December, January, and February—and the summer terms continued well into July, or at least until harvest was close at hand. Quite frequently married people, who were older by many years than the teacher, received instruction during the winter months. The salaries paid were, for male teachers, from ten to twelve dollars a month, and for females from four to five dollars a month, with their boarding provided by the residents or "boarding 'round," as it was called. The hours were from nine in the morning until four in the afternoon, with a short recess at noon for lunch.

There was a full session every day, excepting Saturdays, when the hours lasted till 12 o'clock only, the afternoon session being omitted.

In addition to the regular subscription agreed upon by the residents to be paid, each one was obliged to contribute a certain proportion of wood, the aggregate of which would supply the school during the winter. This was hauled to the school-house in sled lengths, twelve feet long, and the boys were required to cut up, each noon or on Saturdays, sufficient to last during the next day. The duty of kindling the fires devolved upon the boys, and it was frequently the cause of sour looks and bitter thoughts.

About this time exhibitions by the scholars were inaugurated, and on no other occasions was any attempt made to leave the rudimental path of instruction. At these exhibitions, however, some efforts were made towards declamation, generally in the way of dialogues, no pupil having sufficient self-reliance, apparently, to depend entirely upon himself.

The books most used in pursuing the studies were Dillworth's Spelling Book, and Webster's American Spelling Book, which were considered the standard. The New Testament was extensively used as a reading book. The English Reader, American Preceptor, and Columbian orator also occupied places among the acknowledged text books of the schools. For writing copies, the teacher furnished small slips written by himself. Quill pens were used, and in the place of ink a decoction of soft maple bark, copperas and vinegar filled the pots. Pike's & Walker's Arithmetic is the most ancient known in this section, but its popularity was of short duration on account of its abstruseness, and it was quickly followed by Daboll's Arithmetic and the Western Calculator, but both were also "too hard," as the scholars said, and were displaced by Adam's Arithmetic, which made a great stride toward simplifying the study. The latter named of the different classes of books were probably used for a number of years after this date, but how long can not be stated with any degree of certainty.

The furniture of the school-house of these times consisted of a smooth, hewn log, with four pins driven in for legs, upon which the children sat while studying, with no support for their backs, except when allowed to place the bench against the wall, and no desk but their knees for their books. The conveniences for writing consisted of a board placed slanting against the wall, before which was a bench made as before described, with very long legs, upon which the scholars were perched, and so sat in a line, high up in the air around the building, facing the wall and with their feet dangling.

THE ACADEMY.

The second school-house within the limits of the village of Youngstown was a two-story frame structure of considerable pretensions, built in 1823 by Amnii R. Bissell, and paid for by subscription. There is no record of its cost when completed. It was located just off the southwestern side of the Public square, upon the ground now occupied by what is known as "Diamond block." It was used for a school-house until the introduction of the union school system, when it was sold for a Disciple church, and used as a house of worship until 1873, when it was again sold, and is now doing service as a saloon and grocery on East Federal street, at the corner of Basin street. This concludes the first twenty-five years of the history of Youngstown, and finds the village proper in possession of two school houses, in which regular summer and winter sessions were held, and the matter of the proper tuition of youth was receiving the attention which it deserved. It is not known who filled the position of teacher from 1820 to 1827, but it is very probable that Miss Phebe Wick and Jabez P. Manning were the principal incumbents.

There were no persons particularly charged with the care and management of the schools up to this time, but some such arrangement as that exhibited by the agreement, before recited, between Mr. Manning and the residents, was entered into, and then the teachers attended to the carrying out of the contract. At the beginning of the second quarter of the century, a desire for a more elaborate education began to manifest itself, which received great encouragement from the division of the township into school districts, which took place on the 22d of May, 1826.

This step served to invest the matter with a new degree of importance and dignity, and the teacher was thereafter looked upon, not as an employe, purely, of his patrons, but more as the ruler of a little empire, whose boundaries consisted of his district lines. The site of the present city was within the boundaries of the First or Center district. The old log school-house on the Public square seems to have been abandoned about the year 1826, and shortly afterwards another building was erected on the northern side of East Federal street, somewhere in the neighborhood of the present location of Himrod furnaces.

In 1827 John Moore began the erection of a building on what is now the corner of Wood and Champion, for a Presbyterian church, but when he had finished the first story a dissension arose among the members of the congregation that was to occupy it, and the result was an abandonment of the work. This building was purchased by Dr. Manning, by whom it was inclosed and afterwards used as a private school.

In 1827 a Mr. Robinson taught in the building on the southwest side of the public square, and which was honored by the dignified name of academy. He was a good tutor, conscientious and honest in all his actions. While teaching he was also drilling and educating himself for a Methodist minister, and it was his practice to spend much of his leisure time in strolling through the woods soliloquizing. He was a constant visitor to the grove which stood where now the section of the city known as Smoky hollow is situate, where he would preach to the trees as auditors, making all the appropriate expressions of countenance and gesture.

Mr. Robinson was followed by Mr. Black, who in turn gave place in the year 1829 to Hiram B. Floyd. He continued to hold the position until 1833. His companions were Jane Taylor in 1831, and Loraine Marvin and her sister, who taught during 1832 and 1833. From 1834 to 1836 the place of teacher at the academy was filled by a Mr. Stafford, and about the latter date Mr. Metcalf comes into notice. These two gentlemen probably filled the chair until 1838, when Mr. Parret was employed. The names of those who had charge of the lower school seem to have passed out of memory, though it may be that the two last named teachers were in charge of the two schools at the same time. The mention of Mr. Parret brings out pleasant reminiscences. By all he was acknowledged to be as good a teacher as was ever in the district, and the advances in the courses of study made during his tenure of service were exceedingly commendable. He was the first who taught the higher branches of study, having introduced those of Latin and algebra. This was a great step, for at that time those who desired an education other than a mere rudimental one, were compelled to go to Burton, Geauga county; Hudson, Summit county, or Western Reserve seminary, and the village of Youngstown frequently contributed students to all those institutions. Mr. Parret was a man whose influence was felt outside of his particular district.

An atmosphere of genuine scholarship seemed to emanate from the field of his labors, the power of which was manifested in the accomplishments of the students who passed under his care. Teachers in surrounding districts recognized in him a model of their profession, and even those who had never met him could discern in his labors the evidence of true merit.

By the year 1840 the number of scholars had become so great that it was found the accommodations already provided were not sufficient. A subscription list was immediately started, and in a short time sufficient was raised to erect another building. The site chosen was at the southeast corner of Front and Phelps streets, where now the fine brick building of the Union schools stands, and here was built the third schoolhouse of the village then standing--the fourth erected. It was quite a good-sized, commodious structure, built after the plans of those days, as much as the facilities of the times would admit, and was used for a church quite frequently. There were two rooms in this building, one on the south side of the hall, which ran completely through the center of the house. From 1840 to 1845 we were confronted by a blank in the list of teachers, with regard to any certainty as to the dates or length of their administration, but during that time the names of James Thorn, who taught the East Federal street school, Hiram A. Hall, and George Seaton, of the Front-street school appear. Of this latter gentleman it may be said, that he was noted for his genial disposition and strong voice. He was preparing himself for the bar. Mr. Hall was one of the first board of examiners of the county, with John M. Edwards and Reuben McMillan, who were appointed by Judge Newton, of Canfield. In 1845 Mr. Gillespie, Miss Betsey Kirk, and Miss Susan Standish taught. In 1846 Mr. Yates became a tutor. In 1847 we find the name of E. B. Starkweather and Miss Louisa Phillips. In 1848 Miss Thompson was a teacher.

In 1850 there appeared in the village a young man by the name of William Travis, a native of Jefferson county, Ohio, and graduate of Washington college. He organized and conducted for one year the New Lisbon union schools, and to him more than to any one else is the city indebted for the adoption of the system of schools provided for by a practical Legislature. Immediately upon his arrival he set himself to work to accomplish the adoption of the new system, which promised to be and did prove far superior to the manner in which the schools of the city were then being conducted. He was peculiarly fitted for the task undertaken, by reason of the experience had at New Lisbon, and yet it required the exercise of a vast amount of argument to gain the ear of those who were the most influential citizens of the place. The schools at this time were governed by trustees who were able to perform all the functions of the office with little expense, and the youth appeared to the casual observer to be receiving as good an education as could be expected from public education. But this man had seen the improvements the schools were capable of, and the advantages of the changes authorized by the act of 1849.

Possessed of a soul filled with a desire for the advancement of the means of mental culture, he thought not of the obstacles besetting the way, but began boldly the work. At first he sought out singly and alone the several members of the educational interests, and individually laid before them the beauties of the new system. At first they were inflexible, but after a time would listen with some degree of attention, and finally Mr. Travis succeeded, with his clear and convincing arguments, in persuading that the matter was worthy of consideration. In furtherance of the efforts of those in favor of the new system, for Mr. Travis had at last made some converts, John Hutchins, Esq., of Warren, was invited to deliver an address, the result of which may be inferred from the notice of it contained in the issue of the Ohio Republican of March 21, 1850:

A very interesting lecture on the subject of the advantages of the Union school system was delivered before the library association, on March 20th, by John Hutchins, Esq., of Warren. Subsequently the question was discussed by the Literary society, at which time preliminary steps were taken to test the public voice on the subject, according to the statute.

The work now went on bravely, and each day witnessed the conviction of some of the opponents that the new was an improvement over the old system. There were those, however, chronic grumblers, who saw in it nothing but an increased rate of taxation, and the requirement of them to support schools for other people's children. But very soon among its most earnest advocates could be counted men who were looked upon as of sound judgment and discreet foresight. Their very presence in the ranks had its beneficial influence, and many of those who had hitherto been outspoken in their opposition, merely held their peace and allowed the movement to gather strength without remonstrance. Some, however, were inexorable, and did all in their power to hinder the efforts of their opponents.

At last sufficiently large had grown the number relied upon as friends to warrant the promulgators in calling a meeting of the electors to vote upon the adoption of the statute. Notices were written and posted, specifying the 12th day of April, 1851, as the time, and the literary rooms as the place for holding such meeting. The weekly paper having espoused the cause, and the plans of the leaders having proved so successful, nearly all opposition was smothered out by the time of the election, and the advocates being so confident of success, and the opponents so certain of defeat, there was a very light vote polled—eighty in all; seventy-five for, and five against the adoption of the law.

In the issue of the Ohio Republican of the 18th of April, 1851, appears the following notice, which is the first documentary evidence of the existence within the districts named of the union schools, and declares upon its face the prompt manner in which the business of organization was being conducted:

PUBLIC NOTICE.

WHEREAS, The qualified electors of School Districts No. 1, No. 8, and No. 9, of Youngstown, did assemble on Saturday, April 12, 1851, at Literary Society hall, and then, by their votes, did adopt the law for the better regulation of public schools in cities, towns, etc., of the State, passed February 21, 1849;

THEREFORE, The qualified electors of the aforesaid districts are notified to meet at the Literary Society hall in Youngstown on Monday, the 8th day of April, 1851, at 10 o'clock, A. M., for the purpose of electing six directors of the public schools of said district, two of whom shall serve for one year, two for two years, and two for three years, the time that each shall serve to be designated on the ballots.

JOHN R. HOLCOMB,
W. H. FITCH, Clerk. Chairman.
Youngstown, April 12, 1851.

In accordance with this notice the qualified electors met, and the choice of the board of directors clearly evidenced the sincerity with which the matter was considered, and showed a just appreciation of the important work to be done in the premises, for we find it composed of the following named gentlemen: Henry Manning, Dr.

T. Garlick, William J. Edwards, Wilson S. Thorn, Jesse Baldwin, and A. D. Jacobs. They might well be called the representative men of Youngstown, and into no more competent authority could have been intrusted the work of organizing the union schools of the district. On the 5th of May the board of directors elect were qualified, as appears by the following copy of the certificate, which occupies the first page of the record book:

THE STATE OF OHIO, } ss.
MAHONING COUNTY,

Personally appeared before me, a Master Commissioner in Chancery, Henry Manning, Theodatus Garlick, William J. Edwards, Wilson S. Thorn, Jesse Baldwin, and A. D. Jacobs, school directors elect of the borough of Youngstown, and solemnly swore to discharge faithfully, according to the best of their skill and ability, the duties of their said office.

E. S. HUBBARD,
Master Commissioner in Chancery.

May 6, A. D., 1851.

Upon the opposite page, in the handwriting of the secretary, Mr. William J. Edwards, appears the entry of the first regular meeting of the board, as follows:

At a meeting held by the directors-elect, elected under the act of Assembly of February 21, 1849, for the borough of Youngstown and the territory attached thereto, for school purposes, on the evening of the 3d of May, 1851, Dr. H. Manning was elected president of the board of education, William J. Edwards secretary, and Wilson S. Thorn treasurer of said board. Homer Hine was appointed school examiner for one year. R. J. Powers was appointed school examiner for two years and R. W. Taylor for three years. It was ordered by the board that the treasurer give bond and security for the faithful discharge of his duties to the amount of $2,000.

Adjourned to meet on Saturday, the 10th day of May, at 7 o'clock P. M.

Attest: WILLIAM J. EDWARDS,
                                                        Secretary.

And so the first board of education in the then borough of Youngstown was established. Of its officers nothing more need be said at this time than that they were the "right men in the right place." There is no record of the place where this first meeting was held, but it is very probable that the office of Dr. Garlick was used for the purpose, as many of the meetings immediately following are recorded to have been held in that place. It was in the building now occupied by Mrs. Jennie Wick, on the north side of Federal street, just west of the Diamond.

At the next regular meeting, held on June 7th, "it was voted that the auditor of Mahoning county be directed to make out a tax on the property of the district of three mills on the dollar for school purposes in said district." This was the first step in active operations taken by the board.

The next matter to be considered was the procuring of proper and efficient teachers, and an able superintendent. The board after due deliberation unanimously chose Samuel F. Cooper. Mrs. M. J. Cooper, wife of the superintendent, was elected to the position of assistant teacher in the high school. Rev. W. S. Gray was appointed to the secondary department. Positions in the primary department were given to Miss Alice Kirk, Miss Upson, Miss Eliza Powers, and Miss Huldah Holcomb.

The salaries paid to the several teachers were as follows: Superintendent, $500 per year; principal in the grammar school, $300 per year; assistant in high school, $160 per year; primary teachers, $140 per year.

The board did not take exclusive and organized control of the schools until the fall session, which began on Monday, the 15th day of September, 1851. There were three school-houses, the Academy, East Federal-street, and the Middle or Front-street. The furniture had been badly worn, and it was found necessary to obtain a new supply. John Loughridge furnishes one hundred and sixty-five chairs at twenty cents each, and T. G. Phillips furnished fifty desks at twenty-five cents each. The revenue of the schools was derived from the Western Reserve fund, show and other funds, tuition, State Common school fund, and the levy authorized to be made by the board. The schools were divided into four classes—high school, grammar, secondary, and primary. There was taught in the high school geometry, algebra, chemistry, botany, physiology, arithmetic, geography, English grammar, reading, and history. In the grammar school, reading, writing, spelling and arithmetic, with grammar commenced; in secondary, a lower grade of reading, spelling, writing, and elementary arithmetic, and in the primary the A, B, C, and first reading lessons. For a number of years the grammar and high schools were united, that is, the high school branches were taught in the grammar school to those who desired. Such being few in number this could very readily be done without in the least interfering with the duties of the grammar school.

The first term of the school the whole number of scholars was 386, 190 males and 196 females, with an average number 257, 118 males and 139 females. The average daily attendance at the several schools was as follows: High, 21 males and 25 females; grammar, 20 males and 25 females; secondary, 20 males and 23 females; primary, 57 males and 66 females. The first annual report of the superintendent showed an enrollment of 408, 190 males and 218 females. As soon as the system was fully and completely organized and in operation, much of the animosity which had been manifest during its establishment entirely disappeared; in fact, in many instances, gave place to a feeling of encouragement for that which was so obviously superior to the "old style," as the supplanted manner of conducting the schools began to be called. A helping hand was extended by some from whom it was hardly to be expected, so that the board felt they were securing the support of nearly the entire population, which had a tendency to cause extra exertions to secure in practical results a vindication of what they had claimed for the project.

The growth of this system has been very marked, and at the same time substantial and permanent.

The present course of study, which differs but little from that recommended by the Northern Ohio Teachers' association, may be regarded rather as an imperceptible growth than as a creation. There have been many important changes in the methods of teaching. In the early history of the system the scholars were promoted on account of standing manifested by annual examinations; later by the average of term examinations; now by the average of monthly examinations and regular standing in classes. This last method has been found highly satisfactory, giving to the worthy an opportunity of securing to themselves higher positions in study whenever they are fitted therefor.

Vast improvements have been made in school accommodations, buildings, furniture, apparatus, etc. The houses now in use are all of the most approved modern arrangement, and have ample space about them to serve as a play-ground, and secure a free passage of air. Particular mention should be made of the very excellent plan of the large and beautiful buildings on Front and Covington streets. Both of these are models of neatness, convenience, beauty, and utility, and it is doubtful if there exists in the State a public school structure which exceeds the Front street one in these particulars. The city owes a debt of gratitude to the board, consisting of Messrs. Paul Wick, A. B. Cornell, Edward Bell, W. W. McKeown, A. J. Packard, and Dr. Bruchner, under whose administration these two were projected and completed. The furniture is all of the latest and most approved pattern, and the buildings are all well supplied.

In 1877 a substantial four-room building was erected on Oak street, to take the place of an old two-story frame. The same year a fine and convenient brick building of eight rooms was erected on the west side, to take the place of the two-room frame, which was at that time the oldest in the city. In 1881 two large rooms were added to the Covington-street building, and two to the south side building. A two-room structure was built on the west side and occupied in January, 1882. Six more rooms will be added during the present year.

Although the real estate under the control of the board is valued at $150,000, accommodations for the rapidly increasing number of pupils is inadequate. The enrollment is increasing at the rate of twenty per cent. per annum. When the present superintendent took charge of the schools there were five teachers employed; there are at present fifty, besides those giving instruction in private and parochial schools, the whole number being about sixty-five. These figures will give some idea of the organizing work Professor McMillan has been gradually accomplishing.

SCHOOL LIBRARY.

The school library was commenced during the administration of the first commissioner, Hon. H. H. Barney, under the provisions of the law relating thereto. Additions were made to it from time to time till the repeal of the law. Within the last six years funds have been raised by entertainments given by the schools, and there are now in the library a little more than two thousand volumes of interesting and instructive books. The library is now well patronized by both pupils and citizens. It is under the charge of a librarian.

Freeman O. Arms.

RAVEN SCHOOL.

In 1854 Judge William Rayen, an old and highly respected citizen of this city, died leaving a large estate disposed of by will. One of the items set apart a residuary fund, the principal of which was vested in trustees, who were authorized to expend the interest in establishing a school, to be known as the "Rayen school." Legislation was received, and through the influence of Hon. R. W. Tayler, one of the board, an act of incorporation was passed in 1856. In accordance therewith five trustees are appointed, one each year, to serve five years. This appointment is made by the judge of the court of common pleas. As a matter of interest, it may be stated that three of the original five still hold office, and the only change in the board, since the beginning of the school, was caused by the resignation of R. W. Tayler, and the appointment of Robert McCurdy in his stead. The building was completed in 1866, and acting under the direction of the board of education and the Rayen school board, Mr. Reuben McMillan proceeded to employ teachers and organize the school for high school work, it having been deemed the best for the interest of all concerned that the Rayen school should be the high school for the city and township.

Professor E. S. Gregory, who was selected as principal, came to the school with thirteen years experience at the Western Reserve college, as professor of Latin, and principal of the preparatory department, and with an enviable reputation as an instructor and manager of youth. It is no exaggeration to say that he has more than sustained his reputation, and met the expectations of the friends of the school. Finding here a field more congenial to his tastes, and having an enthusiastic love for natural science, he has imparted that love to his pupils, and through them to the community in which he has labored. In 1879 M. S. Campbell was called to the principalship. He has fully sustained the reputation brought with him from Portsmouth, as a ripe scholar, accomplished teacher, and a Christain gentleman. Under his administration the school has been thoroughly efficient. Miss Florence Rayen has been a teacher in the school for thirteen years, and won an enviable reputation. The success of the school is in part due to her. The other two assistants are Mary D. Campbell, and E. D. Kimball, the latter a graduate of Dartmouth, the former an experienced teacher. The present board of the Rayen school consists of A. B. Cornell, Robert McCurdy, John Stambaugh, Cecil D. Wine, and H. O. Bonnell. The building was in 1881 completely remodeled at an expense of $10,000, and is now one of the most convenient and comfortable high school buildings in the State.

The school opened with about forty scholars, and graduated its first class in 1868. Since that time, under the wise management of the public schools of the city, the number of pupils has been doubled. A chemical laboratory, fitted with all the requirements for chemical analysis, is open to the students. A fine binocular compound microscope, with powers from twenty to three thousand diameters, is used to illustrate natural history. Three fine spectroscopes afford ample means for teaching the art of modern spectrum analysis.

The buildings and grounds are valued at $90,000. The apparatus is valued at $25,000.

The courses of study are as follows: First year—mathematics, algebra, elementary or higher language, Latin lessons, Latin grammar, Latin reader, natural science, zoology, English history, compositions and declamations; second year—mathematics, geometry, language, Latin grammar, Cæsar, Virgil, Latin composition, natural science, natural philosophy, physical geography, compositions and declamations; third year—mathematics, trigonometry, mensuration, language (French and German), natural science, chemistry, botany, astronomy, elements in geology, rhetoric, with essays and declamations. In chemistry, qualitative and quantitative analysis is taught to those who desire to make chemistry a special study.

Students are also allowed to take a course of study designed to be preparatory to a college course. Previous to the organization of the Rayen high school, all the higher branches were taught. No pupils were prepared for college in classes, but by special instruction quite a number were fitted for the freshman class. Before the Rayen school was established, in 1866, the superintendent was principal of the high school, but a small portion of his time being devoted to supervision. As the attendance increased and the establishment of addi tional schools became necessary, it was found that a more thorough supervision was desirable, and indeed necessary in order to secure the efficient management of the schools.

The first superintendent was employed in 1851, immediately upon the organization of the schools, and the office has never been abolished. The terms of the several incumbents were as follows: Samuel F. Cooper, 1851 to 1853; Reuben McMillan, 1853 to 1855; Ephraim Miller, 1855 to 1856; Charles H. Lathrop, 1856 to 1857; A. B. Cornell, 1857 to 1859; Dwight Hubbard, 1859 to 1860; Hiram A. Hall, 1860 to 1861; Reuben McMillan, 1861 to 1867; P. T. Caldwell, 1867 to 1872; Reuben McMillan, 1872.

The time devoted to supervision alone was very little at first, not over an hour a day, but as the number of schools increased, and the attendance became larger, more time was given, until at last the superintendent became what his title implied.

By order of the board of education a night school was organized in connection with the winter term of 1873, and continued through that and the next winter. It was patronized by boys necessarily kept at labor during the daytime. Nearly one hundred were in attendance under the instruction of five teachers. The next winter (1875) so many being thrown out of work by reason of the suspension of operations by a number of the manufactories of the city, it was decided to establish an ungraded school in place of the night school. It was well patronized, and produced good results.

It has been thirty one years since the union school system was adopted in Youngstown, and there has been almost perfect harmony in all departments of government during all that time. The board has been for the most part composed of men of business habits and positive character—the only kind of men to be safely trusted.

Particular mention should be made of Dr. Henry Manning, the first president of the board, and Dr. C. C. Cook. Both of these gentlemen were indefatigable in their efforts, and those who followed them in office can and do testify to the efficiency of their labors. The position of superintendent has been filled by competent men, and with but very few exceptions perfect satisfaction in the discharge of duties has been given.

Particular notice was directed to the exalted grade acquired by the schools in the matter of morality during the superintendency of A. B. Cornell, and the firm foundation then laid has had built upon it, by his successors in office, a noble edifice. So marked is the excellency of our schools in this respect that there is a perceptible impression made upon the minds of an observer. That the labors of Mr. P. T. Caldwell, who superintended nearly five years from 1867, were appreciated may be inferred from the testimony of his successor and the following resolutions, passed by the board of education on accepting his resignation March 11, 1872:

Resolved, That in accepting the resignation of P. T. Caldwell, Esq., superintendent of the schools, the board desire to express their appreciation of Mr. Caldwell's able and efficient services in the difficult and responsible position which he has held; to testify to the faithful and careful discharge of his duties, and to return their sincere thanks for his successful and honorable work in the interest of the public school system of this city.

Resolved, That we part with Mr. Caldwell with sincere regret, as his satisfactory conduct of the schools has contributed largely to their increase and efficiency.

Many of the teachers have left behind them tender memories, which will remain in the minds of those who passed under their instruction as long as life lasts. Mrs. Cooper was very superior in many respects, and was one of the most popular and successful teachers that ever taught in Youngstown. Miss Kirk (now Mrs. General Grierson), Eliza Powers, Miss Jane Rayen, Miss Lizzie Loughridge, Miss Helen Ruggles, Miss Susan Bingham, and Miss Juliana Thorn, all deserve honorable mention. Miss Thorn taught nearly seventeen consecutive years as a successful primary teacher, and left the school only when she left the profession. Many of the others are still living among the scenes of their early labors, and hold esteemed places. A large number of teachers, since 1864, received their training in our schools, many of the most successful ones passing through all the grades from primary up, and were emphatically home-made teachers.

MEMBERS OF THE BOARD.

The following named gentlemen have been members of the board of education, either by election or appointment to fill a vacancy, in the order named: Dr. Henry Manning, Dr. Theodatus Garlick, William J. Edwards, Wilson S. Thorn, Jesse Baldwin, A. D. Jacobs, Richard S. Garlick, John Van Fleet, R. S. Powers, Dr. C.

C. Cook, S. F. Burnett, Jonathan Warner, Francis E. Hutchins, William G. Moore, Reuben Carroll, Robinson Truesdale, William Jones, Wilson Thorn (second term), John F. Hollingsworth, Philip Jacobs, Paul Wick, William R. Parmelee, A. McKinnie, F. O. Arms, A. B. Cornell, Edwin Bell, W. W. McKeown, A. J. Packard, Dr. W. I. Beuchner, Homer Hamilton, William Dennison, Jacob Stambaugh, T. R. McEwen, Alexander Adams, W. L. Buechner. The present board consists of J. S. Cunningham, president; Hon. William B. Pollock, Edwin Bell, William Dennison, Henry A. Evans, and David Theobald.

Paul Wick retired in 1879, after nineteen years of consecutive service, the longest period any man has acted on the board, and it may be said, without prejudice to anyone else, no more useful member ever acted.

COMMERCIAL COLLEGES.

The first attempt to establish a commercial college in Youngstown was made in 1872, by Professor Miller. His success was not flattering though sufficient to give encouragement to the enterprise. It changed management several times within a brief period, the successive proprietors being Professors Courtney, Hall, and Beardsley. The latter disposed of his effects in 1880. A second school was opened in 1878, by Professor J. H. Cook, with fifty-eight pupils, which continues in a flourishing condition. The average attendance during the past year was eighty-seven. The college is conveniently located on Federal street. Mr. Cook is well supported by a corps of experienced teachers—Mrs. Callis Cook, penmanship; W. C. Sterling, English department and phonography; B. C. Eddy, telegraphy and type writer. Professor Cook gives instructions in the department of practical bookkeeping.

Besides the public library connected with the public schools, there is the Youngstown reading room, which is an outgrowth of the crusade. A society of about one dozen women was formed in 1876, with a view to founding a reading room and library for the general public. A room on Federal street was fitted up and supplied with papers and magazines of a healthful character. Donations of books have from time to time since been received, which are already forming a library of permanent value.

SUPERINTENDENT M'MILLAN.

Reuben McMillan, superintendent since 1872, was born in Canfield, Ohio, October 7, 1820. His father was a native of Burlington, New Jersey, his mother of Cumberland county, Pennsylvania. Both were of Scotch-Irish descent. His early education was due to his own determination, having received in the public schools and by private tuition some instruction. He, at the age of thirteen years, commenced to learn the trade of harness making, at which he continued four years, and studied Latin and other branches in the meantime. In the year 1837 he determined to obtain an academical education, and during the following two years taught school to obtain means to support his expenses while at the academy. From 1839 till 1843 he employed his time in a similar manner, and in the latter year obtained a position as assistant in the academy, which position he held till 1845. From this time forward he continued teaching and studying. He never attended college but received from Western Reserve college the degree of master of arts.

Mr. McMillan was elected superintendent of the schools at Hanoverton, Columbiana county, in 1849, and subsequently filled the same position in New Lisbon, where he remained two years, when his health broke down. He then lived on a farm near Canfield till 1853, and during the winter season superintended an academy. From 1853 till 1855 he superintended the Youngstown schools; in 1855 he removed to Salem, where the schools were under his charge till 1861, at which time he returned to Youngstown. Failing health in 1867 compelled him to retire from active labor, though he was that year offered the superintendency of the city schools of Cleveland. After a five years' rest Mr. McMillan was recalled to the superintendency at Youngstown and has since filled the position to the entire satisfaction of officers, subordinate teachers and pupils. He gives the closest attention to the duties of his office. The school library has been built up largely by him, and it has been his special care that no poor child should be without instruction because of inability to purchase school books.

Prof. McMillan has been an elder in the First Presbyterian church for several years and is active in all moral and social movements. In

1849 he married Miss Susan Campbell, daughter of John Campbell, late of Salem, Ohio.

CHAPTER V.
PHYSICIANS.

CHARLES DUTTON was born in Wallingford, Connecticut, in 1777. He there studied medicine with Dr. Jared Potter, a distinguished physician, the grandfather, of the late Dr. Jared Potter Kirtland, of Poland, Ohio, and afterwards of Cleveland. As the Western Reserve was opening up for settlement and emigrants were moving there from Connecticut in 1801, Dr. Dutton, being then ready to commence practice, determined to settle in the new country. Turhand Kirtland, the father of Dr. J. P. Kirtland, was a large proprietor of land in the Reserve, and agent for other proprietors. From Old to New Connecticut was, then a long and tedious journey of several weeks. Turhand Kirtland, in April, 1801, was preparing to move a band of emigrants from Wallingford, and had provided three four-horse covered wagons filled with them and their goods ready for starting. Dr. Kirtland then describes Dr. Dutton's start for his future home in the West:

> The Doctor, somewhat eccentric and peculiar in his ways of thinking and acting, sprang upon the driver's seat of one of these wagons, and, at that moment, his aged and widowed mother, with eyes suffused with tears, and other relatives and friends gathered around to bid him "farewell." He, without noticing them, gathered up the reins, cracked his whip, and started off his team, at the same time singing, in an elevated strain, the chorus of "Jefferson and Liberty," the political song of that day:
>
> "Rejoice, Columbia's sons, rejoice!
> To tyrants never bend your knee,
> But join with heart, and soul and voice,
> For Jefferson and Liberty."

The long journey being safely made, the young doctor, as Youngstown was then a prominent place and its prospects promising, selected it for his future residence, and immediately commenced practice. In July, 1802, he purchased a tract of two acres, fronting twenty rods on the south line of West Federal street, a short distance east of Spring common, for which he paid $200, and there erected a log-house, and afterwards a frame-house, in which he resided during his life.

He soon became one of the leading citizens. In July, 1803, he was appointed postmaster of Youngstown, being the second who held the office, and continued the postmaster until March 9, 1818. A copy of the quarterly account from October 1 to December 31, 1817, was preserved among his papers, which, as showing the amount of business of the office at that time, is quite a curiosity, and also interesting historically. The amount collected on letters was $35; on newspapers, $3.79; total, $38.79. Postmaster's commission, $13.19; paid general post-office, $25.60; total, $38.79. He was also occasionally elected a township trustee, and to other township offices.

He became the owner of lands near the village and devoted much attention to farming and stock raising, particularly to raising mules. In later years he practiced his profession only occasionally.

Dr. J. P. Kirtland, who visited Youngstown in 1811 and then made him a visit, speaks of him as the leading physician and surgeon of the vicinity and sustaining a favorable reputation in that capacity for energy and good judgment. Another physician of eminence, who knew him well, in a brief sketch of him says: "Dr. Dutton was regarded by the medical men of the Reserve as an able man, a very good surgeon for those days, and a successful physician; was thought to be somewhat heroic in practice. He was a shrewd man, possessing discriminating judgment, somewhat eccentric, sometimes a little rough, very social, having a large share of those kindly feelings which go into the make up of a good physician, and I may add enter largely into the composition of a good man."

His wife, Cynthia Dutton, died April 26, 1816, aged thirty-one years. They had one child, Jane, who married Dr. Lemuel Wick, son of Henry Wick, an early settler. She died some years since. Dr. Wick died recently.

Dr. Dutton was again married, April 7, 1822, to Miss Cordelia Poole, of Youngstown. He died in March, 1842. She survived him a few years.

HENRY MANNING was born in Lebanon, Connecticut, January 15, 1787. His father was a farmer, and his ancestors were among the earlier settlers of Massachusetts. By the side of his grandmother Manning, whose maiden name was Seabury, he was a descendant of Governor Bradford. He attended for a period Bacon academy, at Colchester, Connecticut, assisting also, when not attending school, in the work on his father's farm. When about twenty years of age he commenced studying medicine with Dr. Hutchinson, of Lebanon, and studied with him about two years. He studied another year with Dr. White, of Cherry Valley, New York. He had taught school at the age of eighteen, and taught at intervals during the time he was pursuing his medical studies. Upon the completion of his studies he removed to Ohio, making the journey on horseback, and arrived in Youngstown, his future home, on July 13, 1811. He commenced practice, and although the place was healthy, the inhabitants not numerous, and not much business for a physician, yet he had, the first year, sufficient practice to sustain himself.

After Hull's surrender in August, 1812, the First regiment, Third brigade, Fourth division of Ohio militia, commanded by Colonel William Rayen, of Youngstown, went to the frontier. Dr. Manning accompanied the regiment as surgeon on Colonel Rayen's staff. The regiment marched, by way of Painesville, to Cleveland, and camped about three-fourths of a mile south of the Public square, on the east side of the river. He stayed there two weeks, and then, at General Perkins' request, went to Huron, where much sickness prevailed among the troops. He there found two surgeons, Dr. Peter Allen, of Kinsman, and Dr. Goodwin, of Burton, both sick. The camp was on the east side of Huron river, near the present village of Milan. He remained there until some time in November. He went from Huron to Lower Sandusky, now Fremont; stayed there until March, when he returned to Youngstown, reaching home March 13, 1813. By his unwearied attention and great kindness to the soldiers who required his services, and the skill he displayed in the treatment of their diseases, he gained the affection and confidence of the men of his regiment, a large share of whom were from Youngstown and its vicinity. His reputation had preceded him, and on his return his practice, which he immediately commenced, occupied his whole time. He continued in active practice until within a few years of his decease, when the infirmities of age and other business avocations induced him to withdraw from it in a great measure, although he was ever ready, when his health permitted, to aid, by his counsel and personal attention, the sick who sought his assistance. When he commenced practice in Youngstown he had not received a diploma as M. D. from any college or medical institution, but afterwards he received several honorary diplomas.

In the fall of 1815, in company with Colonel Caleb B. Wick, he commenced a drug store, afterwards increased to a country store, in which he was interested about ten years. When commenced this was probably the first drug store on the Reserve, although most of the country stores at that time included a few drugs in their stock.

He was several times elected one of the township trustees, and in 1819 he was elected a representative in the State Legislature. In 1825 he was elected State senator, and again a representative in 1843. In 1835 he was elected by the Legislature an associate judge of the court of common pleas for a term of seven years. In 1854 he was elected president of the Mahoning County bank, and in 1862, when the bank was organized as the First National bank of Youngstown, was elected its president, which office he held until 1866, when he declined a re-election, but still continued a director.

He was married to Miss Lucretia Kirtland, of Poland, Ohio, in September, 1814. She was a daughter of Jared Kirtland, an early settler of that place. She died July 13, 1819, aged twenty-two years, leaving one daughter, now married to William J. Edwards, of Youngstown. His second wife was Miss Mary Bingham, daughter of Asa Bingham, of Ellsworth, Ohio, to whom he was married in June, 1821. She died July 21, 1845, aged forty-seven years, leaving three sons and two daughters. He was again married to Mrs. Caroline M. Ruggles, of Canfield, Ohio, in September, 1848. She died May 18, 1862, aged fifty-seven years.

About two years before his death he became blind, but his hearing remained good, and his memory and mental faculties remained unimpaired until near his last. He died January 11, 1869, aged eighty-two years, wanting four days.

From the time he arrived in Youngstown he

was identified with its growth, improvement, and the development of its resources and material interests. The many positions of responsibility and trust with which he was honored by his fellow-citizens, are the best evidence of their estimate of his character as a business man of capacity and strict integrity. As a citizen he was public spirited, and ever ready to aid with his purse and influence in projects of public improvement, and in the promotion of the general welfare.

He was a good surgeon, possessing, in an eminent degree, all the qualities required to make one cool; never excited, with a hand not only steady, but skillful in the use of surgical instruments, and he was a good anatomist. As a physician he ranked with the first on the Reserve in point of professional ability. Among his patients he was regarded with affection as their true friend.

CHARLES C. COOK was born in Wallingford, Connecticut, June 22, 1799. He was a nephew of the late Dr. Charles Dutton, of Youngstown. He received his early education in the schools of his native place, and afterwards in New Haven, Connecticut, to which city his father had removed. He studied medicine with Dr. Eli Ives, of that city, attended the courses of medical lectures in Yale college, and graduated in the Medical department of that institution in 1822. He was married about that time to Miss Mary E. J. Salter, who was born in New Haven, February 15, 1800. He removed to Youngstown about 1824 and commenced practice. He soon gained a reputation as an able practitioner and became one of the prominent and leading physicians in eastern Ohio. Dr. Theodatus Garlick, for many years a prominent physician of Youngstown and afterwards of Cleveland, gives the following just record of his character: "He was a good physician, ranked quite above the average of the medical profession. He did not make much pretension as a surgeon, though he did occasionally make surgical operations. He was quite polished in his manners, a genial, gentlemanly person, and entirely free from every low vice. Added to these he was a fine musician, both vocal and instrumental." He took much interest in educational matters, was for a considerable period a member of the board of education of the union school of Youngstown. In 1857, on the organization of the Rayen school to give effect to the will of Colonel William Rayen, who had left a fund for its establishment and support, he was appointed by the court of common pleas one of the five trustees. His associates were Jonathan Warner, Robert W. Tayler, James Mackey and Charles Howard, all prominent citizens and business men. Although taking a strong interest in public measures, and on all proper occasions expressing decided opinions on political questions, he was not an office seeker and repeatedly declined the offers of his fellow-citizens to support him for public office. He preferred to devote his time to the practice of his profession and acts of friendship and generosity, and in the promotion of measures, educational and otherwise, which would benefit his fellow-citizens and the community in which he had made his home. Mrs. Cook, his estimable wife, died November 3, 1862, mourned by a large circle of friends. He survived her not quite a year, and died September 26, 1863, leaving an unblemished reputation as a physician and citizen.

TIMOTHY WOODBRIDGE was born in Youngstown, Ohio, March, 1810. He was the third son of John E. Woodbridge, who settled in Youngstown in 1807, and is one of the oldest native citizens of that place now living. His father was born in Stockbridge, Massachusetts, and was a grandson of Rev. Jonathan Edwards, the distinguished theologian. When J. E. Woodbridge came to Youngstown, he purchased a tannery at the west end of the village, on the banks of the Mahoning, which was then owned and operated by Joseph Townsend, the first tanner in the township. While quite a small boy, Timothy, with his brother John, a year or two older, were bathing in the Mahoning, near the family residence, and getting beyond their depth John was drowned, and Timothy narrowly escaped. He passed his youth at home, attending school part of the time, and part of the time assisting in the tannery. Arriving near his majority, he determined to pursue the medical profession, and commenced its study with Dr. Henry Manning. He afterwards attended the Jefferson Medical college at Philadelphia, and graduated as M. D. at that institution in 1833. He commenced practice in North Lima, Mahoning county, remained there a few months, and at the solicitation of several prominent citizens returned to Youngstown, and entered into a good practice.

In 1847, by invitation of Hon. David Tod, then appointed by President Polk United States Minister to Brazil, he accompanied Mr. Tod and part of his family to Rio Janeiro as his family physician. He remained there about a year, and returned with Mrs. Tod and the children, to Youngstown; and resumed the practice of his profession. He continued in the practice until 1861, when he was appointed a surgeon of volunteers in the United States army, and took charge of the military post at Johnson's Island in Lake Erie, where he remained until the close of the war in 1865, when he returned to Youngstown and resumed practice. In 1879 he was appointed, by President Hayes, a surgeon in the United States army, and was located at Fort Peck, Montana, where he now remains.

On April 3, 1844, he was married to Miss Isabella McCurdy, a native of Ireland, who removed, in 1842, from that country, with her father, the late Dr. Robert McCurdy, with his family, to Youngstown. She died at Youngstown in September, 1869. He was again married, in 1871, to Mrs. Sarah E. Brewer, of New Lisbon, Ohio, widow of A. I. Brewer, Esq., a lawyer of prominence in that place.

Dr. Woodbridge has long stood in the front rank of Ohio physicians. He has frequently been a member and officer of medical conventions, and, from its organization to his departure to his western appointment, was president of the Mahoning County Medical society. He is eminent, both as a physician and surgeon. He is noted not only for his professional skill but for his kindness and benevolence, never refusing to attend a professional call on account of the poverty of the patient, and many a poor sufferer on a bed of sickness has had occasion to be grateful to him for other than professional aid.

Dr. William I. Buechner was born in the grand duchy of Hesse, Germany, December 3, 1830. He was educated at a public school until fourteen years of age, when he entered the gymnasium at Darmstadt, from which he was graduated in 1848. He then went to the University of Giessen, where he remained five years, graduating in 1853. The doctor very naturally chose the profession of medicine, his father, grandfather, and great-grandfather all having been physicians. His father was one of five brothers, all physicians, who served under Napoleon Bonaparte, the oldest of whom died on the retreat from Russia. In the autumn of 1853 Dr. Buechner came to America, landing in New York after a stormy voyage of two months. He went to Pittsburg, where he practiced his profession the following winter. In the spring of 1854 he came to Youngstown, where he has since been in constant practice, being now the oldest practitioner in the city. March 22, 1858, he was united in marriage to Elvira Hiener, daughter of John Hiener, the first mayor of Youngstown. Mrs. Buechner is a native of Pennsylvania, born February 1, 1832. They are the parents of one daughter and one son, viz: Lucy R., and William H., the latter a student at high school, intending to adopt the profession of his ancestors. Dr. Buechner served one term as councilman about 1870, and is now serving his second term as member of the board of education. He has been a member of the board of health since its organization, and health officer since the office was created. He is a member of the State and County Medical societies, and is local surgeon of the New York, Pennsylvania & Ohio railroad. He is an active Mason, and has been presiding officer of the four different Masonic lodges of Youngstown. He is also member of the Scottish Rite.

Dr. Oliver Dwight Paine, second son of Stephen and Sarah (Strong) Paine, was born in Northampton, Massachusetts, March 7, 1819. His father was a soldier of the War of 1812, and was active in militia affairs in the early day, in which he was an officer. He died June 1, 1834. After the death of her husband Mrs. Paine with her family removed to Springfield, Massachusetts, where she died August 27, 1852. Oliver attended school in Springfield and about 1848 was a student at the Eclectic Medical college, Cincinnati, for one year. He was afterwards for several years in the office of his brother, Professor William Paine, at Warren, Ohio, until recently a professor in a medical college in Philadelphia. He attended the Philadelphia Eclectic Medical college, from which institution he graduated in February, 1860. Previous to that, in 1850, he had located in Youngstown, where he engaged in the practice of his profession until 1875. He then retired from practice, and subsequently became interested in the coal business, in which he was successful. In his profession he was popular and enjoyed an extensive practice. He was married April 27, 1850, to Susan Marstellar, who was born in Mercer county, Pennsylvania, April 4, 1830. They are the parents of five children, three of whom are living, viz: Mary, wife of Hugh S. Scoble, of Steubenville, Ohio, and Ida and Belle, at home. Dr. Paine is an active temperance worker. The doctor was formerly a producer of the mulberry, from which he got a handsome start in life, realizing $5,000 in a short time.

Dr. John McCurdy was born in county Donegal, Ireland, January 21, 1835, and with his parents emigrated to America in 1843. They came directly to Youngstown, Ohio, settling three miles above the city. His father, Robert McCurdy, was a physician. After removing to the Mahoning valley he purchased five hundred acres of land and engaged in stock raising. He was a graduate of Edinburgh university, and was successful and influential in business. He died in 1867. He raised a family of nine children, of whom seven are living. Dr. McCurdy, the subject of this sketch, fitted himself for the practice of his profession at Cleveland, and at Philadelphia, graduating in the former city in 1857, and in the latter in 1858. He began practice under Professor Ackley, at the Marine hospital, Cleveland, coming to Youngstown, Ohio, where he has since resided, in 1858. Early in 1861 he went into the army, was passed before the medical board of examiners, at Columbus, and was ordered to the Twenty-third Ohio volunteer infantry, as assistant surgeon, serving in West Virginia. After acting as assistant surgeon about one year, General J. D. Cox detached him as medical inspector of his district, of West Virginia, in which capacity he served till assigned to duty of surgeon of the Eleventh Ohio volunteer infantry, which occurred on the field of Antietam, immediately after the battle. He was captured at Chickamauga, and remained a prisoner some three months, most of the time in Libby. Being exchanged he rejoined his regiment, and as its surgeon served in the Atlanta campaign. While on that campaign he was requested by General Cox to submit to an examination before the United States examining board for entrance into the United States volunteer corps, which he passed, received his commission, and was ordered on the staff of General Palmer, as assistant medical director of the Fourteenth army corps. He was again captured before Atlanta, and was a prisoner some six weeks, going the rounds of the rebel prisons. After his exchange he was assigned on the staff of General Thomas, as medical inspector, which position he filled until the dispersion of General Hood's force, when he resigned and came home, the war being virtually ended. After the war he was appointed United States examiner for pensions, at Youngstown, and has since filled that position. He was married in 1866 to Miss Mary L. McEwen, and has a family of four children.

Dr. C. N. Fowler is a son of Dr. C. R. Fowler, of Canfield, and was born February 13, 1828. After passing through the course of Canfield academy he began the study of medicine in his father's office. Subsequently he attended lectures at Western Reserve Medical college at Cleveland, graduating in 1850. One year before his graduation, and one year after, he served as clinical assistant in the hospital, under charge of Prof. Ackley, thus fully fitting himself for surgical practice. He entered the profession in association with his father, in Canfield, but a few years later removed to Poland, where he had charge of the anatomical department of the law college, and at the same time engaged in general practice. In August, 1862, Dr. Fowler enlisted in the volunteer service and was commissioned surgeon of the One Hundred and Fifth Ohio volunteer infantry. He attained to the rank of medical inspector in the Fourteenth army corps, under General Beard, and was mustered out of the service in 1865. Soon after returning from the field he began practicing in Youngstown, where he has since remained. He has attained considerable reputation as a surgeon. Dr. Fowler married, in 1853, Mary Snyder, of Canfield, and has one child.

Dr. F. V. Floor was born in Beaver county, Pennsylvania, May 11, 1836. His parents are Jacob and Agnes Floor, who removed to Berlin, Mahoning county, Ohio, in the spring of 1838, where they still reside. Dr. Floor obtained his schooling in the common schools and at Poland academy, which he attended for three years. Taught school for several winters until twenty, and then

John R. Holcomb

commenced to read medicine with Dr. W. H. Brown, of Lordstown. He attended Michigan university, Ann Arbor, one term, and the University of Philadelphia in 1866, from which institution he was graduated. In the meantime he had been practicing his profession, having commenced at New Middletown, Mahoning county, in the spring of 1862. In 1872 he settled in Youngstown and has since built up a good practice. In 1876 he attended a course of lectures at the Cleveland Medical college and received his degree from that college. He is a member of the County Medical association.

In 1858 he was married to Eliza A. Eckis, of Milton. The children now living by this marriage are Dr. Charles L. Floor, a graduate of Cleveland Medical college, Helen V., Lois I., Milton J., and Ola E. His first wife died in 1873 and in 1875 he married Miss Laura A. Davis, by whom he has one daughter, Norma I.

Dr. James F. Wilson was born in Berlin township, Mahoning county, Ohio, in 1847. He is a son of Joseph and Mary (Boyd) Wilson, one of the influential families of that township. His mother's father, Henry Boyd, of Ellsworth, was a member of the State Legislature. Dr. Wilson's education was obtained in the common schools and at Mount Union college. He read medicine under Dr. W. K. Hughes, of Berlin Center, and subsequently graduated at the Western Reserve Medical college, Cleveland, in 1872. He practiced one year in Orwell, Wayne county, Ohio, then located in Youngstown, and has since been engaged in the practice of his profession in this city. Dr. Wilson enjoys an excellent practice, and his standing in the profession is attested by the fact that he is a member of the American Medical association, having been elected in 1877. For several years he was secretary of the Mahoning Medical society. In 1879 he was elected county coroner, and again in 1881. In 1880 he was married to Mrs. Mary A. McGaw, of Youngstown.

Dr. John S. Cunningham, oldest son of Judge Joseph and Jeannette Cunningham, was born in Beaver county, Pennsylvania, February 4, 1833. He attended the common schools, and at fifteen was a student at an academy at Poland, Ohio, after which he was engaged in teaching school for two years. When nineteen he entered Allegheny college, Meadville, Pennsylvania, and remained there some three years. He read medicine for three or four years with Hon. J. W. Wallace, M. D., at New Castle, Pennsylvania, and subsequently graduated from Jefferson Medical college in March, 1860, having previously attended a course of lectures at Cleveland Medical college. He commenced practice at Plain Grove, Pennsylvania, where he remained two years. While there he was married, June, 1861, to Miss Sadie R. Campbell, and has two children: Lulu W., born June 15, 1865, and Frank Campbell, born July 5, 1873. Two children are deceased. In 1862 Dr. Cunningham came to Youngstown, where, with the exception of two years that he resided in Marietta, Ohio, he has since resided. He was county coroner one term, member of the board of health for six years, and for the past five years has been a member of the Youngstown board of education, and is now president of the board, always taking an active part in the promotion of educational interests.

Dr. William J. Wheelan was born in Ireland, September 27, 1840, and emigrated to this country in 1859, locating in Detroit, Michigan. He began the study of medicine in Detroit, continuing for some eighteen months previous to the commencement of the rebellion in 1861, when he went as hospital steward with the First Michigan cavalry. He was in the campaign of the Shenandoah valley, and was captured at Winchester, Virginia, while on detached duty; was paroled in January, 1863. In the spring of 1863 he was sent to Benton Barracks general hospital, St. Louis, and attended two courses of lectures at the St. Louis Medical college, during the winters of 1863-64 and 1864-65. In the spring of 1869 he was sent to Fort Phil. Kearney, Nebraska, where he remained till February, 1866, when he resigned his position in the United States army, returned to Chicago and attended a session at the Chicago Medical college, from which he received a diploma. He began practice in Saratoga county, New York, where his mother and sister then resided. He came to Youngstown, Ohio, in March, 1867, where he has since lived, engaged in the practice of his profession. At the session of 1874-75 he attended a course of lectures at the College of Physicians and Surgeons, New York city, graduating from that institution. He married, in

1867, Miss M. Jennie E. Hewitt. They are the parents of eight children, of whom six are living.

Dr. John E. Woodbridge, oldest son of Henry and Elizabeth (White) Woodbridge, was born in Lawrence county, Pennsylvania, May 7, 1841. His grandfather, John Eliot Woodbridge, was an early settler in Mahoning county, coming here in 1807. He was a grandson, or his mother's side, of Jonathan Edwards, the distinguished New England divine. He was born in Stockbridge, Massachusetts, June 24, 1777, went to Philadelphia in 1798, married in 1803, and the same year removed to Lawrence county, Pennsylvania. Afterwards he moved to Baltimore, Maryland, thence to Youngstown in 1807. He owned a tannery in which the father of General Grant at one time worked. Dr. Woodbridge obtained his primary education in Youngstown. With his parents he removed to Kentucky, where he attended various institutions of learning. He was afterwards a private student under Dr. G. C. E. Weber, the founder of the medical department of Wooster university, Cleveland, from which institution he graduated in 1866. He was house surgeon of United States Marine hospital at Cleveland one year, and was post surgeon at Fort Inge, Texas, serving under General J. H. Reynolds for nearly two years. He came to Youngstown in 1871, where he has since been in active practice. In 1861 he enlisted in the Twenty-seventh Kentucky (Union) regiment, and served until his health failed him. He afterwards enlisted in the One Hundred and Sixty-ninth Ohio National guards, and was stationed at Fort Ethan Allen, Virginia, and was mustered out at Cleveland, September, 1864. April 28, 1881, he was united in marriage to Miss Carlyn C. Price, a native of Detroit, Michigan.

Dr. Isaiah Brothers, son of Jesse Brothers, was born in Lawrence county, Pennsylvania, January 15, 1831. He was brought up to farming, was a pupil at Poland academy for several terms and was engaged in teaching school winters. In 1850 he commenced the study of medicine with Dr. E. F. Davis, of Hillsville, Pennsylvania, with whom he remained three years. He took his first course of lectures in the winter of 1852-53 at Cincinnati, and for three and a half years subsequently practiced in Lancaster, Pennsylvania. He took another course of lectures and in 1857 commenced practice in Hillsville, Pennsylvania, where he remained until 1872, when he removed to Youngstown, where he has since followed his profession. In 1853 he was married to Miss Rhoda Patterson, a native of Lawrence county, Pennsylvania. They are the parents of four children, two sons and two daughters. One son and daughter are married, the other two being still at home.

Dr. M. S. Clark was born in Gallipolis, Ohio, October 9, 1840. He was a student at Hiram college, under General Garfield, from 1855 to 1861, with the exception of the winter months when he was engaged in teaching. He graduated from that institution in 1861 and shortly afterward enlisted in the Forty-first Ohio volunteer infantry. He served one year, being discharged, on account of physical disability, in 1862. Returning to civil life he commenced the study of medicine under Dr. F. C. Applegate, of Windham, Portage county, and attended lectures at the Michigan university, medical department, in the winters of 1863 and 1864. He enlisted as hospital steward in the One Hundred and Seventy-first Ohio National guard, and at the battle of Cynthiana, Kentucky, filled the position of assistant surgeon. With his regiment he was taken prisoner by the rebels, but was afterwards re-captured by the Union forces under General Burbridge. He served out his term of enlistment and was mustered out at Johnson's island. He again attended lectures at Michigan university in the winter of 1864-65 and graduated therefrom March 30, 1865. The same fall he located in Warren, Ohio, and engaged in the practice of his profession. In the spring of 1868 he moved to Bristol, Trumbull county, where he remained until the fall of 1873, engaged in practice, when he removed to Youngstown, where he has since resided. May 9, 1867, he was married to Miss Hettie J. Smith, of Hiram, Ohio, and a graduate of that college. They have two children, viz: Clayton A., born September 25, 1874; and Louis P., July 9, 1880. James A. died when sixteen months old. Dr. Clark is a member of the medical board of the Mahoning Valley Mutual Relief association.

Dr. Benjamin F. Hawn, son of Nathan and Catharine Hawn, was born in North Lima, Mahoning county, July 4, 1848. Nathan Hawn was a well known physician of North Lima, where he located in 1846. He died in 1873. Dr. Hawn, our subject, attended the schools of his native town and was afterwards a student for three years at the Poland academy. He taught school in various places for several years, and during that time was engaged in reading medicine. He finished his course of reading with his father and older brother, Amos, and entered the medical department at Ann Arbor, Michigan, in the winter of 1871-72; was also a student at Bellevue Medical college, New York, in 1873. He began the practice of his profession with his brother Enos at Leetonia, afterwards locating at Newton Falls, Trumbull county, where he remained for one year, coming to Youngstown in October, 1874, where he has since continued to practice. He was married, in May, 1871, to Ella N. Robbins, of Trumbull county, and has one son, Frank S., born February 5, 1874. Dr. Hawn is an active member of the Independent Order of Odd Fellows.

Dr. George S. Peck, second son of L. S. and Sarah T. Peck, was born in Akron, Ohio, July 16, 1851. He graduated from the high school there, and afterwards learned a trade connected with the iron business. He followed that some seven years. In the fall of 1871 he commenced the study of medicine, which he continued for three years, and then attended his first course of lectures at the University of Wooster Medical college, Cleveland. He was appointed assistant house surgeon of Charity hospital, Cleveland, in the spring of 1874, and occupied that position under Drs. Weber and Scott, until the spring of 1876. He graduated from Wooster University Medical college, Cleveland, February, 1875. April, 1876, he came to Youngstown, where he has since been engaged in practice. Dr. Peck is examining surgeon for the United Order of Foresters.

M. L. Davis, son of John and Ann Davis, great-grandson of Sir William Pugh, was born in London, England, July 14, 1845. He first visited America in 1859. His early education was pursued in the Branch Welsh and St. Bartholomew's, the course in the latter embracing the classics, general science, pharmacy, and medicine. He graduated in pharmacy in 1868. He has been a student of Dr. B. Baily, Chicago; Dr. D. L. Ross, Scotland, Connecticut; at Wyoming Medical college, Pennsylvania, and at Starling Medical college, Columbus, Ohio, graduating in 1874 and 1878, respectively. He was naturalized as a citizen of the United States in Luzerne county, Pennsylvania, in 1866. Dr. Davis has been practicing in Youngstown since 1878.

George Edgar Allen, homeopathist, was born at Northfield, Massachusetts, March 2, 1838. His father, Phineas Allen, graduated at Harvard college in 1825. James Allen, the progenitor of the family, emigrated from Scotland to America in 1639, and was one of the founders of Medfield. Dr. Allen received a fair common school education at West Newton, and at the age of fifteen embarked for a voyage around the world on a ship commanded by a friend of his family. At the end of three years difficulties were encountered and hardships suffered on the New England coast, which impaired his health. He became a machinist and steam engineer at Boston. At the opening of the rebellion he enlisted in the navy, and served on board the Nightingale, and subsequently as engineer on the United States gunboat Underwriter, which was captured off the coast of North Carolina, February 2, 1864. For gallant conduct in assisting eighteen sailors to escape, Mr. Allen was made chief engineer of the United States steamer Lockwood, and served in that position till the war closed. While in the navy he made the acquaintance of Dr. Kendall, and under his directions began the study of medicine, but after the war his studies were interrupted by a term of service as superintendent of a type foundry. He entered the medical department of the Boston university in 1873, and graduated in 1877. Since March, 1877, he has been practicing in Youngstown. Dr. Allen married in March, 1867, Fannie Phillips, of Boston. Frank F., their only son, was born June 9, 1868.

Dr. A. M. Clark is a native of Washington county, Pennsylvania, a son of Dr. Matthew Henderson Clark, a well-known physician of Washington county of high standing. Dr. Clark, our subject, when sixteen years of age entered the Washington and Jefferson college, Washington, Pennsylvania, from which he graduated. He subsequently took three courses of lectures at the Medical department of the University of Pennsylvania, graduating from that institution also; was afterwards resident physician and surgeon of West Pennsylvania hospital at Pittsburg one year. He came to Youngstown in the spring of 1881, and is now engaged in practice there.

Dr. Joseph Wilson was born in Youngstown township, Mahoning county, Ohio, September 14, 1836. His father, William J. Wilson, was a native of Pennsylvania, born in 1799; was the son of Joseph Wilson, who purchased property two and a half miles west of Youngstown in 1798, settling there with his family the following year. He cleared up a farm there, and resided upon it until his death. He was born on the ocean during the voyage of his parents to America from the north of Ireland. He was a noted hunter throughout this region, and was a member of the jury in the celebrated McMahon murder case. William J. Wilson married Mary, eldest daughter of Robert Kincaid, a native of Youngstown township, and who still lives on the old homestead near Youngstown. He died there in 1870. They raised a family of seven children, of whom six are still living, most of them in Youngstown and vicinity. Dr. Wilson was reared upon a farm, and remained at home until he was nineteen years of age. He was educated principally in Youngstown and Girard, where he was a pupil for some years. He was engaged as clerk in drug stores in various places for some time. He commenced reading medicine in 1858 with Dr. Isaac Barclay, continuing for three years, during which he attended lectures at the Cleveland Medical college, graduating from that institution in 1862. He commenced practice in North Jackson, Mahoning county; residing there three years, then removed in 1865 to Girard. Remained in Girard till 1879, when he came to Youngstown, occupying at first the former office of Dr. Timothy Woodbridge on the site of the McGillin block. He was married in 1862 to Miss Emily P. Shepherd, born in Milton, Mahoning county, and has one daughter and one son—Blanche M. and William Guy.

The remaining physicians now in practice in Youngstown are Dr. Sloson, W. H. McGranaghan, H. H. Hahn, and W. S. Mathews.

THE MAHONING COUNTY MEDICAL SOCIETY.

On November 13, 1872, a number of gentlemen of the medical fraternity held a meeting in Dr. Cunningham's office, at which place the following business was transacted, Dr. T. Woodbridge acting chairman, and Dr. Whelan secretary: After some consideration a motion prevailed that the physicians then present organize themselves into an association to be known as the Mahoning County Medical society, and a committee of five was appointed to draw up a constitution and by-laws. The committee consisted of Dr. G. W. Brooke, Dr. J. McCurdy, Dr. T. Woodbridge, Jr., and Dr. W. J. Whelan. The society met pursuant to adjournment on October 27, 1872, adopted the constitution and by-laws submitted by the committee appointed at the previous meeting, after which a paper was read by Dr. Cunningham—being the first lecture given for the benefit of the society. This meeting was held at the office of Dr. J. E. Woodbridge, and was adjourned to meet at the office of Dr. Fowler, December 4, 1872, at which time the society proceeded to elect the following officers for a permanent organization: Dr. T. Woodbridge, president; Dr. G. W. Brooke, vice-president; Dr. W. J. Whelan, secretary; Dr. John McCurdy, treasurer. Censors, Dr. C. N. Fowler, Dr. W. L. Buechner, Dr. G. L. Starr. A committee of three, Dr. Fowler, Dr. Buechner, and Dr. Starr, drew up and reported the first fee bill which governed the practice in Youngstown. The society maintains its organization. Its meetings promote friendly feeling and afford opportunity for valuable professional conference.

DENTAL SURGEONS.

Dr. B. F. Gibbons, second son of William and Mary Ann Gibbons, was born in Mahoning county, Ohio, February 12, 1833. William Gibbons was a native of Lancaster county, Pennsylvania, where he was born about 1800. He came to Ohio about 1828, settling in Goshen township, now Mahoning county, where he resided until his death. He met his death suddenly by being run over by his wagon, loaded with saw logs, in the fall of 1844. His widow is living, still owning a portion of the old place. They raised a family of five sons, all of whom are living. The doctor was raised to farming until eighteen, when he served an apprenticeship in Warren at the carriage-making business with his brother, Dr. David Gibbons, now a resident of Warren. He was engaged in that business for five years in West Chester, Pennsylvania, selling out in the winter of 1859-60. He commenced the study of his profession during his business career, and in

1860 attended the Pennsylvania Dental college. Returning to Ohio he suffered from a severe illness for some time, and with his brother made a trip through the South and located at St. Charles, Missouri. The secession sentiment at the outbreak of the rebellion in '61, compelled them to go north. He located in Salem, Ohio, where he practiced for a short time, in 1863 removing to Warren, where he practiced till 1869. In the winter of 1869 he settled in Youngstown, where he is still engaged in the practice of his profession. During his residence in Warren, November 28, 1867, he was married to Miss Martha W., daughter of Edward and Lucy C. Potter, of Warren, born February 3, 1846, and has one son, Edward F., born September 6, 1870. Mrs. Gibbons died January 2, 1878.

Dr. Nathan B. Acheson, only son of Dr. David and Esther B. Acheson, was born in Vienna township, Trumbull county, Ohio, September 3, 1847. His father was an early physician in Vienna, and practiced there for many years, continuing until his death which occurred while on a visit to Iowa in 1851. His wife died in 1853.

Dr. Acheson was brought up under the guardianship of Adam McClurg, and was raised to farming pursuits. He received his primary education at Kingsville, Ashtabula county. Coming to Youngstown, he commenced the printing trade in the Register office, but after working at it a couple of years, he found it did not agree with his health. He soon after commenced studying dentistry under Dr. Whitslar, of Youngstown, subsequently continuing his studies under Dr. Taft, of Cincinnati, where he attended lectures in 1868-69. While there he had charge of the Ohio Dental college. In 1869 he commenced practicing in Sharon, Pennsylvania, in partnership with Dr. Stewart. On account of ill health he sold out to his partner one year afterward, and engaged in mercantile business in Youngstown, which proved disastrous. He resumed the practice of his profession at Cuyahoga Falls, where he continued eighteen months, locating in Youngstown in 1871, where he is still engaged in practice. He is a member of the Ohio State Dental association, and also of the American Dental association. December 25, 1867, he was married to Miss Alice L. Harber, and has three children, viz: Minnie, born April 16, 1870; Maudie, April 15, 1872, and Gracie, February 15, 1874. He is the inventor of a number of contrivances, among others the Acheson Water metre, for measuring water.

Dr. E. A. Clarke, only child of Edwin and Elizabeth Clark, was born in Mesopotamia, Trumbull county, Ohio, April 15, 1847. He remained at home on the farm until twenty-one, after which for three years he was employed in a drug store in Mesopotamia, and for a short time subsequently was a prescription clerk in Sharon, Pennsylvania, returning home during the illness of his father. He afterwards began the study of dentistry at Chardon, Geauga county, Ohio, in the office of Dr. E. D. Richardson, where he completed his profession. He began practice in Jefferson, Ohio, in 1868, remaining one year, then located in Mesopotamia, where he remained in practice seven years. He afterwards followed the profession in Garrettsville, Ohio, until September, 1879, when on account of a protracted illness he suspended practice until the following spring. September, 1880, he came to Youngstown, where he now has an office over the McGillin store. Dr. Clarke is a member of Youngstown lodge Independent Order of Odd Fellows, No. 403.

Dr. F. S. Whitslar was born in Austintown, Mahoning county, Ohio, September 7, 1824. His father, Henry Whitslar, was a native of Pennsylvania, came to Ohio about 1809, and settled in Austintown township, then Trumbull county; married Catharine, daughter of Frederick Shively, one of the early settlers of Austintown, and raised a family of twelve children. He was a contractor and builder, and constructed many of the best residences in Youngstown. He died in 1873, at Mansfield, Ohio. Dr. Whitslar was reared upon a farm. Taught school winters, during which time he was engaged in reading dentistry. March 4, 1849, he was married to Miss Matilda, daughter of John Fox, of Canfield township, and has three children, Alice M., William H., and Grant S. For two or three years after his marriage he itinerated in the practice of his profession, and about 1855 or 1856 commenced practice in Youngstown. In 1861 he was a member of the military committee of the county, and subsequently at the suggestion of Mr. Paul Wick, he recruited company D, One Hundred and Fifty-fifth Ohio National guard, of which he was captain, and was at Cedar Creek, Martinsburg, White House Landing, in front of Petersburgh, and at Bower's Hill, serving out his term of enlistment, and was mustered out at Camp Dennison. Dr. Whitslar was the first president of the city council of Youngstown, after the organization of the city. He continued to practice on Federal street until the spring of 1881, when he removed his office to his residence on West Boardman street. He has been a member of the Disciple church for forty-seven years, of which he has been elder many years.

C. A. Beard opened an office in Youngstown in 1872, and has been practicing dental surgery since that time. He was born in Columbiana, in 1846, studied dentistry at Philadelphia Dental college, and graduated from that institution in 1872.

S. J. Beard was born in Columbiana, in 1853. He graduated from Philadelphia Dental college in 1877, and soon after began the practice with his brother in Youngstown.

CHAPTER VI.
SOLDIERS' MONUMENT.

The project of erecting a monument to perpetuate the names of fallen soldiers and to commemorate their patriotism and suffering, had its inception during the sad and stormy conflict. While appeal after appeal for volunteers was coming from the Government at Washington, and day after day the papers brought accounts of bloody battles and the death of friends, it seemed proper to offer a pledge to all who were willing to risk their lives, that if the worst should befall them a monument would associate their names with the cause for which they had died. The war was not yet over when a committee began to devise plans for the fulfillment of this pledge. A meeting of citizens placed the entire management in the hands of a committee of three, Thomas H. Wells, Governor David Tod, and William S. Crawford. This was in 1864. It was at first proposed to ask for one dollar subscriptions, so that all, rich and poor, should have the opportunity of contributing. More than one thousand two hundred people responded cheerfully to this call. There were at that time probably not more than one thousand five hundred families in the township. The amount thus fell far short of the most parsimonious estimates of the cost of the intended memorial. A second subscription paper was circulated, by which funds to the amount of $6,000 were placed at the disposal of the committee. This amount was deemed sufficient to guarantee action, and artists in different parts of the country were called upon for designs and estimates. It was found, however, that nothing worthy of the township and the cause could be purchased for less than $10,000. A meeting of twenty citizens named by the committee was called at Mr. Wells' office, and all pledged their support to whatever action the committee might take. A contract was subsequently made with James Blattersby, of Hartford, Connecticut, for a shaft and statue of a young soldier, to be made of Westerly granite. It was decided to locate the monument in the old cemetery, where the court-house has since been built. The foundation was built and the corner-stone laid, as is customary, by the Masonic fraternity. Governor Hayes conducted the ceremony on that occasion.

It was subsequently decided, however, to erect the monument in the public square. The foundation was removed. General Garfield secured an appropriation of four cannon, to be selected by the committee, which were in due time placed in position. One of the greatest difficulties encountered by the committee was to get an accurate list of the names of those soldiers who had resided in Youngstown township at the time of their enlistment, and had actually died in the service or from injuries received in the service. The list was several times revised and is believed to be absolutely accurate. The monument was unveiled and dedicated July 4, 1870. Mr. Wells, on the part of the committee, presented it to the citizens of Youngstown township as an enduring memorial of the township's patriotic contribution to the cause of the Union, universal liberty, and equality of rights and privileges. General Garfield removed the flag beneath which the substantial shaft and handsome statue was concealed. He then delivered a touching dedicatory address.

The entire cost of the monument as it stands

was about $15,000. It is one of the finest of its character in Ohio, and reflects credit upon the taste of the members of the committee and the patriotism of the citizens whose liberality enabled them to execute their plans. The base is ten feet square, composed of four pieces, each five feet square and one foot eight inches high. On this rests a second base, being a single stone seven and one-half feet square and a foot and one-half high. On this is the plinth five and a half feet square and two feet eight inches high, the upper part finely moulded, and the lower part facing the north bearing this inscription:

ERECTED BY THE CITIZENS OF YOUNGSTOWN IN MEMORY OF THE HEROES OF THE TOWNSHIP WHO GAVE THEIR LIVES TO THEIR COUNTRY IN THE WAR OF THE REBELLION, 1861-1865.

Above the plinth is the die, a stone four feet square and four feet high, on which the names of the soldiers whose memory and heroism it is designed to perpetuate are inscribed. These names are given below. Above the die is a cap from which rises the spire, and on the cap on the north side extending up the spire in relief is cut the arms of the State of Ohio, partly covering the National, above which on a scroll is the motto, *E pluribus unum*, surmounted by a stand of colors, wreath of flowers, drum, cannon, etc. About one-third up the spire is cut in relief the names Chickamauga, Winchester, Cedar Mountain, Vicksburg, one on each side, and the about the same distance above, Antietam, Shiloh, Stone River, Perryville.

The spire is capped with a stone three feet square, on which, facing north, is the statue of a soldier seven feet high. The soldier is in private's uniform, with his army overcoat thrown over his shoulders, full bearded, cap on and stands with his hands on his gun in the position of "parade rest." The height of the monument is forty-seven feet. It rests on a sandstone foundation sunk several feet in the earth and rising three feet above the level of the earth, to which height the ground around it has been graded.

On the north side of the die the names of the heroic dead of Youngstown township, killed in battle or died from disease contracted in the army, 1861-1865, are inscribed as follows:

FIRST INFANTRY DIVISION, ARMY OF VIRGINIA.
Surgeon-in-chief Thomas J. Shannon, Cedar Creek.

SECOND OHIO VOLUNTEER CAVALRY.
Joseph A. Truesdale, Fort Scott.
William Wakefield, Washington.

SEVENTH OHIO VOLUNTEER INFANTRY.
Lieutenant Joseph H. Ross, Cedar Mountain, Virginia.
Sergeant Andrew J. Kelley, Winchester, Virginia.
Sergeant Robert McClelland, Dallas, Georgia.
Sergeant John McFadden, Frederick, Maryland.
James Bop, Winchester, Virginia.
Michael Campbell, Port Republic, Virginia.
George Fox, Cedar Mountain, Virginia.
James P. Ray, Cedar Mountain, Virginia.
William Waldorf, Cedar Mountain, Virginia.
James L. Stevenson, Cedar Mountain, Virginia.
Lemuel J. Cecil, Charlestown, Virginia.
Abram D. Crooks, Youngstown, Ohio.
Charles L. Cowden, Dallas, Georgia.
Joseph B. Deeds, Dallas, Georgia.
John D. Dicks, Kanawha, Virginia.
Jacob Muller, Murfreesboro, Tennessee.
James C. Shoaff, Charlestown, Virginia.
John Shannon, Brier Hill, Ohio.
Thomas D. Williams, Harper's Ferry, Virginia.
David Williams.

NINETEENTH OHIO VOLUNTEER INFANTRY.
Lieutenant David Donovan, Stone River.
Corporal Daniel Cooper, Stone River.
John Thomas, Shiloh.
Isaac Davis, Stone River.
Charles Jacobs, Chickamauga.
Patrick Murphy, Nashville, Tennessee.
Samuel Vogan, McMinnville, Tennessee.
Peter Allison, Andersonville prison.

East Side.
TWENTY-SIXTH OHIO VOLUNTEER INFANTRY.
Captain William H. Ross, Chickamauga.
Lieutenant David McClelland, Stone River.
Lieutenant Samuel Platt, Atlanta, Georgia.
Lieutenant James C. Morrow, Johnston's Island.
Sergeant John A. Woods, Big Shantee, Georgia.
Sergeant Joseph Fullerton, Chickamauga.
Sergeant James Cochran, Andersonville prison.
Sergeant John Jennings, Stone River.
Corporal Nikolaus Knchbaum, Stone River.
Isaac Rider, Stone River.
John Tagg, Stone River.
John Carney, Stone River.
Joseph Reese, Stone River.
Robert McAuly, Chickamauga.
Daniel Mitchell, Chickamauga.
James Evans, Chickamauga.
William Crum, Chickamauga.
James McIlvey, Chickamauga.
John Llewellyn, Chickamauga.
David Williams, Chickamauga.
Luman Parmele, Kenesaw, Georgia.
Con Duey, Andersonville prison.
William Brown, Andersonville prison.
Samuel Birch, Booneville, Virginia.
John Smith, Greene Lake, Texas.
Francis P. Jones, Chattanooga, Tennessee.

ONE HUNDRED AND EIGHTY-EIGHTH OHIO VOLUNTEER INFANTRY.
George Ague, Camp Chase.

ILLINOIS VOLUNTEER INFANTRY.
Elias A. Crooks, Youngstown, Ohio.
ONE HUNDREDTH PENNSYLVANIA VOLUNTEER INFANTRY.
James W. Bell, James Island, South Carolina.

West Side.

TWENTY-THIRD OHIO VOLUNTEER INFANTRY.
Sergeant Eli Fitch, Cloyd Mountain, West Virginia.
Mayberry Goodman, Antietam.
David Williams, South Mountain, Maryland.
Luther Leslie, Wheeling, West Virginia.
David H. Edwards.
Thomas Moore, Rebel prison.

TWENTY-SEVENTH OHIO VOLUNTEER INFANTRY.
Lieutenant Frederick Dennis, Vicksburg, Mississippi.
John Lamb, Vicksburg, Mississippi.
Ignatius Reuter, Wyoming, Virginia.
Henry Loerer, Wyoming, Virginia.

THIRTY-FOURTH OHIO VOLUNTEER INFANTRY.
Andrew Buchannan.

THIRTY-SIXTH OHIO VOLUNTEER INFANTRY.
Benjamin Kyle, Camp Nelson, Kentucky.
Manly Partridge, Camp Nelson, Kentucky.

SIXTH OHIO VOLUNTEER CAVALRY.
Lieutenant Henry M. Baldwin, Ladd's Farm.
Sergeant John Dunlap, Stevensburg.
William Borts, Wilderness.
Robert Barrett, died in prison.
William Schieble, died in prison.

TENTH OHIO VOLUNTEER CAVALRY.
Corporal Hiram Fifield, Ringgold.
Corporal James E. Johnston, Andersonville prison.

FIFTEENTH OHIO BATTERY.
Milton D. Fellows, Vicksburg, Mississippi.

TWENTY-SECOND OHIO BATTERY.
Healey Powers, Knoxville, Tennessee.

South Side.

ONE HUNDRED AND FIFTH OHIO VOLUNTEER INFANTRY.
Sergeant Lafayette McCoy, Murfreesboro, Tennessee.
Sergeant William H. Craig, Chickamauga, Tennessee.
Sergeant N. W. King, Chickamauga, Tennessee.
John Boyle, Chickamauga, Tennessee.
James Williams, Perryville, Kentucky.
Henry Niblock, Perryville, Kentucky.
Michael McGinty, Perryville, Kentucky.
Albert Miller, Perryville, Kentucky.
Lawrence Kelly, Atlanta, Georgia.
Isaac Morris, Andersonville prison.
Reuben B. Reep, Cowan Station, Tennessee.
John Stewart, Tennessee.
William B. Price, Louisville, Kentucky.
John Thomas, Munfordville, Kentucky.

ONE HUNDRED AND TWENTY-FIFTH OHIO VOLUNTEER INFANTRY.
Sergeant Richard M. Elliott, Youngstown, Ohio.
John W. Powers, Chickamauga.
John C. Stroily, Chickamauga.
John Homer, Kenesaw Mountain.
John Barker, Youngstown, Ohio.
Thomas Jones, Louisville, Kentucky.

ONE HUNDRED AND FIFTY-FIFTH OHIO VOLUNTEER INFANTRY.
Sergeant John W. Brothers, Portsmouth, Virginia.
Myron I. Arms, Youngstown, Ohio.
James C. Miller, Portsmouth, Virginia.
Lawrence Baker, Portsmouth, Virginia.
Manuel Leppard, Portsmouth, Virginia.
Joel B. McCollum, Portsmouth, Virginia.
Thomas Jacobs, Washington, District of Columbia.
Benjamin C. Cunningham, Pittsburg, Pennsylvania.
Alexander K. McClelland, Pittsburg, Pennsylvania.

CHAPTER VII.

THE PRESS—SECRET SOCIETIES.

The county seat contest which resulted in 1846 in the division of Trumbull county and the organization of Mahoning county brought into existence the first paper in Youngstown. It was also the first in the present territory of Mahoning county. The Olive Branch and New County Advocate made its appearance in the fall of 1843. It was a poor supporter of the cause which its title pledged it to support, and it is not improbable that for that reason it was poorly supported. In its files covering a period of three months, only a few items relate to the local issue which was then above all other issues. Under such circumstances little public support could be expected, and there being no official patronage its publication was soon suspended.

THE OHIO REPUBLICAN

made its appearance soon after the county was organized. It was published by A. Medbury and J. M. Webb, the latter being the chief editorial writer. In politics it represented pure Jacksonianism, and supported Polk's administration, opposed Taylor and devoted its energies during the campaign of 1852 to praising Franklin Pierce. It professed to have an eye single to the glory of the party, and if we are to believe the business statement of its publishers contained in the last issue found in the files of the county auditor's office, private funds were drawn upon to maintain its publication. A knowledge of the trials of these pioneers in the journalistic field in Youngstown may temper the appearance of more recent tribulations. The journalist never knows when he has a safe investment. The Republican was removed to Canfield soon after the Presidential election in 1852, and combined with the Mahoning Sentinel under the name Mahoning Republican Sentinel. The Mahoning Sentinel had been established in 1852 by an association of citizens, with Ira Norris as editor. It subsequently passed through several changes of ownership and editorship until finally purchased by John M. Webb, and after a few years removed to Youngstown. It had before this taken its old name, the Mahoning Sentinel. The times were particularly adverse to Mr. Webb's enterprise. He made a strong fight and maintained a respectable standing during the campaign of 1860, but after the election of Lincoln and the secession of Southern States there was little room for an old line Democratic paper on the Reserve. The following appeared at the head of its editorial column in the issue of October 23, 1861:

"The Mahoning Sentinel is now the only Democratic paper in this county, senatorial or judicial district, the only paper on the Western Reserve supporting the regular Democratic ticket. Wealth, influence, and slander, each are being brought to bear to crush it out. The paper is not published purely as a pecuniary speculation, but for the success of genuine Union and Democratic principles, and therefore the unterrified and un-abolitionized people should rally to its support. It should be sustained instead of sustaining any withdrawal of support. Let the friends of the good cause, the honest Union men of this county and valley go to work and spread the old Sentinel.

It seems, however, that the "honest Union men" did not respond enthusiastically to this appeal, for in the next issue we find this announcement:

With this number of the Sentinel its publication is necessarily suspended for the present through circumstances over which we have no control, but with which our patrons have to do.

The presses stood idle until July 10, 1862, when the Sentinel again appeared. Its motto, printed in heavy black letters was: "The Constitution as it is and the Union as it was." If Mr. Webb had understood the axiom "While the battle is raging there is no time to talk," or that the only logic in war is cannon and musketry; he probably would have spared himself the trouble of reviving his paper. Able as it was its political effect was inconsiderable, and its pecuniary returns must have been small. The Sentinel barely survived the Presidential election of 1864. Its place as a Democratic organ was not filled until the Vindicator made its appearance in 1869.

During this time another paper obtained a substantial foothold, and was until recently the organ of the dominant party in the county. The Mahoning Register may be said to have had its beginning in the

FREE DEMOCRAT,

which was the first paper in the county representing abolition sentiment. It made its appearance December 31, 1852, with Edward D. Howard as editor, and M. Cullaton publisher. The paper in typographical make up was creditable, but editorially it lacked strength and vigor of expression. But in this respect it was not unlike most country papers of the period. Long drawn out, obscure editorials took the place of news and strong, direct and concise expressions of current opinion. In the first issue of the Free Democrat a salutatory filled two columns, but the great political issues which were then absorbing public attention are not defined. The following paragraph is the only intimation of what the paper was to represent politically:

The free Democratic party standing alone upon consistent and uncompromising anti-slavery ground; acknowledging no other issue, and preferring honorable defeat to victory with sacrifice of principle; looking to the future as the harvest time of its labors, and waiting patiently for the wintry snows and summer suns to perfect the golden grain; stripped of its meretricious accessions of '48, was felt to be stronger and more vigorous than ever before.

It is always interesting to study business methods. The newspaper man finds nothing more difficult than to push his paper into circulation. Mr. Cullaton's plan is explained by the following notice at the head of the first editorial column:

All persons who receive this number, who are not already subscribers and not wishing to take the paper, will please return it by mail to our address immediately. We shall consider those who retain the copy as subscribers.

The Free Democrat supported Samuel Lewis for Governor in 1853, and announced John P. Hale, of New Hampshire, as its candidate for President in 1856. Mr. Howard retired from the editorship in 1853, and in November of that year D. S. Elliott purchased the establishment. Edward D. Howard again became editor, January 5, 1855, and a few weeks later suspended publication. The political party of which it was the organ had ceased to exist.

THE TRUE AMERICAN

was the follower of the Free Democrat, the latter being merged into the former. D. S. Elliott and J. M. Nash appeared as editors and publishers. It was a true representative of the old order of Know Nothingism in the days of the party of that idea. "Americans should rule America," was the party's platform and the paper's motto. The extension of slavery was incidentally opposed. A few sentences from the salutatory editorial may throw some light upon political history:

In refusing to confer the elective franchise upon aliens we deprive them of no rights they ever had, and consequently no wrong is done to them. We offer them an asylum here from the oppression of their own rulers, but we do not invite them here to rule us, at least not until they have lived long enough among us to understand something of our country, and the principles of true Americanism. In self defense we contend for some check to the vast political influence which is every day placed in foreign hands unfit to wield it intelligently, and which is fast tending to the overthrow of our whole political system, and must, if continued in, ultimately reduce us to a by-word and reproach among the nations of the earth—a people having the power but not the will to govern their own country.

That was a period of political change and it is not strange that a few months should find this paper supporting Chase and the Republican party.

In anti-war times politics was the leading business of a country newspaper. A little agriculture was thrown in for diversion, and a few locals to fill up. It is not strange that this should be the case, for papers were sustained, not as at present, on legitimate business principles, but as party organs, supported as a kind of political beneficiaries.

Mr. Nash withdrew from the True American in the fall of 1855, and Mr. Elliott sold the paper December 1, 1855, to Colonel James Dumars, of the Warren Chronicle. Colonel Dumars was a practical country journalist, a strong thinker, clear writer, and a cultured gentleman. He changed the name of his paper to

MAHONING REGISTER,

and made it the best journal the county had ever had. It was fully identified with the anti-slavery and Republican sentiment of the majority of people within the range of his constituency. During the war the Register was a welcome visitor to the camp of Mahoning soldiers. In its files during the war are contained many incidents from the field of local interest. John M. Edwards was associate editor of the Register during the latter part of Dumars' management. The paper changed hands April 1, 1865. V. E. Smalley & Co. purchased the office, Mr. Smalley assuming the editorship. Mr. Edwards continued as associate editor. Colonel Dumars, in his last issue, said of his successor:

In vacating the chair editorial, the retiring editor asks for his successor that kindness and good will which have uniformly been shown toward himself, feeling confident that it will be well deserved. The future editor, V. E. Smalley, has had considerable experience in the newspaper business, and is not altogether unknown to the readers of the Register, having been its associate editor a few months in 1863, and since that time an occasional correspondent from Washington city. He has also been connected with the editorial management of the Painesville Press and Advertiser and Cleveland Daily Herald, and will bring to the columns of the Register experience, energy, and ability that cannot fail to make it an able, interesting, and popular journal.

Mr. Smalley, with the assistance of Mr. Edwards, fulfilled this prediction. In about one year R. E. Hull was associated with Mr. Smalley, and in September, 1868, J. F. Hudson joined the firm under the firm of Smalley, Hull & Hudson. Colonel Dumars engaged, after leaving Youngstown, in a journalistic venture in Memphis, Tennessee, which resulted unfortunately.

In April, 1869, Mr. Smalley retired from the Register, and in January, 1870, the firm became Hull & Hudson. Mr. Hull retired in December, 1871. During his five years connection with the paper it was enlarged twice and steadily grew in public favor. James F. Hudson continued sole proprietor until December 11, 1873, when C. A. Vaughan, A. R. Seagrave, and W. H. Gault purchased the establishment. In May, 1874, W. L. Campbell purchased Mr. Gault's interest, Messrs. Seagrave & Campbell becoming the editors.

It is necessary now to go back a short time in the chronological order of events to notice the

YOUNGSTOWN TRIBUNE,

a sprightly Republican paper, which made its appearance February 18, 1874, as a daily and weekly. The publishers were James M. Nash, J. R. Johnston, James K. Bailey, and L. F. Shoaf. Mr. Nash assumed editorial management and continued in that capacity until September, 1874, when W. H. Eckman succeeded him. In just one year after its establishment the Tribune was consolidated with the Register under the name Youngstown Register and Tribune, the Register management continuing.

THE MAHONING COURIER

was established just after the war, by Patrick O'Connor & Bro. It was a vigorous Republican paper and divided Republican patronage with the Register until 1869, when its publication was suspended.

THE MAHONING VINDICATOR,

at present a leading Democratic paper in northern Ohio, made its first appearance in June, 1869. Youngstown had been without a Democratic paper for a long time, and the appearance of the Vindicator with the name of J. H. Odell as editor, had an encouraging effect upon the party. After about six months, Mark Shakey was associated with Mr. Odell, but retired in August, 1870. Mr. Odell retired from the paper in September, 1873, being succeeded by O. P. Wharton, an old compositor in the office. J. H. Odell and William A. Edwards purchased the office in April, 1874, Mr Odell taking editorial charge. In February, 1875, S. L. Everett purchased the office. Mr. Brown purchased from Everett in July, 1875, and continued its publication until succeeded by Vallandingham & Clark in April, 1880. O. P. Shaffer and O. P. Wharton were employed on the editorial staff during Mr. Brown's management. Judge L. D. Thoman purchased Vallandingham's interest in April, 1881. The paper is now published and edited by Thoman & Clark. The paper's political expressions are positive and emphatic, especially upon questions of party policy and management.

THE YOUNGSTOWN COMMERCIAL

was issued by Patrick O'Connor and L. F. Shoaf May 5, 1875. It suspended publication in about six months after that time. Patrick O'Connor began the publication of the

NEW STAR

May 28, 1879. It continued as a weekly journal and is the organ in the Mahoning valley of the National Greenback party.

THE YOUNGSTOWN RUNDCHAU

is the only German paper in the Mahoning valley. It was established by Hery Gentz, now of Cleveland, August 1, 1874. R. Wilbrandt had charge of its editorial management during the first year. Since August 1, 1875, William F. Maag has been editor and proprietor. He is a practical printer and before coming to Youngstown was employed in Fort Wayne, Indiana. The Rundchau has a circulation of seventeen hundred and the office has a paying job printing patronage.

THE FREE PRESS

was established in 1881, by O. P. Wharton, formerly of the Vindicator.

The first daily in Youngstown was the

MINER AND MANUFACTURER,

which first made its appearance as a daily in June, 1873. The weekly Miner and Manufacturer had been published for some time in the interest of the laboring men, Mr. A. D. Fassett being editor. During the strikes in 1873 Mr. Fassett took issue in favor of the strikers, which resulted in an attempt on part of a few business men to coerce him into a change of policy, by threatening a withdrawal of patronage. The latter they had a perfect right to do and the editor told them so, but he emphatically denied them the right to interfere with his columns, and to give emphasis to his indignation, ordered them from his office. This circumstance, like all such attempts to interfere with the legitimate liberties of the press, gave the paper prestige by stiffening the confidence of its constituency. A daily issue was shortly after announced, and in due time made its appearance as a five-column folio, which sold at two cents. It attained a circulation of eight hundred, and was soon enlarged to six columns. It was a very respectable local paper and was well received until the daily Tribune was started in 1874, which was enabled by good financial backing to take the lead. The Miner and Manufacturer struggled along till November, 1874, when it suspended publication, the editor being chosen to the city editorship of the Daily Register, which was started in December, 1874.

THE NEWS-REGISTER

has an unusual history; we say unusual, because it seldom happens in journalism that a new aspirant for public favor, however worthy, can long withstand the strong opposition of an established organ unless there be room on the field for both. Experience has abundantly proved that there is not room for two Republican dailies in Youngstown. When, therefore, on the 16th of July, 1877, a six-column, 22x30 inch daily, without dispatches, made its appearance, conservative newspaper men were disposed to remark that history was given another chance to repeat itself. The News first appeared as a local daily, and was published by an association of compositors composed of R. E. Hull, W. S. Styleman, E. K. Hull, Thomas Kerr, and Ellwood Kennedy. The proprietors struggled heroically until January, 1878, when an incorporated company was formed, the corporators being the original proprietors with the exception of J. M. Webb, who had taken the place of Mr. Kennedy. The first board of directors were: R. E. Hull, president; Mason Evans, secretary and treasurer; Thomas W. Sanderson, Jonathan Head, and L. D. Thoman. J. M. Webb took editorial charge and H. C. Schwab was chosen city editor. The paper began the publication of National Associated press dispatches, in July, 1879. In August, 1880, it announced itself squarely Republican in politics. The staff at that time consisted of O. P. Shaffer, managing editor; Charles Gray, assistant editor; and C. A. Smith, city editor. Six months later E. S. Durban took Gray's place as chief editorial writer. The News was published with daily and weekly editions till January 21, 1882, when the Register and News companies consolidated, making the capital stock of the new company $40,000. The News-Register was adopted as the name of the paper. The board of directors is constituted as follows: Frank B. Williams, T. W. Sanderson, Mason Evans, O. P. Shaffer, John Stambaugh, Robert McCurdy, and Thomas H. Wells. The News-Register is the largest two-cent evening daily in the State. October 1, 1855, took possession of the Warren Chronicle. Colonel Hapgood enlarged three years afterwards in 1858, made it the only practical country journalist, a strong and clear writer, and a cultured gentleman. Six years afterwards, in 1864, he changed the name of his paper to

MAHONING REGISTER,

and made it the best journal the county had ever had. It was fully identified with the anti-slavery and Republican sentiment of the majority of people within the range of his constituency. During the war the Register was a welcome visitor to the camp of Mahoning soldiers. In its files during the war are con-

SECRET SOCIETIES.

MASONIC.

Masonry in Mahoning county was first instituted at Canfield. The drafting and adoption of the following petition was the initial movement:

To the right worshipful master of the Grand lodge of the State of Ohio, the petition of the subscribers humbly sueth:

That your petitioners are brethren, members of the Masonic society, and having attained to the third degree in that art are desirous of enjoying the rights, privileges, and benefits resulting from the peculiar advantages of that honorable and ancient institution. That situated as your petitioners are, having residence no less than twenty miles from any regular lodge of Masons, we are prevented of the aforesaid privileges. That your petitioners made application to the brethren of Erie lodge for a letter of recommendation from them, have been there sufficiently vouched for as master Masons of good and respectable standing, and have obtained such letter of recommendation which is hereby transmitted to the R. W. G. M. That for the purpose of placing ourselves in a position where the benefits of Masonry may be reciprocally enjoyed and the practical principles thereof more fully understood and more strictly regarded, we do humbly pray the R. W. G. M. that he would grant us a dispensation of the by-laws of the Grand lodge of Ohio which prohibit any body of men to work as Masons without a charter from said Grand lodge and permit us to become installed a lodge to be known and recognized by the name of Western Star lodge, with all the privileges and powers of a master's lodge, to be holden at Canfield, Trumbull county, State of Ohio, monthly on the evening of the first Thursday preceding the full moon in every month; praying a dispensation in such a form and under such regulation as the constitution and by-laws of said Grand lodge shall prescribe and require, your petitioners pledging their honor as Masons and men in all cases to conform to all constitutional laws and regulations of the Grand lodge.

And we further pray that the R. W. G. M. may be pleased to appoint and install our dutiful and well beloved brother Elijah Wadsworth as our first worshipful grand master; our dutiful and well beloved Trial Tanner as our first senior warden, and our dutiful and well beloved brother Isaac Newton as our first junior warden.

And we further pray that the R. W. G. M. would please to direct our well beloved brother the grand secretary to make out without delay such charter or letter of authority as shall enable us to proceed to the institution of a regular lodge as aforementioned, and your petitioners as in duty bound will ever pray.

Dated at Canfield this 23d day of July, A. L. 5812, A. D. 1812.

Signed,

CHARLES A. BOARDMAN,	HENRY RIPLEY,
ELISHA WHITTLESEY,	CHARLES B. FITCH,
GEORGE STILSON,	RICHARD FITCH,
FRANCIS DOWLER,	WILLIAM LOGAN,
RAID WAY,	ARCHIBALD TANNER,
and AL TANNER,	LEWIS HOYT,
M. N. NEWTON,	JOHN NORTHROP.

and I[n] swer to this petition a dispensation was itorial on the "seventeenth day of January, in capacity of Redemption one thousand eight hun-Eckman sixteen, and of Masonry the five thousand eight hundred and fourteenth," by Henry L. Brush, R. W. G. M. John Leavitt, master of Erie lodge at Warren, was designated to institute the new lodge, but on account of sickness he could not attend. He appointed Judge George Tod his deputy. The following entry is the record of the consecration ceremonies:

CANFIELD, June 8, 1813.

The original petitioners, together with a number of brethren from adjacent lodges, met agreeably to appointment at the house of Zalmon Fitch, from which place they proceeded to the school house, where a very appropriate discourse was delivered by brother Darrow, of Vienna, after which they returned to the house of Mr. Fitch, when brother Tod proceeded to consecrate the lodge and install the following officers:

Elijah Wadsworth, master; Trial Tanner, senior warden; Isaac Newton, junior warden; Elisha Whittlesey, treasurer; John H. Patch, secretary; John Northrop, senior deacon; Richard Fitch, junior deacon; George Stilson, Archibald Tanner, stewards; Charles B. Fitch, Charles A. Boardman, tylers.

The lodge took rank as No. 21. Owing to the war, and other discouraging causes, it made little progress during the first year. Its work, however, in caring for the families of members, made the usefulness of the lodge felt. Shadwick Bostwick was the only member initiated during the first six months. Meetings were held with regularity, and were made clever social occasions. The "bottle" had not yet gone out of style, and was a powerful auxiliary in making meetings interesting. Masons in those days considered refreshments as necessary to a convocation as a room to meet in. But the brethren were among the most progressive members of society, and consequently the lodge was one of the first social organizations to abandon the common use of ardent spirits at meetings.

In the year 1828 this lodge suffered the experience of most other lodges in the United States in consequence of the reported murder of John Morgan. The last four meetings were held at Boardman, November 19th being the last, at which the following members were present: John Northrop, Daniel Titus, Henry Hubbard, Isaac Newton, Thomas T. Payne, Philo Cook, Elisha Blake, Harmon W. Austin.

Yielding to the bitter feeling of opposition, no more meetings were held until May, 1848, when the following brethren convened at Canfield: John Northrop, I. Chidister, I. Newton, A. Collar, William Schmick, William S. Reed, Isaac N. Lane, and Isaac Brookhart. The last four were visitors. Interest in the order revived, and the lodge grew somewhat in membership, though it had a small territory to draw from. Youngstown Masons belonged to Erie lodge, at Warren. Though few in numbers the Canfield lodge was composed of prominent and highly respectable men. It continued to hold its convocations at Canfield until the fall of 1852.

The initial steps toward forming a lodge of Free and Accepted Masons were taken in Youngstown in the year 1851. A dispensation was issued by the grand master March 18, 1852, to Mahoning lodge, in which Theodatus Garlick is designated grand master, John M. Webb senior warden, and Thomas H. Wells junior warden. The following were the dispensation members: Theodatus Garlick, John M. Webb, Thomas H. Wells, P. M. Kelley, W. H. Ross, William Braden, D. B. King, B. E. Betts, Abram A. Dekaff, Isaac Heaton, B. H. Lake, Samuel Cooper, A. J. Gardner, John Stambaugh, James H. Ford, James M. Lauridge, R. J. Price, Thomas Jones, William G. Moore, Reuben Carroll, Franklin Thorn, John Cramer, I. C. Allison. The lodge grew rapidly both in numbers and influence, and has ever since maintained its standing as the leading order in the county.

A charter was never granted to Mahoning lodge, instituted under the dispensation of March, 1852, when the proposition came before the grand lodge at Chillicothe at the regular meeting in October. A charter would have been granted, but the application was withdrawn upon the "occurrence of the facts and proceedings:"

That W. N. Prentice, worshipful master of the Western Star lodge and the delegate from said lodge, in compliance with the wishes of the members of Western Star lodge and of a resolution passed unanimously therein, offered the following resolution for adoption:

Resolved, That Western Star lodge No. 21, now holding its regular communications in Canfield, Mahoning county, be removed to, and hereafter hold its meetings in, Youngstown, provided the following be agreed to and adopted by the Grand lodge:

Resolved, That the petitioners for a new lodge at Youngstown have leave to withdraw their petition, provided the foregoing resolution be agreed to.

These resolutions were adopted, and Western Star lodge was accordingly removed to Youngstown, where its membership was consolidated with Mahoning lodge. The first officers of the consolidated lodge were: W. N. Prentice, W. M.; S. F. Cooper, S. W.; James H. Ford, J. W.;

John Stambaugh, secretary; Thomas Jones, treasurer; William Braden, senior deacon; J. B. King, junior deacon; Andrew J. Gardner, tyler. After the removal of the charter and effects of Western Star lodge to Youngstown, it was the only society of master Masons in the county till Hillman lodge was formed recently.

There are at present in Youngstown two blue lodges, a commandery, council, and chapter. Western Star lodge retains its old number, twenty-one. Hillman lodge, which includes in its membership some of the most prominent men in the city, ranks No. 481.

St. John's commandery No. 20, Knights Templar, draws its membership from Warren, Hartford, and other neighboring lodges. It takes a prominent place among the Ohio commanderies. Mahoning council No. 45, Royal and Select Masters, and Youngstown chapter No. 93, Royal Arch Masons, are in a flourishing condition. The lodge hall in the Savings' Bank building is neatly furnished, and handsomely finished.

HEBRON LODGE NO. 55, I. O. O. F.

Oddfellowship was instituted in Youngstown in the fall of 1845. Several members of the lodge at Warren having received honorable dismissal petitioned and obtained from the Grand lodge a charter. The ceremony of institution took place in the Mansion house, December 2, 1845. The following names appear on the charter: William Braden, Theodatus Garlick, John C. Grierson, R. G. Garlick, Frederick S. Smith, and Daniel J. Wick. William Braden was the first noble grand. His immediate successors were Joseph G. Haney and Joseph Wilder.

The early history of this lodge can be given but imperfectly, in consequence of the early records having been destroyed by fire. Meetings were held in a room in the Mansion house until 1849. During this period the lodge prospered and increased in membership. Among the more conspicuous initiates are found the names of James Calvin, Asahel Medbury, Joseph and Frank Barclay, Peter Ketter, and other prominent citizens. Of the original members, only one survives, Joseph Wilder, whose zeal has grown stronger with ripening age. The effects of the lodge were removed to the Porter block in 1849, which remained the place of meeting till 1865. During this period the lodge experienced many ups and downs, at times commanding attention and exerting an influence and at other times giving its friends reasonable solicitude lest even it should cease to maintain an organized existence. During the first meeting in January, 1864, while Dr. Bronson, of Newton Falls lodge, then acting as deputy grand master, was conducting the ceremony of installation of officers, a fire was discovered in the dressing room. The doctor, followed by several of his frightened brethren, made a rush for the door; but a number of the cooler heads remained to arrest the fire, in which they succeeded, but not until considerable damage had been done. In June, 1865, a second fire occurred, which totally destroyed the block, with all its contents, including all the property of the lodge—furniture, regalia, records, and charter. This loss was not allowed to interfere with the society's prosperity. Occurring just when soldiers were returning from the army and the benefits of Oddfellowship were most needed and most appreciated, no time was lost in securing facilities for carrying on its work. A subscription paper was circulated and more commodious and better furnished apartments than before were soon ready for occupancy. Since occupying Porter's block, these halls have successively been occupied: Chapman and Nash's, Ritter's and the present hall.

Oddfellowship in Youngstown has grown steadily since the war. In 1868 it was deemed expedient to divide the membership and accordingly Youngstown lodge was formed. Hebron may be considered the mother of four other lodges—Niles, Girard, Hubbard, and Mineral Ridge. Niles was formed of members from both Hebron and Mahoning lodge of Warren. On account of the destruction of records we are unable to give a full list of past noble grands. The following is a list since 1868: Henry Onions, Roswell Shurtleff, R. M. Wallace, Thomas Kay, Alexander N. Kay, Thomas Davis, John L. Alexander, Emanuel Guthman, John R. Davis, Samuel N. Smith, Edwin Webb, Volney Rodgers, David M. Osborn, Albert W. Yahus, James J. Harman, Henry M. Thullen, James Parfitt, Thomas Bowdich, Henry Palmer, Rudolph Wilbrandt, Jonathan Oatsy, William Kinsey, Henry Moreman.

YOUNGSTOWN LODGE INDEPENDENT ORDER OF ODD FELLOWS.

The division of Hebron lodge and the institution of Youngstown lodge originated in a belief that two lodges could work more effectually than one. The grand lodge was petitioned and a charter issued to the following members: John M. Edwards, Charles C. Chapman, Ezriah Pratt, Philip A. Palmer, L. R. Roberts, Isaac Fellows, James Sutch, Nelson Crandall, George B. Converse, Elmer O. Woodford, Henry Slosson, Hamson Keen, P. N. Wilder, J. M. Silliman, and James Predmore.

The lodge ranks No. 403 and was instituted by Special Deputy H. Y. Beebe, July 9, 1868. The first officers were John M. Edwards, noble grand; C. C. Chapman, vice-grand; P. A. Palmer, secretary; E. O. Woodford, permanent secretary; Isaac Fellows, treasurer. This lodge has had a steady growth, its present membership being one hundred and eighty-six. It has always maintained good standing since its institution. The following in the order given have passed the chair of noble grand: J. M. Edwards, C. C. Chapman, H. Slosson, E. O. Woodford, A. S. Williams, J. M. Silliman, Isaac Fellows, D. W. Smith, L. J. Jacobs, A. W. Jones, W. T. Hughes, P. Everhart, J. S. Lett, D. C. Daniels, E. Pratt, A. Hawn, M. Petitt, J. J. Morgan, J. C. Muter, G. Noll, E. H. Turner, J. H. Dalzell, L. D. Clark, Thomas Peate, R. Montgomery, J. D. Porter, M. S. Clark. The following members of this lodge were past grands from other lodges: James Sutch, N. Crandall, D. Rodgers, S. Werturf, D. P. Thomas, P. N. Wilder, Nelson Parker, and M. D. McCandless.

OTHER SOCIETIES.

Tod Grand Army Post was organized in Youngstown in November, 1879.

Royal Templars of Temperance, a secret temperance society, with insurance benefits connected, was organized in 1880.

Buckeye council No. 11, Royal Templars of Temperance, was instituted April 18, 1879, a temperance society with insurance connections.

Star of Albion lodge No. 55, Sons of St. George, formed in April, 1881, with thirty members; present membership, one hundred and ten.

Court Flower No. 6266, I. O. F., was established October 25, 1876, with forty members; present membership one hundred and thirty-five.

Crystal Fountain lodge No. 697, I. O. G. Templars, was organized by F. J. Pitney, July 28, 1874.

Youngstown lodge I. O. Rechabites was organized in October, 1880.

Youngstown Mænnerchor was organized January 1, 1863.

Youngstown Turnverein, an organization for physical improvement, was formed April 1, 1878.

Mahoning lodge Amalgamated Association of Iron, Steel, and Tin Workers, was organized in August, 1877.

Youngstown lodge No. 14, Amalgamated Association of Iron, Steel, and Tin Workers, was organized in 1875.

Star lodge No. 3, Amalgamated Association of of Iron, Steel and Tin Workers was organized April 24, 1880.

Wells lodge No. 17, Amalgamated Association of Iron, Steel, and Tin Workers, was organized August 24, 1876.

Enterprise lodge No. 9, was organized October, 1869.

Valley lodge No. 12, Amalgamated Association of Iron, Steel, and Tin Workers, was formed November 1, 1879.

The Royal Arcanum was organized September 25, 1879.

The Harmonics was organized in 1877, an organization for the promotion of dramatic power and intellectual improvement.

The Philharmonics was organized in September, 1880.

Youngstown Temperance Union was formed May, 1877.

Young People's Temperance organization was formed November 21, 1878.

CHAPTER VIII.
BIOGRAPHICAL SKETCHES.
JOHN YOUNG.

In August, 1875, in response to a request from John M. Edwards, corresponding secretary of the Mahoning Valley Historical society, Charles C. Young, of Brooklyn, New York, fourth son of John Young, the founder of Youngstown, and to which he gave his name, furnished a biographical sketch of his father, which is published in the Collections of the society, and from which we have prepared the following:

The family is of Scotch origin, and settled in the north of Ireland, near Londonderry, in the sixteenth or seventeenth century. "Here, in 1623, the first of the family whose record is known to us was born. In 1718, in his ninety-sixth year, with his son and grandson, their brothers and sisters, and sisters' husbands, in all fourteen, formed a part of a Scotch-Irish colony, which sailed away from Ireland and landed in Boston, Massachusetts, the same year." One of the descendants settled in Petersborough, Hillsborough county, New Hampshire, and there "John Young was born in 1763, emigrated to Whitestown, New York, about 1780, and in June, 1792, was married to his life-long wife, Mary Stone White, the youngest daughter of Hugh White, the first settler and original proprietor of a large tract of wild land." Mr. White was of English descent; had moved, in 1785, with his family, from Middletown, Connecticut, to this land, founded a town, to which he gave his name, became, in time, a judge of the court, and died in 1812."

"John Young lived in Whitestown until 1796, when his own land interest was removed to Ohio, and in 1797 he began the settlement of Youngstown. In 1799 he removed with his family, wife and two children, John and George, to Youngstown, where two more were born to him, William, in November, 1799, and Mary, in February, 1802. In 1803 Mrs. Young, finding the trials of her country life there, with the latch-string always out, and a table free to all, too great with her young family, for her power of endurance, Mr. Young, in deference to her earnest entreaties, closed up his business as best he could, and returned with his family to Whitestown, and to the home and farm which her father had provided and kept for them."

"Our father's nominal occupation after his return was that of a farmer, but not much given to manual labor. He soon became interested in the Great Western turnpike, from Utica to Canandaigua, and for many years was engaged in its construction and superintendency; and still later on other public works, such as the Erie canal, which canal ran for miles in sight of our house, and upon which one of my brothers was then employed as civil engineer.

"He was a Mason of high order, and brought back with him from Ohio the prefix of 'judge,' by which he was ever known and addressed. In some incidental way it came to him, and remained a fixture for life." It came in this way: He was one of the justices of the peace and quorum, and, as such, sat upon the bench at the first Territorial court held at Warren in 1800. His name stands on the record first in the list of justices holding the court, and he probably was the president. Hence, the title of judge. "With great strength of will and force of character, he was full of intelligence, courtesy, and kindness, a genial soul, who made many friends and but few enemies that we ever heard of.

"He died quietly at his home, after a long but a severe illness, in April, 1825, aged sixty-two years, twenty-two years after his return from Youngstown. Our mother survived him fourteen years, and died at last full of joyful hope, in September, 1839, in the old home of her father, in the village of Whitestown, New York, aged sixty-seven years."

JAMES HILLMAN.

No man, in the early days of the Reserve, was more widely known than Colonel Hillman, and the name of no one connected with its settlement and the traditions of the pioneer days has been transmitted to these latter days more honored. We shall only attempt a brief biographical sketch, imperfect, especially as to his youth, and only an outline. He was born in Northumberland county, Pennsylvania. He was a soldier in the Revolutionary war, and after the war, with his father, he moved West, and made his home for a time in a cabin on the banks of the Ohio river, about three miles below Pittsburg.

The first authentic account of his early history and the business in which he was engaged, is contained in a letter from him to Judge Barr, of Cleveland, dated November 23, 1843, found on page 363 of Colonel Whittlesey's Early History of Cleveland, from which we make extracts:

In the spring of 1786 Messrs. Duncan & Wilson entered into a contract with Messrs. Caldwell & Elliott, of Detroit, to deliver a quantity of flour and bacon at the mouth of the Cuyahoga river to a man named James Hawder, an Englishman, who had a tent at the mouth of the river for the purpose of receiving it. In May, 1786, I engaged with Duncan & Wilson, at Pittsburg, as a packhorseman, and started immediately. We took the Indian trail for Sandusky, until we arrived at the "Standing Stone," on the Cuyahoga, a little below the mouth of Breakneck creek, where the village of Franklin is now. There we left the Sandusky trail and took one direct to the mouth of Tinker's creek, where was a little town built by Heckewelder and Zeisberger, with a number of Moravian Indians. They were Moravian preachers. Here we crossed the Cuyahoga, and went down the west side to the mouth. In going down we passed a small log tradinghouse, where one Meginnis traded with the Indians. He had left the house in the spring before we were there. . . . We made six trips that summer. On the second trip, one Hugh Blair, a packhorseman, in crossing Breakneck creek fell backwards from his horse and broke his neck. His horse got his foot fast in some beech roots. We called it Breakneck creek, a name, I believe, it has always retained. . . Caldwell & Clark had a small sail-boat to carry the flour and bacon to Detroit. We used to cross the river by means of the Mackinaw, that being the name of the sail boat. . . . There was a spring near where Main street comes to the river. We made collars of our blankets for some of the horses, and took our tent ropes, made of raw elk skin, for tugs, drew small logs and built a hut at the spring, which, I believe, was the first house built on the Cleveland side. At that time there were no traders about the mouth of the river, only Hawder's tent, who was there to receive the flour and bacon.

After this, as perhaps he had done prior, he made a voyage up the Mahoning river trading with the Indians, and it was upon one of these voyages, in 1796 or 1797, that he met John Young, near Spring common, in Youngstown, who had just arrived with his company to survey the townships he had purchased of the Connecticut Land company, into lots. He then made such arrangements with Mr. Young that shortly after he removed, with his wife and a few household goods, from his old home on the Ohio river to his new, future, and lifelong home in Youngstown. He at first built a log house on the east side of the river. Afterwards he moved on a farm of about sixty acres which he purchased of Mr. Young, on the west side of the river, on which, tradition says, he built a frame house and that it was the first frame house in the township. In 1804 he sold about an acre of this farm, extending on the east to the middle of the river, to Caleb Plum, who built thereon a grist- and saw-mill, the first in the village, and it is said that then or afterwards Hillman had some interest in the mill. He removed back to the village about 1808, and kept a tavern in a log house, still standing on Federal street next west of the town hall, but now covered with boards. He went out as wagonmaster in Colonel Rayen's regiment in the War of 1812. On his return he sold out his tavern, purchased a farm east of Crab creek, on which he erected a large frame house, still standing on the north side of East Federal street extension, and in which he kept a tavern. In 1818 he sold this farm to Homer Hine, and removed to a house on the northeast corner of Federal and Walnut streets, where he kept a tavern until about 1824, when he purchased a farm on the west side of the river, to which he removed and where he resided until his death.

On the occurrence, July 20, 1800, of the memorable tragedy at the salt springs, about nine miles northwest of Youngstown, the shooting of Captain George and Spotted John, two Indians, by Joseph McMahon and Richard Storer, consternation spread throughout the sparse settlement, and fear of revenge by the Indians was felt in every cabin. James Hillman came to the rescue. He followed the Indians, who had gone west, pacified them, averted the threatened disaster, and has ever been regarded as the preserver of the infant Reserve.

At the first Territorial court held in Trumbull county, August 25, 1800, he was appointed constable of Youngstown. At the first township election, in April, 1802, he was elected appraiser of houses and was re-elected several times. He was frequently elected township trustee. In 1806 he was elected sheriff of Trumbull county. On February 16, 1808, he was commissioned by the Governor as lieutenant-colonel, commandant of the Second regiment, First brigade, Fourth division Ohio militia, and took the official oath March 19, 1808, before George Tod, judge of the supreme court. On his commission is an indorsement dated November 4, 1809, signed by Samuel Huntington, Governor and Commander-in-chief of the State of Ohio, "That upon the representation of Mr. Hillman that he is about removing out of the State of Ohio, and is of an age that excuses him from military duty in time of peace, and tendered his resignation of his said office, I have thought fit, in consideration of the reason above mentioned, to accept his resignation and he is accordingly discharged from any further service in the office above said." He did not remove from the State as he then contemplated. In 1814 he was elected Representative in the State Legislature, Wilson Elliott being his co-Representative and Turhand Kirtland Senator. In 1825 he was elected justice of the peace and held the office several years.

He was married before he came to Youngstown, and this is the romantic story of his wedding: After his return from his service as a soldier in the Revolutionary war he attended a husking frolic somewhere in western Pennsylvania, and there he met Miss Catharine — (we are unable to learn her maiden name). After the husking there was dancing. James was pleased with Catharine, danced with her several times, proposed marriage, she assented, and a 'squire being one of the company, a halt was made in the dancing, the 'squire assumed the magisterial look and office, the magic words were said, the nuptial knot was tied and Catharine became Mrs. Hillman. She was his partner through his life, and was the first white woman who ever visited Youngstown, the pioneer female settler of the Reserve, and was everywhere known and praised for her hospitality, benevolence, and many estimable traits of character. There were no children of this marriage. She survived her husband about seven years, and, as her tombstone records the date, she died August 7, 1855, at the venerable age of eighty-three years. Colonel Hillman was always known as a strictly moral man. He joined the Methodist Episcopal church in 1820. He was shrewd, active, industrious, brave, kind-hearted, a good neighbor and a good citizen. He had some education, could write a fair hand, and was a good business man. In person he was about five feet eight inches in height, stout and muscular. He was reared a hardy frontiersman and was just the man to be one of the pioneers in the new settlement. A sandstone slab in Oak Hill cemetery records the date of his birth and death:

In Memory of Colonel James Hillman, born October 27, 1762, died November 12, 1848, aged 86 years, 1 month, and 15 days.

CALEB BALDWIN.

Caleb Baldwin was born in October, 1753, in Mendham, New Jersey. We have but little information of his early history. We learn, however, that he enlisted in the army in the Revolutionary war, that he was a gunsmith, and during the war he was sent home to make guns. He removed to Washington county, Pennsylvania, soon after the war, and removed from there to Youngstown, Ohio, in 1799 or in 1800. He was one of the first justices of the peace of Youngstown and was appointed under the Territorial government as early as August, 1880, as appears from the records of the first Territorial court then held at Warren, and was continued in the office for several years. Soon after his arrival in Youngstown he erected a large double log-house on a lot in the town plat which he had purchased (the lot on which E. M. McGillin & Co.'s store now stands), in which he kept tavern for a few years. He was licensed to keep a tavern by the court at its May term, 1801, and was probably the first tavern-keeper in the village. He bought other land in the township and engaged in farming. In those early days he was one of the most prominent and influential men, and was always held in high esteem by his fellow citizens. He was married while residing in New Jersey to Miss Elizabeth Pitney, who was born in Morristown, New Jersey, July 23, 1860. They were the parents of twelve children, a part of whom removed with them to Youngstown, and one or more were born there. Their names were Eunice, married to Eliab Axtell, of Middletown, Mercer county, Pennsylvania, they removed to Youngstown in 1802 and resided there during their lives; Phœbe, married to Thomas Kirkpatrick, of Youngstown; Polly; Amanda; Andrew; Betsey, married to John Kimmel, of Youngstown; Stephen, married at Youngstown, November 3, 1800, to Rebecca Rush, the first marriage in the township, and the first recorded marriage on the Reserve; Elizabeth, married to Andrew Kirkpatrick, and settled in Coitsville, Ohio; Caleb; Byram; Nehemiah, and Benjamin Pitney, born March 24, 1802, now residing on his farm in Milton, Mahoning county, and probably the oldest person living born in Youngstown. Esquire Baldwin, the name by which he was most generally known, lived but a few years after removing to Youngstown. An old and partially defaced sandstone slab, in Oak Hill cemetery, removed from the old and first graveyard in the city, informs us of the date of his death and of his worth:

> In Memory of
> Caleb Baldwin, Esq., who departed this life February 19, 1810, in the 67th year of his age.
> He loved the Church, he loved God,
> He sought no worldly pomp or fame,
> The way of piety he trod,
> And well deserves the Christian's name.

His wife survived him over forty years; she died May 19, 1850, aged nearly ninety years.

WILLIAM RAYEN.

William Rayen was born October 21, 1776, in Kent county, Maryland. He resided in Maryland until his removal to Ohio, and for a few years was clerk in a country store, and after he attained his majority was engaged in the storekeeping business. In 1802 he removed to Youngstown, Ohio, where he shortly after commenced keeping a public house. The first township meeting, as we learn from the records, was held in April of that year, at the inn of William Rayen. He kept public house until about 1812, but continued in mercantile business, in which he engaged some time after his arrival, until 1837, a considerable part of the time without a partner, but from 1814 for a few years in partnership with James Mackey, as Rayen & Mackey. He was postmaster of Youngstown from 1818 to 1839, and kept the post-office in his store. In 1804 he was elected treasurer of Youngstown township. In 1805 he was elected township clerk, and by annual elections continued in that office until 1809, and was again elected in 1810, 1811, 1812, and 1816. In August, 1812, as colonel of the First regiment, Third brigade, Fourth division of Ohio militia, and in command of his regiment, he marched to the western frontier where he spent several months, serving with distinction. On November 22, 1819, he was commissioned a justice of the peace. On August 27, 1820, he was commissioned by Ethan Allen Brown, Governor, as an associate judge of the court of common pleas in Trumbull county. In 1840 he was elected by the Legislature a member of the board of public works of the State for five years from April 1, 1840, and served in that office during his term. In 1850 the Mahoning County bank, located at Youngstown, was organized. He was one of its founders, and one of the largest stockholders. At the first election of officers he was elected president, and annually re-elected during his life.

Soon after his arrival in Youngstown he purchased of John Young, proprietor of the township, a considerable tract of land in and near the village, which he improved, and was thenceforth engaged at times largely in agriculture, and was always active in promoting agricultural improvements. In 1819, with other prominent citizens of Trumbull county, he assisted in forming an agricultural society which was the first on the Reserve, and probably in Ohio. He was elected corresponding secretary of the society. He was always in favor of public improvements and enterprises of a public nature, and ready with his purse to aid them. He was one of the corporators named in the act chartering the Pennsylvania & Ohio Canal company, passed by the Legislature of Ohio in 1827, and was subsequently a stockholder and director of the company. In after years he was one of the original stockholders of the Cleveland & Mahoning Railroad company, whose road has been so efficient in promoting the prosperity of his adopted home.

Although he was not blest with children of his own, yet he was always strongly interested in the education of youth, and was liberal in the support of schools. This liberality and interest was manifested in his will, leaving a large fund to be appropriated to the education of the youth of the township. With this fund was founded the well-known and admirably managed Rayen school. A clause of his will deserves mention and quotation, viz: "As this school is designed for the benefit of all youth of the township, without regard to religious denominations or differences, and that none may be excluded for such or the like reasons or grounds, I hereby prohibit the teaching therein of the peculiar religious tenets or doctrines of any denomination or sect whatever; at the same time I enjoin that no others be employed as teachers than those of good moral character and habits." To enable carrying out the provisions of the will an act was passed by the Legislature "to provide for the government of schools and academies specially endowed." By virtue of the provisions of this act, at the June term, A. D. 1857, of the court of common pleas of Mahoning county, Jonathan Warner, Charles Howard, Charles C. Cook, James Mackey, and Robert W. Tayler, respectively for one, two, three, four, and five years, were appointed and incorporated as trustees of the fund, and it was ordered "that the corporate name of said trustees be the trustees of the Rayen school," each to give bond in five thousand dollars, a new trustee in the place of the one retiring to be appointed yearly by the court. On July 7, 1858, the executors delivered to the trustees money, stocks, etc., amounting to the nominal sum of $31,390.90. A lot was purchased by the trustees, and a large and commodious school building erected with the interest of the fund, as it accrued, the will providing that none of the principal should be used for those purposes, and in 1866 the school was opened with forty scholars, by Professor Edwin S. Gregory as principal, and Miss Emma Cutler as assistant. Professor Gregory continued as principal until 1878; Miss Cutler resigned as assistant some years before that time, and was succeeded by Miss Florence Rayen, a niece of Judge Rayen. Professor Middleton S. Campbell is now (1882) principal, with Miss Florence Rayen, Miss Mary D. Campbell, and Professor F. S. Kimball assistants. The number of scholars in attendance is one hundred and fifteen. The fund bearing interest, through the judicious and careful management of the trustees, has increased to $70,000. The present trustees are Robert McCurdy, John Stambaugh, Augustus B. Cornell, Cecil D. Hine, and Henry O. Bonnell.

JAMES McCAY.

James McCay (or M'Coy as he was more usually called), one of the earliest pioneers, was born on the eastern shore of Maryland, about 1769, on the plantation of his father, who owned about three hundred slaves. Of his early life we know little, but, as he was acquainted with mercantile business when he came, and engaged in it afterwards, it is probable he had been engaged in it, and, as is supposed, in Philadelphia. He crossed the mountains from Philadelphia to Pittsburg and came to Youngstown on horseback, in company with John S. Edwards, afterwards a lawyer of Warren, Ohio. The time of his arrival was probably in the spring of 1799, as letters of Mr. Edwards, still preserved, show that he then made this journey. We can only infer what business Mr. McCay engaged in after his arrival, but the records and such information as we have indicate that he was a man of note.

In August, 1801, with two others, he was appointed, by the Territorial court, to view and lay out a public road from Youngstown, west of the river, through Boardman to Poland. In 1801, when it was contemplated to establish a post-office at Youngstown, he was recommended for postmaster by General Wadsworth, who was corresponding with the department in regard to the matter. But Calvin Pease was appointed January 1, 1802, and the reason why Mr. McCay did not receive the appointment is said, by his daughter, Mrs. Reno, to have been that he declined the appointment, as he was then preparing to remove from the place, which he soon did. At a court held at Warren in February, 1802, it was ordered that a town meeting be held on first Monday of April ensuing, in Youngstown, at the house of James McCay. The township records show that the meeting was held at the house of William Rayen, inn-keeper. It was probably held at the house owned or occupied by Mr. McCay when the order was made, but that Mr. Rayen, who arrived in Youngstown early in 1802, had bought him out before the time came for holding the meeting, and it is also probable that Mr. McCay had kept an inn or place of public entertainment. Another incident is related by Mrs. Reno as having occurred in 1801. She says that when Judge Tod removed his family from Connecticut to Youngstown in the spring of that year, he came with his wife and two children in a wagon; that he was stopped by a swamp in Poland, and sent to Youngstown for help. John Young and Mr. McCay went to his assistance, each with a pair of oxen, and pulled him through.

From this we may infer that Mr. McCay was in some business in which oxen were used. He left Youngstown in 1802 or 1803 and went to New Orleans. He remained there about six months and returned to Philadelphia. There, in 1805, he was married to Miss Sarah Randall, a Quakeress. She is said to have been a very handsome woman, tall and graceful, of a highly cultivated mind, and with pleasing manners and kindly disposition. She always, during life, dressed in the Quaker costume. She survived her husband about ten years and died in 1849. He kept a store in Philadelphia from 1805 to 1814, when he removed to Pittsburg, remained there until 1829, engaged in mercantile business, when he returned to Youngstown. He erected a frame building on the northwest corner of the Diamond and Federal street, in which he kept store for about a year and then sold out his goods, converted the building into a tavern, which he kept until his death in July, 1839. As a tavern-keeper he was very popular. Travelers would often continue their journey to a late hour in the evening to stop at McCay's tavern, and the house was frequently so full of people that many slept on the floor. It was, while he kept it, the chief hotel in the place.

When he came to Youngstown the second time he brought out a Franklin stove to burn bituminous coal. It cost $25 in Pittsburg. Mr. Rayen wanted the stove and Mr. McCay let him have it, and sent to Pittsburg and had a wrought iron grate made, set it in the tavern and burnt coal in it for years. This was the first use of coal in a stove or grate in Youngstown. The coal was obtained from the bank of Mary Caldwell, on the west side of Crab creek, the first coal bank opened in the township. Coal had previously been taken from that bank for blacksmith's use. He was a tall man, over six feet high, well proportioned, fair complexion, sandy hair, well educated, and was a prominent and a leading man in the township, and in this section. As has been mentioned, his father was a slaveholder. When his father's estate was divided among his children, on his decease, McCay gave their freedom on the spot to those slaves who fell to his share. Mr. and Mrs. McCay were the parents of four children, all born in Philadelphia, two sons, who died young, and two daughters, Rachel and Sarah, now living in Youngstown. Rachel was married, in 1837, to Francis Reno, of Beaver, Pennsylvania, a civil engineer, who was employed on the Pennsylvania & Ohio canal, and was a son of Rev. Francis Reno, a pioneer Episcopal clergyman and also a large farmer in Beaver, Pennsylvania. He died September 3, 1863, aged fifty-eight years. Mr. and Mrs. Reno were the parents of six children, viz: James M., Henry, Sallie, Grace, Henrietta (married to John McCurdy, of Danville, New York), and David.

ROBERT MONTGOMERY.

Robert Montgomery was born April 5, 1773, in Danville, Chester county, Pennsylvania. He was of Scotch-Irish descent. He was son of General William Montgomery, who was a colonel in the Revolutionary army, and a member of Congress when it sat in Philadelphia. Of his early history we know but little. His father was a surveyor, and he was also a surveyor, and while a young man was employed as assistant to the surveyor-general of Pennsylvania. While performing the duties of his office in Western Pennsylvania, prior to the settlement of the Reserve, he made a journey of exploration up the Mahoning river, and visited the site of Youngstown. He related to his children that from the mouth of Dry run in the southeast part of Youngstown, east to the township line, or beyond, the land bordering on the Mahoning on the northeast, and back to the rising land, was an Indian cornfield. This cornfield was part of the farm which he afterwards, between 1812 and 1816, purchased, and on which he spent the remainder of his days. It is now part of the manufacturing village of Hazelton, a suburb of Youngstown.

He also, during his younger days, acquired a knowledge of the furnace business, both as regards construction and method of working.

He came to Ohio again as early as 1805, perhaps earlier, selected a suitable site, which he had probably discovered on his first visit, for a furnace, on Yellow creek, in Poland township. This site was on the farm of John Struthers, and iron ore, limestone, and wood for charcoal were abundant in that vicinity, and a good water power was obtained by constructing a dam across the creek. In partnership with Mr. Struthers he erected the furnace, and it was put in blast in 1806 or 1807, and was the first furnace successfully run in Ohio. Dan Eaton had built a furnace on the same stream a year or two before, but it had not worked successfully, and in 1807 Mr. Montgomery and his partners bought the furnace and all the ore and other rights of Mr. Eaton, and it was not run afterwards. James Mackey, Robert Alexander, and David Clendenin became interested as partners in the Montgomery furnace, and it was run successfully until the War of 1812 interrupted the business, and it was not resumed.

After closing up the furnace business, Mr. Montgomery purchased and removed on to his farm in Youngstown. He was elected a justice of the peace in after years and held that office for some time. He was also at some period, either in Pennsylvania or Ohio, major in the militia, and was usually called Major Montgomery. He was well educated and a man of good general information. He was not an aspirant for office, but kept well posted on political matters, was decided in his political opinions and, at all proper times, free to express them. He died in 1857. He was married in Pennsylvania. His wife died young, leaving one child, Mary, now Mrs. Corry, born about 1801. He was again married in 1814, to Mrs. Louisa M. Edwards, widow of John S. Edwards. There were three children born of this marriage, two of whom, Robert Morris and Caroline Sarah (married to Dr. Moses Hazeltine, now deceased), are residents of Youngstown. Ellen Louise, the youngest, married to Samuel Hine, died in June 1854, leaving one son, Cecil Dwight Hine, now a lawyer of Youngstown, Ohio.

ROBERT M. MONTGOMERY.

Robert Morris Montgomery was born in Youngstown, Ohio, October 20, 1815. He was son of Robert and Louisa M. (Morris) Montgomery. He attended the schools in Youngstown and the seminary at Farmington, Ohio, and acquired a good English education. He also worked on his father's farm, became a good, practical farmer, and after attaining his majority took charge, in a measure, of the farm, in company with his father. They made sheep-growing a specialty and were among the most successful in that business in this section of country. The son was at one period president of the Wool Growers' association and of its general convention. He is regarded as an authority in all matters relating to wool growing. In 1862-63 he represented Mahoning county in the State Legislature. He has been elected assessor of real estate and has held other township offices. He is president of the Mahoning Valley Historical society. He has resided all his life on the large paternal farm, of which he inherited a portion, in the southeast part of the township, and is passing the evening of his days quietly in the practice of his favorite avocation of a farmer. He was married at Farmington, Ohio, September 13, 1837, to Miss Nancy H., daughter of Lewis and Mary (Higgins) Wolcott, of that place. They have two children, Lewis W., born November 5, 1838, married June, 1872, to Miss Belle Cushman; and Mary Corry, born November 20, 1843, married December 9, 1868, to Theron McKinley.

JAMES MACKEY.

Among the early settlers of the Western Reserve who became prominent and influential citizens, was James Mackey. He was born in Chester county, Pennsylvania, in 1776. We have but limited information of his history prior to his arrival on the Reserve. It was at that time evident, however, that his early years had been industriously passed, and that his education had been well cared for. He was then a well trained practical surveyor, an excellent accountant, and a good mathematician.

He came from Pennsylvania to Poland, Ohio, about 1805, assisted Robert Montgomery in building a furnace on Yellow creek, became an owner in the furnace, and from his first connection with it until it ceased operations about 1812, was book-keeper of the company. An explanation of the cause of his joining Mr. Montgomery at Poland may be found, probably, in the fact that the latter was a Pennsylvanian and a surveyor, who had been a State surveyor, or one of the assistants of the surveyor-general of Pennsylvania, and while engaged in the duties of that office had become acquainted with Mr. Mackey and his business capacity, and, requiring the aid of a man of that character, had invited Mr. Mackey to join him in his furnace enterprise.

On the declaration of war with Great Britain in 1812 he entered the army, and was promoted to the office of adjutant in the Fourth division of Ohio militia, commanded by Major-general Wadsworth. During the war he was also assistant paymaster of the division, and his accurate rolls, and their careful preservation, was of great aid to the soldiers in after years in enabling them to furnish evidence of their military service, and thereby obtain bounty land warrants and pensions. His early training and business capacity well qualified him for these positions, and his kind and generous treatment of the soldiers won him their gratitude, affection, and respect. His military employments gave him the rank and title of major.

About 1816 he entered into mercantile business, in partnership with Colonel William Rayen, under the firm of Rayen & Mackey, in a log store building on the northeast corner of Federal and Holmes streets, in Youngstown, Ohio. This partnership continued several years and during it he purchased a farm of two hundred and seventy-five acres, northeast of the present city of Youngstown. He was married September 10, 1823, to Miss Margaret Farley, of Coitsville, Ohio, and about that time moved onto his farm, which was thenceforth his home. In addition to the usual business of farming, he devoted great attention to stock raising and its improvement. Colonel Rayen owned a farm in the neighborhood in the adjoining township of Coitsville, and as both were fine grazing farms, there was a lively but friendly rivalry between these farmers in the business of raising fine cattle and swine. Major Mackey's "big yoke of oxen" was well known in the streets of Youngstown, and in the surrounding country, and was the subject of much commendation and admiration. They were the best in this region. In connection with his other business his well known ability as a land surveyor gave him much employment in that line. He was frequently elected by his fellow-citizens of the township and county to public offices. In 1814 he was elected township clerk, in 1822 and 1823, township trustee, and in subsequent years trustee, supervisor of highways, fence viewer, overseer of the poor, and justice of the peace. In 1819 he was elected county commissioner for a term of three years. In 1822 he was elected Representative from Trumbull county in the General Assembly. Cyrus Bosworth was his associate. There were nine candidates. Major Mackey received eight hundred and seven votes, Mr. Bosworth eight hundred and twelve votes. The highest vote received by any other candidate was five hundred and sixty-nine by Isaac Heaton. Tracy Bronson received four hundred and eight votes, Turhand Kirtland three hundred and sixty-seven votes, Calvin Cone one hundred and sixty-eight votes, the others less than one hundred votes each. The candidates, judging from the Western Reserve Chronicle, from which this vote is taken, do not appear to have run on any regular political or party a ticket, but rather on their popularity and merits as men. The Legislature convened in Columbus, December 1, 1822, and Major Mackey traveled from his home in Youngstown to Columbus on horseback, riding his superior, favorite, and well known roan horse, "Bob," which he kept there during the winter, and rode him back in the spring. In 1830 he was elected treasurer of Trumbull county for two years, and in collecting the taxes he each year visited all the thirty-five townships of "Old Trumbull," performing his journeys on horseback on his old favorite, "Bob."

Matters of difference between his neighbors and others, which otherwise might have occasioned long and expensive litigation, were often referred to him for settlement, and his decision, rendered only on full investigation of the facts, was always accepted by them as final.

This is but an outline biographical sketch of a good man. Many interesting anecdotes and incidents of his life are related. He was a man of good general information, always active and industrious, public spirited, of strict integrity, possessing great firmness and decision of character, of good judgment, and standing high in the confidence, respect, and esteem of his fellow-citizens.

He died August 15, 1844, aged sixty-eight years. His wife died May 14, 1870, aged seventy-two years. They were the parents of eight children, of whom three died young. The others, David, Nancy (intermarried with the late Dr. William Breaden), James, Robert, Letitia (intermarried with Andrew Kirk), are among our most valued and respected citizens.

The three brothers have been extensively engaged in partnership, for the last ten years in the real estate business in Youngstown, and to their energy and enterprise the city of Youngstown is indebted for its first street railroad, built on Federal street in the spring of 1875. Robert, whose general business is farming, was a representative from Mahoning county, in 1878-9, in the Ohio Legislature, having been elected to that position by a large majority over a very popular competitor. James, by profession a civil engineer and surveyor, had, for a period of twenty years prior to 1874, when he quit mine surveying, perhaps the most extensive practice in the business of surveying coal mines of any one in the State of Ohio. Recently he was one of the Ohio commissioners, appointed by the Governor of the State to resurvey and establish the boundary line between Ohio and Pennsylvania. He still continues in the practice of his profession, in which he ranks among the most eminent.

DAN EATON.

Dan Eaton was one of two or three brothers who came from Pennsylvania to Ohio soon after the settlement of the Reserve, as early as 1803, and probably earlier. We first find him in Poland township, upon Yellow creek, about one and one-fourth miles south of its junction with the Mahoning river, where he is preparing to construct a furnace, and this, the first authentic information in regard to him, is derived from a contract made June 23, 1807, between him and Robert Alexander and David Clendenin, in which he contracts to sell them the "Hopewell" furnace, as he has named it, and one hundred and two acres of land, on which it stands, which he holds by contract with Turhand Kirtland, and also "his interest in and to the whole of the iron ore on the plantation of Lodwick Ripple, as held by said Dan, under a certain agreement between him and said Lodwick, dated 31st day of August, 1803," also certain other rights to wood, etc. On that day, August 31, 1803, as appears by this document, he made a contract for iron ore preliminary to building a furnace. On October 17, 1804, as further appears by this document, he made contracts with others for wood for charcoal to run the furnace, which probably then was nearly ready to start. But at what time he "blew in" we only learn from tradition, which places it from 1804 to 1806. He was undoubtedly here before making that contract for ore in 1803. Tradition says he came about 1800.

As it may be interesting at this day to learn the purchase price of the furnace, etc., we quote from the contract. The purchasers agree to pay said Dan "$200 then in hand and $300 in sixty days from the date of said articles of agreement, and forty thousand pounds of good castings on the 1st day of July, 1808; forty thousand pounds on the same day of July, 1809; forty thousand pounds on the same day of July, 1810, at the furnace aforesaid, or $85 per two thousand pounds, and to pay Turhand Kirtland the original purchase money of said lot of land not to exceed $350," etc. This makes the price of the furnace, ore rights, etc, $5,600, and of the land not quite $3.50 per acre.

We next learn of him at Niles, Trumbull county, where he and his brother James built a forge and used the pig iron made at the Yellow creek furnaces and paid on the contract as above recited. In 1812 or 1813, with his brother James, and perhaps others of the family, he built a furnace at Niles, which was in operation as late as 1856. About 1825 with his brother James, Reese and Isaac Heaten, sons of James, and Eli Phillips, he built a furnace on Mill creek, in Youngstown, the first in the township, a short distance below the Mahoning falls. About this time and for many years after he resided on a small farm on the west side of Mill creek, near its junction with the Mahoning, part of the tract originally purchased, on which to locate the furnace. His name was originally Daniel Heaton, but he had it contracted by act of Legislature to Dan Eaton, for the reason, as he alleged, that the letters cut off were superfluous. He had not received the benefit of much education in his early life, but he had a good mind, was fond of reading and possessed a fair stock of general information. He published a book called The Christian's Manual, setting forth his religious belief and advocating universal brotherhood. In his younger days he was an ardent Methodist; afterwards he held deistical views, and in his latter years he adopted many of the notions of the Spiritualists. During the fifteen or twenty last years of his life he devoted much of his time to talking and writing on finance. His favorite idea, on which he elaborated at length when he could find a listener, was that banks should not issue currency, but that all paper money should be notes issued by the United States Treasury, and made a legal tender; that offices should be established in the several States for loaning these notes, and that the Government should reap the benefit of the interest on the notes loaned and used as currency instead of the banks, etc. In 1847 he prepared a bill containing fourteen sections, defining his project, which he forwarded to Congress, accompanied by a petition requesting its passage, signed by many of his friends and neighbors. But Congress did not pass the bill.

In 1811, at Niles, he organized the first temperance society known in this region. The constitution contained a pledge of total abstinence from intoxicating drinks, which he and the members of his family with many others signed. He adhered to his pledge, and was a strong advocate of temperance during his life.

As evidencing his standing among his fellow-citizens, the public records show that in 1813 he was Senator from Trumbull county, and in 1820 Representative from the county in the State Legislature, Hon. Elisha Whittlesey being his co-representative.

A friend who was long acquainted with him thus characterizes him:

> He was a man of strong prejudices and fiery passions, which, when aroused, made him fearful to contemplate. He would then consign to the lowest depths of infamy the man who would advocate injustice or tyranny. He was a genuine philanthropist, a warm and ardent advocate of the universal brotherhood of man, a perfect hater of slavery and the slave system, and would do all in his power to overthrow it.

In person he was rather tall, stout, and muscular, and possessed a vigorous constitution. He died at Youngstown about 1857, at an advanced age, at the house of his daughter, Mrs. Hannah E. Kendle, with whom he had lived several years. His wife died several years before him. This is but an imperfect sketch of the pioneer of our industries who, for many years of a long life, was one of the most noted and prominent men of the Mahoning valley.

JOHN E. WOODBRIDGE.

John E. Woodbridge was born in Stockbridge, Massachusetts, June 24, 1777. He was a son of Jahleel Woodbridge, and Lucy (Edwards) Woodbridge, who was a daughter of Rev. Jonathan Edwards. His early years were passed in Stockbridge, where he obtained a good common school education. He then learned the trade of a tanner with William Edwards, a relative, in the northern part of the State of New York, and with whom he remained until attaining the age of twenty-one years. In 1798 he went to Philadelphia and worked at his trade, and afterwards worked in Lancaster, Pennsylvania, and Baltimore, Maryland. He was married in Philadelphia, in 1803, to Miss Mary M. Horner, who was born in Wilmington, Delaware, in September, 1783. In the summer of 1807 he removed with his family, then consisting of his wife and two children, to Youngstown, Ohio, from Baltimore, where had been residing. The journey was made in a big wagon, and consumed two weeks in reaching Pittsburg. At Youngstown he purchased a tannery of Joseph Townsend, who was a relative, who had established it, and who then became a farmer. When Mr. Woodbridge purchased the tannery, it was a small affair. He enlarged it, and pursued the business during his life, in his later years in partnership with some of his sons, they taking the principal charge of the business. During the first year, after he came to Youngstown, Mr. Grant, the grandfather of President Grant, worked in the tannery, in the employ of Mr. Woodbridge, according to the tradition in the family, which is probably correct, as Mr. Grant lived in Youngstown several years, and as stated by his son Roswell, in a letter read at the pioneer reunion in 1874, removed from there in 1810.

In the War of 1812, on the request of Colonel William Rayen, his neighbor and friend, he accepted the position of paymaster of Colonel Rayen's regiment, went with it into the field, and during the six months for which it was called out served with credit to himself and the satisfaction of his superior officers and of the regiment. On his return he resumed his business, and thenceforth passed his days in the quiet discharge of all the duties of a parent, neighbor, and citizen.

He died in Youngstown on December 1, 1844. Rev. Charles A. Boardman, in a funeral discourse, thus speaks of him: "His uniform urbanity, intelligence, integrity, refinement, and morality of deportment commanded the respect of all, and the cordial attachment of those who best knew him, which, unshaken by adversity and trial, he has borne with him to the grave. He was a modest man, with qualifications for official station which won the confidence of his fellow-citizens, but he recoiled from its responsibility, and steadfastly resisted all offers of public favor."

His estimable wife survived him several years. They were the parents of eleven children, viz: Lucy, married to Jonathan Edwards; John, George, Timothy, Henry, William, Walter, Samuel, Elizabeth, married to George Tayler; Louisa Maria, married to Robert W. Tayler, late first comptroller of the United States Treasury, and Stark Edwards.

NATHANIEL G. DABNEY.

Nathaniel Gardner Dabney, one of the pioneer settlers of Mahoning county, was born in Boston, Massachusetts, about the year 1770 or 1771. His parents were highly respectable and influential. His father, Nathaniel Dabney, died in early manhood. He was surgeon of a ship owned by himself and brother, which is believed to have been shipwrecked, as it was never afterward heard from. His mother was a Miss Betsey Gardner, of Connecticut, a very superior woman. He was their only child and received a fine education. Being possessed of considerable means and desirous of seeing the western country he came to Pittsburg, and while there he was induced by a friend to join him in buying a tract of land in Youngstown township suitable for town lots, and they were to engage in the mercantile business. Before their plans were perfected his friend died and young Dabney found himself in possession of a tract of land and without the slightest practical knowledge of agriculture.

In the year 1797 he married Miss Mary Keifer, of Pennsylvania, a farmer's daughter, and came to Ohio and settled upon his land. Having considerable means he soon had erected comfortable buildings. He reared a family of six children, three daughters and three sons. The oldest daughter was born in Youngstown in 1798. In 1813, just as Mr. Dabney was preparing to take his oldest daughter to Boston and leave her with his mother to be educated, he was taken sick and after a short illness died of consumption. His farm was divided among his children. His second daughter, Mary, married Peter Everett, whose ancestors settled in Pennsylvania. They had a large family of children, four of whom are now living. Her portion of the farm was used by them as a homestead and is still in the possession of her daughter, Kate Everett, who in 1858 married John W. Morrison, of Delaware county, Pennsylvania. They have two children, John W., Jr., and Agnes Everett. John graduated at the Rayen school in the class of 1881, and is now engaged in the retail grocery business in Youngstown. Agnes is attending the Rayen school.

Gardner Dabney, the oldest son, who was to inherit the widow's portion, died before coming into possession of the property. His daughter Laura J. (wife of Covington Westlake, of Warren) now owns it.

DANIEL SHEHY.

The subject of this sketch was born in county Tipperary, Ireland. The exact date is not known. He was liberally educated, and when he arrived at man's estate received his share of his father's inheritance and sought a home in the New World. He came over in the first emigrant ship that sailed after the war of the Revolution. He met Mr. Young in Albany, New York, and was induced by him to go to Ohio and locate. Mr. Shehy had $2,000 in gold which he wished to invest, and agreed to his proposal. He came out to Ohio with Young, when he (Young) first came to explore the country, and in company with Mr. Isaac Powers assisted in the survey of the Western Reserve. The only white man who preceded them was Colonel Hillman, whom they met on the banks of the Mahoning. It was a mutual surprise. Mr. Shehy made his selection of land, consisting of one thousand acres, for which he paid $2,000, four hundred acres of which lie east of the city of Youngstown and six hundred on the south bank of the river. Having concluded the bargain in good faith he married Miss Jane McLain, of Beaver county, Pennsylvania, and built for himself a little cabin on the bank of the river, between Youngstown and Hazelton. Here they hoped to prosper and build for themselves and their children a home. In this they succeeded. It was a hard struggle, such as we in these times of modern conveniences cannot realize. They had to do without the comforts and even most of the necessaries of life. For many years their grain had to be carried to Beaver through a trackless wilderness, to be ground, until, as their circumstances improved, they procured a hand-mill which did the grinding for the whole neighborhood. Among the number who often awaited her turn at the mill was that excellent woman, the mother of the late Governor Tod.

In every respect the Shehy's did their full share towards building up the country, and suffered cheerfully the many privations of pioneer life. Theirs would have been a comparatively happy life but for one cloud that darkened their horizon. That was the difficulty in getting a title to their land. After Mr. Shehy had paid the price he agreed to, and in other respects fulfilled his part of the contract, Young would not give him the deed, and, there being no law courts, there was no redress.

Shortly after the settlement of the township Mr. Robert Gibson wanted the tract of land lying on the south side of the river, and gave Young fifty cents per acre more than Shehy had paid for it. This act on the part of Young caused serious trouble between the two parties. Mr. Shehy's indignation arose so high at one time that it is said he took the law in his own hands and gave Young a severe chastisement.

He was arrested for this; had some kind of a rude trial, was fined and imprisoned, but was released the next day on giving bonds to keep the peace. Mr. Shehy determined not to lose his home and started for Connecticut, leaving his brave young wife and tender babes alone in the wilderness, to lay his case before the original land owners, and try to obtain his rights. He made two trips on foot (there being no public conveyance) and succeeded in effecting a compromise. They compelled Young to give Shehy a deed for the remaining four hundred acres. But the severe hardship told on his constitution, though naturally a rugged one, and Shehy became a prematurely old man. He lived, however, to rear a large family and spent a useful life. His wisdom and superior education, together with his knowledge of law, made him a man just suited to the times, his advice being sought for in all emergencies.

Although he was blind for some years before his death, his mind was clear and active, and many a knotty problem in mathematics he solved for the young students of the day.

In faith Mr. Shehy was a Roman Catholic. In politics, in which he took an active part, he was a Whig and high tariff man. In disposition he was warm-hearted, generous, and hospitable, and was public spirited, willing to do what he could for the good of the new settlement.

Mr. Shehy was the father of nine children, as follows: Catherine Shehy Campbell, born February 17, 1799; Robert Shehy, born February 17, 1801; Mary Shehy Woods, born August 12, 1803; John Shehy, born September 27, 1805; Daniel Shehy, born February 12, 1808; Margaret Shehy McAllister, born June 14, 1810; McLain Shehy, born May 17, 1813; James Shehy, born January 13, 1816; Jane Shehy Lett, born August 1, 1818.

Lucius McLain Sheehy, son of Daniel and Jane (McLain) Sheehy, was born in Youngstown, Ohio, May 17, 1813. His father dying when he was about twenty years of age, he and a younger brother took charge of the farm, which then consisted of three hundred and twenty acres. Over twenty acres are now within the city limits of Youngstown and will eventually be sold for city lots. Mr. Sheehy was united in marriage July 5, 1839, to Julia Bedell, born in Alleghany county, Pennsylvania, in 1820. They have three daughters and one son as follows: Emeline A., wife of George Rigby, of Youngstown; Elizabeth Ellen, wife of William Kerr of Youngstown, Lucius McLain at home (married and has one son), Mary Jane, wife of T. M. Hewitt.

JAMES GIBSON AND DESCENDANTS.

James Gibson was born in Ireland in 1747, of Scotch-Irish parentage. At the age of sixteen he came to America with some friends, leaving his parents in Ireland, and settled in Cumberland county, Pennsylvania, in the year 1763. He worked at whatever he could find to do amongst farmers during the farming season, and went to school in the winter, chopping wood and grubbing mornings and evenings, and at the close of the term he would work one week extra to pay for his board.

At the breaking out of the Revolutionary war he enlisted in the American army and was afterwards made captain of a company of volunteers, in which capacity he served for five years, most of the time on scout duty, fighting Indians.

He was married to Anna Belle Dixon in 1777. She had two brothers who were members of Captain Gibson's company, and were both killed in battle with the Indians while under his command. James and his wife had five children born to them, four sons and one daughter. John, the oldest son, was born July 29, 1779. On that same day the whites were attacked by the Indians and a terrible battle took place in the neighborhood where they lived. The mother and infant were carried by their friends to the river, placed in a canoe and floated down stream to a place of safety. Several of Captain Gibson's men were killed in this fight, among them one of Mrs. Gibson's brothers. Their home and its contents were burned. A few days afterwards another brother was killed. Gibson was the owner of a large bloodhound that always went with the company when out on duty, and was always first to discover the presence of an enemy, and many times by stopping and growling he indicated the Indian ambush and saved the volunteers from Indian mercy. Some twenty years after the war was over an old Indian named Jaloway came through Ohio and stayed one day with him. Jaloway had learned to talk English, and told him that had it not been for his big dog he could have had his scalp on two different occasions, when he was lying in ambush and saw him out accompanied only by his dog, but he said he knew that it was not safe unless he could kill both the man and his dog at the same time.

They sold their farm in Cumberland county, in the year 1799, and came over the mountains in wagons through Pittsburg, Beaver, and Poland to Youngstown, Ohio. Coming up the Mahoning, south of Youngstown, they passed a large spring of clear water, which flowed out from the hillside. After examining the spring and viewing the land in that vicinity, they drove on to Youngstown, consisting at that time of three cabin houses. Their destination was Warren, where they arrived the next night. They stayed that night with a man who came from their neighborhood in the early part of the season. His name was Davidson. After looking about Warren for land, the old gentleman thought there was nothing that would suit him as well as the farm with the big spring on it near Youngstown. He went back to Youngstown and bought the spring, with three hundred acres of land, from Daniel Shehy. He immediately returned to Warren and moved their goods back to Youngstown to the farm he had just purchased, arriving there on the 1st day of November, 1799.

There was a floorless cabin on the farm about fifteen feet square, and there had been about an acre of the timber cut off. They at once went to work and built a large cabin near the old one and split out puncheon for floors for both, and split clapboards for roof and doors. In order to provide shelter for their horses, they built sheds. They sold three of their horses and when they were unable to procure any more food for them, they put bells on the other two and turned them out to look for their own provender in the daytime, shutting them up at night. Once they strayed away and John Gibson, the oldest son, after hunting two weeks, found them near Pittsburg.

James Gibson had ten children, four boys and six girls. John Gibson was married to Miss Esther Davidson in 1801, by Rev. William Wick. His father gave him one hundred acres of the south side of lot forty-three in Youngstown township, on which he spent the remainder of his life. He purchased seventy-five acres more from an adjoining farm. They had ten children, four boys and six girls. Three of the girls are yet living. John Gibson died October 28, 1833. His wife died in May, 1848, aged seventy-two years. The other sons of James Gibson, Robert, James, and Samuel, staid with their parents and cleared up the farm. In 1815 they bought two hundred and fifty acres more, lying on the west side of the original purchase. James Gibson, the elder, died in 1817; his wife died in March, 1836, at the age of eighty-eight years. Robert D. Gibson and Lydia Marshall were married April 16, 1818. They had nine children, four of whom are now living, viz: Samuel, John, Mrs. A. O. Hine, and Mrs. James Neilson. Lydia Marshall was the daughter of James Marshall, who came from Hunting-

don county, Pennsylvania, in 1807, and settled in Weathersfield township, Trumbull county, Ohio. In the spring of 1831 Robert D., James, and Samuel Gibson divided their lands. Robert took two hundred acres from the south end, and James and Samuel took three hundred and twenty-five acres on the north, extending to the Mahoning river.

James Gibson was married to Miss Jane Riddle in May, 1833. They had one daughter. He, James Gibson, was drowned in the spring of 1835, while trying to ford the Mahoning on horseback, at what was known as the Gibson furding.

Samuel Gibson, the youngest of the four sons of James Gibson, was a deaf mute. He was a very large and strong man, kind hearted and industrious and systematic in all that he did. He was a great lover of horses and always kept his own in good order, and they were considered the best trained horses in the neighborhood. He conversed by motions of the hands and face, and took pleasure in telling of the privations of pioneer life and of the game he used to kill. He was very expert in the use of the rifle. He died in his seventieth year, never having been married.

Robert D. Gibson died at the old homestead, March, 1863, at the age of seventy-eight years. His wife died at the same place in August, 1873, at the age of seventy-seven years.

After the death of James Gibson by drowning, the lands of James and Samuel, the mute, were divided. Henry Wick bought some two hundred acres of the river farm, and Robert McCartney twenty acres. Samuel kept the balance, including the big spring and the buildings.

Robert's son Samuel afterwards bought the land that his uncle Samuel, the mute, had owned, and in 1870 sold a portion of it to Andrew Hitchcock. He resides on the balance near the spring. John Gibson, Robert's youngest son, lives on the old homestead. There remains of the third generation Mrs. Stephen Saxton, of Poland, Ohio, about seventy years of age. Mrs. George Allen, about sixty-seven years of age, living near New Bedford, Pennsylvania; and Mrs. George Dickson, about sixty-two years of age, daughter of John Gibson; and Mrs. Brindley, living near Wheatland, Pennsylvania, the daughter of James Gibson, aged forty-eight years.

James Gibson served about one year in the War of 1812. Robert D. Gibson served about three months in the same war.

COLONEL CALEB B. WICK.

The name of Wick has been identified with Youngstown from a very early day. One of the first, if not the first, minister of the gospel of any denomination who held religious services in the infant settlement, and was for many years afterwards pastor of the Presbyterian church, and who there solemnized a marriage as early as November, 1800, was Rev. William Wick, an uncle of the subject of this memoir, and elder brother of his father, Henry Wick, who came in 1802 and was one of the earliest merchants.

The family is of English origin. An early ancestor in the United States was Job Wick, of Southampton, Long Island, New York. He was married, as appears by a family record, to Anna Cook December 21, 1721. They were the parents of eleven children, of whom Lemuel, born April 16, 1743, was the ninth. Lemuel was married to Deborah Lupton about 1763. They were the parents of five children, of whom William, the pioneer minister above named, born June 29, 1768, was the third, and Henry, the pioneer merchant, born March 19, 1771, was the fourth.

Henry removed, while a young man, from Southampton, Long Island, to Washington county, Pennsylvania, and was there married December 11, 1794, to Miss Hannah Baldwin, daughter of Caleb Baldwin, of that county. They were the parents of eleven children, of whom Caleb Baldwin Wick, born October 1, 1795, was the eldest.

Henry Wick was engaged in mercantile business in Washington county, Pennsylvania, after his removal there. He first came to Youngstown in 1802, probably at the instance of his father-in-law, Caleb Baldwin, who removed there about 1799. A deed on record shows that on April 29, 1802, Henry Wick purchased of John Young the square bounded on Main (now West Federal), Hill (now Wood), Phelps, and Hazel streets, and a lot of thirty-seven acres outside of the town plat for $235. He erected buildings for residence and store, commenced mercantile business soon after his purchase of land, and removed his family, then consisting of his wife and four children: Caleb B., Thomas L., Betsey, and Lemonel, in the spring of 1804 to Youngstown. He died November 4, 1845. Mrs. Hannah B. Wick, his widow, died April 10, 1849.

Caleb B. Wick was in the ninth year of his age when he came to Youngstown. The settlement at that time, as he related in his after years, consisted of only a few scattered log cabins. On the ground now occupied by the main part of the city the timber had been burnt off by the Indians, and there were only bushes and thick bunches of hazel. Wild deer were frequently to be seen running where are now the most populous and active business streets.

He received such an education in the ordinary branches as was attainable in the schools of that day, and at times assisted his father in his store and other business. In the fall of 1815, in partnership with the late Dr. Henry Manning, he commenced a country store, connecting with it a drug store, the first in this part of the Reserve. This store stood on the north side of West Federal street, next west of the (present) large store building of E. M. McGillin & Co., in a frame building now occupied by J. F. Hollingsworth as a stove and hardware store. He continued in partnership with Dr. Manning in this building about ten years. He continued the mercantile business in another building, next east of the present Excelsior block, part of the time without a partner, and at times with different partners until 1848, when having been a merchant for over thirty years he retired from that business, being then the oldest merchant in business in Youngstown.

During his active life he was honored, at different times, by election and appointment to positions of public trust and honor. On June 2, 1817, having been elected by the company to the office, he was commissioned by Governor Worthington, lieutenant of the Third company, First battalion, First regiment, Fourth division Ohio militia, and qualified by taking the official oath before Hon. George Tod, judge of the common pleas. On September 3, 1818, he was commissioned captain of the same company. On March 22, 1822, he was commissioned lieutenant-colonel of the First regiment, and in the fall of the same year colonel of the regiment, which office he held for a few years.

In 1820 and again in 1824 he was elected township clerk of Youngstown, and subsequently was elected trustee, and held other township offices. During the exciting Presidential campaign of 1840 Colonel Wick was an active supporter of General Harrison, and on November 17, 1841, was commissioned postmaster of Youngstown, which office he held until March 10, 1843, when, not being a supporter of President Tyler, he was removed.

After retiring from mercantile business, in 1848, he did not enter into any active business, but devoted his attention to the care of his estate, which had become large. He died June 30, 1865, aged nearly seventy years. At that time he was, and since the death of Colonel William Rayen, in April, 1854, he had been, the oldest citizen or resident of Youngstown.

He was married, January 1, 1816, to Miss Rachel Kirtland, daughter of Jared Kirtland, of Poland, Ohio. They were the parents of two children, one of whom, Henry K., for some time a merchant of Youngstown, died at about the age of twenty-two years; the other died in infancy. His wife died in 1820. He was again married, November 3, 1828, to Miss Maria Adelia Griffith, of Youngstown, formerly of Caledonia, Livingston county, New York. They were the parents of ten children, seven of whom —Rachel K., intermarried with Robert W. Tayler, late first comptroller of the United States Treasury; Hannah B., intermarried with Charles D. Arms, of Youngstown; Laura E., Caleb B., Henry K., Charles E., and Eliza M.—are now living.

His character as a citizen and in his various relations to the community is sketched in an obituary notice, prepared shortly after his death, by one who knew him well, from which we make extracts:

In social life, as a citizen, a neighbor, and a friend Colonel Wick was liberal, kind, and warm-hearted. In his house everyone felt at home, and his hospitality knew no limit. Indulgent to his own family in social joys, and cheerful to the last, he had great delight in the society of the young as well as the old.

He united with the First Presbyterian church of Youngstown, on profession of faith, on April 6, 1835. For more than thirty years he had been known as a Christian man, devising liberal things for the church of his choice. He had been an invalid for several years, but his end came suddenly, and though it came with little warning, yet he was awaiting the summons from on high and peacefully fell asleep.

WILLIAM JOHNSON EDWARDS.

William Johnson Edwards was born in Warren, Ohio, December 26, 1811. He was a son of Colonel John Stark and Louisa Maria (Morris) Edwards. In 1814 he removed to Youngstown with his mother, after her marriage to her second husband, Major Robert Montgomery. He received, during his early years, such education as the schools at home could furnish, and when about sixteen years of age he went to New Haven, Connecticut, attended the lectures of some of the professors of Yale college, and pursued several of the higher branches of English studies. He then returned home, and on his step-father's farm, southeast of the village of Youngstown, made himself a practical farmer. He was married October 2, 1839, at Youngstown, to Miss Mary Manning, born July 1, 1817, daughter of Dr. Henry and Lucretia (Kirtland) Manning. After their marriage they removed to a farm he owned and was cultivating in Mesopotamia, Trumbull county, and remained there as farmers about nine years, and then returned to Youngstown, to a farm which he had purchased west of the village, but now in the city. A part of this farm he has sold off for city lots, and part of it he still cultivates. When quite young, by sickness his hearing was affected, and he has since suffered the great disadvantage of being "hard of hearing." It has not, however, prevented him from reading and study, and he is, at this day, one of the best informed men in the place, and is generally so regarded. His life has been quiet and uneventful, attending to his own business and not seeking public honors. And yet, on the recommendation of citizens who knew his eminent qualifications for the position, after the establishment of the Rayen school in 1858, he was appointed by the court one of the trustees, and soon after was elected president of the board. He held this office until about a year since, when he declined a further re-appointment as trustee.

Mr. and Mrs. Edwards, on October 2, 1879, celebrated the fortieth anniversary of their marriage. Seven of the guests present, viz: Mrs. Mary Correy, R. M. Montgomery and wife, Mrs. C. M. Garlick, Miss Jane Taylor, Henry Manning, Jr., and John M. Edwards, attended the wedding forty years ago. They have one child, Louisa Maria, a lady of fine personal appearance, fine mind, well educated, and very highly esteemed.

JOHN R. HOLCOMB.

John R. Holcomb was born in Plymouth, Chenango county, New York, September 8, 1805. He served an apprenticeship at the tinner's trade, sheet iron, and copper business in Norwich, New York; came to Poland, now Mahoning county, Ohio, in 1829, where he worked at his trade. July 28th of that year he married Sally Amelia Fitch, daughter of Jedediah Fitch, of Boardman township. Mr. Fitch owned the Wier farm, which he sold in 1834 and moved to Vernon township. The subject of our sketch was in the tinning business for a short time with Asahel Medbury, but in 1830 he lived in a two-story hewed log-house that stood on the southeast corner of the "Diamond," Youngstown, the site now being occupied by the Tod house. In 1832 he moved to Farmington, Ohio, but returned to Youngstown the next year. In 1834 he lived at the mouth of Mill creek, and in 1835 at Warren. In the spring of 1836 he returned and in the fall of that year made a trip down the Ohio and Mississippi rivers, with a tin-shop on board. He sold out at Vicksburg. He afterwards took two other such trips, the last time going to New Orleans. He had met with financial reverses in 1837, and in 1842 made this last trip down the river with a tin and gunsmith boat by which means he hoped to pay his debts, amounting to some $2,000. His trip netted him about $900, $700 of which consisted of gold coin, $50 of silver, and the balance of Southern products, such as sugar, coffee, yams, etc.

He changed his place of residence in Youngstown several times and in the spring of 1838 moved back to the old place on the "Diamond," where he had a tin-shop in the second story, having his dwelling below. He carried on his business quite extensively, keeping from four to six teams on the road.

In the fall of 1839 he bought for $360 the property where the Mahoning National bank and opera house now stands, where he lived until 1848, when he purchased the John L. Johnson property at the foot of Market-street hill. Shortly after moving there his first wife died, leaving him with four children—Henry, born August 28,

1830; Jedediah Fitch, January 8, 1833; Laura Maria, March 5, 1843; Mary Ann, June 26, 1845. Henry was married in 1852 to Emily, daughter of Harvey Sawyer, of Youngstown, and is now living in Painesville; has two daughters. Jedediah F. resides in Laramie City, Wyoming Territory, engaged in the hardware business, and is unmarried. Laura Maria married Abner Reeves, of Warren, Ohio, in the summer of 1876, and is now living in Belmont, Wright county, Iowa, and has one daughter. Mary Ann married William A. Ray, of Warren, in 1865; they now live two or three miles east of Warren on a farm; they have two boys and one girl. November 11, 1848, Mr. Holcomb was married to Sarah Fowler, in Pittsburg, Pennsylvania. She was born in Bradley, Staffordshire, England, September 22, 1819. Of this marriage four children were born, the youngest dying in infancy. The others are John Fowler Holcomb, born December 12, 1850; Addie Louisa, December 24, 1852; Henrietta, September 3, 1854. John F., after acquiring a fair education in the Youngstown schools, commenced to learn the trade of his father, but on account of the death of his father August 23, 1868, changed his plans, and in the spring of 1869 he entered the hardware store of Fowler, Stambaugh & Co., the senior of the firm being his uncle. He remained with that firm until the summer of 1876, when he purchased the stock of stoves and tin-ware where he is now located, starting in business on a cash capital of $600. He has since done a gradually increasing, and is now doing a good business. He was married September 29, 1880, to Miss Emma O., daughter of Dr. D. Beaver, of Liberty, Indiana, who had been living for three years in Youngstown with her uncle, Richard Brown. Addie L. Holcomb was married June 7, 1879, to Joseph N. Evans, of Connellsville, Pennsylvania, and is now residing in Youngstown. Henrietta was married in the fall of 1874 to John E. Reep, of Youngstown, and now lives near Knoxville, Tennessee. Mrs. Holcomb, the widow of the subject of this sketch, is still living in Youngstown, making her home with her son, John F.

Mr. Holcomb, the subject of our sketch, was a strong temperance man and an ultra abolitionist, being at one time one of only four of that political faith in Youngstown, and dined Frederick Douglass on the occasion of his visit to that city to deliver a lecture.

JOHN BROWNLEE.

One of the first miners and shippers of iron ore to Youngstown was John Brownlee, who opened the mines at the mouth of Yellow creek. He was born in Scotland, April 12, 1811. In 1832 he emigrated to America and came direct to Trumbull, now Mahoning county, and settled in Poland township. He became engaged in general farming and stock raising, to which he gave exclusive attention, until the opening of valuable mineral deposits offered a more profitable field of industry. He married June 14, 1842, Eliza L., daughter of Isaac and Leah (Frazee) Powers, who was born in Youngstown township January 22, 1822.

Mr. Brownlee had the Scotch temperament, exact and exacting, conscientious and prompt in all his dealings. It is a credit to his foreign birth that from his first acquaintance with American institutions he had a strong hatred of slavery and his political affiliations were with the anti-slavery sentiment. He was a Free-soiler, Abolitionist and later a Republican.

To carry on his business operations more advantageously, he removed to Youngstown in the spring of 1864. His death occurred the following September. Mr. and Mrs. Brownlee were the parents of six children, of whom four are living, viz: A. B., a well known coal dealer in Youngstown; Isaac P., engaged in the stone trade; Mary L., wife of Lucius Cochran of Youngstown, and Leah M. wife of George McKelvey, of Hubbard township. Mrs. Brownlee continues to reside in Youngstown, being possessed of a comfortable competence and surrounded by kind children.

It was Mr. Brownlee's enterprise that assisted materially in the development of the iron industry, and consequently he should be held in remembrance as one of the number who laid the foundation for the rapid and substantial growth of this city.

ALEXANDER B. BROWNLEE,

son of John and Lettie Brownlee, was born in Struthers, Mahoning county, Ohio, November 2, 1843. He was educated in the common schools of Poland (walking sometimes a distance of five miles), and at the Poland academy. In May, 1863, he enlisted in the Eighty-eighth Ohio volunteer infantry, and was in Virginia and Kentucky with his regiment, serving until November, 1863, when he was mustered out. Returning to Youngstown he entered the employ of Arms, Powers & Co., remaining until 1868. In the fall of that year, having in the meantime had charge of a store in Missouri for J. H. Brown & Co., he engaged in business for himself in Youngstown under the firm name of Odbert & Brownlee, continuing until 1873, when they closed up. He was afterwards the junior member of the firm of Powers & Brownlee, engaged in shipping coal. With Mr. Odbert he became a member of the firm in 1878, purchased the interest of Powers in 1879. In 1880 James Wick was admitted to the firm, now A. B. Brownlee & Co. This firm do an extensive business in flour, feed, and agricultural implements, and also in coal, lime, and cement, aggregating a business of $150,000 per annum. Mr. Brownlee has been twice married, first in 1872 to Mary D. Fowler, who died in 1876. In the fall of 1877 he married Henrietta, daughter of E. G. Hollingsworth, of Youngstown, by whom he has had two children, who died in infancy.

JOHN M. EDWARDS.

John M. Edwards was born in New Haven, Connecticut, October 23, 1805. He is a son of Henry W. and Lydia (Miller) Edwards, a grandson of Judge Pierrepont Edwards, one of the original proprietors of the Western Reserve, as a member of the Connecticut Land company, and great-grandson of Jonathan Edwards, the distinguished divine and an early president of Princeton, New Jersey, college. On his father's side he is of Welsh, English, and Norman descent, on his mother's, of English descent, her father, John Miller, being a native of London, England, who came to America prior to the Revolutionary war, and was a captain in the merchant marine, trading in the China and East India ports.

He was graduated at Yale college in 1824, read law with Judge Bristol at New Haven, was there admitted to the bar of Connecticut in 1826, and to the bar of the circuit court of the United States in 1828. He practiced law at New Haven until 1832, when he removed to Ohio. He arrived in Youngstown July 4, 1832, remained there a few months and removed to the north part of Trumbull county, and engaged in other than law business. He was admitted to the bar of Ohio by the supreme court August 30, 1838, at Warren, Ohio, and soon after there commenced practice. In addition to law practice he was engaged, in 1840 and following years, in editing the Trumbull Democrat, a weekly newspaper. Soon after the passage of the bankrupt law in 1841, he was appointed by the United States district court commissioner of bankrupts for Trumbull county, and held that office until the repeal of the law. In 1842 he was nominated, without solicitation by him, or previous knowledge that it was contemplated, by a Democratic convention, representative in Congress from the old Nineteenth district, to fill the vacancy occasioned by the resignation of Hon. Joshua R. Giddings. The Democratic party in the district being largely in the minority he was not elected, but the majority of Mr. Giddings, who was his opponent, was far less than it had been at any former, or was at any future, election. About 1843 he was appointed by the court of common pleas school examiner for Trumbull county, and held the office until he removed from the county. About 1841 he was elected and commissioned captain of the militia under the old military system.

In 1846 he removed to Canfield on the organization of Mahoning county, practiced law there until 1864, when he removed his office to Youngstown; removed his residence there in 1868, and now there resides in practice. At the first term of the court of common pleas in Mahoning county he was, on motion of Hon. Elisha Whittlesey, with Professors Reuben McMillan and Hiram A. Hall, both school superintendents, appointed school examiner for Mahoning county for three years, and again in 1863 he was appointed by the probate court school examiner, was reappointed and held the office until after

56

he removed his residence to Youngstown, when he declined a reappointment which was tendered him.

In 1846, shortly after his removal to Canfield, he became editor and one of the publishers of the Mahoning Index, the first newspaper published in Mahoning county, and continued as such a few years. From 1855, and shortly after its establishment, he was weekly correspondent, from Canfield, of the Mahoning Register of Youngstown, over the *nom de plume* of "Quill Pen." This correspondence was a marked feature of the paper, and obtained its author much commendation. It was continued until 1864, when he became associate editor of the Register, and was connected with it editorially for several years.

From 1865 to 1879 he was the Youngstown correspondent of the Cleveland Herald, and his communications which he has preserved, filling two large scrap book volumes, furnish a full history of Youngstown and its vicinity during that period. Since 1840 he has been almost constantly connected, as editor, correspondent or occasional contributor, with Warren, Canfield, Youngstown, Cleveland, and other papers, and is, at this time, the oldest editor of Mahoning county, and, with two exceptions (probably), of the Reserve.

At the session of the Ohio Legislature of 1864-65 he was one of the clerks of the Senate.

In April, 1869, he was elected justice of the peace of Youngstown township, re-elected in 1872 and 1875, and held the office three terms or nine years until 1878.

He was one of the founders of the Mahoning Valley Historical society in 1874, and has been one of its corresponding secretaries from its organization. With the late William Powers he was editor of the valuable volume of Historical Collections published by the society in 1876. He has contributed to the press, during many years past, a series of interesting reminiscences of the incidents of the pioneer days, rescuing, and inciting others to assist in rescuing, from impending oblivion, the wonderful history of those eventful times, and preserving the biographies of those heroes and heroines who have made of this Western Reserve, the wilderness of less than one hundred years ago, one of the fairest portions of our beloved Union.

He was married July 14, 1842, at Warren, Ohio, to Miss Mary P. Crail, daughter of Joseph Crail, an early settler. She was an artist of great merit as an amateur, and her paintings are highly commended. She died at Youngstown, May 15, 1877.

Mr. and Mrs. Edwards were the parents of three children, two of whom are living: Henrietta Frances, married to Stanley M. Caspar, and residing in Youngstown; and Henry W., a merchant of Philadelphia, Pennsylvania, of the firm of Hood, Bonbright & Co.

BRAINARD SPENCER HIGLEY.

The record of this family is not accurately known at this time. On account of the tedious means of transportation, and slender postal facilities of the earlier years of the present century, the pioneers who left New England and settled in Ohio in a measure died to the kindred and friends left behind, and lost trace of those records and traditions through which genealogical history is preserved. Beyond doubt B. S. Higley is a lineal descendant of John Higley, who resided in Windsor, Connecticut, and who married Hannah Drake in the year 1671. John Higley seems to have been a man of some prominence in those days. He was justice of the peace, judge of the county court, first captain of military company in 1698, and was a member of the Legislature for many sessions subsequent to that time.

Of the immediate ancestors of B. S. Higley, his great-grandfather, Joseph Higley, was born in Simsbury, Massachusetts, in the year 1741. He married Azabah Gilkt about the year 1773, and during the same year removed to Becket, Berkshire county, Massachusetts, where they both subsequently died, he December 17, 1823, aged eighty-two years, and she February 13, 1825, aged seventy six years. Joseph Higley, the grandfather of B. S. Higley, was born in Becket, Massachusetts, April 25, 1774, and there married Sybil Coggswell, December 4, 1803. They emigrated to Windham, Portage county, Ohio, in September or October, 1815. He was one of the early surveyors of that township. He died of fever in Windham, October 4, 1825, aged fifty-one years. His widow died in the same place, December 1, 1864, aged eighty-eight years. Joseph N. Higley, the father of B. S. Higley, was born in Becket, Massachusetts, September 6, 1806, and removed with his parents to Windham, Ohio, in 1815. May 2, 1832, he was married to Susan W. Spencer, of Aurora, Ohio, who was the daughter of Brainard Spencer, one of the pioneers of that township. He was born at Middlefield, Massachusetts, July 2, 1785. On September 9, 1809, at Aurora Ohio, he married Amy Cannon, who was born at Blanford, Massachusetts, October 10, 1785. He died May 14, 1835, and his widow, October 3, 1864. Joseph N. Higley died at Youngstown, Ohio, in March 1879, aged seventy-three years. His widow is still living.

Brainard S. Higley was born in Windham, Portage county, September 1, 1837, and was three years old when his parents removed to Aurora, Portage county, and twelve when they removed from there to Twinsburg, Summit county. At the latter place he received instruction at the Twinsburg Literary institute, preparatory to entering college. He graduated from Western Reserve college in 1859 with the third honor of his class. The following year he was complimented with the offer of tutorship, and three years after his graduation received the degree of A. M.

Mr. Higley studied law with Hon. Sherlock J. Andrews, and Hitchcock, Mason & Estep, and also attended lectures at the Cleveland Law college. He was admitted to the bar at Wooster, in July, 1860, and came to Youngstown during the winter of 1861-62.

Mr. Higley was soon recognized as a painstaking and reliable counsellor and attorney, qualities which peculiarly fitted him for the settlement of estates and the management of causes growing out of business transactions. There were only five attorneys in Youngstown when Mr. Higley came here, only two of whom are here at present—William G. Moore and Thomas W. Sanderson. With these two exceptions he is the oldest member of the present bar.

His military service was short, but cannot be said to have been strictly easy. After Morgan's raid through Ohio, in 1863, the people, and Legislature as well, awoke to the necessity of greater preparations for the defense of their own homes. The militia were once more organized and mustered for drill. At the first regimental election B. S. Higley was elected lieutenant-colonel of the regiment, composed of Youngstown and Coitsville townships, and Governor Tod forwarded him a commission as such. The National guard, of which there were three companies in Youngstown, were then organizing, and Mr. Higley, thinking it better for the State for him to become a private in one of these companies than to be an officer in the militia, declined to accept the commission of lieutenant-colonel. The National guards were organized, equipped and drilled for home defense, and had no expectation of leaving the State of Ohio. They comprised some of the very best citizens of Youngstown and vicinity, manufacturers, mechanics, merchants, attorneys, doctors, and farmers.

In April, 1864, Governor Brough, thinking the National Government needed these men at that time more than Ohio did, ordered the whole force of Ohio National guards to report on May 10, 1864, for active service for one hundred days, the purpose being to place them upon garrison and guard duty in the rear of the lines and thus release a like number of veterans for service on the field. The Youngstown companies became a part of the One Hundred and Fifty-fifth Ohio volunteer infantry under Colonel H. H. Sage. B. S. Higley was a member of company D, Captain F. S. Whitslar commanding. The regiment was mustered into service at Camp Dennison and immediately afterwards sent to Martinsburg, West Virginia, where it went into camp and was employed in guarding the city and escorting trains up and down the Shenandoah valley. About a month thereafter the regiment was ordered to White House Landing on the Pamunky river, that being then Grant's base of supplies in his advance upon Richmond. It went thither by way of Washington and thence by boat down the Chesapeake bay and up the York and Pamunky rivers. The regiment remained at White House until Grant transferred his base of supplies to City Point, where it was (after having assisted to load the wounded and sick of the army on boats for Washington) transferred by boat down the Pamunky and York rivers, thence to Fortress Monroe and up the James river to Fort Powhatan. Here the river was obstructed by a pontoon bridge over which Grant's army was making a forced march for Petersburg. From this point the regiment marched to City Point and crossed to Bermuda Hundred, being under orders to join General B. F. Butler at Dutch Gap canal. However, much to the satisfaction of all from the colonel down, this order was countermanded and the regiment returned to City Point, went into camp behind the fortifications and relieved a colored regiment who started for the front. At City Point the climate began to tell upon the men and many sickened. Early in July the regiment was transported by boat to Norfolk, Virginia, and there relieved another colored regiment. At this point the regiment remained until ordered back to Camp Dennison to be mustered out, some time in the early part of September, 1864. The only adventure it can be said to have had was a raid through the Dismal swamp to Elizabeth City, North Carolina, said to have been planned to capture cotton, but resulting for the most part in confiscation of watermelons. It was an expedition in which much fun was had and no blood shed.

While at Norfolk the whole regiment and particularly the Youngstown part sickened. The men were mostly between thirty and forty-five years of age, and the climate seemed deadly to them. Very few escaped, many died, and large numbers were completely disabled. B. S. Higley was among the latter class and from the time of his arrival at Norfolk, he was only able to render assistance in taking charge of the ambulance and assisting the hospital steward. These duties, however, were such as will never pass from his memory. Without exception he took every one of the sick to the general hospital who went there; and being the only member of the regiment who visited the hospital daily and therefore who could or did ask for and see the sick ones, it happened that with possibly one exception, his was the last familiar face upon which any of the brave men who died at Norfolk gazed. All the time and strength he had remaining and nerve he gave to his sick comrades. When the Youngstown companies returned home, they deserved and received the commisseration of the entire community. For a long time afterward it was a common occurrence to hear it said of anyone who looked particularly sick and haggard that "he looked as bad as a hundred days man." B. S. Higley was unable to resume his practice for several months after his return and his health was permanently impaired by the terrible ordeal.

Just before entering the service Mr. Higley had been elected mayor; a new marshal and council except one member had also been chosen. They all enlisted before assuming the duties of their respective offices, leaving the town to be governed temporarily by the old officers, whose terms had expired. As soon as the regiment returned the offices were vacated and the incumbents-elect took their places.

Mr. Higley filled the office of mayor two terms. In 1864 he was elected and accepted the office of justice of the peace for Youngstown township, and brought to that position unusual qualifications. He embarked in a business enterprise at Marietta, Ohio, in 1867, having been chosen secretary and treasurer of a rolling-mill company, in which he was a stockholder. The business proved a failure and the stockholders suffered considerable loss.

Mr. Higley returned from Marietta to Youngstown in 1875 and has since devoted himself closely to the practice of his profession. He is a lawyer rather than an advocate and is particularly successful in causes requiring careful preparation and close, tedious study. As a citizen and man he is held in high regard.

Mr. Higley was married at Twinsburgh, January 1, 1861, to Miss Isabella R. Stevens, daughter of Dr. John G. Stevens, a highly respectable physician. She was born in Nelson, Portage county, Ohio.

FREEMAN O. ARMS.

Freeman O. Arms was born in Sodus, Wayne county, New York, April 14, 1824. His parents were Israel and Sarah (Axtell) Arms. He received a good English education and when approaching manhood was clerk in a store. He came to Youngstown in 1845, entered as a clerk the store of J. Warner & Co. (Jonathan Warner and Myron T. Arms, an elder brother who had removed from Sodus in 1844). Here he remained until 1848, when, with a younger brother, Charles D., he opened a store in Brookfield, Trumbull county, Ohio. For about two years with his brother, and then for ten years alone, he conducted this place successfully. He returned to Youngstown about 1860 and entered into partnership with Arms & Murray (Myron T. Arms and George T. Murray), as Arms, Murray & Co. He continued in mercantile business as a member of this and the successive firms of Arms, Powers & Co., and Arms, Wick & Blocksom, in the same building, known as the Arms & Murray block, on the southeast corner of Federal and Phelps streets, until the spring of 1880, when, on account of ill health, he retired from that business.

He was also, during this period following 1860, largely interested in coal mining, being a partner in several companies, owning and operating mines in the Mahoning and Shenango valleys. He was a leading partner in the firm of Arms, Bell & Co., carrying on an extensive nut and washer manufactory. He was a director and vice-president of the First National bank, and one of the founders and president of the Youngstown Savings and Loan association, which became the Mahoning National bank. As captain of a company of the National guards, during the war of 1861, he gallantly responded to the call for ninety days' men, left his large business and marched with his company to the field of war. He was often elected township trustee, and upon the establishment of water-works by the city, he was unanimously elected by his fellow citizens one of the trustees, and was elected by the board its president. He was an active member and for many years a vestryman of St. John's Episcopal church.

On March 1, 1879, he was struck with paralysis, which affected his right side and disabled him from active business. He was slowly recovering and could in a measure attend to business when he suffered a second attack, attributed to exposure to cold on December 8, 1880, and died in a few hours.

We quote from an obituary in one of our city papers this just eulogium:

Mr. Arms was a man for whom too much cannot be said of his sterling worth, strict integrity, and high character. Modest and unassuming in all the intercourse of life, of few words, free from every species of deceit, dishonesty or hypocrisy, he always gave strength to any movement in which he was engaged, or any enterprise he undertook. Though never seeking or desiring office he was, in his quiet way, active in politics, throwing the weight of his character and influence on the side of the right as he saw it. A devoted husband and father, a faithful friend and citizen, he has passed away, leaving behind the memory of a noble man, and a life well lived as a comfort and an inspiration.

He was married at Sodus on September 18, 1849, to Miss Emily S. Proseus, a very estimable lady. After the marriage she came with him to Brookfield, and they there resided until their removal to Youngstown, in 1860, where she died June 10, 1861. They were the parents of two children, Freeman, who died at the age of four years, and Caroline L., now the wife of Tod Ford, Esq., a rising lawyer of Youngstown.

He was married a second time at Youngstown, on November 21, 1865, to Mrs. Emily Wick, widow of John D. Wick. There were no children of this marriage. She survives him. Her maiden name was Emily Lippincott. She was born in Pittsburg, Pennsylvania, June 5, 1826. Her parents were William and Ann (Williamson) Lippincott. She was married to John Dennick Wick, a son of Henry Wick, the pioneer merchant of Youngstown, at Pittsburg on March 30, 1843. Mr. Wick was an extensive wholesale grocer in Pittsburg for many years, and until his death on May 30, 1854. They were parents of six children. Two are deceased. William H., James L., John D., and Fannie, now wife of Warner Arms, are residents of Youngstown. Mrs. Wick, after the decease of Mr. Wick, continued to reside in Pittsburg until 1862, when she removed with her children to Youngstown, and there, as above stated, on November 21, 1865, she was united in marriage to Mr. Freeman O. Arms. She is one of our most highly respected ladies.

PATRICK O'CONNOR.

The subject of this sketch was born in Clonmel, county of Tipperary, Ireland, March 9, 1840. His parents were of the common working class of Irish people. His father mastered the trade of a tanner and finisher of leather, at which were made remunerative wages for those times. He saved sufficient of his earnings to emigrate to America in the spring of 1842.

The family, on their arrival on the shores of the new world, consisted of the parents and their two-year-old son. They came to Quebec, thence to Montreal. They finally settled in what was then called Upper Canada, about midway between Toronto and Lake Simcoe, in Newmarket, a small village through which now runs the Northern railroad. Here, together with two brothers and three sisters, the subject of this article received a common school education; and here also, on the second of March, 1854, he entered a printing office, worked for five years as an apprentice in one office, and thus became a compositor.

From early youth Mr. O'Connor was a lover of books and read with avidity whatever came within his reach. Among other books several volumes of Washington Irving's works, and the juvenile works published by Harper Brothers, embracing history and biography, were eagerly perused.

It was while learning the art of type setting, and toward the close of his five-year apprenticeship that a change occurred in the religious faith of Mr. O'Connor. About that time the question of separate schools for children of Roman Catholic parents was agitated. He took grounds against the measure as being antagonistic to the civilization of the day. Soon afterward the Holy Scriptures became an object of study. The Duay Bible, including the Rheimish New Testament, were compared with King James' version. The study of the Scriptures resulted in the rejection of papal infallibility. This occurred the latter part of 1858, and in January, 1859, two months before Mr. O'Connor was nineteen years of age, he united with the Wesleyan Methodist church of Canada. He had been raised in the bosom of the Church of Rome. His parents were Roman Catholics. This change of religious sentiment, followed so quickly by outward profession was sternly rebuked by his associates and by his mother, who had been widowed three years previously. In June of this year he left the maternal roof to roam, a journeyman printer, from place to place.

On the 30th of June, 1862, he came to Youngstown and at once entered the employment of Mr. John M. Webb, who was at that time publishing the Mahoning Sentinel, a Democratic weekly county paper strongly opposed to the war policy of President Lincoln's administration. Deeply imbued with anti-slavery opinions Mr. O'Connor's convictions upon the subject became more deeply set from contact with Democrats while employed as compositor upon the Sentinel. He knew little of American politics at this time, but was, nevertheless, forcibly struck with the inconsistency of Irishmen voting with the pro-slavery Democratic party while their fellow-countrymen were suffering the oppression of tyranny on their own green isle. Such opinions made him a Republican. Such opinions, and the record of the Democratic party during the war of the Rebellion, led to a distrust of and dislike to the Democratic party that will probably never be shaken off.

In April, 1863, he returned to Canada, but again came to the county in 1864.

On the 30th of June, 1864, he was united in marriage to Miss Lorinda Dorothea Ewing, adopted daughter of the late Cramer Marsteller, and a resident of Youngstown.

In April, 1865, in connection with his brother, Richard O'Connor, he commenced the publication of the Mahoning Courier in Youngstown, which was at first independent, but afterward Republican in politics. He was editor of the Courier until the summer of 1872, when the paper was disposed of to other parties.

It was while editing the Courier, in the year 1868, that his controversy occurred with Rev. E. M. O'Callaghan, who was at the time pastor of the Catholic church in Youngstown, upon the "Errors of Rome," which attracted considerable attention at the time. It was conducted through the columns of the Courier. A reprint of an English publication, upon the subject of the confessional, and entitled the "C. C. C.," was published by Mr. O'Connor the latter part of this year.

Mr. O'Connor and his brother were the first printers to apply steam to a printing press in Youngstown, and the late Mahoning Courier was the first Youngstown paper printed by the application of steam power. This occurred during the winter of 1870–71.

Having sold his interest in the newspaper business in June, 1872, he was admitted to itinerant ministry of the Methodist Episcopal church, and given an appointment by the Erie conference, which was held at Akron, Ohio, in September of the same year.

Failing health caused a return to the newspaper business. He was one of the editors and proprietors of the Youngstown Commercial during 1875, and in January, 1876, was one of the proprietors of the Morning Star. The last named paper was devoted to the Greenback cause, and was the second paper of like political faith started in the United States, the Indianapolis Sun being the first. The Morning Star lived but a short time, and Mr. O'Connor removed with his family to Cleveland in July, 1876. Until August, 1878, he resided in Cleveland, supporting himself and family working as a compositor upon the morning papers and in several of the job printing offices of that city.

In March, 1879, he again embarked in the newspaper enterprise, as the editor and publisher of The New Star, which he still controls.

During the publication of the Mahoning Courier, Mr. O'Connor left the Republican party, having "bolted" from a Republican county convention held at Canfield in 1869, after failing to secure a committal of the convention or its candidates to principles embracing the prohibition of the liquor traffic.

It was during the latter part of 1875 that he espoused the Greenback doctrine, and in the fall of 1876 he recorded his vote for the venerable Peter Cooper for President, as a representative of the political doctrines he had embraced the year before.

BENJAMIN F. HOFFMAN AND FAMILY.

Benjamin F. Hoffman was born January 25, 1812, in East Goshen township, Chester county, Pennsylvania. His parents, Joseph and Catharine Steteler Hoffman, of German descent, were born in America. His grandparents emigrated from Germany to America prior to the Revolutionary war. His ancestors were industrious farmers. During his boyhood and until the age of nineteen, Benjamin Hoffman worked on his father's farm, and during that time received from two and one-half to three months' schooling each winter. His father resolved to remove to Ohio with his family, and during the two years passed in arranging his affairs for that purpose he sent his son to a select boarding school at West Chester, and then at Shadeville, near the same place.

In the spring of 1833, at the age of twenty-one, he came to Ohio with his parents, arriving at Youngstown in May. He intended teaching school and practicing surveying, but at the suggestion of his father in September of the same year he entered the law office of David Tod as a student, without, however, designing to engage in the practice. He remained in Mr. Tod's office two years, during which time he came to like the business, and then attended the law school of the Cincinnati college for six months, at the end of that time receiving the degree of bachelor of laws. He was admitted to the bar in the spring of 1836, at Cincinnati, and returning to Warren entered into partnership with Hon. George Tod, father of David Tod. At the end of six months the partnership was dissolved and he became a partner with David Tod, under the firm name of Tod & Hoffman.

In October, 1838, Mr. Tod was elected to the State Senate and resigned the postmastership of Warren, to which Mr. Hoffman was appointed, and where he served until about July, 1841. Hon. Matthew Birchard became a member of the firm of Tod & Hoffman in the spring of 1841, and remained in that connection about eleven months, when he was elected by the Legislature judge of the supreme court. In 1844 Hon. John Hutchins joined the firm, which became Tod, Hoffman & Hutchins. He was elected to the Legislature in 1849, and ceased to be a member of the firm. Mr. Tod removed to Brier Hill in 1844, and in 1846 ceased the practice of the law. Mr. Hoffman conducted the law business by himself until 1853, when Colonel R. W. Ratliff became his partner.

In 1853 Mr. Hoffman visited England as attorney for persons in this country who supposed themselves heirs to a large estate there, but examination failed to find such estate. While abroad he visited Paris, spending two weeks there. He also visited several large cities in England— York, Leeds, and Liverpool.

In October, 1856, he was elected judge of the common pleas court for the second sub-division of the Ninth judicial district, and served in that capacity five years.

On the election of David Tod as Governor, in 1861, Mr. Hoffman accompanied him to Columbus as private secretary, and gave faithful and laborious work to the cause of the Union in that position for two years.

In 1865 Mr. Hoffman opened a law office in Youngstown, though residing in Warren, and conducted his law business until April, 1870, when he removed to Youngstown.

Benjamin Hoffman was married in December, 1837, to Elizabeth H. Cleveland, daughter of Dr. John Cleveland, formerly of Rutland, Vermont. The children by this marriage were a son, John C. Hoffman, who died of consumption about 1861, and a daughter, Catharine C. Hoffman, who married General Henry L. Burnett, and died in July, 1864, leaving two children, Grace and Kittie. In 1869 Mrs. Hoffman died, at the age of fifty-three, of consumption.

In 1870 Mr. Hoffman was a second time married, to Mrs. Alice W. Hezlep. His family now consists of himself, his wife, and a daughter of his wife by a previous marriage, and a daughter by this union, now five years of age.

Mr. Hoffman in his early life was a strong adherent of Democracy from 1833 to 1841. About that time he became interested in the agitation of the question of slavery, and making up his mind that the system was radically wrong he became an outspoken Abolitionist, when to be an Abolitionist meant much more than it did twenty years later. From the time he espoused the cause of human freedom until the success of the war for the preservation of the Union unloosed the shackles of bondage from four millions of down-trodden slaves, he gave of his strength to the cause of liberty. And now, that freedom is assured to the down-trodden, he feels that he has a right to rest, at his age, from further political action, and leave to the watchful care of the rising generation the preservation of the same.

THE OSBORN FAMILY.

Nicholas Osborn, when a young man, emigrated to this country from England, and settled in Virginia. He married in that State Margaret Cunnard, and raised a family of children as follows: Jonathan, Sarah, Abraham, Richard, John, Elizabeth, Anthony, Mary, Joseph, and Aaron. His occupation was farming and milling. In 1804 he sold out and came to Trumbull county, Ohio, now Mahoning county, and purchased a large tract of land, one thousand acres of which were in Youngstown township, and five hundred acres in Canfield, and he had still other tracts. With him came Abraham, Anthony, Joseph, and their families, Aaron, then single, and the family of William Nier. John and his family came a short time before the rest.

Joseph Osborn was born in Virginia in May, 1775, and when twenty-two years of age he married Margaret, daughter of John Wolfcale, who was born October 7, 1774. They were the parents of ten children, viz: Sarah, Mary, Mahlon, Jonathan, John W., Alfred, Abner, Thomas P., Elizabeth, and Joseph. On the 25th of December, 1804, Joseph Osborn moved upon a part of the thousand acre tract, which contained a log house erected by a man by the name of Parkhurst. The floor consisted of a few loose boards and the door and windows were simply openings cut out of the sides of the house. There was no ceiling, and the fire-place had no hearth.

Upon that place he resided and toiled until his death which occurred February 17, 1846. His wife died July 20, 1854.

Jonathan Osborn, a son of Joseph and Margaret Osborn, was born in Loudoun county, Virginia, May 28, 1804. The same year his parents removed to Ohio, and settled on the land which had been purchased in Trumbull county as previously mentioned. Jonathan had but few early advantages for the acquirement of an education, but he has become by reading and observation a well informed man. He remained upon the farm until after twenty-one. When he started for himself he had only a two-year old colt. For the first five years he worked for Judge Baldwin, commencing at $8.00 per month, and never higher than $12.00. During this time he bought two hundred acres of land, paying $2.30 an acre for it. January 28, 1836, he married Mary Ann Goff, daughter of Humphrey Goff, then of Youngstown. She was born February 15, 1818, near Lewistown, Pennsylvania. This marriage was blessed with six children as follow: George W., Margaret J., Albert M., William N., Mary Alice, and Jonathan W. William and Jonathan died in early childhood. Mr. Osborn resides upon a finely improved farm in the northwestern part of Jackson township.

Mr. Osborn, since 1830, has done a large amount of business as executor and administrator. He has held the office of justice of the peace of Jackson township nine years. He has often been township trustee, was township clerk six years, was county commissioner of Trumbull county, before Mahoning was set off, for one term of three years.

REV. SAMUEL MAXWELL,

was born in Albany, New York, August 6, 1839. He was the oldest child of Samuel and Mary Newcombe (Tullidge) Maxwell, natives of Scotland and England respectively. He graduated July 21, 1857, from the College of the City of New York, receiving the degree of A. B.; remained at the college one year as a resident graduate, and then received the degree of bachelor of science. At the commencement of the college, in 1860, the degree of master of arts was conferred upon him. He attended the regular course of studies at the Episcopal Theological seminary at Alexandria, Fairfax county, Virginia; was admitted to the order of deacons by the Rt. Rev. Horatio Potter, bishop of the diocese of New York, in the church of the Epiphany, on May 23, 1861, and immediately entered upon the duties of assistant minister in St. Mark's church, New York city, Rev. A. H. Vinton, rector, where he remained until April, 1863, when he accepted a call to St. Paul's church at Akron, Ohio. He resided in Akron until April, 1866, when he removed to Youngstown, Ohio, upon his acceptance of a call to St. John's church, of which he has since then been the rector.

At the commencement of his rectorship the number of communicants was fifty-five. It is now two hundred and twenty-five. In 1880 the church edifice was enlarged, improved, and refurnished. It is unincumbered by debt.

On August 6, 1867, he was married, at Akron, Ohio, to Miss Mary Helen, only daughter of Hon. W. W. Goodhue, of that city. They are the parents of two children—Mary Goodhue, born April 24, 1870, and Allen Samuel, born July 9, 1875.

CHAPTER IX.
NOTES OF SETTLEMENT.

Philip Kimmel was born in Somerset county, Pennsylvania, in 1793, and in 1798 came to Trumbull county with his parents. His father settled near Brier Hill, on what is now the Wirt farm. Philip Kimmel learned the blacksmith trade, which was the principal occupation of his life. At one time he kept the American house on West Federal street. He was in the War of 1812, and was at Sandusky under Colonel Musgrove, and was the last survivor of that war from Youngstown. He was also captain of the militia. He died April 3, 1873. He married Sarah J., daughter of Thomas and Phebe (Baldwin) Kirkpatrick. Mrs. Kimmel was born in Youngstown, October 12, 1806. Her parents came to Ohio, and settled a mile south of Youngstown in 1798. When they first settled here, they were obliged to go to Beavertown, Pennsylvania, for flour and salt. They raised a family of fourteen children, eight of whom are yet living. Thomas Kirkpatrick was a blacksmith by trade, and is said to have established the first shop in Youngstown. In 1828 he removed to the vicinity of New Castle, Pennsylvania, where he died in 1856. He was a native of New Jersey, born in 1769. Mrs. Kirkpatrick was a native of Washington county, Pennsylvania. Mrs. Kimmel is still living near Youngstown, and preserves many interesting recollections of early times.

Nathan Ague, one of the earliest settlers, died in the year 1872 at the advanced age of eighty-two years. When about eight years of age he came with his father, Frederick Ague, in 1798 or 1799. John Swazy, with his family, came at the same time, from Washington county, Pennsylvania. All the effects of the two families were brought on two pack-horses. At that time there were no roads but simply paths made by the Indians. One of these they followed from the Ohio river, starting at Georgetown, at which place they crossed over, coming to what is now called Flint Hill. At this place they put up two huts made of poles. Mr. Ague was drafted and served a term on the frontier in 1812 as a private in Captain Joshua L. Cotton's company, First regiment, Third brigade, Fourth division, in the Ohio militia. He lies buried in the Mahoning cemetery.

Joshua Kyle, senior, a native of Westmoreland county, Pennsylvania, came West about 1800, and settled on Mill creek, Youngstown township, then Trumbull county. He bought a large tract of land, and erected one of the first saw-mills in the vicinity. His wife, Mary Stewart, was a native of Ireland, but came to this country with her parents when a small child. Joshua and Mary Kyle were the parents of twelve children, as follows: John, James, Eleanor, Anna, Jane, Thomas, Robert, Hannah, Joshua, William H. Harrison, A. Stewart, and Joseph. Five are living, all residing in Mahoning county, viz: Mrs. Jane Henry, Robert, Mrs. Hannah McCollom, Joshua, and A. S. Mr. and Mrs. Kyle were long members of the Presbyterian church. He was a soldier of the War of 1812, serving under General Harrison. He died April 25, 1842, and his wife March 3, 1844.

Joshua Kyle, junior, was born in Youngstown township, April 2, 1810. He married April 9, 1839, Elizabeth, daughter of Andrew Brickley, who was born October 9, 1815. The result of this union was one child, Otis W. Kyle, an attorney of Youngstown. Mrs. Kyle died October 6, 1845, and April 20, 1848, he married for his second wife Barbara Ann Bowman, who was born in Pennsylvania September 12, 1809. One child was born to this marriage—Joseph, born August 18, 1852. Mrs. Barbara Kyle died October 3, 1877. Mr. Kyle is a farmer of Austintown township. He is a member of the Disciple church which he joined more than forty years ago.

A. S. Kyle was born on the old place in Youngstown township in 1815. He married, in 1843, Mary W. Henderson, who died in 1865. By this marriage he had three children—Mrs. Margaret L. Knox, Anna M. Lett, and John C. He settled on a part of the original farm, removing to his present location about 1854. In October, 1869, he married Mary Baldwin, born October 31, 1821, daughter of Eli Baldwin, who came from Connecticut to Boardman as early as 1810, coming out first as a surveyor in the employ of the Connecticut Land company. He died in Boardman about 1841, in his sixty-fourth year. His wife's maiden name was Mary Newport. Mr. Kyle has for many years operated in coal, while at the same time he has carried on farming.

Hugh Bryson Wick, son of Henry Wick, was born in Youngstown, Ohio, February 5, 1809. He engaged in mercantile business in Youngstown in 1828, which he continued until 1857, when he engaged in banking, being the senior partner of Wick Brothers & Co. Mr. Wick was a prominent business man of Youngstown for many years, widely and favorably known. October 30, 1832, he married Miss Lucretia G., only daughter of Orrin and Laura (Cook) Winchell, who was born in Wallingford, Connecticut, September 5, 1813. Mrs. Wick's parents died in infancy and she was raised in the family of an uncle, Dr. Charles Cook. Until fourteen she was a pupil at a select school in New Haven. In 1827 she came to Ohio and for a year or two afterward resided in Ellsworth, Mahoning county, removing to Youngstown with her uncle, Dr. Cook, in 1829, where she has since resided. Mr. and Mrs. Wick have had a family of ten children, of whom four survive, as follow: John C., of the bank of Wick Brothers & Co.; Mrs. Lucretia H. Bonnell; Henry, of the Youngstown rolling mills, and Mrs. Emily Bonnell, of Chicago. Mr. Wick died April 22, 1880.

Piatt Williamson was born on the old homestead now occupied by his son Horace in Youngstown township, now Mahoning county, March 1, 1801. His father, Joseph, a native of New Jersey, came from Pennsylvania and settled the year before on the place where Piatt was born, which then comprised seventy acres. He was the father of one son and one daughter, viz: Piatt and Betsey. Piatt was married in 1826 to Annie Knox, and reared a family of eight children, of whom six are living. He died January 9, 1877, and his wife October 11, 1879.

Joseph Williamson (son of Piatt) was born July 31, 1827. He learned the trade of carpenter and joiner. He purchased a farm and has since then directed his attention, more or less, to farming. He married, November 23, 1856, Belinda A. Detcheon, born in Boardman township. Two daughters and one son were born, viz: Warren P., now a student at a commercial college in Pittsburg, Mary B., and Martha B.

Isaac Williamson was born January 31, 1833. He learned the trade of carpenter and joiner, and in 1855 went to Tennessee in the employ of a company engaged in the manufacture of windmills, where he remained over four years, the last year as partner in the business. Returning to Youngstown he resumed work at his trade. For the last year or two he has given considerable attention to bee culture. December, 1868, he married Julia McClurg, born in Boardman, and has had three children—William Judd, Addie J., and Olo Blanche.

Horace Williamson was born August 4, 1835. He was reared on the farm, and owing to the crippled condition of his father was obliged to take charge of the home place on reaching majority. He has been quite successful in his business, owning now over one hundred acres adjoining the city of Youngstown.

W. S. Crawford was born in Youngstown, Ohio, May 5, 1819. His father, Moses Crawford, was a native of Mifflin county, Pennsylvania, born in 1769. In 1801 he was married to Isabel Scott, who was born in 1779, and the same year removed to Ohio and settled in Youngstown. He was a carpenter and cabinet-maker by trade and was perhaps the first undertaker in the community. Mr. and Mrs. Crawford were among the first five families in Youngstown to meet and organize for public worship, being members of the Methodist Episcopal church. Mr. Crawford operated what are now the city mills for a number of years. They raised a family of eight children, of whom Mr. W. S. Crawford, now of Cleveland, is the only survivor. Moses Crawford died April 1, 1844, and his wife in 1855. W. S. Crawford, after receiving an ordinary education in the schools in Youngstown, began clerking in Mecca for Daniel Shehy, Jr, and subsequently was in the employ of Francis Barclay, of Youngstown, until 1840. That year he entered into partnership with S. C. Stevens, of Gustavus, with whom he continued for three years. He then removed to Freedom, Portage county, where he resided until 1846. He conducted a store for R. G. Parks, at Girard, for one year and then removed to Beaver, Pennsylvania, for two years, then came back to Girard and was in partnership in the mercantile business with N. Crandall until burned out in 1854. He was employed in Philadelphia two years until 1856. Mr. Crawford then entered the employ of the Cleveland & Mahoning railroad and continued in that position for a period of thirteen years and six months. He ran the first train from Cleveland to Youngstown June 30, 1856. He resigned his position January 1, 1870, and removed to Cleveland, entering into partnership with D. Theobald & Co., of Youngstown, in the sale of sewing machines, in which he continued until 1875. He commenced in his present business as dealer in gas fixtures and gas stoves in 1876, No. 156 Erie street, Cleveland. Mr. Crawford was married first, January 11, 1841, to Miss Jane C., daughter of Colonel Williams, of Gustavus, Trumbull county, and by this marriage had four children, of whom one is living, Isabel J. His first wife died at Girard August 20, 1853, and he was again married May 19, 1857, to Miss Hannah Townsend, his present wife, who was born in Youngstown, of which place her parents were also among the early settlers.

William Fitch was born in New York city, June 15, 1808, came to Ohio in 1822 and was a resident of Canfield, and also of Warren, where he completed his trade, that of cabinet maker. He was engaged in the business for some time in Youngstown but was compelled to give it up on account of ill health. He was then canal collector at Youngstown for some years, and afterwards clerk for Freeman Arms. He then accepted the position of book-keeper in a bank, now the Mahoning National bank, which position he filled until his death, which occurred April 27, 1881. He married, November 8, 1829, Eleanor, daughter of Richard and Sarah Van-Fleet, born in Mercer county, Pennsylvania, December 3, 1805, and had a family of twelve children, eleven of whom are living, namely: William H., born July 21, 1830, residing in Detroit; Charles L., December 27, 1831, in Cleveland; Edward F., August 22, 1833, in Youngstown; Martin B., August 28, 1835, in Youngstown; VanFleet, August 5, 1837, in Youngstown; Mary E., June 22, 1839, wife of G. W. Washburne; Christmas E., December 2, 1840, residing in Wampum, Pennsylvania; John K., June 28, 1843, in Youngstown; Sarah M., August 5, 1845, widow of David Stambaugh, in Youngstown; Hannah L., April 25, 1847, wife of William S. Stigleman, in Youngstown; Homer I. and Helen L., born May 27, 1851. Homer is living in Youngstown and Helen is deceased. Mrs. Fitch has also brought up three children of her son Edward F., their mother dying when they were young. Two of them are married. The oldest,

Edith Jane Fitch, is still with her grandmother. William Fitch was a prominent member of the Disciple church many years, and was active in Sunday-school work, and assisted in organizing the first Sabbath-school in Youngstown.

Norman Andrews was born in Hartford county, Connecticut, May 15, 1799. His parents were Whitely Hunn and Rosanna (Hamblin) Andrews. His father came to Trumbull county as early as 1804, and purchased a tract of land in Vienna township. He afterwards settled in Brookfield township, where he lived until his death. Norman remained at home until seventeen, when he came to Ohio and located in Vienna, and afterwards engaged in mercantile business at Paine's corners, the firm being Andrews & Fuller. He was married about 1822 to Julia, daughter of Isaac Humason. Six children were born of this marriage, five of whom are living—Laura Ann, born August 12, 1822, now wife of William G. Moore, of Youngstown; Chauncy H., December 2, 1823, a prominent business man of Youngstown; Lawrence G., September 12, 1828; Wallace C., June 17, 1833; Phebe R., February 8, 1837, wife of Thomas L. Moore, of Hazelton; Savilla P., born November 30, 1825, died in 1846. His first wife dying, he married, in 1851, Mrs. Lucia Cotton (nee Hutchins), daughter of Samuel Hutchins, of Trumbull county, and by this marriage had two children—Emma R., born March 26, 1852, and Norman C., December 30, 1856. Mr. Andrews came to Youngstown in 1841, and bought the old Mansion House of Governor Tod, which he conducted as a hotel for several years, until the death of his first wife. For the last twenty years he has led a retired life. Mr. Andrews, notwithstanding the limited opportunities enjoyed for the acquirement of an education, is a man of much intelligence, and is familiar with some of the best works of our literature, being particularly fond of Shakespeare.

James McKinnie was born in Pennsylvania in 1793, came to Ohio with his parents in an early day and settled on a place now occupied by his widow in Youngstown. He was a prosperous farmer. He served in the War of 1812, for which his widow now draws a pension. He died March 1, 1843. He married, February 26, 1826, Hannah Fusselman, who was born in Pennsylvania June 25, 1805, and came with her parents, John and Barbara, to Warren, Trumbull county, in 1814. James and Hannah McKinnie have raised nine children, of whom seven are living, six of them residents of Youngstown and vicinity: John F., a farmer, Matthew, a carpenter, Andrew J., Alfred, Mrs. Joseph Bressett, George, a farmer, and Mrs. Alfred Gilmore. Andrew resides at Richmond, Indiana. Mr. Bressett was in the employ of Brown, Bonnell & Co. for fourteen or fifteen years. He died July 7, 1874, leaving a wife and two daughters. Mrs. Bressett resides with her mother.

Philip Bortz, father of George and Philip, now living in Mahoning county, was a native of Pennsylvania, and came to Ohio with his father, Philip Bortz, Sr., about 1805. The family settled in Ellsworth township, and cleared up the place now owned by George Hardman. The family of Philip Bortz, Sr., consisted of three daughters and two sons, of whom one daughter and one son survive. Philip, Jr., was the oldest son. He resided in Ellsworth township until about 1833, when he removed to Youngstown, and settled on the place now owned by his sons George and Philip, then consisting of two hundred and seventy acres. It was then but little improved. A log cabin and a double log barn then stood on the place. He cleared up the place, and put up a good dwelling, which was destroyed by fire about 1855. He died in 1852. He raised seven sons, of whom George and Philip are the only survivors. William, the youngest son, was a member of the Sixth Ohio cavalry, and was killed in the service.

George Bortz was born in Ellsworth, Mahoning county, Ohio, May 31, 1827. November 18, 1847, he was married to Miss Elizabeth Christy, born in Mercer county, Pennsylvania, in 1828. They had six children, as follow: Mary, wife of J. S. Pollock, of Youngstown; Edward, who died at the age of sixteen; Charles A., superintendent of Youngstown rolling mills; California, William, and George C. In the spring of 1848 Mr. Bortz purchased a farm in Berlin township, and resided there until the death of his father in 1852, when he moved onto the home place. He was in California some three years engaged in mining. In the fall of 1861 he returned to Youngstown, and engaged in draying for three years, the first to engage in that business. He is now engaged in farming.

Robert Kyle, son of Joshua and Mary (Stewart) Kyle, was born in Youngstown township, Mahoning county, Ohio, May 13, 1805. He remained at home until twenty-two, when he purchased the site of his present home. In 1829 he was married to Dinah Phillips, who was born in Washington county, Pennsylvania, February 9, 1810. By this marriage there were born ten children, of whom eight are living, as follow: Mary Ann, born October 21, 1831, wife of John Osborn, of Canfield; Kate I., January 12, 1833, wife of Hiram Lynn, of Canfield; Joshua, December 4, 1834, of Canfield; William H. H., October 8, 1836, of Canfield; Lefford T., August 3, 1838, of Kyle's Corners; Alice O., December 10, 1842, wife of David S. Loveland, of Coitsville; Amanda, December 16, 1844, wife of Emory Knox, of Youngstown township; and Ira M., April 19, 1850, residing on the home place. Mr. Kyle has resided upon his present place since his marriage. He discovered coal on his farm about 1870, which has since been profitably mined.

James Smith, oldest son of William and Mary (Wishart) Smith, was born in Youngstown township, March 21, 1808. William Smith was a native of Pennsylvania, born in 1784, and came to Ohio in 1805, settling on the place now owned by James Smith and S. F. Foster. He settled in the woods and occupied the place until his death. He raised a family of eight children, of whom the subject of this sketch is the only survivor. He was an elder in the United Presbyterian church at Liberty for many years. He sent a substitute to the War of 1812. He died in 1879 in his ninety-sixth year. James Smith was raised on the farm and finally took charge of the home place. In 1838 he was married to Miss Mary Ann Gibson, by whom he had two sons—William, a graduate of the Deaf and Dumb asylum at Columbus, Ohio, and now a farmer of Boardman township; John F., a resident of Colorado. His first wife died December 4, 1843, and May 17, 1848, he married Harriet Goorley, a native of West Virginia. By this marriage he had two daughters and four sons, as follow: Hannah Mary Ann, wife of David Houston, of Lowellville, Ohio; Nancy Adaline, James G., both at home; Joseph in business in Youngstown; George B., a student of Westminster college; Eleazer S., attending a commercial college at Pittsburg, Pennsylvania. Mr. Smith located where he now lives in 1858. Besides his large farm of nearly three hundred acres, he has several coal banks in operation. He is an elder in the Presbyterian church in Youngstown of which he was one of the original members.

Philip Jacobs, son of Abraham and Elizabeth Jacobs, was born in Washington county, Pennsylvania, November 18, 1811. His father came to Ohio as early as 1805 or 1806, and was employed in a mill where now stands the city mills. He married Elizabeth Kimmel, and raised a family of nine children, of whom four are living. He died in Coitsville. Philip remained at home on the farm until he was of age, and received an accident which crippled him for life. While assisting his father in cutting down a tree his ankle was broken by the falling tree, which resulted in the amputation of the leg above the knee. He afterwards engaged in teaching school, and also in the mercantile business in Youngstown, keeping a general store, in which he continued until 1865. During those years he was also engaged in the buying and shipping of live stock. Since his retirement from the mercantile business he has been interested in coal mining. In 1836 he was married to Miss Sallie, daughter of John and Betsy Kimmel, born in 1818. Her parents settled in Youngstown township in 1819, and cleared up a farm. Mr. Kimmel was a blacksmith by trade, which he carried on in connection with farming. He and his wife both died in 1881. Mr. and Mrs. Jacobs are the parents of eleven children, of whom nine are living, namely: Amanda, at home; Orrin, in Youngstown; Millard, in Coitsville; Emma, wife of John H. Nash, of Youngstown; Flora, wife of J. H. Thompson, of Fowler, Stambaugh & Co.; Frank, a lawyer by profession; Jennie, at home; Berne and Belle, (born December 1, 1861,) the former residing in Pennsylvania, and the latter at home.

Christopher Kincaid was born in Liberty township, Trumbull county, Ohio, August 10, 1808. His father was Robert Kincaid, who was born in Pennsylvania, February 13, 1784, and came to Ohio in 1802. He was a blacksmith by trade and assisted in building the mill where the Baldwin mill now stands. He married in 1805, Margaret Erwin, and settled on the place now owned by his son Christopher, cleared up the place and occupied it until his death. He was active during the War of 1812 in raising recruits. He died in 1857, and his wife in 1868. Christopher Kincaid remained at home until of age; was weigher of coal for four years and engineer for three years. He married, November 22, 1832, Miss Mary Phillips, born in Washington county, Pennsylvania, January 11, 1806, and has had four children, two of whom are living, as follow: Salome, wife of William Oatstene, who conducts the home place, and Margaret, residing at home with her parents. Julius and Emeline are dead. Julius was a member of the Second Ohio volunteer cavalry during the rebellion and was at Belle Island as prisoner. After his exchange he again returned to the army and was wounded at Cedar Creek. He served three years. He died February 11, 1874. In 1855 Mr. Kincaid purchased the home place of his father, where he has since resided.

Richard Holland, oldest son of Benjamin and Rebecca Holland, was born in Montgomery county, Maryland, April 27, 1805. In the fall of 1806 his parents came to Ohio, and settled in the woods in Youngstown township, on the banks of Dry run, near where Hazelton now is. In the spring of 1807 they moved into Youngstown, and in 1808 located on the site of the present home. Benjamin Holland was a carpenter by trade. He was deputy sheriff, constable, etc. During the War of 1812 he was drafted five times, but on account of sickness provided a substitute. He died in 1847. Richard, only survivor of seven children, learned the trade of carpenter with his father, but adopted that of carriage making, and commenced the business under the firm name of Holland & Upham, December, 1826, continuing the business until 1844. He was then engaged in the clothing and dry goods trade for twelve years, being the first to sell ready made clothing in Youngstown. In 1856 he resumed his former business of carriage making, which he has since carried on. He was married September 13, 1827, to Rosana McLean, a native of county Antrim, Ireland, born in 1807. The result of this union was one son, Andrew, born July 8, 1828; married Miss Dorcas Wilson, June, 1854, and has two children—Ada R. and Harris F.

Mrs. Ann Truesdale, daughter of Isaac and Annie Kimmel, was born in Youngstown, Ohio, November 15, 1809. Her parents settled in what is now West Youngstown, in the early years of the present century. They raised a family of eleven children, of whom two are living. She was married in 1831 to John Shehy, a blacksmith by trade, who was born in Youngstown in 1805, by whom she had the following children, viz: Robert, now engineer of the Youngstown water works; Ellen, wife of George C. Wilson, residing in Youngstown; Lois, wife of James Ross of Youngstown; Anna (now Mrs. T. J. Lewis) is at home, and Daniel J. is at home. John Shehy died in 1844. Mrs. Truesdale was subsequently married to Alexander Truesdale, who died in 1874. Mrs. Truesdale has been a member of the Methodist Episcopal church for many years.

Jesse Price, son of James and Hannah (Kyle) Price, was born in Youngstown township June 8, 1811. James Price was a native of Maryland, born June 8, 1782. He went to Pennsylvania in 1795, married in Westmoreland county in 1803 and came to Ohio in 1809, settling on the place now owned by his son Samuel, which he cleared up and improved. He raised a family of ten children, of whom four daughters and two sons survive. He died April 13, 1869, surviving by nearly two years the death of his wife, which occurred July 11, 1867. Jesse Price married in 1832 Miss Nancy Leach, born in New Jersey in 1813, and has had a family of eleven children, of whom only four are now living, as follow: Rufus J. resides in California; Phebe Maria, wife of William Crowley, of Youngstown; Malvina Florence, wife of William A. Edwards, of Youngstown, and Charles T., in the employ of the Morse Bridge company. Sallie Ann, wife of Thomas P. D'Camp, died February 14, 1867; Eliza Jane, wife of Henry P. Wise, died March 7, 1863; William B. died in hospital at Louisville, Kentucky, November 7, 1864. Mrs. Price died October 25, 1875. After his marriage Mr. Price removed to Champion, Trumbull county, where he was engaged in farming some three years, afterwards lived in Warren township, coming to Youngstown about 1855, where he has since lived, engaged until about 1875 in carpentering and building, a trade that he learned in former years. He was assessor of Youngstown township in 1863.

Milton W. Powers, third son of Abraham and

Elizabeth Powers, was born in Youngstown, Ohio, October 14, 1811. He was brought up on the farm; was married February 14, 1841, to Miss Lucy M., daughter of Abijah Silliman, who was born in Fowler township, Trumbull county, March 6, 1821. They are the parents of eleven children, of whom five are living, two daughters and three sons, as follow: Austin R., foreman in a furnace; Emma E., wife of Frank P. Wick; Emmor P., a resident of Bradford, Pennsylvania, at the present writing; Frank W., and Ada, still at home. After his marriage Mr. Powers located upon the Hayden place, which he had previously purchased and which he continues to own. On this place he opened a coal bank which the Powers' Coal company are still operating. He purchased his present home, consisting of twenty-eight acres, and known as "Parks' place," in 1853. Formerly for some fifteen years Mr. Powers was an extensive livestock dealer, driving at one time five hundred head of cattle to Philadelphia. During the Rebellion he was a large shipper of stock.

William Barclay, son of Francis and Elizabeth (Wilson) Barclay, was born in Poland township, Mahoning county, Ohio, March 9, 1814. Francis Barclay, his father, was a native of Pennsylvania, coming to Ohio about 1805 or 1806, settling in the woods in Poland, where he lived and died. He raised a family of eleven sons and three daughters, of whom eight are living. He served in the War of 1812; died about 1845. William, when about twenty, learned the trade of carpenter and joiner, which he has since followed until his retirement some three years since, residing in Youngstown. In 1840 he married Miss Mary Morley, born in Atwater, Portage county, Ohio, August 18, 1818, daughter of Daniel S. Morley, a former well known resident of Youngstown. He was a mayor in the year 1812. Mr. and Mrs. Barclay are the parents of four children, of whom two survive, viz: Helen, widow of William H. Hall, at home, and Julia H., wife of Cyrus Roose. Mr. Roose and wife are both teachers in the public schools of Youngstown. Mr. Barclay has been a member of the city council of Youngstown for some five years. His wife died January 14, 1882.

Joseph Barclay, son of Francis and Betsey (Wilson) Barclay, was born in Poland, Mahoning county, Ohio, February 11, 1816. He came to Youngstown in 1833, and began clerking for McClurg & Barclay, (the latter a brother) with whom he remained three years. During this time he fitted himself, by reading, for the occupation of a civil engineer, and after leaving the store obtained a position for two years as engineer on the Pennsylvania & Ohio canal. He then went into mercantile business with his brother, under the firm name of F. & J. Barclay. His wife, Lavina Crandall, whom he married September 9, 1838, was born in Chenango county, New York, May 6, 1815. Three children were born, two living, viz: Charles D., April 29, 1839, a surveyor residing in Youngstown, and Lucy Zade, July 2, 1848, wife of Oliver Creed of Youngstown. Mr. Barclay was engaged in conducting business for Wood & Tod for three years, and was in mercantile trade with Dr. Braedon for some years. He was salesman in a wholesale house in New York city two years. Ill health finally compelled him to relinquish active business. He filled the position of book-keeper for Tod & Stambaugh for some time. For three years he conducted a store for William Porter of Austintown. He was elected county surveyor for Trumbull county in 1845 for three years, and afterwards elected to the same office for Mahoning county. In 1875 he was elected to the Legislature. He has also served two years as county treasurer, and as assessor several terms. He is now quite feeble, having had a second stroke of paralysis.

Alexander Barclay, son of Francis and Elizabeth Barclay, was born in Poland township, Mahoning county, Ohio, June 20, 1819. He remained at home until of age, during which he learned the carpenter trade. After becoming of age he took charge of the home farm which he carried on for eight years. He was married April 29, 1842, to Miss Amelia Morse, by whom he had three children, only one of whom is now living, viz: Lois, wife of Porter Watson, of Poland. He married for his second wife in 1853, his first wife having died in 1851, Nancy Liggett, who was born in Pennsylvania in 1823. By this marriage were born the following children, viz: Charles W., Alice J., George W., Willie I., and Frank.

Mr. Barclay commenced the carpenter and joiner trade about 1853, in Lowellville, which he continued about four years. Then for some six years he was clerk in a general store, when he resumed his trade which he still follows. In the fall of 1881 he removed to Youngstown, where he now resides. In 1854 he was elected a justice of the peace, but after filling the position some eighteen months, resigned. He was also township assessor one term.

Samuel Price, son of James and Hannah (Kyle) Price, was born in Youngstown November 2, 1815. He was brought up to farming, and he always resided on the home place. He was married, April 25, 1839, to Miss Lydia Stewart, who was born in Pennsylvania March 11, 1815. Their family numbered five children, three of whom are living, namely: Margaret, wife of Perry Wehr; Lydia E., wife of N. A. Beecher, of Youngstown, and James S. Mr. Price commenced mining coal on his place in 1870, the Reno bank, which is now exhausted. He is also interested in other mines adjoining.

Peter Corll, son of John and Elizabeth (Bailey) Corll, was born in Austintown, Mahoning county, Ohio, August 22, 1817. John Corll was a native of Pennsylvania and came to Ohio in 1812 or 1813. He settled in Austintown on the place now owned by David Greenwald, clearing up that place and spending the balance of his life there. He had a family of seven children, of whom six are living. Peter learned the trade of carpenter and worked at it two years. November 4, 1839, he married Sarah Rubright, who was born October 30, 1822. They are the parents of seven children, of whom six are living, as follow: William, born September 11, 1842, now of Geneva, Ashtabula county; Henry, July 23, 1844, of Boardman; Franklin, November 30, 1858, of Austintown; Freeman, February 3, 1872, of Cornersburg; Levi, February 25, 1855, at home; and Susannah, November 12, 1859, wife of Eli Stidle, of Canfield township. Mary Ann, the eldest, born March 23, 1841, was the wife of Wilson Wehr and died in 1879. Henry enlisted in 1863, and was in the service about eighteen months, making the march to the sea with Sherman. In 1852 Mr. Corll purchased of his father-in-law the place where he now lives.

Jacob Stambaugh was born in Youngstown, November 20, 1820; son of Philip and Rebecca (Bower) Stambaugh. Philip Stambaugh was an early resident of Youngstown, where he kept tavern five years. He raised a family of eight children, of whom one daughter and five sons are living. He died in 1845 or 1846, and his wife in 1857. The subject of this sketch was married in 1850 to Lydia Wise, who was born in Weathersfield, May, 1826. They are the parents of five children, three living—Rachel Priscilla, born January 21, 1853; David W., August 31, 1857; Maggie E., October 5, 1867. Mr. Stambaugh located where he now lives in 1852, his farm consisting of one hundred and fourteen acres.

John F. Hollingsworth, oldest child of Christopher and Elizabeth (Horner) Hollingsworth, was born in Wilmington, Delaware, October 4, 1804. With his parents he removed to Wheeling, Virginia, about 1806, and about 1810 the family removed to Belmont county, Ohio, locating in St. Clairsville. In 1820 they came to Youngstown. Christopher Hollingsworth was a hatter by trade, purchasing the business of John Townsend, of Youngstown, which he continued for many years. He afterwards purchased a farm in Austintown, and still later a farm upon which a portion of Girard is now situated, where he spent the balance of his life. He was a member of the Society of Friends, the nearest place of worship being Salem, Ohio. He died February, 1842. John F., the subject of this sketch, learned the trade of his father and followed that business for a number of years, conducting the business established by his father. He married, December, 1827, Miss Maria Tibbitts, born in Youngstown March 8, 1807, by whom he has had seven children, of whom five are living, viz: Charles, now of Jackson, Michigan; John F., Jr., a merchant of Youngstown; Sheldon, Sarah Ann, and Elizabeth (Lenegan), all living in Youngstown. Mrs. Hollingsworth died August 31, 1880. Mr. Hollingsworth for some thirteen years conducted a general mercantile business in Youngstown, and after quitting that trade has since been engaged in the tin and stove trade. In 1870, in connection with his son-in-law, Mr. Lenegan, he added a general hardware stock, afterwards continuing the business alone and adding agricultural implements. His business now consists of stoves, tinware, agricultural implements, etc. Mr. Hollingsworth is one of the original members of the Methodist Episcopal church of Youngstown. He was a member of the board of education for fourteen years and township treasurer several terms.

Peter Wirt, deceased, born in Carlisle, Pennsylvania, about the year 1793, came to Mahoning county, Ohio, about 1821, and afterwards settled on a farm at Brier Hill. He discovered coal upon his place at an early day, and it was used by him for domestic purposes long before its real value became known. He leased the farm afterwards to Thomas Davis, and still later to William Philpot. It is now owned by Mackey brothers, and is embraced in an addition to the city of Youngstown. Mr. Wirt was a successful farmer and man of business. He was an elder in the Disciple church. He married Margaret Ettenburg, born in Middlesex, Pennsylvania, daughter of William Ettenburg and Betsey Gilmore. He died June 8, 1874. His widow still resides in Youngstown. They were the parents of five daughters and three sons, all of whom are living, viz: William, of Youngstown; Mrs. Elizabeth Mosteller, of Middlesex, Pennsylvania; Sarah, widow of William Shannon, of Youngstown; Josiah, of Youngstown; Jennie, wife of James Irving, of Fredonia, New York; Angeline (Mrs. R. E. Gundy) of Middlesex, Pennsylvania; John P., occupying the old home at Brier Hill, and Emma L., living at home with her mother.

William Wirt, oldest of the family of the subject of the preceding sketch, was born in Brier Hill, Ohio, March 9, 1826. He was brought up to farming, but before becoming of age he learned the trade of carpenter. He was engaged in the coal office of Mr. Philpot for a couple of years, and about the same length of time with Crawford & Price. January 18, 1848, he was married to Miss Eliza Jane Sankey, born in Lordstown, Trumbull county, Ohio, by whom he has one son, B. F., born in Pennsylvania, an attorney of Youngstown. Mr. Wirt came to Youngstown about 1852, having for a year or two previously resided in Middlesex, Pennsylvania, engaged in the foundry business. During his residence in Youngstown he has followed the business of builder and contractor. His wife died in September, 1881, an active member of the Disciple church for many years.

G. A. Young, only child of Robert and Lucinda T. (Day) Young, was born in Baltimore, Maryland, January 5, 1816. With his mother he came to Ohio in October, 1821, and settled in Youngstown. Mrs. Lucinda Young, "Auntie Young," as she was familiarly called, was a native of Maryland, born in 1791, and died December 20, 1863. She was an active Christian woman and the originator of the first Baptist church in Youngstown. The subject of this sketch was raised in the family of Colonel James Hillman, one of the earliest settlers of Youngstown. When sixteen he commenced the trade of glover; subsequently learned the cooper trade and carried on the two trades jointly until seven years ago when he abandoned the former and has since been engaged exclusively in the coopering business in Youngstown, manufacturing flour barrels extensively. October 27, 1842, he was married, at Cambridge, Massachusetts, to Elmira H. Noon, who was born in Boston, Massachusetts, in 1819, and has eight children, as follow: Mary E., wife of W. W. Clark, of Youngstown; Kate, wife of M. L. Andrews, residing in Enon valley, Pennsylvania; Elmira H., wife of James M. Owen, of Steubenville, Ohio; Susan M., wife of Edwin Tidball, of Youngstown; Arthur G., an architect of Youngstown; Dillman, a silversmith of the same city; and Emma and Allie Manning Young, still at home. One died. Mr. Young was a resident of Boston five years prior to his marriage. Of all of his acquaintances in Youngstown when he first came there, in 1821, only five are now living there.

D. J. Wick was born in Austintown, Mahoning county (then Trumbull), December 28, 1814; son of William Wick, one of the early residents of Youngstown. D. J. Wick was for years one of the leading residents of Youngstown, and an influential citizen. He died April 26, 1857. He married, July 19, 1838, Miss Emeline C., daughter of Ebenezer and Delia (Morley) Griffith, who was born in Caledonia, New York, August 28, 1818. When six years of age Mrs. Wick was left an orphan, and with an elder sister came to Ohio, locating in Youngstown. She remained with her sister until her marriage. Mrs. Wick is the mother of one daughter and three sons. The daughter, Caroline I., died November 29, 1858, aged twenty. The sons are Ralph J., in business in Youngstown, Frank P., of the Mahoning Valley Iron company, and Daniel J., residing in Pennsylvania.

William Knox was born in Mifflin county,

Pennsylvania, in 1812. He was a blacksmith by trade, and came to Ohio about 1823. He married, June 12, 1834, Eliza Roberts, by whom he had eight children, five living. His first wife dying, he was again married September 2, 1852, to Margaret A. Rayen, born in Youngstown January 24, 1823. Her father, James Rayen, was a native of Maryland, born March 5, 1797, and came to Ohio in 1806. He married, in 1822, Clarissa Porter, and raised a family of seven children, of whom five survive. He died in Pennsylvania, June, 1860. Mr. Knox had by his second marriage six children—Cyrus A., Lois E., Anna I., Eliza, Ida C., and Grant. Mr. Knox died June 8, 1873.

John Van Fleet, son of Richard and Sarah (Hogue) Van Fleet, was born in what is now Lawrence county, Pennsylvania, October 14, 1807. Richard Van Fleet visited the locality of Youngstown in 1797, where there was then a small settlement. John was brought up on a farm, but in 1825 came to Youngstown and learned the tanner's trade. In 1830 he established a tannery in Youngstown, which he carried on until 1870. He was also engaged in a leather and findings business up to 1878. His successful business life is solely attributable to his industry and ability. He had no start in youth and retired with a competence. During the Rebellion he was active in support of the Government with his means and influence. He was married August 20, 1834, to Miss Jane Douglas, born in Pennsylvania December 28, 1811, and has the following children: Nancy J., James D., Sarah, Mary, Lucretia, Charlotte, and Alfred B.

Jonas Foster was born in Washington county, New York, May 18, 1792; married June 29, 1820, Lovina Pierce, born in Otsego county, New York, December 13, 1797. They came to Ohio in 1825, settling on the place now occupied by German Lanterman. They reared a family of seven children, of whom four daughters and one son are living. The son, Lemuel Talcott, was born October 23, 1824. He acquired a good education and taught school for many years, including eight years in the Fosterville school-house. He married, on the 11th of March, 1869, Florence, daughter of German Lanterman, by whom he had two children, Una L., and Ina W. The mother died June 19, 1873, and the children now live with their grandfather, Mr. Lanterman. He was again married September 11, 1878, his wife being Susannah B. Alexander, granddaughter of Hugh Baird, one of the early settlers of Youngstown township. By this marriage he has had three children—Charles L., born June 14, 1879; Eliza L., July 22, 1880; Alice B., November 6, 1881. Mr. L. T. Foster has been justice of the peace for many years, and was president of the Ohio Poultry association for many years. He owns a farm of over three hundred acres, upon which is located the productive mine known as the Fosterville Coal-bank. He gives much attention to the raising of fine breeds of stock, owning one short-horn cow for which he paid $1,500.

Wilson S. Thorn was for many years one of the prominent business men of Youngstown. He was born in Pittsburg, Pennsylvania, in 1800. His father, William Thorn, was a native of Philadelphia, and resided there until after his marriage, removing to Pittsburg in 1798. In 1812 he came with his family to Youngstown. In 1823 Wilson S. Thorn married Miss Sarah Hogue, of Youngstown, and raised a family of nine children, named as follow: Margaret, Charles, Julia, Harriet, William, John, Emlen, Lydia, and Helen, of whom only John, Emlen, and Helen, now Mrs. J. M. Rany, are now living. Mr. Thorn died January 22, 1872, and his wife the previous year. Although but three of their children are living the total number of their living descendants is twenty-two and all residing in Mahoning county except two. Mr. Thorn was engaged in various kinds of business at different times, and successfully in each. He carried on a tannery for a number of years on what is now Phelps street. He put up many buildings, among others the hotel on the corner of East Federal street and the Diamond. He was also engaged in general farming and especially in wool growing, being one of the most extensive wool growers in the county for a number of years. He was one of the original corporators of the Mahoning County bank of Youngstown, now the First National, and one of the directors for many years. He always manifested a deep interest in educational interests and was an active promoter of the improvement and increased usefulness of the common schools. He was a member of the board of education of Youngstown for a number of years. He gave several of his children a collegiate education. Mr. Thorn was a member of the Methodist church for about twenty years, though at the time of his death was not connected with any church organization. He was a man of great activity of life and energy of character and of a sound and practical judgment. Mrs. Thorn was an active member of the Methodist church from girlhood.

Charles Thorn (deceased), son of Wilson S. Thorn, was born in Youngstown, Ohio, December 6, 1826. He was liberally educated, having attended the colleges at Hudson and Oberlin, and was subsequently engaged in teaching much of his lifetime. He was also a fine musician. He was married August 29, 1852, to Huldah, daughter of Orange and Hannah (Stevens) Holcomb, who was born in Lebanon, New York, March 18, 1829. Mrs. Thorn supplemented her education obtained at the common school by an attendance at a seminary in Hamilton, New York, and afterwards taught school several years in New York State. Her widowed mother died March 7, 1844, and in 1848 she came to Ohio with her uncle, John Holcomb. She commenced teaching in Youngstown immediately after the establishment of the union schools, continuing several years. Mr. and Mrs. Thorn removed to Mercer county, Pennsylvania, some two years after their marriage, where they resided many years, and where he owned a farm. They were the parents of four children, of whom three are living, viz: Ralph E., born September 12, 1856, now a carriage-maker of Greenville, Pennsylvania; Wilson S., February 15, 1858, now clerking in Youngstown; Harriet Edith, April 18, 1861, a music teacher, residing with her mother. Mr. Charles Thorn died December 7, 1874, leaving his widow a handsome property in Youngstown.

John H. Thorn, son of Wilson S. and Sarah Thorn, and younger brother of Charles, was born June 2, 1836. He learned the trade of machinist at Salem, Ohio, which he has since continued to follow. In 1862 he was married to Miss Betsy Jacobs, daughter of Philip Jacobs, an old resident of Youngstown township. By this marriage he had three children—Sallie, Samuel M., and Mabel. His wife died March 10, 1873, and January 6, 1874, he married again, taking for his wife Miss Ella Metz, a native of Pennsylvania, born November 2, 1853. The result of this marriage is one son, Charles W., born February 12, 1875. Mr. Thorn was in the one hundred day service in 1864, being a member of the One Hundred and Fifty-fifth Ohio National guards, serving in Virginia, and was mustered out at Camp Dennison.

Emlen P. Thorn, son of Wilson S., and Sarah (Hogue) Thorn, was born in Youngstown, Ohio, December 21, 1838. He married, April 16, 1873, Miss Mary Baird, of Sandy Lake, Pennsylvania, and has three children. Mr. Thorn is at present United States storekeeper and guager, residing at Ellsworth, Mahoning county.

Clark Woods was born in Youngstown township, Mahoning county, Ohio, February 14, 1827, the youngest son of John and Elizabeth Woods. John Woods was a native of Washington county, Pennsylvania. He was a clothier by trade, and after coming to Ohio was engaged in dressing cloth in Youngstown township. Clark remained at home until about 1851, when he was married to Miss Laura A. Foster, who was born in Youngstown township, August, 1831. They have four daughters—Alma P. and Alice B., born in 1852; Florence D., wife of C. C. Brothers, of Youngstown, and Sarah L. After his marriage Mr. Woods resided in Berlin township for one year, and on returning to Youngstown township purchased a place adjoining the family homestead, where he has since resided.

John Wehr, a native of Pennsylvania, was born in 1807. He came to Ohio about 1830, and subsequently married Elizabeth Nier, who was born in Lehigh county, Pennsylvania, November 28, 1813, and came with her parents to Austintown, Mahoning (then Trumbull) county, in 1827. After his marriage he was employed at Lanterman's mill some three years, and resided in Canfield engaged in farming one year. About 1848 he settled on the place still owned by the family. He died July 8, 1857. Mrs. Wehr continued to reside on the home place until 1872, when she removed to Youngstown, where she now resides. They have eight children living, as follow: Perry, Mrs. Emeline Woodford, Mrs. Henrietta Arnold, Alfred, Mrs. Anna Van-Alstine, Mrs. Florence Horne, Orinda, and Mrs. Celestia Lewis, all residing in or near Youngstown, except Alfred, who lives at Houston, Texas.

Perry Wehr was born in Youngstown township August 22, 1833. On the death of his father he took charge of the home place till 1860. July 4th of that year he married Miss Margaret J., daughter of Samuel Price. The result of this union is three children, as follow: Myron I., born January 7, 1866; Paul H., May 25, 1868; Ranney, September 25, 1879. Soon after his marriage he located where he now lives.

John A. Woods was born in Youngstown, Ohio, March 16, 1828. His father, William Woods, was born in Ireland and came to Ohio about 1822. He married, some two years afterwards, Mary, second daughter of Daniel Shehy. They raised a family of eight children. At one time, for a few years, he was engaged in merchandising on the corner of Phelps and Federal streets. He died in 1850, his wife surviving him until February, 1880, dying in her seventy-seventh year. John A. Woods was reared upon a farm, but learned the trade of carpenter and joiner, which has been his occupation through life, having since marriage engaged in building and contracting. In 1867 he was married to Miss Mary E. Long. The children are Annie E., J. Frank, Mary I., Gertrude I., and Theresa.

John F. McKinnie, son of James and Hannah (Fusselman) McKinnie, was born in Youngstown January 20, 1829. He was married February 17, 1870, to Miss Mary, daughter of Andrew Osborn, of Canfield township, and has one son, John A., born October 20, 1873. When the home place was divided in 1873 he located upon the south part, his place consisting of twenty-four acres adjoining the city limits of Youngstown.

Mrs. Charlotte P. Sheehy was born in East Cornwall, Connecticut, January 13, 1807. Her father, Amos Pierson, was a Revolutionary soldier, and served all through the war. He was present at the execution of Major Andre. He married in Connecticut Sarah, daughter of Captain Nathaniel Johnson, who was also a soldier of the Revolution. They came to Trumbull county, Ohio, about the year 1829, and settled in Mecca township. They raised a family of six children, two of whom are living. Mr. Pierson died April 23, 1842. Mrs. Shechy, the subject of this sketch, was married in 1836 to Daniel Sheehy, son of Daniel Shechy, Sr., the pioneer of Youngstown. Daniel, Jr., was engaged in merchandising in Mecca, Trumbull county, and was also a successful farmer. He returned to Youngstown in 1843; died in 1865. He had no children, and at his death he left a handsome property to the city of Youngstown for the education of the children of the poor. He was a Protestant in his religious faith and was an attendant at the First Presbyterian church of Youngstown. Mrs. Sheehy has been a member of the same church for fifty years. She still resides in Youngstown and notwithstanding her advanced age is smart and active.

Manuel Hamilton, son of William and Mary (Hull) Hamilton, was born in Boardman, Mahoning county, Ohio, February 8, 1812. William Hamilton settled in Boardman township in 1802, being one of the earliest settlers of that township. He raised a family of eight children, of whom five are living. He served in the War of 1812, and was in the battle of the Peninsula. He died in 1847. Manuel remained at home until twenty-one. He commenced the milling trade, and afterwards purchased an interest in a mill with Jesse Baldwin. He was married April 16, 1835, to Catharine Deed, born in Beaver county, Pennsylvania, in 1809, and has four sons —Homer, a manufacturer of Youngstown; Benjamin F., a carriage painter; Nelson S., superintendent of Youngstown water works; Chauncey D., a moulder by trade. Mr. Hamilton helped to build the first mill and dam where the Diamond mill now stands. He has held the position of infirmary director and also that of coroner.

Asahel Medbury, oldest son of Charles Medbury and Esther Sheldon, was born in Rhode Island, August 28, 1799. He removed with his parents to Chenango county, New York, in 1813. He was reared upon a farm and obtained a fair education. When eighteen he commenced to teach school, at which he continued eleven seasons. He was married February 17, 1827, to Almira Crandall, born in Dutchess county, New York, about 1802, and is the father of five children, four of whom are living. He continued to reside in New York until the winter of 1830, when he came to Youngstown, Ohio, were he engaged in the tin and sheet iron business, the first of the kind in the place. In 1846 he founded the Ohio Republican, afterwards the Mahoning Sentinel, in connection with John M.

Webb, of which they were editors and proprietors. He remained in the newspaper business for several years; was engaged in farming in the vicinity of Youngstown for some fifteen years. In 1833 he was elected justice of the peace which office he held two terms—six years. In 1839 he was appointed postmaster of Youngstown, but after holding the position a year and a half he resigned. In 1843 he was elected to the State Legislature. Mr. Medbury has been twice married. His first wife died in 1851, and in 1855 he married Mrs. James Mackey. She died in 1870, and since then Mr. Medbury has led a retired life.

Richard G. Garlick, a native of New England, was born in 1816. He fitted himself for the practice of medicine, and came West about the year 1830. In 1847 he opened a drug store in Youngstown, the first regular drug store in the place. He was also, to some extent, engaged in farming. April 4, 1848, he married Miss Caroline Lord Manning, daughter of Dr. Henry and Mary (Bingham) Manning. Mrs. Garlick was born in Youngstown, Ohio, December 15, 1825. The result of this union was four children, as follows: Henry Manning, born December 28, 1848, cashier of the Second National bank of Youngstown; Mary Adaline, born October 24, 1851, wife of Sidney Strong, an attorney of Youngstown; Anson K., born October 31, 1853, a civil engineer, residing in Youngstown, Alice E, born August 7, 1855, died July 15, 1873.

John W. D'Camp was born in Youngstown township March 25, 1832. His father, Parkis D'Camp was a native of Washington county, Pennsylvania, born January 29, 1799, and came to Ohio with his parents in 1801, the family settling in Boardman township, Mahoning county. He was married June, 1826, to Pleasant Thornburg and had a family of three children. Mr. D'Camp continued to live in Boardman until about 1830 when he removed to Youngstown, locating on the place adjoining the family home. He is still living. His wife died April, 1859. John W. D'Camp obtained a fair education and taught school for six winters. He married, June 26, 1859, Miss Elizabeth Osborn, whose father was an early resident of Canfield township. Mrs. Osborn died at the residence of her daughter, Mrs. D'Camp, January 13, 1877, aged eighty-four. Mr. and Mrs. DeCamp are the parents of three children, two of whom are living, viz: Alice R., born February 11, 1861, and Orril B., March 30, 1865. Lewis D'Camp, the grandfather of the subject of this sketch, was drafted from Boardman in the War of 1812, but did not serve, the war having closed before his services were needed.

Ferdinand Lynn was born in Canfield township, Mahoning county, Ohio, December 1, 1832, youngest son of Adam and Rachel Lynn. Adam Lynn was born in Lehigh county, Pennsylvania, in 1802. He came with his parents to Ohio in 1804, settling in Canfield. He cleared a place there and raised a family of three children. He was a justice of the peace some forty years in Canfield. He died July 11, 1880. Ferdinand was married January 26, 1866, to Miss Mary J. Cooper, born in Perry county, Pennsylvania, February 9, 1833. They have one child, Clarence. After his marriage he lived on the home place one year, purchasing the place in Youngstown township where he now lives in 1867. He was in the service of the Government during the Rebellion several months.

John K. Jacobs, son of Abraham and Elizabeth Kimmel Jacobs, was born in Washington county, Pennsylvania, January 15, 1814. His parents removed with their family to Ohio in 1832, and settled in Coitsville township, Mahoning county. They raised a family of six sons and two daughters, of whom are living one daughter and three sons. Abraham Jacobs died January 6, 1861, and his wife, Elizabeth, December 10, 1869. John K. remained at home until of age, and was engaged in teaching school seven years. November 14, 1837, he was married to Henrietta S. Stilson, born in Coitsville, June 15, 1817. The fruit of this marriage was eleven children, of whom eight are living. His first wife died December 15, 1856. He married again September 28, 1881, Julia A. Clark, born in Lunenburgh county, Virginia, August 20, 1839, where Mr. Jacobs owns a fine property, consisting of five hundred and fourteen acres of land. He had been until the past two years a resident there for several years, and was elected justice of the peace there in 1876, serving one term. After his first marriage he learned the trade of carpenter and joiner of his brother, a business which he carried on successfully until his retirement from active business a few years since.

Stephen F. Burnet, oldest son of Henry and Eunice Burnet, was born in New Jersey, October 15, 1805. With his parents he removed to Pennsylvania in 1816. He learned the trade of gunsmith from his father, and when seventeen went to Cincinnati where he worked as engine finisher. He afterwards returned to Pennsylvania, and in 1827 married Harriet Drake, born in England in 1806, and emigrated to the United States with her parents in 1808. After his marriage he resided in Clarksville, Pennsylvania, till 1831, when he came to Austintown, Mahoning county, where he remained until May, 1832, when he moved to Youngstown. He established there the gunsmith business in which he was engaged for many years. In the fall of 1836 he made his first trip down the Ohio and Mississippi rivers with a flat boat. Besides the trade of gunsmith he was engaged as tin manufacturer, and also in groceries and produce, at intervals until 1844. In 1845-46 he established the first exclusive hardware store in Youngstown, which he carried on for upwards of twenty years. He was the senior member of the firm of Burnet, Fowler & Co., now Fowler, Stambaugh & Co. Soon after the close of the rebellion, in which three of his sons rendered efficient service, he retired from active business. Mr. Burnet was elected mayor of Youngstown soon after its incorporation as a city, and was a member of the board of education ten years, some nine of which he was its treasurer. He has been a member of the Methodist Episcopal church for nearly fifty years, and his residence was used for prayer-meetings, and as a class room for some fifteen years. He has been engaged in buying furs for many years, and is still engaged in it. He is also a great hunter and sportsman. Mr. Burnet has had a family of eight children, of whom five are living —three daughters and two sons.

Dr. Jacob E. Stambaugh was born at Brier Hill, Mahoning county, April 29, 1846. His father, Jeremiah Stambaugh, was a native of Pennsylvania, born May 10, 1817; came to Ohio in 1834, and was engaged in opening the first coal mine at Brier Hill. He married, in 1841, Elizabeth, daughter of Jacob Wise, an early settler in Weathersfield. They were the parents of two sons, the subject of this sketch and Charles H., now residing on the home place. Mr. Stambaugh died June 13, 1880. His widow is still living. Dr. Stambaugh was brought up to farming, and obtained his education at the common schools and the high school in Youngstown. In the winter of 1873-74 he attended a course of lectures at Philadelphia, and in the winter of 1874-75 took a course at Cleveland. He is now engaged in farming.

S. C. K. Griffith was a native of Rutland, Vermont, born in 1802. He married in New York State in 1823, Miss Ruby, daughter of Amos and Olive Skinner, who was born in Lyme, New Hampshire. She removed with her parents to Livingston county, New York, in 1811. After his marriage he remained in New York until 1834, when he removed to Youngstown, Ohio, where he kept the Mansion house for a short time. He was afterwards engaged in the mercantile trade, and was in the grocery business many years, continuing until 1861. He was actively engaged in business until a short time before his death, which took place in March, 1864. He was an active temperance worker. Mr. and Mrs. Griffith were the parents of ten children, seven of whom are living—William E., a resident of Hubbard, Trumbull county; Emeline C., wife of William H. Foster, residing in Wisconsin; Amos S., a physician of Lebanon, Illinois; Fanny W., wife of Isaac Fellows, of Youngstown; Ann Eliza, widow of David Kelley, living in Youngstown; and Clara G., wife of Rufus P. Manning, of Youngstown. Mrs. Griffith has lived with her children since her husband's death.

Job Froggett was born in New Jersey in 1830 and came to Youngstown about 1845. He engaged in the iron business with Brown, Bonnell & Co., and is still in their employ, having charge of the blast furnace. June 20, 1851, he married Miss Nancy J. Woods, born in Youngstown, Ohio, February 2, 1834. She is the daughter of William and Mary (Shehy) Woods, who were among the early settlers of Mahoning county. William Woods was a native of Ireland, a weaver by trade; coming to Youngstown about 1820. He raised a family of eight children, seven daughters and one son, all living. He died in 1848, and his wife February, 1881. Mr. and Mrs. Froggett are the parents of nine children, as follow: Emma A., born April 19, 1852, died March 18, 1854; Susan B., born August 30, 1853; Edwin, August 18, 1855; Willis W., September 16, 1857; Annie L., born April 13, 1860; John A., November 19, 1866, died December 19, 1867; Lucy M., September 23, 1868, died February 16, 1871; Joseph F., August 21, 1870; Mary H., March 3, 1873.

Joseph Harber, son of John and Susan Harper, was born in Berks county, Pennsylvania, September 22, 1818. When in his eleventh year he located with an uncle in Canfield, Mahoning county, where he remained a year and a half. He then, upon the arrival of his mother from Pennsylvania, settled in Austintown. There he began the shoemaker's trade, afterwards following it in Youngstown, where he came in 1834. October 16, 1842, he married Eliza, daughter of Reuben Darrow. Mrs. Harber was born in New York State September 9, 1823. They are the parents of six daughters and four sons, of whom five are living—Theodatus was a member of the Nineteenth Ohio volunteer infantry in the war of the Rebellion, as a musician, serving one year, and was afterwards out in the one hundred day service. He died January 26, 1869, from the effects of his army service. Giles B. is a lieutenant in the United States navy, and was recently (February, 1882) appointed by the Secretary of the Navy to assist in the search for the survivors of the Jeannette, now in the Arctic regions. Lieutenant Harber was appointed to the Naval academy at Annapolis in 1875 through the influence of General Garfield, after passing a rigid examination before a committee at Warren, and graduated in 1879, standing near the head of a class of one hundred and sixty-two. Alice L. is the wife of N. B. Acheson, a dentist of Youngstown; Mary L. is the wife of Harry St. Clair, an attache of the New York Tribune; Caroline B. married O. H. Ballard, and died December 7, 1879. A daughter of Mrs. Ballard lives with her grandparents. Addie E. is the wife of Eugene K. Hull, of Youngstown; Wilmot H. is still at home. After his marriage Mr. Harber began business for himself, manufacturing only. About 1854 he established a boot and shoe store, which he continued until 1874, when he engaged in real estate. The latter business engaged his attention some two years when he retired from active business.

George W. Lodwick, sheriff of Mahoning county, was born in Austintown township, in the year 1834. His grandfather, Conrad Lodwick, removed from Pennsylvania to Austintown during the early settlement of that part of Mahoning county. His family consisted of four sons and one daughter. John was born in Pennsylvania, and was but a boy at the time of the family's immigration to Ohio. He married in Austintown, and had a family of three sons and two daughters. He died in the year 1860. His son George W. learned the blacksmithing trade in Austintown, and worked at the forge twenty-eight years. During the last ten years he connected carriage-making with his general custom work. He married in 1858 Elizabeth Overlander, of Poland. They have a family of five children. Mr. Lodwick served as clerk of Austintown township two years prior to his election to the office of county sheriff in 1880. He has been for some time a local politician of prominence. His election to the office of sheriff is a merited recognition of his party service, and at the same time the office has secured a well-qualified incumbent.

William Cornelius, treasurer of Mahoning county, was born in Lawrence county, Pennsylvania, in 1840. His father, Maxwell Cornelius, is a native of Allegheny county, Pennsylvania, whence he removed to Lawrence county, and again removed in 1873 to Poland, Mahoning county. William Cornelius, before coming to Youngstown engaged in farming. While in that city up to the time of his assuming official duties, he was in the flour and feed trade. He was elected treasurer in 1880, and took charge of the office in 1881. He married in 1862, Miss M. J. Swisher, of Pennsylvania. They have two children, Sadie H. and Ralph Edwin.

Myron J. Arms during his life in Youngstown was prominently identified with mercantile and manufacturing interests. He was born in Wayne county, September 17, 1822. He first engaged in business with Jonathan Warner, in his native town, and with him came to Youngstown. They opened a dry goods store on Federal street, and carried on trade for a number of years. While the iron industry was being developed they transferred their interests to manufacturing. Mr. Arms was chosen superintendent of the Eagle furnace at Brier Hill, and served successfully in that capacity until 1864, when he enlisted. While serving with his regiment at Norfolk, Virginia, his health broke down under an attack of fever. He was brought home sick and survived only two weeks. His death occurred in Youngstown, September 10, 1864. Mr. Arms married November 30, 1848, Emeline E. Warner, a daughter of Jonathan Warner. She was born in Wayne county, New York, September 6, 1830, and came to Youngstown with her father. Their family consists of six children, two sons and four daughters,—Mary, wife of Henry Wick, Warner, Myron J., Emma E., Jennie M., and Harriet E.

David Theobald is the oldest clothing merchant in Youngstown. He was one of the first in the city to open a stock exclusively of gentlemen's wear. This was in 1852. He made enough advance during the first year to add a merchant tailoring department the second, and from that time his business has been steadily increasing with the city until it is now the largest establishment of the kind in northeastern Ohio. Mr. Theobald is the son of David and Catharine Theobald, and was born in Germany in May, 1826. He married, in Philadelphia September 10, 1856, Caroline Ritter, daughter of Abraham Ritter, a sketch of whom appears elsewhere. They have one child—Cassie. Mr. Theobald began his business career a comparatively poor man. His success is the reward of close application and careful attention to details. In 1874 he connected with his business a wholesale department.

Thomas H. Ward, county recorder, was born in Youngstown, March 11, 1848. His father, George Ward, was born in Herefordshire, England, in 1815. He came to America in 1842, and settled near Youngstown on a farm. He died in 1873, in Weathersfield township. His wife, Mrs. Hannah Ward, died in Austintown in 1880. Of their family of eight children four are living. Thomas H., after receiving a common school education, entered the mines and was employed at mining most of the time till elected recorder. He married, April 26, 1874, Mary E. Hively, of Boardman, and has one child—Irene. Mr. Ward was elected assessor of Austintown township in 1877, and in the fall of that year recorder of the county. He was re-elected recorder in 1880 by 276 majority, running about one thousand ahead of his (the Democratic) ticket. This was not an ordinary compliment.

William M. Fisher, son of Frederick and Martha (Wall) Fisher, was born in Girard, Trumbull county, Ohio, May 11, 1835. His father was a native of Wurtemburg, Germany. He settled in Warren township, Trumbull county; raised a family of nine children, and died in Warren about 1850. The subject of this sketch was employed as clerk by J. A. Morgan, in Windham, Portage county, some nine years. He went to Chicago in 1857 where he learned the carpenter trade. In 1861 he came to Youngstown and engaged in the grocery trade, and has been engaged in business in Youngstown since, now conducting a popular restaurant. He married, in 1864, Cynthia Ward, daughter of Benjamin Harmon, of Stark county.

James Fowler was born in Lycoming county, Pennsylvania, in 1814. He came to Youngstown about 1837, and afterwards engaged in the merchant tailoring business in connection with F. O. Arms, a business which he followed during his life. He married, October 10, 1839, Lydia Hamilton, daughter of William and Mary Hamilton. Mrs. Fowler was born in Youngstown township, Mahoning county, February 9, 1815. Mr. Fowler died October 26, 1868. Mrs. Fowler still lives in Youngstown, and has four children living—Mrs. Orinda Medbury; Ralph, an engineer; Caroline A., and Mrs. Sallie Gans, all residing in Youngstown.

Daniel Moyer, son of Gideon and Susan Moyer, was born in Southington township, Trumbull county, Ohio, October 15, 1838. Gideon Moyer was a native of Lehigh county, Pennsylvania, born in 1810, and came to Ohio about 1830. He lived some four years in Southington, afterwards settling on the place in Warren township now owned by his widow. He died there in December, 1852. Mrs. Susan Moyer is still living. Daniel Moyer remained at home until of age, when he entered the store of C. Moser, as clerk, with whom he remained some six years in Warren and Girard. He came to Youngstown in the spring of 1865 and commenced in the grocery trade. In the fall of 1866 the present firm of Reel & Moyer was formed. In 1866 he was married to Elizabeth A., daughter of James McCartney, who settled in an early day in Weathersfield township. Mrs. Moyer was born in Trumbull county in 1842. They have had four children, viz: John W., born July 27, 1867; James E., August 12, 1870; Ella and Elsie, December 11, 1875. John died November 30, 1877. In 1864 Mr. Moyer enlisted in the One Hundred and Seventy-first Ohio National guards, and was mustered out at Johnson's island at close of term of service.

James Mansell, son of Joseph and Sarah Mansell, was born in Liberty township, Trumbull county, Ohio, September 24, 1830. Joseph Mansell was a native of England, married in Pittsburg, and came to Ohio about 1829, settling in Liberty, where he afterwards lived. He died in 1875. Our subject, when about twenty-one, learned the carpenter and joiner trade. December 13, 1854, he married Ellen Amanda, daughter of John and Jane Lett, born in Hubbard, February 14, 1838, and located in Youngstown where he has continued to work at his trade. In the spring of 1864 he enlisted in the One Hundred and Fifty-fifth Ohio National guard, serving one hundred days, and after the expiration of his term of service was mustered out at Camp Dennison. Mr. and Mrs. Mansell are the parents of the following children, all daughters, viz: Ella P., born September 19, 1855; Ida I., July 4, 1857; Lottie J., July 24, 1859; Nettie Wilson, September 27, 1863; Kate C., December 11, 1867; and Alice A., December 18, 1873. Mrs. Mansell died October 30, 1879. Henry Mansell, a brother of the subject of this sketch, born in 1834, has been for twenty years a missionary in India, under the auspices of the Methodist Episcopal church.

George McKinnie, youngest son of James and Hannah McKinnie, was born in Youngstown, January 25, 1840. He has been in the employ of coal companies engaged as driller for the past sixteen years. May 14, 1868, he married Mary E. Mahon, of Liberty township, and has one daughter, Carrie, born February 25, 1872. Upon the division of his father's estate he settled on a portion, owning thirteen acres adjoining the city of Youngstown.

George W. Haney was born in Youngstown, March 29, 1840. His parents, Joseph G. and Sarah Haney, were natives respectively of Virginia and Pennsylvania, born September 5, 1808, and August 19, 1812. They were married in 1832, and raised a family of eight children. He died October 17, 1871, but Mrs. Haney is still living. Mr. Haney was a shoemaker by trade and was a justice of the peace some twelve years, and an original member of Hebron lodge No. 55, Independent Order of Odd Fellows, and also a member of the Disciple church. George W. Haney, when fifteen years of age, learned the printer's trade at the Register office in Youngstown. He was book-keeper for Arms, Murray & Co., and also at Phenix furnace. In 1867 he commenced the insurance business, which he is still engaged in, doing an extensive business in fire insurance. In 1864 he was married to Miss Margaret W. Lord, and has one daughter and one son, Florence and William L. The house in which Mr. Haney was born was the first house (shingle roofed and shingle sided) in which court was held in Mahoning county. It stood nearly opposite the present site of the Mansion house. He died June 2, 1882.

Thomas Davis was born in Wales, August, 1803, emigrated to America in 1830, locating in Pottsville, Pennsylvania. In 1840 he came to Youngstown, Ohio, leased a coal bank of Peter Werts, and engaged in the coal business for five years, sending the first load of coal from Youngstown to Ravenna. In the fall of 1841 he discovered coal on land of Governor Tod, at Brier Hill, and in the spring of 1842 built a railroad from it to the canal. He established a grocery on a place that he owns on the canal, which he kept for some three years. He was an active and successful miner, an occupation which he followed until selling out at Brier Hill in 1858. He settled in Youngstown, and was one of the first to develop the coal interest there. He laid the first flag-stone walk in the place. Mr. Davis is a useful, public-spirited, and enterprising citizen, and has done much promotive of the interests of Youngstown. In 1850 he was united in marriage to Mary Turner, born in Mahoning county, Ohio, in 1812. Three children were born, of whom but one is living—Elizabeth, born April 16, 1853, now the wife of Bostwick Raney, of Franklin Square, Ohio. His first wife died in 1856, and in 1858 he was married to Phebe James, a native of Pembrokeshire, Wales. In 1867 he visited the land of his nativity in company with his daughter, and visited London. He is still hale and hearty, and is held in high esteem in the community where he has so long resided.

Thomas H. Wilson was born in Liberty township, Trumbull county, Ohio, October 9, 1841. He was brought up on a farm, and in 1860 entered as a clerk the banking house of Wick Brothers & Co., of which he is now cashier. He was elected a member of the State Legislature in 1879. He married in 1863 Miss Louise E. Fellows, daughter of Isaac Fellows, of Youngstown, and has a family of two sons, Willard and Henry B.

Lloyd Fording, oldest son of Ewing and Christiana Fording, was born in New Lisbon, Columbiana county, Ohio, February 10, 1834. His father was born in Pennsylvania in 1810, came to Ohio in an early day and settled in Mahoning county about 1842. He still resides in Smith township, where he located in 1846. The subject of this sketch was brought up to farming. He was educated at Mount Union college, and at Greensburg, Summit county. In 1861 he enlisted in the Sixty-fifth Ohio volunteer infantry, and participated in the battles of Pittsburg Landing, Corinth, Green River, Stone River. At the latter battle he was severely wounded and permanently disabled. He was discharged at Louisville, Kentucky, April, 1863. He resumed his former occupation of teaching in Iowa and in this State, continuing until the fall of 1881, when he was elected county clerk of Mahoning county. He was married in 1869 to Miss Elizabeth Wehr, by whom he has four children, as follows: Mary C., born August 4, 1870; Oscar E., November 13, 1873; Susan C., September 9, 1876; Garfield, July 8, 1881.

E. G. Hollingsworth, younger brother of John F., was born in St. Clairsville, Ohio, February 10, 1820. When seventeen years of age he learned the trade of tinner at which he worked as journeyman for some time. In the fall of 1842 with his brother he engaged in the tinning business in Youngstown, the previous year having made a trip to New Orleans on a boat with a tin shop on board. In later years he made three similar trips. He engaged in business alone about 1852. November 17, 1843, he married Mary E. Shepard, daughter of Henry Shepard of Poland, by whom he had two daughters and a son, viz: Elizabeth (Mrs. Theodore Williams), born November 19, 1844, residing with her father; E. S., in business with his father; and Henrietta, wife of A. B. Brownlee of Youngstown. His first wife died in 1856. October 25, 1860, he married Isabel Fusselman, who was born in Hubbard, Trumbull county, Ohio, in 1830. By this marriage he has one son, Ceylon E., born January 22, 1869. Mr. Hollingsworth is still engaged in business in Youngstown, having occupied his present location for the last thirty-eight years, and carries a large stock of stoves, tinware, and general hardware. He and his brother are the only merchants now doing business in Youngstown who were in trade forty years ago.

William Dennison, oldest son of Henry and Frances Dennison, was born in Liberty township, Trumbull county, February 25, 1820. When about seventeen he commenced an apprenticeship at the carpenter and joiner trade. May 4, 1842, he married Miss Susannah, daughter of Joseph Applegate, an early resident of Liberty township. He located in Youngstown and engaged in building and contracting until 1856, when he removed to Crawford county, Pennsylvania, where he resided some ten years engaged in farming and dairying, but returned to Youngstown in 1866, where he has since resided. His first wife died January 17, 1851. By this marriage were born three children, two living, viz: Rachel, wife of John Manchester, of Mercer county, Pennsylvania; and Sarah, still at home. Henry, a carpenter by trade, died November 7, 1881. He married for his second wife, November 23, 1852, Miss Priscilla, daughter of Abram Jordan, of Youngstown. She died March 21, 1866. The result of this union was five children, four of whom are living, as follow: Mary Elizabeth, wife of Frank Ray, a merchant of Hubbard; Emma Alice, at home; Myron E., and William S. Mr. Dennison was a member of the city council of Youngstown in 1874, and has been a member of the board of education five or six years.

Rees Herbert was born in Wales June 27, 1804. He was brought up to farming and was also engaged in mining. He married May 26, 1834, Miss Jane Davis, who was born in Wales June 10, 1812. They have a family of four children, four having died. The survivors are: Mary, wife of Thomas James, living in Liberty township, Trumbull county; Ann, wife of Job Morgan, of Youngstown; Margaret, wife of William Phillips, of Akron, Ohio; and William, a moulder by trade, of Youngstown. Mr. Herbert with his family emigrated to this country in 1842, and came direct to Ohio, reaching Youngstown in December of the above year. He entered the employ of Governor Tod and remained in his employ thirty-three years. He located where he now lives in 1846.

Samuel E. Holland was born in Youngstown, June 20, 1843; oldest child of Samuel and Margaret Holland. Samuel, Sr., was a tinner by trade. Samuel E., when fourteen years of age, began to learn the trade of watchmaker, and was thus engaged at the breaking out of the war in 1861. He enlisted as a musician in the Nineteenth Ohio volunteer infantry band, and was at the battle of Shiloh. He was mustered out of the service in 1862, and in 1863 re-enlisted in the Eighty-sixth Ohio volunteer infantry, company A, as private, and after serving out his term of enlistment was mustered out in 1864 at Cleveland. He also served for one hundred days in the One Hundred and Fifty-fifth Ohio National guard. For one year following his army service he was a resident of Nashville, Tennessee, working at watchmaking. Returning to Youngstown he was in the employ of Harry Quarteer for several years, and also of William Jonas for twelve years. October, 1880, he entered the employ of the Forsyth Scale works. December 31, 1867, he was married to Miss Mary E., daughter of John S. Probst, of Youngstown. She was born in Pittsburg in 1845. Mr. and Mrs. Holland are the parents of three children—Grace E., Charles P., and Bessie.

Rev. David Probert, pastor of the Welsh Baptist church, Youngstown, was born in Wales, December 25, 1813. His educational advantages during his youth were limited, being engaged most of the time in assisting his father in his duties of iron worker. After his father's death, with his mother and two brothers he came to this country in 1833, settling in Pottsville, Pennsylvania. He afterwards resided in Pittsburg for some years, during which he fitted himself for the ministry. He was ordained to the ministry of the Baptist church July 10, 1841, and was in charge of a church at Sugar creek some two years. In 1844 he came to Youngstown and in 1846 organized a Welsh Baptist church at Brier Hill, the society being removed to Youngstown in 1866, where a house of worship was soon after built. Mr. Probert was married in 1836 to Ellen Davis, born in Wales, and had ten children, of whom four survive, viz: John, born April 5, 1842, now living in Hubbard township, Trumbull county; Frederick, born March 24, 1845, a resident of Girard; Morgan, born February 2, 1848, residing in Hubbard; and Thomas, born August 5, 1850, a Baptist clergyman of Cincinnati. William, a twin brother of Frederick, died January 15, 1874, leaving one son, Willie, now being brought up by his grandfather, the subject of this sketch. Mary J., born July 23, 1853, died June 22, 1871.

Hon. W. B. Pollock, oldest son of Thomas Pollock and Susanna Morrow, born December 7, 1832. Thomas Pollock came to Poland township, Mahoning county, in 1844, where he operated a grist-mill, removing to Youngstown in 1854 and erecting the Phœnix mills of that city. He was also engaged in the iron business more or less until his death, which occurred in 1879. W. B. Pollock, our subject, was educated in the schools of Poland, completing his education at Bland academy. He learned the trade of machinist and engineer, and was first employed as engineer in a blast furnace. He was afterwards connected with various furnaces as engineer, book-keeper, manager, and proprietor, until commencing his present boiler works in 1864, a sketch of which is given elsewhere. Mr. Pollock's splendid success as a business man is due to his native energy, and ability and foresight, and to these alone. In the fall of 1880 he was elected a member of the Sixty-fifth General Assembly of Ohio from his district on the Republican ticket. He was married in 1860 to Miss Alice K. Jones, of Youngstown, and has had four children, of whom two survive, a son and a daughter.

David L. Stambaugh was born in Youngstown, Ohio, March 29, 1844. In 1861 he enlisted in the Nineteenth Ohio volunteer infantry for three years. He was at the front one year, and was at Pittsburg Landing; was in hospital for some time, after which he was transferred to the quartermaster department, and continued in the service until the close of the war, being mustered out at Columbus, Ohio, August, 1865. October 11, 1866, he married Miss Sarah, daughter of W. H. and Eleanor Fitch, who was born in Youngstown, Ohio, August 12, 1845. He engaged in the flour and feed business, and was interested in coal. In the fall of 1867, he moved with his family to Girard, where he engaged in the hardware business, and afterward buying an interest in a foundry. October 12, 1869, he was injured by the bursting of a gun and died the next day. Mrs. Stamburg afterwards engaged in the millinery trade in Girard, removing to Youngstown to reside permanently in 1876. She has two children: William H., born May 12, 1867, and David L., March 15, 1870.

German Lanterman, son of Peter and Elizabeth Lanterman, was born in Austintown township, Mahoning county, Ohio, February 6, 1814. His father was a native of New Jersey, born February 28, 1779; was married September 19, 1802, in Washington county, Pennsylvania, and raised a family of six children, of whom German is the only survivor. He died December 28, 1841. His wife survived him many years, dying in the ninety-seventh year of her age. They came to Ohio in 1802, and settled in Austintown, on the place on which is situated the Leadville coal mine, where he spent the balance of his life. He was justice of the peace for many years. He was an extensive dealer in live stock, driving them to the Eastern markets. He sent a substitute to the War of 1812. German Lanterman was united in marriage February 3, 1842, to Miss Sally Ann Woods, daughter of John and Elizabeth Woods, early settlers in Youngstown township. She was born July 12, 1821. Mr. and Mrs. Lanterman have two children: Florence E., born February 12, 1843, was the wife of L. T. Foster, died June 19, 1873, leaving two daughters, now living with their grandparents; and John, born February 15, 1844, is a physician now living in Colorado. In 1845 Mr. Lanterman located where he still lives, and immediately commenced building the flouring-mill which is still standing there, and which he operated until within the past year or two. He has also been engaged in stock-raising. At a reunion held a few years ago five generations of the family were present.

John W. Smith, son of Michael and Eve Smith, was born in Bavaria, Germany, September 13, 1828. He learned the trade of tanner and currier in his native country. He emigrated to America in June, 1845, and came to Ohio in the fall of 1846, settling in Warren, Trumbull county. He purchased a tannery in Windham, Portage county, in 1847, which he carried on until 1854: was afterwards a resident of Michigan for some nine years engaged in farming. He came to Youngstown in March, 1864, and was engaged in the provision business until December of the same year, when he was burned out and commenced in the boot and shoe business, the firm being Smith & Stine until 1869. He was in company with E. M. McGillin from 1873 until 1875, since which time he has carried on business alone. He married, April 27, 1850, Miss Catherine E. Fisher, a native of Germany, born October 19, 1828. They have five children, as follow: Mary E., wife of Rev. J. S. Trauger, of Columbus, Ohio; Henry H., assistant in the management of the store; William E., Caroline, and Henrietta.

A. H. Rice was born in Poland, Mahoning county, Ohio, January 19, 1846, youngest son of Chauncey and Jane (Scott) Rice. Chauncey Rice was born in 1773, came to Ohio from Pennsylvania, about 1837, purchasing the Dr. Kirtland place where he spent the balance of his life. He raised a family of six children, all of whom are living; one daughter and five sons. He was an active Presbyterian. He died in 1852. A. H. Rice attended the academy at Poland, and also the university at Lewisburg, Pennsylvania, came to Youngstown in 1864, and was in the employ of Parks & Case some four years, afterwards conducting a merchant tailoring business for two years. He commenced the insurance business in 1870 and also real estate, in which he is still engaged. He was married in 1867 to Miss Ada Lord, who was born in Youngstown August 1, 1850. The fruit of this union is two daughters, Fannie L. and Amy A.

Calvin Shook was born in Warren, Trumbull county, November, 1818. November 16, 1847, he was married to Julia A. Stambaugh, daughter of John Stambaugh. He located on the Governor Tod farm, afterwards settling on the Stambaugh homestead, where he resided till 1864 when he removed to Youngstown, where he was engaged in mercantile pursuits for several years. His first wife died in 1866. By this marriage he had three children,—John W., now of New Orleans; Silas, conducting the Brier Hill farm, and Sarah, at home. He was married again April 25, 1867, to Mary Gray, born in Fowler township, in 1834. He died November 11, 1881, and his wife is living in Youngstown.

William Pollock, son of William and Delilah (Thompson) Pollock, was born in Brownsville, Washington county, Pennsylvania, May 8, 1812. When sixteen years of age he commenced an apprenticeship of four years as machinist. He was on the Ohio and Mississippi rivers as engineer for fourteen years, until 1847, when he came to Mahoning county and entered the employ of James Wood & Co. Soon after this he became interested in the Brier Hill Coal company, with which he is still connected, being a director in the corporation. The business of the company since Mr. Pollock's first connection with it has increased to large proportions, and has principally occupied his attention since. He was one of the first to engage in the iron business, which was then an experiment. He was married in Pittsburg, Pennsylvania, about 1842, to Miss Mary Hynes, a native of Ireland, and has had four children, as follows: Thomas H., a well known resident of Youngstown; Mrs. Henry Tod, who died in 1878; William G., residing in Cleveland, and Temp, still at home.

General J. H. Ford was born in Painesville, Ohio, in 1829. In May, 1850, he was united in marriage to Arabella Stambaugh, youngest daughter of John and Sarah (Beaver) Stambaugh. She was born in Brier Hill, September 11, 1832. General Ford came to Youngstown, Ohio, a year or two prior to his marriage and built where Brown, Bonnell & Co.'s works now are one of the finest furnaces in the country. He also operated in coal. In 1862 he raised a company and was afterwards appointed colonel of the Second Colorado cavalry, which he commanded during the war. A year before the close of the war he was breveted brigadier-general for gallant and meritorious service during Price's raid. Returning to Youngstown he became a member of the firm which originated the present firm of William Tod & Co. His army service impaired his health and he died at Akron, Ohio, January 12, 1867. Mrs. Ford, who still resides in Youngstown, is a lady of much enterprise and public spirit. She founded the reading room in 1874, and the industrial school in 1878. She takes an active part in all temperance reform movements. She has three children living and residing in Youngstown—Mrs. H. M. Garlick; D. Tod, an attorney-at-law; and John S., private secretary to his uncle, John Stambaugh. James R. Ford died January 29, 1878.

J. E. Knox was born in Boardman township, Mahoning county, July 29, 1840. His father, John Knox, was born in Pennsylvania in 1806. About 1836 he married Catherine E., daughter of Abraham and Phebe Bow, early settlers in Boardman. She was born in Massachusetts in 1810. John and Catherine Knox raised a family of one daughter—Harriet, wife of William Fesler, residing in Ashtabula, and a son, the subject of this sketch. They settled where the son now lives about 1849, where he spent the balance of his life. He died February 18, 1861. Mrs. Knox is still living. J. E. Knox was married November 13, 1864, to Miss Amanda Kyle, born in Youngstown township, December 16, 1844. They are the parents of four children—Wilbur S., born August 22, 1865; Nettie C., September 28, 1868; James Herbert, August 9, 1873; Daisy M., September 14, 1877. Mr. Knox is a successful farmer, having one hundred and twelve acres.

Jenkin T. Jenkins was born in Wales September 8, 1813. In early years he followed the occupation of coal miner. He married in 1835 Jane M. Jones, born in Wales in 1815, and has a family of four children, three having died. The survivors are as follow: Richard M., residing on the home place; Hannah, wife of Thomas Childs, of Liberty township; Mary Ann, wife of Thomas D. Jenkins of Liberty, and John M., on the home place. Mr. Jenkins settled on his present place in 1849 in the woods. His wife died September, 1881.

Allen Helawell was born in Yorkshire, England, May 9, 1834, the youngest of a family of nine children. He came to America with his parents in 1842, the family settling in Wisconsin. He came to Youngstown, Ohio, in 1851 and commenced as clerk in Wood's store at Brier Hill, where he remained two years. He was afterwards in the employ of Arms & Murray, of Youngstown, and for several years book-keeper at Wood's furnace. Was engaged in mining coal in Weathersfield, and then became interested in a furnace at Lowellville, returning to Youngstown in 1874 and entering the employ of Arms, Bell & Co., as book-keeper.

In 1878 he commenced the stove and tinware business, which he has since continued, recently removing to No. 12 West Federal street, the firm being Allen Hellawell & Co. In 1879 he was elected by the council city clerk of Youngstown and is still filling that position. He was married February, 1858, to Miss Ellen Richards, a native of Staffordshire, England. They are the parents of three children—Ada, George A., and David Tod. Mr. Hellawell also does an extensive business in fire insurance.

John L. Gallagher, a native of Ireland, was born in 1820. He emigrated to the United States with his family in 1852, locating in Youngstown. He was in the employ of M. W. Powers four or five years, and in that of others until purchasing the present home in 1864. He died March 27, 1880. His wife, Bridget M., whom he married January 18, 1844, is still living. She was born in county Donegal, Ireland, November, 1824. Their children are John, born December 19, 1847, residing with his mother on the home place, a carpenter by trade; Sarah Ann, wife of Charles Erb; Mary, wife of Thomas Welsh; Maggie, Lida B., Susan, Elizabeth, Alice, Agnes, all living in Youngstown.

M. T. Jewell was born in Sodus, Wayne county, New York, June 20, 1825, only son of Dr. M. T. and Dorcas (St. John) Jewell. Early in life he was employed in a general store, and when fifteen entered, as clerk, a bank in Lambertsville, New Jersey, where he remained for two years, the last year being teller of the bank. Returning to New York he engaged in mercantile business in various places, commencing a general business, including drugs, in Sodus in 1845. He was afterwards for two years employed as salesman in New York city. In 1853 he came to Ohio and subsequently engaged in the grocery and drug business in Youngstown. About 1857 he purchased the corner where he now does business. He was burnt out in 1867 and afterwards erected the building which he now occupies, doing an extensive business in drugs and medicines. He was married, in 1855, to Maria F. Edwards, daughter of William Edwards, and granddaughter of Colonel Peregrine Fitzhugh, one of the old and prominent families of New York State. Mrs. Jewell was born in 1826. Dr. M. T. Jewell, the father of the subject of this sketch, was a surgeon in the War of 1812,
contracting a disease from which he died in 1825.

S. K. Shedd, youngest son of Simon and Lovina Shedd, was born in Genessee county, New York, August 14, 1823. He was reared upon a farm, and when eighteen began an apprenticeship of three years at the trade of tanner and currier, and also shoemaking. He worked as journeyman from 1845 to 1854 in various places. In January of the latter year he came to Ohio, and found his way to Youngstown the following summer. He was engaged in the boot and shoe trade one year, and afterwards entered the employ of John Jehu, a grocer, as clerk, subsequently going into partnership with him, and continuing in the grocery trade about seven years. In 1863, with James Cartwright, William Clark, and John Lundy, he organized the Enterprise Rolling Mill company for the manufacture of hoop iron as a specialty. The firm was Shedd, Clark & Co. for some three years when Mr. Clark sold his interest, and the firm was then Shedd, Cartwright & Co. He retained his connection with the concern in all about seven years, acting as financial manager. He was superintendent of a branch establishment in Cleveland until 1871, when he returned to Youngstown, and has since been engaged principally in real estate and insurance. In 1858 he was married to Elizabeth Price, daughter of James Price, an early resident of Youngstown township. She was born May 25, 1825, died October 19, 1881.

John S. Probst, son of John and Rebecca Probst, was born in Northumberland county, Pennsylvania, May 1, 1820. When eighteen he commenced an apprenticeship of four years at the harness-making trade at Greensburg, Pennsylvania, and subsequently worked as journeyman at Pittsburg eleven years. In 1854 he came to Youngstown, and at once commenced the business for himself, and still continues the same, doing a fine custom trade. He married May, 1841, Elizabeth Ewing, a native of Pennsylvania, and has had eight children, of whom six are living—Lydia, Mary Elizabeth (wife of Samuel E. Holland), John W., a resident of Warren, Albert M., James A., and F. E.

Thomas C. Conroy was born in county Leitrim, Ireland, January 22, 1836, only son of Luke and Ann Conroy. He came to this country in 1855, and for about three years engaged in mercantile business in Rochester, New York, and also for a year in Albion, New York; was afterwards a resident of Cleveland, Ohio, Akron, and New Philadelphia, coming to Youngstown in 1872, where he commenced the grocery trade with a partner, the firm being Kielty & Conroy. After continuing in the grocery business about a year and a half he engaged for nearly two years in other pursuits. He again resumed the grocery business and has continued in it since. In 1881, in connection with E. H. Turner, he built the Conroy & Turner block, in which their respective business is located.

Roswell Shurtleff was born in Carver, Plymouth county, Massachusetts, July 7, 1816; oldest son of Luther and Hannah (Fuller) Shurtleff, natives of Massachusetts. His mother was a descendant of John Fuller, who came over in the Mayflower. Roswell, when fifteen, learned the trade of nailer, having a few years before lost his father. In 1838 he went to Pennsylvania. In 1842 he was married to Miss Margaret Ruby, and has had a family of eight children, of whom two daughters and two sons are living. He resided in Pennsylvania some seventeen years, coming to Youngstown in 1855. He entered the employ of Brown, Bonnell & Co., of Youngstown, with whom he still remains. He was superintendent of the nail department for some time, but was obliged to give it up on account of ill health. In April, 1861, he enlisted in company I, Seventh Ohio volunteer infantry, and was elected captain of the company. He was ordered by the Governor to take command of Tod artillery, and went to Cleveland, but soon after returned home. He was subsequently elected captain of company B, Nineteenth Ohio volunteer infantry, and served in West Virginia, participating in the battle of Rich Mountain; was mustered out at Camp Chase, in the fall of 1861. He was afterwards in company B, Eighty-fourth Ohio volunteer infantry, and stationed at Cumberland, Maryland. Was mustered out at Delaware, Ohio. In 1863 he was made captain of company D, One Hundred and Fifty-fifth Ohio National Guards; was promoted to the command of the Forty-fourth battalion, Ohio National Guard, ranking as lieutenant-colonel. Was at Martinsburg, West Virginia, where they had some skirmishing, at City Point, and at Norfolk. He has always taken great interest in military affairs and is now lieutenant-colonel of the Eighth Ohio National guard. The regiment was highly complimented for their efficient service at the Garfield obsequies. After his service in the army Mr. Shurtleff resumed his former occupation in Youngstown.

Alexander Caufield was born in county Cavan, Ireland, May 12, 1820. When seventeen he learned the cooper's trade. He married February 19, 1846, Miss Elizabeth Mineley, of the same nativity, born July 18, 1827. They have six children living, as follow: John, born in Canada, November 23, 1847, now residing in Colorado; George W., born February 2, 1851, a merchant of Youngstown; Margaret Ann, February 10, 1853, wife of Benjamin Cartwright, of Youngstown; Emma, wife of S. Brown Claig, born March 20, 1857; Ella, September 8, 1860; Grace, March 6, 1869. John enlisted in 1863 in the Tenth Ohio volunteer cavalry, and was in numerous engagements, taking part in Sherman's raid. He was taken prisoner, and was confined at Richmond several months. Upon his release he returned home, where he remained some eighteen months, when he enlisted in the regular army. Mr. Caufield, the subject of this notice, came to America in the summer of 1846, and resided in Canada for two or three years. In 1849 he settled in Crawford county, Pennsylvania, and in the fall of 1856 came to Youngstown, and engaged in the coopering business as contractor in Brown, Bonnell & Co.'s mill for some eight or ten years, doing an extensive business. In 1878 he was elected city commissioner, and again in 1880, filling the position two terms. He is an active temperance man.

John Jehu was born in North Wales, Montgomeryshire, July 6, 1827. In 1844 he came to America. He remained in Lowell and Lawrence, Massachusetts, some six years, coming to Ohio about 1850. He resided in Portage county a few years engaged in clerking. While there he married, August 15, 1852, Miss Catharine A. Wartman, born in Reading Pennsylvania, in 1830. They have had four children, who grew up of whom one is living,—Mrs. E. G. Peterson, of Youngstown, born October 30, 1855. She has one child, Ethel Grace, born December 2, 1878, at Fort Worth, Texas. David M. Jehu, born March 6, 1858, died

December 30, 1879, was engaged in merchandising at time of his death. David and Robert were in the Union army during the rebellion. Robert was a lieutenant in the Eleventh Illinois volunteer infantry; was killed at Yazoo City, Mississippi. David died after the war, from injuries received in the army. Mr. Jehu, our subject, came to Youngstown in 1856, and began in the grocery and provision business, the first house of the kind which delivered goods in Youngstown. He carried on an extensive business until 1861, when he sold out. In 1862 he made a trip to Europe and after his return again entered the grocery business, continuing until 1877, when he retired from active business. When he first came to Youngstown, he says there was little or no cash in circulation. Orders were given by Brown, Bonnell & Co., on merchants, which were paid by them in goods. Mr. Jehu also took iron and nails which he exchanged for goods. There was no railroad in Youngstown until the year after his arrival and his first goods were brought by canal.

Sheldon Jacobs, son of Nicholas and Phebe (Kirk) Jacobs, was born in Coitsville, Mahoning county, Ohio, October 15, 1839. His grandfather, Abraham Jacobs, was one of the earliest settlers of Youngstown. He died about 1860. Nicholas Jacobs was born in Youngstown, and followed the trade of carpenter and joiner. He removed to Coitsville and engaged in farming, clearing up a place there, and was among the early settlers of that township. He raised a family of fourteen children, ten of whom are living. He died in November, 1880. When eighteen Mr. Sheldon commenced an apprenticeship of three years at the carriage manufacturing and blacksmith trade; afterwards worked as journeyman some eight years in Youngstown, and also at Warren. June 24, 1862, he married Lucy Truesdale, daughter of Alexander Truesdale, born October 30, 1838. They are the parents of six children—Frederick T., Charles R., Clyde Baldwin, and William S. April 7, 1861, he enlisted in the Nineteenth Ohio volunteer infantry, serving out his enlistment, and was afterward a member of the One Hundred and Fifty-fifth Ohio National guard. He is now a carriage manufacturer.

George Turner, oldest son of Robert and Elizabeth (Richardson) Turner, was born in Nottinghamshire, England, September 3, 1827. When sixteen he commenced an apprenticeship at the blacksmith trade, and worked as journeyman six or seven years. He married October 5, 1846, Miss Jane Horridge, and has two sons and two daughters, as follow: Robert R., residing in Middlesex, Pennsylvania; William G., Elizabeth A., and Ida, still at home. He came to America in 1854, and resided in Cleveland three or four years, coming to Youngstown in 1857. He was in the employ of Brown, Bonnell & Co. some ten years as foreman blacksmith. About 1869, in connection with his son, he engaged in the manufacture of railroad spikes in which he did an extensive business until 1876. In the spring of 1877 he started in his present business, the manufacture of wrought iron fences, and is doing a large business.

John M. Raney was born in Crawford county, Pennsylvania, February 18, 1839, son of John D. and Jane Raney. He was occupied in assisting in his father's flouring-mill during his youth, and was also for some years with Hiram Parks, in Edinburg, Pennsylvania, in the mercantile business. He became owner, with his brother, of Pearl steam flouring-mills in 1864, which he conducted until 1872. In 1846 he was married to Helen A. Thorn, of Youngstown. The result of this marriage was five children, of whom four are living, as follow: William T., Howard E., Helen A., and Julia. Mr. Raney has continued to reside in Youngstown since 1859. After disposing of his milling business he engaged in real estate and the flour and feed business.

Ira McCollum was born in Austintown township, Mahoning county, January 17, 1810, son of John and Jane McCollum, natives of Washington county, Pennsylvania. John McCollum settled in Austintown in 1800, clearing up the place on which he afterwards lived until his death. He raised a family of seven children, only two of whom are now living. He died about 1850. He was a soldier of the War of 1812. Ira McCollum, when sixteen years of age, learned the shoemaking trade, serving an apprenticeship of two years. In 1831 he married Miss Hannah, daughter of Joshua and Mary Kyle. He resided in Austintown until 1859, when he removed to Youngstown township, locating on the Kyle homestead. Mrs

McCollum was born November 17, 1807. They are the parents of seven children, of whom four are living, viz: Thompson C., a resident of Austintown; Mary K., widow of John Barclay, of Austintown; Alexandra, on the home place, and Lois, wife of James A. Rayney, residing in Pennsylvania. The eldest child died young. Angelina died in 1856, at the age of twenty-two, and Elizabeth, who was the wife of B. I. Pierce, died in 1876.

C. H. Gilman was born in South Berwick, Maine, December 28, 1843. His parents were George S. and Susan G. Gilman. He was thrown upon his own resources at the early age of twelve years. He came to Youngstown, Ohio, in the spring of 1860, and was employed as a dry goods clerk for some three years, and was subsequently for four years engaged in the same business for himself in a neighboring town. In the summer of 1867 the firm of C. H. Gilman & Co. was formed and engaged in the furniture business. He married in 1867, Miss Kate R. Robertson, of New Lisbon, the result of this union being one son, Levinne R., born September 1, 1872. Mr. Gilman was a member of the One Hundred and Fifty-fifth Ohio National guards.

Dr. George Lloyd Hogue, son of Wesley and Ann Hogue, was born in Fowler township, Trumbull county, Ohio, April 24, 1834. His grandfather, John Hogue, was a native of Ireland, a tailor by trade, and one of the early settlers of Youngstown. He afterwards settled on the place now owned by J. O. Edwards. Wesley Hogue was a dentist by profession, one of the first in Youngstown. He was an anti-slavery man and prominent in that cause. He raised a family of eight children. Two daughters and three sons are living. He died in 1868. His first wife died November, 1851, and he married for his second wife Milcah Lamb and had four children by this marriage. Dr. Hogue obtained his early education at the common schools in Mercer county, Pennsylvania, where the family had removed about 1838. His father owned a grist-mill, etc., which occupied his attention, and had paid some attention to dentistry. With his father he came to Youngstown about 1852, opening an office in connection with Dr. Garlick. Dr. Hogue was married March 21, 1856, to Sarah Crowley, a native of Washington, District of Columbia, and has three children: Cora N., Anna M., and Kate L. Subsequent to this marriage he resided in Illinois for about four years, coming to Youngstown in 1860, where he soon after commenced the practice of dentistry. He was in the employ of Dr. F. S. Whitslar some ten years.

D. N. Simpkins, second son of Enoch and Mary (Neely) Simpkins, was born in Mercer county, Pennsylvania, October 2, 1833; was brought up to mercantile pursuits, and was also engaged in teaching school. He engaged in mercantile business in Ashtabula county about 1860. He disposed of his business and went to Youngstown in the fall of 1861, and was engaged in clerking for various firms until the winter of 1865; when he entered the employ of the Atlantic & Great Western railway (now the New York, Pennsylvania & Ohio), as cashier. In this position he remained until August, 1872, when he resigned and commenced the flour and feed business, under the firm name of E. Miller & Co. He was elected justice of the peace in April, 1878. He was elected city clerk in 1868, but resigned the position on account of other duties. He was a member of the One Hundred and Fifty-fifth Ohio National guard, and was detached on special service, and was mustered out at Camp Dennison, September, 1864. He was married, February 28, 1856, to Miss Emily S. Ward, of Wayne, Ashtabula county. By this marriage he has one son—Frederick A., of Youngstown, born September 30, 1859. His first wife died in 1861, and April 9, 1862, he was married to Jennie Gilmore, born in Ravenna, Ohio, December 15, 1838. Three children were born of this marriage, two of whom are living— Maggie May, born February 1, 1866, and F. Gertrude, born July 10, 1870. Squire Simpkins is now serving as justice of the peace in Youngstown.

Joseph B. Couch, son of John and Mary Ann Couch, was born in Pittsburg, Pennsylvania, October 11, 1842. When seventeen he served an apprenticeship of three years at the carpenter and joiner trade, and in 1861 came to Ohio, locating in Youngstown, and worked with his brother in the manufacture of nail kegs. In 1862 he enlisted in the Eighty-fourth Ohio volunteer infantry, served out his term, and was mustered out at Camp Chase; was also out in in the one hundred day service in the One Hundred and Fifty-fifth Ohio National guard, first as adjutant, which position he resigned, and was then appointed first lieutenant of company B. In 1866 he commenced the grocery trade in Youngstown, but was burnt out in 1869; then engaged as clerk for some five or six years, and in the spring of 1878 again engaged in the trade of general groceries in his present location, in which he is doing an extensive business. He married, March 20, 1863, Cora D. Hughes, daughter of Captain William Hughes.

J. D. Raney was born in Poland, now Mahoning county, Ohio, January 5, 1810. His father, Alexander Raney, was a native of Pennsylvania, born October 25, 1789; came to Ohio in 1806, married in 1808 Nancy Dickson and settled in Poland township, then Trumbull county, clearing up a farm there of two hundred acres. He was a soldier of the War of 1812, in command of a company from Poland, and was in the battle of the Peninsula. He raised a family of four sons and four daughters, all of whom are living. He died February 28, 1844. J. D. Raney was engaged at farming until nineteen, after which he was engaged during winters for some four years in a distillery; also taught school one winter. He was married April 22, 1832, to Miss Jane Park, daughter of James and Elizabeth Park, of Mercer county, Pennsylvania, and has had a family of nine children, of whom six are living, as follow: Almon, born November 6, 1834, residing in Tennessee; Bostick, December 21, 1836, residing in Columbiana county, Ohio, operating a flouring mill; John M., February 18, 1839, in Youngstown; Nancy Elizabeth, April 15, 1841, at home; James Alexander, August 26, 1843, a resident of Lawrence county, Pennsylvania; Mary Jane, April 9, 1849, wife of Henry J. Morris, of Youngstown. Mr. Raney was, for twenty-one years, engaged in mercantile pursuits. He was also a contractor on the Pennsylvania & Ohio canal, building one and a half miles. He then built a flouring mill and operated it for over twenty years, until 1862, when he came to Youngstown, Ohio. He had met with serious business reverses in Pennsylvania. From 1869 to 1872 he was mail agent from Sharon, Pennsylvania, to Cleveland. In the latter year he was elected mayor of Youngstown, and in the fall of the same year was elected justice of the peace, serving three years. He was a member of the Pennsylvania Legislature one term, in 1852-53, and held various minor offices. He visited Youngstown about 1818 in company with his father, who was a military officer. There were then but two frame houses in the place, and about twenty-five in all. Mr. Raney is now engaged in buying and shipping flour and grain, and also in insurance. He has been a member of the Disciple church for fifty-one years, and his wife about the same time.

William T. Hughes was born in Pembrokeshire, Wales, February 6, 1840, and the same year came to America with his parents who settled at Palmyra, Portage county, Ohio; engaged in agricultural pursuits. In 1847 they removed to Youngstown. William T., the subject of this sketch, followed the occupation of a miner until 1861, assisting in the care of the family (his father having died when he was eleven years of age). He then engaged as salesman in a dry goods store at Austintown, Mahoning county, coming to Youngstown in 1863, where he was engaged in the same capacity with various firms. In 1865 he took a commercial course at the Iron City Commercial college, Pittsburg, Pennsylvania, and on his return to Youngstown was in the employ of Thomas & Owen. In the spring of 1867 he engaged in the general store and dry goods trade, being the junior member of the firm of Richards, Davis & Hughes, later as Davis & Hughes. From 1872 till 1875 he carried on the business alone. In 1876 he was elected infirmary director, a position which he still holds. In 1870 he was elected justice of the peace for three years, and township trustee for three years, from 1873 to 1876. He was married in 1867 to Miss Mary Richards, and has two children—Anna S., born February 27, 1876, and Lydia R., born September, 1881.

Lucius E. Cochran was the son of Robert and Nancy Humason Cochran, and was born in Delaware, Ohio, June 12, 1841. He was educated in the public schools of Lawrence county, Pennsylvania, where he resided with an aunt. He graduated from Duff's Business college, Pittsburg, Pennsylvania, in 1864, and in the fall of that year came to Youngstown, and engaged as book-keeper for Andrews & Hitchcock at their Hubbard mines. He was then promoted to their general office at Youngstown as book-keeper, and remained there until 1867, when he became book-keeper and financial manager for Andrews Brother & Co. In 1882 he purchased an interest in the furnace and mines of Andrews Brother & Co., at Hazelton. He has been a stockholder in the Niles Iron company since its organization in 1872, and has held the position of secretary and treasurer of the company. He has also been a stockholder in the Booth Coal company, a director in the Commercial National bank, a director in the Pittsburg, Youngstown & Chicago railroad, and a director in the Youngstown Carriage and Wagon works. Mr. Cochran was married January 9, 1868, to Mary Isabella, daughter of John and Letitia Brownlee. Their family consists of two sons—Robert Bruce, born January 8, 1869, and Chauncey A., born August 28, 1873. Both Mr. and Mrs. Cochran are members of the First Presbyterian church.

John R. Davis, son of Rev. Rees and Esther Davis, was born in Paris, Portage county, Ohio, July 26, 1840. His father was a native of Wales, emigrated to this country about the year 1830 and settled in Portage county, where he married and raised a family of three children. Two of the three children are living and reside in Mahoning county. John R., the subject of this sketch, who resides in Youngstown, Ohio, was educated in the common schools and at an academy at Newton Falls, where he was a student some three years. He was brought up to farming and remained at home until 1863, when he went to Youngstown and obtained employment in a leading business house as book-keeper. In the spring of 1864 he went into the army as a member of the One Hundred and Fifty-fifth Ohio volunteer infantry, and was at the front with his regiment. After his return from the army he engaged in his former occupation which he followed some three years. For about six months thereafter he was superintendent of a coal mine in Illinois. January 1, 1867, he was married to Miss Maria S. Richards, sister of the present Lieutenant-governor of Ohio, and in April of the same year came to Youngstown, and for the next five years was engaged in general merchandise, the firm being Davis & Hughes. He sold out in the spring of 1872, and in the fall of the same year he was elected to the office of sheriff of Mahoning county and held that office two terms (four years), being re-elected in the fall of 1874, on the "removal" ticket by over three thousand majority. The removal of the county seat from Canfield to Youngstown took place during the last term of his office and he thus had the honor of opening the first court in Youngstown in September, 1876. The first year after his term expired he spent in traveling extensively through the Western States and upon his return he entered into the business of insurance and real estate, his office being No. 47, West Federal street (up stairs). He has a family of four children, three sons and one daughter.

Abraham Hubler was born in Coitsville, Mahoning county, Ohio, January 23, 1834. His father, Moses Hubler, was born in Center county, Pennsylvania, in 1803. In 1825 he married Miss Sarah Newberry, who was born in Northumberland county, Pennsylvania, in 1807. They were the parents of twelve children, of whom nine are living. They came to Ohio in 1833, and settled in Coitsville, where they lived many years. He died March 16, 1855, but his widow is still living. The youth of our subject was spent at home on the farm. The death of the father threw the care of the farm upon him for some six years. November 21, 1862, he was married to Miss Sarah Jane, daughter of Piatt Williamson, born in Youngstown township in 1838. They are the parents of seven children, six of whom survive—Frank E., Myron G., Piatt W., Jesse L., Alice May, and Howard C. In 1864 Mr Huber moved on to the Williamson addition, where he still lives. After his marriage he worked in a rolling mill until the spring of 1880, when he commenced the grocery business. He is now largely interested in real estate, and also engaged in the insurance business.

William Jonas was born in Merklenberg, Germany, May 8, 1828. When fifteen, he commenced an apprenticeship of five years at the jeweler's trade, after which he was employed at his trade in Dresden and other cities until 1851, when he emigrated to America. He was subsequently in the employ of a wholesale house in Philadelphia until 1854, and for three years afterwards resided in Minersville, Pennsylvania, engaged in business. May, 1857, he married Miss Amelia, daughter of Abraham Ritter, an old resident of Youngstown. After his marriage he was a resident of Virginia a number of years, coming to Youngstown in 1864, and engaging in the business, which he has since carried on. He is now doing an extensive trade in jewelry, watches, and musical instruments. Mr. Jonas has a family of ten children living, and two deceased. The survivors are Louisa, wife of Solomon Lazarus, of Youngstown; Carrie B., wife of Morris Huffman, living in Missouri; David, city editor of the Youngstown Vindicator; Hattie, Herman, Ida, Emma, Julius, Emill, and Eddie.

James H. Thompson was born in Chatham, England, September 20, 1844, son of William H. and Mary W. Thompson. He came to the United States with his parents in 1849, locating in Cleveland. In 1862, being then but seventeen years of age, he enlisted in company A, Twenty-third Ohio volunteer infantry. He participated in the battle of Cloyd Mountain, was in the Lynchburg raid, and served under Sheridan in the Shenandoah campaign; was at Berryville, Fisher Hill, Cedar Creek, and other engagements, serving out his enlistment; was mustered out as quartermaster sergeant in September 1865. Returning home he engaged in mercantile pursuits, entering the employ of Fowler, Matherson & Co., in the hardware trade. He continued as employe till 1868, when the present firm of Fowler, Stamburg & Co., wholesale and retail hardware, was formed, of which he became a partner. Mr. Thompson was married in 1870 to Miss Flora, daughter of Philip Jacobs of Youngstown. They have three children, Philip J., George F., and Florence.

David Reel was born in Weathersfield township, Trumbull county, Ohio, December 15, 1838, being the youngest son of Peter and Elizabeth Reel. His father was a native of Pennsylvania, born about 1789, and removed to Ohio in 1807, settling in Weathersfield. He raised a family of eight children, of whom five are living. He died in 1865. The subject of this sketch obtained his education in the schools of Lordstown and Girard, completing it at a commercial college in Pittsburg. He was engaged in teaching school some seven years. He was book-keeper for some time for Park & Patch, of Warren, and came to Youngstown in 1866. In partnership with Daniel Moyer he founded the present grocery house of Reel & Moyer. He was married, in 1867, to Miss Emma McKee, who was born in Lordstown township, Trumbull county. They are the parents of five children—Harry M., Ella May, Effie Bell, Fred Bliss, and Jay Garfield. Mr. Reel served as city treasurer two years previous to removal of county seat, after which the office was abolished. He was elected councilman from the first ward of Youngstown in the spring of 1881, and is chairman of the finance committee. During the Rebellion he twice offered his services in behalf of the Union, but was rejected on account of physical disability.

J. J. Hamman, oldest son of John and Hannah (Reiss) Hamman, was born in Allentown, Pennsylvania, November 5, 1841. When a boy he learned the trade of cigar maker, and in 1856 went to Philadelphia, and worked as journeyman afterwards in other cities, coming to Youngstown in 1866. In 1871 he commenced the business of the manufacture of cigars under the firm name of Hamman & Bernd. In 1876 he purchased his partner's interest and has since carried on the business alone, having two stores and doing a wholesale and retail business. Mr. Hamman has been twice married, first in 1866 to Miss Ophelia Knapp, a native of Danbury, Connecticut. By this marriage two children were born, both of whom died young. His wife died in 1871, and September 16, 1875, he married Miss Ella J. Arner, who was born in Ellsworth township, Mahoning county, Ohio, in 1853, daughter of Eli T. Arner. The result of this union is two sons—Paul N., born in 1877, and James, born in 1880. In 1861 Mr. Hamman enlisted in the Fifty-third Pennsylvania volunteer infantry, and was in the battles of Fair Oaks, Gaines Mill, Peach Orchard, Malvern Hill, and others. He was discharged in 1862 on account of physical disability. He was elected councilman from the Fourth ward of Youngstown in the spring of 1880 and is at present filling that position. He was one of the original members of the first fire company in Youngstown, and was foreman of the same; is a member of the Independent Order of Odd Fellows.

George Rudge was born in England February 6, 1824. He was brought up to mercantile pursuits and was salesman in London and Birmingham. He married, in March, 1852, Miss Jane Stork, and in April of the same year came to the United States, and immediately afterwards to Mahoning county. He purchased a farm in Boardman and resided there until 1866, when he removed to Youngstown where he engaged in mercantile business, also in real estate for a short time. In June, 1872, he was appointed to his present position, that of secretary to water-works board of trustees, and was a member of the city council one term about 1871. His family consists of eight children, as follow: George, Jr., J. Frederick, Mary L. (wife of William A. Maline), J. Edgar, Mary Beatrice, Elizabeth A., Charles Eugene, and William Henry.

Frank McMaster was born in county Antrim, Ireland, November 25, 1843. He emigrated to this country in 1863, and in the fall of 1864 came to Ohio, locating in the spring of 1866 in Youngstown. He was subsequently engaged as foreman in a brickyard for over a year. In the fall of 1867 he began contracting stone and brick work, building the foundation of the Opera house and other business blocks in Youngstown. In the fall of 1878 Mr. McMaster was elected county commissioner, and in the fall of 1881 was re-elected to the same position. He was married April 4, 1867, to Miss Matilda McIlray, who was born in Ontario, Canada, in 1847.

Edwin Webb was born in Gloucestershire, England, November 21, 1843, and emigrated with his parents to America in 1854, locating in Schuylkill county, Pennsylvania. When sixteen he commenced to learn the shoemaking trade, at which he continued until 1862, when he enlisted in the One Hundred and Twenty-ninth Pennsylvania volunteer infantry, under Colonel Freck. He was at Antietam, Bull Run, and Fredericksburg, where he was taken prisoner. He was soon paroled and for some time thereafter was in hospital. He was mustered out at Harrisburg, Pennsylvania, May 19, 1863. He resumed his trade of shoemaking, completing it at Philadelphia. He was in Meadville, Pennsylvania, some fifteen months, part of the time in business for himself. Came to Youngstown, Ohio, in the spring of 1867 and engaged in trade with Mr. Clark, the firm being Clark & Webb. After continuing two years Mr. Edward Turner purchased Clark's interest, the firm being then Webb & Turner. In 1874 he disposed of his interest to Mr. Turner. In March, 1869, he was married to Miss Emma Copeland, who was born in London, England. They are the parents of four children, as follow: Alice B., Edwin H., and Eva. Carrie died when four years old.

George J. Williams, postmaster at Youngstown, was born in Medina, Ohio, January 6, 1841; oldest son of John and Susan Williams, natives of New York State. In 1861 he enlisted in the Forty-second Ohio volunteer infantry, and participated in the battles of Middle Creek, Chickasaw Bayou, Arkansas Post, and Champion Hills. At the latter place he was severely wounded, losing a leg. After recovering sufficiently to leave the hospital he was discharged in the fall of 1863, having been in active service some nineteen months. In 1867 he came to Youngstown, and until 1870 was in the employ of the Pittsburg, Fort Wayne, and Chicago railroad as telegraph operator; was engaged in the grocery business until 1873, and was city clerk of Youngstown for some time. In 1881 he was appointed postmaster by President Garfield, which position he now holds. In 1873 he was married to Mrs. Eliza G. Pinney, daughter of William P. Ladd, of Portage county, Ohio, and has two daughters, Blanche A. and Georgiana.

Amos Pitts, second son of Henry and Mary Ann (Myers) Pitts, was born in Springfield township, Mahoning county, Ohio, March 11, 1846. He was raised upon a farm, and remained at home until of age. He came to Youngstown in 1868, and for some eight years engaged in teaming. In 1875, with Mr. Ferrin, he engaged in the livery business under the firm name of Pitts & Ferrin. Married in 1875, Miss Kate Baker, and has four children living—two sons and two daughters.

Edward H. Turner was born in Minersville, Pennsylvania, June 19, 1845. He partially learned the shoemaker's trade with his father when young, and when sixteen went to Philadelphia, where he continued it. In February, 1863, he enlisted in the Forty-eighth Pennsylvania volunteer infantry, and was at the battles of Spottsylvania Court House, where he was wounded, Shady Grove, and at the front before Petersburg. He served until the close of the war, and was discharged at Alexandria, Virginia, in June, 1865. He returned to Philadelphia, where he completed his trade afterwards following it in various places. He came to Youngstown in 1868, and afterwards bought the interest of Mr. Clark, of the firm of Clark & Webb, the new firm being known as Webb & Turner. In June, 1874, he purchased the interest of Mr. Webb, and carried on the business alone until August, 1881, when the firm of Turner & Cornelius was formed, the junior being William Cornelius, the county treasurer of Mahoning county. In 1869 Mr. Turner was married to Miss B. Lenahan, and has a family of three daughters and three sons.

B. S. Decker, son of Jeremiah and Elsie (Newkirk) Decker, was born in Orange county, New York, August 15, 1815. When about sixteen he served an apprenticeship of five or six years at the tanning and currier trade in Orange county. In 1835 he came to Ohio, locating in Cleveland, and engaged in farming. He returned again to Orange county, and on May 23, 1836, was married to Sarah Harlow, born in Ulster county, New York, August 25, 1812. He returned to Cleveland and engaged in buying and selling live stock, and engaged also in the mercantile business. In 1856 he removed to Wayne, Ashtabula county, where he carried on a cheese factory, a store, and was also postmaster. In the spring of 1868 he came to Youngstown, and engaged in the grocery trade for some time, soon after building, on the street where he is now located, and commenced in the business of flour, feed, coal, lime, cement, etc., in which he is still engaged. His first wife died January 31, 1847, leaving two daughters and two sons, who are living. He was married the second time in 1850 to Sophia M. Billings, born in East Cleveland, Ohio, in 1832. By this marriage have been born two sons and one daughter —Charles N., of Youngstown; Rosa Virginia, at home with her parents, and Lewis E., who assists his father in his business. Mr. Decker was a member of the city council one term, and assessor for the Fourth ward one year.

Abraham Ritter was the oldest person living in the Mahoning valley. The following sketch of him from the pen of David Jones is taken from the Evening News of November 29, 1880:

There lives in this city one of the few living witnesses of the greatness of Napoleon, and who served with him that ancient dynasties and old forms of tyranny might be crushed out. Although nearly three quarters of a century have passed since these events shook the thrones of the Old World, this gentleman, Mr. Abraham Ritter, possesses all the faculties of a middle-aged man, and can converse clearly and explicitly upon subjects which are known to most people through the inanimate record of books. Upon these subjects he delights to talk, especially to the Frenchmen, although for more than fifty years he has had little opportunity of putting his knowledge of that language to use. Yesterday (November 28, 1880) he celebrated his ninety-sixth birthday.

. . . He was born in the village of Luntuch, Germany, and at the age of sixteen went to France where he remained two years and then returned to his native village. In 1810 he joined the imperial army and in 1811 went to Spain. He did not remain there long but returned with the army and in 1812 started with it in the Russian campaign, memorable for the great destruction it wrought in Napoleon's forces. At Wilna, although not a single battle was fought, over ten thousand horses had died of hunger, and over twenty-five thousand of Napoleon's best and most experienced men were starving in the hospitals. On the 13th of August the army was put in motion and on the 16th began the terrible battle of Smolensk. All day and all night they fought, though weak from exhaustion and want of food, and in the morning a division of the French army entered Smolensk and found it in ashes and deserted, the fleeing Russians not even taking time to care for their dead and wounded. In this battle Mr. Ritter was wounded in the leg and had his horse shot from under him. This of course caused him to be taken to the hospital.

On the 2d day of May, 1813, he was with his comrades again at Lutzen, in Saxony, where they met the allied armies, one hundred thousand strong, and experienced men. Napoleon, however, at Wilna, and Smolensk, and Moscow had lost his old and trusty soldiers, and now had only eighty thousand young and inexperienced men. He could be seen in the thickest of the fight at Lutzen and compelled the allies to retreat to Dresden. There they remained about a week, while peace negotiations were pending, and then removed to Bautzen, where the allies were entrenched, and in the terrible conflict which ensued Mr. Ritter was again wounded in the leg and compelled to go to the hospital, and in 1814 he was mustered out.

On leaving the army he went to Katzenheim, and in 1855 came to this country. For twelve years he lived in Philadelphia, and then removed to this city, where his sons and daughters were living, and two years later his wife died at the age of seventy years. Mr. Ritter has five children living —Edward Ritter, Ferdinand Ritter, Mrs. Theobald, and Mrs. William Jones, of this city, and Mrs. A. Waldrun, of Chillicothe, Maryland. He has twenty-four grandchildren. The memory of Mr. Ritter is as remarkable as the firmness with which he walks. He remembers distinctly the days of Napoleon's greatness and delights to talk of them. He says that never was a commander so loved as was the mighty Corsican. "Frequently," Mr. Ritter says, "he would pass through our tents, and with iron spoon in hand would taste our food to see if it was palatable or not."

Mr. Ritter in 1882 was as hale and hearty as Mr. Jones describes him to have been on his ninety-sixth birthday. His death occurred on June 7, 1882, at the age of ninety-eight.

Lippman Liebman, son of Rev. Joshua and Rosa Liebman, was born in Baden, Germany, September 24, 1832. He was under the care of a private tutor until he was seventeen, and then entered a seminary at Karlsruhe, from which he graduated in 1852. For two years subsequently he was minister and teacher at Malsh, Baden, and in August, 1854, came to the United States. He settled in Cincinnati, filling the position of teacher in a congregation for two years. In 1856 he accepted a call to Dayton, Ohio, to officiate as minister and teacher, where he remained one year. He then returned to Cincinnati, accepting a position as teacher and cantor to the congregation of Dr. Lilienthal, remaining until 1860; also conducting a private school, continuing until 1864, being obliged to decline a call as minister and teacher to Washington, District of Columbia, on account of his wife's ill health. He was subsequently located in Cleveland as minister, during which he was a teacher in the public schools in Brooklyn for two years. In 1868 he came to Youngstown in the capacity of minister and teacher. In 1872 he engaged also in the real estate business and insurance, to which he now devotes his entire attention, having resigned his position as minister and teacher in January, 1882. The firm is Liebman & Son. Mr. Liebman married, January 20, 1855, Fanny Hess. They are the parents of twelve children, of whom eleven, six daughters and five sons, are living.

Christian Mauser was born in Bartenbach, Koenigreich, Wurtemburg, Germany, February 21, 1847, and came to this country in 1866. He came to Youngstown and engaged at work in 1867. In 1868, 1869, and 1870 he was in Pittsburg, and in 1871 commenced as contractor in Youngstown. In the latter year he was married to Lucinda Krum, who was born in Springfield township, Mahoning county, January 22, 1847. They have three children—Emma Rosina, born April 20, 1872, Louis Karl, February 5, 1874, Alice Maria, July 12, 1880. Mr. Mauser has a stone yard on Walnut street, Youngstown, and deals in block, cut, flagging, and building stone. He learned his trade of builder and contractor in Germany. He was naturalized in 1873.

S. D. Currier was born in East Kingston, New Hampshire, October 23, 1846, youngest son of R. W. and Lois S. Currier. Early in life he had an inclination for mercantile pursuits and first engaged in peddling goods, traveling on foot. In 1863 he was employed in the store of his brother, O. G. Currier, a merchant in Boston, with whom he remained a few years. Subsequently he entered the employ of the New England Carpet company remaining until 1872. In this year he removed to Youngstown, Ohio, and at once commenced business for himself on East Federal street, removing to his present location in 1881. Mr. Currier has built up a large establishment from a small beginning, it being now the most extensive store of the kind in any city the size of Youngstown in the country, dealing principally in carpets, oil-cloths, upholsterers' goods, wall paper, lace curtains, etc., employing sixteen hands. Mr. Currier was married in 1881 to Miss Ella M. Pendleton, born in Massachusetts in 1849.

Henry Wendler was born in Brookfield township, Trumbull county, Ohio, November 29, 1836. His father, Adam Wendler, emigrated to this country from Germany about 1833 with his family, came to Trumbull county, and settled in Brookfield, being one of the first foreign families that located in that township. He raised a family of one daughter and four sons, all of whom are living in Trumbull and Mahoning counties. He died about 1867. His widow, Mrs. Caroline Wendler, is still living in Brookfield, at the advanced age of eighty-four. Adam Wendler was a soldier under Napoleon for twelve years, and was with the army at the time of its retreat from Moscow. Henry Wendler, when fifteen, learned the cabinet-making trade in Hartford, Trumbull county, and worked as journeyman until 1859. In the fall of that year he went to California, and engaged in that business in Nevada City till 1864. Shortly before his return his business was destroyed by fire, losing everything. In the spring of that year he returned to Trumbull county, and commenced business in Warren. March 28, 1865, he was married to Miss Margaret Smith, born in New York city in 1845. They are the parents of three children, as follows: George Adam, Charles Henry, and Emma Lilian. He continued in business in Warren until 1869. He was engaged in furniture manufacturing in Tecumseh, Michigan, for some years, removing to Youngstown in 1872, where he commenced the undertaking business. About two years since he added the picture frame business, in which he is doing an extensive trade.

Ferrin Gardener was born in Concord township,

Erie county, New York, May 30, 1832; was brought up to farming, but when twenty commenced the livery business at Springville, New York, continuing until 1861; was afterwards engaged for some five years in practice as veterinary surgeon in Chicago, having fitted himself for that profession at the Veterinary institute, Chicago, receiving a diploma from that institution. He resided in Meadville, Pennsylvania, for some time, engaged in the livery business and also in the practice of his profession. Came to Youngstown in the spring of 1874, and in 1875 went into partnership with Amos Pitts in the livery business in which he is still engaged. Married July 2, 1856, to Jane Morse. Has had five children of whom two survive.

J. K. Wolf was born in Springfield township, Mahoning county, Ohio, December 29, 1841; oldest son of Andrew and Barbara Wolf. Andrew Wolf was born in Germany, January 9, 1814, and came to this country with his parents in 1819. They settled in Tioga county, Pennsylvania, came to Ohio about 1826, and to Mahoning county about two years later. He married January 12, 1841, and raised a family of ten children, of whom five are living. J. K. Wolf was married Feburary 25, 1868, to Miss Maria Yarian, born in Beaver township, Mahoning county. They are the parents of three children, viz: Laura L., Orrin C., and an infant born December 29, 1881. Mr. Wolf was engaged in mercantile business in Woodworth, Boardman township, some seven months, selling out in the spring of 1875; came to Youngstown and commenced the grocery business in which he has since continued. While residing in Boardman he was postmaster for one year.

Jared Huxley, second son of Socrates S. and Paulina (Spaulding) Huxley, was born in Mahoning county, Ohio, July 23, 1840. After the usual attendance at the common schools, and at an academy, teaching at intervals, when about twenty he entered a commercial college at Cleveland. He afterwards took a scientific course at Oberlin college, graduating from that institution, and in 1869 went to Lafayette, Indiana, where he had charge of a commercial college for one year. He then returned to Cleveland and engaged in the same duties there, during which he began the study of law in the office of McNutt & Grubbs. He returned to LaFayette, but after residing there one year came again to Cleveland, where he resumed the study of law under Palmer & DeWolf. He was admitted to the bar at Norwalk, Ohio, April, 1871, and engaged in practice at Canfield, Mahoning county, until the removal of the county seat to Youngstown, when he located in the latter place and has since been in active practice there. His father, who died in 1868, was long a resident of Mahoning county. His mother is still living on the home place in Ellsworth township.

J. R. Baird, oldest son of David and Mary Baird, was born in Virginia, March 15, 1832. He remained at home, employed in his father's merchant-mill, until 1860, when he came to Ohio, locating at Zanesville, where he learned the art of photography. While there, in 1861, he was married to Miss Jennie Munro. They have three sons—William C., Mortimer M., and Robert R. Mr. Baird continued to reside in Zanesville, conducting a photograph gallery until the fall of 1876, when he removed to Youngstown, where he has since been engaged in the same business, and where he has built up a good trade.

J. O. McGowan, youngest of the family of David and Mary McGowan, was born in Steubenville, Jefferson county, Ohio, December 23, 1847. He was employed in the post-office in Steubenville until 1862, when he enlisted in the Eighty-fourth Ohio volunteer infantry, and served out his term of enlistment. He re-enlisted in the Seventeenth Virginia volunteer infantry, and served in the Shenandoah valley campaign. He held the position of second lieutenant, and was on the staff of General Duvall; was mustered out at Wheeling, West Virginia. After his return home was engaged in railroading for four or five years. He was engaged in mercantile business in Steubenville until his removal to Youngstown in the fall of 1878, where he commenced the grocery trade, which he is still engaged in. He is one of the charter members of the first post, Grand Army of the Republic, in Youngstown, and was elected senior commander for the State of Ohio in January, 1882. Mr. McGowen was married May 10, 1877, to Miss Emma V. Myers, of Steubenville, Ohio, and has two sons—William Lawrence, born March 17, 1878, and Robert M., June 15, 1881.

J. A. Espy was born in Mercer county, Pennsylvania, July 9, 1836, youngest son of Samuel Allen and Sarah (McDonald) Espy. He was engaged as clerk in a general store at the commencement of the Rebellion, and during the first year of the war enlisted in the Sixty-first Pennsylvania volunteer infantry. He was in the Peninsula campaign during the seven days' fight. At the battle of Fair Oaks he was severely wounded and was disabled for further service. He was discharged in 1862. The following year he commenced the drug business in Middlesex, Pennsylvania. He was afterwards engaged in the same business in Sharon, Pennsylvania, and in Toledo, carrying on a wholesale business in the latter place under the firm name of Reno, Espy & Co. He was burnt out there in 1872 but continued business until 1873, when the firm sold out. He engaged in the business again in Sharon and continued there till 1877. In 1879 he came to Youngstown, where he has since been engaged in the drug trade. He married, in 1866, Miss Eugenia Reeves, daughter of Jesse Reeves. They have three children living—Guila, Charles A., and Eugenia.

James H. Cook, oldest son of Henry C. and Maria (Hollister) Cook, was born in Great Barrington, Berkshire county Massachusetts, May 20, 1829. In 1834 his parents removed to Illinois, where he attended the common schools until seventeen, when he attended an academy at Chicago. In 1847 he entered Michigan university, Ann Arbor, Michigan, and remained there two years and a half, completing his education there. He was engaged with his father in the lumber trade at Chicago until 1861, when he enlisted in the Eleventh Illinois cavalry. He was shortly afterwards detached on other duty, and was connected with the secret service during the war, serving some seven months after its close, receiving his discharge in the fall of 1865. After his return he resumed his former occupation at Chicago, residing there until 1870; afterwards resided in Nebraska, where he engaged in teaching. Returning to Chicago, he was married, October 8, 1875, to Miss C. A. Allis, a native of Vermont, and settled in their home in Rockford, Illinois, where he had charge of a commercial college for a few years. In 1879 he came to Youngstown, where he founded the Youngstown Commercial college and Institute of Penmanship, which he is still conducting.

J. M. Bowman, son of John and Jane (Scott) Bowman, was born in Virginia, April 9, 1824. John Bowman was a native of Pennsylvania, coming to Ohio in 1832 or 1833, and locating on Mill creek, where he spent the balance of his life. He was a soldier of the War of 1812. He raised a family of eight children, of whom five are living. He died February 28, 1864. Mrs. Jane Bowman died in September, 1860. J. M. Bowman, when sixteen, learned the trade of the manufacture of edge tools, serving an apprenticeship of three years, and afterwards worked as journeyman. He commenced the edge tool business with his brother in Warren. August 22, 1847, he married Amanda Dunn, a native of Vermont, and has one child—Etta May, born December 25, 1862. After his marriage Mr. Bowman located in Chagrin Falls, Ohio; was also a resident of Michigan some three years engaged in farming. Returning to Ohio, after living in Portage county engaged at farming a year or two, he entered the employ of Andrews Brothers, first conducting a store for them across the line in Pennsylvania. He has since been in their employ, being now in charge of their store at Hazelton.

O. J. Simpkins was born in Pennsylvania, August 25, 1841, and is a son of Enoch and Mary (Mealey) Simpkins. His education was obtained in the common schools and qualified himself to teach, which vocation he followed until the second call for troops in October, 1861, when he enlisted in the Sixth Ohio volunteer cavalry. He was afterward transferred to company H, Second Ohio volunteer cavalry, and took part in many engagements. September 19, 1864, he was mustered out at Columbus, Ohio, and on October 19th of the same year married Ellen Hammond Crandall, who was born June 20, 1843, in Pittsfield, Lorain county, Ohio, to which place her parents removed from Cleveland in 1839. She came from a family noted for patriotism. Her great-grandfather served all through the war of the Revolution, her grandfather in 1812, and her three brothers in the Rebellion; one of the latter was killed at Cumberland Gap. Mr. and Mrs. Simpkins have had two daughters, Grace, born February 2, 1867, and Minnie M., December 26, 1868, and died December 3, 1874. Mr. Simpkins has been employed as baggage-master for the New York,

Pennsylvania & Ohio railroad, at Youngstown, for the past fifteen years. He is a member of the Masonic order, and a genial and pleasant gentleman.

James Wilson was born in Youngstown September 22, 1800, and is supposed to be the first white child born in the settlement. His parents were William and Temperance Wilson, natives of Baltimore, Maryland, and of Scotch ancestry. The boy remained at home with his parents until he attained his twenty-fourth year, assisting in clearing up the farm, and obtaining such education as the subscription schools of that day afforded. He was married December 27, 1827, to Miss Nancy Welty, of Stark county, Ohio. To them were born fourteen children, nine of whom are yet living. Six of his sons are ministers in the Methodist Episcopal church; two of the daughters are residents of Warren; the other resides in Portage county. James Wilson was a successful farmer, and lived to celebrate the fiftieth anniversary of his wedding. He died June 9, 1879. His wife survives him. Rev. Corwin Wilson, their son, was born in Warren in 1841, obtained an education in the common schools and graduated from the Warren high school; was three years a pupil at Meadville college, from which he was graduated.' He received an appointment to preach in 1868; was a minister in Pennsylvania four years, then for three years at Braceville and Newton Falls, then at Ravenna and Niles, and came to Youngstown in 1881. He was married in 1867 to Miss Martha Hughes, and has had a family of six children, of which four are now living.

Joel K. Applegate was born in Liberty township, Trumbull county, April 15, 1831. His parents were Joseph and Rachel (Tomson) Applegate. His father was born in Allegheny county, Pennsylvania, December 27, 1789, and came to this vicinity at an early day with his father, settling in Liberty township. The father was a captain in the War of 1812, and the son, Joseph, was a non-commissioned officer at the same time. Joseph Applegate died November 21, 1847; his wife died February 15, 1871. Joel K. Applegate remained on the farm until he became of age, when he went to the Pacific coast and engaged in mining, and as lighthouse-keeper in Washington Territory for one year. He returned in 1859. September 2, 1862, he was married to Miss Eliza Dennison, whose father, Samuel Dennison, was an early settler in Liberty township. She was born January 19, 1827. After marriage they lived six years in Liberty, and removed to Youngstown in 1867, since which time Mr. Applegate has been engaged in coal drilling. While in the West Mr. Applegate served seventy days in the First Oregon regiment against the Indians.

James B. Drake, son of Simeon and Elvina (Houk) Drake, was born in Howland township, June 10, 1835. His father died in 1845 or 1846, and soon after he purchased of the heirs the home place, on which he remained until 1869, when he removed to Mahoning county and engaged in milling with his uncle, James Brown. In 1875 he was elected sheriff, and was re-elected in 1877, and since the expiration of his term of office has been a member of the livery firm of N. R. Miller & Co. Mr. Drake was married, in 1862, to Catharine Jane, daughter of Robert Kerr. They have had a family of four children, three of them now living—Simeon D., Annie A., and Ella K.

R. D. Burnett was born in Weathersfield township, March 22, 1841. His father, Henry Burnett, was born in 1801, near the present town of Hudson, where his parents had settled in 1798. He died in August, 1876, in the suburbs of Youngstown, after participating in the many and varied incidents of pioneer life; and living to see cities, towns, and villages, and waving fields of grain take the place of the wilderness of wood and swamp. His children were eight in number—Caroline, Sarah Ann, Hattie, Hiram, Henry L. (who became a major-general during the war of the Rebellion), and R. D. The latter read medicine when seventeen years of age with Dr. Wilcox, of Mount Jackson, Pennsylvania, and afterwards took some part in the Kansas troubles. In 1862 he enlisted in the Second Ohio volunteer cavalry as hospital steward, and was discharged for injuries received from a fall. He afterwards engaged in coal mining, and became president of the Hocking Valley Iron, Coal, and Coke company; was later engaged in the limestone business. He was married in 1860 to Eliza M., daughter of Henry Clark, an old resident of Hubbard.

A SKETCH OF THE
LIFE OF JAMES A. GARFIELD.

JAMES A. GARFIELD.

HIS ANCESTORS AND BIRTHPLACE.

On both his father's and his mother's side General Garfield comes of a long line of New England ancestry. The first of the American Garfields was Edward, who came from Chester, England, to Massachusetts bay as early as 1630, settled at Watertown, and died June 14, 1672, aged ninety-seven. One of the family, Abraham Garfield, a great uncle of General Garfield, was in the fight at Concord Bridge, and was one of the signers of the affidavits sent to the Continental Congress at Philadelphia to prove that the British were the aggressors in that affair, and fired twice before the patriots replied. After the Revolutionary war several members of the family left Massachusetts and settled in Central New York. General Garfield's father, Abram Garfield, was born there in 1799. He lived there till his eighteenth year, when he went to Newburg, Ohio, and soon after settled near Zanesville. He was a tall, robust young fellow, of very much the same type as his famous son, but a handsomer man, according to the verdict of his wife. He had a sunny, genial temper, like most men of great physical strength, was a great favorite with his associates, and was a natural leader and master of the rude characters with whom he was thrown in his forest-clearing work and his later labors in building the Ohio canal. His education was confined to a few terms in the Worcester district school, and the only two specimens of his writing extant show that it was not thorough enough to give him much knowledge of the science of orthography. He was fond of reading, but the hard life of a poor man in a new country gave him little time to read books, if he had had the money to buy them. The weekly newspapers and a few volumes borrowed from neighbors formed his intellectual diet.

On the 3d of February, 1819, Abram Garfield and Eliza Ballou were married in the village of Zanesville by a justice of the peace named Richard H. Hogan. The bridegroom lacked nine months of being twenty-one years of age, and the bride was only eighteen. Eliza Ballou's father was a cousin of Hosea Ballou, the founder of Universalism in this country. Eliza was born in 1801. The Ballous are of Huguenot origin, and are directly descended from Maturin Ballou, who fled from France on the revocation of the edict of Nantes, and with other French Protestants joined Roger Williams' colony in Rhode Island, the only American colony founded on the basis of full religious liberty. The gift of eloquence was undoubtedly derived by General Garfield from the Ballous, who were a race of preachers.

The newly wedded pair went to Newburg, Cuyahoga county, Ohio—now a part of the city of Cleveland—and began life in a small log house on a new farm of eighty acres. In January, 1821, their first child, Mehitabel, was born. In October, 1822, Thomas was born, and Mary in October, 1824. In 1826 the family moved to New Philadelphia, Tuscarawas county, where the father had a contract to construct three miles of canal. In 1827 the fourth child, James B., was born. This was the only one of the children that the parents lost. He died in 1830, after the family returned to the lake country. In January, 1830, Abram went to Orange township, Cuyahoga county, where lived Amos Boynton, his half-brother—the son of his mother by her second husband—and bought eighty acres of land at $2 an acre. The country was nearly all wild, and the new farm had to be carved out of the forest. Boynton purchased at the same time a tract of the same size adjoining, and the two families lived together for a few weeks in a log house built by the joint labors of the men. Soon a second cabin was reared across the road. The dwelling of the Garfields was built after the standard pattern of the houses of poor Ohio farmers in that day. Its walls were of logs, its roof was of shingles split with an axe, and its floor of rude thick planking split out of tree-trunks with a wedge and maul. It had only a single room, at one end of which was the big cavernous chimney, where the cooking was done, and at the other a bed. The younger children slept in a trundle-bed, which was pushed under the bedstead of their parents in the daytime to get it out of the way, for there was no room to spare; the older ones climbed a ladder to the loft under the steep roof. In this house James A. Garfield was born, November 19, 1831.

The father worked hard early and late to clear his land and plant and gather his crops. No man in all the region around could wield an axe like him. Fenced fields soon took the place of the forest; an orchard was planted, a barn built, and the family was full of hope for the future when death removed his strong support. One day in May, 1833, a fire broke out in the woods, and Abram Garfield, after heating his blood and exerting his strength to keep the flames from his fences and fields, sat down to rest where a cold wind blew, and was seized with a violent sore throat. A country doctor put a blister on his neck, which seemed only to hasten his death. Just before he died, pointing to his children, he said to his wife: "Eliza, I have planted four saplings in these woods. I leave them to your care." He was buried in a corner of a wheat-field on his farm. James, the baby, was eighteen months old at the time.

HIS BOYHOOD.

The childhood of James A. Garfield was passed in almost complete isolation from social influences save those which proceeded from the home of his mother and that of his uncle Boynton. The farms of the Garfields and Boyntons were partially separated from the settled country around by a large tract of forest on one side and a deep rocky ravine on another. For many years after Abram Garfield and his half-brother Boynton built their log cabins, the nearest house was seven miles distant, and when the country became well settled the rugged character of the surface around their farms kept neighbors at a distance too great for the children of the two families to find associates among them, save at the district school. The district school-house stood upon a corner of the Garfield farm, and it was there, when nearly four years old, that James conned his Noah Webster's Spelling Book, and learned his "a-b ab's."

James was put to farm work as soon as he was big enough to be of any use. The family was very poor, and the mother often worked in the fields with the boys. She spun the yarn and wove the cloth for the children's clothes and her own, sewed for the neighbors, knit stockings, cooked the simple meals for the household in the big fireplace, over which hung an iron crane for the pothooks, helped plant and hoe the corn and gather the hay crop, and even assisted the oldest boy to clear and fence land. In the midst of this toilsome life the brave little woman found time to instil into the minds of her children the religious and moral maxims of her New England ancestry. Every day she read four chapters of the Bible—a practice she keeps up to this time, and has never interrupted for a single day save when lying upon a sick bed. The children lived in an atmosphere of religious thought and discussion. Uncle Boynton, who was a second father to the Garfield family, flavored all his talk with Bible quotations. He carried a Testament in his pocket wherever he went, and would sit on his plough-beam at the end of a furrow to take it out and read a chapter. It was a time of religious ferment in Northern Ohio. New sects filled the air with their doctrinal cries. The Disciples, a sect founded by the preaching of Alexander Campbell, an eloquent and devout man of Scotch descent, who ranged over Kentucky, Ohio, Virginia, and Pennsylvania, from his home at Bethany in the "Pan Handle," had made great progress. They assailed all creeds as made by men, and declared the Bible to be the only rule of life. Attacking all the older denominations, they were vigorously attacked in turn. James' mind was filled at an early day with the controversies this new sect excited. The guests at his mother's house were mostly traveling preachers, and the talk of the neighborhood, when not about the crops and farm labors, was usually on religious topics.

At the district school James was known as a

fighting boy. He found that the larger boys were disposed to insult and abuse a little fellow who had no father or big brother to protect him, and he resented such imposition with all the force of a sensitive nature backed by a hot temper, great physical courage, and a strength unusual for his age. His big brother, Thomas, had finished his schooling and was much away from home, working by the day or month to earn money for the support of the family. Many stories are told in Orange of the pluck shown by the future major-general in his encounters with the rough country lads in defense of his boyish rights and honor. They say he never began a fight and never cherished malice, but when enraged by taunts or insults would attack boys of twice his size with the fury and tenacity of a bulldog. A few years after the death of his father the house was enlarged in a curious fashion. The log school-house was abandoned for a new frame building, and the old structure was bought by Thomas Garfield for a trifle, and he and James, with the help of the Boynton boys, pulled it down and put it up again on a site a few steps in the rear of the Garfield dwelling. Thus the family had two rooms and were tolerably comfortable, as far as household accommodations were concerned. In these two log buildings they lived until James was fourteen, when the boys built a small frame house for their mother. It was painted red and had three rooms below and two under the roof.

FARM BOY AND BOATMAN.

James often got employment in the haying and harvesting season from the farmers of Orange. When he was sixteen he walked ten miles to Aurora, in company with a boy older than himself, looking for work. They offered their services to a farmer who had a good deal of hay to cut. "What wages do you expect?" asked the man. "Man's wages—a dollar a day," replied young Garfield. The farmer thought they were not old enough to earn full wages. "Then let us mow the field by the acre," said the young man. The farmer agreed; the customary price per acre was fifty cents. By 4 o'clock in the afternoon the hay was down and the boys earned a dollar apiece. Then the farmer engaged them for a fortnight. James' first wages were earned from a merchant who had an ashery where he bleached ashes and made black salts, which were shipped by the lake and canal to New York. He got $9 a month and his board, and stuck to the business for two months, at the end of which his hair below his cap was bleached and colored by the fumes until it assumed a lively red hue. Afterwards he went to Newburg, where an uncle lived who had a piece of oak-timbered land to clear on the edge of Independence township. James agreed to chop one hundred cords of wood at fifty cents a cord. He boarded with one of his sisters, who was married and lived near by. He was a good chopper and easily cut two cords a day.

The view of Lake Erie and the passing sails stirred afresh in him the ambition to be a sailor, which almost every sturdy farmer's boy feels who reads tales of sea fights and adventures in the quiet monotony of his inland home. He resolved to ship on one of the lake craft, and with this purpose he walked to Cleveland and boarded a schooner lying at the wharf and told the captain he wanted to hire out as a sailor. The captain, a brutal, drunken fellow, was amazed at the impudence of the green country lad, and answered him with a torrent of profanity. Escaping as quickly as he could from the vessel, the lad walked up the river along the docks. Soon he heard himself called by name from the deck of a canalboat, and turning round, recognized a cousin, Amos Letcher, who told him he commanded the craft, and proposed to engage him to drive horses on the towpath. The would-be sailor thought that here was a chance to learn something of navigation in a humble way, preparatory to renewing his application for service on the lakes. He accepted the offer and the wages of "$10 a month and found," and next day the boat started for Pittsburg with a cargo of copper ore. It was called the Evening Star, was open amidships, and had a cabin at the bow for the horses and one at the stern for the men. On the return trip the Evening Star stopped at Brier Hill on the Mahoning river, and loaded with coal at the mines of David Tod, afterwards Governor of Ohio, and a warm friend of Garfield, the major-general and member of Congress. The boating episode in Garfield's life lasted through the season of 1848. After the first trip to Pittsburg the boat went back and forth between Cleveland and Brier Hill with cargoes of coal and iron.

Late in the fall the young driver, who had risen to the post of steersman, was seized with a violent attack of ague, which kept him at home all winter and in bed most of the time. All his summer's earnings went for doctor's bills and medicines. When he recovered, his mother, who had never approved of his canal adventure, dissuaded him from carrying out his project of shipping on the lakes. To master one passion she stimulated another—that of study. She brought to her help the district school teacher, an excellent, thoughtful man named Samuel D. Bates, who fired the boy's mind with a desire for a good education, and doubtless changed the course of his life. He went to the Geauga academy, at Chester, a village a few miles distant, and began a new career.

He repulsed all efforts to persuade him to join the church, and when pressed hard stayed away from meetings for several Sundays. Apparently, he wanted full freedom to reach conclusions about religion by his own mental processes. It was not until he was eighteen and had been two terms at the Chester school that he joined his uncle's congregation. He was baptised in March, 1850, in a little stream putting into the Chagrin river. His conversion was accomplished by a quiet, sweet-tempered man who held a series of meetings in the school-house near the Garfield homestead, and told in the plainest and most straightforward manner the story of the Gospel. A previous perusal of Pollock's Course of Time had made a deep impression upon him and turned his thoughts to religious subjects.

FIGHT FOR AN EDUCATION.

The country school-master who helped Mrs. Garfield dissuade her son from going as a sailor on the lakes in the spring of 1849 was a student at Geauga academy, a Free-will Baptist institution in the village of Chester, ten miles away from the home of the Garfields in Orange. The argument which finally turned the robust lad from his cherished plan of adventure was advanced by his mother, and was that, if he fitted himself for teaching by a few terms in school, he could teach winters and sail summers, and thus have employment the year round. In the month of March, with $17 in his pocket, got together by his mother and his brother Thomas, James went to Chester with his cousins, William and Henry Boynton. The boys took a stock of provisions along, and rented a room with two beds and a cook-stove in an old unpainted house where lived a poor widow woman, who undertook to prepare their meals and do their washing for an absurdly small sum. The academy was a two-story building, and the school, with about a hundred pupils of both sexes, drawn from the farming country around Chester, was in a flourishing condition. It had a library of perhaps one hundred and fifty volumes—more books than young Garfield had ever seen before. A venerable gentleman named Daniel Branch was principal of the school, and his wife was his chief assistant. At the end of the term of twelve weeks he went home to Orange, helped his brother build a barn for their mother, and then worked for day wages at haying and harvesting. With the money he earned he paid off some arrears of doctors' bills left from his long illness. When he returned to Chester in the fall he had one silver sixpence in his pocket. Going to church next day he dropped the sixpence in the contribution box.

He had made an arrangement with Heman Woodworth, a carpenter in the village, to live at his house and have lodging, board, washing, fuel, and light for $1.06 a week, and this sum he expected to earn by helping the carpenter on Saturdays and at odd hours on school days. The carpenter was building a two-story house, and James' first work was to get out siding at two cents a board. The first Saturday he planed fifty-one boards, and so earned $1.02, the most money he had ever got for a day's work. That term he paid his way, bought a few books, and returned home with $3 in his pocket. He now thought himself competent to teach a country school, but in two days' tramping through Cuyahoga county failed to find employment. Some schools had already engaged teachers, and where there was still a vacancy the trustees thought him too young. He returned home completely discouraged and greatly humiliated by the rebuffs he had met with. He made a resolution that he would never again ask for a position of any sort, and the resolution was kept, for every public place he has since had came to him unsought.

Next morning, while still in the depths of despondency, he heard a man call to his mother from the road, "Widow Gaffield," (a local corruption of the name Garfield), "where's your boy Jim? I wonder if he wouldn't like to teach our school at the Ledge." James went out and found a neighbor from a district a mile away, where the school had been broken up for two winters by the rowdyism of the big boys. He said he would like to try the school, but before deciding must consult his uncle, Amos Boynton. That evening there was a family council. Uncle Amos pondered over the matter, and finally said, "You go and try it. You will go into that school as the boy, 'Jim Gaffield;' see that you come out as Mr. Garfield, the school-master." The young man mastered the school, after a hard tussel in the school-room with the bully of the district, who resented a flogging and tried to brain the teacher with a billet of wood. His wages were $12 a month and board, and he "boarded around" in the families of the pupils.

He had $48 in the spring—more money than had ever been in his possession before. Before returning to Chester he joined the Disciples' church, and his religious experience, together with his new interest in teaching, caused him to abandon his boyhood ambition of becoming a sailor. During his third term at the academy he and his cousin Henry boarded themselves. At the end of six weeks the boys found their expenses for food had been just thirty-one cents per week apiece. Henry thought they were living too poorly for good health, and they agreed to increase their outlay to fifty cents a week apiece. James had up to this time looked upon a college course as wholly beyond his reach, but he met a college graduate who told him he was mistaken in supposing that only the sons of rich parents were able to take such a course. A poor boy could get through, he said, but it would take a long time and very hard work. The usual time was four years in preparatory studies and four in the regular college course. James thought that by working part of the time to earn money he could get through in twelve years. He then resolved to bend all his energies to the one purpose of getting a college education.

From this resolution he never swerved a hair's breadth. Until it was accomplished it was the one overmastering idea of his life. The tenacity and single-heartedness with which he clung to it and the sacrifices he made to realize it unquestionably exerted a powerful influence in molding and solidifying his character. He began to study Latin, philosophy, and botany. When the spring term ended he went home again and worked through the summer at haying and carpentering. Next fall he was back at Chester for a fourth term, and in the winter he got a village school to teach in Warrensville, at $16 a month and board.

Returning to Orange in the summer, he decided to go on with his education at a new school just established by the Disciples at Hiram, Portage county, a petty cross-roads village, twelve miles from the town and a railroad. His religious feeling naturally called him to the young institution of his own denomination. In August, 1851, he arrived at Hiram, and found a plain brick building standing in the midst of a cornfield, with perhaps a dozen farm houses near enough for boarding places for the students. He lived in a room with four other pupils, studied harder than ever, having now his college project fully anchored in his mind, got through his six books of Cæsar that term, and made good progress in Greek. In the winter he again taught school at Warrensville, and earned $18 a month. Next spring he was back at Hiram, and during the summer vacation he helped build a house in the village, planing all the siding and shingling the roof.

At the beginning of his second year at Hiram, Garfield was made a tutor in place of one of the teachers who fell ill, and thenceforward he taught and studied at the same time, working tremendously to fit himself for college. His future wife recited to him two years in Greek, and when he went to college she went to teach in the Cleveland schools, and to wait patiently the realization of their hopes. When he went to Hiram he had studied Latin only six weeks and had just begun Greek, and was therefore in a condition to fairly begin the four years' preparatory course ordinarily taken by students before entering college in the freshman class. Yet in three years' time he fitted himself to enter the junior class, two years further along, and at the same time earned his own living, thus crowding six years' study into three, and teaching for his support at the same time. To accomplish this he shut the world out from his mind save that little portion of it within the range of his studies, knowing nothing of politics or the news of the day, reading no light literature, and engaging in no social recreations that took his time from his books.

In the spring of 1854 he wrote to the presidents of Yale, Brown, and Williams, telling what books he had studied, and asked what class he could enter if he passed a satisfactory examination in them. All three wrote that he could enter the junior year. President Hopkins, of Williams, added this sentence to the business part of his letter: "If you come here, we shall do what we can for you." This seemed like a kindly hand held out, and it decided him to go to Williams. He had been urged to go the Disciples' college, in Bethany, Virginia, founded by Alexander Campbell, but with a wisdom hardly to be expected in a country lad devotedly attached to the sect represented by the Bethany school, he sought the wider culture and broader opportunities of a New England college.

LIFE AT COLLEGE.

When Garfield reached Williams college, in June, 1854, he had about $300 which he had saved while teaching in the Hiram school. With this money he hoped to manage to get through a year. A few weeks remained of the closing school year, and he attended the recitations of the sophomore class in order to get familiar with the methods of the professors before testing his ability to pass the examinations for the junior year. The examination for entering the junior class was passed without trouble. Although self-taught, his knowledge of the books prescribed was thorough. A long summer vacation followed his examination, and this time he employed in the college library, the first large collection of books he had ever seen. His absorption in the double work of teaching and fitting himself for college had hitherto left him little time for general reading, and the library opened a new world of profit and delight. He had never read a line of Shakespeare, save a few extracts in the school reading-books. From the whole range of fiction he had voluntarily shut himself off at eighteen, when he joined the church, having serious views of the business of life, and imbibing the notion, then almost universal among religious people in the country districts of the West, that novel reading was a waste of time, and therefore a sinful, worldly sort of intellectual amusement. When turned loose in the college library, with weeks of leisure to range at will over the shelves, he began with Shakespeare, which he read through from cover to cover. Then he went to English history and poetry. Of the poets Tennyson pleased him best, which is not to be wondered at, for the influence of the laureate was then at its height.

Garfield studied Latin and Greek, and took up German as an elective study. One year at college completed his classical studies, on which he was far advanced before he came to Williams. German he carried on successfully until he could read Goethe and Schiller readily, and acquired considerable fluency in the conversational use of the language. He entered with zeal into the literary work of the school, joined the Philologian society, was a vigorous debater, and in his last year was one of the editors of the Williams Quarterly, a college periodical of a high order of merit.

At the end of the fall term of 1854 came a winter vacation of two months, which Garfield employed in teaching a writing-school at North Pownal, Vermont. He wrote a bold, handsome, legible hand, not at all like that in vogue nowadays in the systems taught in the commercial colleges, but a hand that was strongly individual, and was the envy of the boys and girls who tried to imitate it in his Vermont class. It is said that a year or two before Garfield taught his writing-class in the North Pownal school-house, Chester A. Arthur taught the district school in the same building.

At the end of the college year, in June, Garfield went back to Ohio and visited his mother, who was then living with a daughter in Solon. His money was exhausted, and he had to adopt one of two plans, either to borrow enough to take him through to graduation at the end of the next year, or to go to teaching in order to earn the money, and thus break the continuity of his college course. He then hit upon a plan of insuring his life, and assigning the policy as a security for a loan. His brother Thomas undertook to furnish the funds in instalments, but becoming embarrassed was not able to do so, and a neighbor, Dr. Robinson, assumed the obligation. Garfield gave his notes for the loan, and regarded the transaction as on a fair business basis, knowing that if he lived he would repay the money, and that if he died his creditor would be secure.

His second winter vacation Garfield spent in Poestenkill, New York, a country neighborhood about six miles from Troy, where a Disciple minister from Ohio, named Streeter, was preaching, and where he soon organized a writing-school to employ his time and bring him in a little money. Occasionally Garfield preached in his friend's church. During a visit to Troy he became acquainted with the teachers and directors of the public schools of that city, and was one day surprised by the offer of a position in them at a salary far beyond his expectation of what he could earn after his graduation and return to Ohio. It was a turning-point in his life. If he accepted, he could soon pay his debts, marry the girl to whom he was engaged, and live a life of comfort in an attractive eastern city; but he could not finish his college course, and he would have to sever the ties with his friends in Ohio and with the struggling school at Hiram, to which he was a deeply attached. Had he taken the position, his whole subsequent career would no doubt have been different.

During his last term at Williams he made his first political speech, an address before a meeting gathered in one of the class-rooms to support the nomination of John C. Fremont. Although he had passed his majority nearly four years before, he had never voted. The old parties did not interest him; he believed them both corrupted with the sin of slavery; but when a new party arose to combat the designs of the slave power it enlisted his earnest sympathies. His mind was free from all his bias concerning the parties and statesmen of the past, and he could equally admire Clay or Jackson, Webster or Benton. He is the first man nominated for the Presidency whose political convictions and activities began with the birth of the Republican party. He was graduated August, 1856, with a class honor established by President Hopkins, and highly esteemed in the college—that of metaphysics—reading an essay on The Seen and the Unseen.

TEACHER AND PREACHER.

Before Garfield graduated at Williams college the trustees of the Hiram Eclectic institute elected him teacher of ancient languages, and the post was ready for him as soon as he got back to Ohio. It was not a professorship, because the institution was not a college, and did not became one until 1869, long after his connection with it ceased. A year later, when only twenty-six years old, he was placed at the head of the school with the title of chairman of the board of instruction, the board waiting another year before conferring upon him the full honors of the principalship. He continued to hold the position of principal until he went into the army in 1861. He was nominal principal two years longer, the board hoping he would return and manage the school after the war ended. When he went to Congress he was made advising principal and lecturer, and his name was borne upon the catalogues in this capacity until 1864.

Before he went to college Garfield had begun to preach a little in the country churches around Hiram, and when he returned he began to fill the pulpit in the Disciples' church in Hiram with considerable regularity. In his denomination no ordination is required to become a minister. Any brother having the ability to discourse on religious topics to a congregation is welcomed to the pulpit. His fame as a lay preacher extended throughout the counties of Portage, Summit, Trumbull, and Geauga, and he was often invited to preach in the towns of that region.

One of his former pupils says of his peculiarities as a teacher:

No matter how old the pupils were, Garfield always called us by our first names, and kept himself on the most familiar terms with all. He played with us freely, scuffled with us sometimes, talked with us in walking to and fro, and we treated him out of the class-room just about as we did one another. Yet he was a most strict disciplinarian and enforced the rules like a martinet. He combined an affectionate and confiding manner with respect for order in a most successful manner. If he wanted to speak to a pupil, either for reproof or approbation, he would generally manage to get one arm around him and draw him close to him. He had a peculiar way of shaking hands, too, giving a twist to your arm and drawing you right up to him. This sympathetic manner had helped him to advancement. When I was janitor he used some times to stop me and ask my opinion about this and that, as if seriously advising with me. I can see that my opinion could not have been of any value, and that he probably asked me partly to increase my self-respect, and partly to show me that he felt an interest in me. I certainly was his friend all the firmer for it.

ENTRANCE INTO POLITICS.

He cast his first vote in 1856 for John C. Fremont, his own political career thus beginning with the first National campaign of the Republican party. Before leaving Williams college he made a speech to the students on the question of slavery in the Territories, and during the fall, after he returned to Hiram, he spoke in the Disciples' church, in reply to Alphonso Hart, of Ravenna, who had delivered a Democratic address there a few nights before. Then a joint debate was arranged at Garrettsville, between Hart and Garfield, which attracted a good deal of local attention, and is well remembered to this day by the older farmers of Portage county. This debate launched Garfield as a political speaker. His reputation as a stump orator widened steadily from that debate until it embraced first the State of Ohio and then the Nation.

A year after he took charge of the Hiram school Garfield married Lucretia Rudolph, his fellow-student and pupil in former years, to whom he had engaged himself before he went to Williams college. Their love had stood the test of time and absence, and now that he had made his place in the world and felt that he could support a family, there was nothing to hinder its consummation. The marriage took place at the house of the bride's parents, November 11, 1858.

His labors upon the stump, beginning in 1856, with perhaps a score of speeches for Fremont and Dayton in country school-houses and town-halls in the region around Hiram, were extended in 1857 and 1858 over a wider area of territory, and in 1859 he began to speak at county mass-meetings. His first appearance at a big meeting was at Akron, where his name was put upon the bill below that of Salmon P. Chase. There the young teacher met for the first time the great anti-slavery leader whom he had honored and admired from his boyhood, and a friendship sprang up between the two which endured until Chase's death.

In January, 1860, he went to Columbus, and took his seat in the State Senate. The campaign of 1860 made him widely known throughout the State. He found time to read law assiduously while he was in the Legislature. In 1858 he made up his mind that his future career should be at the bar. He therefore entered his name as a law student in the office of Williamson & Riddle, in Cleveland, and got from Mr. Riddle a list of books to be studied. In 1861 he applied to the supreme court at Columbus for admission to the bar, was examined by a committee composed of Thomas M. Key, a distinguished lawyer of Cincinnati, and Robert Harrison, afterward a member of the supreme court commission, and admitted. His intention was to open an office in Cleveland, but the breaking out of the war changed his plans.

HIS RECORD IN THE WAR.

The most complete and comprehensive account of General Garfield's military career is found in Whitelaw Reid's "Ohio in the War," which was written many years before Garfield's nomination for the Presidency. When the time came, says this account, for appointing the officers for the Ohio troops, the Legislature was still in session. Garfield at once avowed his intention of entering the service. He was offered the lieutenant-colonelcy of the Forty-second Ohio regiment, but it was not until the 14th of December that orders for the field were received. The regiment was then sent to Catlettsburg, Kentucky, and Garfield, then made colonel, was directed to report in person to General Buell. On the 17th of December he assigned Colonel Garfield to the command of the Seventeenth brigade, and ordered him to drive the rebel forces under Humphrey Marshall out of Sandy valley, in Eastern Kentucky. Up to this date no active operations had been attempted in the great department that lay south of the Ohio river. The spell of Bull Run still hung over our armies. Save the campaign in Western Virginia and the unfortunate attack by General Grant at Belmont, not a single engagement had occurred over all the region between the Alleghanies and the Mississippi. General Buell was preparing to advance upon the rebel position at Bowling Green when he suddenly found himself hampered by two co-operating forces skillfully planted within striking distance of the flank. General Zollicoffer was advancing from Cumberland Gap toward Mill Spring; and Humphrey Marshall moving down the Sandy valley, was threatening to overrun eastern Kentucky. Till these could be driven back an advance upon Bowling Green would be perilous, if not actually impossible. To General George H. Thomas, then just raised from his colonelcy of regulars to a brigadier-generalship of volunteers, was committed the task of repulsing Zollicoffer; to the untried colonel of the raw Forty-second Ohio, the task of repulsing Humphrey Marshall, and on their success the whole army of the department waited.

Colonel Garfield thus found himself, before he had ever seen a gun fired in action, in command of four regiments of infantry, and some eight companies of cavalry, charged with the work of driving out of his native State the officer reputed the ablest of those, not educated to war, whom Kentucky had given to the Rebellion. Marshall had under his command nearly five thousand men, stationed at the village of Paintville, sixty miles up the Sandy valley. He was expected by the rebel authorities to advance toward Lexington, unite with Zollicoffer, and establish the authority of the provisional government at the State capital. These hopes were fed by the recollection of his great intellectual abilities, and the soldierly reputation he had borne ever since he led the famous charge of the Kentucky volunteers at Buena Vista. But Garfield won the day. Marshall hastily abandoned his position, fired his camp equipage and stores, and began a retreat which was not ended until he reached Abingdon, Virginia. A fresh peril, however, now beset the little force. An unusually violent rain storm broke out, the mountain gorges were all flooded, and the Sandy rose to such a height that steamboat men pronounced it impossible to ascend the stream with supplies. The troops were almost out of rations, and the rough, mountainous country was incapable of supporting them. Colonel Garfield had gone down the river to its mouth. He ordered a small steamer, which had been in the quartermaster's service, to take on a load of supplies and start up. The captain declared it was impossible. Efforts were made to get other vessels, but without success.

Finally Colonel Garfield ordered the captain and crew on board, stationed a competent army officer on deck to see that the captain did his duty, and himself took the wheel. The captain still protested that no boat could possibly stem the raging current, but Garfield turned her head up the stream and began the perilous trip. The water in the usually shallow river was sixty feet deep, and the tree tops along the bank were almost submerged. The little vessel trembled from stem to stern at every motion of the engines; the water whirled her about as if she were a skiff; and the utmost speed that steam could give her was three miles an hour. When night fell the captain of the boat begged permission to tie up. To attempt to ascend that flood in the dark, he declared was madness. But Colonel Garfield kept his place at the wheel.

Finally, in one of the sudden bends of the river, they drove, with a full head of steam, into the quicksand of the bank. Every effort to back off was in vain. Garfield at last ordered a boat to be lowered to take a line across to the opposite bank. The crew protested against venturing out in the flood. The Colonel leaped into the boat himself and steered it over. The force of the current carried them far below the point they sought to reach; but they finally succeeded in making fast to a tree, and rigging a windlass with rails sufficiently powerful to draw the vessel off and get her once more afloat.

It was on Saturday that the boat left the mouth of the Sandy. All night, all day Sunday, and all through Sunday night they kept up that struggle with the current, Garfield leaving the wheel only eight hours out of the whole time, and that during the day. By 9 o'clock Monday morning they reached the camp, and were received with tumultuous cheering. Garfield himself could scarcely escape being borne to headquarters on the shoulders of the delighted men.

These operations in the Sandy valley had been conducted with such energy and skill as to receive the special commendation of the commanding general and the Government. General Buell had been moved to words of unwonted praise. The War Department had conferred the grade of brigadier-general, the commission bearing the date of the battle of Middle Creek. And the country, without understanding very well the details of the campaign—of which indeed, no satisfactory account was published at the time—fully appreciated the satisfactory result. The discomfiture of Humphrey Marshall was a source of special chagrin to the rebel sympathizers of Kentucky, and of amazement and admiration throughout the loyal West, and Garfield took rank in the public estimation among the most promising of the younger volunteer generals.

On his arrival at Louisville, from the Sandy valley, General Garfield found that the army of the Ohio was already beyond Nashville, on its march to Grant's aid at Pittsburg Landing. He hastened after it, reported to General Buell about thirty miles from Columbia, and, under his order, at once assumed command of the Twentieth brigade, then a part of the division under General Thomas J. Wood. He reached the field of Pittsburg Landing about 1 o'clock on the second day of the battle, and participated in the closing scenes.

The old tendency to fever and ague, contracted in the days of his tow-path service on the Ohio canal, was now aggravated in the malarious climate of the South, and General Garfield was finally sent home on sick leave about the 1st of August. Near the same time the Secretary of War, who seems at this early day to have formed the high estimate of Garfield which he continued to entertain throughout the war, sent him orders to proceed to Cumberland Gap and relieve General George W. Morgan of his command. But when they were received he was too ill to leave his bed. A month later the Secretary ordered him to report in person at Washington as soon as his health would permit. On his arrival it was found that the estimate placed on his knowledge of law, his judgment, and his loyalty had led to his selection as one of the first members of the court-martial for the noted trial of Fitz John Porter. In the duties connected with this detail most of the autumn was consumed. Early in January he was ordered out to General Rosecrans. From the day of his appointment, General Garfield became the intimate associate and confidential adviser of his chief. But he did not occupy so commanding a station as to be able to put restraint upon him. From the 4th of January to the 24th of June General Rosecrans lay at Murfreesboro. Through five months of this delay General Garfield was with him. The War department demanded an advance, and, when the spring opened, urged it with unusual vehemence. Finally General Rosecrans formally asked his corps, division, and cavalry generals as to the propriety of a movement. With singular unanimity, though for diverse reasons, they opposed it. Out of seventeen generals not one was in favor of an immediate advance, and not one was even willing to put himself on record as in favor of an early advance. General Garfield collated the seventeen letters sent in from the generals in reply to the questions of their commander, and fairly reported their substance, coupled with a cogent argument against them and in favor of an immediate movement. This report we venture to pronounce the ablest military document known to have been submitted by a chief of staff to his superior during the war. General Garfield stood absolutely alone, every general commanding troops having, as we have seen, either openly opposed or failed to approve an advance. But his statements were so clear and his arguments so forcible, that he carried conviction.

Twelve days after the reception of this report the army moved—to the great dissatisfaction of its leading generals. One of the three corps commanders, Major-general Thomas L. Crittenden, approached the chief of staff at the headquarters on the morning of the advance: "It is understood, sir," he said, "by the general officers of the army, that this movement is your work. I wish you to understand it is a rash and fatal move, for which you will be held responsible." This rash and fatal move was the Tullahoma campaign--a campaign perfect in its conception, excellent in its general execution, and only hindered from resulting in the complete destruction of the opposing army by the delays which had too long postponed its commencement. It might even yet have destroyed Bragg but for the terrible season of rains which set in on the morning of the advance and continued uninterruptedly for the greater part of a month. With a week's earlier start it would have ended the career of Bragg's army in the war.

At last came the battle of Chickamauga. Such by this time had come to be Garfield's influence that he was nearly always consulted and often followed. He wrote every order issued that day—one only excepted. This he did rarely as an amanuensis, but rather on the suggestions of his own judgment, afterward submitting what he had prepared to Rosecrans for approval or change. The one order which he did not write was the fatal order to Wood which lost the battle. The meaning was correct; the words, however, did not clearly represent what Rosecrans meant, and the division commander in question so interpreted them as to destroy the right wing. The general commanding, and his chief of staff were caught in the tide of disaster and borne back toward Chattanooga. The chief of staff was sent to communicate with Thomas, while the general proceeded to prepare for the reception of the routed army. Such at least were the statements of the reports, and, in a technical sense, they were true. It should never be forgotten, however, in Garfield's praise, that it was on his own earnest representations that he was sent—that, in fact, he rather procured permission to go to Thomas, and so back into the battle, than received orders to do so. He refused to believe that Thomas was routed or the battle lost. He found the road environed with dangers; some of his escort were killed, and they all narrowly escaped death or capture. But he bore to Thomas the first news that officer had received of the disaster on the right, and gave the information on which he was able to extricate his command. At 7 o'clock that evening, under the personal supervision of General Gordon Granger and himself, a shotted salute from a battery of six Napoleon guns was fired into the woods after the last of the retreating assailants. They were the last shots of the battle of Chickamauga, and what was left of the Union army was master of the field. For the time the enemy evidently regarded himself as repulsed; and Garfield said that night, and has always since maintained, that there was no necessity for the immediate retreat on Rossville.

SERVICE IN CONGRESS.

Practically this was the close of General Garfield's military career. A year before, while he was absent in the army, and without any solicitation on his part, he had been elected to Congress from the old Giddings district, in which he resided. He was now, after a few weeks' service with General Rosecrans at Chattanooga, sent on to Washington as the bearer of dispatches. He there learned of his promotion to a major-generalship of volunteers, "for gallant and meritorious conduct at the battle of Chickamauga." He might have retained this position in the army; and the military capacity he had displayed, the high favor in which he was held by the Government, and the certainty of his assignment to important commands, seemed to augur a brilliant future. He was a poor man, too, and the major-general's salary was more than double that of the Congressman. But on mature reflection he decided that the circumstances under which the people had elected him to Congress bound him up to an effort to obey their wishes. He was furthermore urged to enter Congress by the officers of the army, who looked to him for aid in procuring such military legislation as the country and army required. Under the belief that the path of usefulness to the country lay in the direction in which his constituents pointed, he sacrificed what seemed to be his personal interests, and on the 5th of December, 1863, he resigned his commission, after nearly three years' service.

General Garfield continued his military service up to the day of the meeting of Congress. Even then he seriously thought of resigning his position as a Representative rather than his major-general's commission, and would have done so had not Lincoln urged him to enter Congress. He has often expressed regret that he did not fight the war through. Had he done so he would no doubt have ranked at its close among the foremost of the victorious generals of the Republic, for he displayed in his Sandy valley campaign and at the battle of Chickamauga the highest qualities of generalship. A brilliant opening awaited him in the Army of the Cumberland. General Thomas wanted him to take command of a corps. President Lincoln told him he greatly needed the influence in the House of one who had had practical military experience to push through the needed war legislation. He yielded, and on the 5th of December, 1863, gave up his generalship and took his seat in the House.

He was appointed on the military committee, under the chairmanship of General Schenck, and was of great service in carrying through the measures which recruited the armies during the closing years of the war.

In the summer of 1864 a breach occurred between the President and some of the most radical of the Republican leaders in Congress over the question of the reconstruction of the States of Arkansas and Louisiana. Congress passed a bill for the organization of loyal governments within the Union lines of these States, but Lincoln vetoed it, and appointed governors. Senator Ben Wade, of Ohio, and Representative Henry Winter Davis, of Maryland, united, in a letter to the New York Tribune, sharply criticising the President for defeating the will of Congress. The letter became known as the Wade-Davis manifesto, and created a great sensation in political circles. The story got about in the Nineteenth district that General Garfield had expressed sympathy with the position of Wade and Davis. His constituents condemned the document, and were strongly disposed to set him aside and nominate another man for Congress. When the convention met the feeling against Garfield was so pronounced that he regarded his nomination as hopeless. He was called upon to explain his course. He went upon the platform, and everybody expected something in the nature of an apology, but he boldly defended his position, approved the manifesto, justified Wade, and said he had nothing to retract, and could not change his honest convictions for the sake of a seat in Congress. He had great respect, he said, for the opinions of his constituents, but greater regard for his own. If he could serve them as an independent representative, acting on his own judgment and conscience, he would be glad to do so, but if not, he did not want their nomination; he would prefer to be an independent private citizen. Probably no man ever talked that way before or since to a body of men who held his political fate in their hands. Leaving the platform, he strode out of the hall and down the stairs, supposing that he had effectually cut his own throat. Scarcely had he disappeared when one of the youngest delegates sprang up and said: "The man who has the courage to face a convention like that deserves a nomination. I move that General Garfield be nominated by acclamation." The motion was carried with a shout that reached the ears of the Congressman, and arrested him on the sidewalk as he was returning to the hotel. He was elected by a majority of over twelve thousand.

At the beginning of the Thirty-ninth Congress in December, 1865, General Garfield asked Speaker Colfax to transfer him from the committee on military affairs to that of ways and means, saying that in the near future financial questions would occupy the attention of the country, and he desired to be in a position to study them carefully in advance. The military committee having on its hands the work of reorganizing the regular army on a peace basis, was the more important of the two at the time, but Garfield foresaw the storm of agitation and delusion concerning the debt and the currency which was soon to break upon the country, and wisely prepared to meet it. He began a long and severe course of study, ransacking the Congressional library for works that threw light on the experience of other countries, and that gave the ideas of the thinkers and statesmen of all nations on these subjects; his membership of the ways and means also opened up a line of congenial work in connection with the tariff and the system on internal revenue taxation. These two sources of income, gauged to the needs of the war, had to be changed to conform to the conditions of peace. In the course of this work and of the investigations which accompanied it, reached a conclusion upon the tariff question from which he never departed—namely, that whatever may be the truth or falsity of abstract theories about free trade, the interests of the United States require a moderate protective system. In March, 1866, he made his first speech on the currency question, and took strong ground in favor of a speedy return to specie payments.

In the summer of 1867 General Garfield went to Europe and made a rapid tour through Great Britain and the Continent. His health failed under the pressure of too much brain work and he took this means of recuperating. This was the only year since he entered public life that he had been absent from a political campaign. He returned late in the fall to find that Pendletonism —a demand for the payment of the bonded debt in irredeemable greenback notes—had run rampant in Ohio, and had taken possession of the Republican party as well as of the Democracy. A reception was given him at Jefferson, in his district, which assumed the form of a public meeting. He was told that he had better say nothing about his financial views, for his constituents had made up their minds that the bonds ought to be redeemed in greenbacks. He made a speech in which he told his friends plainly that they were deluded, that there could be no honest money not redeemable in coin, and no honest payment of the debt could be made save in coin, and that as long as he was their representative he should stand on that ground, whatever might be their views. The speech produced a deep impression throughout the district. The next June the National Republican Convention took sound ground on the debt and currency questions, and most Republicans who had been carried away by Pendletonism grew ashamed of their folly.

A LEADER IN FINANCE.

In the Fortieth Congress General Garfield was put back on the military committee and made its chairman. In 1868 he was renominated without opposition, and chosen a fourth time to represent his district. On the organization of the Forty-first Congress, in December, 1869, General Garfield was made chairman of the committee on banking and currency. The inflation movement was rapidly gathering force in the country, and men of both parties in Congress were swept into it by fear of their constituents. A cry was set up that times were getting bad because there was not money enough to do the business of the people. The West, particularly, clamored for more currency. General Garfield led the opposition to inflation. Fnally, after a long fight in his committee with the men who wanted to throw out a flood of new greenbacks, he brought in and carried through Congress a bill allowing an addition of $54,000,000 to the National bank circulation, and giving preference in the assignment of the new issue to the States which had less than their quota of the old circulation. This measure was a stunning blow to the inflation movement. The new issue was not all taken up for four years, and during all that time it was a sufficient answer to all demands for "more money" to call attention to the fact that there was currency waiting in the Treasury for any one who would organize a bank. Soon after the $54,000,000 was applied for National banking was made perfectly free. The New York gold panic came during General Garfield's chairmanship of the banking committee. Under orders of the House he conducted with great sagacity and thoroughness an investigation which exposed all the secrets of the gold gamblers' plot which culminated in "Black Friday." He made a report which was a complete history of the affair, and the lesson he drew from it was that the only certain remedy against the occurrence of such transactions was to be found in the resumption of specie payments. He became the recognized leader of the honest-money party in the House and the most potent single factor in the opposition to inflation. He helped work up the bill to strengthen the public credit, which failed to get through during the closing days of Johnson's administration, but was passed as soon as Grant came in, and was the first measure to which the new President put his signature. This bill committed Congress fully to the payment of the public debt in coin, and was the fortress around which the financial battle raged in subsequent years.

In December, 1871, General Garfield was placed at the head of the important committee on appropriations, a position which made him a leader of the majority side of the House. With his old habit of doing everything he undertook with the utmost thoroughness, he made a laborious study of the whole history of appropriation bills of this country and of the English budget system. He found a great deal of looseness and confusion in the practice concerning estimates and appropriations. Unexpended balances were lying in the Treasury, amounting to $130,000,000, beyond the supervision of Congress and subject to the drafts of Government officers. There were besides what was called permanent appropriations, which ran on from year to year without any legislation. Garfield instituted a sweeping reform. He got laws passed covering all old balances back into the Treasury, making all appropriations expire at the end of the fiscal year for which made, unless needed to carry out contracts, and covering in all appropriations at the end of every second year. At the same time he required the executive committee to itemize their estimates of the money needed to run the Government much more fully than had been done before, so that Congress would know just how every dollar it voted was to be expended. The four years of his chairmanship of appropriations were years of close and unremitting labor. He worked habitually fifteen hours a day. In addition to the demands of his own department of legislation he took part in all the debates involving the principles of the Republican party, fought without cessation a brave battle against inflation and repudiation, and omitted no opportunity to aid in educating the public mind to a comprehension of the importance of returning to specie payments.

Five times had General Garfield been chosen to represent the old Giddings district without serious opposition in his own party, and without a breath of suspicion being cast upon his personal integrity. With one exception his nominations had been made by acclamation. In his sixth canvass, however, a storm of calumny broke upon him. A concerted attack was made upon him for the purpose, if possible, of defeating him in the convention, and failing in that, to beat him at the polls. He was charged with bribery and corruption in connection with the Credit Mobilier affair and the DeGolyer pavement contract, and with responsibility for the salary grab. His people, however, resented the slanders, and in the convention he was nominated by a majority of three to one. The opposition to him did not bring forward a candidate, but merely cast blank votes. His enemies then nominated a second Republican candidate. General Garfield met the charges against him before the jury of his constituents. He visited all parts of the district, speaking day and night at township meetings. The verdict of the election was a complete vindication of his character and actions, and in 1876 and 1878 his constituents nominated him by acclamation and elected him by increased majorities.

HEADING THE MINORITY.

The result of the election of 1874 was to give the Democrats control of the House, which met in December, 1875. Hitherto the legislative work of General Garfield had been constructive. Now he was called upon to defend this work against the assaults of the party which step by step had opposed its accomplishment, and which, by the aid of the solid support of the late rebel element, had gained power in Congress. One of the first movements of the Democrats was for universal amnesty. Mr. Blaine offered an amendment to their bill, excluding Jefferson Davis. Then followed the famous debate about the treatment of prisoners of war, opened by Blaine's dashing attack on Hill, continued by Hill's reply charging that Confederates had been starved in Northern prisons, and closing with Garfield's response to Hill. Garfield, by a brilliant stroke of parliamentary strategy, forced a Democrat to testify to the falsity of Hill's charge. He said that the Elmira, New York, district, where was located during the war the principal prison for captured rebels, was represented in the House by a Democrat. He did not know him, but he was willing to rest his case wholly on his testimony. He called upon the member from Elmira to inform the House whether the good people of his city had permitted the captured Confederate soldiers in their midst to suffer for want of food and clothing during their imprisonment. The gentleman rose promptly and said that to his knowledge the prisoners had received exactly the same rations as the Union soldiers guarding them. While this statement was being made, a telegraph dispatch was handed to General Garfield. Holding it up he said: "The lightnings of heaven are aiding me in this controversy." The dispatch was from General Elwell, of Cleveland, who had been the quartermaster at the Elmira prison, and who telegraphed that the rations issued to the rebel prisoners were in quantity and quality exactly the same as those issued to their guards. Garfield's speech killed the Democrats' bill. They withdrew it rather than risk a vote. Mr. Blaine's transfer to the Senate soon after this debate left Garfield the recognized leader of the Republicans in the House. Mr. Kerr, the Democratic speaker, died in the midst of his term, and in the election of his successor General Garfield received the unanimous Republican vote. Soon after, in August, 1876, came the dispute with Lamar. Lamar was the greatest orator the Democrats had, and was selected by them to make a keynote campaign speech. It was a sharp attack upon the Republican party, an appeal for sympathy for the "oppressed South," and an argument to show that peace and prosperity could come only through Democratic rule. General Garfield took notes of the speech. All his colleagues insisted that he alone was competent to break the force of Lamar's masterly effort. This speech is usually accounted the greatest of his life. It created a furore in the House. All business was suspended for ten minutes after he finished, so great was the excitement. One hundred thousand copies of the speech were subscribed for at once by members who wanted to circulate it in their districts, and during the campaign over a million copies were distributed. It contributed powerfully to the success of the Republican party in the Presidential campaign of that year.

After the election arose the dispute about the count of the votes of South Carolina, Florida, and Louisiana. President Grant telegraphed to General Garfield, under date of November 10th, as follows:

I would be gratified if you would go to New Orleans and remain there until the vote of Louisiana is counted. Governor Kellogg requests that reliable witnesses be sent to see that the canvass of the vote is a fair one.

U. S. GRANT.

Garfield went to Washington, consulted with the President, and then proceeded to New Orleans in company with John Sherman, Stanley Matthews, and a number of other prominent Republicans. While on his way back to Washington, returning from New Orleans, he was again chosen by the unanimous vote of the Republicans of the House as their candidate for speaker.

General Garfield opposed the electoral commission bill, but in spite of his opposition, when the bill passed he was selected as a member of the tribunal. The Republicans of the House were to have two members. They met in caucus and were about to ballot, when Mr. McCreary, of Iowa, said that there was one name on which they were all agreed, and which need not be submitted to the formality of a vote—that of James A. Garfield. Garfield was chosen by acclamation. The second commissioner was George F. Hoar, of Massachusetts, who afterwards presided over the Chicago convention which nominated General Garfield for the Presidency. As a member of the electoral commission General Garfield delivered two opinions, in which he brought out with great clearness the point that the Constitution places in the hands of the Legislatures of the States the power of determining how their electors shall be chosen, and that Congress had no right to go behind the final decision of a State. If there was nothing in the constitution or laws of a State touching the matter, its Legislature could appoint electors as Vermont did, after her admission to the Union.

Immediately after President Hayes' inauguration the Republicans in the Ohio Legislature desired to elect General Garfield to the United States Senate in place of John Sherman, who had resigned his seat to enter the Cabinet. Mr. Hayes made a personal appeal to him to decline to be a candidate and remain in the House to lead the Republicans in support of the Administration. General Garfield acceded, in the belief that his services would be of more value to the party in the House than in the Senate, and withdrew his name from the canvass, greatly to the disappointment of his friends in Ohio, who had already obtained pledges of the support of a large majority of the Republican members of the Legislature.

In the session of 1878 General Garfield led the long struggle in defence of the resumption act, which was assailed by the Democrats with a vigor born of desperation. He also made a remarkable speech on the tariff question, in opposition to Wood's bill, which sought to break down the protective system. During the extra session of 1879, forced by the Democrats, for the purpose of bringing the issue of the repeal of the Federal election laws prominently before the country, General Garfield led the Republican minority with consummate tact and judgment. The plan of the Democrats was to open the debate with a general attack on the Republican party in order to throw their adversaries upon the defensive as apologists for the course of their party. McMahon, of Ohio, was selected to make the opening speech. Garfield did not wait for him to make his argument, but securing the floor ahead of him, delivered his famous Revolution in Congress speech, in which he attacked the Democrats with such vigor and exposed with so much force their scheme for withholding appropriations for the support of the Government, to compel the President to sign their political measures, that they were thrown into confusion, and instead of taking the offensive, were obliged to resort to a weak, defensive campaign. Driven from position to position by successive vetoes and by the persistent assaults of the Republican minority, they ended with a ridiculous fiasco. Instead of refusing $45,000,000 of appropriations, as they threatened at the beginning, they ended by appropriating $44,000,000 of the amount, leaving only $400,000 unprovided for. The following winter the Democrats recommenced the fight, but in a feeble, disheartened way. They set out to refuse all pay to the United States marshals unless the President would let them wipe out the election laws. General Garfield met them with a powerful speech on Nullification in Congress, in which he showed that while it was clearly the foremost duty of the law-makers in Congress to obey, the Democrats had become leaders in an attempt to disobey them and break them down. General Garfield's last work in Congress was a report on the Tucker tariff bill. In January, 1880, General Garfield was chosen to the Senate by the Legislature of Ohio for the term of six years, beginning March 4, 1881. He received the unanimous vote of the Republican caucus, an honor never before conferred upon a citizen of Ohio by any party.

NOMINATION FOR PRESIDENT.

General Garfield went to the Republican National convention at Chicago as a delegate at large from the State of Ohio. His great experience in National politics made him very naturally the leader of the delegation. Ohio had agreed to present the name of Secretary Sherman to the convention as its candidate for President. His speech presenting Sherman's name was universally applauded as a model of dignified oratory, and as a timely effort to prevent the sharp differences of feeling in the convention from weakening the party in the approaching campaign. His short speeches on questions arising before the convention during its long and turbulent session were all couched in the same vein of wise moderation, while adhering firmly to the principle of district representation and the right of every individual delegate to cast his own vote.

When the balloting began, a single delegate from Pennsylvania voted for Garfield. No attention was paid to this vote, which was thought to be mere eccentricity on the part of the man who cast it. Later on a second Pennsylvania delegate joined the solitary Garfield man. So the balloting continued, the fight being a triangular one between Grant, Blaine, and Sherman, with Washburne, Edmunds, and Windom in the field, ready for possible compromises. General Garfield's plan, as leader of the Sherman forces, was to keep his candidate steadily in the field, in the belief that the Blaine men, seeing the impossibility of the success of their favorite, would come to Sherman and thus secure his nomination. After a whole day voting, however, it became plain that a union of the Blaine and Sherman forces in favor of Sherman could not be effected, and that an attempt in that direction would throw enough additional votes to Grant to give him the victory. Some unsuccessful efforts were made on the second day's voting to rally on Edmunds and Washburne.

Finally, on the thirty-fourth ballot, the Wisconsin men determined to make an effort in an entirely new direction to break the deadlock. They threw their seventeen votes for Garfield. General Garfield sprang to his feet and protested against this proceeding, making the point of order that nobody had a right to vote for any member of the convention without his consent, and that consent, he said, "I refuse to give." The chairman declared that the point of order was not well taken, and ordered the Wisconsin vote to be counted. On the next ballot nearly the whole Indiana delegation swung over to Garfield, and a few scattering votes were changed to him from other States, making a total of fifty votes cast for him in all. Now it became plain that, by a happy inspiration, a way out of the difficulty had been found. On the thirty-sixth ballot, State after State swung over to Garfield amidst intense excitement, and he was nominated by the following vote: Garfield, 399; Grant, 306; Sherman, 3; Washburne, 5. The nomination was accepted on all hands as an exceedingly fortunate one, and both the friends and opponents of General Garfield vied with each other in the enthusiasm with which they indorsed it. Congratulations poured in from all parts of the country, and on his way from Chicago to his farm in Ohio General Garfield was the recipient of a popular ovation, which repeated itself at every town and railroad station.

Outside of his political work, General Garfield was a frequent platform speaker on topics connected with education, finance and social science. In 1878 he delivered a notable address in Faneuil hall, Boston, on Honest Money. In 1874 he delivered six lectures on social science at Hiram college. In 1869 he spoke on the value of statistics before the American Social Science association in New York. In late years he was an occasional contributor to the pages of the Atlantic Monthly and the North American Review.

HOME AND FAMILY LIFE.

The first years of General Garfield's married life were passed in Hiram, boarding with families of friends, and it was not until he went to the war that he saved money enough to buy a home. In 1862 he purchased a small frame cottage facing the college green, paying for it $800. About $1,000 more was spent in enlarging it by a wing and fitting it up. The rooms were small and the ceilings low, as was the fashion in village houses of moderate pretensions, but the young housewife soon made the place cosy and homelike. This was the only home of the family for many years. While in Washington they lived in apartments. The lack of a settled home at the capital, where the children could grow up amid wholesome influences, was seriously felt early in

General Garfield's Congressional career, but it was not until he had been three times elected that he began to regard that career as likely to continue for an indefinite period, and sought the means of escaping from the disagreeable features of hotel and boarding-house life. He bought a lot on the corner of Thirteenth and I streets, facing Franklin square, and with money loaned him by an old army friend put up a plain, square, substantial brick house, big enough to hold his family and two or three guests. As the boys grew older, however, and needed more range for their activities than the city house could afford, the desire to own a farm which he had always felt grew upon him. When he had paid off the mortgage on his house and had a little money ahead, he thought he could safely gratify his desire, and after a good deal of thought about localities, decided to settle in the vicinity of the Lake Shore railroad on one of the handsome productive ridges that run parallel to Lake Erie. A farm of one hundred and sixty acres was bought in the town of Mentor, Lake county, a mile from a railway and telegraph station, and half a mile from a post-office. The buildings consisted of a tumble-down barn and an ancient farm house a story and a half high; but the land was fertile, the summer climate, tempered by breezes from the neighboring lake, was delightful, and the people in the vicinity were of the best class of farmers to be found in Ohio. Here the General revived all the farming skill of his boyhood days, holding the plow or loading the hay wagon or driving the ox team. Draining, fencing, and other improvements absorbed all the money the place brought in, and the time spent upon it was highly enjoyed by all the members of the household, and every winter they looked forward to the adjournment of Congress and their release from Washington with pleasant anticipations.

General Garfield had seven children and five are living. The oldest, Mary, died when he was in the army, and the youngest, Edward, died in Washington about four years ago. Of the surviving children, the oldest, Harry, is fifteen; after him comes James, Molly, Irwin (named after General McDowell), and Abraham. Harry and James are preparing for college at St. Paul's school, in Concord, New Hampshire. Harry is the musician of the family, and plays the piano well. James, who more resembles his father, is the mathematician. Molly, a handsome girl of thirteen, is ruddy, sweet-tempered, vivacious, and blessed with perfect health. The younger boys are still in the period of boisterous animal life. All the children have quick brains and are strongly individualized. All learned to read young except Abe, who hearing that his father had years ago said in a lecture on education, that no child of his should be forced to read until he was seven years old, took refuge behind the theory and declined to learn his letters until he had reached that age.

The manner of life in the Garfield household, whether in Washington or on the Mentor farm, was simple and quiet. The long table was bountifully supplied with plainly cooked food, and there was always room for any guest who might drop in at meal-time. No alcoholic drinks were used. There was no effort at following fashions in furniture or at table service. No carriage was kept at Washington, but on the farm there were vehicles of various sorts, and two teams of stout horses. Comfort, neatness, and order prevailed, without the least attempt at keeping up with style of dress and living, or any desire to sacrifice the healthful regularity of household customs adopted before the General won fame and position, to the artificial usages of what is called good society.

CANDIDATE AND PRESIDENT.

General Garfield's conduct during the campaign greatly strengthened his candidacy. He remained upon his farm in Mentor, receiving all who came to see him in a frank, open-handed way, and expressing with clearness and dignity his views on the main lines of topics entering into the canvass. A series of extempore speeches made to various delegations representing many interests and many classes of people, which called upon him, gave new proof of the breadth of his mind, his self control, and his patriotic impulses. All these addresses added to his popularity. In past campaigns candidates had usually been bridled by their friends for fear they would injure their chances. General Garfield allowed no one to be the judge of when he should speak or what he should say, and no word he spoke, from the day of his nomination to that of his election, lost him a vote. He left his farm on two or three occasions to attend reunions of his old army comrades, and in August went to New York to confer with the leaders of the Republican party. The rest of the time he kept open house, receiving during the campaign many thousands of people representing every State in the Union.

After his election, of which, by the way, he never had serious doubt, he continued to live in his farm house until the time for his journey to Washington. He was overwhelmed with advice and importuned in regard to his Cabinet appointments, but the advice was welcome whenever it was honest and unselfish, and the importunities he bore with the usual patient courtesy. When the time came for action he made up his Cabinet to suit himself according to his own best judgment. It was generally approved by the public.

The administration began with the hearty support of the country, and with high hopes for its success. The President's inaugural was an admirable production. It was eloquent, high-minded, courageous, and patriotic. His bearing and behavior in the White House showed that his strength of mind, knowledge of government and conception of the dignity of his position were such as to fill the full measure of the highest requirements of the executive office. He gave promise of being an ideal President. No one ever came to the Presidential chair before him with such wide knowledge of public men and public affairs. All went smoothly until the unhappy conflict began over the Federal patronage in New York, for which Senator Conkling was responsible. In that controversy President Garfield bore himself with firmness and dignity. It was his right to make appointments in New York as in other States, and he quietly and unyieldingly insisted upon exercising that right. The Senate sustained him by a unanimous vote after the resignation of the two New York Senators, and the people stood by him with almost equal unanimity.

President Garfield gave the closest attention to his duties The little time he took for rest he spent in the midst of his family or in the society of a few friends. He gave the customary receptions but he had no love of ceremonies or display. He was serious and sad. The office which had come to him without seeking he regarded as a grave responsibility and a heavy burden. If he ever thought it involved a peril to his life he did not speak on the subject. He was a brave man, who had faced death on many battle-fields, and he was not, like timorous persons, in the habit of dwelling upon possible dangers. No pains were taken to shield him from assassination, although he had received warning that the animosities his action created in the minds of a small political faction might end in an attempt on his life. He was so thoroughly a man of the people, and so firm a believer in the orderly working of Republican institutions in this country, that he suspected no danger to himself from freely mingling with crowds. When he left the White House he went like an ordinary citizen, and no effort was made to protect his person. He visited Long Branch with his family and a single officer; he returned to Washington accompanied by one friend only. A little precaution would have saved him from the assassin's bullet, but nobody thought precaution necessary.

During the few days General Garfield spent at Long Branch the rapid recovery of his wife from her serious illness and his own comparative rest from the official work produced a marked effect upon him. He spoke of his excellent physical health and talked cheerfully of having got through with the severest strain likely to come upon him during his administration. Much of his old, hearty, genial, frank manner, of which the cares of office had seemed to be robbing him, came back in his intercourse with his friends. He showed much pleasure at the near prospect of revisiting the scenes of his college life in Williamstown, Massachusetts, and promised himself the delight of reviving old memories with his classmates, and being for a little time in thought a boy again. His habitual mental state at that time was, however, one of great gravity. A friend who saw him said to him: "I saw the roof of your house the other day while traveling on the Lake Shore railroad." "I wish I could see it again," replied the President in a solemn tone of voice, as if he felt for the moment he was destined never to see the home that was so dear to him.

ASSASSINATION AND DEATH.

By close attention to the duties of her position as hostess of the Executive mansion and assistant to the President in the onerous duties devolving upon him in putting into active operation the machinery of the new Government, in a building subject to the influence of the malaria arising from the low grounds near the Whitehouse, Mrs. Garfield was attacked by a wellnigh fatal disease that finally compelled her removal to the sea shore for complete recovery. She was taken to Long Branch before June was fairly opened, leaving the President to his multifarious duties, which he carried on with his wonted vigor, his mind at the same time filled with thoughts of her he missed in his every task. A few weeks of rest and quiet at the sea shore had almost restored her to her usual health, and preparations had been made by the President to take a short respite from the daily cares of official life. Arrangements had been made for his trip to Long Branch on the morning of the 2d of July, accompanied by Secretary Blaine and Colonel Rockwell, as well as his two sons, Harry and James Garfield, and their tutor, with two others of the family, members of the Cabinet also being of the party. The carriage containing the President, Secretary Blaine, and Colonel Rockwell arrived at the depot a short time before departure of the train. The Secretary preceded the President into the ladies' waiting room. The President had advanced but a few steps into the room when a man stepped behind him, drew a revolver, and fired directly at his back. The President threw his hand to his back, tottered, and fell forward upon his face. As he fell the assassin fired a second shot, but with no further injury. He was immediately seized and hurried away to close confinement.

Sympathizing hands lifted the stricken President, placed him on a mattress, and conveyed him up the stairs to a private room connected with the officers' quarters of the railroad. There his wound was examined by Dr. Townsend, health officer of Washington, Surgeon-general Barnes of the United States army, and Dr. D. W. Bliss, of Washington. It was thought best to at once remove the President to the White house, and an ambulance was called in which, guarded by a force of police, he was quickly conveyed to the place he had so lately left in perfect health, and in the full strength of his manhood. A telegraph message was at once sent to Mrs. Garfield, at Long Branch, acquainting her with the disaster that had befallen the President. A special train conveyed the grief-stricken wife to the bedside of her husband, which she left only when absolutely necessary during the eleven long and sad weeks that followed.

The report of the assassination of President Garfield produced great demonstrations of sorrow throughout the country, as well as in foreign lands. In no place was the grief deeper or more heartfelt than among his friends and neighbors in the district he had for so many years represented in Congress. The premature report of his death came like a clap of thunder in a clear sky. No one could imagine any cause why such a man should be laid low by an assassin's bullet, and the report could not be believed. Subsequent reports confirmed the shooting, but as life continued hope began to revive, and many expressed the belief that he might yet recover and resume his place among men.

The wearisome watching and hope against hope were prolonged week after week, the stricken man gradually growing weaker as day followed day. As the weeks passed by the President frequently expressed a desire to return to his home near the quiet country village of Mentor, where he might rest. A consultation of the attending surgeons was held on the 4th of September, and on the morning of the 6th he was carefully conveyed in an express wagon to the car prepared to take him to the seaside cottage at Elberon. In the afternoon of the same day he was resting quietly in the cottage, listening to the ceaseless murmur of the waves upon the shore, and from his cot watching through the window the white sails of passing vessels. The days resumed their wearisome round, the sufferer each day becoming weaker. At length the end came. On the 12th of September it became evident to the attendants that the dreaded change was not far distant. Still he lingered on, brave and patient through all, until the night of the 19th. He had rested as well as usual during the day and at evening fell asleep. About 10 o'clock he was awakened by a terrible pain in the region of the heart. All was done that could be done, and at 10:35 the end had come. The noble, self-sacrificing man and President, James A. Garfield, had breathed his last.

The rest is soon told. A post mortem examination demonstrated that death must surely have taken place from the nature of the wound.

The ball had fractured the right eleventh rib, passed through the spinal column in front of the spinal canal, fracturing the body of the first lumbar vertebra, driving pieces of bone into the adjacent soft parts, and finally became encysted. Death was immediately caused by hemorrhage of one of the mesenteric arteries, a large quantity of blood finding its way into the abdominal cavity, which was probably the cause of the pain in the chest complained of a few moments before death.

The body of the dead President was embalmed, and lay in view in the cottage where he passed his last hours until Wednesday morning, September 21st, when it was taken to the capitol at Washington. There the honors due the Chief Magistrate of a great nation were shown by his successor, his Cabinet, the members of both houses of Congress, besides vast multitudes of people—his friends and admirers. Friday the funeral train left the capital of the Nation for Cleveland, where the last resting place of the dead statesman had been selected.

Along the line of the sad journey were gathered sympathizing men, women, and children to drop a tear to his memory as the swiftly-moving train passed by. The procession reached Cleveland Saturday, the 24th, and debarking at Euclid Avenue station, proceeded to the Public square, where appropriate arrangements had been made to render honor to him who living was honored and dead was not forgotten. The final exercises were held Monday, the 26th of September, the greatest concourse of people ever gathered in Cleveland being present on the occasion. The remains were deposited in a vault in the beautiful Lake View cemetery, where they were placed under the watchful guardianship of a company of United States soldiers.

The man who fired the fatal shot, Charles J. Guiteau, was confined under a strong guard, and in due course of law was tried for the crime of murder, found guilty after a fair and impartial trial, and sentenced to be hung on the 30th of June, almost a year after the fatal shot was fired.

While the memory of the assassin Guiteau will be forever execrated, the memory of the good and noble Garfield will be revered and kept fresh in the minds of childrens' children of those who knew and loved him.

www.ingramcontent.com/pod-product-compliance
Lightning Source LLC
Chambersburg PA
CBHW031943290426
44108CB00011B/651